Mobil ✪✪

Travel Guide

Northwest

2003

ExxonMobil Travel Publications

ACKNOWLEDGMENTS

We gratefully acknowledge the help of our representatives for their efficient and perceptive inspection of the lodging and dining establishments listed; the establishments' proprietors for their cooperation in showing their facilities and providing information about them; the many users of previous editions of the Mobil Travel Guides who have taken the time to share their experiences; and for their time and information, the thousands of chambers of commerce, convention and visitors bureaus, city, state, and provincial tourism offices, and government agencies who assisted in our research.

Mobil, Mobil 1, Exxon, Speedpass, and Mobil Travel Guide are trademarks of Exxon Mobil Corporation or one of its subsidiaries. All rights reserved. Reproduction by any means including but not limited to photography, electrostatic copying devices, or electronic data processing is prohibited. Use of the information contained herein for solicitation of advertising or listing in any other publication is expressly prohibited without written permission from Exxon Mobil Corporation. Violations of reserved rights are subject to prosecution.

PHOTO CREDITS

Alan Bisson/Spokane Area Convention and Visitors Bureau: 325; Folio, Inc.: David R. Frazier: 77; Mark Newman: 293; **FPG/Getty Images:** Walter Bibikow:157, 439; Dave Gleiter: 108; Jeri Gleiter: 168; H. Richard Johnston: 185; Alan Kearney: 434; Harvey Lloyd: 368; Buddy Mays: 32; Stan Osolinski: 375; Gary Randall: 182, 230; Ken Ross: 360; Gail Shumway: 84; John Taylor: 19; Travelpix: 402; VCG: 395; **Kelly-Mooney Photography/Corbis:** 296; **Robert Holmes Photography:** 426; **Markham Johnson/Backroads:**116, 142; **Super-Stock:** 1, 6, 14, 44, 54, 59, 93, 100, 125, 148, 217, 224, 232, 240, 249, 259, 267, 270, 278, 313, 342, 344, 356, 364, 392, 398, 411, 433, 445, 454, 549, 463, 470, 478, 480, 486.

Maps © MapQuest 2002, www.mapquest.com

Printed by Publications International, Ltd.
7373 North Cicero Avenue
Lincolnwood, Illinois 60712

info@mobiltravelguide.com

ISBN 0-7627-2611-3

Manufactured in China.

10 9 8 7 6 5 4 3 2 1

CONTENTS

Northwest

Maps

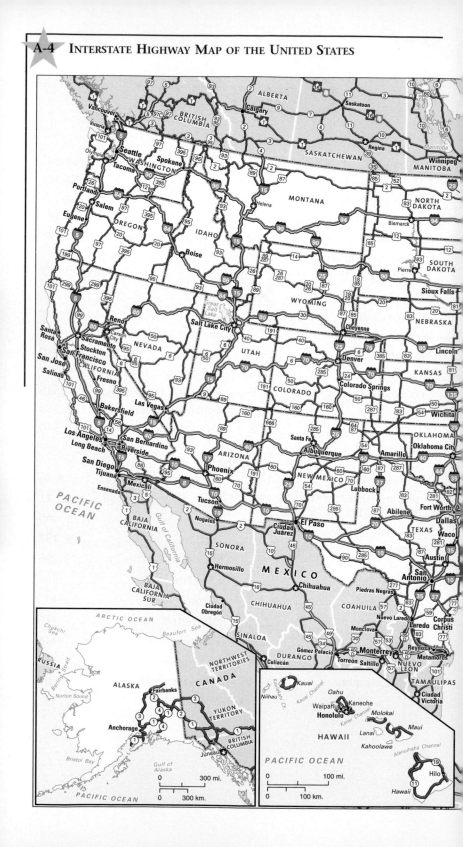

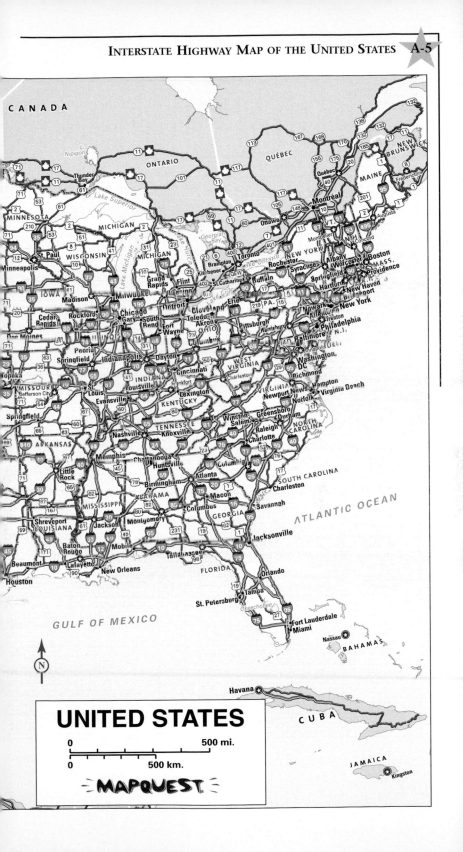

A-6 MILEAGE CHART

Distances in chart are in miles. To convert miles to kilometers, multiply the distance in miles by 1.609 Example: New York, NY to Boston, MA = 215 miles or 346 kilometers (215 x 1.609)	ALBUQUERQUE, NM	ATLANTA, GA	BALTIMORE, MD	BILLINGS, MT	BIRMINGHAM, AL	BISMARCK, ND	BOISE, ID	BOSTON, MA	BUFFALO, NY	BURLINGTON, VT	CHARLESTON, SC	CHARLESTON, WV	CHARLOTTE, NC	CHEYENNE, WY	CHICAGO, IL	CINCINNATI, OH	CLEVELAND, OH	DALLAS, TX	DENVER, CO	DES MOINES, IA	DETROIT, MI	EL PASO, TX	HOUSTON, TX	INDIANAPOLIS, IN	JACKSON, MS	KANSAS CITY, MO	LAS VEGAS, NV
ALBUQUERQUE, NM		1490	1902	991	1274	1333	966	2240	1808	2178	1793	1568	1649	538	1352	1409	1619	754	438	1091	1608	263	994	1298	1157	894	578
ATLANTA, GA	1490		679	1889	150	1559	2218	1100	910	1158	317	503	238	1482	717	476	726	792	1403	967	735	1437	800	531	386	801	2067
BALTIMORE, MD	1902	679		1959	795	1551	2401	422	370	481	583	352	441	1665	708	521	377	1399	1690	1031	532	2045	1470	600	1032	1087	2445
BILLINGS, MT	991	1889	1959		1839	413	626	2254	1796	2181	2157	1755	2012	455	1246	1552	1597	1433	554	1007	1534	1255	1673	1432	1836	1088	965
BIRMINGHAM, AL	1274	150	795	1839		1509	2170	1215	909	1241	466	578	389	1434	667	475	725	647	1356	919	734	1292	678	481	241	753	1852
BISMARCK, ND	1333	1559	1551	413	1509		1039	1846	1388	1773	1749	1347	1604	594	838	1144	1189	1342	693	675	1126	1597	1582	1024	1548	801	1378
BOISE, ID	966	2218	2401	626	2170	1039		2697	2239	2624	2520	2182	2375	737	1708	1969	2040	1711	833	1369	1977	1206	1952	1852	2115	1376	760
BOSTON, MA	2240	1100	422	2254	1215	1846	2697		462	214	1003	741	861	1961	1003	862	654	1819	2004	1326	741	2465	1890	940	1453	1427	2757
BUFFALO, NY	1808	910	370	1796	909	1388	2239	462		375	899	431	695	1502	545	442	197	1393	1546	868	277	2039	1513	508	1134	995	2299
BURLINGTON, VT	2178	1158	481	2181	1241	1773	2624	214	375		1061	782	919	1887	930	817	567	1763	1931	1253	652	2409	1916	878	1479	1366	2684
CHARLESTON, SC	1793	317	583	2157	466	1749	2520	1003	899	1061		468	204	1783	907	622	724	1109	1705	1204	879	1754	1110	721	703	1102	2371
CHARLESTON, WV	1568	503	352	1755	578	1347	2182	741	431	782	468		265	1445	506	209	255	1072	1367	802	410	1718	1192	320	816	764	2122
CHARLOTTE, NC	1649	238	441	2012	389	1604	2375	861	695	919	204	265		1637	761	476	520	1031	1559	1057	675	1677	1041	575	625	956	2225
CHEYENNE, WY	538	1482	1665	455	1434	594	737	1961	1502	1887	1783	1445	1637		972	1233	1304	979	100	633	1241	801	1220	1115	1382	640	843
CHICAGO, IL	1352	717	708	1246	667	838	1708	1003	545	930	907	506	761	972		302	346	936	1015	337	283	1543	1108	184	750	532	1768
CINCINNATI, OH	1409	476	521	1552	475	1144	1969	862	442	817	622	209	476	1233	302		253	958	1200	599	261	1605	1079	116	700	597	1955
CLEVELAND, OH	1619	726	377	1597	725	1189	2040	654	197	567	724	255	520	1304	346	253		1208	1347	669	171	1854	1328	319	950	806	2100
DALLAS, TX	754	792	1399	1433	647	1342	1711	1819	1393	1763	1109	1072	1031	979	936	958	1208		887	752	1218	647	241	913	406	554	1331
DENVER, CO	438	1403	1690	554	1356	693	833	2004	1546	1931	1705	1367	1559	100	1015	1200	1347	887		676	1284	701	1127	1088	1290	603	756
DES MOINES, IA	1091	967	1031	1007	919	675	1369	1326	868	1253	1204	802	1057	633	337	599	669	752	676		606	1283	992	481	931	194	1429
DETROIT, MI	1608	735	532	1534	734	1126	1977	741	277	652	879	410	675	1241	283	261	171	1218	1284	606		1799	1338	318	960	795	2037
EL PASO, TX	263	1437	2045	1255	1292	1597	1206	2465	2039	2409	1754	1718	1677	801	1543	1605	1854	647	701	1283	1799		758	1489	1051	1085	717
HOUSTON, TX	994	800	1470	1673	678	1582	1952	1890	1513	1916	1110	1192	1041	1220	1108	1079	1328	241	1127	992	1338	758		1033	445	795	1474
INDIANAPOLIS, IN	1298	531	600	1432	481	1024	1852	940	508	878	721	320	575	1115	184	116	319	913	1088	481	318	1489	1033		675	485	1843
JACKSON, MS	1157	386	1032	1836	241	1548	2115	1453	1134	1479	703	816	625	1382	750	700	950	406	1290	931	960	1051	445	675		747	1735
KANSAS CITY, MO	894	801	1087	1088	753	801	1376	1427	995	1366	1102	764	956	640	532	597	806	554	603	194	795	1085	795	485	747		1358
LAS VEGAS, NV	578	2067	2445	965	1852	1378	760	2757	2299	2684	2371	2122	2225	843	1768	1955	2100	1331	756	1429	2037	717	1474	1843	1735	1358	
LITTLE ROCK, AR	900	528	1072	1530	381	1183	1808	1493	1066	1437	900	745	754	1076	662	632	882	327	984	567	891	974	447	587	269	382	1478
LOS ANGELES, CA	806	2237	2705	1239	2092	1702	1033	3046	2572	2957	2554	2374	2453	1116	2042	2215	2374	1446	1029	1703	2310	801	1558	2104	1851	1632	274
LOUISVILLE, KY	1320	419	602	1547	369	1139	1933	964	545	915	610	251	464	1197	299	106	356	852	1118	595	366	1499	972	112	594	516	1874
MEMPHIS, TN	1033	389	933	1625	241	1337	1954	1353	927	1297	760	606	614	1217	539	493	742	466	1116	720	752	1112	586	464	211	536	1611
MIAMI, FL	2155	661	1109	2554	812	2224	2883	1529	1425	1587	583	994	730	2147	1382	1141	1250	1367	2069	1632	1401	1959	1201	1196	915	1466	2733
MILWAUKEE, WI	1426	813	805	1175	763	767	1748	1100	642	1027	1003	601	857	1012	89	398	443	1010	1055	378	380	1617	1193	279	835	573	1808
MINNEAPOLIS, MN	1339	1129	1121	839	1079	431	1465	1417	958	1343	1319	918	1173	881	409	714	760	999	924	246	697	1530	1240	596	1151	441	1677
MONTRÉAL, QC	2172	1241	564	2093	1289	1685	2535	313	397	92	1145	822	1003	1799	841	815	588	1772	1843	1165	564	2363	1892	872	1514	1359	2596
NASHVILLE, TN	1248	242	716	1648	194	1315	1976	1136	716	1086	543	395	397	1240	474	281	531	681	1162	725	541	1328	801	287	423	559	1826
NEW ORLEANS, LA	1276	473	1142	1955	351	1734	2234	1563	1254	1588	783	926	713	1502	935	820	1070	525	1409	1117	1079	1118	360	826	185	932	1854
NEW YORK, NY	2015	869	192	2049	985	1641	2491	215	400	299	773	515	631	1755	797	636	466	1589	1799	1121	622	2235	1660	715	1223	1202	2552
OKLAHOMA CITY, OK	546	944	1354	1227	729	1136	1506	1694	1262	1632	1248	1022	1102	773	807	863	1073	209	681	546	1062	737	449	752	612	348	1124
OMAHA, NE	973	989	1168	904	941	616	1234	1463	1005	1390	1290	952	1144	497	474	736	806	669	541	136	743	1236	910	618	935	188	1294
ORLANDO, FL	1934	440	904	2333	591	2003	2662	1324	1221	1383	379	790	525	1926	1161	920	1045	1146	1847	1411	1180	1738	980	975	694	1245	2512
PHILADELPHIA, PA	1954	782	104	2019	897	1611	2462	321	414	371	685	454	543	1725	768	576	437	1501	1744	1091	592	2147	1572	655	1135	1141	2500
PHOENIX, AZ	466	1868	2366	1199	1723	1662	993	2706	2274	2644	2184	2035	2107	1004	1819	1876	2085	1077	904	1558	2074	432	1188	1764	1482	1360	285
PITTSBURGH, PA	1670	676	246	1719	763	1311	2161	592	217	587	642	217	438	1425	467	292	136	1246	1460	791	292	1893	1366	370	988	857	2215
PORTLAND, ME	2338	1197	520	2352	1313	1944	2795	107	560	233	1101	839	959	2059	1101	960	751	1917	2102	1424	838	2563	1988	1038	1550	1525	2855
PORTLAND, OR	1395	2647	2830	889	2599	1301	432	3126	2667	3052	2948	2610	2802	1166	2137	2398	2469	2140	1261	1798	2405	1767	2381	2280	2544	1805	1188
RAPID CITY, SD	841	1511	1626	379	1463	320	930	1921	1463	1848	1824	1422	1678	305	913	1219	1264	1077	404	629	1201	1105	1318	1101	1458	710	1035
RENO, NV	1020	2440	2623	960	2392	1372	430	2919	2460	2845	2741	2403	2595	959	1930	2191	2262	1933	1054	1591	2198	1315	2072	2073	2337	1598	442
RICHMOND, VA	1876	527	152	2053	678	1645	2496	572	485	630	428	322	289	1760	802	530	471	1309	1688	1126	627	1955	1330	641	914	1085	2444
ST. LOUIS, MO	1051	549	841	1341	501	1053	1628	1181	749	1119	850	512	704	892	294	350	560	635	855	436	549	1242	863	239	505	252	1610
SALT LAKE CITY, UT	624	1916	2100	548	1868	960	342	2395	1936	2322	2218	1880	2072	436	1406	1667	1738	1410	531	1067	1675	864	1650	1549	1813	1074	417
SAN ANTONIO, TX	818	1000	1671	1500	878	1599	1761	2092	1665	2036	1310	1344	1241	1046	1270	1231	1481	271	946	1009	1490	556	200	1186	644	812	1272
SAN DIEGO, CA	825	2166	2724	1302	2021	1765	1096	3065	2632	3020	2483	2393	2405	1179	2105	2234	2437	1375	1092	1766	2373	730	1487	2122	1780	1695	337
SAN FRANCISCO, CA	1111	2618	2840	1176	2472	1749	646	3135	2677	3062	2934	2620	2759	1176	2146	2407	2478	1827	1271	1807	2415	1181	1938	2290	2232	1814	575
SEATTLE, WA	1463	2705	2775	816	2657	1229	500	3070	2612	2997	2973	2571	2827	1234	2062	2368	2413	2208	1329	1822	2350	1944	2449	2249	2612	1872	1256
TAMPA, FL	1949	455	960	2348	606	2018	2677	1380	1276	1438	434	845	581	1941	1176	935	1101	1161	1862	1426	1194	1753	995	990	709	1259	2526
TORONTO, ON	1841	958	565	1762	958	1354	2204	570	106	419	1006	537	802	1468	510	484	303	1441	1512	834	233	2032	1561	541	1183	1028	2265
VANCOUVER, BC	1597	2838	2908	949	2791	1362	633	3204	2745	3130	3106	2705	2960	1368	2196	2501	2547	2342	1463	1956	2483	2087	2583	2383	2746	2007	1390
WASHINGTON, DC	1896	636	38	1953	758	1545	2395	458	384	517	539	346	397	1659	701	517	370	1362	1686	1025	526	2008	1433	596	996	1083	2441
WICHITA, KS	707	989	1276	1067	838	934	1346	1616	1184	1554	1291	953	1145	613	728	785	995	367	521	390	984	898	608	674	771	192	1276

	LITTLE ROCK, AR	LOS ANGELES, CA	LOUISVILLE, KY	MEMPHIS, TN	MIAMI, FL	MILWAUKEE, WI	MINNEAPOLIS, MN	MONTRÉAL, QC	NASHVILLE, TN	NEW ORLEANS, LA	NEW YORK, NY	OKLAHOMA CITY, OK	OMAHA, NE	ORLANDO, FL	PHILADELPHIA, PA	PHOENIX, AZ	PITTSBURGH, PA	PORTLAND, ME	PORTLAND, OR	RAPID CITY, SD	RENO, NV	RICHMOND, VA	SALT LAKE CITY, UT	SAN ANTONIO, TX	SAN DIEGO, CA	SAN FRANCISCO, CA	SEATTLE, WA	ST. LOUIS, MO	TAMPA, FL	TORONTO, ON	VANCOUVER, BC	WASHINGTON, DC	WICHITA, KS
LITTLE ROCK, AR	900	806	1320	1033	2155	1426	1339	2172	1248	1276	2015	546	973	1934	1954	466	1670	2338	1395	841	1020	1876	1051	624	818	825	1111	1463	1949	1841	1597	1896	707
LOS ANGELES, CA	528	2237	419	389	661	813	1129	1241	242	473	869	944	989	440	782	1868	676	1197	2647	1511	2440	527	549	1916	1000	2166	2618	2705	455	958	2838	636	989
LOUISVILLE, KY	1072	2705	602	933	1109	805	1121	564	716	1142	192	1354	1168	904	104	2366	246	520	2830	1626	2623	152	2100	1671	2724	2840	2775	960	565	2908	38	1276
MEMPHIS, TN	1530	1239	1547	1625	2554	1175	239	2093	1648	1955	2049	1227	904	2333	2019	1199	1719	2352	889	379	960	2053	1341	548	1500	1303	1341	1868	878	2348	1762	949	1953	1067
MIAMI, FL	381	2092	369	241	812	763	1079	1289	194	351	985	729	941	591	897	1723	763	1313	2599	1463	2392	678	501	1868	878	2021	2412	2657	606	958	2791	758	838
MILWAUKEE, WI	1183	1702	1139	1337	2224	767	431	1685	1315	1734	1641	1136	616	2003	1611	1662	1311	1944	1301	320	1372	1645	1053	960	1599	1765	1749	1229	2018	1354	1362	1545	934
MINNEAPOLIS, MN	1808	1033	1933	1954	2883	1748	1465	2535	1976	2241	1506	1234	2662	2462	993	2161	2795	432	930	430	2496	1628	342	1761	1096	546	2677	2204	633	2395	1346
MONTRÉAL, QC	1493	3046	964	1353	1529	1100	1417	313	1136	1563	215	1694	1463	1324	321	2706	592	107	3126	1921	2919	572	1181	2395	2092	3065	3135	3070	1380	570	3204	458	1616
NASHVILLE, TN	1066	2572	545	927	1425	642	958	397	716	1254	400	1262	1005	1221	414	2274	217	560	2667	1463	2460	485	749	1936	1665	2632	2677	2612	1276	106	2745	384	1184
NEW ORLEANS, LA	1437	2957	915	1297	1587	1027	1343	92	1086	1588	299	1632	1390	1383	371	2644	587	233	3052	1848	2845	630	1119	2322	2036	3020	3062	2997	1438	419	3130	517	1554
NEW YORK, NY	2005	2554	610	760	583	1003	1319	1145	543	783	773	1248	1290	379	685	2184	642	1101	2448	2741	428	850	2218	1310	2483	2934	2913	434	1006	3106	539	1291
OKLAHOMA CITY, OK	745	2374	251	606	994	601	918	822	395	926	515	1022	952	790	454	2035	217	839	2610	1422	2405	322	512	1880	1344	2393	2620	2571	845	537	2705	346	953
OMAHA, NE	754	2453	404	614	730	857	1171	1003	797	713	1107	1144	525	543	2107	438	959	2802	1678	2595	289	704	2072	1241	2405	2759	2827	581	802	2960	397	1145
ORLANDO, FL	4076	1197	1217	2147	1012	881	1799	1240	1502	1755	773	497	1926	1725	1004	1425	2059	1166	305	959	1760	892	436	1046	1179	1176	1234	1941	1468	1368	1699	613
PHILADELPHIA, PA	662	2042	299	539	1382	89	405	841	474	935	797	907	474	1161	768	1819	467	101	2137	913	1930	802	294	1406	1270	2046	2062	1176	510	2196	701	728
PHOENIX, AZ	811	1111	106	473	1111	399	714	815	781	820	636	863	736	920	576	1876	292	960	2398	1219	2191	530	350	1667	1231	2234	2407	2368	935	484	2501	517	783
PITTSBURGH, PA	882	2374	356	742	1250	443	760	588	531	1070	466	1073	806	1045	437	2085	136	151	2409	1204	1104	1101	1478	1411	1101	2203	627	270	995
PORTLAND, ME	327	1416	852	466	1361	1003	100	999	1772	681	525	1589	209	646	1146	1501	1077	1246	1917	7140	1077	1933	1309	635	1410	271	1375	1822	2208	1161	1441	2342	1362	367
PORTLAND, OR	984	1029	1110	1116	2069	1055	974	1844	1162	1409	1799	601	541	1847	1744	904	1460	2102	1261	404	1054	1688	833	331	946	1092	1271	1729	1867	1517	1463	1686	521
RAPID CITY, SD	567	1703	595	720	1632	378	240	1165	728	771	1171	488	138	1011	1091	1300	720	101	1176	436	1061	1009	1766	1807	1033	446	101
RENO, NV	891	2360	366	752	1401	580	607	564	541	1079	622	1047	743	1100	592	2074	292	838	2405	1201	2198	627	549	1675	1490	2373	2415	2350	1194	233	2483	526	904
RICHMOND, VA	974	801	1499	1112	1959	1617	1530	2363	1328	1118	2235	737	1236	1738	2147	432	1893	2563	1767	1105	1315	1955	1242	864	556	730	1181	1944	1753	2032	2087	2008	890
SALT LAKE CITY, UT	447	1558	972	586	1201	1193	1240	1892	801	760	1660	449	910	980	1572	1188	1366	1988	2381	1318	2012	1330	863	1650	200	1487	1938	2449	995	1561	2583	1433	608
SAN ANTONIO, TX	381	118	161	1108	270	596	877	787	876	715	752	618	975	655	1764	370	1038	2280	1101	2073	641	239	1549	1106	2122	2290	2249	990	541	2383	596	674
SAN DIEGO, CA	269	1851	594	211	915	835	1151	1514	423	185	1223	612	935	694	1135	1482	988	1550	2544	1458	2337	914	505	1813	644	1100	2233	2012	789	1102	2416	006	771
SAN FRANCISCO, CA	382	1632	516	536	1466	573	441	1359	559	932	1202	348	188	1245	1141	1360	851	1625	1803	710	1590	1005	262	1074	817	1695	1814	1872	1259	1028	2007	1033	192
SEATTLE, WA	1478	274	1874	1611	2733	1808	1677	2596	1826	1854	2552	1194	926	2512	2500	285	2215	2855	1188	1035	442	2610	1610	417	1272	337	575	2364	878	589	2947	2441	1276
ST. LOUIS, MO	1706	140	1190	707	814	1446	355	1262	355	570	969	1175	1367	920	1590	2237	1093	2030	983	416	1507	600	1703	2012	2305	984	1115	2439	1036	464
TAMPA, FL	2126	1839	2759	2082	1951	2869	2054	1917	2820	1352	2538	2760	369	2476	3144	971	1309	519	2682	1856	691	1356	124	385	1148	2553	2538	1291	2702	1513
TORONTO, ON	526	2126	386	1084	394	611	920	75	714	1174	376	764	1631	125	2144	2372	2364	878	589	2497	596	705
VANCOUVER, BC	140	1839	386	1051	624	940	1306	215	396	1123	487	724	830	1035	1500	780	1451	2382	1247	2175	843	294	1652	739	1841	2144	2440	845	975	2574	896	597
WASHINGTON, DC	1190	2759	1084	1051	1478	1794	1671	907	874	1299	1609	1654	232	1211	2390	1167	1627	3312	2176	3105	954	1214	2581	1401	2688	3140	3370	274	1532	3504	1065	1655
WICHITA, KS	747	2082	394	624	1478	337	939	569	1020	894	880	514	1257	865	1892	564	1198	2063	842	1897	899	367	1446	1343	2145	1286	1991	1272	657	1446	1588	924	1788	1115	637

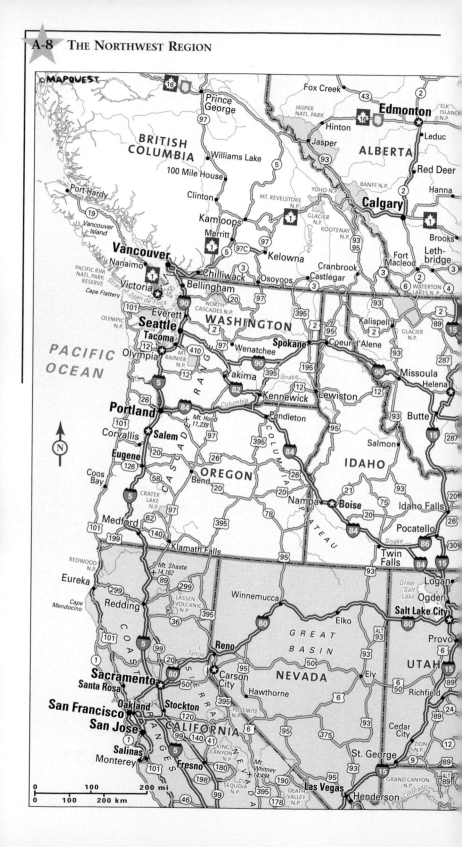

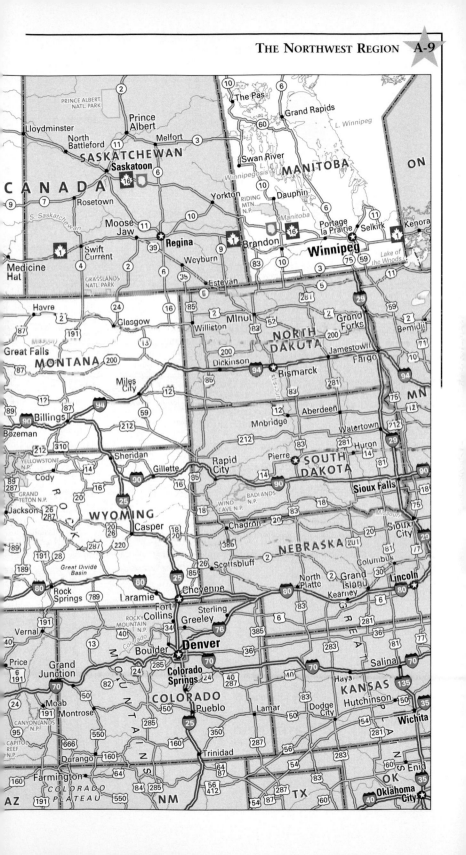

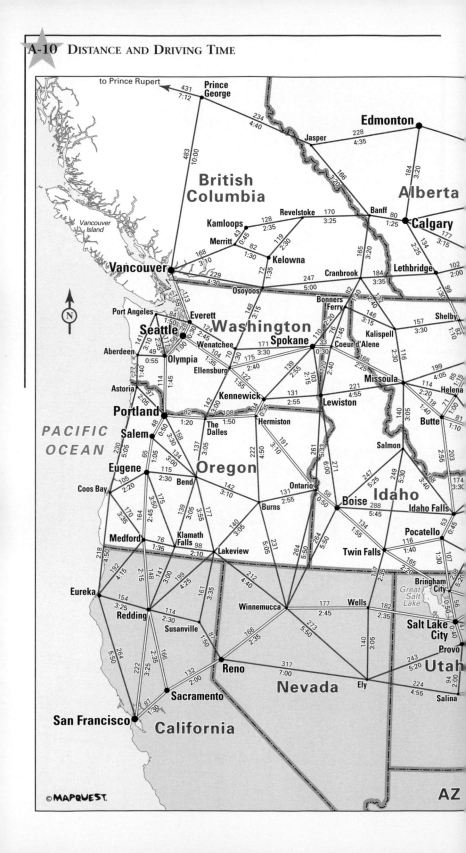

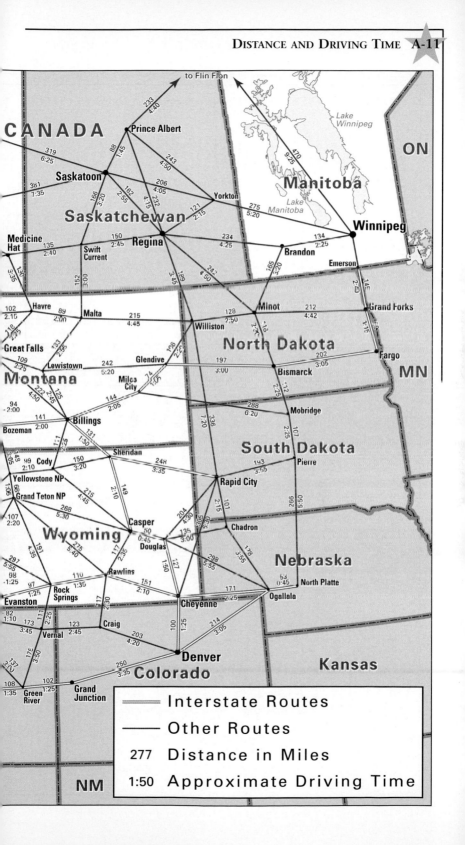

PARTIAL INDEX TO CITIES AND TOWNS

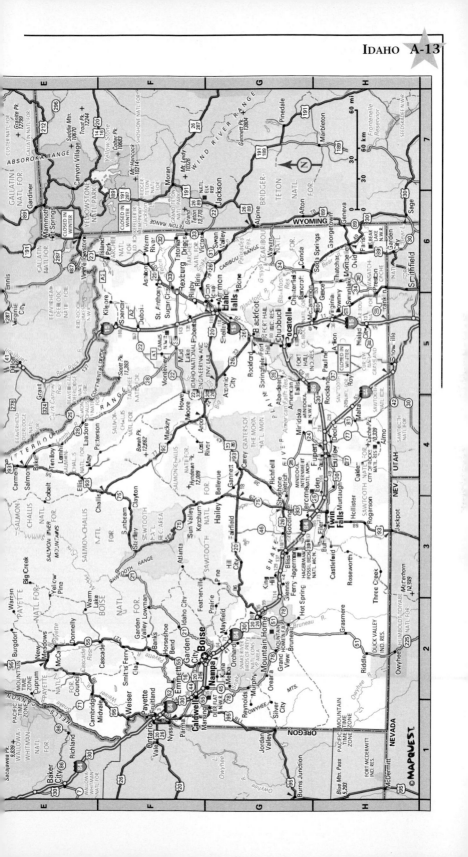

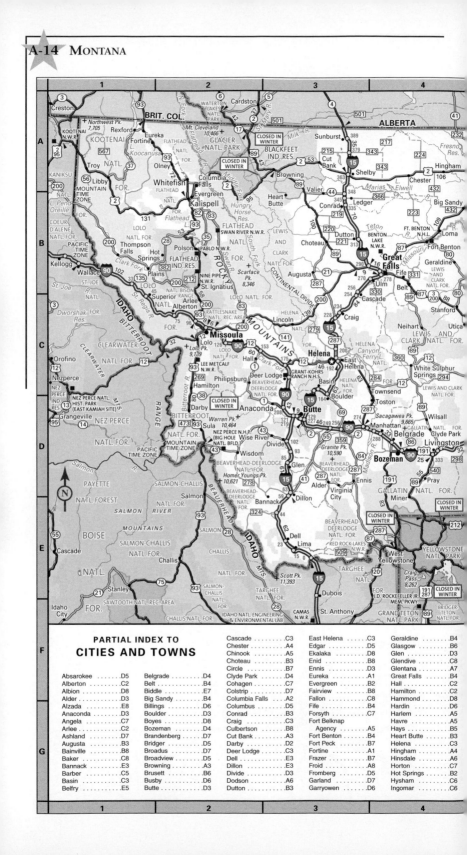

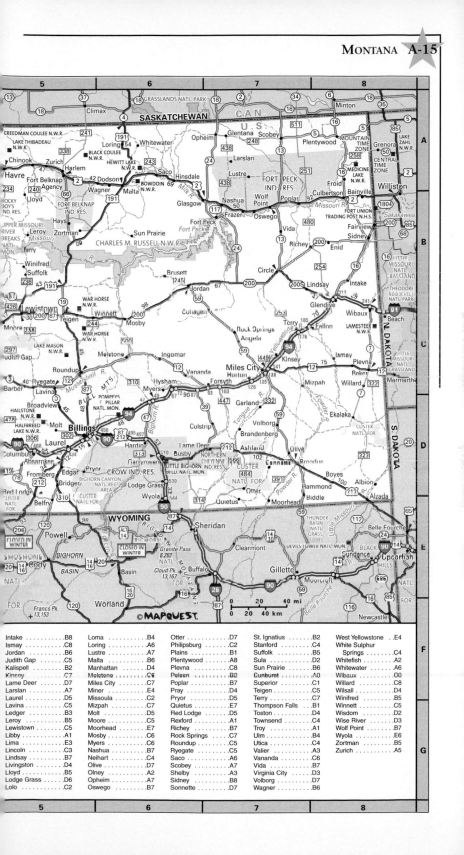

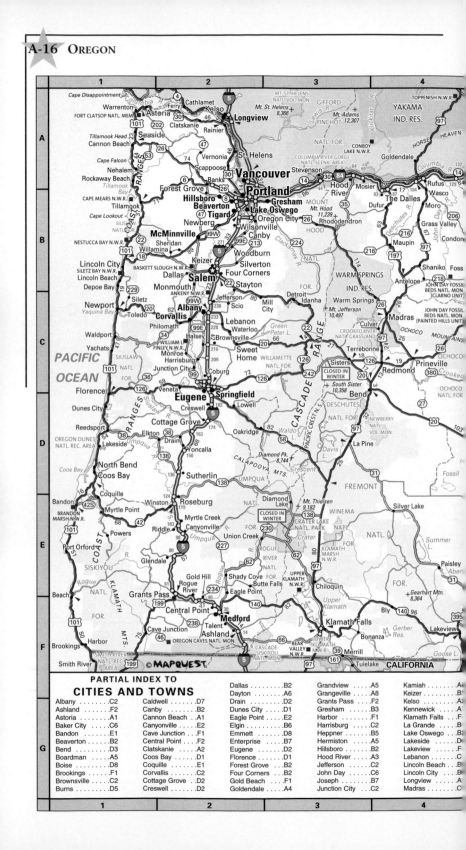

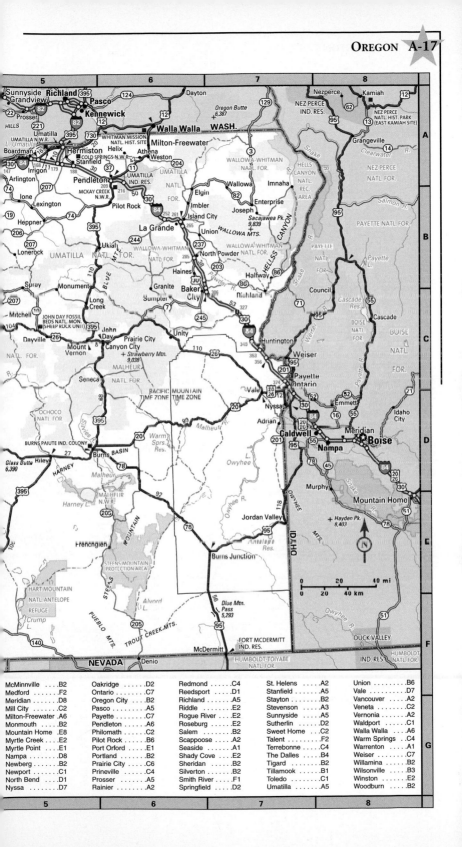

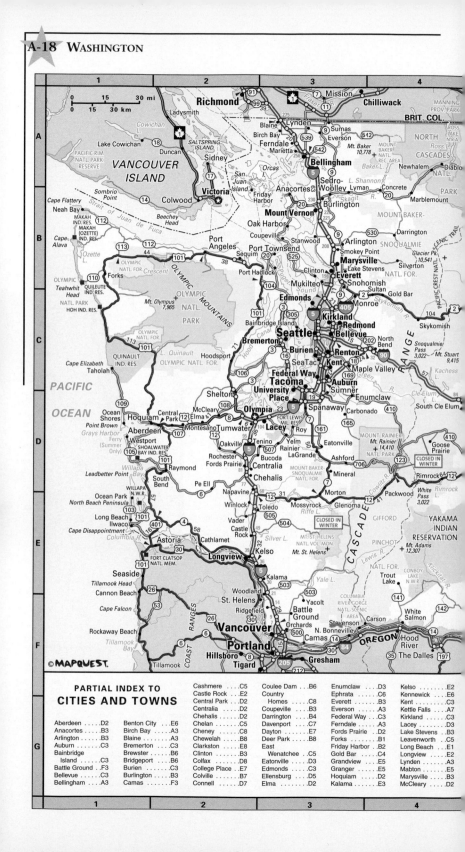

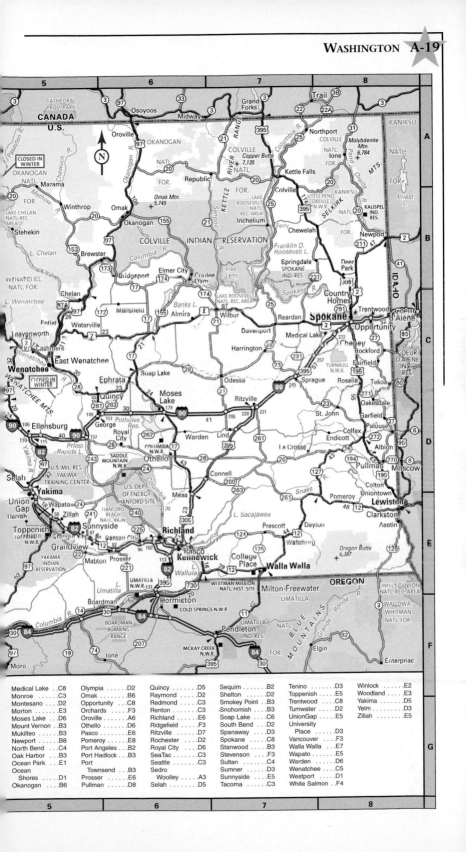

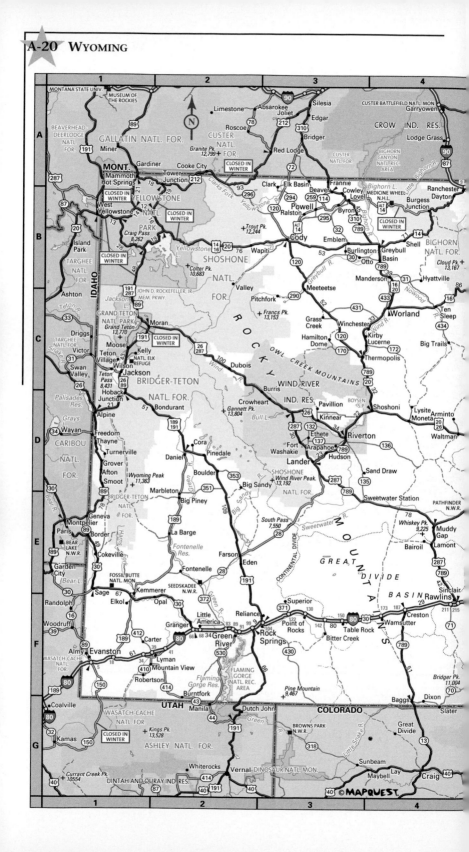

PARTIAL INDEX TO CITIES AND TOWNS

Absarokee	A2
Afton	D1
Ashton	C1
Ault	G7
Bar Nunn	D5
Basin	B4
Belle Fourche	B7
Bridger	A3
Broadus	A6
Buffalo	B5
Casper	D5
Cheyenne	F7
Coalville	G1
Cody	B3
Craig	G4
Custer	C7
Dayton	B4
Deadwood	B7
Douglas	D6
Driggs	C1
Dubois	C2
Edgemont	D7
Evanston	F1
Evansville	D5
Fort Collins	G6
Gering	F8
Gillette	B6
Glenrock	D6
Greeley	G7
Green River	F2
Greybull	B4
Guernsey	E7
Hanna	E5
Hot Springs	C8
Jackson	C1
Joliet	A3
Kamas	G1
Kemmerer	E1
Kimball	F8
Lander	D3
Laramie	F6
Lead	B7
Lodge Grass	A4
Loveland	G6
Lovell	B3
Lusk	D7
Lyman	F2
Marbleton	E2
Mills	D5
Mitchell	E7
Montpelier	E1
Moorcroft	B6
Mountain View	F2
Newcastle	C7
Paris	E1
Pine Bluffs	F7
Pinedale	D2
Powell	B3
Ranchester	B4
Rawlins	F4
Red Lodge	A3
Riverton	D3
Rock Springs	F3
Saratoga	F5
Scottsbluff	E8
Sheridan	B4
Sinclair	E4
Spearfish	B7
Steamboat Springs	G5
Sturgis	B8
Sundance	B7
Thermopolis	C3
Torrington	E7
Upton	C7
Vernal	G2
Walden	G5
Wellington	G6
West Yellowstone	B1
Wheatland	E6
Windsor	G6
Worland	C4
Wright	C6

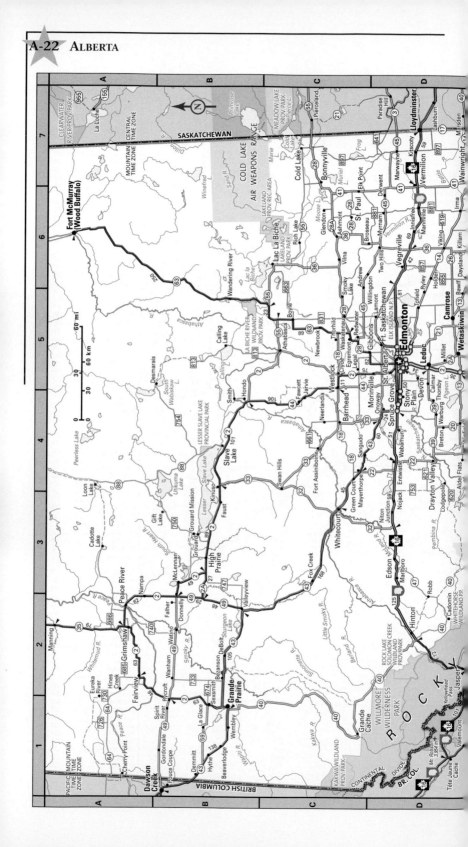

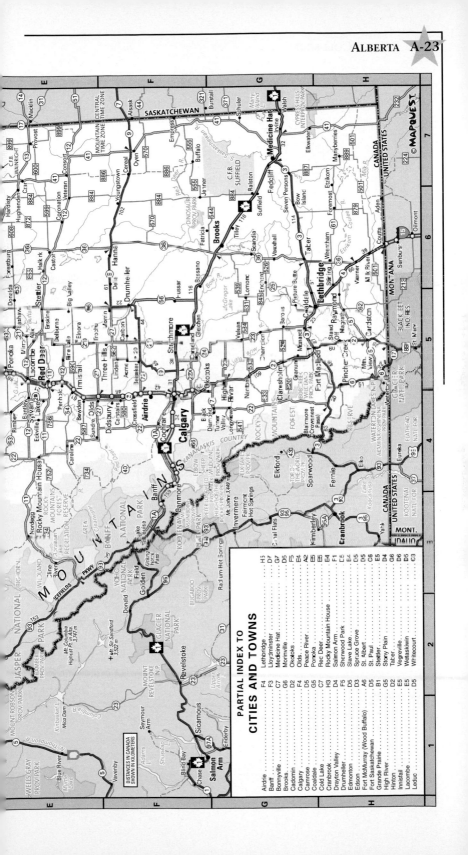

DISTANCES IN CANADA
SHOWN IN KILOMETERS

© MAPQUEST

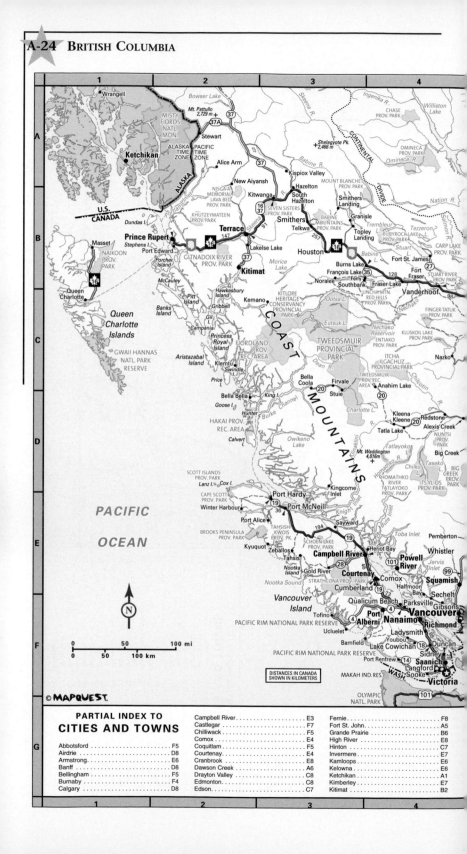

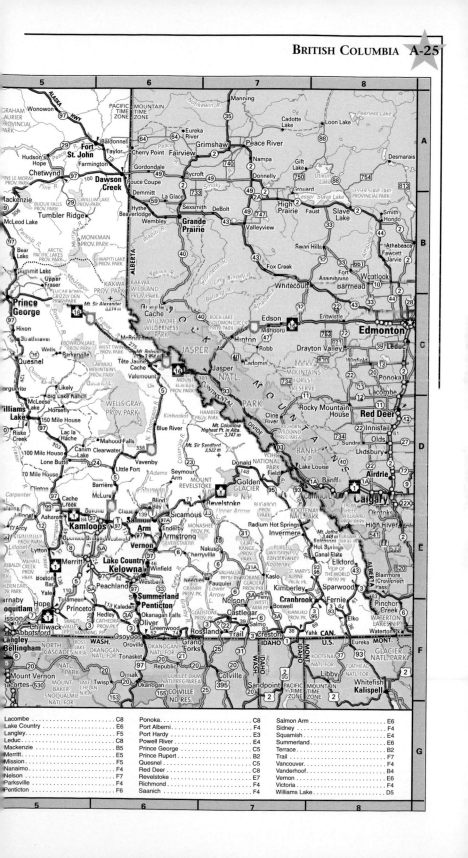

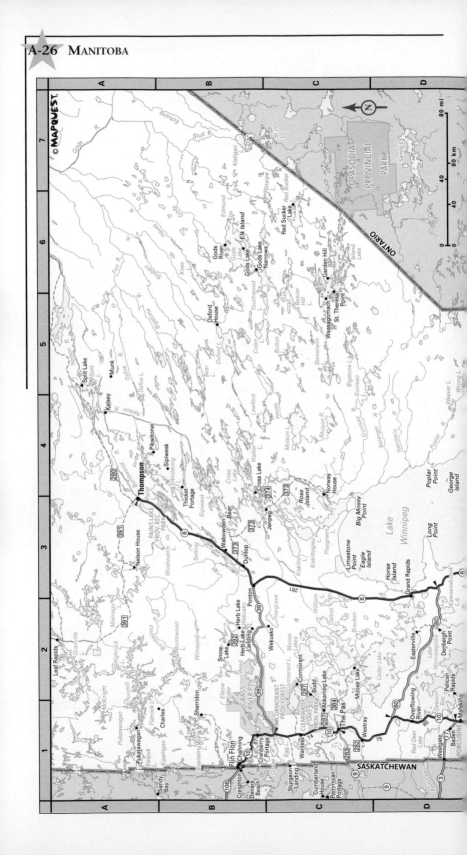

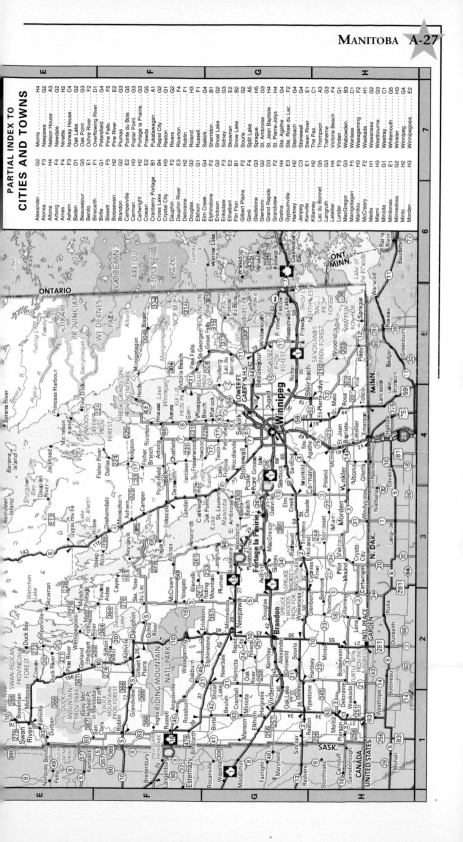

MAP LEGEND

TRANSPORTATION

CONTROLLED ACCESS HIGHWAYS

Free

Toll; Toll Booth

Under Construction

Interchange and Exit Number

Ramp
Downtown maps only

OTHER HIGHWAYS

Primary Highway

Secondary Highway

Multilane Divided Highway
Primary and secondary highways only

Other Paved Road

Unpaved Road
Check conditions locally

HIGHWAY MARKERS

Interstate Route

US Route

State or Provincial Route

County or Other Route

Business Route

Trans-Canada Highway

Canadian Provincial Autoroute

Mexican Federal Route

OTHER SYMBOLS

Distances Along Major Highways
Miles in US; kilometers in Canada and Mexico

Tunnel; Pass

One-Way Street

Airport

Railroad
Downtown maps only

Auto Ferry; Passenger Ferry

RECREATION AND FEATURES OF INTEREST

National Park

National Forest; National Grassland

Other Large Park or Recreation Area

Military Lands

Indian Reservation

Small State Park with and without Camping

Public Campsite

Trail

Point of Interest

Golf Course
Professional tournament location

Hospital
City maps only

Ski Area

CITIES AND TOWNS

National Capital; State or Provincial Capital

County Seat
State maps only

Cities, Towns, and Populated Places
Type size indicates relative importance

Urban Area
State and province maps only

Large Incorporated Cities

OTHER MAP FEATURES

County Boundary and Name

Time Zone Boundary

Mountain Peak; Elevation
Feet in US; meters in Canada and Mexico

Perennial; Intermittent River

Perennial; Intermittent or Dry Water Body

Dam

Swamp

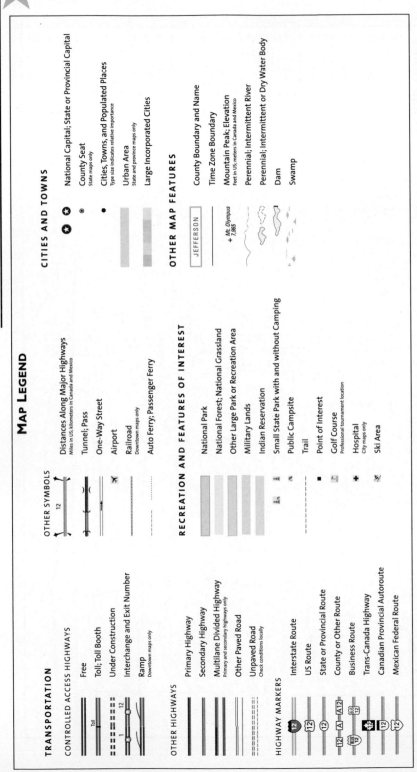

WELCOME

Dear Traveler,

Since its inception in 1958, Mobil Travel Guide has served as a trusted aid to auto travelers in search of value in lodging, dining, and destinations. Now in its 45th year, Mobil Travel Guide is the hallmark of our ExxonMobil family of travel publications, and we're proud to offer an array of products and services from our Mobil, Exxon, and Esso brands in North America to facilitate life on the road.

Whether business or pleasure venues, our nationwide network of independent, professional evaluators offers their expertise on thousands of travel options, allowing you to plan a quick family getaway, a full service business meeting, or an unforgettable Five-Star celebration.

Your feedback is important to us as we strive to improve our product offerings and better meet today's travel needs. Whether you travel once a week or once a year, please take the time to complete the customer feedback form at the back of this book. Or, contact us at www.mobiltravelguide.com. We hope to hear from you soon.

Best wishes for safe and enjoyable travels.

Lee R Raymond

Lee R. Raymond
Chairman
Exxon Mobil Corporation

A WORD TO OUR READERS

In this day and age the travel industry is ever-changing, and having accurate, reliable travel information is indispensable. Travelers are back on the roads in enormous numbers. They are going on day trips, long weekends, extended family vacations, and business trips. They are traveling across the country- stopping at National Parks, major cities, small towns, monuments, and landmarks. And for 45 years, the Mobil Travel Guide has been providing this invaluable service to the traveling consumer and is committed to continuing this service well into the future.

You, the traveler, deserve the best food and accommodations available in every city, town, or village you visit. But finding suitable accommodations can be problematic. You could try to meet and ask local residents about appropriate places to stay and eat, but that time-consuming option comes with no guarantee of getting the best advice.

The Mobil Travel Guide One- to Five-Star rating system is the oldest and most respected lodging and restaurant inspection and rating program in North America. This trusted, well-established tool directs you to satisfying places to eat and stay, as well as to interesting events and attractions in thousands of locations. Mobil Corporation (now known as Exxon Mobil Corporation, following a 1999 merger) began producing the Mobil Travel Guides in 1958, following the introduction of the US Highway system in 1956. The first edition covered only 5 southwestern states. Since then, the Mobil Travel Guide has become the premier travel guide in North America, covering the 48 contiguous states and major cities in Canadian provinces. Now, ExxonMobil presents the latest edition of our annual Travel Guides series.

For the past 45 years, Mobil Travel Guide has been inspecting and rating lodging and restaurants throughout the United States and Canada. Each restaurant, motel, hotel, inn, resort, guest ranch, etc., is inspected and must meet the basic requirements of cleanliness and service to be included in the Mobil Travel Guide. Highly trained quality assurance team members travel across the country generating exhaustive inspections reports. Mobil Travel Guide management's careful scrutiny of findings detailed in the inspection reports, incognito inspections, where we dine in the restaurant and stay overnight at the lodging to gauge the level of service of the hotel and restaurant, review of our extensive files of reader comments and letters are all used in the final ratings determinations. All of this information is used to arrive at fair, accurate, and useful assessments of lodgings and restaurants. Based upon these elements, Mobil Travel Guide determines those establishments eligible for listing. Only facilities meeting Mobil Travel Guide standards of cleanliness, maintenance and stable management are listed in the Guide. Deteriorating, poorly managed establishments are deleted. A listing in the Mobil Travel Guide constitutes a positive quality recommendation; every rating is an accolade; a recognition of achievement. Once an establishment is chosen for a listing, Mobil's respected and world-famous one- to five-star rating system highlights their distinguishing characteristics.

Although the ten-book set allows us to include many more hotels, restaurants, and attractions than in past years, space limitations still make it impossible for us to include every hotel, motel, and restaurant in America. Instead, our database consists of a generous, representative sampling, with information about places that are above-average in their type. In essence, you can confidently patronize any of the restaurants, places of lodging, and attractions contained in the *Mobil Travel Guide* series.

What do we mean by "representative sampling"? You'll find that the *Mobil Travel Guide* books include information about a great variety of establishments. Perhaps you favor rustic lodgings and restaurants, or perhaps you're most comfortable with elegance and high style. Money may be no object or, like most of us, you may be on a budget. Some travelers place a high premium on 24-hour room service or special menu items. Others look for quiet seclusion. Whatever your travel needs and desires, they will be reflected in the *Mobil Travel Guide* listings.

Allow us to emphasize that we have charged no establishment for inclusion in our guides. We have no relationship with any of the businesses and attractions we list and act only as a consumer advocate. In essence, we do the investigative legwork so you won't have to.

Look over the "How to Use This Book" section that follows. You'll discover just how simple it is to quickly and easily gather all the information you need—before your trip or while on the road. For terrific tips on saving money, travel safety, and other ways to get the most out of your travels, be sure to read our special section, "Making the Most of Your Trip."

Keep in mind that the hospitality business is ever-changing. Restaurants and places of lodging—particularly small chains or stand-alone establishments—can change management or even go out of business with surprising quickness. Although we have made every effort to double-check information during our annual updates, we nevertheless recommend that you call ahead to be sure a place you have selected is open and still offers all the features you want. Phone numbers are provided, and, when available, we also list fax and Web site information.

We hope that all your travel experiences are easy and relaxing. If any aspects of your accommodations or dining motivate you to comment, please drop us a line. We depend a great deal on our readers' remarks, so you can be assured that we will read and assimilate your comments into our research. General comments about our books are also welcome. You can write us at Mobil Travel Guides,

1460 Renaissance Drive, Suite 401, Park Ridge, IL 60068, or send email to info@mobiltravelguide.com.

Take your *Mobil Travel Guide* books along on every trip. You'll be pleased by their convenience, ease of use, and breadth of dependable coverage.

Happy travels in the new millennium!

EDITORIAL CONTRIBUTOR AND CONSULTANT FOR DRIVING TOURS, WALKING TOURS, ATTRACTIONS, EVENTS, AND PHOTOGRAPHY:

Clark Norton is a freelance travel writer and a longtime San Francisco resident who now splits his time between California and New York. He is the author of *Where Should We Take the Kids?: California* and *Around San Francisco with Kids* and has contributed to several other California guides, including *California's Best Bed and Breakfasts*. Clark has also written about traveling in California for *San Francisco Magazine, Los Angeles,* and *West.*

HOW TO USE
THIS BOOK

The *Mobil Travel Guides* are designed for ease of use. Each state has its own chapter. The chapter begins with a general introduction, which provides both a general geographical and historical orientation to the state; it also covers basic statewide tourist information, from state recreation areas to seatbelt laws. The remainder of each chapter is devoted to the travel destinations within the state—cities and towns, state and national parks, and tourist areas—which, like the states, are arranged alphabetically.

The following is an explanation of the wealth of information you'll find regarding those travel destinations—information on the area, on things to see and do there, and on where to stay and eat.

Maps and Map Coordinates

Next to most destinations is a set of map coordinates. These are referenced to the appropriate state map in the front of this book. In addition, we have provided maps of selected larger cities.

Destination Information

Because many travel destinations are close to other cities and towns where visitors might find additional attractions, accommodations, and restaurants, cross-references to those places are included whenever possible. Also listed are addresses and phone numbers for travel information resources—usually the local chamber of commerce or office of tourism—as well as pertinent vital statistics and a brief introduction to the area.

What to See and Do

Almost 20,000 museums, art galleries, amusement parks, universities, historic sites and houses, plantations, churches, state parks, ski areas, and other attractions are described in the *Mobil Travel Guides*. A white star on a red background ◼ signals that the attraction is one of the best in the state. Because municipal parks, public tennis courts, swimming pools, and small educational institutions are common to most towns, they are generally not represented within the city.

Following the attraction's description, you'll find the months and days it's open, address/location and phone number, and admission costs (see the inside front cover for an explanation of the cost symbols). Note that directions are given from the center of the town under which the attraction is listed, which may not necessarily be the town in which the attraction is located. Zip codes are listed only if they differ from those given for the town.

Driving and Walking Tours

The driving tours are usually day trips—though they can be longer—that make for interesting side trips. This is a way to get off the beaten track and visit an area often overlooked. These trips frequently cover areas of natural beauty or historical significance. The walking tours focus on a particularly interesting area of a city or town. Again, these can be a break from more everyday tourist attractions. The tours often include places to stop for a meal or snack.

Special Events

Special events can either be annual events that last only a short time, such as festivals and fairs, or longer, seasonal events such as horse racing, summer theater and concerts, and professional sports. Special event listings might also include an infrequently occurring occasion that marks a certain date or event, such as a centennial or other commemorative celebration.

Major Cities

Additional information on airports and ground transportation, and suburbs may be included for large cities.

Lodging and Restaurant Listings

ORGANIZATION

For both lodgings and restaurants, when a property is in a town that does not have its own heading, the listing appears under the town nearest its location with the address and town immediately after the establishment name. In large cities, lodgings located within five miles of major commercial airports are listed under a separate "Airport" heading, following the city listings.

LODGING CLASSIFICATIONS

Each property is classified by type according to the characteristics below. Because the following features and services are found at most motels and hotels, they are not shown in those listings:

- Year-round operation with a single rate structure unless otherwise quoted
- European plan (meals not included in room rate)
- Bathroom with tub and/or shower in each room
- Air-conditioned/heated, often with individual room control
- Cots
- Daily maid service
- In-room phones
- Elevators

Motels/Motor Lodges. Accommodations are in low-rise structures with rooms easily accessible to parking (which is usually free). Properties have outdoor room entry and small, functional lobbies. Service is often limited, and dining may not be offered in lower-rated motels and lodges. Shops and businesses are found only in higher-rated properties, as are bellhops, room service, and restaurants serving three meals daily.

Hotels. To be categorized as a hotel, an establishment must have most of the following facilities and services: multiple floors, a restaurant and/or coffee shop, elevators, room service, bellhops, a spacious lobby, and recreational facilities. In addition, the following features and services not shown in listings are also found:

- Valet service (one-day laundry/cleaning service)
- Room service during hours restaurant is open
- Bellhops
- Some oversize beds

Resorts. These specialize in stays of three days or more and usually offer American plan and/or housekeeping accommodations. Their emphasis is on recreational facilities, and a social director is often available. Food services are of primary importance, and guests must be able to eat three meals a day on the premises, either in restaurants or by having access to an on-site grocery store and preparing their own meals.

All Suites. All Suites' guest rooms consist of two rooms, one bedroom and one living room. Higher rated properties offer facilities and services comparable to regular hotels.

B&Bs/Small Inns. Frequently thought of as a small hotel, a bed-and-breakfast or an inn is a place of homelike comfort and warm hospitality. It is often a structure of historic significance, with an equally interesting setting. Meals are a special occasion, and refreshments are frequently served in late afternoon. Rooms are usually individually decorated, often with antiques or furnishings representative of the locale. Phones, bathrooms, or TVs may not be available in every room

Guest Ranches. Like resorts, guest ranches specialize in stays of three days or more. Guest ranches also offer meal plans and extensive outdoor activities. Horseback riding is usually a feature; there are stables and trails on the ranch property, and trail rides and daily instruction are part of the program. Many guest ranches are working ranches, ranging from casual to rustic, and guests are encouraged to participate in ranch life. Eating is often family style and may also include cookouts. Western saddles are assumed; phone ahead to inquire about English saddle availability.

Extended Stay. These hotels specialize in stays of three days or more and usually offer weekly room rates. Service is often limited and dining might not be offered at lower-rated extended-stay hotels.

Villas/Condos. Similar to Cottage Colonies, these establishments are usually found in recreational areas. They are often separate houses, often luxuriously furnished, and rarely offer restaurants and only a small variety of services on the premises.

Conference Centers. Conference Centers are hotels with extended meeting space facilities designed to house multiday conferences and seminars. Amenities are often geared toward groups staying for longer than one night and often include restaurants and fitness facilities. Larger Conference Center Hotels are often referred to as Convention Center Hotels.

Casinos. Casino Hotels incorporate areas that offer games of chance like Blackjack, Poker, Slot machines, etc. and are only found in states that legalize gambling. Casino Hotels offer a wide range of services and amenities, comparable to regular hotels.

Cottage Colonies. These are housekeeping cottages and cabins that are usually found in recreational areas. Any dining or recreational facilities are noted in our listing.

DINING CLASSIFICATIONS

Restaurants. Most dining establishments fall into this category. All have a full kitchen and offer table service and a complete menu. Parking on or near the premises, in a lot or garage, is assumed. When a property offers valet or other special parking features, or when only street parking is available, it is noted in the listing.

Unrated Dining Spots. These places, listed after Restaurants in many cities, are chosen for their unique atmosphere, specialized menu, or local flavor. They include delis, ice-cream parlors, cafeterias, tearooms, and pizzerias. Because they may not have a full kitchen or table service, they are not given a *Mobil Travel Guides* rating. Often they offer extraordinary value and quick service.

QUALITY RATINGS

The *Mobil Travel Guides* have been rating lodgings and restaurants on a national basis since the first edition was published in 1958. For years the guide was the only source of such ratings, and it remains among the few guidebooks to rate restaurants across the country.

All listed establishments were inspected by experienced field representatives or evaluated by a senior staff member. Ratings are based upon their detailed inspection reports of the individual properties, on written evaluations of staff members who stay and dine anonymously, and on an extensive review of comments from our readers.

You'll find a key to the rating categories, ★ through ★★★★★, on the inside front cover. All establishments in the book are recommended. Even a ★ place is clean, convenient, limited service, usually providing a basic, informal experience. Rating categories reflect both the features the property offers and its quality in relation to similar establishments.

For example, lodging ratings take into account the number and quality of facilities and services, the luxury of appointments, and the attitude and professionalism of staff and management. A ★ establishment provides a comfortable night's lodging. A ★★ property offers more than a facility that rates one star, and the decor is well planned and integrated. Establishments that rate ★★★ are well-appointed, with full services and amenities; the lodging experience is truly excellent, and the range of facilities is extensive. Properties that have been given ★★★★ not only offer many services but also have their own style and personality; they are luxurious, creatively decorated, and superbly maintained. The ★★★★★ properties are among the best in North America, superb in every respect and entirely memorable, year in and year out.

Restaurant evaluations reflect the quality of the food and the ingredients, preparation, presentation, service levels, as well as the property's decor and ambience. A restaurant that has fairly simple goals for menu and decor but that achieves those goals superbly might receive the same number of stars as a restaurant with somewhat loftier ambitions, but the execution of which falls short of the mark. In general, ★ indicates a restaurant that's a good choice in its area, usually fairly simple and perhaps catering to a clientele of locals and families; ★★ denotes restaurants that are more highly recommended in their area; ★★★ restaurants are of national caliber, with professional and attentive service and a skilled chef in the kitchen; ★★★★ reflect superb dining choices, where remarkable food is served in equally remarkable surroundings; and ★★★★★ represent that rare group of the best restaurants in the country, where in addition to near perfection in every detail, there's that special something extra that makes for an unforgettable dining experience.

A list of the four-star and five-star establishments in each region is located just before the state listings.

Each rating is reviewed annually and each establishment must work to maintain its rating (or improve it). Every effort is made to assure that ratings are fair and accurate; the designated ratings are published purely as an aid to travelers. In general, properties that are very new or have recently undergone major management changes are considered difficult to assess fairly and are often listed without ratings.

LODGINGS

Each listing gives the name, address, directions (when there is no street address), neighborhood and/or directions from downtown (in major cities), phone number (local and 800), fax number, number and type of rooms available, room rates, and seasons open (if not year round). Also included are details on recreational and dining facilities on the property or nearby, the presence of a luxury level, and credit card information. A key to the symbols at the end of each listing is on the inside front cover. (Note that Exxon or Mobil Corporation credit cards cannot be used for payment of meals and room charges.)

All prices quoted in the *Mobil Travel Guide* publications are expected to be in effect at the time of publication and during the entire year; however, prices cannot be guaranteed. In some localities there may be short-term price variations because of special events or holidays. Whenever possible, these price charges are noted. Certain resorts have complicated rate structures that vary with the time of year; always confirm listed rates when you make your plans.

RESTAURANTS

Each listing gives the name, address, directions (when there is no street address), neighborhood and/or directions from downtown (in major cities), phone number, hours and days of operation (if not open daily year-round), reservation policy, cuisine (if other than American), price range for each meal served, children's menu (if offered), specialties, and credit card information. In addition, special features such as chef ownership, ambience, and entertainment are noted. By carefully reading the detailed restaurant information and comparing prices, you can easily determine whether the restaurant is formal and elegant or informal and comfortable for families.

TERMS AND ABBREVIATIONS IN LISTINGS

The following terms and abbreviations are used throughout the listings:

A la carte entrees With a price, refers to the cost of entrees/main dishes that are not accompanied by side dishes.

AP American plan (lodging plus all meals).

Bar Liquor, wine, and beer are served in a bar or cocktail lounge and usually with meals unless otherwise indicated (e.g., "wine, beer").

Business center The property has a designated area accessible to all guests with business services.

Business servs avail The property can perform/arrange at least two of the following services for a guest: audiovisual equipment rental, binding, computer rental, faxing, messenger services, modem availability, notary service, obtaining office supplies, photocopying, shipping, and typing.

Cable Standard cable service; "premium" indicates that HBO, Disney, Showtime, or similar cable services are available.

Ck-in, ck-out Check-in time, check-out time.

Coin lndry Self-service laundry.

Complete meal Soup and/or salad, entree, and dessert, plus nonalcoholic beverage.

Continental bkfst Usually coffee and a roll or doughnut.

Cr cds: A, American Express; C, Carte Blanche; D, Diners Club; DS, Discover; ER, enRoute; JCB, Japanese Credit Bureau; MC, MasterCard; V, Visa.

D Followed by a price, indicates room rate for a "double"—two people in one room in one or two beds (the charge may be higher for two double beds).

Downhill/X-country ski Downhill and/or cross-country skiing within 20 miles of property.

Each addl Extra charge for each additional person beyond the stated number of persons at a reduced price.

Early-bird dinner A meal served at specified hours, typically around 4:30-6:30 pm.

Exc Except.

Exercise equipt Two or more pieces of exercise equipment on the premises.

Exercise rm Both exercise equipment and room, with an instructor on the premises.

Fax Facsimile machines available to all guests.

Golf privileges Privileges at a course within ten miles.

Hols Holidays.

In-rm modem link Every guest room has a connection for a modem that's separate from the phone line.

Kit. or Kits. A kitchen or kitchenette that contains stove or microwave, sink, and refrigerator and that is either part of the room or a separate room. If the kitchen is not fully equipped, the listing will indicate "no equipt" or "some equipt."

Luxury level A special section of a lodging, covering at least an entire floor, that offers increased luxury accommodations. Management must provide no less than three of these four services: separate check-in and check-out, concierge, private lounge, and private elevator service (key access). Complimentary breakfast and snacks are commonly offered.

MAP Modified American plan (lodging plus two meals).

Movies Prerecorded videos are available for rental.

No cr cds accepted No credit cards are accepted.

No elvtr In hotels with more than two stories, it's assumed there are elevators; only their absence is noted.

No phones Phones, too, are assumed; only their absence is noted.

Parking There is a parking lot on the premises.

Private club A cocktail lounge or bar available to members and their guests. In motels and hotels where these clubs exist, registered guests can usually use the club as guests of the management; the same is frequently true of restaurants.

Prix fixe A full meal for a stated price; usually one price is quoted.

Res Reservations.

S Followed by a price, indicates room rate for a "single," i.e., one person.

Serv bar A service bar, where drinks are prepared for dining patrons only.

Serv charge Service charge is the amount added to the restaurant check in lieu of a tip.

Table d'hôte A full meal for a stated price, dependent upon entree selection; no a la carte options are available.

Tennis privileges Privileges at tennis courts within five miles.

TV Indicates color television.

Under certain age free Children under that age are not charged if staying in room with a parent.

Valet parking An attendant is available to park and retrieve a car.

VCR VCRs in all guest rooms

VCR avail VCRs are available for hookup in guest rooms.

Special Information for Travelers with Disabilities

The *Mobil Travel Guides* Ⓓ symbol shown in accommodation and restaurant listings indicates establishments that are at least partially accessible to people with mobility problems.

The *Mobil Travel Guides* criteria for accessibility are unique to our publication. Please do not confuse them with the universal symbol for wheelchair accessibility. When the Ⓓ symbol appears following a listing, the establishment is equipped with facilities to accommodate people using wheelchairs or crutches or otherwise needing easy access to doorways and rest rooms. Travelers with severe mobility problems or with hearing or visual impairments may or may not find facilities they need. Always phone ahead to make sure that an establishment can meet your needs.

All lodgings bearing our Ⓓ symbol have the following facilities:

- ISA-designated parking near access ramps
- Level or ramped entryways to building
- Swinging building entryway doors minimum 39"
- Public rest rooms on main level with space to operate a wheelchair; handrails at commode areas
- Elevators equipped with grab bars and lowered control buttons
- Restaurants with accessible doorways; rest rooms with space to operate wheelchair; handrails at commode areas
- Minimum 39" width entryway to guest rooms
- Low-pile carpet in rooms
- Telephone at bedside and in bathroom
- Bed placed at wheelchair height
- Minimum 39" width doorway to bathroom
- Bath with open sink—no cabinet; room to operate wheelchair
- Handrails at commode areas; tub handrails

- Wheelchair-accessible peephole in room entry door
- Wheelchair-accessible closet rods and shelves

All restaurants bearing our Ⓓ symbol offer the following facilities:

- ISA-designated parking beside access ramps
- Level or ramped front entryways to building
- Tables to accommodate wheelchairs
- Main-floor rest rooms; minimum 39" width entryway
- Rest rooms with space to operate wheelchair; handrails at commode areas

In general, the newest properties are apt to impose the fewest barriers.

To get the kind of service you need and have a right to expect, do not hesitate when making a reservation to question the management in detail about the availability of accessible rooms, parking, entrances, restaurants, lounges, or any other facilities that are important to you, and confirm what is meant by "accessible." Some guests with mobility impairments report that lodging establishments' housekeeping and maintenance departments are most helpful in describing barriers. Also inquire about any special equipment, transportation, or services you may need.

MAKING THE MOST OF YOUR TRIP

A few hardy souls might look with fondness upon the trip where the car broke down and they were stranded for a week. Or maybe even the vacation that cost twice what it was supposed to. For most travelers, though, the best trips are those that are safe, smooth, and within their budget. To help you make your trip the best it can be, we've assembled a few tips and resources.

Saving Money

ON LODGING

After you've seen the published rates, it's time to look for discounts. Many hotels and motels offer them—for senior citizens, business travelers, families, you name it. It never hurts to ask—politely, that is. Sometimes, especially in late afternoon, desk clerks are instructed to fill beds, and you might be offered a lower rate, or a nicer room, to entice you to stay. Look for bargains on stays over multiple nights, in the off-season, and on weekdays or weekends (depending on location). Many hotels in major metropolitan areas, for example, have special weekend package plans that offer considerable savings on rooms; they may include breakfast, cocktails, and meal discounts. Prices can change frequently throughout the year, so phone ahead.

Another way to save money is to choose accommodations that give you more than just a standard room. Rooms with kitchen facilities enable you to cook some meals for yourself, reducing restaurant costs. A suite might save money for two couples traveling together. Even hotel luxury levels can provide good value, as many include breakfast or cocktails in the price of the room.

State and city sales taxes, as well as special room taxes, can increase your room rates as much as 25 percent per day. We are unable to include this specific information in the listings, but we strongly urge that you ask about these taxes when placing reservations to understand the total cost of your lodgings.

Watch out for telephone-usage charges that hotels frequently impose on long-distance calls, credit-card calls, and other phone calls—even those that go unanswered. Before phoning from your room, read the information given to you at check-in, and then be sure to read your bill carefully before checking out. You won't be expected to pay for charges that they did not spell out. (On the other hand, it's not unusual for a hotel to bill you for your calls after you return home.) Consider using your cell phone; or, if public telephones are available in the hotel lobby, your cost savings may outweigh the inconvenience.

ON DINING

There are several ways to get a less expensive meal at a more expensive restaurant. Early-bird dinners are popular in many parts of the country and offer considerable savings. If you're interested in sampling a 4- or 5-star establishment, consider going at lunchtime. While the prices then are probably relatively high, they may be half of those at dinner and come with the same ambience, service, and cuisine.

ON PARK PASSES

Although many national parks, monuments, seashores, historic sites, and recreation areas may be used free of charge, others charge an entrance fee (ranging from $1 to $6 per person to $5 to $15 per carload) and/or a "use fee" for special services and facilities. If you plan to make several visits to federal recreation areas, consider one of the following National Park Service money-saving programs:

Park Pass. This is an annual entrance permit to a specific unit in the National Park Service system that normally charges an entrance fee. The pass admits the permit holder and any accompanying passengers in a private noncommercial vehicle or, in the case of walk-in facilities, the holder's spouse, children, and parents. It is valid for entrance fees only. A Park Pass may be purchased in person or by mail from the National Park Service unit at which the pass will be honored. The cost is $15 to $20, depending upon the area.

Golden Eagle Passport. This pass, available to people who are between 17 and 61, entitles the purchaser and accompanying passengers in a private noncommercial vehicle to enter any outdoor National Park Service unit that charges an entrance fee and admits the purchaser and family to most walk-in fee-charging areas. Like the Park Pass, it is good for one year and does not cover use fees. It may be purchased from the National Park Service, Office of Public Inquiries, Room 1013, US Department of the Interior, 18th and C sts NW, Washington, D.C. 20240, phone 202/208-4747; at any of the ten regional offices throughout the country; and at any National Park Service area that charges a fee. The cost is $50.

Golden Age Passport. Available to citizens and permanent residents of the United States 62 years or older, this is a lifetime entrance permit to fee-charging recreation areas. The fee exemption extends to those accompanying the permit holder in a private noncommercial vehicle or, in the case of walk-in facilities, to the holder's spouse and children. The passport also entitles the holder to a 50 percent discount on use fees charged in park areas but not to fees charged by concessionaires. Golden Age Passports must be obtained in person. The applicant must show proof of age, i.e., a driver's license, birth certificate, or signed affidavit attesting to age (Medicare cards are not acceptable proof). These passports are available at most park service units where they're used, at National Park Service headquarters (see above), at park system regional offices, at National Forest Supervisors' offices, and at most Ranger Station offices. The cost is $10.

Golden Access Passport. Issued to citizens and permanent residents of the United States who are physically disabled or visually impaired, this passport is a free lifetime entrance permit to fee-charging recreation areas. The fee exemption extends to those accompanying the permit holder in a private noncommercial vehicle or, in the case of walk-in facilities, to the holder's spouse and children. The passport also entitles the holder to a 50 percent discount on use fees charged in park areas but not to fees charged by concessionaires. Golden Access Passports must be obtained in person. Proof of eligibility to receive federal benefits is required (under programs such as Disability Retirement, Compensation for Military Service-Connected Disability, Coal Mine

Safety and Health Act, etc.), or an affidavit must be signed attesting to eligibility. These passports are available at the same outlets as Golden Age Passports.

FOR SENIOR CITIZENS

Look for the senior-citizen discount symbol in the lodging and restaurant listings. Always call ahead to confirm that the discount is being offered, and be sure to carry proof of age. At places not listed in the book, it never hurts to ask if a senior-citizen discount is offered. Additional information for mature travelers is available from the American Association of Retired Persons (AARP), 601 E St NW, Washington, D.C. 20049, phone 202/434-2277.

Tipping

Tipping is an expression of appreciation for good service, and often service workers rely on tips as a significant part of their income. However, you never need to tip if service is poor.

IN HOTELS

Door attendants in major city hotels are usually given $1 for getting you a cab. Bellhops expect $1 per bag, usually $2 if you have only one bag. Concierges are tipped according to the service they perform. It's not mandatory to tip when you've asked for suggestions on sightseeing or restaurants or help in making reservations for dining. However, when a concierge books you a table at a restaurant known to be difficult to get into, a gratuity of $5 is appropriate. For obtaining theater or sporting event tickets, $5-$10 is expected. Maids, often overlooked by guests, may be tipped $1-$2 per days of stay.

AT RESTAURANTS

Coffee shop and counter service waitstaff are usually given 8 percent–10 percent of the bill. In full service restaurants, tip 15 percent of the bill, before sales tax. In fine restaurants, where the staff is large and shares the gratuity, 18 percent–20 percent for the waiter is appropriate. In most cases, tip the maitre d' only if service has been extraordinary and only on the way out; $20 is the minimum in upscale properties in major metropolitan areas. If there is a wine steward, tip him or her at least $6 a bottle, more if the wine was decanted or if the bottle was very expensive. If your bus person has been unusually attentive, $2 pressed into his hand on departure is a nice gesture. An increasing number of restaurants automatically add a service charge to the bill instead of a gratuity. Before tipping, carefully review your check. If you are in doubt, ask your server.

AT AIRPORTS

Curbside luggage handlers expect $1 per bag. Car-rental shuttle drivers who help with your luggage appreciate a $1 or $2 tip.

Staying Safe

The best way to deal with emergencies is to be prepared enough to avoid them. However, unforeseen situations do happen, and you can prepare for them.

IN YOUR CAR

Before your trip, make sure your car has been serviced and is in good working order. Change the oil, check the battery and belts, and make sure tires are inflated properly (this can also improve gas mileage). Other inspections recommended by the car's manufacturer should be made, too.

Next, be sure you have the tools and equipment to deal with a routine breakdown: jack, spare tire, lug wrench, repair kit, emergency tools, jumper cables, spare fan belt, auto fuses, flares and/or reflectors, flashlights, first-aid kit, and, in winter, windshield wiper fluid, a windshield scraper, and snow shovel.

Bring all appropriate and up-to-date documentation—licenses, registration, and insurance cards—and know what's covered by your insurance. Also bring an extra set of keys, just in case.

En route, always buckle up! In most states it is required by law.

If your car does break down, get out of traffic as soon as possible—pull well off the road. Raise the hood and turn on your emergency flashers or tie a white cloth to the roadside door handle or antenna. Stay near your car. Use flares or reflectors to keep your car from being hit.

IN YOUR LODGING

Chances are slim that you will encounter a hotel or motel fire. The 🏨 in a listing indicates that there were smoke detectors and/or sprinkler systems in the rooms we inspected. Once you've checked in, make sure that any smoke detector in your room is working properly. Ascertain the locations of fire extinguishers and at least two fire exits. Never use an elevator in a fire.

For personal security, use the peephole in your room's door.

PROTECTING AGAINST THEFT

To guard against theft wherever you go, don't bring anything of more value than you need. If you do bring valuables, leave them at your hotel rather than in your car, and if you have something very expensive, lock it in a safe. Many hotels have one in each room; others will store your valuables in the hotel's safe. And of course, don't carry more money than you need; use traveler's checks and credit cards, or visit cash machines.

For Travelers with Disabilities

A number of publications can provide assistance. The most complete listing of published material for travelers with disabilities is available from The Disability Bookshop, Twin Peaks Press, Box 129, Vancouver, WA 98666, phone 360/694-2462.

The Reference Section of the National Library Service for the Blind and Physically Handicapped (Library of Congress, Washington, D.C. 20542, phone 202/707-9276 or 202/707-5100) provides information and resources for persons with mobility problems and hearing and vision impairments, as well as information about the NILS talking program (or visit your local library).

IMPORTANT TOLL-FREE NUMBERS AND ONLINE INFORMATION

Hotels and Motels

Adams Mark 800 444-2326
www.adamsmark.com
Amerisuites 800 833-1516
www.amerisuites.com
AMFA Parks & Resorts 800 236-7916
www.amfac.com
Baymont Inns 800 229-6668
www.baymontinns.com
Best Western 800 780-7234
www.bestwestern.com
Budget Host Inn 800 283-4678
www.budgethost.com
Candlewood Suites 888 226-3539
www.candlewoodsuites.com
Clarion Hotels 800 252-7466
www.choicehotels.com
Clubhouse Inns 800 258-2466
www.clubhouseinn.com
Coast Hotels & Resorts 800 663-1144
www.coasthotels.com
Comfort Inns 800 252-7466
www.choicehotels.com
Concorde Hotels 800 888-4747
www.concorde-hotel.com
Country Hearth Inns 800 848-5767
www.countryhearth.com
Country Inns 800 456-4000
www.countryinns.com
Courtyard by Marriott 888 236-2437
www.courtyard.com
Crown Plaza Hotels 800 227-6963
www.crowneplaza.com
Days Inn 800 544-8313
www.daysinn.com
Delta Hotels 800 268-1133
www.deltahotels.com
Destination Hotels & Resorts
800 434-7347
www.destinationhotels.com
Doubletree 800 222-8733
www.doubletree.com
Drury Inns 800 378-7946
www.druryinn.com
Econolodge 800 553-2666
www.econolodge.com
Embassy Suites 800 362-2779
www.embassysuites.com
Fairfield Inns 800 228-2800
www.fairfieldinn.com
Fairmont Hotels 800 441-1414
www.fairmont.com

Family Inns of America 800 251-9752
www.familyinnsofamerica.com
Forte Hotels 800 300-9147
www.fortehotels.com
Four Points by Sheraton
www.starwood.com 888 625-5144
Four Seasons 800 545-4000
www.fourseasons.com
Hampton Inns 800 426-7866
www.hamptoninn.com
Hilton 800 774-1500
www.hilton.com
Holiday Inn 800 465-4329
www.holiday-inn.com
Homestead Studio Suites
www.stayhsd.com 888 782-9473
Homewood Suites 800 225-5466
www.homewoodsuites.com
Howard Johnson 800 406-1411
www.hojo.com
Hyatt 800 633-7313
www.hyatt.com
Inn Suites Hotels & Suites
www.innsuites.com 800 842-4242
Inter-Continental 888 567-8725
www.interconti.com
Jameson Inns 800 526-3766
www.jamesoninns.com
Kempinski Hotels 800-426-3135
www.kempinski.com
Kimpton Hotels 888-546-7866
www.kimptongroup.com
La Quinta 800-531-5900
www.laquinta.com
Leading Hotels of the World
www.lhw.com 800-223-6800
Loews Hotels 800-235-6397
www.loewshotels.com
Mainstay Suites 800-660-6246
www.choicehotels.com
Mandarin Oriental 800-526-6566
www.mandarin-oriental.com
Marriott 888-236-2427
www.marriott.com
Nikko Hotels 800-645-5687
www.nikkohotels.com
Omni Hotels 800-843-6664
www.omnihotels.com
Preferred Hotels & Resorts Worldwide
800-323-7500
www.preferredhotels.com
Quality Inn 800-228-5151
www.qualityinn.com

Radisson Hotels   800-333-3333
  www.radisson.com
Ramada   888-298-2054
  www.ramada.com
Red Lion Inns   800-733-5466
  www.redlion.com
Red Roof Inns   800-733-7663
  www.redroof.com
Regal Hotels   800-222-8888
  www.regal-hotels.com
Regent International   800-545-4000
  www.regenthotels.com
Renaissance Hotels   888-236-2427
  www.renaissancehotels.com
Residence Inns   888-236-2427
  www.residenceinn.com
Ritz Carlton   800-241-3333
  www.ritzcarlton.com
Rodeway Inns   800-228-2000
  www.rodeway.com
Rosewood Hotels & Resorts
                           888-767-3966
  www.rosewood-hotels.com
Sheraton   888-625-5144
  www.sheraton.com
Shilo Inns   800-222-2244
  www.shiloinns.com
Shoney's Inns   800-552-4667
  www.shoneysinn.com
Sleep Inns   800-453-3746
  www.sleepinn.com
Small Luxury Hotels   800-525-4800
  www.slh.com
Sofitel   800-763-4835
  www.sofitel.com
Sonesta Hotels & Resorts
  www.sonesta.com   800-766-3782
SRS Worldhotels   800-223-5652
  www.srs-worldhotels.com
Summerfield Suites   800-833-4353
  www.summerfieldsuites.com
Summit International   800-457-4000
  www.summithotels.com
Swissotel   800-637-9477
  www.swissotel.com
The Peninsula Group
  www.peninsula.com
Travelodge   800-578-7878
  www.travelodge.com
Westin Hotels & Resorts
  www.westin.com   800-937-8461
Wingate Inns   800-228-1000
  www.wingateinns.com
Woodfin Suite Hotels   800-966-3346
  www.woodfinsuitehotels.com
Wyndham Hotels & Resorts
  www.wyndham   800-996-3426

Airlines

Air Canada   888-247-2262
  www.aircanada.ca
Alaska   800-252-7522
  www.alaska-air.com
American   800-433-7300
  www.aa.com
America West   800-235-9292
  www.americawest.com
British Airways   800-247-9297
  www.british-airways.com
Continental   800-523-3273
  www.flycontinental.com
Delta   800-221-1212
  www.delta-air.com
Island Air   800-323-3345
  www.islandair.com
Mesa   800-637-2247
  www.mesa-air.com
Northwest   800-225-2525
  www.nwa.com
Southwest   800-435-9792
  www.southwest.com
United   800-241-6522
  www.ual.com
US Air   800-428-4322
  www.usair.com

Car Rentals

Advantage   800-777-5500
  www.arac.com
Alamo   800-327-9633
  www.goalamo.com
Allstate   800-634-6186
  www.bnm.com/as.htm
Avis   800-831-2847
  www.avis.com
Budget   800-527-4000
  www.budgetrentacar.com
Dollar   800-800-3665
  www.dollarcar.com
Enterprise   800-325-8007
  www.pickenterprise.com
Hertz   800-654-3131
  www.hertz.com
National   800-227-7368
  www.nationalcar.com
Payless   800-729-5377
  www.800-payless.com
Rent-A-Wreck.com   800-535-1391
  www.rent-a-wreck.com
Sears   800-527-0770
  www.budget.com
Thrifty   800-847-4389
  www.thrifty.com

It pays for all kinds of fuel.

Speedpass: today's way to pay. Don't go on the road without *Speedpass*. You can pay for gas at the pump or just about anything inside our store. It's fast, free, and links to a check card or major credit card you already have. To join the millions who use *Speedpass*, call **1-87-SPEEDPASS** or visit speedpass.com.

 **Mobil**

We're drivers too.

With the right gas, a kid could go pretty far.

Next time you stop at an Exxon or Mobil station, consider a new destination: college. ExxonMobil is working with Upromise to help you save for a child's education. How do you start saving? Just join at upromise.com and register your credit cards. It's FREE to join. Then when you buy Exxon or Mobil gas with a credit card registered with Upromise, one cent per gallon will be contributed to your Upromise account.* This account helps you pay for the college education of any child you choose. Contributions from other Upromise participants, like GM, AT&T and Toys"R"Us, are also added to this account.** One more thing: be sure to register the credit card you linked to your *Speedpass*. That way, *Speedpass* gasoline purchases can also contribute to your account. To get your FREE *Speedpass*, go to speedpass.com or call toll free 1-87-SPEEDPASS. Upromise is an easy way to help you save for a child's education. How do we know? We're drivers too.

Join Upromise for FREE at upromise.com
For your FREE *Speedpass*, call 1-87-SPEEDPASS
or visit speedpass.com.
You must have Internet access and a valid email address to join Upromise.
*No contributions are made for diesel fuel purchases.
** Specific terms and conditions apply for each company's contributions.
   Visit upromise.com for details.
Available at Exxon and Mobil stations that accept *Speedpass*.
©2002 Exxon Mobil Corporation. All rights reserved.

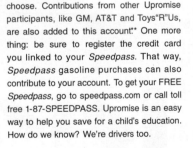

FOUR-STAR ESTABLISHMENTS IN THE NORTHWEST

Montana
★★★★ **Lodging**
Averill's Flathead Lake Lodge, *Bigfork*

Oregon
★★★★ **Restaurants**
Couvron, *Portland*
Genoa, *Portland*

Washington
★★★★ **Lodgings**
Bellevue Club Hotel, *Bellevue*
Four Seasons Hotel Seattle, *Seattle*
Woodmark Hotel on Lake
    Washington, *Bellevue*
★★★★ **Restaurants**
Brasa, *Seattle*
The Georgian, *Seattle*
The Herbfarm, *Bellevue*
Rover's, *Seattle*

Wyoming
★★★★ **Lodging**
Lost Creek Ranch, *Grand Teton
    National Park*

Alberta
★★★★ **Restaurant**
Post Hotel Dining Room, *Lake Louise*

British Columbia
★★★★ **Lodgings**
The Aerie Resort, *Victoria*
Four Seasons Hotel Vancouver,
    Vancouver
Hastings House, *Victoria*
The Metropolitan Hotel, *Vancouver*
The Sutton Place Hotel, *Vancouver*
The Wickaninnish Inn, *Victoria*
★★★★ **Restaurants**
The Aerie Dining Room, *Victoria*
Bishop's, *Vancouver*
La Belle Auberge, *Vancouver*
Lumiere, *Vancouver*
Restaurant Matisse, *Victoria*

IDAHO

When Idaho Territory was created (it included much of Montana and Wyoming as well as the present state), President Abraham Lincoln had difficulty finding a governor who was willing to come to this wild and rugged land. Some appointees, including Gilman Marston and Alexander H. Conner, never appeared.

They had good reason to be timorous—the area was formidable and still is. For there is not just one Idaho; there are at least a half dozen: a land of virgin rain forests (more than ⅓ of the state is wooded); a high desert covering an area bigger than Rhode Island and Delaware combined; gently sloping farmland, where soft Pacific winds carry the pungency of growing alfalfa; an alpine region of icy, isolated peaks and densely forested valleys hiding more lakes and streams than have been named, counted, or even discovered; an atomic energy testing station as modern as tomorrow, only a few miles from the Craters of the Moon, where lava once poured forth and congealed in fantastic formations; and the roadless, nearly uninhabited, 2.3-million-acre Frank Church—River of No Return Wilderness, where grizzly bear, moose, and bighorn sheep still run wild.

Population: 1,251,700
Area: 82,413 square miles
Elevation: 710-12,662 feet
Peak: Borah Peak (Custer County)
Entered Union: July 3, 1890 (43rd state)
Capital: Boise
Motto: It is forever
Nickname: The Gem State
Flower: Syringa
Bird: Mountain Bluebird
Tree: White Pine
Fair: Eastern, August 29-September 5, 2003, in Blackfoot; Western, August 16-23, 2003, in Boise
Time Zone: Mountain and Pacific
Website: www.visitid.org

Stretching southward from Canada for nearly 500 miles and varying dramatically in terrain, altitude, and climate, Idaho has the deepest canyon in North America (Hell's Canyon, 7,913 feet), the largest stand of white pine in the world (in Idaho Panhandle National Forests), the finest big game area in the country (Chamberlain Basin and Selway), the largest wilderness area in the United States (the Frank Church—River of No Return Wilderness), and the largest contiguous irrigated area in the United States (created by American Falls and several lesser dams). Idaho's largest county, named after the state itself, would hold the entire state of Massachusetts; its second-largest county, Owyhee, would hold New Jersey.

In addition to superlative scenery, fishing, and hunting, the visitor will find such diversions as buried bandit treasure, lost gold mines, hair-raising boat trips down the turbulent Salmon River (the "River of No

The Sawtooth Mountains, Stanley

Return"), and ghost mining towns. For those who prefer something less strenuous, Sun Valley and Coeur d'Alene have luxurious accommodations.

Millions of years ago mammoths, mastodons, camels, and a species of enormous musk ox roamed the Idaho area. When Lewis and Clark entered the region in 1805, they found fur-bearing animals in such great numbers that they got in each other's way. The promise of riches in furs brought trappers, who fought the animals, the Native Americans, the country, and each other with equal gusto. They were aided and abetted by the great fur companies, including the legendary Hudson's Bay Company. The first gold strike in the Clearwater country in 1860, followed by rich strikes in the Salmon River and Florence areas, the Boise Basin, and Coeur d'Alene (still an important mining area in the state), brought hordes of miners who were perfectly willing to continue the no-holds-barred way of life initiated by fur trappers. Soon afterward the shots of warring sheepmen and cattlemen mingled with those of miners.

Mining, once Idaho's most productive and colorful industry, has yielded its economic reign, but the state still produces large amounts of silver, zinc, pumice, antimony, and lead. It holds great reserves (268,000 acres) of phosphate rock. Copper, thorium, limestone, asbestos, graphite, talc, tungsten, cobalt, nickel, cinnabar, bentonite, and a wealth of other important minerals are found here. Gems, some of the finest quality, include agate, jasper, garnets, opals, onyx, sapphires, and rubies.

Today, Idaho's single largest industry is farming. On more than $3^{1}/_{2}$ million irrigated acres, the state produces an abundance of potatoes, beets, hay, vegetables, fruit, and livestock. The upper reaches of the Snake River Valley, once a wasteland of sagebrush and greasewood, are now among the West's most fertile farmlands. Manufacturing and processing of farm products, timber, and minerals is an important part of the state's economic base. Tourism is also important to the economy.

When to Go/Climate

Summer and fall are usually pleasant times to visit Idaho, although it can snow at almost any time of year here. The state's varied topography makes for a wide range of weather conditions. Winter temperatures are cold but not so cold as to make outdoor acitivities uncomfortable.

AVERAGE HIGH/LOW TEMPERATURES (°F)

BOISE

Jan 36/22	May 71/44	Sept 77/48
Feb 44/28	June 81/58	Oct 65/39
Mar 53/32	July 90/58	Nov 49/31
Apr 61/37	Aug 88/57	Dec 38/23

POCATELLO

Jan 32/14	May 68/40	Sept 75/43
Feb 38/20	June 78/53	Oct 63/34
Mar 47/26	July 88/53	Nov 45/26
Apr 58/32	Aug 86/51	Dec 34/16

Parks and Recreation Finder

Directions to and information about the parks and recreation areas below are given under their respective town/city sections. Please refer to those sections for details.

NATIONAL PARK AND RECREATION AREAS

Key to abbreviations. I.H.S. = International Historic Site; I.P.M. = International Peace Memorial; N.B. = National Battlefield; N.B.P. = National Battlefield Park; N.B.C. = National Battlefield and Cemetery; N.C.A. = National Conservation Area; N.E.M. = National Expansion Memorial; N.F. = National Forest; N.G. = National Grassland; N.H.P. = National Historical Park; N.H.C. = National

Heritage Corridor; N.H.S. = National Historic Site; N.L. = National Lakeshore; N.M. = National Monument; N.M.P. = National Military Park; N.Mem. = National Memorial; N.P. = National Park; N.Pres. = National Preserve; N.R.A. = National Recreational Area; N.R.R. = National Recreational River; N.Riv. = National River; N.S. = National Seashore; N.S.R. = National Scenic Riverway; N.S.T. = National Scenic Trail; N.Sc. = National Scientific Reserve; N.V.M. = National Volcanic Monument.

Place Name	Listed Under
Boise N.F.	BOISE
Caribou N.F.	MONTPELIER , POCATELLO
Challis N.F.	CHALLIS
City of Rocks National Reserve	BURLEY
Clearwater N.F.	LEWISTON
Craters of the Moon N.M.	same
Idaho Panhandle N.F.	COEUR D'ALENE, PRIEST LAKE AREA, ST. MARIE'S
Nez Perce N F	GRANGEVILLE
Nez Perce N.H.P.	LEWISTON
Payette N.F.	McCALL
Salmon N.F.	SALMON
Sawtooth N.F.	BELLEVUE, BURLEY, STANLEY
Targhee N.F.	ASHTON

STATE PARK AND RECREATION AREAS

Key to abbreviations. I.P. = Interstate Park; S.A.P. = State Archaeological Park; S.B. = State Beach; S.C.A. = State Conservation Area; S.C.P. = State Conservation Park; S.Cp. = State Campground; S.F. = State Forest; S.G. = State Garden; S.H.A. = State Historic Area; S.H.P. = State Historic Park; S.H.S. = State Historic Site; S.M.P. = State Marine Park; S.N.A. = State Natural Area; S.P. = State Park; S.P.C. = State Public Campground; S.R. = State Reserve; S.R.A. = State Recreation Area; S.Res. = State Reservoir; S.Res.P. = State Resort Park; S.R.P. = State Rustic Park.

Place Name	Listed Under
Bear Lake S.P.	MONTPELIER
Bruneau Dunes S.P.	MOUNTAIN HOME
Eagle Island S.P.	BOISE
Farragut S.P.	COEUR D'ALENE
Harriman S.P.	ASHTON
Hell's Gate S.P.	LEWISTON
Henry's Lake S.P.	ASHTON
Heyburn S.P.	ST. MARIE'S
Lucky Peak S.P.	BOISE
Malad Gorge S.P.	JEROME
Massacre Rocks S.P.	AMERICAN FALLS
Old Mission S.P.	KELLOGG
Ponderosa S.P.	McCALL
Priest Lake S.P. (Dickensheet, Indian Creek, and Lionhead units)	PRIEST LAKE AREA
Round Lake S.P.	SANDPOINT

Water-related activities, hiking, riding, various other sports, picnicking, visitor centers, and camping are available in most of these areas. Camping: $16/site/night with all hookups; $12/site/night with water; $10/site/night for primitive site. Extra vehicle $7/night. There is a 15-day maximum stay at most parks. Reservations available only at Bear Lake, Farragut, Hell's Gate, Ponderosa, and Priest Lake parks ($8 fee). Motorized vehicle entrance fee (included in camp-

CALENDAR HIGHLIGHTS

FEBRUARY

Pacific Northwest Sled Dog Championship Races (Priest Lake Area). At Priest Lake Airport. Approximately 100 teams from the US and Canada compete in various races from ½ mi to 35 mi. Phone Chamber of Commerce, 208/443-3191.

Lionel Hampton/Chevron Jazz Festival (Moscow). University of Idaho. Four-day festival hosted by Lionel Hampton featuring all-star headliners and student performers. Phone 208/885-6765.

APRIL

Cowboy Poet Festival (St. Anthony). Entertainment, clogging demonstrations. Phone South Fremont Chamber of Commerce, 208/624-4870.

JUNE

Western Days (Twin Falls). Three-day event featuring shoot-out, barbecue contests, dances, parade. Phone 800/255-8946.

National Oldtime Fiddlers' Contest (Weiser). One of the oldest such contests in the country, attracting some of the nation's finest fiddlers. Also parade, barbecue, arts and crafts. Phone 800/437-1280.

Boise River Festival (Boise). Night-time parade, contests, entertainment, fireworks. Phone 208/338-8887.

JULY

smART Festival (St. Marie's). St. Marie's City Park. Paintings and crafts by local and regional artists. Food; entertainment; swimming. Phone 208/245-3417.

Snake River Stampede (Nampa). Among nation's top professional rodeos. All seats reserved. Phone 208/466-8497.

AUGUST

Shoshone-Bannock Indian Festival (Blackfoot). Fort Hall Indian Reservation. Tribes from many western states and Canada gather for this festival. Dancing, parades, rodeo, Native American queen contest, buffalo feast, and other events. Phone 208/785-2080.

Western Idaho Fair (Boise). Largest fair in state. Four entertainment stages, grandstand for nationally known musicians. Livestock, rodeo, agricultural pavilion, antique tractors, indoor and outdoor commercial exhibits, midway rides. Phone 208/376-3247.

SEPTEMBER

Eastern Idaho State Fair (Blackfoot). Seventy-acre fairground. Livestock, machinery exhibits, four-, six-, and eight-horse hitch competition, racing (pari-mutuel betting), rodeo, tractor pull, demolition derby, parade, nightly outdoor musical shows. Phone 208/785-2480.

ing fee), $2/day or $35 annual pass; no entrance fee for persons walking, riding a bicycle, or horseback riding. All camping parks in the Idaho system feature at least one site designed for use by the disabled. Most visitor centers and restrooms also accommodate the disabled. For further information contact the Idaho Department of Parks & Recreation, PO Box 83720, Boise 83720-0065; phone 208/334-4199 or 800/VISIT-ID.

SKI AREAS

Place Name	Listed Under
Bogus Basin Ski Resort	BOISE
Brundage Mountain Ski Area	McCALL
Grand Targhee Ski and Summer Resort	DRIGGS

Lookout Pass Ski Area	WALLACE
Pebble Creek Ski Area	POCATELLO
Pomerelle Ski Area	BURLEY
Schweitzer Mountain Resort	SANDPOINT
Silver Mountain Ski Area	KELLOGG
Snowhaven Ski Area	GRANGEVILLE
Soldier Mountain Ski Area	MOUNTAIN HOME
Sun Valley Resort	SUN VALLEY AREA

FISHING AND HUNTING

Nowhere in Idaho is the outdoor enthusiast more than an hour's drive from a clearwater fly-fishing stream. From 2,000 lakes, 90 reservoirs, and 16,000 miles of rivers and streams, anglers take several million fish each year. Kokanee, trout (steelhead, rainbow, Kamloops, cutthroat, brown, brook, Dolly Varden, and Mackinaw), bass, perch, channel catfish, and sunfish are the most common varieties, with trout the most widespread and certainly among the scrappiest. Big game including whitetail and mule deer, elk, antelope, bighorn sheep, mountain goat, and black bear. There are 12 kinds of upland game birds; ducks, Canada geese, and doves in season.

Nonresident fishing license: season $53; one-day $10; each additional day $3/day; three-day salmon/steelhead $31.50. Nonresident hunting license: game $110; turkey tag $40; deer tag $240; elk tag $340; other tag fees required for some game. There are nonresident quotas for deer and elk, apply mid-December. State permit validation is required for hunting waterfowl and some upland bird species, $6.50; archery and muzzleloader permits, $9. Prices may vary; for full information contact the Idaho Department of Fish and Game, 600 S Walnut St, Box 25, Boise 83707; phone 208/334-3700 or 800/635-7820.

RIVER EXPEDITIONS

See Grangeville, Lewiston, Pocatello, Salmon, Stanley, Sun Valley Area, and Weiser. Contact Idaho Outfitters and Guides Association, PO Box 95, Boise 83701; phone 800/71-IDAHO.

Driving Information

Safety belts are mandatory for all persons in front seat of vehicle. Children under four years must be in an approved safety seat anywhere in vehicle. For further information phone 208/334-8100.

INTERSTATE HIGHWAY SYSTEM

The following alphabetical listing of Idaho towns in *Mobil Travel Guide* shows that these cities are within ten miles of the indicated Interstate highways. A highway map, however, should be checked for the nearest exit.

Highway Number	Cities/Towns within ten miles
Interstate 15	Blackfoot, Idaho Falls, Lava Hot Springs, Pocatello.
Interstate 84	Boise, Burley, Caldwell, Jerome, Mountain Home, Nampa, Twin Falls.
Interstate 86	American Falls, Pocatello.
Interstate 90	Coeur d'Alene, Kellogg, Wallace.

Additional Visitor Information

Idaho Travel Council, PO Box 83720, 700 W State St, Boise 83720-0093, publishes a number of attractive and helpful pamphlets, among them an Idaho Travel Guide. Phone 208/334-2470 or 800/71-IDAHO.

Visitor centers in Idaho are located in or near the Oregon/Idaho, Washington/Idaho, and Utah/Idaho borders, as well as throughout the state. Visitors who stop by will find information and brochures helpful in planning stops at points of interest.

THE WILDS OF IDAHO

This route begins in the Snake River Canyon and follows a series of dramatic river valleys into the very heart of the Rockies, finally climbing up to crest the Continental Divide. Lewiston sits at the junction of the Snake and Clearwater rivers, which meet beneath 1,000-foot desert cliffs. (Lewiston is the starting point for jet boat trips to popular Hell's Canyon, the gorge formed by the Snake River.) Highway 30 follows the Clearwater River east, where the valley quickly turns forested and green. This portion of the route passes through the Nez Perce National Historic Park, where several sites of mythic and historic interest to the Nez Perce people are highlighted and interpreted. As the route continues east, the valley becomes more narrow and dramatic, with small, venerable fishing resorts clinging to the rocky river bank. East from Kooskia, Highway 12 wedges into the canyon of the Lochsa River, a mountain terrain so formidable (and scenically dramatic) that completion of this section of the highway was not possible until 1962, when modern engineering and construction processes became available. This near-wilderness area is popular with experienced whitewater rafters, who are often seen on the coursing river. Near the pass into Montana, easy hiking trails lead to undeveloped, natural hot springs.
(APPROX 172 MI)

ICE-AGE LAKES AND DEEP RIVER CANYONS

This tour starts at a gold rush town at the heart of the Rockies, passes an ice-age glacial lake, and drops down through farm country to the desert canyons of the Snake River.

Stately Wallace sits in the shadows of a steep Rocky Mountain valley that contains some of the richest silver and lead veins in the world. There has been extensive industrial mining here since the 1880s, and the town of Wallace possesses one of the best-preserved Victorian town centers in Idaho. The entire town is listed on the National Historic Register. Visit the Wallace District Mining Museum, which tells the story of the region's silver boom. Then walk to the Northern Pacific Depot Railroad Museum, located in the town's lovely old depot.

A number of silver mines still operate in the Wallace area. If you're interested in what goes on underground in a silver mine, take a tour of the Sierra Silver Mine. From downtown Wallace, old trolleys drive you to the mine, where underground tours demonstrate the techniques and equipment of hard-rock mining.

Continue west on I-90 to Cataldo. The Mission of the Sacred Heart, now a state park, is Idaho's oldest building. Built by Catholic "Blackrobe" Jesuits in 1848, this simple church, constructed of mortised and tenoned beams, sits above a bluff on the Coeur d'Alene River. For decades, this was the spiritual and educational center of northern Idaho. The state park now includes a visitor center with interpretive information, picnic area, and a self-guiding nature trail.

Continue west on I-90, climbing up over Fourth of July Pass before dropping down onto Lake Coeur d'Alene, a large glacier-dug lake flanked by green-forested mountains. The town of Coeur d'Alene sits at the west end of the lake and is the center of a large resort community. The heart of Coeur d'Alene is City Park and Beach at the edge of downtown. During summer, a crush of people enjoy the sun and water here, indulging in such pastimes as swimming, sailing, jet-skiing, and windsurfing. From the marina in front of the Coeur d'Alene Resort, lake cruises depart to explore the lake. The streets behind the beachfront preserve period storefronts with good casual restaurants and shops.

From Coeur d'Alene, turn south on Highway 95 and pass through the Coeur d'Alene Indian Reservation. The landscape transforms from pine and fir forests to rolling farmland. Amid the wheat fields are more curious crops: this is the center of lentil production in the United States. Moscow is home to the University of Idaho. The compact downtown area has a pleasant alternative feel, with bookstores, coffee shops, food co-ops, and brew pubs.

From Moscow south on Highway 95, the farmland begins to fall away and the road begins to wind down the Snake River canyon. During the early settlement days, the canyon wall north of Lewiston was an impediment to transport and commerce for farms in the Moscow area. Finally in 1914, with improved engineering and technology, a road was devised that snaked down Lewiston Hill, slowly dropping 2,000 feet in 9 miles, with 64 switchbacks, to reach the valley floor. Nowadays, a freeway zips up and down the hill, but the old road is preserved as the Old Spiral Highway. Take this side road for more leisurely and scenic views onto Lewiston and the confluence of the Snake and Clearwater rivers.

Lewiston is the departure point for jet boat trips up the Hell's Canyon of the Snake River, the deepest river canyon in North America. The tours depart from Hell's Gate Park, south of the city on Snake River Avenue. **(APPROX 164 MI)**

American Falls

(G-5) *See also Pocatello*

Pop 3,757 **Elev** 4,404 ft
Area code 208 **Zip** 83211
Information Chamber of Commerce, 239 Idaho St, PO Box 207; 208/226-7214

After a party of American Fur Company trappers was caught in the current of the Snake River and swept over the falls here, the fur company gave its name to both the community and the falls. American Falls boasts an important hydroelectric plant and is the capital of a vast dry-farming wheat belt; agricultural reclamation projects stretch westward for 170 miles.

What to See and Do

American Falls Dam. Impounds 25-mi-long lake; Willow Bay Recreation Area has swimming (beaches), fishing, boating (ramp; fee); picnicking, camping (hookups; fee). I-86 exit 40, follow signs on ID 39 Bypass. Phone 208/226-7214.

Indian Springs. Hot mineralized springs, pools, and baths; camping. (May-Labor Day, daily) 4 mi S on ID 37. Phone 208/226-2174. ¢¢

Massacre Rocks State Park. Nine hundred ninety-five acres. Along the Old Oregon Trail, emigrants carved their names on Register Rock. Nearby, at Massacre Rocks, is the spot where a wagon train was ambushed in 1862. River, juniper-sagebrush area; extensive bird life. Waterskiing, fishing, boating (ramps); hiking, bird-watching, picnicking. Fifty-two tent and trailer sites (dump station). Interpretive programs; info center. Standard fees. (Daily) 12 mi SW on I-86 at exit 28. Phone 208/548-2672. ¢

Trenner Memorial Park. Honors engineer who played key role in development of area; miniature power station, fountain, lava terrace. Near Idaho Power Co plant, SW of dam. **FREE**

Special Event

Massacre Rocks Rendezvous. Massacre Rocks State Park. Reenactment of Wild West past with black powder shoots and knife-throwing contest. First wkend June. Phone 208/548-2672.

Arco (F-4)

Settled 1879 **Pop** 1,016 **Elev** 5,318 ft
Area code 208 **Zip** 83213

Arco, seat of Butte County, was the first town to be lighted by power derived from atomic energy. Wildcat Peak casts its shadow on this pleasant little community located in a bend of the Big Lost River. Visitors pause here while exploring the Craters of the Moon National Monument (see), 20 miles southwest.

What to See and Do

Experimental Breeder Reactor Number I (EBR-I). The first nuclear reactor developed to generate electricity (Dec 20, 1951). Visitor center exhibits incl the original reactor and three other nuclear reactors, equipment, and control rm, as well as displays on the production of electricity. Self-guided or one-hr tours (Memorial Day wkend-Labor Day, daily; rest of yr, by appt). 18 mi SE via US 20/26. Contact INEL Tours, PO Box 1625, Idaho Falls 83415-3695. Phone 208/526-0050. **FREE**

Ashton

(F-6) *See also Driggs, Rexburg, St. Anthony*

Pop 1,114 **Elev** 5,260 ft
Area code 208 **Zip** 83420
Information Chamber of Commerce, City Hall, 64 N 10th St, PO Box 689; 208/652-3987

Ashton's economy is centered on the flow of products from the rich agricultural area that extends to Blackfoot. Equally important to the town, which has a view of the Twin Teton Peaks in Wyoming, is the influx of vacationers bound for the Targhee National Forest, Warm River recreation areas, and Bear Gulch winter sports area. A Ranger District office of the forest is located here.

What to See and Do

Harriman State Park. Located in the heart of a 16,000-acre wildlife refuge; home of the rare trumpeter swan. Nature is the main attraction here with Golden and Silver lakes, wildflowers, lodgepole pines, and thriving wildlife. The world-famous fly-fishing stream, Henry's Fork of the Snake River, winds through the park. Historic Railroad Ranch. Hiking, horseback riding, cross-country skiing. (Daily) Standard fees. 19 mi N on US 20/191, S of Island Park. Phone 208/558-7368. Per vehicle ¢

Henry's Lake State Park. This 586-acre park offers waterskiing, boating (ramp); hiking, picnicking, 50 campsites (26 with hookups, 24 without hookups; dump station). (Mid-May-Oct, daily) Standard fees. 37 mi N on US 20, then 1 mi W; N of Island Park, on the S shore of famous fishing area, Henry's Lake. Phone 208/558-7368. Per vehicle ¢

✪ **Targhee National Forest.** Approx 1.8 million acres incl two wilderness areas: Jedediah Smith (W slope of the Tetons, adj to Grand Teton National Park) and Winegar Hole (grizzly bear habitat, bordering Yellowstone National Park); no motorized vehicles allowed in wilderness areas. Fishing (incl trout fishing on Henry's Fork of the Snake River and Henry's Lake Reservoir), big game hunting, camping (fee), picnicking, winter sports; Grand Targhee Resort (see DRIGGS) ski area. Float trips on the Snake River; boating, sailing, waterskiing, and canoeing on the Palisades Reservoir; outfitters and guides for the Jedediah Smith Wilderness. Closed Sat and Sun. Phone 208/523-3278. In the forest are

Big Springs. Source of N Fork of Snake River which gushes from subterranean cavern at constant 52°F; it quickly becomes 150 ft wide. Schools of salmon and rainbow trout can be seen from bridge. The stream was designated the first National Recreation Water Trail. Moose, deer, sandhill cranes, trumpeter swans, and bald eagles can be seen along the banks. 33 mi N on

US 20/191 to Mack's Inn, then 5 mi E on paved road.

Lower Mesa Falls. N Fork drops another 65 ft here; scenic overlook; camping. 14 mi NE on ID 47.

Upper Mesa Falls. N Fork of Snake River takes a 114-ft plunge here; scenic overlook. 18 mi NE on ID 47 on Forest Service land.

Bellevue

(G-4) See also Shoshone, Sun Valley Area

Pop 1,275 **Elev** 5,190 ft
Area code 208 **Zip** 83313

What to See and Do

Sawtooth National Forest. Elevations from 4,500-12,100 ft. Swimming, water sports, fishing, boating; nature trails, downhill and cross-country skiing, snowmobiling, picnicking, saddle and pack trips, hunting, camping. Fee at certain designated campgrounds. N and W. Contact Forest Supervisor, 2647 Kimberly Rd E, Twin Falls 83301-7976. Phone 208/737-3200. **FREE**

Blackfoot

(G-5) See also Idaho Falls, Pocatello

Founded 1878 **Pop** 9,646 **Elev** 4,504 ft **Area code** 208 **Zip** 83221
Information Chamber of Commerce, Riverside Plaza, #1, PO Box 801; 208/785-0510

Blackfoot's economy has been stimulated by the establishment of an atomic reactor center, about 45 miles west (see ARCO), and deep-well drilling techniques that have increased agricultural productivity. The town, once called Grove City, was established in anticipation of the Utah Northern Railroad's arrival on Christmas Day. Its present name is linked to a legend about Native Americans who crossed a fire-blackened range. To the south is the 528,000-acre Fort Hall Indian Reservation. Excellent Shoshone and Bannock handicraft work is available at local stores and at the tribal office in Fort Hall agency on US 91.

What to See and Do

Bingham County Historical Museum. Restored 1905 homestead of Brown family containing gun collection, Native American artifacts, early 20th-century furnishings and kitchen utensils. (Mar-Nov, Wed-Fri; closed hols) 190 N Shilling Ave. Phone 208/785-8065. **Donation**

Parks. Airport. Racetrack; picnicking, playground, golf, BMX track. **Jensen Grove.** Boating, waterskiing, paddle-boat rentals, varied water activities, disc golf, skateboard park, hockey. Airport Rd, on Snake River. Parkway Dr, ½ mi N via I-15 Exit 93.

Special Events

Blackfoot Pride Days. Late June. Phone 208/785-0510.

Shoshone-Bannock Indian Festival. Fort Hall Indian Reservation, S on I-15, Simplot Rd exit 80, then 2 mi W. Tribes from many western states and Canada gather for this festival. Dancing, parades, rodeo, Native American queen contest, buffalo feast, and other events. Phone 208/238-3700. Early Aug.

Eastern Idaho State Fair. Seventy-acre fairground, N of town. Live-stock, machinery exhibits, four-, six-, and eight-horse hitch competition, racing (pari-mutuel betting), rodeo, tractor pull, demolition derby, parade, nightly outdoor musical shows. Phone 208/785-2480. Sept.

Boise

(F-2) *See also Nampa*

Settled 1862 **Pop** 125,738 **Elev** 2,726 ft **Area code** 208

Information Convention and Visitors Bureau, 312 S 9th St, Suite 100, PO Box 2106, 83701; 208/344-7777 or 800/635-5240

Web www.boise.org

Capital and largest city in Idaho, Boise (BOY-see) is also the business, financial, professional, and trans-portation center of the state. It is home to Boise State University (1932) and the National Interagency Fire Center, the nation's logistical support center for wildland fire sup-pression. Early French trappers labeled this still tree-rich area as *les bois* (the woods). Established during gold rush days, Boise was overshad-owed by nearby Idaho City until des-ignated the territorial capital in 1864. Abundant hydroelectric power stimulated manufacturing, with elec-tronics, steel fabrication, and mobile homes the leading industries. Several major companies have their head-quarters here. Lumber, fruit, sugar beets, and livestock are other main-stays of the economy; the state's main dairy region lies to the west of Boise. Natural hot water from the underground springs (with tempera-tures up to 170°F) heats some of the homes in the eastern portion of the city. A Ranger District office and the headquarters of the Boise National Forest are located here.

Extending alongside the Boise River is the Greenbelt, a trail used for jogging, skating, biking, and walk-ing. When complete, the 22-mile trail will connect Eagle Island State Park on the west side of the city with Lucky Peak State Park on the east side of the city.

What to See and Do

Basque Museum and Cultural Center. (1864) The only museum in North America dedicated solely to Basque heritage; historical displays, paint-ings by Basque artists, changing exhibits, restored boarding house used by Basque immigrants in 1900s. (Tues-Sat, limited hrs) Phone 208/343-2671. ¢¢

Bogus Basin Ski Resort. Four double chairlifts, two high-speed quad, pad-dle tow; patrol, school, rentals; two lodges, restaurants, bar; day care. Longest run 1½ mi; vertical drop 1,800 ft. Night skiing. (Nov-Apr, daily) Cross-country trails. 16 mi N on Bogus Basin Rd. ¢¢¢¢

Boise National Forest. This 2,646,341-acre forest incl the head-waters of the Boise and Payette rivers, two scenic byways, abandoned mines and ghost towns, and access to the Sawtooth Wilderness and the

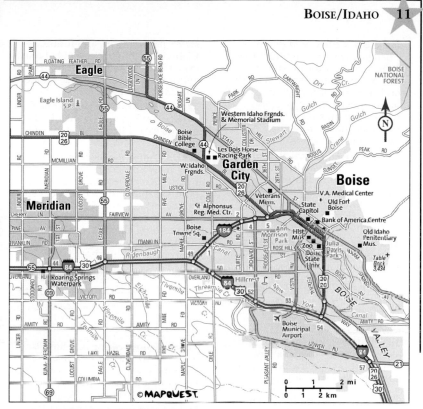

Frank Church—River of No Return Wilderness. Trout fishing, swimming, rafting; hunting, skiing, snowmobiling, mountain biking, motorized trail biking, hiking, picnicking, camping. Visitor Center. For further info contact the Supervisor, 1387 S Vinnell Way. Phone 208/373-4007.

Discovery Center of Idaho. Hands-on exhibits explore various principles of science; large bubblemaker, catenary arch, magnetic sand. (Tues-Sun; closed hols) 131 Myrtle St. Phone 208/343-9895. ¢¢

Eagle Island State Park. This 546-acre park was once a prison farm. Situated between the N and S channels of the Boise River, the park has cottonwoods, willows, and a variety of native flowers, as well as an abundance of wildlife incl the great blue heron, eagle, hawk, beaver, muskrat, fox, and weasel. Facilities incl 15-acre man-made lake (no fishing), swimming beach, water slide (fee); picnicking, concession. No pets. No glass beverage bottles. (Memorial Day-Labor Day, daily) 8 mi W via ID 20/26 to Linder Rd. Phone 208/939-0696. ¢¢

Idaho Botanical Gardens. Twelve theme and display gardens incl meditation, cactus, rose, water, and butterfly/hummingbird gardens; ¾-mi nature trail, plaza. (Daily) 2355 N Penitentiary Rd. Phone 208/343-8649. ¢¢

☑ **Julia Davis Park.** Rose garden, tennis courts, picnicking, (shelters), playground. Boat rentals, Gene Harris bandshell. Between Capitol Blvd and Broadway on the Boise River. Phone 208/384-4240. On grounds are

Boise Art Museum. Northwest, Asian, and American art featured in changing and permanent exhibits. (Tues-Sun; closed hols) 670 S Julia Davis Dr. Phone 208/345-8330. ¢¢

Boise Tour Train. Narrated, one-hr tour of the city and historical areas aboard motorized 1890s-style tour train. Departure point in Julia Davis Park. (Memorial Day-Labor Day, daily; early May-Memorial Day and after Labor Day-Oct, wkends) Phone 208/342-4796. ¢¢¢

Idaho Black History Museum.
Changing exhibits highlight the history and culture of African Americans, with special emphasis on Idaho African Americans. Lectures, films, workshops, storytelling, and musical performances. (Summer, Tues-Sun; winter, Wed-Sat) Phone 208/443-0017.

Idaho State Historical Museum.
History of Idaho and Pacific Northwest. Ten historical interiors; Native American exhibits; fur trade, mining, ranching, forestry displays. (Daily) 610 N Julia Davis Dr. Phone 208/334-2120. ¢

Zoo Boise. Home to 285 animals; large birds of prey area; otter exhibit, primates, variety of cats, petting zoo. Education center; gift shop. (Daily; closed Jan 1, Thanksgiving, Dec 25) 355 N Julia Davis Dr. Phone 208/384-4260. ¢¢

Lucky Peak State Park. A 237-acre park comprised of three units: Spring Shores Marina (boating, day use), Sandy Point (swimming beach below dam), and Discovery unit (picnicking, three group shelters, river). Standard fees. 10 mi SE on ID 21. Phone 208/334-2679. Per vehicle ¢¢

M-K Nature Center. River observatory allows visitors to view activities of fish life; aquatic and riparian ecology displays; also visitor center with hands-on computerized exhibits; nature trails. (Tues-Sun) 600 S Walnut St. Phone 208/334-2225. Visitor center ¢¢

Old Idaho Penitentiary. (1870) Self-guided tour through the cells, compounds, and other areas of the prison. Guided tours by appt (Memorial Day-Labor Day). Displays about famous inmates, lawmen, and penal methods. Slide show on history. (Daily; closed hols) Under 13 only with adult. 2½ mi E via Warm Springs Ave (ID 21) to 2445 Old Penitentiary Rd. Phone 208/368-6080. ¢¢

St. Michael's Episcopal Cathedral.
(1900) Tiffany window in S transept is fine example of this type of stained glass. (Mon-Fri, call for schedule) 518 N 8th St. Phone 208/342-5601.

State Capitol. (1905-22) Neo-classical design, faced with Boise sandstone; mounted statue of George Washington in lobby on second floor. Murals on fourth floor symbolically tell state's past, present, and future. Changing exhibits. Self-guided tours (Mon-Sat). Guided tours (Mon-Fri, by appt). 8th and Jefferson Sts. Phone 208/334-5174. **FREE**

Table Rock. Provides panoramic view of entire valley, 1,100 ft below. Road may be closed in winter. 4 mi E at end of Shaw Mtn Rd.

World Center for Birds of Prey.
Originally created to prevent extinction of peregrine falcon; scope has been expanded to incl national and intl conservation of birds of prey and their environments. Visitors can see breeding chamber of California condors and other raptors at interpretive center; gift shop. (Daily; closed Jan 1, Thanksiving, Dec 25) 5668 W Flying Hawk Ln, I-84, exit 50 to S Cole Rd, then 6 mi S. Phone 208/362-TOUR. ¢¢

Special Events

Thoroughbred racing. Les Bois Park. 5610 Glenwood Rd. Wed and Sat eves; matinees Sun. Simulcast racing yr-round (daily). Phone 208/376-RACE (7223). May-mid-Aug.

Idaho Shakespeare Festival.
Amphitheater. Repertory theater. Phone 208/429-9908. June-Sept.

Boise River Festival. Night parade, contests, entertainment, fireworks. Phone 208/338-8887. Last full wkend June.

Western Idaho Fair. Largest fair in state. Phone 208/376-3247. Aug.

Motels/Motor Lodges

★★ **BEST REST INN.** *8002 Overland Rd (83709). 208/322-4404; fax 208/322-7487; toll-free 800/733-1481.* 87 rms, 2 story. June-mid-Sept: S, D $49-$95; under 18 free; ski plans; lower rates rest of yr. Crib free. Pet accepted. TV; cable (premium), VCR (movies). Pool; whirlpool. Ck-out noon. Business servs avail. Sundries. Gift shop. Cr cds: A, D, DS, MC, V.

⬛ 🛁 🖼 🏃 🔄 🐾

★★ **BEST WESTERN AIRPORT MOTOR INN.** *2660 Airport Way (83705). 208/384-5000; fax 208/384-5566; res 800/780-7234. www. bestwestern.com.* 50 rms, 2 story. S $49-$65; D $56-$72; each addl $4; under 18 free. Crib free. TV; cable (premium). Pool. Complimentary

EXPLORING DOWNTOWN BOISE

Boise is a high-spirited city that manages to meld the vestiges of the cowboy Old West with the sophistication of the urban Pacific Northwest. The downtown core is relatively small, which makes it fun to explore on foot. There's plenty of street life and activity, and much of the late-19th-century architecture—born of a gold rush—is still intact.

Begin at the state capitol building, at Boulevard and Jefferson Street. This vast structure is constructed of local sandstone and faced on the interior with four kinds of marble and mahogany paneling. On the first floor, wander across the rotunda and gaze upward at the interior of the 200-foot dome, ringed with 43 stars (Idaho was the 43rd state in the Union). The legislative chambers are on the third floor. The Idaho capitol is the only geothermally heated statehouse in the country: water from hot springs five blocks away is pumped into the building's radiators.

From the capitol, proceed down Capitol Boulevard to Main Street. From this corner east on Main Street to about 3rd Street is a district of fine old homes—many renovated into shops and restaurants—that recalls Boise's early-20th-century opulence. Referred to as Old Boise, this street is home to the Egyptian Theatre (at Main and Capital Boulevard), an architecturally exuberant early vaudeville theater and movie palace in full King Tut drag.

One block farther west, at Grove and 8th Street, is The Grove, Boise's unofficial city center. The Grove is a brick-lined plaza with a large fountain, public art, and a pedestrian area. Summer concerts are held here, and it's the place to gather for skateboarders, cyclists, and lunchtime office workers.

Continue down Grove to 6th Street to the Basque Museum and Cultural Center (611 Grove Street). Idaho contains one of the largest Basque settlements outside of Europe, and this interesting museum tells the story of their culture and settlement in southwest Idaho. Next door, and part of the museum, is the Cyrus Jacobs-Uberuaga House, built as a boarding house for Basque immigrants in 1864.

Continue up Capitol Boulevard to Julia Davis Park, a large park along the Boise River that contains many of the city's important museums and cultural institutions. Follow the posted sign trails to the Idaho Historical Museum (610 North Julia Davis Drive), which gives an excellent overview of the state's rich historic heritage. Especially good are the exhibits devoted to Idaho native Indian history and to Oregon Trail pioneers. Immediately next door is Pioneer Village, a re-created town with vintage buildings dating from the late 19th century. Also in the park is the Boise Art Museum (670 Julia Davis Drive), with a permanent collection that focuses on American Realism.

At the center of Julia Davis Park is Zoo Boise. In addition to the traditional exotic zoo animal favorites from Africa, the zoo is home to a collection of large Rocky Mountain mammals like moose, mountain lions, elk, and bighorn sheep. Zoo Boise has the largest display of birds of prey in the Northwest. Return to the downtown area along 5th Street.

continental bkfst. Restaurant opp open 24 hrs. Ck-out 1 pm. In-rm modem link. Coin lndry. Free airport, bus depot transportation. Some refrigerators. Cr cds: A, C, D, DS, MC, V.

★★ **BEST WESTERN SAFARI INN.**
1070 Grove St (83702). 208/344-6556; *fax 208/344-7240; res 800/541-6556.* *www.bestwestern.com.* 103 rms, 3 story. May-mid-Sept: S $59; D $75; each addl $5; suites $73-$125; under 18 free; higher rates special events; lower rates rest of yr. Crib free. TV; cable (premium). Heated pool; whirlpool. Complimentary continental bkfst. Complimentary coffee in rms. Restaurant nearby. Ck-out 1 pm.

Meeting rms. Business servs avail. Free airport, RR station, bus depot transportation. Exercise equipt; sauna. Downhill/x-country ski 16 mi. Refrigerators. Cr cds: A, C, D, DS, MC, V.

□ 🦆 ♒ ✈ ⛷ 🔥

★★ **BEST WESTERN VISTA INN.** *2645 Airport Way (83705).* 208/336-8100; fax 208/342-3060; res 800/727-5006. www.bestwestern.com. 87 rms, 2 story. S $55-$75; D $65-$85; each addl $4; under 18 free. Crib free. TV; cable (premium). Indoor pool; whirlpool. Complimentary continental bkfst. Restaurant nearby. Ck-out 1 pm. Meeting rms. Business servs avail. In-rm modem link. Free airport, RR station, bus depot transportation. Exercise equipt. Some refrigerators. Cr cds: A, C, D, DS, MC, V.

□ ♒ ⛷ 🔥

★ **BOISE CENTER GUEST LODGE.** *1314 Grove St (83702).* 208/342-9351; fax 208/336-5828. 48 rms, 41 with shower only, 2 story. May-mid-Sept: S $45-53; D $50-$60; each addl $5; under 18 free; lower rates rest of yr. Crib free. Pet accepted. TV; cable (premium). Pool. Complimentary continental bkfst. Complimentary coffee in rms. Restaurant nearby. Ck-out noon. Free airport transportation. Cr cds: A, C, D, DS, ER, JCB, MC, V.

🦆 ♒ ⛷ 🔥 SC

★ **COMFORT INN.** *2526 Airport Way (83705).* 208/336-0077; fax 208/342-6592; toll-free 800/228-5150. www.comfortinn.com. 62 rms, 2 story. Apr-Oct: S $49; D $62; each addl $6; suites $62-$76; under 18 free; lower rates rest of yr. Crib $2. TV; cable (premium), VCR avail. Indoor pool; whirlpool. Complimentary continental bkfst. Restaurant adj open 24 hrs. Ck-out 11:30 am. In-rm modem link. Free airport transportation. Downhill ski 20 mi. Refrigerator in suites. Cr cds: A, DS, MC, V.

♒ ⛷ 🔥

★ **ECONO LODGE.** *4060 Fairview Ave (83706).* 208/344-4030; fax 208/342-1635; toll-free 800/553-2666. www.econolodge.com. 52 rms, 3 story. S $40-$45; D $45-$50; each addl $6; under 18 free. Crib free. Pet accepted, some restrictions. TV; cable (pre-mium), VCR avail. Complimentary continental bkfst. Restaurants nearby. Ck-out 11 am. Cr cds: A, DS, MC, V.

🦆 🔥

★★ **HOLIDAY INN.** *3300 Vista Ave (83705).* 208/344-8365; fax 208/343-9635; res 800/465-3249. www.holiday-inn.com. 265 rms, 2 story. S, D $79-$109; under 18 free; wkend rates. Crib free. Pet accepted. TV; cable (premium). Pool. Coffee in rms. Restaurant 5:30 am-2 pm; 5-11 pm. Bar noon-1 am. Ck-out noon. Coin lndry. Meeting rms. Business servs avail. Bellhops. Sundries. Free airport transportation. Downhill ski 20 mi. Exercise equipt. Cr cds: A, C, D, DS, ER, JCB, MC, V.

□ ♒ ♒ ♒ 🕊 ⛷ SC

★★ **INN AMERICA.** *2275 Airport Way (83705).* 208/389-9800; fax 208/338-1303; toll-free 800/469-4667. www.innamerica.com. 73 rms, 3 story. S $39-$49; D $45-$56; each addl $5; under 18 free; higher rates: Boise River Fest, NCAA events. Crib free. TV; cable (premium). Heated pool. Restaurant nearby. Ck-out 1 pm. Coin lndry. Business servs avail. In-rm modem link. Valet serv. Sundries. Free airport transportation. Downhill/x-country ski 20 mi. Some refrigerators. Cr cds: A, D, DS, MC, V.

♒ 🗡 ⛷ 🔥

Rafting on the Owyhee River

★★★ **OWYHEE PLAZA HOTEL.**
1109 Main St (83702). 208/343-4611; fax 208/336-3860; toll-free 800/233-4611. www.owyheeplaza.com. 100 rms, 3 story. S $79; D $118; each addl $10; suites $225-$425; under 18 free. Crib free. Pet accepted. TV; cable (premium), VCR avail. Heated pool; poolside serv. Restaurants 6 am-10 pm. Bars; entertainment. Ck-out noon. Meeting rms. Business servs avail. In-rm modem link. Bellhops. Valet serv. Sundries. Beauty shop. Free airport transportation. Downhill/x-country ski 20 mi. Balconies. Built 1910. Cr cds: A, MC, V.

★ **QUALITY INN AIRPORT SUITES.** *2717 Vista Ave (83705). 208/343-7505; fax 208/342-4319; res 800/228-5151. www.qualityinn.com.* 79 suites, 2 story, 50 kit. units. May-Oct: suites, kit. units $57-$64; under 18 free; wkly rates; lower rates rest of yr. Crib $2. Pet accepted, some restrictions; $10. TV; cable (premium), VCR avail. Pool. Complimentary continental bkfst. Restaurant nearby. Ck-out noon. Coin lndry. Free airport transportation. Refrigerators. Cr cds: A, C, D, DS, ER, JCB, MC, V.

★ **RODEWAY INN.** *1115 N Curtis Rd (83706). 208/376-2700; fax 208/377-0324; res 800/228-2000. www.rodeway.com.* 98 rms, 2 story. S $65-$70; D $70-$80; each addl $10; suites $80-$100, under 18 free. Crib free. Pet accepted; $25 refundable. TV; cable (premium). Indoor/outdoor pool; whirlpool. Sauna. Complimentary full bkfst. Coffee in rms. Restaurant 6:30 am-10 pm. Bar; entertainment. Ck-out noon. Meeting rms. Business servs avail. In-rm modem link. Bellhops. Valet serv. Free airport, RR station, bus depot transportation. Private patios, balconies. Cr cds: A, C, D, DS, MC, V.

★★ **SHILO INN AIRPORT.** *4111 Broadway Ave (83705). 208/343-7662; fax 208/344-0318; res 800/222-2244. www.shiloinns.com.* 125 rms, 4 story. S, D $79.95-$99.95; each addl $10; suites $85-$89; under 13 free. Pet accepted; $10. TV; cable (premium), VCR. Pool; whirlpool. Complimentary continental bkfst. Coffee in rms.

Restaurant adj open 24 hrs. Ck-out noon. Coin lndry. Meeting rms. Business servs avail. Valet serv. Free airport, bus depot transportation. Exercise equipt; sauna. Refrigerators, microwaves, bathrm phones; some wet bars. Cr cds: A, D, DS, MC, V.

★★ **SHILO INN RIVERSIDE.** *3031 Main St (83702). 208/344-3521; fax 208/384-1217; res 800/222-2244. www.shiloinns.com.* 112 rms, 3 story. S, D $49.95-$95; each addl $10; under 12 free. Crib free. Pet accepted; $10. TV; cable (premium), VCR (movies). Indoor pool. Complimentary continental bkfst. Restaurant nearby. Ck-out noon. Coin lndry. Meeting rms. Business servs avail. Valet serv. Free airport, RR station, bus depot transportation. Downhill/x-country ski 15 mi. Exercise equipt; sauna, steam rm. Refrigerators, microwaves. Private patios, balconies (many overlook river). Cr cds: A, C, D, DS, ER, JCB, MC, V.

★ **SLEEP INN.** *2799 Airport Way (83705). 208/336-7377; fax 208/336-2035; toll-free 800/753-3746. www.sleepinn.com.* 69 rms, shower only, 2 story. S $60; D $67; each addl $5; under 18 free. Crib free. TV; cable (premium), VCR (movies). Complimentary continental bkfst. Coffee in rms. Restaurant nearby. Ck-out 1 pm. Business servs avail. In-rm modem link. Free airport, bus depot transportation. Some refrigerators. Cr cds: A, C, D, DS, ER, JCB, MC, V.

★ **SUPER 8.** *2773 Elder St (83705). 208/344-8871; res 800/800-8000. www.super8.com.* 110 rms, 3 story. S, D $43-$67; each addl $5; under 13 free. Crib free. Pet accepted, some restrictions. TV; cable (premium), VCR avail. Heated pool. Restaurant opp 6 am-10 pm. Ck-out 11 am. Business servs avail. Cr cds: A, C, D, DS, MC, V.

★★ **UNIVERSITY INN.** *2360 University Dr (83706). 208/345-7170; fax 208/345-5118; toll-free 800/345-7170. www.universityinnboise.com.* 82 rms, 2 story. S $46.50-$65.50; D $55.50-$65; each addl $6; suites

$80-$100; under 18 free. Crib free. TV; cable (premium). Heated pool; whirlpool, poolside serv. Complimentary bkfast. Lounge. Ck-out noon. Business servs avail. Valet serv. Free airport transportation. Cr cds: A, C, D, DS, MC, V.

★★ **WEST COAST PARKCENTER SUITES.** *424 E Parkcenter Blvd (83706). 208/342-1044; fax 208/342-2763. www.westcoasthotels.com.* 238 kit. units, 3 story. S, D $99-$140; under 12 free; wkend, wkly rates; higher rates Boise River Festival. Crib free. Pet accepted; $100. TV; cable (premium). Pool; whirlpool. Complimentary continental bkfst. Complimentary coffee in rms. Restaurant nearby. Bar 5-10 pm. Ck-out noon. Coin lndry. Meeting rms. Business center. In-rm modem link. Valet serv. Free airport, RR station, bus depot transportation. Exercise equipt. Minibars. Cr cds: A, D, DS, MC, V.

Hotels

★★ **DOUBLETREE.** *1800 Fairview Ave (83702). 208/344-7691; fax 208/336-3652; res 800/222-8733. www.doubletree.com.* 182 rms, 3-7 story. S $104-$109; D $114-$119; each addl $15; suites $195; under 18 free; wkend rates. Crib free. TV; cable. Heated pool. Restaurant 6 am-10 pm. Bar 4 pm-2 am. Ck-out noon. Meeting rms. Business servs avail. Bellhops. Valet serv. Free airport, RR station, bus depot transportation. Downhill ski 16 mi. Exercise equipt. Balconies. Cr cds: A, C, D, DS, ER, JCB, MC, V.

★★ **DOUBLETREE CLUB HOTEL - BOISE.** *475 Parkcenter Blvd (83706). 208/345-2002; fax 208/345-8354; res 888/444-2582. www.doubletree.com.* 158 rms, 6 story. S $79; D $89; each addl $10; suites $165; under 12 free; wkend rates. Crib free. TV; cable (premium). Heated pool. Coffee in rms. Bar. Ck-out 1 pm. Meeting rm. Business center. Free airport, RR station, bus depot transportation. Downhill/x-country ski 20 mi. Exercise equipt. Refrigerator in suites. Opp river. Cr cds: A, C, D, DS, ER, JCB, MC, V.

★★ **DOUBLETREE HOTEL RIVERSIDE.** *2900 Chinden Blvd (83714). 208/343-1871; fax 208/344-4994; res 800/222-8733. www.doubletree.com.* 304 rms, 2 story. S, D $104-$130; each addl $15; suites $170-$395; under 18 free. Crib $10. Pet accepted, some restrictions. TV; cable. Heated pool; wading pool, whirlpool, poolside serv. Restaurant 6 am-11 pm. Bar. Ck-out noon. Convention facilities. Business servs avail. In-rm modem link. Bellhops. Sundries. Free airport, RR station, bus depot transportation. Downhill ski 16 mi. Exercise equipt. Some bathrm phones, refrigerators. Private patios, balconies. Beautifully landscaped grounds; on Boise River. Cr cds: A, C, D, DS, ER, JCB, MC, V.

★★ **PLAZA SUITE HOTEL.** *409 S Cole Rd (83709). 208/375-7666; fax 208/376-3608; toll-free 800/376-3608. www.lexres.com.* 39 suites, 4 story. S, D $95; suites $70-$200; each addl $9; under 5 free. Crib free. TV; cable (premium), VCR avail. Indoor pool. Coffee in rms. Ck-out 1 pm. Meeting rms. Business servs avail. In-rm modem link. Free airport transportation. Downhill ski 20 mi. Cr cds: A, D, DS, MC, V.

★★ **STATEHOUSE INN.** *981 Grove St (83702). 208/342-4622; fax 208/344-5751; toll-free 800/243-4622. www.statehouse-inn.com.* 88 rms, 6 story. S $90-$95; D $100-$110; each addl $10; suites $175; under 18 free. Crib free. TV; cable (premium), VCR. Complimentary full bkfst. Restaurant 6 am-10 pm. Bar 4 pm-midnight. Ck-out 1 pm. Meeting rms. Business servs avail. Free garage parking. Free airport, RR station, bus depot transportation. Exercise equipt; sauna. Some refrigerators. Cr cds: A, DS, MC, V.

B&B/Small Inn

★★ **IDAHO HERITAGE INN.** *109 W Idaho St (83702). 208/342-8066; fax 208/343-2325. www.idheritageinn.com.* 6 rms, 2 with shower only, 3 story. S $65; D $70; each addl $10. TV; cable in 3 rms. Complimentary full bkfst; afternoon refreshments. Complimentary coffee in rms. Restaurants nearby. Ck-out 11 am, ck-in 3 pm.

Downhill/x-country ski 20 mi. Built 1904; many antiques. Former home of Senator Frank Church. Cr cds: A, DS, MC, V.

Extended Stay

★★ RESIDENCE INN BY MARRIOTT. *1401 Lusk Ave (83706). 208/344-1200; fax 208/384-5354; res 800/331-3131. www.residenceinn.com.* 104 rms, 2 story. S $100-$110; D $115-$140. Crib free. Pet accepted, some restrictions; $10/day. TV; cable (premium). Pool; whirlpool. Complimentary coffee. Restaurant nearby. Ck-out noon. Coin lndry. Meeting rms. Business servs avail. Free airport, RR station, bus depot transportation. Downhill/x-country ski 20 mi. Lawn games. Refrigerators. Private patios, balconies. Picnic tables, grills. Cr cds: A, DS, MC, V.

Restaurants

★★ MILFORD'S FISH HOUSE. *405 S 8th St #100 (83702). 208/342-8382.* Hrs: 5 pm-10 pm; Sun-Mon to 9 pm. Closed hols. Res accepted. Bar. Dinner $15-$30. Specializes in fresh Northwest seafood. Outdoor dining. Former railroad freight warehouse. Cr cds: A, DS, MC, V.

★ ONATI-THE BASQUE RESTAURANT. *3544 Chinden Blvd (83714). 208/343-6464.* Hrs: 5-9:30 pm, Sat from 5:30 pm. Closed Fri; Jan 1, July 4, Dec 24. Res accepted. Bar. Dinner complete meals: $9.95-$17. Basque-style dancing. Basque artwork on display. Cr cds: A, D, DS, MC, V.

★ RICK'S CAFE AMERICAN AT THE FLICKS. *646 Fulton St (83702). 208/342-4288. www.theflicksboise.com.* Hrs: 4-9:45 pm; Fri-Sun from noon. Wine, beer. Lunch, dinner $5-$15. Specializes in grilled Italian sandwiches. Outdoor dining. Designed after Humphrey Bogart's famous cafe in Casablanca; movie memorabilia, directors chairs, hologram image. Totally nonsmoking. Cr cds: A, DS, MC, V.

Bonners Ferry

(A-2) *See also Sandpoint*

Settled 1864 **Pop** 2,193 **Elev** 1,777 ft
Area code 208 **Zip** 83805
Information Visitors Center, PO Box X; 208/267-5922

E.L. Bonner offered ferry service from this point on the Kootenai River, near the northern tip of the state, and gave this community its name. Today Bonner's Ferry services the agricultural and lumbering districts of Boundary County, of which it is the county seat. From here the broad, flat, and fertile Kootenai Valley stretches north to British Columbia. This is a scenic area featuring many lakes and streams; fishing, hunting, and hiking are popular pastimes. A Ranger District office of the Idaho Panhandle National Forest-Kaniksu (see PRIEST LAKE AREA) is located here.

What to See and Do

Kootenai National Wildlife Refuge. This 2,774-acre refuge was created as a resting area for waterfowl during migration. Its wide variety of habitat supports many species of birds and mammals, incl bald eagles. Auto tour (4½ mi). Hunting, fishing. 5 mi W on Riverside Rd. For further info contact Refuge Mgr, HCR 60, Box 283. Phone 208/267-3888. **FREE**

Moyie Falls. Park and look down into 400-ft canyon at spectacular series of plunges. Greater flow during the spring runoff. 9 mi E on US 2, then N at Moyie Springs on small road; watch for sign for overlook just E of first bridge over Moyie River.

Special Event

Kootenai River Days. June. Phone 208/267-3888.

Motels/Motor Lodges

★ KOOTENAI VALLEY MOTEL. *Hwy 95 (83805). 208/267-7567; fax 208/267-2600.* 22 rms, 2 kit. units, some with showers only. June-Sept: S

$55; D $65-$125; each addl $5; kit. units $75-$95; higher rates special events; lower rates rest of yr. Crib free. TV; cable (premium). Whirlpool. Playground. Restaurant adj 4:30 am-8 pm. Ck-out 11 am. Business servs avail. Picnic tables. Cr cds: MC, V.

★ **SUNSET MOTEL.** *2705 Canyon St (Hwy 3E), Creston (V0B 1G0). 250/428-2229; fax 250/428-2251; toll-free 800/663-7082. www.kootenay. com/~sunset/iframe/index.htm.* 24 rms, 2 story, 7 kit. units. June-mid-Sept: S $58; D $64; each addl $5; kit. units $5 addl; golf packages; lower rates rest of yr. Crib $5. Pet accepted; $5. TV; cable (premium). Heated pool. Complimentary coffee in rms. Ck-out 11 am. Refrigerators; microwaves avail. Cr cds: A, C, D, DS, ER, MC, V.

★ **TOWN & COUNTRY MOTEL.** *US 95 S (83805). 208/267-7915.* 11 rms, some with shower only, 5 kits. S $35-$60; D, kit. units $40-$65; each addl $5. TV; cable. Restaurant nearby. Ck-out 11 am. Cr cds: A, C, D, DS, MC, V.

Restaurant

★ **PANHANDLE RESTAURANT.** *230 Main St (83805). 208/267-2623.* Hrs: 6 am-8 pm; Sat, Sun from 7 am. Closed hols. Bkfst $3-$6.95, lunch $3.50-$6.95, dinner $6-$12. Specialties: chicken-fried steak, fish and chips. Own soups. Cr cds: DS, MC, V.

Buhl

(H-3) *See also Twin Falls*

Pop 3,516 **Elev** 3,793 ft
Area code 208 **Zip** 83316
Information Chamber of Commerce, 716 US 30 E; 208/543-6682

Named for Frank Buhl, an early empire builder, this community processes the outpouring of farm goods produced in the farmlands of "Magic Valley." A Ranger District

office of Nevada's Humboldt National Forest is located here.

What to See and Do

Balanced Rock. This 40-ft rock tower, resembling the mushroom cloud of an atomic bomb, rests on an 18-by-36-inch base; picnic area nearby. 12 mi SW on local roads.

Special Events

Farmers Market. Phone 208/733-3974. Last wk June-Sept.

Sagebrush Days. Sidewalk sales, arts in the park, fireworks, parade. Phone 208/543-6682. Early July.

Twin Falls County Fair and Magic Valley Stampede. 6 mi E in Filer. Carnival, 4-H exhibits, flower, art, and antique shows; RCA rodeo. Phone 208/326-4396. First wkend in Sept.

Burley

(H-4) *See also Twin Falls*

Pop 8,702 **Elev** 4,165 ft
Area code 208 **Zip** 83318
Information Mini-Cassia Chamber of Commerce, 324 Scott Ave, Rupert, 83350; 208/678-7230 or 800/333-3408

Web http:www.cyberhighway. net/~mcidcham/

Created by a 210,000-acre irrigation project that turned a near-desert area into a thriving agricultural center ideal for alfalfa, grain, sugar beet, and potatoes. Burley is a center for potato processing and has one of the largest sugar beet processing plants in the world. A Ranger District office of the Sawtooth National Forest is located here.

What to See and Do

Boating. Thirty mi of the Snake River, with constant water levels, provide great boating opportunities throughout the summer.

Cassia County Historical Museum. Railroad cars, pioneer cabins, wagon collection, other pioneer relics. (Apr-mid-Nov, Tues-Sat; closed July 4) E Main and Hiland Ave. Phone 208/678-7172. **Donation**

Needle Rock, City of Rocks

City of Rocks National Reserve. A pioneer stopping place, this 25-sq-mi area of granite spires and sculptured rock formations resembles a city carved from stone; granite walls are inscribed with messages and names of westward-bound settlers, and remnants of the California Trail are still visible. Well known for technical rock climbing, Hiking, picnicking, primitive camping. 22 mi S on ID 27 to Oakley, then 16 mi S and follow signs; or 32 mi S on ID 77 to Almo, then 2 mi W and follow signs. Phone 208/824-5519.

Sawtooth National Forest. Fishing, camping, hiking, horseback riding, snowmobiling, cross-country and downhill skiing, scenic views. Includes Howell Canyon, Lake Cleveland and four other glacial lakes. Fee for certain designated campgrounds. 9 mi E on US 30 to Declo, then 15 mi S on ID 77; other areas E and W. For further info contact the Supervisor, 2647 Kimberly Rd E, Twin Falls 83301-7976; Phone 208/737-3200. In forest is

Pomerelle Ski Area. Double, triple chairlifts, rope tow; patrol, school, rentals; cafeteria. Longest run 2.2 mi; vertical drop 1,000 ft. (Mid-Nov-Mar, daily; Apr, wkends) Night skiing (Jan-mid-Mar, Tues-Sat). 25 mi SE on ID 77, off I-84 Exit 216. ¢¢¢¢

Special Events

Idaho Powerboat Regatta. Burley Marina. Boat racers from throughout the western US compete in this American Power Boat Association's national championship series event. Last wkend June. Phone 208/436-4793.

Cassia County Fair and Rodeo. County Fairgrounds, E end of E 10th & E 12th Sts. Racing, pari-mutuel betting. Third wk Aug. Phone 208/678-9150.

Motel/Motor Lodge

★★ **BEST WESTERN BURLEY INN & CONVENTION CENTER.** *800 N Overland Ave (83318). 208/678-3501; fax 208/678-9532; toll-free 800/599 1849. www.bestwestern.com.* 126 rms, 2 story. S $59-$69; D $69-$79; each addl $6; suites $88. Crib free. Pet accepted. TV; cable (premium). Heated pool. Playground. Restaurant 6-1.30 am. Bar 4 pm 1 am. Ck-out noon. Coin lndry. Meeting rms. Business servs avail. Lawn games. Trailer facilities. Cr cds: A, C, D, DS, MC, V.

Caldwell

(F-2) *See also Boise, Nampa*

Founded 1883 **Pop** 18,400 **Elev** 2,369 ft **Area code** 208 **Zip** 83605
Information Chamber of Commerce, 300 Frontage Rd, PO Box 819, 83606; 208/459-7493
Web www.caldwellid.org

Caldwell, seat of Canyon County, is situated in the triangle formed by the confluence of the Snake and Boise rivers. Founded by the Idaho and Oregon Land Improvement Company, the town was named for the company's president, C.A. Caldwell. Livestock, diversified agriculture, and vegetable-processing plants are mainstays of the economy.

What to See and Do

Albertson College of Idaho. (1891) 800 students. Oldest four-yr college in state. Private liberal arts college.

Evans Mineral Collection, the Orma J. Smith Natural Science Museum, and a planetarium are in Boone Science Hall; Blatchley Hall houses the Rosenthal Gallery of Art (Sept-May, inquire for hrs). On Cleveland Blvd at 20th St. Phone 208/459-5500.

Ste. Chapelle Winery and Vineyards. Vineyards spread over slopes of the beautiful Snake River Valley. Reception area; tasting rm; 24-ft cathedral windows offer spectacular view of valley and distant Owyhee Mts. Half-hr tours. (Daily) 12 mi S via ID 55. Phone 208/459-7222. **FREE**

Succor Creek Canyon. Two-mi stretch of spectacular canyon scenery and interesting earth formations. An abundance of prehistoric fossils has been found here. 33 mi W on ID 19, just across Oregon line.

Warhawk Air Museum. Displays WWII aviation artifacts. (Tues-Sun; call for schedule) 4917 Aviation Way, Caldwell Industrial Airport. Phone 208/465-6446. ¢¢

Special Events

Caldwell Exchange Youth Rodeo. Second wk July. Phone 208/459-7493.

Canyon County Fair. Late July. Phone 208/455-8500.

Night Rodeo. Second or third wk Aug. Phone 208/459-2060.

Motels/Motor Lodges

★★ **LA QUINTA INN.** *901 Specht Ave (83605). 208/454-2222; fax 208/454-9334; res 800/228-5150.* 59 rms, 3 story. Mid-May-mid-Sept: S $58-$69; D $66-$74; each addl $8; suites $84-$112; under 18 free. Crib free. Pet accepted. TV; cable (premium). Indoor pool; whirlpool. Complimentary continental bkfst. Coffee in rms. Restaurant adj open 6 am-midnight. Ck-out 1 pm. Coin lndry. Meeting rms. Sundries. Gift shop. Exercise equipt; sauna. Health club privileges. Some refrigerators, minibars. Volleyball, basketball, lawn games. Picnic tables, grills. Cr cds: A, D, DS, MC, V.

D ⊸ ≈ 大 ⊠ ⊛ SC

★ **SUNDOWNER MOTEL.** *1002 Arhtur (83605). 208/459-1585; fax 208/454-9487; res 800/454-9487.* 65 rms, 2 story. S, D $42.95-$55.95; TV; cable (premium). Pet accepted, some

restrictions; $10. Complimentary continental bkfst. Restaurant nearby. Ck-out 11 am. Cr cds: A, D, DS, MC, V.

⊸ ⊠ ⊛

Challis (F-4)

Founded 1876 **Pop** 1,073 **Elev** 5,288 ft **Area code** 208 **Zip** 83226

Cloud-capped mountains, rocky gorges, and the Salmon River make this village one of the most picturesque in the Salmon River "Grand Canyon" area. This is the seat of Custer County and the headquarters for Challis National Forest. Two Ranger District offices of the forest are also located here.

What to See and Do

Challis National Forest. More than 2½ million acres of forestland surrounds Challis on all sides, crossed by US 93 and ID 75. Hot springs, ghost towns, nature viewing via trails; portion of the Frank Church—River of No Return Wilderness; trout fishing; camping, picnicking, hunting. Guides, outfitters avail in Challis and vicinity. Idaho's highest point is here—Mt Borah (12,665 ft). For further info contact the Recreation Staff Officer, Forest Supervisor Building, HC 63, Box 1671. Phone 208/879-2285. Flowing through the forest is the

> **Middle Fork of the Salmon Wild and Scenic River.** One of the premier whitewater rafting rivers in the US. Permits are required to float this river (apply Oct-Jan, permits issued June-Sept by lottery; fee). For permit info contact Middle Fork Ranger, PO Box 750. Phone 208/879-4101.

Grand Canyon in miniature. Walls cut 2,000 ft down on either side. Best seen at dusk. 10-13 mi S and SE on US 93.

Motels/Motor Lodges

★ **NORTHGATE INN.** *Hwy 93 (83226). 208/879-2490; fax 208/879-5767.* 56 rms, 3 story. S $36-$43; D $47-$57; each addl $4; under 12

free. Crib free. Pet accepted; $4. TV;
cable. Ck-out 11 am. Cr cds: A, D,
DS, MC, V.

[D] [icons]

★ **VILLAGE INN.** *US 93 (83226).*
208/879-2239; fax 208/879-2813. 54
rms, 6 kits. S $30-$45; D $42-$55;
each addl $2; kit. units $2 addl;
under 3 free. Pet accepted; $3. TV;
cable (premium). Whirlpool. Restaurant 6 am-10 pm. Ck-out 11 am.
Meeting rm. Downhill ski 7 mi; x-
country ski 10 mi. Some refrigerators.
Cr cds: A, D, DS, MC, V.

[D] [icons]

Coeur d'Alene

(B-2) *See also Kellogg, also see Spokane,*
WA

Settled 1878 **Pop** 24,563 **Elev** 2,152 ft
Area code 208 **Zip** 83814
Information Coeur d'Alene Area
Chamber of Commerce, PO Box 850,
83816; 208/664-3194
Web www.coeurdalene.com

Nestled amid lakes and rivers, Coeur
d'Alene (cor-da-LANE) is a tourist
and lumbering community, but particularly a gateway to a lush vacation
area in the Idaho Panhandle. Irrigation has opened vast sections of
nearby countryside for agricultural
development; grass seed production
is of major importance. This is the
headquarters for the three Idaho
Panhandle National Forests, and
there are three Ranger District offices
here.

What to See and Do

Coeur d'Alene Greyhound Park. Pari-
mutuel betting; clubhouse, restaurant, concessions. (Daily) 11 mi W
via I-90, at Idaho/Washington state
line. Phone 208/773-0545. **FREE**

Farragut State Park. Four thousand
acres on S end of Lake Pend Oreille;
some open landscape, heavy woods.
Swimming, bathhouse, fishing, boating (ramps); hiking and bicycle
route, cross-country skiing, sledding,
and snowshoeing in winter. Model
airplane field. Picnicking. Tent and
trailer sites (hookups Apr-mid-Oct,
dump station; res recommended).
Campfire programs; interpretive displays and talks; info center. (Daily)
Standard fees. 20 mi N on US 95,
then 4 mi E on ID 54, in Athol.
Phone 208/683-2425. Per vehicle ¢

**Idaho Panhandle National Forests—
Coeur d'Alene.** Boating, fishing;
camping (fee), cabins, picnicking,
hiking, x-country skiing, snowmobil-
ing trails. Visitors are welcome at the
Coeur d'Alene Tree Nursery, 1 mi
NW on Ramsey Rd. Contact the For-
est Supervisor, 3815 Schreiber Way.
Other national forests that lie in the
Panhandle are Kaniksu (see PRIEST
LAKE AREA) and St. Joe (see ST.
MARIE'S). Phone 208/765-7223. **Lake
Coeur d'Alene.** Partially adj to the
Idaho Panhandle National Forest.
This lake, 26 mi long with a 109-mi
shoreline, is considered one of the
loveliest in the country. Popular for
boating, fishing, swimming. Municipal
beach, picnic grounds at point where
lake and town meet. At S end of lake is

Lake Coeur d'Alene Cruises, Inc.
Makes 6-hr trip up Lake Coeur d'A-
lene into the St. Joe River (Mid-
June-early Sept, Wed and Sun; late
Sept-Oct, Sun only). Also 90-min
lake cruises (Mid-May-mid-Oct,
daily). Dinner cruises (June-mid-
Sept, Sun-Thurs). Sun brunch
cruises (Mid-June-Sept). 1115 S Second St. Phone 208/765-4000. ¢¢¢¢

St. Joe River. One of the rivers that
feed Lake Coeur d'Alene. Trout and
lovely scenery abound. Stretch
between Lake Chatcolet and
Round Lake is said to be the
world's highest navigable river.

Museum of North Idaho. Exhibits
feature steamboating, timber industry, and Native American history.
Also, a big game trophy collection.
(Apr-Oct, Tues-Sat) 115 NW Blvd, adj
to City Park, near waterfront. Phone
208/664-3448. ¢ Admission incl

Fort Sherman Museum. North
Idaho College campus. Housed in
old powder house of Fort Coeur
d'Alene (ca 1880). Exhibits incl log
cabin once used by US Forest Service firefighters. Logging, mining,
and pioneer implements are
among featured exhibits. (May-
Sept, Tues-Sat) Phone 208/664-
3448.

⭐ **Scenic drives.** Some of the most spectacular drives are S on US 97, along E shore of Lake Coeur d'Alene; E on US 10, through Fourth of July Canyon; and N, along US 95. In any direction from city.

Silverwood Theme Park. Turn-of-the-century park and village with Victorian buildings incl restaurants, saloon, general store, theater featuring old newsreels and classic movies, aircraft museum, air shows, and entertainment; adj to amusement park with rides and attractions. (Memorial Day wkend-Labor Day, daily) 15 mi N on I-95, in Athol. Phone 208/683-3400. ¢¢¢¢

Special Events

Art on the Green. First wkend Aug. Phone 208/667-9346.

Northern Idaho Fair. Late Aug. Phone 208/765-4969.

Motels/Motor Lodges

★★ **BEST INN & SUITES.** *280 W Apple Way (83814). 208/765-5500; fax 208/664-0433; res 800/228-5150. www.bestinn.com.* 51 rms, 2 story. June-Sept: S $$89; D $109; each addl $10; higher rates special events; lower rates rest of yr. Crib free. Pet accepted. TV; cable (premium). Pool; wading pool, whirlpool. Sauna. Playground. Complimentary continental bkfst. Restaurant adj open 24 hrs. Ck-out noon. Coin lndry. Meeting rm. Gift shop. Lawn games. Refrigerator, minibar in suites. Picnic tables. Cr cds: A, C, D, DS, ER, JCB, MC, V.
🄳 ⭐ ≈ ⊠ 🕭

★★ **COEUR D'ALENE INN & CONFERENCE CENTER.** *414 W Appleway Ave (83814). 208/765-3200; fax 208/664-1962; toll-free 800/251-7829. www.cdainn.com.* 122 rms, 2 story. S, D $64-$144; each addl $10; under 18 free. Crib free. Pet accepted; $10. TV; cable (premium). Heated pool. Spa. Coffee in rms. Restaurant 6 am-10 pm. Bar; entertainment. Ck-out noon. Meeting rms. Business servs avail. In-rm modem link. Sundries. Airport, RR station, bus depot transportation. Exercise equipt. Cr cds: A, C, D, DS, JCB, MC, V.
🄳 ⭐ 🔥 ⸸ ≈ 🕈 ✕ ⊠ 🕭 SC

★ **DAYS INN.** *2200 Northwest Blvd (83814). 208/667-8668; fax 208/765-0933; res 800/329-7466. www.daysinn.com.* 62 rms, 2 story. June-Aug: S $65; D $70; each addl $5; under 18 free; lower rates rest of yr. Crib free. Pet accepted. TV; VCR avail. Complimentary continental bkfst. Ck-out noon. Meeting rm. Sundries. Exercise equipt; sauna. Cr cds: A, D, DS, MC, V.
🄳 ⭐ 🕈 ⊠ 🕭

★ **FLAMINGO MOTEL.** *718 E Sherman Ave (83814). 208/664-2159; fax 208/667-8576.* 13 rms, 2 kits. May-Sept: S, D $65.50-$80; each addl $5; suites $89-$95; under 12 free; lower rates rest of yr. Crib free. TV; cable (premium). Coffee avail. Restaurant nearby. Ck-out 11 am. Airport transportation. Cr cds: A, C, D, DS, MC, V.
≈ 🕈 ⊠ 🕭

★ **HOWARD JOHNSON EXPRESS INN.** *3705 W 5th Ave, Post Falls (83854). 208/773-4541; fax 208/773-0235; toll-free 800/829-3124. www.hojo.com.* 99 rms, 2-4 story, 2 suites. June-Sept: S, D $70-$75; each addl $5; under 18 free; package plans; lower rates rest of yr. Crib $5. Pet accepted; $10. TV; cable (premium), VCR avail. Indoor pool; whirlpool. Complimentary continental bkfst. Restaurant opp open 24 hrs. Ck-out noon. Game rm. Cr cds: A, C, D, DS, MC, V.
🄳 ⭐ ≈ ⊠ 🕭

★ **MOTEL 6.** *416 W Appleway Ave (83814). 208/664-6600; fax 208/667-9446; res 800/466-8356. www.motel6.com.* 109 rms, 2 story. S $39.99; D $45.99; each addl $3; under 18 free. Crib free. Pet accepted. TV; cable (premium). Pool. Restaurant adj 6 am-10 pm. Ck-out noon. Cr cds: A, C, D, DS, MC, V.
🄳 ⭐ ≈ ⊠ 🕭

★★ **RIVERBEND INN.** *4105 W Riverbend Ave, Post Falls (83854). 208/773-3583; fax 208/773-1306; toll-free 800/243-7666.* 71 rms, 2 story. S $39; D $49; each addl $5; under 12 free. Crib free. TV; cable (premium). Heated pool; whirlpool. Ck-out noon. Coin lndry. Cr cds: A, DS, MC, V.
≈ 🕭

★★ **SHILO INN.** *702 W Appleway Ave (83814). 208/664-2300; fax 208/667-2863; res 800/222-2244. www.shiloinns.com.* 139 rms, 4 story. May-Oct: S, D $80-$179; each addl $12; under 13 free; ski plans; lower rates rest of yr. Crib free. Pet accepted; $7. TV; cable (premium), VCR avail. Indoor pool; whirlpool. Complimentary continental bkfst. Restaurant adj 6 am-11 pm. Ck-out noon. Coin lndry. Meeting rms. Business servs avail. Valet serv. Airport, bus depot transportation. Exercise equipt; sauna. Bathrm phones, wet bars. Cr cds: A, C, D, DS, ER, JCB, MC, V.

🄳 ⃠ 🛇 ⃠ ⃠ 🛇 ⃠ ⃠ 🛇 **SC**

★ **SUPER 8 MOTEL.** *505 W Appleway Ave (83814). 208/765-8880; res 800/800-8000. www.super8.com.* 95 units, 3 story. June-Sept: S $36-$60; D $43-$68; each addl $5; suites $48-$73; under 12 free; wkly rates winter; lower rates rest of yr. Crib free. Pet accepted. TV; cable (premium), VCR avail. Complimentary coffee. Ck-out 11 am. Cr cds: A, C, D, DS, JCB, MC, V.

🄳 🛇 ⃠ 🛇 **SC**

★★ **WESTCOAST TEMPLIN'S RESORT.** *414 E 1st Ave, Post Falls (83854). 208/773-1611; fax 208/773-4192; toll-free 800/325-4000. www.westcoasthotels.com.* 167 rms, 2-3 story. May-mid-Sept: S $93-$112; D $100-$121; each addl $15; suites $119-$269; under 12 free; lower rates rest of yr. Crib $10. Pet accepted, some restrictions. TV; cable (premium). Indoor pool. Restaurant 6 am-10 pm. Bar 10 pm-1 am; entertainment. Ck-out noon. Meeting rms. Business servs avail. In-rm modem link. Airport transportation. Tennis. Exercise equipt; sauna. Lawn games. Some refrigerators. Private patios, balconies. Picnic tables. On river; marina, guest docking, boat rentals. Cr cds: A, D, DS, MC, V.

🄳 🛇 ⃠ 🛇 ⃠ 🛇 🛇

Resort

★★★ **THE COEUR D'ALENE - A RESORT ON THE LAKE.** *115 S 2nd St (83814). 208/765-4000; fax 208/664-7276. www.cdaresort.com.* 336 rms, 18 story. Mid-June-Sept: S,

D $150-$390; each addl $10; suites $600-$2,500; under 18 free; lower rates rest of yr. Crib free. TV; cable (premium), 2 heated pools, 1 indoor; wading pool, whirlpool, poolside serv. Playground adj. Supervised children's activities. Restaurants (see also BEVERLY'S). Bars; entertainment. Ck-out noon, ck-in after 4 pm. Convention facilities. Business center. Valet serv. Shopping arcade. Airport, bus depot transportation. Tennis. 18-hole golf. Marina. Boat rentals. Tour boats. Seaplane rides. X-country ski on site. Bowling. Exercise rm; sauna, steam rm. Massage. Spa. Refrigerators. Balconies. Atrium areas. Cr cds: A, D, DS, MC, V.

🄳 🛇 ⃠ 🛇 ⃠ 🛇 ⃠ 🛇 ⃠ 🛇 🛇

B&B/Small Inn

★★ **THE ROOSEVELT.** *105 E Wallace Ave (83814). 208/765-5200; fax 208/664-4142; res 800/290-3358. www.therooseveltinn.com.* 16 rms, 4 story, 4 suites. May-Oct: S $99; D $175; each addl $20; suites $199-$249; package plans; lower rates rest of yr. Children over 6 yrs only. TV in common rm; VCR avail. Complimentary full bkfst; afternoon refreshments. Ck-out noon, ck-in 3 pm. Street parking. Downhill ski 20 mi; x-country ski 1 mi. Built in 1905; was an old elementary school named after Theodore Roosevelt. Totally nonsmoking. Cr cds: A, DS, MC, V.

🛇 🛇 🛇

Restaurants

★★★ **BEVERLY'S.** *115 S 2nd St (83816). 208/765-4000. www.cdaresort.com.* Hrs: 11 am-10 pm; Sun from 5 pm. Res accepted. Northwestern cuisine. Bar. Wine cellar. A la carte entrees: lunch $8.95-$15.95, dinner $19.95-$29.95. Child's menu. Specialties: broiled salmon with shitake mushrooms, rack of lamb, tenderloin of beef. Cr cds: A, D, DS, MC, V.

🄳

★ **IRON HORSE.** *407 Sherman Ave (83814). 208/667-7314.* Hrs: 7 am-10 pm; Sat from 8 am; Sun 9 am-9 pm. Closed Jan 1, Dec 25. Bar 11-2 am. Bkfst $3.65-$7.95, lunch $4.75-

$10.95, dinner $6.95-$25.95. Children's meals. Specializes in prime rib, burgers. Outdoor dining. RR train decor. Cr cds: MC, V.

SC

★★ **JIMMY D'S CAFE.** *320 Sherman Ave (83814). 208/664-9774. www.jimmyds.com.* Hrs: 11 am-10 pm. Closed Jan 1, Thanksgiving, Dec 25. Bar. Bkfst, lunch $6-$8.95, dinner $9.95-$19.95. Specializes in fresh seafood, steaks. Outdoor dining. Sidewalk cafe atmosphere. Cr cds: A, DS, MC, V.

D

Craters of the Moon National Monument

(18 mi SW of Arco on US 20/26/93)

So named because it resembles the surface of the moon as seen through a telescope, this 83-square-mile monument has spectacular lava flows, cinder cones, and other volcanic creations. Geologists believe a weak spot in the earth's crust permitted outbursts of lava at least eight times during the last 15,000 years. These eruptions produced the lava flows, the 25 cinder cones, spatter cones, lava tubes, natural bridges, and tree molds within the monument. Geological and historical exhibits are on display at the visitor center (Daily; closed winter hols). Autos may follow the seven-mile loop drive; closed by snow in winter. Interpretive programs of nature walks, campfire talks (Mid-June-Labor Day). Campground (no hookups) near entrance (Mid-May-Oct; fee). Golden Eagle, Golden Age, Golden Access passports accepted (see MAKING THE MOST OF YOUR TRIP). For further information contact PO Box 29, Arco 83213; 208/527-3257. Per vehicle ¢¢

Driggs

(F-6) *See also Ashton, Rexburg, St. Anthony*

Pop 846 **Elev** 6,116 ft **Area code** 208 **Zip** 83422

A Ranger District office of the Targhee National Forest (see ASHTON) is located here.

What to See and Do

Grand Targhee Ski and Summer Resort. Three chairlifts, surface lift; patrol, school, rentals; three lodges, three restaurants, cafeteria, bar; nursery; hot tubs, heated outdoor pool. Longest run 2.7 mi; vertical drop 2,200 ft. (Mid-Nov-early Apr, daily) Second mountain for powder skiing only. Cross-country trails; snowboard half-pipe. Summer activities incl fishing, rafting; horseback riding, biking, hiking, golf, tennis, music festivals (July-Aug); chairlift rides (June-Aug, daily). Half-day rates. 12 mi E on county road, in Alta, WY. Phone 307/353-2300. ¢¢¢¢¢

Motels/Motor Lodges

★★ **BEST WESTERN TETON WEST.** *476 N Main St (83422). 208/354-2363; fax 208/354-2962; res 800/780-7234. www.bestwestern.com.* 42 rms, 2 story, 2 kits. S $49-$79; D $59-$89; each addl $4; kit. units $100; under 12 free; ski plans. Crib $4. TV; cable (premium). Indoor pool; whirlpool. Complimentary continental bkfst. Restaurant nearby. Ck-out noon. Meeting rm. Downhill ski 10 mi; x-country ski 5 mi. Cr cds: A, C, D, DS, MC, V.

D

★ **INTERMOUNTAIN LODGE.** *34 Ski Hill Rd (98403). 208/354-8153.* 20 rms. Dec-Jan, July-Sept: S, D $49-$69; each addl $5; lower rates rest of yr. Crib avail. TV; VCR avail. Complimentary coffee in lobby. Ck-out 11 am. Coin lndry. Downhill/x-country ski 10 mi. Whirlpool. Picnic tables. Totally nonsmoking. Cr cds: A, DS, MC, V.

D

★ **SUPER 8 TETON WEST.** *133 State Hwy 33 (83422). 208/354-8888; fax*

208/354-2962; res 800/800-8000. www.
super8.com. 46 rms, 2 story. Mid-
June-mid-Sept: S, D $48-$70; under
12 free; higher rates wk of Dec 25;
lower rates rest of yr. Crib avail. TV;
cable (premium). Pool; whirlpool.
Complimentary continental bkfst.
Ck-out noon. Coin lndry. Down-
hill/x-country ski 13 mi. Refrigerators, microwaves. Cr cds: A, C, DS,
MC, V.

★ **TETON MOUNTAIN VIEW
LODGE.** 510 Egbert Ave, Tetonia
(83452). 208/456-2741; fax 208/456-
2232; res 800/625-2232. www.teton
mountainlodge.com. 24 rms, 10 with
shower only, 2 story. July-Sept: S
$79.95, D $89.95; each addl $5; suite
$109.95; under 16 free; wkly rates;
lower rates rest of yr. Crib free. Pet
accepted, some restrictions. TV;
cable. Complimentary continental
bkfst. Restaurant nearby. Ck-out noon.
Whirlpool. Cr cds: A, DS, MC, V.

Resort

★★★ **GRAND TARGHEE.** 3300 E
Ski Hill Rd, Alta (83342). 307/353-
2300; fax 307/353-8148; toll-free
800/827-4433. www.grandtarghee.com.
96 rms, 1 1 story, 32 kit. units. Late
Nov-late Apr: S, D $103-$200; kit.
units $150-$398; ski plans; lower
rates June-Sept. Closed rest of yr.
Crib free. TV, VCR avail (movies).
Heated pool; whirlpools. Supervised
children's activities, ages 6-12. Complimentary coffee in rms. Dining rms
7:30 am-9 pm. Box lunches. Picnics.
Bar 11:30 am-10 pm; entertainment.
Ck-out 11 am, ck-in 4 pm. Grocery.
Coin lndry. Package store. Meeting
rms. Business servs avail. Concierge.
Gift shops. Airport transportation.
Tennis. Downhill/x-country ski on
site (rentals). Dogsled rides (winter).
Horse stables. Hiking. Rec rm. Game
rm. Child day care (2 months-5 yr).
Exercise equipt; sauna. Spa. Bal-
conies. Picnic tables. In Targhee
National Forest, adj to Grand Teton
National Park. Cr cds: A, DS, MC, V.

Guest Ranch

★★★ **TETON RIDGE RANCH.** 200
Valley View Rd, Tetonia (83452). 208/
456-2650; fax 208/456-2218. 7 units.
June-Oct, AP: S $435; D $550; each
addl $125; lower rates rest of yr.
Closed Nov-mid-Dec, Apr-May. Chil-
dren over 12 yrs only. Pet accepted,
some restrictions. TV in public rms;
cable (premium). Box lunches.
Setups. Ck-out, ck-in noon. Grocery.
Guest lndry. Package store 9 mi.
Meeting rms. Airport transportation.
Downhill ski 20 mi; x-country ski on
site. Sleighing. Horse stables. Hiking.
Mountain bikes (rentals). Rec rm.
Fishing/hunting guides, clean and
store. Balconies. Secluded mountain
valley ranch situated on west side of
Grand Tetons. Cr cds: MC, V.

Fort Hall (G-5)

(see Blackfoot)

Grangeville (D-2)

Founded 1876 **Pop** 3,226 **Elev** 3,390
ft **Area code** 208 **Zip** 83530
Information Chamber of Commerce,
US 95 & Pine St, PO Box 212;
208/983-0460

Grangeville is a light industry and
agricultural community. It was a
focal point in the Nez Perce Indian
War and a gold rush town in the
1890s when rich ore was found in
the Florence Basin and the Elk City
areas. The seat of Idaho County, it is
also the gateway to several wilderness areas. The headquarters and two
Ranger District offices of the Nez
Perce National Forest are located
here.

What to See and Do

**Hell's Canyon National Recreation
Area.** Created by the Snake River, at
the Idaho/Oregon border, Hell's
Canyon is the deepest gorge in

North America—1½ mi from He Devil Mt (elevation 9,393 ft) to the Snake River at Granite Creek (elevation 1,408 ft). Overlooks at Heaven's Gate, W of Riggins, and in Oregon (see JOSEPH, OR). The recreation area incl parts of the Nez Perce and Payette National Forests in Idaho and the Wallowa-Whitman National Forest in Oregon. Activities incl float trips, jet boat tours; auto tours, backpacking, and horseback riding; boat trips into canyon from Lewiston, Grangeville, and Riggins, also via Pittsburg Landing or the Hell's Canyon Dam (see WEISER). Developed campgrounds in Oregon and Idaho; much of the area is undeveloped, some is designated wilderness. Be sure to inquire about road conditions before planning a trip; some roads are rough and open for a limited season. Access approx 16 mi S on US 95 to White Bird, then W on County 493 to Pittsburg Landing; access also from Riggins, from US 95 take Rd 241 (Race Creek) N of Riggins; paved access via ID 71 from Cambridge (see WEISER). For further information contact Hell's Canyon National Recreation Area, 88401 Hwy 82, Enterprise, OR 97828. Phone 541/426-4978; or 2535 Riverside Dr, Box 699, Clarkston, WA 99403, phone 509/758-0616. For river information and float res, phone 509/758-1957.

🟦 **Nez Perce National Forest.** More than 2.2 million acres with excellent fishing; camping, cabins (fee at some campgrounds), picnicking, cross-country skiing, and snowmobiling. The Salmon (the River of No Return), Selway, South Fork Clearwater, and Snake rivers, all classified as wild and scenic, flow through or are adj to the forest. Pack and float trips are avail; contact the Idaho Outfitters and Guides Assn, PO Box 95, Boise 83701; Phone 208/342-1438. High elevations are open only in summer and fall; low elevations are open Mar-Nov. For further info contact Office of Information, Rte 2, Box 475. S on US 95. Phone 208/983-1950.

Snowhaven. T-bar, rope tow; patrol, school, rentals; cafeteria. Vertical drop 400 ft. (Dec-early Mar, Fri-Sun) Night skiing; half-day rates. 7 mi SE via Fish Creek Rd. Phone 208/983-3866.

White Bird Hill. Site of the famous Whitebird Battle of the Nez Perce Indian Wars. View of Camas Prairie, canyons, mountains, and Seven Devils Peaks. Self-guided tour brochures avail from Chamber of Commerce. 5 mi S on US 95. Phone 208/983-0460.

Special Events

Border Days. Three-day rodeo and parades, dances. Art-in-the-park; food. Phone 208/983-0460. July 4 wkend.

Oktubberfest. Three-day event features tub races on Main St, arts and crafts, street dance, entertainment. Last wkend Sept. Phone 208/983-0460.

Idaho City

(F-2) *See also Boise*

Settled 1862 **Pop** 322 **Elev** 3,906 ft
Area code 208 **Zip** 83631
Information Chamber of Commerce, PO Box 70; 208/392-4148

Flecks of gold persist in the gravel beneath most of Idaho City, and the community is steeped in gold rush lore. From the 18-square-mile Boise Basin, said to have produced more gold than all of Alaska, Idaho City's fame once spread far and wide. Idaho City also is home to the state's first Pioneer Lodge (established 1864) and the birthplace of the Grand Lodge of Idaho (established 1867).

What to See and Do

Boise Basin Museum. (1867) Restored bldg houses artifacts of gold rush era. Walking tours of Idaho City avail (fee). (Memorial Day-Labor Day, daily; May and Sept, wkends only; rest of yr, by appt) Montgomery and Wall Sts. Phone 208/392-4550. ¢

Boise National Forest. Surrounding area. Fishing, hunting, swimming; camping, skiing, and snowmobiling. A Ranger District office of the forest is located here. Contact the Supervisor, 1750 Front St, Boise 83702.

Boot Hill. Restored 40-acre cemetery, last resting place of many gunfight victims. Phone 208/392-4148.

Gold Hill. Rich Boise Basin placer ground. 1 mi N on Main St. Phone 208/392-4148.

Idaho Falls

(G-5) *See also Blackfoot, Pocatello, Rexburg*

Pop 43,929 **Elev** 4,710 ft
Area code 208
Information Chamber of Commerce, 505 Lindsay Blvd, PO Box 50498, 83405, 208/523-1010 or 800/634-3246

An industrial, transportation, and trading center in the upper Snake River Valley, Idaho Falls is a center of potato production and headquarters for the Idaho Operations Office of the Department of Energy. The Idaho National Engineering Laboratory is located on the Lost River Plains, 30 miles west on US 20. Potato processing is important; stockyards here are the state's largest; and one of the nation's leading safety research centers for nuclear reactors is located here. A Ranger District office of Targhee National Forest (see ASHTON) is also in Idaho Falls.

What to See and Do

Bonneville Museum. Displays of early county, state, and city history; natural history; Native American artifacts; early settler and mountain-man relics; replica of early (ca 1890) Idaho Falls (Eagle Rock); 30-min video on county history and other subjects of local interest. Art exhibits featuring works of area artists; special and traveling exhibits. (Mon-Fri; also Sat afternoons; closed Jan 1, Thanksgiving, Dec 25) 200 N Eastern Ave. Phone 208/522-1400. ¢

Heise Hot Springs. Mineral water pool, freshwater pools, water slide, fishing; golf, camping. (Mid-May-Sept) Fee for activities. 23 mi E on US 26, in Ririe. Phone 208/538-7312.

Idaho Falls. Falls run for 1,500 ft along Snake River. Picnic tables nearby. Phone 208/523-1010.

The Lavas. Lava-created caves, fissures, and rock flows, fringed by dwarf trees. Native American relics are also plentiful. 10 mi S via US 91 to Shelley, then 4 mi W on local road. Phone 208/523-1010.

Tautphaus Park. Zoo (fee); amusement rides (Memorial Day wkend-Labor Day wkend; fee); picnic and barbecue areas; lighted tennis courts and softball diamonds; horseshoe pits; ice-skating, hockey (seasonal). Park (Daily; closed Jan 1, Thanksgiving, Dec 25). Rollandet Ave or South Blvd. **FREE**

Special Event

War Bonnet Roundup. Sandy Downs Park Rodeo Grounds. Rodeo. Four nights early Aug.

Motels/Motor Lodges

★★ **AMERITEL INN.** *645 Lindsay Blvd (83402). 208/523-1400; fax 208/523-0004; res 800/600-6001. www.ameritelinns.com.* 126 rms, 4 story. June-Sept: S, D $99.75; each addl $8; suites $119-$229; under 12 free; lower rates rest of yr. Crib free. TV; cable (premium). Complimentary full bkfst. Complimentary coffee in rms. Restaurant nearby. Ck-out noon. Meeting rms. Business servs avail. In-rm modem link. Sundries. Free airport transportation. Exercise equipt. Indoor pool; whirlpool. Bathrm phones; some refrigerators, microwaves. Cr cds: A, C, D, DS, JCB, MC, V.
D ⊶ 🛉 🏋 🕥 🖵

★★ **BEST WESTERN COTTON TREE INN.** *900 Lindsay Blvd (83402). 208/523-6000; fax 208/523-0000; toll-free 800/662-6886. www.bestwestern. com.* 94 rms, 3 story, 9 suites, 6 kit. units. S, D $65-$75; each addl $5; suites $90-$110; kit. units $90-$110; under 18 free. Crib $8. TV; cable (premium). Indoor pool; whirlpool. Complimentary continental bkfst. Restaurant nearby. Ck-out noon. Coin lndry. Meeting rms. Business servs avail. Valet serv. Free airport transportation. Exercise equipt. Microwaves avail. Near river. Cr cds: A, C, D, DS, MC, V.
D ⊶ 🛉 🕥 🔥

★★ **COMFORT INN.** *195 S Colorado Ave (83402). 208/528-2804; fax 208/522-3083; res 800/228-5150. www.comfortinn.com.* 56 rms, 2 story, 14 suites. June-Sept: S $59.99; D $69.99; each addl $7; suites $74.99-$120; under 12 free; lower rates rest of yr. Crib free. Pet accepted, some restrictions. TV; cable. Indoor pool; whirlpool. Complimentary continental bkfst. Restaurant nearby. Ck-out 11 am. Refrigerators. Cr cds: A, D, DS, MC, V.
🄳 🐾 ⇌ ✕ 🖳 🔥

★★ **HAMPTON INN.** *2500 Channing Way (83404). 208/529-9800; fax 208/529-9455; res 800/426-7866. www.hamptoninn.com.* 63 rms, 3 story, 7 suites. Late May-Aug: S $64; D $69; suites $74-$99; under 18 free; lower rates rest of yr. Crib free. TV; cable (premium). Complimentary continental bkfst. Restaurant nearby. Ck-out noon. Meeting rm. Business servs avail. Bellhops. Exercise equipt. Indoor pool; whirlpool. Refrigerator, microwave in suites. Cr cds: A, C, D, DS, MC, V.
🄳 ⇌ 🕺 🖳 🔥

★★ **SHILO INN.** *780 Lindsay Blvd (83402). 208/523-0088; fax 208/522-7420; res 800/222-2244. www.shiloinns.com.* 161 rms, 4 story. S, D $80-$99; each addl $10; under 12 free. Crib free. Pet accepted, some restrictions; $7/day. TV; cable (premium). Indoor pool; whirlpool. Complimentary full bkfst. Coffee in rms. Restaurant 6 am-10 pm. Bar. Ck-out noon. Coin lndry. Meeting rms. Business servs avail. Sundries. Free airport transportation. Exercise equipt; sauna. Refrigerators, microwaves. Some balconies. On river. Cr cds: A, C, D, DS, ER, JCB, MC, V.
🄳 🐾 ⇌ 🕺 ✕ 🖳 🔥 🆂🅲

Restaurant

★ **JAKERS.** *851 Lindsay Blvd (83402). 208/524-5240.* Hrs: 11:30 am-2 pm, 5-10 pm; Fri, Sat to 10:30 pm; Sun 4-9 pm. Closed Jan 1, Thanksgiving, Dec 25. Res accepted. Bar 11:30 am-midnight. Lunch $5.95-$11.95, dinner $8.95- $22.95. Child's menu. Specialties: pan-fried shrimp, prime rib, steaks and ribs. Contemporary rustic decor. Cr cds: A, D, DS, MC, V.
🄳

Jerome

(G-3) *See also Shoshone, Twin Falls*

Pop 6,529 **Elev** 3,781 ft
Area code 208 **Zip** 83338
Information Chamber of Commerce, 101 W Main St, Suite 6; 208/324-2711

What to See and Do

Jerome County Historical Museum. Located in historic Pioneer Hall building. Changing displays. Guided tours. (May-Sept, Mon-Sat; rest of yr, Tues-Sat) 220 N Lincoln. Phone 208/324-5641. **FREE**

Malad Gorge State Park. More than 650 acres with the 2½-mi-long, 250-ft-deep Malad Gorge. Footbridge spans waterfall at Devil's Washbowl. Interpretive trails, picnicking. (Schedule varies) Phone 208/837-4505.

Special Events

Horse racing. Jerome County Fairgrounds. Pari-mutuel racing. Phone 208/324-7211. Two wkends mid-June.

Jerome County Fair & Rodeo. Concert, rodeo, carnival, parade. Phone 208/324-7211. First wk Aug.

Chariot Races. Jerome County Fairgrounds. Phone 208/324-7211. Wkends, Dec-Feb.

Motels/Motor Lodges

★★ **BEST WESTERN SAWTOOTH INN.** *2653 S Lincoln Ave (83338). 208/324-9200; fax 208/324-9292; toll-free 800/780-7234. www.bestwestern.com.* 57 rms, 2 story. June-Sept: S $54-$69; D $64-$89; each addl $10; suites $69-$79; under 17 free; higher rates: Jerome County Fair, 1st wk July; lower rates rest of yr. Crib free. Pet accepted, some restrictions. TV; cable (premium). Complimentary continental bkfst. Restaurant nearby. Ck-out noon. Meeting rms. Business servs avail. Bellhops. Coin lndry. Exercise equipt. Indoor pool; whirlpool. Some refrigerators, microwaves. Cr cds: A, C, D, DS, MC, V.
🄳 🐾 ⇌ 🕺 🖳 🔥 🆂🅲

★ **DAYS INN.** *1200 S Centennial Spur (83338). 208/324-6400; fax 208/324-9207; res 800/329-7466. www.daysinn.*

com. 73 rms, 3 story. May-Sept: S $52; D $58; under 12 free; lower rates rest of yr. Crib free. Pet accepted. TV; cable (premium), VCR (movies). Restaurant adj open 24 hrs. Ck-out noon. Meeting rm. Business servs avail. In-rm modem link. Sundries. Coin lndry. Whirlpool. Cr cds: A, C, D, DS, JCB, MC, V.

D ▢ ▢ ▢ SC

Kellogg

(B-2) *See also Coeur d'Alene, Wallace*

Pop 2,591 **Elev** 2,308 ft
Area code 208 **Zip** 83837
Information Greater Kellogg Area Chamber of Commerce, 608 Bunker Ave; 208/784-0821
Web www.nidlink.com/~kellogg

In this rich mining region are the country's largest silver and lead mines. One of the state's most violent miners' strikes took place here in 1899. Today, the former mining town is being transformed into a ski resort.

What to See and Do

Old Mission State Park. (1830) A 100-acre park. Tours of the Coeur d'Alene Mission of the Sacred Heart, a restored Native American mission; oldest existing building in state. Picnicking; information center; interpretive programs; history trail. Standard fees. (Daily) 10 mi W off I-90 exit 39, in Cataldo. Phone 208/682-3814.

Skiing. Silver Mountain Ski Area. Double, quad, three triple chairlifts, surface lift; patrol, school, rentals; lodges, restaurants, cafeteria, bar, nursery. Fifty trails, longest run 2.5 mi; vertical drop 2,200 ft. (Mid-Nov-Apr, Wed-Sun) ½ mi SW, off I-90 exit 49. Phone 208/783-1111. ¢¢¢

Sunshine Mine Disaster Memorial. Double-life-size statue constructed of steel is memorial to all miners; created by Kenn Lonn, a native of Kellogg. The helmet's light burns perpetually and the miner holds a typical jackleg drill. 3 mi E on I-90, exit 54, Big Creek. Phone 208/784-0821.

Special Event

Christmas Dickens Festival. 608 Bunker Ave. Entire town dressed in period costume. Plays, skits, puppet shows, parade. Second wkend Dec. Phone 208/784-0821.

Motels/Motor Lodges

★ **SILVERHORN MOTOR INN & RESTAURANT.** *699 W Cameron Ave (83837).* 208/783-1151; fax 208/784-5081; toll-free 800/437-6437. 40 rms. S $55; D $60; each addl $5; under 12 free. Crib $3. Pet accepted. TV; cable. Restaurant 6 am-9 pm. Rm serv. Ck-out noon. Business servs avail. Free lndry facilities. Gift shop. Downhill/x-country ski 3 mi. Whirlpool. Cr cds: A, C, D, DS, MC, V.

D ▢ ▢ ▢ ▢ ▢ ▢ SC

★ **SUPER 8 MOTEL.** *601 Bunker Ave (83837).* 208/783-1234; fax 208/784-0461; res 800/785-5443. www.super8. *com.* 61 rms, 2 story. Mid June-mid Sept: S, D $40-$63; each addl $5; suites $75-$90; under 13 free; ski plans; lower rates rest of yr. Crib free. Pet accepted. TV; cable (premium), VCR avail. Complimentary continental bkfst. Restaurant opp 11 am-10 pm. Ck-out 11 am. Meeting rms. Business servs avail. Downhill ski on site. Indoor pool; whirlpool. Some refrigerators, microwaves. Picnic tables. Cr cds: A, C, DS, MC, V.

▢ ▢ ▢ ▢

Ketchum (F-3)

(see Sun Valley Area)

Lava Hot Springs

(G-5) *See also Pocatello*

Pop 420 **Elev** 5,060 ft **Area code** 208
Zip 83246

Hot water pouring out of the mountains and bubbling up in springs, believed to be the most highly mineralized water in the world, makes Lava Hot Springs a busy year-round resort. Fishing, swimming; hunting, camping, and golf are available in the surrounding area.

What to See and Do

Lava Hot Springs. Outdoor mineral pools, fed by 30 different springs, range from 104-112°F. Olympic-size swimming pool with diving tower (Memorial Day-Labor Day). (Daily; closed Thanksgiving, Dec 25) ½ mi E on US 30N. Phone 208/776-5221. ¢¢

South Bannock County Historical Center. Museum artifacts, photographs, transcripts, and memorabilia trace history of town from the era of Native American and fur trappers to its development as a resort area. Slide show and guided walking tour (by appt). (Daily) 110 Main St. Phone 208/776-5254. **Donation**

Lewiston

(D-1) *See also Moscow, also see Clarkston, WA*

Founded 1861 **Pop** 28,082 **Elev** 739 ft
Area code 208 **Zip** 83501
Information Chamber of Commerce, 111 Main St, Suite 120; 208/743-3531 or 800/473-3543
Web www.lewistonchamber.org

The Clearwater River, starting in the Bitterroot Mountains and plunging through the vast Clearwater National Forest, joins the Snake River at Lewiston. The two rivers and the mountains that surround the town give it one of the most picturesque settings in the state. A thriving tourist trade supplements Lewiston's grain, lumber, and livestock industries.

What to See and Do

◻ **Auto tours.** The Lewis and Clark Hwy (US 12) parallels the famous Lewis and Clark Trail E to Montana. Interpretive signs along the way explain the human and natural history of the canyon. A Forest Service Information Station is at Lolo Pass

on the Idaho/Montana border. The Chamber of Commerce has maps for other tours.

Castle Museum. Three-story, hand-made cement block house built in 1906 and patterned after Scottish castle; embossed metal ceilings, antiques. (By appt) 23 mi N on ID 3 in Juliaetta; 1 blk off main hwy. Phone 208/276-3081. **Donation**

Clearwater National Forest. About 1,850,000 acres with trout fishing; hunting, skiing and snowmobiling trails, camping (fee for some developed campsites), cabins, picnicking, lookout towers (fee). Pack trips. Higher elevations accessible July-Sept; lower elevations accessible Mar-Oct or Nov. Lolo Pass Visitor Center and Lochsa Historical Ranger Station on US 12 (Mid-May-mid-Sept; daily). US 12 in Orofino. For further info contact the Supervisor, 12730 US Hwy 12, Orofino 83544. Phone 208/476-4541.

Hell's Canyon Excursions. Jet boat trips and fishing charters into Hell's Canyon National Recreation Area (see GRANGEVILLE). For info contact the Chamber of Commerce.

Hell's Gate State Park. Nine hundred sixty acres on Snake River, 40 mi N of Hell's Canyon National Recreation Area (see GRANGEVILLE). Swimming, fishing, boating (marina, concession, ramp); hiking and paved bicycle trails, horseback riding area, picnicking, playground, tent and trailer campsites (hookups, dump station; 15-day max). Info center, interpretive programs, exhibits; excursion boats. Park (Mar-Nov). Standard fees. 4 mi S on Snake River Ave. Phone 208/799-5015.

Luna House Museum. On site of first hotel in town (1861). Exhibits on Nez Perce and pioneers; displays on town and county history. (Tues-Sat; closed hols) 3rd and C Sts. Phone 208/743-2535. **FREE**

Nez Perce National Historical Park. The park is composed of 38 separate sites scattered throughout Washington, Oregon, Montana, and Idaho. All of the sites relate to the culture and history of the Nez Perce; some relate to the westward expansion of the nation into homelands. Headquarters has visitor center and museum, 39063 US 95, Lapwai, ID 83540. (Daily; closed Jan 1, Thanksgiving, Dec 25). Phone 208/843-2261. **FREE**

Special Events

Lewiston Round-Up. Lewiston Round-Up grounds, 7000 Tammany Creek Rd. Wkend after Labor Day. Phone 208/746-6324.

Nez Perce County Fair. Four days late Sept. Phone 208/743-3302.

Motels/Motor Lodges

★ **HOWARD JOHNSON.** *1716 Main St (83501). 208/743-9526; fax 208/746-6216; res 800/446-4656. www. hojo.com.* 66 rms, 1-2 story, 4 kit. units. S $62-$67; D $62-$82; under 18 free. Pet accepted. TV; cable (premium). Complimentary continental bkfst. Coffee in rms. Heated pool. Ck-out noon. Free lndry facilities. In-rm modem link. Refrigerators. Cr cds: A, C, D, DS, JCB, MC, V.
🄳 🐾 ≈ ⛏ ⛲ 🔥

★★ **INN AMERICA - A BUDGET MOTEL.** *702 21st St (83501). 208/746-4600; fax 208/746-7756; res 800/469-4667. www.lewiston. innamerica.com.* 61 rms, 3 story. S $48-$52; D $56-$62; each addl $5; kit. units $61.95; under 18 free; golf plans; higher rates special events. Crib free. TV; cable (premium). Complimentary coffee in lobby. Restaurant opp 8 am-10 pm. Ck-out 1 pm. Business servs avail. In-rm modem link. Sundries. Coin lndry. Pool. Some refrigerators. Cr cds: A, C, D, DS, ER, JCB, MC, V.
🄳 ⛏ ≈ ✈ ⛲ 🔥

★★ **RED LION HOTEL.** *621 21st St (83501). 208/799-1000; res 800/232-6730. www.redlionlewiston.com.* 134 rms, 4 story. S, D $79-$89; each addl $10; suites $89-$130; under 18 free; wkly rates; golf plans. Crib free. Pet accepted. TV; cable (premium). 2 pools, 1 indoor; whirlpool, poolside serv. Coffee in rms. Restaurant 6 am-10 pm. Bar 4 pm-1:30 am. Ck-out noon. Coin lndry. Meeting rms. Valet serv. Concierge. Sundries. Free airport, RR station, bus depot transportation. Some bathrm phones. Cr cds: A, C, D, DS, ER, JCB, MC, V.
🄳 🐾 ⛏ ≈ ⛲ 🔥 🆂🅲

★★ **RIVERVIEW INN.** *1325 Main St (83501). 208/746-3311; fax 208/746-7955; toll-free 800/806-7666.* 75 rms, 4 story. S $39.95; D $48.95; each addl $6; under 12 free. Crib free. Pet accepted. TV; cable (premium). Heated pool. Complimentary continental breakfast. Coffee in rms. Restaurant nearby. Ck-out noon. Meeting rm. In rm modem link. Exercise equipt. Refrigerators; some microwaves. Cr cds: A, D, DS, MC, V.
🄳 🐾 ≈ ⛏ ⛲ 🔥

★★ **SACAJAWEA SELECT INN.** *1824 Main St (83501). 208/746-1393; fax 208/743-3620; toll-free 800/333-1393. www.selectinn.com.* 78 rms, 2 story, 12 suites. S $49; D $58; each addl $3; suites $63; under 13 free. Crib avail, fee. Pet accepted, some restrictions; fee. TV; cable (premium). Heated pool; whirlpool. Complimentary continental bkfst. Restaurant 6 am-10 pm. Bar 11-1 am; closed Sun. Ck-out noon. Coin lndry. Meeting rms. In-rm modem link. Valet serv. Airport transportation. Exercise equipt. Refrigerators. Cr cds: A, C, D, DS, MC, V.
🄳 🐾 ≈ ⛏ ⛲ 🔥

★ **SUPER 8 MOTEL.** *3120 North & South Hwy (83501). 208/743-8808; fax 208/743-8808; res 800/800-8000. www. super8.com.* 62 rms, 2 story. Apr-Sept: S $37-$49; D $55-$75; each addl $5; under 12 free; higher rates special events; lower rates rest of yr. Crib free. TV; cable (premium), VCR. Complimentary coffee. Ck-out 11 am. Refrigerators, microwaves avail. On river. Cr cds: A, C, D, DS, ER, JCB, MC, V.
🄳 ⛲ 🔥 🆂🅲

McCall (E-2)

Pop 2,005 **Elev** 5,030 ft
Area code 208 **Zip** 83638

Information Chamber of Commerce, PO Box D; 208/634-7631 or 800/260-5130

At the southern tip of Payette Lake, McCall is a resort center for one of the state's chief recreational areas. Fishing, swimming, boating, and waterskiing are available on Payette Lake. McCall is also the headquarters for Payette National Forest, and three Ranger District offices of the forest are located here.

What to See and Do

Brundage Mountain Ski Area. Two triple chairlifts, Quadlift, Pomalift, platter tow; patrol, school, rentals; bar, cafeteria; nursery. (Mid-Nov-mid-Apr, daily) 8 mi NW via ID 55, unnumbered road. Phone 634/415-1888. ¢¢¢¢

Cascade Dam Reservoir. Fishing, boating. 25 mi S on ID 55, in Cascade.

Pack trips into Idaho primitive areas. Check with Chamber of Commerce for list of outfitters. Phone 208/634-7631.

Payette National Forest. More than 2.3 million acres surrounded by the Snake and Salmon rivers, the River of No Return Wilderness, Hell's Canyon National Recreation Area, and the Boise National Forest. Trout and salmon fishing in 300 lakes and 3,000 mi of streams, boating; 2,100 mi of hiking trails, hunting, camping, and picnic areas; winter sports. For further info contact the Supervisor, PO Box 1026. 800 W Lakeside, PO Box 1026. Phone 208/634-0700.

Ponderosa State Park. Approx 1,280 acres. Large stand of ponderosa pines. Swimming, waterskiing, fishing, boating (ramps); hiking; cross-country skiing, picnicking, camping (exc winter; res accepted Memorial Day-Labor Day); tent and trailer sites (hookups; 15-day max; dump station). Park (Daily). 2 mi NE, on Payette Lake. Standard fees. Contact Park Manager, PO Box A. Phone 208/634-2164.

River rafting. Salmon River Outfitters. Offers five- and six-day guided raft trips along the Salmon River. For information and res, contact PO Box 307, Columbia, CA 95310. Phone 209/795-4041. ¢¢¢¢

Special Events

Winter Carnival. Parades, fireworks; ice sculptures, snowmobile and ski races, snowman-building contest, carriage and sleigh rides, ball. Ten days early Feb. Phone 208/634-7631.

McCall Folk Music Festival. Fiddle music; Western, swing, Irish, folk, blues, and jazz; square dancing. Third wkend July. Phone 208/634-7631.

Motels/Motor Lodges

★★ **BEST WESTERN MCCALL.** *415 N 3rd St (83638). 208/634-6300; fax 208/634-2967; toll-free 800/780-7234. www.bestwestern.com.* 79 rms, 2 story. Mid-June-mid-Sept: S $70-$120; D $75-$125; under 18 free; lower rates rest of yr. Crib free. Pet accepted, some restrictions. TV; cable (premium), VCR avail. Indoor pool; whirlpool. Complimentary coffee in lobby. Ck-out 11 am. Coin lndry. Meeting rms. In-rm modem link. Exercise equipt. Downhill/x-country ski 10 mi. Refrigerators, microwaves. Cr cds: A, C, D, DS, MC, V.
🄳 🐾 🖃 🛏 🎿 🏊 🐾 SC

★ **WOODSMAN MOTEL AND CAFE.** *402 N 3rd St (83638). 208/634-7671; fax 208/634-3191.* 60 rms, 1-2 story. No A/C. S $46; D $56. TV, some B/W; cable. Restaurant 7 am-9:30 pm. Ck-out 11 am. Airport, bus depot transportation. Downhill ski 10 mi; x-country ski on site. Cr cds: A, DS, MC, V.
🖃 🎿 🐾

"The River of No Return"

B&B/Small Inn

★★ **HOTEL MCCALL.** *1101 N 3rd St (83638). 208/634-8105; fax 208/634-8755.* 36 rms, 3 story, 2 suites. S, D $55-$350; each addl $10; under 10 free; ski plan. TV; cable (premium), VCR avail. Complimentary continental bkfst. Ck-out 11 am, ck-in 2 pm. In rm modem link. Downhill ski 10 mi; x-country ski 1 mi. Garden patio, sun deck. Overlooks Payette Lake. Totally nonsmoking. Cr cds: A, DS, MC, V.

D **t** **⚥** **►** **🔥**

Restaurant

★★ **MILL STEAKS & SPIRITS.** *324 N 3rd St (83638). 208/634-7683. www.themillmccallidaho.com.* Hrs: 6-10 pm; Fri, Sat to 11 pm. Closed Thanksgiving, Dec 25. Bar. Dinner $8.45-$25.95. Child's menu. Specializes in steak, prime rib, seafood. Entertainment wkends. Photo collection of history of the Northwest. Family-owned. Cr cds: A, D, DS, MC, V.

◪

Montpelier (H-6)

Founded 1864 **Pop** 2,656 **Elev** 5,964 ft **Area code** 208 **Zip** 83254

Information Bear Lake Convention and Visitors Bureau, PO Box 26, Fish Haven 83287; 208/945-2072 or 800/448-2327

Located in the highlands of Bear Lake Valley, Montpelier is surrounded by lakes, rivers, creeks, and grazing ranges. The average yearly temperature is 46°F. First called Clover Creek, then Belmont, it was finally designated by the Mormon leader, Brigham Young, as Montpelier, after the capital of Vermont. There are Mormon tabernacles throughout this area. Phosphate is mined extensively nearby. A Ranger District office of the Caribou National Forest is located here.

What to See and Do

Bear Lake. Covering 71,000 acres, this 20-mi-long, 200-ft-deep body of water lies across the Idaho/Utah border. Fishing for Mackinaw, cutthroat, whitefish, and the rare Bonneville cisco. 20 mi S on US 89. On N shore is

Bear Lake State Park. Provides swimming beach, waterskiing, fishing, boating (ramp); picnicking, park (Mid-May-mid-Sept), camping on E shore (dump station, hookups). Standard fees. Phone 208/945-2790.

Bloomington Lake. Spring-fed lake of unknown depth. Camping, fishing. 12 mi S on US 89, then W on local road, W of Bloomington.

Caribou National Forest. Fishing; camping (fee at certain designated campsites), hunting, picnicking, winter sports. W, N, and S of US 89; N and S of US 30. For further info contact Ranger District, 431 Clay St. Phone 208/945-2407. Within the forest is

Minnetonka Cave. Cave is ½ mi long and has 9 rms; 40°F. Guided tours (Mid-June-Labor Day, daily). 10 mi W of St. Charles off US 89. Phone 208/847-0375. ¢¢

Special Events

Oregon Trail Rendezvous Pageant. Fri closest to July 24. Phone 800/448-2327.

Bear Lake County Fair and Rodeo. Third wkend Aug. Phone 208/945-2072.

Motels/Motor Lodges

★★ **BEST WESTERN CLOVER CREEK INN.** *243 N 4th St (83254). 208/847-1782; fax 208/847-3519; res 800/780-7234. www.bestwestern.com.* 65 rms, 2 story. May-Oct: S $56; D $73; each addl $6; suites $101; under 12 free; lower rates rest of yr. Crib $6. Pet accepted, some restrictions. TV; cable (premium), VCR avail (movies). Complimentary continental bkfst. Coffee in rms. Restaurant opp 6 am-10 pm. Ck-out 11 am. Meeting rm. Business servs avail. Exercise equipt. Whirlpool. Some refrigerators, microwaves. Cr cds: A, C, D, DS, MC, V.

D **🐾** **🛐** **⬚** **🔥**

★ **SUPER 8.** *276 N 4th St (83254). 208/847-8888; fax 208/847-3888; res*

800/800-8000. www.super8.com. 50 rms, 2 story, 5 suites. June-Sept: S $35-$40; D $45-$50; each addl $4; suites $55-$60; under 12 free; lower rates rest of yr. Crib free. TV; cable. Complimentary continental bkfst. Restaurant nearby. Ck-out 11 am. Meeting rms. Business servs avail. Gift shop. Exercise equipt. Some refrigerators, microwaves. Cr cds: A, D, DS, MC, V.

Moscow (C-1)

Pop 18,519 **Elev** 2,583 ft
Area code 208 **Zip** 83843
Information Chamber of Commerce, PO Box 8936; 208/882-1800 or 800/380-1801
Web www.moscow.com/chamber

Moscow is the seat of Latah County in the heart of the Palouse Hills country and beautiful Paradise Valley. It is known as the "Dry Pea and Lentil Capital of the Nation."

What to See and Do

Appaloosa Museum and Heritage Center. Exhibit of paintings and artifacts relating to the Appaloosa horse; early cowboy equipt; saddle collection; Nez Perce clothing, tools. (June-Aug, Mon-Sat; rest of yr, Mon-Fri; closed hols) Also houses national headquarters of the Appaloosa Horse Club, Inc. Moscow-Pullman Hwy. Phone 208/882-5578. **FREE**

Latah County Historical Society. Historic rms, exhibits, and artifacts depicting local history. Local history and genealogy library, children's activities. Museum (Tues-Sat, limited hrs; closed hols); library, 327 E 2nd St (Tues-Fri). McConnell Mansion (1886), 110 S Adams St. Phone 208/882-1004. **Donation**

University of Idaho. (1889) 11,000 students. Graduate and undergraduate programs. On campus is a major collection of big game specimens from the estate of well-known hunter Jack O'Connor; art gallery and performing arts center; mining, forestry, and wildlife exhibits in the mining and forestry bldgs; 18,000-seat, covered Kibbie-ASUI Activities Center with award-winning barrel-arch dome. Tours (daily). W off US 95. Phone 208/885-6424.

Special Events

Lionel Hampton/Chevron Jazz Festival. Univ of Idaho. Four-day festival hosted by Lionel Hampton featuring all-star headliners and student performers. Phone 208/885-6765. Late Feb.

Idaho Repertory Theater. E.W. Hartung Theater, Univ of Idaho. Shakespeare, musicals, dramas, comedies. Phone 208/885-7212 or 800/345-7402. June-early Aug. Phone 208/885-7986.

Rendezvous in the Park. In East City Park. Arts and crafts festival, juried art shows, silent movies, concerts under the stars. Phone 208/882-1178. Two wkends July.

Latah County Fair. Fairgrounds, E of town. Phone 208/883-5722. Second wk Sept, after Labor Day.

Motels/Motor Lodges

★★ **BEST WESTERN UNIVERSITY INN.** 1516 Pullman Rd (83843). 208/882-0550; fax 208/883-3056; toll-free 800/325-8765. www.bestwestern.com. 173 units, 2 story. S $74; D $84; each addl $7; suites $150-$350; under 18 free. TV; cable. Crib $10. Pet accepted; $10. Indoor pool; wading pool; whirlpool. Coffee in rms. Restaurant open 24 hrs. Bar 11-2 am. Ck-out noon. Meeting rms. Business servs avail. In-rm modem link. Valet serv. Gift shop. Airport, bus depot transportation. Exercise equipt; sauna. Some refrigerators, microwaves. Cr cds: A, C, D, DS, MC, V.

★ **HILLCREST MOTEL.** 706 N Main St (83843). 208/882-7579; fax 208/882-0310; toll-free 800/368-6564. 35 rms, some with showers only. S $36; D $41; each addl $4; suites $58; under 6 free; family, wkly rates; higher rates: special events, university football games. Pet accepted; $5. TV; cable. Continental bkfst. Restaurant nearby. Ck-out 11 am. Coin lndry. Business servs avail. Some refrigerators, microwaves. Cr cds: A, MC, V.

★★ **MARK IV MOTOR INN.** *414 N Main St (83843). 208/882-7557; fax 208/883-0684; res 800/833-4240. www.ark4motorinn.com.* 86 units, 2 story. S $39-$49; D $49-$69; each addl $5; suites $59-$99; higher rates special events. Pet accepted; $10. TV; cable (premium). Indoor pool; whirlpool. Restaurant 6 am-9 pm. Bar 3:30 pm-midnight. Ck-out noon. Meeting rm. Business servs avail. In-rm modem link. Free airport, bus depot transportation. Cr cds: A, C, D, DS, MC, V.

D ⬛ ⬛ ⬛ ⬛ SC

★ **SUPER 8.** *175 Peterson Dr (83843). 208/883-1503; fax 208/883-4769; res 800/800-8000. www.super8.com.* 60 rms, 3 story. No elvtr. S $42-$78; D $52-$72; each addl $3; under 12 free; higher rates special events. Crib free. TV; cable (premium). Ck-out 11 am. Meeting rms. Cr cds: A, C, D, DS, MC, V.

D ⬛ ⬛ ⬛ SC

Mountain Home

(G-2) *See also Boise*

Pop 7,913 **Elev** 3,143 ft
Area code 208 **Zip** 83647
Information Desert Mountain Visitor Center, 2900 American Legion Blvd, PO Box 3; 208/587-4464

A transportation center in the Boise-Owyhee Valley of southwest Idaho, Mountain Home affords a fine starting point for side trips. Within a few hours' drive are forested ranges of the Boise National Forest, sand dunes, ghost towns, reservoirs, and canyons; a Ranger District office of the forest (see BOISE) is located here.

What to See and Do

Bruneau Canyon. A 61-mi gorge, 800 ft deep but narrow enough in places to toss a rock across. **Bruneau Dunes State Park** (4,800 acres) has small lakes, sand dunes, and the highest single-structured dune in North America (470 ft). Fishing for bass and bluegill, boating (ramps; no motors); nature trails, picnicking, tent and trailer sites (15-day max; hookups, dump station). Info center, public observatory, interpretive programs (by appt). Standard hrs, fees. 20 mi S on ID 51 to Bruneau, then SE on local road, near Bruneau. Phone 208/366-7919.

Elmore County Historical Foundation Museum. Contains historical info about Mountain Home and Elmore County. (Mar-Dec, Fri and Sat afternoons) 180 S 3rd St E. Phone 208/587-2104. **Donation**

Fishing, swimming, boating, camping. Strike Reservoir, 23 mi S on ID 51, or Anderson Ranch Reservoir, 22 mi NE on ID 20.

Skiing. Soldier Mountain Ski Area. Two double chairlifts, rope tow; patrol, school, rentals; snowmaking; cafeteria, concession. Longest run two mi; vertical drop 1,400 ft. Half-day rates. (Mid-Nov-Apr, Thurs-Sun and hols; Christmas and Easter wks, daily) NE on US 20 to Fairfield, then 10 mi N on Soldier Creek Rd. Phone 208/764-2300. ¢¢¢¢

Three Island Crossing State Park. On 513 acres. Site was once a river crossing on the Oregon Trail. Camping (res recommended; fee). Interpretive center; gift shop. 35 mi SE in Glenns Ferry. 35 mi SE in Glenns Ferry, I-84 at Glenns Ferry exit. Phone 208/366-2394.

Motels/Motor Lodges

★★ **BEST WESTERN FOOTHILLS MOTOR INN.** *1080 Hwy 20 (83647). 208/587-8477; fax 208/587-5774; res 800/780-7234. www.bestwestern.com/ foothillsmotorinn.* 76 rms, 2 story. S $60; D $70; each addl $5; suites $130; under 13 free. Crib $5. TV; cable. Pool; whirlpool. Complimentary continental bkfst. Complimentary coffee in rms. Ck-out noon. Business servs avail. In-rm modem link. Cr cds: A, C, D, DS, ER, JCB, MC, V.

D ⬛ ⬛ ⬛

★ **HILANDER MOTEL & STEAK HOUSE.** *615 S 3rd W (83647). 208/ 587-3311; fax 208/580-2152.* 33

rms, 2 story. June-Aug: S $36; D
$44; each addl $4; Crib avail. Pet
accepted, some restrictions, $4.TV;
cable. Pool. Restaurant 4-10 pm.
Bar. Ck-out 11 am. Cr cds: A, D, DS,
MC, V.

★ **SLEEP INN.** *1180 US 20 (83647).*
208/587-9743; fax 208/587-7382; toll-
free 800/753-3746. www.sleepinn.com.
60 rms, shower only, 2 story. S $55;
D $60; each addl $5; under 13 free.
Crib $5. TV; cable, VCR. Pool privi-
leges. Complimentary continental
bkfst. Coffee in rms. Restaurant 6
am-11 pm. Exercise equipt. Ck-out
noon. In-rm modem link. Guest
lndry. Refrigerators. Cr cds: A, C, DS,
MC, V.

Nampa

(G-2) *See also Boise*

Founded 1885 **Pop** 28,365 **Elev** 2,490
ft **Area code** 208
Information Chamber of Commerce,
1305 3rd St S, PO Box A, 83653;
208/466-4641
Web www.nampa.com

Nampa, the largest city in Canyon
County, is located in the heart of the
agriculturally rich Treasure Valley of
southwestern Idaho.

What to See and Do

**Canyon County Historical Society
Museum.** Historical artifacts and
memorabilia inside a 1903 train
depot once used as offices of the
Union Pacific Railroad. (Tues-Sat,
limited hrs) 1200 Front St. Phone
208/467-7611. **Donation**

Deer Flat National Wildlife Refuge.
Thousands of migratory waterfowl
pause at this 10,500-acre refuge
while on their journey (Oct-Dec).
Wildlife observation. Fishing, hunting in season. Visitor center (Mon-
Fri; closed hols). 5 mi SW off I-84.
Phone 208/467-9278. **FREE** Within
the refuge is

Lake Lowell. Approx 8,800 acres.
Boating, sailing, waterskiing; pic-
nicking (mid-Apr-Sept, daily).
Phone 208/467-9278.

Lakeview Park. A 90-acre park with
gardens, sports facilities, tennis, picnic areas. Pool (June-Labor Day; fee).
Antique fire engine, locomotive,
steam roller, jet fighter plane on display. Amphitheater. Park (Daily).
Garrity Blvd and 16th Ave N. Phone
208/465-2215. **FREE**

Special Event

Snake River Stampede. Among
nation's top professional rodeos. All
seats reserved. For tickets contact PO
Box 231, 83653; 208/466-8497. Tues-
Sat, third wk July.

Motels/Motor Lodges

★ **DESERT INN.** *115 9th Ave S*
(83651). 208/467-1161; fax 208/467-
5268; res 800/588-5268. www.sun-
downerinc.com. 40 rms, 2 story. S, D
$42.95-$55.95; under 12 free. TV;
cable (premium). Pet accepted; $10.
Pool. Complimentary continental
bkfst. Ck-out 11 am. Some refrigerators, microwaves. Cr cds: A, D, DS,
MC, V.

★★ **INN AMERICA.** *130 Shannon Dr*
(83687). 208/442-0800; fax 208/442-
0229; res 800/469-4667. www.
innamerica.com. 61 rms, 3 story. S
$42-$50; D $49-$62; each addl $5;
kit. units $52-$57; under 18 free. Crib
free. TV; cable (premium). Complimentary coffee in lobby. Restaurant
nearby. Ck-out 1 pm. Business servs
avail. In-rm modem link. Valet serv.
Sundries. Coin lndry. Pool. Some
refrigerators. Cr cds: A, D, DS, MC, V.

★★ **SHILO INN.** *617 Nampa Blvd*
(83687). 208/466-8993; fax 208/465-
3239; res 800/222-2244. www.
shiloinns.com. 61 rms, 3 story. No
elvtr. S, D $56.95-$79.95; each addl
$10; under 12 free. Crib free. Pet
accepted; $10. TV; cable (premium).
Heated pool; whirlpool. Complimentary continental bkfst. Coffee in rms.
Ck-out noon. Coin lndry. Valet serv.
Sauna, steam rm. Refrigerators,
microwaves. Cr cds: A, D, DS, JCB,
MC, V.

★★ **SHILO INN SUITES.** *1401 Shilo Dr (83687). 208/465-3250; fax 208/465-5929; res 800/222-2244. www.shiloinns.com.* 83 suites, 4 story. S, D $89.95-$109.95; each addl $10; under 13 free. Crib free. Pet accepted; $10. TV; cable (premium). Indoor pool; whirlpool. Coffee in rms. Complimentary continental bkfst. Restaurant adj 6 am-10 pm. Ck-out noon. Coin lndry. Meeting rms. Sundries. Free airport, RR station, bus depot transportation. Exercise equipt; sauna. Bathrm phones, refrigerators, microwaves; many wet bars. Cr cds: A, C, JCB, MC, V.

Pocatello

(G-5) See also Blackfoot, Idaho Falls

Founded 1882 **Pop** 46,080 **Elev** 4,464 ft **Area code** 208

Information Greater Pocatello Chamber of Commerce, 343 W Center St, PO Box 626, 83204; 208/233-1525

At the heart of the intermontane transportation system is Pocatello. Once the site of a reservation, the city was named for the Native American leader who granted the railroad rights of way and building privileges. A Ranger District office and the headquarters of the Caribou National Forest are located here.

What to See and Do

Caribou National Forest. Scenic drives, pack trips, camping (fee in some designated developed campgrounds), picnic grounds, hunting, fishing, downhill and cross-country skiing, snowmobiling. S, W and E of city. For further info contact the Forest Supervisor, 670 Broadway Ave, Idaho Falls, 83401. Phone 208/523-3278. In forest is

Pebble Creek Ski Area. Two triple, one double chairlifts; beginner-to-expert trails; patrol, school, rentals; restaurant, bar. Longest run 1½ mi; vertical drop 2,200 ft. Night skiing. Half-day rates. (second wk Dec-early Apr; daily) 10 mi SE on I-15 to Inkom, then 5 mi E on Green Canyon Rd. Phone 208/775-4452. ¢¢¢¢

Idaho State University. (1901) 13,500 students. Undergraduate and graduate programs. Art gallery in Fine Arts Building has changing exhibits (academic yr, daily; summer by appt, phone 208/236-3532); art gallery in Student Union Building (Daily); both galleries free. On campus is 12,000-seat Holt Arena, indoor football stadium and sports arena. Tours. 741 S 7th Ave. Phone 208/236-3620. Also here is

Idaho Museum of Natural History. Exhibits on Idaho fossils, especially large mammals of the Ice Age; Native American basketry and beadwork; "Discovery Room" for educational activities; museum shop. (Mon-Sat; closed hols) Phone 208/282-3168 or 208/236-2262. ¢¢

Rocky Mountain River Tours. Six-day wilderness rafting tours; equipt provided. Middlefork Salmon River Canyon. Phone 208/345-2400.

Ross Park. Zoo; swimming pool (June-Aug); water slide; playground; picnic area with shelter, band shell. Park (Daily). Fee for some activities. S 2nd Ave. Phone 208/234-6232. On upper level are

Bannock County Historical Museum. Relics of the early days of Pocatello and Bannock County; Bannock and Shoshone display. (Memorial Day-Labor Day, daily; rest of yr, Tues-Sat, limited hrs; closed hols, also mid-Dec-mid-Jan) Phone 208/233-0434. ¢

Old Fort Hall Replica. Reproduction of 1834 Hudson's Bay Trading Post; period displays. (June-mid-Sept, daily; Apr-May, Tues-Sat) ¢

Special Events

Summer Band Concert Series. Guy Gates Memorial Band Shell, in lower level of Ross Park. Sun, July-Aug. Phone 208/234-6232.

Shoshone-Bannock Indian Festival. Begins second Wed Aug. Phone 208/237-1340.

Bannock County Fair and Rodeo. North: Bannock County Fairgrounds. South: Downey Fairgrounds. Carnival, rodeo, exhibits, food booths, livestock and horse shows. Mid-Aug. Phone 208/237-1340.

Motels/Motor Lodges

★★ **AMERITEL INN.** *1440 Bench Rd (83201). 208/234-7500; fax 208/234-0000. www.ameritelinns.com.* 148 rms, 3 story. June-Aug: S, D $79; each addl $8; suites, kit. units $109-$189; under 13 free; lower rates rest of yr. Crib free. TV; cable (premium). Indoor pool; whirlpool. Complimentary continental bkfst. Restaurant nearby. Ck-out noon. Coin lndry. Meeting rms. In-rm modem link. Valet serv. Free airport transportation. Exercise equipt. Some refrigerators; microwaves avail. Cr cds: A, D, DS, MC, V.

🄳 ⛱ 🏃 🖼 🔥

★★ **BEST WESTERN COTTON TREE INN.** *1415 Bench Rd (83201). 208/237-7650; fax 208/238-1355; res 800/780-7234. www.cottontree.net.* 149 rms, 3 story. S, D $66; studio rms $78-$84; each addl $6; suites $110-$150; under 18 free. Crib free. Pet accepted. TV; cable (premium). Indoor pool; whirlpool. Restaurant 6 am-11 pm. Bar 3:30 pm-1 am. Ck-out noon. Coin lndry. Meeting rms. Business servs avail. Bellhops. Valet serv. Free airport transportation. Health club privileges. Some refrigerators; microwaves avail. Cr cds: A, C, D, DS, MC, V.

🄳 🐾 ⛱ 🏃 🖼 🔥

★ **COMFORT INN.** *1333 Bench Rd (83201). 208/237-8155; fax 208/237-5695; res 800/228-5150. www.comfortinn.com.* 52 rms, 2 story, 14 suites. June-Sept: S $59; D $69; suites $74; under 18 free; lower rates rest of yr. Crib free. Pet accepted. TV; cable (premium). Indoor pool; whirlpool. Complimentary continental bkfst. Restaurant nearby. Ck-out 11 am. Microwaves avail. Cr cds: A, DS, MC, V.

🐾 ⛱ 🖼

★★ **HOLIDAY INN.** *1399 Bench Rd (83201). 208/237-1400; fax 208/238-0225; toll-free 800/200-8944. www.holiday-inn.com.* 190 rms, 2 story, 20 suites. S, D $69; each addl $6; suites $139; under 18 free; wkly, wkend, hol rates. Crib free. Pet accepted, some restrictions; $25 deposit. TV; cable (premium), VCR avail. Complimentary continental bkfst. Complimentary coffee in rms. Restaurant 6 am-2 pm, 5-10 pm. Rm serv 6 am-10 pm. Bar 5 pm-1 am. Ck-out noon. Meeting rms. Business servs avail. Bellhops. Sundries. Coin lndry. Free airport transportation. Indoor putting green. Exercise equipt; sauna. Indoor pool; whirlpool. Game rm. Cr cds: A, C, D, DS, JCB, MC, V.

🐾 ⛱ 🏃 🖼 🔥 SC

★ **POCATELLO SUPER 8.** *1330 Bench Rd (83201). 208/234-0888; fax 208/232-0347; res 800/800-8000. www.super8.com.* 80 rms, 3 story, 8 suites. S, D $50-$70; each addl $4; suites $66-$78; under 12 free. Crib free. Pet accepted, some restrictions; $2. TV; cable. Complimentary continental bkfst. Ck-out 11 am. Microwaves avail. Cr cds: A, C, D, DS, MC, V.

🄳 🐾 🖼 🔥 SC

★★ **WESTCOAST POCATELLO HOTEL.** *1555 Pocatello Creek Rd (83201). 208/233-2200; fax 208/234-4524; toll-free 800/325-4000. www.westcoasthotels.com.* 150 rms, 2 story. S, D $79; suites $125; each addl $5; under 18 free. Crib free. Pet accepted, some restrictions; $10. TV; cable. Indoor pool; wading pool, whirlpool. Coffee in rms. Restaurant open 24 hrs. Bar. Ck-out noon. Coin lndry. Meeting rms. Business center. Valet serv. Free airport transportation. Exercise equipt; sauna. Microwaves avail. Some balconies. Cr cds: A, C, D, DS, MC, V.

🄳 🐾 ⛱ 🏃 ✈ 🖼 SC 🏃

Priest Lake Area

(A-2) *See also Sandpoint*

(25 mi N of Priest River via ID 57)

Among the few remaining unspoiled playgrounds of the Pacific Northwest are lovely and spectacular Priest Lake and the Idaho Panhandle National Forest. North of the confluence of the Pend Oreille and Priest rivers, giant lake trout, big game, towering mountains, waterfalls, lakes, and tall trees make this area one of the most attractive in the country. Mountain ranges and Pacific breezes keep the climate moderate.

This entire water and forest domain was explored by a Jesuit priest, Father Peter John DeSmet, also known as "great black robe" and the "first apostle of the Northwest." Priest Lake and Priest River were both named in his honor. A Ranger District office of the Idaho Panhandle National Forests-Kaniksu is located at Priest Lake.

What to See and Do

Idaho Panhandle National Forests—Kaniksu. Surrounds Priest Lake and Lake Pend Oreille; other areas NE. Rich with huge trees, wildflowers, fishing streams. Boating, swimming, fishing in Pend Oreille and Priest lakes; big game hunting, cross-country skiing, snowmobiling trails, picnicking, 12 forest-run campgrounds on the W side of Priest Lake (possible fee); other state-run campgrounds in the area. Contact the Priest Lake Ranger District, 32203 Hwy 57, Priest River 83856. Phone 208/443-2512.

Priest Lake. Lower Priest, the main lake, is 18½ mi long, about four mi wide, and has a 63-mi shoreline. Upper Priest (inaccessible by road; best reached by boat) is 3¼ mi long, one mi wide and has an 8-mi shoreline. The area is very popular for picnics, overnight cruises, and campouts. There are three state-run campgrounds on the E side: Dickensheet, Indian Creek, and Lionhead; the US Forest Service operates other campgrounds in the area, on the W side. Nearby is the Roosevelt Grove of ancient cedars with 800-yr-old trees standing as tall as 150 ft. Granite Falls is within the grove. Priest Lake is famous for its giant-size lake trout (Mackinaw trout) and cutthroat trout. The main lake contains six islands ideal for picnicking and camping (ten-day max). Recreation around the lake incl swimming, boating (ramp), ice fishing; cross-country skiing, snowmobiling, ice-skating, sledding. 22 mi N of town of Priest River via ID 57, then approx 6 mi E on East Shore Rd; or approx 6 mi farther on ID 57, then 1 mi E on Outlet Bay Rd. On the E side of the lake is

Priest Lake State Park. This park comprises three state-run campgrounds: **Dickensheet** unit is one mi off ID 57, on the Coolin Rd (46 acres; 11 campsites); **Indian Creek** unit is 11 mi N of Coolin, on the Eastshore Rd (park headquarters; 295 acres; 93 campsites, two camper cabins, store, boating facilities, RV hookups, trails); and **Lionhead** unit is 23 mi N of Coolin, on the Eastshore Rd (415 acres; 47 tent sites, group camp, boating facilities, trails). Res are avail for Indian Creek campsites; res are required for the group camp at Lionhead. Phone 208/443-6710.

Priest River. Old logging roads parallel much of it. Only at N and S stretches is it easily reached from ID 57. Long whitewater stretches provide adventure for canoe experts; riffles, big holes, smooth-flowing sections make it a tantalizing trout stream (fishing: June-Oct). Winds for 44 mi S of lake through wild, forested country.

Special Events

Pacific Northwest Sled Dog Championship Races. On ID 57 at Priest Lake Airport, W shore. Last wkend Jan.

Spring Festival. Auction, parade. Memorial Day wkend. Phone 208/443-3191.

Resorts

★ ★ **ELKINS ON PRIEST LAKE.** *404 Elkins Rd, Nordman (83848). 208/443-2432; fax 208/443-2527. www. elkinsresort.com.* 31 air-cooled kit. cottages. July-Aug (1 wk min), Sept-June (2-day min): S, D $75-$280; wkly rates; higher rates hol wkends; lower rates rest of yr. Crib free. Pet accepted; $5. Restaurant 8 am-9 pm; closed Mar and Apr. Box lunches, picnics. Bar. Ck-out 11 am, ck-in 4 pm. Gift shop. Grocery. Coin lndry 2 mi. Meeting rms. Game rm. Private beach. Boats. X-country ski on site. Picnic tables. Cr cds: DS, MC, V.

🄳 🐾 ⚓ 🎿 🔥

★ ★ **GRANDVIEW LODGE AND RESORT.** *3492 Reeder Bay Rd, Nordman (83848). 208/443-2433; fax 208/443-3033; res 888/806-3033. www.gvr.com.* 8 rms, 2 story, 11 suites, 9 cottages. June-Aug: S, D $95; suites $165; lower rates rest of yr. TV; cable. Complimentary coffee in rms, newspaper. Restaurant, Bar. Pool. Coin lndry, gift shop. Meeting rms. Beach access, hiking trail. Picnic facilities. Cr cds: MC, V.

★★ **HILLS RESORT.** *4777 W Lakeshore Rd, Priest Lake (83856). 208/ 443-2551; fax 208/443-2363. www. hillsresort.com.* 50 kit. chalets, cabins, 1-2 story. No A/C. Last wk June-Labor Day: $800-$1,850/wk; lower rates rest of yr. Crib $5. Pet accepted; $25. Dining rm 8 am-9:30 pm. Box lunches. Bar 1 pm-1 am. Ck-out 10 am. Grocery. Coin lndry. Meeting rms. Business servs avail. Tennis. Beach, boats, rowboats, canoes, waterskiing. X-country ski on site. Sleighing, tobogganing, snowmobiles. Bicycles (rentals). Lawn games. Entertainment, dancing, movies. Game rm. Housekeeping units. Fireplaces. Balconies. Picnic tables, grills. Cr cds: DS, MC, V.

Rexburg

(F-6) *See also Ashton, Idaho Falls, St. Anthony*

Founded 1883 **Pop** 14,302 **Elev** 4,865 ft **Area code** 208 **Zip** 83440
Information Chamber of Commerce Tourist & Information Center, 420 W 4th S; 208/356-5700
Web www.rexcc.com

Rexburg enjoys its position as a farm and trading center. Founded on instructions of the Mormon Church, the community was named for Thomas Ricks; usage changed it to Rexburg.

What to See and Do

Idaho Centennial Carousel. Restored Spillman Engineering carousel. (June-Labor Day, daily) Porter Park. Phone 208/359-3020. ¢

Parks.

Beaver Dick. A 12-acre preserve on W bank of the N Fork of Snake River. Fishing, boating, ramp; picnic facilities, primitive camping. (Mar-Dec) 7 mi W on ID 33.

Twin Bridges. A 30-acre preserve on N bank of the S Fork of Snake River. Fishing, boating, ramp; picnic facilities, camping. (Apr-Nov) 13 mi SE on Archer-Lyman Rd. Phone 208/356-3102.

Teton Flood Museum. Artifacts, photographs, and films document the 1976 flood caused by the collapse of the Teton Dam, which left 11 persons dead and $1 billion in damage. Also various historical displays. (May-Aug, Mon-Sat; rest of yr, Mon-Fri, limited hrs; closed hols exc July 4) 51 N Center. Phone 208/359-3063. ¢

Yellowstone Bear World. Drive-through preserve near Yellowstone National Park (see WYOMING) features bears, wolves, other wildlife; "Cub Yard" shows bear cubs at play; "Duck Deck" waterfowl observation/ feeding deck. (May-Oct, daily) 5 mi S on Hwy 20. Phone 208/359-9688. ¢¢¢

Special Event

Idaho International Folk Dance Festival. Dance teams from around the world, events. Last wk July-first wkend Aug. Phone 208/356-5700.

Motels/Motor Lodges

★★ **BEST WESTERN COTTON TREE INN.** *450 W 4th St S (83440). 208/356-4646; fax 208/356-7461; toll-free 800/662-6886. www.bestwestern. com.* 101 rms, 2 story. S $64; D $69-$74; each addl $5; suite $195; under 18 free. Crib free. Pet accepted. TV; cable. Indoor pool; whirlpool. Restaurant adj 7 am-10 pm. Ck-out noon. Coin lndry. Meeting rms. Business servs avail. Health club privileges. Some refrigerators, microwaves. Balconies. Cr cds: A, D, DS, MC, V.

★ **COMFORT INN.** *1565 W Main St (83440). 208/359-1311; fax 208/359-1387; toll-free 800/228-5150. www. comfortinn.com.* 52 rms, 2 story. June-mid-Sept: S, D $59-$69; suites $94; under 18 free; lower rates rest of yr.

Crib $5. Pet accepted. TV; cable. Indoor pool; whirlpool. Complimentary continental bkfst. Ck-out 11 am. Meeting rms. Exercise equipt. Refrigerator, microwave in suites. Cr cds: A, C, D, DS, JCB, MC, V.

★ **SUPER 8.** *215 W Main St (83440). 208/356-8888; fax 208/356-8899; res 800/800-8000. www.super8.com.* 41 rms, 2 story. June-Sept: S, D $40-$59; each addl $4; under 12 free; lower rates rest of yr. Crib free. TV; cable. Complimentary continental bkfst. Restaurant nearby. Ck-out 11 am. Business servs avail. Cr cds: A, C, D, DS, MC, V.

Restaurant

★ **FRONTIER PIES RESTAURANT.** *460 W 4th St (83440). 208/356-3600.* Hrs: 6:30 am-10 pm; Fri, Sat to 11 pm. Closed Dec 25. Bkfst $2.95-$5.59, lunch $4.59-$7.29, dinner $4.99- $10.99. Child's menu. Specialties: Navajo taco, broiled chicken Hawaiian. Own soups, pies. Rustic decor; Old West antiques. Totally nonsmoking. Cr cds: A, D, DS, MC, V.

St. Anthony

(F-6) *See also Ashton, Idaho Falls, Rexburg*

Pop 3,010 **Elev** 4,972 ft
Area code 208 **Zip** 83445
Information Chamber of Commerce, City Hall, 114 N Bridge St; 208/624-3494

Seat of Fremont County, headquarters for the Targhee National Forest and a center of the seed potato industry, St. Anthony is named for Anthony Falls, Minnesota. Tourists make it a base for exploring Idaho's tiny (30 miles long, one mile wide) "sahara desert," the St. Anthony Sand Dunes.

What to See and Do

Fort Henry Trading Post Site. (1810) First fort on what early voyageurs called the "accursed mad river." 7 mi W along Henry's Fork of Snake River.

St. Anthony Sand Dunes. 12 mi W. Phone 208/624-3494.

Special Events

Cowboy Poet Festival. Entertainment, clogging demonstrations. Apr. Phone 208/624-4870.

Fremont County Pioneer Days. Rodeo, parade, carnival. Late July. Phone 208/624-4870.

Fremont County Fair. Fairgrounds. Features demolition derby. Aug. Phone 208/624-4870.

Summerfest. Main St Booth fair. Aug. Phone 208/624-4870.

St. Marie's

(B-2) *See also Coeur d'Alene*

Pop 2,442 **Elev** 2,216 ft
Area code 208 **Zip** 83861
Information Chamber of Commerce, 906 Main, PO Box 162; 208/245-3563

St. Marie's (St. Mary's) is a center for lumbering and the production of plywood, a crossroads for lake, rail, and road transportation, and the jumping-off place for exploring the shadowy St. Joe River country. A Ranger District office of the Idaho Panhandle National Forests-St. Joe is located in St. Marie's.

What to See and Do

Benewah, Round, and Chatcolet lakes. Famous as one of state's best bass fishing and duck hunting areas. The three lakes became one lake with the construction of Post Falls Dam. Along St. Joe River. Also here is

Heyburn State Park. More than 7,800 acres. Swimming beach, fishing, boating (ramps, fee); ice-skating, ice fishing; hiking and bridle trails, mountain biking, self-guided nature walks, picnicking, concession, tent and trailer campsites (15-day max; hookups), dump station.

Campfire and interpretive programs. Dinner and interpretive cruises. Park (Daily). 7 mi W on ID 5. Phone 208/686-1308.

Idaho Panhandle National Forests—St. Joe. Hunting, fishing, hiking, camping, cabins, picnicking, summer and winter sports areas, cross-country skiing, snowmobiling trails; digging for garnets; scenic drives. Phone 208/245-2531; or the Avery Ranger District, HC Box 1, Avery 83802, Phone 208/245-4517; or the Supervisor, 3815 Schreiber Way, Coeur d'Alene, 83815, phone 208/765-7223. Access from US 95 and I-90; other areas E on local roads. Contact the St. Marie's Ranger District, PO Box 407. Other forests in the Panhandle are Coeur d'Alene (see COEUR D'ALENE) and Kankisu (see PRIEST LAKE AREA).

St. Joe Baldy Mountain. Lookout at top has view of Washington and Montana. 8 mi E on St. Joe River Rd (Forest Hwy 50).

St. Joe River. Called "the river through the lakes," one of the world's highest navigable rivers. Connects St. Marie's with Lake Coeur d'Alene. Just E on ID 5.

Special Events

smART Festival. St. Marie's City Park. Paintings and crafts by local and regional artists. Food, entertainment, swimming. Phone 208/245-3417. Third wkend July.

Paul Bunyan Days. Incl parade, fireworks, logging events, water show, carnival. Labor Day wkend. Phone 208/245-3563.

Salmon (E-4)

Settled 1866 **Pop** 2,941 **Elev** 4,004 ft **Area code** 208 **Zip** 83467
Information Salmon Valley Chamber of Commerce, 200 Main St, Suite 1; 208/756-2100 or 800/727-2540

This town, at the junction of the Salmon and Lemhi rivers, serves as a doorway to the Salmon River country. It has towering mountains, lush farmland, timberland, and rich mines. The Salmon River runs through the town on its way to the Columbia River and the Pacific Ocean. Fishing and boating are available along the Salmon and Lemhi rivers and in more than 250 lakes. The headquarters and two Ranger District offices of the Salmon National Forest are located here.

What to See and Do

River rafting, backpack, fishing, and pack trips. Along the Lemhi, Salmon, Middle Fork, and other rivers can be arranged. Contact the Chamber of Commerce for a list of outfitters in the area.

Salmon National Forest. Approx 1.8 million acres. Boat trips, fishing; hunting, picnicking, camping. Incl portion of the Frank Church—River of No Return Wilderness. N, E, and W of town along US 93. For further info contact the Supervisor, 50 Hwy 93 S. Phone 208/756-2215.

Special Events

High School Rodeo. First wkend June. Phone 208/756-2100.

Salmon River Days. July 4. Phone 208/756-2100.

The Great Salmon BalloonFest. Hot-air balloon festival. Aug. Phone 208/727-2540.

Lemhi County Fair & Rodeo. Third wk Aug.

Motel/Motor Lodge

★★ **STAGECOACH INN MOTEL.** *201 Hwy 93 N (83467). 208/756-4251; fax 208/756-3456.* 100 rms, 3 story. S $57; D $64; each addl $6; under 12 free; Crib avail, fee. TV; cable. Pool. Complimentary continental bkfst. Ck-out 11 am. Coin lndry. Meeting rms. Free airport transportation. Picnic facilities. Beach access. Cr cds: A, C, D, MC, V.
🄳 🐾 ➿ ✈ 🔌 🔥

Restaurant

★ **SALMON RIVER COFFEE SHOP.** *606 Main St (83467). 208/756-3521.* Hrs: 5 am-10 pm. Closed Jan 1, Thanksgiving, Dec 25. Bar. Bkfst $3-$6.95, lunch from $3.75, dinner $6.25-$20. Child's menu. Specializes in steak, seafood. Salad bar. Entertainment Mon-Sat. Cr cds: A, C, D, MC, V.

D ⟶

Sandpoint

(A-2) *See also Priest Lake Area*

Pop 5,203 **Elev** 2,085 ft
Area code 208 **Zip** 83864
Information Chamber of Commerce, 900 N 5th, PO Box 928; 208/263-2161 or 800/800-2106
Web www.sandpointchamber.com

At the point where the Pend Oreille River empties into Lake Pend Oreille (pon-da-RAY, from a Native American tribe given to wearing pendant ear ornaments), Sandpoint straddles two major railroads and three US highways. All of these bring a stream of tourists into town. In the surrounding area are dozens of smaller lakes and streams. A Ranger District office of the Idaho Panhandle National Forests-Coeur d'Alene (see COEUR D'ALENE) is located here.

What to See and Do

Bonner County Historical Society Museum. Exhibits depict history of Bonner County. Research library with newspaper collection dating from 1899. (Apr-Oct, Tues-Sat; rest of yr, Thurs; closed hols) In Lakeview Park, Ontario and Ella Sts. Phone 208/263-2344. ¢

Coldwater Creek on the Cedar Street Bridge. Shopping mall built on a bridge over Sand Creek. Inspired by the Ponte Vecchio in Florence, Italy, the Coldwater Creek shops provide panoramic views of Lake Pend Oreille and nearby mountains. (Daily) Phone 208/263-2265.

Lake Pend Oreille. Largest in Idaho, one of the largest natural lakes wholly within US; more than 43 mi long, six mi wide, with more than 111 mi of shoreline. Approx 14 varieties of game fish incl famous Kamloops, largest rainbow trout in world (avg 16-26 lbs). Boating, swimming, waterskiing; camping, picnicking.

Round Lake State Park. Approx 140 acres of coniferous woods. Swim-

ming, skin diving, fishing, ice fishing, ice-skating, boating (ramp, no motors); hiking, cross-country skiing, sledding, tobogganing, snowshoeing in winter, picnicking. Camping (15-day max; no hookups), dump station. Campfire programs. Park (Daily). Standard fees. 10 mi S on US 95, then 2 mi W, near Sagle. Phone 208/263-3489.

Sandpoint Public Beach. Nearly 20 acres. Bathhouse, swimming, waterskiing, boat docks, ramps; picnic tables, fireplaces, volleyball and tennis courts; concession (seasonal). Park (Daily). Foot of Bridge St, E edge of town. **FREE**

Skiing. Schweitzer Mountain Resort. Five chairlifts, high-speed quad; school, rentals; lodging, restaurants, bars, cafeteria; nursery. Longest run 2.7 mi; vertical drop 2,400 ft. (Nov-Apr, daily) Summer chairlift rides (fee). 11 mi NW off US 2 and US 95, in Selkirk Mts of Idaho Panhandle National Forests. Phone 800/831-8810.

Special Event

Winter Carnival. Two wkends of festivities incl snow sculpture, snowshoe softball, and other games, races, torchlight parade. Mid-Jan. Phone 208/263-2161

Motels/Motor Lodges

★ ★ ★ **CONNIE'S HAWTHORN INN.** 415 Cedar St (83864). 208/263-9581; fax 208/263-3395; res 800/527-1133. www.hotels-west.com. 70 rms, 3 story. July-Aug: S $99; D $109; each addl $8; suites $199-$299; under 17 free; golf, ski plans; lower rates rest of yr. Crib $8. TV; cable (premium), VCR avail. Heated pool; whirlpool. Restaurant 6 am-10 pm; Fri, Sat to midnight. Rm serv 7 am-10 pm. Bar 11-1 am. Ck-out 1 pm. Meeting rm. Business servs avail. In-rm modem link. Valet serv. Downhill/x-country ski 9 mi. Health club privileges. Some bathrm phones, refrigerators. Balconies. Cr cds: A, DS, MC, V.
🏊 ⊶ 🔥

★ ★ **EDGEWATER RESORT.** 56 Bridge St (83864). 208/263-3194; toll-free 800/635-2534. www.sandpoint hotels.com/edgewater. 55 rms, 3 story.

No elvtr. S $106-$115; D $110-$119; each addl $10; suites $120-$150; under 16 free; package plans. Crib $5. Pet accepted; $5. TV; cable, VCR avail. Restaurant 11 am-10 pm; Sun to 9 pm. Complimentary bkfst. Bar. Ck-out noon. Meeting rms. Business servs avail. Whirlpool. Sauna. Private patios, balconies. On Lake Pend Oreille; swimming beach. Cr cds: A, C, D, DS, ER, JCB, MC, V.

★ **LAKESIDE INN.** *106 Bridge St (83864). 208/263-3717; fax 208/265-4781; toll-free 800/543-8126. www. keokee.com/lakeside.* 60 units, 2-3 story, 10 kits. No elvtr. July-Aug: S $49-$74; D $54-$79; each addl $5; suites $125; kits. $105; under 12 free; ski, golf plans; higher rates hols; lower rates rest of yr. Crib free. Pet accepted, some restrictions; $5/day. TV; cable. Whirlpool; sauna. Complimentary continental bkfst. Restaurant nearby. Ck-out 11 am. Coin lndry. Free airport, RR station transportation. Lawn games. Balconies. Picnic tables, grills. On Lake Pend Oreille. Cr cds: A, D, DS, MC, V.

★ **SANDPOINT QUALITY INN.** *807 N 5th Ave (83864). 208/263-2111; fax 208/263-3289; res 800/635-2534. www. qualityinn.com.* 62 rms, 2 story. S $59-$88; D $65-$95; each addl $6; under 18 free; ski plan. Crib free. Pet accepted; $5. TV; cable, VCR avail. Indoor pool; whirlpool. Coffee in rms. Restaurant 5:30 am-10 pm. Bar 11-2 am. Ck-out noon. Business servs avail. Coin lndry. Sundries. Downhill/x-country ski 11 mi. Cr cds: A, C, D, DS, MC, V.

★ **SUPER 8 MOTEL.** *476841 Hwy 95 N (83864). 208/263-2210; res 800/800-8000. www.super8.com.* 61 rms, 2 story. Mid-June-mid Aug: S, D $35-$75; D $55-$80; each addl $5; under 13 free; family rates; package plans; higher rates special events; lower rates rest of yr. Crib free. Pet accepted. TV; cable (premium). Complimentary coffee in lobby. Restau-

rant adj 8 am-9 pm. Ck-out 11 am. Business servs avail. In-rm modem link. Downhill ski 9 mi; x-country ski 1 mi. Microwaves avail. Cr cds: A, C, D, DS, MC, V.

Restaurants

★★ **BANGKOK CUISINE.** *202 N 2nd Ave (83864).* 208/265-4149. Hrs: 11:30 am-9 pm. Closed Sun; also Labor Day, Thanksgiving, Dec 25. Res accepted. Thai menu. A la carte entrees: lunch $5.25-$6.25, dinner $6.95-$12.95. Specializes in vegetarian dishes, curries. Street parking. Some Thai decor; fish tank. Cr cds: D, DS, MC, V.

★★ **FLOATING RESTAURANT.** *ID 200 E, Hope (83836).* 208/264-5311. Hrs: 11 am-9 pm; Sun 10 am-9 pm; Sun brunch 10 am-2 pm. Closed

Lake Pend Oreille

Nov-Mar. Res accepted. Seafood menu. Bar. A la carte entrees: lunch $4.25-$9, dinner $4.95-$8.95. Dinner $11.95-$18.95. Sun brunch $8.95. Child's menu. Specializes in fish, pasta. Own baking. Parking. Outdoor dining. On lake. Totally nonsmoking. Cr cds: A, DS, MC, V.

★ **HYDRA.** *115 Lake St (83864).* 208/263-7123. Hrs: 11:30 am-10 pm; Fri, Sat to 10:30 pm; Sat, Mon from 5 pm; Sun 10 am-9 pm; Sun brunch to 2 pm. Closed Thanksgiving, Dec 25. Bar 4-11 pm. Buffet: lunch $5.95. Dinner $5.25-$16.95. Sun brunch

$7.50. Eclectic decor. Cut-glass by local artist. Cr cds: A, D, DS, MC, V.
D ⊣

★★ **IVANO'S RISTORANTE.** *124 S 2nd Ave (83864). 208/263-0211.* Hrs: 5-10 pm. Closed Easter, Thanksgiving, Dec 25. Res accepted. Italian menu. Bar. Dinner $7.95-$19.95. Child's menu. Specializes in pasta, seafood. Outdoor dining. Cathedral ceiling in main dining rm. Cr cds: A, D, DS, MC, V.
D

★ **JALAPENO'S.** *314 N 2nd Ave (83864). 208/263-2995. www.jalapenos restaurant.com* Hrs: 11 am-11 pm. Closed some major hols. Mexican menu. Lunch $5-$9, dinner $5-$11. Child's menu. Specialties: garlic shrimp, pork carnitas, carne asada. Street parking. Outdoor dining. Wall murals. Totally nonsmoking. Cr cds: A, DS, MC, V.
D

Shoshone

(G-3) *See also Jerome, Twin Falls*

Founded 1882 **Pop** 1,249 **Elev** 3,970 ft **Area code** 208 **Zip** 83352
Information City Hall, 207 S Rail St W, Box 208; 208/886-2030

Shoshone (sho-SHOWN or sho-SHO-nee) is the seat of Lincoln County and the marketplace for a farming and livestock area fed by irrigation.

What to See and Do

Mary L. Gooding Memorial Park. Playground, pool (May-Aug, daily), picnic area along Little Wood River. (Daily) 300 N Rail St. Phone 208/886-2030.

⊠ **Shoshone Indian Ice Caves.** Natural refrigerator, with temperatures ranging from 18-33°F. Cave is three blks long, 30 ft wide, and 40 ft high. On grounds are statue of Shoshone Chief Washakie and a museum of Native American artifacts; minerals, gems (free). 45-min guided tours (May-Sept, daily). 17 mi N on ID 75. Phone 208/886-2058. ¢¢¢

Special Events

Arts in the Park. Arts and crafts fair. Second wkend July.

Manty Shaw Fiddlers' Jamboree. Second wkend July. Phone 208/886-2030.

Lincoln County Fair. Third wk July. Phone 208/886-2030.

Stanley (F-3)

Pop 71 **Elev** 6,260 ft **Area code** 208 **Zip** 83278
Information Chamber of Commerce, PO Box 8; 208/774-3411
Web www.stanleycc.org

Situated on the Salmon River (the famous "river of no return"), Stanley is located at the center of the Sawtooth Wilderness, Sawtooth Valley, and scenic Stanley Basin. A Ranger District office of the Sawtooth National Forest (see BELLEVUE, BURLEY) is located here.

What to See and Do

Salmon River. Rafting, kayaking, fishing; camping. Phone 208/879-4101.

River Expeditions. Many outfitters offer wilderness float trips on the Middle Fork of the Salmon River. Along the river are Native American pictographs, caves, abandoned gold mines, and abundant wildlife. Activities incl boating, fishing, hiking, natural hot water springs, and photography. For a list of outfitters contact the Chamber of Commerce or the Idaho Company Outfitters and Guides Assn. Phone 208/774-3411.

Sawtooth National Recreation Area. Fishing, boating, waterskiing; hiking, biking, camping (fee). Many lakes are here, incl Stanley, Redfish, and Alturas. (Also see SUN VALLEY AREA). In Sawtooth National Forest. Contact Area Ranger, HC 64, Box 8291, Ketchum 83340. Phone 208/727-5000. In recreation area are

Redfish Lake Visitor Center. Historical, geological, naturalist displays and dioramas. Self-guided trails. Campfire programs, guided tours. (Memorial Day-Labor Day, daily) 5

mi S on ID 75, then 2 mi SW.
Phone 208/774-3376. **FREE**

Sawtooth Wilderness. Many lakes;
wilderness hiking, backpacking,
and mountain climbing. 8 mi N,
in Ketchum. Phone 208/727-5000.

Sawtooth Valley and Stanley Basin.
Fishing; cross-country skiing, snowmobiling, mountain biking, backpacking, hunting. Dude ranches
featuring pack trips; big game guides.
Contact Chamber of Commerce.
Phone 208/774-3411.

Special Events

**Sawtooth Mountain Mamas Arts and
Crafts Fair.** Third wkend July. Phone
208/774-3411.

Sawtooth Quilt Festival. Community
Building. Third wkend Sept. Phone
208/774-3411.

Motel/Motor Lodge

★★ **MOUNTAIN VILLAGE LODGE.**
*Hwys 75 and 21 (83278). 208/774-
3661; fax 208/774-3761. www.
mountainvillage.com.* 61 rms, 2 story.
S, D $59-$74; each addl $5; suites
$80-$115; under 5 free; package plan.
Pet accepted; $5. TV; cable (pre-
mium), VCR avail. Coffee in rms.
Restaurant 7 am-11 pm. Bar 11-1 am;
entertainment. Ck-out 11 am. Coin
lndry. Meeting rms. Business servs
avail. Airport transportation. Lawn
games. Panoramic view of Sawtooth
Mtns. Near Salmon River. Cr cds: A,
D, DS, MC, V.

Guest Ranch

★★ **IDAHO ROCKY MOUNTAIN
RANCH.** *HC 64 Box 9934 (83278).
208/774-3544; fax 208/774-3477.
www.idahorocky.com.* 4 rms in lodge,
17 cabins. No phones. June-Sept:
MAP S, D $71; each addl $30-$71;
under 2 free; wkly rates. Nov-Apr:
kit. cabins $85-$220. Pool. Dining
rm 7-10 am, 6:30-8:30 pm. Box
lunches. Ck-out 11 am, ck-in 3 pm.
Grocery store 9 mi. Guest lndry. X-
country ski on site. Horse stables.
Hiking. Bicycle rentals. Stone fireplace in cabins. On Salmon River.
View of Sawtooth Mtns. Totally nonsmoking. Cr cds: DS, MC, V.

Sun Valley Area

(F-3)

Elev 5,920 ft **Area code** 208
Information Sun Valley/Ketchum
Chamber of Commerce, PO Box
2420, Sun Valley 83353; 208/726-
3423 or 800/634-3347
Web www.visitsunvalley.com

In a sun-drenched, bowl-shaped valley, this is one of the most famous
resorts in the world. Developed by
the Union Pacific Railroad, this area
was established after an extensive
survey of the West. Sheltered by surrounding ranges, it attracts both winter and summer visitors and offers
nearly every imaginable recreational
opportunity. Powder snow lasts until
late spring, allowing long skiing seasons, and there is hunting, mountain
biking, and superb fly fishing. Two
Ranger District offices of the Sawtooth National Forest (see BELLE-
VUE, BURLEY) are located in
Ketchum.

What to See and Do

Sawtooth National Recreation Area.
Fishing, boating, waterskiing; hiking,
camping (fee). Many lakes are here,
incl Stanley, Redfish, and Alturas.
(Also see STANLEY). NW via ID 75,
in Sawtooth National Forest. Contact
Area Ranger, HC 64, Box 8291,
Ketchum 83340. Phone 208/727-
5000. In recreation area on ID 75 is

> **Headquarters Visitor Information
> Center.** Orientation exhibits,
> maps, brochures, interpretive
> material. Evening programs (sum-
> mer). Center (Daily; schedule may
> vary) Phone 208/727-5013. **FREE**

**Sun Valley Resort. Year-round activi-
ties.** Sports director, supervised recreation for children; three outdoor
pools (two glass-enclosed), lifeguard;
sauna, massage, bowling, indoor and
outdoor ice-skating, movies, dancing; Sun Valley Center for the Arts
and Humanities. Special activities.
Contact Sun Valley Resort. 1 Sun
Valley Rd.

> **Summer.** Three outdoor pools,
> fishing, boating, whitewater river
> raft trips; tennis (school), 18-hole
> Robert Trent Jones golf course

(pro), Olympic ice show, skeet and trap shooting, lawn games, horse-back riding (school), mountain biking, hiking, pack trips, hay rides. Auto trips may be arranged to Redfish Lake near Stanley.

Winter. Seventeen ski lifts to slopes for every level of skier; ski school, rentals. Longest run three mi; vertical drop 3,400 ft. Ice-skating, sleigh rides, and groomed cross-country trails. (Thanksgiving-Apr, daily)

Special Event

Wagon Days. Celebration of the area's mining history; large, non-motorized parade, band concerts, entertainment, arts and crafts fair, dramas. Labor Day wkend. Phone 208/726-3423.

Motels/Motor Lodges

★ **AIRPORT INN.** *820 S 4th St, Hailey (83333). 208/788-2477; fax 208/788-3195. www.taylorhotelgroup. com.* 29 rms, 1-2 story. S, D $73-$89; each addl $8; suites $90-$101; under 12 free. Crib free. TV; cable. VCR avail. Restaurant nearby. Ck-out 11 am. Coin lndry. Downhill ski 12 mi; x-country ski adj. Whirlpool. Some refrigerators, microwaves. Cr cds: A, C, D, DS, MC, V.
🐾 ⛷ 🐾 SC

★★ **BEST WESTERN KENTWOOD LODGE.** *180 S Main St, Ketchum (83340). 208/726-4114; fax 208/726-2417; toll-free 800/805-1001. www. bestwestern.com.* 57 rms, 3 story. Feb-mid-Apr, mid-June-mid-Sept, mid-Dec-early Jan: S, D $145; each addl $10; suites, kit. units $145; under 12 free; 2-day min some wkends, 3-day min some hols; lower rates rest of yr. Crib $5. TV; cable. Indoor pool; whirlpool. Restaurant adj 8 am-3 pm. Ck-out 11 am. Coin lndry. Meeting rm. Business servs avail. Valet serv. Exercise equipt. Refrigerators; microwaves avail. Some balconies. Totally nonsmoking. Cr cds: A, DS, MC, V.
⛷ 🕺 🐾 🔥

★★ **BEST WESTERN TYROLEAN LODGE.** *260 Cottonwood Ave, Ketchum (83353). 208/726-5336; fax 208/726-2081; toll-free 800/333-7912. www.bestwestern.com.* 56 rms, 3 story,

7 suites. No A/C. Mid-Dec-early Jan: S $85; D $90-$100; each addl $8; suites $125-$155; under 12 free; ski plan; lower rates rest of yr. Crib free. Pet accepted, some restrictions; fee. TV; cable. Pool; whirlpool. Complimentary continental bkfst. Restaurant nearby. Ck-out 11 am. Coin lndry. Meeting rms. Business servs avail. Downhill/x-country ski adj. Exercise equipt; sauna. Game rm. Microwaves avail. Cr cds: A, C, D, DS, MC, V.
🐾 ⛷ 🔥

★ **TAMARACK LODGE.** *Sun Valley Rd and Walnut Ave, Ketchum (83353). 208/726-3344; fax 208/726-3347; toll-free 800/521-5379. www.tamaracksun valley.com.* 26 rms, 3 story. No elvtr. Dec-Mar: S, D $69-$96; each addl $10; suites $119; under 13 free; lower rates rest of yr. Crib $5. TV; cable (premium). Indoor pool; whirlpool. Complimentary coffee in rms. Restaurant nearby. Ck-out 11 am. Downhill/x-country ski 1 mi. Refrigerators, microwaves, fireplaces. Cr cds: A, C, D, DS, JCB, MC, V.
🐾 🕺 ⛷ 🛏 🛏 🔥 SC

Hotel

★★★ **KNOB HILL INN.** *960 N Main St, Ketchum (83340). 208/726-8010; fax 208/726-2712. www.knobhillinn. com.* 16 rms, 4 story, 8 suites. Jan-Mar, June-Dec: S, D $185-$385; each addl $15. TV; cable (premium); VCR avail. Complimentary continental bkfst. Ck-out noon. Meeting rms. Business serv avail. Exercise rm; whirlpool. Cr cds: A, MC, V.
🕺 🔥

Resorts

★★★ **ELKHORN RESORT.** *100 Elkhorn Rd, Sun Valley (83353). 208/622-4511; fax 208/622-3261; toll-free 800/355-4676. www.elkhornresort. com.* 90 condos, 4 story; 7 suites. Jan-Mar, S, D $139; suites $299. each addl $10; under 18 free; ski, golf plans; lower rates rest of yr. Crib free. TV; cable. Pools; whirlpool, lifeguard. Supervised children's activities (June-Aug); ages 4-12. Bar. Ck-out 10 am-noon, ck-in 4 pm. Meeting rms. Business servs avail. In-rm modem link. Gift shop. Free airport trans-

WANDERING THE SUN-DRENCHED SUN VALLEY AREA

Begin a tour of the resort towns of Ketchum and Sun Valley at the Ketchum-Sun Valley Heritage and Ski Museum, in Ketchum's Forest Service Park at 1st Street and Washington Avenue. The museum tells the story of the indigenous Tukudeka tribe, the early mining settlement, and the building of Sun River Resort. There is also information on past and present residents like Ernest Hemingway, Olympic athletes, and the Hollywood glitterati who come here to ski. Walk north along Washington Avenue, passing coffee shops and gift boutiques, to the Sun Valley Center for the Arts and Humanities (191 5th Street East), the hub of the valley's art world. The center presents exhibits, lectures, and films and is a great place to find out what's going on in Ketchum.

Walk one block east to Main Street. Downtown Ketchum has, for a city of its size, an enormous number of art galleries, restaurants, and high-end boutiques. It would be easy to spend a day wandering the small town center, looking at art, trying on sheepskin coats, and stopping for lattes. While you wander, be sure to stop at the Chapter One Bookstore (160 Main), which offers a good selection of regional titles. Charles Stuhlberg Furniture (571 East Avenue North) is filled with the faux-rustic New West furniture and accessories popular with the area's upscale residents. For art galleries, go to the corner of Sun Valley Road and Walnut Avenue. The Walnut Avenue Mall (620 Sun Valley Road) is a boutique development with four independent galleries. Directly across the street is the Colonnade Mall (601 Sun Valley Road) with four more top-notch galleries.

Continue east on Sun Valley Road, picking up the walking and biking trail north of the road. Follow the trail one mile east through forest to the Sun Valley Resort, a massive complex with an imposing central lodge, condominium developments, home tracts, and golf courses. The lodge was built in 1936 by Averill Harriman, chairman of the Union Pacific Railroad, and was modeled after European ski resorts in Switzerland and Austria. Harriman hired an Austrian count to tour the western United States in search of a suitable locale; the count chose the little mining town of Ketchum for the resort.

Wander the interior of the vast lodge, looking at the photos of the celebrities who have skied here. In its heyday, Sun Valley hosted the likes of Lucille Ball, the Kennedys, Gary Cooper, and dozens of other stars of film and politics. Hundreds of photos line the hallways, commemorating the famous guests who have skied here. Just west of the lodge, and easily glimpsed through the windows that look out onto the Bald Mountain ski area, is an outdoor skating rink. Kept frozen even in summer, the rink is usually a-spin with novice ice-skaters. On Saturday evenings, professional ice-skaters take to the ice to perform.

For a longer hike, return to Sun Valley Road and walking trail, and continue east up Trail Creek, past golf courses and meadows. In a mile, the valley narrows. Here, in a grove of cottonwoods overlooking the river, is the Hemingway Memorial, a simple stone bust that commemorates the author who died in Ketchum in 1961. Etched in the stone are the words Hemingway wrote at the death of a friend: "Best of all he loved the fall. The leaves yellow on the cottonwoods. Leaves floating on the trout streams. And above the hills the high blue windless skies...now he will be a part of them forever."

portation. Tennis, pro. 18-hole golf, greens fee (incl cart) $98, pro, putting green, driving range, golf school. Downhill ski on site. Bicycles, bike trails. Lawn games. Entertainment. Music concerts in summer. Exercise equipt; sauna, steam rm. Massage. Fishing/hunting guides. Fly fishing lessons. Luxury level. Cr cds: A, C, D, DS, MC, V.

★★★ **SUN VALLEY RESORT.** *1 Sun Valley Rd, Sun Valley (83353). 208/ 726-3344; fax 208/726-3347; toll-free*

800/521-5379. www.sunvalley.com. 262 rms, 4 story; 193 condo units, 2-4 story. No A/C. Jan-Mar: S $89-$159; D $99-$229; each addl $15; suites $349; condos (1-4-bedrm) $184-$399; under 12 free; lower rates rest of yr. Crib free. TV; cable. 3 pools, heated; wading pool, poolside serv. Supervised children's activities. Dining rms 7 am-10 pm (see also GRETCHEN'S). Bars noon-1 am. Ck-out 11 am, ck-in 4 pm. Grocery. Package store. Convention facilities. Business servs avail. Bellhops. Valet serv. Concierge. Barber, beauty shop. Free airport transportation. Sports dir. Tennis, pro. 18-hole golf, greens fee $83, pro, putting green, driving range. Paddle boats. Downhill/x-country ski on site. Sleigh rides. 2 ice-skating rinks; ice shows. River rafting. Bicycles. Roller blades (rentals). Lawn games. Trap and skeet shooting. Entertainment, movies. Bowling. Game rm. Exercise equipt; sauna. Massage. Fishing/hunting guides. Refrigerator, microwave in condos; some fireplaces. Some private patios, balconies. Picnic tables. Cr cds: A, D, DS, MC, V.

B&Bs/Small Inns

★★★ **IDAHO COUNTRY INN.** 134 Latigo Ln, Sun Valley (83353). 208/727-4000; fax 208/725-0193; toll-free 800/635-4444. www.premierresorts sv.com. 11 rms, 2 story. Jan-Mar and June-Sept: S, D $125-$185; higher rates wk of Dec 25, lower rates rest of yr. TV; cable. Complimentary full bkfst, cookies in the afternoon. Restaurant nearby. Ck-out 10 am, ck-in 5 pm. Downhill/x-country ski 1½ mi. Whirlpool. Refrigerators. Balconies. Library, warming rm; individually decorated rms. Stone fireplace. View of Bald Mountain. Totally nonsmoking. Cr cds: A, MC, V.

★★★ **THE RIVER STREET INN.** 100 River St, Ketchum (83340). 208/726-3611; fax 208/726-2439; toll-free 888/746-3611. www.theriverstreet inn.com. 8 rms, 2 story. Jan-Apr, June-July, Sep: S, D $135-$185; each addl $25; lower rates rest of yr. TV; cable (premium), VCR avail. Complimentary full bkfst; coffee in rms. Restau-

rant nearby. Ck-out 11 am, ck-in 2 pm. Bike rentals nearby. Hiking Trail. Picnic facilities. Cr cds: A, MC, V.

Restaurants

★★ **CHANDLER'S RESTAURANT.** 200 S Main St, Ketchum (83340). 208/726-1776. www.chandlers restaurant.com. Hrs: 6-10 pm. Res accepted. Wine, beer. Dinner $14-$29. Prix fixe: dinner $19.95. Child's menu. Specialties: fresh Hawaiian ahi, elk loin, Yankee pot roast. Outdoor dining. 1940s home has antique furnishings, open beamed ceilings. Cr cds: A, DS, MC, V.

★★★ **EVERGREEN BISTRO.** 171 First Ave (83340). 208/726-3888. Hrs: 6-10 pm. Closed May, Nov. Res accepted. French, American menu. Beer. Wine cellar. Dinner $16.95-$30. Specializes in venison, rack of lamb, fresh fish. Outdoor dining. In converted house; view of Mt Baldy. Totally nonsmoking. Cr cds: A, MC, V.

★★★ **GRETCHEN'S.** Sun Valley Rd, Sun Valley (83353). 208/622-2144. www.sunvalley.com. Hrs: 7 am-10 pm. (located in Sun Valley Lodge) Res accepted. Continental menu. Bar noon-1 am. Bkfst $5-$8, lunch $6.25-$9.75, dinner $14.50-$22. Child's menu. Specialties: hazelnut-crusted elk loin, spicy farfalle pasta with roasted roma tomatoes, raspberry chocolate mousse. Own baking. Outdoor dining. Cozy, country-French atmosphere. Totally nonsmoking. Cr cds: A, D, DS, MC, V.

★★ **WARM SPRINGS RANCH RESTAURANT.** 1801 Warm Springs Rd, Ketchum (83340). 208/726-2609. Hrs: 6-10 pm. Res accepted. Bar 5 pm-1 am. Dinner $10.95-$25.95. Child's menu. Specializes in scones, seafood, barbecued ribs. Parking. Outdoor dining. Overlooks mountains and stocked, spring-fed ponds. Family-owned. Cr cds: A, MC, V.

Twin Falls

(H-3) *See also Buhl, Burley, Jerome, Shoshone*

Founded 1904 **Pop** 27,591 **Elev** 3,745 ft **Area code** 208 **Zip** 83301
Information Chamber of Commerce, 858 Blue Lakes Blvd N; 208/733-3974 or 800/255-8946
Web www.cyberhighway.net/ ~tfidcham/

After rising "like magic" on the tide of irrigation that reached this valley early in the century, Twin Falls has become the major city of south central Idaho's "Magic Valley" region. Seat of agriculturally rich Twin Falls County, it is also a tourist center, boasting that visitors in the area can enjoy almost every known sport. The headquarters and a Ranger District office of the Sawtooth National Forest (see BELLEVUE, BURLEY, STANLEY) are located here.

What to See and Do

Fishing. In Snake River and numerous other rivers, lakes. Sturgeon of up to 100 pounds may be caught, but by law cannot be removed from the water. Twin Falls Chamber of Commerce can provide detailed info.

Herrett Center. Exhibits on archaeology of North, Central, and South America; gallery of contemporary art; Faulkner Planetarium. (Tues-Sat; closed hols) 315 Falls Ave, on College of Southern Idaho campus. Phone 208/733-9554.

Perrine Memorial Bridge. Bridge, 486 ft high and 1,500 ft long, crosses the Snake River canyon. 1½ mi N on US 93. Phone 208/733-3974.

Sawtooth Twin Falls Ranger District. Fishing; camping (fee at some designated campgrounds), picnicking, hiking trails, snowmobile trails, downhill and cross-country skiing. 9 mi E on US 30 to Hansen, then 28 mi S on local roads, in Sawtooth National Forest. Phone 208/737-3200.

◾ **Shoshone Falls.** "Niagara of the West" drops 212 ft (52 ft more than Niagara Falls). During irrigation season, the flow is limited; it is best during spring and fall. 5 mi NE, on Snake River. Access to the falls is avail through

Shoshone Falls Park. Picnic tables, stoves, fireplace, trails, waterskiing. (Mar-Nov, daily) S bank of river. Phone 208/736-2265 or 208/736-2266. ¢¢

Twin Falls. 5½ mi NE. These 132-ft falls are accessible via

Twin Falls Park. Boating (dock, ramp), fishing, waterskiing; picnic area. (Daily) S bank of river. Phone 208/423-4223.

Special Events

Western Days. Three-day event featuring shoot-out, barbecue contests, dances, parade. Dates may vary, phone 800/255-8946 for schedule; usually wkend following Memorial Day.

Twin Falls County Fair and Magic Valley Stampede. County Fairgrounds, 6 mi W via US 30 in Filer. One wk starting Wed before Labor Day. Phone 208/326-4396.

Motels/Motor Lodges

★★ **AMERITEL INN-TWIN FALLS.** *1377 Blue Lakes Blvd N (83301). 208/736-8000; fax 208/734-7777; toll-free 800/600-6001. www.ameritelinns. com.* 118 rms, 3 story. June-Aug: S, D $63-$100; each addl $5; suites $110; kit. units $98.75; under 12 free; lower rates rest of yr. Crib $5. TV; cable (premium). Indoor pool; whirlpool. Complimentary continental bkfst. Restaurant adj 6 am-10 pm. Ck-out 11 am. Coin lndry. Meeting rms. Free airport transportation. Exercise equipt. Microwaves avail. Cr cds: A, D, DS, MC, V.
🄳 ⇌ 🕴 ✈ ⊠ 🔥

★★ **BEST WESTERN CANYON SPRINGS PARK HOTEL.** *1357 Blue Lakes Blvd N (83301). 208/734-5000; fax 208/733-3813; toll-free 800/780-7234. www.bestwestern.com.* 112 rms, 2 story. S $69.75; D $75.75; each addl $6; under 12 free. Crib free. TV; cable (premium). Heated pool. Restaurant 6 am-10 pm; Fri, Sat to 11 pm. Bar 4 pm-1 am. Ck-out 1 pm. Meeting rms. Bellhops. Valet serv. Free airport transportation. Exercise equipt. Balconies. Cr cds: A, C, D, DS, MC, V.
🄳 ⇌ 🕴 ⊠ 🔥 SC

★★ **COMFORT INN TWIN FALLS.**
1893 Canyon Springs Rd (83301).
208/734-7494; fax 208/735-9428; res
800/228-5150. www.comfortinn.com.
52 rms, 2 story, 15 suites. S $52.99; D
$59.99; each addl $7; suites $67.99;
under 18 free. Crib free. Pet accepted.
TV; cable (premium). Indoor pool;
whirlpool. Complimentary continental bkfst. Ck-out 11 am. Health club
privileges. Cr cds: A, D, DS, MC, V.

★★ **SHILO INN.** *1586 Blue Lakes*
Blvd N (83301). 208/733-7545; fax
208/736-2019; res 800/222-2244.
www.shiloinns.com. 128 rms, 4 story.
S, D $69.95-$140.95; each addl $10;
kit. units $109-$149; under 12 free.
Crib free. Pet accepted, some restrictions; $10/day. TV, cable (premium),
VCR (movies). Complimentary continental bkfst. Coffee in rms. Restaurant nearby. Ck-out noon. Meeting
rms. Business servs avail. In-rm
modem link. Sundries. Coin lndry.
Exercise equipt; sauna. Indoor pool;
whirlpool. Refrigerators, microwaves,
wet bars. Cr cds: A, C, D, DS, ER,
JCB, MC, V.

Restaurant

★★ **JAKER'S.** *1598 Blue Lakes Blvd*
(83301). 208/733-0400. www.jakers.
com. Hrs: 11:30 am-2 pm; 5-10 pm;
Sat to 10:30 pm; Sun to 9:30 pm.
Closed hols. Bar. Lunch $2.95-$9.95,
dinner $7.95-$29.95. Child's menu.
Specializes in prime rib, pasta,
seafood. Outdoor dining. Cr cds: A,
D, DS, MC, V.

Wallace

(B-2) *See also Coeur d'Alene, Kellogg*

Founded 1884 **Pop** 1,010 **Elev** 2,744
ft **Area code** 208 **Zip** 83873
Information Chamber of Commerce,
10 River St, PO Box 1167; 208/753-
7151

Gold was discovered in streams near
here in 1882; lead, zinc, silver, and
copper deposits were found in 1884.
A Ranger District office of the Idaho
Panhandle National Forests-Coeur
d'Alene (see COEUR D'ALENE) is
located in nearby Silverton.

What to See and Do

Auto tour. Fifteen-mi drive through
spectacular scenery in Idaho Panhan-
dle National Forests—Coeur d'Alene
and St. Joe. Local roads follow Nine
Mile Creek, Dobson Pass, and Two
Mile Creek to Osburn. This trip may
be extended by traveling N and E out
of Dobson Pass along Beaver and
Trail creeks to Murray, then W to
Prichard; then follow Coeur d'Alene
River W and S to Kingston; return to
Wallace on US 10, I-90.

Lookout Pass Ski Area. Chairlift,
rope tow; patrol, school, rentals;
cafeteria; bar. Longest run one mi;
vertical drop 850 ft. Half-day rate
(Mid-Nov-mid-Apr, Thurs-Sun) Cross-
country skiing is also avail. Snowmobiling. 12 mi E on I-90, in Idaho
Panhandle National Forests. Phone
208/744-1301. ¢¢¢¢

**Northern Pacific Depot Railroad
Museum.** (1901) Houses artifacts,
photographs, and memorabilia that
portray railroad history of the Coeur
d'Alene Mining District; display of
railroad depot (ca 1910). (May-Oct,
hrs vary) 219 6th St. Phone 208/752-
0111. ¢

Oasis Bordello Museum. Former bor
dello (ca 1895); moonshine still.
(May-Oct, daily) 605 Cedar St. Phone
208/753-0801. ¢¢

Sierra Silver Mine Tour. Offers 1¼-hr
guided tour through actual silver
mine. Demonstrations of mining
methods, techniques, and operation
of modern-day equipt. Departs every
30 min. (May-mid-Oct, daily) 420
5th St. Phone 208/752-5151. ¢¢

Wallace District Mining Museum.
Material on the history of mining,
20-min video, old mining machinery. Information on mine tours and
old mining towns in the area. (May-
Sept, daily; rest of yr, Mon-Sat) 509
Bank St. Phone 208/556-1592. ¢

Motels/Motor Lodges

★★ **BEST WESTERN WALLACE INN.** *100 Front St (83873). 208/752-1252; fax 208/753-0981; res 800/780-7234. www.bestwestern.com.* 63 rms, 2 story. S $70-$75; D $80-$85; each addl $8; suites $225-$250; under 12 free. Crib $8. TV; cable (premium), VCR avail. Indoor pool; whirlpool, poolside serv. Restaurant 7 am-9 pm. Bar. Ck-out noon. Meeting rms. Business servs avail. Gift shop. Bus depot transportation. Exercise equipt; sauna. Refrigerator, minibar in suites. Cr cds: A, C, D, DS, MC, V.

★ **STARDUST MOTEL.** *410 Pine St (83873). 208/752-1213; fax 208/753-0981; toll-free 800/643-2386.* 42 rms, 22 A/C, 2 story. S $46.00; D $54.00; each addl $8; under 12 free. Crib $6. Pet accepted; $10 deposit. TV; cable (premium). Restaurant nearby. Ck-out noon. Airport transportation. Downhill ski 10 mi; x-country ski 11 mi. Cr cds: A, DS, MC, V.

Weiser

(F-1) *Also see Ontario, OR*

Founded 1888 **Pop** 4,571 **Elev** 2,117 ft **Area code** 208 **Zip** 83672
Information Chamber of Commerce, 8 E Idaho St; 208/549-0452 or 800/437-1280

Located at the confluence of the Weiser and Snake rivers, the town of Weiser (WEE-zer) is both a center for tourism for Hell's Canyon National Recreation Area to the north and a center for trade and transportation for the vast orchards, onion, wheat, and sugar beet fields of the fertile Weiser Valley to the east. Lumbering, mining, the manufacture of mobile homes, and the raising of cattle also contribute to the town's economy. A Ranger District office of the Payette National Forest (see McCALL) is located in Weiser.

What to See and Do

Fiddlers' Hall of Fame. Mementos of past fiddle contests, pictures of champion fiddlers, state winners; collection of old-time fiddles; state scrapbook on view. (Mon-Fri; also wkend during Fiddlers' Contest; closed hols) 10 E Idaho St. Phone 208/549-0452.

Hell's Canyon National Recreation Area. Spanning the Idaho/Oregon border, this canyon, the deepest in North America, was created by the Snake River, which rushes nearly 8,000 ft below Seven Devils rim on the Idaho side. Three dams built by the Idaho Power Company have opened up areas that were once inaccessible and created man-made lakes that provide boating, fishing, and waterskiing. Whitewater rafting and jet boat tours are avail below the dams, on the Snake River. Stretching N for 100 mi; access approx 55 mi NW via US 95 to Cambridge, then via ID 71. Also here are

Brownlee Dam. The southernmost dam of the three, at end of ID 71. This 395-ft rockfill dam creates Brownlee Lake, 57½ mi long, reaching to 10 mi N of Weiser. Woodhead Park, a short distance S, and McCormick Park, a short distance N, provide picnicking, boat ramps; tent and trailer sites, showers. ¢¢

Hell's Canyon Dam. This structure (330 ft high) creates another water recreation area. The improved Deep Creek trail, Idaho side, provides angler and other recreational access to the Snake River below Hell's Canyon Dam. 23 mi N of Oxbow Dam.

Oxbow Dam. This 205-ft-high barrier makes a 12½-mi-long reservoir. Copperfield Park, just below the dam on the Oregon side, has trailer and tent spaces, showers, and day-use picnicking; 9 mi N of dam on the Idaho side is Hell's Canyon Park, offering boat ramp; tent and trailer sites, showers, picnicking. 12½ mi N of Brownlee Dam. ¢¢

Snake River Heritage Center. Artifacts and memorabilia portray the history of Snake River Valley. (By appt only) 2295 Paddock Ave, in Hooker Hall. Phone 208/549-0205. ¢

Trips into Hell's Canyon. Several companies offer river rafting, jet boat, and pack trips into and around Hell's Canyon National Recreation

Area. For info on additional outfitters, contact the Chamber of Commerce.

Hell's Canyon Adventures. Jet boat tours; rafting. Contact PO Box 159, Oxbow, OR 97840. Phone 503/785-3352.

Hughes River Expeditions. Outfitters for whitewater and fishing trips on backcountry rivers of Idaho and eastern Oregon, incl three-, four-, and five-day trips on the Snake River through Hell's Canyon. (May-Oct, several dates) Advance res required. 26 mi N on US 95, at 95 First St in Cambridge. Phone 208/257-3477. ¢¢¢¢

Special Event

National Oldtime Fiddlers' Contest. One of the oldest such contests in the country, attracting some of the nation's finest fiddlers. Also parade, barbecue, arts and crafts. Phone 800/437-1280. Mon-Sat, third full wk June.

MONTANA

This magnificent state took its name from the Spanish *montaña* —meaning mountainous. The altitude of about half the state is more than 5,000 feet, and the sprawling ranges of the Continental Divide rise more than two miles into air so clear photographers must use filters to avoid overexposure. The names of many towns, though, indicate that Montana has more than mountains. Grassrange, Roundup, and Buffalo tell of vast prairie regions, where tawny oceans of wheat stretch to the horizon and a cattle ranch may be 30 miles from front gate to front porch. Big Timber and Highwood suggest Montana's 22 million acres of forests; Goldcreek and Silver Gate speak of the roaring mining days (the roaring is mostly over, but you can still pan for gold in almost any stream); and Jim Bridger reminds us of the greatest mountain man of them all. Of special interest to the vacationing visitor are Antelope, Lame Deer, and Trout creeks, which indicate hunting and fishing *par excellence*.

First glimpsed by French traders Louis and François Verendrye in 1743, Montana remained unexplored and largely unknown until Lewis and Clark crossed the region in 1805. Two years later, Manuel Lisa's trading post at the mouth of the Big Horn ushered in a half century of hunting and trapping.

The Treasure State's natural resources are enormous. Its hydroelectric potential is the greatest in the world—annual flow of the four major rivers is enough to cover the whole state with six inches of water. The 25 major dams include Fort Peck, one of the world's largest hydraulic earthfill dams. Near Great Falls, one of the world's largest freshwater springs pours out nearly 400 million gallons of water every day. In more than 1,500 lakes and 16,000 miles of fishing streams the water is so clear you may wonder if it's there at all.

For a hundred years the state has produced gold and silver, with Virginia City (complete

Yellowstone River

Population: 799,065
Area: 145,392 square miles
Elevation: 1,800-12,799 feet
Peak: Granite Peak (Park County)
Entered Union: November 8, 1889 (41st state)
Capital: Helena
Motto: Oro y Plata ("Gold and Silver" in Spanish)
Nickname: The Treasure State, Big Sky Country
Flower: Bitterroot
Bird: Western Meadowlark
Tree: Ponderosa Pine
Fair: July 27-August 3, 2003, in Great Falls
Time Zone: Mountain
Website: www.visitmt.com or www.travel.state.mt.us

with Robbers' Roost situated within convenient raiding distance) probably the most famous mining town. Montana produces about $1 billion worth of minerals a year. Leading resources are coal, copper, natural gas, silver, platinum, and palladium. Montana also produces more gem sapphires than any other state. Farms and ranches totaling 67 million acres add $2 billion a year to the state's economy.

Along with the bounty of its resources, Montana's history has given us Custer's Last Stand (June 25, 1876), the last spike in the Northern Pacific Railroad (September 8, 1883), the country's first Congresswoman (Jeannette Rankin of Missoula, in 1916), the Dempsey-Gibbons fight (July 4, 1923), and a state constitution originally prefaced by the Magna Carta, the Declaration of Independence, the Articles of Confederation, and the US Constitution.

If you come in winter, bring your mittens. Temperatures can drop below zero, but the climate is milder than perceived because of the state's location in the interior of the continent. Snowmobiling and downhill and cross-country skiing are popular sports here. Summer days are warm, dry, and sunny.

When to Go/Climate

Montana's weather is changeable and temperatures are cold for much longer than they are warm. To the east of the divide, weather is more extreme than in the west, due to winds blowing unhindered across the plains. There is heavy snowfall in the mountains and summer doesn't really begin until July. Summer is tourist season; early fall is less crowded and temperatures are still good for outdoor adventures.

AVERAGE HIGH/LOW TEMPERATURES (°F)

BILLINGS

Jan 32/14	May 67/43	Sept 72/47
Feb 39/19	June 78/58	Oct 61/38
Mar 46/25	July 87/58	Nov 45/26
Apr 57/34	Aug 85/57	Dec 34/17

MISSOULA

Jan 30/15	May 66/38	Sept 71/40
Feb 37/21	June 74/50	Oct 57/31
Mar 47/25	July 83/50	Nov 41/24
Apr 58/31	Aug 82/50	Dec 30/16

Parks and Recreation Finder

Directions to and information about the parks and recreation areas below are given under their respective town/city sections. Please refer to those sections for details.

NATIONAL PARK AND RECREATION AREAS

Key to abbreviations. I.H.S. = International Historic Site; I.P.M. = International Peace Memorial; N.B. = National Battlefield; N.B.P. = National Battlefield Park; N.B.C. = National Battlefield and Cemetery; N.C.A. = National Conservation Area; N.E.M. = National Expansion Memorial; N.F. = National Forest; N.G. = National Grassland; N.H.P. = National Historical Park; N.H.C. = National Heritage Corridor; N.H.S. = National Historic Site; N.L. = National Lakeshore; N.M. = National Monument; N.M.P. = National Military Park; N.Mem. = National Memorial; N.P. = National Park; N.Pres. = National Preserve; N.R.A. = National Recreational Area; N.R.R. = National Recreational River; N.Riv. = National River; N.S. = National Seashore; N.S.R. = National Scenic

CALENDAR HIGHLIGHTS

JANUARY

Montana Pro Rodeo Circuit Finals (Great Falls). Four Seasons Arena. Best riders in the state compete for a chance to reach the nationals. Phone 406/727-8115.

FEBRUARY

Chocolate Festival (Anaconda). Chocolate baking contest with winners sold at charity bake sale. Free chocolates at local merchants. Various "sweetheart" activities throughout town. Phone 406/563-2422.

JULY

Wild Horse Stampede (Wolf Point). One of Montana's best and oldest rodeos. Phone Chamber of Commerce & Agriculture, 406/653-2012.

State Fair (Great Falls). Fairgrounds. Rodeo, livestock exhibits, horse racing, petting zoo, commercial exhibits, entertainment, carnival. Phone 406/727-8900.

AUGUST

Western Montana Fair and Rodeo (Missoula). Fairgrounds. Live horse racing, three-night rodeo, nightly fireworks. Carnival, livestock, commercial exhibits. Musical performance, demolition derby, blacksmith competition. Phone 406/721-FAIR.

Montana Cowboy Poetry Gathering (Lewistown). Modern-day cowboys and admirers of Western folklore relate life "down on the range" through original poetry. Phone 406/538-5436.

OCTOBER

Bridger Raptor Festival (Bozeman). Bridger Bowl ridge area. View birds of prey, including the largest concentration of migrating Golden Eagles in the contiguous 48 states, on their trip south. Phone 406/585-1211.

Riverway; N.S.T. = National Scenic Trail; N.Sc. = National Scientific Reserve; N.V.M. = National Volcanic Monument.

Place Name	Listed Under
Bear's Paw Battleground	CHINOOK
Beaverhead N.F.	DILLON
Big Hole N.B.	same
Bitterroot N.F.	HAMILTON
Custer N.F.	HARDIN
Deerlodge N.F.	BUTTE
Flathead N.F.	KALISPELL
Fort Union Trading Post N.H.S.	SIDNEY
Gallatin N.F.	BOZEMAN
Glacier N.P.	same
Grant-Kohrs Ranch N.H.S.	DEER LODGE
Helena N.F.	HELENA
Kootenai N.F.	LIBBY
Lewis and Clark N.F.	GREAT FALLS
Little Bighorn Battlefield N.M.	same
Lolo N.F.	MISSOULA

The national forests of Montana are part of the more than 25,000,000 acres that make up the Northern Region of the Forest Service. The terrain runs from rugged mountains to rolling hills, from lodgepole pine and Douglas fir to grass.

The highest point in the region is Granite Peak in the Beartooth Mountains, 12,799 feet. Recreation opportunities abound: hiking, rock hounding, fishing, boating, mountain camping, hunting, and horseback riding. For further information contact the Forest Service, Northern Region, Federal Building, PO Box 7669, Missoula 59807; phone 406/329-3511. For reporting forest fires, phone 406/329-3857.

STATE PARK AND RECREATION AREAS

Key to abbreviations. I.P. = Interstate Park; S.A.P. = State Archaeological Park; S.B. = State Beach; S.C.A. = State Conservation Area; S.C.P. = State Conservation Park; S.Cp. = State Campground; S.F. = State Forest; S.G. = State Garden; S.H.A. = State Historic Area; S.H.P. = State Historic Park; S.H.S. = State Historic Site; S.M.P. = State Marine Park; S.N.A. = State Natural Area; S.P. = State Park; S.P.C. = State Public Campground; S.R. = State Reserve; S.R.A. = State Recreation Area; S.Res. = State Reservoir; S.Res.P. = State Resort Park; S.R.P. = State Rustic Park.

Place Name	Listed Under
Bannack S.P.	DILLON
Canyon Ferry S.P.	HELENA
Deadman's Basin Fishing Access Site	HARLOWTON
Flathead Lake S.P. (Big Arm, Elmo, and Finley Point units)	POLSON
Flathead Lake S.P. (Wayfarers and Yellow Bay units)	BIGFORK
Fort Owen S.P.	HAMILTON
Giant Springs S.P.	GREAT FALLS
Hell Creek S.P.	GLASGOW
Lewis and Clark Caverns S.P.	THREE FORKS
Lost Creek S.P.	ANACONDA
Makoshika S.P.	GLENDIVE
Missouri River Headwaters S.P.	THREE FORKS
Painted Rocks S.P.	HAMILTON
Pictograph Cave S.P.	BILLINGS
Whitefish S.P.	WHITEFISH

Water-related activities, hiking, riding, various other sports, picnicking, and visitor centers, as well as camping, are available in many of these areas. Parks are open approximately May-September. Day-use fee, $5 per vehicle, $1 per walk-in visitor. Camping (limited to 14 days), $10-$14/site/night. Additional fees may be charged at some areas for other activities. Pets on leash only. For information on state parks write Parks Division, Montana Department of Fish, Wildlife, and Parks, 1420 E Sixth Ave, Helena 59620; phone 406/444-3750.

SKI AREAS

Place Name	Listed Under
Big Mountain Ski and Summer Resort	WHITEFISH
Big Sky Ski and Summer Resort	BIG SKY
Bridger Bowl Ski Area	BOZEMAN
Discovery Basin Ski Area	ANACONDA
Lost Trail Powder Mountain Ski Area	HAMILTON
Marshall Mountain Ski Area	MISSOULA
Maverick Mountain Ski Area	DILLON
Montana Snowbowl Ski Area	MISSOULA
Red Lodge Mountain Ski Area	RED LODGE
Showdown Ski Area	WHITE SULPHUR SPRINGS
Turner Mountain Ski Area	LIBBY

FISHING AND HUNTING

Game fish includes all species of trout as well as salmon, whitefish, grayling, sauger, walleye, paddlefish, sturgeon, pike, burbot, channel catfish, and bass. Nonresident fishing license: annual, $50; two-day consecutive license, $12; nonfee permit needed in Glacier or Yellowstone national parks.

Big game includes moose, elk, deer, antelope, bighorn sheep, mountain goat, mountain lion, and black bear; game birds includes both mountain and prairie species. Nonresident hunting license: game birds, $125; various types of elk and deer combination licenses are available. Licenses for moose, sheep, goat, antelope are awarded through special drawings. License for mountain lion must be purchased by August 31.

A $5 conservation license is a prerequisite to hunting or fishing license. For detailed information write Montana Fish, Wildlife, and Parks, 1420 E Sixth Ave, PO Box 200701, Helena 59620-0701; phone 406/444-2535 (general information) or 406/444-2950 (special licensing).

Driving Information

Safety belts are mandatory for all persons anywhere in vehicle. Children under four years or under 40 pounds in weight must be in an approved safety seat anywhere in vehicle. For information phone 406/444-3412.

INTERSTATE HIGHWAY SYSTEM

The following alphabetical listing of Montana towns in *Mobil Travel Guide* shows that these cities are within ten miles of the indicated Interstate highways. A highway map, however, should be checked for the nearest exit.

Highway Number	Cities/Towns within ten miles
Interstate 15	Butte, Dillon, Great Falls, Helena.
Interstate 90	Anaconda, Big Timber, Billings, Bozeman, Butte, Deer Lodge, Hardin, Livingston, Missoula, Three Forks.
Interstate 94	Billings, Glendive, Miles City.

Additional Visitor Information

Several pamphlets and brochures, which comprise a "Vacation Planning Guide," list points of interest, motels, campgrounds, museums, events, and attractions. They may be obtained from Travel Montana, 1424 9th Ave, PO Box 200533, Helena, 59620-0533; phone 800/VISIT-MT.

Three periodicals are recommended to the Montana visitor. They are: *Montana: Magazine of Western History,* quarterly, Montana Historical Society, 225 N Roberts St, Helena 59601; *Montana Magazine Inc,* bimonthly, 3020 Bozeman, Helena 59624; and *Montana Outdoors,* bimonthly, Department of Fish, Wildlife, and Parks, 1420 E Sixth Ave, PO Box 200701, Helena 59620-0701.

EXPLORING MONTANA'S BITTERROOT RIVER VALLEY

Take this scenic alternative to freeway driving along I-15 and I-90. From Missoula, follow Highway 93 south along the Bitterroot River. At first, the valley is wide and filled with farms, then the mountains close in: the jagged Bitterroot Range rears to the west and the gentle Sapphire Range rises to the east. This is one of Montana's most scenic valleys, and holds some of its best fishing. Near Florence, visit the Daly Mansion, which was home to one of the super-rich Copper Kings in the 1880s. Just below the Continental Divide, stop at Lost Trail Hot Springs. After climbing up to

Lost Trail Pass, turn back toward Montana on Highway 43 and drop by Big Hole National Battlefield where the Battle of the Big Hole, one of the West's most dramatic Army/Indian battles, was fought. Paths lead to the battle site, where Chief Joseph and the Nez Perce defeated the US Army; there's also a good interpretive center. The little ranch town of Wisdom, with its excellent fine-art gallery, is the fishing capital of Big Hole (the Big Hole River is a "blue ribbon" fishing river), a very broad prairielike valley filled with historic cattle ranches flanked by towering mountain ranges. Continue along Highway 278 through lovely high prairies, stopping by Bannack, the territorial capital of Montana and one of the best-preserved ghost towns in the West (also a state park). Join I-15 at Dillon, a handsome Victorian town that is home to Montana's oldest college and considerable historic architecture. (**APPROX 207 MI**)

MONTANA'S UNIQUE LANDMARKS

Stanford is in the center of the Judith Basin, an area of high prairie ringed by low-slung mountain ranges. This was one of the centers of the old open-range cattle ranches, and cowboy artist Charlie Russell painted many of the unique, monumental buttes and mountains in the area. From the farm and ranch lands around Stanford, leave Highway 200 and cut north on Highway 80. The horizon is filled with odd, blocklike buttes rising directly out of the plains. The largest is Square Butte, which from a distance looks like a completely square block of rock towering thousands of feet above the range. These odd formations are lava batholiths, which formed as subterranean lakes of molten rock that cooled and were later exposed by erosion. Square Butte is protected by the Bureau of Land Management, but anyone with a high-clearance vehicle can climb up the side to a plateau 1,000 feet above the prairie for views that stretch hundreds of miles. The prairie ecosystem on the butte is considered pristine, an example of the flora that once greeted Lewis and Clark. Past Square Butte, the road dips into a vast abandoned river channel that once carried the Ice-Age Missouri River. As the route approaches the present-day river, you can see glimpses of the famed White Cliffs of the Missouri, which so impressed Lewis and Clark. (This section of the Missouri is protected as a Wild and Scenic River and is otherwise essentially roadless.) The route drops onto the Missouri at Fort Benton, the upper terminus of the Missouri riverboat trade of the 1850s. Fort Benton is one of the oldest towns in the state and has several good museums and historic buildings. Here the route joins Highway 87. (**APPROX 48 MI**)

Anaconda

(D-3) *See also Butte, Deer Lodge*

Founded 1883 **Pop** 10,278 **Elev** 5,265 ft **Area code** 406 **Zip** 59711
Information Chamber of Commerce, 306 E Park St; 406/563-2400

Chosen by Marcus Daly, a copper king, as the site for a copper smelter, the city was first dubbed with the tongue-twisting name of Copperopolis, but was later renamed. In 1894, the "war of the copper kings" was waged between Daly and W.A. Clark over the location of the state capital. Clark's Helena won by a small margin. After his rival's death, the world's largest copper smelter was built, standing 585 feet 1½ inches.

What to See and Do

Anaconda's Old Works. 18-hole Jack Nicklaus signature golf course located on developed grounds of former copper smelters. Also features fully accessible trail that skirts the foundations of the old works and allows interpretation of town's smelting heritage (free). Clubhouse, dining room; pro shop. (Late May-Oct, daily, weather permitting) 1205 Pizzini Way. Phone 406/563-5989. ¢¢¢¢

Big Hole Basin. Fishing, hunting; raft races; lodge, skiing. 25 mi SW on MT 274.

Big Hole National Battlefield. (see). 22 mi SW on MT 274, then 40 mi SW on MT 43.

Copper Village Museum and Arts Center. Local and traveling art exhibitions; theater, music, films; museum of local pioneer and industrial history. (Summer, daily; rest of yr, Tues-Sat; closed hols) 401 E Commercial St. Phone 406/563-2422. **FREE**

Discovery Basin. Two triple lifts, three double chairlifts, two beginner lifts, snowmaking; patrol, school, rentals; restaurant, bar. Longest run 1½ mi; vertical drop 1,300 ft. (Thanksgiving-Apr, daily) Cross-country trail. 18 mi NW on MT 1. Phone 406/563-2184. ¢¢¢¢

Georgetown Lake. Waterskiing, boating, fishing, swimming, camping, picnicking, wilderness area; skiing, snowmobiling. 15 mi W on Pintler Scenic Route (MT 1).

Ghost towns and Sapphire mines. Near Georgetown Lake on Pintler Scenic Route (MT 1). Inquire at local chambers or visitor centers.

Lost Creek State Park. Lost Creek Falls is feature of a deep canyon carved through mountains of limestone. Hiking. Picnicking, grills. Camping. Interpretive display. Standard fees. 1½ mi E on MT 1, then 2 mi N on MT 273, then 6 mi W on unnumbered road. Phone 406/542-5500.

◪ **Visitor Center.** Display of smelter works photographs; outdoor railroad exhibit; self-guided walking tours; historic bus tours (Memorial Day-Labor Day, daily); video presentation (20 min) showing area attractions; tourist info for both city and state. (Summer, daily; rest of yr, Mon-Fri) 306 E Park St. Bus tours ¢¢

Special Event

Wayne Estes Memorial Tournament. One of the largest basketball tournaments in the NW. Slamdunk, three-point contest. Last wkend Mar. Phone 406/563-2400.

Resort

★★ **FAIRMONT HOT SPRINGS RESORT.** *1500 Fairmont Resort Rd (59711). 406/797-3241; fax 406/797-3337; toll-free 800/332-3272. www. fairmontmontana.com.* 152 rms, 3 story. May-Sept: S, D $119; each addl $15; suites, kit. units $139-$349; under 12 free; ski plan; lower rates rest of yr. Crib free. TV; cable, VCR avail (movies). 4 pools, 2 indoor; lifeguard. Restaurants 6:30 am-10 pm. Bar to 1:30 am; entertainment Tues-Sat. Ck-out 11 am. Ck-in 3 pm. Meeting rms. Business servs avail. Gift shop. Airport transportation. Tennis. 18-hole golf, greens fee $19-$39, driving range. Bicycle rentals. Exercise equipt. Massage. Game rm. Lawn games. Hayrides. Private patios, balconies. Cr cds: A, C, D, DS, MC, V.

Restaurant

★★ **BARCLAY II.** *1300 E Commercial (59711). 406/563-5541.* Hrs: 5-10 pm; Sun 4-9:30 pm. Closed Mon; some major hols. Bar. Complete meals: dinner $9-$60. Specialties: tenderloin steak, halibut, breaded veal. Cr cds: A, DS, MC, V.

D

Bigfork

See also Kalispell, Polson

Pop 1,080 **Elev** 2,968 ft
Area code 406 **Zip** 59911
Information Chamber of Commerce, PO Box 237; 406/837-5888

Surrounded by lakes, a river, and a dam, Bigfork's businesses are electric power and catering to tourists who visit the east shore of Flathead Lake (see POLSON). A Ranger District office of the Flathead National Forest (see KALISPELL) is located here.

What to See and Do

Bigfork Art and Cultural Center. Exhibits of artists and crafters of northwestern Montana; gift shop. (Spring and fall, Wed-Sat; summer, Tues-Sat) 525 Electric Ave. Phone 406/837-6927. **FREE**

Flathead Lake Biological Station, The University of Montana. Laboratories for teaching and research in natural sciences; museum; self-guided nature trips. (Mon-Fri; closed major hols) MT 35, milepost 17½, midway between Bigfork and Polson. Phone 406/982-3301. **FREE**

Flathead Lake State Park. On Flathead Lake (see POLSON). At all units: swimming; fishing; boating (ramp). Picnicking. Camping (no hookups). Standard fees. Phone 406/837-4196.

Wayfarers Unit. Hiking trails. Camping (dump station, patrons only). Off MT 35. Phone 406/837-4196.

Yellow Bay Unit. Joint state/tribal fishing license required. No RVs or trailers permitted. 10 mi S on MT 35. Phone 406/752-5501.

Swan Lake. About 10 mi long. Swimming, waterskiing; fishing, boating. 14 mi SE of Big Fork on MT 83. Phone 406/837-5081.

Special Events

Bigfork Summer Playhouse. 526 Electric Ave. Broadway musicals. Nightly exc Sun. For res contact PO Box 456; 406/837-4886. May-late Aug.

Wild West Day. Sept. Phone 406/837-5888.

Motels/Motor Lodges

★ **SWAN VALLEY SUPER 8 MOTEL.** *Hwy 83, Mile Marker 46.5, Condon (59826). 406/754-2688; fax 406/754-2651; res 800/800-8000. www.super8.com.* 22 rms, 2 story. No A/C. June-Sept: S $58.88; D $69.88; each addl $2; under 18 free; lower rates rest of yr. Crib free. TV; cable. Complimentary coffee in lobby. Ck-out 11 am. Business servs avail. Some refrigerators. Cr cds: A, D, DS, JCB, MC, V.

D ⬥ ⬥ ⬥ ⬥

★ **TIMBERS MOTEL.** *8540 Hwy 35 S (59911). 406/837-6200; fax 406/837-6203; toll-free 800/821-4546. www.timbersmotel.com.* 40 rms, 1-2 story. June-Sept: S $74; D $79; lower rates rest of yr. Crib $7. Pet accepted; $5, $50 deposit. TV; cable. Heated pool; whirlpool. Complimentary continental bkfst. Complimentary coffee in rms. Restaurant nearby. Ck-out 11 am. X-country ski 7 mi. Sauna. Cr cds: A, DS, MC, V.

D ⬥ ⬥ ⬥ ⬥ ⬥ ⬥

Resort

★★★ **MARINA CAY RESORT & CONFERENCE CENTER.** *180 Vista Ln (59911). 406/837-5861; fax 406/837-1118; toll-free 800/433-6516. www.marinacay.com.* 119 rms, 3 story. Mid-June-Sept: S, D $82-$120; studio rms $104.50-$125.50; suites $182-$350; lower rates rest of yr. Crib $10. TV; cable. Heated pool; whirlpool, poolside serv. Dining rm 7 am-9:30 pm. Bar. Ck-out 11 am, ck-in 3 pm. Meeting rms. Business servs avail. X-country ski 6 mi. Rental boats, canoes, water cycles. Fishing trips, whitewater rafting. Refrigerators, fireplaces; microwaves avail. Some private patios, balconies. Picnic table, grill. On Bigfork Bay of Flathead Lake. Cr cds: A, D, DS, MC, V.

[D] [symbols]

B&Bs/Small Inns

★★ **COYOTE ROADHOUSE INN.**
600 & 602 Three Eagle Ln (54521).
406/837-4250. 5 rms, 5 cabins, 2 with shower only, 2 story. No A/C. No rm phones. June-Sept: S $75; D $75-$150; lower rates Apr-May, Oct. Closed rest of yr. Complimentary full bkfst. Ck-out 11 am, ck-in 3 pm. Many in-rm whirlpools. On Swan River. Many antiques. Totally non-smoking. Cr cds: MC, V.

[D] [symbols]

★★ **O'DUACHAIN COUNTRY INN.**
675 Ferndale Dr (59911). 406/837-6851; fax 406/837-0778; res 800/837-7460. *www.montanainn.com.* 5 rms, 2 share bath, 3 story, 1 guest house. No A/C. No rm phones. June-Sept: S, D, guest house $120; each addl $20; under 5 free. Crib free. Pet accepted, some restrictions. Complimentary full bkfst. Ck-out 11 am, ck-in 2 pm. Luggage handling. Whirlpool. Sauna. Authentic log home. Totally non-smoking. Cr cds: A, DS, MC, V.

[D] [symbols]

Guest Ranch

★★★★ **AVERILL'S FLATHEAD LAKE LODGE.** *150 Flathead Lake Lodge Rd (59911).* 406/837-4391; fax 406/837-6977. *www.averills.com.* This 2,000-acre Rocky Mountain ranch, just south of Glacier National Park, is family operated and provides a casual, down-to-earth vacation for guests of all ages. Rates include meals and various recreations, such as horseback riding, lake cruising, and trail hiking. Visitors can even learn the inner workings of an authentic dude ranch by roping cattle and helping out around the corral. 19 rms in 2-story lodge, 22 cottages. No A/C. AP, mid-June-Sept, wkly: S, D $2,275; 13-19 yrs $1,687; 6-12 yrs $1,526; 3-5 yrs $996; under 3 yrs $101. Closed rest of yr. Crib free. Heated pool. Free supervised children's activities (June-Sept); ages 6-teens. Dining rm 8 am-6:30 pm. Patio barbecues. Ck-out 11 am, ck-in 1 pm.

Grocery, package store 1 mi. Coin lndry. Business servs avail. Valet serv. Gift shop. Airport, RR station transportation. Tennis. Private beach; boats, motors, canoes, sailboats, raft trips, waterskiing, instruction. Lake cruises. Fly-fishing instruction. Hiking. Whitewater rafting. Mountain bike rental. Soc dir. Indoor, outdoor games. Rec rm. Health club privileges. Many private patios, balconies. Picnic tables, grills. Cr cds: A, MC, V.

[D] [symbols]

Restaurants

★★ **BIGFORK INN.** *604 Electric Ave (59911).* 406/837-6680. Hrs: 5-10 pm. Closed Thanksgiving, Dec 25. Res accepted. Bar to midnight. Dinner $12-$18. Child's menu. Specializes in fresh seafood, chicken. Entertainment Fri, Sat. Outdoor dining. Swiss chalet country inn. Cr cds: A, DS, MC, V.

[symbol]

★★★ **COYOTE RIVERHOUSE.** *600 Three Eagle Ln, Ferndale (59911).* 406/837-1233. Hrs: 5:30-8:30 pm. Closed Mon, Tues. Res accepted. No A/C. Continental menu. Bar. Dinner $17-$20. Child's menu. Specialties: Cajun stuffed breast of chicken, sauteed Provimi veal. Own desserts. Outdoor dining. Secluded country dining with view of Swan River; flower gardens. Totally nonsmoking. Cr cds: MC, V.

[D]

★★ **SHOWTHYME.** *548 Electric Ave (59911).* 406/837-0707. *www. showthyme.com.* Hrs: 5-10 pm; May-Sept hrs vary. Closed Sun; Dec 25. A la carte entrees: dinner $10.95-$18.95. Child's menu. Specializes in fresh seafood, duck, lamb. Outdoor dining. In old bank building (1910). Cr cds: A, DS, MC, V.

Big Hole National Battlefield

(10 mi W of Wisdom on MT 43 or 16 mi E of Lost Trail Pass on MT 43, off MT 93, near Idaho border.)

Fleeing the US Army from what is now Idaho and Oregon, five "non-treaty" bands of Nez Perce were attacked here before dawn by US troops and citizen volunteers on August 9, 1877. More than 655 acres of the battlefield are preserved today. The Nez Perce escaped, but were pursued by the army to what is now called Bear Paw Battleground (see CHINOOK), where Chief Joseph and the surviving Nez Perce surrendered after a six-day battle. Ironically, the tribe had previously been on good terms with the settlers until a treaty, forced on them in 1863, diminished the land originally granted to them in 1855. Those left out refused to recognize the 1863 treaty.

Three self-guided trails lead through the Siege Area, the Nez Perce Camp, and the Howitzer Capture Site. Wildlife roam the area; fishing is permitted with a license. Visitor Center Museum exhibits firearms and relics of the period (Summer, daily; winter, Mon-Sat; closed Jan 1, Thanksgiving, Dec 25). Interpretive walks presented daily in summer. Some access roads are closed in winter. For further info contact PO Box 237, Wisdom 59761; 406/689-3155. Per vehicle (Memorial Day-Labor Day) ¢¢

Big Sky (Gallatin County)

See also Bozeman

Pop 450 **Elev** 5,934 ft **Area code** 406 **Zip** 59716

Information Sky of Montana Resort, PO Box 160001; 406/995-5000 or 800/548-4486

Web www.bigskyresort.com

Located 45 miles southwest of Bozeman in Gallatin National Forest, Big Sky is a resort community developed by the late newscaster and commentator, Chet Huntley. Golf, tennis, skiing, fishing, whitewater rafting, and horseback riding are among the many activities available in the area.

What to See and Do

Big Sky Resort. Quad, three high-speed quads, four triple, five double chairlifts, four surface tows; patrol, school, rentals; bar, concession area, cafeteria; nursery. Longest run six mi; vertical drop 4,350 ft. (Mid-Nov-mid-Apr, daily) Fifty mi of x-country trails. Gondola. Tram. Also summer activities. Phone 406/995-5000. ¢¢¢¢

River trips. Yellowstone Raft Company. Half- and full-day whitewater raft trips on Gallatin and Madison rivers. No experience necessary. Paddle or oar powered rafts. For res contact PO Box 160262. Phone 406/995-4613.

Motels/Motor Lodges

★★ **BEST WESTERN BUCK'S T-4 LODGE.** *Hwy 191, 46625 Gallatin Rd, Big Sky (59716). 406/995-4111; fax 406/995-2191; toll-free 800/822-4484. www.buckst4.com.* 72 rms, 2½ story. Some A/C. May-Nov: S $69-$139; D $99-$159; each addl $6; suites $159-$219; under 12 free; ski plan; higher rates late Dec. Closed rest of yr. Crib $5. TV; cable, VCR avail (movies $3). Complimentary coffee in rms. Complimentary bkfst. Restaurant 7-10 am, 5-10 pm. Bar 5 pm-2 am. Ck-out 11 am. Coin lndry. Gift shop. Meeting rms. Business servs avail. Downhill/x-country ski 9 mi. Whirlpools. Game rm. Refrigerators, microwaves avail. Cr cds: A, C, D, DS, MC, V.

★ **COMFORT INN.** *47214 Gallatin Rd, Big Sky (59716). 406/995-2333; fax 406/995-2277; res 877/466-7222. www.comfortinnbigsky.com.* 62 rms, 3 story, 17 suites. No elvtr. June-mid-Sept: S, D $79-$129; each addl $10; suites $130-$240; under 18 free; ski plans; higher rates special events; lower rates rest of yr. Crib free. Pet accepted; $50 deposit. TV; cable (premium), VCR avail. Complimentary continental bkfst. Complimentary coffee in rms. Restaurant nearby. Ck-out 11 am. Meeting rms. Business servs avail. Gift shop. Coin lndry. Downhill ski 10 mi; x-country ski 2 mi. Exercise equipt. Indoor pool; whirlpool, water slide. Some refrigerators, microwaves. Cr cds: A, C, D, DS, JCB, MC, V.

⊡ ◻ ⬧ ⬚ ⬚ ⬚ ⬚ ⬚ SC

★★ **RAINBOW RANCH.** *42950 Gallatin Rd, Big Sky (59716). 406/995-4132; fax 406/995-2861; res 800/937-4132. www.rainbowranch. com.* 16 rms. No A/C. No rm phones. June-Oct: D $135-$280; each addl $30; package plans; lower rates rest of yr. TV; cable, VCR (movies). Complimentary continental bkfst. Restaurant 6 am-9:30 pm. Bar 5-11 pm; entertainment Thurs. Ck-out 11 am. Business servs avail. Bellhops. Sundries. Downhill ski 15 mi; x-country ski 11 mi. Many in-rm whirlpools, fireplaces. Many balconies. On river. Totally nonsmoking. Cr cds: A, DS, MC, V.

⊡ ◻ ⬧ ⬚ ⬚ ⬚ SC

★★ **RIVER ROCK LODGE.** *3080 Pine Dr, Big Sky (59716). 406/995-2295; fax 406/995-2447; toll-free 800/548-4488. www.bigskylodging.com.* 29 rms, 2 story. Mid-Nov-mid-Apr: S $115; D $130; each addl $15; suite $230; under 12 free; lower rates rest of yr. Crib $15. TV; cable, VCR (movies). Restaurant nearby. Ck-out 10:30 am. Meeting rms. Business servs avail. Concierge. Sundries. Downhill/x-country ski 6 mi. Refrigerator. Totally nonsmoking. Cr cds: A, C, D, DS, MC, V.

⊡ ◻ ⬧ ⬚ ⬚ ⬚ SC

Resort

★★★ **BIG SKY RESORT.** *1 Lone Mountain Tr, Big Sky (59716). 406/995-5000; fax 406/995-5001; toll-free 800/548-4486. www.bigsky resort.com.* 298 rms. Some A/C. Thanksgiving-mid-Apr: S, D $143-$340; each addl $22; ski plan; higher rates late Dec; lower rates rest of yr. Crib $10. TV; cable (premium). 2 heated pools; 3 whirlpools. Playground. Coffee in rms. Dining rm 7-10 am, 6-9 pm. Box lunches. Picnics. Rm serv. Bar 4 pm-2 am; entertainment. Ck-out noon, ck-in 3-5 pm. Coin lndry. Convention facilities. Concierge. Shopping arcade. Airport transportation. Tennis. 18-hole golf, pro, putting green, driving range. Mountain biking; rentals. Sleigh rides. Exercise equipt; sauna, steam rm. Downhill/x-country ski on site. Ski storage, school. Ski and sports

shops. Refrigerators; some fireplaces. Picnic tables. Established by famed newscaster Chet Huntley. Cr cds: A, D, DS, MC, V.

⊡ ◻ ⬧ ⬚ ⬚ ⬚ ⬚ ⬚ ⬚ ⬚

Guest Ranches

★★★ **LONE MOUNTAIN.** *Lone Mtn Access Rd, Big Sky (59716). 406/995-4644; fax 406/995-4670; toll-free 800/514-4644. www.lmranch.com.* 30 cabins. No A/C. AP, Dec-Apr, June-Oct: S $2,500-$3,970/wk; D $4,300/wk; each addl $1,650/wk. Children age 2-3 addl $485/wk, age 4-5 addl $1,150/wk. Closed rest of yr. Crib free. Whirlpool. Playground. Supervised children's activities (June-Labor Day). Restaurant (see LONE MOUNTAIN RANCH DINING ROOM). Bar 3:30 pm-midnight. Ck-out 11 am, ck-in 3 pm. Coin lndry. Meeting rms. Sundries. Gift shop. Free airport transportation. Downhill ski 6 mi; x-country ski on site. Ski rentals, lessons. Sleigh ride dinners. Massage. Soc dir; entertainment. Game rm. Fishing guides. Fireplaces. Private porches. Picnic tables, boxed lunches avail. Rustic setting. Totally nonsmoking. Cr cds: DS, MC, V.

⊡ ◻ ⬧ ⬚ ⬚ ⬚ ⬚

★★ **NINE QUARTER CIRCLE RANCH INC.** *5000 Taylor Fork Rd, Gallatin Gateway (59730). 406/995-4276. www.ninequartercircle.com.* 15 cabins (1-bedrm), 8 cabins (2-bedrm). No A/C. AP, mid-July-Sept: S $1,680/wk; D $2,800/wk; family rates. Closed rest of yr. Crib free. Pool. Playground. Free supervised children's activities (mid-June-mid-Sept). Dining rm sittings: 7 am, noon, 6:30 pm. Ck-out varies, ck-in noon. Coin lndry. Meeting rms. Airport transportation. Lawn games. Some fireplaces. 4,000-ft landing strip. Cr cds: A, DS, MC, V.

⊡ ◻ ⬧ ⬚ ⬚

Restaurants

★ **CAFE EDELWEISS.** *1005 Big Sky Spur Rd, Big Sky (59716). 406/995-4665.* Hrs: 11:30 am-9:30 pm; winter 6-10 pm. Closed Apr-mid-June, Oct-Nov. Res accepted. German, American menu. Bar. Lunch $4.50-$8, dinner $14-$22. Child's menu. Specialties: Wiener schnitzel, rack of lamb, chicken lienz. Outdoor dining. Original Austrian wood carvings. World Cup ski trophies on display. Cr cds: A, MC, V.

D

★★ **FIRST PLACE.** *Little Coyote Rd, Big Sky (59716).* 406/995-4244. Hrs: 6-10 pm. Closed mid-Apr-May. Res accepted. No A/C. Bar 5 pm-2 am. Dinner $12.50-$22.75. Child's menu. Specializes in fresh fish, wild game. Scenic mountain view. Cr cds: A, C, D, DS, ER, MC, V.

★★★ **LONE MOUNTAIN RANCH DINING ROOM.** *Lone Mtn Access Rd, Big Sky (59716).* 406/995-2782. *www. lmranch.com.* Hrs: 7-9 am, noon-2 pm, 6-8·30 pm. Closed Memorial Day, Thanksgiving. Res accepted; required dinner. No A/C. Continental menu. Bar 3:30 pm-midnight. Buffet: bkfst $7.95, lunch $9.95. Prix fixe: dinner $32. Specialties: symphony of lamb, beef tenderloin tournedos. Outdoor dining. Western ranch atmosphere. Totally non-smoking. Cr cds: DS, MC, V.

D

Big Timber

See also Bozeman, Livingston

Pop 1,557 **Elev** 4,081 ft
Area code 406 **Zip** 59011

Some of the tall cottonwoods that gave this settlement its name and the grasses that endowed the county with the name Sweet Grass remain. Livestock ranches make Big Timber their selling and shopping center. This is also a popular dude ranch area, with good hunting and fishing facilities. The Yellowstone and Boulder rivers provide good trout fishing. The first dude ranch in the state was started here around 1911. Natural bridge and falls area is located approximately 25 miles south of town.

A Ranger District office of the Gallatin National Forest (see BOZEMAN) is located here.

Special Event

NRA/MRA Rodeo. Phone 406/252-1122. Mid-May-mid-Sept.

Motel/Motor Lodge

★ **SUPER 8 MOTEL.** *I-90 & Hwy 10 W (59011).* 406/932-8888; fax 406/932-4103; res 800/800-8000. *www.super8.com.* 41 rms, 2 story. May-Sept: S $77; D $81; each addl $4; lower rates rest of yr. Crib free. Pet accepted; $15 deposit. TV; cable. Complimentary continental bkfst. Restaurant adj 6 am-10 pm. Ck-out 11 am. Coin lndry. Cr cds: A, D, DS, MC, V.

D ◄ ➘ ▧ SC

Restaurant

★★ **THE GRAND.** *139 McLeod St (59011).* 406/932-4459. *www. thegrand-hotel.com.* Hrs: 5-10 pm; Sun brunch 11 am-2 pm. Res accepted. Bar 11-1 am. Dinner $13.95-$42. Sun brunch $8.95. Child's menu. Specialties: pan-roasted salmon, rack of lamb, tenderloin. 1890 hotel dining rm. Cr cds: DS, MC, V.

D

Billings

(D-6) See also Hardin

Founded 1882 **Pop** 81,151 **Elev** 3,124 ft **Area code** 406

Information Billings Area Chamber of Commerce, 815 S 27th St, PO Box 31177, 59107; 406/252-4016 or 800/735-2635

Web www.billingscvb.visitmt.com

On the west bank of the Yellowstone River, Billings, seat of Yellowstone County, was built by the Northern Pacific Railway and took the name of railroad President Frederick K. Billings. Today, it is the center of a vast trade region. Billings is a major distribution point for Montana's and Wyoming's vast strip-mining operations. Industries include agriculture, tourism, and oil trade. Billings offers excellent medical facilities and is a regional convention center. It is also the headquarters of the Custer National Forest (see HARDIN).

What to See and Do

Boothill Cemetery. Final resting place of Billings' gunmen and lawmen who died with their boots on. E end of Chief Black Otter Trail.

Chief Black Otter Trail. Drive above city, past Boothill Cemetery, up Kelly Mt and down along edge of sheer cliff. Excellent view of Billings. Starts at E end of city.

Geyser Park. 18-hole mini golf course; water bumper boats, Lazer-Tag, Go-Karts and track; concessions. (May-Oct, daily; closed hols) 4910 Southgate Dr. Phone 406/254-2510. ¢¢¢

Moss Mansion. In 1901 architect H. J. Hardenbergh created the three-story estate. Original furnishings. (Daily) 914 Division St. Phone 406/256-5100. ¢¢¢

Peter Yegen, Jr.—Yellowstone County Museum. Native American artifacts, antique steam locomotive, horse-drawn vehicles; dioramas depict homesteading days and Native American sacrificial ceremony; vast display of valuable guns, saddles, precious stones. Breathtaking view of Yellowstone Valley and the mountains. (Mon-Sat; closed hols) At Logan Field Airport, on MT 3. Phone 406/256-6811. **Donation**

Pictograph Cave State Park. Inhabited 4,500 yrs ago; pictographs on walls. Picnicking. (Mid-Apr-mid-Oct) I-90 at Lockwood Exit, 6 mi S on county road. Phone 406/245-0227. ¢¢

Range Rider of the Yellowstone. Life-size bronze statue of cowboy and his mount; posed for by William S. Hart, an early silent film cowboy star. Near airport, off Chief Black Otter Trail.

Rocky Mountain College. (1878) 850 students. First college in Montana. Sandstone buildings are some of Billings's oldest permanent structures. 1511 Poly Dr. Phone 406/657-1000.

Western Heritage Center. Featuring rotating exhibits relating to the history of the Yellowstone Valley from prehistoric to modern times. (Tues-Sat; closed major hols) 2822 Mon-

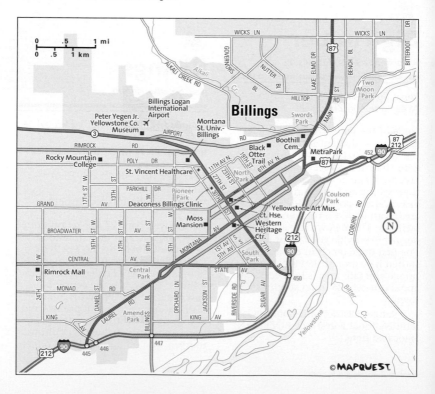

tana Ave. Phone 406/256-6809.
Donation

Yellowstone Art Museum. Contemporary and historic art exhibitions, lectures, chamber concerts, films. (Tues-Sun; closed Jan) 401 N 27th St. Phone 406/256-6804. ¢¢

ZooMontana. The state's only wildlife park features homestead petting zoo. (Mid-Apr-mid-Oct, daily; rest of yr, wkends, weather permitting) 2100 S Shiloh Rd. Phone 406/652-8100. ¢¢

Special Events

Montana Fair. MetraPark. Phone 406/256-2400. Mid-Aug.

Northern International Livestock Exposition. MetraPark. Oct. Phone 406/256-2400.

Motels/Motor Lodges

★★ **BEST WESTERN BILLINGS.** *5610 S Frontage Rd (59101). 406/248-9800; fax 406/248-2500; res 800/780-7234. www.bestwestern.com.* 80 rms, 3 story, 12 suites. June-Aug: S $54-$64; D $66-$76; each addl $5; suites $78-$110; under 18 free; lower rates rest of yr. Crib free. Pet accepted, some restrictions. TV; cable (premium). Indoor pool; whirlpool. Complimentary continental bkfst. Coffee in rms. Restaurant adj open 24 hrs. Ck-out noon, ck-in 2 pm;. Coin lndry. Meeting rms. Business servs avail. Valet serv. Sauna. Some refrigerators; microwave avail in suites. Airport transportation avail. Cr cds: A, C, D, DS, MC, V.

★★ **BEST WESTERN PONDEROSA INN.** *2511 1st Ave N (59101). 406/259-5511; fax 406/245-8004; toll-free 800/628-9081. www.bestwestern. com.* 132 rms, 2 story. S $58-$65; D $67-$75; each addl $5; under 12 free. Crib free. Pet accepted, some restrictions. TV; cable (premium). Pool. Complimentary coffee in rms. Restaurant open 24 hrs. Bar 3 pm-2 am; closed Sun. Ck-out 11 am. Coin lndry. Meeting rm. Business servs avail. Valet serv. Free airport transportation. Exercise equipt; sauna. Cr cds: A, C, D, DS, MC, V.

★★ **THE BILLINGS INN.** *880 N 29th St (59101). 406/252-6800; toll-free 800/231-7782.* 60 rms, 4 story. S $49; D $53; each addl $5; under 12 free. Crib $5. Pet accepted, some restrictions; $5. TV; cable. Complimentary continental bkfst. Ck-out 11 am. Coin lndry. Valet serv. Sundries. Airport transportation. Some refrigerators, microwaves. Cr cds: A, DS, MC, V.

★★ **C'MON INN.** *2020 Overland Ave (59102). 406/655-1100; fax 406/652-7672; toll-free 800/655-1170.* 72 rms, 2 story, 8 suites. May-Aug: S $63.99; D $66.99-$74.99; each addl $5; suites $140.99; under 13 free; lower rates rest of yr. Crib free. TV; cable (premium). Indoor pool; wading pool, whirlpool. Complimentary continental bkfst. Restaurant nearby. Ck-out noon. Meeting rms. Business servs avail. Exercise equipt. Valet serv. Game rm. Minibars; refrigerator, microwave in suites. Cr cds: A, DS, MC, V.

★ **COMFORT INN.** *2030 Overland Ave (59102). 406/652-5200; toll-free 800/228-5150. www.comfortinn.com.* 60 rms, 2 story. June-mid-Sept: S $69.95; D $79.95; each addl $5; suites $84-$90; under 18 free; lower rates rest of yr. Crib free. Pet accepted, some restrictions. TV; cable (premium). Indoor pool; whirlpool. Complimentary continental bkfst. Ck-out 11 am. Business servs avail. Game rm. Some refrigerators. Cr cds: A, C, D, DS, ER, JCB, MC, V.

★ **DAYS INN.** *843 Parkway Ln (59101). 406/252-4007; fax 406/896-1147; res 800/329-7466. www.daysinn. com.* 63 rms. S $43.99-$67.50; D $57-$78; each addl $5; under 12 free. Crib free. Pet accepted, some restrictions. TV; cable, VCR avail (movies). Complimentary continental bkfst. Coffee in rms. In-rm modem link. Restaurant nearby. Ck-out noon. Coin lndry. Sundries. Whirlpool. Cr cds: A, C, D, DS, JCB, MC, V.

★★ **FAIRFIELD INN.** *2026 Overland Ave (59102). 406/652-5330; fax 406/652-5330; res 800/228-2800.*

www.fairfieldinn.com. 63 rms, 3 story. June-mid-Sept: S $64.95-$74.95; D $69.95-$79.95; each addl $5; under 18 free; lower rates rest of yr. Crib free. TV; cable (premium). Indoor pool; whirlpool. Complimentary continental bkfst. Restaurant nearby. Ck-out noon. Meeting rms. Business servs avail. Game rm. Some refrigerators. Cr cds: A, D, DS, JCB, MC, V.

⬜ 🏊 🔆 🔥

★★ **HILLTOP INN.** *1116 N 28th St (59101). 406/245-5000; fax 406/245-7851; toll-free 800/878-9282.* 45 rms, 3 story. S $75-$85; D $75-$89; each addl $5; under 12 free. Crib $5. Pet accepted. TV; cable. Complimentary continental bkfst. Restaurant nearby. Ck-out 11 am. Sundries. Valet serv. Coin lndry. Business servs avail. Some refrigerators, microwaves. Cr cds: A, D, DS, MC, V.

🔆 ✖ 🔆 🔥

★ **HOWARD JOHNSON EXPRESS INN.** *1001 S 27th St (59101). 406/248-4656; fax 406/248-7268; res 800/446-4656. www.hojo.com.* 173 rms, 3 story. June-Sept: S $59-$75; D $79; each addl $4; under 18 free. Crib free. Pet accepted, some restrictions; deposit. TV; cable. Complimentary continental bkfst. Coffee in rms. Ck-out noon. Coin lndry. Meeting rms. Business servs avail. In-rm modem link. Free airport transportation. Cr cds: A, C, D, DS, MC, V.

⬜ 🔆 🕊 🔆 🔆 🔥

★ **QUALITY INN.** *2036 Overland Ave (59102). 406/652-1320; toll-free 800/228-5151. www.qualityinn.com.* 119 rms, 2 story. S, D $62.95-$79.95; each addl $5; suites $67.95-$84.95; under 18 free. Crib free. Pet accepted; $25 deposit. TV; cable (premium), VCR avail (movies). Indoor pool; whirlpool. Complimentary full bkfst. Coffee in rms. Restaurant nearby. Ck-out noon. Coin lndry. In-rm modem link. Business servs avail. Bellhops. Valet serv. Free airport transportation. Golf privileges. Sauna. Health club privileges. Some refrigerators. Cr cds: A, D, DS, MC, V.

⬜ 🔆 🏊 🔆 🏊 ✈ 🔆 🔥 SC

★ **RAMADA LIMITED.** *1345 Mullowney Ln (59101). 406/252-2584; res 888/298-2054. www.ramada.com.* 116 rms, 2 story. S $55-$65; D $65-$75; each addl $5; under 18 free. Crib

free. Pet accepted, some restrictions. TV; cable (premium). Pool. Playground. Complimentary continental bkfst. Restaurant nearby. Ck-out noon. Coin lndry. Business servs avail. Exercise equipt. Cr cds: A, C, D, DS, MC, V.

⬜ 🔆 🏊 🔆 🔆 🔥

★ **SLEEP INN.** *4904 Southgate Dr (59101). 406/254-0013; fax 406/254-9878; res 800/753-3746. www.sleep inn.com.* 75 rms, shower only, 2 story. S $47.95; D $53.95; each addl $6; under 18 free. Crib free. TV; cable (premium). Complimentary continental bkfst. Restaurant nearby. In-rm modem link. Ck-out 11 am. Cr cds: A, DS, MC, V.

🔥

★ **SUPER 8 MOTEL.** *5400 Southgate Dr (59102). 406/248-8842; toll-free 800/800-8000. www.super8.com.* 114 rms, 3 story. S $43-$57; D $56-$63; each addl $5; suites $65-$75; under 12 free. Crib free. Pet accepted, some restrictions; $20. TV; cable (premium), VCR avail (movies). Restaurant nearby. Ck-out 11 am. Cr cds: A, C, D, DS, MC, V.

⬜ 🔆 🔆 🔥 SC

Hotels

★★ **HOLIDAY INN GRAND MONTANA.** *5500 Midland Rd (59101). 406/248-7701; fax 406/248-8954; toll-free 877/554-7263. www.holiday-inn. com/billings-west.* 315 rms, 34 suites, 7 story. June-Oct: S, D $69-$99; each addl $10; suites $106-$250; under 18 free; family rates; package plans; lower rates rest of yr. Crib $5. Pet accepted, some restrictions; $10. TV; cable (premium). Complimentary coffee in rms. Restaurant 6 am-10 pm. Bar 11-1 am; entertainment Fri night. Ck-out noon. Convention facilities. In-rm modem link. Business center. Gift shop. Free airport transportation. Exercise equipt; sauna. Indoor pool; whirlpool. Game rm. Some refrigerators, minibars. Cr cds: A, C, D, DS, JCB, MC, V.

⬜ 🔆 🏊 🔆 ✈ 🔆 🔥 🏃

★★ **RADISSON NORTHERN HOTEL.** *19 N 28th St (59101). 406/245-5121; fax 406/259-9862; toll-free 800/542-5121. www.radisson.com.* 160 rms, 10 story. S, D $79-$119; each addl $10; under 18 free. Crib free. Pet accepted, some restrictions. TV; cable (premium). Restaurant 6:30 am-10 pm. Bar 11-1 am. Ck-out noon, ck-in 3 pm. Meeting rms. Business servs avail. Gift shop. Free covered parking. Airport transportation. Exercise equipt. Some refrigerators. Cr cds: A, DS, MC, V.

★★★ **SHERATON.** *27 N 27th St (59101). 406/252-7400; fax 406/252-2401; toll-free 800/588-7666. www. sheraton.com.* 282 rms, 23 story. S, D $69-$109; each addl $10; suites $150-$200; under 18 free. Crib free. Pet accepted, some restrictions. TV; cable (premium). Indoor pool; wading pool, whirlpool. Coffee in rms. Restaurant 6:30 am-10 pm. Bar 11-2 am. Ck-out noon. Convention facilities. Business servs avail. In-rm modem link. Gift shop. Free airport transportation. Exercise rm; sauna. Game rm. Some refrigerators. Cr cds: A, C, D, DS, ER, JCB, MC, V.

Restaurants

★★ **GEORGE HENRY'S.** *404 N 30th St (59101). 406/245-4570.* Hrs: 11 am-2 pm, 5:30-9 pm; Sat from 5:30 pm. Closed Sun; hols. Res accepted. Continental menu. Beer, wine. Lunch $5.75-$7.75, dinner $8.95-$18.95. Child's menu. Specializes in chicken, steaks, seafood. Own soups, desserts. Parking. Built 1882; former boardinghouse and tearoom; some original fixtures. Totally nonsmoking. Cr cds: A, DS, MC, V.

★★ **GREAT WALL.** *1309 Grand Ave (59102). 406/245-8601.* Hrs: 11 am-9:30 pm; Fri, Sat to 10 pm. Closed Thanksgiving, Dec 25. Res accepted. Chinese menu. Wine, beer. Lunch $5.25-$8.25, dinner $5.75-$16.95. Lunch buffet $6.25. Child's menu. Specialties: marinated crisp duck, Taiwanese seafood in bird's nest, hot amazing chicken. Parking. Cr cds: A, DS, MC, V.

★★★ **JULIANO'S.** *2912 N 7th Ave (59101). 406/248-6400.* Hrs: 11:30 am-2 pm, 5:30-9 pm; Wed-Sat from 5:30 pm. Closed Sun; Thanksgiving, Dec 25. Res accepted. Continental menu. Bar. Wine list. Lunch $6.95-

$7.95, dinner $13.95-$21.95. Specialties: peppered Montana ostrich, seared sesame-crusted (rare) tuna. Own baking. Parking. Outdoor dining. Converted Victorian home (1902); turn-of-the-century decor. Totally nonsmoking. Cr cds: A, C, D, DS, MC, V.

★★ **MATTHEW'S TASTE OF ITALY.** *1233 N 27th (59101). 406/254-8530.* Hrs: 11 am-10 pm; Sat, Sun from noon. Closed Thanksgiving, Dec 25. Res accepted. Italian menu. Bar. Lunch $5.95-$9.95, dinner $7.95-$16.95. Child's menu. Specialties: scallopini di pollo, pasta con pollo al sugo bianco. Italian bistro decor. Cr cds: A, MC, V.

★★ **REX.** *2401 Montana Ave (59101). 406/245-7477.* Hrs: 5:30-10 pm; Fri, Sat to 10:30 pm. Closed Thanksgiving, Dec 25. Res accepted. Bar 11:30-1 am; Sat, Sun from 5 pm. Dinner $12.95-$27.95. Specializes in hand-cut steak, prime rib, fresh seafood. Outdoor dining. In National Historic District. Totally nonsmoking. Cr cds: A, D, DS, MC, V.

★★★ **WALKER'S GRILL.** *301 N 27th St (59101). 406/245-9291. www. walkersgrill.com.* Hrs: 5:30-10:30 pm; Sat from 5. Closed Sun; some major hols. Res accepted. Bar from 4 pm. Dinner $12.95-$22.50. Child's menu. Specializes in dry-aged beef, fresh fish, pasta. Jazz Fri, Sat. Parking. Bistro atmosphere. Cr cds: A, DS, MC, V.

Bozeman

(D-4) See also Livingston, Three Forks, White Sulphur Springs

Settled 1864 **Pop** 22,660 **Elev** 4,810 ft
Area code 406

Information Chamber of Commerce, 2000 Commerce Way, 59718; 406/586-5421 or 800/228-4224

Web www.bozemanchamber.com

Blazing a trail from Wyoming, John M. Bozeman led a train of immigrants who settled here and named the town for their leader. The first settlements in the Gallatin Valley were agricultural, but were economically surpassed by the mines nearby. Today, small grain farming, livestock, dairying, tourism, and the state university are important sources of income. The city is the marketplace for the cattle-producing Gallatin Valley.

What to See and Do

Gallatin National Forest. 1,735,412 acres. Mountain peaks, pine and fir forest, winter sports, pack trips, picnicking, camping, fishing, hunting; 574,788-acre Absaroke-Beartooth Wilderness south of Livingston, 253,000-acre Lee Metcalf Wilderness, Gallatin Gateway to Yellowstone. Forest rangers provide interpretive programs in summer at the Madison River Canyon Earthquake Area (see WEST YELLOWSTONE); exhibits. N and S of town. For info contact Supervisor, 10 E Babcock St, PO Box 130, 59771. Phone 406/587-6701.

Montana State University. (1893) (11,000 students). 11th Ave, College St, 7th Ave, and Lincoln St, at S edge of town. Phone 406/994-0211. On campus is

Museum of the Rockies. Pioneer, Native American exhibits; dinosaurs; art and science displays. Taylor Planetarium. (Daily; closed hols) 600 W Kagy Blvd. Phone 406/994-2251. ¢¢

Skiing. Bridger Bowl Ski Area. Quad, triple, five double chairlifts, ski school, patrol, rentals; half-day rates; lodge, cafeteria, bar. Longest run 3 mi; vertical drop 2,000 ft. (Mid-Dec-Apr, daily) 16 mi NE via MT 86, in Gallatin National Forest. Phone 406/587-2111. ¢¢¢¢

Special Events

Montana Winter Fair. Late Jan or early Feb. Phone 406/585-1397.

Gallatin County Fair. Third wkend July. Phone 406/582-3270.

Sweet Pea Festival. First full wkend Aug. Phone 406/586-4003.

Bridger Raptor Festival. Bridger Bowl ridge area. View birds of prey, including the largest concentration of

migrating Golden Eagles in the contigous 48 states, on their trip south. Usually late Sept or early Oct. Phone 406/585-1211.

Motels/Motor Lodges

★★ **BEST WESTERN GRANTREE INN.** 1325 N 7th Ave (59715). 406/587-5261; fax 406/587-9437; res 800/624-5865. www.bestwestern.com/ grantreeinn. 120 rms, 2 story. May-Aug: S, D $79-$105; each addl $4; suites $96-$125; under 17 free; family rates; package plans; lower rates rest of yr. Crib free. TV; cable. Complimentary coffee in rms. Restaurant 6 am-10 pm. Bar 9-2 am. Ck-out noon. Meeting rms. Business servs avail. Bellhops. Coin lndry. Free airport transportation. Downhill/x-country ski 16 mi. Exercise equipt. Indoor pool; whirlpool. Game rm. Cr cds: A, C, D, DS, MC, V.
🄳 🐾 ⊠ ⛌ 🏃 ✈ 🚱 🔥 SC

★★ **BOZEMAN'S WESTERN HERITAGE INN.** 1200 E Main St (59715). 406/586-8534; fax 406/587-8729; toll-free 800/877-1094. www.avicom.net/ westernheritage. 38 rms, 3 story. June-Sept: S $46-$63; D $49-$73; each addl $7; suites $85-$135; under 15 free; ski plan; higher rates Sweet Pea Festival; lower rates rest of yr. Crib $7. Pet accepted. TV; cable (premium). Complimentary continental bkfst. Restaurant adj 6 am-10:30 pm. Ck-out 11 am. Coin lndry. Meeting rms. Business servs avail. Valet serv. Sundries. Downhill/x-country ski 16 mi. Exercise equipt; steam rm. Some in-rm whirlpools. Cr cds: A, C, D, DS, MC, V.
🔁 ⊠ 🏃 🚱 🔥 SC

★ **COMFORT INN.** 1370 N 7th Ave (59715). 406/587-2322; fax 406/587-2423; toll-free 800/587-3833. www. comfortinnbozeman.com. 87 rms, 3 story. June-Sept: S $73-$89; D $77-$92; each addl $4; suites $92-$106; under 18 free; lower rates rest of yr. Crib $4. Pet accepted, some restrictions. TV; cable. Indoor pool; whirlpool. Complimentary continental bkfst. Coffee in rms. Restaurant opp 6:30 am-11 pm. Ck-out 11 am. Coin lndry. Meeting rm. Business center. In-rm modem link. Exercise equipt; sauna. Cr cds: A, DS, MC, V.
🄳 🔁 🐾 🔆 ⊠ 🏃 ✈ 🔥 🏃

★ **DAYS INN.** *1321 N 7th Ave (59715). 406/587-5251; fax 406/587-5351; toll-free 800/329-7466. www.the. daysinn.com/bozeman06765.* 79 rms, 2 story. S, D $69-$99; suites $90-$100; each addl $5; under 17 free. Crib free. Pet accepted; $25 deposit. TV; cable (premium), VCR avail (movies). Complimentary full bkfst. Restaurant adj 6 am-10 pm. Ck-out 11 am, ck-in 3:30. Business servs avail. Coin lndry. Downhill/x-country ski 17 mi. Exercise equipt. Whirlpool, sauna. Cr cds: A, DS, JCB, MC, V.

★ ★ **FAIRFIELD INN.** *828 Wheat Dr (59715). 406/587-2222; toll-free 800/228-2800. www.fairfieldinn.com.* 57 rms, 3 story. June-Aug: S $89; D $89-$99; each addl $5; suites $94-$99; under 18 free; lower rates rest of yr. Crib free. TV; cable (premium). Indoor pool; whirlpool. Complimentary continental bkfst. Restaurant opp open 24 hrs. Ck-out noon. Business servs avail. In rm modem link. Valet serv, Sundries. Downhill/x-country ski 16 mi. Game rm. Refrigerator, microwave in suites. Cr cds: A, C, D, DS, MC, V.

★ ★ **HAMPTON INN.** *75 Baxter Ln (59715). 406/522-8000; fax 406/522-7446; res 800/426-7866. www. hamptoninn.com.* 70 rms, 2 story. June-mid-Sept: S, D $95-$115; under 18 free; lower rates rest of yr. Crib free. TV; cable (premium). Complimentary continental bkfst. Compli- mentary coffee in rms. Restaurant adj 6:30 am-10 pm. Ck-out 11 am. Meeting rms. Business servs avail. In- rm modem link. Bellhops. Coin lndry. Free airport transportation. Downhill/x-country ski 16 mi. Exercise equipt. Indoor pool; whirlpool. Cr cds: A, C, D, DS, ER, JCB, MC, V.

★ ★ **HOLIDAY INN.** *5 Baxter Ln (59715). 406/587-4561; fax 406/587-4413; toll-free 800/366-5101. www. sixcontinentshotels.com/holiday-inn.* 179 rms, 2 story. S, D $79-$109; suite $149; under 18 free. Crib free. Pet accepted. TV; cable. Indoor pool; whirlpool. Coffee in rms. Restaurant 6 am-2 pm, 5-10 pm. Bar 4 pm-mid- night. Ck-out noon. Coin lndry. Meeting rms. Business servs avail. Bellhops. Valet serv. Free airport, bus

depot transportation. Downhill/x-country ski 16 mi. Lawn games. Exer- cise equipt. Massage. Rec rm. Picnic tables. Cr cds: A, DS, MC, V.

★ ★ **HOLIDAY INN EXPRESS.** *6261 Jackrabbit Ln, Belgrade (59714). 406/388-0800; fax 406/388-0804; toll-free 800/542-6791. www.holiday-inn.com.* 67 rms, 3 story. June-Aug: S, D $59.95-$69.95; under 12 free; lower rates rest of yr. Crib free. Pet accepted. TV; cable (premium). Com- plimentary coffee in lobby. Restau- rant adj open 24 hrs. Ck-out 11 am. Exercise equipt. Cr cds: A, C, D, DS, JCB, MC, V.

★ **MOTEL 6.** *817 Wheat Dr (59715). 406/585-7888; fax 406/585-8842; res 800/466-9356. www.motel6.com.* 56 rms, shower only. 5 suites, 2 story. Early July-mid-Sept: S $44-$79; D $49-$89; suites $105; under 17 free; lower rates rest of yr. Crib free. Pet accepted. TV; cable. Indoor pool; whirlpool. Complimentary continen- tal bkfst. Restaurant nearby. Ck-out 11 am. Downhill/x-country ski 16 mi. Sauna. Game rm. Some refrigera- tors, microwaves. Cr cds: A, C, D, DS, ER, JCB, MC, V.

★ **RAMADA INN.** *2020 Wheat Dr (59715). 406/585-2626; fax 406/585-2727; res 888/298-2054. www.ramada. com.* 50 rms, shower only. 2 story. June-Aug: S $79; D $99-$109; suites $119-$139; lower rates rest of yr. Crib free. Pet accepted. TV; cable (pre- mium). Indoor pool; whirlpool, water slide. Complimentary continental bkfst. Restaurant nearby. Ck-out noon. Valet serv. Downhill/x-country ski 16 mi. Cr cds: A, C, D, DS, MC, V.

★ **ROYAL 7.** *310 N 7th Ave (59715). 406/587-3103; toll-free 800/587-3103.* 47 units. S $30-$42; D $37-$49; kit. unit $63.75. Crib $4. Pet accepted. TV; cable (premium). Play- ground. Restaurant adj 7 am-10 pm. Ck-out noon. Business servs avail. Downhill/x-country ski 16 mi. Whirlpool. Picnic tables. Cr cds: A, D, DS, MC, V.

★ **TLC INN.** *805 Wheat Dr (59715). 406/587-2100; fax 406/587-4941; toll-free 877/466-7852. www.tlc-inn.com. 42 rms, 3 story. No elvtr. June-Aug: S* $346-$56; D $68; each addl $4; under 18 free; lower rates rest of yr. Crib free. Pet accepted, $5. TV; cable. Complimentary continental bkfst.

THE RICHEST HILL ON EARTH

Butte, the quintessential Old West mining town, was the nation's largest single source of silver in the late 19th century and the largest source of copper until the 1930s. Butte's magnificent homes and commercial and civic buildings attest to its early wealth and importance. Its massive smokestacks, soot-grimed brick buildings, and the yawning Berkeley Pit mine also serve as historic reminders of the environmental damage of rabid, unregulated mining.

Butte contains the nation's second-largest National Historic Landmark District, with over 4,500 historic structures within 2,700 acres—from elegant mansions of Copper Kings to humble miner's cottages, boarding houses, and hotels that once housed an estimated 100,000 people.

Begin a tour of Butte at the Copper King Mansion (219 West Granite Street). This private home was built in 1888 by William Clark, one of the three Copper Kings of Butte, at a time when he was one of the world's richest men. This three-story brick High Victorian mansion contains 30 rooms, many with frescoed ceilings, carved staircases, inlaid floors, and Tiffany windows. Clark spent $300,000 on the building and imported many craftsmen from Europe. The third floor boasts a 60-foot-long ballroom and a chapel. The mansion is open for tours daily.

Walk one block south on Washington Street. Clark's son Charles was so taken by a chateau he visited in France that he procured the plans and had it reconstructed in Butte. Now known as the Arts Chateau (321 Broadway Street), the building serves as Butte's community arts center.

Continue one block south on Washington, and turn west on Park Street. Another gem of old Butte architecture is the Mother Lode Theater (316 West Park Street). This magnificent old vaudeville theater has been refurbished and serves as Butte's performing arts center. The theater is home to the Butte Symphony and a regional theater troupe.

Walk east on Park Street toward the core of downtown, which is found along Park and Broadway streets. Be sure to stop at Butte Hill Bakery (7 South Montana) to order a pasty, a form of meat pie that was a lunchtime staple for miners.

The showpiece of Butte civic architecture is the Butte-Silver Bow Courthouse (155 West Granite Street), built in 1910. A lovely stained-glass dome tops the four-story rotunda, murals decorate the ceilings, and oak fixtures predominate throughout. Butte leaders spent almost twice as much on this courthouse as the state spent on the Montana Capitol.

Continue along Park or Broadway to Main Street, and turn south. The Dumas Brothel (45 East Mercury) was Butte's longest-lived house of ill repute, in operation from 1890 until 1982. Now a museum, the two-story brick building still has quite a few architectural features distinctive to a house of prostitution, such as windows onto the corridors and "bedrooms" that the miners more appropriately called cribs. This is the only surviving building from Butte's once thriving red-light district.

Also unusual is Mai Wah (17 West Mercury), a museum dedicated to telling the story of Chinese miners and workers who pioneered in Butte. The Mai Wah building once housed a number of Chinese-owned businesses; Butte's China Alley, the heart of the old Chinatown, is adjacent.

Ck-out 11 am. Whirlpool. Sauna. Cr
cds: A, C, D, DS, JCB, MC, V.

B&Bs/Small Inns

★★★ **FOX HOLLOW BED &
BREAKFAST.** 545 Mary Rd (59718).
406/582-8440; fax 406/582-9752; res
800/431-5010. www.bozeman-mt.com.
5 rms, 2 story, 2 suites, 1 kit. unit.
No A/C. No rm phones. S, D $89-
$99; each addl $25; suites $109, kit.
unit $108. Children over 10 yrs only.
TV in some rms; cable (premium),
VCR avail (movies). Complimentary
full bkfst. Ck-out 11 am, ck-in 4-7
pm. Luggage handling. Downhill/x-
country ski 20 mi. Lawn games. Picnic tables. View of Rockies.
Contemporary and Western art.
Totally nonsmoking. Cr cds: A, DS,
MC, V.

★★★ **GALLATIN GATEWAY.**
76405 Gallatin Rd (US 191), Gallatin
Gateway (59718). 406/763-4672; toll-
free 800/676-3522. www.gallatin
gatewayinn.com. 35 rms, 2 story.
Some A/C. July-early Sept: S $70-
$105; D $85-$120; each addl $15;
suites $160-$175; under 12 free;
lower rates rest of yr. Crib $5. TV;
cable (premium). Heated pool; whirlpool. Complimentary continental
bkfst. Restaurant (see also GALLATIN
GATEWAY INN). Bar 5 pm-midnight.
Concierge serv. Airport transportation. Tennis. Lawn games. Mountain
bike rentals. On river. Restored railroad hotel (1927); many antiques. Cr
cds: A, DS, MC, V.

★★ **SILVER FOREST.** 15325 Bridger
Canyon Rd (59715). 406/586-1882;
fax 406/582-0492; res 888/835-5970.
www.silverforestinn.com. 6 rms, some
share bath, 5 with shower only. No
A/C. No rm phones. S, D $115-$150;
each addl $10; under 12 free; pack-
age plans. Crib free. TV; cable (premium), VCR avail (movies). Ck-out
noon, ck-in 4-6 pm. Luggage handling. Guest lndry. Downhill/x-coun-
try ski ¼ mi. Built in 1931; rustic
decor. Totally nonsmoking. Cr cds: A,
MC, V.

★★ **VOSS INN.** 319 S Willson Ave
(59715). 406/587-0982; fax 406/585-
2964. www.bozeman-vossinn.com. 6
rms, 2 A/C, 2 story. S $85-$105; D
$105-$125; each addl $10. TV in sit-
ting rm. Complimentary full bkfst;
afternoon refreshments. Ck-out
noon, ck-in 2 pm. Downhill/x-coun-
try ski 16 mi. Built 1883; Victorian
decor, antiques; brass and iron beds.
Totally nonsmoking. Cr cds: A, DS,
MC, V.

Restaurants

★★ **BOODLES.** 215 E Main St
(59715). 406/587-2901. Hrs: 11:30
am-2 pm, 5:30-9:30 pm; Sat, Sun
5:30-9:30 pm. Closed Thanksgiving,
Dec 25. Res accepted. Continental
menu. Bar. Lunch $6-$9, dinner $13-
$27. Specializes in fish, steaks. Jazz
Fri, Sat. Street parking. In 1880s
saloon building old English club
decor. Cr cds: A, DS, MC, V.

★★★ **GALLATIN GATEWAY INN.**
76405 Gallatin Rd, Gallatin Gateway
(59730). 406/763-4672. www.gallatin
gatewayinn.com. Hrs: 6-9:30 pm. Res
accepted. Bar to midnight. Wine list.
Dinner $13.50-$25. Child's menu.
Specializes in pasta, fresh seafood,
wild game. Spanish decor. Totally
nonsmoking. Cr cds: A, DS, MC, V.

★★ **JOHN BOZEMAN'S BISTRO.**
125 W Main St (59715). 406/587-
4100. Hrs: 11 am-2:30 pm, 5-9:30
pm; Sun 8 am-2 pm. Closed Mon.
Res accepted. Continental menu.
Wine, beer. Bkfst $4.95-$9.95, lunch
$4.95-$8.95, dinner $13.95-$24.95.
Child's menu. Specializes in fresh
seafood, Montana steaks, fresh sushi.
Parking. Eclectic decor; original art.
Totally nonsmoking. Cr cds: A, D,
DS, MC, V.

★★ **SPANISH PEAKS BREWERY.** 14
N Church Ave (59772). 406/585-2296.
www.spanishpeaks.com. Hrs: 11:30
am-10:30 pm; Sun noon-10 pm. Res
accepted. Italian menu. Bar to 2 am.
Lunch $5.95-$8.95, dinner $7.95-
$18.95. Specializes in homemade
pasta, wood-fired pizza. Parking.

Own beer brewed on site. Contemporary decor. Cr cds: MC, V.

Unrated Dining Spots

LEAF & BEAN COFFEE HOUSE. *35 W Main St (59715). 406/587-1580.* Hrs: 6:30 am-10 pm; wkends to 11 pm. Closed Thanksgiving, Dec 25. No A/C. Pastries/desserts $1-$3. Selection of specialty coffees, teas and desserts. Entertainment Fri, Sat. Totally nonsmoking. Cr cds: MC, V.

MACKENZIE RIVER PIZZA. *232 E Main St (59715). 406/587-0055.* Hrs: 11:30 am-10 pm; Sun from 5 pm. Closed hols. Lunch, dinner $4.95-$16.75. Specializes in gourmet pizza. Cr cds: A, DS, MC, V.

Browning

(A-3) *See also East Glacier Area, under Glacier National Park*

Pop 1,170 **Elev** 4,362 ft
Area code 406 **Zip** 59417

Eastern gateway to Glacier National Park (see), Browning is the capital of the Blackfeet Nation. The town was named for a US Commissioner of Indian Affairs. The reservation itself covers 2,348,000 acres.

What to See and Do

Museum of Montana Wildlife and Hall of Bronze. Miniature dioramas, mounted specimens; paintings; sculpture. (May-Sept, daily) Just E of Museum of the Plains Indian on US 2, 89. Phone 406/338-5425. ¢

Museum of the Plains Indian. Collection of Blackfeet and Northern Plains Native American tribal artifacts plus history of tribes of the northern Great Plains. Administered by Dept of Interior, Indian Arts and Crafts Board. (June-Sept, daily; rest of yr, Mon-Fri; closed Jan 1, Thanksgiving, Dec 25) W at jct US 2, 89; 13 mi from Glacier National Park. Phone 406/338-2230. ¢¢

Special Event

North American Native American Days Powwow. Blackfeet Reservation. Phone 406/338-7276. Mid-July.

Butte

(D-3) *See also Anaconda, Three Forks*

Settled 1864 **Pop** 33,336 **Elev** 5,549 ft
Area code 406 **Zip** 59701
Information Butte-Silver Bow Chamber of Commerce, 1000 George St; 800/735-6814
Web www.butteinfo.org

Settled more than 100 years ago, Butte, atop the "richest hill on earth," harvests treasures of copper along with by-product gold, silver, and other metals from 1,000 acres of mines. Although mined for more than a century, this treasure chest seems to be inexhaustible. Butte's famous old properties continue to produce high-grade ores. Modern mining techniques have exposed vast new low-grade mineral resources.

Butte was born as a bonanza silver camp. When the silver ores became lower grade at comparatively shallow depths, copper ores were discovered. Although development of the copper mines was a slow process, culminating in the "war of the copper kings," fortunes were made and lost and battles were fought in court for control of ore on surface and underground.

The brawny, colorful mining-camp days of Butte are over. Although copper mining still plays an important role in the Butte economy, it is also a retailing, distribution, and diversified industrial center. A Ranger District office of the Deerlodge National Forest is located here.

What to See and Do

Arts Chateau. (1898). Originally home of Charles Clark, now a heritage museum and arts center. Stairway leads from first floor galleries to fourth floor ballroom. Stained-glass windows, intricate moldings. (Mon-Sat) 321 W Broadway. Phone 406/723-7600. ¢¢

Berkeley Pit. Located just outside of downtown Butte, the former open-pit copper mine is over 1,800 ft deep and more than one mi across. When filled, it is Montana's deepest and most toxic body of water. Can be seen from viewing stand (Mar-Nov). 200 Shields St. Phone 406/723-3177.

Copper King Mansion. (ca 1888) Restored 32-rm home of Senator W.A. Clark, prominent political figure of Montana's early mining days; of particular interest are frescoed ceilings and walls, stained-glass windows, nine hand-carved fireplaces, antique pipe organ; silver and crystal collections. (May-Sept, daily) 219 W Granite St. Phone 406/782-7580. ¢¢

Deerlodge National Forest. 1,176,152 acres incl 158,516-acre Anaconda-Pintler Wilderness, alpine lakes, ghost towns. Fishing, hunting. Bridle trails. Winter sports. Picknicking. Camping. Sections surround town, reached by I-90, I-15, MT 2, MT 1 (Pintler scenic route). Contact Forest Supervisor, 400 N Main St, PO Box 400. Phone 406/496-3400.

Dumas Brothel Museum. Listed on the National Register of Historic Places, museum is one of the few remaining buildings in the West purposely built as a brothel. Various brothel-related exhibits. Gift shop. Not recommended for children. Tours (Memorial Day-Labor Day, daily; rest of yr by appt) 45 E Mercury St. Phone 406/723-6128. ¢¢

Montana Tech of the University of Montana. (1893) 1,900 students. Mineral energy-oriented college near mining operations. On W Park St. Phone 406/496-4266. On campus is

> **Mineral Museum.** Mineral display; some fossils; specimens from collection of 15,100 rotate periodically; special fluorescent and Montana minerals. Guided tours. (Mon-Fri; also by appt; closed hols) Phone 406/496-4414. **FREE**

Old No. 1. Tour of city aboard replica of early-day streetcar departs from Chamber of Commerce office. (Memorial Day-Labor Day, daily) Phone 800/735-6814. ¢¢

Our Lady of the Rockies. 90-ft likeness of Mary, Mother of Jesus, sits atop Continental Divide overlooking town. Trips to mountaintop avail in summer. Phone 406/494-2656. ¢¢¢

World Museum of Mining and 1899 Mining Camp. Outdoor and indoor displays of mining mementos; turn-of-the-century mining camp, Hell Roarin' Gulch. Picnic area. (Memorial Day-Labor Day, daily; rest of yr, daily exc Mon) W Park St. Phone 406/723-7211. ¢

Special Event

Butte Vigilante Rodeo. July. Phone 406/494-3002.

Motels/Motor Lodges

★ **COMFORT INN OF BUTTE.** *2777 Harrison Ave (59701). 406/494-8850; fax 406/494-2801; res 800/228 5150. www.townpump.com.* 150 rms, 3 story. No elvtr. Mid-May-Sept: S $65-$75; D $70 $80; each addl $5; suites $89-$132; under 18 free; lower rates rest of yr. Pet accepted; $5. TV; cable (premium), VCR avail (movies). Complimentary continental bkfst. Restaurant nearby. Ck-out 11 am. Coin lndry. Meeting rms. Business servs avail. Airport transportation. Exercise equipt; sauna. Whirlpool. Cr cds: A, C, D, DS, ER, JCB, MC.

⬛ 🔌 🐾 ✕ ⬛ 🔥 **SC**

★ **DAYS INN.** *2700 Harrison Ave (59701). 406/494-7000; fax 406/494-7000; res 800/329-7466. www.daysinn. com.* 74 rms, 3 story. Mid-May-mid-Sept· S $60-$72; D $70 $89; each addl $8; suites $150; under 18 free; lower rates rest of yr. Crib free. Pet accepted. TV; cable, VCR avail. Complimentary continental bkfst. Restaurant nearby. Ck-out 11 am. Meeting rms. Business servs avail. Bellhops. Exercise equipt; sauna. Cr cds: A, C, D, DS, ER, JCB, MC, V.

⬛ 🔌 🦅 ✂ 🧍 ✕ ⬛ 🔥 **SC**

★★ **HOLIDAY INN EXPRESS-PARKSIDE.** *One Holiday Park (59701). 406/494-6999; fax 406/494 1300; res 800/465-4329.* 83 rms, 5 story, 17 suites. June-Sept: S, D $72; suites $85-$99; under 18 free; lower rates rest of yr. Crib free. TV; cable (premium). Complimentary continental bkfst. Restaurant adj open 24 hrs. Ck-out noon. Meeting rms. Business center. Coin lndry. Free airport transportation. Exercise equipt. Bathrm phones; refrigerator in suites. Cr cds: A, DS, MC, V.

★ **RAMADA INN.** *4655 Harrison Ave (59701). 406/494-6666; fax 406/494-3274; toll-free 800/332-8600. www. ramada.com.* 146 rms, 2 story. S, D $88-$98; each addl $10; suites $165; under 18 free. Crib free. Pet accepted. TV; cable. Indoor pool. Coffee in rms. Restaurants 6 am-9 pm. Bar 11-2 am; entertainment Fri, Sat. Ck-out noon. Coin lndry. Meeting rms. Business servs avail. Bellhops. Free airport transportation. Indoor tennis. Exercise equipt; sauna. Private patios. Cr cds: A, C, D, DS, MC, V.

★ **SUPER 8 MOTEL.** *2929 Harrison Ave (59701). 406/494-6000; toll-free 800/800-8000. www.super8.com.* 106 rms, 3 story. No elvtr. Mid-May-mid-Sept: S $52.88; D $56.88-$60.88; each addl $4; suites $70.88; under 12 free; lower rates rest of yr. Crib free. TV; cable, VCR avail (movies). Complimentary continental bkfst. Restaurant opp 6 am-11 pm. Ck-out 11 am. Cr cds: A, C, D, DS, MC, V.

Restaurants

★★★ **LYDIA'S.** *4915 Harrison Ave (59701). 406/494-2000.* Hrs: 5:30-10:30 pm. Closed hols. Italian, American menu. Complete meals: dinner $9.25-$18.50. Child's menu. Specializes in tenderloin steaks, homemade ravioli, seafood. Victorian decor; stained-glass windows. Family-owned. Cr cds: A, D, DS, MC, V.

★★ **SPAGHETTINI'S.** *805 Utah Ave (59701). 406/782-8855.* Hrs: 11 am-2 pm, 5:30-10:30 pm. Closed most major hols. Res accepted. Italian menu. Wine, beer. Lunch $4-$5, dinner $7-$16. Specializes in seafood, chicken, fresh pasta. Outdoor dining. Former 1890s warehouse with Italian decor. Cr cds: A, C, D, DS, MC, V.

★★★ **UPTOWN CAFE.** *47 E Broadway (59701). 406/723-4735. www. montana.com/uptown.* Hrs: 11 am-2 pm, 5-10 pm; early-bird dinner 5-6:30 pm. Closed hols. Res accepted. Serv bar. Buffet: lunch $5. Complete meals: dinner $8.95-$29. Specializes in beef, fresh seafood. Own desserts. Monthly art display. Totally non-smoking. Cr cds: A, DS, MC, V.

Chinook

(A-5) *See also Havre*

Pop 1,512 **Elev** 2,438 ft
Area code 406 **Zip** 59523
Information Chamber of Commerce, PO Box 744; 406/357-2100

Gas wells, farming, and grazing are the main concerns of this town, which takes its name from the much-desired January and February winds that melt the snow, exposing grass for cattle.

What to See and Do

Bear's Paw Battleground. Scene of final battle and surrender of Chief Joseph of the Nez Perce following trek N from the Big Hole River, ending Montana's Native American wars in 1877. It was here that Chief Joseph spoke the eloquent words "From where the sun now stands, I will fight no more forever." This is the newest addition to the Nez Perce National Historic Park system. Picnicking. (See BIG HOLE NATIONAL BATTLEFIELD) 16 mi S on MT Sec 240.

Blaine County Museum. Local historical exhibits. (Memorial Day-Labor Day, daily; rest of yr, Mon-Fri) 501 Indiana. Phone 406/357-2590. **FREE**

Special Event

Blaine County Fair. July. Phone 406/357-3205.

Motel/Motor Lodge

★ **BEAR PAW COURT.** *114 Montana St (59523). 406/357-2221; toll-free 888/357-2224.* 16 rms. S $36-$41; D $47; each addl $5. Crib $2. TV; cable. Restaurant nearby. Ck-out 11 am. Cr cds: A, DS, MC, V.

Columbia Falls

(A-2) *See also Kalispell, Whitefish*

Pop 2,942 **Elev** 3,087 ft
Area code 406 **Zip** 59912
Information Flathead Convention &
Visitor Bureau, 15 Depot Park,
Kalispell, 55901; 406/756-9091 or
800/543-3105
Web www.fcvb.org

A gateway to Glacier National Park
(see), and the north fork of the Flathead River, this is an area of superb
hunting and fishing. Here also is the
Hungry Horse News, Montana's only
Pulitzer Prize-winning newspaper.

What to See and Do

Big Sky Water Slide. Ten water slides,
inner tube river run, hot tubs. Picnicking, concessions. (Memorial Day-
Labor Day, daily) Jct US 2, MT 206; 1
mi SE via US 2. Phone 406/892-5025.
¢¢¢¢¢

Glacier Maze. A two-level, 3-D maze
with passages more than one mi
long; also 18-hole miniature golf
course. Picnicking, concessions.
(May-Labor Day, daily) 10 mi NE on
US 2E. Phone 406/387-5902. ¢¢

Hungry Horse Dam and Power Plant.
One of world's largest concrete dams
(564 ft), set in a wooded canyon near
Glacier National Park. The reservoir
is approximately 34 mi long and 3½
mi at its widest point. Pictorial and
interactive displays; video (mid-May-
late Sept, daily). Several recreation
and camping sites of the Flathead
National Forest (see KALISPELL) are
on the reservoir. US 2 E 6 mi. Phone
406/387-5241. **FREE**

Special Event

Heritage Days. July. Phone 406/892-
2480.

Resort

★ ★ ★ **MEADOW LAKE.** *100 Saint
Andrews Dr (59912). 406/892-8700;
fax 406/892-0330; toll-free 800/321-
4653. www.meadowlake.com.* 24 rms,
1-3 story, 60 condos. June-Sept: D
$89-$149; each addl $15; condos
$159-$229; townhouses $259-$439;
lower rates rest of yr. Crib $5. Pet
accepted, some restrictions. TV; cable
(premium), VCR (movies). 2 pools, 1
indoor; wading pool, whirlpools.
Playground. Supervised children's
activities. Restaurant 7 am-10 pm.
Ck-out 10 am, ck-in 4 pm. Meeting
rms. Business servs avail. Free airport,
RR station transportation. Tennis. 18-
hole golf, greens fee $36, pro,
putting green, driving range. Downhill ski 18 mi; x-country ski on site.
Ice-skating. Rec rm. Exercise equipt.
Some wood-burning fireplaces. Balconies. Cr cds: A, D, DS, MC, V.

Hungry Horse Dam

B&B/Small Inn

★ ★ ★ **BAD ROCK COUNTRY BED
& BREAKFAST.** *480 Bad Rock Dr
(59912). 406/892-2829; fax 406/892-
2930; res 800/422-3666. www.
badrock.com.* 7 rms, 5 A/C, 5 with
shower only, 1-2 story. June-Sept: S
$105-$165; D $149-$169; each addl
$20; lower rates rest of yr. TV in
common rm; cable, VCR avail. Complimentary full bkfst. Ck-out 11 am,

ck-in 3 pm. Business servs avail. Luggage handling. Free airport, RR station transportation. X-country ski 10 mi. Whirlpool. Game rm. Some fireplaces. Old West atmosphere. Totally nonsmoking. Cr cds: A, C, D, DS, MC, V.

Cooke City

See also Red Lodge; also see Cody, WY

Settled 1873 **Pop** 100 **Elev** 7,651 ft
Area code 406 **Zip** 59020
Information Chamber of Commerce, PO Box 1071; 406/838-2272

Once the center of a gold rush area in which $1 million was panned from the rushing streams, Cooke City today is busy serving tourists on their way to Yellowstone National Park (see WYOMING). Available locally are jeep, horse, and snowmobile trips.

What to See and Do

Grasshopper Glacier. One of the largest icefields in US; so named because of the millions of grasshoppers frozen in its 80-ft ice cliff. Accessible only by trail, the last two mi reached only by foot; be prepared for adverse weather. Grasshoppers are visible only during brief time periods; glacial ice must be exposed by snow melt, which generally does not occur until mid-Aug, while new snow begins to accumulate late Aug. 14 mi NE on mountain trail in the Absaroka-Beartooth Wilderness, Custer National Forest (see HARDIN).

Motels/Motor Lodges

★ **HIGH COUNTRY MOTEL.** *113 Main (59020). 406/838-2272.* 15 rms, 1-2 story, 4 kits. No A/C. S, D $49; each addl $5; kit. units $52-$65. Crib $2. Pet accepted. TV. Restaurant nearby. Ck-out 10 am. X-country ski 1 mi. Some refrigerators. Cabins avail. Cr cds: A, D, DS, MC, V.

★ **HOOSIER'S MOTEL & BAR.** *Corner Hwy 212 and Huston N (59020). 406/838-2241.* 12 rms, 1-2 story. No A/C. S, D $50-$60; each addl $5. TV;

cable (premium). Restaurant nearby. Bar 6 pm-2 am. Ck-out 10 am. Totally nonsmoking. Cr cds: DS, MC, V.

Restaurant

★ **LOG CABIN CAFE.** *US 212, Silver Gate (59081). 406/838-2367.* Hrs: 7 am-10 pm. Closed Sept-May. Bkfst $1.75-$7.45, lunch $1.95-$8.95, dinner $9.95-$23.95. Specializes in rainbow trout, steak, hickory-smoked barbecue. Own desserts. Rustic Western log cabin (1938). View of mountains. Totally nonsmoking. Cr cds: MC, V.

Deer Lodge

(C-3) *See also Anaconda, Helena*

Settled 1862 **Pop** 3,378 **Elev** 4,521 ft
Area code 406 **Zip** 59722
Information Powell County Chamber of Commerce, 1171 S Main St; 406/846-2094

Near Montana's first important gold discovery at Gold Creek, this town was first a trapping and trading center, later an important stage and travel station between the early gold camps. Remnants of old mining camps are a few miles from town.

What to See and Do

Deerlodge National Forest. (See BUTTE) A Ranger District office is located here. Self-guided auto tour (inquire locally). W and E of town.

Frontier Montana. Museum houses western memorabilia incl weapons, clothing, bar. (Memorial Day-Labor Day) 1106 Main St. Phone 406/846-3111. ¢¢

Grant-Kohrs Ranch National Historic Site. Preserved in its pioneer state, this was once headquarters for more than a million acres of ranchland. The house was called the "finest home in Montana Territory." Original furniture, horse-drawn vehicles and buildings provide an authentic look into history. Visitors may tour the house, barns and bunkhouse. In season, see blacksmith and ranch hands at work, 19th-century style. (Daily; closed Jan 1, Thanksgiving, Dec 25) N edge of town. Phone 406/846-2070. **FREE**

Montana Territorial Prison. Montana prison from 1871 to 1979. A sandstone wall, built in 1893, surrounds the five-acre complex. The 1912 castlelike cell block remains intact and offers the visiting public a rare view of early prison life. Montana Law Enforcement Museum on grounds. (Daily) 1106 Main St. Phone 406/846-3111.

Powell County Museum. Displays reflecting the history of Powell County and SW Montana. (June-Labor Day, daily) 1193 Main St. Phone 406/846-3111. **FREE**

Towe Ford Museum. Collection of antique Ford cars. 100 on display, dating from 1903. Picnic area. (Daily) 1106 Main St. Phone 406/846-3111.

Yesterday's Playthings. Extensive doll collection from different time periods and cultures. Antique toys. (Mid May-mid-Sept, daily) 1017 Main St. Phone 406/846-1480.

Special Events

Powell County Territorial Days. Third wkend June. Phone 406/846-2094.

Tri-County Fair. Third wkend Aug. Phone 406/846-3627.

Motel/Motor Lodge

★ **SUPER 8 MOTEL.** *1150 N Main (59722). 406/846-2370; fax 406/846-2373; res 800/800-8000. www.super8. com.* 54 rms, 2 story. June-Aug: S $52.68; D $57.88-$62.88; each addl $5; suites $70.88; under 6 free; lower rates rest of yr. Crib free. Pet accepted; $5. TV; cable. Complimentary coffee in lobby. Restaurant adj open 24 hrs. Ck-out 11 am. Meeting rms. Cr cds: A, DS, MC, V.

Dillon (E-3)

Founded 1880 **Pop** 3,991 **Elev** 5,096 ft **Area code** 406 **Zip** 59725

Information Tourist Information Center and Chamber of Commerce, 125 S Montana, PO Box 425; 406/683-5511

Named after a president of the Union Pacific Railroad, Dillon is in a ranching community. Its farms and ranches produce more than 200,000 tons of hay each year. Livestock raising is also important.

What to See and Do

Bannack State Park. First territorial capital, now ghost town. Created by big gold strike on Grasshopper Creek (1862). Fishing. Picnicking. Camping (no hookups). Standard fees. 5 mi S on I-15, then 21 mi W on MT 278, then 4 mi S on county road. Phone 406/834-3413.

Beaverhead County Museum. Geological displays, mining, livestock and commercial artifacts, pioneer housewares, outdoor interpretive area. (Apr-early Nov, daily; closed hols and rest of yr) 15 S Montana St. Phone 406/683-5027. **FREE**

Beaverhead National Forest. More than two million acres. Rugged mountains, alpine lakes, hot springs. Fishing, hunting. Skiing, snowmobiling. Picnicking. Camping (standard fees). E and W off US 91, I-15. For info contact Supervisor, 420 Barrett St; Phone 406/683-3900.

Maverick Mountain Ski Area. Double chairlift, pony lift; school, rentals, patrol; half-day rates; cafeteria and bar. Longest run 2¼ mi; vertical drop 2,100 ft. (Dec-Apr, Thurs-Sun; closed Dec 25) Cross-country trails. 40 mi NW on MT 278 at 475 Maverick Mountain Rd. Phone 406/834-3454.

Special Events

Bannack Days. Bannack State Park. Reliving of gold rush days in Bannack. Gold panning; demonstrations. Third wkend July. Phone 406/834-3413.

Beaverhead County Fair & Jaycee Rodeo. Five days before Labor Day. Phone 406/683-5511.

Motels/Motor Lodges

★★ **BEST WESTERN PARADISE INN.** *650 N Montana St (59725). 406/683-4214; fax 406/683-4216; res*

800/780-7234. www.bestwestern.com.
65 rms, 2 story. Mid-May-Oct: S $49-$51; D $55-$57; each addl $2; suites $70-$80; some lower rates rest of yr. Crib $6. TV; cable. Heated pool; whirlpool. Restaurant 6 am-10 pm; summer hrs vary. Bar 4 pm-2 am. Ck-out 11 am. Business servs avail. Cr cds: A, C, D, DS, ER, MC, V.

★ **COMFORT INN OF DILLON.** *450 N Interchange (59725). 406/683-6831; fax 406/683-2021; res 800/228-5150. www.townpump.com.* 48 rms, 2 story. June-mid-Oct: S $53-$56; D $63-$66; each addl $4; under 18 free; lower rates rest of yr. Crib $3. Pet accepted; $3. TV; cable (premium). Indoor pool. Restaurant nearby. Bar. Ck-out 11 am. Coin lndry. Sundries. Cr cds: A, C, D, DS, ER, JCB, MC, V.

★ **SUPER 8 MOTEL.** *550 N Montana St (59725). 406/683-4288; fax 406/683-4288; toll-free 800/800-8000. www.super8.com.* 48 rms, 3 story. No elvtr. May-Aug: S $50; D $60; each addl $5; under 12 free; lower rates rest of yr. Crib free. Pet accepted; $25. TV; cable (premium). Restaurant opp open 24 hrs. Ck-out 11 am. Cr cds: A, C, D, DS, MC, V.

B&B/Small Inn

★ **THE CENTENNIAL INN.** *122 S Washington St (59725). 406/683-4454. www.bmt.net/~centenn.* 4 rms, 2 story. No A/C. May-Sept: S $69-$79; D $70-$159; each addl $15; under 6 free; family rates; package plans; lower rates rest of yr. Crib free. TV in common rm; cable. Complimentary full bkfst. Restaurant 11 am-2 pm, 5-10 pm. Ck-out 11 am. Luggage handling. Guest lndry. Built in 1905; rancher's townhouse. Turn-of-the-century antiques. Totally nonsmoking. Cr cds: A, DS, MC, V.

Restaurant

★★ **THE OLD HOTEL.** *101 E 5th Ave, Twin Bridges (59754). 406/684-5959. www.theoldhotel.com.* Hrs: 7:30 am-4 pm, 6-10 pm; Sun (brunch) 7:30 am-2 pm. Closed Mon; hols. Res required. Continental menu. Wine, beer. Bkfst $2-$8, lunch $3-$12, din-

ner $15-$30. Sun brunch $2-$15. Specialties: Scottish potted eggs, parmesan-encrusted halibut, chili honey-glazed pork. Parking. Outdoor dining. In 1890 hotel building; unique Scottish atmosphere. Totally nonsmoking. Cr cds: DS, MC, V.

Ennis

(D-3) See also Three Forks, Virginia City

Settled 1864 **Pop** 773 **Elev** 4,939 ft
Area code 406 **Zip** 59729

Surrounded by three Rocky Mountain ranges in the Madison River valley and encircled by cattle ranches, Ennis has good trout fishing and big-game hunting. Beartrap Canyon offers whitewater floats. Swimming, boating, snowmobiling, and Nordic skiing are popular. A Ranger District office of the Beaverhead National Forest (see DILLON) is located here.

What to See and Do

National Fish Hatchery. Raises rainbow trout. (Daily) 12 mi S off US 287. Phone 406/682-4847. **FREE**

Motels/Motor Lodges

★★ **EL WESTERN RESORT.** *US 287 S (59729). 406/682-4217; fax 406/682-5207; toll-free 800/831-2773. www.elwestern.com.* 29 units, 18 kits. No A/C. May-mid-Oct: S, D $55-$65; each addl $5-$10; kit. units $85-$325. Closed rest of yr. Crib $5. Pet accepted; $5. TV; cable. Restaurant nearby. Ck-out 11 am. Some fireplaces. Patios. Western decor. Cr cds: A, DS, MC, V.

★ **FAN MOUNTAIN INN.** *204 N Main St (59729). 406/682-5200; fax 406/682-5266; toll-free 877/682-5200.* 28 rms, 2 story. S $39.50; D $48-$56; each addl $5; suite $75. Pet accepted; $5. TV; cable (premium), VCR avail (movies). Complimentary coffee in lobby. Restaurant nearby. Ck-out 11 am. Meeting rm. Cr cds: A, C, D, DS, MC, V.

★ **RAINBOW VALLEY LODGE.** *S US Hwy 287 (59729). 406/682-4264; fax*

406/682-5012. www.rainbowvalley. com. 24 rms, 6 kits. June-Nov: S $55; D $70; each addl $5; kit. units $55-$100; lower rates rest of yr. TV; cable (premium). Heated pool. Restaurant nearby. Ck-out noon. Coin lndry. River float trips. Refrigerators avail. Picnic tables. Grills. Cr cds: A, C, D, DS, MC, V.

Fort Benton

(B-4) *See also Great Falls*

Founded 1846 **Pop** 1,660 **Elev** 2,632 ft **Area code** 406 **Zip** 59442
Information City Clerk, PO Box 8; 406/622-5494

Established as a fur-trading post and named in honor of Senator Thomas Hart Benton of Missouri, this famous frontier outpost at the head of navigation on the Missouri River became a strategic commercial stronghold. Supplies were received here and shipped overland to trappers and miners throughout Montana. The seat of Chouteau County and one of the oldest communities in the state, it continues as a trading center. The Lewis and Clark State Memorial in Fort Benton Park honors the surveyors who opened the area for trade and commerce.

What to See and Do

Museum of the Northern Great Plains. Agricultural and homestead history displays. (Memorial Day-Labor Day, daily) 20th and Washington. Phone 406/622-5494. ¢¢
Museum of the Upper Missouri River. Displays of steamboats, freighting, stagecoaches, fur and Canadian trade. (Mid-May-mid-Sept, daily) 18th and Front Sts. Phone 406/622-5494. ¢¢
Ruins of Old Fort Benton. (1847) One building and parts of another remain of old trading post and blockhouse. On riverfront, near Main St.

Special Events

Summer Celebration. Last wkend June. Phone 406/622-3351.

Chouteau County Fair. Late Aug. Phone 406/622-5282.

Gardiner

Founded 1883 **Pop** 600 **Elev** 5,314 ft **Area code** 406 **Zip** 59030

Gardiner was established as the original entrance to Yellowstone Park. Named for a trapper who worked this area, Gardiner is the only gateway open throughout the year to Yellowstone National Park (see WYOMING). A Ranger District office of the Gallatin National Forest (see BOZEMAN) is located here.

What to See and Do

Rafting. Yellowstone Raft Company. Half- and full-day whitewater raft trips on the Yellowstone, Gallatin and Madison rivers. Departures from Gardiner and Big Sky (see). Res recommended. Phone 406/848-7777. ¢¢¢¢

Special Event

Gardiner Summer Series Rodeo. NRA sanctioned rodeo. Phone 406/848-7971. June.

Motels/Motor Lodges

★ **ABSAROKA LODGE.** *US 89 and Yellowstone River Bridge (59030). 406/848-7414; fax 406/848-7560; toll-free 800/755-7414. www.yellowstone motel.com.* 41 rms, 2 story, 8 kit. units. June-mid-Sept: S, D $40-$90; each addl $5; kit. units $100; under 12 free; lower rates rest of yr. Pet accepted; $5. TV; cable. Complimentary coffee in lobby. Restaurant nearby. Ck-out 11 am. Balconies overlooking Yellowstone River. Cr cds: A, C, D, DS, MC, V.

★★ **BEST WESTERN BY MAMMOTH HOT SPRINGS.** *Hwy 89 W (59030). 406/848-7311; fax 406/848-7120; toll-free 800/828-9080. www. bestwestern.com.* 86 rms, 2 story, 4 kits. June-Sept: S, D $45-$87; each addl $5; kit. units $145-$165; under

13 free; lower rates rest of yr. Crib
$5. Pet accepted. TV; cable. Indoor
pool; whirlpool. Restaurant adj.
Meeting rm. Business servs avail.
Sauna. Some in-rm whirlpools,
microwaves, refrigerators. Some balconies. On the Yellowstone River. Cr
cds: A, C, D, DS, MC, V.

★★ **COMFORT INN.** *107 Hellroaring
St (59030). 406/848-7536; fax 406/
848-7062; res 800/228-5150. www.
comfortinn.com.* 80 rms, 3 story. Mid-
June-mid-Aug: S $35-$99; D $40-
$139; each addl $8; suites $129-$149;
under 16 free; lower rates rest of yr.
TV; cable. Complimentary continental bkfst. Ck-out 10 am. Coin lndry.
Business servs avail. Cr cds: A, C, D,
DS, MC, V.

★ **MOTEL 6 GARDINER.** *109 Hell
Roaring Rd (59030). 406/848-7520;
fax 406/848-7555; res 877/266-8356.*
40 rms, 3 story. July-Aug: S $40-$75;
D $46-$81; each addl $6; under 17
free; lower rates rest of yr. Crib free.
Pet accepted. TV; cable. Complimen-
tary coffee in rms. Ck-out 10 am.
Business servs avail. Cr cds: A, C, D,
DS, MC, V.

★ **YELLOWSTONE SUPER 8.** *US 89
S (59030). 406/848-7401; fax
406/848-9410; toll-free 800/800-8000.
www.super8.com.* 66 rms, 3 story, 1
suite. June-Sept: S, D $59-$89; suites
$79-$165; each addl $5; lower rates
rest of yr. Crib free. Pet accepted,
some restrictions. TV; cable (premium). Indoor pool. Complimentary
continental bkfst. Restaurant nearby.
Ck-out 10 am. Opp river. Cr cds: A,
C, D, DS, MC, V.

★★ **YELLOWSTONE VILLAGE
INN.** *Yellowstone Park North Entrance
(82190). 406/848-7417; fax 406/848-
7418; toll-free 800/228-8158. www.
yellowstoneinn.com.* 43 rms, 3 condos, 2 story. June-Sept: S $30-$69; D
$35-$69; condos $135-$155; each
addl $5; lower rates rest of yr. Crib
free. TV; cable (premium). Indoor
pool. Complimentary coffee in
lobby. Restaurant nearby. Ck-out 11
am. Coin lndry. Business servs avail.
Sauna. Refrigerators, microwaves
avail. Cr cds: A, DS, MC, V.

Restaurant

★★ **YELLOWSTONE MINE.** *US 89
(59030). 406/848-7336.* Hrs: 6-11 am,
5-10 pm; Sat to 11 pm; Sun to noon.
Bar 11-2 am. Bkfst buffet $6.50, dinner
$6.95-$19.95. Child's menu. Specializes
in prime rib, seafood, stuffed chicken.
Old West mining decor. Totally nonsmoking. Cr cds: A, DS, MC, V.

Glacier National Park

Big, rugged, and primitive, Glacier
National Park is nature's unspoiled
domain. Human civilization is
reduced to insignificance by the wild
grandeur of these million acres. It's
the place for a snowball fight in midsummer, for glacial solitude, for
fishing, for alpine flowers, lonely and
remote campgrounds along fir-
fringed lakes. The park is also a living
textbook in geology.

Declared a national park on May
11, 1910, these 1,013,595 acres of
spectacular scenery are preserved
year after year much as they were
when Meriwether Lewis saw them in
the distance in 1806. The United
States and Canada share these treasures of nature; the 204 square miles
of Canada that are linked to Glacier
are known as the Waterton-Glacier
International Peace Park. Glacier
National Park contains 50 glaciers,
among the few in the United States,
some of which are comparatively
accessible. There are more than 200
lakes and 1,400 varieties of plants, 63
species of animals—from mice to
moose—and 272 varieties of birds.

Visitors here can choose a variety of
activities during their stay; they can
enjoy the scenery from the shadow of
a hotel or chalet, share the cama-
raderie of a community campground,
or seek solitude in the wilderness. The
delights of Glacier, however, should
be savored cautiously. Rangers recommend that visitors stay on the trails
and never hike alone. The behavior of
wild animals can be unpredictable.

This is a land where winter does
not beat a full retreat until mid-June,
and sometimes returns in mid-Sep-

tember. The summer season extends between those periods, but until July, high snowbanks line the roads and the mountains are capped with snow. Late June is a time of cascading waterfalls and profuse wildflowers. In the fall, the dense forests are a blaze of colors set against a background of snow-covered peaks. Winter brings deep-snow peace, which only the most hardy invade for cross-country skiing or photography.

Spectacular views of the park may be seen from your car, particularly when crossing the Continental Divide on the Going-to-the-Sun Road; it is 50 miles long and one of the most magnificent drives in the world (approximately mid-June-mid-October). As of January, 1994, vehicles in excess of 21 feet in length (including combinations of units) and 8 feet in width (including mirrors) are prohibited on the Going-to-the-Sun Road between Avalanche and Sun Point. Vehicles exceeding these restrictions may use US 2 or can be parked at Avalanche or Sun Point parking areas. The road continuously winds up and down in tight curves and requires caution. This unforgettable ride links the east and west sides of the park, passing over Logan Pass (a visitor center with exhibits is here; June-September, daily; closed rest of year) for a 100-mile view from an elevation of 6,646 feet. It connects with US 89 at St. Mary (here is a visitor center with exhibits, programs, May-September, daily) and with US 2 at West Glacier. US 89 on the east side of the park is the Blackfeet Highway, extending from Browning to Canada. The road to Many Glacier Valley branches from US 89, nine miles north of St. Mary. The road to Two Medicine Lake leaves MT 49, four miles north of East Glacier Park. Chief Mountain International Highway (MT 17) leads to Waterton Lakes National Park in Canada (see).

Most of the park, however, including the glaciers, is accessible only by trail. There are 732 maintained miles of trails penetrating to remote wilderness areas. By foot or on horseback, magnificent and isolated parts of Glacier await discovery.

There are eight major and five semiprimitive campgrounds. The camping limit is seven days. Most campgrounds are available on a first come, first served basis. Fish Creek and St. Mary campgrounds may be reserved ahead of time through the National Park Reservation System by calling 800/365-2267. A fee is charged for camping. Visitors planning to camp overnight in Glacier's backcountry must obtain a Backcountry User Permit and camp in designated sites; 406/888-7800.

Place-name signs and roadside exhibits mark the major roads from late May-September 15. Also, ranger-naturalists conduct daily walks and campfire programs that are both rewarding and scenic. Park-wide guided hikes for day and overnight trips available through Glacier Wilderness Guides, PO Box 535, West Glacier 59936. Guided bus tours available through Glacier Park, Inc, Dial Tower, Dial Corporate Center, Phoenix, AZ 85077 (October-mid-May); or East Glacier Park 59434 (rest of year). Saddle horses available through Mule Shoe Outfitters, LLC, PO Box 322, Kila 59920; also at Many Glacier, Lake McDonald Lodge and Apgar Village Lodge. Launch service operates on Two Medicine, Swiftcurrent, Josephine, St. Mary, and McDonald lakes through Glacier Park Boat Co, PO Box 5262, Kalispell 59903; and between the townsite in Waterton Lakes National Park, Canada, and the head of Waterton Lake in Glacier National Park through Waterton Shoreline Cruises, PO Box 126, Waterton, Alberta, Canada TOK 2MO (June-August).

Contact the Superintendent, Glacier National Park, West Glacier 59936; 406/888-9800, for detailed information. Golden Eagle Passport accepted (see MAKING THE MOST OF YOUR TRIP). Seven-day pass: per vehicle ¢¢¢; Per person ¢¢

What to See and Do

Avalanche Creek. Flows through deep gorge filled with spray. Two-mi hike to Avalanche Lake Basin with waterfalls, 2,000-ft-high cliffs. Camping; picnicking.

Belly River Country. Trails, lake fishing, backcountry camping, glacial valleys.

Sunrise against the beautiful backdrop of Glacier National Park

Cut Bank. A primitive, densely wooded valley. At head of valley is 8,011-ft Triple Divide Peak. Hiking, camping.

Flattop Mountain. Between the Lewis Range and the Livingston Range; meadows and groves of trees contrast with dense forest growth elsewhere.

Granite Park. Trails, glacial valleys, alpine flowers. Accessible only by foot. Res required. Phone 800/521-7238.

⭐ **Lake McDonald.** Largest in park: 10 mi long, 1 mi wide; heavily forested shores with peaks rising 6,000 ft above lake. Trail to Sperry Glacier. One-hr boat tours, horseback riding trips leave from Lake McDonald Lodge (mid-June-mid-Sept, daily). Phone 800/521-7238.

Many Glacier Area. Fishing, boating (trips), camping, hiking, riding; trails to Morning Eagle Falls, Cracker Lake, Grinnell Glacier and Lake, Iceberg Lake. Footpaths go around Swiftcurrent and Josephine lakes and to Appekunny Falls and Cirque. Self-guided trail from hotel. Phone 602/207-2600.

Red Eagle Lake. Located in a glacially carved basin with dramatic falls and gorge. Backcountry camping. Phone 406/888-7800.

River Rafting. Four companies offer several half- to six-day trips on the Middle and North forks of the Flathead River. Guided fishing trips, com-

bination trips. Phone 406/888-7800. For information and res contact:

Glacier Raft Co. Phone 406/888-5454.

Great Northern Whitewater. Phone 406/387-5340. ¢¢¢¢

Montana Raft Company & Glacier Wilderness Guides. Phone 406/387-5555. ¢¢¢¢

Wild River Adventures. Phone 406/387-9453. ¢¢¢¢

St. Mary Lake. Emerald green, with peaks on three sides. Fishing, boating, hiking. 1½-hr boat tours leave from Rising Sun Boat Landing (mid-June-mid-Sept, daily). Self-guided trail from Sun Point.

Sperry and Grinnell Glaciers. Largest in the park. Inquire about trips to Grinnell. Phone 406/888-7800.

Two Medicine Valley. Deep valleys, towering peaks surround mountain lake. Brook, rainbow trout; trails for hiking; boating; camping. Phone 406/888-7800.

East Glacier Area

Motels/Motor Lodges

★ **JACOBSON'S COTTAGES.** *1204 MT 49, PO Box 454, East Glacier (59534). 406/226-4422; fax 406/226-*

5551; toll-free 888/226-4422. 12 cottages, 1 kit. No A/C. No rm phones. Mid-May-Oct: S $48; D $52-$58; each addl $3; kit. cottage $65; under 6 free. Closed rest of yr. Crib free. TV; cable. Restaurant adj 6:30 am-10:30 pm. Ck-out 11 am. Picnic table. Cr cds: A, DS, MC, V.

D ⬛ ⬛ ✈ ⬛ ⬛

★★ **MOUNTAIN PINE.** *MT 49, East Glacier Park (59934). 406/226-4403; fax 406/226-9290.* 26 rms. No A/C. Mid-June-mid-Sept: S $51; D $56; each addl $3; family units $98-$110; log house $175; lower rates May-mid-June, late Sept. Closed rest of yr. Crib free. TV; cable. Restaurant nearby. Ck-out 11 am. Free RR station transportation. Picnic tables. Cr cds: A, D, DS, MC, V.

D ⬛ ⬛

★★ **THE RESORT AT GLACIER.** *Jct Hwy 89 and Going to Sun Rd, St. Mary (59417). 406/732-4431; fax 406/732-9265; res 800/368-3689. www.glcpark. com.* 106 rms, 3 story, 18 suites. July-Aug: S $99; D $109; each addl $10; under 12 free; lower rates rest of yr. Crib avail, fee. TV, cable. Restaurant (see also SNOW GOOSE GRILLE). Bar. Ck-out 11 am. Meeting rms. Cr cds: A, DS, MC, V.

⬛ ⬛

★ **SWIFTCURRENT MOTOR INN.** *12 mi W of Babb Mtn, East Glacier (59434). 406/732-5531; fax 406/732-5595. www.glacierparkinc.com.* 88 units, 26 cottages. No A/C. Mid-June-mid-Sept: S $29-$75; D $35-$81; each addl $10. Closed rest of yr. Restaurant 7 am-9:30 pm. Ck-out 11 am. Coin lndry. Sundries. Trail center for hikers. Cr cds: A, DS, MC, V.

D ⬛ ⬛ ⬛

Hotel

★ **VILLAGE INN.** *Apgar Village - West Glacier, East Glacier Park (59434). 406/756-2444. www.glacier parkinc.com.* 210 rms, 5 story. No A/C. No elvtr. Early June-mid-Sept: S $95; D $120; each addl $10; suites $163-$174; under 12 free. Closed rest of yr. Crib free. Restaurant 6:30 am-9:30 pm. Bar 11:30 am-midnight; entertainment. Ck-out 11 am. Gift shop. Hiking. Overlooks Swiftcurrent Lake. A Glacier Park, Inc. hotel. Cr cds: A, D, DS, MC, V.

⬛ ⬛ ⬛ ⬛ ⬛

Restaurants

★★ **GLACIER VILLAGE.** *304-308 Hwy 2E (59434). 406/226-4464.* Hrs: 6 am-10 pm. Closed late Sept-early May. Res accepted. Wine, beer. Bkfst $2.25-$6.95, lunch $4.50-$6.95, dinner $5.95-$13.95. Specializes in broiler items, seafood, roast turkey. Own bread, desserts. Family-owned since 1954. Cr cds: DS, MC, V.

D

★★ **SNOW GOOSE GRILLE.** *St. Mary (East Glacier Area) (59417). 406/732-4431. www.glcpark.com.* Hrs: 7 am-10 pm. Closed Oct-mid-May. Bar. Bkfst $3.75-$7.50, lunch $4.95-$8.95, dinner $9.95-$18.95. Child's menu. Specialties: sourdough scones, range-ted buffalo, locally caught whitefish. Family-owned. Totally nonsmoking. Cr cds: A, D, DS, MC, V.

D

West Glacier Area

Hotel

★ **LAKE MCDONALD LODGE.** *Going To the Sun Rd, West Glacier (59434). 602/207-6000; fax 602/207-5589.* 32 rms in lodge, 38 cabins, 30 motel rms, 1-2 story. No A/C. Early June-late Sept: lodge: S $115; D $121; each addl $10; under 12 free; cabins: S $65-$113; D $71-$119; each addl $10; motel: S $78; D $83; each addl $10. Closed rest of yr. Crib free. Restaurant. Bar 11 am-midnight. Ck-out 11 am. Gift shop. Boating; launch cruises. Hiking. Camp store. Rustic hunting lodge amid giant cedars. Lodge totally nonsmoking. Cr cds: DS, MC, V.

D ⬛ ⬛ ⬛ ⬛

B&B/Small Inn

★★ **IZAAK WALTON INN.** *290 Izaak Walton Inn Rd, Essex (59916). 406/888-5700; fax 406/888-5200.* 33 rms, 3 story. No A/C. No rm phones.

S, D $98; each addl $5; suites $150; caboose kit. cottages (3-day min) $475; wkly rates; package plans. Crib free. Dining rm 7 am-8 pm. Bar. Ck-out 11 am, ck-in 3 pm. Coin lndry. Meeting rm. Business servs avail. X-country ski on site; rentals. Sauna. Game rm. Rec rm (movies). Lawn games. Bicycle rentals. Picnic tables. Old railroad hotel (1939); restored sleeper cars avail for rental (3-day min). Adj to Glacier National Park. Totally nonsmoking. Cr cds: A, DS, MC, V.

Glasgow (B-6)

Founded 1887 **Pop** 3,572 **Elev** 2,090 ft **Area code** 406 **Zip** 59230

Information Glasgow Area Chamber of Commerce & Agriculture, 740 US 2E, PO Box 832; 406/228-2222

Glasgow has had four booms in its history. The first was opening of land to white settlement in 1888, the second when another 18,000,000 acres were opened around 1910. In the 1930s, Glasgow was headquarters for the 10,000 construction workers on Fort Peck Dam. Glasgow AFB made its home 18 miles northeast of town from 1954-68; the flight facilities are now owned by Boeing and the residential area is being developed into a military retirement community. Wheat and livestock are raised in Valley County.

What to See and Do

Fort Peck Dam and Lake. Built by Army Corps of Engineers. Largest hydraulic earthfill dam in the world, forming huge reservoir with 1,600-mi lakeshore. Dam rises 280½ ft above Missouri River; total length 21,026 ft; road follows crest of the dam, leading to mile-long concrete spillway. Information center; museum. Guided tours of power plant (Memorial Day-Labor Day, daily; rest of yr, by appt). Self-guided nature trail. There are several recreation areas with fishing, camping (fee), trailer sites, boating (ramps), concession. 20 mi SE on MT 24.

Hell Creek State Park. Swimming, fishing, boating (ramp, rentals); picnicking, camping (no hookups). Standard fees. 50 mi S on MT 24, then 6 mi W on county road. Phone 406/232-4365.

Valley County Pioneer Museum. Displays of Native American artifacts; photos of pioneers and events of their time; pioneer farm machinery. Also fossils and aviation display. (Memorial Day-Labor Day, daily) ½ mi W on US 2. Phone 406/228-8692. **FREE**

Special Events

Longest Dam Run. Kiwanis Park, foot of Fort Peck Dam. 5K and 10K run/walk crosses 1.8 mi of Dam. Refreshments, prizes. Phone 406/228-2222. Third wk June.

Fort Peck Summer Theater. 17 mi SE on MT 24 in Fort Peck. Professional cast performs musicals, comedies. Fri-Sun. Historical landmark. Phone 406/228-9219. Late June-Labor Day.

Montana Governor's Cup Walleye Tournament. Fort Peck Lake. Phone 406/228-2222. Early July.

Northeast Montana Fair and Rodeo. Fairgrounds at W edge of city. Exhibits, midway, rodeo, nightly shows. Three days Late July or early Aug. Phone 406/228-8221.

Highland Games Festival. Scottish games and music. Mid-Sept. Phone 406/228-2222.

Motel/Motor Lodge

★ **COTTONWOOD INN.** US 2 E (59230). 406/228-8213; fax 406/228-8248; toll-free 800/321-8213. 92 rms, 2 story. S $44-$50; D $55-$60; each addl $5; studio rms $75-$80; under 12 free. Pet accepted, some restrictions. TV; cable (premium). Indoor pool; whirlpool. Restaurant 6 am-10 pm. Bar 11-2 am. Ck-out 11 am. Coin lndry. Business servs avail. Valet serv. Airport, RR station transportation. Exercise equipt; sauna. Some refrigerators. Cr cds: A, C, D, DS, MC, V.

Restaurant

★★ **SAM'S SUPPER CLUB.** 307 Klein (US 2) (59230). 406/228-4614. Hrs: 11 am-2 pm, 5-10:30 pm; Sat from 4 pm. Closed Sun, Mon; July 4,

Thanksgiving, Dec 25. Res accepted. Bar to 2 am. Lunch $2-$6.75, dinner $6-$19.50. Child's menu. Specializes in char-broiled steak, walleye pike, fresh pasta. Cr cds: A, MC, V.

[D]

Glendive (C-8)

Settled 1864 **Pop** 4,802 **Elev** 2,078 ft **Area code** 406 **Zip** 59330

Information Chamber of Commerce & Agriculture, 313 S Merrill Ave; 406/365-5601

Web www.midrivers.com/chamber

Glendive is the shipping center for the crops of Dawson County. It also serves the oil wells, railroad yards, and natural gas fields that ring the city.

What to See and Do

Fishing. The unusual spatula-nosed paddlefish (*Polyodon spathula*) is found here in the Yellowstone River. Fishing for this rare, prehistoric species is permitted mid-May-June only.

Frontier Gateway Museum. Collection depicts Glendive and early Dawson County; "Main Street 1881" exhibit in basement; one-room schoolhouse, blacksmith shop, display of early farm machinery on grounds and five other buildings in complex. (June-Aug, daily) Belle Prairie Frontage Rd, 1 mi E off I-94, Exit 215. Phone 406/365-8168. **FREE**

Hunt moss agates. Along Yellowstone River.

Makoshika. (Ma-KO-she-ka) **State Park.** Spectacular badlands scenery; fossils. The eroded sandstone cliffs are particularly striking at sunrise and sunset. Visitor Center. Hiking. Picnicking. Camping (no hookups). Standard fees. ¼ mi SE on Snyder Ave. Phone 406/365-8596.

Special Events

Buzzard Day. Makoshika State Park. Day-long activities; softball tourna-

ments, concerts, BBQ. Early June. Phone 406/365-6256.

Dawson County Fair and Rodeo. Four days mid-Aug. Phone 406/377-6781.

Motel/Motor Lodge

★ **DAYS INN.** *2000 N Merrill Ave (59330). 406/365-6011; fax 406/365-2876; res 800/329-7466. www.daysinn. com.* 59 rms, 2 story. S $38-$50; D $55-$65; each addl $5; under 12 free; lower rates winter. Crib free. TV; cable (premium). Complimentary continental bkfst. Restaurant adj 6 am-10 pm. Ck-out 11 am. Cr cds: A, C, D, DS, MC, V.

[D] [≡] [▨]

Great Falls

(B-4) *See also Fort Benton*

Founded 1884 **Pop** 55,097 **Elev** 3,333 ft **Area code** 406

Information Chamber of Commerce, 710 1st Ave N, PO Box 2127, 59403; 406/761-4434

Web www.greatfallschamber.org

Great Falls's growth has been powered by thriving diversified industry, agriculture and livestock, construction, and activity at nearby Malmstrom AFB. The city takes its name from the falls of the Missouri River, a source of electric power.

What to See and Do

✪ **C.M. Russell Museum Complex and Original Log Cabin Studio.** Charles Russell paintings, bronzes, original models and illustrated letters; exhibits of Russell's contemporaries. Browning Firearms Collection. (Daily; winter, Tues-Sun) 400 13th St N. Phone 406/727-8787. ¢¢

Giant Springs State Park and State Trout Hatchery. One of the largest freshwater springs in the world produces nearly 390 million gallons of water every 24 hrs. The hatchery next to the springs raises trout. Picnic grounds. (Daily) 4 mi NE on River Dr. Phone 406/454-5840. ¢

Lewis and Clark National Forest.
More than 1.8 million acres of canyons, mountains, meadows and wilderness. Parts of the Scapegoat Wilderness and the Bob Marshall Wilderness (384,407 acres), with the 15-mi-long, 1,000-ft-high Chinese Wall are here. Activities incl scenic drives, stream and lake fishing, big-game hunting, hiking, camping (fee), picnicking, winter sports. E on US 87, 89, MT 200. For info contact Supervisor, 1101 15th St N, PO Box 869, 59403; Phone 406/791-7700.

Lewis and Clark National Historical Trail Interpretive Center.
Exhibits follow the historical expedition's journey, incl canoe-pulling simulation, Mandan Indian earth lodge, Shoshone tepee, and replicas of the boats used in the expedition. Twenty-min film on the expedition in 158-seat theater. (Daily) 3 mi NW on Giant Springs Rd. Phone 406/727-8733. ¢¢

Malmstrom AFB.
Home of the 341st Space Wing and center of one of the largest intercontinental ballistic missile complexes in the world. Museum featuring historical military displays. Tours by appt. 1 mi E of 2nd Ave N and Bypass Rd. Phone 406/731-4046. **FREE**

Paris Gibson Square Museum of Art.
Historical school building contains a gallery with changing displays of contemporary regional art. Gift shop; lunchtime cafe. (Memorial Day-Labor Day, Mon-Sat, rest of yr Tues-Sun) 1400 1st Ave N. Phone 406/727-8255. **FREE**

University of Great Falls.
(1932) (1,000 students). A 40-acre campus. Chapel sculpture and stained-glass windows designed and produced at college. The pool in McLaughlin Memorial Center is open to public (inquire for days, hrs, fees). 1301 20th St S. Phone 406/761-8210.

Special Events

Montana Pro Rodeo Circuit Finals.
Four Seasons Arena. Phone 406/727-8900. Mid-Jan.

State Fair.
Fairgrounds. Rodeo, livestock exhibits, horse racing, petting zoo, commercial exhibits, entertainment, carnival. Phone 406/727-8900. July 27-Aug 3.

Motels/Motor Lodges

★★ BEST WESTERN HERITAGE INN.
1700 Fox Farm Rd (59404). 406/761-1900; fax 406/761-0136; toll-free 800/548-8256. www.best western.com/heritageinngreatfalls. 239 rms, 2 story. S, D $89-$99; each addl $6; suites $85-$125; under 18 free. Crib free. Pet accepted, some restrictions. TV; cable. Indoor pool; whirlpool. Coffee in rms. Restaurant 6 am-10 pm. Bar 9-2 am. Ck-out noon. Business servs avail. Coin lndry. Bellhops. Valet serv. Gift shop. Free airport, bus depot transportation. Exercise equipt; sauna. Microwaves avail. Cr cds: A, C, D, DS, MC, V.
D ⌀ ⛷ ≈ 🕴 ✈ ⬗ 🔥 SC

★ BUDGET INN.
2 Treasure State Dr (59404). 406/453-1602; toll-free 800/362-4842. www.budgetinns.com. 60 rms, 2 story. S $51-$55; each addl $4; under 16 free; lower rates winter. Crib free. Pet accepted, some restrictions. TV; cable. Complimentary continental bkfst. Coffee in rms. Restaurant adj 6 am-11 pm. Ck-out noon. Airport transportation. Valet serv. Health club privileges. Cr cds: A, C, D, DS, MC, V.
D ⌀ ⛷ ✈ ⬗ 🔥 SC

★ COMFORT INN.
1120 9th St S (59405). 406/454-2727; res 800/228-5150. www.comfortinn.com. 64 rms, 3 story. S, D $69.95; each addl $5; suites $79.95; under 18 free. Crib free. Pet accepted; $5. TV; cable (premium). Indoor pool; whirlpool. Complimentary continental bkfst. Restaurant nearby. Ck-out 11 am. Business servs avail. Health club privileges. Cr cds: A, D, DS, MC, V.
D ⌀ ⛷ 🏊 ≈ ⬗ 🔥

★ DAYS INN OF GREAT FALLS.
101 NW 14th Ave (59404). 406/727-6565; fax 406/727-6308; res 800/329-7466. www.daysinn.com. 62 rms, 2 story. June-Sept: S $59; D $65; each addl $6; under 13 free. Crib free. Pet accepted. TV; cable. Complimentary continental bkfst. Ck-out 11 am. Coin lndry. Cr cds: A, DS, JCB, MC, V.
D ⌀ 🔥

★★ FAIRFIELD INN.
1000 9th Ave S (59405). 406/454-3000; toll-free 800/228-2800. www.fairfieldinn.com. 63 rms, 3 story, 16 suites. S $69.95; D $74.95; each addl $5; suites $79.95;

under 18 free. Crib free. TV; cable. Indoor pool; whirlpool. Complimentary continental bkfst. Restaurant opp open 24 hrs. Ck-out noon. Valet serv. Game rm. Refrigerator, microwave in suites. Cr cds: A, D, DS, MC, V.

★ TOWN HOUSE INN OF GREAT FALLS. *1411 S 10th Ave (59405). 406/761-4600; fax 406/761-7603; toll-free 800/442-4667. www.townpump. com.* 109 rms, 2 story, May-Sept: S $65-$70; D $71-$76; each addl $5; under 13 free; lower rates rest of yr. Crib free. Pet accepted; $5. TV; cable (premium). Indoor pool; whirlpool. Restaurant 7 am-10 pm. Bar. Ck-out 11 am. Coin lndry. Meeting rms Business servs avail. Bellhops. Sundries. Valet serv. Free airport transportation. Sauna. Game rm. Cr cds: A, C, D, DS, ER, JCB, MC.

Hotel

★★ HOLIDAY INN. *400 10th Ave S (59405). 406/727-7200; fax 406/268-0472; res 800/257-1998. www.holiday-inn.com.* 168 rms, 7 story. S, D $75; suites $145. Crib free. Pet accepted, some restrictions. TV; cable (premium). Indoor pool; whirlpool Coffee in rms. Restaurant 6 am-10 pm. Bar noon-2 am. Ck-out noon. Meeting rms. Business servs avail. Free airport, bus depot transportation. Sauna. Health club privileges. Cr cds: A, C, D, DS, ER, JCB, MC, V.

Restaurants

★ EDDIE'S SUPPER CLUB. *38th and N 2nd Ave (59401). 406/453-1616.* Hrs: 9:30 am-11 pm; Fri, Sat to midnight. Italian, American menu. Bar. Lunch $3-$7, dinner $9.95-$20.95. Specializes in steak, hamburgers. Entertainment Fri, Sat. Cr cds: DS, MC, V.

★★ JAKER'S STEAK, RIBS & FISH HOUSE. *1500 10th Ave S (59405). 406/727-1033. www.jakers.com.* Hrs: 11:30 am-10 pm; Fri to 11 pm; Sat 4-11 pm; Sun from 4 pm. Closed Dec 25. Res accepted. Lunch $4.95-$7.95, dinner $6.45-$19.95. Child's

menu. Specializes in prime rib, baby-back ribs, seafood. Cr cds: A, D, DS, MC, V.

Hamilton

(C-2) *See also Missoula*

Pop 2,737 **Elev** 3,572 ft
Area code 406 **Zip** 59840
Information Bitterroot Valley Chamber of Commerce, 105 E Main; 406/363-2400
Web www.bvchamber.com

Hamilton is the county seat and main shopping center for Ravalli County and headquarters for the Bitterroot National Forest.

What to See and Do

Big Hole National Battlefield. (see) S on US 93.

Bitterroot National Forest. (1,579,533 acres) Lake and stream fishing, big-game hunting; Anaconda-Pintler Wilderness, Selway-Bitterroot Wilderness, and River of No Return Wilderness. Mountain lakes, hot springs. Scenic drives in Bitterroot Valley; Skalkaho Falls. Hiking and riding trails, winter sports, camp and picnic sites. Inquire locally for wilderness pack trips. Fees may be charged at recreation sites. Surrounding Hamilton with access by US 93, MT 38. Contact Supervisor, 1801 N 1st St; Phone 406/363-7161.

Daly Mansion. (ca 1890) This 42-rm mansion was the home of Marcus Daly, an Irish immigrant who became one of Montana's "copper kings" through the copper mines near Butte. Seven Italian marble fireplaces, original furniture, transplanted exotic trees, "dollhouse" built for Daly children. Tours (Apr-Oct, daily; rest of yr, by appt). 2 mi NE on County 269. Phone 406/363-6004. ¢¢

Fort Owen State Park. Restoration of Montana's first white settlement, more a trading post than a fort. Day use only. 20 mi N, off US 93 to Stevensville, then 5 mi E on MT 269.

Painted Rocks State Park. Swimming; fishing; boating (ramp). Picnicking. Camping (no hookups). Standard fees. 20 mi S on US 93, then 23 mi SW on MT 473, in the Bitterroot Mts. Phone 406/542-5500. ¢¢

St. Mary's Mission. (1841) Picturesque log church and residence; one of the oldest churches in Northwest (present structure built in 1866); also old pharmacy (1868). Restored and furnished to period. Pioneer relics, Chief Victor's house and cemetery. Site is first in religion, education, agriculture, music in Montana. Gift shop. Guided tours. Park, picnicking. (Mid-Apr-mid-Oct, daily) 20 mi N off US 93; W end of 4th St in Stevensville. Phone 406/777-5734. ¢¢

Skiing. Lost Trail Powder Mountain. Three chairlifts, three rope tows; patrol, ski school, rentals, concession area. Vertical drop 1,200 ft. (Dec-Apr, Thurs-Sun, hols) Cross-country trails. 50 mi S at 7674 Hwy 93S, in Sula. Phone 406/821-3508.

Special Events

Chief Victor Days. Victor Park. July. Phone 406/363-2400.

Good Nations Powwow. Daly Mansion Grounds. July. Phone 406/363-5383.

Ravalli County Fair. Late Aug. Phone 406/363-3411.

McIntosh Apple Days. Ravalli County Museum. Oct. Phone 406/363-3338.

Motels/Motor Lodges

★★ **BEST WESTERN HAMILTON INN.** *409 S 1st St (59840). 406/363-2142; toll-free 800/426-4586. www. bestwestern.com.* 36 rms, 2 story. May-Sept: S $49-$63; D $56-$66; each addl $5; lower rates rest of yr. Crib free. TV; cable (premium). Restaurant nearby. Ck-out 11 am. Outdoor whirlpool. Cr cds: A, C, D, DS, MC, V.
🄳 ♿ 🛐 🔌 🐾 SC

★ **COMFORT INN OF HAMILTON.** *1113 N 1st St (59840). 406/363-6600; fax 406/363-5644; res 800/228-5150. www.townpump.com.* 64 rms, 2 story. May-Sept: S $54-$57; D $60-$64; each addl $5; under 18 free; lower rates rest of yr. Crib $4. Pet accepted. TV; cable (premium), VCR avail (movies). Complimentary coffee in lobby. Restaurant adj 8 am-10 pm. Ck-out 11 am. Meeting rm. Business servs avail. Coin lndry. Whirlpool. Sauna. Cr cds: A, C, D, DS, ER, JCB, MC, V.
🄳 ♿ 🛐 🐾 SC

B&B/Small Inn

★ **DEER CROSSING BED & BREAKFAST.** *396 Hayes Creek Rd (59840). 406/363-2232; toll-free 800/763-2232. www.wtp.net/go/deercrossing.* 2 rms, 3 story, 2 suites, 2 cabins. Apr-Sept: S, D $80; suites $129; each addl $15; cabins $129-$149; lower rates rest of yr. Complimentary full bkfst. Ck-out 11 am, ck-in 3 pm. Cr cds: A, MC, V.
🐴 🔌 🛐 🐾

Guest Ranch

★★★ **TRIPLE CREEK RANCH.** *5551 W Fork Rd, Darby (59829). 406/821-4600; fax 406/821-4666; toll-free 800/654-2943.* 20 cabins, showers only, 2 kit. cabins. AP: S $460-$945; D, kit. cabins $510-$995; each addl $200. Children over 16 yrs only. TV; cable (premium), VCR (movies). Pool; poolside serv. Complimentary coffee in lobby. Restaurant 8-2 pm, 6-8:30 pm. Box lunches, picnics. Bar 6-11 pm; entertainment Wed, Sat, Sun. Ck-out noon, ck-in 3 pm. Gift shop. Meeting rms. Business servs avail. In-rm modem link. Airport transportation. Sports dir. Tennis. Putting green. X-country ski on site. Horse stables. Snowmobiles. Hiking. Lawn games. Soc dir. Exercise equipt. Massage. Refrigerators, wetbars, fireplaces; some in-rm whirlpools. Picnic tables. Cr cds: A, DS, MC, V.
🐴 🔌 🎿 ⛷ 🏊 🎯 🐾

Hardin

(D-6) *See also Billings*

Pop 2,940 **Elev** 2,902 ft
Area code 406 **Zip** 59034
Information Chamber of Commerce, 21 E 4th St; 406/665-1672
Web www.mcn.net/~custerfight/

Hardin became the seat of Big Horn County after the area was opened to white settlers in 1906. It is the trading center for ranchers, farmers, and

Native Americans from the Crow
Reservation.

What to See and Do

**Bighorn Canyon National Recreation
Area.** (See LOVELL, WY) 43 mi S on
MT 313.

Custer National Forest. Approx 1.2
million acres in Montana and South
Dakota; Little Missouri Grasslands,
an additional 1.2 million acres in
North Dakota, is also included.
Rolling pine hills and grasslands; picnicking; saddle and pack trips; big-
game hunting; camping. E via US
212; includes Beartooth Hwy, a
National Forest Scenic Byway (see
RED LODGE). Headquarters: 2602 1st
Ave N, Billings 59103. Phone
406/657-6361.

Special Events

Little Bighorn Days. Custer's last
stand reenactment. Military Ball,
rodeo, street dance, bed races, children's games. Third wkend June.
Phone 406/665-1672.

Crow Fair. Crow Reservation, S on
MT 313. Features largest all-Native
American rodeo in the country. Aug.
Phone 406/638-2601.

Motels/Motor Lodges

★ **AMERICAN INN.** *1324 N Crawford Ave (59034). 406/665-1870; fax
406/665-1615; toll-free 800/582-
8094.* 42 rms, 2 story. May-Oct: S
$45; D $56-$63; each addl $5; lower
rates rest of yr. Crib $2. TV; cable.
Pool; whirlpool; water slide. Playground. Restaurant adj 7 am-10 pm.
Ck-out 11 am. Coin lndry. Exercise
equipt. Game rm. Cr cds: A, C, D,
DS, MC, V.
🄳 🗫 🏃 🛏 🐾 **SC**

★ **SUPER 8 MOTEL.** *201 W 14th St
(59034). 406/665-1700; fax 406/665-
2746; toll-free 800/800-8000. www.
super8.com.* 53 rms, 2 story. May-Sept:
S $47.88; D $49.88-$53.88; each addl
$4; under 12 free; higher rates special
events; lower rates rest of yr. Crib $2.
Pet accepted. TV; cable. Complimentary continental bkfst. Ck-out 11 am.
Coin lndry. Meeting rms. Cr cds: A,
C, D, DS, MC, V.
🄳 🗫 🛏 🐾 **SC**

Harlowton

Pop 1,049 **Elev** 4,167 ft
Area code 406 **Zip** 59036
Information Chamber of Commerce,
PO Box 694; 406/632-4694

A Ranger District office of the Lewis
and Clark National Forest (see
GREAT FALLS) is located here.

What to See and Do

**Deadman's Basin Fishing Access
Site.** Swimming; fishing; boating.
Picnicking. Standard fees. 23 mi E
on US 12 to milepost 120, then 1
mi N on county road. Phone
406/247-2940.

**Fishing, camping. Martinsdale, Harris
and North Fork lakes.** W on US 12.
Lebo Lake, 9 mi W on US 12 to
Twodot, then 7 mi S on County 296.

Special Event

Harlowtown Rodeo. Chief Joseph
Park. NRA approved; parade, conces-
sions, campgrounds. Early July.
Phone 406/632-4694.

Havre

(A-5) *See also Chinook*

Founded 1887 **Pop** 10,201 **Elev** 2,494
ft **Area code** 406 **Zip** 59501
Information Chamber of Commerce,
518 1st St, PO Box 308; 406/265-
4383
Web www.nmclites.edu/havre

Center of a cattle and wheat-produc-
ing area, Havre (HAVE-er) is an
important retail and wholesale distribution point for northern Montana.
It is one of the oldest and largest
division points on the Burlington
Northern Santa Fe (formerly Great
Northern) Railway.

What to See and Do

Beaver Creek Park. 10,000 acres.
Swimming; fishing; boating. Skiing,
cross-country skiing, snowmobiling.

Camping (fee). **Fresno Lake.** Water-skiing, boating, camping. 15 mi NW. About 10 mi S, in Bear Paw Mtns. Phone 406/395-4565. **FREE**

Fort Assinniboine. Built in 1879-1883 and used as a military fort until 1911. In 1913 it became an agricultural experiment station. Some original buildings still stand. Tours (June-Sept). 6 mi SW on US 87. Phone 406/265-4383. ¢¢

Havre Beneath the Streets. Tour an "underground mall" where many of the first businesses in the town were established. Includes turn-of-the-century Sporting Eagle Saloon; Holland and Son Mercantile; Wah Sing Laundry; even an Opium den. Tours take approx one hr. Res required. (Daily) 100 3rd Ave. Phone 406/265-8888. ¢¢

H. Earl Clack Memorial Museum. Regional history. (Apr-Oct, Wed-Sun; rest of yr, by appt) 306 3rd Ave, in Havre Heritage Center. Phone 406/265-4000. **FREE** Museum manages

> **Wahkpa Chu'gn.** Archealogical excavation of prehistoric bison jump site. Also campground (fee). Tours (Memorial Day-Labor Day, Tues-Sun). ½ mi W on US 2. Phone 406/265-6417. ¢¢

Special Events

Rocky Boy Powwow. Rocky Boy Indian Reservation. First wkend Aug. Phone 406/395-4282.

Great Northern Fair. Phone 406/265-7121. Second wk Aug.

Havre Festival Days. Third wkend Sept. Phone 406/365-4383.

Motel/Motor Lodge

★ **TOWNHOUSE INN.** *601 W 1st St (59501). 406/265-6711; fax 406/265-6213; toll-free 800/442-4667. www.townpump.com.* 104 rms, 1-2 story. S $58; D $62-$66; each addl $4; suites $88-$170. Crib free. Pet accepted, some restrictions; $4. TV; cable (premium). Indoor pool; whirlpool. Restaurant opp open 24 hrs. Bar 8-2 am. Ck-out noon. Coin lndry. Meeting rm. Free airport, RR station, bus depot transportation. Cr cds: A, C, D, DS, MC, V.

Helena

(C-3) See also Deer Lodge, White Sulphur Springs

Settled 1864 **Pop** 24,569 **Elev** 4,157 ft **Area code** 406 **Zip** 59601

Information Helena Area Chamber of Commerce, 225 Cruse Ave, Suite A; 406/442-4120 or 800/7-HELENA (outside MT)

Web www.helenachamber.com

Montana's state capital and fourth largest city, Helena was the site of one of the state's largest gold rushes. In 1864, a party of discouraged prospectors decided to explore a gulch—now Helena's Main Street—as their "last chance." This gulch and the area surrounding it produced more than $20 million in gold. A hundred cabins soon appeared. The mining camp, known as "Last Chance," was renamed Helena, after a town in Minnesota. Besides being the governmental center for Montana, today's Helena hosts agricultural and industrial business, including an important smelting and ore-refining plant in East Helena.

What to See and Do

The Archie Bray Foundation. Internationally recognized resident program, workshop, gallery, and classroom. 2915 Country Club Ave. Phone 406/443-3502.

Canyon Ferry State Park. (Chinamans Unit). There are numerous recreation sites around this reservoir, which was created in 1954 by the construction of the Canyon Ferry Dam. Swimming, waterskiing, fishing, boating; picnicking, camping (no hookups). Standard fees. 10 mi E on US 12/287, then 6 mi N on MT 284. Phone 406/475-3319.

Cathedral of St. Helena. Gothic cathedral with 230-ft spires and 68 stained-glass windows made in Germany. Modeled after cathedral in Cologne. (Daily) Lawrence and Warren Aves.

Frontier Town. Rustic pioneer village shaped with solid rock and built with giant logs. 75-mi view of the

State Capitol

Continental Divide. Restaurant, bar. (Mother's Day-early Oct, daily) 15 mi W on US 12, atop MacDonald Pass. Phone 406/442-4560. **FREE**

Gates of the Mountains. Twelve-mi, two-hr Missouri River cruise explores deep gorge in Helena National Forest, discovered and named by Lewis and Clark. Views of cliffs, canyons, wildlife and wilderness. (Memorial Day wkend mid Sept, daily) Launching facilities (Apr-Nov). 16 mi N, off I-15. Phone 406/458-5241. ¢¢¢

Gold Collection. Collection incl nuggets, wire and leaf gold, gold dust and coins. (Mon-Fri; closed hols) Wells Fargo Helena, 350 N Last Chance Gulch. Phone 406/447-2000. **FREE**

Helena National Forest. Approx 975,000 acres incl part of the Scapegoat Wilderness and the Gates of the Mountains Wilderness, camp and picnic sites. Scenic drives, fishing, hunting for deer and elk. Adj to Helena, accessible from US 12, 91, 287, I-15, MT 200. For information contact Forest Supervisor, 2880 Skyway Dr, 59601. Phone 406/449-5201.

Holter Museum of Art. Changing exhibits featuring paintings, sculpture, photography, ceramics, weaving. (Tues-Sun; closed hols) 12 E Lawrence. Phone 406/442-6400. **Donation**

⭐ **Last Chance Tour Train.** Departs from historical museum. Covered trains tour the city's major points of interest, incl Last Chance Gulch. (Mid-May-Sept, Mon-Sat) Phone 406/442-1023. ¢¢

Marysville Ghost Town. A ghost town with abandoned saloons, churches, etc., complete with a fully functioning restaurant—Marysville House amidst the ruins. (Restaurant Wed-Sat; summer, Tues-Sat). No phone number avail for restaurant. 7 mi N, off Hwy 279.

⭐ **Montana Historical Society Museum.** History of Montana in Montana Homeland exhibit; notable collection of Charles M. Russell's art, Haynes Gallery on Montana Photography; changing exhibits. Montana Historical Library is on second floor. (Memorial Day-Labor Day, daily; rest of yr, Mon-Sat; closed Jan 1, Thanksgiving, Dec 25) 225 N Roberts St. Phone 406/444-2694. ¢¢

Original Governor's Mansion. (1888) Restored 22-rm brick house used as governor's residence 1913-1959. 304 N Ewing St. Phone 406/444-4789.

Pioneer Cabin. (1864) Depicts frontier life (1864-1884); many authentic furnishings. (Memorial Day-Labor Day, Mon-Fri; rest of yr, by appt) 212 S Park Ave. Phone 406/443-7641. ¢

LAST CHANCE GULCH

Montana's capital city straddles one of history's richest gold strikes—Last Chance Gulch—and consequently the city has a rich legacy of monuments and architecture.

Begin at the Montana Historical Society (225 North Roberts Street), across from the state capitol. Montana's premier museum, this captivating complex mixes fine art and exhibits charting the state's history. Of special interest is the MacKay Gallery of Charles M. Russell Art, one of the nation's largest public collections of Russell's painting and sculpture.

Walk west on 6th Street to the Montana State Capitol at 1301 6th Avenue. This imposing structure, domed with a cupola of Butte copper, was built in 1899 and enlarged in 1912 by the extensions containing the present legislative wings. Significant paintings and murals decorate the interior. In the House Chambers hangs Lewis and Clark Meeting the Flathead Indians at Ross' Hole by Charley Russell, one of his largest and most acclaimed works. In the lobby of the House of Representatives are six paintings by E. S. Paxson, which detail the state's history. Tours of the Capitol are given daily on the hour, 9 am-5 pm.

Continue walking down 6th Street to the Old Governor's Mansion (304 North Ewing). Built in 1883 by a local entrepreneur, the 20-room residence served as the governor's home from 1913 to 1959. The building is now owned by the Montana Historical Society, which has restored the ornate building to its historic splendor. Free tours are offered.

Continue down Ewing Street to Lawrence Street, and turn west. The Cathedral of St. Helena (509 North Warren) was begun in 1908 but wasn't finished until 1924. Modeled after Cologne Cathedral, Helena's largest church dominates the skyline with its 230-foot twin spires. Its stained glass was fashioned in Germany.

Continue west on Lawrence Street to Last Chance Gulch, the site of Helena's gold rush. In the 1860s, Prickly Pear Creek snaked down from the mountains through a thicket of mining claims called Last Chance Gulch. As mining gave way to commerce, the gulch remained the main street; its winding path, and especially the one-claim-sized business buildings, still reflect its mining past. The old business district of Helena is still impressive, even after a 1933 earthquake destroyed some of its buildings.

The Power Block (58-62 North Last Chance Gulch) was built in 1889; note that on the southeast corner, each of the five floors has windows grouped in corresponding numbers of panes. The Securities Building (101 North Last Chance Gulch), built in 1886, is a Romanesque former bank with curious carved thumbprints between the first-floor arches. The Montana Club (24 West 6th Avenue) was Montana's most prestigious private club: membership was open only to millionaires. The club's present building was designed by Cass Gilbert, the designer of the US Supreme Court Building.

Be certain to stop in at The Parrot (42 Last Chance Gulch), an old-fashioned ice-cream parlor and chocolate confectioner that's one of Helena's longest operating businesses. The Atlas Building (7-9 North Last Chance Gulch) is one of Helena's most fanciful; on a cornice upheld by Atlas, a salamander and lizards do symbolic battle.

Reeder's Alley. This area previously housed miners, muleskinners and Chinese laundry workers, now houses specialty shops and a restaurant. Near S end of Last Chance Gulch. Phone 406/442-3222.

State Capitol. Neoclassic structure faced with Montana granite and sandstone, topped with a copper dome. Murals by Charles M. Russell, E.S. Paxson and other artists on display inside. (Daily; guided tours mid-June-Labor Day) Bounded by Lockey and Roberts Sts, 6th and Montana Aves. Phone 406/444-2511. **FREE**

Special Events

"Race to the Sky" Dog Sled Races.
Feb. Phone 406/442-4008.

Governor's Cup Marathon. Early
June.

**Montana Traditional Dixieland Jazz
Festival.** Mid-June. Phone 406/442-
4120.

Last Chance Stampede and Fair.
Lewis and Clark County Fairgrounds.
Rodeo. July. Phone 406/442-1098.

Western Rendezvous of Art. Mid-
Aug. Phone 406/442-4263.

Eagle Watch. Bald eagles migrate to
nearby Missouri River to feed on
salmon. Mid-Nov-mid-Dec. Phone
406/442-4120.

Motels/Motor Lodges

★★ **BEST WESTERN HOTEL.** *2301
Colonial Dr (59601). 406/443-2100;
fax 406/442-0301; toll-free 800/422-
1002. www.bestwestern.com.* 149 rms,
2 story. S $72-90; D $79-$102; under
18 free. Crib free. TV; cable (premium). 2 heated pools, 1 indoor;
poolside serv. Coffee in rms. Restaurant 6 am-9 pm. Bar 5 pm-1:30 am.
Ck-out 1 pm. Coin lndry. Meeting
rms. Business servs avail. Bellhops.
Valet serv. Gift shop. Barber, beauty
shop. Free airport transportation.
Exercise equipt. Some bathrm
phones, in-rm whirlpools, refrigerators; microwaves avail. Cr cds: A, C,
D, DS, MC, V

★ **COMFORT INN.** *750 Fee St
(59601). 406/443-1000; fax 406/443-
1000; toll-free 800/228-5150. www.
comfortinn.com.* 56 rms, 2 story, 14
suites. June-Aug: S $70; D $75; each
addl $5; suites $80-$85; under 18
free; lower rates rest of yr. Crib free.
Pet accepted. TV; cable (premium).
Indoor pool; whirlpool. Complimentary continental bkfst. Complimentary coffee in lobby. Restaurant opp
open 24 hrs. Ck-out 11 am, ck-in 2
pm. Business servs avail. Cr cds: A, C,
D, DS, ER, JCB, MC, V.

★★ **FAIRFIELD INN.** *2150 11th Ave
(59601). 406/449-9944; fax 406/449-
9949; res 800/228-2800. www.fairfield
inn.com.* 60 rms, 3 story. June-Aug: S
$64; D $69-$79; each addl $5; under

18 free; lower rates rest of yr. Crib
free. TV; cable (premium). Complimentary continental bkfst. Restaurant nearby. Ck-out noon, ck-in 3
pm. Business servs avail. Coin lndry.
Exercise equipt. Indoor pool. Many
refrigerators, microwaves. Cr cds: A,
C, D, DS, MC, V.

★★ **HOLIDAY INN EXPRESS.** *701
Washington Ave (59601). 406/449-
4000; fax 406/449-4522; res 800/465-
4329.* 75 rms. Mid-June-mid-Sept: S,
D $72-$85; suites $89-$99; under 19
free; wkend rates; lower rates rest of
yr. Crib $8. TV; cable (premium).
Complimentary continental bkfst.
Restaurant nearby. Ck-out noon.
Coin lndry. Meeting rms. Business
servs avail. Exercise equipt. Some
refrigerators. Totally nonsmoking. Cr
cds: A, C, D, DS, JCB, MC, V.

★★ **JORGENSON'S INN AND
SUITES.** *1714 11th Ave (59601).
406/442-1770; fax 406/449-0155; toll-
free 800/272-1770.* 117 rms, 3 story.
June-Sept: S $46-$62; D $51-$82;
each addl $5; suites $92-$99; under
12 free; lower rates rest of yr. Crib
$3. TV; cable (premium). Indoor
pool. Complimentary coffee in
lobby. Restaurant 6:30 am-10 pm.
Bar 11:30 am-11 pm. Ck-out noon.
Meeting rms. Business servs avail.
Free airport transportation. Exercise
equipt. Health club privileges. Many
bathrm phones; refrigerator in suites.
Cr cds: A, D, DS, MC, V.

★ **SHILO INN.** *2020 Prospect Ave
(59601). 406/442-0320; fax 406/449-
4426; res 800/222-2244. www.shilo
inns.com.* 48 rms, 3 story, 3 kits. No
elvtr. S, D $59-$109; each addl $10;
kit. units $85. Crib free. Pet accepted;
$7. TV; cable (premium); VCR
(movies $5). Indoor pool; whirlpool.
Sauna, steam rm. Complimentary
continental bkfst. Coffee in rms.
Restaurant adj open 24 hrs. Ck-out
noon. Coin lndry. Meeting rm. Valet
serv. Free airport, bus depot transportation. Bathrm phones, refrigerators. Cr cds: A, C, D, DS, ER, JCB,
MC, V.

★ **SUPER 8 MOTEL.** *2200 11th Ave (59601). 406/443-2450; toll-free 800/800-8000. www.super8.com.* 102 rms, 3 story. No elvtr. S $49.88-$62.99; D $58.99-$62.99; each addl $5. Crib free. TV; cable (premium). Restaurant adj 11 am-10 pm. Ck-out 11 am. Coin lndry. Meeting rm. Exercise equipt. Cr cds: A, C, D, DS, MC, V.

🏋 ➦ 🐾 SC

B&Bs/Small Inns

★★ **APPLETON INN BED & BREAKFAST.** *1999 Euclid Ave (59601). 406/449-7492; fax 406/449-1261; res 800/956-1999. www.appleton inn.com.* 5 rms, 3 with A/C, 3 with shower only, 3 story, 1 suite. No elvtr. May-Oct: S $90-$98; D $95-$125; each addl $15; suites $105-$145; lower rates rest of yr. Cable TV in common rm. Complimentary full bkfst; afternoon refreshments. Ck-out 11 am, ck-in 4-8 pm. Business servs avail. Luggage handling. Health club privileges. Built in 1890. Historic elegance; turn-of-the-century antiques. Totally nonsmoking. Cr cds: A, D, DS, MC, V.

✈ ➦ 🐾

★★ **BARRISTER BED & BREAKFAST.** *416 N Ewing St (59601). 406/443-7330; fax 406/442-7964; toll-free 800/823-1148. www.wtp.net/go/ montana/sites/barrister.html.* 5 rms, 2 story. No rm phones. S, D $90; each addl $15. Pet accepted. TV; cable, VCR avail. Complimentary full bkfst. Restaurant nearby. Ck-out 10:30 am, ck-in 4-7 pm. Guest lndry. Luggage handling. Business servs avail. Free airport transportation. Built in 1880; antiques. Totally nonsmoking. Cr cds: A, D, DS, MC, V.

🐾 💈 ✈ 🔌

★★★ **THE SANDERS - HELENA'S BED & BREAKFAST.** *328 N Ewing (59601). 406/442-3309; fax 406/443-2361. www.sandersbb.com.* 7 rms, 2 story. S $80; D $90-$105; each addl $15. TV; VCR avail (movies). Complimentary full bkfst; afternoon refreshments. Restaurant nearby. Ck-out 11 am, ck-in 4-7 pm. In-rm modem link. Built 1875 by Senator Wilbur Fisk Sanders. Many original furnishings. Totally nonsmoking. Cr cds: A, D, DS, V.

➦ 🐾

Restaurants

★ **JADE GARDEN.** *3128 N Montana Ave (59602). 406/443-8899.* Hrs: 11 am-9:30 pm; Fri, Sat to 10 pm. Chinese menu. Wine, beer. Lunch $5.50-$8.75, dinner $4.50-$17.95. Child's menu. Specialties: broccoli beef, imperial shrimp, Mandarin pork. Parking. Contemporary Chinese decor. Totally nonsmoking. Cr cds: A, DS, MC, V.

D

★★ **ON BROADWAY.** *106 Broadway (59601). 406/443-1929.* Hrs: 5:30-9:30 pm. Fri, Sat to 10 pm. Closed Sun; hols. Bar from 5 pm. Dinner $9.75-$17.75. Specialties: oven-roasted fresh salmon, pan-blackened tuna, fresh East Coast mussels. In 1889 grocery store. Totally nonsmoking. Cr cds: A, DS, MC, V.

★★ **STONEHOUSE.** *120 Reeder's Alley (59601). 406/449-2552.* Hrs: 11:30 am-2 pm, 5-9 pm; Fri to 10 pm; Sat 5-10 pm. Closed Sun; some major hols. Res accepted. Wine, beer. Lunch $4.95-$7, dinner $11.95-$19.95. Buffet: lunch $6.95. Child's menu. Specialties: wild game, sauteed salmon, bread pudding with rum sauce. Turn-of-the-century house. Totally nonsmoking. Cr cds: A, DS, MC, V.

D SC

★ **WINDBAG SALOON.** *19 S Last Chance Gulch (59601). 406/443-9669.* Hrs: 11 am-2:30 pm, 5-9:30 pm; Sun 5-9 pm (June-Sept); Closed Sun (Oct-May); hols. Bar. Lunch $5-$7.75, dinner $6.25-$18.95. Specializes in Northwestern seafood, prime rib, fresh cobb salads. In former bordello; antique bar. Cr cds: A, DS, MC, V.

D 🔌

(⛽)

Kalispell

(B-2) *See also Bigfork, Columbia Falls, Whitefish*

Founded 1891 **Pop** 11,917 **Elev** 2,955 ft **Area code** 406 **Zip** 59901

Information Flathead Convention & Visitor Bureau, 15 Depot Park; 406/756-9091 or 800/543-3105

Web www.fcvb.org

Center of a mountain vacationland, Kalispell is the convention center of the Flathead Valley. Seed potatoes and sweet cherries are grown and processed in great quantities. Recreational activities abound in the area.

What to See and Do

Conrad Mansion. (1895) A 23-rm Norman-style mansion, authentically furnished and restored. Tours (Mid-May-mid-Oct, daily). Six blks E of Main St on 4th St E. Phone 406/755-2166. ¢¢¢

Flathead Lake. (See POLSON) 9 mi S on US 93. Phone 406/837-4196.

Flathead National Forest. A 2.3 million acre forest; incl part of 1,009,356-acre Bob Marshall Wilderness; 286,700-acre Great Bear Wilderness, and the 73,573-acre Mission Mts Wilderness; 15,368-acre Jewel Basin hiking area and the 219-mi Flathead National Wild and Scenic river system. Spectacular geological formations; glaciers, wild areas. Swimming, fishing, boating, canoeing; riding, picnicking, camping (June-Sept; fee), hunting, outfitters and guides, winter sports; recreation resorts, scenic drives. Near US 2, 93, adj to west and south sides of Glacier National Park. Contact Supervisor, 1935 3rd Ave E. Phone 406/755-5401.

Glacier National Park. (see)

Hockaday Center for the Arts. Changing exhibits; sales gallery. (Tues-Sat; closed hols) 3rd St and 2nd Ave E. Phone 406/755-5268. ¢¢

Lawrence Park. Preserved in natural state. Picnic, playground facilities. E off N Main St. Phone 406/758-7700. **FREE**

Woodland Park. On 37 acres. Flower and rock gardens; mile-long lagoon; skating rink (winter); picnicking, kitchen; playground; pool, wading pool (fees). (Daily) 8 blks E of Main St on 2nd St E. Phone 406/758-7700. **FREE**

Special Events

Agriculture-Farm Show. Two days mid-Feb. Phone 406/758-4423.

Youth Horse Show. May. Phone 406/758-2800.

Flathead Music Festival. July. Phone 406/758-2800.

Quarter Horse Show. July. Phone 406/758-2800.

Northwest Montana Fair and Rodeo. Flathead County Fairgrounds. Mid-Aug. Phone 406/758-5810.

Glacier Jazz Stampede. Oct. Phone 406/862-3814.

Motels/Motor Lodges

★★ **BEST WESTERN OUTLAW HOTEL.** *1701 Hwy 93 S (59901). 406/755-6100; fax 406/756-8994; res 800/780-7234. www.bestwestern.com.* 220 rms, 3 story. S $82-$135; D $92-$175; each addl $10; under 12 free; package plans. Crib $7. Pet accepted; $10. TV; cable (premium). 2 indoor pools; wading pool, whirlpool. Playground. Coffee in rms. Restaurant 6 am-10 pm. Bar 11-2 am. Ck-out 11 am. Coin lndry. Meeting rms. Business servs avail. Bellhops. Valet serv. Sundries. Gift shop. Barber, beauty shop. Tennis. Exercise equipt, sauna. Game rm. Microwaves avail. Some balconies. Casino. Western art gallery. Cr cds: A, C, D, DS, MC, V.
🄳 🕊 🖾 🏊 🗶 🖳 🐾 SC

★ **DAYS INN.** *1550 Hwy 93 N (59901). 406/756-3222; fax 406/756-3277; toll-free 800/329-7466. www.daysinn.com.* 53 rms, 2 story. Mid-May-Sept: S $59-$69; D $74-$79; each addl $5; suites $75-$85; under 12 free; lower rates rest of yr. Crib free. TV; cable (premium). Complimentary continental bkfst. Restaurant nearby. Ck-out 11 am. Meeting rm. Cr cds: A, C, D, DS, JCB, MC, V.
🄳 🖳 🐾 SC

★★ **HAMPTON INN.** *1140 W US 2 (59901). 406/755-7900; fax 406/755-5056; res 800/426-7866. www.northwestinns.com.* 120 rms, 3 story. June-Sept: S $83; D $93; suites $155-$205; under 19 free; lower rates rest of yr. Crib free. Pet accepted. TV; cable (premium), VCR. Complimentary continental bkfst. Complimentary coffee in rms. Restaurant adj 7 am-10 pm. Ck-out noon. Meeting rms. Business center. Bellhops. Valet serv. Sundries. Gift shop. Coin lndry. Free airport transportation. Downhill/x-country ski 16 mi. Exercise equipt. Indoor pool; whirlpool.

Rec rm. Refrigerators; in-rm whirlpool, microwave, wet bar, fireplace
in suites. Cr cds: A, C, D, DS, JCB,
MC, V.

★★ **WESTCOAST KALISPELL
CENTER.** *20 N Main St (59901).
406/752-6660; fax 406/752-6628.* 132
rms, 3 story, 14 suites. Mid-May-Sept:
S $98; D $105; each addl $12; suites
$120-$190; kit. units $150, under 18
free; ski, golf plans; lower rates rest
of yr. Crib free. Pet accepted, some
restrictions. TV; cable. Indoor pool;
whirlpools. Coffee in rms. Restaurant
6:30 am-10 pm. Bar 4 pm-2 am;
entertainment Fri, Sat. Ck-out noon.
Meeting rms. Business servs avail.
Bellhops. Shopping arcade. Barber,
beauty shop. Downhill ski 20 mi; x-
country ski 15 mi. Exercise equipt;
sauna. Casino. Adj to 50-store indoor
shopping mall. Cr cds: A, D, DS, MC,
V.

Hotel

★ **KALISPELL GRAND HOTEL.** *100
Main St (59901). 406/755-8100; fax
406/752-8012; toll-free 800/858-7422.
www.kalispellgrand.com.* 40 rms, 38
with shower only, 3 story. No elvtr.
June-Aug: S $58-$74; D $68-$81;
each addl $7; suites $79-$115; under
12 free; lower rates rest of yr. Crib
free. Pet accepted, some restrictions.
TV; cable. Complimentary continental bkfst. Bar 8-2 am; entertainment
Thurs-Sat. Ck-out 11 am. Business
servs avail. Exercise equipt. Casino.
Cr cds: A, D, DS, MC, V.

B&B/Small Inn

★★★ **ANGEL POINT GUEST
SUITES.** *829 Angel Point Rd, Lakeside
(59922). 409/844-2204; toll-free
800/214-2204. www.mtcondos.com.* 2
kit. suites. No A/C. June-Sept (3-day
min): S, D $85-$100; each addl $40;
lower rates rest of yr. Complimentary
full bkfst. Ck-out 11 am, ck-in 3 pm.
X-country ski 7 mi. Lawn games.
Refrigerators. Balconies. Picnic tables,
grill. Gazebo. Secluded, elegant lodging on lake; antiques, original art.
Totally nonsmoking.

Restaurant

★★ **FIRST AVENUE WEST.** *139 1st
Ave W (59901). 406/755-4441.* Hrs:
11 am-3 pm, 5:30-10 pm; Sat, Sun
from 5:30 pm. Closed Thanksgiving,
Dec 25. Res accepted. Bar to 1 am.
Lunch $3.95-$7.95, dinner $4.95-
$16.95. Child's menu. Specializes in
grilled fresh seafood, pasta. Outdoor
dining. Casual, bistro atmosphere. Cr
cds: MC, V.

Lewistown (C-5)

Founded 1881 **Pop** 6,051 **Elev** 3,963
ft **Area code** 406 **Zip** 59457
Information Chamber of Commerce,
PO Box 818; 406/538-5436
Web www.lewistown.net/~lewchamb

At the geographic center of the state,
amid some of Montana's finest farming and ranching country, Lewistown
is a farm trade community. The area
is famous for hard, premium wheat
and high-grade registered cattle.
Originally a small trading post on
the Carroll Trail, it was first called
"Reed's Fort," and later renamed to
honor a Major Lewis who established
a fort two miles south in 1876.

What to See and Do

Big Spring Creek. One of the top rainbow trout streams in the country. Picnic grounds. Runs north and south.

**Charles M. Russell National Wildlife
Refuge.** Missouri River "Breaks" and
prairie lands; wildlife incl pronghorn, elk, mule and whitetail deer;
bighorn sheep, sage and sharptail
grouse. Refuge (Daily, 24 hrs). Lewistown headquarters (Mon-Fri; closed
hols). 70 mi NE via US 191 or MT
200. Phone 406/538-8706. **FREE**

Fort Maginnis. Ruins of 1880 frontier post. 15 mi E on US 87, then
10 mi N.

**Historical points of 19th-century gold
mining. Maiden.** 10 mi N on US 191,
then 6 mi E. **Kendall.** 16 mi N on US
191, then 6 mi W on gravel road.
Giltedge. 14 mi E on US 87, then
6 mi NW.

Special Events

Drag Races. Quarter-mile races. NHRA sanctioned. May-late Sept. Phone 406/453-7555.

Charlie Russell Chew-Choo. 3½-hr dinner train runs through rugged beauty of Central Montana. Sat June-Sept. Phone 406/538-5436.

Central Montana Horse Show, Fair, Rodeo. Fergus County Fairgrounds. Last full wk in July. Phone 406/538-8841.

Montana Cowboy Poetry Gathering. Modern-day cowboys and admirers of Western folklore relate life "down on the range" through original poetry. Third wkend Aug. Phone 406/538-5436.

Motel/Motor Lodge

★ **SUPER 8 MOTEL.** 102 Wendell Ave (59457). 406/538-2581; fax 406/538-2702; res 800/800-8000. www.super8. com. 44 rms, 2 story. June-Sept: S $42.88; D $45.88-$48.88; each addl $4; under 12 free; lower rates rest of yr. Crib free. TV; cable (premium). Complimentary coffee in lobby. Restaurant opp 7 am-10 pm. Ck-out 11 am. Coin lndry. Non-smoking. Cr cds: A, DS, MC, V.
[D] [icon]

Restaurant

★ **WHOLE FAMDAMILY.** 206 W Main St (59457). 406/538-5161. Hrs: 11 am-8 pm; Sat to 5 pm. Closed Sun; hols. Res accepted. Wine, beer. Lunch $4-$7, dinner $5.95-$6.50. Child's menu. International specials each day. Own desserts. Decorated with family portraits. Totally non-smoking. Cr cds: A, DS, MC, V.
[D]

Libby

(A-1) *See also Kalispell; also see Bonners Ferry and Sandpoint, ID*

Settled 1863 **Pop** 2,532 **Elev** 2,086 ft
Area code 406 **Zip** 59923

Information Chamber of Commerce, 905 W 9th St, PO Box 704; 406/293-4167
Web www.libby.org

Nestled in the Cabinet Mountains, Libby, formerly a gold town, is now busy processing logs. It is headquarters for Kootenai National Forest which has three Ranger District offices.

What to See and Do

Camping. Libby Ranger District;. 406/293-7773 includes three campgrounds. **Howard Lake Campground;** 26 mi S on Hwy 2, 5 mi on W Fisher Rd. **McGillvray Campground;** 13 mi NE, near Lake Koocanusa. **McGregor Lake;** 53 mi SE on Hwy 2.

Heritage Museum. Located in 12-sided log building and features various exhibits on area pioneers; animal exhibits; art gallery; exhibits by the Forest Service, mining interests, the lumber industry. (June-Aug, Mon-Sat, also Sun afternoons) 1¼ mi S via US 2. Phone 406/293-7521. **Donation**

Kootenai National Forest. More than 2.2 million acres. Includes 94,360-acre Cabinet Mts Wilderness. Scenic drives along Yaak River, Lake Koocanusa Reservoir, Fisher River, Bull River; Giant Cedars Nature Trail. Ross Creek Cedars. Fishing. Boating, canoeing. Hiking trails. X-country skiing. Picnicking. Camping. Surrounds Libby, accessible on US 2, MT 37 and Hwy 56. For info contact Supervisor's Office, 1101 W Hwy 2; Phone 406/293-6211. In the forest is

> **Turner Mountain Ski Area.** T-bar, rope tow; patrol, school, rentals; snack bar. (Dec-Apr, Sat and Sun) 23 mi NW on Pipe Creek Rd.

Libby Dam. Lake Koocanusa extends 90 mi upstream. A US Army Corps of Engineers project. Fishing; boating (dock). Picnicking. (Daily) Visitor center and gift shop; tours of dam and powerhouse; viewpoints (Memorial Day-Labor Day, daily). 17 mi NE on MT 37. Phone 406/293-5577. **FREE**

Special Events

Logger Days. Adult and child logging contests. Carnival, parade, karaoke contest. Vendors, food. Early July. Phone 406/293-4167.

Nordicfest. Scandinavian festival, parade, dances, food, melodrama. Third wkend Sept. Phone 406/293-4167.

Little Bighorn Battlefield National Monument

See also Billings, Hardin

(2 mi SE of Crow Agency. Entrance 1 mi E of I-90 on US 212.)

Scene of Custer's "last stand," this monument memorializes one of the last armed clashes between Northern Plains tribes, fighting to preserve their traditional way of life, and the forces of the United States, charged with safeguarding westward expansion. Here, on June 25, 1876, Lieutenant Colonel George A. Custer and approximately 263 men of the US Army Seventh Cavalry and attached personnel were killed in a battle against an overwhelming force of Lakota and Cheyenne warriors. Also here are a national cemetery, established in 1879; and the Reno-Benteen Battlefield, five miles southeast, where the remainder of the Seventh Cavalry withstood until late on June 26. Headstones show where the soldiers fell and a large obelisk marks the mass grave of the Seventh Cavalry. A visitor center contains a bookstore and museum with dioramas and exhibits (Daily; closed Jan 1, Thanksgiving, Dec 25). National Park Service personnel provide interpretive programs (Memorial Day-Labor Day), guided tours of Custer National Cemetery. For further info contact PO Box 39, Crow Agency 59022; 406/638-2621. ¢¢-¢¢¢

Livingston

(D-4) *See also Big Timber, Bozeman*

Settled 1882 **Pop** 6,701 **Elev** 4,503 ft **Area code** 406 **Zip** 59047

Information Chamber of Commerce, 208 W Park; 406/222-0850

Web www.livingston.avicom.net

Custer National Cemetery

Railroading has been a key to the town's history and economy since railroad surveyors first named it Clark City; later the present name was adopted to honor a director of the Northern Pacific Railway. Today agriculture, ranching, and tourism are the chief industries. Farm products from Paradise and Shields valleys also pass through the town. Trout fishing is excellent in the Yellowstone River. A Ranger District office of the Gallatin National Forest (see BOZEMAN) is located here.

What to See and Do

Depot Center. Changing exhibits and cultural art shows. Gift shop. (Mid-May-mid Oct, Mon-Sat, also Sun afternoons) Park and 2nd Sts. Phone 406/222-2300. ¢¢

Emigrant Gulch. Gold was discovered here in 1862. Chico and Yellowstone City boomed busily but briefly—the gold supply was limited and the Crow were aggressive. Both are ghost towns now. 37 mi S, off US 89.

Park County Museum. "House of Memories;" pioneer tools, library, old newspapers, sheep wagon, stagecoach, Native American and archaeological exhibits. Northern Pacific Railroad Room. (Memorial Day-Labor Day, afternoons, rest of yr by appt) 118 W Chinook. Phone 406/222-4184. ¢¢

Special Event

Rodeo Days. Fairgrounds. Early July. Phone 406/222-0850.

Motels/Motor Lodges

★★ **BEST WESTERN YELLOW-STONE INN & CONFERENCE CENTER.** *1515 W Park St (59047). 406/222-6110; fax 406/222-3357; toll-free 800/770-1874. www.bestwestern. com.* 98 rms, 3 story. Mid-May-mid-Sept: S, D $72-$99; each addl $7; kit. unit $144; under 13 free; wkly rates; lower rates rest of yr. Crib free. Pet accepted; $8. TV; cable. Complimentary coffee in lobby. Restaurant 6 am-10 pm. Bar noon-2 am. Ck-out noon. Meeting rms. Business servs avail. Bellhops. Sundries. Barber, beauty shop. Indoor pool. Cr cds: A, C, D, DS, MC, V.

D ⬦ ≋ ⬧ ⬧ SC

★★ **CHICO HOT SPRINGS RESORT.** *1 Chico Rd, Pray (59065). 406/333-4933; fax 406/333-4694; toll-free 800/468-9232. www.chicohot springs.com.* 49 lodge rms, 3 story, 29 motel units, 16 cottages. No A/C. Some rm phones. June-Sept: (lodge) S, D $69-$85; (motel) S, D $105; cabins $75-$85; chalets (1-5 bedrm) $129-$300; under 7 free; lower rates rest of yr. Crib free. Pet accepted; $5. Heated pool. Supervised children's activities (summer only). Dining rm 7-11 am, 5:30-10 pm. Box lunches. Bar 11-2 am; entertainment Fri, Sat. Ck-out 11 am, ck-in 3 pm. Grocery. Coin lndry 5 mi. Meeting rms. Business servs avail. Gift shop. Exercise equipt. X-country ski 3 mi. Hiking. Bicycle rentals. Lawn games. Fishing/hunting guides. Massage. Some refrigerators. Picnic tables. Rustic surroundings; secluded in Paradise Valley. Cr cds: A, DS, MC, V.

D ⬦ ⬧ ⬧ ⬧ ⬧ ⬧ ⬧ ≋ ⬧ ⬧ ⬧

★ **COMFORT INN.** *114 Love Ln (59047). 406/222-4400; fax 406/222-7658; res 800/228-5150. www.comfort inn.com.* 49 rms, 2 story. July-Aug: S $74.95; D $79.95-$84.95; each addl $3; suites $96.95-$106.95; under 18 free; lower rates rest of yr. Crib free. TV; cable (premium). Complimentary continental bkfst. Retaurant nearby. Ck-out 11 am. Meeting rm. Bellhops. Sundries. Coin lndry. Indoor pool; whirlpool. Game rm. Refrigerator, wet bar in suites. Cr cds: A, C, D, DS, MC, V.

D ≋ ⬧ ⬧ SC

★ **LIVINGSTON SUPER 8.** *105 Centennial Dr (59047). 406/222-7711; toll-free 800/800-8000. www.super8. com.* 36 rms. June-Sept: S $42-$57; D $50-$65; each addl $4; under 12 free; lower rates rest of yr. Crib free. TV; cable (premium). Complimentary coffee in lobby. Restaurant adj 6 am-11 pm. Ck-out 11 am. Coin lndry. Cr cds: A, D, DS, JCB, MC, V.

D ⬧ ⬧ ⬧

★ **PARADISE INN.** *Park Rd and Rogers Ln (59047). 406/222-6320; fax 406/222-6481; toll-free 800/437-6291.* 43 rms. Mid-May-Sept: S, D $79-$89;

each addl $5; suites $99-$129; lower rates rest of yr. Crib $5. Pet accepted; $5. TV; cable (premium). Indoor pool. Restaurant 6 am-10:30 pm. Bar 3 pm-2 am. Ck-out 11 am. Cr cds: A, MC, V.

[D] [icons]

Guest Ranch

★★★ **MOUNTAIN SKY GUEST RANCH.** *Big Creek Rd, Emigrant (59027). 406/333-4911; fax 406/587-3397; toll-free 800/548-3392. www. mtnsky.com.* 27 cabins, 1-3 bedrm. No rm phones. AP, June-Sept: S, D $2,030-$2,450/wk; family rates; 50 percent deposit required to confirm res. Closed rest of yr. Heated pool; whirlpool. Playground. Free supervised children's activities (mid-June-Aug). Coffee in rms. Ck-out 10 am, ck-in 3 pm. Guest lndry. Meeting rms. Business servs avail. Airport transportation. Tennis, pro. Sauna. Float trips. Lawn games. Hiking. Soc dir; entertainment. Rec rm. Refrigerators. 30 mi N of Yellowstone National Park. Cr cds: MC, V.

[icons]

Restaurant

★★★ **CHATHAMS LIVINGSTON BAR AND GRILL.** *130 N Main St (59047). 406/222-7909.* Hrs: 11:30 am-2 pm, 5:30-10 pm; Sun to 9 pm. Closed Thanksgiving, Dec 25. Res accepted. Continental menu. Bar. Wine list. Lunch $4.75-$11.50, dinner $18-$20. Child's menu. Specialties: baked poussin, fresh grouper, New York strip steak. Own baking. Street parking. Turn-of-the-century bldg has 100-yr-old mahogany bar; overlooks downtown. Cr cds: A, DS, MC, V.

[D] [icon]

Malta (B-6)

Pop 2,340 **Elev** 2,255 ft
Area code 406 **Zip** 59538
Information Malta Area Chamber of Commerce, PO Box 1420; 406/654-1776 or 800/704-1776

What to See and Do

Bowdoin National Wildlife Refuge. Approx 15,500 acres provide excellent nesting, resting, and feeding grounds for migratory waterfowl. The refuge also supports whitetailed deer and pronghorns. Use of the self-guided drive-through trail is recommended. (Daily; weather permitting) 7 mi E via Old US 2. Phone 406/654-2863. **FREE**

Phillips County Museum. Features Native American, homestead, and dinosaur exhibits. (Mid-May-Labor Day, daily) US 2 E. Phone 406/654-1037. **Donation**

Motel/Motor Lodge

★ **MALTANA.** *138 S 1st Ave W (59538). 406/654-2610; fax 406/654-1663; toll-free 800/735-9278.* 19 rms. S $37; D $44; each addl $3. Crib $3. TV; cable. Complimentary coffee in rms. Restaurant nearby. Ck-out 11 am. Airport, RR station transportation. Cr cds: A, C, D, DS, MC, V.

[icons]

[gas pump icon]

Miles City (C-7)

Pop 8,461 **Elev** 2,358 ft
Area code 406 **Zip** 59301
Information Chamber of Commerce, 901 Main St; 406/232-2890
Web www.mcchamber.com

This trade, industrial, and energy-concerned city is also a livestock and agricultural center. Seat of Custer County, the city is named for a US infantry general. Here are the Livestock Auction Saleyards where about 25 percent of Montana's livestock is processed.

What to See and Do

Custer County Art Center. Housed in former holding tanks of old Miles City Water Works, overlooking the Yellowstone River. Contemporary art exhibits. Gift shop. (Tues-Sun afternoons; closed hols) Water Plant Rd, W via US 10, 12. Phone 406/232-0635. **FREE**

Range Riders Museum and Pioneer Memorial Hall. Exhibits and memorabilia of the days of the open range. Bert Clark gun collection is one of the largest in the Northwest. (Apr-Oct) West end of Main St. Phone 406/232-6146. ¢¢

Special Events

Bucking Horse Sale. Fairgrounds. Exit 135 off I-94. Born in 1951, it grew out of the Miles City Roundup. Features Wild Horse Stampede, bronc and bull riding, and the sale of both bucking horses and bulls. Third wkend May. Phone 406/234-2890.

Ballon Roundup. Fourth wkend June. Phone 406/232-2890.

Eastern Montana Fair. Fairgrounds. Exit 135 off I-94. Four days late Aug. Phone 406/234-2890.

Motels/Motor Lodges

★★ **BEST WESTERN WAR BONNET INN.** *1015 S Haynes Ave (59301). 406/232-4560; fax 406/232-0363; toll-free 800/528-1234. www. bestwestern.com.* 54 rms, 2 story. May-Sept: S $66; D $71; each addl $6; suites $100; under 18 free; higher rates Bucking Horse Sale; lower rates rest of yr. Crib $6. Pet accepted. TV; cable (premium). Indoor pool; whirlpool. Complimentary continental bkfst. Ck-out noon. Meeting rms. Cr cds: A, C, D, DS, JCB, MC, V.

★ **COMFORT INN.** *1615 S Haynes Ave (59301). 406/232-3141; fax 406/232-2924; toll-free 800/228-5150. www.comfortinn.com.* 49 rms, 2 story. May-Aug: S $52.95; D $57.95-$62.95; each addl $5; under 18 free; higher rates Bucking Horse Sale; lower rates rest of yr. Crib free. TV; cable (premium). Indoor pool; whirlpool. Complimentary continental bkfst. Ck-out 11 am. Coin lndry. Meeting rms. Business servs avail. Cr cds: A, D, DS, MC, V.

★★ **HOLIDAY INN EXPRESS.** *1720 S Haynes (59301). 406/232-1000; fax 406/232-1365; toll-free 888/700-0402. www.holiday-inn.com.* 52 rms, 2 story, 6 suites. Mid-May-early Sept: S, D $69-$85; suites $99; under 18 free; higher rates special events; lower

rates rest of yr. TV; cable (premium). Complimentary continental bkfst. Ck-out 11 am. Meeting rms. Business servs avail. Coin lndry. Indoor pool; whirlpool. Bathrm phone, refrigerator, microwave, wet bar in suites. Totally nonsmoking. Cr cds: A, C, D, DS, JCB, MC, V.

Missoula

(C-2) *See also Hamilton*

Settled 1860 **Pop** 42,918 **Elev** 3,200 ft **Area code** 406
Information Chamber of Commerce, 825 E Front, PO Box 7577, 59807; 406/543-6623

Since the days of the Lewis and Clark Expedition, Missoula has been a trading and transportation crossroads. It is a lumber and paper manufacturing center, the hub of large reserves of timber, and the regional headquarters of the US Forest Service and Montana State Forest Service.

What to See and Do

Aerial Fire Depot. Forest Service headquarters for aerial attack on forest fires in western US. Smokejumpers trained and based here during summer. 7 mi W on US 10, I 90, ½ mi W of Johnson Bell Airport. Phone 406/329-4900.

Rocky Mountain Research Station Fire Sciences Laboratory. Conducts research in fire prevention and control and the beneficial uses of fire in forest management. Tours by appt. Phone 406/329-4934.

Smokejumper Center. Training and dispatching center for airborne fire crews; parachute and fire training. Phone 406/329-4934. **FREE**

Visitor Center. Fire management exhibits, guided tour of parachute loft and training facilities; films, information on recreational facilities in 13 national forests in region. (Memorial Day-Labor Day, daily; rest of yr, by appt) Phone 406/329-4934. **Donation**

Art Museum of Missoula. Art of the western states. Changing exhibits. Educational programs. 335 N Pattee. Phone 406/728-0447. **FREE**

Historical Museum at Fort Missoula. Established to interpret the history of Missoula County, and the forest management and timber production in western Montana. The museum features indoor galleries with permanent and changing exhibits; outdoor area incl ten historic structures, four are restored. Located in the core of what was originally Fort Missoula (1877-1947). Several original buildings remain. Other areas incl railroad and military history. (Summer, daily; winter, Tues-Sun) 5 mi S from I-90 via Reserve St to South Ave, then 1 mi W. Phone 406/728-3476.

Lolo National Forest. Foot trails to 100 lakes and peaks, camping (mid-May-Sept, full-service campgrounds, some free); picnicking, fishing, hunting, winter sports, scenic drives through 2,062,545 acres. Incl Welcome Creek Wilderness and Rattlesnake National Recreation Area and Wilderness, part of Scapegoat Wilderness, and Selway-Bitterroot Wilderness. The Pattee Canyon Recreation Area is five mi from town. Historic Lolo Trail and Lewis and Clark Hwy (US 12) over Bitterroot Mtns take visitors along route of famed exploration. Surrounds Missoula, accessible on US 10, 12, 93, MT 200, 83, I-90. Contact Supervisor, Fort Missoula, Building 24, 59801. Phone 406/329-3750.

Missoula Carousel. Carousel features hand-carved horses—the first such carousel in the US to do so in over 60 yrs. Gift shop. (Daily) In Caras Park, just W of the Higgins Bridge. Phone 406/549-8382.

Missoula Public Library. Outstanding collection of historical works on Montana and the Northwest and genealogical materials. 301 E Main St. Phone 406/721-2665.

Paxson Paintings. Eight murals depicting Montana's history by one of the West's outstanding artists. (Mon-Fri; closed hols) County Courthouse, 200 W Broadway between Orange and Higgins sts. Phone 406/721-5700. **FREE**

St. Francis Xavier Church. (1889). Steeple highlights this structure built the same year Montana became a state. (Daily) 420 W Pine St. Phone 406/542-0321.

Ski areas.

Marshall Mountain Ski Area. Triple chairlift, T-bar, rope tow; school, patrol, rentals, snowmaking; half-day rates; cafeteria, bar, snack bar. Longest run 2½ mi; vertical drop 1,500 ft. Night skiing. (Dec-Mar, daily exc Mon) 7 mi NE via I-90, E Missoula exit. Phone 406/258-6000.

Montana Snowbowl. Two double chairlifts, T-bar, rope tow; patrol, school, rentals; cafeteria, bar. Longest run three mi; vertical drop 2,600 ft. (Late Nov-Apr, Mon and Wed-Sun) Lifts fee; tow free. Summer chairlift. Hiking trails; mountain biking. (July-Aug, Fri-Sun) 3 mi NW on I-90 (Reserve St Exit), then 9 mi N on Grant Creek Rd to Snow Bowl Rd. Phone 406/549-9777. ¢¢¢¢

University of Montana. (1893) 10,000 students. At the foot of Mt Sentinel. University Center Gallery and Gallery of Visual Arts. University and Arthur aves. Campus tours. Phone 406/243-2522.

Special Events

International Wildlife Film Festival. Downtown. Phone 406/728-9380. Apr.

Western Montana Quarter Horse Show. Fairgrounds. Late June. Phone 406/543-6623.

Western Montana Fair & Rodeo. Fairgrounds. Mid-Aug. Phone 406/721-3247.

Motels/Motor Lodges

★ **BEST INN.** *4953 N Reserve St (59808). 406/542-7550; fax 406/721-5931; toll-free 800/272-9500. www. bestinn.com.* 67 rms, 3 story. Mid-May-mid-Sept: S, D $59-$69; under 12 free. Crib $6. Pet accepted. TV; cable (premium). Complimentary coffee in lobby. Restaurant adj open 24 hrs. Ck-out 11 am. Coin lndry. Whirlpool. Some refrigerators. Cr cds: A, C, D, DS, MC, V.

D 🐾 ✕ ⊟ 🐾 SC

★ **BEST INN AND CONFERENCE CENTER.** *3803 Brooks St (59804). 406/251-2665; fax 406/251-5733; toll-free 800/272-9500. www.bestinn.*

com. 91 rms, 3 story. Mid-May-mid-Sept: S $45-69; lower rates rest of yr. Crib $6. TV; cable (premium). Restaurant adj open 24 hrs. Ck-out 11 am. Coin lndry. Meeting rms. Business servs avail. Whirlpool. Cr cds: A, DS, MC, V.

⬜ ✕ 🔲 🔥 SC

★★ **BEST WESTERN GRANT CREEK INN.** *5280 Grant Creek Rd (59808). 406/543-0700; fax 406/543-0777; res 888/543-0700. www.best western.com/grantcreekinn.* 126 rms, 4 story. Late May-early Sept: S, D $79-$99; each addl $10; suites $150; under 12 free; lower rates rest of yr. Crib free. Pet accepted, some restrictions. TV; cable, VCR avail (movies). Complimentary continental bkfst. Complimentary coffee in rms. Ck-out 11 am. Meeting rms. Business servs avail. In-rm modem link. Gift shop. Coin lndry. Free airport transportation. Downhill/x-country ski 5 mi. Exercise equipt; steam rm. Indoor pool; whirlpool. Refrigerator, fireplace in suites. Some balconies. Cr cds: A, C, D, DS, MC, V.

⬜ 🔲 ⬇ 🔲 🔲 ✕ 🔲 🔥 SC

★★ **HAMPTON INN.** *4805 N Reserve St (59802). 406/549-1800; fax 406/549-1737; toll-free 800/426-7866. www.hamptoninn.com.* 60 rms, 4 story. S $69-$79; D $79-$89; under 18 free. Crib free. Pet accepted; $5. TV; cable (premium). Indoor pool; whirlpool. Complimentary continental bkfst. Restaurant nearby. Ck-out noon. Meeting rms. Business servs avail. Bellhops. Valet serv. Free airport transportation. Exercise equipt. Cr cds: A, C, D, DS, MC, V.

⬜ 🔲 🔲 ✕ 🔲 🔥 SC

★★ **HOLIDAY INN EXPRESS.** *1021 E Broadway St (59802). 406/549-7600; fax 406/543-2223; res 800/465-4329. www.holiday-inn.com.* 95 rms, 5 with shower only, 4 story, 14 suites. May-Aug: S, D $65-$85; suites $99; under 18 free; higher rates special events; lower rates rest of yr. Crib free. TV; cable (premium). Complimentary continental bkfst. Restaurant nearby. Ck-out noon. Meeting rms. Business center. In-rm modem link. Bellhops. Coin lndry. Free airport transportation. Downhill/x-country ski 5 mi. Exercise equipt. Pool privileges. Bathrm phones. Refrigerator,

microwave, wet bar in suites. Some balconies. On river. Cr cds: A, DS, MC, V.

⬜ 🔲 🔥 🔲 🔲 ✕ 🔲 SC 🔲

★★ **HOLIDAY INN PARKSIDE.** *200 S Pattee St (59802). 406/721-8550; toll-free 800/379-0408.* 200 rms, 4 story. S, D $88-$99; suites $125-$150; under 18 free. Pet accepted. TV; cable. Indoor pool; whirlpool. Restaurant 6:30 am-2 pm, 5:30-10:30 pm. Bar 2 pm-2 am; entertainment Fri, Sat. Ck-out noon. Meeting rms. Business servs avail. Bellhops. Gift shop. Free airport transportation. Downhill ski 12 mi; x-country ski 5 mi. Exercise equipt; sauna. Balconies. Open atrium, outside patio dining. On Clark Fork River and park. Cr cds: A, DS, MC, V.

⬜ 🔲 🔲 🔲 ✕ 🔲 🔥 SC

★ **ORANGE STREET BUDGE MOTOR INN MISSOULA.** *801 N Orange St (59806). 406/721-3610; fax 406/721-8875; toll-free 800/328-0801.* 81 rms, 3 story. May-Sept: S $43-$46; D $46-$50; each addl $5; lower rates rest of yr. Crib $3. Pet accepted; $5. TV; cable (premium), VCR avail (movies). Complimentary continental bkfst. Restaurant nearby. Ck-out 11 am. Meeting rms. Business servs avail. Free airport transportation. Exercise equipt. Cr cds: A, C, D, DS, MC, V.

⬜ 🔲 ✕ 🔲 🔲

★★ **RED LION INN.** *700 W Broadway (59802). 406/728-3300; fax 406/728-4441. www.redlion.com.* 76 rms, 2 story. S, D $59-$99; each addl $10; under 18 free. Crib free. Pet accepted; $5. TV; cable (premium). Heated pool. Complimentary coffee in rms. Restaurant adj 6:30 am-10 pm. Ck-out noon. Meeting rm. Business servs avail. Sundries. Free airport, bus depot transportation. Downhill/x-country ski 20 mi. Cr cds: A, C, D, DS, MC, V.

⬜ 🔲 🔲 🔲 🔲 🔥 SC

★ **SLEEP INN.** *3425 Dore Ln (59801). 406/543-5883; fax 406/543-5883; toll-free 800/228-5050. www. sleepinn.com.* 59 rms, 3 story, 10 suites. Mid-May-Aug: S $59.95; D $64.95-$69.95; each addl $5; suites $74.95-$79.95; under 18 free; higher rates University of Montana graduation; lower rates rest of yr. Crib free. Pet accepted, some restrictions. TV; cable (premium). Complimentary continental bkfst. Restaurant opp 6:30 am-10 pm. Ck-out 11 am. Business servs avail. Bellhops. Indoor pool; whirlpool. Cr cds: A, D, DS, JCB, MC, V.

[D] [🐾] [⤢] [⛄] [🔥] [SC]

★ **SUPER 8.** *4703 N Reserve St (59802). 406/549-1199; fax 406/549-0677; res 888/900-9022. www. super8mt.com.* 58 rms, 2 story. May-Sept: S $45-$60; D $55-$65; each addl $3; under 13 free; lower rates rest of yr. Crib free. TV; cable (premium). Complimentary continental bkfst. Restaurant nearby. Ck-out 11 am. Sundries. Coin lndry. Free airport transportation. Cr cds: A, C, D, DS, MC, V.

[D] [✈] [⤢] [🔥]

★ **SUPER 8.** *3901 Brooks St (59801). 406/251-2255; fax 406/251-2989; toll-free 888/900-9010. www.super8mt. com.* 104 rms, 3 story. No elvtr. S $44.88; D $49.88-$54.88; each addl $3; ski plan. Crib free. TV; cable (premium). Restaurant nearby. Ck-out 11 am. Downhill/x-country ski 20 mi. Cr cds: A, DS, MC, V.

[D] [♿] [⤢] [✈]

★ **TRAVELODGE.** *420 W Broadway St (59802). 406/728-4500; fax 406/543-8118; toll-free 800/578-7878. www.travelodge.com.* 60 rms, 3 story, no ground floor rms. Mid-May-mid-Sept: S $49-$55; D $55-$62; each addl $2; suites $68-$82; under 18 free; lower rates rest of yr. Crib free. TV; cable (premium). Ck-out noon. Sundries. Downhill/x-country ski 10 mi. Balconies. Cr cds: A, C, D, DS, MC, V.

[⤢] [⤢] [🔥] [SC]

★ **VAL-U INN.** *3001 SW Brooks St (59801). 406/721-9600; fax 406/721-7208; toll-free 800/443-7777. www. valuinn.com.* 84 rms, 3 story. S $45-$55; D $60-$70; each addl $4; suites $90; under 12 free. Crib free. TV; cable (premium), VCR avail (movies). Complimentary continental bkfst. Restaurant nearby. Ck-out noon. Coin lndry. Meeting rm. Business servs avail. Airport transportation. Downhill/x-country ski 11 mi. Whirlpool. Sauna. Cr cds: A, C, D, DS, MC, V.

[⤢] [⤢] [🔥]

Hotel

★★ **DOUBLETREE HOTEL MISSOULA/EDGEWATER.** *100 Madison (59802). 406/728-3100. www. doubletree.com.* 182 rms, 2 story. S, D $125-$275; each addl $20; under 17 free. Crib avail. TV; cable (premium), VCR avail. Complimentary coffee, newspaper in rms. Restaurant 6 am-10 pm. Ck-out noon. Meeting rms. Business center. Gift shop. Exercise rm. Some refrigerators, minibars. Cr cds: A, D, DS, MC, V.

[🏃] [🔥] [🏃]

B&Bs/Small Inns

★★★ **THE EMILY A. BED & BREAKFAST.** *Mile Marker 20 Hwy 83 N, Seeley Lake (59868). 406/677-3474; res 800/977-4639. www.theemilya.com.* 5 rms, 3 share bath, 2 story, 1 suite, 1 guest house. No A/C. No rm phones. S, D $115; each addl $15; suite $150; guest house $150. Crib free. Pet accepted, some restrictions. Premium cable TV in common rm; VCR avail (movies). Complimentary full bkfst. Ck-out 11 am, ck-in 2-7 pm. Business servs avail. Luggage handling. Coin lndry. Airport transportation. X-country ski on site. Rec rm. Some balconies. Picnic tables, grills. Log interior and exterior; Western artworks. Totally nonsmoking. Cr cds: A, DS, MC, V.

[♿] [⤢] [⤢] [🔥]

★★ **GOLDSMITH'S BED & BREAKFAST INN.** *809 E Front St (59802). 406/721-6732; fax 406/543-0045. www.goldsmithsinn.com.* 7 rms, 2 story. May-Sept: S $60-$70; D $69-$89; suites $104-$114; under 10 free; lower rates rest of yr. Crib free. TV; cable. Complimentary full bkfst. Restaurant nearby. Ck-out 11 am, ck-in 1 pm. Picnic tables. Built 1911; Victorian decor; antiques. On Clark Fork river. Totally nonsmoking. Cr cds: DS, MC, V.

[♿] [⤢] [🔥]

Restaurants

★★ **DEPOT.** *201 W Railroad St (59801). 406/728-7007.* Hrs: 5:30-10:30 pm; Fri, Sat to 11 pm. Closed Thanksgiving, Dec 25. Res accepted. Bar 4 pm-2 am; Sun from 5 pm. Dinner $10.95-$22.95. Specializes in fresh seafood, prime rib, hand-cut steak. Salad bar. Parking. Outdoor dining. Cr cds: A, D, DS, MC, V.

D

★★ **ZIMORINO RED PIES OVER MONTANA.** *424 N Higgins Ave (59807). 406/721-7757. www. zimorinos.com.* Hrs: 5-10 pm. Closed hols. Italian menu. Bar. Dinner $8-$15. Child's menu. Specializes in pizza, chicken, manicotti. Italian bistro decor. Totally nonsmoking. Cr cds: A, DS, MC, V.

D

Polson

(B-2) *See also Bigfork*

Pop 3,283 **Elev** 2,931 ft
Area code 406 **Zip** 59860
Information Chamber of Commerce, 7 Third Ave W, PO Box 667; 406/883-5969
Web www.polsonchamber.com

At the south edge of Flathead Lake, Polson is the trade center for a productive farming area and a provisioning point for mountain trips. According to legend, Paul Bunyan dug the channel from Flathead Lake to Flathead River.

What to See and Do

Flathead Lake Cruise. *Port Polson Princess* departs from Kwataqnuk Resort for sightseeing around Flathead Lake. View the Narrows, Bird Island and Wildhorse Island. (June-Sept, daily) Res recommended. Phone 406/883-3636. ¢¢¢¢¢

Flathead Lake State Park. 28 mi long, 15 mi wide, average depth 220 ft; formed by glacial action. Fishing best in early spring, late fall; swimming, boating, waterskiing. There are six state park units surrounding the lake (also see BIGFORK). Phone 406/837-4196.

Big Arm Unit. Also fishing (joint state/tribal license required). Camping (no hookups, dump sta-

tion). 13 mi N, along W shore on US 93.

Elmo Unit. 16 mi N on US 93.

Finley Point Unit. 12 mi N off MT 35.

National Bison Range. Visitor center, exhibits, nature trails; picnic grounds near headquarters. Bison, antelope, bighorn sheep, deer, elk, and other big-game species roam over 18,500 acres of fenced-in range. A 19-mi self-guided tour route rises 2,000 ft over Mission Valley (mid-May-mid-Oct, daily). Motorcycles and bicycles are not permitted on the drives. 32 mi S on US 93, then 13 mi SW on US 212 to main entrance in Moiese. Phone 406/644-2211. ¢¢

Ninepipe and Pablo National Wildlife Refuges. More than 180 species of birds have been observed on these waterfowl refuges, incl ducks, geese, grebes, great blue herons and cormorants. Fishing permitted at certain times and areas in accordance with tribal and state regulations. Joint state/tribal recreation permit and fishing stamp required. Portions of (or all) refuges may be closed during waterfowl season and nesting period. Visitors may obtain more information, incl regulations, from Refuge Manager at National Bison Range, 132 Bison Range Rd, Moiese 59824. Pablo is 7 mi S on US 93; Ninepipe is 18 mi S on US 93. Phone 406/644-2211.

Polson-Flathead Historical Museum. Native American artifacts, farm and household items from the opening of the Flathead Reservation in 1910; home of Rudolph, a Scotch-Highland steer, who appeared in over 136 parades in five states and Canada; wildlife display and old stagecoach. (Summer, daily) 8th Ave and Main St. Phone 406/883-3049. **Donation**

River Rafting. Flathead Raft Company. Offers half-day whitewater trips on Lower Flathead River, leaving from Port Polson, S end of Flathead Lake. Phone 406/883-5838. ¢¢¢¢

Resort

★★ **BEST WESTERN KWATAQNUK RESORT.** *303 US Hwy 93 E (59860). 406/883-3636; fax 406/883-5392; res 800/882-6363. www.kwataqnuk.com.* 112 rms, 3 story.

Mid-June-mid-Sept: S $92-$113; D $102-$123; each addl $10; suites $179; under 12 free; lower rates rest of yr. Crib free. TV; cable (premium), VCR avail. 2 pools, 1 indoor; whirlpool. Coffee in rms. Restaurant 6 am-11 pm. Ck-out 11 am. Meeting rms. Business servs avail. Bellhops. Sundries. Gift shop. Game rm. Many balconies. On Flathead Lake; swimming, boat cruises (fee). Cr cds: A, C, D, DS, MC, V.

Red Lodge

(D-5) *See also Cooke City; also see Cody, WY*

Pop 1,958 **Elev** 5,553 ft
Area code 406 **Zip** 59068
Information Chamber of Commerce, PO Box 988; 406/446-1718
Web www.wtp.net/redlodge

The seat of Carbon County and a busy resort town, Red Lodge was, according to legend, named for a Native American band whose tepees were painted red. It is a most magnificent approach to Yellowstone National Park (see WYOMING) and gateway to the half-million-acre Beartooth-Absaroka Wilderness Area. A Ranger District office of the Custer National Forest (see HARDIN) is located here.

What to See and Do

Beartooth Highway (National Forest Scenic Byway). US 212 travels 64 mi over an 11,000-ft pass in the Beartooth Mts to the NE entrance of Yellowstone National Park. Includes Rock Creek Vista Point; Granite Peak, highest point in Montana (12,799 ft); a 345,000-acre portion of the Absaroka-Beartooth Wilderness; Grasshoper Glacier (see COOKE CITY). The area is characterized by alpine plateaus, rugged peaks, and hundreds of lakes. Offers winter sports and trout fishing. Views of glaciers, lakes, fields of alpine flowers, peaks and canyons. There are no service areas or gas stations on the 64-mi (2½-hr) stretch between Red Lodge and Cooke City. Beartooth Hwy is closed each winter between Red Lodge and Cooke City (closing dates depend on snow conditions) and is open approx June-Sept.

Skiing. Red Lodge Mountain Ski Area. Triple, two high-speed detachable quads, four double chairlifts, mitey-mite; patrol, school, rentals; snowmaking; restaurant, cafeteria, bar, daycare. Longest run 2½ mi; vertical drop 2,400 ft. (Thanksgiving-Apr, daily) 6 mi W off US 212, in Custer National Forest. Phone 406/446-2610.

Special Events

Winter Carnival. Red Lodge Mountain Resort. Ski races, snow sculpting, entertainment. Mar. Phone 406/446-1718.

Music Festival. Red Lodge Civic Center. Features performances by faculty members from schools throughout the country. June. Phone 406/446-1718.

Top of the World Bar. 30 mi SW via US 212. Citizens of Red Lodge welcome travelers with free beverages served from bar carved from snow bank atop 11,000-ft Beartooth Pass. July.

Scenic Beartooth Highway

Festival of Nations. Red Lodge Civic Center. Exhibits, nightly entertainment reflecting several European cultures. Art demonstrations and displays. Early-mid-Aug. Phone 406/446-1718.

Motels/Motor Lodges

★★ **BEST WESTERN LUPINE INN.** *702 S Hauser Ave (59068). 406/446-1321; fax 406/446-1465; res 888/567-1321. www.bestwesternlupine.com.* 46 rms, 2 story. S, D $49-$89; kit. unit $4 addl; under 12 free; higher rates special events; lower rates May and Labor Day-Thanksgiving. Crib free. Pet accepted, some restrictions. TV; cable (premium). Indoor pool, whirlpool. Playground. Complimentary continental bkfst. Restaurant nearby. Ck-out noon. Coin lndry. Meeting rms. Business servs avail. Bundles. Downhill/x-country ski 6 mi. Exercise equipt; sauna. Game rm. Some in-rm whirlpools. Some balconies. Cr cds: A, C, D, DS, MC, V.

★ **COMFORT INN.** *612 N Broadway (59068). 406/446-4469; fax 406/446-4669; toll-free 800/228-5150. www.comfortinn.com.* 55 rms, 2 story. July-Aug: S, D $50-$90; each addl $10; suites $99-$109; under 18 free; ski plans; lower rates rest of yr. Crib free. Pet accepted; $25 deposit. TV; cable, VCR avail. Complimentary continental bkfst. Ck-out 11 am. Meeting rms. Business servs avail. Downhill/x-country ski 6 mi. Indoor pool; whirlpool. Cr cds: A, C, D, DS, JCB, MC, V.

★ **SUPER 8.** *1223 S Broadway Ave (59068). 406/446-2288; fax 406/446-3162; res 800/813-8335. www.super8.com.* 50 rms, 2 story. S, D $39-$69; suites $59-$88. Crib free. Pet accepted, some restrictions. TV; cable (premium). Indoor pool; whirlpool. Complimentary continental bkfst. Ck-out 11 am. Coin lndry. Meeting rm. Downhill/x-country ski 5 mi. Some refrigerators, in-rm whirlpools; microwaves avail. Some rms with view of mountains. Cr cds: A, D, DS, MC, V.

Hotel

★★ **POLLARD HOTEL.** *2 N Broadway (59068). 406/446-0001; fax 406/446-0002; toll-free 800/765-5273. www.pollardhotel.com.* 39 rms, 5 with shower only, 3 story. Mid-June-mid-Sept, mid-Dec-mid-Apr: S, D $85-$110; each addl $20; suites $170-$185; ski plan; lower rates rest of yr. Crib free. TV; cable. Complimentary full bkfst. Restaurant (see GREENLEE'S). No rm serv. Ck-out noon. Meeting rms. Business servs avail. Concierge. Gift shop. Downhill/x-country ski 6 mi. Exercise rm; sauna. Whirlpool. Racquetball courts. Some in rm whirlpools. Restored hotel built 1893. Totally nonsmoking. Cr cds: A, DS, MC, V.

Resort

★★★ **ROCK CREEK RESORT.** *HC 49 (59068). 406/446-1111; fax 406/446-3688; res 800/667-1119.* 90 rms, 2-3 story, 39 kits. No A/C. S $88; D $88-$93; kit. units $99-$285. Crib free. TV; cable (premium), VCR avail. Indoor pool; whirlpool. Playground. Dining rm 7 am-2 pm. Ck-out 11 am, ck-in 3 pm. Coin lndry. Meeting rms. Business servs avail. Gift shop. Tennis. Downhill ski 11 mi. Exercise equipt. Lawn games. Some in-rm whirlpools; microwaves avail. Balconies. Cr cds: A, D, DS, MC, V.

Restaurants

★★★ **GREENLEE'S.** *2 N Broadway (59068). 406/446-0001. www.pollardhotel.com.* Hrs: 7 am-1:30 pm, 6-9 pm. Res accepted. French, American menu. Bar. Wine cellar. Bkfst $3.50-$5.75, lunch $5.50-$7.50, dinner $14.25-$27. Child's menu. Specialties: pistachio salmon, Montana ostrich, steaks, chops. Own desserts. Victorian hotel dining rm; original art. Totally nonsmoking. Cr cds: A, DS, MC, V.

★★ **OLD PINEY DELL.** *US 212 (59068). 406/446-1196.* Hrs: 5-10 pm; Sun 3-9 pm. Res accepted. No A/C. Continental menu. Bar. Dinner

$13.50-$22. Child's menu. Specializes in steak, seafood, chicken. View of Beartooth Mtns. Family-owned. Cr cds: A, D, MC, V.

D

Sidney (B-8)

Pop 5,217 **Elev** 1,931 ft
Area code 406 **Zip** 59270
Information Chamber of Commerce, 909 S Central; 406/482-1916
Web www.mtsid.mt1ib.org

Irrigation in Richland County produces bountiful crops of sugar beets and wheat, which are marketed at Sidney, the county seat. Oil fields, open-pit coal mining, and livestock feeding contribute to the town's economy.

What to See and Do

Fort Union Trading Post National Historic Site. (In Williston, ND) 7 mi W of Williston, North Dakota. 19 mi SW Hwy 1804. Phone 701/572-9083.

MonDak Heritage Center. Seventeen-unit street scene displaying historical artifacts of the area; changing art exhibits; historical and art library, gift shop. (Tues-Sun afternoons; daily in summer; closed hols) 120 3rd Ave SE. Phone 406/482-3500. ¢¢

Special Events

Peter Paddlefish Day. The sighting of Peter on his spawning run up the Yellowstone River indicates a normal run-off on the Yellowstone and a normal season. Phone 406/482-1916. Last Sat Apr.

Sunrise Festival of the Arts. Central Park. Second Sat July. Phone 406/433-1916.

Richland County Fair and Rodeo. Exhibits, livestock shows, petting zoo, carnival, PRCA rodeos, country western show. Phone 406/433-2801. Early Aug.

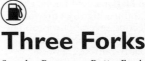

Three Forks

See also Bozeman, Butte, Ennis

Pop 1,203 **Elev** 4,080 ft
Area code 406 **Zip** 59752

In 1805, Lewis and Clark discovered the source of the Missouri River, beginning of the world's largest river chain, at the confluence of the Jefferson, Madison, and Gallatin rivers here. Native Americans resisted settlement of the valley, a favorite bison hunting ground, but before long it became a trading post headquarters for hunters and trappers.

What to See and Do

Lewis and Clark Caverns State Park. Underground wonderland of colorful rock formations; ¾-mi lighted path; 50°F. Two-hr (two-mi) guided tour (May-Sept, daily) Picnicking. Camping (no hookups, dump station). Visitor center. Standard fees. 19 mi W on MT 2, milepost 271. Phone 406/287-3541. ¢¢¢

Madison Buffalo Jump State Monument. Native American hunting technique of herding charging buffalo over cliffs is illustrated. Hiking. Picnicking. Day use only. E on I-90, then 7 mi S on Buffalo Jump Rd. Phone 406/285-4880. ¢¢

Missouri Headwaters State Park. Where Lewis and Clark discovered the source of the Missouri. Fishing; boating (ramp). Picnicking. Camping (no hookups, dump station). Standard fees. 3 mi E on I-90, then E on MT Secondary 205, then 3 mi N on MT Secondary 286. Phone 406/994-4042.

Motel/Motor Lodge

★ **FORT THREE FORKS.** *10776 US 287 (59752). 406/285-3233; fax 406/285-4362; toll-free 800/477-5690. www.fortthreeforks.com.* 25 rms, 2 story. June-Sept: S $38-$42; D $46-$50; each addl $4; suites $75; under 12 free; lower rates rest of yr. Crib $5. Pet accepted; $5. TV; cable (premium). Complimentary continental bkfst. Restaurant adj 6 am-8 pm. Ck-out 11 am. Coin lndry. Meeting rm.

Business servs avail. Cr cds: A, D, DS, MC, V.

Virginia City

(D-3) *See also Ennis*

Settled 1863 **Pop** 142 **Elev** 5,822 ft **Area code** 406 **Zip** 59755

Information Bovey Restoration, PO Box 338; 406/843-5377 or 800/648-7588. Chamber of Commerce; 800/829-2969

On May 26, 1863, gold was found in Alder Gulch. The old days of the rough 'n' tough West are rekindled in this restored gold boomtown, once the capital of the territory. Alder Gulch (Virginia and Nevada cities) sprouted when six men who had escaped from Native Americans discovered history's richest placer deposit. Ten thousand gold miners arrived within a month, followed by bands of desperadoes; 190 murders were committed in seven months. Vigilantes hunted down 21 road agents and discovered that the sheriff was the leader of the criminals. Nearly $300 million in gold was washed from Alder Gulch, but the area faded as the diggings became less productive and Nevada City became a ghost town. In 1946 a restoration program began, which has brought back much of the early mining-town atmosphere.

What to See and Do

Boot Hill. Graves of five criminals hanged by the vigilantes.

Restored buildings. Includes the offices of the Montana *Post*, first newspaper in the state; the Gilbert Brewery, dressmaker's shop, Wells Fargo Express office, livery stable, barbershop, blacksmith shop, general store, many others. Phone 406/843-5377. Includes

> **Gilbert's Brewery.** Virginia City's first brewery was built in 1864. The main building has been restored and original brewery is still inside. Musical variety shows (Mid-June-mid-Sept, Mon and Wed-Sun). E Cover St. Phone 406/843-5377. ¢¢¢

Nevada City. Authentic buildings incl early mining camp stores, homes, school, offices. Music Hall has large collection of mechanical musical machines. (Memorial Day-mid-Sept, daily) 1½ mi W on MT 287. **FREE**

Nevada City Depot. Houses steam railroad museum (fee) of early-day engines and cars. Train ride to Virginia City. (Early June-Labor Day, daily; fee)

Robbers' Roost. Old-time stage station often used by outlaws. 15 mi W on MT 287.

St. Paul's Episcopal Church. (Elling Memorial) (1902). Built on site of 1867 building; oldest Protestant congregation in state. Tiffany windows. Idaho St.

Thompson-Hickman Memorial Museum. Relics of the gold camps. (May-Sept, daily) Wallace St. Phone 406/843-5238. **Donation**

Virginia City-Madison County Historical Museum. Traces western Montana history. (Early June-Labor Day, daily) Wallace St. ¢¢

Special Event

Classic melodramas. In Old Opera House, foot of Wallace St. Virginia City Players present 19th-century entertainment. Tues-Sun. Res required. Phone 406/843-5314. Early June-Labor Day.

West Yellowstone (E-4)

Pop 913 **Elev** 6,666 ft **Area code** 406 **Zip** 59758

Information Chamber of Commerce, 30 Yellowstone Ave, PO Box 458; 406/646-7701

At the west entrance to Yellowstone National Park (see WYOMING), this town serves as a hub for incoming tourists. Not too long ago, West Yellowstone was abandoned and snowbound in the winter; today winter sports and attractions allow the town to serve visitors all year. A Ranger District office of the Gallatin National Forest (see BOZEMAN) is located here.

What to See and Do

Grizzly Wolf & Discovery Center. Bear and wolf preserve and educational facility. Interactive exhibits, films, presentations. Wildlife-themed gift shop. (Daily; closed hols) 201 S Canyon St. Phone 406/646-7001. ¢¢¢

Interagency Aerial Fire Control Center. A US Forest Service facility. Guided tour by smokejumpers who explain firefighting techniques. (Late June-Labor Day, daily) 2 mi N on US 191. Phone 406/646-7691. **FREE**

Madison River Canyon Earthquake Area. Incl Quake Lake, formed by earthquake Aug 17, 1959. This area, with its slides and faults, is a graphic demonstration of earthquake damage. Camping (Mid-June-mid-Sept; Beaver Creek Campground, fee/night). Visitor Center (on US 287, 22 mi W of US 191) with talks, exhibits; list of self-guided tours (Memorial Day-Labor Day, daily). Road through area (all yr). 8 mi N on US 191, then 17 mi W on US 287, in Gallatin National Forest (see BOZEMAN). For details inquire at the Chamber of Commerce or at the US Forest Service Office on US 191/287 N of town; or contact PO Box 520. Phone 406/646-7369. ¢¢

Sightseeing tours.

Buffalo Bus Lines. Phone 406/646-9564.

Gray Line bus tours. For info Phone 800/523-3102.

Xanterra Parks & Resorts. Offers guided snowcoach tours and cross-country ski trips through Yellowstone National Park (see WYOMING) departing from West Yellowstone and other locations surrounding the park (Mid-Dec-early Mar). Summer season offers full-day bus tours, boat tours and horseback rides in the park (June-Aug). Res recommended. Phone 307/344-7311.

Yellowstone IMAX Theatre. Six-story-high screen shows "Yellowstone," a film interpreting the history, wildlife, geothermal activity and grandeur of America's first national park. Exhibits incl wildlife photography, props used

in film, and "Effects of the Yellowstone Hot Spot." (Daily, shows hrly) 101 S Canyon St. Phone 406/646-4100. ¢¢¢

Special Events

Yellowstone Rendezvous Marathon Ski Race. Rendezvous Ski Trails. Mar. Phone 406/646-7701.

World Snowmobile Expo. Third wkend Mar. Phone 406/646-7701.

Playmill Theater. 29 Madison Ave. Musical comedies and melodramas. Daily exc Sun. Phone 406/646-7757. Memorial Day-Labor Day.

Motels/Motor Lodges

★ **COMFORT INN.** *638 Madison Ave, W Yellowstone (59758).* 406/646-4212; fax 406/646-4212; toll-free 888/264-2466. www.comfortinn.com. 79 rms, 3 story, 7 suites. June-Sept: S, D $59-$129; each addl $8; suites $189; under 18 free; lower rates rest of yr. Crib avail. TV; cable (premium). Complimentary continental bkfst. Ck-out 10 am. Meeting rms. Business servs avail. Bellhops. Sundries. Coin lndry. Exercise equipt. Indoor pool; whirlpool. Microwave, wet bar in suites. Cr cds: A, C, D, DS, JCB, MC, V.
🄓 ⬤ ✦ ≈ 🛍 ✈ ⊠ 🐾 SC

★ **DAYS INN.** *301 Madison (59758).* 406/646-7656; fax 406/646-7965; toll-free 800/548-9551. www.daysinn.com. 45 rms, 2 story. June-Oct, Dec-mid-Mar: S, D $89; each addl $8; suites $165; kit. unit $152; under 13 free; lower rates rest of yr. Crib free. TV; cable (premium). Indoor pool; whirlpool. Restaurant adj 7 am-10 pm. Ck-out 11 am. Business servs avail. Some refrigerators. Cr cds: A, D, DS, MC, V.
🄓 ⬤ ✦ ≈ ⊠ 🐾

★★ **FAIRFIELD INN.** *105 S Electric St, W Yellowstone (59758).* 406/646-4892; fax 406/646-4893; res 800/565-6803. www.fairfieldinn.com. 77 rms, 3 story, 4 suites. Mid-June-mid-Sept: S, D $120-$130; each addl $8; suites $150-$160; under 18 free; lower rates rest of yr. Crib free. TV; cable (premium). Complimentary continental bkfst. Restaurant nearby. Ck-out noon. Business servs avail. In-rm modem link. Coin lndry. X-country ski ½ blk. Indoor pool; whirlpool. Cr cds: A, DS, MC, V.

★★ **GRAY WOLF INN & SUITES.** *250 S Canyon St (59758). 406/646-0000; fax 406/646-4232; res 800/852-8602. www.graywolf-inn.com.* 102 rms, 3 story, 19 suites. June-Sept: S, D $129; each addl $10; suites $190; under 18 free; higher rates special events; lower rates rest of yr. Crib free. TV; cable (premium), VCR in suites. Complimentary continental bkfst. Complimentary coffee in rms. Restaurant nearby. Ck-out 11 am. Meeting rm. Business servs avail. Bellhops. Sundries. Coin lndry. Free garage parking. X-country ski 3 blks. Indoor pool; whirlpool. Sauna. Refrigerator, microwave, wet bar in suites. Cr cds: A, C, D, DS, JCB, MC, V.

★★ **HOLIDAY INN SUNSPREE RESORT.** *315 Yellowstone Ave (59758). 406/646-7365; fax 406/646-4433; res 800/465-4329. www.yellowstone-conf-hotels.com.* 123 rms, 3 story, 36 suites. Mid-June-Sept: S, D $129-$200; each addl $8; under 12 free; lower rates rest of yr. Crib free. TV; cable. Indoor pool; whirlpool. Complimentary coffee in rms. Restaurant 6:30 am-10 pm. Bar 11-2 am. Ck-out 11 am. Coin lndry. Meeting rms. Business servs avail. Bellhops. Valet serv. Gift shop. Exercise equipt; sauna. Refrigerators, microwaves; some in-rm whirlpools. Cr cds: A, DS, MC, V.

★★ **KELLY INN.** *104 S Canyon (59758). 406/646-4544; fax 406/646-9838. www.wyellowstone.com/kellyinn.* 78 rms, 3 story. June-Sept: S, D $120-$130; each addl $8; under 12 free; lower rates rest of yr. Crib free. Pet accepted. TV; cable. Complimentary continental bkfst. Restaurant nearby. Ck-out 11 am. Business servs avail. Coin lndry. X-country ski 3 blks. Indoor pool; whirlpool. Sauna. Many refrigerators, microwaves. Cr cds: A, D, DS, MC, V.

★★ **STAGECOACH INN.** *209 Madison Ave (59758). 406/646-7381; fax 406/646-9575; toll-free 800/842-2882; res 800/800-8000. www.yellowstone*

inn.com. 89 rms, 1-2 story. Early June-mid-Sept: S $79-$125; D $79-$131; each addl $6; under 12 free; lower rates rest of yr. Crib free. TV; cable. Restaurant 6:30 am-10 pm. Bar 5 pm-2 am; entertainment Tues-Sat (in season). Ck-out 11 am. Coin lndry. Meeting rms. Gift shop. X-country ski ¼ mi. Sauna. Whirlpools. Snowmobiling. Cr cds: A, C, D, DS, MC, V.

★ **SUPER 8 LIONSHEAD RESORT.** *1545 Targhee Pass Hwy, W Yellowstone (59758). 406/646-9584; fax 406/646-7404; res 800/800-8000. www.super8.com.* 44 rms, 2 story. Memorial Day-Labor Day: S, D $46-$104; each addl $5; suites $85-$131. under 13 free; lower rates rest of yr. Crib $5. TV; cable (premium). Playground. Restaurant 7-11 am, 5-9:30 pm. Ck-out 11 am. Coin lndry. Sauna. Whirlpool. Cr cds: A, C, D, DS, MC, V.

Restaurant

★★ **THREE BEAR.** *205 Yellowstone Ave (59758). 406/646-7811.* Hrs: 7-11 am, 5-10 pm. Closed Dec 25; mid-Mar-early-May, mid-Oct-mid-Dec. No A/C. Bar 4 pm-midnight. Bkfst $3.25-$8.75, dinner $10.95-$20.95. Child's menu. Specializes in seafood, hand-cut steaks, pasta. Family-owned. Totally nonsmoking. Cr cds: MC, V.

Whitefish

(A-2) *See also Columbia Falls, Kalispell*

Pop 4,368 **Elev** 3,036 ft
Area code 406 **Zip** 59937

Information Flathead Convention & Visitor Bureau, 15 Depot Park, Kalispell, 59901; 406/756-9091 or 800/543-3105
Web www.fcvb.org

On the shore of Whitefish Lake, this community prospers from tourism and railroading. The town is headquarters for a four state summer vacation area and is a winter ski center. A growing forest products industry and the railroad constitute the other side of Whitefish's economy. A Ranger District office of the Flathead National Forest (see KALISPELL) is located here.

What to See and Do

Big Mountain Ski and Summer Resort. Double, four triple, two high-speed quad chairlifts, T-bar, platter lift, patrol; school, rentals; hotels, restaurants, bars, cafeteria, concession area; sleigh rides; nursery. Longest run 3½ mi; vertical drop 2,500 ft. (Late Nov-mid-Apr, daily) Cross-country trails. Gondola (also operates in summer) provides views of Rockies, Flathead Valley; travels 6,800 ft to summit of Big Mt. Summer activites (June-early Oct): gondola rides overlooking Glacier National Park (see), hiking, mountain biking, tennis; outdoor theater, events. 8 mi N on County 487 in Flathead National Forest (see KALISPELL); shuttle bus trips daily in winter. Phone 800/858-5439.

Glacier National Park. (see)

⊠ **Whitefish Lake.** Seven mi long, two mi wide. Studded with resorts, particularly on E shore; swimming, waterskiing; fishing; sailing; picnicking. On lake is

Whitefish State Park. Swimming; fishing; boating (ramp). Picnicking. Camping (no hookups). Standard fees. ½ mi W on US 93, milepost 129, then 1 mi N. Phone 406/862-3991.

Special Event

Winter Carnival. First wkend Feb. Phone 406/862-3501.

Motels/Motor Lodges

★★ **BEST WESTERN ROCKY MOUNTAIN LODGE.** *6510 US 93 S (59937). 406/862-2569; fax 406/862-1154; toll-free 800/862-2569. www.rockymtnlodge.com.* 79 rms, 3 story. July-Aug: S $69-$129; D $79-$139; each addl $10; suites $149; under 12 free; ski, golf plans; lower rates rest of yr. Crib free. TV; cable. Heated pool; whirlpool. Complimentary continental bkfst. Restaurant nearby. Ck-out 11 am. Coin lndry. Meeting rms. Downhill ski 8 mi; x-country ski

1 mi. Exercise equipt. Some in-rm whirlpools, fireplaces; microwaves avail. Cr cds: A, C, D, DS, MC, V.

★★ **KANDAHAR LODGE.** *3824 Big Mountain Rd (59937). 406/862-6098; fax 406/862-6095; toll-free 800/862-6094. www.kandaharlodge.com.* 48 rms, 4 story, 10 suites. Feb-Mar, July-Aug: S, D 129-$229; each addl $10; suite $275; kit. $179; under 12 free; higher rates wk of Dec 25, last 2 wks of Feb; lower rates rest of yr. Crib avail. TV; cable, VCR avail. Restaurant 7 am-9:30 pm. Bar 4 pm-midnight. Ck-out 11 am. Coin lndry. Meeting rms. Business servs avail. Downhill/x-country ski on site. Sauna. Whirlpool. Cr cds: A, DS, MC, V.

★★ **PINE LODGE.** *920 Spokane Ave (59937). 406/862-7600; fax 406/862-7616; res 800/305-7463. www.the pinelodge.com.* 76 rms, 4 story, 25 suites. June-Sept: S $60-$120; D $70-$130; suites $125-$195; under 18 free; ski plan; lower rates rest of yr. Crib $5. Pet accepted, some restrictions. TV; cable. Indoor pool; whirlpool. Complimentary continental bkfst. Ck-out 11 am. Coin lndry. Meeting rms. Business servs avail. Valet serv. Free airport transportation. Exercise equipt. Game rm. Refrigerator, microwave in suites. Cr cds: A, C, D, DS, ER, MC, V.

★ **SUPER 8 MOTEL.** *800 Spokane Ave (59937). 406/862-8255; res 800/800-8000. www.super8.com.* 40 rms, 3 story. No elvtr. July-Aug: S, D $40-$80; each addl $5; lower rates rest of yr. Crib free. Pet accepted, some restrictions; $5. TV; cable (premium). Complimentary coffee in lobby. Ck-out 11 am. Whirlpool. Grill. Cr cds: A, C, D, DS, MC, V.

Resort

★★ **GROUSE MOUNTAIN LODGE.** *2 Fairway Dr (59937). 406/862-3000; fax 406/862-0326; toll-free 800/321-8822. www.montanasfinest.com.* 133 rms, 3 story, 12 suites. July-Aug, Dec: D $189; each addl $10; suites $229; under 12 free; ski, golf, rafting plans; lower rates rest of yr. Crib free. TV;

cable (premium). Indoor pool; whirlpools. Dining rm 7 am-2 pm, 5-10 pm. Box lunches. Bar 11-2 am; entertainment Fri, Sat. Ck-out 11 am, ck-in 4 pm. Grocery 1 mi. Coin lndry. Package store ½ mi. Meeting rms. Business servs avail. Bellhops. Airport, RR station, ski area transportation. Tennis. 36-hole golf, greens fee $38, pro, putting green, driving range. Downhill ski 8 mi; x-country ski adj. Sauna. Game rm. Some refrigerators, in-rm whirlpools. Some balconies. Rustic, elegant lodge. Cr cds: A, C, D, DS, ER, MC, V.

B&B/Small Inn

★★ **GOOD MEDICINE LODGE.** 537 Wisconsin Ave (59937). 406/862-5488; fax 406/862-5489; toll-free 800/860-5488. www.wtp.net/go/goodrx. 9 rms, 2 with shower only, 2 story. Some A/C. Mid-May-Oct: S $85-95; D $95-$105; each addl $30; suites $135-$190; under 11 free; ski plan; lower rates rest of yr. Closed Nov. Complimentary full bkfst. Restaurant nearby. Ck-out 11 am, ck-in 3 pm. Lawn games. Some balconies. Rustic mountain decor. Totally nonsmoking. Cr cds: A, DS, MC, V.

Restaurant

★★ **FENDERS.** US 93 N (59937). 406/752-3000. Hrs: 11 am-3 pm, 5-10 pm. Res accepted. Bar. Dinner $10-$40. Child's menu. Specializes in prime rib, seafood. Many collectibles, old cars. Totally nonsmoking. Cr cds: A, DS, MC, V.

White Sulphur Springs

(C-4) See also Bozeman, Helena

Pop 963 **Elev** 5,100 ft **Area code** 406 **Zip** 59645

Mineral springs, as well as fine hunting and fishing, make this a popular summer and fall resort town. It lies in a mile-high valley ringed by mountains—the Castles, Crazies, and Big and Little Belts. Agates may still be found in the area. A Ranger District office of the Lewis and Clark National Forest (see GREAT FALLS) is located here.

What to See and Do

Skiing. Showdown Ski Area. Triple, double chairlift, Pomalift, free beginners tow; patrol, school, rentals; cafeteria, bar; day care. Longest run two mi; vertical drop 1,400 ft. (Late Nov-mid-Apr, Tues-Sun) 29 mi N on US 89, in Lewis and Clark National Forest. Phone 236/552-2800. ¢¢¢¢

Wolf Point (B-7)

Pop 2,880 **Elev** 1,997 ft
Area code 406 **Zip** 59201

Information Chamber of Commerce & Agriculture, 218 3rd Ave S, Suite B; 406/653-2012

During the winters of the 1870s, trappers poisoned wolves and hauled the frozen carcasses to this point on the Missouri River for spring shipment to St. Louis. Wolf Point is the seat of Roosevelt County and a trading point for oil, wheat, and cattle. Hunting for antelope, deer, and sharp-tailed and sage grouse is popular here.

Special Events

Wild Horse Stampede. One of Montana's best and oldest rodeos. Contact Chamber of Commerce and Agriculture for info. Second wkend July. Phone 406/653-2200.

Wadopana Powwow. Phone 406/653-3476. First wkend Aug.

OREGON

This is the end of the famous Oregon Trail, over which came scores of pioneers in covered wagons. The state abounds in the romance of the country's westward expansion. Meriwether Lewis and William Clark, sent by President Thomas Jefferson to explore the vast area bought in the Louisiana Purchase, ended their explorations here. This was also the scene of John Jacob Astor's fortune-making fur trade and that of Hudson's Bay Company, which hoped to keep the area for England, as well as gold rushes and the traffic of stately clippers of the China trade.

English Captain James Cook saw the coast in 1778. Others had seen it before him and others after him, but it remained for Lewis and Clark to discover what a prize Oregon was. On their return to St. Louis in 1806 they spread the word. In 1811, Astor's Pacific Fur Company built its post at Astoria, only to be frightened into selling to the British North West Company during the War of 1812. (In 1818 it again became US territory.) Other fur traders, missionaries, salmon anglers, and travelers followed them, but the Oregon territory was far away and hard to reach. The first true settlers did not make their way there until 1839, four years before a great wagon train blazed the Oregon Trail.

Cattle and sheep were driven up from California and land was cleared for farms. Oregon was settled not by people hungry for gold, but by pioneers looking for good land that could support them. The Native Americans resented the

Population: 2,842,321
Area: 97,060 square miles
Elevation: 0-11,239 feet
Peak: Mount Hood (Between Clackamas, Hood River Counties)
Entered Union: February 14, 1859 (33rd state)
Capital: Salem
Motto: The Union
Nickname: Beaver State
Flower: Oregon Grape
Bird: Western Meadowlark
Tree: Douglas Fir
Fair: August 21-September 1, 2003, in Salem
Time Zone: Mountain and Pacific
Website:
www.traveloregon.com

An afternoon of cycling along the coast of Oregon

early settlers and fought them until 1880. The Oregon Territory, established in 1848, received a flood of immigrants; they continued to arrive after statehood was proclaimed, under President James Buchanan, 11 years later.

The rich forests grew rapidly in the moist climate west of the mountains called the Cascades, and lumber was an early product of this frontier. The streams were full of fish, the woods offered nuts and berries, and the lush, green scenery lifted hearts and hopes at the end of the weary journey. The rivers—Columbia, Willamette, Rogue, and many others—offered transportation to the sea. Steamboats plied the Willamette and Columbia as early as 1850. The first full ship's cargo of wheat went from Portland to Liverpool in 1868, and when the railroad reached Portland in 1883, the world began receiving the fish, grain, lumber, and livestock that Oregon was ready to deliver.

Vast rivers provide more than transportation. Dammed, they are the source of abundant electric power and of water used to irrigate farms east of the Cascades. Timber is still important; a quarter of Oregon is national forest land. Sustained yield practices by the big lumber companies ensure a continuing supply.

One of the most beautiful drives in Oregon extends from Portland (see) to The Dalles (see) along the Columbia River. Here is the spectacular Columbia Gorge, designated a National Scenic Area, where waterfalls, streams, and mountains abound. The area offers many recreational activities such as camping—the Cascade Locks Marina Park lies four miles east of the Bonneville Dam (see HOOD RIVER), skiing (see MOUNT HOOD NATIONAL FOREST), snowmobiling, windsurfing, and hiking.

Whether one's taste is for an ocean beach, a ski slope, a mountain lake, or ranch life with riding and rodeos, the visitor who loves the outdoors or the American West loves Oregon. Each year, millions of tourists enjoy the state's magnificent coastline, blue lakes, mountains, and forests.

When to Go/Climate

Temperatures along the Pacific coast are mild, while Portland and the Willamette Valley experience more extreme weather conditions. Heavy snow falls in the Cascades; and to the east there's a high desert area that experiences typical desert heat and dry conditions.

AVERAGE HIGH/LOW TEMPERATURES (°F)

BURNS

Jan 34/13	May 66/36	Sept 74/36
Feb 40/19	June 74/42	Oct 62/28
Mar 48/25	July 85/47	Nov 45/22
Apr 57/29	Aug 83/45	Dec 35/15

PORTLAND

Jan 45/34	May 67/47	Sept 75/52
Feb 51/36	June 74/53	Oct 64/45
Mar 56/39	July 80/57	Nov 53/40
Apr 61/41	Aug 80/57	Dec 46/35

Parks and Recreation Finder

Directions to and information about the parks and recreation areas below are given under their respective town/city sections. Please refer to those sections for details.

NATIONAL PARK AND RECREATION AREAS

Key to abbreviations. I.H.S. = International Historic Site; I.P.M. = International Peace Memorial; N.B. = National Battlefield; N.B.P. = National Battlefield Park; N.B.C. = National Battlefield and Cemetery; N.C.A. = National Conservation

Area; N.E.M. = National Expansion Memorial; N.F. = National Forest;
N.G. = National Grassland; N.H.P. = National Historical Park; N.H.C. = National
Heritage Corridor; N.H.S. = National Historic Site; N.L. = National Lakeshore;
N.M. = National Monument; N.M.P. = National Military Park;
N.Mem. = National Memorial; N.P. = National Park; N.Pres. = National Preserve;
N.R.A. = National Recreational Area; N.R.R. = National Recreational River;
N.Riv. = National River; N.S. = National Seashore; N.S.R. = National Scenic
Riverway; N.S.T. = National Scenic Trail; N.Sc. = National Scientific Reserve;
N.V.M. = National Volcanic Monument.

Place Name	Listed Under
Crater Lake N.P.	same
Deschutes N.F.	BEND
Fort Clatsop N.Mem.	same
Fremont N.F.	LAKEVIEW
Hells Canyon N.R.	JOSEPH
John Day Fossil Beds N.M.	JOHN DAY
Malheur N.F.	JOHN DAY
Mount Hood N.F.	same
Newberry N.V.M.	BEND
Ochoco N.F.	PRINEVILLE
Oregon Caves N.M.	same
Oregon Dunes N.R.	REEDSPORT
Rogue River N.F.	MEDFORD
Siskiyou N.F.	GRANTS PASS
Siuslaw N.F.	CORVALLIS
Umatilla N.F.	PENDLETON
Umpqua N.F.	ROSEBURG
Wallowa-Whitman N.F.	BAKER CITY
Willamette N.F.	EUGENE
Winema N.F.	KLAMATH FALLS

STATE PARK AND RECREATION AREAS

Key to abbreviations. I.P. = Interstate Park; S.A.P. = State Archaeological Park;
S.B. = State Beach; S.C.A. = State Conservation Area; S.C.P. = State Conservation
Park; S.Cp. = State Campground; S.F. = State Forest; S.G. = State Garden;
S.H.A. = State Historic Area; S.H.P. = State Historic Park; S.H.S. = State Historic
Site; S.M.P. = State Marine Park; S.N.A. = State Natural Area; S.P. = State Park;
S.P.C. = State Public Campground; S.R. = State Reserve; S.R.A. = State Recreation
Area; S.Res. = State Reservoir; S.Res.P. = State Resort Park; S.R.P. = State Rustic
Park.

Place Name	Listed Under
Benson S.R.A.	PORTLAND
Beverly Beach S.P.	NEWPORT
Bullards Beach S.P.	BANDON
Cape Arago S.P.	COOS BAY
Cape Blanco S.P.	PORT ORFORD
Cape Lookout S.P.	TILLAMOOK
Cape Sebastian S.P.	GOLD BEACH
Carl G. Washburne Memorial S.P.	FLORENCE
Catherine Creek S.P.	LA GRANDE
Champoeg S.H.A.	NEWBERG
Cline Falls S.P.	REDMOND
Collier Memorial S.P.	KLAMATH FALLS
The Cove Palisades S.P.	MADRAS

CALENDAR HIGHLIGHTS

MAY

Boatnik Festival (Grants Pass). Riverside Park. Parade, concessions, carnival rides, boat races, entertainment. A 25-mile whitewater hydroboat race from Riverside Park to Hellgate Canyon and back. Square dance festival at Josephine County Fairgrounds. Phone 800/547-5927.

JUNE

Return of the Sternwheeler Days (Hood River). Celebration of the sternwheeler *Columbia Gorge's* return to home port for the summer. Wine and cheese tasting, crafts, food. Phone 541/374-8619.

Sandcastle Contest (Cannon Beach). Nationally known event features sand sculptures on beach. Phone 503/436-2623.

Portland Rose Festival (Portland). Held for more than 80 years, this festival include the Grand Floral Parade (reservations required for indoor parade seats) and two other parades; band competition; rose show; championship auto racing; hot-air balloons; air show; carnival; Navy ships. Phone 503/227-2681.

Scandinavian Midsummer Festival (Astoria). Parade, folk dancing, display booths, arts and crafts demonstrations, Scandinavian food. Phone Astoria Warrenton Chamber of Commerce, 503/325-6311.

Bach Festival (Eugene). Numerous concerts by regional and international artists; master classes, family activities. Phone 800/457-1486.

JULY

Oregon Coast Music Festival (Coos Bay). Variety of musical presentations ranging from jazz and dance to chamber and symphonic music. Phone 877/897-9350.

Da Vinci Days (Corvallis). Festival celebrating the relationship between art, science, and technology. Phone 541/757-6363.

Salem Art Fair and Festival (Salem). Bush's Pasture Park. Arts and crafts booths and demonstrations, children's art activities and parade, ethnic folk arts, performing arts, street painting, 5K run, food; tours of historic Bush House. Phone 503/581-2228.

AUGUST

Oregon State Fair (Salem). Fairgrounds. Horse racing, wine competition and tastings, agricultural exhibits, horse show, livestock, food, carnival, entertainment. Phone 503/378-FAIR.

SEPTEMBER

Pendleton Round-Up (Pendleton). Stadium. Rodeo and pageantry of Old West, annually since 1910. Gathering of Native Americans, PRCA working cowboys, and thousands of visitors. Phone 800/457-6336.

Crown Point S.P.	PORTLAND
Dabney S.P.	PORTLAND
Darlingtonia S.P.	FLORENCE
Devil's Elbow S.P.	FLORENCE
Devil's Lake S.P.	LINCOLN CITY
Devil's Punch Bowl S.P.	NEWPORT
Ecola S.P.	CANNON BEACH
Emigrant Springs S.P.	PENDLETON
Face Rock S.P.	BANDON

Farewell Bend S.P.	ONTARIO
Fogarty Creek S.P.	DEPOE BAY
Fort Stevens S.P.	ASTORIA
Guy W. Talbot S.P.	PORTLAND
Harris Beach S.P.	BROOKINGS
Hat Rock S.P.	UMATILLA
Hilgard Junction S.R.A.	LA GRANDE
Humbug Mountain S.P.	PORT ORFORD
Jackson F. Kimball S.P.	KLAMATH FALLS
Jessie M. Honeyman Memorial S.P.	FLORENCE
Joseph P. Stewart S.P.	MEDFORD
Lake Owyhee S.P.	ONTARIO
LaPine S.P.	BEND
Lewis and Clark S.P.	PORTLAND
Loeb S.P.	BROOKINGS
Mayer S.P.	THE DALLES
Milo McIver S.P.	OREGON CITY
Neptune S.P.	YACHATS
Ona Beach S.P.	NEWPORT
Ontario S.P.	ONTARIO
Oswald West S.P.	CANNON BEACH
Peter Skene Ogden Wayside S.P.	REDMOND
Pilot Butte S.P.	BEND
Rooster Rock S.P.	PORTLAND
Saddle Mountain S.P.	SEASIDE
Samuel H. Boardman S.P.	BROOKINGS
Shore Acres S.P.	COOS BAY
Silver Falls S.P.	SILVERTON
Smith Rock S.P.	REDMOND
South Beach S.P.	NEWPORT
Sunset Bay S.P.	COOS BAY
Tou Velle S.P.	MEDFORD
Tumalo S.P.	BEND
Ukiah-Dale Forest S.P.	PENDLETON
Umpqua Lighthouse S.P.	REEDSPORT
Unity Lake S.P.	BAKER CITY
Valley of the Rogue S.P.	GRANTS PASS
Wallowa Lake S.P.	JOSEPH
Willamette Stone S.P.	PORTLAND
William M. Tugman S.P.	REEDSPORT
Yachats S.R.A.	YACHATS
Yaquina Bay S.P.	NEWPORT

Water-related activities, hiking, riding, various other sports, picnicking, and visitor centers, as well as camping, are available in many of these areas. Many camping facilities in state parks stay open year-round, while others remain open as long as weather permits, usually March-October. All campgrounds are open mid-April-late October. Campers are limited to 10 days in any 14-day period from May 15-September 14; and 14 days out of 18 the rest of the year. Discount rates are available at most campgrounds October-April. Summer fees per night: primitive campsite $8-$14; tent sites $14-$17; electrical sites $13-$19; full hookup sites $17-$20; extra vehicle $7; firewood is available (fee varies). Campsites may be reserved at 25 state parks throughout the year with a $6 fee plus first night's camping rate. A day-use fee of $3 is charged for each motor vehicle entering 24 state parks. For more information, contact Oregon Parks and Recreation Department, 1115 Commercial St NE, Salem 97301. For campsite reservations phone 800/452-5687; for information phone 503/378-6305 or 800/551-6949.

SKI AREAS

Place Name	Listed Under
Anthony Lakes Ski Area	BAKER CITY
Mount Ashland Ski Area	ASHLAND
Mount Bachelor Ski Area	BEND
Mount Hood Meadows Ski Area	MOUNT HOOD NATIONAL FOREST
Spout Springs Ski Area	PENDLETON
Timberline Lodge	MOUNT HOOD NATIONAL FOREST
Williamette Pass Ski Area	EUGENE

FISHING AND HUNTING

Nonresident fishing license, annual $48.50; seven day license $34.75; combined angling harvest card, $16.50; one-day license, $8. Nonresident hunting license, annual $58.50. Special tags required in addition to license for big game. All licenses include agent-writing fee.

Oregon has 15,000 miles of streams, hundreds of lakes, and surf and deep-sea fishing. Fishing is good for Chinook and coho salmon, steelhead, rainbow and cutthroat trout, striped bass, perch, crappies, bluegill, catfish, and many other varieties. The hunter will find mule and blacktail deer, elk, ring-necked pheasant, Hungarian and chukar partridge, quail, blue and ruffed grouse, band-tailed pigeons, mourning doves, waterfowl, jackrabbits, coyote, fox, and bear.

For synopses of the latest angling and big-game regulations, contact Oregon Department of Fish and Wildlife, PO Box 59, Portland 97207; 503/872-5268.

Driving Information

Safety belts are mandatory for all persons anywhere in vehicle. Under age four (or 40 lbs) must use an approved safety seat. For further information phone 503/986-4190 or 800/922-2022 (OR).

INTERSTATE HIGHWAY SYSTEM

The following alphabetical listing of Oregon towns in *Mobil Travel Guide* shows that these cities are within ten miles of the indicated Interstate highways. A highway map, however, should be checked for the nearest exit.

Highway Number	Cities/Towns within ten miles
Interstate 5	Albany, Ashland, Beaverton, Corvallis, Cottage Grove, Eugene, Grants Pass, Jacksonville, Medford, Oregon City, Portland, Roseburg, Salem.
Interstate 84	Baker City, Beaverton, Biggs, Hermiston, Hood River, La Grande, Ontario, Oregon City, Pendleton, Portland, The Dalles, Umatilla.

Additional Visitor Information

The Oregon Tourism Commission, 775 Summer St NE, Salem 97301; 800/547-7842, will provide visitors with an Oregon travel guide and other informative brochures on request.

There are nine staffed state welcome centers in Oregon (April-October). They are: Astoria (downtown); Brookings (OR-CA border, S on US 101); Lakeview (downtown); Siskiyou (OR-CA border, S on I-5); Ontario (OR-ID border, E on I-84); Seaside (at Chamber of Commerce on US 101); Umatilla (on Brownell Blvd); Jantzen Beach-Portland (I-5 exit 308); Klamath Falls (OR-CA border, S on US 97).

DRIVING OREGON'S CENTRAL COAST

Oregon's central coast has some of the state's most dramatic scenery, with volcanic mountains dropping into the pounding Pacific surf. Along this route, you'll encounter many enchanting small towns, as well as an excellent aquarium and a sand dune recreation area.

Begin in Newport, Oregon's second-largest commercial port. Dominated by the high-arching Yaquina Bay Bridge, old downtown Newport is still a very lively seafront, complete with seafood markets, the smells of a working port, and the bark of seals. Bay Boulevard is lined with fish-processing plants on one side; chandlers, fish restaurants, art galleries, and brew pubs on the other. A number of ship owners offer boat excursions around Yaquina Bay and trips out into the Pacific to view whales.

Besides Newport's mile-long beaches, the city's biggest draw is the Oregon Coast Aquarium. Exhibits are grouped by ecosystem with interactive displays to explain the dynamics of the various forms of life found there. Outside, trails lead around natural-looking enclosures for seals, sea lions, and sea otters; the seabird aviary includes puffins and murres.

Drive south along Highway 101 to Seal Rock State Park, where a massive hump of rock protects a beach and tide pools, making this a good place for young children to explore the coast. Waldport is a quiet town on the mouth of the Alsea River with an unusual museum of transport. Travel along Oregon's rugged coast was not always simple, as The Alsea Bay Bridge Historical Interpretive Center makes evident. The facility traces the history of transportation routes along the coast, beginning with

trails used by Native Americans and moving on to the sea, rail, and road routes now in use. From Waldport south to Yachats (pronounced Ya-HOTS) are more wide sandy beaches, easily accessed at state park access points.

Some of Oregon's most spectacular shoreline begins at Yachats and continues south about 20 miles. This entire area was once a series of volcanic intrusions, which resisted the pummeling of the Pacific long enough to rise as oceanside peaks and promontories. Tiny beaches lined by cliffs seem almost serendipitous; acres of tide pools appear and disappear according to the fancy of the tides and are home to starfish, sea anemones, and sea lions. Picturesque lighthouses rise above the surf.

Cape Perpetua, two miles south of Yachats, was first sited and named by England's Captain James Cook in 1778. This volcanic remnant is one of the highest points on the Oregon coast. Views from the cape are incredible, taking in coastal promontories from Cape Foulweather to Cape Arago. Deep fractures in the old volcano allow waves to erode narrow channels into the headland, creating the compelling Devil's Churn. Waves race up a deep trench between basalt ledges, then shoot up the 30-foot inlet only to explode against the narrow sides of the channel. From the base of the Devil's Churn trail, turn south to explore acres of tide pools.

To continue, follow Highway 101 south. Stop at Devil's Elbow State Park and the Hecata Head Lighthouse, complete with an 1893 lighthouse keeper's house. From here, the road tunnels through mountains and edges along cliffs to reach Sea Lion Caves, an enormous natural sea grotto filled with smelly, shrieking sea lions. A 208-foot elevator drops down a small natural shaft that opens onto the larger grotto. From this observation point 50 feet above the surging waves, watch Steller's sea lions clambering onto rocks, jockeying for position at the top of ledges, and letting loose with mighty roars.

From the Sea Lion Caves, Highway 101 drops down from the volcanic peaks to a broad sandy plain fronted by extensive beaches preserved in state parks. Florence is an old fishing port that boomed in the 1890s. Detour from the Highway 101 strip to Old Town Florence, the historic port area on the Siuslaw River. The town's small fishing fleet ties at the base of restored Victorian storefronts, now filled with restaurants, coffee shops, and galleries.

From Florence southward to Reedsport is the Oregon Dunes National Recreation Area. These massive dunes front the Pacific Ocean but undulate east as much as three miles to meet coastal forests, with a succession of curious ecosystems and formations between. A number of hiking trails, bridle paths, and boating and swimming areas have been established throughout this unique place, and the entire region is noted for its abundant wildlife, especially birds.

Reedsport, once an important fishing and log milling town, is home to the Umpqua Lighthouse State Park. The still-operating lighthouse was built in 1894 and is open for tours. Directly opposite the lighthouse is a whale-watching platform with displays that explain various whale species and their habits. **(APPROX 75 MI)**

THE COLUMBIA RIVER HIGHWAY AND BEYOND

The magnificent canyon of the Columbia River slices through the spine of the Cascade Range just east of Portland. The Columbia, over a mile wide, winds through a 3,000-foot-deep gorge flanked by volcanic peaks and austere bands of basalt. The gorge contains one of the greatest concentrations of waterfalls in North America—chutes of water tumble from its edge to fall hundreds of feet to the river.

Begin in Portland, driving east on I-84. As the walls of the river canyon rise in the distance, take exit 22 and climb up the forested valley to join Highway 30, the Historic Columbia River Highway, atop the gorge wall. Modeled on European mountain roads, the Columbia River Highway was built in the 1910s as a scenic automobile route through the Gorge—quite an engineering feat at that time.

Famous as the western entry to the Gorge, Crown Point is a viewpoint and interpretive center atop a craggy 800-foot-high point of basalt. To the east, as far as the eye can see, the Columbia River unfurls between green cliffs. The famed Columbia Gorge waterfalls start almost immediately. Latourell Falls is the first major falls, a chute of water dropping 249 feet into a misty pool. To see churning Bridal Veil Falls requires a mile round-trip walk through deep forest and odd rock formations. Hike up the trail at Wahkeena Falls to see why it is named after an Indian term meaning "the most beautiful."

Half a mile east of Oneonta Gorge is Horsetail Falls, which drops out of a notch in the rock to fall 176 feet. While the waterfall is easily seen from the turnout along Highway 30, hikers should consider the three-mile Horsetail-Oneonta Loop Trail, an easy hike that takes in another waterfall and the narrow Oneonta chasm.

From there, continue east on Highway 30, rejoining I-84 at Dodson. Built in 1937 at the height of the Depression, Bonneville Dam was one of the largest of the New Deal projects and was the first major hydropower dam on the Columbia. The visitor center, at exit 40, has a good collection of Native American artifacts, as well as exhibits about the building of the dam. From the lower floors of the visitor center, you can watch through underwater windows as fish negotiate the dam's fish ladders. Walk to the Bonneville Fish Hatchery, where salmon and sturgeon are reared to restock the Columbia River. Nearby, the Columbia River Sternwheeler offers cruises through the Columbia River Gorge departing from Cascade Lock's Marine Park.

Continue on I-84 to Hood River, an old orchard town on the Columbia River that has found new life as a world capital of windsurfing. From Hood River, turn south on Highway 35. As you climb out of the Gorge, Mount Hood—Oregon's highest peak at 11,240 feet—fills the skyline, a slim white incisor towering above a valley filled with apple, pear, and cherry orchards. As the orchards thin, Highway 35 winds up around the base of Mount Hood, through fir forests and along rushing streams. At Government Camp, turn north into Timberline Lodge, and climb six steep miles to 6,000 feet. Here, at the foot of soaring Mount Hood, sits one of the unquestioned masterpieces of WPA-funded Depression-era public works, Timberline Lodge (phone 503/272-3311). The interior of this 43,700 square-foot lodge is spectacular: the central stone fireplace rises 92 feet through three open stories of lobby. The third floor bar and cafe is a wonderful place to take in the inspiring handiwork that created this architectural gem.

The ski lifts at Timberline operate almost all year, so strap on skis or a snowboard and head to the lifts. Hiking trails lead out from the lodge in almost all directions. For food, check out the Blue Ox Pub, tucked away in a cavernlike corner, or splurge at the wood-beamed Cascade Dining Room.

Return to Highway 30, and continue west to the Portland suburbs.
(APPROX 75 MI)

Albany

(C-2) *See also Corvallis, Salem, Sweet Home*

Founded 1848 **Pop** 29,462 **Elev** 212 ft
Area code 541 **Zip** 97321

Information Visitors Convention & Association, 300 SW 2nd Ave, PO Box 965; 541/928-0911 or 800/526-2256

Web www.albanyvisitors.com

Gateway to Oregon's covered bridge country, Albany was founded by Walter and Thomas Monteith and named for their former home, Albany, New York. The city boasts the largest collection of Victorian homes in the state. Albany is nestled in the heart of the Willamette Valley along the I-5 corridor of the Cascades. The Calapooia River joins the Willamette here. The seat of Linn County, Albany has diversified industry ranging from agriculture, timber, and wood products to rare metals.

What to See and Do

Flinn's Heritage Tours. Twenty different narrated tours take visitors through historic areas in the Mid Willamette Valley. Tours range from 45 min-six hrs; feature covered bridges of Linn County, Albany's three historic districts, ghost towns, 100-yr-old apple orchard, and historic homes. (Daily; closed Dec 25) 222 First Ave W. Phone 541/928-5008. ¢¢¢¢

Special Events

Veteran's Day Parade. One of the nation's largest. Phone 541/451-5799. Mid-Nov. Phone 541/367-8323.

Historic Interior Homes Tours. Phone 541/928-0911 or 800/526-2256. Summer and late Dec.

Motels/Motor Lodges

★★ **BEST WESTERN PONY SOLDIER INN.** *315 Airport Rd SE (97321). 541/928-6322, fax 511/928 8124; toll-free 800/634-7669. ponysoldierinns.com.* 72 rms, 2 story. S, D $69-$89; under 17 free. Crib avail. Pet accepted. TV; cable. Pool; whirlpool. Complimentary bkfst. Coffee in rms. Restaurant adj. Ck-out noon. Free guest lndry. Exercise equipt. Meeting rms. In-rm modem link. Free airport shuttle. Refrigerators, microwaves. Cr cds: A, C, D, DS, JCB, MC, V

Covered bridge over Crabtree Creek, Linn County

★★ LA QUINTA INN AND SUITES
ALBANY. *251 Airport Rd SE (97321). 541/928-0921; fax 541/928-8055. www.laquinta.com.* 62 rms, 2 story. Apr-Aug: S $60-$75; D $67-$82; each addl $7; suites $150; kit. units $70-$107; under 18 free; package plans; higher rates special events; lower rates rest of yr. Crib free. Pet accepted. TV; cable. Indoor pool; whirlpool. Complimentary continental bkfst. Restaurant opp 5 am-11 pm. Ck-out 1 pm. Coin lndry. Meeting rms. Business servs avail. Gift shop. Exercise equipt; sauna. Refrigerators avail. Cr cds: A, C, DS, V.

Ashland

(F-2) *See also Jacksonville, Medford*

Founded 1852 **Pop** 16,234 **Elev** 1,951 ft **Area code** 541 **Zip** 97520

Information Chamber of Commerce, 110 E Main St, PO Box 1360; 541/482-3486

Web www.ashlandchamber.com

When the pioneers climbed over the Siskiyou Mountains and saw the green expanse of the Rogue River Valley ahead of them, many decided to go no further. Later, when mineral springs were found, their Lithia water was piped in and now gushes from fountains on this city's plaza. Tourism, education, and small industry support the town. Southern Oregon University College (1926) makes this a regional education center. Rogue River National Forest (see MEDFORD) is on three sides; a Ranger District office is located here.

What to See and Do

Lithia Park. Has 100 acres of woodlands and ponds. Nature trails, tennis, picnicking, sand volleyball. Rose and Japanese gardens. Concerts. (Daily) Adj to City Plaza. Phone 541/488-5340. **FREE**

Skiing. Mount Ashland Ski Area. Area has two triple, two double chairlifts; patrol, school, rentals; cafeteria, bar. Longest run one mi; vertical drop 1,150 ft. (Thanksgiving-Apr) 8 mi S on I-5, then 9 mi W on access road. Phone 541/482-2897.

Special Events

Oregon Cabaret Theatre. 1st and Hargadine sts. Musicals, revues, and comedies in dinner club setting. Schedule varies. Phone 541/488-2902. Feb-Dec.

Oregon Shakespeare Festival. Elizabethan Theater (outdoor); Angus Bowmer Theater (indoor); Black Swan Theater (indoor). Series of 12 classic and contemporary plays. Tues-Sun. Wheelchair seating by advance arrangement. Phone 541/482-4331. Mid-Feb-Oct.

Motels/Motor Lodges

★★ BEST WESTERN BARD'S INN. *132 N Main St (97520). 541/482-0049; fax 541/488-3259; toll-free 800/533-9627. www.bestwestern.com.* 91 rms, 2-3 story. June-Oct: S $92-$115; D $106-$128; each addl $10; lower rates rest of yr. Crib $10. Pet accepted; $10. TV; cable (premium). Pool; whirlpool. Complimentary continental bkfst. Restaurant adj. Ck-out 11 am. Meeting rms. Downhill/x-country ski 20 mi. Refrigerators. Near Shakespeare Festival theater. Cr cds: A, C, D, DS, MC, V.

★★ BEST WESTERN WINDSOR INN. *2520 Ashland St (97520). 541/488-2330; fax 541/482-1068; toll-free 800/334-2330. www.bestwestern.com.* 92 rms, 2 story, 5 kit. units. Mid-May-Sept: S $60.75-$93.75; D $65.75-$93.75; each addl $6; under 18 free; kit. units $93.75-$103.75; lower rates rest of yr. Crib $6. Pet accepted; $15/night/pet. TV; cable. Heated pool. Complimentary continental bkfst. Restaurant adj open 24 hrs. Coffee in rms. Ck-out 11 am. Business servs avail. In-rm modem link. Valet serv. Airport transportation 7 am-11 pm. Downhill/x-country ski 15 mi. Refrigerators. Cr cds: A, C, D, DS, MC, V.

★ CEDARWOOD INN. *1801 Siskiyou Blvd (97520). 541/488-2000; fax 541/482-2000; res 800/547-4141. www.brodeur-inns.com.* 64 rms, 14 with shower only, 2-3 story, 24 kit.

units. Mid-May-mid-Oct: S, D $82-$148; kit. units $78-$125; under 2 free; ski plans; lower rates rest of yr. Crib avail. Pet accepted, some restrictions. TV; cable, VCR avail (movies). Complimentary coffee in rms. Restaurant nearby. Bar. Ck-out 11 am. Business servs avail. Downhill/x-country ski 15 mi. 2 pools, 1 indoor; whirlpool; sauna; steam rm. Microwaves avail. Picnic tables, grills. Cr cds: A, D, DS, MC, V.

D 🔧 ⤢ ≈ 🐾 SC

★ **KNIGHTS INN.** 2359 Hwy 66 (97520). 541/482-5111; fax 541/488-1589; res 800/547-4566. www.brodeur-inns.com. 40 rms, 1-2 story. Mid-May-mid-Oct: S, D $68-$78; ski plans; lower rates rest of yr. Crib $6. Pet accepted, some restrictions; $6. TV; cable. Heated pool; whirlpool. Complimentary coffee in rms. Restaurant 7 am-10 pm. Bar 11 am-midnight. Ck-out 11 am. Downhill ski 15 mi. Cr cds: A, D, DS, MC, V.

🔧 ⚓ ⤢ ≈ ≈ 🐾

★ **RODEWAY INN.** 1193 Siskiyou Blvd (97520). 541/482-2641; fax 541/488-1656; toll-free 800/547-6414. www.rodewayinn.com. 64 rms, 1-3 story. S $72-$80; D $72-$82; each addl $6. Crib $6. Pet accepted, some restrictions; $6. TV; cable (premium). Heated pool. Coffee in rms. Restaurant adj. Ck-out 11 am. Business servs avail. Downhill/x-country ski 18 mi. Microwaves avail. College opp. Cr cds: A, C, D, DS, MC, V.

D 🔧 ⤢ ≈ ≈ 🐾

★★ **STRATFORD INN.** 555 Siskiyou Blvd (97520). 541/488-2151; fax 541/482-0479; toll-free 800/547-4741. 55 rms, 3 story, 6 kits. June-Sept: S, D $85-$165; each addl $5; lower rates rest of yr. Crib free. TV; cable (premium). Indoor pool; whirlpool. Complimentary continental bkfst. Restaurant nearby. Ck-out 11 am. Downhill/x-country ski 18 mi. Refrigerators; some microwaves. Locker rm for skis and bicycles. Cr cds: A, D, DS, MC, V.

D ⚓ 🎿 ⤢ ≈ ≈ 🐾

★★★ **WINDMILL INN & SUITES.** 2525 Ashland St (97520). 541/482-8310; fax 541/488-1783; toll-free 800/547-4747. www.windmillinns.com. 230 rms, 3 story. June-Sept: S, D $52-

$89; each addl $6-$11; suites $142-$260; under 18 free; lower rates rest of yr. Crib $3.50. Pet accepted. TV; cable. Heated pool; whirlpool. Complimentary continental bkfst. Restaurant 6:30 am-9 pm. Bar. Ck-out 11 am. Meeting rms. Business servs avail. Coin lndry. Bellhops. Valet serv. Sundries. Beauty shop. Airport transportation. Tennis. Downhill/x-country ski 13 mi. Exercise equipt. Some refrigerators; microwaves avail. Balconies. Bicycles. Cr cds: A, D, DS, MC, V.

B&Bs/Small Inns

★★★ **CHANTICLEER INN.** 120 Gresham St (97520). 541/482-1919; fax 541/488-4810; toll-free 800/898-1950. www.ashland bed breakfast.com. 6 rms, 3 story. June-Oct: S, D $135-$195; each addl $20; lower rates rest of yr. Complimentary full bkfst; afternoon refreshments. Restaurant nearby. Ck-out 11 am, ck-in 3-6 pm. Free local airport, bus depot transportation. Downhill/x-country ski 14 mi. Lawn games. Country French inn; river rock fireplace. Patio. Cr cds: A, DS, MC, V.

⤢ ≈ 🐾

★★★ **COUNTRY WILLOWS BED & BREAKFAST INN.** 1313 Clay St (97520). 541/488-1590; fax 541/488-1611; res 800/945-5697. www.willows inn.com. 9 rms, 2 with shower only, 2 story, 3 suites. Mar-Oct: S $110-$160, D $115-$185; each addl $30; suites $225-$245; lower rates rest of yr. Children over 12 yrs only. TV in common rm; cable (premium). Complimentary full bkfst. Complimentary coffee in rms. Ck-out 11 am, ck-in 3-5 pm. Business servs avail. In-rm modem link. Luggage handling. Concierge serv. Gift shop. Downhill/x-country ski 14 mi. Heated pool; whirlpool. Some refrigerators, microwaves, wet bars, fireplaces. Many balconies. Opp river. Built in 1896; country inn atmosphere and decor. Totally nonsmoking. Cr cds: A, DS, MC, V.

D ⤢ ≈ ≈ 🐾

★★ **MCCALL HOUSE BED & BREAKFAST.** 153 Oak [...] 541/482-9296; fax 54[...]

800/808-9749. www.mccallhouse.com.
9 rms, 2 story. Rm phones avail.
May-Oct: S, D $145-$225; each addl
$30; varied lower rates rest of yr.
Children over 12 yrs only. Complimentary full bkfst; afternoon refreshments. Restaurant nearby. Ck-out 11
am, ck-in 3-6 pm. Former residence
(1883) of Civil War veteran and
mayor of Ashland. Totally nonsmoking. Cr cds: MC, V.

★★★ **MOUNT ASHLAND INN.** *550
Mt Ashland Rd (97520). 541/482-8707;
res 800/830-8707. www.mtashlandinn.
com.* 5 suites, 4 story. No rm phones.
S $130; D $135; each addl $30; suites
$120-$190; ski plan. Children over 10
yrs only. Complimentary full bkfst;
afternoon refreshments. Restaurant
nearby. Ck-out 11 am, ck-in 3-5 pm.
Downhill/x-country ski 3 mi. Sauna.
Whirlpool. Refrigerators, microwaves,
fireplaces. Cedar log lodge; handmade furnishings, antiques. View of
Mt Shasta. Totally nonsmoking. Cr
cds: DS, MC, V.

★★ **OAK HILL BED & BREAKFAST.**
*2190 Siskiyou Blvd (97520). fax
541/482-1378; toll-free 800/888-7434.
www.oakhillbb.com.* 6 rms, 2 story. No
rm phones. May-Oct: S, D $129-
$159; D $95-$120. Children over 12
yrs only. Complimentary full bkfst.
Ck-out 11 am, ck-in 3-6 pm. Luggage
handling. Downhill/x-country ski 15
mi. Built 1910 as farmhouse. Many
antiques. Totally nonsmoking. Cr
cds: DS, MC, V.

★★ **PEDIGRIFT HOUSE B&B.** *407
Scenic Dr (97520). 541/482-1888; fax
541/482-8867; res 800/262-4073.
www.pedigrift.com.* 4 rms, 2 story.
May-mid-Oct: S, D $135; each addl
lower rates rest of yr. Children
ly TV. Complimentary
arby. Ck-out

rms, 2 story. May-Oct: D $130-$185;
lower rates rest of yr. Children over
12 yrs only. Heated pool; whirlpool.
Complimentary full bkfst; refreshments. Ck-out 11 am, ck-in 3-6 pm.
Downhill ski 14 mi; x-country ski 15
mi. Private patios. Cape Cod-style
house; fireplaces, hand-stitched
Amish quilts; gardens. Totally nonsmoking. Cr cds: DS, MC, V.

★★ **THE WOODS HOUSE BED &
BREAKFAST.** *333 N Main St (97520).
541/488-1598; fax 541/488-2027; toll-
free 800/435-8260. www.woodshouse.
com.* 6 rms, 2 story. No rm phones.
May-Oct: S $115-$135; D $120-$140;
each addl $35; lower rates rest of yr.
Complimentary full bkfst; refreshments. Restaurant nearby. Ck-out 11
am, ck-in 2-5 pm. Airport transportation. Downhill/x-country ski
15 mi. Rms in original Ashland
house (1908); antiques; terraced gardens. Totally nonsmoking. Cr cds:
DS, MC, V.

★★★ **THE WINCHESTER INN &
RESTAURANT.** *35 S Second St
(97520). 541/488-1113; fax 541/488-
4604; toll-free 800/972-4991. www.
winchesterinn.com.* 18 rms, 3 story.
June-Oct: S $145-$220; D $150-$225;
each addl $30; under 8 free; some
wkend rates off-season; lower rates
rest of yr. Complimentary full bkfst;
afternoon refreshments. Restaurant
(see WINCHESTER COUNTRY INN).
Ck-out 11 am, ck-in 3 pm. Down-
hill/x-country ski 15 mi. Some
whirlpools, fireplaces in suites. Some
balconies. Patio tables. Restored Victorian house (1886) once served as
the area's first hospital. Individually
decorated rms; period furnishings.
Gazebo, flower gardens. Totally nonsmoking. Cr cds: A, DS, MC, V.

Restaurants

★ **ASHLAND BAKERY & CAFE.** *38
E Main St (97520). 541/482-2117.
www.ashlandbakery.com.* Hrs: 7 am-9
pm; Fri, Sat to 10 pm. Closed
Thanksgiving, Dec 25. Wine, beer.
Bkfst $3.25-$10.50, lunch $2.75-
$10.95, dinner $2.75-$10.95. Special-
izes in baked goods, vegetarian

dishes. Totally nonsmoking. Cr cds: MC, V.

D

★★ **CHATEAULIN.** *50 E Main St (97520). 541/482-2264. www. chateaulin.com.* Hrs: 5-9:30 pm. Closed Thanksgiving, Dec 24-25. Res accepted. French menu. Bar. Dinner $16-$30. Child's meals. Specializes in fresh seafood, lamb, roast duckling. Totally nonsmoking. Cr cds: A, D, MC, V.

D

★ **MACARONI'S.** *58 E Main St (97520). 541/488-3359.* Hrs: 5-9 pm; Fri, Sat to 10 pm. Closed Jan 1, Thanksgiving, Dec 25. Italian menu. Bar. Dinner $9.50-$15.95. Specializes in pizza, pasta, salad. Cr cds: A, D, DS, MC, V.

D

★★ **WINCHESTER COUNTRY INN.** *35 S Second St (97520). 541/488 1113. www.winchesterinn.com.* Hrs: 5:30-9 pm; Nov-May 5:30-8:30 pm; Sun brunch 9:30 am-1 pm. Continental menu. Serv bar. Dinner $14.95-$22.95. Sun brunch $8.50-$12.95. Specializes in fresh salmon, beef, lamb. Outdoor dining. Built 1886. Cr cds: A, DS, MC, V.

Astoria

(A-1) See also Cannon Beach, Seaside

Settled 1811 **Pop** 10,069 **Elev** 18 ft
Area code 503 **Zip** 97103
Information Astoria-Warrenton Chamber of Commerce, 111 W Marine Dr, PO Box 176; 503/325-6311 or 800/875-6807
Web www.el.com/to/astoria

John Jacob Astor's partners sailed around Cape Horn and picked this point of land ten miles from the Pacific, overlooking the mouth of the Columbia River, for a fur trading post. The post eventually lost its importance, but the location and the natural resources attracted immigrants, and the town continued to grow. A four-mile-long bridge crosses the mouth of the Columbia.

What to See and Do

Astoria Column. (1926) A 125-ft tower commemorates first settlement; observation deck at top. Gift shop.(Daily) Information booth (Memorial Day-Labor Day, daily). Follow scenic drive signs to Coxcomb Hill. Phone 503/325-7275. **FREE**

Columbia River Maritime Museum. Rare maritime artifacts and memorabilia of Columbia River, its tributaries, and the Northwest coast. *Columbia,* Lightship 604 at moorage in Maritime Park. Fishing industry, discovery and exploration, steamship, shipwreck, navigation, and steamboat exhibits. Coast Guard and Navy exhibits. (Daily; closed Thanksgiving, Dec 25) 17th and Marine Dr. Phone 503/325-2323. ¢¢

Flavel House. (1883-1887) Built by Captain George Flavel, pilot and shipping man, outstanding example of Queen Anne architecture. Restored Victorian home houses antique furnishings and fine art; collection of 19th- and 20th-century toys. Carriage house, museum store, orientation film.(Daily; closed hols) 441 8th St. Phone 503/325-2203. ¢

🟫 **Fort Clatsop National Memorial.** (see) 6 mi SW on US 101A.

Fort Stevens State Park. A 3,763-acre park adj to old Civil War fort. Wreck of the *Peter Iredale* (1906) is on the ocean shore. Fort Stevens is the only military post in the lower 48 states to be fired upon by foreign forces since 1812. On June 21, 1942, a Japanese submarine fired several shells from its five-inch gun; only one hit land while the others fell short. Visitor center and self-guided tour at the Old Fort Stevens Military Complex. Ocean beach, lake swimming, fishing, clamming on beach, boating (dock, ramp); bicycling, picnicking at Coffenbury Lake. Improved tent and trailer sites (daily; standard fees, dump station) 5 mi W on US 101, then 5 mi N on Ridge Rd. Phone 503/861-1671.

SLEEPY ASTORIA

The oldest American settlement in the Pacific Northwest, Astoria was founded as a fur-trading fort in 1811. Thereafter, thanks to its fortuitous location at the mouth of the mighty Columbia River, the town became a prosperous shipping and fishing port. During the 1880s, sea captains and other captains of industry built magnificent homes overlooking the Columbia River. Astoria contains some of the most lovingly restored and precipitously poised Victorian homes outside of San Francisco.

Begin a walking tour of Astoria at the Columbia River Maritime Museum (1792 Marine Drive), a modern 25,000-square-foot facility that tells the story of the city's two centuries of seafaring history. The galleries explore Astoria's maritime past with exhibits on the salmon-packing industry, local lighthouses, the evolution of boat design, and delicate ivory scrimshaw work. There is also a creepy display on harpoons.

From the museum, follow Highway 30/Marine Drive to the west, and turn south on 16th Street. Housed in the former City Hall building, the Astoria Heritage Museum (1618 Exchange Street) contains a commemoration of Astoria's fishing past, as well as an exhibit dedicated to the various ethnic communities that came together to form the city; take note of the Tong shrine. Another room is dedicated to the Clatsop Indians and the early days of exploration.

A block to the west, at 15th and Exchange streets, is the site of old Fort Astoria, founded in 1811 by the Pacific Fur Company. While nothing remains of the original structure, volunteers have rebuilt the blockhouse and stockade to original drawings.

Astoria's landmark Victorian mansions line the steep hills behind downtown. Climb up 16th Street to Grand Avenue. One block east is the Foard House (690 17th Street), an elaborate Queen Anne mansion that is now a wildly painted bed-and-breakfast. Walk back west, past more restored mansions and below the St. Mary's Catholic Church (1465 Grand Avenue), built in 1902.

Drop down to Franklin Street and continue walking westward past street after street of mammoth Victorian homes. At 137 Franklin Avenue is the oldest surviving house in Astoria, built in 1853. Other notable homes, now bed-and-breakfasts, include the Columbia River Inn (1681 Franklin Street) and the Rosebriar Hotel (636 14th Street), formerly a convent.

At 8th Street, turn north and walk downhill to Duane Street. Captain George Flavel was one of Astoria's leading citizens during the 1870s and 1880s. He built a highly ornamented mansion, Flavel House (441 8th Street), with great views over the harbor (especially from the three-story corner tower) to keep an eye on his ships. The house is now a museum that has been restored throughout and repainted with its original colors; the grounds have been returned to Victorian-era landscaping. Tours are offered daily.

From the Flavel House, drop down to Commercial Street, and walk west through sleepy downtown Astoria to again reach the Maritime Museum.

Special Events

Astoria-Warrenton Crab and Seafood Festival. Hammond Mooring Basin on Columbia River. Crab feast, Oregon wines, food and craft booths. Carnival, water taxi, crabbing and fishing boats. Last wkend Apr. Phone 503/325-6311.

Scandinavian Midsummer Festival. Parade, folk dancing, display booths, arts and crafts demonstrations, Scandinavian food. Phone 503/325-4600. Mid-June.

Astoria Regatta. Parade, arts festival, public dinner, barbecue, boating competition. Mid-Aug. Phone 503/325-2353.

Great Columbia Crossing Bridge Run. One of the most unusual and scenic runs; eight-mi course begins at

Chinook, WA and ends at Astoria port docks. Phone 503/325-6311. Mid-Oct.

Motels/Motor Lodges

★ **ASTORIA DUNES MOTEL.** *288 W Marine Dr (97103). 503/325-7111; fax 503/325-0804; toll-free 800/441-3319. astoriadunes.uswestdex.com.* 58 rms, 18 A/C, 2-3 story. No elvtr. June-Sept: S, D $60-$95; each addl $7; lower rates rest of yr. TV; cable (premium). Indoor pool; whirlpool. Complimentary coffee. Restaurant nearby. Ck-out 11 am. Coin lndry. Business servs avail. Some refrigerators. Opp river. Cr cds: A, DS, MC, V.

![icons]

★ **BAYSHORE MOTOR INN.** *555 Hamburg Ave (97103). 503/325-2205; fax 503/325-5550; toll-free 800/621-0641.* 76 rms, 4 story. Some A/C. June-Oct: S, D $39-$69; each addl $7, under 10 free; lower rates rest of yr. Crib avail. Pet accepted, some restrictions; $5. TV; cable. Indoor pool; whirlpool. Sauna. Complimentary continental bkfst. Ck-out 11 am. Coin lndry. Meeting rm. Business servs avail. In-rm modem link. Sundries. Some refrigerators. On river. Cr cds: A, D, DS, JCB, MC, V.

![icons]

★★ **CREST MOTEL.** *5366 Leif Erickson Dr (97103). 503/325-3141; toll-free 800/421-3141. www.crest-motel. com.* 40 rms, 1-2 story. No A/C. Mid May mid-Oct: S $46-$55; D $62-$73; each addl $7; under 10 free; lower rates rest of yr. Crib free. Pet accepted. TV; cable (premium). Complimentary continental bkfst, coffee in rms. Ck-out noon. Coin lndry. Business servs avail. Whirlpool. Some refrigerators. Balconies. On high bluff overlooking Columbia River. Cr cds: A, DS, MC, V.

![icons]

★★ **RED LION INN.** *400 Industry St (97103). 503/325-7373; fax 503/325-5786; toll-free 800/733-5466. www. redlion.com.* 124 rms, 2 story. No A/C. May-early Oct: S, D $79-$139; each addl $10; under 18 free; lower rates rest of yr. Crib free. Pet accepted, some restrictions; $10. TV; cable. Restaurant 6 am-10 pm. Bar 11-2 am; entertainment Tues-Sat. Ck-out

noon. Coin lndry. Valet serv. Meeting rms. Business servs avail. Free airport transportation. Private balconies. Overlooks harbor; on Columbia River. Cr cds: A, C, D, DS, MC, V.

![icons]

★★ **SHILO INN SUITES.** *1609 E Harbor Dr, Warrenton (97146). 503/861-2181; fax 503/861-2980; toll-free 800/222-2244. www.shiloinns.com.* 63 rms, 4 story, 11 kit. units. May-Sept: S, D $59-$249; each addl $15; kit. units $109-$185; under 12 free; lower rates rest of yr. Crib free. Pet accepted; $10. TV; cable (premium), VCR (movies). Indoor pool; whirlpool. Restaurant 7 am-10 pm. Bar. Ck-out noon. Coin lndry. Meeting rms. Business servs avail. Sundries. Free airport transportation. Exercise equipt; sauna. Refrigerators, microwaves, wet bars. Cr cds: A, D, DS, ER, JCB, MC, V.

![icons]

B&Bs/Small Inns

★ **COLUMBIA RIVER INN.** *1681 Franklin Ave (97103). 503/325-5044; toll-free 800/953-5044. www.moriah. com/columbia.* 5 rms, 3 story. No rm phones. S, D $75-$125; each addl $10. Children over 12 yrs only. Complimentary full bkfst. Restaurant nearby. Ck-out 11 am, ck-in 3-6 pm. Gift shop. Free airport, bus depot transportation. Victorian house (ca 1870); many antiques. Totally nonsmoking. Cr cds: A, DS, MC, V.

![icons]

★ **FRANKLIN STREET STATION BED & BREAKFAST INN.** *1140 Franklin St (97103). 503/325-4314; toll-free 800/448-1098. www.franklin-st-station-bb.com.* 6 rms, 3 story, 2 suites. No A/C. No rm phones. Mid-May-mid-Oct: S $80-$99; D, suites, kit. unit $95-$135; each addl $10; lower rates rest of yr. TV; cable, VCR. Complimentary full bkfst. Ck-out 11 am, ck-in 3 pm. Some refrigerators. Balconies. Victorian house built in 1900. Totally nonsmoking. Cr cds: A, DS, MC, V.

![icons]

★★ **ROSE BRIAR HOTEL.** *636 14th St (97103). 503/325-7427; fax 503/325-6937; toll-free 800/487-0224.*

www.rosebriarhotel.com. 10 rms, 2 story. No A/C. S, D $65-$139; each addl $10. Complimentary bkfst. Restaurant nearby. Ck-out 11 am, ck-in 3 pm. Business servs avail. Some fireplaces. Built in 1902 as a residence; was also used as a convent. Many antiques. Overlooks town and river. Totally nonsmoking. Cr cds: A, D, DS, MC, V.

D ⬡ ⬡ ⬡ ⬡

Restaurants

★★ **PIER II FEED STORE.** *77 11th St (97103). 503/325-0279.* Hrs: 7 am-10 pm; winter to 9 pm. Closed Thanksgiving, Dec 25. Res accepted. Bar to midnight wkends. Bkfst $2.95-$8.50, lunch $5.50-$9, dinner $8-$24.50. Specializes in seafood, steak. Salad bar. Old feed store on pier (late 1800s); natural beamed ceilings. View of Columbia River. Totally nonsmoking. Cr cds: A, D, MC, V.

D

★★ **SHIP INN.** *1 2nd St (97103). 503/325-0033.* Hrs: 11:30 am-9:30 pm. Closed major hols. Bar. Lunch, dinner $5-$12. Complete meals: lunch, dinner $8.50-$16.50. Specializes in Cornish and chicken pasties, seafood. Salad bar. View of Columbia River. Cr cds: C, MC, V.

D

Baker City

(C-6) *See also La Grande*

Pop 9,140 **Elev** 3,443 ft
Area code 541 **Zip** 97814
Information Baker County Visitor & Convention Bureau, 490 Campbell St; 541/523-3356 or 800/523-1235
Web www.neoregon.com/visitBaker.html

The Baker City Historic District includes more than 100 commercial and residential buildings, many built from stone quarried in town at the same place where gold was found. A 15-block area, from the Powder River to 4th Street and from Estes to Campbell streets, has many structures built between 1890 and 1910 that are being restored. Baker City,

on the "old Oregon trail," is also the home of the Armstrong Gold Nugget found June 19, 1913, by George Armstrong. It weighs more than 80 ounces. A Ranger District office and the office of the supervisor of the Wallowa-Whitman National Forest is located here.

What to See and Do

Eastern Oregon Museum. Large collection of relics and implements used in the development of the West; turn-of-the-century logging and mining tools; period rms; doll collection; children's antique furniture. On grounds is 1884 railroad depot. (Mid-Apr-mid-Oct, daily) 9 mi NW on old US 30. Phone 541/856-3233. **Donation**

National Historic Oregon Trail Interpretive Center. Exhibits, living history presentations, multi-media displays. (Daily; closed Jan 1, Dec 25) 5 mi E on OR 86, at summit of Flagstaff Hill. Phone 800/523-1235. ¢¢

Oregon Trail Regional Museum. Houses one of the most outstanding collections of rocks, minerals, and semiprecious stones in the West. Also, an elaborate sea-life display; wildlife display; period clothing and artifacts of early Baker County. (Late Mar-Oct, daily) 2490 Grove St. Phone 800/523-1235. ¢

Sumpter Valley Railroad. Restored gear-driven Heisler steam locomotive and two observation cars travel seven mi on narrow-gauge track through a wildlife game habitat area where beaver, muskrat, geese, waterfowl, herons, and other animals may be seen. Also passes through the Sumpter mining district, location of the Sumpter Dredge which brought up more than $10 million in gold between 1913 and 1954 from as far down as 20 ft. (May-Sept, Sat, Sun, hols) 30 mi SW on OR 7. Phone 800/523-1235. ¢¢

Unity Lake State Park. A 39-acre park with swimming, fishing, boat ramp on Unity Lake; picnicking, tent and improved-site camping. Standard fees. 45 mi SW on OR 245, near jct US 26. Phone 541/575-2773.

Wallowa-Whitman National Forest. Reached via OR 7, 26, 86, 203, 82, I-84. More than two million acres with 14,000-acre North Fork John Day

Wilderness; 7,000-acre Monument Rock Wilderness; 358,461-acre Eagle Cap Wilderness; 215,500-acre Hells Canyon Wilderness. Snowcapped peaks, Minam River; alpine meadows, rare wildflowers; national scenic byway, scenic drive Hells Canyon Overlook, which overlooks deepest canyon in North America—Hells Canyon National Recreation Area (see JOSEPH); Buckhorn Lookout; Anthony Lake and Phillips Lake. Stream and lake trout fishing; elk, deer, and bear hunting; float and jet boat trips; saddle and pack trips. Picnic area. Camping. Sections west, northeast, and south. For further information contact Supervisor, PO Box 907. Phone 541/523-6391. In forest is

Anthony Lakes Ski Area. Triple chairlift, Pomalift; patrol, school, rentals; nursery; day lodge, cafeteria, concession area, bar. Longest run 1½ mi; vertical drop 900 ft. (Mid-Nov-mid Apr, Thurs-Sun) X-country trails. Fishing, hiking, cabin rentals, store (summer). 35 mi NW, off I-84 at 17500 Anthony Lake Hwy, in North Powder. Phone 541/856-3277. ¢¢¢¢

Special Event

Miner's Jubilee. Third wkend July. Phone 541/523-5855.

Motels/Motor Lodges

★★ **BEST WESTERN SUNRIDGE INN.** 1 Sunridge Ln (97814). 541/523-6444; fax 541/523-6446; toll-free 800/233-2468. www.bestwestern.com. 155 rms, 2 story. S $54-$64; D $58-$68; each addl $4; suites $150-$175; under 12 free. Crib $5. TV; cable (premium), VCR avail. Heated pool; whirlpool. Coffee in rms. Restaurant 5:30 am-10 pm. Ck-out noon. Meeting rms. Business servs avail. In-rm modem link. Sundries. Free airport transportation. Some microwaves, refrigerators. Private patios, balconies. Cr cds: A, C, D, DS, MC, V.
[D] [≈] [🐾] [SC]

★★ **ELDORADO INN.** 695 Campbell St (97814). 541/523-6494; toll-free 800/537-5756. 56 rms, 2 story. S, D $43-$55; family rates. Crib $3. Pet accepted; $2/day. TV; cable, VCR avail. Indoor pool. Complimentary

coffee. Restaurant open 24 hrs. Ck-out noon. Business servs avail. Refrigerators avail. Cr cds: A, C, D, DS, MC, V.
[🐾] [≈] [☒] [🐾] [SC]

★ **QUALITY INN.** 810 Campbell St (97814). 541/523-2242; res 800/228-5151. www.qualityinn.com. 54 rms, 2 story. Mid-May-mid-Sept: S $50-$54; D $57-$61; each addl $5; under 19 free; lower rates rest of yr. Crib $3. Pet accepted; $2/day. TV; cable. Pool privileges. Complimentary continental bkfst. Restaurant nearby. Ck-out noon. Meeting rms. Some refrigerators. Cr cds: A, DS, MC, V.
[🐾] [≈] [🐾]

★ **SUPER 8 MOTEL.** 250 Campbell St (97814). 541/523-8282; fax 541/523-9137; res 888/726-2466. www.super8.com. 72 rms, 2 story, 2 kit. units. Apr-Sept: S $43.88; D $49.88; each addl $4; kit. units $71.88; under 13 free; lower rates rest of yr. Crib $4. TV; cable (premium), VCR avail (movies). Indoor pool; whirlpool. Complimentary continental bkfst. Restaurant nearby. Ck-out 11 am. Coin lndry. Business servs avail. Refrigerators. Cr cds: A, C, D, DS, JCB, MC, V.
[D] [≈] [☒] [🐾] [SC]

Bandon

(E-1) See also Coos Bay, North Bend, Port Orford

Pop 2,215 **Elev** 67 ft **Area code** 541 **Zip** 97411

Information Chamber of Commerce, PO Box 1515; 541/347-9616

A fine beach, known for its picturesque beauty, legendary rocks, and a harbor at the mouth of the Coquille River attracts many tourists to Bandon. From November through March, the town is known for its short-lived storms followed by sunshine, and even has a group called the Storm Watchers. Popular seashore activities include beachcombing, hiking, fishing from the south jetty, and crabbing from the docks. Summer and early autumn bring the salmon run in the Coquille River. Rockhounds search for agate, jasper, and petrified wood.

What to See and Do

Bandon Museum. Exhibits on maritime activities of early Bandon and Coquille River; coastal shipwrecks, Coast Guard operations; extensive collection of Native American artifacts; old photos. (Schedule varies) US 101 and Filmore Ave. Phone 541/347-2164. ¢

Bullards Beach State Park. A 1,266-acre park with four mi of ocean beach. Fishing; boating (dock, ramp with access to Coquille River). Picnicking. Improved trailer campsites (dump station). Coquille River Lighthouse (1896); interpretive plaques (May-Oct, daily). Standard fees. 2 mi N on US 101. Phone 541/347-3501. **FREE**

Face Rock State Park. An 879-acre park on coastal dune area with access to beach; fishing. Picnicking. 4 mi S on US 101, then 1 mi W on Bradley Lake Rd. Phone 541/347-3501. **FREE**

West Coast Game Park. A 21-acre park with more than 450 exotic animals and birds. Visitors meet and walk with free-roaming wildlife. Animal keepers demonstrate the personalities of many large predators residing at the park. (Mar-Nov, daily; rest of yr, wkends and hols) 7 mi S on US 101. Phone 541/347-3106. ¢¢

Special Events

Wine & Food Festival. Memorial Day wkend. Phone 541/347-9616.

Cranberry Festival. Parade, barbecue, square dances, harvest ball, sports events. Sept. Phone 541/347-9616.

Motels/Motor Lodges

★ **HARBOR VIEW MOTEL.** *355 Hwy 101 (97411). 541/347-4417; fax 541/347-3616; toll-free 800/526-0209. www.harborviewmotelbandon.com.* 59 rms, 3 story. No elvtr. July-late Sept: S $93-$108; D $98-$113; each addl $5; cottage $142; lower rates rest of yr. Crib $3. TV; cable (premium). Whirlpool. Coffee in rms. Restaurant nearby. Ck-out noon. Refrigerators. Many balconies. On Coquille River. Cr cds: A, C, D, DS, MC, V.

★ **SUNSET OCEANFRONT ACCOMMODAT.** *1865 Beach Loop Dr (97411). 541/347-2453; fax 541/347-3636; toll-free 800/842-2407. www.sunsetmotel.com.* 70 rms, 1-3 story, 8 kits. S, D $45-$105; suites $110-$215; kit. units $66-$120; cottages w/kits $125-$215. Crib free. Pet accepted, some restrictions; $5/day. TV; cable. Indoor pool. Restaurant 11 am-3 pm, 5-9 pm. Ck-out 11 am. Coin lndry. Meeting rm. Business servs avail. Gift shop. Free airport transportation. Whirlpool. Ocean view; beach access. Totally non-smoking. Cr cds: A, DS, MC, V.

Restaurants

★★ **BANDON BOATWORKS.** *275 Lincoln Ave SW (97411). 541/347-2111. www.destinationbandon.com.* Hrs: 11:30 am-2:30 pm, 5-9 pm; Sun 11 am-8:30 pm. Closed Dec 25. Res accepted. Wine, beer. Lunch $5-$8.45, dinner $9-$21.95. Children's meals. Specializes in seafood, steak, chicken. Salad bar. View of jetty, lighthouse. Totally nonsmoking. Cr cds: A, D, MC, V.

★★★ **LORD BENNETT'S.** *1695 Beach Loop Dr (97411). 541/347-3663.* Hrs: 11 am-3 pm, 5-9 pm; Sun brunch to 2 pm. Closed Dec 25. Res accepted. Serv bar. Lunch $4.50-$8.25, dinner $10-$18. Sun brunch $4.50-$8.75. Children's meals. Specializes in fresh seafood. Overlooks ocean. Cr cds: A, D, MC, V.

★ **WHEELHOUSE.** *125 Chicago Ave (97411). 541/347-9331.* Hrs: 11:30 am-9 pm; June-Sept to 10 pm. Bar to 11 pm. Lunch $5-$10, dinner $8-$20. Specializes in seafood, local lamb. In restored fish warehouse. View of boat harbor and fishing boats. Cr cds: A, MC, V.

Beaverton

(B-2) *See also Forest Grove, Hillsboro, Oregon City, Portland*

Pop 53,310 **Elev** 189 ft **Area code** 503 **Zip** 97005
Information Beaverton Area Chamber of Commerce, 4800 SW Griffith Dr, Suite 100; 503/644-0123
Web www.beaverton.org

Motels/Motor Lodges

★★ COURTYARD BY MARRIOTT.
8500 SW Nimbus Dr (97008). 503/641-3200; fax 503/641-1287; toll-free 800/831-0224. www.courtyard. com. 149 rms, 3 story. S, D $79; suites $118-$128; under 12 free. Crib free. TV; cable (premium). Indoor pool; whirlpool. Complimentary coffee in rms. Bkfst avail. Bar 5-10 pm. Ck-out noon. Coin lndry. Meeting rms. Business servs avail. Valet serv. Sundries. Exercise equipt. Refrigerator in suites. Balconies. Cr cds: A, D, DS, MC, V.

★★ FAIRFIELD INN & SUITES.
15583 NW Gateway Ct (97006). 503/972-0048; fax 503/972-0049; res 800/228-2800. www.fairfieldinn.com/ pdxfh. 106 rms, 4 story. Feb-Nov: S, D $74-$94; under 18 free; lower rates rest of yr. Crib free. TV; cable (premium), VCR avail. Complimentary buffet bkfst. Complimentary coffee in rms. Restaurant nearby. Ck-out noon. Meeting rm. Business servs avail. Valet serv. Sundries. Coin lndry. Exercise equipt. Indoor pool; whirlpool. Some refrigerators, microwaves. Cr cds: A, D, DS, MC, V.

★★★ GREENWOOD INN.
10700 SW Allen Blvd (97005). 503/643-7444; fax 503/626-4545; toll-free 800/289-1300. www.greenwoodinn.com. 250 rms, 2 story, 24 kits. S $99-$133; D $114-$148; each addl $10; kit. suites $180-$400; under 12 free; wkend rates. Crib free. Pet accepted; $10. TV; cable (premium). Pools; whirlpool. Complimentary coffee in rms. Restaurant (see PAVILION). Bar 4 pm-1:30 am; entertainment Mon-Sat. Ck-out 1 pm. Meeting rms. Business center. In-rm modem link. Sundries.

Gift shop. Exercise equipt; sauna. Some refrigerators. Cr cds: A, DS, MC, V.

★★ PEPPERTREE INN.
10720 SW Allen Blvd (97005). 503/641-7477; fax 503/643-5899; toll-free 800/453-6219. www.peppertreeinn.com. 73 rms, 2 story. S $65; D $70; each addl $5; under 12 free. TV; cable (premium), VCR (movies $5). Heated pool; whirlpool. Complimentary continental bkfst. Coffee in rms. Restaurant adj 6:30 am-10 pm. Ck-out 11 am. Coin lndry. Business servs avail. Valet serv. Exercise equipt. Health club privileges. Refrigerators. Cr cds: A, D, DS, JCB, MC, V.

★★ PHOENIX INN TIGARD.
9575 SW Locust St, Tigard (97223). 503/624-9000; fax 503/968-8184; res 800/624-6884. www.phoenixinn.com. 101 rms, 3 story. S $72-$77; D $79-$89; each addl $10; under 18 free; wkend rates. Crib free. TV; cable (premium). Complimentary continental bkfst. Complimentary coffee in rms. Restaurant nearby. Ck-out noon. Meeting rms. Business servs avail. Valet serv. Sundries. Coin lndry. Exercise equipt. Indoor pool; whirlpool. Refrigerators, microwaves; some wet bars. Cr cds: A, D, DS, MC, V.

★ RAMADA INN.
13455 SW Canyon Rd (97005). 503/643-9100; fax 503/643-0514; res 800/228-2828. www.ramada.com. 143 rms, 3 story, 18 kits. S, D $115-$144; each addl $10; kit. units $120-$150; under 18 free. Crib free. TV, cable (premium). Heated pool. Complimentary continental bkfst. Coffee in rms. Restaurant adj open 24 hrs. Ck-out noon. Meeting rms. Business servs avail. Exercise equipt. Cr cds: A, C, D, DS, MC, V.

Restaurants

★★★ PAVILION TRATTORIA.
10700 SW Allen Blvd (97005). 503/626-4550. www.paviliontrattoria. citysearch.com. Hrs: 6:30 am-10 pm; Sun, Mon 7 am-9 pm; early-bird dinner Sun-Thurs 4-6 pm; Sun brunch

10 am-2 pm. Res accepted. Northwestern menu. Bar. Bkfst $4-$9.25, lunch $5.95-$9.50, dinner $8-$19. Sun brunch $19.95. Children's meals. Specializes in salmon, prime rib. Entertainment Thurs-Sat. Outdoor dining. Casual decor. Cr cds: A, D, DS, MC, V.

D

★★ **SAYLER'S OLD COUNTRY KITCHEN.** *4655 SW Griffith Dr (97005).* *503/644-1492.* Hrs: 4-11 pm; Fri to midnight; Sat 3 pm-midnight; Sun noon-11 pm. Closed July 4, Thanksgiving, Dec 24, 25. Bar from 2:30 pm. Dinner $8.95-$21.95. Children's meals. Specializes in steak, prime rib, chicken. Family-owned. Cr cds: A, MC, V.

D SC

★★ **SHANGHAI TO TOKYO RESTAURANT & BAR.** *11995 SW Beaverson (Hillsdale Hwy) (97005).* *503/646-5697. www.koji.com.* Hrs: 11:30 am-11 pm. Closed most major hols. Japanese menu. Bar. Lunch $6-$13, dinner $12-$23. Specializes in sushi, Japanese-style noodles. Japanese decor. Cr cds: A, MC, V.

D

Bend

(D-3) *See also Prineville, Redmond*

Settled 1900 **Pop** 20,469 **Elev** 3,628 ft **Area code** 541

Information Chamber of Commerce, 63085 N US 97, 97701; 541/382-3221 or 800/905-2363

Web www.bendchamber.org

The early town was named Farewell Bend after a beautiful wooded area on a sweeping curve of the Deschutes River, where pioneer travelers had their last view of the river. The Post Office Department shortened it, but there was good reason for this nostalgic name. As westward-bound settlers approached, they found the first lush, green forests and good water they had seen in Oregon.

Tourists are attracted year-round to the region by its streams and lakes, mountains, great pine forests, ski

slopes, and golf courses. There is also much of interest to the geologist and rockhound in this area. Movie and television producers take advantage of the wild western scenery.

Two Ranger District offices of the Deschutes National Forest are located here.

What to See and Do

★ **Driving Tour In Deschutes National Forest.** An 89-mi paved loop (Century Dr, Cascade Lakes Hwy) provides a clear view of Three Sisters peaks, passes many mountain lakes and streams. Go W on Franklin Ave past Drake Park, follow the signs. Continue S past Mt Bachelor, Elk Lake, Lava Lakes, and Cultus Lake. After passing Crane Prairie Reservoir, turn left (E) on Forest Rd 42 to US 97, then left (N) for return to Bend. Also in the forest are Newberry National Volcanic Monument, the Lava Cast Forest and Lava Butte Geological Area, Mt Bachelor Ski Area, Crane Prairie Osprey Management Area, as well as Mt Jefferson, Diamond Peak, Three Sisters, and Mt Washington wildernesses. Fishing, hiking, camping, picnicking, and rafting are popular. The forest incl 1.6 million acres with headquarters in Bend. 10 mi S of Bend, at the base of Lava Butte, is Lava Lands Visitor Center, operated by the US Forest Service, with dioramas and exhibits on history and geology of volcanic area. For further information contact Supervisor, 1645 US 20E, 97701. Phone 541/388-2715.

The High Desert Museum. Regional museum with indoor/outdoor exhibits featuring live animals and cultural history of Intermountain Northwest aridlands; hands-on activities; on-going presentations. Galleries house wildlife, Western art, and Native American artifacts; landscape photography; walk-through dioramas depicting opening of American West. Desertarium showcases seldom-seen bats, burrowing owls, amphibians, and reptiles. Visitor center. (Daily; closed Jan 1, Thanksgiving, Dec 25) 6 mi S on US 97. Phone 541/382-4754. ¢¢¢

Lava Butte and Lava River Cave. Lava Butte is an extinct cinder cone. Paved road to top provides view of Cascades; interpretive trails through pine forest and lava flow. One mi south, Lava River Cave offers a lava tube 1.2 mi long (fee); ramps and stairs ease walking. 11 mi S on US 97. Visitor center has audiovisual shows (May-Sept, daily). Phone 541/593-2421. ¢¢

Newberry National Volcanic Monument. Wide range of volcanic features and deposits similar to Mt Etna; obsidian flow, pumice deposits. On same road are East and Paulina lakes. There is a view of entire area from Paulina Peak. Both lakes have excellent fishing, boat landings; hiking, picnicking (stoves, fireplaces), resorts, tent and trailer sites. 24 mi S on US 97, then 14 mi E on Forest Rd 21, in Deschutes National Forest. Phone 541/383-5300. ¢¢¢

Pine Mount Observatory. University of Oregon astronomical research facility. Visitors may view stars, planets, and galaxies through telescopes. (Memorial Day-Sept, Fri and Sat) 26 mi SE near Millican, via US 20, then 9 mi S. Phone 541/382-8331. ¢¢

Skiing. Mount Bachelor Ski Area. Panoramic, scenic view of forests, lakes, and Cascade Range. Facilities at base of 6,000 ft; 6,000 acres. Ten chairlifts; patrol, school, rentals; cafeterias, concession areas, bars, lodges; day care. Longest run 1½ mi; vertical drop 3,365 ft. (Mid-Nov-May, daily) 56 mi of x-country trails. 22 mi SW on Century Dr. Phone 541/382-2442. ¢¢¢¢¢

State parks and recreation areas.

LaPine. A 2,333-acre park on Deschutes River in Ponderosa pine forest. Scenic views. Swimming, bathhouse, fishing, boating; picnicking, improved trailer campsites (dump station). Standard fees. 22 mi S on US 97, then 4 mi W. Phone 541/388-6055.

Pilot Butte. A 101-acre park noted for a lone cinder cone rising 511 feet above the city. Summit affords an excellent view of the Cascade Range. No water, no camping. 1 mi E on US 20. Phone 541/388-6055.

Tumalo. A 320-acre park situated along the banks of the Deschutes River; swimming nearby, fishing; hiking, picnicking, tent and trailer campsites; solar-heated showers. Standard fees. 5½ mi NW off US 20. Phone 541/382-3586.

Tumalo Falls. A 97-ft waterfall deep in pine forest devastated by 1979 fire. W via Franklin Ave and Galveston Ave, 12 mi beyond city limits, then 2 mi via unsurfaced forest road. Phone 541/383-5300.

Whitewater Rafting. Sun Country Tours. Choose from two-hr or all-day trips. Also canoeing and special programs. (May-Sept) Phone 541/382-6277. ¢¢¢¢¢

Motels/Motor Lodges

★★ **BEST WESTERN ENTRADA LODGE.** *19221 Century Dr (97702). 541/382-4080; res 800/528-1234. www.bestwestern.com/entradalodge.* 79 rms. S, D $59-$89; each addl $5; ski plans; some higher rates major hols. Crib $5. Pet accepted; $10/day. TV; cable. Pool; whirlpool. Complimentary continental bkfst. Coffee in rms. Ck-out noon. Meeting rm. Business servs avail. In-rm modem link. Downhill/x-country ski 17 mi. Health club privileges. On 31 acres. Whitewater rafting. Cr cds: A, C, D, DS, MC, V.

⊠ 🐾 🏊 ➰ 🚭 ♨

★★ **HAMPTON INN.** *15 NE Butler Market Rd (97701). 541/388-4114; fax 541/389-3261; res 800/426-7866. www.hamptoninn.com.* 99 rms, 2 story. S $69-$84, D $79-$89; under 18 free. Crib free. Pet accepted. TV; cable (premium). Heated pool; whirlpool. Complimentary continental bkfst. Coffee in rms. Ck-out noon. Business servs avail. In-rm modem link. Cr cds: A, C, D, DS, MC, V.

🄳 🐾 🐾 ⅃ ➰ 🚭 ♨ 🆂🅲

★ **MOTEL 6.** *201 NE 3rd St (97701). 541/382-8282; fax 541/388-6833; res 800/466-8357. www.motel6.com.* 60 rms, 2 story. S $39-$59; D $49-$69; each addl $5. Crib avail. Pet accepted, some restrictions; $10. TV; cable (premium). Heated pool. Complimentary continental bkfst. Restaurant nearby. Ck-out noon. Business servs avail. Downhill/x-country ski 20 mi. Some microwaves. Cr cds: A, D, DS, MC, V.

⊠ 🏊 ➰ 🚭 ♨

★★ **MOUNT BACHELOR VILLAGE RESORT.** *19717 Mt Bachelor Dr (97701). 541/389-5900; fax 541/388-7820; toll-free 800/452-9846. www.*

mountbachelorvillage.com. 130 condos, some A/C, 2 story. Condos $97-$329; ski, golf plans. Crib $5. TV; cable. Heated pool; whirlpools. Complimentary coffee in lobby. Restaurant 11:30 am-10 pm. Ck-out noon. Coin lndry. Meeting rm. Business center. Downhill ski 18 mi; x-country ski 14 mi. Tennis. Health club privileges. Refrigerators, fireplaces; some microwaves. Private patios, balconies. Picnic tables. Woodland setting along Deschutes River. Cr cds: A, DS, MC, V.

★★ **RED LION INN NORTH.** *1415 NE 3rd St (97701). 541/382-7011; fax 541/382-7934; res 800/733-5466. www.redlion.com.* 75 rms, 2 story. S, D $79; each addl $10; under 18 free. Crib free. Pet accepted. TV; cable (premium). Heated pool; whirlpool. Restaurant 6 am-10 pm. Ck-out noon. Meeting rms. Business servs avail. In-rm modem link. Sundries. Saunas. Some refrigerators, microwaves. Cr cds: A, D, DS, MC, V.

★★★ **THE RIVERHOUSE RESORT.** *3075 N Hwy 97 (97701). 541/389-3111; fax 541/389-0870; toll-free 800/547-3928. www.riverhouse.com.* 220 rms, 2 story, 29 suites, 39 kits. S $57-$77; D $69-$89; each addl $8; suites $87-$195; kit. units $87-$119; under 6 free; ski, golf plans. Crib $10. Pet accepted. TV; cable (premium), VCR (movies). 2 heated pools, 1 indoor; poolside serv. Coffee in rms. Restaurant 6 am-10 pm. Ck-out noon. Coin lndry. Meeting rms. Business servs avail. In-rm modem link. Bellhops. Sundries. 18-hole golf, greens fee $28-$42, pro, putting green, driving range. Exercise equipt. Some microwaves. Balconies. On the Deschutes River. Cr cds: A, D, DS, MC, V.

★★ **SHILO INN.** *3105 NE O. B. Riley Rd (97701). 541/389-9600; fax 541/382-4310; res 800/222-2244. www.shiloinns.com.* 151 rms, 2 story, 54 kit. units. S, D $99-$199.95; each addl $10; under 12 free. Crib free. Pet accepted, some restrictions; $10/day. TV; cable (premium). 2 pools, 1 indoor; whirlpools. Coffee in rms. Restaurant 7 am-9 pm. Bar. Ck-out noon. Coin lndry. Meeting rms. Business servs avail. Sundries. Free airport transportation. Downhill/x-country ski 20 mi. Exercise equipt; sauna. Refrigerators, microwaves. On Deschutes River. Cr cds: A, C, D, DS, ER, JCB, MC, V.

Resorts

★★ **BLACK BUTTE RANCH.** *13653 Hawks Beard Rd, Redmond (97759). 541/595-6211; fax 541/595-2077; toll-free 800/452-7455. www.blackbutte ranch.com.* 132 condo and house units (1-4 bedrm), 69 with kit. Condo units $85-$178; houses $130-$280; golf, ski plans. Crib $5. TV; VCR (movies $3-$5). 4 heated pools; wading pool, lifeguard. Playground. Supervised children's activities (June-Labor Day). Dining rm 8 am-3 pm, 5-9 pm. Snack bar. Bar 11 am-10 pm. Ck-out 11 am, ck-in 4 pm. Meeting rms. Business servs avail. Grocery. Sports dir. Lighted tennis, pro. Two 18-hole golf courses, pro, greens fee $55, putting green, driving range. Downhill/x-country ski 15 mi; x-country rental equipt. Exercise equipt. Massage. Game rm. Bicycles. Many microwaves, fireplaces. Private patios. On 1,830 wooded acres. Cr cds: A, D, DS, MC, V.

★★★ **THE INN OF THE SEVENTH MOUNTAIN.** *18575 SW Century Dr (97702). 541/382-8711; fax 541/382-3517. www.7thmtn.com.* 300 rms, 3 story, 200 kits. No elvtr. Dec-Mar, June-Aug: S $64-$74; D $94-$104; kit. units $89-$109; kit. suites $169-$269; package plans. Crib $3. TV; cable, VCR avail (movies). 2 pools, wading pool, whirlpools, poolside serv, lifeguard (summer). Playgrounds. Supervised children's activities (June-Sept); ages 4-11. Dining rms 7 am-10 pm. Box lunches. Bar 4 pm-1 am. Ck-out noon. Coin lndry. Meeting rms. Business servs avail. Grocery. Sports dir. Tennis, pro. Canoeing, rafting trips. Downhill/x-country ski 14 mi. Outdoor ice/roller rink; horse-drawn sleigh rides. Snowmobile, bike tours. Bicycles. Lawn games. Sauna. Movies. Rec rm. Some refrigerators, microwaves, fireplaces. Private patios. Picnic tables, grills. Cr cds: A, D, DS, MC, V.

★★★ **SUNRIVER RESORT.** *1 Center Dr, Sunriver (97707). 541/593-1000; fax 541/593-4167; toll-free 800/801-8765. www.sunriverresort.com.* 211 units (1-3 bedrm) in 2-story lodge units, 77 kits., 230 houses (1-4 bedrm). Mid-June-Sept: S, D $130-$139; kit. suites $190; houses (up to 8 persons) $165-$325; higher rates hols; lower rates rest of yr. TV; cable (premium), VCR avail (movies $3). 3 pools; 3 wading pools, outdoor whirlpools, lifeguard. Playground. Supervised children's activities (June-Sept); ages 3-14. Dining rms 7 am-10 pm (see also MEADOWS). Ck-out 11 am, ck-in 4 pm. Coin lndry. Meeting rms. Business center. Gift shop. Grocery. Barber, beauty shop. Airport transportation. Ski bus. Sports dir. 28 tennis courts. Three 18-hole golf courses, 6 pros, putting greens, driving ranges, pro shops. Canoes; whitewater rafting. Downhill ski 18 mi; x-country ski on site. Skating rink, equipt (fee). Racquetball. Bicycles; 30 mi of bike trails. Nature center. Stables. Indoor, outdoor games. Game rm (fee). Entertainment. Massage. Health club privileges. Fishing guide service. 5,500-ft airstrip. Marina. Houses with full amenities and private patios. Some microwaves. Balconies. Picnic tables. 3,300 acres on Deschutes River. Cr cds: A, DS, MC, V.

⬛ 🛋 🔥 ▶ 🎿 ➿ 🏃 ⛷ 🔥 **SC** 🎿

Guest Ranch

★★ **ROCK SPRINGS GUEST RANCH.** *64201 Tyler Rd (97701). 541/382-1957; fax 541/382-7774; toll-free 800/225-3833. www.rocksprings.com.* 26 cottages. S $1,430/wk; family rates; AP late June-Aug; MAP Thanksgiving. TV in sitting rm. Heated pool; whirlpool. Free supervised child's activities (late June-Aug); ages 3-16. Dining rm (sittings) 8-9 am, noon-1 pm, 6:30-7:30 pm. Box lunches. Picnics. Ck-out 11 am, ck-in 4:30 pm. Grocery 3 mi. Guest lndry. Meeting rm. Business servs avail. Free airport transportation. Lighted tennis, pro. Downhill/X-country ski 20 mi. Exercise equipt. Massage. Lawn games. Western trail rides. Game rm. Fish

pond. Refrigerators, fireplaces. Picnic tables. Cr cds: A, C, D, DS, MC, V.

⬛ 🛋 🔥 ▶ 🎿 ➿ 🏃 ➿ 🔥

Restaurants

★★★ **ERNESTO'S ITALIAN RESTAURANT.** *1203 NE 3rd St (97701). 541/389-7274.* Hrs: 4:30-9:30 pm; Fri, Sat to 10 pm. Italian menu. Bar. Dinner $7.95-$15.50. Children's meals. Specializes in pizza, calzone. Parking. Housed in former church. Cr cds: A, D, DS, MC, V.
SC

★★★ **MEADOWS.** *1 Center Dr, Sunriver (97707). 541/593-1000. www.sunriverresort.com.* Northwest High Desert menu. Own pastries, desserts. Hrs: 6-10 pm. Res accepted. Owl's Nest pub 11-2 am. Extensive wine list. A la carte entrees: dinner $11-$25. Totally nonsmoking. Cr cds: A, C, D, DS, MC, V.
D

★★ **PINE TAVERN.** *967 NW Brooks St (97701). 541/382-5581. www.pinetavern.com.* Hrs: 11:30 am-9:30 pm; Sun from 5:30 pm. Res accepted. Bar. Lunch $5.95-$8.95, dinner $10.50-$17.50. Children's meals. Specializes in fresh trout, prime rib, seafood. Salad bar (lunch). Garden dining. 100-ft pine tree in dining rm. Overlooks Deschutes River, garden. Totally nonsmoking. Cr cds: A, D, MC, V.
D

★ **ROSZAK'S FISH HOUSE.** *1230 NE 3rd St (97701). 541/382-3173.* Hrs: 11:30 am-2:30 pm, 4-10 pm; Sat, Sun 4-9 pm. Closed Memorial Day, Labor Day. Res accepted. Bar. Lunch $6.25-$8.95, dinner $10.95-$22.95. Children's meals. Specializes in prime rib, seafood. Parking. Totally nonsmoking. Cr cds: A, D, DS, MC, V.
D

★ **TONY'S.** *415 NE 3rd St (97701). 541/389-5858.* Hrs: 6 am-9:30 pm. Closed Dec 25. Res accepted. Italian, American menu. Bar 3-10 pm. Bkfst $2.75-$6.95, lunch $2.95-$5.95, dinner $6.95-$12.95. Children's meals. Specializes in pizza. Parking. Early Amer building; original paintings, fireplace. Family-owned. Cr cds: D, DS, MC, V.

D SC

Unrated Dining Spot

WESTSIDE BAKERY & CAFE. *1005 NW Galveston Ave (97701). 541/382-3426.* Hrs: 7 am-3 pm; Sun to 2 pm. Closed Thanksgiving, Dec 25. Bkfst, lunch $5-$8. Children's meals. Specializes in baked goods, omelettes. Parking. 3 dining rms; many antiques and toys. Cr cds: DS, MC, V.

D

Biggs

See also The Dalles

Pop 30 **Elev** 173 ft **Area code** 541
Zip 97065

What to See and Do

John Day Locks and Dam. A $487-million unit in the US Army Corps of Engineers Columbia River Basin project. Visitors may view turbine generators from powerhouse observation rm; fish-viewing stations. Self-guided tours (daily; guided tours by appt; closed hols). 5 mi E off I-84 N. **FREE** The dam creates

> **Lake Umatilla.** A 100-mi reservoir. The eastern part of the lake is a national wildlife management area for the preservation of game waterfowl and fish.

Motel/Motor Lodge

★★ **RIVIERA.** *91484 Biggs (97065). 541/739-2501; fax 541/739-2091; toll-free 800/528-1234. www.biggsjct. com.* 40 rms, 1-2 story. S $53; D $62; each addl $5; suites $69-$93. Crib $5. Pet accepted; $7. TV. Pool. Complimentary continental bkfst. Restaurant adj 6 am-10 pm. Ck-out noon. Business servs avail. Cr cds: A, C, D, DS, MC, V.

Brookings

(F-1) *See also Coos Bay, Gold Beach*

Pop 4,400 **Elev** 130 ft **Area code** 541
Zip 97415

Information Brookings-Harbor Chamber of Commerce and Information Center, 16330 Lower Harbor Rd, PO Box 940; 800/535-9469

Beachcombers, whale watchers, and fishermen find this coastal city a haven for their activities. A commercial and sportfishing center, Brookings lies in an area that produces a high percentage of the nation's Easter lily bulbs. A Ranger District office of the Siskiyou National Forest (see GRANTS PASS) is located here.

What to See and Do

Azalea Park. A 36-acre city park with five varieties of large native azaleas, some blooming twice a yr (see SPECIAL EVENT). Observation point. Hiking. Picnicking. Just E off US 101. Phone 541/469-2021.

State parks.

> **Harris Beach.** A 171-acre park with scenic rock cliffs along ocean. Ocean beach, fishing; hiking trails, observation point, picnicking, improved tent and trailer campsites (dump station). Standard fees. 2 mi N on US 101. Phone 541/469-2021.

> **Loeb.** A 320-acre park on the Chetco River with an area of beautiful old myrtle trees; also redwoods. Swimming, fishing; picnicking, improved camping. Standard fees. 10 mi NE off US 101. Phone 541/469-2021.

> **Samuel H. Boardman.** A 1,473-acre park with observation points along 11 mi of spectacular coastline. Fishing, clamming; hiking, picnicking. 4 mi N on US 101. Phone 541/469-2021.

Special Event

Azalea Festival. Azalea Park. Parade, seafood, art exhibits, street fair, crafts fair, music. Memorial Day wkend. Phone 541/469-2021.

Motel/Motor Lodge

★ **SPRINDRIFT MOTOR INN.** *1215 Chetco Ave (97415). 541/469-5345; fax 541/469-5213; toll-free 800/292-1171.* 35 rms, 2 story. Mid-May-Sept: S $45-$52; D $49-$69; each addl $5; lower rates rest of yr. Crib $5. TV; cable (premium). Complimentary coffee in lobby. Restaurant opp 7 am-10 pm. Ck-out 11 am. Business servs avail. Refrigerators. Cr cds: A, C, D, DS, MC, V.

🐾 ✕ ⊠ 🔥

Burns (D-5)

Pop 2,913 **Elev** 4,170 ft
Area code 541 **Zip** 97720
Information Harney County Chamber of Commerce, 18 West D St; 541/573-2636
Web www.oregon1.org/harney/

This remote trading center and county seat serves a livestock-raising and forage production area bigger than many eastern states. Ranger District offices of the Malheur National Forest (see JOHN DAY) and Ochoco National Forest (see PRINEVILLE) are located here.

What to See and Do

Harney County Historical Museum. Displays incl arrowheads, quilts, wildlife, artifacts, furniture, clothing, cut glass, old-fashioned kitchen, Pete French's safe and spurs. The Hayes Room contains a bedrm and dining rm furnished in antiques. Also old wagons, tools, and machinery. (Apr-Oct, Mon-Sat; closed July 4) 18 West D St. Phone 541/573-5618. ¢¢

Malheur National Wildlife Refuge. Established in 1908 by Theodore Roosevelt, the 185,000-acre refuge was set aside primarily as a nesting area for migratory birds. It is also an important fall and spring gathering point for waterfowl migrating between the northern breeding grounds and the California wintering grounds. More than 320 species of birds and 58 species of mammals have been recorded on the refuge. Headquarters has museum. (Daily)

32 mi S on OR 205. Phone 541/493-2612. **FREE**

Special Events

John Scharff Migratory Bird Festival. Incl bird-watching and historical tours, films, arts and crafts. First wkend Apr. Phone 541/573-2636.

Steens Mountain Rim Run. In Frenchglen, approx 48 mi S on OR 205. Six-mi run at high elevation, pit barbecue, all-night street dance, team-roping, horse cutting. First Sat Aug. Phone 541/573-2636.

Harney County Fair, Rodeo and Race Meet. Incl rodeo and pari-mutuel racing. Tues-Sun after Labor Day. Phone 541/573-6166

Motels/Motor Lodges

★ **DAYS INN PONDEROSA.** *577 W Monroe St (97720). 541/573-2047; fax 541/573-3828 res 800/325-2525. www.daysinn.com.* 52 rms, 2 story. S $48-$53, D $53-$63; each addl $5. Pet accepted; $10. TV; cable (premium). Pool. Complimentary continental bkfst. Restaurant nearby. Ck-out 11 am. Business servs avail. Cr cds: A, C, D, DS, MC, V.

D 🐾 ⊠ ⊠ 🐾 SC

★ **SILVER SPUR MOTEL.** *789 N Broadway Ave (97720). 541/573-2077; fax 541/573-3921; res 800/400-2077.* 26 rms, 2 story. S $35-$40; D $45-$55; each addl $5. Crib $5. TV; cable (premium). Pet accepted; $5. Complimentary continental bkfst. Complimentary coffee in rms. Ck-out 11:30 am. Free airport transportation. Health club privileges. Refrigerators, microwaves. Cr cds: A, DS, MC, V.

D 🐾 ✕ 🔥

Restaurant

★★ **PINE ROOM CAFE.** *543 W Monroe (97720). 541/573-6631.* Hrs: 5-10 pm; winter to 9 pm. Closed Sun, Mon; hols. Res accepted. Bar 4 pm-2:30 am. Dinner $7.25-$17.25. Specialties: brochette of tenderloin, stuffed prawns Mornay. Pictures of Harney County by local artist. Family-owned. Cr cds: A, DS, MC, V.

D ⊠

Cannon Beach

(A-1) *See also Astoria, Seaside*

Pop 1,221 **Elev** 25 ft **Area code** 503
Zip 97110
Information Visitor Information Center, 207 N Spruce, PO Box 64;
503/436-2623

The cannon and capstan from the schooner USS *Shark,* which was washed ashore near here in 1846, are now on a small monument four miles south of this resort town. Swimming (lifeguard on duty in summer), surfing, and surf fishing can be enjoyed here and the seven-mile stretch of wide beach is wonderful for walking. Among the large rocks offshore is the 235-foot Haystack Rock, third-largest monolith in the world.

What to See and Do

Ecola State Park. End of the trail for Lewis and Clark expedition. A 1,303-acre park with six mi of ocean frontage; sea lion and bird rookeries on rocks and offshore islands; Tillamook Lighthouse. Beaches, fishing; hiking (on the Oregon Coast Trail), picnicking at Ecola Point. Whale-watching at observation point. 2 mi N off US 101. Phone 503/861-1671.

Oswald West State Park. A 2,474-acre park with outstanding coastal headland; towering cliffs; low dunes; rain forest with massive spruce and cedar trees; road winds 700 ft above sea level and 1,000 ft below peak of Neahkahnie Mtn. Surfing (at nearby Short Sands Beach), fishing; hiking trails (on the Oregon Coast Trail), picnicking, primitive campgrounds accessible only by ¼-mi foot trail. 10 mi S on US 101. Phone 503/368-5943.

Special Event

Sandcastle Contest. Nationally known event features sand sculptures on beach. Early June. Phone 503/436-2623.

Motels/Motor Lodges

★★★ **HALLMARK RESORT.** *1400 S Hemlock St (97110). 503/436-1566;* fax 503/436-0324; toll-free 800/345-5676. www.hallmarkinns.com.* 132 rms, 3 story, 63 kits., 5 cottages. July-Sept: S, D $109-$189; suites $125-$229; kit. units $125-$229; cottages $265-$425; lower rates rest of yr. Crib free. Pet accepted; $8/day. TV; cable (premium), VCR avail (movies). Indoor pool; wading pool, whirlpool. Complimentary coffee. Restaurant adj 8 am-9 pm. Ck-out noon, ck-in 4 pm. Coin lndry. Meeting rms. Business servs avail. Gift shop. Exercise equipt; sauna. Health club privileges. Refrigerators; some in-rm whirlpools, fireplaces. Balconies. On beach. Cr cds: A, DS, MC, V.

★★★ **HEARTHSTONE INN.** *107 Jackson St E (97110). 503/436-1392; fax 503/436-1396; res 800/238-4107. www.oregoncoastlodgings.com/cannonbeach/cbhl/hearthstone.* 26 rms, 2 story. No A/C. June-Oct: S, D $69-$125; each addl $10; lower rates rest of yr. TV; cable, VCR avail. Complimentary continental bkfst. Restaurant 8 am-10 pm. Ck-out 11 am. Business servs avail. Totally nonsmoking. Cr cds: A, C, D, DS, MC, V.

★★ **SCHOONERS COVE OCEAN FRONT MOTEL.** *188 N Larch (97110). 503/436-2300; fax 503/436-2156; toll-free 800/843-0128. www.*

Oswald West State Park

schoonerscove.com. 30 kit. units, 2 story, 16 kit. suites. No A/C. Mid-June-Labor Day: S, D $99-$149; each addl $10; kit. suites $149-$199; lower rates rest of yr. Crib $10. TV; cable (premium), VCR. Restaurant nearby. Ck-out 11 am. Coin lndry. Meeting rm. Whirlpool. Fireplaces. Balconies. Picnic tables, grills. On beach. Cr cds: A, C, D, DS, MC, V.

D 🔌 🐾 SC

★★★ **SURFSAND RESORT HOTEL.** *Oceanfront (97110). 503/436-2274; fax 503/436-9116; toll-free 800/547-6100. www.surfsand.com.* 82 rms, 2 story, 38 kits. No A/C. June-mid-Oct: S, D $159-$249; suites, kit. units $159-$299; lower rates rest of yr. Crib $5. Pet accepted; $5/day. TV; cable (premium), VCR (movies $3). Indoor pool; whirlpool. Coffee in rms. Restaurant 8 am-midnight. Bar to 1 am. Ck-out noon. Lndry facilities. Meeting rms. Gift shop. Health club privileges. Refrigerators, fireplaces; some in-rm whirlpools. Balconies. On ocean, beach. View of Haystack Rock. Cr cds: A, DS, MC, V.

D 🔌 ⛱ 🔌 🔥

★★ **TOLOVANA INN.** *3400 S Hemlock (97145). 503/436-2211; fax 503/436-0134; toll-free 800/333-8890. www.tolovanainn.com.* 175 rms, 3 story, 96 kits. No A/C. No elvtr. S, D $61-$71; suites $153-$249; kit. units $150-$249; studio rms $104-$150. Crib free. Pet accepted, some restrictions; $10. TV; cable, VCR avail (movies). Indoor pool; whirlpool. Ck-out noon. Coin lndry. Meeting rms. Business servs avail. Game rm. Health club privileges. Refrigerators; some fireplaces. Private patios, balconies. Overlooks Haystack Rock. Cr cds: A, D, DS, MC, V.

D 🔌 🏋 ⛷ ⛱ 🔌 🐾

B&B/Small Inn

★ **GREY WHALE INN.** *164 Kenai St (97110). 503/436-2848.* 5 rms, shower only, 3 kit. units. No A/C. June-Sept: S, D $74-$94; each addl $10; lower rates rest of yr. TV; cable, VCR. Complimentary coffee in rms. Ck-out 11 am, ck-in 3 pm. Totally nonsmoking. Cr cds: MC, V.

⛱ 🔥

Restaurant

★★ **DOOGER'S.** *1371 S Hemlock (97110). 503/436-2225.* Hrs: 8 am-10 pm. Closed Thanksgiving, Dec 25; also 2 wks Jan. Bar. Bkfst $2.75-$8.95, lunch $3-$9.50, dinner $7.95-$34.95. Children's meals. Specializes in steak, seafood. Totally nonsmoking. Cr cds: A, D, DS, MC, V.

D

Cave Junction

(F-1) *See also Grants Pass*

Pop 1,126 **Elev** 1,295 ft
Area code 541 **Zip** 97523
Information Illinois Valley Chamber of Commerce, 201 Caves Hwy, PO Box 312; 541/592-3326

A Ranger District office of the Siskiyou National Forest (see GRANTS PASS) is located here.

What to See and Do

Kerbyville Museum. Home (ca 1870) furnished in the period; outdoor display of farm, logging, and mining tools; Native American artifacts; rock display; log schoolhouse, blacksmith shop, general store. Picnic tables. (Mar-Dec, daily) 2 mi N on US 199 in Kerby. Phone 541/592-2076. ¢¢

Oregon Caves National Monument. (see) 20 mi E on OR 46.

Special Events

Annual Moon Tree Country Run. Siskiyou Smoke Jump Base. Phone 541/596-2621. Mid-June.

Wild Blackberry Festival. Blackberry foods, cooking, games, crafts and music. Mid-Aug. Phone 541/592-3326.

Motel/Motor Lodge

★★ **OREGON CAVES LODGE.** *20000 Cave Hwy (97523). 541/592-3400; fax 541/592-3800.* 22 rms, 3 story, 3 suites. No A/C. No elvtr. No rm phones. S, D $89; each addl $10; suites $119; under 6 free. Closed Nov-Apr. Crib $10. Restaurants from 7 am. Ck-out 11 am. Meeting rms.

Business center. Sundries. Gift shop. X-country ski on-site. Picnic tables, grills. Totally nonsmoking. Cr cds: A, DS, MC, V.

Coos Bay

(D-1) *See also Bandon, Brookings, North Bend, Reedsport*

Founded 1854 **Pop** 15,076 **Elev** 11 ft
Area code 541 **Zip** 97420
Information Bay Area Chamber of Commerce, 50 E Central, PO Box 210; 541/269-0215 or 800/824-8486
Web www.ucinet.com/~bacc

Coos Bay, one of the world's largest shipping ports for forest products, is also a deep-sea fishing haven. Dairy herds graze in the surrounding area, providing milk for the production of butter and cheddar cheese. Local cranberry bogs supply fruit for processing.

What to See and Do

Charleston Marina Complex. Charter boats; launching and moorage facilities (fee); car and boat trailer parking (free); dry boat storage, travel park; motel; marine fuel dock; tackle shops; restaurants. Office (Mon-Fri). 9 mi SW in Charleston. Phone 541/888-2548.

The Oregon Connection/House of Myrtlewood. Manufacturing of myrtlewood gift items. Tours. (Daily; closed hols) 1125 S 1st St, just off US 101 in S Coos Bay. Phone 541/267-7804. **FREE**

South Slough National Estuarine Research Reserve. A 4,400-acre area reserved for the study of estuarine ecosystems and life. Previous studies here incl oyster culture techniques and water pollution. Special programs, lectures, and exhibits at Interpretive Center. Trails and waterways (daily); guided trail walks and canoe tours (June-Aug; fee). Interpretive Center (June-Aug, daily; rest of yr, Mon-Fri). 4 mi S on Seven Devils Rd, in Charleston. Phone 541/888-5558. **FREE**

State parks.

Cape Arago. This 134-acre promontory juts ½ mi into ocean. Two beaches, fishing; hiking (on Oregon Coast Trail), picnicking. Observation point (whale and seal watching). 14 mi SW off US 101 on Cape Arago Hwy. Phone 541/888-8867.

Shore Acres. Former grand estate of Coos Bay lumberman, noted for its unusual botanical and Japanese gardens and spectacular ocean views (743 acres). Ocean beach; hiking (on the Oregon Coast Trail), picnicking. Standard fees. 13 mi SW off US 101 on Cape Arago Hwy. Phone 541/888-3732.

Sunset Bay. A 395-acre park with swimming beach on sheltered bay, fishing; hiking, picnicking, tent and trailer sites. Observation point. Standard fees. 12 mi SW off US 101 on Cape Arago Hwy. Phone 541/888-4902.

Special Events

Oregon Coast Music Festival. Variety of musical presentations ranging from jazz and dance to chamber and symphonic music. Also free outdoor picnic concerts. Phone 877/897-9350. Last two full wks July.

Blackberry Arts Festival. Fourth wkend Aug. Phone 541/267-1022.

Bay Area Fun Festival. Third wkend Sept. Phone 800/738-4849 or 541/267-3341.

Motels/Motor Lodges

★★ **BEST WESTERN HOLIDAY MOTEL.** *411 N Bayshore Dr (97420). 541/269-5111; res 800/528-1234. www.bestwestern.com.* 77 rms, 2 story. July-Aug: S, D $71-$91; each addl $5; suites $100-$140; kits. units $69-$99; lower rates rest of yr. Crib avail. TV; cable (premium). Indoor pool; whirlpool. Complimentary coffee in lobby. Restaurant adj open 24 hrs. Guest lndry. Ck-out noon. Exercise equipt. Microwaves avail. Whirlpools in suites. Cr cds: A, C, D, DS, MC, V.

★★ **RED LION HOTEL.** *1313 N Bayshore Dr (97420). 541/267-4141; fax 541/267-2884; res 800/733-5466. www.redlion.com.* 143 rms, 1-2 story. S $64-$79; D $69-$84; each addl

$15; under 18 free. Crib free. Pet accepted, some restrictions. TV; cable (premium). Pool. Coffee in rms. Restaurant 6 am-9 pm. Bar; entertainment Fri, Sat. Ck-out noon. Guest lndry. Meeting rms. Business servs avail. In-rm modem link. Free airport transportation. Exercise equipt. Refrigerators, microwaves avail. On Coos Bay. Cr cds: A, C, D, DS, MC, V.

🅓 🐾 🏖 🕴 ✈ 🔌 🐾 SC

Restaurant

★ ★ **PORTSIDE.** *8001 Kingfisher Rd, Charleston (97420). 541/888-5544. www.portsidebythebay.com.* Hrs: 11:30 am-11 pm. Res accepted. Bar. Lunch $4.95-$22.95, dinner $10.95-$24.95. Children's meals. Specialties: bouillabaisse, live lobster, fresh salmon. Own desserts. Entertainment Fri-Sun. Outdoor dining. Cr cds: A, DS, MC, V.

🅓

Corvallis

(C-2) *See also Albany, Eugene, Salem*

Settled 1845 **Pop** 44,757 **Elev** 225 ft
Area code 541
Information Convention and Visitors Bureau, 420 NW 2nd, 97330; 541/757-1544 or 800/334-8118
Web www.visitcorvallis.com

Located in the heart of Oregon's fertile Willamette Valley and built on the banks of the Willamette River, Corvallis is a center for education, culture, and commerce. It is the home of Oregon State University, the state's oldest institution of higher education. A prosperous business environment is supported by several international firms located here. Siuslaw National Forest headquarters is here.

What to See and Do

Avery Park. A 75-acre park on the Marys River. Bicycle, x-country, and jogging trails. Picnicking, playground, ballfield. Rose and rhododendron gardens, community gardens; 1922 Mikado locomotive. Playground (accessible to the disabled). (Daily) S 15th St and US 20. Phone 541/757-6918. **FREE**

Benton County Historical Museum. Located in the former Philomath College building. Features displays on history of the county; art gallery. Reference library (by appt). (Tues-Sat) 6 mi W at 1101 Main St in Philomath. Phone 541/929-6230. **FREE**

Oregon State University. (1868) 14,500 students. On its 400-acre campus are Memorial Union Concourse Gallery (daily). Phone 541/737-2416. **FREE**

Siuslaw National Forest. Incl 50 mi of ocean frontage with more than 30 campgrounds; public beaches, sand dunes and overlooks; visitor center and nature trails in the Cape Perpetua Scenic Area. Marys Peak, highest peak in the Coast Range, has a road to picnic grounds and campground near the summit. Swimming; ocean, lake, and stream fishing; hunting for deer, bear, elk, and migratory birds; clam digging; boating. Hiking. Picnicking. Camping (fee in most areas); dune buggies (in designated areas). Forest contains 630,000 acres incl the Oregon Dunes National Recreation Area. W via OR 34. Contact Forest Supervisor, 97333. Phone 541/750-7000.

Tyee Wine Cellars. Located on 460-acre Century farm. Offers tastings, tours, interpretive hikes, picnicking. (July-Aug, Fri-Mon; Apr-June and Oct-Dec, wkends; also by appt) 7 mi S via US 99 W, 3 mi W on Greenberry Rd. Phone 541/753-8754. **FREE**

Special Events

Oregon Folklife Festival. Traditional and contemporary folk music; crafts. Phone 541/758-3243 or 541/754-3601. Late-June.

Da Vinci Days. Festival celebrating the relationship between art, science, and technology. Phone 541/757-6363. Third wkend July.

Benton County Fair and Rodeo. Phone 541/757-1521. Late July-early Aug.

Fall Festival. Phone 541/752-9655. Last wkend Sept.

Motels/Motor Lodges

★★ **BEST WESTERN GRAND MANOR INN.** *925 NW Garfield Ave (97330). 541/758-8571; fax 541/758-0834; toll-free 800/626-1900. www. bestwestern.com.* 55 rms, 3 story. S $71-$160; D $78-$160; each addl $6; suites $98-$160; under 12 free. Crib $6. TV; cable (premium). Heated pool. Complimentary continental bkfst. Restaurant nearby. Ck-out 11 am. Business servs avail. In-rm modem link. Exercise equipt. Refrigerators; some microwaves. Cr cds: A, D, DS, MC, V.

D ⟰ 🛪 ⟱ 🐾

★ **MOTEL ORLEANS.** *935 NW Garfield Ave (97330). 541/758-9125; fax 541/758-0544; res 800/626-1900.* 61 rms, 3 story. No elvtr. S $45-$50; D $51-$54; each addl $4; suites $56-$64; under 12 free. Crib $5. Pet accepted, some restrictions. TV; cable. Pool privileges. Complimentary coffee in lobby. Restaurant nearby. Ck-out 11 am. Coin lndry. Whirlpool. Microwaves avail. Cr cds: A, C, D, DS, MC, V.

D ⟰ ⟰ ⟰ ⟰ 🐾

★★ **SHANICO INN.** *1113 NW 9th St (97330). 541/754-7474; toll-free 800/432-1233. www.shanicoinn.com.* 76 rms, 3 story. S $49; D $57-$67; each addl $5; suites $67; under 12 free. Crib free. Pet accepted, some restrictions. TV. Heated pool. Complimentary continental bkfst. Restaurant adj open 24 hrs. Ck-out noon. Meeting rm. Cr cds: A, C, D, DS, MC, V.

D ⟰ ⟰ ⟰ ⟰ 🐾

B&B/Small Inn

★★★ **HARRISON HOUSE BED & BREAKFAST.** *2310 NW Harrison Blvd (97330). 541/752-6248; fax 541/754-1353; res 800/233-6248. www.corvallis-lodging.com.* 4 rms, 2 share bath, 2 with A/C, 2 story. S, D $100; each addl $15; under 8 free; wkly, monthly rates. TV in some rms; cable (premium), VCR avail (movies). Complimentary full bkfst; afternoon refreshments. Rm serv 10 am-10 pm. Ck-out 11 am, ck-in 4 pm. Business servs avail. In-rm modem link. Luggage handling. Concierge serv. X-country ski 10 mi. Built in 1939;

antiques. Totally nonsmoking. Cr cds: A, C, D, DS, JCB, MC, V.

⟰ 🛪 ⟱ 🐾

Restaurants

★★ **GABLES.** *1121 NW 9th St (97330). 541/752-3364. www.b-sphere. com/gables.html.* Hrs: 5-9 pm; early-bird dinner Mon-Fri 5-6 pm. Res accepted. Continental menu. Bar 4:30-11 pm. Dinner $10.95-$25.95. Children's meals. Specializes in fresh seafood, steak, prime rib. Own desserts. Wine cellar dining area. Family-owned. Cr cds: A, D, DS, MC, V.

D

★★ **MICHAEL'S LANDING.** *603 NW Second St (97330). 541/754-6141. www.michaelslanding.com.* Hrs: 11:30 am-9 pm; Fri, Sat to 9:30 pm. Closed Dec 25. Res accepted. Bar to 11 pm; wkends to midnight. Lunch $5.25-$10.25, dinner $10.95-$18.95. Children's meals. Specializes in prime rib, pasta, seafood. Old RR depot overlooking river, built 1909. Cr cds: A, C, D, DS, MC, V.

D

⛽

Cottage Grove

(D-2) *See also Eugene*

Pop 7,402 **Elev** 641 ft **Area code** 541 **Zip** 97424

Information Cottage Grove Area Chamber of Commerce, 330 Hwy 99 S, PO Box 587; 541/942-2411

Cottage Grove is the lumber, retail, and distribution center for south Lane County. A Ranger District office of the Umpqua National Forest (see ROSEBURG) is located here.

What to See and Do

Chateau Lorane Winery. 30-acre vineyard located on 200-acre wooded estate features lakeside tasting room in which to enjoy great variety of traditional, rare and handmade wines. (June-Oct, daily; Mar-May and Nov-Dec, wkends and hols; also by appt) 12 mi W on Cottage Grove-

Lorane Rd to Siuslaw River Rd. Phone 541/942-8028. **FREE**

Cottage Grove Lake. Three-mi-long lake. Lakeside (west shore) and Wilson Creek (east shore) parks have swimming, boat launch, and picnicking. Shortridge Park (east shore) has swimming, waterskiing, fishing, and picnicking. Primitive and improved camping (showers, dump station) at Pine Meadows on east shore (Mid-May-mid-Sept, 14-day limit; no res; fee). S via I-5, Cottage Grove Lake exit 170, turn left, then 5 mi S on London Rd. Phone 541/942-8657. ¢¢¢

Cottage Grove Museum. Displays of pioneer homelife and Native American artifacts housed in a former Roman Catholic Church (1897), octagonal, with stained-glass windows made in Italy. Adj to annex houses model of ore stamp mill showing how gold was extracted from the ore; working model of a green chain; antique tools. (Mid-June-Labor Day, Wed-Sun afternoons; rest of yr, wkends) Birch Ave and H St. Phone 541/942-3963. **FREE**

Covered Bridges. Five old-time covered bridges within ten-mi radius of town. Inquire at Chamber of Commerce. Phone 541/942-2411.

Dorena Lake. Five-mi-long lake. Schwarz Park (camping fee), on Row River below dam, has fishing, picnicking, and camping (dump station). Lane County maintains Baker Bay Park, on south shore, and offers swimming, waterskiing, fishing, boating (launch, marina, rentals); picnicking, concession, camping (fee). Harms Park, on north shore, offers boat launching and picnicking. For further information inquire at Cottage Grove project office. 5 mi E on Row River Rd. Phone 541/942-1418. ¢¢¢

Special Event

Bohemia Mining Days Celebration. Commemorates area's gold-mining days; parades; flower, art shows; rodeo, entertainment. Third wk July. Phone 541/942-5064.

Motel/Motor Lodge

★★ **BEST WESTERN VILLAGE GREEN.** 725 Row River Rd (97424). 541/942-2491; fax 541/942-2386; toll-free 800/343-7666. www.bestwestern. com. 96 rms. June-Oct: S $69-$99; D $79-$110; each addl $5; suites $99-$165; under 12 free; lower rates rest of yr. Crib free. Pet accepted. TV; cable (premium). Heated pool; whirlpool. Playground. Restaurant 6:30 am-9 pm. Bar 4 pm-midnight. Ck-out 11 am. Coin lndry. Meeting rms. Business servs avail. Sundries. Covered parking. Tennis. Some refrigerators. Private patios. 18-hole golf course adj. Cr cds: A, D, DS, MC, V.

⊡ 🏌 🐾 🛥 🍴 🎿 🏃 🛎 🚲

Restaurant

★ **COTTAGE.** 2915 Row River Rd (97424). 541/942-3091. Hrs: 11 am-9 pm. Closed Sun; wk of Thanksgiving. Bar. Lunch, dinner $2.75-$19. Children's meals. Specializes in fresh seafood, steak, chicken. Salad bar. Own desserts. Bldg solar heated. Cr cds: A, MC, V.

⊡

Crater Lake National Park

(57 mi N of Klamath Falls on US 97, OR 62)

One of Crater Lake's former names, Lake Majesty, probably comes closest to describing the feeling visitors get from these deep blue waters in the caldera of dormant Mount Mazama. More than 7,700 years ago, following climactic eruptions, this volcano collapsed and formed a deep basin. Rain and snow accumulated in the empty caldera, forming the deepest lake in the United States (1,932 ft). Surrounded by 25 miles of jagged rim rock, the 21-square-mile lake is broken only by Wizard and Phantom Ship islands. Entrance by road from any direction brings you to the 33-mile Rim Drive (July-mid-October or first snow), leading to all observation points, park headquarters, and a visitor center at Rim Village (June-September, daily). The Sinnott Memorial Overlook with broad terrace permits a beautiful view of the area. On sum-

Crater Lake National Park

mer evenings, rangers give campfire talks at Mazama Campground (late June-September, phone 541/594-2211). The Steel Center located at Park Headquarters (daily) has exhibits about the natural history of the park and a movie is shown daily.

The park can be explored on foot or by car, by following spurs and trails extending from Rim Drive. Going clockwise from Rim Village, to the west, The Watchman Peak is reached by a trail almost one mile long that takes the hiker 1,800 feet above the lake with a full view in all directions; Mount Shasta in California, 105 miles away, is visible on a clear day. The road to the north entrance passes through the Pumice Desert, once a flood of frothy debris from the erupting volcano.

On the northeast side, Cleetwood Trail descends one mile to the shore and a boat landing where two-hour launch trips depart hourly each day in summer (fee). From the boats, Wizard Island, a small volcano, and Phantom Ship, a craggy mass of lava, can be seen up close.

Six miles farther on Rim Drive, going clockwise, is the start of a 2½-mile hiking trail, 1,230 feet to Mount Scott, soaring 8,926 feet, the highest point in the park. Just to the west of the beginning of this trail is a one-mile drive to the top of Cloudcap, 8,070 feet high and 1,600 feet above

the lake. Four miles beyond this point, a road leads seven miles from Rim Drive to The Pinnacles, pumice spires rising like stone needles from the canyon of Wheeler Creek.

Back at Rim Village, two trails lead in opposite directions. Counterclockwise, a 1½-mile trek mounts the top of Garfield Peak. The other trail goes to Discovery Point, where in 1853 a young prospector, John Hillman, became the first settler to see the lake.

In winter, the south and west entrance roads are kept clear in spite of the annual 45-foot snowfall; the north entrance road and Rim Drive are closed from mid-October-June, depending on snow conditions. A cafeteria is open daily at Rim Village for refreshments and souvenirs.

Depending on snow, the campground (fee) is open from late-June-mid-October. Mazama, at the junction of the south and west entrance drives, has a camper store, fireplaces, showers, laundry facilities, toilets, water, and tables; no reservations. There are six picnic areas on Rim Drive. The wildlife includes black bears—keep your distance and never feed them. There are also deer, golden-mantled ground squirrels, marmots, and coyotes. Do not feed any wildlife in park.

The park was established in 1902 and covers 286 square miles. For park information contact Superintendent, Crater Lake National Park, PO Box 7, Crater Lake 97604; 541/594-2211 ext 402. Golden Eagle Passport (see MAKING THE MOST OF YOUR TRIP). Per vehicle ¢¢¢

Note: Conservation measures may dictate the closing of certain roads and recreational facilities. In winter, inquire locally before attempting to enter the park.

Motel/Motor Lodge

★ ★ ★ **CRATER LAKE LODGE.** *565 Rim Village Dr, Crater Lake (97604). 541/594-2255; fax 541/594-2342; res 541/830-8700, www.crater-lake.com.* 71 rms, 4 story. No A/C. No rm phones. S, D $99-$120, under 12 free. Closed mid-Oct-mid-May. Complimentary coffee in lobby. Restaurant 7-10:30 am, 11:30 am-2:30 pm, 5-10 pm. Ck-out 11 am. Bellhops. Picnic tables, grills. On lake. Totally nonsmoking. Cr cds: MC, V.

The Dalles

(B 4) *See also Biggs, Hood River*

Founded 1851 **Pop** 10,200 **Elev** 98 ft **Area code** 541 **Zip** 97058
Information Chamber of Commerce, 404 W 2nd St; 541/296-2231 or 800/255-3385

Once The Dalles was the end of the wagon haul on the Oregon Trail. Here the pioneers loaded their goods on boats and made the rest of their journey westward on the Columbia River. The falls and rapids that once made the river above The Dalles unnavigable are now submerged under water backed up by the Columbia River dams. The Dalles Dam is part of a system of dams extending barge traffic inland as far as Lewiston, Idaho, and Pasco, Washington. The port has berthing space for all types of shallow draft vessels. The chief source of income in the area is agriculture. The Dalles is noted for its cherry orchards and wheat fields located in the many canyons along the river.

What to See and Do

☒ **Columbia Gorge Discovery Center.** Over 26,000-sq-ft building is official interpretive center for the Columbia River Gorge National Scenic Area. Hands-on and electronic exhibits detail the volcanic upheavals and raging floods that created the Gorge, describe the history and importance of the river, and look to the Gorge's future. Also Early Explorers, Steamboats and Trains, Industry and Stewardship exhibits. Guided tours, seminars, classes, and workshops (some fees). Library and collections (by appt). Cafe. (Daily; closed Jan 1, Thanksgiving, Dec 25) 3 mi NW at Crate's Point, 5000 Discovery Dr. Phone 541/296-8600. ¢¢¢ Admission incl

Oregon Trail Living History Park. Incl 80,000 sq ft of outdoor exhibits and gardens. Costumed interpreters demonstrate life of Oregon Trail emigrants, members of Lewis and Clark expedition, and Native Americans. Footpaths wind through park; offers stunning views of river from high bluff. (Schedule and phone same as Center)

Wasco County Historical Museum. Reveals colorful history of over 10,000 yrs of county's occupation and importance of Columbia River on area history. Artifacts and exhibits feature Native Americans, missionaries, early pioneers and explorers; history of area railroad industry, farming, and shipping. Interactive displays incl a late-19th-century town, railroad depot and barn. (Schedule and phone same as Center)

The Dalles Dam and Reservoir. Two-mi train tour with views of historic navigation canal, visitor center, petroglyphs, and fish ladder facilities (Memorial Day-Labor Day, daily; Apr-May and Oct-Mar, Wed-Sun). 3 mi E of town off I-84 and 1 mi E of The Dalles Hwy Bridge, which crosses the Columbia just below the dam (use I-84 exit 87 in summer, exit 88 off-season). Phone 541/296-1181. **FREE** On south shore, 8-1/2 mi east of dam is

Celilo Park. Swimming, sailboarding, fishing, boating (ramp); picnicking, playground. Comfort station. Recreational areas with similar facilities also are on north and south shores. Adj to ancient fishing grounds, now submerged under waters backed up by The Dalles Dam.

Fort Dalles Museum. Only remaining building of the 1856 outpost is the Surgeon's Quarters. Rare collection of pioneer equipment; stagecoaches, covered wagons. (Mar-Oct, daily; rest of yr, Wed-Sun; closed hols, also first two wks Jan) 15th and Garrison sts. Phone 541/296-4547.

Mayer State Park. A 613-acre park comprised of an undeveloped area with overlook on Rowena Heights; and a developed area, on the shores of the Columbia River, with swimming beach, windsurfing, dressing rms, fishing, boat ramp. Picnicking. 10 mi W, off I-84 exit 77. Phone 541/695-2261.

Mount Hood National Forest. (see) W of city.

Sorosis Park. This 15-acre park overlooks the city from the highest point on Scenic Dr, with view of the Columbia River, Mt Adams, and Mt Hood. Located on part of the bottom of ancient Lake Condon. The bones of three types of camels, the ancient horse, and mastodons were found near here. Jogging trail; tennis courts. Picnic area. Rose Garden.

Riverfront Park. Swimming beach, windsurfing, fishing, boating (launch), jet boat excursions; picnicking. Off I-84, exit 85.

Special Events

Northwest Cherry Festival. Fourth wkend Apr. Phone 541/296-5481.

Fort Dalles Rodeo. CASI sanctioned. Thurs-Sun, third wk July. Phone 541/296-2231.

Motels/Motor Lodges

★★ **BEST WESTERN UMATILLA HOUSE.** *112 W 2nd St (97058). 541/296-9107; fax 541/296-3002; toll-free 888/935-2378. www.bestwestern. com.* 65 rms, 2-4 story. S $51-$56; D $59-$63; each addl $7; under 12 free. Crib free. Pet accepted; $5. TV; cable (premium). Heated pool. Restaurant 6:30 am-9 pm. Bar 11 am-11 pm. Ck-out 11 am. Meeting rms. Business servs avail. In-rm modem link. Health club privileges. Some refrigerators. Cr cds: A, C, D, DS, ER, JCB, MC, V.

🄳 🦐 🖼 ⊠ 🔥 SC

★★★ **COMFORT INN.** *351 Lone Pine Dr (97058). 541/298-2800; fax 541/298-8282; toll-free 800/955-9626. www.comfortinn.com.* 56 rms, 2 story. June-Sept: S $56-$60; D $69-$74; each addl $6; suites $109; under 12 free; lower rates rest of yr. Pet accepted, some restrictions; $6. TV; cable (premium). Indoor pool; whirlpool. Complimentary full bkfst. Restaurant adj 6 am-10 pm. Bar 4 pm-2 am. Ck-out noon. Coin lndry. Meeting rms. Business servs avail. Sundries. Gift shop. Free airport transportation. Golf privileges, pro, driving range. Exercise equipt. Lawn games. Refrigerators, microwaves. Cr cds: A, D, DS, MC, V.

🄳 🦐 ⓛ 🈦 🖼 🛪 ⊠ 🔥

★ **INN AT THE DALLES.** *3550 SE Frontage Rd (97058). 541/296-1167; fax 541/296-3920.* 45 rms, 4 kits. S, D $34-$57; each addl $5; suites, kit. units $45-$75. Crib $5. Pet accepted. TV; cable. Indoor pool. Coffee in lobby. Restaurant nearby. Ck-out 11 am. Business servs avail. Free airport transportation. View of Columbia River, Mt Hood, The Dalles Dam. Cr cds: A, C, D, DS, MC, V.

🦐 ⓛ 🖼 🛪 ⊠ 🔥

★ **QUALITY INN.** *2114 W 6th St (97058). 541/298-5161; fax 541/298-6411; toll-free 800/848-9378. www. qualityinn-thedalles.com.* 85 rms, 2 story, 16 kits. S $59-$90; D $65-$90; kit. units $72-$85; each addl $5. Crib $5. Pet accepted; $2. TV; cable. Heated pool; whirlpool. Restaurant 6 am-10 pm; Fri, Sat to 11 pm. Ck-out 11 am. Coin lndry. Meeting rms. Business servs avail. In-rm modem link. Health club privileges. Some fireplaces. Cr cds: A, C, D, DS, MC, V.

🄳 🦐 ⓛ 🈺 🖼 🛪 ⊠ 🔥

Restaurant

★ **COUSIN'S.** *2115 W 6th St (97058). 541/298-2771. www. qualityinn.com.* Hrs: 6 am-10 pm; Fri, Sat to 11 pm. Closed Dec 25. Bar. Bkfst $1.95-$7.95, lunch $4.25-$6.25, dinner $6.50-$11.50. Children's meals. Specialties: pot roast, turkey and dressing. Frontier motif. Cr cds: A, C, D, DS, MC, V.

D

Depoe Bay

(B-I) *See also Lincoln City, Newport*

Pop 870 **Elev** 58 ft **Area code** 541 **Zip** 97341
Information Chamber of Commerce, PO Box 21; 541/765-2889

The world's smallest natural navigable harbor, with six acres, Depoe Bay is a base for the US Coast Guard and a good spot for deep-sea fishing. The shoreline is rugged at this point. Seals and sea lions inhabit the area, and whales are so often seen that Depoe Bay claims to be the "whale watching capital of the Oregon coast." In the center of town are the "spouting horns," natural rock formations throwing geyserlike sprays high in the air. There are nine state parks within a few miles of this resort community.

What to See and Do

Depoe Bay Park. Covers three acres. Ocean observation building with view of bay, spouting horn, and fishing fleets. Small picnic area. N on US 101. Phone 541/765-2361.

Fogarty Creek State Park. A 142-acre park with beach area and creek, swimming (dressing rms), fishing; hiking, picnicking. Standard fees. 2 mi N on US 101. Phone 541/265-9278. ¢¢

Thundering Seas. (Oregon State University School for the Crafts) Professional school for goldsmiths and silversmiths lies 60 ft above the Pacific Ocean; unusual museum. Tours (Daily). Phone 541/765-2604. FREE

Special Events

Classic Wooden Boat Show and Crab Feed. Last wkend Apr. Phone 541/765-2889.

Fleet of Flowers Ceremony. After services on shore, flowers are cast on the water to honor those who lost their lives at sea. Memorial Day. Phone 541/765-2889.

Salmon Bake. Depoe Bay Park. Salmon prepared in the Native American manner. Third Sat Sept. Phone 541/765-2889.

Motels/Motor Lodges

★★ **INN AT OTTER CREST.** *301 Otter Crest Loop Rd, Otter Rock (97369). 541/765-2111; fax 541/765-2047; toll-free 800/452-2101. www. innatottercrest.com.* 120 units. S, D $99-$299. Crib free. TV; cable (premium), VCR avail. Heated pool; whirlpool. Restaurant 8 am-10 pm; mid-Oct-mid-June to 8 pm. Bar. Ck-out noon. Coin lndry. Meeting rms. Business servs avail. Bellhops. Sundries. Gift shop. Outdoor tennis. Exercise equipt; sauna. Lawn games. Sun deck. Refrigerators; some microwaves. Private balconies. On 35 acres; duck pond. Ocean view; beach access. Cr cds: A, DS, MC, V.

D

★★ **SURFRIDER RESORT.** *3115 NW Hwy 101 (97341). 541/764-2311; fax 541/764-4634; toll-free 800/662-2378. www.surfriderresort.com.* 52 rms, 2 story, 20 kits. No A/C. June-Sept, wkends, hols: S, D $75-$95; each addl $10; studio rms, suites, kit. units $105-$125; under 12 free; lower rates rest of yr. Crib $5. TV; cable (premium). Indoor pool; whirlpool. Restaurant 7 am-10 pm. Bar 11-1 am. Ck-out 11 am. Gift shop. Free airport transportation. Sauna. Many fireplaces; some in-rm whirlpools. Many private patios, balconies. All rms with ocean view. Cr cds: A, C, D, DS, MC, V.

D

B&B/Small Inn

★★ **CHANNEL HOUSE.** *35 Ellingson St (97341). 541/765-2140; fax 541/765-2191; toll-free 800/447-2140. www.channelhouse.com.* 14 rms, 3 story, 9 suites, 2 kit. units. No elvtr. Mar-Dec: S, D $80-$150; each addl $30; suites $175-$225; kit. units $225; lower rates rest of yr. Children over 12 yrs only. TV; cable (premium). Complimentary bkfst. Restaurants nearby. Ck-out 11 am, ck-in 4 pm. Business servs avail. Street parking. Some balconies. Modern oceanfront building overlooking Depoe Bay. Totally nonsmoking. Cr cds: A, DS, MC, V.

Enterprise (B-7)

(see Joseph)

Eugene

(D-2) *See also Corvallis, Cottage Grove*

Settled 1846 **Pop** 112,669 **Elev** 419 ft
Area code 541
Information Lane County Convention & Visitors Association, 115 W 8th, Suite 190, PO Box 10286, 97440; 541/484-5307 or 800/547-5445
Web www.cvalco.org/travel.html

Eugene sits on the west bank of the Willamette (Wil-AM-et) River, facing its sister city Springfield on the east bank. The Cascade Range rises to the east, mountains of the Coast Range to the west. Bicycling, hiking, and jogging are especially popular here, with a variety of trails to choose from. Forests of Douglas fir support a lumber industry that accounts for 40 percent of the city's manufacturing. Eugene-Springfield is at the head of a series of dams built for flood control of the Willamette River Basin. Willamette National Forest headquarters are located here.

What to See and Do

Armitage County Park. A 57-acre park on partially wooded area on the south bank of the McKenzie River. Fishing, boating (ramp); hiking, picnicking. Standard fees. 6 mi N off I-5 on Coburg Rd. Phone 541/682-2000.

Camp Putt Adventure Golf Park. Eighteen-hole course with challenging holes like "Pond O' Peril," "Thunder Falls," and "Earthquake." Lakeside patio with ice cream bar. (Late Mar-

mid-Nov, daily) 4006 Franklin Blvd. Phone 541/741-9828. ¢¢

Fall Creek Dam and Lake. Winberry Creek Park has swimming beach, fishing, boating (ramp); picnicking. (May-Sept) Some fees. North Shore Ramp has fishing, boat launching facilities; picnicking. (Daily with low-level ramp) Cascara Campground has swimming, fishing, boating (ramp); camping (May-Sept). Some fees. 20 mi SE on OR 58 to Lowell, then follow signs to Big Fall Creek Rd. N county road. Phone 541/937-2131.

Hendricks Park Rhododendron Garden. A 20-acre, internationally known garden features more than 6,000 aromatic plants, incl rare species and hybrid rhododendrons from the local area and around the world (peak bloom mid-Apr-mid-May). Walking paths, hiking trails, picnic area. (Daily) Summit and Skyline Drs. Phone 541/682-5324. **FREE**

Hult Center. Performing arts center offering more than 300 events each yr ranging from Broadway shows and concerts to ballet. 7th Ave and Willamette St; 1 Eugene Center. Phone 541/682-5000.

Lane County Historical Museum. Changing exhibits depict history of county from mid-19th century to 1930s; incl artifacts of pioneer and Victorian periods; textiles; local history research library. (Wed-Fri, also Sat afternoons) 740 W 13th Ave. Phone 541/682-4242. ¢

Lookout Point and Dexter Dams and Lakes. The 14-mi-long Lookout Point Lake has Black Canyon Campground (May-Oct; fee) with trailer parking. Fishing; picnicking. Hampton Boat Ramp with launching facilities and four camp sites (all yr; fee) with trailer parking, picnicking; fishing, closed to launching during low water (usually Oct-Apr). **Lowell Park** on three-mi-long Dexter Lake has swimming, waterskiing, boating (moorage, ramp), sailboating; picnicking. **Dexter Park** has waterskiing, fishing, boating (ramp), sailboating; picnicking. The Powerhouse at Lookout Point Dam is open to the public (by appt). 20 mi SE on OR 58. For further information inquire at Project Office, Lookout Point Dam. Phone 541/937-2131.

Owen Municipal Rose Garden. A five-acre park with more than 300 new and rare varieties of roses, as well as wild species (best blooms late June-early July); a recognized test garden for experimental roses. Also here is a collection of antiques and miniatures. Picnic area. (Daily) North end of Jefferson St, along the Willamette River. Phone 541/682-5025. **FREE**

Skiing. Willamette Pass Ski Area. Double, three triple chairlifts; patrol, school, rentals (ski and snowboard). Lodge, restaurant, lounge. Longest run 2.1 mi; vertical drop 1,583 ft. Also 20 km of groomed nordic trails. (Late-Nov-mid-Apr) Night skiing (late Dec-late Feb, Fri-Sat). S via I-5, E on OR 58. Phone 541/345-7669. ¢¢¢¢

Spencer Butte Park. Park has 305 acres of wilderness, with Spencer Butte Summit, at 2,052 ft, dominating the scene. Hiking trails. Panoramic views of Eugene, Cascade Mtns. (Daily) 2 mi S of city limits on Willamette St. Phone 541/682-4800. **FREE** Starting at edge of park is

> **South Hills Ridgeline Trail.** A five-mi trail extending from Blanton Rd east to Dillard Rd; a spur leads to top of Butte. Trail offers magnificent views of the Cascade Mtns, Coburg Hills and Mt Baldy; wildflowers along the trail reach peak bloom late Apr. Begins at 52nd St and Willamette St. Phone 503/325-7275.

University of Oregon. (1876) 19,000 students. The 250-acre campus incl more than 2,000 varieties of trees. Points of interest incl the Museum of Natural History, Robinson Theatre, Beall Concert Hall, Hayward Field, and the Erb Memorial Union. Campus tours depart from Information and Tour Services, Oregon Hall (Mon-Sat). Bounded by Franklin Blvd and Agate St, Alder and 18th sts. Phone 541/346-3014. Also on campus are

> **Knight Library.** With more than two million volumes, this is the largest library in Oregon. Main lobby features changing exhibits of rare books, manuscripts; Oregon Collection on second floor. Fine arts pieces, wrought iron gates and carved panels. (Daily) Phone 541/346-3054.

> **Museum of Art.** Diverse collections incl large selection of Asian art representing cultures of China, Japan, Korea, Cambodia, and American and British works of Asian influence; official court robes of the *Ch'ing* dynasty (China, 1644-1911); Russian icon paintings from the 17th-19th centuries; Persian miniatures and ceramics; photography; works by contemporary artists and craftsmen from the Pacific Northwest, incl those of Morris Graves. Special exhibits. Gift shop. (Wed-Sun afternoons; closed hols). Phone 541/346-3027. **FREE**

Whitewater rafting. Numerous companies offer trips on the McKenzie, Deschutes, and Willamette rivers. Trips range from two hrs to five days. Contact Convention and Visitors Association for details. Phone 800/547-5445.

Willamette National Forest. More than 1½ million acres. Home to more than 300 species of wildlife; incl Cascade Mtn range summit; Pacific Crest National Scenic Trail with views of snowcapped Mt Jefferson, Mt Washington, Three Fingered Jack, Three Sisters, Diamond Peak; Koosah and Sahalie Falls on the Upper McKenzie River; Clear Lake; the lava beds at summit of McKenzie Pass; Waldo Lake near summit of Willamette Pass. Fishing; hunting, hiking, skiing, snowmobiling, camping (fee at some sites). E via US 20, OR 126. Contact Supervisor, 211 E 7th Ave, 97401. Phone 541/225-6300.

Willamette Science and Technology Center. Participatory science center encourages hands-on learning; features exhibits illustrating physical, biological, and earth sciences and related technologies. Planetarium shows. (Wed-Sun) 2300 Leo Harris Pkwy. Phone 541/682-7888. ¢¢

Special Events

Bach Festival. Numerous concerts by regional and international artists; master classes; family activities. Phone 800/457-1486. Mid-June-early July.

Lane County Fair. Mid-Aug. Phone 541/682-4292.

Motels/Motor Lodges

★ **BEST INN AND SUITES.** *3315 Gateway St, Springfield (97477).*

541/746-1314; fax 541/746-3884; toll-free 800/626-1900. www.bestinn.com. 72 rms, 3 story. No elvtr. S $42-$46; D $46-$54; each addl $5; suites $58-$66; under 12 free. Crib $5. TV; cable. Complimentary coffee in lobby. Restaurant nearby. Ck-out 11 am. Coin lndry. Business servs avail. In-rm modem link. Health club privileges. Whirlpool. Microwaves avail. Cr cds: A, C, D, DS, MC, V.

D ⊠ ⚑ SC

★★ **BEST WESTERN GRAND MANOR.** 971 Kruse Way, Springfield (97477). 541/726-4769; fax 541/744-0745; toll-free 800/626-1900. www. bestwestern.com. 65 suites, 3 story. S $84; D $89; each addl $6; under 12 free. Crib $6. TV; cable. Indoor pool. Complimentary continental bkfst. Restaurant adj open 24 hrs. Ck-out 11 am. Coin lndry. Meeting rms. Business servs avail. In-rm modem link. Exercise equipt; sauna. Refrigerators; some wet bars; microwaves avail. Some balconies. Cr cds: A, D, DS, MC, V.

⊠ ⚑

★★ **BEST WESTERN NEW ORE-GON MOTEL.** 1655 Franklin Blvd (97403). 541/683-3669; fax 541/484-5556; toll-free 800/528-1234. www. bestwestern.com/neworegonmotel. 129 rms, 1-2 story. S $62-$68; D $70-$74; each addl $2; suites $89-$125. Crib free. Pet accepted, some restrictions; $25 deposit. TV; cable (premium). Indoor pool; whirlpool. Complimentary coffee in lobby. Restaurant adj 6 am-11 pm. Ck-out noon. Coin lndry. Business servs avail. In-rm modem link. Exercise equipt; saunas. Refrigerators. Cr cds: A, C, D, DS, ER, JCB, MC, V.

D ⚑ ⊠ 🖈 ⊠ ⚑

★ **CAMPUS INN.** 390 E Broadway (97401). 541/843-3376; fax 541/343-3376. campus-inn.com. 58 rms, 2 story. S $46; D $48-$70; each addl $8; under 18 free. Pet accepted; $20 refundable. TV; cable (premium). Complimentary continental bkfst. Restaurant nearby. Ck-out 11 am. In-rm modem link. Cr cds: A, DS, MC, V.

D ⚑ ⊠ ⚑ SC

★★ **HOLIDAY INN EXPRESS.** 3480 Hutton St, Springfield (97477). 541/746-8471; fax 541/747-1541; res

800/363-8471. www.hiexpress.com. 58 rms, 3 story. S, D $79-$89; each addl $6; under 18 free. Pet accepted; $10. TV; cable, VCR avail (movies). Indoor pool; whirlpool. Complimentary continental bkfst. Restaurant adj open 24 hrs. Ck-out noon. Coin lndry. Meeting rms. Business servs avail. In-rm modem link. Exercise equipt. Microwaves avail. Cr cds: A, C, D, DS, JCB, MC, V.

D ⚑ ⊠ 🖈 ⊠ ⚑ SC

★ **PACIFIC 9 MOTOR INN.** 3550 Gateway St, Springfield (97477). 541/726-9266; fax 541/744-2643; toll-free 800/722-9462. www.pacific9.com. 119 rms, 3 story. S $34-$48; D $40-$60; each addl $6; under 18 free. Crib free. TV; cable. Pool. Complimentary continental bkfst. Restaurant opp 24 hrs. Ck-out 11 am. Health club privileges. Cr cds: A, C, D, DS, MC, V.

D ⊠ ⊠ ⚑ SC

★★ **PHOENIX INN.** 850 Franklin Blvd (97403). 541/344-0001; fax 541/686-1288; res 800/344-0131. www.phoenixinn.com. 97 rms, 4 story. S $89; D $99; each addl $5; suites $129; under 17 free; wkly rates. Crib avail. TV; cable. Complimentary continental bkfst. Complimentary coffee in rms. Restaurant nearby. Ck-out noon. Meeting rms. Business servs avail. Valet serv. Coin lndry. RR station transportation. Exercise equipt. Indoor pool; whirlpool. Refrigerators, microwaves; some bathrm phones. Cr cds: A, D, DS, MC, V.

D ⊠ 🖈 ⊠ ⚑

★★ **RED LION HOTEL EUGENE.** 205 Coburg Rd (97401). 541/342-5201; fax 541/485-2314; toll-free 800/733-5466. www.redlion.com. 137 rms, 2 story. S, D $59-$99; each addl $15; studio rms $80-$100; under 18 free. Crib free. Pet accepted, some restrictions. TV; cable, VCR avail. Heated pool; whirlpool. Restaurant 6 am-10 pm. Bar 3 pm-2 am, Sun to midnight. Ck-out noon. Meeting rms. Business servs avail. In-rm modem link. Bellhops. Sundries. Free airport, RR station, bus depot transportation. Exercise equipt. Some private patios, balconies. Cr cds: A, C, D, DS, ER, JCB, MC, V.

D ⚑ ⊠ 🖈 ✈ ⊠ ⚑ SC

★★ **SHILO INN.** *3350 Gateway St, Springfield (97477). 541/747-0332; fax 541/726-0587; toll-free 800/222-2244. www.shiloinn.com.* 143 rms, 2 story, 43 kits. S, D $49.95-$109.95; each addl $10; kit. units $79-$89; under 12 free; package plans. Pet accepted, some restrictions; $10/day. TV; cable (premium), VCR avail (movies). Pool. Complimentary continental bkfst. Restaurant 6 am-11 pm. Bar 11-2 am. Ck-out noon. Coin lndry. Meeting rms. Business servs avail. Free airport transportation. Some microwaves. Cr cds: A, C, D, DS, ER, JCB, MC, V.

⬛ 🍴 ≈ ⬛ 🐾 SC

★ **TRAVELODGE.** *1859 Franklin Blvd (97403). 541/342-6383; toll-free 800/444-6383. www.travelodge.com.* 60 rms, 2-3 story. S $52-$61; D $70-$80; each addl $5; suites $80-$85; under 12 free. Crib free. Pet accepted, some restrictions. TV; cable. Complimentary continental bkfst. Coffee in rms. Restaurant adj 7 am-11 pm. Ck-out 11 am. Business servs avail. Sauna. Whirlpool. Microwaves avail; refrigerator in suites. Cr cds: A, C, D, DS, MC, V.

⬛ 🍴 ⬛ 🐾 SC

★★★ **VALLEY RIVER INN.** *1000 Valley River Way (97401). 541/687-0123; fax 541/683-5121; toll-free 800/543-8266. www.valleyriverinn. com.* 257 rms, 2-3 story. S $140-$180; D $160-$200; suites $175-$300; under 18 free. Crib free. Pet accepted, some restrictions. TV; cable (premium), VCR avail. Heated pool; whirlpool, wading pool, poolside serv. Restaurant (see SWEETWATERS). Bar 11:30 am-midnight, Sun 9 am-11 pm; entertainment. Ck-out 11 am. Meeting rms. Business servs avail. In-rm modem link. Bellhops. Valet serv. Concierge. Gift shop. Free airport, RR station, bus depot transportation. Exercise equipt; sauna. Health club privileges. Private patios, balconies. Logging memorabilia. Some rms have views of Willamette River. Cr cds: A, D, DS, MC, V.

⬛ 🍴 ⬛ ≈ 🕴 ✈ ⬛ 🐾

Hotel

★★★ **HILTON.** *66 E 6th Ave (97401). 541/342-2000; fax 541/342-6661. www.eugene.hilton.com.* 272 rms, 12 story. S $130; D $145; each addl $15; suites $290-$360; under 18 free. Pet accepted, some restrictions; $25. TV; cable (premium). Indoor pool; whirlpool. Restaurant 6:30 am-10 pm. Rm serv to 1 am. Bar; entertainment. Ck-out noon. Convention facilities. Business center. Concierge. Gift shop. Free covered parking. Free airport, RR station, bus depot transportation. Exercise equipt. Health club privileges. Some refrigerators; microwaves avail. Balconies. Luxury level. Cr cds: A, C, D, DS, MC, V.

⬛ 🍴 ⬛ ≈ 🕴 ⬛ 🐾 🕴

B&B/Small Inn

★★★ **THE CAMPBELL - A CITY INN.** *252 Pearl St (97401). 541/343-1119; fax 541/343-2258; toll-free 800/264-2519. www.campbellhouse. com.* 18 rms, 3 story. May-Oct: S, D $129-$149; each addl $15; lower rates rest of yr. TV; cable, VCR (movies avail). Complimentary full bkfst. Coffee in rms. Restaurant nearby. Ck-out noon, ck-in 4 pm. Concierge serv. Luggage handling. Business servs avail. In-rm modem link. Health club privileges. Lawn games. Refrigerators; some microwaves. Built in 1892; on hill with views of city. Totally nonsmoking. Cr cds: A, DS, MC, V.

⬛ 🐾 ⬛ 🐾

Restaurants

★★ **AMBROSIA.** *174 E Broadway (97401). 541/342-4141.* Hrs: 11:30 am-10 pm; Fri, Sat to 11 pm; Sun 4:30-10 pm. Closed hols. Italian menu. Bar. Lunch $8-$10, dinner $10-$17. Specializes in regional Italian dishes. Outdoor dining. Many antiques. Cr cds: MC, V.

⬛

★ **CAFE NAVARRO.** *454 Willamette St (97401). 541/344-0943.* Hrs: 11 am-2 pm, 5-9:30 pm; Sat from 9 am; Sun 9 am-2 pm. Closed Mon; also July 4, Thanksgiving, Dec 25. No A/C. Caribbean, Latin menu. Wine, beer. Bar. Bkfst $4.95-$7.95, lunch $4.50-$8, dinner $14.95. Totally nonsmoking. Cr cds: MC, V.

⬛ SC

★★★ **CHANTERELLE.** *207 E 5th Ave (97401). 541/484-4065.* Hrs: 5-10 pm. Closed Sun, Mon; major hols. Res accepted. Continental menu. Serv bar. Complete meals: dinner $16.95-$23.95. Specializes in wild game, rack of lamb, seafood. Casual, intimate dining. Totally nonsmoking. Cr cds: A, JCB, MC, V.
D

★ **EXCELSIOR INN.** *754 E 13th (97401). 541/342-6963. www. excelsiorinn.com.* Hrs: 7 am-midnight; Sun brunch 10 am-2 pm. Res accepted. Continental, Italian menu. Bar until 1 am. Bkfst $3-$8, lunch $6-$12.50, dinner $13.95-$21.95. Sun brunch $6.95-$13.95. Children's meals. Specializes in fresh seafood. Patio dining. Intimate, informal dining. Totally nonsmoking. Cr cds: A, C, D, DS, MC, V.
D

★★ **NORTH BANK.** *22 Club Rd (97401). 541/343-5622. www.teleport. com/~casado/northbank.* Hrs: 11:30 am-9:30 pm; Fri to 10 pm; Sat 5-10 pm; Sun 4:30-9 pm. Closed Dec 25. Res accepted. Bar. A la carte entrees: lunch $3.25-$8.95, dinner $9.95-$19.95. Specializes in fresh seafood, steak, prime rib. Parking. Outdoor deck overlooks Willamette River and Ferry St Bridge. Cr cds: A, DS, MC, V.
D

★★ **OREGON ELECTRIC STA-TION.** *27 E Fifth St (97401). 541/485-4444.* Hrs: 11:30 am-2:30 pm, 5-10 pm; Fri to 10:30 pm; Sat 4:30-10:30 pm; Sun 4:30-9:30 pm. Closed July 4, Dec 25. Res accepted. Bar 11:30-1 am; Fri to 2 am; Sat 4 pm-2 am; Sun 4 pm-midnight. Lunch $3.75-$10.95, dinner $10.95-$29.95. Children's meals. Specializes in prime rib, seafood, chicken. Parking. Outdoor dining. Former RR station (1912); memorabilia. Cr cds: A, C, D, DS, MC, V.
D

★★★ **SWEETWATERS.** *1000 Valley River Way (97401). 541/687-0123. www.valleyriverinn.com.* Hrs: 6:30 am-2 pm, 5:30-9:30 pm; Sun from 7:30 am; Sun brunch 9 am-2 pm. Res accepted. Bar 11:30 am-midnight. Wine list. Bkfst $4-$8, lunch $7-$9, dinner $15-$22. Sun brunch $15.75. Children's meals. Specializes in

seafood, fowl, Pacific Northwest regional cuisine. Parking. Outdoor dining. Fireplace. Overlooks Willamette River; view from every table. Cr cds: A, D, DS, MC, V.
D

★★ **ZENON CAFE.** *898 Pearl St (97401). 541/343-3005.* Hrs: 8 am-11 pm; Fri, Sat to midnight; Sun from 9:30 am; Sun brunch to 2 pm. Closed Thanksgiving, Dec 25. Wine, beer. Bkfst $5.25-$8, lunch $5.75-$9.50, dinner $8.75-$17.50. Sun brunch $5.75-$9.75. Specializes in local pork, lamb. Own desserts. Outdoor dining. Totally nonsmoking. Cr cds: MC, V.
D

Unrated Dining Spot

GOVINDA'S VEGETARIAN BUFFET. *270 W 8th St (97401). 541/686-3531.* Hrs: 11:30 am-2:30 pm, 5-8 pm; Sat from 5 pm. Closed Sun; Jan 1, July 4, Dec 25. Res accepted. International vegetarian menu. A la carte entrees: lunch $2-$4, dinner $2-$4.50. Buffet: lunch, dinner $5-$6. Children's meals. Specializes in vegetable, rice and pasta dishes. Salad bar. Parking. Far Eastern atmosphere. Totally nonsmoking. Cr cds: A, DS, MC, V.
D SC

Florence

(D-1) See also Reedsport, Yachats

Settled 1876 **Pop** 5,162 **Elev** 23 ft **Area code** 541 **Zip** 97439

Information Florence Area Chamber of Commerce, PO Box 26000; 541/997-3128

Web www.presys.com/wtc/discover-florence

At the northern edge of the National Dunes Recreation Area, with some of the highest sand dunes in the world, Florence is within reach of 17 lakes for fishing, swimming, and boating. River and ocean fishing, crabbing, and clamming are also popular. Along the Siuslaw River is "Old

Town," an historic area with galleries, restaurants, and attractions.

What to See and Do

C&M Stables. Experience spectacular scenery of Oregon coast on horseback. Beach (1½-2 hrs), dune trail (1-1½ hrs), sunset (two hr, with or without meal), and coast range (½-day or all day) rides. Must be eight yrs or older. (Daily; closed Thanksgiving, Dec 25) 8 mi N on US 101. Phone 541/997-7540. ¢¢¢¢

Heceta Head Lighthouse. (1894) Picturesque beacon set high on rugged cliff. 12 mi N on US 101. Phone 541/547-3696.

Sand Dunes Frontier. Excursions aboard 20-passenger dune buggies or drive-yourself Odysseys; miniature golf; flower garden; gift shop, snack bar. (Daily) 3½ mi S on US 101. Phone 541/997-3544. ¢¢¢¢¢

⭐ **Sea Lion Caves.** Descend 208 ft under basaltic headland into cavern (1,500 ft long); home of wild sea lions. These mammals (up to 12 ft long) are generally seen on rocky ledges outside the cave in spring and summer and inside the cave in fall and winter. Self-guided tours; light jacket and comfortable shoes suggested. (Daily; closed Dec 25) 12 mi N on US 101. Phone 541/547-3111. ¢¢

Siuslaw Pioneer Museum. Exhibits preserve the history of the area; impressive display of artifacts and items from early settlers and Native Americans. Library rm; extensive genealogy records; hundreds of old photographs. (Jan-Nov, Tues-Sun; closed hols) 85294 US 101S, 1 mi S. Phone 541/997-7884. ¢

State parks.

Carl G. Washburne Memorial. This 1,089-acre park is a good area for study of botany. Two-mi-long beach, swimming, fishing, clamming; hiking, picnicking, tent and trailer campsites with access to beach. Elk may be seen in campgrounds and nearby meadows. 14 mi N on US 101. Phone 541/547-3416.

Darlingtonia. An 18-acre park with short loop trail through bog area noted for Darlingtonia, a carnivorous, insect-eating plant also known as cobra lily. Picnicking, viewing deck. 5 mi N on US 101. Phone 541/997-3641.

Devil's Elbow. A 545-acre park. Ocean beach, fishing; hiking, picnicking. Observation point. 13 mi N on US 101, below Heceta Head Lighthouse. Phone 541/997-3641. ¢¢

Jessie M. Honeyman Memorial. Park has 522 coastal acres with wooded lakes and sand dunes, an abundance of rhododendrons and an excellent beach. Swimming, waterskiing, fishing, boat dock and ramps; hiking, picnicking, improved camping, tent and trailer sites (dump station). (Daily) Standard fees. 3 mi S on US 101. Phone 541/997-3641.

***Westward Ho!* Stern-wheeler.** One-hr historical cruise, ½-hr afternoon cruises; Sunday brunch cruises (Fri-Sat eves, res

Haceta Head Lighthouse

required) (Apr-Oct, daily) Bay &
Maple. Phone 541/997-9691.

Special Event

Rhododendron Festival. Third wkend
May. Phone 541/997-3128.

Motels/Motor Lodges

★★ **BEST WESTERN PIER POINT
INN.** *85625 Hwy 101 (97439).
541/997-7191; fax 541/997-3828; res
800/528-1234. www.bestwestern.com.*
55 rms, 3 story. Mid-May-early Sept:
S $75-$99; D $95-$129; each addl
$10; lower rates rest of yr. TV; cable
(premium). Complimentary continental bkfst. Coffee in rms. Ck-out
11 am. Meeting rms. Sauna. Whirlpool. Balconies. Overlooks Siuslaw
River. Cr cds: A, D, DS, MC, V.
[D] [🐾] [🔥] [➥] [🔥]

★★ **HOLIDAY INN EXPRESS.** *2475
Hwy 101 (97439). 541/997-7797; fax
541/997-7895; res 800/465-4329.
www.holiday-inn.com.* 51 rms, 2 story.
S, D $55-$99; each addl $10; under
19 free. TV; cable (premium). Complimentary continental bkfst. Restaurant adj 6 am-9 pm. Ck-out 11 am.
Meeting rms. Exercise equipt. Whirlpool. Cr cds: A, C, D, DS, MC, V.
[D] [🐾] [🔥] [🧍] [➥] [🔥]

★ **MONEY SAVER MOTEL.** *170 Hwy
101 (97439). 541/997-7131; fax
541/902-2303; toll-free 877/997-7131.*
40 rms, 2 story. No A/C. June-Sept: S,
D $44-$59; each addl $6; lower rates
rest of yr. Crib $6. Pet accepted,
some restrictions; $5. TV; cable.
Complimentary coffee in lobby.
Restaurant nearby. Ck-out 11 am. Cr
cds: A, DS, MC, V.
[D] [✕] [➥] [🔥] [SC]

★ **RIVER HOUSE MOTEL.** *1202 Bay
St (97439). 541/997-3933; toll-free
877/997-3933. www.riverhouseflorence.
com.* 40 rms, 2 story. No A/C. June-
Sept: S, D $64-$120; each addl $6;
higher rates hols; lower rates rest of
yr. Crib $6. TV; cable. Complimen-
tary coffee in lobby. Restaurant
nearby. Ck-out 11 am. Coin lndry.
On river. Cr cds: A, DS, MC, V.
[✕] [🔥]

Restaurant

★★ **CLAWSON WINDWARD INN.**
*3757 US 101N (97439). 541/997-
8243.* Hrs: 7 am-9 pm; Fri-Sun to
9:30 pm. Closed Dec 25. Res
accepted. Bar. Bkfst $2.95-$8.95,
lunch $3.95-$10.95, dinner $6.95-
$18.95. Children's meals. Specializes
in steak, fresh seafood. Own baking.
Pianist wkends. Cr cds: DS, MC, V.
[D] [SC]

Forest Grove

*(B-2) See also Beaverton, Hillsboro, Port-
land*

Settled 1845 **Pop** 13,559 **Elev** 175 ft
Area code 503 **Zip** 97116
Information Chamber of Commerce,
2417 Pacific Ave; 503/357-3006
Web www.grovenet.org/forestgrove/
chamber/index.html

Forest Grove traces its beginning to
missionaries who brought religion to
what they called the "benighted
Indian." The town is believed to
have been named for a forest of firs
which met a grove of oaks.

What to See and Do

Pacific University. (1849) 1,600 students. Founded as Tualatin Academy,
it is one of the Northwest's oldest
schools. On campus is art gallery and
Old College Hall (academic yr, Tues,
Thurs; also by appt). Tours of campus. Main entrance on College Way.
Phone 503/357-6151.

Scoggin Valley Park and Hagg Lake.
Features 11 mi of shoreline. Swimming, windsurfing, fishing, boating
(ramps); picnic sites. (Feb-Nov) 7 mi
SW via OR 47, Scoggin Valley Rd
exit. Phone 503/359-5732.

Special Events

Barbershop Ballad Contest. Phone
503/357-3006. First wkend Mar.

Hawaiian Luau. Pacific University.
Hawaiian traditions celebrated in
food, fashions and dance. Phone
503/357-6151. Mid-Apr.

Concours d'Elegance. Pacific University. Classic and vintage auto display.

Phone 503/357-2300. Third Sun June.

Founders Day Corn Roast. Phone 503/357-3006. Late Sept.

Motels/Motor Lodges

★ **FOREST GROVE INN.** *4433 Pacific Ave (97116).* 503/357-9700; fax 503/357-3135; toll-free 800/240-6504. 20 rms, 2 story, 4 kit. units. S $41-$46; D $46-$49; each addl $7; kit. units $70. Crib free. TV; cable (premium). Complimentary coffee in rms. Restaurant nearby. Ck-out 11 am. Business servs avail. Refrigerators. Cr cds: A, D, DS, MC, V.

★ **TRAVELODGE SUITES.** *3306 Pacific Ave (97116).* 503/357-9000; fax 503/359-4134; toll-free 800/578-7878. www.travelodge.com. 41 rms, 3 story. May-Sept: S $55-$65; D $60-$70; each addl $6; under 12 free; lower rates rest of yr. Crib free. TV; cable (premium). Indoor pool; whirlpool. Complimentary continental bkfst. Coffee in rms. Restaurant adj 6-1 am. Bar 11 am 11 pm. Ck out 11 am. Coin lndry. Meeting rms. Business servs avail. In-rm modem link. Exercise equipt. Refrigerators. Cr cds: A, C, D, DS, ER, JCB, MC, V.

Fort Clatsop National Memorial

See also Astoria, Cannon Beach, Seaside

(6 mi SW of Astoria off US 101A)

This site marks the western extremity of the territory explored by Meriwether Lewis and William Clark in their expedition of 1804-1806. The fort is a reconstruction of their 1805-1806 winter quarters. The original fort was built here because of its excellent elk hunting grounds, its easy access to ocean salt, its protection from the westerly coastal storms, and the availability of fresh water.

The expedition set out on May 14, 1804, to seek "the most direct and practicable water communication across this continent" under orders from President Thomas Jefferson. The first winter was spent near Bismarck, North Dakota. In April, 1805, the party, then numbering 33, resumed the journey. On November 15, they had their first view of the ocean from a point near McGowan, Washington. The company left Fort Clatsop on March 23, 1806, on their return trip and was back in St. Louis on September 23 of the same year. The Lewis and Clark Expedition was one of the greatest explorations in the history of the United States, and its journals depict one of the most fascinating chapters in the annals of the American frontier. The visitor center has museum exhibits and provides audiovisual programs. The canoe landing has replicas of dugout canoes of that period. Ranger talks and living history demonstrations are presented mid-June-Labor Day. (Daily; closed Dec 25) For further information contact Superintendent, Rte 3, Box 604 FC, Astoria 97103; phone 503/861-2471. April-September ¢¢; Rest of year **FREE**

Gleneden Beach

(see Lincoln City)

Gold Beach

(F-1) *See also Brookings, Port Orford*

Pop 1,546 **Elev** 51 ft **Area code** 541 **Zip** 97444

Information Chamber of Commerce & Visitors Center, 29279 Ellensburg Ave #3; 541/247-7526 or 800/525-2334

Web www.goldbeach.org

Until floods in 1861 washed the deposits out to sea, placer mining in the beach sands was profitable here;

hence the name. There is still some mining farther up the Rogue River. Gold Beach is at the mouth of the Rogue River, on the south shore; Wedderburn is on the north bank. Agate hunting is popular at the mouth of the Rogue River. The river is also well-known for steelhead and salmon fishing. Surf fishing and clamming are possible at many excellent beaches. The Siskiyou National Forest (see GRANTS PASS) is at the edge of town and a Ranger District office of the forest is located here.

What to See and Do

Boat trips.

Jerry's Rogue River Jet Boat Trips. A six-hr (64-mi) round trip into wilderness area; two-hr lunch or dinner stop at Agness. Also eight-hr (104-mi) and six-hr (80-mi) round-trip whitewater excursions. Rogue River Museum and Gift Shop (all yr). (May-Oct, daily). South end of Rogue River Bridge at port of Gold Beach Boat Basin. Phone 541/247-4571. ¢¢¢¢

Mail Boat Whitewater Trips. A 104-mi round trip by jet boat into wilderness and whitewater of the upper Rogue River. Narrated 7½-hr trip. (Mid-May-mid-Oct, daily) Also 80-mi round trip to the middle Rogue River. Narrated 6¾-hr trip departs twice daily. (Mid-June-Sept) Res advised for all trips. Mail Boat Dock. Phone 800/458-3511. ¢¢¢¢¢

Official Rogue River Mail Boat Hydro-Jet Trips. A 64-mi round trip by jet boat up the wild and scenic Rogue River; two-hr lunch stop at Agness. (May-Oct, daily) Res advised. Mail Boat Dock, ¼ mi upstream from north end of Rogue River Bridge in Wedderburn, on north bank of the Rogue River. Phone 800/458-3511. ¢¢¢¢¢

Cape Sebastian State Park. Approx 1,143 acres of open and forested land. Cape Sebastian is a precipitous headland, rising more than 700 ft above tide with a view of many mi of coastline. 1.5 mi trail to tip of the cape; beach access. A short roadside through the forest area is marked by wild azaleas, rhododendrons, and blue ceanothus in season. Trails; no rest rms or water. 7 mi S on US 101. Phone 541/469-2021.

Curry County Historical Museum. Collections and interpretive displays of early life in Curry County. (June-Sept, Tues-Sat afternoons; rest of yr, Sat afternoons) Fairgrounds. Phone 541/247-6113. **Donation**

Prehistoric Gardens. Life-size sculptures of dinosaurs and other prehistoric animals that disappeared more than 70 million yrs ago are set among primitive plants, which have survived. (Daily) 14 mi N on US 101, located in Oregon's rain forest. Phone 541/332-4463. ¢¢

Special Events

Spring Flower, Art, & Clam Chowder Festival. First wkend May. Phone 541/247-6550.

Whale of an Art and Wine Festival. Mid-May. Phone 541/247-7526.

Curry County Fair. Last wkend July.

Festival of Quilts. Sept. Phone 541/247-7526.

Motels/Motor Lodges

★★ **SHORE CLIFF INN.** *29346 Ellensburg Ave (97444). 541/247-7091; fax 541/247-7170; toll-free 888/663-0608. www.shorecliffinn.com.* 38 rms, 1-2 story. S, D $59-$75; each addl $5. TV; cable (premium). Complimentary coffee in lobby. Restaurant adj 6 am-10 pm. Ck-out 11 am. Balconies. On beach. Cr cds: MC, V.

🄳 🖉 🐾

★★★ **TU TU' TUN LODGE.** *96550 N Bank Rogue (97444). 541/247-6664; fax 541/247-0672.* 16 rms, 2 suites, 1 garden house. S, D $135-$325; each addl $25 ; suites $185-$225; garden house $235, $125 off season. Heated Pool. Complimentary hors d'oeuvres. Dining rm open May-Oct (public by res): bkfst 7:30-9:30 am, lunch sitting (registered guests only) 1 pm; dinner sitting 7 pm. Bar. Ck-out 11 am, ck-in 3 pm. Business center. In-rm modem link. Free airport transportation. Dock; guides, whitewater boat trips. 4-hole pitch and putt golf; horseshoes. Private patios, balconies. Library. Cr cds: DS, MC, V.

🄳 🐾 ⚡ 🍴 🏊 ✈ 🖉 🐾 🚶

B&B/Small Inn

★★ **INN AT NESIKA BEACH.** *33026 Nesika Rd (97444). 541/247-*

6434. *www.moriah.com.* 4 rms, 2 story. No rm phones. S, D $125-$160. Complimentary full bkfst. Ck-out 11 am, ck-in 3 pm. Game rm. Lawn games. On bluff overlooking Pacific Ocean. Victorian-style house; antiques. Totally nonsmoking.

Restaurant

★★ **NOR'WESTER SEAFOOD.** *10 Harbor Way (97444). 541/247-2333.* Hrs: 5-10 pm. Closed Dec, Jan. Continental menu. Bar. Dinner $12.95-$22.95. Children's meals. Specializes in seafood, steak. Overlooks bay and ocean. Cr cds: A, MC, V.

Grants Pass

(F-2) *See also Cave Junction, Jacksonville, Medford*

Pop 17,488 **Elev** 948 ft **Area code** 541
Information Visitor & Convention Bureau, PO Box 1787, 97528; 541/476-5510 or 800/547-5927
Web www.visitgrantspass.org

Grants Pass was named by the rail constructors who were here when news reached them of General Grant's victorious siege of Vicksburg in 1863. On the Rogue River, Grants Pass is the seat of Josephine County. Tourism is the chief source of income; agriculture and electronics are next in importance. Fishing in the Rogue River is a popular activity. A Ranger District office and headquarters of the Siskiyou National Forest is located here.

What to See and Do

Grants Pass Museum of Art. Permanent and changing exhibits of photography, paintings, art objects. (Tues-Sat afternoons; closed hols) 229 SW G St in Grants Pass. Phone 541/479-3290. **FREE**

Oregon Caves National Monument. (see). 28 mi SW on US 199 to Cave Junction, then 20 mi E on OR 46.

Rogue River Raft Trips. One- to five-day whitewater scenic or fishing trips through the wilderness, past abandoned gold-mining sites; overnight lodges or camping en route. Some of these are seasonal; some all yr. For details contact the Visitor and Convention Bureau. Phone 800/547-5927. Also avail is

Hellgate Jetboat Excursions. Interpretive jet boat trips down the Rogue River: two-hr scenic excursion (May-Sept, daily); four-hr country dinner excursion (Mid-May-Sept); four-hr champagne brunch excursion (Mid-May-Sept, wkends); five-hr whitewater trip (May-Sept, daily). Depart from Riverside Inn. Phone 800/648-4874. ¢¢¢¢

Siskiyou National Forest. Over one million acres. Famous for salmon fishing in lower Rogue River gorge and early-day gold camps. Many species of trees and plants are relics of past ages; a botanist's paradise. An 84-mi stretch of Rogue River between Applegate River and Lobster Creek Bridge is designated a National Wild and Scenic River; nearly half is in the forest. Boat, pack, and saddle trips into rugged backcountry. Picnic sites. Camping. North, south, and west off US 199 or W of I-5. For further information contact Visitor Information Office, PO Box 440, 200 NE Greenfield Rd. Phone 541/471-6516.

Valley of the Rogue State Park. A 275-acre park with fishing, boat ramp to Rogue River; picnicking, improved tent and trailer sites (Daily; dump station). Standard fees. 8 mi S on I-5. Phone 541/582-1118.

Special Events

Amazing May. Eclectic mixture of events heralding the arrival of spring. May. Phone 541/476-7717.

Pari-mutuel Horse Racing. Fairgrounds. Phone 541/476-3215. Late May-early July.

Boatnik Festival. Riverside Park. Parade, concessions, carnival rides, boat races; entertainment. A 25-mi whitewater hydroboat race from Riverside Park to Hellgate Canyon and back. Square dance festival at Josephine County Fairgrounds.

Memorial Day wkend. Phone 541/474-2361.

Jedediah Smith Mountain Man Rendezvous. Sportsman Park. Muzzleloader/black powder shoots, costume contests, exhibits. Phone 541/476-5020. Early Aug.

Josephine County Fair. Fairgrounds, Redwood Hwy and W Park St. Phone 541/476-3215. Mid-Aug.

Heritage Days. Historical and ethnic related events of the pioneers that settled the southern Oregon territory. Sept-mid-Oct. Phone 541/476-7717.

Josephine County Air Fair. Airport, Brookside Dr. Antique aircraft, contests, airplane and helicopter rides. Phone 541/474-5285 or 541/474-0665. Early Sept.

Motels/Motor Lodges

★★ **BEST WESTERN GRANTS PASS INN.** *111 NE Agness Ave (97526). 541/476-1117; fax 541/479-4315; toll-free 800/553-7666. www. bestwestern.com.* 84 rms, 2 story. June-Sept: S $65-$82; D $75-$90; each addl $5; suites $110-$129; under 19 free; lower rates rest of yr. Crib $5. TV; cable (premium), VCR avail. Heated pool; whirlpool. Coffee in rms. Restaurant 6 am-10 pm. Bar. Ck-out 11 am. Coin lndry. Business servs avail. In-rm modem link. Health club privileges. Some refrigerators. Whirlpool in suites. Rogue River 1 mi. Cr cds: A, D, DS, MC, V.

[D] [symbols]

★★ **BEST WESTERN INN AT THE ROGUE.** *8959 Rogue River Hwy (97527). 541/582-2200; fax 541/582-1415; toll-free 800/238-0700. www. bestwestern.com.* 54 rms, 2 story. June-Sept: S, D $55-$79; each addl $5; suites $129-$179; under 12 free; lower rates rest of yr. Crib $5. Pet accepted, some restrictions; $10. TV; cable (premium), VCR avail. Heated pool; whirlpool. Complimentary continental bkfst. Restaurant adj 6 am-10 pm. Bar 5-10 pm. Ck-out 11 am. Coin lndry. Meeting rms. Business servs avail. Exercise equipt. Some refrigerators, microwaves, minibars. Balconies. Cr cds: A, C, D, DS, MC, V.

[D] [symbols]

★ **COMFORT INN.** *1889 NE 6th St (97526). 541/479-8301; fax 541/955-9721; toll-free 800/626-1900. www. comfortinn.com.* 59 rms, 2 story. S $49.99; D $59.99-$64.99; each addl $5. Crib $5. TV; cable (premium). Heated pool. Complimentary continental bkfst. Restaurant adj open 24 hrs. Ck-out 11 am. Microwaves avail. Cr cds: A, DS, MC, V.

[D] [symbols] [SC]

★★ **HOLIDAY INN EXPRESS GRANTS PASS.** *105 NE Agness Ave (97526). 541/471-6144; fax 541/471-9248; toll-free 800/838-7666. www. rogueweb.com/holiday.* 80 rms, 4 story. Mid-May-mid-Sept: S $67-$85; D $72-$90; each addl $5; suites $129; under 19 free; higher rates Boatnik Festival; lower rates rest of yr. Crib free. Pet accepted, some restrictions; $5/day. TV; cable (premium). Heated pool; whirlpool. Complimentary continental bkfst. Restaurant adj 6 am-11 pm. Ck-out 11 am. Guest lndry. Meeting rms. Business center. In-rm modem link. Sundries. Cr cds: A, C, D, DS, JCB, MC, V.

[D] [symbols]

★★ **MORRISON'S ROGUE RIVER LODGE.** *8500 Galice Rd, Merlin (97532). 541/476-3825; fax 541/476-4953; toll-free 800/826-1963. www. morrisonslodge.com.* 13 units, 2 with shower only, 4 rms in lodge, 9 cottages. July-Aug, MAP: S $75-$175; D $120-$300; each addl $90; AP rates avail mid-Sept-Nov; family rates; lower rates May-June. Closed rest of yr. TV; VCR. Heated pool. Restaurant. Ck-out 11 am. Meeting rms. Business center. Gift shop. Tennis. Lawn games. Guided raft trips. Some balconies. Picnic tables. On river. Cr cds: DS, MC, V.

[symbols]

★ **MOTEL DEL ROGUE.** *2600 Rogue River Hwy (97527). 541/479-2111. www.moteldelrogue.com.* 14 rms, 1-2 story, 13 kits. (oven in 10). S $40; D $65; each addl $5-$10; suites, kit. units $45-$65; lower rates rest of yr. TV; cable. Restaurant nearby. Ck-out 11 am. Coin lndry. Many microwaves. Porches. Picnic tables, grills. Shaded grounds; on river. Cr cds: MC, V.

[symbols]

★★ **REDWOOD MOTEL.** *815 NE 6th St (97526). 541/476-0878; fax 541/476-1032; toll-free 888/535-8824.*

www.redwoodmotel.com. 26 rms, 9
kits. Mid-May-Sept: S $55-$80; D
$60-$82; each addl $5; kit. units $68-
$95; whirlpool suites $97; lower rates
rest of yr. Crib $5. Pet accepted,
some restrictions; $10. TV; cable (pre-
mium). Heated pool; whirlpool. Playground. Complimentary continental
bkfst. Restaurant opp 6 am-10 pm.
Guest lndry. Ck-out 11 am. Many
refrigerators, microwaves. Picnic
tables. Cr cds: A, D, DS, MC, V.

★★★ **RIVERSIDE INN.** 971 SE 6th
St (97526). 541/476-6873; fax
541/474-9848; toll-free 800/334-4567.
www.riverside-inn.com. 174 rms, 3
story. S $69-$99; D $99-$109; each
addl $10; suites $140-$275; cottage
$350; under 11 free. Crib $10. Pet
accepted, some restrictions; $15. TV;
cable, VCR avail (movies). 2 heated
pools. Complimentary coffee in rms.
Restaurant 7 am-10 pm. Bar 11-1 am.
Ck-out 11 am. Meeting rms. Business
servs avail. Sundries. Gift shop.
Health club privileges. Some in-rm
whirlpools; microwaves avail. Balconies. Jet boat trips May-Sept. Cr
cds: A, D, DS, JCB, V.

★ **ROGUE VALLEY MOTEL.** 7799
Rogue River Hwy (97527). 541/582-
3762. 8 rms, 6 with shower only, 1
story. June-Sept: S $45-$49; D $72;
each addl $5; lower rates rest of yr.
Crib free. Pet accepted, some restrictions. TV; cable. Heated pool. Complimentary coffee in rms. Ck-out 11
am. Refrigerators; many microwaves. Picnic tables. On river. Cr
cds: MC, V.

★ **ROYAL VIEW MOTOR HOTEL.**
110 NE Morgan Ln (97526). 541/479-
5381; toll-free 800/547-7555. www.
royalview.com. 58 rms, 2 story. S $40-
$44; D $49-$66; suites $64. Crib $4.
Pet accepted. TV; cable (premium),
VCR avail. Heated pool; whirlpool,
poolside serv. Coffee in rms. Restaurant 6 am-10 pm. Bar 11-2 am; entertainment Thurs-Sun. Ck-out noon.
Coin lndry. Sauna, steam rm. Refrigerator, minibar in suites. Balconies.
Cr cds: A, C, D, DS, MC, V.

★★ **SHILO INN.** 1880 NW 6th St
(97526). 541/479-8391; fax 541/474-
7344; res 800/222-2244. www.
shiloinn.com. 70 rms, 2 story. May-
Sept: S, D $49.95-$89.95; each addl
$10; under 12 free; lower rates rest of
yr. Crib free. Pet accepted; $7. TV;
cable (premium). Pool. Continental
bkfst. Restaurant adj open 24 hrs.
Ck-out noon. Meeting rm. Sauna,
steam rm. Microwaves avail. Cr cds:
A, D, DS, MC, V.

B&Bs/Small Inns

★★ **FLERY MANOR.** 2000 Jumpoff
Joe Creek Rd (97526). 541/476-3591;
fax 541/471-2303. www.flerymanor.
com. 4 rms, 3 story. No elvtr. S, D
$75-$125; wkly rates. Children over
10 yrs only. TV in common rm; VCR
avail (movies). Complimentary full
bkfst; afternoon refreshments. Ck-
out 11 am, ck-in 4-6 pm. Business
servs avail. Luggage handling. Picnic
tables, grills. Country decor; fireplace, antiques. Totally nonsmoking.
Cr cds: A, DS, MC, V.

★★ **PINE MEADOW INN.** 1000
Crow Rd (97532). 541/471-6277; toll-
free 800/554-0806. www.pinemeadow
inn.com. 4 rms, 2 story. D $85-$100.
Complimentary full bkfst. Ck-out 11
am, ck-in 4 pm. Luggage handling.
Whirlpool. Midwest-style farm house
furnished with turn-of-the-century
antiques. 9 acres of meadow and private forest. Totally nonsmoking. Cr
cds: A, DS, MC, V.

★★★ **WEASKU INN.** 5560 Rogue
River Hwy (97527). 541/476-4190; fax
541/471-7038; res 800/493-2758.
www.weasku.com. 17 rms, many with
A/C, 2 story, 3 suites. S, D $85-$250;
suites $195-$295. TV; cable, VCR
(movies). Complimentary continental bkfst; afternoon refreshments. Ck-
out noon, ck-in 3 pm. Business servs
avail. Luggage handling. Gift shop.
Health club privileges. Lawn games.
Some fireplaces. Some balconies. On
river. Built in 1924; antiques. Cr cds:
A, DS, MC, V.

Restaurant

★★ **YANKEE POT ROAST.** *720 NW Sixth St (97526). 541/476-0551. www.yankee-potroast.com.* Hrs: 11 am-2 pm, 5-9 pm. Closed Mon, Tues; Dec 25. Serv bar. Dinner $7.95-$16.95. Children's meals. Specializes in Yankee pot roast, fresh halibut. Restored historic home; built 1905. Cr cds: A, MC, V.

Hermiston

(A-5) *See also Pendleton, Umatilla*

Pop 10,040 **Elev** 457 ft **Area code** 541 **Zip** 97838
Information Greater Hermiston Chamber of Commerce, 415 S US Hwy 395, PO Box 185; 541/567-6151 or 541/564-9109

Centrally located between the major cities of the Northwest, Hermiston offers an abundant array of recreational opportunities. The Columbia River, second largest river in the country, flows five miles to the north and the Umatilla River skirts the city limits; both are popular for fishing. The nearby Blue Mountains offer a variety of summer and winter activities. Agriculture, processing, and production form the economic base of this community, which has become a trading center for this area of the Columbia River Basin.

Special Event

Stock Car Racing. Race City, USA, on US 395. Phone 541/564-8674. Apr-Oct.

Motel/Motor Lodge

★ **ECONOMY INN.** *835 N 1st St (97838). 541/567-5516; res 888/567-9521.* 39 rms, 3 kit, 1-2 story. S $35; D $42; each addl $5; suites $65; wkly rates. Crib $10. Pet accepted; $5. TV; cable (premium). Pool. Restaurant adj 6 am-10 pm. Bar adj. Ck-out 11 am. Business servs avail. Refrigerators, microwaves. Cr cds: A, D, DS, MC, V.

Hillsboro

(B-2) *See also Beaverton, Forest Grove, Oregon City, Portland*

Pop 37,520 **Elev** 165 ft **Area code** 503
Information Greater Hillsboro Chamber of Commerce, 334 SE 5th Ave, 97123; 503/648-1102
Web www.hilchamber.org

Motel/Motor Lodge

★ **TRAVELODGE.** *622 SE 10th St (97123). 503/640-4791; fax 503/640-8127; res 800/578-7878. www. travelodge.com.* 58 rms, 2 story. S $60; D $65; each addl $10. Crib $10. TV; cable (premium). Complimentary coffee in rms. Restaurant adj 6 am-10 pm. Ck-out 11 am. Coin lndry. Business servs avail. Refrigerators. Cr cds: A, DS, MC, V.

Hood River

(A-3) *See also The Dalles*

Settled 1854 **Pop** 4,632 **Elev** 155 ft **Area code** 541 **Zip** 97031
Information Chamber of Commerce Visitor Center, 405 Portway Ave; 541/386-2000 or 800/366-3530
Web www.gorge.net/hrccc

Hood River, located in the midst of a valley producing apples, pears, and cherries, boasts a scenic view of Oregon's highest peak, Mount Hood; its slopes are accessible in all seasons by road. OR 35, called the Loop Highway, leads around the mountain and up to the snowline. The Columbia River Gorge provides perfect conditions for windsurfing in the Hood River Port Marina Park.

What to See and Do

Bonneville Lock & Dam. The dam consists of three parts, one spillway and two powerhouses. It has an overall length of 3,463 ft and extends across the Columbia River to Washington. It was a major hydroelectric project of the US Army Corps of

Engineers. On the Oregon side is a five-story visitor center with underwater windows into the fish ladders and new navigation lock with viewing facilities. Audiovisual presentations and tours of fish ladders, and the original powerhouse (June-Sept, daily or by appt; closed Jan 1, Thanksgiving, Dec 25). State salmon hatchery adj. Fishing (salmon and sturgeon ponds); picnicking. Powerhouse II and Visitor Orientation Building on Washington side, WA 14; underwater fish viewing, audiovisual presentations, fish ladder and powerhouse tours (June-Sept, daily or by appt; closed Jan 1, Thanksgiving, Dec 25); accessible via Bridge of the Gods from I-84, 23 mi W on I-84. Phone 541/374-8820. **FREE**

Columbia Gorge. Sternwheeler makes daytime excursions, sunset dinner and brunch cruises, harbor tours, and special holiday cruises. Res required exc for daily excursions (mid-June-Sept). Port of Cascade Locks. 10 mi W on I-84, exit 44. Phone 541/374-8427.

Hood River County Museum. Items from early settlers to modern residents. An outdoor display incl sternwheeler paddle wheel, beacon light used by air pilots in the Columbia Gorge, steam engine from the *Mary.* (Apr-Oct, daily) Port Marina Park. Phone 541/386-6772. **Donation**

Lost Lake. Swimming, fishing, boat rentals; hiking, picnicking, concession, day lodge, camping. 28 mi SW off I-84 on Dee Secondary Hwy and paved Forest Service road in Mt Hood National Forest (see). Phone 541/386-6366.

Mount Hood National Forest. (see) South and west of city.

Mount Hood Scenic Railroad. Historic railroad (1906); 44-mi round-trip excursions. Dinner, brunch and murder mystery excursions avail. (Apr-Dec, schedule varies) 110 Railroad Ave. Phone 541/386-3556.

Panorama Point. Observation point for Hood River Valley and Mt Hood. ½ mi S on OR 35 to Eastside Rd. Phone 800/366-3530.

Winery tours.

Flerchinger Vineyards. Tours; tasting rm. (Daily) 4200 Post Canyon Dr. Phone 541/386-2882. **FREE**

Hood River Vineyards. Tours; tasting rm. (Mar-Dec, daily) 4693 Westwood Dr. Phone 541/386-3772. **FREE**

Special Events

Blossom Festival. Third wkend Apr.

Hood River Valley Sternwheeler Days. Celebration of the sternwheeler *Columbia Gorge*'s return to home port for the summer. Wine and cheese tasting, crafts, food. Phone 541/386-2000. June.

Hood River County Fair. July. Phone 541/354-2865.

Cross Channel Swim. Labor Day. Phone 800/366-3530.

Hood River Valley Harvest Fest. Fresh local fruit, art and crafts, wine tasting, contests. Third wkend Oct. Phone 800/366-3530.

Motels/Motor Lodges

★★ **BEST WESTERN HOOD RIVER INN.** *1108 E. Marina Way (97031). 541/386-2200; fax 541/386-8905; res 800/828-7873. www.hoodriverinn.com.* 149 rms, 2-3 story. May-Sept: S $54-$84; D $89-$119; each addl $12; suites $129-$200; under 16 free; lower rates rest of yr. Crib free. Pet accepted. TV; cable (premium). Heated pool. Coffee in rms. Restaurant 6 am-9 pm. Bar; entertainment. Ck-out noon. Coin lndry. Business servs avail. In-rm modem link. Private patios. Beach access; windsurfing. In Columbia River Gorge. Cr cds: A, C, D, DS, MC, V.

⬛ 🐾 ⬛ ⬛ ⬛ ⬛

★ **LOVE'S RIVERVIEW LODGE.** *1505 Oak St (97031). 541/386-8719; fax 541/386-6671; res 800/789-9568. www.lovesriverview.com.* 20 rms, 2 story, 2 kit. units. June-mid-Sept: S $55-$62; D $69-$72; each addl $6; kit. units $79-$145; under 12 free; ski plans; lower rates rest of yr. Crib free. TV; cable (premium). Complimentary coffee in rms. Restaurant nearby. Ck-out 11 am. Business servs avail. Indoor pool; whirlpool. Refrigerators, microwaves. Some balconies. Cr cds: A, DS, MC, V.

⬛ ⬛ ⬛ ⬛ **SC**

★★ **VAGABOND LODGE HOOD RIVER.** *4070 Westcliff Dr (97031).*

541/386-2992; fax 541/386-3317; toll-free 877/386-2992. www.vagabond lodge.com. 42 rms, 7 suites. S $43-$53; D $52-$75; each addl $7; suites $63-$85; lower rates winter. Crib $5. Pet accepted. TV; cable. Playground. Restaurant adj 7 am-midnight. Ck-out 11 am. Picnic tables. On 5 wooded acres; overlooks Columbia River Gorge. Cr cds: A, DS, MC, V.

🄳 🐾🐘 🕭 ≍ 🈲 🔥

Hotel

★★★ **COLUMBIA GORGE HOTEL.** 4000 Westcliff Dr (97031). 541/386-5566; fax 541/387-5414; toll-free 800/345-1921. www.columbiagorge hotel.com. 40 rms, 3 story. S, D $175-$275; each addl $30. Pet accepted; $15. TV; cable, VCR avail. Complimentary full bkfst. Restaurant (see COLUMBIA RIVER COURT DINING ROOM). Bar 8 am-midnight. Ck-out noon. Business servs avail. Free RR station, bus depot transportation. Health club privileges. Restored building (1920s) with formal gardens. Jazz Age atmosphere. Windsurfing nearby. Overlooks river, waterfall. Cr cds: A, C, D, DS, JCB, MC, V.

🐘 🐘 🕭 ≍ 🈲 🔥

Resort

★★★ **SKAMANIA LODGE.** 1131 SW Skamania Lodge Way, Stevenson (98648). 509/427-7700; fax 509/427-2547; toll-free 800/376-9116. skamania.com. 195 rms, 4 story. May-Sept: S, D $129-$169; each addl $15; suites $185-$255; under 12 free. Crib free. TV; cable. Indoor pool; whirlpool. Playground. Complimentary coffee in rms. Restaurant 7 am-10 pm. Bar. Ck-out noon. Meeting rms. Business center. In-rm modem link. Bellhops. Sundries. Gift shop. Tennis. Mountain bike rentals. 18-hole golf, pro, greens fee $40, putting green, driving range. Exercise rm; sauna. Massage. Game rm. Lawn games. Refrigerators. Some balconies. Picnic tables. Cr cds: A, D, DS, JCB, MC, V.

🄳 🐘 🕭 🏋 🎿 ≍ 🎾 ≍ 🈲 🔥 🏃

B&B/Small Inn

★★ **INN OF THE WHITE SALMON.** 172 W Jewett Blvd, White Salmon (98672). 509/493-2335; toll-free

800/972-5226. www.innofthewhite salmon.com. 16 rms, 2 story, 5 suites. S $87; D $112; suites $109-$129. Crib free. Pet accepted. TV. Whirlpool. Complimentary full bkfst. Restaurant nearby. Ck-out noon, ck-in 3 pm. Luggage handling. Picnic tables. European-style inn built in 1937; antique decor, original art. Cr cds: A, C, D, DS, JCB, MC, V.

🐘 🐘 🕭 🈲 🔥

Restaurant

★★★ **COLUMBIA RIVER COURT DINING ROOM.** 4000 Westcliff Dr (97031). 541/386-5566. www.columbiagorgehotel.com. Hrs: 8 am-10 pm. Res accepted; required hols. Continental menu. Bar to midnight. Wine list. Complete meals: bkfst $24.74. Prix fixe: 3-course lunch $13.50. A la carte entrees: dinner $18-$30. Specialties: wilted spinach salad with apple smoked duck, fresh salmon, Hood River apple tarte. Own baking. Pianist evenings. View of river gorge. Totally nonsmoking. Cr cds: A, D, DS, MC, V.

🄳

Jacksonville

See also Ashland, Grants Pass, Medford

Founded 1852 **Pop** 1,896 **Elev** 1,569 ft **Area code** 541 **Zip** 97530

Information Historic Jacksonville Chamber of Commerce, PO Box 33; 541/899-8118

Web www.budget.net/~jville/chamber

Gold was discovered here in 1851 and brought prospectors by the thousands. An active town until the gold strike played out in the 1920s, Jacksonville lost its county seat to the neighboring town of Medford (see) in 1927. Now a national historic landmark, the town is one of the best preserved pioneer communities in the Pacific Northwest. Approximately 80 original buildings can be seen and some visited. A Ranger District office of the Rogue River National Forest (see MEDFORD) is located about 20 miles southwest of town, in Applegate Valley.

What to See and Do

⭐ **Jacksonville Museum.** In Old County Courthouse (1883), has exhibits of southern Oregon history, pioneer relics, early photographs, Native American artifacts, quilts, natural history. (Wed-Sun; closed Jan 1, Thanksgiving, Dec 25) Children's Museum is in Old County Jail. (1911), 206 N 5th St. Phone 541/773-6536. ¢¢ Also maintained by the Southern Oregon Historical Society is

Beekman House. (1875) Country Gothic house; former home of a prominent Jacksonville citizen. Living history exhibit. (Memorial Day-Labor Day, Wed-Sun) 352 E California St. ¢¢

The Oregon Vortex Location of the House of Mystery. The Vortex is a spherical field of force half above the ground, half below. Natural, historical, educational, and scientific phenomena are found in former assay office and surrounding grounds. Guided lecture tours (Mar-Oct, daily). Approx 10 mi NW on county road, at 4303 Sardine Creek Rd, in Gold Hill. Phone 541/855-1543. ¢¢

Special Event

Britt Musical Festivals. Hillside estate of pioneer photographer Peter Britt forms a natural amphitheatre. Festivals in classical, jazz, folk, country, dance, and musical theater. Phone 541/779-0847 or 800/882-7488. Mid-June-Sept.

B&Bs/Small Inns

★★ **JACKSONVILLE INN.** *175 E California St (97530). 541/899-1900; fax 541/899-1373; res 800/321-9344. www.jacksonvilleinn.com.* 11 rms, 8 with shower only, 2 story, 3 suites, 3 cottages. S $112; D $125; each addl $10; suites, cottages $205-$245. Crib $10. TV in cottages; cable. Complimentary full bkfst. Restaurant (see JACKSONVILLE INN). Bar. Ck-out 11 am (cottages 1:30 pm), ck-in 3 pm (cottages 4:30 pm). Meeting rms. Business servs avail. In-rm modem link. Sundries. Shopping arcade. Free airport transportation. Refrigerators; some bathrm phones, in-rm whirlpools, microwaves, fireplaces.

Built in 1860s; gold-rush era atmosphere. Cr cds: A, C, D, DS, V.

🄳 ⬤ ✈ ⬤ ⬤

★ **STAGE LODGE.** *830 N 5th St. (97530). 541/899-3953; fax 541/899-7556; toll-free 800/253-8254. www.stagelodge.com.* 27 rms, 2 suites, 2 story. Late May-Sept: S $65-$69; D $73-$79; each addl $5; suites $135; under 10 free; lower rates rest of yr. Crib $3. Pet accepted, some restrictions; $10. TV; cable. Complimentary continental bkfst. Ck-out 11 am, ck-in 2 pm. Some refrigerators, microwaves. Cr cds: A, D, DS, MC, V.

🄳 ⬤ ⬤

★★ **TOUVELLE HOUSE BED & BREAKFAST.** *455 N Oregon St (97530). 541/899-8938; fax 541/899-3992; res 800/846-8422. www.touvellehouse.com.* 6 rms, 3 story, 1 suite. May-Sept: S, D $85-$140; each addl $30; hols (2-day min); lower rates rest of yr. Children over 12 yrs only. TV in common rm; cable (premium). Complimentary full bkfst. Restaurant nearby. Ck-out 11 am, ck-in 3 pm. Business servs avail. In-rm modem link. Luggage handling. Concierge serv. Gift shop. Free airport transportation. Heated pool; whirlpool. Picnic tables, grills. Built in 1916; antiques. Cr cds: A, DS, MC, V.

⬤ ⬤ ⬤ ⬤

Restaurants

★★★ **JACKSONVILLE INN.** *175 E California St (97530). 541/899-1900. www.jacksonvilleinn.com.* Hrs: 7:30-10:30 am, 11:30 am-2 pm, 5-10 pm; Mon 7:30-10:30 am, 5-10 pm; Sun 10 am-2 pm (brunch), 5-9 pm. Closed Thanksgiving, Dec 24, 25. Res accepted. Continental menu. Bar 11:30 am-midnight. Wine list. Bkfst $5.95-$9.95, lunch $6.95-$14.95, dinner $13.95-$41.95. Specialties: prime rib, fresh salmon in season, veal scallopini. Patio dining. Building dates to gold-rush era. Totally nonsmoking. Cr cds: A, C, D, DS, MC, V.

★★★ **MCCULLY HOUSE.** *240 E California St (97530). 541/899-1942. www.mccullyhouseinn.com.* Hrs: 5-10 pm. Res accepted. Bar. Dinner $10.95-$24.95. Specializes in international, New Orleans cuisine. Outdoor dining. Rose garden. One of first houses built in town (1861). 3 guest rms avail. Totally nonsmoking. Cr cds: A, D, DS, MC, V.

D

John Day (C-6)

Pop 1,836 **Elev** 3,085 ft
Area code 541 **Zip** 97845
Information Grant County Chamber of Commerce, 281 W Main; 541/575-0547 or 800/769-5664

John Day, named for a heroic scout in the first Astor expedition, was once a Pony Express stop on trail to The Dalles. Logging and cattle raising are the major industries in the area. Headquarters for the Malheur National Forest is located here; two Ranger District offices of the forest are also located here.

What to See and Do

Grant County Historical Museum. Mementos of gold-mining days, Joaquin Miller cabin, Greenhorn jail (1910). (Mid-May-Sept, Mon-Sat, also Sun afternoons) 2 mi S on US 395 at 101 S Canyon City Blvd in Canyon City. Phone 541/575-0362. ¢

John Day Fossil Beds National Monument. The monument consists of three separate units in Wheeler and Grant counties of north central Oregon; no collecting within monument. Wayside exhibits at points of interest in each unit. 40 mi W on US 26, then 2 mi N on OR 19. Phone 541/987-2333. **FREE** These units incl

Clarno Unit. Consists of hills, bluffs, towering rock palisades, and pinnacles. Self-guided Trail of the Fossils features abundant plant fossils visible in the 35-50 million-yr-old rock. Picnicking. 20 mi W of Fossil on OR 218. Phone 541/763-2203.

Painted Hills Unit. Displays a colorful, scenic landscape of buff and red layers in the John Day Formation. Self-guided Painted Cove Trail and Leaf Hill Trail. Exhibits; picnicking. 9 mi NW of Mitchell, off US 26 on a county road. Phone 541/462-3961.

Sheep Rock Unit. Here are outstanding examples of the buff and green layers of the fossil-bearing John Day Formation, Mascall Formation, and Rattlesnake Formation. Visitor center offers picnicking and browsing among fossil displays. Self-guided Island in Time Trail and Story in Stone Trail

John Day Fossil Beds National Monument

incl exhibits. 7 mi W of Dayville on OR 19. Phone 541/987-2333.

Kam Wah Chung and Co Museum. Originally constructed as a trading post on The Dalles Military Rd (1866-1867). Now houses Chinese medicine herb collection, shrine, kitchen, picture gallery, Doc Hay's bedroom. (May-Oct, Mon-Thurs, Sat and Sun) 250 NW Canton, adj to city park. Phone 541/575-0028.

Malheur National Forest. Nearly 1½ million acres in southwestern part of Blue Mtns incl Strawberry Mtn and Monument Rock wilderness areas. Trout fishing in Magone and Yellowjacket Lakes, stream fishing, elk and deer hunting. Hiking. Winter sports. Picnicking. N and S on US 395; E and W on US 26. Camping. For further information contact Supervisor, PO Box 909. Phone 541/575-3000. **FREE**

Special Events

"62" Day Celebration. Canyon City, 1 mi S. Celebrates the discovery of gold in 1862. Medicine wagon and fiddling shows, parade, booths, barbecue, dancing, selection of queen. Second wkend June. Phone 541/575-0329.

Grant County Fair and Rodeo. Grant County Fairgrounds. Oregon's oldest continuous county fair. Early Aug. Phone 541/575-1900.

Motels/Motor Lodges

★ **DREAMERS LODGE MOTEL.** *144 N Canyon Blvd (97845). 541/575-0526; fax 541/575-2733; toll-free 800/654-2849.* 25 rms, 2 story. S $44-$46; D $48-$50; each addl $2; suites $60-$80. Crib $4. Pet accepted. TV; cable (premium). Complimentary coffee in rms. Restaurant nearby. Ckout 11 am. Business servs avail. Free airport transportation. X-country ski 20 mi. Refrigerators. Cr cds: A, D, DS, MC, V.

★ **JOHN DAY SUNSET INN.** *390 W Main St (97845). 541/575-1462; fax 541/575-1471; toll-free 800/452-4899.* 43 rms, 2 story. S $45-$55; D $55-$65; each addl $5; suites $110. Crib $5. Pet accepted, some restrictions. TV, cable (premium). Indoor pool;

whirlpool. Restaurant 5 am-11 pm. Bar. Ck-out 11 am. Meeting rms. Business servs avail. Free airport transportation. Cr cds: A, C, D, DS, ER, JCB, MC, V.

Joseph (B-7)

Pop 1,073 **Elev** 4,190 ft
Area code 541 **Zip** 97846
Information Wallowa County Chamber of Commerce, 107 SW First St, PO Box 427, Enterprise 97828; 541/426-4622 or 800/585-4121
Web www.eoni.com/~wallowa/

Joseph is located in the isolated wilderness of northeast Oregon. Remote from industry, the town attracts vacationers with its beautiful surroundings. There are fishing lakes here and hunting in the surrounding area. At the north end of Wallowa Lake is Old Joseph Monument, a memorial to the Nez Perce chief who resisted the US government. A Ranger District office of the Wallowa-Whitman National Forest (see BAKER) is located in nearby Enterprise.

What to See and Do

Hells Canyon National Recreation Area. Created by the Snake River, at the Idaho/Oregon border, Hells Canyon is the deepest river-carved gorge in North America—1½ mi from Idaho's He Devil Mtn (elevation 9,393 ft) to the Snake River at Granite Creek (elevation 1,408 ft). Overlooks at Hat Point, southeast of Imnaha, and in Idaho (see GRANGEVILLE, ID); both are fire lookouts. The recreation area incl parts of the Wallowa-Whitman National Forest in Oregon, and the Nez Perce and Payette national forests in Idaho. Activities incl float trips, jet boat tours, boat trips into canyon from Lewiston, ID (see) or the Hells Canyon Dam (see WEISER, ID); auto tours; backpacking and horseback riding. Developed campgrounds in Oregon and Idaho; much of the area is undeveloped, some is designated wilderness. Be sure to inquire about road conditions before planning a trip; some are rough and open for a limited season. 30 mi NE on County Rd 350 in Wallowa-Whitman National Forest (see BAKER). For a commercial outfitters guide list and further information contact Hells Canyon National Recreation Area Office, 88401 OR 82, Enterprise 97828. Phone 541/426-5546.

Valley Bronze of Oregon. Company produces finished castings of bronze, fine and sterling silver, and stainless steel. Showroom displays finished pieces. Tours of foundry depart from showroom (by res). (May-Nov, daily; rest of yr, by appt) 018 S Main. Phone 541/432-7445. ¢¢

Wallowa Lake State Park. Park has 201 forested acres in an alpine setting formed by a glacier at the base of the rugged Wallowa Mtns. Swimming, water sport equipment rentals, fishing, boating (dock, motor rentals); picnicking, concession, improved tent and trailer sites (dump station). Standard fees. Park at edge of Eagle Cap wilderness area; hiking and riding trails begin here. Horse stables nearby. 6 mi S on OR 82. Phone 541/432-4185.

Wallowa Lake Tramway. Gondola rises from valley to Mt Howard summit. Snack bar at summit. (June-Sept, daily; May, wkends, weather permitting) 6 mi S on OR 82. Phone 541/432-5331. ¢¢¢¢

Special Event

Chief Joseph Days. PRCA rodeo, parades, Native American dances, cowboy breakfasts. Contact Chamber of Commerce. Last full wkend July. Phone 541/432-1015.

Motels/Motor Lodges

★ **FLYING ARROW RESORT.** *59782 Wallowa Lake Hwy (97846). 541/432-2951. www.flyingarrowresort.com.* 20 cottages. Memorial Day-Sept: cottages $130-$145; each addl $5; 5-day min stay; higher rates 1-day stay; lower rates rest of yr. TV; cable. Heated pool; whirlpool. Ck-out 11 am. Fireplaces. Picnic tables, decks, grills. On river. Cr cds: DS, MC, V.

★ **INDIAN LODGE MOTEL.** *201 S Main (97846). 541/432-2651; fax 541/432-4949; toll-free 888/286-5484.* 16 rms. Apr-Oct: S $30-$35; D $40-$50; each addl $5; lower rates rest of yr. TV; cable (premium). Pet accepted; $5-$10. Complimentary coffee in rms. Restaurant nearby. Ck-out 11 am. Lake 1 mi. Cr cds: DS, MC, V.

★★ **WALLOWA LAKE LODGE.** *60060 Wallowa Lake Hwy (97846). 541/432-9821; fax 503/432-4885. www.wallowalake.com.* 22 units, 3 story, 2 suites, 8 kit. cottages. No A/C. No elvtr. No rm phones. No TVs. May-mid Oct: S, D $75-$165; family rates; lower rates rest of yr. Restaurant 7 am-1 pm, 5:30-9 pm. Ck-out 11 am. Meeting rms. Downhill ski 16 mi. On Wallowa Lake; swimming. Totally nonsmoking. Cr cds: DS, MC, V.

B&B/Small Inn

★★ **CHANDLERS BED BREAD TRAIL INN.** *700 S Main St (97846). 541/432-9765; fax 541/432-4303; toll-free 800/452-3781. www.eoni.com/ ~chanbbti.* 5 rms, 2 share bath, 2 story. No A/C. No rm phones. S $50-$70; D $60-$80; each addl $10. Children over 11 yrs only. Whirlpool. Complimentary full bkfst. Ck-out 11 am, ck-in 2 pm. Downhill/x-country ski 6 mi. Picnic tables. Cedar and log interiors with high vaulted ceilings. Outdoor gazebo. Totally nonsmoking. Cr cds: MC, V.

Klamath Falls (F-3)

Settled 1867 **Pop** 17,737 **Elev** 4,105 ft
Area code 541

Information Klamath County Department of Tourism, 1451 Main St, 97601; 541/884-0666 or 800/445-6728

Web www.klamathcountytourism. com

The closest sizable town to Crater Lake National Park (see) with more than 100 good fishing lakes nearby, Klamath Falls is host to sports-minded people. Upper Klamath Lake, the largest body of fresh water in Oregon, runs north of town for 30 miles. White pelicans, protected by law, nest here each summer, and a large concentration of bald eagles winter in the Klamath Basin. Headquarters and a Ranger District office of the Winema National Forest are located here.

What to See and Do

Collier Memorial State Park and Logging Museum. A 655-acre park located at the confluence of Spring Creek and Williamson River. Open-air historic logging museum with display of tools, machines, and engines; various types of furnished 1800s-era pioneer cabins; gift shop (daily; free). Fishing; hiking, picnicking. Tent and trailer campsites (hookups, dump station). Standard fees. 30 mi N, on both sides of US 97. Phone 541/783-2471.

Favell Museum of Western Art and Native American Artifacts. Contemporary Western art; working miniature gun collection; extensive display of Native American artifacts. Also art and print sales galleries. Gift shop. (Tues-Sat) 125 W Main. Phone 541/882-9996. ¢

Jackson F. Kimball State Park. A 19-acre pine and fir-timbered area at headwaters of Wood River, noted for its transparency and deep blue appearance. Fishing; picnicking, primitive campsites. Standard fees. 40 mi N on US 97, OR 62 to Fort Klamath, then 3 mi N on OR 232. Phone 541/783-2471.

Klamath County Baldwin Hotel Museum. Restored turn-of-the-century hotel contains many original furnishings. Guided tours (June-Sept, Tues-Sat; closed hols). 31 Main St. Phone 541/883-4208. ¢¢

Klamath County Museum. Local geology, history, wildlife, and Native American displays; research library has books on history, natural history, and anthropology of Pacific Northwest. (Tues-Sat; closed hols) 1451 Main St. Phone 541/883-4208. ¢

Migratory Bird Refuge. (In OR and CA) Major stopover on Pacific Flyway. There are six national wildlife refuges in the Klamath Basin. Upper Klamath and Klamath Marsh refuges lie to the north, and Lower Klamath, Bear Valley, Tule Lake, and Clear Lake lie to the south of the city. There is a visitor center with exhibits at refuge headquarters at Tule Lake (Daily). Waterfowl (Mar-Apr, Oct-Nov); bald eagles (Dec-Mar); migratory birds (Mar-Apr); waterfowl and colonial bird nesting (summer). S on OR 39 and CA 139 to Tulelake, CA, then 5 mi W on East-West Rd. Phone 530/667-2231. **FREE**

Winema National Forest. This forest (more than one million acres) incl former reservation lands of the Klamath Tribe; high country of Sky Lakes; portions of Pacific Crest National Scenic Trail; recreation areas in Lake of the Woods, Recreation Creek, Mountain Lakes Wilderness, and Mt Theilson Wilderness. Swimming, boating; picnicking, camping (some areas free). North, east, and west, reached by US 97, OR 62 or OR 140. For information contact Supervisor, 2819 Dahlia St. Phone 541/883-6714. ¢¢

Special Events

Bald Eagle Conference. Mid-Feb. Phone 800/445-6728.

Klamath Memorial Powow and Rodeo. Late May. Phone 800/524-9787.

Jefferson State Stampede. Early Aug. Phone 541/883-3796.

Klamath County Fair. Early Aug. Phone 541/883-3796.

Motels/Motor Lodges

★★ **BEST WESTERN KLAMATH INN.** 4061 S 6th St (97603). 541/882-1200; fax 541/882-2729; toll-free 877/882-1200. www.bestwestern.com/klamathinn. 52 rms, 2 story. S $73-$79; D $77-$83; each addl $8. Crib $4. Pet accepted, some restrictions. TV; cable (premium), VCR avail. Indoor pool. Complimentary continental bkfst. Coffee in rms. Restaurant adj 6 am-10:30 pm. Ck-out noon. Meeting rms. Microwaves; some in-rm whirlpools, refrigerators. Cr cds: A, C, D, DS, MC, V.

D 🐾 🛌 ⌗ ⌗ 🖐 SC

★★ **BEST WESTERN OLYMPIC INN.** *2627 S 6th St (97603). 541/882-9665; fax 541/884-3214; toll-free 800/600-9665. www.bestwestern.com.* 71 rms, 3 story. June-Sept: S, D $79-$99; each addl $10; under 12 free; lower rates rest of yr. TV; cable (premium). Complimentary continental bkfst. Complimentary coffee in rms. Restaurant opp open 24 hrs. Ck-out 11 am. Meeting rms. Business servs avail. In-rm modem link. Exercise equipt. Heated pool; whirlpool. Refrigerators, microwaves. Cr cds: A, D, DS, MC, V.

D 🏌 🏊 🎿 🛟 🔥 SC

★ **CIMARRON MOTOR INN.** *3060 S 6th St (97603). 541/882-4601; fax 541/882-6690; toll-free 800/742-2648.* 163 rms, 2 story. S $45; D $50-$55; each addl $5; under 10 free. Crib avail. Pet accepted; $5. TV; cable (premium). Heated pool. Continental bkfst. Restaurant adj open 24 hrs. Ck-out noon. Meeting rm. Business servs avail. Cr cds: A, DS, MC, V.

D 🍽 🏊 🛟 🔥 SC

★★ **HOLIDAY INN EXPRESS.** *2500 S 6th St (97601). 541/884-9999; fax 541/882-4020; res 800/465-4329. www.holiday-inn.com.* 57 rms, 2 story, 15 suites. S, D $62-$80; each addl $8; suites $95-$125; under 17 free; family rates. Crib free. TV; cable (premium), VCR avail. Indoor pool; whirlpool. Complimentary continental bkfst. Restaurant nearby. Ck-out noon. Coin lndry. Meeting rms. Business servs avail. Exercise equipt. Refrigerators, microwaves. Cr cds: A, C, D, DS, MC, V.

D 🏊 🎿 🛟 🔥

★ **QUALITY INN & SUITES.** *100 Main St (97601). 541/882-4666; fax 541/883-8795; toll-free 800/732-2025. www.qualityinn.com.* 80 rms, 2 story, 4 suites. S $63; D $63-$95.50; each addl $5; suites $93.50; under 18 free. Crib free. Pet accepted, some restrictions. TV; cable (premium). Heated pool. Complimentary continental bkfst. Coffee in rms. Restaurant adj. Ck-out noon. Coin lndry. Meeting rms. Business servs avail. In-rm modem link. Some in-rm whirlpools, microwaves. Cr cds: A, C, D, DS, JCB, MC, V.

D 🍽 🏊 🛟 🔥 SC

★★ **SHILO INN SUITES HOTEL.** *2500 Almond St (97601). 541/885-7980; fax 541/885-7959; toll-free 800/222-2244. www.shiloinn.com.* 143 suites, 4 story. June-Sept: S, D $89-$129; each addl $10; kit. units $149; under 12 free; golf plans; lower rates rest of yr. Crib free. Pet accepted, some restrictions; $7. TV; cable (premium), VCR (movies). Complimentary continental bkfst. Complimentary coffee in rms. Restaurant 6 am-11 pm. Bar 11-2 am. Ck-out noon. Meeting rms. Business center. In-rm modem link. Bellhops. Valet serv. Sundries. Coin lndry. Free airport, RR station transportation. Exercise equipt; sauna. Health club privileges. Indoor pool; whirlpool. Bathrm phones, refrigerators, microwaves, wet bars. Cr cds: A, D, DS, MC, V.

D 🍽 🏊 🎿 🛟 🔥 SC 🏌

★ **SUPER 8.** *3805 Hwy 97 (97601). 541/884-8880; fax 541/884-0235; res 800/800-8000. www.super8.com.* 61 rms, 3 story. No elvtr. June-mid-Sept: S $47.88-$51.88; D $51.88-$61.88; each addl $4; lower rates rest of yr. Crib free. TV; cable. Complimentary coffee in lobby. Restaurant nearby. Ck-out noon. Coin lndry. Whirlpool. Cr cds: A, D, DS, JCB, MC, V.

D 🏌 🔆 🎿 🔥

Restaurant

★★ **FIORELLA'S.** *6139 Simmer Ave (97603). 541/882-1878.* Hrs: 5-9 pm. Closed Sun, Mon; Dec 25. Res accepted. Northern Italian menu. Bar. Dinner $8.50-$19.95. Complete meals: dinner $12-$22. Children's meals. Specialties: pasticico, gnocchi, filet mignon. Large wine selection. Cr cds: A, DS, MC, V.

D

La Grande

(B-6) *See also Baker City, Pendleton*

Settled 1861 **Pop** 11,766 **Elev** 2,771 ft
Area code 541 **Zip** 97850
Information La Grande/Union County Visitors & Conventions

Bureau, 1912 Fourth Ave, #200; 541/963-8588 or 800/848-9969

Web www.eoni.com/~visitlg

Located in the heart of Northeast Oregon amid the Blue and Wallowa mountains, La Grande offers visitors breathtaking scenery and numerous exhilarating activities. Rafting and fishing enthusiasts enjoy the Grande Ronde River; hikers and mountain bikers navigate the Eagle Cap Wilderness and the tracks of the Oregon Trail. A Ranger District office of the Wallowa-Whitman National Forest (see BAKER) is located here.

What to See and Do

Catherine Creek State Park. A 160-acre park in pine forest along creek. Fishing; biking, hiking, picnicking, camping. Standard fees. 8 mi SE on OR 203. Phone 541/963-0430.

Eastern Oregon University. (1929) 2,000 students. Campus overlooks the town. Liberal arts college. Rock and mineral collection displayed in science building (Mon-Fri; closed hols; free). Nightingale Gallery, concerts, theatrical productions, in Loso Hall; changing exhibits. 1 University Blvd. Phone 541/962-3672.

Hilgard Junction State Recreation Area. A 233-acre park on the old Oregon Trail. Fishing; picnicking, camping (daily). Exhibits at Oregon Trail Interpretive Center (Memorial Day-Labor Day, daily). Standard fees. 8 mi W off I-84 N. Phone 541/963-0430.

Turns of the Brick. Self-guided walking tour of 30 turn-of-the-century buildings and ghost signs. Approx one-hr tour incl McGlasson's Stationery (1890), Masonic Lodge and JC Penney Company (ca 1900), Fire Station Building (1898) and Helm Building (1891). Unique brickwork and architecture explained in brochure avail from La Grande Downtown Development Association. 105 Fir, Suite 321. Phone 503/963-2411. **FREE**

Special Event

Union County Fair. Union County Fairgrounds. Early Aug. Phone 800/848-9969.

Motels/Motor Lodges

★ **HOWARD JOHNSON INN.** *2612 Island Ave (97850). 541/963-7195; fax 541/963-4498; res 800/446-4656. hojo.com.* 146 rms, 2 story. S, D $67-$77; each addl $8; under 18 free; lower rates rest of yr. Pet accepted. TV; cable (premium). Heated pool; whirlpool. Complimentary continental bkfst. Coffee in rms. Restaurant adj open 24 hrs. Ck-out noon. Free lndry. Meeting rms. Business servs avail. Exercise equipt; sauna. Refrigerators. Private patios, balconies. Cr cds: A, DS, MC, V.

⊡ ➹ ⚹

★ **ROYAL MOTOR INN.** *1510 Adams Ave (97850). 541/963-4154; fax 541/963-3588; res 800/990-7575.* 43 rms, 2 story. S, D $40-$52; each addl $5; under 17 free. Crib free. TV; cable (premium). Coffee in rms. Restaurant nearby. Ck-out 11 am. Cr cds: A, C, D, DS, MC, V.

⊠ ⯐ SC

B&B/Small Inn

★★ **STANG MANOR BED & BREAKFAST.** *1612 Walnut St (97850). 541/963-2400; toll-free 888/286-9463. www.stangmanor.com.* 4 rms, 2 story. No A/C. S $77; D $85; each addl $15. Children over 10 yrs only. TV in some rms, living room, VCR avail. Complimentary full bkfst; afternoon refreshments. Restaurant nearby. Ck-out 11 am, ck-in 3:30 pm. Picnic tables. Georgian Colonial design; grand staircase; antique furnishings. Totally nonsmoking. Cr cds: MC, V.

⊠ ⯐

Lakeview (F-4)

Founded 1876 **Pop** 2,526 **Elev** 4,798 ft **Area code** 541 **Zip** 97630

Information Lake County Chamber of Commerce, 126 N E St; 541/947-6040

Web www.triax.com/lakecounty/lakeco.htm

General John C. Fremont and Kit Carson passed through what is now

Lake County in 1843. There are antelope and bighorn sheep in the area, many trout streams, and seven lakes nearby. A supervisor's office of the Fremont National Forest is located here; also here is a district office of the Bureau of Land Management and an office of the US Department of Fish and Wildlife.

What to See and Do

Drews Reservoir. Fishing, boating (launch); camping. 15 mi W on Dog Lake Rd. Phone 541/947-3334.

Fremont National Forest. More than five million acres. Incl remnants of ice-age lava flows and the largest and most defined exposed geologic fault in North America, Abert Rim, on east side of Lake Abert. Abert Rim is most spectacular at the east side of Crooked Creek Valley. Many of the lakes are remnants of post-glacial Lake Lahontan. Gearhart Mtn Wilderness is rough and forested with unusual rock formations, streams and Blue Lake. Fishing; hunting, picnicking, camping. E and W via OR 140, N and S via US 395 and OR 31. For information contact Supervisor. Phone 541/947-2151.

Geyser and Hot Springs. "Old perpetual," said to be largest continuous hot water geyser in the Northwest. Spouts as high as 70 ft occur approx every 90 seconds. Hot springs nearby. 1 mi N on US 395. Phone 541/947-2817.

Paisley. Unspoiled old Western town. 45 mi N on OR 31. Phone 541/943-3114.

Schminck Memorial Museum. Pressed-glass goblets, home furnishings, dolls, toys, books, clothing, quilts, guns, saddles, tools, and Native American artifacts. (Feb-Nov, Tues-Sat; also by appt; closed hols) 128 S E St. Phone 541/947-3134. ¢

Special Events

Irish Days. Mid-Mar. Phone 877/947-6040.

Junior Rodeo. Last wkend June. Phone 877/947-6040.

Festival of Free-Flight. July 4 wkend. Phone 877/947-6040.

Lake County Fair and Roundup. Labor Day wkend. Phone 877/947-6040.

Motels/Motor Lodges

★★ **BEST WESTERN INN.** *414 N G St (97630). 541/947-2194; fax 541/947-3100; res 800/528-1234. www.bestwestern.com.* 38 rms, 2 story. S $48-$56; D $54-$60; each addl $6; suites $70-$110; higher rates special events. Crib $10. TV; cable (premium). Indoor pool; whirlpool. Complimentary continental bkfst. Complimentary coffee in rms. Restaurant adj 6 am-8 pm. Ck-out 11 am. Business servs avail. In-rm modem link. Coin lndry. Downhill/x-country ski 10 mi. Refrigerators, microwaves avail. Cr cds: A, C, D, DS, MC, V.
🐾 🐱 ⛷ 🏊 ▨ 🔥

★ **LAKEVIEW LODGE.** *301 N G St (97630). 541/947-2181; fax 541/947-2572.* 40 rms. S, D $40-$50; each addl $4; family units $42-$60; kit. units $4-$6 addl; under 18 free; higher rates Labor Day wkend. Crib free. Pet accepted. TV; cable (premium). Complimentary coffee in rms. Restaurant nearby. Ck-out 11 am. Downhill/x-country ski 8 mi. Exercise equipt; sauna. Whirlpool. Microwaves avail. Cr cds: A, C, D, DS, MC, V.
🄳 🐾 ⛷ 🏃 ✈ ▨ 🔥 SC

Lincoln City

(B-1) *See also Depoe Bay, Newport, Tillamook*

Pop 5,892 **Elev** 11-115 ft
Area code 541 **Zip** 97367
Information Visitor and Convention Bureau, 801 SW US 101, Suite #1; 541/994-8378 or 800/452-2151

Nicknamed the "kite capital of the world," Lincoln City is a popular recreation, art, and shopping area offering many accommodations with ocean view rooms.

What to See and Do

Alder House II. Set in a grove of alder trees, this is the oldest glass-blowing studio in Oregon. Watch molten glass drawn from a furnace and shaped into pieces of traditional or modern design. (Mid-Mar-Nov;

daily) 611 Immonen Rd, ½ mi E off
US 101. **FREE**

Devil's Lake State Park. A 109-acre
park with swimming, fishing, boating (ramp on east side of Devil's
Lake). Tent and trailer sites (on
northwest side of lake). Standard
fees. South of town, off US 101.
Phone 541/994-2002.

Theatre West. Community theater
featuring comedy and drama. (Thurs-
Sat) 3536 SE US 101. Phone 541/994-
5663.

Motels/Motor Lodges

★★ **BEST WESTERN LINCOLN
SANDS.** 535 NW Inlet Ave (97367).
541/994-1227; fax 541/994-2282; res
800/528-1234. www.bestwestern.com
33 kit. suites, 3 story. Suites $99-
$369. Crib $10. Pet accepted, some
restrictions. TV; cable (premium),
VCR. Heated pool; whirlpool. Complimentary continental bkfst. Complimentary coffee in rms. Restaurant
nearby. Ck-out 11 am. In-rm modem
link. Exercise equipt; sauna. Microwaves. Balconies. On beach. Cr cds:
A, DS, MC, V.
D ⬛ ⬛ ⬛ ⬛ SC

★ **COHO INN.** 1635 NW Harbor Ave
(97367). 541/994-3684; fax 541/994-
6244; toll-free 800/848-7006. www.
thecohoinn.com. 50 rms, 3 story, 31
kits. No A/C. No elvtr. June-Oct: S, D
$100; each addl $6; suites $104-$128;
lower rates rest of yr. Pet accepted,
some restrictions; $6. TV; cable (premium). Complimentary coffee in
lobby. Ck-out 11 am. Business servs
avail. Sauna. Whirlpool. Some fire
places. Some private patios, balconies. Oceanfront; beach nearby. Cr
cds: A, DS, MC, V.
⬛ ⬛ ⬛ ⬛ ⬛

★ **COZY COVE BEACH FRONT
RESORT.** 515 NW Inlet Ave (97367).
541/994-2950; fax 541/996-4332,
toll-free 800/553-2683. 70 rms, 2-3
story, 33 kits. S, D $55-$145; suites
$145-$250; kit. units $79-$100. TV;
cable; VCR avail (free movies).
Heated pool; whirlpool. Complimentary coffee in lobby. Restaurant
nearby. Ck-out 11 am. Business servs
avail. Sauna. Some in-rm whirlpools,
fireplaces. Some private patios, bal-

conies. Picnic tables. On beach. Cr
cds: A, DS, MC, V.
D ⬛ ⬛ SC

★★ **DOCK OF THE BAY MOTEL.**
1116 SW 51st St (97367). 541/996-
3549; fax 541/996-4759; toll-free
800/362-5229. dockofthebay-or.com. 24
kit. suites, 3 story. No elvtr. Mid-
June-mid-Sept: 1-bedrm $119-$139;
2-bedrm $139-$179; lower rates rest
of yr. Crib avail. TV, VCR avail.
Restaurant nearby. Ck-out 11 am.
Whirlpool. Balconies. On bay; beach.
Cr cds: DS, MC, V.
⬛ ⬛ ⬛ ⬛ ⬛ SC

★★ **D SANDS MOTEL.** 171 SW Hwy
101 (97367). 541/994-5244; fax
541/994-7484; toll-free 800/527-3925.
www.dsandsmotel.com. 63 kit. units, 3
story. No elvtr. May-Oct: S, D $124-
$149; each addl $10; under 8 free;
lower rates mid-wk off-season. Crib
free. TV; cable (premium), VCR
(movies). Indoor pool; whirlpool.
Complimentary coffee in lobby.
Restaurant nearby. Ck-out 11 am.
Business servs avail. Some fireplaces.
Some private balconies. On ocean,
beach. Cr cds: A, DS, MC, V.
⬛ ⬛ ⬛ SC

★★★ **INN AT SPANISH HEAD.**
4009 S Hwy 101 (97367). 541/996-
2161; fax 541/996-4089; toll-free
800/452-8127. 120 kit. units, 10
story. S, D $129-$169; each addl
$15; suites $199-$289; under 16
free. Crib free. TV; cable, VCR avail
(movies). Heated pool; whirlpool.
Restaurant 8 am-2 pm, 5-9 pm; Sun-
Thurs in winter to 8 pm. Bar 2 pm
to close; winter from 5 pm. Ck-out
noon. Meeting rms. Business servs
avail. Bellhops. Valet parking. Exercise equipt; sauna. Game rm. Many
private balconies. Built on side of
cliff; ocean view. Cr cds: A, C, D,
DS, MC, V.
⬛ ⬛ ⬛ ⬛ ⬛

★★ **NORDIC MOTEL.** 2133 NW
Inlet Ave (97367). 541/994-8145; fax
541/994-2329; toll-free 800/452-3558.
www.nordicmotel.com. 52 rms, 3 story,
24 kits. No elvtr. June-Aug: S, D $59-
$79; each addl $7; suites $97; kit.
units $85-$97; lower rates rest of yr.
Crib $7. TV; cable, VCR. Indoor pool;
whirlpool. Complimentary continental bkfst. Restaurant nearby. Ck-out

noon. Meeting rm. Business servs avail. Saunas. Game rm. Microwaves avail. Cr cds: A, C, D, DS, MC, V.

⊡ ⬛ 🔆 ⬛ ⬛ ⬛

★ **PELICAN SHORES INN.** *2645 NW Inlet Ave (97367). 541/994-2134; fax 541/994-4963; toll-free 800/705-5505. www.pelicanshores.com.* 34 rms, 3 story, 19 kits. No elvtr. May-Sept: S, D $59-$79; each addl $5; suites, kit. units $99-$119; lower rates Sun-Thurs rest of yr. Crib free. TV; cable, VCR avail. Indoor pool. Coffee in rms. Restaurant nearby. Ck-out 11 am. Business servs avail. Some fireplaces. On ocean; beach access. Cr cds: A, C, D, DS, MC, V.

⊡ ⬛ ✈ ⬛ ⬛ SC

★ **QUALITY INN.** *136 NE Hwy 101 (97367). 541/994-8155; fax 541/994-5581; toll-free 800/423-6240. www. qualityinn.com.* 30 rms, 3 story, 4 kits. May-Oct: S $49-$149; D $59-$159; each addl $10; lower rates rest of yr. Crib avail. TV; cable (premium). Complimentary continental bkfst. Coffee in rms. Restaurant nearby. Ck-out 11 am. Business servs avail. Microwaves. Many balconies. Cr cds: A, C, D, DS, ER, MC, V.

⬛ ⬛

★★ **SHILO INN OCEANFRONT RESORT.** *1501 NW 40th Pl (97367). 541/994-3655; fax 541/994-2199; res 800/222-2244. www.shiloinn.com.* 247 rms, 3-4 story. Mid-June-mid-Sept: S $49-$269; under 12 free; lower rates rest of yr. Crib free. Pet accepted, some restrictions; $10/day. TV; cable (premium), VCR avail. Indoor pool; whirlpool. Restaurant adj 7-2 am. Bar 11-1 am. Ck-out noon. Coin lndry. Meeting rms. Business center. Free airport, bus depot transportation. Exercise equipt; sauna. Health club privileges. Refrigerators, microwaves; some bathrm phones. Picnic tables. On beach. Cr cds: A, C, D, DS, ER, JCB, MC, V.

⊡ ⬛ ⬛ ⬛ ⬛ ⬛ SC ⬛

Resort

★★★ **WESTIN SALISHAN LODGE.** *7760 Hwy 101 N, Gleneden Beach (97388). 541/764-2371; fax 541/764-3663; toll-free 800/452-2300. salishan.com.* 205 rms, 2-3 story. S, D $99-$199; each addl $20; under 17 free; Crib free. Pet accepted, some restrictions; $25. TV; cable (premium), VCR avail. Indoor pool; whirlpool, hydrotherapy pool. Restaurants (see also THE DINING ROOM AT SALISHAN). Rm serv. Bar 4pm-midnight; entertainment wkends. Ck-out noon. Meeting rms. Business servs avail. Bellhops. Shopping mall. Indoor/outdoor lighted tennis, pro. 18-hole golf, greens fee $35-$50, pro, putting greens, covered driving range. Self-guided nature trail. Exercise rm; sauna. Massage. Game rm. Refrigerators. Art gallery. Library. Cr cds: A, C, D, ER, JCB, MC, V.

⊡ ⬛ ⬛ 🔆 ⬛ ⬛ ⬛ ⬛ ⬛ ⬛

Restaurants

★★★ **BAY HOUSE.** *5911 SW US 101 (97367). 541/996-3222.* Hrs: 5:30-9 pm; Sat from 5 pm. Closed Dec 25; also Mon, Tues Nov-Apr. Res accepted. Serv bar. Dinner $18-$26. Specializes in fresh seafood, game, pasta. Overlooking Siletz Bay. Cr cds: A, DS, MC, V.

⊡

★★ **CHEZ JEANNETTE.** *7150 Old US 101, Gleneden Beach (97388). 541/764-3434.* Hrs: 5:30-10 pm. Res accepted. French, Northwestern menu. Bar. Dinner $20-$29. Children's meals. Specializes in seafood, rack of lamb, game. French cottage decor; built 1920. Cr cds: A, DS, MC, V.

⊡

★★ **THE DINING ROOM AT SALISHAN.** *7760 N Hwy 101, Gleneden Beach (97388). 541/764-2371. www. salishan.com.* Regional American menu. Specializes in Oregon lamb, fresh seafood, regional cuisine. Own baking. Hrs: 7 am-10 pm; Fri, Sat to 10:30 pm; Sun brunch 10 am-2 pm. Res accepted. Serv bar. Wine cellar. A la carte entrees: bkfst $6-$9, lunch $8-$12, dinner $10-$28. Sun brunch $23.50. Children's meals. Valet parking. Cr cds: A, D, DS, MC, V.

⊡

★ **DORY COVE.** *5819 Logan Rd (97367). 541/994-5180. www.dorycove. com.* Hrs: 11:30 am-8 pm; Sun from noon; summer to 9 pm. Wine, beer. Lunch $4-$10, dinner $9-$20. Children's meals. Specializes in seafood.

Some tables have ocean view. Cr cds:
A, DS, MC, V.
D SC

Madras

(C-4) See also Prineville, Redmond

Pop 3,443 **Elev** 2,242 ft
Area code 541 **Zip** 97741
Information Chamber of Commerce,
197 SE 5th St, PO Box 770; 541/475-
2350 or 800/967-3564

Although the area was explored as
early as 1825, settlement here was
difficult because of Native American
hostility. Settlement east of the Cascades, considered a wall of separation
between the Native Americans and
the settlers, was officially forbidden
in 1856. In 1858 the order was
revoked, and in 1862 the first road
was built across the Cascades to provide a passage for traders. Shortly
thereafter, settlement began in
earnest.

What to See and Do

The Cove Palisades State Park. A
4,130-acre park on Lake Billy Chinook behind Round Butte Dam;
scenic canyon of geological interest;
spectacular views of the confluence
of the Crooked, Deschutes, and
Metolius rivers forming Lake Billy
Chinook in a steep basaltic canyon.
Swimming, fishing, boating (ramp,
dock, rentals, marina with restaurant, groceries), houseboat rentals;
hiking, picnicking, tent and trailer
sites (dump station). Standard fees.
15 mi SW off US 97. Phone 541/546-
3412.

Jefferson County Museum. Located in
the old courthouse; old-time doctor's
equipment; military memorabilia;
homestead and farm equipment.
(May-Oct, Mon-Fri) 34 SE D St, 1 blk
off Main St. Phone 541/475-3808. ¢

**Rockhounding. Richardson's Recre-
ational Ranch.** All diggings accessible
by road; highlight of ranch are
famous agate beds, featuring Thunder Eggs and ledge agate material.

Rockhound campground area (no
hookups). Digging fee. 11 mi N on
US 97, then right 3 mi to ranch
office. Phone 541/475-2680.

Special Event

Collage of Culture. Friendship Park.
Music and balloon festival celebrat-
ing cultural diversity. Mid-May.
Phone 541/475-2350.

Motel/Motor Lodge

★ ★ **SONNY'S MOTEL.** *1539 SW
Hwy 97 (97741). 541/475-7217; fax
541/475-6547. www.sonnysmotel.com.*
44 rms, 2 story, 2 suites, 2 kits. S $47;
D $55; each addl $8; suites $80-$105;
kit. units $95; under 6 free. Crib $4.
Pet accepted, $10. TV; cable (pre-
mium). Heated pool; whirlpool.
Complimentary continental bkfst.
Restaurant 3-10 pm. Bar to midnight.
Ck-out 11 am. Coin lndry. Business
servs avail. Lawn games. Some micro-
waves; refrigerators avail. Cr cds: A,
DS, MC, V.
D ⊁ ≈ 🖎

Resort

★ ★ ★ **KAH-NEE-TA LODGE.** *100
Main St, Warm Springs (97761).
541/553-1112; fax 541/553-1071; toll
free 800/554-1786. www.kah-nee-
taresort.com.* 139 rms in 3-4 story
lodge, 32 condos, 20 unfurnished
teepees in village. Lodge: S, D $115-
$140; suites $170-$275; condos:
$109.95; village teepees for 5, $55;
under 6 free in lodge; mid-wk packages (off season). Pet accepted. TV;
cable (premium). 2 heated pools;
whirlpools, poolside serv, private hot
mineral baths at village. Dining rm 7
am-10 pm. Snacks. Salmon Bake Sat
(Memorial Day-Labor Day). Bars 11
am-2 pm. Ck-out 11:30 am, ck-in
4:30 pm. Lodge meeting rms. Gift
shop. Tennis. 18-hole golf, greens fee
$32, pro, putting green, driving
range. Exercise rm; sauna. Massage.
Kayak float trips. Trails. Bicycles. Rec
dir; entertainment. Game rm.
Authentic Native American dances
Sun May-Sept. Varied accommodations. Owned by Confederated Tribes
of Warm Springs Reservation. RV and

trailer spaces avail. Casino. Cr cds: A, C, D, DS, MC, V.

[icons]

McKenzie Bridge

Pop 200 **Elev** 1,337 ft **Area code** 541 **Zip** 97413

Information McKenzie River Chamber of Commerce and Information Center, MP 24 McKenzie Hwy East (OR 126), PO Box 1117, Leaburg 97489; 541/896-3330 or -9011
Web www.el.com/to/Mckenzierivervalley/

McKenzie Bridge and the neighboring town of Blue River are located on the beautiful McKenzie River, with covered bridges, lakes, waterfalls, and wilderness trails of the Cascades nearby. Fishing, float trips, skiing, and backpacking are some of the many activities available. Ranger District offices of the Willamette National Forest (see EUGENE) are located here and in Blue River.

What to See and Do

Blue River Dam and Lake. Saddle Dam Boating Site offers boat ramp. Mona Campground offers swimming; fishing. Picnicking (fee). Dam is a US Army Corps of Engineers project. Recreation areas administered by the US Forest Service. Camping (mid-May-mid-Sept; fee). 7 mi W on OR 126, then N on Forest Rd 15 in Willamette National Forest. Phone 541/822-3317.

Carmen-Smith Hydroelectric Development. Salmon spawning facility near Trail Bridge Dam; three stocked reservoirs—Trail Bridge, Smith and Carmen (daily). Boat launching (free). Picnicking. Camping at Lake's End, N end of Smith Reservoir, at Ice Cap Creek on Carmen Reservoir and at Trail Bridge (ten-day limit). 14 mi NE on OR 126, on Upper McKenzie River. Phone 541/484-2411. ¢¢

Cougar Dam and Lake. Six-mi-long reservoir. Echo Park is a day-use area with boat ramp (free). Slide Creek campground offers swimming, water-skiing; fishing; boat ramp. Picnicking

(free). Camping (fee). Delta and French Pete campgrounds offer fishing, picnicking. Campgrounds maintained and operated by US Forest Service. Dam is a US Army Corps of Engineers project. (May-Sept; most areas closed rest of yr, inquire) For further info inquire at Blue River Ranger Station. 5 mi W on OR 126, then S on Forest Rd 19 (Aufderheide Forest Dr) in Willamette National Forest (see EUGENE). Phone 541/822-3317.

Motel/Motor Lodge

★ **SLEEPY HOLLOW MOTEL.** *54791 McKenzie Hwy, Blue River (97413). 541/822-3805.* 19 rms, 2 story. Apr-Oct: S $48; D $55; each addl $10.80. Closed rest of yr. TV in some rms. Restaurant nearby. Ck-out 11 am. Refrigerators. Cr cds: MC, V.
[icons]

Restaurant

★ ★ **LOG CABIN INN.** *56483 McKenzie Hwy (97413). 541/822-3432. www.logcabininn.com.* Hrs: May-Nov noon-9 pm; Sun brunch 10 am-2 pm; winter hrs vary. Res accepted. Bar 5 pm-midnight. Lunch $5.95-$8.95, dinner $10.95-$17.95. Sun brunch $8.95. Children's meals. Specializes in mesquite-smoked barbecued fish, game. Outdoor dining. Built as stagecoach stop in 1906. Cr cds: A, MC, V.
[D]

McMinnville

(B-2) *See also Newberg, Oregon City, Salem*

Pop 17,894 **Elev** 160 ft **Area code** 503 **Zip** 97128
Information Chamber of Commerce, 417 N Adams; 503/472-6196
Web www.mcminnville.org

McMinnville is in the center of a wine-producing area. Many of the wineries offer tours.

What to See and Do

Community Theater. Musical, comedy and drama productions by the

Gallery Players of Oregon (Fri-Sun). Phone 503/472-2227.

Linfield College. (1849) 2,100 students. Liberal arts. On the 100-acre campus are Miller Fine Arts Center, Linfield Anthropology Museum and the Linfield Theater. The music department offers concerts. Lectures and events throughout the yr. Phone 503/883-2200.

Special Events

Wine & Food Classic. Mid-Mar. Phone 503/472-6196.

Turkey Rama. Mid-July. Phone 503/472-6196.

Yamhill County Fair & Rodeo. Late July-early Aug. Phone 503/434-7524.

Motel/Motor Lodge

★★ **SAFARI MOTOR INN, INC.** 345 NE Hwy 99W (97128). 503/472-5187, fax 503/434-6380. 90 rms, 2 story. S $54; D $58; each addl $3. Crib $3. TV; cable. Restaurant 6 am-9 pm; Sun 7 am-3 pm. Bar from 4 pm. Ck-out noon. Meeting rms. Business servs avail. Whirlpool. Exercise equipt. Cr cds: A, C, D, DS, MC, V.

🄳 🏋 ⊠ 🐾

B&B/Small Inn

★★ **STEIGER HAUS BED & BREAKFAST.** 360 SE Wilson St (97128). 503/472-0821; fax 503/472-0100. www.steigerhaus.com. 5 rms, 3 story. No A/C. No rm phones. S, D $70-$80; suite $95-$130; each addl $20. Children over 10 yrs only. Complimentary full bkfst. Coffee in rms. Ck-out 11 am, ck-in 3-6 pm. Business servs avail. Luggage handling. Lawn games. Balconies. Some refrigerators, microwaves, fireplaces. Picnic tables. Northern European country-style house; stained-glass windows. Totally nonsmoking. Cr cds: DS, MC, V.

⊠ 🐾

Guest Ranch

★★ **FLYING M RANCH.** 23029 NW Flying M Rd, Yamhill (97148). 503/662-3222; fax 503/662-3202. www.flying-m-ranch.com. 24 rms in main building, 6 kit. cottages, 1 cottage. S, D $60; kit. cottages $85-$200; cottage $150. Pet accepted, some restrictions. TV in lounge; TVs in some cottages. Dining rm 8 am-8 pm; Fri, Sat and hols to 10 pm. Box lunches. Picnics. Bar; entertainment Sun. Ck-out 11 am, ck-in 4 pm. Package store 10 mi. Meeting rms. Business servs avail. Gift shop. Swimming pond. Hiking. Overnight trail rides. Lawn games. Fishing. Balconies. Picnic tables, grills. Cr cds: A, D, DS, MC, V.

🄳 🐾 🏋 ⚡ ⊠ 🐾

⛽ Medford

(F-2) See also Ashland, Grants Pass, Jacksonville

Founded 1885 **Pop** 46,951 **Elev** 1,380 ft **Area code** 541

Information Visitors and Convention Bureau, 101 E 8th St, 97501; 541/779-4847 or 800/469-6307

Medford is a name known throughout the US for pears: Comice, Bartlett, Winter Nellis, Bosc, and d'Anjou. The city, on Bear Creek 10 miles from its confluence with the Rogue River, is surrounded by orchards. Trees make the city park-like; lumbering provides a large share of the industry. Mild winters and warm summers favor outdoor living and also encourage outdoor sports: boating and fishing on the Rogue River, fishing in 153 stocked streams and 17 lakes; camping and hunting in 56 forest camps within an 80-mile radius. The Rogue River National Forest headquarters is here.

What to See and Do

Butte Creek Mill. Water-powered grist mill (1872) grinds whole grain products with original millstones. Museum (summer, Sat). Mill (Mon-Sat; closed hols). 10 mi N on OR 62 in Eagle Point. Phone 541/826-3531. **FREE**

Crater Rock Museum. Gem and mineral collection; Native American artifacts; fossils, geodes and crystals. Gift shop. (Tues, Thurs and Sat; closed major hols) N on I-5, exit 35 then S on OR 99 in Central Point at 2002 Scenic Ave. Phone 541/664-6081. **Donation**

Joseph P. Stewart State Park. A 910-acre park located on lake formed by Lost Creek Dam. Swimming; fishing; boat dock and ramp to Rogue River. Hiking, bike trails. Picnicking. Tent and improved campsites (Daily; dump station). Some fees. 35 mi NE on OR 62. Phone 541/560-3334.

⭐ **Rogue River National Forest.** Forest has 632,045 acres with extensive stands of Douglas fir, ponderosa, and sugar pine. Rogue-Umpqua National Forest Scenic Byway offers a day-long drive through southern Oregon's dramatic panorama of mountains, rivers, and forest; viewpoints. A part of the Pacific Crest National Scenic Trail and portions of three wilderness areas are incl in the forest. For fishermen, the upper reaches of the Rogue River, and other streams and lakes yield rainbow, cutthroat, and brook trout. Union Creek Historic District, on OR 62 near Crater Lake National Park. Forest is in two separate sections, located in the Siskiyou Mtns (W of I-5) and Cascade Range (E of I-5). Swimming; hiking, backpacking, downhill and x-country skiing, picnic areas, camping. Some fees. S off I-5 and NE on OR 62, 140. Contact Information Receptionist, PO Box 520, 333 W 8th St. Phone 541/776-3600.

Southern Oregon History Center. More than 2,000 items from Southern Oregon Historical Society's cultural history collection. Exhibits, public programs, research library. (Mon-Fri) 106 N Central Ave. Phone 541/773-6536. **FREE**

Tou Velle State Park. A 51-acre park. Fishing on Rogue River; boat ramp to Rogue River. Picnicking. 3 mi NE on I-5, then 6 mi N on Table Rock Rd. Phone 541/582-1118. ¢

Special Events

Pear Blossom Festival. Parade; ten-mi run; band festival. Second wkend Apr. Phone 541/779-4847.

Jackson County Fair. Jackson County Fairgrounds. Entertainment, dance, music, 4-H fair. Third wkend July. Phone 541/774-8270.

Motels/Motor Lodges

★★ **BEST INN & SUITES.** *1015 S Riverside Ave (97501). 541/773-8266; fax 541/734-5447; toll-free 800/237-8466. www.bestinn.com.* 112 rms, 2 story, 14 suites. May-Oct: S $69-$73; D $75-$79; each addl $6; suites $102; under 18 free. Crib free. Pet accepted; some restrictions; $100 deposit (refundable). TV; cable (premium). Pool. Complimentary continental bkfst. Complimentary coffee in rms. Restaurant adj. Bar 10-2 am. Ck-out 11 am. Meeting rms. Business servs avail. Downhill/x-country ski 20 mi. Refrigerators, microwaves, wet bars in suites. Cr cds: A, D, DS, MC, V.
🔲 🔫 🏨 🔥 🏊 🛄 🛶 🐾

★★ **BEST WESTERN HORIZON INN.** *1154 E Barnett Rd (97504). 541/779-5085; fax 541/772-6878; toll-free 800/452-2255. www.bestwestern. com.* 123 rms, 2 story. S, D $80-$89; each addl $5; suites $100-$150; under 17 free. Crib free. Pet accepted; $10. TV; cable (premium), VCR avail (movies). Heated pool; whirlpool. Complimentary coffee in rms. Restaurant 6 am-midnight. Bar. Ck-out 11 am. Meeting rm. Business center. In-rm modem link. Valet serv. Airport transportation. Downhill/x-country ski 20 mi. Exercise equipt; sauna. Some refrigerators, microwaves in suites. Cr cds: A, C, D, DS, MC, V.
🔲 🔫 🛄 🏊 🛋 🔥 🐾 SC

★★ **BEST WESTERN PONY SOLDIER INN.** *2340 Crater Lake Hwy (94504). 541/779-2011; fax 541/779-7304; toll-free 800/634-7669. www. bestwestern.com.* 74 rms, 2 story. May-Sept: S $87-$92; D $89-$94; each addl $5; under 18 free; lower rates rest of yr. Crib $3. Pet accepted, some restrictions; $10. TV; cable (premium), VCR avail (movies). Heated pool; whirlpool. Complimentary continental bkfst, newspaper. Coffee in rms. Restaurant adj open 24 hrs. Bar. Ck-out noon. Free guest lndry. Business servs avail. In-rm modem link. Downhill/x-country ski 20 mi. Health club privileges. Refrigerators, microwaves. Cr cds: A, C, D, DS, MC, V.
🔫 🏊 🛄 🛶 🐾 SC

★ **CEDAR LODGE MOTOR INN.** *518 N Riverside (97501). 541/773-*

7361; fax 541/776-1033; toll-free 800/282-3419. www.ore.fishing.com. 79 rms, 1-2 story. May-Oct: S $40-$45; D $46-$53; each addl $5; suites $45-$62; kit. unit $52; under 12 free; wkly rates; lower rates rest of yr. Crib $5. Pet accepted, some restrictions. TV; cable. Heated pool. Complimentary continental bkfst. Restaurant adj 6 am-10 pm. Bar 10-2 am. Ck-out 11 am. Downhill/x-country ski 20 mi. Some refrigerators, microwaves. Cr cds: A, C, D, DS, MC, V.

★ **KNIGHTS INN.** *500 N Riverside Ave (97501). 541/773-3676; fax 541/857-0493; toll-free 800/531-2655.* 83 rms, 2 story. S $35; D $39 $46; each addl $4. Crib $4. Pet accepted, some restrictions. TV; cable. Pool. Restaurant adj 6 am-9 pm. Ck-out 11 am. Downhill/x-country ski 20 mi. Microwaves avail. Cr cds: A, C, D, DS, MC, V.

★★ **RED LION HOTEL MEDFORD.** *200 N Riverside Ave (97501). 541/779-5811; fax 541/779-7961. www. redlionmedford.com.* 185 rms, 2 story. S, D $89-$94; each addl $10; suites $250; under 18 free. Crib free. Pet accepted; $50 deposit. TV; cable (premium). 2 heated pools. Restaurant 6 am-10 pm; dining rm 11:30 am-2 pm, 5-10 pm; Sun 10 am-2 pm. Rm serv. Bar 3 pm-midnight; Fri, Sat to 2 am; entertainment. Ck-out noon. Coin lndry. Valet serv. Meeting rms. Business center. In-rm modem link. Bellhops. Sundries. Free airport transportation. Downhill/x-country ski 20 mi. Health club privileges. Some private patios, balconies. Cr cds: A, C, D, DS, JCB, MC, V.

★★ **RESTON HOTEL.** *2300 Crater Lake Hwy (97504). 541/779-3141; fax 541/779-2623; toll-free 800/779-7829. www.restonhotel.com.* 164 rms, 2 story. S, D $65-$75; each addl $10; suites $100; under 17 free. Crib free. Pet accepted, some restrictions; $10. TV; cable. Indoor pool. Complimentary continental bkfst. Restaurant 6:30-11 am, 5-10 pm. Bar 5 pm-midnight; Thurs-Sat to 2 am. Ck-out noon. Convention facilities. Business servs avail. Free airport transportation. Health club privileges. Exercise

equipt. Microwaves avail. Cr cds: A, D, DS, MC, V.

★★★ **ROGUE REGENCY INN.** *2345 Crater Lake Hwy (97504). 541/770-1234; fax 541/770-2466; toll-free 800/535-5805. www.rogueregency. com.* 203 rms, 9 suites, 4 story. S $95-$97; D $105-$107; each addl $10; suites $185-$210; under 18 free. Crib free. TV; cable (premium). Heated pool; whirlpool. Coffee in rms. Restaurant 6 am-10 pm. Bar 4 pm-midnight; Sat, Sun from 11 am. Ck-out 11 am. Meeting rms. Business center. In-rm modem link. Free airport, bus depot transportation. Health club privileges. Exercise equipt. Gift shop. Coin lndry. Refrigerators, microwaves, wet bars. Whirlpools, fireplaces in suites. Cr cds: A, D, DS, JCB, MC, V.

★★ **WINDMILL INN.** *1950 Biddle Rd (97504). 541/779-0050; toll-free 800/547-4747. www.windmillinns.com.* 123 rms, 2 story. S, D $79-$90; kit. units $95; under 18 free. Crib $3.50. Pet accepted. TV; cable (premium). Heated pool; whirlpool. Complimentary continental bkfst, newspaper. Restaurant adj 6 am-11 pm. Ck-out 11 am. Meeting rm. Business servs avail. In rm modem link. Coin lndry. Valet serv. Sundries. Free airport, bus depot transportation. Exercise equipt; sauna. Health club privileges. Bicycles. Refrigerators, microwaves avail. Library. Cr cds: A, D, DS, MC, V.

Restaurant

★★ **MON DESIR DINING INN.** *4615 Hanrick Rd, Central Point (97502). 541/664-7558.* Hrs: 11 am-2 pm, 4-9 pm; Sat from 4 pm. Closed Sun, Mon. Res accepted. Continental menu. Bar. Lunch $4.95-$8.95, dinner $12.95-$24.95. Specializes in international cuisine. Outdoor dining. Converted mansion; fireplace, antiques; garden. Totally nonsmoking. Cr cds: D, MC, V.

Mount Hood National Forest

(B-2) *See also Hood River, The Dalles*

Web www.mthood.org

Mount Hood (11,235 ft) is the natural focal point of this 1,064,573-acre forest with headquarters in Sandy. Its white-crowned top, the highest point in Oregon, can be seen for miles on a clear day. It is also popular with skiers, who know it has some of the best slopes in the Northwest. There are five winter sports areas. Throughout the year, however, visitors can take advantage of the surrounding forest facilities for camping (1,600 camp and picnic sites), hunting, fishing, swimming, mountain climbing, golfing, horseback riding, hiking, and tobogganing. The Columbia Gorge, which cuts through the Cascades here, has many spectacular waterfalls, including Multnomah (620 ft). There are nine routes to the summit, which has fumed and smoked several times since the volcanic peak was discovered. Only experienced climbers should try the ascent and then only with a guide. For further information contact the Mount Hood Information Center, 65000 E US 26, Welches 97067; phone 503/622-7674, 503/622-4822, or 888/622-4822.

What to See and Do

River cruise. Two-hr narrated cruise of Columbia Gorge aboard the 599-passenger *Columbia Gorge,* an authentic sternwheeler. (Mid-June-Sept, three departures daily; res required for dinner cruise) Also here: museum; marina; travel information; picnicking; camping. 45 mi E of Portland via I-84 in Cascade Locks. Phone 503/223-3928. ¢¢¢¢

Ski Areas.

Mount Hood Meadows. Quad, triple, seven double chairlifts, free rope tow; patrol, school, rentals; restaurant, cafeteria, concession, bar, daycare, two day lodges. Longest run three mi; vertical drop 2,777 ft. Also 550 acres of expert canyon skiing. (Nov-May, daily) Groomed, ungroomed x-country trails; night skiing (Wed-Sun). 11 mi NE of Government Camp on OR 35. Phone 503/337-2222.

Timberline Lodge. Four Quads, triple, one double chairlift; patrol, school, rentals; restaurant, cafeteria, concession, bar, lodge. Longest run more than two mi; vertical

Mount Hood, the highest point in Oregon

drop 3,580 ft. (Mid-Nov-June, daily) Chairlift also operates (Daily, weather permitting; fee). 6 mi N of US 26. Phone 503/272-3311. ¢¢¢¢¢

Motel/Motor Lodge

★ **MOUNT HOOD INN.** *87450 E Government Camp Loop, Government Camp (97028). 503/272-3205; fax 503/272-3307; toll-free 800/443-7777. www.mounthoodinn.com.* 56 rms, 2 story, 4 suites. No A/C. S, D $125-$195; each addl $10; suites $145; under 12 free. Crib $5. Pet accepted; $5. TV; cable (premium), VCR avail. Complimentary continental bkfst. Restaurant nearby. Ck-out noon. Coin lndry. Meeting rms. Business servs avail. Downhill ski ¼ mi; x country ski adj. Whirlpool. Some refrigerators, wet bars. Picnic tables. Cr cds: A, C, D, DS, MC, V.
D ⬛ 🔧 📶 🛶 🎿 🔥

Resorts

★★★ **THE RESORT AT THE MOUNTAIN.** *68010 E Fairway Ave, Welches (97067). 503/622-3101; fax 503/622-2222; toll-free 800/669-7666. www.theresort.com.* 160 rms, 2 story, 60 kit. units. Mid-June-Oct: S, D $119-$149; each addl $20; kit. units from $169; under 18 free; ski, golf plans; lower rates rest of yr. Crib free. TV; VCR (movies). Heated pool; whirlpool. Restaurant (see HIGHLANDS DINING ROOM). Rm serv. Box lunches. Picnics. Bar 3 pm-midnight; entertainment Sat, Sun. Ck-out noon, ck-in 4 pm. Business servs avail. In-rm modem link. Gift shop. Grocery 1 mi. Coin lndry. Bellhops. Concierge. Valet serv. Sports dir. Social dir. Lighted tennis. 27-hole golf, greens fee $40, pro, putting green. Downhill/x-country ski 18 mi. Hiking trails. Bicycle rentals. Exercise equipt. Massage. Lawn games. Rec rm. Balconies. Picnic tables. 300-acres of forest at Salmon River. Scottish amenities reminiscent of Highlands. Cr cds: A, DS, MC, V.
D ⬛ 🎿 🔧 ⛷ 🛶 🎾 🔥

★★ **TIMBERLINE LODGE.** *Timberline, Timberline Lodge (97028). 503/272-3311; fax 503/272-3710; toll-free 503/231-7979. www.timberline*

lodge.com. 70 rms, 4 story. No A/C. S, D $65-$180; each addl $15; under 11 free; ski plans. Crib free. TV in most rms; cable, VCR avail (movies). Pool; whirlpool. Sauna. Supervised children's activities (Dec-Mar); ages 4-12. Dining rm 8-10 am, noon-2 pm, 6-8:30 pm. Snack bar. Bars 11 am-11 pm. Ck-out 11 am, ck-in 4 pm. Business servs avail. Downhill ski on site. Some fireplaces. Rustic rms; hand-carved furniture. Totally nonsmoking. Cr cds: A, D, DS, MC, V.
D ⬛ 🔧 🎿 🛶 🎿 🔥

Restaurants

★★ **DON GUIDO'S ITALIAN CUISINE.** *73330 E US 26, Rhododendron (97049). 503/622-5111. www.don guidos.com.* Hrs: 5-10 pm. Closed hols. Res accepted. Italian menu. Bar. A la carte entrees: dinner $9.95-$21.95. Children's meals. Specialties: chicken marsala, halibut piccata, seafood fettucine. Parking. Built in 1928. Romantic atmosphere. Totally nonsmoking. Cr cds: A, DS, MC, V.
D

★★★ **HIGHLANDS DINING ROOM.** *68010 E Fairway Ave, Welches (97067). 503/622-2214. www.theresort. com.* Hrs: 7 am-9 pm; Sun brunch 10 am-2 pm. Res accepted. Bar to midnight. Wine list. Bkfst $3.95-$7.95, lunch $5.50-$12, dinner $13.95-$17.95. Sun brunch $17.95. Children's meals. Specializes in prime rib, salmon, Northwest cuisine. Pianist Fri, Sat. Outdoor dining. Bright and cheerful atmosphere; view of pool and gardens. Totally nonsmoking. Cr cds: A, C, D, DS, ER, MC, V.
D

Newberg

(B-2) *See also Beaverton, Hillsboro, McMinnville, Oregon City, Portland, Salem*

Founded 1889 **Pop** 13,086 **Elev** 176 ft
Area code 503 **Zip** 97132

Information Chamber of Commerce, 115 N Washington; 503/538-2014

Quakers made their first settlement west of the Rockies here and established Pacific Academy in 1885. Herbert Hoover was in its first graduating class (1888).

What to See and Do

Champoeg State Historic Area. A 615-acre park on site of early Willamette River settlement, site of settlers' vote in 1843 for a provisional territorial government, swept away by flood of 1861. Fishing, boat dock on Willamette River; hiking, picnicking, improved camping (dump station). Standard fees. Visitor information, interpretive center; monument. French Prairie Loop 40-mi auto or bike tour begins and ends here. (See SPECIAL EVENT) 5 mi W off I-5. Phone 503/678-1251. ¢¢ In the area are

Newell House Museum. Reconstructed home of Robert Newell, one-time mountain man and friend of the Native Americans. Contains period furnishings, quilts, coverlets and examples of fine handiwork; collection of inaugural gowns worn by wives of Oregon governors; Native American artifacts. Old jail (1850) and typical pioneer one-rm schoolhouse. (Feb-Nov, Wed-Sun; closed Thanksgiving) Just W of park entrance at 8089 Champoeg Rd NE. Phone 503/678-5537. ¢

Pioneer Mother's Memorial Log Cabin. A replica, much enlarged, of the type of log cabin built by early pioneers. Constructed of peeled hand-hewn logs, with a shake roof, it has a massive stone fireplace in the living rm, a sleeping loft and two small bedrms; many pioneer items incl an old Hudson's Bay heating stove, collection of guns and muskets dating from 1777-1853, a fife played at Lincoln's funeral, china and glassware and original furnishings from pioneer homes. (Feb-Nov, Wed-Sun; closed Thanksgiving) Located in the park, on the banks of the Willamette River, at 8035 Champoeg Rd NE. Phone 503/633-2237. ¢

Visitor Center. Interpretive historical exhibits tell the story of "Champoeg: Birthplace of Oregon"; films; tours. (Daily) 8239 Champoeg Rd NE. Phone 503/678-1251. **Donation**

George Fox University. (1891) 2,600 students. Founded as Friends Pacific Academy; renamed in 1949 for English founder of the Society of Friends. Herbert Hoover was a student here; Hoover Building has displays. Brougher Museum has Quaker and pioneer exhibits. Campus tours. 414 N Meridian. Phone 503/538-8383.

Hoover-Minthorn House Museum. Herbert Hoover lived here with his uncle, Dr. Henry Minthorn. Quaker house built in 1881 contains many original furnishings, photographs and souvenirs of Hoover's boyhood. (Mar-Nov, Wed-Sun; Dec and Feb, Sat and Sun; closed Jan) 115 S River St. Phone 503/538-6629. ¢

Special Event

Vintage Celebration. Classic automobiles and airplanes, arts and crafts, wine tasting. Phone 503/538-2014. Sat, Sun after Labor Day.

Motel/Motor Lodge

★ ★ **SHILO INN.** *501 Sitka Ave (97132). 503/537-0303; fax 503/537-0442; toll-free 800/222-2244. www. shiloinn.com.* 60 rms, 3 story. S, D $49.95-$99.95; each addl $10; suites $75; kit. units $79; under 13 free. Crib free. Pet accepted; $10/day. TV; cable (premium), VCR avail. Pool; whirlpool. Complimentary continental bkfst. Restaurant adj. Ck-out noon. Coin lndry. Meeting rms. Business servs avail. Sundries. Exercise equipt; sauna. Bathrm phones, refrigerators, microwaves, wet bars. Cr cds: A, D, DS, MC, V.

D ✈ 🕈 🎝 🐾 SC

Newport

(C-1) *See also Depoe Bay, Lincoln City, Yachats*

Settled 1882 **Pop** 8,437 **Elev** 160 ft **Area code** 541 **Zip** 97365
Information Chamber of Commerce, 555 SW Coast Hwy; 541/265-8801 or 800/262-7844
Web www.newportchamber.org

This fishing port at the mouth of the Yaquina River has been a resort for more than 100 years. Crabbing is a popular activity here; Dungeness crabs can be caught in the bay year-round.

What to See and Do

Hatfield Marine Science Center of Oregon State University. Conducts research on oceanography, fisheries, water quality, marine science education and marine biology; research vessel *Wecoma;* nature trail; aquarium-museum; films; special programs in summer. Winter and spring grey whale programs. Braille text and other aids for the hearing and visually impaired. (Daily; closed Dec 25) Marine Science Dr, S side of Yaquina Bay, just E of Newport Bridge, off US 101. Phone 541/867-0100. **Donation**

Lincoln County Historical Society Museums. Log Cabin Museum. Artifacts from Siletz Reservation; historical, pioneer and maritime exhibits. (Tues-Sun; closed Jan 1, Thanksgiving, Dec 25) 545 SW 9th St. Also **Burrows House Museum.** Victorian-era household furnishings, clothing; history of Lincoln County. (Same days as log cabin museum) 579 SW 9th St. Phone 541/265-7509. **FREE**

Marine Discovery Tours. Whale-watching and river cruises. Hands-on activities. (Hrs vary seasonally; closed Dec 25) 345 SW Bay Blvd. Phone 541/265-6200. ¢¢¢¢¢

Mineral collecting. Gemstones, marine fossils, other stones are found on beaches to N and S of Newport, particularly at creek mouths. Phone 800/262-7844.

Oregon Coast Aquarium. Houses 15,000 animals representing 500 species in unique habitats. (Daily; closed Dec 25) S side of Yaquina Bay. 2820 SE Ferry Slip Rd. Phone 541/867-3474. ¢¢

Ripley's—Believe It or Not. Exhibits incl replicas of a backwards fountain; King Tut's tomb; the *Titanic;* the Fiji mermaid. (Daily; closed Dec 25) 250 SW Bay Blvd. Phone 541/265-2206. ¢¢¢

State parks.

Beverly Beach. A 130-acre park with beach access; fishing. Hiking. Picnicking. Tent and trailer sites (dump station). Standard fees. 7 mi N on US 101. Phone 541/265-9278.

Devil's Punch Bowl. An eight-acre park noted for its bowl-shaped rock formation that fills at high tide; ocean-carved caves, marine gardens. Beach Trails. Picnicking. Observation point. 8 mi N off US 101. Phone 541/265-9278.

Devil's Punch Bowl

Ona Beach. A 237-acre day-use park with ocean beach, swimming; fishing, boat ramp on creek. Picnicking. 8 mi S on US 101. Phone 541/867-7451.

South Beach. Over 400 acres. Botanically interesting area, sandy beach, dunes. Fishing. Hiking. Picnicking. Improved campsites (dump station). Standard fees. 2 mi S on US 101. Phone 541/867-7451.

Yaquina Bay. Over 30 acres. Ocean beach, fishing, picnicking. Agate beaches nearby. Old Yaquina Bay Lighthouse (1871) has been restored; exhibits. (Memorial Day-Labor Day, daily; rest of yr, wkends) N end of bridge on US 101. Phone 541/867-7451. **Donation**

Undersea Gardens. Visitors descend beneath the sea for underwater show. Watch native sea life through viewing windows; guides narrate as scuba divers perform; features Armstrong, the giant octopus. (Daily; closed Dec 25) 250 SW Bay Blvd, on Yaquina Bay just off US 101 in the Bay Front district. Phone 541/265-2206. ¢¢

Wax Works. Events of the past and future shown with animation and special effects. (Daily; closed Dec 25) 250 SW Bay Blvd. Phone 541/265-2206. ¢¢

Yaquina Head. Lighthouse here is a popular spot for whale-watching and fully accessible tidal pool viewing. Also interpretive center. ½ mi N on US 101. Phone 541/574-3100.

Special Events

Seafood and Wine Festival. Last full wkend Feb. Phone 541/265-8801.

Loyalty Days and Sea Fair Festival. Military ships, parade, sailboat races; entertainment. Phone 541/265-8801. First wkend May. Phone 541/867-3798.

Motels/Motor Lodges

★★ **EMBARCADERO RESORT HOTEL.** *1000 SE Bay Blvd (97365). 541/265-8521; fax 541/265-7844; toll-free 800/547-4779. www.embarcadero-resort.com.* 85 units, 3 story, 50 kits., 36 patio suites. No elvtr. May-Oct: S, D $129-$289; lower rates rest of yr; package plans. TV; cable, VCR avail. Indoor pool; whirlpools. Restaurant 7 am-9 pm. Bar 11 am-midnight. Ck-out 11 am. Coin lndry. Meeting rms. Business servs avail. Sundries. Airport transportation. Exercise equipt; sauna. Marina; boat rentals. Private balconies; some fireplaces, kitchens. View of bay. Cr cds: A, D, DS, MC, V.
🔧 🛏 🏋 🖪 🐾

★★ **LITTLE CREEK COVE.** *3641 NW Oceanview Dr (97365). 541/265-8587; fax 541/265-4576; toll-free 800/294-8025. www.newportnet. com/lcc.* 29 kit. units, 2-3 story. No elvtr. S, D $99-$215; each addl $10. TV; cable (premium), VCR. Restaurant nearby. Ck-out noon. Business servs avail. Microwaves, fireplaces. Beach access. Cr cds: A, C, D, DS, MC, V.
🐾

★★ **SHILO INN.** *536 SW Elizabeth St (97365). 541/265-7701; fax 541/265-5687; res 800/222-2244. www. shiloinns.com.* 179 rms, 4 story. S, D $99-$109; each addl $15; under 13 free. Crib free. Pet accepted, some restrictions; $10/day. TV; cable (premium), VCR. Indoor pool. Complimentary refreshments in lobby. Coffee in rms. Restaurant 7 am-9 pm. Bar 11-2 am; entertainment Fri, Sat. Ck-out noon. Meeting rms. Coin lndry. Business servs avail. Refrigerators, microwaves. Covered parking. On beach. Cr cds: A, C, D, DS, ER, JCB, MC, V.
D 🔧 🖋 🛏 🖪 🐾 SC

★ **WHALER MOTEL.** *155 SW Elizabeth St (97365). 541/265-9261; fax 541/265-9515; toll-free 800/433-9444. www.whalernewport.com.* 73 rms, 3 story. No elvtr. S, D $89-$119; package plans off-season; under 18 free. Crib $5. TV; cable (premium). Heated indoor pool; whirlpool. Complimentary continental bkfst, refreshments, newspaper. Coffee in rms. Restaurant nearby. Ck-out noon. Coin lndry. Exercise equipt. Free airport, bus depot transportation. Some refrigerators, microwaves, wet bars. Balconies. Ocean view. Cr cds: A, D, DS, MC, V.
D 🛏 🏋 🖈 🖪 🐾 SC

Restaurant

★ **WHALE'S TALE.** *452 SW Bay Blvd (97365). 541/265-8660.* Hrs: 8 am-10 pm; Sat, Sun from 9 am. Closed Dec 24, 25; Jan 2-Feb 14; Wed in spring, fall, winter. Wine, beer. Bkfst $4-$8, lunch $4-$7, dinner $10.95-$18.95. Children's meals. Specializes in seafood, natural foods. Own baking. Nautical decor. Local artwork. Cr cds: A, C, D, DS, MC, V.

⛽

North Bend

(D-1) *See also Bandon, Coos Bay, Reedsport*

Settled 1853 **Pop** 9,614 **Elev** 23 ft
Area code 541 **Zip** 97459

Information Bay Area Chamber of Commerce, PO Box 210, Coos Bay 97420; 541/269-0215 or 800/824-8486. North Bend Info Center is

located at 1380 Sherman Ave in town, phone 541/756-4613
Web www.coos.or.us/~nbend

Commercial fisheries, lumbering, and manufacturing thrive in this city on a peninsula in Coos Bay.

What to See and Do

Coos County Historical Society Museum. Local history; permanent and changing exhibits. (Tues-Sat) In Simpson Park, on US 101, N edge of town. Phone 541/756-6320. ¢

Oregon Dunes National Recreation Area. Area is two mi wide and 40 mi long. One of largest bodies of sand outside of the Sahara. (See REED-SPORT) Phone 541/271-3611.

The Real Oregon Gift. Manufacturers of myrtlewood products. Tour of factory; gift shop. (Daily) 5 mi N on US 101. Phone 541/756-2220. **FREE**

Motel/Motor Lodge

★ **BAY BRIDGE MOTEL.** *33 Coast Hwy (97459).* 541/756-3151; fax 541/756-0749; toll-free 800/557-3156. 16 rms, 3 kit. units. May-Oct: S $42-$52; D $52-$60; each addl $5; kit. units $59-$65; under 3 free; lower rates rest of yr. Crib $2. Pet accepted, some restrictions; $5/day. TV; cable. Complimentary coffee in lobby. Restaurant nearby. Ck-out 11 am. Some refrigerators. On Pacific Bay. Cr cds: A, DS, MC, V

Restaurant

★ ★ **HILLTOP HOUSE.** *166 N Bay Dr (97459).* 541/756-4160. Hrs: 11:30 am-2:30 pm, 4-10 pm. Res accepted. Lunch $4.25-$14.95, dinner $7.25-$29.95. Specializes in steak, seafood, pasta. View of bay harbor and sand dunes. Cr cds: A, D, MC, V.

Ontario

(C-7)

Founded 1883 **Pop** 9,392 **Elev** 2,154 ft **Area code** 541 **Zip** 97914
Information Visitors and Convention Bureau, 88 SW 3rd Ave; 541/889-8012 or 888/889-8012

Ontario, the largest town in Malheur County, is a trading center at the eastern border of Oregon. Irrigation from the Snake River has made possible the cultivation of sugar beets, potatoes, onions, corn, hay, and alfalfa seed, but there is still a vast wilderness of rangeland, lakes and reservoirs, mountains, and canyons. Quartz crystals, jaspers, thundereggs, marine fossils, petrified wood, and obsidian are abundant in the area.

What to See and Do

Fishing and hunting. Rainbow trout, crappie and bass are plentiful. Mallard and Canada geese are found on the Snake River; sage grouse, chukars, antelope, mule deer in the sagebrush areas; pheasant on irrigated land. Phone 541/384-3300.

Owyhee Canyon. Fossils and utensils of Native Americans; petroglyphs. Boating. Fishing and hunting. Contact office, 3948 Development Ave, Boise, ID, 83705. Phone 541/384-3300.

State parks.

Farewell Bend. A 72-acre park named by pioneers who left the Snake River at this point in their trek west. Swimming beach (bathhouse); fishing; boat ramp. Picnicking. Primitive and improved camping (dump station). Standard fees. 25 mi NW on I-84. Phone 541/869-2365.

Lake Owyhee. A 730-acre park with 52-mi-long lake created by Owyhee Dam. Fishing; boating (ramp). Picnicking. Improved camping (dump station). Standard fees. 33 mi SW off OR 201. Phone 541/339-2331.

Ontario. A 35-acre day-use area. Fishing; boat ramp. Picnicking. On I-84 at N end of town. Phone 541/869-2365.

Special Events

American Musical Jubilee. Early June. Phone 888/889-8012.

Obon Festival. Japanese dancing, food; art show. Mid-July. Phone 888/889-8012.

Malheur County Fair. First wk Aug. Phone 541/889-3431.

Motels/Motor Lodges

★★ **BEST WESTERN.** *251 Goodfellow St (97914). 541/889-2600; fax 541/889-2259; res 800/828-0364. www.best western.com.* 61 rms, 2 story, 14 suites. S, D $57-$81; each addl $4; suites $100; under 12 free. Crib free. Pet accepted, some restrictions; $25. TV; cable (premium). Heated indoor pool; whirlpool. Complimentary continental bkfst. Restaurant nearby. Ck-out 11 am. Coin lndry. Exercise equipt. Refrigerators, microwaves; some mini-bars. Cr cds: A, C, D, DS, MC, V.
🄳 🐾 🛉 ≈ 🏊 🔥 SC

★★ **HOLIDAY INN.** *1249 Tapadera Ave (97914). 541/889-8621; fax 541/889-8023; toll-free 800/525-5333. www.holiday-inn.com.* 98 rms, 2 story. S, D $74; under 18 free. Crib free. Pet accepted; $10. TV; cable. Heated pool; whirlpool. Coffee, tea in rms. Restaurant 6 am-11 pm. Bar 5 pm-12:30 am. Ck-out noon. Meeting rms. Business servs avail. Coin lndry. Valet serv. In-rm modem link. Local airport, RR station, bus depot transportation. Health club privileges. Exercise equipt. Some patios, balconies. Cr cds: A, C, D, DS, JCB, MC, V.
🄳 🐾 🛉 🛉 ≈ 🏊 🔥

★ **HOLIDAY MOTOR INN.** *615 E Idaho Ave (97914). 541/889-9188; fax 541/889-4303.* 72 rms, 2 story. S $30-$35; D $40-$45; each addl $5; under 12 free. Crib $5. Pet accepted. TV; cable (premium). Heated pool. Coffee in lobby. Restaurant open 24 hrs, Sun, Mon 6 am-11 pm. Ck-out 11 am. Meeting rm. Business servs avail. Cr cds: A, D, DS, MC, V.
🄳 🐾 ≈ 🔥 SC

★ **MOTEL 6.** *275 NE 12th St (97914). 541/889-6617; fax 541/889-8232; res 800/466-8356. www.motel6.com.* 126 rms, showers only, 2 story. S, D $36.99-$42.99; each addl $3; under 18 free. Crib free. Pet accepted. TV; cable (premium). Pool. Restaurants nearby. Ck-out noon. Coin lndry. In-rm modem link. Cr cds: A, C, D, DS, MC, V.
🄳 🐾 🛉 🛉 ≈ 🏊 🔥

★ **SUPER 8.** *266 Goodfellow St (97914). 541/889-8282; fax 541/881-1400; res 800/800-8000. www.super8. com.* 63 rms, 2 story. S, D $43-$59; each addl $4; under 13 free. TV; cable (premium). Indoor pool; whirlpool. Complimentary continental bkfst. Restaurant nearby. Ck-out 11 am. Meeting rm. Coin lndry. Exercise equipt. Cr cds: A, D, DS, MC, V.
🄳 🛉 ≈ 🛉 🏊 🔥 SC

★ **YE OLDE COLONIAL MOTOR INN.** *1395 Tapadera Ave (97914). 541/889-9615; toll-free 800/727-5014.* 84 rms, 2 story. S $27-$36; D $42-$45. Crib $2. TV; cable. Pet accepted, some restrictions. Indoor pool; whirlpool. Restaurant adj 6 am-noon. Ck-out 11 am. Business servs avail. In-rm modem link. Sundries. Cr cds: A, DS, MC, V.
🄳 🐾 ≈ 🏊 🔥 SC

Restaurant

★★ **NICHOLS STEAK HOUSE.** *411 SW 3rd St, Fruitland (83619). 541/452-3030.* Hrs: 11 am-9 pm; Fri to 10 pm; Sat 4-10 pm; Sun noon-8 pm. Closed Mon; hols. Wine, beer. Lunch $3-$10, dinner $9-$25. Children's meals. Specializes in prime rib, 22-oz T-bone. Salad bar. Western decor; antiques. Paintings by local artists. Cr cds: DS, MC, V.
🄳 🏊

Oregon Caves National Monument

See also Cave Junction, Grants Pass

(20 mi E of Cave Junction on OR 46)

This area was discovered in 1874, when hunter Elijah Davidson's dog followed a bear into the cave. After a visit in 1907, frontier poet Joaquin Miller called this "The Marble Halls of Oregon." In 1909 the cave and 480 acres of the Siskiyou Mts were made a national monument.

The cave has many chambers—Paradise Lost, Joaquin Miller's Chapel, Ghost Room, and others. Guide service is required. The average temperature is 42°F. Evening talks are given by National Park Service naturalists in summer.

On the surface, the area is covered with a beautiful old growth forest with abundant wildlife, birds, wildflowers, and an interesting variety of trees and shrubs. A maintained and marked system of trails provides access to these areas; stay on the trail. Dogs aren't allowed on trails.

Forest Service campgrounds (fee) are located 4 mi and 8 mi NW on OR 46 in Siskiyou National Forest (see GRANTS PASS). (Mid-May-Labor Day) Phone 541/592-3400.

Cave tours (daily; closed Thanksgiving, Dec 25). Children must be at least 3' 6" (42 inches) in height and complete a step test to be permitted into the cave. Cave tours are strenuous; recommended only for those in good physical condition. A jacket and walking shoes with nonslip soles should be worn. Lodge, dining room (May-mid-Oct). For further information contact Oregon Caves Co, 19000 Caves Hwy, Cave Junction 97523; 541/592-2100. Cave tours ¢¢¢

Oregon City

(B-2) *See also Beaverton, Forest Grove, Newberg, Portland, Salem*

Settled 1829 **Pop** 14,698 **Elev** 55 ft **Area code** 503 **Zip** 97045

Information Oregon City Chamber of Commerce and Visitors Center, PO Box 226; 503/656-1619 or 800/424-3002

Below Willamette Falls, where the river spills over a 42-foot drop, is historic Oregon City. Steamers were built here in the 1850s and locks around the falls opened the upriver

to navigation in 1873. Salmon fishing in the Willamette and Clackamas rivers is from early March-mid-May. The city is built on terraces and there is an enclosed elevator to an observation platform.

What to See and Do

End of the Oregon Trail Interpretive Center. Exhibits on journey made by early settlers over the Oregon Trail. (Daily; closed hols) 1726 Washington St. Phone 503/657-9336. ¢¢

Holmes Family Home. (Rose Farm). Oldest standing American home in Oregon City, built in 1847. First Territorial governor gave his first address here in 1849; the upstairs ballroom was the scene of many social events. (Apr-Oct, Sun; closed hols and rest of yr) Holmes Ln and Rilance St. Phone 503/656-5146. ✓

John Inskeep Environmental Learning Center. Eight acres developed on former industrial site to demonstrate wildlife habitat in an urban setting. Includes extensive birds of prey exhibits, various plant and wildlife displays and plant nursery. Haggart Astronomical Observatory (Wed, Fri, Sat; fee). 19600 S Molalla on N side of Clackamas Community College's campus. Phone 503/657-6958. ¢

McLoughlin House National Historic Site. Georgian frame building built in 1845-1846 by Dr. John McLoughlin, chief factor of the Hudson's Bay Company, who ruled the Columbia River region from 1824-1846. Period furnishings; many are original pieces, most having come around Cape Horn on sailing ships. (Tues-Sun; closed hols, also Jan) 713 Center St between 7th and 8th sts. Phone 503/656-5146. ¢¢

Milo McIver State Park. On the Clackamas River, this 937-acre park offers a panoramic view of Mt Hood. Fishing, boating (ramp to river). Hiking, horseback trails. Picnicking. Improved campsites (dump station, electric hook-ups). Standard fees. 4 mi N on OR 213, then 12 mi SE via OR 212, 211. Phone 503/630-7150.

The Old Aurora Colony Museum. Complex of buildings forming historical museum of the Aurora Colony, a German religious communal society, founded by Dr. William Keil (1856-

1883). Includes Kraus House (1863), a colony house with original artifacts; Steinbach Cabin (1876); wash house used by colony women for washing, soapmaking and canning; herb garden divided into various uses—teas, cooking, medicinal, fragrances. Exhibits of furniture, musical instruments, quilts, tools. Tours. (May-mid-Oct, Tues-Sun; mid-Oct-Dec, & Mar-Apr, Fri-Sun; Jan-Feb by appt only) 15 mi SW via OR 99E at 15018 2nd St NE in Aurora. Phone 503/678-5754. ¢¢

Stevens Crawford Heritage House. (Mertie Stevens Residence, 1908). Fifteen fully-furnished period rms. Working kitchen, bedrms, living rm, dining rm; doll collection. (Feb-Dec, Wed-Sun) 603 6th St. Phone 503/655-2866. ¢¢

Willamette Falls Locks. National Historical site; oldest multilift navagation lock, built 1873. Four locks, canal basin and guard lock operated by US Army Corps of Engineers. Picnic areas. Information Center. (Daily) On Willamette River, in West Linn. Phone 503/656-3381. **FREE**

Motel/Motor Lodge

★ **RIVERSHORE HOTEL.** *1900 Clackamette Dr (97045). 503/655-7141; fax 503/655-1927; toll-free 800/443-7777. www.rivershore.com.* 120 rms, 4 story. S $65; D $73; each addl $5; suites $122; under 12 free. Crib $5. Pet accepted, some restrictions; $5. TV; cable (premium). Heated pool; whirlpool. Restaurant 6 am-10 pm; Sun 7 am-9 pm. Bar noon-1 am. Ck-out noon. Most balconies overlook river. Cr cds: A, DS, MC, V.

Pendleton

(A-6) *See also Hermiston, La Grande, Umatilla*

Founded 1868 **Pop** 15,126 **Elev** 1,068 ft **Area code** 541 **Zip** 97801
Information Chamber of Commerce, 501 S Main; 541/276-7411 or 800/547-8911

Located on the old Oregon Trail, Pendleton is a trading center for the extensive cattle, wheat, and green pea production in the area. Seat of Umatilla County, it is famous for its annual Round-up.

What to See and Do

Emigrant Springs State Park. A 23-acre park near summit of Blue Mts (nearly 4,000 ft); ponderosa pine forest. Winter sports. Picnicking, lodge. Tent and trailer sites. Oregon Trail display. Standard fees. 26 mi SE off I-84. Phone 541/983-2277.

Pendleton Woolen Mills. Woolen manufacturing; carding, spinning, rewinding and weaving processes. Guided tours (30 min; Mon-Fri; closed hols). 1307 SE Court Place. Phone 541/276-6911. **FREE**

Ukiah-Dale Forest State Park. A 3,000-acre scenic forest canyon extending along Camas Creek and N Fork of John Day River. Fishing. Camping. Standard fees. 50 mi S on US 395. Phone 541/983-2277.

✪ **Umatilla Indian Reservation.** Created by the Walla Walla Valley Treaty of 1855. Firsthand view and understanding of a Native American community in transition. Historic significance as well as a lifestyle different from modern-day, American-style development. One of the first Catholic missions in the US is here. Reservation always open for unguided touring. Indian Lake has good fishing, camping and beautiful scenery. The foothills and lowlands of the Blue Mts provide excellent upland game and waterfowl hunting. In addition, the Umatilla Tribes have reestablished runs of chinook salmon and steelhead within the Umatilla River. Some fees. 5 mi E via Mission Hwy (US 30). Phone 541/276-3873.

Umatilla National Forest. More than one million acres, partly in Washington. Lewis and Clark passed through this region on the Columbia River in 1805. Includes spectacular views of the Tucannon, Umatilla, Grande Ronde, N Fork John Day, and Wenaha River canyons. Remnants of historic gold mining can be found in the Granite, OR, area in sight of the Greenhorn Mt Range. N Fork John Day, N Fork Umatilla and the Wenaha-Tucannon wilderness areas may be reached on horseback or on foot. Stream fishing (steelhead, rainbow trout), big-game hunting (elk, deer); boating, river rafting. Hiking. Skiing, snowmobiling. Picnicking. Camping (fee at some campgrounds). NE & S of Pendleton. Reached by I-84, US 395, OR 11, 204, 82, 244, 207 and WA 12. For further info Phone 541/276-3811. In forest are

Skiing. Spout Springs. Ski Bluewood. 45 mi NE to Walla Walla, WA, 29 mi NE on WA 12 to Dayton, then 23 mi SE on country road. 21 mi NE on OR 11 to Weston, then 20 mi E on OR 204 to Tollgate (see LA GRANDE). Phone 541/276-7411.

Special Event

Pendleton Round-up. Stadium. Rodeo and pageantry of Old West, annually since 1910. Gathering of Native Americans, PRCA working cowboys and thousands of visitors. Phone 800/457-6336. Mid-Sept.

Motels/Motor Lodges

★ **ECONO LODGE.** *620 SW Tutilla Rd (97801). 541/276-8654; fax 541/276-5808; res 800/446-6900. www.econolodge.com.* 51 rms, 1-3 story, 2 kits. S $45.95-$55.95; D $50.95-$66.95; each addl $5; kit units $57-$60; under 12 free. Crib $4. Pet accepted, some restrictions; $5. TV; cable (premium). Complimentary continental bkfst, coffee in rms. Restaurant adj open 24 hrs. Ck-out 11 am. Business servs avail. Health club privileges. Refrigerators. Some microwaves. Cr cds: A, D, DS, JCB, MC, V.

★ **ECONOMY INN.** *201 SW Court Ave (97801). 541/276-5252; fax 541/278-1213; res 800/522-1555.* 51 rms, 2 story June-Sept; S $32-$36; D $40-$46; each addl $6; under 16 free; lower rates rest of yr. Closed during Pendleton Roundup. Crib free. Pet accepted; $5. TV; cable, VCR avail. Pool. Complimentary continental bkfst. Restaurant nearby. Ck-out noon. Refrigerators avail. Cr cds: A, D, DS, JCB, MC, V.

★★★ **RED LION HOTEL.** *304 SE Nye Ave (97801). 541/276-6111; fax 541/278-2413. www.redlionhotel.com.* 168 rms, 3 story. S, D $63-$73; each addl $10; under 18 free; wkend rates. Crib free. Pet accepted. TV. Heated pool. Coffee in rms. Restaurant 6 am-10:30 pm. Bar; entertainment. Ck-out noon. Meeting rms. Business servs avail. Free airport, RR station, bus depot transportation. Health club privileges. Private patios, balconies. Cr cds: A, C, D, DS, ER, JCB, MC, V.

★ **TAPADERA MOTEL.** *105 SE Court Ave (97128). 541/276-3231; fax 541/276-0754; toll-free 800/722-8277.* 47 rms, 2 story. Mid-May-mid-Sept: S $35-$45, D $49-$55; each addl $5; under 12 free; lower rates rest of yr. Crib $5. Pet accepted; $5. TV; cable (premium). Restaurant 7 am-9 pm. Bar 11-2 am. Ck out noon. Meeting rms. Business servs avail. Health club privileges. Cr cds: A, C, D, DS, MC, V.

Restaurant

★★ **CIMMIYOTTI'S.** *137 S Main St (97801). 541/276-4314.* Hrs: 4-10 pm; Fri, Sat to 11 pm. Closed Sun. Res accepted. Bar. Dinner $12-$20. Children's meals. Specializes in steak, chicken, fish. Western motif. Cr cds: A, C, D, MC, V.

Portland (B-2)

Founded 1851 **Pop** 437,319 **Elev** 77 ft **Area code** 503

Information Portland Oregon Visitors Association, 26 SW Salmon St, 97204; 503/222-2223 or 1-87PORTLAND

Web www.pova.com

Suburbs Beaverton, Forest Grove, Hillsboro, Newburg, Oregon City; also Vancouver, WA.

Oregon's largest city sprawls across both banks of the Willamette River, just south of its confluence with the

Columbia. The lush and fertile Willamette Valley brings it beauty and riches. Portland's freshwater harbor is visited by more than 1,400 vessels annually from throughout the world. The city enjoys plentiful electric power, captured from river waters, which drives scores of industries with minimal amounts of smoke or smog.

Portland is surrounded by spectacular scenery. The Columbia River Gorge, Mount Hood, waterfalls, forests, ski slopes, fishing streams, and hunting and camping areas are within easy access. It attracts many conventions, for which it is well-equipped with four large auditoriums, the Memorial Coliseum Complex, the Metropolitan Exposi-

tion Center, and the Oregon Convention Center. Portland's reputation as "The City of Roses" is justified by its leadership in rose culture, as seen in its International Rose Test Garden and celebrated during the annual Portland Rose Festival, which attracts visitors worldwide. Mount St. Helens (see WASHINGTON), in Washington's Gifford Pinchot National Forest, 50 miles to the northeast, can be seen from numerous vantage points in Portland.

Portland is also an educational center with Portland State University, the University of Portland (1901), Lewis & Clark College (1867), and Reed College (1911).

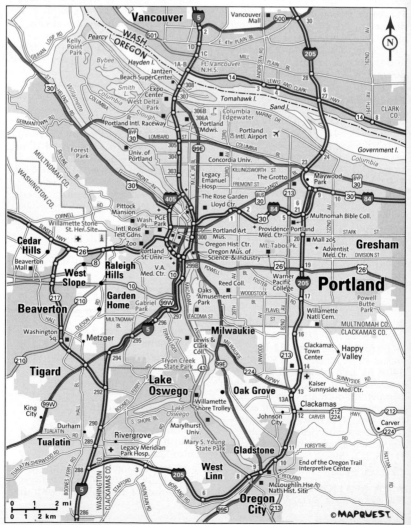

Additional Visitor Information

For further information contact the Portland Oregon Visitors Assn, 26 SW Salmon, 97204, phone 503/222-2223. For a recorded message describing major theater, sports and music events in Portland for the current month, phone 503/225-5555.

Transportation

Car Rental Agencies. See IMPORTANT TOLL-FREE NUMBERS.

Public Transportation. Buses, MAX light rail trains (Tri-County Metropolitan Transportation District), phone 503/238-RIDE.

Rail Passenger Service. Amtrak 800/872-7245.

Airport Information

Portland International Airport. Portland Intl Airport. Information 503/460-4234; lost and found 503/460-4277, weather 503/275-9792; cash machines, Main Terminal, N and S ends of Oregon Market Place.

What to See and Do

American Advertising Museum. Museum devoted to the history and evolution of advertising and its impact on culture. Permanent and changing exhibits on print and broadcast advertising; reference library. (Wed-Sat) 211 NW 5th Ave. Phone 503/226-0000. ¢¢

Benson State Recreation Area. A 272-acre park with lake. Swimming; fishing; boating (no motors). Picnicking. E on I-84, exit 30. Phone 503/695-2261. ¢¢

Children's Museum. Hands-on play spaces incl grocery store, baby rm and clay shop. (Daily; closed major hols) 3037 SW 2nd Ave. Phone 503/823-2227. ¢¢

Council Crest Park. Highest point in Portland (1,073 ft) for views of Tualatin Valley, Willamette River, Mt Hood, Mt St. Helens. S on SW Greenway Ave (follow blue and white scenic tour signs). Phone 503/823-2223. **FREE**

Crystal Springs Rhododendron Garden. Approx 2,500 rhododendrons of 1,000 varieties and other woodland plants in woodland setting (more than six acres) and formal gardens with lake. (Daily) SE 28th Ave, N of SE Woodstock Blvd. Phone 503/823-2223. ¢¢

Forest Park. Park has 4,800 acres of wilderness with 50 mi of hiking trails. Wildwood Trail begins at the Vietnam Veterans Living Memorial in Hoyt Arboretum and extends 27 mi, ending deep in the park beyond Germantown Rd. Bird-watching; small wild animals. Picnicking. (Daily) Off US 30, NW of Fremont Bridge. Phone 503/228-8733. **FREE**

Gray Line bus tours. Contact 4320 N Suttle Rd, PO Box 17306, 97217; Phone 503/285-9845.

Grotto—The National Sanctuary of Our Sorrowful Mother. Religious sanctuary and botanical garden on 62 acres and two levels, created in 1924. Grotto carved in 110-ft cliff is surrounded by gardens. Elevator to the Natural Gallery in the woods featuring more than 100 statues. Landscaped top level with meditation chapel overlooking the Columbia River and Mt St Helens (fee). (Daily; closed Thanksgiving, Dec 25) NE 85th Ave at Sandy Blvd, on OR 30. Phone 503/254-7371. ¢¢

Howell Territorial Park and The Bybee House. (1858). Restored house of early settlers; period furnishings. Pioneer orchard, agricultural museum on grounds. (June-Labor Day, wkend afternoons) 12 mi N via US 30, cross bridge to Sauvie Island, 1 mi W to Howell Territorial Park Rd. Phone 503/222-1741. **DONATION**

Hoyt Arboretum. More than 214 acres, with displays of more than 700 kinds of woody plants and one of the nation's largest collections of needle-bearing trees; self-guided trails with Vietnam Veterans Living Memorial. Also guided nature walk (Apr-Oct, Sat and Sun afternoons). Park and visitor center (Daily). Picnicking. 4000 SW Fairview Blvd. Phone 503/228-8733. **FREE**

Lewis and Clark College. (1867) 3,400 students. Memorial Rose Garden with 1,500 plants; Tudor mansion (Mon-Fri), formal gardens. Tours of campus. SW Palatine Hill Rd, 3 mi E of I-5 Terwilliger Exit. Phone 503/768-7000.

Mount Hood-Columbia Gorge Loop Scenic Drive. This 163-mi scenic drive along the Columbia River and through Mt Hood National Forest (see) offers splendid views of the river basin, visits to waterfalls, many state parks, and spectacular mountain scenery. Drive E 17 mi on US 30, I-84 to Troutdale. At this point, for approx 24 mi, there are two routes: you may turn right and take the mountainous upper-level scenic route or continue on the main river-level freeway. The two roads rejoin about 10 mi W of Bonneville Dam (see HOOD RIVER). Continue E on US 30, I-84 for 23 mi to Hood River, turning S on OR 35 for 47 mi through Mt Hood National Forest to US 26. Drive NW on US 26, 56 mi back to Portland. A description of this tour may be found in a free visitors guide from the Portland Visitors Association.

Mount Tabor Park. Extinct volcano; view of city and mountains. Picnicking. Summer concerts. (Daily) SE 60th Ave and Salmon St. Phone 503/823-2223.

Multnomah Falls. Chief among the 11 waterfalls along 11 mi of this highway; 620-ft drop in two falls, fourth-highest in US. Hiking. Restaurant. Visitor center. 32 mi E on I-84. (See MOUNT HOOD NATIONAL FOREST) Phone 503/695-2372.

Oaks Amusement Park. (1905). Thrill rides, children's area, roller rink (Tues-Sun; rentals), miniature golf; waterfront picnicking. Separate fees for activities. Park (two wks end of Mar, Apr-May, wkends; mid-June-Sept, Tues-Sun). SE Oaks Park Way, E end of Sellwood Bridge. Phone 503/233-5777.

Oregon History Center. Regional repository of Northwest history; permanent and special exhibits; museum store; publishing house; regional research library (Wed-Sat). (Tues-Sun; closed hols) 1200 SW Park Ave. Phone 503/222-1741. ¢¢

Oregon Museum of Science and Industry. Six exhibit halls incl interactive exhibits on space, biological, life, Earth, physical and computer science. Omnimax Theater (daily; fee); planetarium shows; laser light shows (fee). (Labor Day-Memorial Day, Tues-Sun; rest of yr, daily; closed Dec 25) 1945 SE Water Ave. Phone 503/797-4000. ¢¢¢

Oregon Zoo. Specializes in breeding rare and endangered species. Features Asian elephants, Humboldt penguins, chimpanzees, Oregon native plants and animals; bears; musk oxen; wolves; animals of the African plains and rain forests. Train travels through zoo to Washington Park, stopping near the International Rose Test Garden and Japanese gardens (fee). (Daily; closed Dec 25) 4001 SW Canyon Rd. Phone 503/226-1561. ¢¢

Peninsula Park and Community Center. Sunken formal rose gardens with 15,000 rose bushes; reflecting pond. Swimming (fee), wading pools. Tennis. Picnic grove, playground. Community Center (Mon-Fri). (Daily) N Portland Blvd and Albina Ave. Phone 503/823-2223. **FREE**

Pittock Mansion. (1914) Restored and furnished French Chateau-esque mansion surrounded by 46 forested and landscaped acres. Spectacular views of rivers, the city and snow-capped mountains, incl Mt St. Helens and Mt Hood. (Daily; closed most hols) 3229 NW Pittock Dr. Phone 503/823-3624. ¢¢

Police Historical Museum. Collection of early police uniforms, badges, photos, and other police memorabilia. (Mon-Thurs; closed some hols) 1111 SW 2nd Ave, 16th floor. **FREE**

⭐ **Portland Art Museum.** Features 35 centuries of world art: European painting and sculpture from the Renaissance to the present; 19th- and 20th-century American art; noted collections of Northwest Coast Native American art, Asian, pre-Columbian, West African and classical Greek and Roman art; British silver; major print and drawings collection. Changing exhibits. Lectures, films, concerts, special events. Gift shop; rental sales gallery. (Tues-Sun; closed major hols) 1219 SW Park Ave at Jefferson St. Phone 503/226-2811. ¢¢¢

Portland Saturday Market. One of largest, oldest open-air community markets in the US, arts, crafts, food booths, produce, and street entertainers. (Sat-Sun, Mar-Dec) W Burnside St, under the Burnside Bridge. Phone 503/222-6072.

Portland State University. (1946) 21,185 students. Art and photography exhibits in Smith Memorial Center and Neuberger Hall. Campus tours. Visitor information center at SW Broadway and College Sts. Phone 503/725-3000.

Professional sports.

Portland Fire (WNBA). Rose Garden. One Center Ct. Phone 503/797-WNBA.

Portland Trailblazers (NBA). Rose Garden, 1 Center Ct. Phone 503/224-4400.

State parks.

Crown Point. A 307-acre park with 725-ft-high point affords view of Columbia River Gorge with its 2,000-ft-high rock walls. Historic Vista House (1918), pioneer memorial of stone and marble. Visitor information service (summer). E on I-84, exit 22; on US 30 Scenic Rte. Phone 503/695-2230. **FREE**

Dabney. A 135-acre park with fishing in Sandy River. Hiking. Picnicking, 19 mi E off I-84 exit 18, at Stark St Bridge on US 30 Scenic Rte. Phone 503/695-2261. ¢¢

Guy W. Talbot. A 371-acre park. Latourell Falls, second-highest falls in the Columbia Gorge, drops 250 ft. Hiking. Picnicking. Observation point. E on I-84, exit 27; on US 30 Scenic Rte. Phone 503/695-2261. **FREE**

Lewis and Clark. A 56-acre park with fishing; boating (ramp). Hiking. Picnicking. 16 mi E on I-84, exit 18. Phone 503/695-2261. **FREE**

Rooster Rock. A 1½-mi beach on Columbia River in 927-acre park. Swimming; fishing; boating (ramp, docks). Hiking. Picnicking. Clothing optional beach area. E on I-84, milepost 25. Phone 503/695-2261. ¢¢

Willamette Stone. This two-acre historic site marks the initial point of all government land surveys of Oregon and Washington; trail to stone monument. No water, rest rms. 4 mi W at Skyline Blvd and W Burnside. Phone 877/678-5263. **FREE**

Sternwheeler Columbia Gorge. Riverboat scenic and dinner cruises on the Willamette River (Fri-Sun, Oct-mid-June), incl dinner dance cruises, champagne brunch cruises, narrated excursion trps, and special-event cruises. Leaves from Waterfront Park, Portland. Phone 503/223-3928. ¢¢¢¢

⭐ **Washington Park.** A 129-acre park on hill above city. Includes the International Rose Test Garden, with 8,000 bushes of more than 400 varieties (free); the Shakespeare Garden; Lewis and Clark monument; Sacajawea Memorial Statue. Two reservoirs. Archery, tennis. Picnic area. Rose garden amphitheater has music productions, usually Aug (fee). Accessible via W Burnside St, SW Park Place, or Canyon Rd. Phone 503/823-2223. Also here is

Japanese Garden. 5½ acres; acclaimed one of the most authentic Japanese gardens outside of Japan. Traditional gardens incl the Flat Garden (Hiraniwa), Strolling Pond Garden (Chisen-Kaiyu-Shiki), Tea Garden (Rojiniwa), Natural Garden (Shukeiyen) and the Dry Landscape Garden (Karesansui); also an authentic Japanese pavilion. Special events incl ikebana and bonsai exhibits. Gift shop. (Daily; closed hols.) Phone 503/223-1321. ¢¢¢

Water Tower in Johns Landing. Former three-story furniture factory (1903) with cobblestone courtyard; houses specialty shops and restaurants. (Daily; closed major hols) 5331 SW Macadam Ave. Phone 503/242-0022.

World Forestry Center. Educational exhibits on regional and international forests; 70-ft talking tree. Special exhibits, shows. (Daily; closed Dec 25) 4033 SW Canyon Rd. Phone 503/228-1367. ¢¢

Special Events

St. Patrick's Irish Festival. One of the largest Irish festivals in the Pacific NW. Phone 503/227-4057. Three days Mar.

Greyhound Racing. Multnomah Greyhound Park, NE 223rd Ave between NE Halsey and Glisan Sts, 12 mi E off I-84, exit 13 or 16A. Parimutuel betting. Matinee and evening races. Under 12 yrs not permitted at evening races. For schedule phone 503/667-7700. May-Oct.

Portland Rose Festival. Held for more than 90 yrs, this festival incl the

Grand Floral Parade (res required for indoor parade seats) and two other parades; band competition; rose show; championship auto racing; hot-air balloons; air show; carnival; Navy ships. Phone 503/227-2681. Late May-June.

Chamber Music Northwest. Catlin Gabel School and Reed College. Nationally acclaimed summer chamber music festival offers 25 concerts featuring 40-50 artists (Mon, Tues, Thurs-Sat). Catered picnic preceeding each concert. Children under seven only permitted at Family Concert. Phone 503/294-6400. Mid-June-late July.

Portland Scottish Highland Games. 15 mi E at Mt Hood Community College in Gresham. Phone 503/293-8501. Mid-July.

Multnomah County Fair. Agricultural and horticultural exhibits; entertainment. Phone 503/289-6623. Mid-July. Phone 503/761-7577.

Mount Hood Jazz Festival. 15 mi E on I-84, in Gresham. International, national and local jazz acts presented in outdoor festival. Phone 503/219-9833. First wkend Aug.

Portland Center Stage. Portland Center for the Performing Arts. Series of contemporary and classical plays. Tues-Sun. For fees, performance and title schedules phone 503/274-6588. Sept-Apr.

Portland Marathon. World-class running event featuring international competition. Phone 503/226-1111. Early Oct. Phone 503/823-4000.

Horse racing. Portland Meadows, 1001 N Schmeer Rd, 6 mi N on I-5. Parimutuel betting. Thoroughbred and quarter horse racing. (Fri evenings, Sat and Sun matinee) Under 12 yrs not permitted at evening races. Phone 503/285-9144. Late Oct-Apr.

Holiday Parade of Christmas Ships. Along Willamette and Columbia rivers. More than 50 boats cruise the two rivers in a holiday display. Phone 503/225-5555, code 2065. Early-mid-Dec.

Motels/Motor Lodges

★★ **ALDERWOOD INN HOTEL.** *7025 NE Alderwood Rd (97218). 503/255-2700; fax 503/255-4700; res 888/987-2700. www.alderwoodinn.*

com. 150 rms, 4 story. June-Sept: S, D $63-$74; each addl $7; suites $84-$99; under 12 free; lower rates rest of yr. Crib free. TV; cable. Complimentary full bkfst. Restaurant 6:30-9:30 am, 11:30 am-2 pm, 5-10 pm; Sun brunch 7 am-1 pm. Bar. Ck-out 11 am. Meeting rm. Business servs avail. In-rm modem link. Valet serv. Sundries. Coin lndry. Free airport transportation. Exercise equipt. Indoor pool; whirlpool. Refrigerators, microwaves. Cr cds: A, C, D, DS, MC, V.

D ⚡ 🏃 ✕ 🔄 🔥 SC

★★ **BEST WESTERN INN AT THE MEADOWS.** *1215 N Hayden Meadows Dr (97217). 503/286-9600; fax 503/286-8020; toll-free 800/780-7234. www.bestwestern.com.* 146 rms, 3 story. S, D $99-$109; suites $150; under 12 free; family rates; package plans. Crib free. Pet accepted, some restrictions; $21.80. TV; cable (premium). Outdoor whirlpool. Complimentary continental bkfst. Complimentary coffee in rms. Restaurant adj 6 am-11 pm. Bar adj. Ck-out noon. Meeting rms. Business servs avail. Valet serv. Sundries. Coin lndry. Health club privileges. Free RR station transportation. Refrigerators, microwaves, wet bars avail. Cr cds: A, C, D, DS, JCB, MC, V.

D ⚡ 🔄 🔥 SC

★★ **BEST WESTERN PONY SOLDIER INN AIRPORT.** *9901 NE Sandy Blvd (97220). 503/256-1504; fax 503/256-5928; res 800/528-1234. www.bestwestern.com.* 103 rms, 3 story, 15 suites. S, D $101-$109; each addl $5; suites, kit. units $126; under 18 free. Crib free. TV; cable (premium). Heated pool; whirlpool. Complimentary continental bkfst. Coffee in rms. Restaurant adj 6 am-10 pm. Bar adj. Ck-out noon. Free lndry facilities. Meeting rms. Business servs avail. Valet serv. Sundries. Free 24-hr airport transportation. Exercise equipt; sauna. Refrigerators, microwaves. Some whirlpools. Balconies. Cr cds: A, C, D, DS, MC, V.

D ⚡ 🏃 ✕ 🔄 🔥

★ **CHESTNUT TREE INN.** *9699 SE Stark St (97216). 503/255-4444; res 888/236-5660.* 58 rms, 2 story. S $42; D $50; each addl $3. Crib free. TV; cable (premium). Complimentary coffee. Restaurant adj 6 am-11 pm.

PORTLAND'S OUTSTANDING PARKS

The glory of Portland is its parks. Settled by idealistic New Englanders, Portland had an extensive park system in the 1850s, decades before other West Coast cities were even founded. Begin at Portland State University in the North Park Blocks, a swath of twenty blocks of parkland that cuts right through the heart of the city. The park was established in the 1850s and for generations was the best address for civic structures. Numerous historic churches, plus the Portland Art Museum, the Oregon History Center, the Portland Center for the Performing Arts, and the Schnitzer Concert Hall (home to the Oregon Symphony) flank the park. The park is also home to the largest remaining stand of American elm (killed elsewhere by Dutch elm disease), numerous heroic statues, and a farmers market (on Wednesdays and Saturdays).

Drop down to Pioneer Courthouse Square at 6th and Morrison, often referred to as Portland's living room. This is where many outdoor festivals, concerts, and demonstrations take place. (Dan Quayle got such a raucous reception here that he thenceforward refused to visit Portland, referring to the city as America's Beirut.) The Square is a great place for people-watching and sunbathing, and there are many food carts and cafes here. In the blocks around Pioneer Courthouse Square are many of Portland's major shopping venues. Adjacent is the Pioneer Courthouse itself, built in 1875.

Follow 5th Avenue south, noting the abundance of public art along the pedestrian friendly bus mall. At 5th Avenue and Main Street is the Portland Building, a noted postmodern structure designed by Michael Graves. The front is surmounted by a massive statue called Portlandia. This is the second-largest hammered copper statue in the world, the largest being the Statue of Liberty.

Drop down onto the Willamette River waterfront. The park that runs the length of downtown along the river is recent. In the 1970s, the city ripped out a freeway that ran along the river and replaced it with this park, which in summer is loaded with joggers, sun worshipers, and any number of summer festivals. Also along the river are boat tour operators, a large marina with some shops and cafes, and, at the north end, a memorial to Japanese-American internment during World War II. Under the Burnside Bridge, adjacent to Waterfront Park, is the Portland Saturday Market (open both Saturday and Sunday), which is reputed to be the largest open air crafts market in the nation.

Turn north along 3rd Avenue, and walk through Portland's Old Town (most buildings date from the 1880s) to Chinatown. Here, between 2nd and 3rd avenues and Everett and Flanders streets is the Portland Chinese Garden, a brand-new traditional Chinese garden that is a joint project of Portland and the city of Suzhou. It is the largest Chinese-style garden outside of China itself.

Ck-out noon. Business servs avail. Refrigerators. Cr cds: A, C, D, MC, V.
D ⬚ ⬚

★★ **COURTYARD BY MARRIOTT.**
11550 NE Airport Way (97220). 503/252-3200; fax 503/252-8921; toll-free 800/321-2211. www.courtyard. com. 150 rms, 6 story. June-Aug: S, D $104; suites $129; under 18 free; wkly rates; lower rates rest of yr. Crib free. TV; cable (premium), some VCRs. Heated pool; whirlpool, poolside serv. Coffee in rms. Restaurant 6-11 am, 4-10 pm. Rm serv 5-10 pm.

Bar 4-11 pm. Ck-out noon. Coin lndry. Valet serv. Business servs avail. In-rm modem link. Exercise equipt. Free airport transportation. Refrigerator, wet bar in suites. Cr cds: A, C, D, DS, JCB, MC, V.
D ⬚ ⬚ ⬚ ⬚ ⬚ SC

★ **DAYS INN.** *9930 N Whitaker Rd (97217). 503/289-1800; fax 503/289-3778; toll-free 800/329-7466. www. daysinn.com.* 214 rms, 4 story. S, D $65-$75; each addl $5; under 12 free; wkly rates. Crib free. Pet accepted; $10/day. TV; cable (premium). Complimentary continental bkfst. Restaurant adj 6 am-11 pm. Ck-out noon. Coin lndry. Meeting rm. Business servs avail. In-rm modem link. Sundries. Microwaves avail. Free airport, RR station, bus depot transportation. Park adj. Cr cds: A, C, D, DS, JCB, MC, V.

★ **DAYS INN.** *1414 SW 6th Ave (97201). 503/221-1611; fax 503/226-0447; toll-free 800/329-7466. www. daysinn.com.* 173 rms, 5 story. S, D $109-$129; each addl $5; under 12 free. Crib free. TV; cable (premium). Heated pool. Restaurant 6:30 am-10 pm; Sat, Sun from 7 am. Bar 11 am-midnight. Coffee in lobby. Ck-out noon. Meeting rms. Business servs avail. In-rm modem link. Valet serv. Health club privileges. Cr cds: A, C, D, DS, ER, JCB, MC, V.

★ **DAYS INN PORTLAND SOUTH.** *9717 SE Sunnyside Rd, Clackmans (97015). 503/654-1699; fax 503/659-2702; res 800/329-7466. www.daysinn. com.* 110 rms, 3 story. S, D $79; each addl $7; studio rms $65-$130; under 12 free. Crib free. TV; cable (premium). Heated pool; whirlpool. Sauna. Restaurant nearby. Bar. Complimentary continental bkfst. Ck-out noon. Meeting rms. Business servs avail. In-rm modem link. Health club privileges. Coin lndry. Valet serv. Some refrigerators. Cr cds: A, C, D, DS, JCB, MC, V.

★★ **FAIRFIELD INN.** *11929 NE Airport Way (97220). 503/253-1400; fax 503/253-3889; res 800/228-2800. www.fairfieldinn.com.* 106 rms, 3 story. Apr-Sept: S, D $74-$89; each addl $10; under 18 free; lower rates rest of yr. Crib free. TV; cable (premium). Pool; whirlpool. Complimentary continental bkfst. Restaurant nearby. Coffee in rms. Ck-out noon. Business servs avail. In-rm modem link. Valet serv. Sundries. Free airport transportation. Exercise equipt. Cr cds: A, C, D, DS, MC, V.

★★ **FOUR POINTS BY SHERATON PORTLAND DOWNTOWN.** *50 SW Morrison; Front Ave (97204). 503/221-0711; fax 503/484-1414; toll-free 800/325-3535. www.fourpoints.com.* 140 rms, 5 story. S, D $114-$240; each addl $10; under 18 free. Crib free. Pet accepted, some restrictions. TV; cable (premium). Coffee in rms. Restaurant 6 am-10 pm; Sat, Sun from 7 am. Rm serv 5-10 pm. Bar 4 pm-midnight. Ck-out noon. Meeting rm. Business servs avail. Health club privileges. Balconies. Refrigerators avail. Cr cds: A, D, DS, MC, V.

★★ **HAMPTON INN.** *8633 NE Airport Way (97220). 503/288-2423; fax 503/288-2620; toll-free 800/426-7866. www.hamptoninn.com.* 130 rms, 4 story. S $95; D $99; under 18 free; wkend rates. Crib $10. TV; cable (premium). Complimentary continental bkfst. Complimentary coffee in rms. Restaurant adj 6 am-10 pm. Ck-out noon. Meeting rms. Business servs avail. In-rm modem link. Valet serv. Sundries. Free airport transportation. Gift shop. Pet accepted. Health club privileges. Pool privileges. Cr cds: A, C, D, DS, ER, JCB, MC, V.

★★ **HAWTHORN INN & SUITES.** *2323 NE 181st Ave (97230). 503/492-4000; fax 503/492-3271; res 800/527-1133. www.hawthorn.com.* 71 rms, 3 story, 23 suites. May-Sept: S $70-$75; D $85-$90; each addl $7; suites $90-$150; under 18 free; lower rates rest of yr. Crib free. Pet accepted, some restrictions; $10. TV; cable (premium), VCR avail (movies). Indoor pool; whirlpool. Complimentary bkfst buffet. Coffee in rms. Restaurant nearby. Ck-out 1 pm. Coin lndry. Meeting rms. Business servs avail. In-rm modem link. Sundries. Valet serv. Exercise equipt; sauna. Some refrigerators. Cr cds: A, C, D, DS, ER, JCB, MC, V.

★★ **IMPERIAL HOTEL.** *400 SW Broadway at Stark (97205). 503/228-7221; fax 503/223-4551; toll-free 800/452-2323. www.hotel-imperial. com.* 128 rms, 9 story. S $100; D $125; each addl $5; under 12 free. Crib free. TV; cable (premium). Pet accepted; $10. Restaurants 6:30 am-9 pm. Bar 11-1 am; Sat, Sun 1-9 pm. Ck-out 2 pm. Meeting rms. Business servs avail. In-rm modem link. Valet parking. Cr cds: A, C, D, DS, ER, JCB, MC, V.

★★ **PHOENIX INN.** *477 NW Phoenix Dr, Troutdale (97060). 503/669-6500; fax 503/669-3500; toll-free 800/824-6824. www.phoenix inn.com.* 73 rms, 3 story. Mid-May-Sept: S $55-$65, D $60-$70; each addl $7; under 18 free; lower rates rest of yr; package plans. Crib free. Pet accepted; $10. TV; cable (premium). Indoor pool; whirlpool. Complimentary bkfst buffet. Restaurant adj open 24 hrs. Bar 11-2 am. Coffee in rms. Ck-out noon. Coin lndry. Meeting rms. Business servs avail. In-rm modem link. Free airport transportation. Exercise equipt. Health club privileges. Refrigerators, microwaves. Cr cds: A, C, D, DS, MC, V.

◼ ◼ ◼ ◼ ◼ ◼ ◼ SC

★★ **PHOENIX INN.** *14905 SW Bangy Rd, Lake Oswego (97034). 503/624-7400; fax 503/624-7405, toll-free 800/824-9992. www.phoenixinn. com.* 62 rms, 4 story. June-Sept: S, D $94; each addl $5; suites $119-$129; under 18 free; lower rates rest of yr; package plans. Crib free. TV; cable (premium). Indoor pool; whirlpool. Complimentary bkfst buffet. Coffee in rms. Restaurant adj 11 am-11 pm. Bar 11 am-10 pm. Ck-out noon. Coin lndry. Meeting rms. Business servs avail. In-rm modem link. Valet serv. Sundries. Airport transportation avail. Exercise equipt. Refrigerators, microwaves; some minibars. Cr cds: A, C, D, DS, MC, V.

◼ ◼ ◼ ◼ ◼ SC

★ **RAMADA INN.** *6221 NE 82nd Ave (97220). 503/255-6511; fax 503/255-8417, res 800/272-6232. www.ramada. com.* 202 rms, 2 story. S, D $69; each addl $10; suites $95-$250; under 18 free; wkend rates. Crib free. TV; cable (premium). Heated pool; whirlpool. Coffee in rms. Restaurant 6:30 am-11 pm. Bar. Ck-out noon. Coin lndry. Meeting rms. Business center. Bellhops. Valet serv. Free airport transportation. Exercise equipt; sauna. Some private patios, balconies. Cr cds: A, C, D, DS, ER, JCB, MC, V.

◼ ◼ ◼ ◼ ◼ ◼

★★ **RAMADA INN AT ROSE QUARTER.** *10 N Weidler St (97227). 503/287-9900; fax 503/287-3500; toll-free 888/298-2054. www.ramada.com.* 181 rms, 5 story. S, D $69-$99; each

addl $5; suites $175; under 12 free. TV; cable (premium). Indoor pool. Restaurant 6:30 am-9:30 pm. Bar 11-2 am. Coffee in rms. Ck-out 11 am. Meeting rms. Business servs avail. Valet serv. In-rm modem link. Health club privileges. Covered parking. Free RR station, bus depot transportation. Refrigerators avail. Cr cds: A, C, D, DS, MC, V.

◼ ◼ ◼ ◼ SC

★★ **SHILO INN.** *9900 SW Canyon Rd (97225). 503/297-2551; fax 503/297-7708; toll-free 800/222-2244. www.shiloinns.com.* 142 rms, 2-3 story. S, D $69.95-$99.95; each addl $10; under 13 free; wkly rates. Crib free. Pet accepted; $10. TV; cable (premium), VCR avail (movies). Heated pool; whirlpool. Complimentary bkfst buffet. Coffee in rms. Restaurant 6 am-10 pm. Bar 11-2 am, entertainment Mon-Sat. Ck-out noon. Meeting rms. Business servs avail. Valet serv. Sundries. Free airport transportation. Exercise equipt. Refrigerators, microwaves. Private patios, balconies. Cr cds: A, C, D, DS, ER, JCB, MC, V.

◼ ◼ ◼ ◼ ◼ ◼ SC

★★ **SHILO INN.** *10830 SW Greenburg Rd, Tigard (97223). 503/620-4320; fax 503/620-8277; res 800/222-2244. www.shiloinns.com.* 77 rms, 4 story, 6 kits. S, D $59.95-$75.95; each addl $10; kit. units $85; under 13 free; wkly, monthly rates. Crib free. Pet accepted; $10/day. TV; cable (premium), VCR avail (movies). Complimentary continental bkfst. Coffee in rms. Restaurant nearby. Ck-out noon. Coin lndry. Meeting rm. Business servs avail. Valet serv. Free airport transportation. Exercise equipt; sauna, steam rm. Refrigerators, microwaves. Cr cds: A, C, D, DS, ER, JCB, MC, V.

◼ ◼ ◼ ◼ ◼

★★ **SHILO INN PORTLAND AIRPORT.** *11707 NE Airport Way (97220). 503/252-7500; fax 503/254-0794; res 800/222-2244. www.shilo inn.com.* 200 suites, 4 story. S, D $99-$129; each addl $10; under 13 free; higher rates Rose Festival. Crib free. TV; cable (premium), VCR (movies $3.50). Indoor pool; whirlpool. Complimentary continental bkfst; afternoon refreshments. Coffee in rms.

Restaurant 5:30 am-10 pm; Fri, Sat to 11 pm. Rm serv to 10 pm. Bar 11-2:30 am; entertainment. Ck-out noon. Coin lndry. Meeting rms. Business center. In-rm modem link. Concierge. Free airport, RR station, bus depot transportation. Exercise equipt; sauna, steam rm. Bathrm phones, refrigerators, microwaves, wet bars in suites. Cr cds: A, C, D, DS, MC, V.

🄳 ≍ 🏋 ✈ 🏊 🔥 🚶

★ **SUPER 8 WILSONVILLE.** *25438 SW Parkway Ave, Wilsonville (97070). 503/682-2088; fax 503/682-0453; res 800/800-8000. www.super8.com.* 72 rms, 4 story. S $49.88; D $60.88-$67.88; each addl $4. Crib free. Pet accepted; $25 refundable. TV; cable (premium). Complimentary coffee in lobby. Restaurant opp open 24 hrs. Ck-out noon. Coin lndry. Meeting rm. Business servs avail. Cr cds: A, DS, MC, V.

🄳 🐾 🔥

★★ **THE SWEET BRIER INN.** *7125 SW Nyberg Rd, Tualatin (97062). 503/692-5800; fax 503/691-2894; toll-free 800/551-9167. www.sweetbrier. com.* 131 rms, 32 suites. S, D $74-$99; suites $89-$125; each addl $10; under 17 free; wkend rates. Crib free. Pet accepted; $35 refundable. TV; cable (premium). Heated pool. Playground. Complimentary continental bkfst. Coffee in rms. Restaurant 6:30 am-10 pm. Bar; entertainment Tues-Sat. Ck-out noon. Meeting rms. Business servs avail. In-rm modem link. Sundries. Valet serv. Exercise equipt. Health club privileges. Refrigerator in suites. Some balconies, patios. Picnic tables. Cr cds: A, C, D, DS, JCB, MC, V.

🄳 🐾 ≍ 🏋 🏊 🔥

★ **TRAVELODGE.** *2401 SW 4th Ave (97201). 503/226-1121; fax 503/274-2681; res 800/578-7878. www. travelodge.com.* 42 rms in 2 buildings, 2 story. S $55-$65; D $65-$75; each addl $7. Crib $7. TV; cable (premium). Heated pool. Complimentary coffee in lobby. Restaurant 7 am-10 pm. Bar 11-2 am. Ck-out noon. Business servs avail. Some refrigerators, microwaves. Balconies. Cr cds: A, C, D, DS, ER, JCB, MC, V.

✈ ≍ 🏊 🔥

Hotels

★★★ **BENSON HOTEL.** *309 SW Broadway (97205). 503/228-2000; fax 503/471-3920; res 888/523-6766. www.bensonhotel.com.* 287 units, 14 story, 56 suites. S, D $149-$255; each addl $25; suites $250-$900; under 18 free; wkend rates. Crib free. Pet accepted; $50. Garage, valet $22/day. TV; cable, VCR avail. Restaurant (see LONDON GRILL). Rm serv 24 hrs. Bar 11-1 am; entertainment. Coffee in rms. Ck-out 1 pm. Convention facilities. Business center. In-rm modem link. Concierge. Gift shop. Complimentary coffee in rms. Airport transportation. Exercise rm. Minibars. Bathrm phone in suites. Some CD players, fireplaces. Cr cds: A, D, DS, JCB, MC, V.

🄳 🐾 🏋 🔥 🚶

★★★ **CROWNE PLAZA.** *14811 Kruse Oaks Blvd, Lake Oswego (97035). 503/624-8400; fax 503/684-8324; toll-free 800/465-4329. www.basshotels. com/crowneplaza.* 161 rms, 6 story. June-Aug: S, D $129; suites $161-$275; under 18 free; lower rates rest of yr. Crib free. Pet accepted; $10. Valet parking $5. TV; cable (premium). Indoor/outdoor pool; whirlpool. Complimentary coffee, tea in rms. Restaurant 6 am-2 pm, 5-10 pm. Rm serv to midnight. Bar 2 pm-midnight. Ck-out noon. Meeting rms. Business center. In-rm modem link. Concierge. Sundries. Gift shop. Coin lndry. Exercise equipt; sauna. Refrigerators. Luxury level. Cr cds: A, C, D, DS, JCB, MC, V.

🄳 🐾 ≍ 🏋 🏊 🔥 SC 🚶

★★ **DOUBLETREE HOTEL COLUMBIA RIVER.** *1401 N Hayden Island Dr (97217). 503/283-2111; fax 503/283-4718; toll-free 800/222-8733. www.doubletree.com.* 352 rms, 3 story. S, D $99-$109; each addl $15; suites $225-$350; under 18 free. Crib free. Pet accepted; $15. TV; cable (premium). Heated pool. Restaurants 6 am-10 pm. Bars 11-2 am. Coffee in rms. Ck-out noon. Convention facilities. Business center. In-rm modem link. Bellhops. Coin lndry. Valet serv. Gift shop. Beauty shop. Free airport, RR station, bus depot transportation. Tennis adj. Putting green. Some refrigerators, bathrm phones. Whirlpool in some suites. Private patios, balconies. On Columbia River. Cr cds: A, C, D, DS, ER, JCB, MC, V.

★★ **DOUBLETREE HOTEL JANTZEN BEACH.** *909 N Hayden Island Dr (97217). 503/283-4466; fax 503/283-4743; res 800/222-8733. www.doubletree.com.* 320 rms, 4 story. S $119-$139; D $134-$154; each addl $15; suites $195-$350; under 18 free; package plans; wkend rates. Crib free. Pet accepted; $20. TV; cable (premium), VCR avail. Heated pool; whirlpool. Coffee in rms. Restaurant 6 am-10 pm. Bar 10-2:30 am; entertainment. Ck-out 11 am. Convention facilities. Business center. Bellhops. Coin lndry. Valet serv. Beauty shop. Concierge. Gift shop. Sundries. Free airport transportation. Lighted tennis. Exercise equipt. Some bathrm phones, in-rm whirlpools. Private patios, balconies. On river, boat dock. Cr cds: A, C, D, DS, ER, JCB, MC, V.

★★ **DOUBLETREE PORTLAND - LLOYD CENTER.** *1000 NE Multnomah St (97232). 503/281-6111; fax 503/249-3137; toll-free 800/222-8733. www.doubletreehotels.com.* 476 rms, 15 story. S $149-$159 D $159-$169; each addl $15; suites $269-$575; under 18 free. Self parking $18, valet $21. Crib free. Pet accepted, some restrictions. TV; cable (premium), VCR avail. Pool; poolside serv. Coffee in rms. Restaurant 6 am-midnight. Bar. Ck-out 11 am. Convention facilities. Business center. Valet serv. Concierge. Gift shop. Free airport transportation. Exercise equipt. Some bathrm phones, in-rm whirlpools, refrigerators, minibars. Many private patios, balconies. Cr cds: A, C, D, DS, MC, V.

★★★ **5TH AVENUE SUITES HOTEL.** *506 SW Washington St (97204). 503/222-0001; fax 503/222-0004; res 800/711-2971. www. 5thavenuesuites.com.* 221 rms, 10 story, 139 suites. S, D $165-$185; each addl $15; suites $170-$235; under 18 free; wkend, hol rates; package plans. Crib free. Pet accepted, some restrictions. Garage/valet parking $17. TV; cable (premium), VCR avail (movies). Pool privileges. Com-

plimentary coffee in rms. Restaurant 6:30-10 am, 11:30 am-2:30 pm, 5-9:30 pm; Fri 5-10:30 pm; Sat 8 am-3 pm, 5-10:30 pm; Sun 8 am-3 pm, 5-9:30 pm. Rm serv 24 hrs. Bar 11-1 am. Ck-out noon. Meeting rms. Business center. In-rm modem link. Concierge. Exercise equipt. Health club privileges. Refrigerators. Cr cds: A, C, D, DS, ER, JCB, MC, V.

★★★ **GOVERNOR HOTEL.** *611 SW 10th Ave (97205). 503/224-3400; fax 503/241-2122; toll-free 800/554-3456. www.govhotel.com.* 100 rms, 6 story, 24 suites. S $165; D $185; each addl $20; suites $200-$500; under 12 free; wkend rates. Crib free. Valet parking $13-$15. TV; cable, VCR avail. Indoor pool; whirlpool. Restaurant 6:30 am-11 pm (see also JAKE'S GRILL). Rm serv 24 hrs. Bar 11 am-midnight. Valet serv. Ck-out noon. Meeting rms. Business center. Concierge. Barber, beauty shop. Exercise rm; sauna, steam rm. Refrigerators, minibars; some in-rm whirlpools, fireplaces. Some balconies. Cr cds: A, C, D, DS, ER, JCB, MC, V.

★★★ **THE HEATHMAN HOTEL.** *1001 SW Broadway (97205). 503/241-4100; fax 503/790-7110; toll-free 800/551-0011. www.heathmanhotel. com.* 150 rms, 10 story. S, D $159-$169; each addl $20; suites $199-$775; under 6 free; wkend rates. Crib $7. Valet parking. TV; cable (premium), VCR avail (movies). Restaurant (see HEATHMAN). Rm serv 24 hrs. Afternoon tea. Bars 11-2 am; entertainment Wed-Sat. Valet serv. Ck-out noon. Meeting rms. Business servs avail. In-rm modem link. Concierge. Gift shop. Exercise equipt. Health club privileges. Minibars. Library. Cr cds: A, C, D, DS, JCB, MC, V.

★★★ **HILTON PORTLAND.** *921 SW Sixth Ave (97204). 503/226-1611; fax 503/220-2565; res 800/774-1500. www.portland.hilton.com.* 455 rms, 23 story. S, D $185-$195; each addl $30; suites $400-$950; family, wkend rates. Garage in/out $17; valet $3 addl. Crib free. TV; cable (premium). Indoor pool; whirlpool; poolside serv. Restaurant 5:30 am-10 pm;

closed Sun. Bar 5-11 pm; Fri, Sat to 11:45 pm; entertainment Tues-Sat. Closed Sun. Coffee in rms. Ck-out noon. Convention facilities. Business center. Valet serv. In-rm modem link. Concierge. Children's activities. Gift shop. Barber, beauty shop. Exercise equipt; sauna, steam rm. Cr cds: A, C, D, DS, JCB, MC, V.

★ **MALLORY HOTEL.** *729 SW 15th Ave (97205).* 503/223-6311; fax 503/223-0522; toll-free 800/228-8657. www.malloryhotel.com. 136 rms, 8 story. S $90-$100; D $95-$155; each addl $5; suites $145-$155; under 12 free. Crib free. Pet accepted; $10. TV; cable (premium). Free garage parking. Restaurant 6:30 am-9 pm; Sun from 7 am. Bar 11:30-1 am; Sun 1-9 pm. Ck-out 1 pm. Meeting rm. Business servs avail. In-rm modem link. Some refrigerators. Cr cds: A, D, DS, JCB, MC, V.

★ **MARK SPENCER HOTEL PORTLAND.** *409 SW 11th Ave (97205).* 503/224-3293; fax 503/223-7848; toll-free 800/548-3934. www.markspencer.com. 101 kit. units, 6 story. S, D $76-$119; each addl $10; suites $104-$119; studio rms $76; under 12 free; wkly, monthly rates. Crib free. Pet accepted; $200 refundable. TV; cable, VCR avail (free movies). Complimentary continental bkfst, afternoon tea. Restaurant nearby. Ck-out noon. Coin lndry. Valet serv. Meeting rm. Business servs avail. Health club privileges. Refrigerators; microwaves avail. Rooftop garden. Cr cds: A, C, D, DS, JCB, MC, V.

★★★ **MARRIOTT DOWNTOWN PORTLAND.** *1401 SW Naito Parkway (97201).* 503/226-7600; fax 503/221-1789; toll-free 800/228-9290. www.marriott.com. 503 rms, 16 story. S $160-$190; D $170-$200; suites $400-$600; under 18 free. Crib free. Pet accepted. Valet parking in/out

$14/day. TV; cable (premium), VCR avail. Indoor pool; whirlpool, poolside serv. Restaurant 6 am-11 pm; Fri, Sat to midnight. Bar 11:30-1 am; entertainment. Coffee in rms. Ck-out noon. Coin lndry. Convention facilities. Business center. In-rm modem link. Concierge. Gift shop. Exercise equipt; sauna. Massage. Some bathrm phones, wet bar in suites. Some private patios, balconies. Japanese garden at entrance. Luxury level. Cr cds: A, C, D, DS, ER, JCB, MC, V.

★★★ **MARRIOTT PORTLAND CITY CENTER.** *520 SW Broadway (97205).* 503/226-6300; fax 503/227-7515; res 800/228-9290. www.marriott.com. 249 rms, 20 story. S, D $125-$275; each addl $20; under 17 free. Crib avail. Pet accepted, some restrictions. TV; cable (premium), VCR avail. Complimentary coffee, newspaper in rms. Restaurant 6 am-10 pm. Bar. Coffee in rms. Ck-out noon. Meeting rms. Business center. Coin lndry. Valet serv. Gift shop. Exercise rm. Some refrigerators, mini-bars. Luxury level. Cr cds: A, C, D, DS, JCB, MC, V.

★★ **RADISSON HOTEL.** *1441 NE 2nd Ave (97232).* 503/233-2401; fax 503/238-0498; toll-free 800/333-3333. www.radisson.com. 238 rms, 10 story. S, D $129-$149; under 18 free. Crib free. TV; cable (premium). Pet accepted, some restrictions. Heated pool. Complimentary coffee in rms.

Portland at Dusk

Restaurant 6:30 am-2 pm, 5:30-10 pm. Rm serv 24 hrs. Bar. Ck-out noon. Meeting rms. Business center. Free airport transportation. Exercise equipt. Luxury level. Cr cds: A, D, DS, JCB, MC, V.

D 🍴 🏋 ✕ 🏊 🔥 SC 🏋

★★★ **RIVER PLACE HOTEL.** *1510 SW Harbor Way (97201). 503/228-3233; fax 503/295-6190; toll-free 800/227-1333. www.riverplacehotel. com.* 84 rms, 4 story. S, D $219-$239; condos $345-$495; suites $220-$750; under 18 free. Valet, garage parking in/out $15. Crib free. Pet accepted, some restrictions; $100. TV; cable (premium), VCR avail. Complimentary continental bkfst. Restaurant (see ESPLANADE AT RIVERPLACE). Rm serv 24 hrs. Bar 11 am-midnight; entertainment Wed-Sun evenings. Ck-out 1 pm. Meeting rms. Business servs avail. Valet serv. In-rm modem link. Concierge. Shopping arcade. Whirlpool. Sauna. Spa. Health club privileges. Minibars; some bathrm phones, refrigerators; fireplaces in suites. Balconies. On river. Skyline, marina views. Cr cds: A, C, D, DS, ER, JCB, MC, V

D 🍴 🏋 🛟 🏊 🔥 🏋

★★★ **SHERATON PORTLAND AIRPORT HOTEL.** *8235 NE Airport Way (97220). 503/281-2500; fax 503/249-7602; res 800/325-3535. www.sheratonpdx.com.* 214 rms, 5 story. S $89-$139; D $89-$149; each addl $10; suites $165-$395; under 18 free; wkend rates. Crib $5. TV; cable (premium). Indoor pool; whirlpool. Coffee in rms. Restaurant 5 am-10:30 pm; Sat, Sun 6 am-10 pm. Rm serv 5:30 am-11 pm. Bars. Ck-out noon. Meeting rms. Business center. Concierge. Free airport transportation. Exercise equipt; sauna. Minibars. Cr cds: A, C, D, DS, ER, JCB, MC, V.

D 🛟 🏋 ✕ 🏊 🔥 SC 🏋

★★ **SILVER CLOUD INN PORT-LAND.** *2426 NW Vaughn St (97210). 503/242-2400; fax 503/242-1770; toll-free 800/205-6939. www.scinns.com.* 63 rms, 4 story. S, D $85; each addl $10; suites $105; under 18 free. Crib free. Pet accepted, some restrictions; $100. TV; cable (premium). Complimentary continental bkfst. Coffee in

rms. Restaurant nearby. Ck-out noon. Business servs avail. In-rm modem link. Free lndry. Exercise equipt. Whirlpool. Refrigerators. Cr cds: A, D, DS, MC, V.

D 🍴 🏋 🛟 🔥 SC

★★★ **VINTAGE PLAZA.** *422 SW Broadway (97205). 503/228-1212; fax 503/228-3598; toll-free 800/263-2305. www.vintageplaza.com.* 107 rms, 10 story, 23 suites. S, D $99-$180; each addl $15; suites $210-$300; under 18 free; wkend rates. Crib free. Pet accepted. Valet parking $17. TV; cable (premium), VCR avail. Restaurant (see PAZZO RISTORANTE). Rm serv 24 hrs. Bar 11-1 am. Ck-out noon. Meeting rms. Business center. In-rm modem link. Concierge. Exercise equipt. Minibars. Cr cds: A, C, D, DS, ER, JCB, MC, V.

D 🍴 🏋 🔥 🏋

★★★ **THE WESTIN PORTLAND.** *750 SW Alder St (97205). 503/294-9000; fax 503/241-9565; res 800/937-8461. www.westin.com.* Located in the center of downtown Portland, this hotel is within walking distance to such area attractions as the Portland Convention Center. This facility offers guests Internet access, coffee makers, in-room safes, and dual-line direct-dial telephones with fax and data ports. 205 rms, 18 story, 17 suites. June-Nov: S $220; D $245; each addl $25; suites $270; under 17 free; lower rates rest of yr. Crib avail. Pet accepted, fee. Valet parking avail. TV; cable (premium). Complimentary coffee, tea in rms, newspaper. Restaurant 6:30 am-11 pm. 24-hr rm serv. Bar. Ck-out noon, ck-in 3 pm. Meeting rms. Business center. Bellhops. Concierge. Dry cleaning. Exercise equipt. Golf. Downhill skiing. Supervised children's activities. Video games. Minibars. Some fireplaces. Cr cds: A, C, D, DS, ER, JCB, MC, V.

D 🍴 ⛷ 🏌 🏋 🔥 🏋

B&Bs/Small Inns

★★ **HERON HAUS.** *2545 NW Westover Rd (97210). 503/274-1846; fax 503/248-4055. www.heronhaus.com.* 6 rms, 3 story. S $95-$105; D $135-$350; each addl $65. TV; cable (premium), VCR avail (movies). Pool. Complimentary continental bkfst.

Restaurant nearby. Ck-out 11 am, ck-in 4-6 pm. Business servs avail. In-rm modem link. Some fireplaces. Restored house (1904) in NW hills overlooking city; library, morning rm. Totally nonsmoking. Cr cds: MC, V.
⊠ ⊠ ⊠

★★ **MCMENAMINS EDGEFIELD.**
2126 SW Halsey St, Troutdale (97060). 503/669-8610; fax 503/665-4209; toll-free 800/669-8610. www.mcmenamins.com/edge. 103 rms, 100 share bath, 3 story. No rm phones. S, D $50-$105; suite $115-$130; family rm $200; package plans; each addl $15; under 6 free. Crib free. Complimentary full bkfst. Restaurant (see BLACK RABBIT). Bar 11-1 am. Ck-out 11 am. Business servs avail. Massage. 18-hole golf course. Built 1911 as county poor farm; was converted to nursing home in 1960s. Renovated in style of European village complete with theater, winery, distillery, and brewery. Herb gardens, vineyard. Totally nonsmoking. Cr cds: A, DS, MC, V.
D ⊠ ⊠ ⊠ ⊠

★★★ **PORTLAND'S WHITE HOUSE BED AND BREAKFAST.**
1914 NE 22nd Ave (97212). 503/287-7131; fax 503/249-1641; res 800/272-7131. www.portlandswhitehouse.com. 9 rms, 2 story. S $116; D $125; each addl $20; under 6 free. Crib free. Complimentary full bkfst. Restaurant nearby. Ck-out 11 am, ck-in 2 pm. Business servs avail. In-rm modem link. Luggage handling. Street parking. Free airport, RR station, bus depot transportation. Game rm. Some balconies. White Southern Colonial mansion with Greek columns and fountain at entrance. Ballroom; antique stained-glass windows. Totally nonsmoking. Cr cds: A, DS, MC, V.
⊠ ⊠ ⊠

All Suite

★★★ **EMBASSY SUITES DOWNTOWN.** *319 SW Pine St (97204). 503/279-9000; fax 503/497-9051; res 800/362-2779. www.embassyportland.com.* 276 suites, 8 story. S $149-$169; D $179-$199; June-Oct: suites $149-$229; under 18 free; family rates; package plans; lower rates rest of yr. Crib free. Valet parking $19; garage parking $15. TV; cable (premium), VCR avail. Complimentary full bkfst.

Complimentary coffee in rms. Restaurant (see also PORTLAND STEAK AND CHOPHOUSE). Rm serv 24 hrs. Bar 11 am-11 pm; piano Fri, Sat. Ck-out noon. Convention facilities. Business center. In-rm modem link. Concierge. Shopping arcade. Barber, beauty shop. Coin lndry. Airport transportation. Exercise equipt; sauna. Massage. Indoor pool; whirlpool, poolside serv. Game rm. Bathrm phones, refrigerators, microwaves, wet bars. Cr cds: A, C, D, DS, JCB, MC, V.
D ⊠ ⊠ ⊠ ⊠ SC ⊠

Extended Stays

★★ **RESIDENCE INN BY MARRIOTT.** *1710 NE Multnomah St (97232). 503/288-1400; fax 503/288-0241; res 800/331-3131. www.residenceinn.com.* 168 suites, 3 story. June-Sept: suites $111-$159; package plans. Crib free. Pet accepted, some restrictions; $50, $10/day. TV; cable (premium). Complimentary continental bkfst. Complimentary coffee in rms. Restaurant nearby. Ck-out noon. Meeting rms. Business servs avail. In-rm modem link. Valet serv. Sundries. Coin lndry. Free airport, RR station transportation. Lighted tennis. Heated pool; whirlpools. Refrigerators, microwaves. Many fireplaces. Picnic tables. Cr cds: A, DS, MC, V.
D ⊠ ⊠ ⊠ ⊠

★★ **RESIDENCE INN BY MARRIOTT.** *15200 SW Banby Rd, Lake Oswego (97035). 503/684-2603; fax 503/620-6712; res 800/331-3131. www.residenceinn.com.* 112 kit. units, 2 story. 1 and 2-bedrm suites $130-$175. Crib $5. Pet accepted; $10/day. TV; cable (premium), VCR avail (free movies). Heated pool; whirlpool. Complimentary continental bkfst. Restaurant adj. Ck-out noon. Coin lndry. Business servs avail. Valet serv. Health club privileges. Fireplace in suites. Private patios, balconies. Picnic tables, grills. Cr cds: A, DS, MC, V.
D ⊠ ⊠ ⊠ ⊠ SC

Restaurants

★★ **AL-AMIR LEBANESE RESTAURANT.** *223 SW Stark St (97204). 503/274-0010. www.savydiner.com.* Hrs: 11 am-10 pm; Fri to 1 am; Sat 4 pm-1 am; Sun 4-9 pm. Closed Jan 1, Thanksgiving, Dec 25. Res required Fri, Sat. Lebanese menu. Bar. Lunch $5-$8, dinner $8.50-$16.50. Children's meals. Specialties: maza al-amir, kebab. Entertainment Fri, Sat. Lebanese decor. Totally nonsmoking. Cr cds: A, DS, MC, V.

★ **ALESSANDRO'S.** *301 SW Morrison (97204). 503/222-3900. www. citysearch.com.* Hrs: 11:30 am-10 pm; Sat to 11 pm. Closed Sun; hols. Res accepted. Italian menu. Bar. Lunch $5.75-$11, dinner $10.50-$19.95. Complete meals: dinner $32. Specializes in Roman-style Italian seafood, poultry, veal. Parking. Totally nonsmoking. Cr cds: A, D, MC, V.
D

★ **ALEXIS.** *215 W Burnside (97209). 503/224-8577.* Hrs: 11:30 am-2 pm, 5-10 pm; Fri to 11 pm; Sat 5-11 pm; Sun 4:30-9 pm. Closed hols. Greek menu. Bar. Lunch $5.95-$8.95, dinner $8.95-$13.95. Specialties: deep fried squid, eggplant casserole, grape leaves stuffed with ground lamb. Belly dancer Fri, Sat. Greek decor. Cr cds: A, D, DS, MC, V.
D

★★★ **ATWATER'S.** *111 SW 5th Ave (97204). 503/275-3600. www.atwaters. com.* Hrs: 5-9:30 pm; Fri, Sat to 10 pm; Sun 5-9 pm. Closed hols. Res accepted. Contemporary American menu. Bar to 1:30 am on wkends. Wine list. Dinner $18-$33. Children's meals. Specializes in salmon, game, fowl. Jazz Tues-Sat. Totally nonsmoking. Cr cds: A, D, DS, MC, V.
D

★★ **BLACK RABBIT.** *2126 SW Halsey, Troutdale (97060). 503/492-3086. www.mcmenamins.com.* Hrs: 7 am-11 am. Res accepted. Bar 11-1 am. Bkfst $5.25-$9.25, lunch $6.25-$12.50, dinner $13.50-$21. Children's meals. Specializes in fresh Northwestern cuisine. Parking. Outdoor dining. Totally nonsmoking. Cr cds: A, D, DS, MC, V.
D

★★ **BREWHOUSE TAP ROOM & GRILL.** *2730 NW 31st Ave (97210). 503/228-5269. www.portlandbrew.*

com/portland. Hrs: 11 am-10 pm; Mon to 9 pm; Fri to 11 pm; Sat noon-11 pm; Sun noon-9 pm. Closed hols. Northwestern, German cuisine. Bar. Lunch $4.75-$9.95, dinner $5.50-$12.95. Children's meals. Specialties: MacTarnahan's fish and chips, haystack-black baby ribs. Outdoor dining. Copper beer-making equipment at entrance. Totally nonsmoking. Cr cds: A, MC, V.
D

★★ **BUGATTI'S.** *18740 Williamette Dr, West Linn (97068). 503/636-9555.* Hrs: 5-9 pm; Fri, Sat to 10 pm. Closed hols. Res accepted. Italian menu. Beer, wine. A la carte entrees: dinner $8.95-$16.95. Children's meals. Specialties: granchio, pollo capperi, prawns. Parking. Outdoor dining. Totally nonsmoking. Cr cds: MC, V.
D

★★ **BUSH GARDEN.** *900 SW Morrison (97205). 503/226-7181. www. bushgardencitysearch.com.* Hrs: 11:30 am-1:45 pm, 5-9:45 pm; Sat 5-9:45 pm; Sun 5-8:45 pm. Closed hols. Res accepted. Japanese menu. Bar to 12:45 am; Fri, Sat to 1:45 am. Lunch $5.75-$11.95, dinner $11.50-$24.95. Specialties: sashimi, sukiyaki. Sushi bar. Karaoke singing. Parking. Dining in tatami rms. Cr cds: A, D, DS, MC, V.
D

★★ **CAFE AZUL.** *112 NW 9th Ave (97209). 503/525-4422.* Hrs: 5-10 pm. Closed Sun, Mon; hols. Res accepted. Mexican menu. Bar. Dinner $15-$30. Specialties: codornices y empanada, mole. Street parking. Outdoor dining. Totally nonsmoking. Cr cds: D, DS, MC, V.
D

★★★ **CAFE DES AMIS.** *1987 NW Kearney St (97209). 503/295-6487. www.citysearch.com.* Hrs: 5:30-10 pm. Closed Sun; hols. Res accepted. Country French menu. Serv bar. Dinner $13-$25. Specialty: filet of beef with port garlic. Own baking. Parking. Country French decor. Totally nonsmoking. Cr cds: A, MC, V.
D

★★ **CAPRIAL'S BISTRO.** *7015 SE Milwaukee Ave (97202). 503/236-6457.* Hrs: 11 am-3:15 pm; also 5-9:30 pm Sat. Closed Sun, Mon; major hols. Res required. Eclectic menu. Wine, beer. Lunch $4.50-$10, dinner $17-$22. Specializes in pasta, seafood. Casual decor. Totally nonsmoking. Cr cds: MC, V.

D

★★ **CHART HOUSE.** *5700 SW Terwilliger Blvd (97201). 503/246-6963. www.chart-house.com.* Hrs: 11:30 am-3 pm, 5-10 pm; Sat from 5 pm; Sun 5-9 pm. Res accepted. Bar. Lunch $6-$13, dinner $15-$25. Children's meals. Specializes in prime rib, steak, fresh seafood. Valet parking. Fireplace. 1,000 ft above Willamette River; panoramic view of Portland, Mt Hood and Mt St Helens. Cr cds: A, D, DS, MC, V.

D

★★★★ **COUVRON.** *1126 SW 18th Ave (97205). 503/225-1844. www. couvron.com.* Husband and wife team Anthony Demes and Maura Jarach preside over this tiny, French-inspired dining room where the dishes are near perfect and the pace is luxuriously relaxed—a rare quality in this day of multiple, nightly seatings. Chef Demes's passionate commitment to quality ingredients comes to light in three menus offered each evening: one based on the freshest of local ingredients, a vegetarian dinner, and the Grand Options—truly a culinary symphony. Contemporary French menu. Specialties: foie gras, cherrywood-smoked Oregon quail, halibut, roasted salmon mignon, Maine black sea bass, venison, roasted lamb loin. Hrs: 5:30-9 pm; Fri, Sat to 10 pm. Closed Sun, Mon; hols. Res accepted. Wine list. Dinner: $30-$36. Prix fixe: 7-course $75. Cr cds: A, MC, V.

D

★ **DAN & LOUIS OYSTER BAR.** *208 SW Ankeny St (97204). 503/227-5906. www.danandlouiscitysearch.com.* Hrs: 11 am-10 pm; Fri, Sat to 11 pm. Closed hols. Lunch $2.75-$7.25, dinner $5.95-$18.95. Children's meals. Beer, wine. Specialties: stewed, broiled, fried, pan-fried, and raw oysters. Antique seafaring decor. Ship models. 19th-century bldg (1907).

Family-owned. Cr cds: A, C, D, DS, MC, V.

D SC

★ **ESPARZA'S TEX MEX CAFE.** *2725 SE Ankeny St (97214). 503/234-7909.* Hrs: 11:30 am-10 pm. Closed Sun, Mon; hols. Tex-Mex menu. Bar. Lunch $5.50-$10.50; dinner $7.25-$12.50. Children's meals. Specialties: stuffed porkloin with buffalo spicy cactus, carne asada rib-eye steak. Western decor. Totally nonsmoking. Cr cds: A, D, DS, MC, V.

★★ **ESPLANADE AT RIVERPLACE.** *1510 SW Harbor Way (97201). 503/228-3233. www.riverplace.com.* Hrs: 6:30 am-2 pm; 5-10 pm; Sat 6:30-11 am, 5-10 pm; Sun 6:30 am-2 pm, 5-9 pm; Sun brunch 11 am-2 pm. Res accepted. Continental menu. Bar 11-1 am. Wine cellar. Bkfst $3.50-$10.50, lunch $6.95-$15, dinner $13.50-$28. Sun brunch $9-$13. Children's meals. Specializes in Northwestern regional cuisine. Own desserts. Outdoor dining. Split-level dining; view of Willamette River and marina. Totally nonsmoking. Cr cds: A, C, D, DS, MC, V.

D

★★ **FERNANDO'S HIDEAWAY.** *824 SW First Ave (97204). 503/248-4709. www.fernandoshideaway.com.* Hrs: 4:30-10 pm; Fri, Sat to 11 pm; Sun to 9 pm. Closed Mon; Memorial Day, July 4. Res accepted. Spanish menu. Bar to 2:30 am (Thurs-Sat). Lunch, dinner $15.50-$19.50. Specialties: picanton catalan, churrasco, zarzuela de mariscos. Street parking. Outdoor dining. Cr cds: A, C, D, DS, MC, V.

D

★★★★ **GENOA.** *2832 SE Belmont St (97214). 503/238-1464. www.genoa restaurant.com.* It's worth more than two hours out of anyone's busy schedule to experience this northern Italian restaurant's seven-course, prix-fixe extravaganza and warm, cozy atmosphere. This establishment, founded in 1971 by the late restauranteur Michael Vidor, is now co-owned by Cathy Whims and Kerry DeBuse and still carries on the tradition of highlighting a different region of Italy every two to three weeks. Northern Italian menu. Specializes in authentic regional Italian dishes. Own baking. Hrs: 5:30-9:30 pm. Closed Sun; hols. Res accepted.

Prix fixe: 7-course dinner $60, 4-course dinner (Mon-Thurs) $50. Menu changes every two wks. Restaurant nonsmoking; separate room for smoking. Cr cds: A, D, DS, MC, V.
D

★★★ **HEATHMAN.** *1001 SW Broadway (97205). 503/241-4100. www. heathmanhotel.com.* Hrs: 6:30 am-11 pm. Res accepted. French, American menu. Bar 11-1 am. Wine cellar. Bkfst $4-$11, lunch $8-$18, dinner $13-$29. Specialties: Chinook salmon, halibut confit, Oregon lamb. Own baking. Entertainment. Valet parking. Outdoor dining. Cr cds: A, D, DS, MC, V.
D

★★★ **HIGGINS.** *1239 SW Broadway (97205). 503/222-9070. www. citysearch.com.* Hrs: 11:30 am-2 pm, 5-10:30 pm. Closed hols. Res accepted. Northwestern regional menu. Bar to 2 am. A la carte: lunch $7-$13.50; dinner $14.50-$20.50. Children's meals. Specializes in seafood, hamburger. Contemporary decor. Cr cds: A, D, DS, MC, V.
D

★ **HUBER'S CAFE.** *411 SW 3rd Ave (97204). 503/228-5686. www.hubers. com.* Hrs: 11 am-midnight; Fri to 1 am; Sat noon-1 am. Closed Sun; major hols. Res accepted. Bar. Lunch $4.95-$9, dinner $6.50-$18.95. Specialties: roast turkey, flaming Spanish coffees. Originally a saloon established in 1879 that became a restaurant during Prohibition. Arched stained-glass skylight, mahogany paneling and terrazzo floor. Cr cds: A, D, DS, MC, V.
D

★★ **IL FORNAIO.** *115 NW 22nd Ave (97210). 503/248-9400. www.ilfornaio. com.* Hrs: 11:30 am-10 pm; Fri to 11 pm; Sat 10:30 am-11 pm; Sun from 10:30 am; Sat, Sun brunch 10:30 am-2 pm. Closed Thanksgiving, Dec 25. Res accepted. Italian menu. Bar. Lunch $5-$15, dinner $6-$19. Children's meals. Specialties: pizza con la luganega, pollo toscano, ravioli pomodoro. Menu changes monthly. Free valet parking. Show kitchen; wood-burning pizza oven and rotisserie. Cr cds: A, MC, V.
D

★★★ **JAKE'S FAMOUS CRAW-FISH.** *401 SW 12th Ave (97205). 503/226-1419. www.mccormickand schmicks.com.* Hrs: 11:30 am-11 pm; Fri to midnight; Sat 5 pm-midnight; Sun 5-10 pm. Closed July 4, Thanksgiving, Dec 25. Res accepted. Bar. Wine list. A la carte entrees: lunch $4.95-$10, dinner $8.95-$28.95. Specializes in fresh regional seafood. Own baking. Turn-of-the-century decor. Cr cds: A, D, DS, MC, V.
D

★★★ **JAKE'S GRILL.** *611 SW 10th St (97205). 503/220-1850. www. mccormickandschmicks.com.* Hrs: 6:30 am-midnight; Fri to 1 am; Sat 7:30-1 am; Sun 7:30 am-11 pm. Res accepted. Bar. Bkfst $2.50-$11.95, lunch $4.95-$11.95, dinner $4.95-$18.50. Children's meals. Specializes in steak, salmon. Outdoor dining. Casual decor. Cr cds: A, D, DS, MC, V.
D

★★ **L'AUBERGE.** *2601 NW Vaughn St (97210). 503/223-3302. www. laubergepdx.com.* Hrs: 5-11 pm; Fri, Sat to midnight. Closed hols. Res accepted. French menu. Bar. Wine list. Complete meals: dinner $9.75-$36. Prix fixe: dinner $42, $60. Specializes in seafood, steak, lamb. Own baking. Parking. Outdoor dining. Tri level dining; wall hangings, 2 fireplaces. Family-owned. Cr cds: A, D, DS, MC, V.

★★★ **LONDON GRILL.** *309 SW Broadway (97205). 503/295-4110. www.bensonhotel.com.* Hrs: 6:30 am-2 pm, 5-9 pm; Fri, Sat to 10 pm; Sun brunch 9:30 am-2 pm. Res accepted. Continental menu. Bar 11-1 am. Wine cellar. Bkfst $7.75-$14.50, lunch $7.95-$14.95, dinner $25-$35. Sun brunch $27. Children's meals. Specialties: Northwest salmon, rack of lamb, ostrich. Harpist Wed-Sat. Valet parking. Elegant dining in historic hotel. Jacket (dinner). Cr cds: A, D, DS, JCB, MC, V.
D

★★ **MANDARIN COVE.** *111 SW Columbia (97201). 503/222-0006.* Hrs: 11 am-2 pm, 4:30-10 pm; Sat noon-

11 pm; Sun 4-10 pm. Res accepted. Mandarin, Chinese menu. Bar. Lunch $5.25-$7.50, dinner $6.50-$25.50. Specializes in Hunan and Szechwan meats and seafood. Cr cds: A, D, DS, MC, V.
D

★ **MAZZI'S ITALIAN-SICILIAN FOOD.** *5833 SW MacAdam Ave (97201). 503/227-3382. www.mazzis. com.* Hrs: 11:30 am-10 pm; Fri to 11 pm; Sat 5-11 pm; Sun 4-10 pm. Closed Thanksgiving, Dec 24, 25. Italian menu. Bar. Lunch $3.25-$7.95, dinner $6.95-$16.95. Specializes in fresh seafood, homemade pasta. Salad bar (lunch). Parking. Mediterranean decor; fireplaces. Totally nonsmoking. Cr cds: A, MC, V.
D

★★★ **MORTONS OF CHICAGO.** *213 Southwest Clay St (97201). 503/248-2100. www.mortons.com.* Specializes in double-cut filet mignon, porterhouse steak, lobster. Hrs: 5-11 pm. Closed hols. Res accepted. Wine list. Dinner $26.95-$32.95. Entertainment. Cr cds: A, D, JCB, MC, V.
D

★★ **MURATA.** *200 SW Market St (97201). 503/227-0080.* Hrs: 11:30 am-2 pm, 5:30-10 pm. Closed Sat, Sun; also hols. Res accepted. Japanese menu. Wine, beer. Lunch $5.95-$14.75, dinner $15.50-$26.50. Complete meal: $45. Specialties: sushi ban, kaiseki. Parking. Japanese atmosphere. Cr cds: A, D, MC, V.
D

★ **OLD SPAGHETTI FACTORY.** *0715 SW Bancroft St (97201). 503/222-5375. www.osf.com.* Hrs: 11:30 am-2 pm, 5-10 pm; Fri to 11 pm; Sat noon-11 pm; Sun noon-10 pm. Closed Thanksgiving, Dec 24-25. Italian menu. Bar. Lunch $3.50-$5.75, dinner $4.75-$8.50. Children's meals. Specializes in pasta. Own sauces. Parking. 1890s decor; dining in trolley car. Family-owned. Cr cds: A, D, DS, MC, V.
D

★★★ **ORITALIA.** *750 SW Alder St (97205). 503/295-0680. www.oritalia. net.* Specializes in seared eastern sea scallops, ginger steamed halibut. Hrs: 6:30 am-10 pm. Res accepted. Wine, beer. Lunch $3-$6.75; dinner $16-

$26. Brunch $5.75-$14. Entertainment. Cr cds: A, D, DS, MC, V.
D

★★★ **PALEY'S PLACE.** *1204 NW 21st Ave (97209). 503/243-2403. www.paleysplace.citysearch.com.* Hrs: 5:30-10 pm; Fri, Sat to 11 pm; Sun 5-10 pm; closed hols. Res accepted. French northwestern menu. Serv bar. Wine list. Dinner $18-$25. Specializes in local foods. Outdoor dining. Smoke-free interior dining. Cr cds: A, MC, V.
D

★★★ **PAZZO RISTORANTE.** *627 SW Washington (97205). 503/228-1515.* Hrs: 7-10:30 am, 11:30 am-2:30 pm, 5-10 pm; Fri, Sat 8-10:30 am, 11:30 am-2:30 pm, 5-11 pm; Sun from 8 am. Closed hols. Res accepted. Italian menu. Bar 11:30 am-midnight; Fri, Sat to 1 am. A la carte entrees: bkfst $4-$8, lunch $8-$15, dinner $8-$18. Specializes in hardwood oven-baked seafood, meat, fowl. Own bread, pasta. Outdoor dining. Italian marble floors, mahogany bar; also dining in wine cellar. Cr cds: A, D, DS, MC, V.
D

★★★ **PLAINFIELD'S MAYUR.** *852 SW 21st Ave (97205). 503/223-2995. www.plainfields.com.* Hrs: 5:30-10 pm. Closed Thanksgiving, Dec 25. Res accepted. East Indian menu. Serv bar. Wine cellar. A la carte entrees: dinner $7.95-$15.95. Specialties: spiced lamb, rack of lamb, duck in almond sauce. Own baking. Parking. Patio dining. In 1901, shingle-style mansion; centerpiece of dining room is functioning Indian clay oven (tandoor). Cr cds: A, D, DS, MC, V.
D

★ **POOR RICHARDS.** *3907 NE Broadway (97232). 503/288-5285. www.poorrichardstwofer.com.* Hrs: 11:30 am-11 pm; Sat 4-11 pm; Sun noon-9 pm. Closed hols. Res accepted. Bar. Lunch $5.50-$8, dinner $6.50-$16. Children's meals. Specializes in steak, seafood. Parking. Colonial decor; fireplace. Family-owned. Cr cds: A, DS, MC, V.
D

★★★ **PORTLAND STEAK & CHOPHOUSE.** *121 SW 3rd Ave (97204). 503/223-6200. www.portland*

chophouse.com. Hrs: 11 am-11 pm; Fri, Sat to midnight. Res accepted. Steakhouse menu. Bar. Lunch $8.95-$15, dinner $10-$30. Children's meals. Specialties: cedar plank salmon, filet mignon, double cut pork chop. Valet parking (dinner). Outdoor dining. Cr cds: A, D, DS, MC, V.
D

★★★ **RED STAR TAVERN & ROAST HOUSE.** *503 SW Alder St (97204). 503/222-0005. www. opentable.com.* Hrs: 6:30 am-2:30 pm, 5-10 pm; Fri to 11 pm; Sat 8 am-2:30 pm, 5-11 pm; Sun 8 am-10 pm. Closed hols. Res accepted. Bar. Bkfst $5.50-$8.25, lunch $8.95-$12.95, dinner $13-$20. Children's meals. Specialties: sage-roasted chicken with buttermilk mashed potatoes, rotisserie pork loin with sweet potato hash and roasted pear-onion jam. Wood-burning oven. Contemporary decor Cr cds: A, DS, MC, V.
D

★★ **RHEINLANDER.** *5035 NE Sandy Blvd (97213). 503/288-5503.* Hrs: 11 am-10 pm; Sat to midnight; early-bird dinner 4:30-6 pm, Sat from 4 pm, Sun from 3:30 pm. Closed Labor Day, Dec 24, 25. Res accepted. German menu. Bar. Lunch, dinner $10-$20. Children's meals. Specialties: hasenpfeffer, homemade sausage, rotisserie chicken. Strolling accordionist; group singing. Parking. Family-owned. Cr cds: A, MC, V.
D

★★ **RINGSIDE.** *2165 W Burnside St (97210). 503/223-1513. www.ringside steakhouse.com.* Hrs: 5 pm-midnight; Sun 4-11:30 pm. Closed July 4, Thanksgiving, Dec 24-25. Res accepted. Bar. Dinner $13.20-$39.95. Specializes in steak, prime rib, seafood. Valet parking. Fireplace. Prizefight pictures; sports decor. Family-owned. Cr cds: A, D, DS, MC, V.
D

★ **RINGSIDE EAST.** *14021 NE Glisan (97230). 503/255-0750.* Hrs: 11:30 am-2:30 pm, 5 pm-midnight; Sat from 5 pm; Sun from 4 pm. Closed hols. Res accepted. Bar. Lunch $4.50-$10.95, dinner $10.50-$36.75. Spe-

cializes in prime rib, steak, seafood. Parking. Cr cds: A, DS, MC, V.
D

★★ **SALTY'S ON THE COLUMBIA.** *3839 NE Marnie Dr (97211). 503/288-4444. www.saltys.com.* Hrs: 11:15 am-11 pm; Sun 2-10 pm; Fri, Sat June-Sept to midnight; Sun brunch 9:30 am-2 pm. Closed Dec 25. Res accepted. Bar. Lunch $7.25-$18.95, dinner $14-$37. Sun brunch buffet $8.95-$17.95. Children's meals. Specialties: halibut supreme, blackened salmon. Free valet parking. Outdoor dining. Overlooks Columbia River. Cr cds: A, D, DS, MC, V.
D

★★ **SAUCEBOX.** *214 SW Broadway (97205). 503/241-3393. www. citysearch.com.* Hrs: 11:30 am-2:30 pm, 6-10 pm; Sat 6-10 pm. Closed Sun; hols. Res accepted (dinner). Pan-Asian menu. Bar to 2 am. Lunch $7-$11, dinner $9-$13. Specialties: roast Japanese salmon, steamed shrimp dumplings, hamachi and avocado. Street parking. Outdoor dining. Contemporary decor. Cr cds: A, MC, V.
D

★ **SAYLER'S OLD COUNTRY KITCHEN.** *10519 SE Stark (97216). 503/252-4171.* Hrs: 4-11 pm; Fri to midnight; Sat 3 pm-midnight; Sun noon-11 pm. Closed hols. Bar. Complete meals: dinner $9.50-$45. Children's meals. Specializes in steak, seafood, chicken. Parking. Family-owned. Cr cds: A, DS, MC, V.
D SC

★ **SWAGAT INDIAN CUISINE.** *2074 NW Lovejoy (97209). 503/227-4300.* Hrs: 11:30 am-2:30 pm, 5-10 pm. Closed Thanksgiving, Dec 25. Southern and northern Indian menu. Bar. Dinner $9.95-$12.95. Buffet: lunch $5.95. Specialties: chicken tandoori, dosa. Parking. Outdoor dining. Indian atmosphere and decor. Cr cds: A, DS, MC, V.
D

★ **SYLVIA'S.** *5115 NE Sandy Blvd (97213). 503/288-6828. www.sylvias. net.* Hrs: 4-10 pm; Fri, Sat to 11 pm; early-bird dinner 4-6 pm. Closed Thanksgiving, Dec 24, 25. Res accepted; required for theater. Italian

menu. Bar. Dinner $7.75-$15.50. Children's meals. Specialties: lasagne, fettucine Alfredo, veal parmigiana. Parking. Dinner theater adj. Family-owned. Cr cds: A, DS, MC, V.
[D]

★★ **TYPHOON!.** *2310 NW Everett St (97201). 503/243-7557.* Hrs: 11:30 am-2:30 pm, 5-10 pm; Sun 4:30-9 pm. Closed hols. Res accepted. Thai menu. Wine, beer. Lunch $5.95-$8.95, dinner $6.95-$17.95. Specialties: miang kum, drunken noodles. Outdoor dining. Thai decor. Cr cds: A, D, DS, MC, V.
[D]

★ **WIDMER GASTHAUS.** *955 N Russell St (97227). 503/281-3333. www.widmer.com.* Hrs: 11 am-11 pm; Fri, Sat to 1 am; Sun noon-9 pm. Closed Jan 1, Thanksgiving, Dec 25. Res accepted. German, regional menu. Bar. Lunch $6.25-$8.50, dinner $6.25-$13.95. Specialties: schnitzel, sauerbraten. Outdoor dining. Totally nonsmoking. Cr cds: A, DS, MC, V.
[D]

★★★ **WILDWOOD.** *1221 NW 21st Ave (97209). 503/248-9663. www.citysearch.com/pdx/wildwood.* Pacific Northwest menu. Specialties: mussels, breast of duck, salmon. Hrs: 11:30 am-2:30 pm, 5:30-10 pm; Fri, Sat to 10:30 pm; Sun 10 am-2 pm (brunch), 5-8:30 pm. Closed Jan 1, Dec 25. Res accepted. Bar. Wine cellar. Lunch $8-$13, dinner $16-$27. Sun brunch $5.50-$13. Outdoor dining. Totally nonsmoking. Cr cds: A, MC, V.
[D]

★★ **WINTERBORNE.** *3520 NE 42nd (97213). 503/249-8486.* Hrs: 5:30-9:30 pm. Closed Sun-Tues; also Dec 25. Res accepted. French menu. Serv bar. Dinner $13.50-$19. Children's meals. Specializes in seafood. Contemporary decor. Totally nonsmoking. Cr cds: A, DS, MC, V.
[D]

Unrated Dining Spots

IVY HOUSE. *1605 SE Bybee (97202). 503/231-9528. www.ivyhouse.citysearch.com.* Hrs: 11 am-11 pm; Sat 9 am-11 pm; Sun 9 am-10 pm; Sat, Sun brunch 9 am-4 pm. Closed Tues, Wed; Thanksgiving, Dec 24, 25. Res accepted. Continental menu. Wine, beer. A la carte entrees: lunch $3.65-$6.50. Dinner $7.95-$18.95. Sat, Sun brunch $3.25-$9.95. Specializes in European pastries, creamed soups, sandwiches. Parking. Outdoor dining. Cr cds: MC, V.

ORIGINAL PANCAKE HOUSE. *8601 SW 24th Ave (97219). 503/246-9007. www.originalpancakehouse.com.* Hrs: 7 am-3 pm. Closed Mon, Tues. Bkfst, lunch $5-$10. Specialties: omelettes, apple pancakes, cherry crépes. Parking. Colonial decor.

PAPA HAYDN. *5829 SE Milwaukie (97202). 503/232-9440. www.papahaydn.citysearch.com.* Hrs: 11:30 am-11 pm; Fri, Sat to midnight. Closed Sun, Mon; hols. Continental menu. Wine, beer. Lunch $4.95-$6.95, dinner $6.95-$13.95. Specializes in European pastries, desserts. Outdoor dining. Cr cds: A, MC, V.

PERRY'S ON FREMONT. *2401 NE Fremont (97212). 503/287-3655.* Hrs: 4-9 pm; Fri, Sat to 10 pm. Closed Sun, Mon; hols. Bar. Lunch, dinner $9-$22. Children's meals. Specializes in desserts, fish and chips, steak. Outdoor dining. Murals. Totally nonsmoking. Cr cds: DS, MC, V.
[D]

Port Orford

(E-1) *See also Bandon, Gold Beach*

Founded 1851 **Pop** 1,025 **Elev** 56 ft **Area code** 541 **Zip** 97465

Information Chamber of Commerce, 502 Battle Rock City Park, PO Box 637; 541/332-8055

Web www.portorfordoregon.com

Westernmost incorporated city in the contiguous United States, Port Orford overlooks the Pacific Ocean with spectacular views. This was the first settlement in Coos and Curry counties. Captain George Vancouver sighted this area in 1792 and named it for the Earl of Orford. The cedar trees that grow in the area (sometimes called Lawson cypress and later named for the Earl) are highly favored for boat construction.

What to See and Do

Battle Rock Wayside. Site of one of the fiercest Native American battles on the Oregon Coast (1851); explanation of battle is inscribed on a marker in the park. Battle Rock offers one of the best seascapes in the state and has an ocean beach, surfing. Hiking trail. S edge of town on US 101. Phone 541/332-4106.

Cape Blanco State Park. A 1,880-acre park with ocean beach, observation point; historic lighthouse (1870). Fishing; river access for boats. Hiking. Picnicking. Horse camp, beach access/horse trails, rustic cabins. Improved campsites. Standard fees. 9 mi N off US 101. Phone 541/332-6774. In the park is the

> **Historic Hughes House.** (1898). Restored Victorian house. (May-Sept, Thurs-Mon and hols) Phone 541/332-4106. **Donation**

Fishing. Ocean fishing provides salmon, ling cod, perch, snapper and crabs. Fall fishing in the Elk and Sixes rivers provides catches of chinook salmon and trout. **Garrison Lake**, at the NW edge of town, is open all yr for trout and bass fishing. Also swimming, waterskiing; boat ramp. Phone 541/332-7121.

Humbug Mountian State Park. A 1,842-acre park with winding trail leading to summit (1,750 ft); peak looks out on virgin forest, trout streams, sand beach. Fishing. Hiking. Picnicking. Tent and trailer sites (dump station). Standard fees. 6 mi S on US 101. Phone 541/332-6774.

Prineville

(C-4) *See also Bend, Madras, Redmond*

Founded 1868 **Pop** 5,355 **Elev** 2,864 ft **Area code** 541 **Zip** 97754
Information Prineville-Crook County Chamber of Commerce, 390 N Fairview; 541/447-6304

Two-thirds of the population of Crook County lives in or near Prineville. Livestock, alfalfa, wheat, mint, sugar beets, and lumbering are important in this county. Hunting, fishing, and rockhounding are popular. The City of Prineville Railroad, 19 miles of main line connecting the Union Pacific and Oregon Trunk Railway, is one of the few municipally-owned railroads in the United States. Two Ranger District offices and headquarters of the Ochoco National Forest are located here.

What to See and Do

Mineral collecting. Agates of various types, obsidian, petrified wood, geodes and other stones. More than 1,000 acres of digging space in Eagle Rock, Maury Mtn, White Rock Springs, and other areas. Obtain info from Chamber of Commerce. Phone 541/447-6304.

Ochoco Lake Campground. A 10-acre juniper-covered promontory on the N shore of Ochoco Reservoir. Fishing; boating (ramp). Hiking. Picnicking. Improved tent and trailer sites. Standard fees. 7 mi E on US 26. Phone 541/447-1209.

Ochoco National Forest. An approx 848,000-acre forest plus 111,000-acre Crooked River National Grassland; central Oregon high desert; thunderegg deposits; stands of ponderosa pine. Fishing in streams, Walton and Delintment lakes, Haystack and Antelope reservoirs; hunting. Hiking trails. Winter sports. Picnicking. Camping (fee). E on US 26. Phone 541/447-6247.

Redmond

(C-4) *See also Bend, Madras, Prineville*

Pop 7,163 **Elev** 2,997 ft
Area code 541 **Zip** 97756
Information Chamber of Commerce, 446 SW 7th St; 541/923-5191 or 800/574-1325
Web www.nt.empnet.com/rchamber/

Popular with sports enthusiasts and tourists, this is also the agricultural, lumbering, and industrial center of central Oregon. A Ranger District office of the Deschutes National Forest (see BEND) is located here. The US Forest Service Redmond Regional Air Center is located at Roberts Field.

What to See and Do

Firemen's Lake. Children's fishing pond. Three-acre lake stocked with bass, bluegill. Children under 14 and disabled persons only. (Mid-Apr-mid-Oct, daily) Lake Rd and Sisters Ave. Phone 541/548-6068. **FREE**

Petersen Rock Gardens. Model castles and bridges built with rock specimens; lagoons and flower beds; picnicking, fireplaces; museum. (Daily) 7930 SW 77th St, 7 mi S on US 97, then 2½ mi W. Phone 541/382-5574. ¢¢

State parks.

    Cline Falls. A nine-acre park on the banks of the Deschutes River. Fishing. Picnicking. 4 mi W on OR 126. Phone 541/388-6055.

    Peter Skene Ogden Wayside. A 98-acre park with canyon 400 ft wide, 304 ft deep. Picnicking. Observation point. 9 mi N on US 97. Phone 541/548-7501.

    Smith Rock. A 623-acre park with view of unusual multicolored volcanic and sedimentary rock formations and the Crooked River Canyon. Crooked River Gorge (403 ft deep) is 3 mi N. Fishing. Hiking, rock climbing. Picnicking. 9 mi NE off US 97. Phone 541/548-7501.

Special Event

Deschutes County Fair and Rodeo. First wk Aug. Phone 541/548-2711.

Motels/Motor Lodges

★★ **BEST WESTERN RAMA INN.** *2630 SW 17th Pl (97756). 541/548-8080; fax 541/548-3705; res 800/528-1234. www.bestwestern.com.* 49 rms, 2 story. S $57-$110; D $62-$130; under 12 free. Crib $4. TV; cable (premium), VCR avail. Indoor pool; whirlpool. Complimentary continental bkfst. Restaurant nearby. Ck-out 11 am. Coin lndry. Business servs avail. In-rm modem link. Free airport transportation. Exercise equipt. Refrigerators. Cr cds: A, DS, MC, V.
✕ ≈ ☂ ♨

★ **REDMOND INN.** *1545 Hwy 97 S (97756). 541/548-1091; fax 541/548-*0415; *toll-free 800/833-3259.* 46 rms, 3 story, 6 kits. No elvtr. Mid-May-Sept: S $39.99-$53; D $49-$63; each addl $5; kit. units $63; under 12 free; lower rates rest of yr. Crib free. Pet accepted, some restrictions; $5. TV; cable. Heated pool. Complimentary continental bkfst. Restaurant opp 7 am-11 pm. Ck-out 11 am. Refrigerators, microwaves. Cr cds: A, C, D, DS, MC, V.
D ♪ ≈ ✕ ☂ ♨ SC

★ **TRAVELODGE NEW REDMOND HOTEL.** *521 S 6th St (97756). 541/923-7378; fax 541/923-3949; toll-free 800/726-2466. www.travelodge. com.* 48 rms, 3 story. S, D $48-$70; each addl $5; suites $65-$80; under 12 free. TV; cable. Complimentary continental bkfst. Restaurant 11 am-10 pm. Bar to midnight. Ck-out 11 am. Meeting rms. Shopping arcade. Free airport transportation. Exercise equipt. Built 1927. Grand lobby; fireplace, wood beam ceiling, grandfather clock. Cr cds: A, C, D, DS, MC, V.
D ☂ ✕ ☂ ♨

★ **VILLAGE SQUIRE MOTEL.** *629 SW 5th St (97756). 541/548-2105; fax 541/548-5427; toll-free 800/548-2102. www.villagesquiremotel.com.* 24 rms, 2 story. S $40-$45; D $45-$50; each addl $5. Crib $5. TV; cable (premium), VCR avail. Complimentary coffee in lobby. Restaurant nearby. Ck-out 11 am. Some refrigerators, microwaves. Cr cds: A, DS, MC, V.
♨

Resort

★★ **EAGLE CREST RESORT.** *1522 Cline Falls Rd (97756). 541/923-2453; fax 541/923-1720; toll-free 800/682-4786. www.eagle-crest.com.* 100 rms, 2 story, 43 kit. suites. Mid-Mar-Oct: S $69-$96; D $76-$101; kit. suites $93-$128; ski, golf plans; higher rates national hols; lower rates rest of yr. Crib free. TV; cable (premium), VCR avail. Heated pool; whirlpool. Playground. Supervised children's activities (mid-June-early Sept); ages 6-12. Dining rm 7 am-9 pm. Bar from 4 pm. Ck-out noon, ck-in 4 pm. Coin lndry. Business servs avail. Grocery. Meeting rms. Gift shop. Beauty shop. Free airport transportation. Lighted tennis, pro. Two 18-hole golf, greens fee $42, pro, putting green, driving range. Hiking, bicycle trails. Exercise rm. Lawn games. Microwave in suites. Balconies. Picnic tables, grills. On Deschutes River. Cr cds: A, D, DS, MC, V.

Restaurant

★★ **MRS. BEASLEY'S.** *1555 S Hwy 97 (97756).* 541/548-4023. Hrs: 6:30 am-10 pm; Sun brunch 9:30 am-2 pm. Closed Dec 25. Bar from 11:30 am. Bkfst $3-$6, lunch $4-$7, dinner $5-$24. Children's meals. Specializes in seafood, prime rib. Salad bar. Own baking. Cr cds: A, D, DS, MC, V.

Reedsport

(D-1) *See also Coos Bay, Florence, North Bend*

Pop 4,796 **Elev** 10 ft **Area code** 541 **Zip** 97467

Information Chamber of Commerce, PO Box 11; 541/271-3495 or 800/247-2155

Web www.coos.or.us/~reewbycc

Surrounded by rivers, lakes, and the ocean, the area has an abundance and variety of fish, particularly striped bass, steelhead, and salmon. Two of the best bass fishing lakes in Oregon are nearby. Reedsport was originally marshland subject to flooding at high tides, so the earliest buildings and sidewalks were built 3-8 feet above ground. A dike was built after the destructive Christmastime flood of 1964 to shield the lower part of town.

What to See and Do

Dean Creek Elk Viewing Area. Area has 440 acres of pasture and bottomland where Roosevelt elk (Oregon's largest land mammal) and other wildlife can be viewed. Interpretive center. No hunting. (Daily) 3 mi E on OR 38. Contact Bureau of Land Management, 1300 Airport Ln, North Bend 97459; Phone 541/756-0100. **FREE**

Oregon Dunes National Recreation Area. Large coastal sand dunes, forests and wetlands comprise this 32,000-acre area in Siuslaw National Forest (see CORVALLIS). Beachcombing; fishing; boating. Hiking, horseback riding, off-road vehicle areas. Picnicking. Camping (fee; some campgrounds closed Oct-May). Visitors center and headquarters in Reedsport at US 101 and OR 38 (daily). W off US 101. Phone 541/271-3611.

Salmon Harbor. Excellent boat basin for charter boats, pleasure and fishing craft. Fishing for silver and chinook salmon in ocean, a short run from mouth of the Umpqua River (May-Sept, daily; rest of yr, Mon-Fri). Phone 541/271-3407.

Umpqua Discovery Center. Interpretive displays centering on cultural and natural history of area. (Daily; closed Jan 1, Thanksgiving, Dec 25) 409 Riverfront Way. Phone 541/271-4816. ¢¢

Umpqua Lighthouse State Park. This 450-acre park touches the mouth of the Umpqua River, borders the Umpqua Lighthouse Reservation, and skirts the ocean shore for more than two mi with sand dunes rising 500 ft (highest in US). Noted for its marvelous, seasonal display of rhododendrons. Swimming; fishing. Hiking; trail to beach and around Lake Marie. Picnicking. Tent and trailer sites. Whale watching area. Standard fees. 6 mi S off US 101. Phone 541/271-4118.

William M. Tugman State Park. A 560-acre park in scenic coastal lake region. Swimming; bathhouse; fishing; boating (ramp to Eel Lake). Picnicking. Improved tent and trailer sites (dump station). Standard fees. 8 mi S on US 101. Phone 541/759-3604.

Motels/Motor Lodges

★ **ANCHOR BAY INN.** *1821 Hwy 101 (97467).* 541/271-2149; fax 541/271-1802; toll-free 800/767-1821. 21 rms, 2 story, 4 kits. S $48; D $59; kit. units $60-$65. Pet accepted, some restrictions; $5/day. TV; cable (premium), VCR avail. Pool. Complimentary continental bkfst. Restaurant nearby. Ck-out 10 am. Coin lndry. Business servs avail. Some refrigerators, microwaves. Cr cds: A, C, D, DS, MC, V.

★★ **BEST WESTERN.** *1400 Hwy Ave (97467). 541/271-4831; fax 541/271-4832; res 800/528-1234. www. bestwestern.com.* 56 rms, 2 story, 9 suites, 2 kit. units. Late May-mid-Sept: S $64-$79; D $78-$98; each addl $5; suites $95-$130; kit. units $95-$120; lower rates rest of yr. Crib free. Pet accepted; $5. TV; cable (premium), VCR avail. Indoor pool; whirlpool. Complimentary continental bkfst. Restaurant nearby. Ck-out 11 am. Coin lndry. Meeting rms. Business servs avail. Exercise equipt. Minibars; refrigerators. Near Scholfield River. Cr cds: A, C, D, DS, MC, V.

★ **BEST WESTERN SALBASGEON INN AND SUITES.** *1400 Hwy Ave 101 (97467). 541/271-4831; fax 541/271-4832; res 800/528-1234. www.bestwestern.com.* 12 rms, 2 story, 1 suite, 4 kit. units. Late May-mid-Sept: S $52-$68; D $65-$78; each addl $5; suite $71-$94; kit. units $73-$99; lower rates rest of yr. Pet accepted, some restrictions; $5/day. TV; cable (premium). Ck-out 11 am. Picnic tables. On Umpqua River. All rms have river views. Cr cds: A, C, D, DS, MC, V.

Rockaway

(A-1) *See also Cannon Beach, Seaside, Tillamook*

Pop 970 **Elev** 16 ft **Area code** 503 **Zip** 97136

Information Rockaway Beach Chamber of Commerce 103 S First St, PO Box 198; 503/355-8108 or 800/331-5928

Rockaway is an attractive resort area with a fine, wide beach.

Motel/Motor Lodge

★ **SURFSIDE MOTEL.** *101 NW 11th Ave, Rockaway Beach (97136). 503/355-2312; toll-free 800/243-7786.* 79 units, 1-2 story. No A/C. Mid-

May-mid-Sept: S $48.50-$98.50; D $110.50-$149.50; kit. units $79.50-$149.50; lower rates rest of yr. Crib $5. Pet accepted; $10. TV; cable. Indoor pool. Restaurant nearby. Ck-out noon. Many fireplaces. On ocean; beach access. Cr cds: A, DS, MC, V.

Roseburg (E-2)

Settled 1853 **Pop** 17,032 **Elev** 459 ft **Area code** 541 **Zip** 97470

Information Visitors and Convention Bureau, 410 Spruce St, PO Box 1262; 541/672-9731 or 800/444-9584

Web www.oregonnews.com/visitroseburg.html

Roseburg is in one of Oregon's big stands of virgin timber that supports lumbermills and plywood plants. Although roses were the local pride, the town's name came not from the flower but from Aaron Rose, an early settler. This is the seat of Douglas County and headquarters for Umpqua National Forest.

What to See and Do

Douglas County Museum of History and Natural History. Exhibits incl early history and natural history displays of the region; photographic collection; research library. Also Regional Tourist Information. (Daily) 1 mi S via I-5, exit 123 at fairgrounds. Phone 541/440-4507. ¢¢

Umpqua National Forest. Paved scenic byway takes one through magnificent scenery to Diamond Lake, which offers fishing (rainbow, steelhead trout) and forest camps. Mt Thielsen (9,182 ft) and Mt Bailey (8,363 ft) tower above the lake. The Colliding Rivers Visitor Information Center (daily) is located along OR 138 in Glide; Diamond Lake Visitor Center (summer) is located opp entrance to Diamond Lake Campground. The forest (nearly one million acres), named for Native Americans who once fished in the rivers, incl three wilderness areas: Boulder Creek, 19,100 acres, Mt

Thielsen, 22,700 acres, and Roque-Umpqua Divide, 29,000 acres. Also the Oregon Cascades Recreation Area, 35,500 acres. Picnicking, lodging, hiking, camping (fee). Direct access from OR 138, along North Umpqua River. Contact Forest Supervisor, 2900 NW Stewart Pkwy, PO Box 1008. Phone 541/672-6601.

Wildlife Safari. A 600-acre drive-through animal park; 600 exotic specimens of African, Asian and North American wildlife in natural habitats; petting zoo; elephant and train rides (seasonal); guided and walk-through tours by res; restaurant. (Daily) 6 mi S on I 5, exit 119 to OR 42 for 4 mi, in Winston. Phone 541/679-6761. ¢¢¢¢

Wineries.

   Callahan Ridge Winery. Tasting rm. (Apr-Oct, daily; other times call for appt) W of I-5; Garden Valley exit 125, 2 mi W to Melrose then 1 mi S to Busenbark Ln, then right. Phone 541/673-7901. **FREE**

   Henry Estate Winery. Tours, tasting rm; picnic area. (Daily; closed major hols) 13 mi NW via I-5, 1 mi W of Umpqua on County 6. Phone 541/459-5120. **FREE**

   Hillcrest Vineyard. Wine tastings; tours. (Daily; closed hols) Approx 10 mi W; I-5 exit 125, W on Garden Valley Rd, Melrose Rd, Doerner Rd then N on Elgarose and follow signs. Phone 541/673-3709. **FREE**

Special Events

Greatest of the Grape. Mid-Feb. Phone 541/672-9731.

Spring Craft Fair. Late Mar. Phone 541/672-9731.

Umpqua Valley Roundup. Wkend mid-June. Phone 541/672-5777.

Roseburg Graffiti Week. '50's car show & activities. First wk July. Phone 541/672-9731.

Douglas County Fair. Early Aug. Phone 541/957-7010.

Wildlife Safari Wildlights. Dec. Phone 541/679-9210.

Motels/Motor Lodges

★ **BEST INN & SUITES.** 427 NW Garden Valley Blvd (97470). 541/673-5561; fax 541/957-0318. 72 rms, 1-2 story. S $39-$55; D $49-$65; each addl $5; under 12 free. Crib $5. Pet accepted. TV; cable. Pool. Complimentary continental bkfst. Ck-out 11 am. Meeting rm. Business servs avail. Some microwaves. Cr cds: A, D, DS, MC, V.

★★ **BEST WESTERN DOUGLAS INN.** 511 SE Stephens St (97470). 541/673-6625; fax 541/677-9610; toll-free 877/368-4466. www.bestwestern.com. 52 rms, 2 story. June-Sept: S $49-$68; D $60-$76; each addl $5; lower rates rest of yr. Crib $5. TV; cable (premium). Complimentary coffee. Restaurant opp 6 am-10 pm. Ck-out noon. Business servs avail. In-rm modem link. Exercise equipt; sauna. Whirlpool. Cr cds: A, DS, MC, V.

★★ **BEST WESTERN GARDEN VILLA MOTEL.** 760 NW Garden Valley Blvd (97470). 541/672-1601; fax 541/672-1316; res 800/547-3446. www.bestwestern.com. 122 rms, 2 story. June-Sept: S $51-$69; D $57-$76; each addl $7; under 12 free; lower rates rest of yr. Crib $5. Pet accepted, some restrictions. TV; cable (premium), VCR avail (movies). Heated pool. Complimentary continental bkfst. Restaurant adj 5 am-midnight. Ck-out noon. Coin lndry. Meeting rms. Sundries. Exercise equipt. Microwaves avail. Cr cds: A, C, D, DS, ER, JCB, MC, V.

★ **TRAVELODGE.** 315 W Harvard Ave (97470). 541/672-4836; toll-free 800/578-7878. www.travelodge.com. 40 rms, 1-2 story. S $47-$65; D $63-$80; each addl $5; under 17 free. Crib free. TV; cable (premium). Heated pool. Complimentary coffee in rms. Restaurant adj 5 am-midnight. Ck-out 11 am. Valet serv. Balconies. Picnic tables. On river. Cr cds: A, D, DS, MC, V.

★★ **WINDMILL INN OF ROSE-BURG.** 1450 NW Mulholland Dr (97470). 541/673-0901; toll-free 800/547-4747. www.windmillinns.com. 128 rms, 2 story. June-Sept: S, D $65-$72; each addl $6; under 18 free; lower rates rest of yr. Crib $3.50. Pet accepted, some restrictions. TV; cable (premium). Pool; whirlpool. Complimentary continental bkfst. Restaurants 6 am-midnight. Bar. Ck-out 11 am. Guest lndry. Meeting rms. Business servs avail. In-rm modem link. Valet serv. Sundries. Free airport, bus depot transportation. Exercise equipt; sauna. Microwaves avail. Some balconies. Cr cds: A, C, D, DS, MC, V.

D ♠ ⓛ ⌷ 𝍐 ✈ ⊠ 🐾 SC

Salem

(B-2) *See also Albany, McMinnville, Newberg, Oregon City, Portland, Silverton*

Settled 1840 **Pop** 107,786 **Elev** 154 ft
Area code 503

Information Convention and Visitors Association, 1313 Mill St SE, 97301; 503/581-4325 or 800/874-7012

Web www.scva.org

Capital and third-largest city in Oregon, Salem's economy is based on the state government, food processing, light manufacturing, agriculture, and wood products. Salem shares Oregon's sports attractions with other cities of the Willamette Valley.

What to See and Do

A.C. Gilbert's Discovery Village. Hands-on exhibits related to art, drama, music, science and nature. (Mon-Sat, also Sun afternoons) 116 Marion St. Phone 503/371-3631. ¢¢

Bush House. Victorian mansion (1878) with authentic furnishings. (Tues-Sun; closed hols) Bush's Pasture Park. 600 Mission St SE, 6 blks S of capitol. Phone 503/363-4714. ¢¢ Also here is

> **Bush Barn Art Center.** Remodeled barn houses two exhibit galleries with monthly shows and a sales gallery featuring Northwest artists. (Tues-Sun; closed hols) Phone 503/581-2228. **FREE**

Enchanted Forest. Features storybook theme. Other exhibits incl reproduction of early mining town, haunted house (fee), log flume ride (fee), ice mountain bobsled ride (fee), kiddie bumper boats & kiddie ferris wheel (fee), old world village, theater featuring live comedy and children's shows, water and light show. Picnic area; refreshments; gift stores. (Mid-Mar-Mar 31, May 1-Labor Day, daily; Apr and Sept, wkends only) 7 mi S, off I-5 Sunnyside-Turner exit 248, at 8462 Enchanted Way SE. Phone 503/363-3060. ¢¢¢

Historic Deepwood Estate. (1894) Queen Anne-style house and carriage house designed by W.C. Knighton. Povey Brothers stained-glass windows, golden oak woodwork; solarium; Lord and Schryver gardens with wrought-iron gazebo from 1905, boxwood gardens, perennial garden with English teahouse; nature trail. House (May-Sept, Mon-Fri, Sun; rest of yr, Tues-Sat; closed major hols). 1116 Mission St SE. Phone 503/363-1825. ¢

Honeywood Winery. Oregon's oldest producing winery. Tours, tasting rm, gift shop. (Daily; closed Thanksgiving, Dec 25) 1350 Hines St SE. Phone 503/362-4111. **FREE**

Mission Mill Museum. Thomas Kay Woolen Mill Museum (1889) shows process of processing fleece into fabric. Jason Lee House (1841), John D. Boon House (1847), Methodist Parsonage (1841), and Pleasant Grove-Presbyterian Church (1858) help interpret missionary family life. Shops, park, picnicking. Tours of woolen mill, historic houses (Mon-Sat, daily; closed Jan 1, Thanksgiving, Dec 25). 1313 Mill St SE. Phone 503/585-7012. ¢¢¢

State Capitol. (1938) Marble, of modern Greek design. Atop the capitol is a fluted tower topped by a bronze, gold-leafed statue symbolic of the pioneers who carved Oregon out of the wilderness. Tours of capitol (June-Aug, daily; rest of yr by appt). Capitol building (daily; closed Thanksgiving, Dec 25). Video; gift shop. 900 Court St NE Phone 503/986-1388. **FREE** N of here is the

> **Capitol Mall.** Flanked by four state buildings in modern Greek style, including the Public Service, Transportation, Labor and Industries and State Library buildings. The grounds are an arboretum with historical statuary and monuments. Phone 503/986-1388.

Multnomah Falls, Columbia River Gorge

Willamette University. (1842) 2,500 students. Oldest institution of higher learning west of Missouri River, with several historic buildings on campus incl Waller Hall (1867) and the Art Building (1905) with the Hallie Brown Ford Art Gallery. The Mark O. Hatfield Library has special area for research and viewing of Senator Hatfield's public papers. Campus tours; picnic area. 900 State St, between 12th and Winter Sts. Phone 503/370-6300.

Special Events

Salem Art Fair and Festival. Bush's Pasture Park. Arts and crafts booths and demonstrations, children's art activities and parade, ethnic folk arts, performing arts, street painting, 5K run, food; tours of historic Bush House. Phone Salem Art Association 503/581-2228. July 21-23.

West Salem Waterfront Parade. Mid-Aug. Phone 503/362-3601.

Oregon State Fair. Fairgrounds, 2330 17th St NE. Horse racing, wine competition and tasting, agricultural exhibits, horse show, livestock, food, carnival, entertainment. Phone 503/947-3247. End of Aug through first week of Sept.

Motels/Motor Lodges

★ ★ **BEST WESTERN NEW KINGS INN.** *1600 Motor Ct NE (97301). 503/581-1559; fax 503/364-4272; toll-free 877/594-1110. www.bestwestern.com.* 101 rms, 2 story. Mid-May-Oct: S $61-$63; D $63-$68; each addl $6; some lower rates rest of yr. Crib $4. TV; cable (premium). Indoor pool; whirlpool. Playground. Restaurant adj open 24 hrs. Ck-out noon. Coin lndry. Meeting rm. Business servs avail. Free airport, RR station, bus depot transportation. Tennis. Exercise equipt; sauna. Refrigerators, microwaves. Cr cds: A, C, D, DS, MC, V.

🄳 ⌨ 🏊 🍴 ✈ 🛏 🔥 SC

★ **PHOENIX INN.** *4370 Commercial St SE (97302). 503/588-9220; fax 503/585-3616; toll-free 800/445-4498. www.phoenixinn.com.* 89 rms, 4 story. S $62-$90; D $67-$90; each addl $5; suites $115-$125; under 17 free. Crib free. Pet accepted, some restrictions; $10. TV; cable (premium). Indoor pool; whirlpool. Complimentary continental bkfst. Ck-out noon. Coin lndry. Meeting rms. Business servs avail. Exercise equipt. Refrigerators. Some suites with whirlpool. Cr cds: A, C, D, DS, MC, V.

🄳 🕊 🏊 🍴 🛏 🔥 SC

★ ★ **RED LION HOTEL SALEM.** *3301 Market St (97301). 503/370-7888; fax 503/370-6305; toll-free 800/248-6273. www.redlion.com.* 150 rms, 4 story. S, D $80; each addl $5; suites $107-$112; under 18 free. Crib free. Pet accepted; $25. TV; cable (premium), VCR avail. Indoor pool; whirlpool. Complimentary coffee in rms. Restaurant 6:30 am-10 pm. Bar 11-1 am; entertainment Sat. Ck-out 11 am. Coin lndry. Meeting rms. Business servs avail. Bellhops. Sundries. Valet serv. Exercise equipt; sauna. Balconies. Cr cds: A, C, D, DS, ER, JCB, MC, V.

★★ **SHILO INN.** *3304 Market St NE (97301). 503/581-4001; fax 503/399-9385; toll-free 800/222-2244. www. shiloinns.com.* 89 rms, 4 story. S, D $59.95-$94.95; each addl $10; under 12 free. Crib free. TV; cable (premium), VCR. Heated pool; whirlpool. Complimentary continental bkfst. Ck-out noon. Business servs avail. In-rm modem link. Free airport transportation. Exercise equipt; sauna. Refrigerators, wet bars. Cr cds: A, C, D, DS, ER, JCB, MC, V.

★ **TIKI LODGE.** *3705 Market St NE (97305). 503/581-4441.* 50 rms, 20 with shower only, 2 story. Mid-May-Sept: S $49-$52; D $52-$58; each addl $4; under 12 free; wkly rates; lower rates rest of yr. Crib $2. Pet accepted. TV; cable (premium). Heated pool. Sauna. Complimentary coffee in lobby. Restaurant adj open 24 hrs. Ck-out noon. Meeting rms. Business servs avail. Cr cds: A, D, DS, MC, V.

B&B/Small Inn

★★ **A CREEKSIDE INN THE MAR-QUEE HOUSE.** *33 Wyatt Ct NE (97301). 503/391-0837; fax 503/391-1713; res 800/949-0837. www. marqueehouse.com.* 5 rms, 2 share bath, 1 with shower only. No A/C. S $70; D $75; each addl $15; ski plans; hols, special events: 2-day min. Children over 14 yrs only. Cable TV in common rm; movies. Ck-out 11 am, ck-in 4-6 pm. In-rm modem link. Concierge serv. Airport, RR station transportation. Lawn games. Built in 1938. Totally nonsmoking. Cr cds: D, DS, MC, V.

Restaurants

★★★ **ALESSANDRO'S.** *120 NE Commercial St (97301). 503/370-9951. www.alessandros120.com.* Hrs: 11:30

am-2 pm, 5:30-9 pm; Fri, Sat 5:30-10 pm. Closed Sun; major hols. Res accepted. Italian menu. Bar. Wine cellar. Lunch $6.25-$10.50, dinner $9.50-$18.50. Prix fixe: dinner $32. Children's meals. Specializes in seafood, poultry, veal. Overlooks park, waterfall. Cr cds: A, DS, MC, V.

★★ **KWAN ORIGINAL CUISINE.** *835 Commerical St SE (97302). 503/362-7711.* Hrs: 11:30 am-10 pm; Fri, Sat to 11 pm; Sun to 9:30 pm. Closed hols. Res accepted. Chinese menu. Bar. Lunch $5-$8, dinner $7-$12. Children's meals. Specialties: emu, mango chicken with plum sauce, barbecue duck. Parking. Chinese decor; wooden Buddha. Cr cds: A, D, DS, MC, V.

Seaside

(A-1) *See also Astoria, Cannon Beach*

Pop 5,359 **Elev** 13 ft **Area code** 503 **Zip** 97138

Information Chamber of Commerce, 7 N Roosevelt, PO Box 7; 503/738-6391 or 800/444-6740

Web www.clatsop.com/seaside

Seaside is the largest and oldest seashore town in Oregon. It has a concrete promenade two miles long; ocean beaches provide clam digging, surfing, surf fishing, and beachcombing.

What to See and Do

Saddle Mountain State Park. A 2,922-acre park with trail to 3,283-ft summit, one of the highest in the Coastal Range. Hiking. Picnicking. Primitive campsites. Standard fees. 13 mi SE on US 26, then 9 mi N. Phone 503/368-5154.

Seaside Aquarium. Deep-sea life and trained seals; seal feeding (fee); (Mar-Nov, daily; rest of yr, Wed-Sun; closed Thanksgiving, Dec 24, 25) 200 N Prom, on beach. Phone 503/738-6211. ¢¢

Motels/Motor Lodges

★★ **BEST WESTERN OCEAN VIEW RESORT.** *414 N Prom (97138). 503/738-3334; fax 503/738-3264; res 800/234-8439. www.oceanviewresort. com.* 104 rms, 5 story, 20 suites, 45 kit. units. No A/C. June-Aug: S, D, kit. units $60-$250; suites $195-$265; under 18 free; lower rates rest of yr. Crib free. Pet accepted, some restrictions; $15. TV. Indoor pool; whirlpool. Restaurant 7 am-10 pm. Bar 4 pm-midnight. Ck-out 11 am. Coin lndry. Meeting rms. Business servs avail. In-rm modem link. Many refrigerators. Balconies. On beach. Cr cds: A, C, D, DS, MC, V.

★★ **EBB TIDE MOTEL.** *300 N Prom (97138). 503/738-8371; fax 503/738-0938; toll-free 800/468-6232. www. ebbtide.citysearch.com.* 99 rms, 3-4 story, 48 kits. No A/C. May-Sept: S, D $80-$120; kit. units $70-$120; lower rates rest of yr. Crib $5. TV; cable (premium), VCR avail. Indoor pool; whirlpool. Restaurant nearby. Ck-out noon. Coin lndry. Business servs avail. In-rm modem link. Exercise equipt; sauna. Refrigerators. On beach. Cr cds: A, D, DS, MC, V.

★★ **GEARHART BY THE SEA RESORT.** *1157 N Marion Ave, Gearhart (97138). 503/738-8331; fax 503/738-0881; toll-free 800/547-0115. www.gearhartresort.com.* 80 condominiums, 1-5 story. No A/C. Condos $119-$184; each addl $10. Crib $5. TV; cable, VCR avail (movies). Indoor pool. Restaurant 7 am-9 pm; off-season hrs vary. Bar to 2:30 am. Ck-out 11 am. Coin lndry. Meeting rm. 18-hole golf, greens fee $27, pro, putting green. Balconies. Ocean view. Cr cds: A, DS, MC, V.

★★ **HI-TIDE MOTEL.** *30 Ave G (97138). 503/738-8414; fax 503/738-0875; toll-free 800/621-9876. www. hitide.citysearch.com.* 64 rms, 3 story, 64 kits. (no ovens). No A/C. No elvtr. May-Sept: S, D, kit. units $85-$120; lower rates rest of yr. Crib $5. TV; cable (premium), VCR avail. Indoor pool; whirlpool. Restaurant nearby. Ck-out noon. Business servs avail. On ocean. Cr cds: A, C, D, DS, MC, V.

★★ **SHILO INN.** *30 N Prom (97138). 503/738-9571; fax 503/738-0674; res 800/222-2244. www.shiloinn.com.* 112 rms, 5 story, 60 kit. units. No A/C. July-Labor Day: S, D $69-$209; each addl $15; under 12 free; lower rates rest of yr. Crib free. Free garage parking. TV; cable (premium), VCR avail (movies). Indoor pool; whirlpool. Restaurant 7 am-9 pm. Bar 11-2 am. Ck-out noon. Coin lndry. Meeting rms. Business servs avail. Valet serv. Sundries. Free airport transportation. Exercise equipt; sauna. Game rm. Some balconies. On ocean. Cr cds: A, C, D, DS, ER, JCB, MC, V.

★★ **SHILO INN SEASIDE EAST.** *900 S Holladay Dr (97138). 503/738-0549; fax 503/738-0532. www. shiloinn.com.* 58 rms, 3 story. Mid-Apr-early Sept: S, D $45-$135; under 12 free; higher rates hols; lower rates rest of yr. Crib free. TV; cable (premium), VCR avail. Indoor pool; whirlpool. Steam rm, sauna. Complimentary continental bkfst. Restaurant nearby. Ck-out noon. Coin lndry. Business servs avail. Airport transportation. Health club privileges. Bathrm phones. Cr cds: A, C, D, DS, MC, V.

B&Bs/Small Inns

★★ **CUSTER HOUSE BED & BREAKFAST.** *811 1st Ave (97138). 503/738-7825; fax 503/738-4324; res 800/738-7852. www.clatsop.com/ custer.* 6 rms, 5 with shower only, 2 story, 3 cottages. No A/C. Mid-May-mid-Oct: S, D $65-$75; each addl $10; package plans; wkends 2-day min; lower rates rest of yr. Cable TV in some rms; VCR avail. Complimentary full bkfst (main house only). Complimentary coffee in rms (cottages only). Restaurant nearby. Ck-out 11 am, ck-in 3 pm. Business servs avail. Luggage handling. Concierge serv. Refrigerator, microwave, fireplace in cottages. Picnic tables, grills. Built in 1900.

Totally nonsmoking. Cr cds: A, C, D, DS, JCB, MC, V.

★ ★ ★ **GILBERT INN BED & BREAKFAST.** *341 Beach Dr (97138). 503/738-9770; fax 503/717-1070; toll-free 800/410-9770. www.gilbertinn. com.* 10 rms, 3 story, 1 suite. No A/C. S $100-$120; D $105-$125; each addl $10; suite $105. Closed Jan. Crib free. TV; cable. Complimentary full bkfst. Restaurant nearby. Ck-out 11 am, ck-in 3 pm. Bellhops. Free airport, bus depot transportation. Queen Anne/Victorian house (1892); antiques. Totally nonsmoking. Cr cds: A, DS, MC, V.

Restaurants

★ **CAMP 18.** *42362 Hwy 26 (97138). 503/755-1818.* Hrs: 7 am-8 pm; Sun brunch 10 am-2 pm. Closed Dec 25. Bar. Bkfst $3.25-$8.95, lunch $3.95-$8.95, dinner $10.95-$18.95. Sun brunch $11.95. Children's meals. Specializes in omelettes, family-style dinners. In log bldg. Cr cds: A, DS, MC, V.
D

★ ★ **DOOGER'S SEAFOOD & GRILL.** *505 Broadway (97138). 503/738-3773.* Hrs: 11 am-10 pm; winter to 9 pm. Wine, beer. Lunch $4-$10.95, dinner $7.95-$22.95. Children's meals. Specializes in seafood, steak. Own clam chowder. Totally nonsmoking. Cr cds: A, DS, MC, V.
D

Silverton

(B-2) *See also Newberg, Oregon City, Salem*

Pop 5,635 **Elev** 249 ft **Area code** 503
Zip 97381
Information Chamber of Commerce, City Hall, 421 S Water St, PO Box 257; 503/873-5615

What to See and Do

Cooley's Gardens. Largest producer of bearded iris in the world. Display gardens feature many varieties; over one million blossom in fields (Mid-May-early June). 11553 Silverton Rd NE. Phone 503/873-5463. **FREE**

Country Museum/Restored Train Station. Ames-Warnock House (1908) contains local historical items dating from 1846. Southern Pacific Station (1906) contains larger items. (Mar-Dec, Thurs and Sun) Contact Chamber of Commerce. 428 S Water St. **Donation**

Silver Falls State Park. Oregon's largest state park, 8,706 acres, has ten waterfalls, of which five are more than 100 ft high; four may be viewed from road, the others from forested canyon hiking trail. Swimming. Bridle, bicycle trails. Picnicking. Tent and improved sites (dump station). Conference center. Standard fees. 15 mi SE on OR 214. Phone 503/873-8681.

Sweet Home

(C-2) *See also Albany*

Pop 6,850 **Elev** 525 ft **Area code** 541
Zip 97386
Information Chamber of Commerce, 1575 Main St; 541/367-6186
Web www.sweet-home.or.us

Gateway to Santiam Pass and the rugged Oregon Cascades, the area around Sweet Home is popular for fishing, boating, skiing, hiking, and rock hounding. A Ranger District office of Willamette National Forest (see EUGENE) is located here.

What to See and Do

East Linn Museum. Nearly 5,000 artifacts of pioneer life in the area (1847). Period rms; rock collection and mining equipment; logging tools; maps, photos, portraits; guns, dolls, bottles; saddlery and blacksmith shop. (May-Sept, Tues-Sun; rest of yr, Thurs-Sun; also by appt; closed hols) 746 Long St, at jct OR 228, US 20. Phone 541/367-4580. **Donation**

Foster Lake. Swimming, water sports; fishing; boating. 2 mi E on US 20 at Foster. Phone 541/367-5124.

Special Events

The Sweet Home Rodeo. Bull riding, barrel racing, bronco riding, mutton bustin'. Phone 541/367-6186. Second wkend July.

The Oregon Jamboree. Three-day country music and camping festival. Phone 541/367-8800. Second wkend Aug.

Tillamook

(B-1) *See also Lincoln City, Rockaway*

Founded 1851 **Pop** 4,001 **Elev** 16 ft
Area code 503 **Zip** 97141
Information Tillamook Chamber of Commerce, 3705 US 101N; 503/842-7525

Located at the southern end of Tillamook Bay, this is the county seat. Dairying, cheese and butter making, timber, and fishing are the main industries. There are many beaches for swimming, crabbing, clamming, beachcombing; boat landings, camping, picnicking, and fishing sites are also in the area.

What to See and Do

Cape Lookout State Park. A 1,974-acre park with virgin spruce forest, observation point; one of most primitive ocean shore areas in state. Hiking trail to end of cape. Picnicking. Tent and trailer sites (dump station). Standard fees. 12 mi SW off US 101 on Whiskey Creek Rd. Phone 503/842-4981.

🟩 **Capes Scenic Loop Drive to Cape Meares and Oceanside.** (Approx 10 mi) W on 3rd St, NW on Bay Ocean Rd to Cape Meares; go S on Loop Rd to Cape Meares State Park. See Tillamook Bay County Boat Landing, Cape Meares Lake, beach with beachcombing; also Cape Meares Lighthouse; Native American burial Sitka spruce tree known as "Octopus Tree." Continue S to Oceanside, site of Three Arch Rocks Federal Sea Lion and Migratory Bird Refuge, and beach area with beachcombing and agates. Continue S to Netarts; see Netarts Bay Boat Landing and Whiskey Creek Fish Hatchery. Go S

on Cape Lookout Rd to Pacific City and Cape Kiwanda, then back to US 101S. (Or take Whiskey Creek Rd from Netarts boat launching site, continue over Cape Lookout Mt through Sandlake, Tierra Del Mar to Pacific City. Exceptionally scenic, it also avoids traffic on US 101.)

Tillamook County Pioneer Museum. Possessions of early settlers, replica of pioneer home and barn; blacksmith shop; logging displays; war relics; relics from Tillamook Naval Air Station and Blimp Base; minerals, guns, books, vehicles, natural history and wildlife exhibits incl nine dioramas; "great grandma's kitchen." (Daily; closed Thanksgiving, Dec 25) 2106 2nd St at Pacific Ave. Phone 503/842-4553. 🗲

Special Events

Tillamook Dairy Parade and Rodeo. Fairgrounds; 4603 3rd St. Fourth wkend June. Phone 503/842-7525.

Tillamook County Fair. Fairgrounds, 4603 3rd St. First full wk Aug. Phone 503/842-2272.

Motels/Motor Lodges

★★ **MARCLAIR INN.** *11 Main Ave (97141). 503/842-7571; fax 503/842-4654; toll-free 800/331-6857. www. marclairinn.com.* 47 rms, 1-2 story, 6 kits. No A/C. Mid-May–mid-Oct: S $60-$72; D $69-$80; suites, kit. units $85-$105; under 12 free; lower rates rest of yr. Crib $6. TV; cable. Heated pool; whirlpool. Sauna. Restaurant 7 am-9 pm. Ck-out 11 am. Sun deck. Cr cds: A, D, DS, MC, V.
🐾 🅵 🛏 ⛆ 🔥

★★ **SHILO INN.** *2515 N Main St (97141). 503/842-7971; fax 503/842-7960; toll-free 800/222-2244. www. shiloinn.com.* 101 rms, 2 story. July-Oct: S, D $59.95-$129.95; each addl $10; kit. units $120; under 12 free; higher rates County Fair; lower rates rest of yr. Crib free. Pet accepted, some restrictions; $10. TV; cable (premium), VCR avail (movies). Indoor pool; whirlpool. Restaurant 6 am-11 pm. Bar 11-2 am. Ck-out noon. Coin lndry. Meeting rms. Business servs avail. Exercise equipt. Refrigerators. Cr cds: A, C, D, DS, ER, JCB, MC, V.
🅳 🐾 🐾 🛏 🏃 🛫 ⛆ 🔥

B&B/Small Inn

★★ **SANDLAKE COUNTRY INN.**
8505 Galloway Rd, Cloverdale (97112).
503/965-6745; fax 503/965-7425.
www.sandlakecountryinn.com. 4 rms, 2
story, 1 suite, 1 kit. unit. No A/C.
Some rm phones. S, D $90-$135. TV;
cable, VCR. Complimentary full
bkfst. Ck-out 11 am, ck-in 3 pm.
Concierge. In-rm whirlpools, fireplaces. Balconies. Farmhouse built of
timbers washed ashore from a ship
wreck in 1890. Antiques. Totally
nonsmoking. Cr cds: A, DS, MC, V.
🄳 ⛵ 🏞

Umatilla

(A-5) *See also Hermiston, Pendleton*

Founded 1863 **Pop** 3,046 **Elev** 296 ft
Area code 541 **Zip** 97882
Information Chamber of Commerce,
PO Box 67; 541/922-4825 or
800/542-4944

What to See and Do

Columbia Crest Winery. Located
amidst 2,000 acres of European-style
vinifera grapes. Tours, incl wine production, cellar, and tastings. Picnicking; gardens. (Self-guided tours,
Mon-Fri; guided tours, Sat-Sun;
closed hols) 18 mi NW via WA 14, in
Paterson, WA. Phone 509/875-2061.
FREE

Hat Rock State Park. A 735-acre park
on lake formed by McNary Dam.
Swimming beach; fishing; boat ramp
to the Columbia River. Hiking. Picnicking. Hat Rock is a large monolith
that looks like a man's top hat; a
landmark often referred to in diaries
of early-day explorers and travelers. 9
mi E off US 730 near jct OR 207.
Phone 541/567-5032.

McNary Lock and Dam. Single lift
navigation lock. Dam is 7,365 ft
long, 92 ft high. The Columbia River
forms Lake Wallula, a 61-mi waterway partly in Washington. Swimming, waterskiing; fishing, hunting;
boating (marinas). Picnicking. Primitive camping (two areas; free). Tours
of power, navigation and fish passage
facilities (June-Sept, daily). 2 mi E on
US 730. Phone 541/922-4388. **FREE**

Umatilla Marina Park. Swimming
beach; boating (launch, storage, gas,
oil). Picnicking. RV trailer camping
(fee). (Daily) NE edge of town on
Columbia River. Phone 541/922-
3939.

Special Event

Sage Riders Rodeo. NRA sanctioned,
second wkend June. Phone 541/922-
4825.

Yachats

(C-1) *See also Florence, Newport*

Pop 533 **Elev** 15 ft **Area code** 541
Zip 97498

Information Yachats Area Chamber
of Commerce, US 101; PO Box 728;
541/547-3530

Web www.pioneer.net/~yachat

Yachats (YA-hots) is a resort area on
the central Oregon coast, west of
Siuslaw National Forest. Derived
from a Native American phrase
meaning "waters at the foot of the
mountain," Yachats is along a rocky
shore with a fine sandy beach.

What to See and Do

Cape Perpetua Campground. Beachcombing; fishing. Hiking. Camping.
Summer campfire programs (Sat,
Sun). 3 mi S on US 101. Phone
541/563-3211. ¢¢¢ Nearby is

Cape Perpetua Visitor Center.
Interpretive displays of oceanogra-
phy, natural history of coastal area,
movies. Nature trails, auto tour.
(May, Wed-Sun; Memorial Day-
Labor Day, daily; closed winter) In
Siuslaw National Forest. Phone
541/547-3289. ¢¢

Neptune State Park. This 302-acre
park features Cook's Chasm (near N
end), a long, narrow, deep fissure
where the sea falls in with a spectacular fury; wind-depressed forest trees
(near N end); slopes covered with
huckleberry shrubs. A community of
harbor seals makes its home on the
rocks below Strawberry Hill. Surf
fishing. Hiking. Picnicking. Observation point. 3 mi S on US 101. Phone
541/547-3416.

Tillicum Beach Campground. Ocean view, beachcombing. Camping. Summer evening campfire programs Sat and Sun. Camping 3½ mi N on US 101. Phone 541/563-3211. ¢¢¢

Yachats State Recreation Area. A 93-acre day-use park bordering the Yachats River, in the shadow of Cape Perpetua. Small picnic area. Observation point. On US 101. Phone 541/997-3851.

Motels/Motor Lodges

★★ **ADOBE RESORT MOTEL.** *1555 Hwy 101 N (97498). 541/547-3141; fax 541/547-4234; toll-free 800/522-3623. www.adoberesort.com.* 93 rms, 2-3 story, 5 kits. S, D $58-$100; each addl $8; suites $150; kit. units $110 $135. Crib $8. Pet accepted, some restrictions. TV; cable (premium), VCR. Complimentary coffee in rms. Restaurant 8 am-2:30 pm, 5-9 pm. Bar. Ck-out 11 am. Meeting rm. Business servs avail. Gift shop. Exercise equipt; sauna. Whirlpool. Refrigerators; some fireplaces. Whirlpool in suites. Some balconies. On ocean. Cr cds: A, C, D, DS, MC, V.
🅳 🔌 ♿ 🏃 ⛵ 🐾 SC

★ **FIRESIDE MOTEL.** *1881 Hwy 101 N (97498). 541/547-3636; fax 541/547-3152; toll-free 800/336-3573. www.overleaflodge.com/fireside.* 43 rms, 2 story. Mid-May-Sept: S, D $77-$99; each addl $7; kit. cottages $99-$135; some lower rates rest of yr. Crib $5. Pet accepted, some restrictions; $7/day. TV; cable, VCR avail. Complimentary coffee in rms. Restaurant nearby. Ck-out 11 am. Health club privileges. Refrigerators; some fireplaces. View of ocean. Cr cds: A, DS, MC, V.
🅳 🔌 ♿ ⛵ 🐾 SC

★★ **SHAMROCK LODGETTES.** *105 Hwy 101 S (97498). 541/547-3312; fax 541/547-3843; toll-free 800/845-5028. www.shamrocklodgettes.com.* 19 rms, 11 kit. cottages. S, D, kit. units $71-$100; each addl $8; kit. cottages $91-$112; wkly rates. Crib $7. Pet accepted, some restrictions; $3/day. TV; cable (premium). Complimentary coffee in rms. Restaurant nearby. Ck-out 11 am. Massage. Refrigerators; some in-rm whirlpools; microwaves

avail. Some private patios, balconies. Beach adj. Cr cds: A, D, DS, MC, V.
🐾 ♿

B&B/Small Inn

★★ **SEA QUEST BED & BREAKFAST.** *95354 Hwy 101 S (97498). 541/547-3782; fax 541/547-3719; res 800/341-4878. www.seaq.com.* 5 rms, 1 with shower only, 2 story. No rm phones. S, D $150-$160; each addl $20; wkends, hols (2-3-day min). Children over 14 yrs only. Complimentary full bkfst. Ck-out 11 am, ck-in 3 pm. Gift shop. Many in-rm whirlpools. On beach. Ocean view. Totally nonsmoking. Cr cds: MC, V.
🅳 ♿ 🏃 ⛵ 🐾

WASHINGTON

The Stillaguamish, Steilacoom, and Hoh, Puyallup, Tulalip, and La Push, the Duckabush, the Dosewallips, and the Queets, the Skookumchuck, the Sol Duc, and the Pysht—all these are Washington towns and rivers. There are many more like them, named by Native Americans.

Ruggedly handsome Washington is like a bank in which nature has deposited some of her greatest resources. In addition to dramatic mountain ranges, expansive forests, and inviting harbors, it is also a cornerstone of American hydroelectric technology. Here are the majestic spectacles of mighty Mount Rainier—revered as a god by the Native Americans—and the Olympic Peninsula, where one of the wettest and one of the driest parts of the country are only a mountain away from each other; also here is Puget Sound, a giant inland sea where 2,000 miles of shoreline bend into jewel-like bays.

Population: 4,866,692
Area: 68,192 square miles
Elevation: 0-14,410 feet
Peak: Mount Rainier (Pierce County)
Entered Union: November 11, 1889 (42nd state)
Capital: Olympia
Motto: Al-ki (By and By)
Nickname: Evergreen State
Flower: Rhododendron
Bird: Willow Goldfinch
Tree: Western Hemlock
Time Zone: Pacific
Website: www.tourism.wa.gov

Although British and Spanish navigators were the first Europeans to explore Washington's serrated shoreline, the first major discoveries were made in 1792, when an American, Captain Robert Gray, gave his name to Grays Harbor and the name of his ship, *Columbia,* to the great river. An Englishman, Captain George Vancouver, explored and named Puget Sound and christened Mount Baker and Mount Rainier, which he could see far inland. Fort Vancouver was the keystone of the British fur industry, dominating a Northwest empire. After conflicting US and British claims were resolved, Americans surged into this area by ship and wagon train.

Puget Sound

Part of the Oregon Territory until it separated in 1853, the state's eastern boundary was established in 1863, when Idaho became a territory. Entering the last decade of the 19th century as a state of the Union, Washington found itself no longer America's last territorial frontier.

Civilization has not dissipated Washington's natural wealth. On the contrary, after more than a century of logging operations, Washington retains 24 million acres of superb forests, and miracles of modern engineering have almost completely erased the wastelands through which the wagon trains of the pioneers passed on their way to the sea.

The mighty but capricious Columbia River meanders through the heart of northeast and central Washington, then runs for 300 miles along the Oregon-Washington border. Through a series of dams and the Grand Coulee Reclamation Project, the energies of the Columbia have been harnessed and converted into what is presently one of the world's great sources of water power. Irrigation and a vast supply of inexpensive power gave a tremendous push to Washington's economy, sparking new industries and making possible the state's production of huge crops of grains, vegetables, and fruit.

Central Washington is the apple barrel of the country; dairying is a big industry in the western valleys. Forestry and wood products as well as the production of paper and allied products are of major importance in the western and northern sections of the state; 1/3 of the state is covered by commercial forests. In recent years Washington wines have enjoyed great popularity around the nation.

Since 1965, more than 25 percent of Washington's total manufacturing effort has been devoted to the production of transportation equipment, of which a large portion is involved in commercial jet aircraft. Along Puget Sound, industry means canning plants, lumber mills and pulp and paper plants; but even here there is a new economic dimension: petroleum refineries of four major companies have a daily capacity of 366,500 barrels of crude oil and gasoline; biotechnology and software development are growing industries. Tourism is the state's fourth largest industry, amounting to more than $8.8 billion a year.

When to Go/Climate

Moist air off the Pacific Ocean and Puget Sound creates the rainy conditions in western Washington and heavy snowfall in the Cascades. While the western slopes of the Cascades and Olympic Mountains are soaked with moisture, the eastern slopes and, indeed, the entire eastern part of the state is almost desert dry. Temperatures are seasonally mild, except for high in the mountains.

AVERAGE HIGH/LOW TEMPERATURES (°F)

SEATTLE

Jan 46/36	May 64/48	Sept 69/53
Feb 51/38	June 70/53	Oct 60/47
Mar 54/40	July 74/56	Nov 52/41
Apr 58/43	Aug 74/57	Dec 46/37

SPOKANE

Jan 33/21	May 66/42	Sept 72/46
Feb 41/26	June 75/49	Oct 59/36
Mar 48/30	July 83/54	Nov 41/29
Apr 57/35	Aug 83/54	Dec 34/22

Parks and Recreation Finder

Directions to and information about the parks and recreation areas below are given under their respective town/city sections. Please refer to those sections for details.

NATIONAL PARK AND RECREATION AREAS

Key to abbreviations. I.H.S. = International Historic Site; I.P.M. = International Peace Memorial; N.B. = National Battlefield; N.B.P. = National Battlefield Park; N.B.C. = National Battlefield and Cemetery; N.C.A. = National Conservation Area; N.E.M. = National Expansion Memorial; N.F. = National Forest; N.G. = National Grassland; N.H.P. = National Historical Park; N.H.C. = National Heritage Corridor; N.H.S. = National Historic Site; N.L. = National Lakeshore; N.M. = National Monument; N.M.P. = National Military Park; N.Mem. = National Memorial; N.P. = National Park; N.Pres. = National Preserve; N.R.A. = National Recreational Area; N.R.R. = National Recreational River; N.Riv. = National River; N.S. = National Seashore; N.S.R. = National Scenic Riverway; N.S.T. = National Scenic Trail; N.Sc. = National Scientific Reserve; N.V.M. = National Volcanic Monument.

Place Name	Listed Under
Colville N.F.	COLVILLE
Coulee Dam	same
Fort Vancouver N.H.S.	VANCOUVER
Gifford Pinchot N.F.	VANCOUVER
Klondike Gold Rush N.H.P.	SEATTLE
Mount Baker-Snoqualmie N.F.	BELLINGHAM, SEATTLE
Mount Rainier N.P.	same
Mount St. Helens N.V.M.	same
North Cascades N.P.	SEDRO WOOLLEY
Okanogan N.F.	OMAK
Olympic N.F.	OLYMPIA
Olympic N.P.	same
San Juan Island N.H.P.	SAN JUAN ISLANDS
Umatilla N.F.	CLARKSTON
Wenatchee N.F.	WENATCHEE
Whitman Mission N.H.S.	WALLA WALLA

STATE PARK AND RECREATION AREAS

Key to abbreviations. I.P. = Interstate Park; S.A.P. = State Archaeological Park; S.B. = State Beach; S.C.A. = State Conservation Area; S.C.P. = State Conservation Park; S.Cp. = State Campground; S.F. = State Forest; S.G. = State Garden; S.H.A. = State Historic Area; S.H.P. = State Historic Park; S.H.S. = State Historic Site; S.M.P. = State Marine Park; S.N.A. = State Natural Area; S.P. = State Park; S.P.C. = State Public Campground; S.R. = State Reserve; S.R.A. = State Recreation Area; S.Res. = State Reservoir; S.Res.P. = State Resort Park; S.R.P. = State Rustic Park.

Place Name	Listed Under
Alta Lake S.P.	CHELAN
Bay View S.P.	MOUNT VERNON
Belfair S.P.	BREMERTON
Birch Bay S.P.	BLAINE
Blake Island S.P.	BREMERTON
Bogachiel S.P.	FORKS
Brooks Memorial S.P.	GOLDENDALE
Conconully S.P.	OMAK
Deception Pass S.P.	ANACORTES
Federation Forest S.P.	ENUMCLAW
Fields Spring S.P.	CLARKSTON
Flaming Geyser S.P.	ENUMCLAW
Fort Canby S.H.P.	LONG BEACH
Fort Casey S.P.	COUPEVILLE

Fort Columbia S.H.P.	LONG BEACH
Fort Flagler S.P.	PORT TOWNSEND
Fort Simcoe S.H.P.	TOPPENISH
Fort Worden S.P.	PORT TOWNSEND
Ginkgo/Wanapum S.P.	ELLENSBURG
Illahee S.P.	BREMERTON
Kitsap Memorial S.P.	PORT GAMBLE
Lake Chelan S.P.	CHELAN
Lake Cushman S.P.	UNION
Lake Sammamish S.P.	ISSAQUAH
Lake Sylvia S.P.	ABERDEEN
Larrabee S.P.	BELLINGHAM
Lewis and Clark Trail S.P.	DAYTON
Millersylvania S.P.	OLYMPIA
Moran S.P.	SAN JUAN ISLANDS
Moses Lake S.P.	MOSES LAKE
Mount Spokane S.P.	SPOKANE
Old Fort Townsend S.P.	PORT TOWNSEND
Olmstead Place S.P.	ELLENSBURG
Potholes S.P.	MOSES LAKE
Rainbow Falls S.P.	CHEHALIS
Riverside S.P.	SPOKANE
Sacajawea S.P.	PASCO
Scenic Beach S.P.	BREMERTON
Schafer S.P.	ABERDEEN
Seaquest S.P.	KELSO
Sequim Bay S.P.	SEQUIM
Squilchuck S.P.	WENATCHEE
Steamboat Rock S.P.	COULEE DAM
Twanoh S.P.	UNION
Twenty-Five Mile Creek S.P.	CHELAN
Twin Harbors S.P.	WESTPORT
Wenberg S.P.	MARYSVILLE
Yakima Sportsman S.P.	YAKIMA

Water-related activities, hiking, riding, various other sports, picnicking, and visitor centers, as well as camping, are available in many of these areas. The 248,882 acres owned or managed by the Washington State Parks and Recreation Commission provide unusually good camping and trailer facilities at most locations, with a camping fee of $15/site; hookups $21; ten-day limit in summer; 20 days rest of year. Most parks are open daily: April-mid-October, 6:30 am-dusk; some are closed rest of year. Pets on leash only. Further information may be obtained from the Washington State Parks and Recreation Commission, 7150 Cleanwater Lane, PO Box 42650, Olympia 98504-2650; phone 360/902-8844 or 888/226-7688.

SKI AREAS

Place Name	Listed Under
Alpental Ski Area	NORTH BEND
Crystal Mountain Resort	MOUNT RAINIER NATIONAL PARK
Hurricane Ridge Winter Use Ski Area	OLYMPIC NATIONAL PARK
Hyak Ski Area	NORTH BEND
Mission Ridge Ski Area	WENATCHEE

Mount Baker Ski Area	BELLINGHAM
Mount Spokane Ski Area	SPOKANE
Ski Acres Ski Area	NORTH BEND
Ski Bluewood Ski Area	DAYTON
Snoqualmie Ski Area	NORTH BEND
White Pass Village Ski Area	MOUNT RAINIER NATIONAL PARK

FISHING AND HUNTING

With 10,000 miles of bay and Pacific shoreline, 8,000 lakes, and rivers that stretch from Oregon to Canada, Washington provides something for every

---

CALENDAR HIGHLIGHTS

MARCH

Chocolate Fantasy (Yakima). Chocolate manufacturers from across the nation showcase candy, cookies, and pies; sampling, "chocolate bingo." Phone 509/966-6309.

APRIL

Daffodil Festival (Tacoma). In Tacoma and Puyallup Valley. Flower show, coronation, four-city floral parade of floats, marine regatta, bowling tournament. Phone 253/627-6176.

MAY

Wooden Boat Festival (Olympia). Percival Landing in Harbor. Wooden boats on display, some open for public viewing. Wooden crafts fair. Phone 360/943-5404.

Ski to Sea Festival (Bellingham). Parades, carnival, art show, special events. Ski to Sea race; starts on Mount Baker, ends in Bellingham Bay, and involves skiers, runners, canoeists, bicyclists, and kayakers. Memorial Day weekend. Phone 360/734-1330.

JULY

San Juan Island Jazz Festival (San Juan Islands). Indoor/outdoor jazz festival featuring Dixieland, swing, zydeco, and blues/jazz. Friday Harbor. Phone 360/378-5509.

AUGUST

Seafair (Seattle). Citywide marine festival. Regattas, speedboat races, shows at Aqua Theater, parades, sports events, exhibits. Phone 206/728-0123.

Stampede and Suicide Race (Omak). Rodeo events; horses and riders race down a cliff and across the Okanogan River. Western art show. Native American dance contests. Encampment with more than 100 teepees. Phone 509/826-1002.

Southwest Washington Fair (Centralia). First held in 1909, the state's second-oldest fair and one of the largest. Phone 360/736-6072.

SEPTEMBER

Northeast Washington Fair (Colville). Stevens County Fairgrounds. Parade, livestock and horse shows, arts and crafts exhibits, carnival. Phone 509/684-2585.

Western Washington Fair (Puyallup). Pacific Northwest's largest fair; incl three statewide youth fairs, livestock shows, agricultural and commercial exhibits, free entertainment, midway, rodeo, top-name grandstand acts. Phone 253/841-5045.

Central Washington State Fair and Rodeo (Yakima). Fairgrounds. Thoroughbred racing. Pari-mutuel wagering. Phone 509/248-7160.

angler's whim. Fish hatcheries dot the state, stocking nature's waterways and those artificially created by irrigation and navigation dams. If you like salmon and steelhead, Washington is the state to try your luck.

Nonresident freshwater fishing license $40; two-day license. A food fish license is required for salmon and saltwater bottomfish; nonresident food fish license, $20; nonresident saltwater fish license, $36; nonresident combination fresh water/saltwater fish license, $72. A shellfish/seaweed license is required for shellfish; nonresident license, $20. Razor clam season varies; contact the Department of Fish and Wildlife for season dates, phone 360/902-2200. Nonresident small-game hunting license $165; three-day $50; big game, $200-$725. Get hunting and freshwater fishing regulations and a complete list of license fees from Department of Fish and Wildlife, 500 Capitol Way N, Olympia 98504. Fishing and hunting regulation pamphlets are available in local sporting goods stores.

Driving Information

Safety belts are mandatory for all persons anywhere in vehicle. Children under 40 pounds in weight must be in an approved safety seat anywhere in vehicle. For further information phone 360/753-6197.

INTERSTATE HIGHWAY SYSTEM

The following alphabetical listing of Washington towns in *Mobil Travel Guide* shows that these cities are within ten miles of the indicated Interstate highways. A highway map, however, should be checked for the nearest exit.

Highway Number	Cities/Towns within ten miles
Interstate 5	Bellingham, Blaine, Centralia, Chehalis, Everett, Kelso, Longview, Marysville, Mount Vernon, Olympia, Puyallup, Seattle, Sedro Woolley, Snohomish, Tacoma, Vancouver.
Interstate 82	Ellensburg, Kennewick, Pasco, Richland, Sunnyside, Toppenish, Yakima.
Interstate 90	Bellevue, Ellensburg, Issaquah, Moses Lake, North Bend, Ritzville, Seattle, Spokane.
Interstate 182	Pasco, Richland.

Additional Visitor Information

Washington travel information and brochures on the state are available from the Washington State Tourism Department of Community, Trade, and Economic Development, 101 General Administration Building, PO Box 42500, Olympia 98504-2500. Phone 800/544-1800 for a copy of *Washington State Lodging and Travel Guide;* phone 800/638-8474 or 360/586-2088 for tourism information. *This is Washington* (Superior Publishing Co, Seattle) and *Sunset Travel Guide to Washington* (Sunset Publishing, Menlo Park, CA) are also helpful.

There are 180 visitor information centers in Washington; most are open May-September. Visitors who stop by will find information and brochures most helpful in planning stops to points of interest. The locations for the official state visitor centers at points of entry are as follows: 7 mi S of Blaine, near the Canadian border; E of Spokane at the Idaho/Washington border, I-90 exit 299 westbound; 404 E 15th St, Vancouver; in Oroville on US 97, near the Canadian border; at the Oregon border on US 97, near Maryhill State Park and Sam Hill Bridge; and on WA 401 near the Astoria Bridge.

MOUNT RAINIER AND NORTHWEST WILDLIFE

A very popular day trip from Seattle, this route rounds the imposing volcanic cone of Mount Rainier, the centerpiece of Mount Rainier National Park. Take Highway 410 east and climb along the White River with the towering white cone of 14,412-foot Mount Rainier rising above the forest. The park itself has a number of different viewpoints for taking in the peak, and each has its own personalities. Sunrise—the

highest point reached by road in the park—is on the drier, east side of the peak; there are hikes to wildflower meadows and glacial overlooks, and mountain goats are often seen in the area. The aptly named Paradise area—on the southern side of the mountain, atop a broad timberline shoulder—shares postcard views of the peak with the Paradise Inn, a vast historic stone-and-log lodge built in classic Arts-and-Crafts style. An extensive trail system explores flower-filled meadows and tumbling waterfalls. Other highlights of this route are Ohanapecosh, a riparian wetland with a stand of massive old-growth cedar trees, and Longmire, the original park headquarters with several turn-of-the-century structures and another heritage hotel. A highlight of the return trip near Eatonville (on Highway 161) is the Northwest Trek Wildlife Park, a private refuge that rehabilitates wolves, cougars, and other wildlife native to the area that have been injured or must be removed from the wild for other reasons. (**APPROX 142 MI**)

MOUNTAIN WATERWAYS IN THE CASCADES

This route passes through spectacular mountain scenery in one of the West's most rugged national parks. Starting on the moist Pacific side of the Cascade range at Sedro-Wooley, Highway 20 follows the increasingly narrow Skagit River valley inland through dripping fir and cedar forests. Near Rockport, the landscape becomes wilder and steeper; this is a major wintering area for bald eagles, who come here to dine on migrating salmon. As the route enters the park near Marblemount, the Skagit is dammed in quick succession in a precipitous canyon by three early-20th-century hydrodams (this is where Seattle gets its power). Tours of the largest dam are the most popular activity in the park; getting up to the dam itself involves riding an incline railroad up a sheer cliff face. Around the dams are hikes to waterfalls and mist gardens. After climbing Rainy Pass, which has incredible views of tooth-edged mountain ranges and volcanoes in good weather, Highway 20 drops onto the dry side of the Cascades, where the forests are suddenly dominated by ponderosa pines and juniper. The highway follows the Methow River, a very lovely, semiarid valley that was once the province of cattle ranches but is now lined with resort homes and golf courses. The town of Winthrop, which just 15 years ago was filled with feed stores and tractor dealerships, now epitomizes the wealthy New West culture with its art galleries, fine restaurants, and home-decor boutiques. From the delightfully named town of Twisp, follow Highway 153 through ranch land, which slowly gives way to apple orchards as the route joins Highway 97 and the Columbia River at Pateros. (**APPROX 168 MI**)

Aberdeen

(D-2) *See also Hoquiam, Ocean Shores, Westport*

Settled 1878 **Pop** 16,565 **Elev** 19 ft
Area code 360 **Zip** 98520
Information Grays Harbor Chamber of Commerce, 506 Duffy St; 360/532-1924 or 800/321-1924
Web www.graysharbor.org

Aberdeen and Hoquiam are twin cities on the eastern tip of Grays Harbor. Born as a cannery named for the city in Scotland, Aberdeen later blossomed as a lumber town, with one of the greatest stands of Douglas fir ever found in the Pacific Northwest at its back. Many Harbor residents are descendants of Midwestern Scandinavians who came here to fell the forests. Today, the town's commerce consists of wood-processing, fishing, and shipbuilding. The Port of Grays Harbor is located along the waterfront of the two towns.

What to See and Do

Aberdeen Museum of History. Special exhibits with 1880s-1940s furnishings and implements incl kitchen and bed, general mercantile store, one-rm school; farm and logging equipt and displays; blacksmith shop; pioneer church; fire trucks. Slide show, photographs. (June-Labor Day, Wed-Sun; rest of yr, wkends) 111 E 3rd St. Phone 360/533-1976. **DONATION**

Grays Harbor Historical Seaport. Historical interpretive center; classes in long boat building. Incl a museum with informational and active exhibits on the history of sailing in the Pacific Northwest. Also replica of Robert Gray's ship *Lady Washington* (seasonal; fee). (Daily; closed hols) 813 E Heron St. Phone 360/532-8611. **FREE**

Lake Sylvia State Park. Approx 235 acres of protected timber. Swimming, fishing; hiking, picnicking, concession, camping. Standard fees. 10 mi E on US 12, then 1 mi N on unnumbered road. Phone 360/249-3621.

Samuel Benn Park. Named for pioneer settler. Rose and rhododendron gardens; picnic facilities, playground, tennis. (Daily) E 9th and N I Sts. Phone 360/533-4100. **FREE**

Schafer State Park. Approx 120 acres on Satsop River. Swimming, fishing; hiking, picnicking, camping (hookups; dump station). (Apr-mid-Dec, daily; rest of yr, wkends and hols) Standard fees. 13 mi E on US 12, then 10 mi N on unnumbered road. Phone 360/482-3852.

Motels/Motor Lodges

★ **OLYMPIC INN.** *616 W Heron St (98520). 360/533-4200; fax 360/533-6223; toll-free 800/562-8618.* 55 rms, 2 story, 3 kits. No A/C. S $43-$70; D $53-$73; each addl $7; suites, kit. units $65-$97. Crib $7. TV; cable (premium). Complimentary continental bkfst. Restaurant nearby. Ck-out noon. Coin lndry. Meeting rm. Business servs avail. Many refrigerators. Cr cds: A, C, D, DS, MC, V.
D 🐾 🐕

★★ **RED LION INN.** *521 W Wishkah St (98520). 360/532-5210; fax 360/533-8483; toll-free 800/RED-LION. www.redlion.com.* 67 rms, 2 story. June-Sept: S $68-$78; D $78-$98; each addl $10; under 18 free; lower rates rest of yr. Crib free. Pet accepted. TV; cable. Complimentary continental bkfst. Restaurant nearby. Ck-out noon. Sundries. Cr cds: A, C, D, DS, ER, JCB, MC, V.
D 🐾 🐕 🌳 🐾 🐕

B&B/Small Inn

★★ **ABERDEEN MANSION BED AND BREAKFAST.** *807 N M St (98520). 360/533-7079; toll-free 888/533-7079. www.aberdeenmansion bb.com.* 5 rms, 2 story. No A/C. No rm phones. May-Oct: S, D $95-$140, lower rates rest of yr. Children over 12 yrs only. TV; cable. Complimentary full bkfst. Restaurant nearby. Ck-out 11 am, ck-in 4-6 pm. Luggage handling. Victorian house built in 1905; antiques. Totally nonsmoking. Cr cds: A, DS, MC, V.
🐕 🐾 **SC**

Restaurants

★★ **BILLY'S RESTAURANT.** *322 E Heron (98520). 360/533-7144.* Hrs: 8 am-11 pm; Fri, Sat to midnight; Sun to 9 pm. Closed Easter, Thanksgiving, Dec 25. Bar. Lunch, dinner $4.50-$13.95. Children's meals. Specializes in burgers, salad. In 1904 building with antique furnishings. Cr cds: A, D, MC, V.
D ⌐

★★ **BRIDGES RESTAURANT.** *112 N G St (98520). 360/532-6563.* Hrs: 11 am-9 pm; Fri and Sat to 10 pm; Sun 4-9 pm. Bar. Lunch $4.50-$10.95, dinner $6.50-$25.95. Children's meals. Specializes in prime rib, seafood, steak. Solarium. Family-owned. Cr cds: A, D, DS, MC, V.
D

Anacortes

(B-3) *See also Coupeville, La Conner, Mount Vernon, Oak Harbor, San Juan Islands, Sedro Woolley*

Settled 1860 **Pop** 11,451 **Elev** 24 ft
Area code 360 **Zip** 98221
Information Visitor Information Center at the Chamber of Commerce, 819 Commercial Ave, Suite G; 360/293-3832
Web www.anacortes-chamber.com

Anacortes, at the northwest tip of Fidalgo Island, houses the San Juan Islands ferries. The town's name honors Anna Curtis, wife of one of the founders.

What to See and Do

Deception Pass State Park. More than 3,000 acres of sheltered bays and deep forests with fjordlike shoreline. Swimming (lifeguards in summer), scuba diving, fishing, clamming, boating (ramp, dock); hiking trails, picnicking, camping. Standard fees. 9 mi S on WA 20. Phone 360/675-2417.

San Juan Islands Trip. Ferry boats leave several times daily for major islands of the group. Either leave car at dock in Anacortes or disembark at any point and explore from paved roads. For schedules, fares contact the Visitor Information Center. Phone 360/293-3832.

Washington Park. Approx 220 acres. Sunset Beach; saltwater fishing, boating (ramps; fee); picnicking, camping (14-day limit; electricity and water). Coin showers. Park (Daily). 4 mi W on 12th St (Oakes Ave). Phone 360/293-1927. ¢¢¢

Tulip Farm, Skagit Valley

Special Events

Skagit Valley Tulip Festival. First three wkends Apr. Phone 360/428-5959.

Waterfront Festival. Mid-May. Phone 360/293-7911.

Shipwreck Day. Mid-July. Phone 360/293-7911.

Barbershop Concert and Salmon Barbecue. Last wkend July. Phone 360/293-1282.

Motels/Motor Lodges

★★ **ANACORTES INN.** *3006 Commercial Ave (98221). 360/293-3153; fax 360/293-0209; toll-free 800/327-7976. www.anacortesinn.com.* 44 rms, 2 story, 5 kits. May-mid-Oct: S $70; D $70-$115; each addl $5; kit. units $10 addl; under 12 free. Pet accepted. TV; cable (premium). Heated pool. Coffee in rms. Restaurant nearby. Ck-out 11 am. Business servs avail.

Refrigerators, microwaves. Cr cds: A, D, DS, MC, V.

★ **SHIP HARBOR INN.** *5316 Ferry Terminal Rd (98221). 360/293-5177; fax 360/299-2412; toll-free 800/852-8568. www.shipharborinn.com.* 16 rms, 10 cottages, 1-2 story. No A/C. May-Sept: S $50-$75; D $80-$100; each addl $5; under 12 free; lower rates rest of yr. Crib free. TV; cable. Playground. Complimentary continental bkfst. Restaurant adj 11 am-10 pm. Bar. Ck-out 11 am. Coin lndry. Meeting rm. Some refrigerators; microwaves avail. Private patios, porches. Picnic tables, grills. Cr cds: A, C, D, DS, MC, V.

D&D/Small Inn

★★ **CHANNEL HOUSE BED & BREAKFAST.** *2902 Oakes Ave (98221). 360/293-9382; fax 360/299-9208; toll-free 800/238-4353. www.channel-house.com.* 6 air-cooled rms, 2 story. No rm phones. S $79; D $95; each addl $20. Children over 12 yrs only. Complimentary full bkfst; afternoon refreshments. Restaurant nearby. Ck-out 11 am, ck-in 3-9 pm. Whirlpool. Victorian-style residence (1902) built for an Italian count; many antiques, stained-glass windows. Views of Puget Sound. Totally nonsmoking. Cr cds: A, DS, MC, V.

Bellevue

(C-3) *See also Issaquah, Seattle*

Pop 86,874 **Elev** 125 ft
Information Bellevue Chamber of Commerce, 10500 NE 8th St, Suite 212, 98004; 425/454-2464
Web www.bellevuechamber.org

Incorporated in 1953, Bellevue has rapidly become the state's fourth largest city. It is linked across Lake Washington to Seattle by the Evergreen Floating Bridge.

What to See and Do

Bellevue Art Museum. Contemporary Northwest art and craft exhibits and programs. (Tues-Sun) Bellevue Way NE at Sixth St. Phone 425/519-0770. ¢¢

Bellevue Botanical Garden. Thirty-six acres feature woodlands, meadows, and display gardens incl Waterwise Garden, Japanese Gardens, and Fuchsia Display. Garden shop. Visitor Center. (Daily) 12001 Main St. Phone 425/452-2749. **FREE**

Chateau Ste. Michelle. Located on an 87-acre estate; tours; wine tasting; summer concert series. Picnic area, gardens, gift shop with wine and picnic supplies. (Daily; closed hols) N on I-405 to exit 23B, at 14111 NE 145th St in Woodinville. Phone 425/415-3300

Rosalie Whyel Museum of Doll Art. Features curated collection of dolls, teddy bears, toys, and miniatures. Museum shop. (Daily; closed hols) 1116 108th Ave NE. Phone 425/455-1116. ¢¢¢

Motels/Motor Lodges

★★★ **BEST WESTERN BELLEVUE INN.** *11211 Main St (98004). 425/455-5240; fax 425/455-0654; res 800/421-8193. www.bestwestern.com.* 180 rms, 2 story. S, D $118-$179; under 18 free; wkend rates. Crib free. TV; cable (premium). Heated pool; poolside serv. Coffee in rms. Restaurant 6:30 am-2 pm, 5-10 pm. Bar; entertainment Thurs-Sat. Ck-out noon. Meeting rms. Business servs avail. Bellhops. Valet serv. Sundries. Exercise equipt. Refrigerators. Balconies. Cr cds: A, D, DS, MC, V.

★★ **SILVER CLOUD INN.** *12202 NE 124th St, Kirkland (98034). 425/821-8300; fax 425/823-1218; res 800/205-6933. www.silvercloud.com.* 99 rms, 3 story. May-Sept: S $79-$105; D $91-$119; suites $105-$168; under 18 free; lower rates rest of yr. Crib free. TV; cable (premium). Complimentary continental bkfst. Restaurant adj open 24 hrs. Ck-out noon. Business servs avail. Concierge. Sundries. Guest lndry. Exercise equipt. Heated

pool; whirlpool. Refrigerators. Microwaves avail. Cr cds: A, D, DS, MC, V.
[D] [icons]

★★ **WESTCOAST BELLEVUE HOTEL.** *625 116th Ave (98004). 425/455-9444; fax 425/455-2154; toll-free 800/325-4000. www.westcoast hotels.com.* 176 rms, 6 story. S, D $139-$159; ; each addl $10; suites $189; under 18 free. Crib free. TV; cable (premium). Heated pool; poolside serv. Complimentary coffee in rms. Restaurant 6 am-10 pm; Sat, Sun from 7 am. Rm serv. Bar 4-11 pm. Ck-out noon. Meeting rms. Business servs avail. Sundries. Exercise equipt. Cr cds: A, D, DS, MC, V.
[D] [icons]

Hotels

★★★★ **BELLEVUE CLUB HOTEL.** *11200 SE 6th St (98004). 425/454-4424; fax 425/688-3101; toll-free 800/579-1110. www.bellevueclub.com.* On Seattle's east side, this beautifully appointed hotel and private club (open to registered guests) has a clean, award-winning West Coast design with subtle multicultural influences. The interiors are decorated in light earth tones, blond wood finishes, and exotic artwork. Each of the 67 guest rooms has an exquisite bathroom, rich in limestone, marble, and granite with a deep soaking tub and separate glass-enclosed shower, as well as a view of either Mount Rainier, the plaza fountain, or the tennis courts. 67 rms, 2 with shower only, 4 story. S, D $195-$245; suites $575-$1450; under 18 free; wkend rates. Crib free. Valet parking $5. TV; cable (premium), VCR avail. Indoor pool; whirlpool, poolside serv, lifeguard. Supervised children's activities; ages 1-12. Complimentary coffee in lobby. Restaurant (see also POLARIS). Rm serv 24 hrs. Bar 11 am-midnight; entertainment Thurs-Sat. Ck-out 1 pm. Valet serv. Meeting rms. Business center. In-rm modem link. Concierge. Gift shop. Indoor tennis, pro. Extensive exercise rm; sauna, steam rm. Massage. Minibars. Cr cds: A, C, D, JCB, MC, V.
[D] [icons]

★★ **DOUBLETREE HOTEL.** *300 112th Ave (98004). 425/455-1300; fax 425/455-0466; toll-free 800/222-8733.* www.doubletree.com. 353 rms, 10 story. S, D $79-$269; each addl $15; suites $265-$445; under 17 free. Parking; $11. Crib avail. TV; cable (premium). Pool; whirlpool; spa. Complimentary coffee, newspaper in rms. Restaurant 6 am-10 pm. Ck-out noon. Meeting rms. Business center. Gift shop. Exercise equipt. Some refrigerators, minibars. Balconies. Cr cds: A, C, D, DS, ER, JCB, MC, V.
[D] [icons]

★★★ **HILTON HOTEL BELLEVUE.** *100 112th Ave NE (98004). 425/455-3330; fax 425/451-2473; res 800/445-8667. www.hilton.com.* 180 rms, 7 story. S,D $129-$199; each addl $10; family, wkend rates. Crib free. TV; cable (premium). Indoor pool; whirlpool. Complimentary coffee in rms. Restaurants 6 am-10 pm. Bar 10-2 am. Ck-out noon. Meeting rms. Business center. In-rm modem link.Concierge. Sundries. Health club privileges. Exercise equipt; sauna. Refrigerators avail. Cr cds: A, D, DS, JCB, MC, V.
[D] [icons]

★★★ **HYATT REGENCY BELLEVUE.** *900 Bellevue Way NE (98004). 425/462-1234; fax 425/646-7567; toll-free 800/233-1234. www.hyatt.com.* 382 rms, 24 story, 29 suites. S, D $99-$215; suites $199-$315; under 18 free. Crib free. Self parking $11; valet. TV; cable (premium). Coffee in rms. Restaurant 6 am-11pm. Bar 11-1 am. Ck-out noon. Indoor pool; whirlpool. Convention facilities. Business center. Internet access. Concierge. Valet serv. Shopping arcade. Barber, beauty shop. Exercise rm; steam rm. Refrigerators. Hotel connected to office/retail complex. Luxury level. Cr cds: A, C, D, DS, JCB, MC, V.
[D] [icons]

★★ **SILVER CLOUD INN-BELLEVUE.** *10621 NE 12th St, Bellvue (98004). 425/637-7000; fax 425/455-0531; toll-free 800/205-6937. www. scinns.com.* 97 rms, 11 suites, 18 with shower only, 4 story. June-Sept: S $112-$139, D $143-$179; each addl $10; suites $145-$189; under 18 free. Crib free. TV; cable (premium). Heated pool; whirlpool. Complimentary continental bkfst. Restaurant nearby. Coffee in rms. Ck-out noon. Concierge. Business servs avail. In-rm modem link. Guest lndry. Valet serv. Exercise equipt. Refrigerators; microwaves avail. Some balconies, kitchenettes. Cr cds: A, C, MC, V.

[D] [≈] [✕] [≥] [SC]

★★★★ **WOODMARK HOTEL ON LAKE WASHINGTON.** *1200 Carillon Point, Kirkland (98033). 425/822-3700; fax 425/822-3699; res 800/822-3700. www.thewoodmark.com.* Located on the shores of Lake Washington, seven miles east of Seattle, this low-lying hotel is part of a 32-acre community that offers specialty shops, restaurants, a fitness center and spa, a scenic marina, and much more for visitors to enjoy. 100 rms, 4 story, 21 suites. S, D $205-$275; suites $320-$1,800; wkend rates; each addl $20; under 18 free. Crib free. Overnight parking $11; valet parking $14. TV; cable; VCR avail. Pool; poolside serv. Complimentary evening refreshments, coffee in rms. Restaurant 6:30 am-9:30 pm; Sat 7 am-9:30 pm; Sun 7 am 2 pm. Rm serv 24 hrs. Bar 11 am-midnight. Ck-out noon, ck-in 4 pm. Meeting rms. Business servs avail. In-rm modem link. Valet serv. Microwave avail. Concierge. Gift shop. Health club privileges. Full-service, 5,000-sq ft spa. Refrigerators, minibars. Balconies. Fireplace in suites. Marina; 3 lakeside parks. Cr cds: A, D, DS, JCB, MC, V.

[D] [≥] [🔥] [≈]

Resort

★★★ **WILLOWS LODGE.** *14580 NE 145th St, Woodinville (98072). 425/424-3900; fax 425/424-2585; toll-free 877/424-3930. www.willowslodge. com.* 88 rms, 2 story. S, D $260-$320; each addl $15; suites $360-$750. TV; cable (premium), VCR avail. Pet accepted; fee. Complimentary continental bkfst. Valet serv. Concierge serv. Complimentary coffee in rms, newspaper. Ck-out noon. Meeting rms. Business serv avail. Exercise rm; whirlpool. Cr cds: A, D, DS, ER, JCB, MC, V.

[D] [🐕] [✕] [🔥] [SC]

B&B/Small Inn

★★ **SHUMWAY MANSION.** *11410 99th Pl NE, Kirkland (98033). 425/823-2303; fax 425/822-0421.*

www.shumwaymansion.com. 8 rms, 2 story. No A/C. S, D $85-$120; each addl $12; suite $120. Children over 12 yrs only. TV avail. Complimentary full bkfst; evening refreshments. Restaurant nearby. Ck-out 11 am, ck-in 3 pm. Business servs avail. 24-rm historic mansion (1909), restored and moved to present site in 1985. Overlooks Juanita Bay. Totally non-smoking. Cr cds: A, MC, V.

[D] [≥]

Extended Stay

★★ **RESIDENCE INN BY MARRIOTT.** *14455 NE 29th Pl (98007). 425/882-1222; fax 425/885 9260; res 800/331-3131. www.residenceinn.com.* 120 suites, 2 story. S, D $160-$240. Crib free. Pet accepted; $15/day. TV; cable (premium), VCR avail (free movies). Heated pool. Complimentary bkfst. Complimentary coffee in rms. Ck-out noon. Coin lndry. Business servs avail. In-rm modem link. Valet serv. Lawn games. Private patios, balconies. Picnic tables, grills. Cr cds: A, D, DS, MC, V.

[D] [🐕] [≈] [≥] [🔥]

Restaurants

★★★ **CAFE JUANITA.** *9702 120th Pl NE, Kirkland (98034). 425/823-1505. www.cafejuanita.com.* Hrs: 5-10 pm. Closed Mon; hols. Res accepted. Northern Italian menu. Serv bar. Wine cellar. A la carte entrees: dinner $15-$29. Specialties: roasted rabbit, handmade and housemade pastas. Outdoor dining. Casual dining in converted private home; open kitchen. Family-owned. Totally non-smoking. Cr cds: A, JCB, MC, V.

[D]

★★★★ **THE HERBFARM.** *195 NE Gilman Blvd, Woodinville (98024). 206/784-2222. www.herbfarm.com.* Yards of billowing fabric and an open kitchen give this elegant wine country restaurant an atmosphere that can only be described as "country chic." It took several years after a devastating fire for the Zimmerman's to rebuild their beloved shrine to herbs and fresh produce. But it was definitely worth the wait—and the extra few minutes' drive to the new location. Chef Jerry Traunfeld turns out extraordinarily creative and sophisticated herb-based fare for his ever-changing seasonal prix-fixe menu. Local wines, friendly service, and a lovely setting complete this unique dining experience. Hrs: 5-9 pm. Closed Mon-Wed; hols. Wine list. Res required. Complete meals: 6-course dinner with wine $175. Parking. Totally nonsmoking. Cr cds: A, MC, V.

★ ★ **POLARIS.** *11200 SE 6th (98004). 425/637-4608. www. bellevueclub.com.* Hrs: 6:30 am-2:30 pm, 5:30-9 pm; Sat to 10 pm. Res accepted. Continental menu. Dinner $7.50-$32.50. Child's meals. Specializes in pasta, seafood, lamb. Cr cds: A, JCB, MC, V.
D

★ ★ **SPAZZO MEDITERRANEAN GRILL.** *10655 NE 4th St (98004). 425/454-8255. www.schwartzbros.com.* Hrs: 11:30 am-10 pm; Fri to 11 pm; Sat 5-10:30 pm; Sun 5-9 pm. Closed Thanksgiving, Dec 25. Res accepted. Mediterranean menu. Bar. Lunch $6.95-$15.95, dinner $18-$35. Children's meals. Specializes in Italian, Greek and Spanish dishes. View of Lake Washington and downtown. Cr cds: A, D, DS, JCB, MC, V.
D

★ ★ **THIRD FLOOR FISH CAFE.** *205 Lake St S, Kirkland (98033). 425/822-3553. www.fishcafe.com.* Hrs: 5-9:30 pm; Fri, Sat to 10 pm; Sun 4:30-9 pm. Closed Jan 1, Thanksgiving, Dec 25. Res accepted. Bar 4 pm-midnight; Sun to 10 pm. Wine list. A la carte entrees: dinner $17-$35. Specialties: spice-crusted Pacific halibut, pan-seared sturgeon, lamb shank. Own pastries. Pianist. Three window-walls overlook Lake Washington and marina; dark woods create intimate atmosphere. Totally nonsmoking. Cr cds: A, D, DS, MC, V.
D

Bellingham

(A-3) *See also Blaine, Sedro Woolley; also see Vancouver, BC, Canada*

Founded 1853 **Pop** 52,179 **Elev** 68 ft
Area code 360

Information Bellingham/Whatcom County Convention & Visitors Bureau, 904 Potter St, 98226; 360/671-3990 or 800/487-2032 (order information). The Bureau operates a Visitor Information Center off I-5 exit 253; daily; closed hols.
Web www.bellingham.org

This city, located on Bellingham Bay, has the impressive Mount Baker as its backdrop and is the last major city before the Washington coastline meets the Canadian border. The broad curve of the bay was charted in 1792 by Captain George Vancouver, who named it in honor of Sir William Bellingham. When the first settlers arrived here, forests stretched to the edge of the high bluffs along the shoreline. Timber and coal played major roles in the town's early economy.

Today, Bellingham has an active waterfront port, which supports fishing, cold storage, boat building, shipping, paper processing, and marina operations. Squalicum Harbor's commercial and pleasure boat marina accommodates more than 1,800 vessels, making it the second-largest marina on Puget Sound. The marina is a pleasant area to dine, picnic, and watch the fishermen at work. The downtown area contains a mix of restaurants, art galleries, specialty shops, and other stores. Bellingham is also home to Western Washington University, located on Sehome Hill, which affords a scenic view of the city and bay.

What to See and Do

Chuckanut Drive. A ten-mi drive, mostly along highway cut into mountain sides; beautiful vistas of Puget Sound and San Juan Islands. S from Fairhaven Park on WA 11 along Chuckanut Bay to Larrabee State Park.

City recreation areas. More than 2,000 acres of parkland offer a wide variety of activities. (Daily) Fee for some activities. Phone 360/676-6985. Areas incl

Arroyo Park. Approx 40 acres of dense, second-growth forest in a canyon setting. Creek fishing. Hiking, nature, and bridle trails. Off Chuckanut Dr on Old Samish Rd.

Bloedel Donovan Park. Swimming beach, fishing, boat launch; picnicking, playground, concession (summer). Community center with gym. 2214 Electric Ave, NW area of Lake Whatcom.

Boulevard Park. Fishing, boat dock; bicycle paths, picnicking, playground. Craft studio. S State St and Bayview Dr.

Civic Field Athletic Complex. Contains multiple athletic fields and indoor community pool. Lakeway Dr and Orleans St.

Cornwall Park. Approx 65 acres. Wading pool, steelhead fishing in Squalicum Creek; fitness trail, tennis, other game courts and fields, picnicking, playground. Extensive rose garden in park. 3424 Meridian.

Fairhaven Park. Wading pool; hiking trails, tennis, picnicking, playground. 107 Chuckanut Dr.

Lake Padden Park. Approx 1,000 acres with 152-acre lake. Swimming beach, fishing, boat launch (no motors), hiking and bridle trails, 18-hole golf course (fee), tennis, athletic fields, picnicking, playground. 4882 Samish Way.

Sehome Hill Arboretum. The 165-acre native plant preserve contains hiking and interpretive trails; scenic views of city, Puget Sound, San Juan Islands, and mountains from observation tower atop hill. 25th St and McDonald Pkwy.

Whatcom Falls Park. Approx 240 acres. Children's fishing pond, state fish hatchery; hiking trails, tennis, athletic fields, picnicking, playground. 1401 Electric Ave, near Lake Whatcom.

⭐ **Fairhaven District.** In the late 1800s, this area was a separate city that had hopes of becoming the next Chicago. The 1890s buildings are now restaurants and shops. Brass plaques detail history of the area. Walking tour brochures at the information gazebo, 12th and Harris.

Ferndale. Community founded in mid-1800s, with several preserved areas. **Hovander Homestead**, on Neilson Rd, is a county park with working farm and museum; interpretive center with nature trails and observation tower. Approx 9 mi NW

off I-5, exit 262. Phone 360/384-3444. ¢¢

Larrabee State Park. Approx 2,000 acres. Scuba diving, fishing, clamming, crabbing, tide pools, boating (ramp); hiking, picnicking, camping (hookups). Mountain viewpoints. Standard fees. 7 mi S on WA 11. Phone 360/676-2093.

Lynden Pioneer Museum. Exhibits on history of this Dutch community; antique car and buggy, farm equipt. (Mon-Sat) Approx 12 mi N via WA 539, at 217 Front St, Lynden. Phone 360/354-3675. ¢

Maritime Heritage Center. Salmon life-cycle facility and learning center. Outdoor rearing tanks; indoor displays detail development from egg to adult. Park (Daily). Learning Center (Mon-Fri; closed hols). 1600 C St. Phone 360/676-6806. **FREE**

Mount Baker-Snoqualmie National Forest. Mt Baker and Snoqualmie National Forest were combined under a single forest supervisor in July, 1974. Divided into five ranger districts, the combined forest encompasses nearly two million acres. The Snoqualmie section lies east and southeast of Seattle (see); the Mt Baker section lies east on WA 542 and incl the Mt Baker Ski Area. The forest extends from the Canadian border south to Mt Rainier National Park and incl rugged mountains and woodlands on the western slopes of the Cascades, the western portions of the Glacier Peak and Alpine Lakes, Henry M. Jackson, Noisy-Diobsud, Boulder River, Jackson, Clearwater, and Norse Peak wildernesses; seven commercial ski areas; 1,440 mi of hiking trails; picnic areas and campsites. Mt Baker rises 10,778 ft in the north, forming a center for recreation all yr, famous for deep-powder snow skiing and snowboarding. Snoqualmie Pass (via I-90) and Stevens Pass (via US 2) provide yr-round access to popular, scenic destinations; Baker Lake provides excellent boating and fishing. Contact Forest Service/National Park Service Information. Phone 360/599-2714. East of forest is

North Cascades National Park. (See SEDRO WOOLLEY)

Skiing. Mount Baker Ski Area. Four quad, three double chairlifts, rope tow; patrol, school, rentals; restaurant, cafeteria, bar; lodge. Longest run 1½ mi; vertical drop 1,500 ft. (Nov-Mar, daily; Apr, Fri-Sun; closed Dec 25) Also x-country trails. Half-day rates (wkends, hols). 55 mi E on WA 542. Phone 360/734-6771.

Western Washington University. (1893) 11,500 students. A 189-acre campus; internationally acclaimed outdoor sculpture collection; contemporary art at Western Gallery. Phone 360/650-3963.

Whatcom Museum of History and Art. Regional and historic displays; also changing art exhibits; in former city hall (1892) and three adj buildings. Fee for special exhibitions. (Tues-Sun; closed hols) 121 Prospect St. Phone 360/676-6981. **FREE**

Special Events

Ski to Sea Festival. Parades, carnival, art show, special events. Ski to Sea race starts on Mt Baker, ends in Bellingham Bay and involves skiers, runners, canoeists, bicyclists, and kayakers. Memorial Day wkend. Phone 360/734-1330.

Deming Logging Show. Log show grounds, in Deming. Log chopping, tree climbing, logger rodeo, salmon barbecue. Second wkend June. Phone 360/592-2423.

Lummi Stommish. Lummi Reservation, 15 mi NW via I-5, exit 260 to WA 540. Water carnival with war canoe races, arts and crafts; salmon bake, Native American dancing. Wkend June. Phone 360/384-1489.

Motels/Motor Lodges

★★ **BEST WESTERN INN.** *151 E Mcleod Rd (98226). 360/647-1912; fax 360/671-3878; toll-free 800/780-7234. www.bestwestern.com.* 90 rms, 3 story. No elvtr. S $67-$80; D $77-$86; each addl $5; suites $135-$155; studio rms $67-$89; under 12 free. Crib free. TV; cable (premium), VCR avail. Heated pool; whirlpool. Complimentary continental bkfst. Restaurant 6 am-11 pm. Ck-out noon. Meeting rms. Business servs avail. Valet serv. Free airport transportation. Health club privileges. Some refrigerators, wet bars; microwaves avail. Cr cds: A, C, D, DS, MC, V.
[D] [≋] [⊠] [火] [SC]

★★ **BEST WESTERN LAKEWAY INN.** *714 Lakeway Dr (98226). 360/671-1011; fax 360/676-8519; res 888/671-1011. www.bellingham-hotel.com.* 132 rms, 4 story. S $69-$89; D $79-$99; each addl $10; suites $99-$119; under 13 free. Crib $5. Pet accepted, some restrictions. TV; cable (premium). Indoor pool; whirlpool. Coffee in rms. Restaurant 6 am-10 pm. Bar; entertainment Thurs-Sat. Ck-out noon. Coin lndry. Meeting rms. Business center. Valet serv. Beauty shop. Free airport, bus depot transportation. Exercise equipt; sauna. Cr cds: A, C, D, DS, ER, JCB, MC, V.
[D] [🏋] [≋] [🏋] [✈] [⊠] [🔥] [SC] [🏋]

★ **DAYS INN.** *125 E Kellogg Rd (98226). 360/671-6200; fax 360/671-9491; toll-free 800/831-0187. www.daysinn.com.* 70 rms, 3 story. July-Sept: S $49.95; D $54.95; each addl $5; suites $79-$99; under 12 free; lower rates rest of yr. Crib free. Pet accepted; $5. TV; cable (premium). Heated pool; whirlpool. Complimentary continental bkfst. Restaurant nearby. Ck-out 11 am. Coin lndry. Meeting rms. Health club privileges. Some refrigerators; microwaves avail. Cr cds: A, C, D, DS, JCB, MC, V.
[D] [🏋] [≋] [⊠] [🔥]

★★ **HAMPTON INN.** *3985 Bennett Dr (98225). 360/676-7700; fax 360/671-7557. www.hamptoninn.com.* 132 rms, 4 story. June-Sept: S $69-$74; D $79-$89 (up to 4); under 18 free; lower rates rest of yr. Crib free. TV; cable (premium). Pool. Complimentary continental bkfst. Complimentary coffee in rms. Ck-out noon. Meeting rms. Business center. In-rm modem link. Free airport, RR station transportation. Exercise equipt. Cr cds: A, C, D, DS, MC, V.
[D] [≋] [✈] [⊠] [🔥] [🏋]

★ **QUALITY INN.** *100 E Kellogg Rd (98226). 360/647-8000; fax 360/647-8094; res 800/228-5151. www.qualityinn.com.* 86 suites, 3 story. June-mid-Sept: S $69.95-$89.95; D $79.95-$99.95; each addl $10; under 18 free; suites $109-$265; lower rates rest of yr. Crib free. TV; cable (premium), VCR avail. Heated pool; whirlpool. Complimentary continental bkfst. Coffee in rms. Restaurant nearby. Ck-out noon. Coin lndry. Meeting rms. Business center. In-rm modem link.

Free airport, bus depot transportation. Exercise equipt. Refrigerators; microwaves avail. Balconies. Cr cds: A, D, DS, JCB, MC, V.

★ **RAMADA INN.** *215 N Samish Way (81008).* 360/734-8830; fax 360/647-8956; res 888/298-2054. *www.ramada. com.* 66 rms, 3 story. June-Sept: S, D $79-$120; each addl $6; under 18 free; higher rates sporting events; lower rates rest of yr. Crib free. TV; cable (premium), VCR avail. Heated pool. Complimentary continental bkfst. Complimentary coffee in rms. Restaurant nearby. Ck-out noon. Business servs avail. Valet serv. Refrigerators. Balconies. Cr cds: A, C, D, DS, MC, V.

★★ **TRAVELERS INN.** *3750 Meridian St (98225).* 360/671-4600; fax 360/671-6487; toll-free 800/633-8300. 124 rms, 3 story. June-Sept: S $59; D $69; each addl $7; suites $74-$89; under 19 free; lower rates rest of yr. Crib free. TV; cable (premium). Heated pool; whirlpool. Complimentary coffee in lobby. Restaurant nearby. Ck-out 11 am. Coin lndry. Meeting rms. Business servs avail. Some refrigerators. Cr cds: A, C, D, DS, MC, V.

★ **VAL-U INN MOTEL.** *805 Lakeway Dr (98226).* 360/671-9600; fax 360/671 8323; toll free 800/443 7777. *www.valuinn.com.* 82 rms, 3 story. June-Sept: S $51-$54; D $59-$62; each addl $5; suites $75-$90; under 12 free; lower rates rest of yr. Crib $5. Pet accepted; $5. TV; cable (premium), VCR avail. Whirlpool. Complimentary continental bkfst. Restaurant nearby. Ck-out noon. Coin lndry. Meeting rms. Business servs avail. Valet serv. Free airport, RR station, ferry terminal transportation. Some refrigerators; microwaves avail. Cr cds: A, C, D, DS, MC, V.

Restaurants

★★ **CHUCKANUT MANOR.** *3056 Chuckanut Dr, Bow (98232).* 360/766-6191. Hrs: 11:30 am-10 pm; Sun from 10:30 am; Sun brunch to 2:30 pm. Closed Mon; hols. Res accepted.

Bar. Lunch $6-$12, dinner $14-$23. Sun brunch $17.50. Children's meals. Specializes in seafood, steak. Overlooks Samish bay, San Juan Islands. Guest rms avail. Cr cds: A, C, MC, V.

★★ **MARINA.** *7 Bellwetherway (98225).* 360/733-8292. *www. themarinarestaurant.com.* Hrs: 11:30 am-10:30 pm. Closed Dec 25. Res accepted. Bar. A la carte entrees: lunch $5.95-$12.95, dinner $10.95-$29.95. Children's meals. Specializes in seafood, steak. Outdoor dining, views of bay. Cr cds: A, D, MC, V.

Blaine

(A-3) *See also Bellingham; also see Vancouver, BC, Canada*

Pop 2,489 **Elev** 41 ft **Area code** 360 **Zip** 98231

Information Visitor Information Center, 215 Marine Dr, PO Box 4680, 360/332-4544 or 800/487-2032

Web www.blaine.net

What to See and Do

Birch Bay State Park. Approx 190 acres. Swimming, scuba diving, fishing, crabbing, clamming, picnicking, camping (Daily, res advised Memorial Day-Labor Day; hookups; dump station). Standard fees. 10 mi SW via I-5, exit 266, then 7 mi W via Grandview Rd, N via Jackson Rd to Helwig Rd. Phone 360/371-2800.

International Peace Arch. (1921) The 67-ft-high arch is on the boundary line between the US and Canada and marks more than a century of peace and friendship between the two countries. The surrounding park is maintained by the state of Washington and Province of British Columbia; gardens, picnicking, playground. N at point where I-5 reaches Canadian border.

Semiahmoo Park. A cannery once located on this 1½-mi-long spit was the last port of call for Alaskan fishing boats on Puget Sound. Restored buildings now house museum, gallery, and gift shop (June-mid-Sept, Sat and Sun afternoons). Park (daily) offers clam digging, picnicking, bird-watching. Off I-5, exit 274, on Semi-ahmoo Sandspit, Drayton Harbor. Phone 360/371-2000. ¢¢

Special Event

Peace Arch Celebration. International Peace Arch. Ceremony celebrates the relationship between the US and Canada; scouts and veterans from both nations. Second Sun June. Phone 360/332-4544.

Resort

★★★ **RESORT SEMIAHMOO.** *9565 Semiahmoo Pkwy (98230). 360/318-2000. www.semiahmoo.com.* 198 units, 4 story, 14 suites. May-Oct: S, D $99-$189; each addl $20; suites $269-$499; under 18 free; golf plans; lower rates rest of yr. Crib free. TV; cable. Indoor/outdoor pool; whirlpool, poolside serv. Complimentary coffee in rms. Dining rms 6:30 am-2:30 pm, 5:30-11 pm. Box lunches, snack bar. Rm serv 6:30 am-11 pm. Bar 11-1 am; entertainment (seasonal). Ck-out noon, ck-in 4 pm. Grocery 2 blks. Coin lndry, package store 7 mi. Meeting rms. Business servs avail. In-rm modem link. Concierge. Beauty shop. Sports dir. Indoor and outdoor tennis courts, pro. 18-hole golf, greens fee $75, pro, putting green, driving range. Beachcombing. 300-slip marina; boat and water sports. San Juan Island cruise

yacht. Charter fishing, clam digging, oyster picking (seasonal). Bicycle rentals. Lawn games. Game rm. Exercise rm; sauna, steam rm. Spa. Some fireplaces. Some private patios, balconies. On 1,100-acre wildlife preserve. Cr cds: A, D, DS, MC, V.

Bremerton

(C-3) *See also Seattle*

Founded 1891 **Pop** 38,142 **Elev** 60 ft

Information Bremerton Chamber of Commerce, 301 Pacific Ave, PO Box 229, Port Gamble, 98364; 360/479-3579

Web www.bremerton.org

The tempo of the Puget Sound Naval Shipyard is the heartbeat of Bremerton, a community surrounded on three sides by water. The six dry docks of the Naval Shipyard make Bremerton a home port for the Pacific fleet.

What to See and Do

✪ **Bremerton Naval Museum.** Ship models, pictures, display of navy and shipyard history. Naval artifacts. (Tues-Sun; closed hols) 130 Washington Ave. **FREE**

Kitsap County Historical Society Museum. Re-creation of 1800s pioneer settlements. Photos and documents of history to WWII era. (Tues-Sat; closed hols) 280 4th St. Phone 360/692-1949. ¢

State parks.

Belfair. Approx 80 acres. Swimming; picnicking, camping (hookups; res Memorial Day-Labor Day, by mail only). Standard fees. 15 mi SW via WA 3 in Belfair. Phone 360/275-0668.

Blake Island. More than 475 acres. Saltwater swimming

Washington's natural beauty

beach, scuba diving, fishing, boating (dock); hiking, picnicking, primitive camping. Standard fees. 6 mi SE, accessible only by boat. Phone 360/731-8330.

Illahee. Approx 75 acres. Swimming, scuba diving; fishing, clamming; boating (ramp, dock). Hiking. Picnicking. Primitive camping. Standard fees. 3 mi NE off WA 306. Phone 360/478-6460.

Scenic Beach. Approx 90 acres. Swimming, scuba diving; limited fishing, oysters in season. Nature trail. Picnicking. Primitive camping. Standard fees. 12 mi NW on WA 3. Phone 360/830-5079.

USS Turner Joy. Tours of Vietnam War era US Navy destroyer. (May-Sept, daily; rest of yr, Mon, Thurs-Sun; closed Dec 25) 300 Washington Beach Ave. Phone 360/792-2457.

Special Events

Armed Forces Day Parade. Mid May. Phone 360/479-3579.

Mountaineers' Forest Theater. 8 mi W via WA 3, Kitsap Way, Seabeck Hwy, watch for signs. Oldest outdoor theater in the Pacific Northwest. Natural amphitheater surrounded by hundreds of rhododendrons beneath old-growth Douglas fir and hemlock. Log-terraced seats. Family-oriented play. The ⅓-mile walk to theater is difficult for the physically disabled or elderly (assistance avail). Picnicking; concession. Contact 300 Third Ave W, Seattle 98119; 206/284-6310. Late May-early June.

Blackberry Festival. Late Aug. Phone 360/479-3579.

Kitsap County Fair and Stampede. Fairgrounds in Tracyton. Late Aug. Phone 360/337-5376.

Motels/Motor Lodges

★★ **BEST WESTERN BREMERTON INN.** 4303 Kitsap Way (98312). 360/405-1111; fax 360/377-0597; toll-free 800/780-7234. www.bestwestern.com. 103 rms, 2-3 story, 77 kits. No elvtr. S $71; D $79-$86; each addl $7; suites $90-$190; under 13 free. Crib free. TV; cable (premium), VCR avail (movies $5). Heated pool; whirlpool. Playground. Complimentary continental bkfst. Ck-out 11 am. Coin

lndry. Meeting rm. Business servs avail. In-rm modem link. Exercise equipt. Picnic tables, grills. Cr cds: A, C, D, DS, ER, JCB, MC, V.

D ⊷ 🏃 ⊠ 🔥

★★ **FLAGSHIP INN.** 4320 Kitsap Way (98312). 360/479-6566; fax 360/479-6745; res 800/447-9396. www.flagship-inn.com. 29 rms, 3 story. No elvtr. S $65; D $69-$89; each addl $6. Crib $6. TV; cable (premium), VCR (movies $2). Heated pool. Complimentary continental bkfst. Restaurant nearby. Ck-out noon. Business servs avail. In-rm modem link. Refrigerators. Balconies. On Oyster Bay. Cr cds: A, D, DS, MC, V.

⊷ ⊠ 🔥

★★ **MIDWAY INN.** 2909 Wheaton Way (98310). 360/479-2909; fax 360/479-1576; toll-free 800/231-0575. www.midway-inn.com. 60 rms, 3 story, 12 kit. units. S $59; D $64; each addl $5; kit. units $69-$74; under 12 free; wkly rates. Crib $5. Pet accepted, some restrictions; $10. TV; cable (premium), VCR (free movies). Complimentary continental bkfst. Complimentary coffee in rms. Restaurant adj 4 pm-midnight. Ck-out 11 am. Coin lndry. Meeting rms. Business servs avail. Refrigerators; microwaves avail. Cr cds: A, C, D, DS, MC, V.

D 🐾 ⊠ 🔥 SC

★★ **WESTCOAST SILVERDALE HOTEL.** 3073 NW Bucklin Hill Rd, Silverdale (98383). 360/698-1000; fax 360/692-0932; toll-free 800/544-9799. www.westcoasthotels.com. 150 units, 2-3 story. S $85-$115; D $95-$125; each addl $10; suites $135-$325; under 18 free. Crib free. TV; cable. Indoor pool; whirlpool, poolside serv. Coffee in rms. Restaurant 6 am-11 pm. Bar 11-2 am; entertainment Fri-Sat. Ck-out noon. Meeting rms. Business servs avail. Bellhops. Valet serv. Lighted tennis. Exercise equipt; sauna. Game rm. Rec rm. Lawn games. Microwaves avail; refrigerator in suites. Private patios, balconies. Cr cds: A, DS, MC, V.

D 🏌 ⊷ ⊠ 🔥 🏃

Restaurants

★★ **BOAT SHED.** 101 Shore Dr (98310). 360/377-2600. Hrs: 11 am-9 pm; Fri, Sat to 10 pm; Sun 10 am-8 pm. Closed hols. Lunch $5.95-$11.95, dinner $5.95-$26.95. Specializes in seafood, steak, pasta. Outdoor dining. On waterfront. Cr cds: A, MC, V.

★★ **YACHT CLUB BROILER.** *9226 Bay Shore Dr, Silverdale (98383). 360/698-1601.* Hrs: 11 am-11 pm; Sun from 10 am; Sun brunch to 3 pm. Closed hols. Res accepted. Bar. Lunch $6-$12, dinner $10-$26. Sun brunch $4.95-$12. Children's meals. Specializes in prime steak, fresh salmon and halibut. Outdoor dining. Overlooks Silverdale Bay. Cr cds: A, D, MC, V.

Cashmere

(C-5) *See also Leavenworth, Wenatchee*

Founded 1881 **Pop** 2,544 **Elev** 853 ft
Area code 509 **Zip** 98815
Information Chamber of Commerce, PO Box 834; 509/782-7404
Web www.visitcashmere.com

Cashmere's history dates back to the 1860s when a Catholic missionary came to the area to set up a school for Native Americans. Cashmere is located in the Wenatchee Valley in the center of the state on the North Cascade Loop. It has strong timber and fruit industries.

What to See and Do

Cashmere Museum. Pioneer relics, Native American artifacts; Columbia River archaeology exhibit; water wheel (1891); mineral exhibit; "pioneer village" with 21 cabins, mining displays. Great Northern Railroad depot, passenger car and caboose. (See SPECIAL EVENTS) (Mar-Nov, daily; rest of yr, by appt) 600 Cottage Ave, east edge of town. Phone 509/782-3230. ¢¢

Liberty Orchards Company, Inc. Makes fruit-nut confections known as "aplets," "cotlets," "grapelets," and "fruit festives." Tour, samples. (May-Dec, daily; rest of yr, Mon-Fri;

closed hols) Children with adult only. 117 Mission St, off US 2. Phone 509/782-2191.

Special Events

Founders' Day. Chelan County Historical Museum. Last wkend June. Phone 509/782-3230.

Chelan County Fair. First wkend after Labor Day. Phone 509/782-0708.

Apple Days. Chelan County Historical Museum. Apple pie contest, old-time crafts, Pioneer Village in operation, cider making. First wkend Oct. Phone 509/782-3230.

Motels/Motor Lodges

★ **VILLAGE INN MOTEL.** *229 Cottage Ave (98815). 509/782-3522; fax 509/782-8190; res 800/793-3522.* 21 rms, 2 story. S $45-$51; D $50-$60; each addl $5; higher rates festivals. Pet accepted, some restrictions; $5. TV; cable. Complimentary coffee in lobby. Restaurant nearby. Ck-out 11 am. Business servs avail. X-country ski 11 mi. Cr cds: MC, V.

★★ **WEDGE MOUNTAIN INN.** *7335 WA 2 (98815). 509/548-6694; toll-free 800/666-9664. www.wedge mountaininn.com.* 28 rms, 2 story. May-Dec: S $70; D $79; each addl $10; under 18 free; lower rates rest of yr. Crib $5. TV; cable. Heated pool. Complimentary coffee in lobby. Restaurant adj 6 am-9 pm. Ck-out 11 am. Coin lndry. Balconies. Cr cds: A, DS, MC, V.

Centralia

(D-2) *See also Chehalis*

Founded 1875 **Pop** 12,101 **Elev** 189 ft
Area code 360 **Zip** 98531
Information The Centralia, Chehalis, and Greater Lewis County Chamber of Commerce, 500 NW Chamber of Commerce Way, Chehalis 98532; 360/748-8885 or 800/525-3323
Web www.chamberway.com

Centralia was founded by a former slave named George Washington. George Washington Park is named for the founder, not for the country's first president.

What to See and Do

Schaefer County Park. Swimming in the Skookumchuck River; fishing; hiking trails, picnicking (shelter), playground, horseshoe pits, volleyball. ½ mi N on WA 507. Phone 360/740-1135. **FREE**

Special Event

Southwest Washington Fair. 1 mi S on I 5. First held in 1909, this is the state's second-oldest fair and one of the largest. Third wk Aug. Phone 360/736-6072.

Motel/Motor Lodge

★★ **INN AT CENTRALIA.** *702 W Harrison Ave (98531). 360/736-2875; fax 360/736-2651; toll-free 800/459-0035.* 89 rms, 2 story. June-Sept: S $55-$65; D $65-$75; each addl $4; suites $80; under 12 free; lower rates rest of yr. Crib $4. Pet accepted. TV; cable. Heated pool. Complimentary continental bkfst. Restaurant opp open 24 hrs. Ck-out 11 am. Business servs avail. Cr cds: A, C, D, DS, MC, V

Chehalis

(D-2) *See also Centralia*

Settled 1873 **Pop** 6,527 **Elev** 226 ft
Area code 360 **Zip** 98532
Information The Centralia, Chehalis, and Greater Lewis County Chamber of Commerce, 500 NW Chamber of Commerce Way; 360/748-8885 or 800/525-3323
Web www.chamberway.com

First called Saundersville, this city takes its present name, Native American for "shifting sands," from its position at the point where the Newaukum and Chehalis rivers meet. Farms and an industrial park give economic sustenance to Chehalis and neighboring Centralia.

What to See and Do

Historic Claquato Church. (1858) Oldest church in state, original building on original site; handmade pews, pulpit. (Schedule varies) 3 mi W on WA 6, on Claquato Hill. Phone 360/748-4551.

Lewis County Historical Museum. Restored railroad depot (1912). Pioneer displays; Native American exhibits. Cemetery, genealogical history; artifacts, newspapers, books, photographs, written family histories, oral histories of pioneers. (Tues-Sun; closed hols) 599 NW Front Way. Phone 360/748-0831. ¢

Rainbow Falls State Park. Approx 125 acres of woodland. Fishing; hiking trails, picnicking, camping (dump station). Standard fees. 18 mi W on WA 6. Phone 360/291-3767.

Special Event

Music and Art Festival. Arts and craft vendors, food. Late July. Phone 360/748-8885.

Restaurant

★ **MARY MC CRANK'S DINNER HOUSE.** *2923 Jackson Hwy (98532). 360/748-3662. www.marymccranks. com.* Hrs: 11:30 am 8:30 pm; Sun noon-8 pm. Closed Mon; Dec 25. Res accepted. Beer, wine. Lunch $5.25-$10.25, dinner $6.95-$21.95 Children's meals. Own jams, jellies, breads, pies. Farmhouse atmosphere; fireplace; antiques. Established 1935. Totally nonsmoking. Cr cds: DS, MC, V.

Chelan

(C-5) *See also Wenatchee*

Settled 1885 **Pop** 2,969 **Elev** 1,208 ft
Area code 509 **Zip** 98816
Information Lake Chelan Chamber of Commerce, 102 E Johnson, Box 216; 509/682-3503 or 800/4-CHELAN
Web www.lakechelan.com

Located in an apple-growing region, Chelan is a gateway to Lake Chelan and the spectacular northern Cascade mountains. A Ranger District office of the Wenatchee National Forest (see WENATCHEE) is located here.

What to See and Do

Lake Chelan. This fjordlike lake, the largest and deepest lake in the state, stretches northwest for approx 55 mi through the Cascade Mnts to the community of Stehekin in the North Cascades National Park (see SEDRO WOOLLEY); lake is nearly 1,500 ft deep in some areas. There are two state parks and several recreation areas along the lake. Phone 360/902-8844.

Lake cruises. The passenger boats *Lady of the Lake II* and *Lady Express* make daily cruises on Lake Chelan to Stehekin. For details contact Lake Chelan Boat Co, 1418 W Woodin Ave, Box 186. Phone 509/682-4584. ¢¢¢¢

State parks.

Alta Lake. More than 180 acres. Swimming, fishing, boating (ramps); hiking, snowmobiling, ice-skating, camping (hookups). Standard fees. 20 mi N on US 97, then 2 mi W on WA 153. Phone 509/923-2473.

Lake Chelan. Approx 130 lakefront acres. Swimming, fishing, boating (ramps, dock); picnicking, camping (hookups; res required late May-Aug). (Apr-Oct, daily; rest of yr, wkends and hols) Standard fees. 9½ mi W via US 97 and South Shore Dr or Navarre Coulee Rd. Phone 800/452-5687.

Twenty-Five Mile Creek. Approx 65 acres. Fishing, boating (launch, mooring, gas); hiking, concession, camping (hookups). Standard fees. 18 mi NW on South Shore Dr. Phone 800/452-5687.

Special Events

Apple Blossom Festival. 8 mi W via WA 150 in Manson. Second wkend May. Phone 509/687-3071.

Taste of Chelan Street Fair. Late June. Phone 509/682-9384.

Lake Chelan Rodeo. Last wkend July. Phone 509/682-5526.

Motels/Motor Lodges

★★★ **CAMPBELL'S RESORT CONFERENCE CENTER.** *104 W Woodin (98816). 509/682-2561; fax 509/682-2177; toll-free 800/553-8225. www.campbellsresort.com.* 170 rms, 1-4 story, 5 cottages, 22 kits. Mid-June-Labor Day: S, D $80-$90; each addl $10; suites $215-$325; cottages $182-$240; family rates; higher rates Memorial Day wkend, Labor Day wkend; lower rates rest of yr. Crib $5. TV; cable. 2 heated pools; whirlpool, poolside serv. Restaurant 6:45 am-9:30 pm. Bar 11 am-11 pm. Ck-out noon. Meeting rms. Business servs avail. In-rm modem link. Sundries. X-country ski 6 mi. Refrigerators; some minibars. Private patios, balconies. Sand beach; boat. Cr cds: A, D, ER, JCB, MC, V.

⊡ 🐾 ⚓ 🏊 ⛷ 🔥 SC

★★ **CARVEL RESORT MOTEL.** *322 W Woodin Ave (98816). 509/682-2582; fax 509/682-3551; toll-free 800/962-8723.* 93 rms, 1-4 story, 40 kits. Mid-June-mid-Sept: S, D $137-$165; suites $193-$500; wkly rate for kit. units; lower rates rest of yr. Crib $5. TV; cable. Heated pool. Restaurant nearby. Ck-out 11 am. Some refrigerators, fireplaces. Boat moorage. Cr cds: A, MC, V.

⊡ 🏊 ⛷ 🔥

Cheney

(C-8) *See also Spokane*

Pop 7,723 **Elev** 2,350 ft
Area code 509 **Zip** 99004
Information Chamber of Commerce, 201 First St, PO Box 65; 509/235-8480
Web www.cheneychamber.org

Cheney, on a rise of land that gives it one of the highest elevations of any municipality in the state, has been a university town since 1882. It is also a farm distribution and servicing center.

What to See and Do

Cheney Historical Museum. Features pioneer artifacts. (Mar-Nov, Tues and

Sat afternoons) 614 3rd St. Phone
509/235-4343. **FREE**

Eastern Washington University.
(1882) 9,000 students. Tours of campus. Phone 509/359-2397. On campus are a theater, recital hall, and

Gallery of Art. Changing exhibits.
(Academic yr, Mon-Fri; closed hols)
Phone 509/359-2493. **FREE**

Museum of Anthropology.
Teaching-research facility concerning Native Americans of North America. Phone 509/359-2433.
FREE

Turnbull National Wildlife Refuge.
Located on the Pacific Flyway; more than 200 species of birds have been observed in the area; also a habitat for deer, elk, coyotes, beaver, mink, chipmunks, red squirrels, and Columbia ground squirrels. Refuge named after Cyrus Turnbull, an early settler. A 2,200-acre public use area (Daily). 4 mi S on Cheney-Plaza Rd, then 2 mi E. Phone 509/235-4723

Special Event

Rodeo Days. Rodeo, parade. Second wkend July. Phone 509/235-4848.

Motel/Motor Lodge

★ **WILLOW SPRINGS MOTEL.** 5 B
St (99004). 509/235-5138; fax
509/235-4528. www.nebsnow.com/
manager. 44 rms, 3 story, 12 kits. No
elvtr. S $39-$45; D $44-$50; each
addl $5; kit. units $5 addl; under 12
free. Pet accepted; $5/day. TV; cable.
Complimentary coffee in lobby.
Restaurant opp 6 am-10 pm. Ck-out
11 am. Coin lndry. Cr cds: A, D, DS,
MC, V.

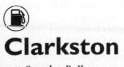

Clarkston

(E-8) *See also Pullman*

Founded 1896 **Pop** 6,753 **Elev** 736 ft
Area code 509 **Zip** 99403
Information Chamber of Commerce,
502 Bridge St; 509/758-7712 or
800/933-2128
Web www.clarkstonchamber.org

Clarkston is located on the Washington-Idaho boundary at the confluence of the Clearwater and Snake rivers. The town became a shipping center when the construction of four dams on the lower Snake River brought barge transportation here. Many recreation areas are located near Clarkston, especially along the Snake River and in the Umatilla National Forest. River trips are available into Hell's Canyon.

What to See and Do

Asotin County Museum. Main museum contains sculptures, pioneer equipt, pictures, and clothing. On grounds are furnished pioneer house, shepherd's cabin, one-rm schoolhouse, 1882 log cabin, blacksmith shop, a windmill, and Salmon River barge. (Tues-Sat; closed hols) Approx 6 mi S on WA 129, at 215 Filmore St, Asotin. Phone 509/243-4659. **FREE**

Fields Spring State Park. Approx 800 forested acres in the Blue Mtns. A one-mi uphill hike from parking lot to Puffer Butte gives view of three states. Wide variety of wildflowers and birdlife. Picnicking, primitive camping. Standard fees. 30 mi S on WA 129. Phone 509/256-3332.

Petroglyphs. Ancient writings inscribed in cliffs of Snake River near Buffalo Eddy. Near town of Asotin. Phone 800/933-2128.

Umatilla National Forest. Approx 319,000 acres of heavily forested mountain area extending into Oregon. Many recreation areas offer fishing; hunting, hiking, camping. Downhill skiing (see DAYTON). S of US 12, access near Pomeroy. For further information contact Supervisor, 2517 SW Hailey Ave, Pendleton, OR 97801. Phone 503/276-3811.

Valley Art Center. Various types of art and crafts; changing monthly exhibits with featured artists and special showings. (Mon-Fri, closed major hols) Northwest Heritage Show is held for two months in summer. 842 6th St. Phone 509/758-8331. **FREE**

Special Events

Asotin County Fair. Incl cowboy breakfast, barbecue, parade. Last Thurs-Sun Apr. Phone 509/758-7712.

Sunflower Days. Second Fri-Sat Aug. Phone 509/758-7712.

Motels/Motor Lodges

★★ **BEST WESTERN RIVERTREE INN.** *1257 Bridge St (99403). 509/758-9551; res 800/780-7234. www.best western.com.* 61 units, 2 story, 20 kits. (no equipt). S $69; D $79; each addl $5; suites $89-$130; kit. units $85 addl; higher rates university football games. Crib $5. TV; cable (premium). Heated pool; whirlpool. Restaurant opp 6-3 am. Ck-out noon. Business servs avail. Exercise equipt; sauna. Refrigerators. Balconies. Picnic tables, grills. Many rms with spiral staircase to loft. Cr cds: A, C, D, DS, MC, V.

🄳 ⊠ 🛩 🐾 SC 🕅

★ **QUALITY INN.** *700 Port Dr (99403). 509/758-9500; fax 509/758-5580; res 800/228-5151. www.quality inn.com.* 75 rms, 3 story. No elvtr. S $65-$89; D $85-$100; each addl $5; suites $105-$135; under 18 free. Crib free. TV; cable (premium). Pool. Coffee in rms. Restaurant 6 am-2 pm, 5-10 pm. Bar from 4 pm. Ck-out noon. Coin lndry. Meeting rms. Business servs avail. Exercise equipt. Valet serv. Balconies. On river. Convention center adj. Cr cds: A, D, DS, JCB, MC, V.

🄳 ⊠ 🛩 🔥 🕅

Restaurant

★ **ROOSTER'S LANDING.** *1550 Port Dr (99403). 509/751-0155.* Hrs: 11 am-10 pm; Fri, Sat to 11 pm. Closed Thanksgiving, Dec 24. Bar to midnight. Lunch, dinner $5.95-$16.95. Children's meals. Specialties: steak calypso, deer valley tenderloin, fish and chips. Parking. Outdoor dining. On river; view of countryside. Totally nonsmoking. Cr cds: A, DS, MC, V.

🄳 SC

Colville

(B-7) *See also Spokane*

Pop 4,360 **Elev** 1,635 ft
Area code 509 **Zip** 99114

Information Chamber of Commerce, 121 E Astor, PO Box 267; 509/684-5973
Web www.colville.com

Once a brawling frontier town, Colville, the seat of Stevens County, has quieted down and now reflects the peacefulness of the surrounding hills and mountains. Many towns flourished and died in this area—orchards, mills, and mines all had their day. The portage at Kettle Falls, a fort, and the crossing of several trails made Colville a thriving center.

What to See and Do

Colville National Forest. This million-acre forest is located in the northeast corner of Washington bordering Canada. The forest extends along its western boundary from the Canadian border south to the Colville Reservation and east across the Columbia River to Idaho. Comprising conifer forest types, small lakes, and winding valleys bounded by slopes leading to higher mountainous areas, the forest offers good hunting and fishing and full-service camping. Also here is Sullivan Lake, offering recreation opportunities incl boating, fishing, swimming; developed and dispersed campground settings, hiking trails, sightseeing. The bighorn sheep that inhabit adj Hall Mt can be viewed at a feeding station near the lake, which is cooperatively managed by the forest and the Washington Department of Wildlife. For more information, contact the Forest Supervisor, Federal Building, 765 S Main St. Phone 509/684-7000. Also located here are a Ranger District office and

> **Lake Gillette Recreation Area.** Boating, swimming, fishing; picnicking, amphitheater with programs, camping (fee). (Mid-May-Sept) E via Tiger Hwy, WA 20. Phone 509/684-5657. **FREE**

Keller Heritage Center. Site of three-story Keller home (1910), carriage house; blacksmith shop; farmstead cabin; gardens; museum; schoolhouse; machinery building; lookout tower. Local records, Native American artifacts. (May-Sept; daily) 700 N Wynne St. Phone 509/684-5968.
Donation

St. Paul's Mission. A chapel was built by Jesuit priests assisted by Native

Americans near here in 1845, followed by the hand-hewn log church in 1847. It fell into disuse in the 1870s and in 1939 was restored to its original state. Self-guided tour. Located at Kettle Falls in Lake Roosevelt National Recreation Area (see COULEE DAM). (All yr) 12 mi NW, near intersection of Columbia River and US 395. Phone 509/738-6266.

Special Events

Colville PRCA Rodeo. Father's Day wkend. Phone 509/684-4849.

Rendezvous. Arts and crafts, entertainment. First wkend Aug. Phone 509/684-5973.

Northeast Washington Fair. Stevens County Fairgrounds. Parade, livestock and horse shows; arts and crafts exhibits; carnival. Aug. Phone 509/684-2585.

B&B/Small Inn

★★★ **MY PARENTS ESTATE BED & BREAKFAST.** *719 Hwy 395 N, Kettle Falls (99141). 509/738-6220.* 3 rms, 1 suite. Suite $100. Adults only. TV in cottage. Complimentary continental bkfst. Ck-out 11 am, ck-in 4-6 pm. Built in 1873 as a convent for a mission. On 47 acres with gazebo, barn, and gymnasium. Totally nonsmoking. Cr cds: MC, V.

🐾 SC 📶

Coulee Dam (B-6)

Founded 1934 **Pop** 1,087 **Elev** 1,145 ft **Area code** 509 **Zip** 99116

Information Grand Coulee Dam Area Chamber of Commerce, 306 Midway Ave, PO Box 760, Grand Coulee, 99133-0760; 509/633-3074 or 800/COULEE2

Web www.grandcouleedam.org

Established as a construction community for workers on the Grand Coulee Dam project, this town now is the home of service and maintenance employees of the dam and headquarters for the Lake Roosevelt National Recreation Area.

What to See and Do

Colville Tribal Museum. More than 8,000 yrs of history on 11 tribes. (Late May-Sept, daily; rest of yr, schedule varies) Mead Way. Phone 509/633-0751. **FREE**

⭐ **Grand Coulee Dam.** Major structure of multipurpose Columbia Basin Project, built by Bureau of Reclamation. Water is diverted from the Columbia River to what in prehistoric days was its temporary course down the Grand Coulee (a deep water-carved ravine). The project will reclaim more than a million acres through irrigation and already provides a vast reservoir of electric power. One of the largest concrete structures in the world, the dam towers 550 ft high, has a 500-ft-wide base and a 5,223-ft-long crest. Power plants contain some of world's largest hydro-generators. Major exhibits along tour route. Laser show (Memorial Day-Sept, nightly). Near jct WA 155, 174. Phone 509/633-9265. **FREE**

Lake Roosevelt National Recreation Area. Totals 100,059 acres incl Franklin D. Roosevelt Lake. Lake formed by Grand Coulee Dam serves as storage reservoir with 630-mi shoreline; extends 151 mi northeast, reaching the Canadian border. Southern part is semi-arid; northern part mountainous, forested with ponderosa pine, fir, tamarack. Excellent for all sizes of motorboats with 151-mi waterway along reservoir and 200 mi of cruising water in Canada provided by Arrow Lakes, reached from Lake Roosevelt by the Columbia River. Thirty-eight areas have been specially developed; most provide camping (fee), picnicking; swimming, boating and launching sites (fee). Fishing all yr in Roosevelt Lake. Contact Superintendent, 1008 Crest, 99116. Phone 509/633-9441. Within is

Fort Spokane. One of the last frontier military outposts of the 1800s. Four of 45 buildings remain; brick guardhouse is now visitor center and small museum. Built to maintain peace between the settlers and Native Americans; no shot was ever fired. Self-guided trail around old parade grounds; interpretive displays. (Mid-June-Labor Day;

daily) Living history programs performed on wkends in summer. Nearby are beach and camping (fee). Phone 509/725-2715.

Steamboat Rock State Park. Approx 900 acres. Swimming, fishing, boating (launch); hiking, picnicking, camping (hookups; res recommended Memorial Day-Labor Day wkends). Standard fees. 11 mi S of Electric City on WA 155. Phone 509/633-1304.

Special Events

Colorama Festival & PWRA Rodeo. Second wkend May. Phone 800/268-5332.

Laser Light Festival. Memorial Day wkend. Phone 800/268-5332.

Motels/Motor Lodges

★ **COLUMBIA RIVER INN.** *10 Lincoln Ave (99116). 509/633-2100; toll-free 800/633-6421. www.columbia riverinn.com.* 34 rms, 2 story. S, D $49-$95; suite $190; under 12 free. Crib $5. TV; cable (premium). Pool; whirlpool. Complimentary coffee in rms. Restaurant nearby. Ck-out 11 am. Coin lndry. Business servs avail. In-rm modem link. Gift shop. Some refrigerators, microwaves. Private patios, balconies. View of dam. Cr cds: A, DS, MC, V.

★ **COULEE HOUSE MOTEL.** *110 Roosevelt Way (99116). 509/633-1101; fax 509/633-1416; toll-free 800/715-7767. www.couleehouse.com.* 61 units, 2 story, 17 kits. S $66-$77; D $77-$88; each addl $4; suites $104-$120; kit. units $54-$74; under 18 free. Crib $4. Pet accepted. TV; cable (premium). Heated pool; whirlpool. Complimentary coffee in lobby. Restaurant adj 6 am-10 pm. Ck-out 11 am. Coin lndry. Business servs avail. Sundries. Some refrigerators, balconies. View of dam. Cr cds: A, C, D, DS, MC, V.

Coupeville

(B-3) *See also Oak Harbor, Port Townsend*

Pop 1,377 **Elev** 80 ft **Area code** 360 **Zip** 98239

Information Visitor Information Center, 107 S Main St; 360/678-5434

One of the oldest towns in the state, Coupeville was named for Thomas Coupe, a sea captain and early settler, the only man to ever sail a full-rigged ship through Deception Pass. Fortified to protect the settlers and for the defense of Puget Sound, Coupeville was once the home of the only seat of higher education north of Seattle, the Puget Sound Academy. Today it is near Whidbey Island Naval Air Station, home of Naval Aviation for the Pacific Northwest.

What to See and Do

Alexander Blockhouse. (1855) One of four such buildings built on Whidbey Island to protect settlers' homes from Native Americans during the White River Massacre. Near Front St, on waterfront. Phone 360/678-5434.

Fort Casey State Park. Approx 140 acres. Scuba diving, saltwater fishing, boating (launch); picnicking, camping. Museum (Early May-mid-Sept). Standard fees. 3 mi S. Phone 360/678-4519.

Motel/Motor Lodge

★ **HARBOUR INN.** *1606 Main St, Freeland (98249). 360/331-6900.* 20 rms, 2 story. No A/C. S $73; D $82; each addl $6. Crib $6. Pet accepted, some restrictions; $6. TV; cable. Complimentary continental bkfst. Restaurant nearby. Ck-out 11 am. Refrigerators; microwaves avail. Cr cds: A, MC, V.

B&Bs/Small Inns

★★ **CAPTAIN WHIDBEY INN.** *2072 W Captain Whidbey Inn Rd (98239). 360/678-4097; toll-free 800/366-4097. www.captainwhidbey. com.* 32 units, 20 with bath, 3 kits. No A/C. S $85; D $135; each addl

$15; suites $135-$195; kit. cottages $175-$285. Complimentary full bkfst. Bar noon-midnight. Ck-out noon, ck-in 4 pm. Meeting rms. Business servs avail. Private beach; dock; boats, sailboats; clamming. Lawn games. Library. Fireplace in cottages. Turn-of-the-century log inn (1907) on sheltered cove. Cr cds: A, C, D, DS, MC, V.

★★★ **GUEST HOUSE BED & BREAKFAST COTTAGES.** *24371 State Rd 525, Greenbank (98253). 360/678-3115. www.whidbey.net/ logcottages.* 5 kit. cottages, 1 luxury log house, 1 and 2 story. A/C in 1 unit. No rm phones. Mar-mid-Oct: cottages: S, D $165-$210; log house $325; wkly rates; lower rates rest of yr. Adults only. TV; cable, VCR (free movies). Heated pool. Complimentary full bkfst. Restaurant nearby. Ck-out 11 am, ck-in 4 pm. Exercise equipt. Lawn games. In-rm whirlpools, microwaves. Fireplace in cottages. Private patios, balconies. Picnic tables, grills. Located on 25 acres with forest and meadows; marine and mountain views. Totally nonsmoking. Cr cds: A, DS, MC, V.

★★★ **INN AT LANGLEY.** *400 First St, Langley (98260). 360/221-3033. www.innatlangley.com.* 24 rms, 4 story. No A/C. No elvtr. S, D $225-$250; each addl $35; suites $395; wkends, hols (2-day min); cottage $575. Children over 12 yrs only. TV, cable (premium), VCR (movies). Complimentary continental bkfst. Complimentary coffee in rms. Dining rm, 1 sitting: 7 pm Fri, Sat. Restaurant nearby. Ck-out noon, ck-in 3 pm. In-rm modem link. Luggage handling. In-rm whirlpools, refrigerators, fireplaces. Balconies. On ocean. Elegant atmosphere. Totally nonsmoking. Cr cds: A, MC, V.

Restaurant

★★ **CAFE LANGLEY.** *113 1st St, Langley (98260). 360/221-3090. www.langley-wa.com/cl.* Hrs: 11:30 am-2:30 pm, 5-9:30 pm. Closed Dec 25. Res accepted. Mediterranean, Greek menu. Wine, beer. Lunch $5-$9, dinner $13.50-$25. Specialties: fresh seafood, locally grown products, Washington lamb. Totally nonsmoking. Cr cds: A, MC, V.

Crystal Mountain

(see Mount Rainier National Park)

Dayton (Columbia County)

(E 7) *See also Walla Walla*

Settled 1859 **Pop** 2,468 **Elev** 1,613 ft **Area code** 509 **Zip** 99328

Information Chamber of Commerce, 166 E Main St; 509/382-4825 or 800/882-6299

Web www.historicdayton.com

Palouse Falls

Once an important stagecoach depot and stopping-off place for miners, Dayton is now the center of a farm area in which sheep, cattle, wheat, apples, peas, asparagus, and hay are raised. Little Goose Lock and Dam, a multipurpose federal project and one of four such developments on the Snake River, is about 35 miles north of town. Vegetable canning and lumbering are local industries.

Dayton has many historic homes and buildings, including the Columbia County Courthouse (1886), oldest courthouse in the state still used for county government, and the Dayton Historic Depot (oldest in state).

What to See and Do

Kendall Skyline Drive. Scenic route through Blue Mtns and Umatilla National Forest (see CLARKSTON). Usually open by July. Contact Chamber of Commerce for details. S of town.

Lewis and Clark Trail State Park. Approx 40 acres. Swimming, fishing; hiking, picnicking, camping. Standard fees. 5 mi SW on US 12. Phone 509/337-6457.

Palouse River Canyon. Deeply eroded gorge pierces wheatlands of region; cliffs rise hundreds of feet above river. At Palouse Falls, river roars over 198-ft cliff into deep ravine of basaltic rock, continues south to join Snake River. Nearby are Lyons Ferry and Palouse Falls state parks. 18 mi N on US 12, then 22 mi NW on unnumbered roads.

Ski Bluewood. Two triple chairlifts, platter pull, half pipe; patrol, school, rentals; cafeteria, bar. Longest run 2¼ mi; vertical drop 1,125 ft. (Jan-Feb, daily; mid-Nov-Dec and Feb-Apr, Tues-Sun) Snowboarding. Half-day rates. 22 mi S via 4th St (North Touchet Rd), in Umatilla National Forest. Phone 509/382-4725. ¢¢¢¢

Special Events

Dayton Depot Festival. Third wkend July. Phone 509/382-2026.

Columbia County Fair. Dayton Fairgrounds. Second wkend Sept. Phone 800/882-6299.

Ellensburg

(D-5) *See also Yakima*

Settled 1867 **Pop** 12,361 **Elev** 1,508 ft
Area code 509 **Zip** 98926
Information Chamber of Commerce, 609 N Main; 509/925-3137 or 888/925-2204
Web www.ellensburg-wa.com

Although this community has long abandoned its first romantic name, Robber's Roost, it cherishes the tradition and style of the West, both as a center for dude ranches and as the scene of one of the country's best annual rodeos. At the geographic center of the state, Ellensburg processes beef and dairy products. The county ranges from lakes and crags in the west through irrigated farmlands to sagebrush prairie along the Columbia River to the east.

A Ranger District office of the Wenatchee National Forest (see WENATCHEE) is located here.

What to See and Do

Central Washington University. (1890) 7,000 students. Liberal arts and sciences, business, technology, education. 8th Ave and Walnut St. Phone 509/963-1111.

CWU Library. Regional depository for federal documents; collection of microforms, maps, general materials. (Daily) 14th Ave and D St. Phone 509/963-1777. **FREE**

Sarah Spurgeon Art Gallery. Features national, regional, and advanced students' art exhibits in all media. (Sept-June, Mon-Fri; closed school hols) In Randall Hall. Phone 509/963-2665. **FREE**

Clymer Museum of Art. Changing gallery exhibits; local artists. (Daily; Sat, Sun afternoons) 416 N Pearl. Phone 509/962-6416. ¢¢

Ginkgo/Wanapum State Park. One of world's largest petrified forests (7,600 acres), with more than 200 species of petrified wood, incl prehistoric ginkgo tree. Waterskiing, fishing, boating; hiking, picnicking, camping (hookups). Standard fees. 28 mi E on

I-90 exit 136, in Vantage. Phone
509/856-2700. **FREE**

✪ **Olmstead Place State Park-Heritage Site.** Turn-of-the-century Kittitas Valley farm, being converted to a
living historical farm. Originally
homesteaded in 1875. Eight buildings; wildlife, flowers and trees;
½-mi interpretive trail. Farm
machinery. Tours. (June-Sept,
wkends; rest of yr, by appt) (See SPECIAL EVENTS). 4 mi E via Kittitas
Hwy on Squaw Creek Trail Rd. Phone
509/925-1943. **FREE**

Wanapum Dam Heritage Center.
Self-guided tour of center; fish-viewing rm; petroglyph rubbings;
exhibits detail life of the Wanapum,
fur traders, ranchers, miners. (Daily)
29 mi E on I-90, then 3 mi S on WA
243. Phone 509/754-5088. **FREE**

Special Events

National Western Art Show and Auction. Phone 509/962-2934. Third
wkend May.

Kittitas County Fair & Rodeo. Carnival, exhibits, livestock, crafts, contests, entertainment. Four days Labor
Day wkend. Phone 509/962-7639.

Threshing Bee and Antique Equipment Show. Olmstead Place State
Park. Steam and gas threshing, blacksmithing demonstrations, horse-drawn equipment, old-time plowing.
Third wkend Sept. Phone 509/925-1943.

Motel/Motor Lodge

★★ **ELLENSBURG INN.** *1700
Canyon Rd (98926). 509/925-9801;
fax 509/925-2093; res 800/321-8791.*
105 rms, 2 story. S $55-$65; D $60-
$70; each addl $5; suites $77; under
12 free; higher rates rodeo. Crib free.
Pet accepted. TV; cable (premium).
Indoor pool; wading pool, whirlpools.
Coffee in rms. Restaurant 6:30 am-10
pm. Bar 11-2 am. Ck-out noon.
Meeting rms. Business servs avail.
Exercise equipt. Refrigerators. Cr cds:
A, C, D, DS, ER, JCB, MC, V.

Restaurant

★★ **CASA DE BLANCA.** *1318 S
Canyon Rd (98926). 509/925-1693.*

Hrs: 10:30 am-10:30 pm. Closed
Thanksgiving, Dec 25. Res accepted.
Mexican, American menu. Bar.
Lunch $3.99-$9, dinner $6.50-$15.
Children's meals. Specializes in prime
rib, steak. Cr cds: A, D, DS, MC, V.
D

Enumclaw

(D-3) *See also Puyallup, Tacoma*

Pop 7,227 **Elev** 750 ft **Area code** 360
Zip 98022

Information Chamber of Commerce/Visitor Information, 1421
Cole St; 360/825-7666
Web chamber.enumclaw.wa.us

A Ranger District office of the Mount
Baker-Snoqualmie National Forest
(see BELLINGHAM, SEATTLE) is
located here.

What to See and Do

Federation Forest State Park.
Approx 620 acres of old-growth timber. Catherine Montgomery Interpretive Center has displays on the state's
seven life zones. Three interpretive
trails, hiking trails, and part of the
Naches Trail, one of the first pioneer
trails between eastern Washington
and Puget Sound. Fishing; hiking,
picnicking. 18 mi SE on WA 410.
Phone 360/663-2207. **FREE**

**Green River Gorge Conservation
Area.** Protects a unique 12-mi corridor of the Green River, which cuts
through unusual rock areas, many
with fossils. Views of present-day
forces of stream erosion through
caves, smooth canyon walls. 12 mi N
on WA 169. **FREE** One of the many
areas in the gorge is

Flaming Geyser State Park. Two
geysers (actually old test holes for
coal), one burning about six inches
high and the other bubbling
methane gas through a spring.
Fishing, boating, rafting; hiking,
picnicking, playground. Abundant
wildlife, wildflowers. No camping.
Standard fees. (Daily) Phone
253/931-3930.

Mud Mountain Dam. One of the world's highest earth core and rock-fill dams. 7 mi SE via WA 410. Phone 360/825-3211.

Special Events

King County Fair. Fairgrounds. Phone 360/825-7777. Third wk July.

Pacific NW Scottish Highland Games. Fairgrounds. Phone 360/825-7777. Fourth wkend July.

Pickles & Ice Cream Festival Street Fair. Downtown. Phone 360/825-1448. Fourth wkend July.

Motel/Motor Lodge

★★ **BEST WESTERN PARK CENTER.** *1000 Griffin Ave (98022). 360/825-4490; fax 360/825-3686; res 800/780-7234. www.bestwestern.com.* 40 rms, 2 story. June-Oct: S, D $63-$75; each addl $5; under 12 free; lower rates rest of yr. Crib $10. Pet accepted; $10. TV; cable. Complimentary coffee in lobby. Restaurant 7 am-9 pm. Bar from 4 pm. Ck-out 11 am. Meeting rms. Business servs avail. In-rm modem link. Exercise equipt. Whirlpool. Some refrigerators, microwaves. Picnic tables. Cr cds: A, C, D, DS, MC, V.

Ephrata

(C-6) *See also Moses Lake, Quincy, Soap Lake*

Settled 1882 **Pop** 5,349 **Elev** 1,275 ft
Area code 509 **Zip** 98823
Information Chamber of Commerce, 90 Alder NW, PO Box 275; 509/754-4656
Web www.ephratawachamber.com

Growth of this area is the result of the development of surrounding farmland, originally irrigated by wells, now supplied by the Columbia Basin irrigation project. Ephrata is the center of an area containing a series of lakes that offer fishing and water sports. There is excellent upland game bird hunting.

What to See and Do

Grant County Historical Museum and Village. Displays trace natural history, early pioneer development of area. Native American artifacts. Pioneer homestead and country village with 31 buildings (some original, restored), incl church, schoolhouse, saloon, barbershop, Krupp-Marlin Jail, photography studio, bank, firehouse, livery stable, blacksmith shop; farm machinery exhibit. Guided tour. (Early May-Sept, Mon, Tues, Thurs-Sun; rest of yr, guided tour by appt) 742 Basin St NW. Phone 509/754-3334. ¢¢

Oasis Park. Picnicking; nine-hole, par three golf (fee); children's fishing pond; playground; miniature golf (fee). Camping (fee); swimming pool (free to campers). (Daily) 1½ mi SW on WA 28. Phone 509/754-5102.

Special Event

Sage and Sun Festival. Parade, sports events, arts and crafts shows. Second wkend June. Phone 509/754-4656.

Motel/Motor Lodge

★ **SHARLYN MOTEL.** *848 Basin St SW (98823). 509/754-3575; toll-free 800/292-2965.* 12 rms, showers only, 2 story. S, D $70-$90; each addl $10. TV; cable. Coffee in rms. Restaurant nearby. Ck-out 11 am. Refrigerators. Cr cds: A, C, D, DS, ER, MC, V.

B&B/Small Inn

★★ **IVY CHAPEL INN BED & BREAKFAST.** *164 D St SW (98823). 509/754-0629. www.ivychapelinn.com.* 6 rms, 1 with shower only, 3 story, 1 suite. No elvtr. No rm phones. S, D $75; suites $100. Children over 10 yrs only. Cable TV in many rms; VCR avail (movies). Complimentary full bkfst. Restaurant nearby. Ck-out 11 am, ck-in 3 pm. In-rm modem link. Street parking. Free airport, RR station, bus depot transportation. Game rm. Microwaves avail. Picnic tables, grills. Built in 1948; was first Presbyterian church in Ephrata. Totally nonsmoking. Cr cds: A, D, DS, MC, V.

Everett

(B-3) See also Marysville, Seattle

Founded 1890 **Pop** 69,961 **Elev** 157 ft
Area code 425
Information Everett/Snohomish
County Convention and Visitor
Bureau, 11400 Airport Rd, Suite B;
425/438-1487
Web www.everettchamber.com

This lumber, aircraft, electronics, and
shipping city is on a sheltered harbor
where the Snohomish River empties
into Port Gardner Bay. To the east is
the snowcapped Cascade Mountain
Range; to the west are the Olympic
Mountains. Developed by Eastern
industrial and railroad money,
Everett serves as a major commercial
fishing port and receives and dis-
patches a steady stream of cargo vessels. The Boeing 747 and 767 are
assembled here.

Along the waterfront is an 1890s-
style seaside marketplace, the Everett
Marina Village.

What to See and Do

Boat tours. For information on companies offering sightseeing, dinner,
and whale-watching cruises, contact
the Convention and Visitors Bureau.
Phone 425/438-1487.

Boeing Everett Facility. Audiovisual presentation; bus tour of assembly facility. Gift shop. (Mon-Fri;
closed hols) No children under ten.
I-5 exit 189, approx 3 mi W on WA
526. Phone 800/464-1476. **FREE ¢¢¢**

Mukilteo. This town, just west of
Everett, is the major ferry point from
the mainland to the southern tip of
Whidbey Island. Its name means
"good camping ground." A lighthouse built in 1905 is open for tours
(Sat). Phone 425/347-1456.

Recreation areas. There are many
recreation areas in and near the city
that offer swimming (fee), fishing,
boat launch; hiking, picnicking,
camping, nature centers, tennis, golf
(fee). Phone 425/257-8300. **FREE**

Totem Pole. 80 ft high, carved by
Tulalip Chief William Shelton.
Rucker Ave and 44th St.

Special Events

Auto racing. Evergreen Speedway, 15
mi SE via US 2, exit 194 off I-5.
NASCAR super and mini stocks,
SVRA modifieds, hobby stocks, figure
eights; demolition events. Phone
360/794-7711 or 360/805-6100. Apr-
Sept.

Salty Sea Days. Festival, parade, displays, food, and carnival. Early June.
Phone 425/339-1113.

Motels/Motor Lodges

★★ **BEST WESTERN CASCADIA
INN.** *2800 Pacific Ave (98201).
425/258-4141; fax 425/258-4755; res
800/780-7234. www.bestwestern
cascadia.com.* 134 rms, 3 story. S $69;
D $99; each addl $4; suites $149-
$249; under 18 free. Crib free. TV;
cable (premium). Heated pool; whirlpool. Complimentary continental
bkfst. Coffee in rms. Restaurant
nearby. Bar 11-1 am. Ck-out noon.
Coin lndry. Meeting rms. Business
servs avail. Health club privileges.
Some refrigerators; microwaves avail.
Cr cds: A, D, DS, MC, V.
🅳 ⬛ ➰ 🔀 🔥 🐾

★ **HOWARD JOHNSON PLAZA
HOTEL.** *3105 Pine St (98201).
425/339-3333; fax 425/259-1547; res
800/446-4656. www.hojo.com.* 247
rms, 7 story. S $99-$139; D $109-
$149; each addl $10; suites $195-
$350; under 18 free. Crib free. TV;
VCR avail. Indoor pool; whirlpool,
poolside serv. Coffee in rms. Restaurant 6:30 am-10 pm. Bar 11-1:30 am;
entertainment. Ck-out noon. Convention facilities. Business servs
avail. Free covered parking. Exercise
equipt; sauna. Some refrigerators;
microwaves avail. Cr cds: A, C, D,
DS, JCB, MC, V.
🅳 ➰ 🕇 🔀 🐾 **SC**

★ **WELCOME MOTOR INN.** *1205
Broadway (98201). 425/252-8828; fax
425/252-8880; toll-free 800/252-5512.
www.welcomemotorinn.com.* 42 rms, 2
story. July-Aug: S $38-$43; D $48-
$52; each addl $5-$10; lower rates
rest of yr. Crib $7. TV; cable (pre-
mium). Restaurant adj 5:30-10:30

pm. Ck-out 11 am. Microwaves avail.
Cr cds: A, C, D, DS, MC, V.

Hotel

★★★ **MARINA VILLAGE INN.** *1728
W Marina View Dr (98201).* 425/259-
4040; fax 425/252-8419; toll-free
800/281-7037. www.marinavillageinn.
net. *26 rms, 2 story, 16 suites. S, D
$95; each addl $20; suites $140-$229;
under 18 free. Crib free. TV; VCR
avail. Complimentary continental
bkfst. Complimentary coffee in rms.
Restaurant adj 7 am-10 pm. Ck-out
noon. Business servs avail. Valet serv.
Bathrm phones; many in-rm whirlpools. On Port Gardner Bay; view
from many rms through large bay
windows. Cr cds: A, D, DS, MC, V.*

Forks (B-1)

Pop 2,862 **Elev** 375 ft **Area code** 360
Zip 98331
Information Chamber of Commerce,
1411 S Forks Ave, PO Box 1249;
360/374-2531 or 800/44-FORKS

The major town in the northwest
section of the Olympic Peninsula,
Forks takes its name from the nearby
junction of the Soleduck, Bogachiel,
and Dickey rivers. Timber processing
is a major industry. A Ranger District
office of the Olympic National Forest
(see OLYMPIA) is located here.

What to See and Do

Bogachiel State Park. Approx 120
acres, on the shores of the Bogachiel
River with swimming, fishing; hiking, camping (hookups, dump station). Standard fees. (Daily) 6 mi S
on US 101. Phone 360/374-6356.

Olympic National Park. (see) 3 mi E
on unnumbered road.

Motels/Motor Lodges

★★ **FORKS MOTEL.** *351 S Forks Ave
(98331).* 360/374-6243; fax 360/374-
6760; toll-free 800/544-3416. www.
forksmotel.com. *73 rms, 1-2 story,*

9 kits. Some A/C. June-Sept: S, D
$52-$72; each addl $5; kit. from $85;
suite $135; lower rates rest of yr. Crib
$5. TV; cable. Heated pool; wading
pool. Restaurant nearby. Ck-out 11
am. Coin lndry. Business servs avail.
Cr cds: A, DS, MC, V.

★ **PACIFIC INN MOTEL.** *352 S Forks
Ave (98331).* 360/374-9400; toll-free
800/235-7344. www.pacificinnmotel.
com. *34 rms, 2 story. Mid-May-Sept: S
$55; D $60-$75; each addl $5; under
13 free; lower rates rest of yr. Crib
$5. TV; cable. Complimentary coffee
in lobby. Restaurant nearby. Ck-out
11 am. Coin lndry. Business servs
avail. Microwaves, refrigerators. Cr
cds: A, DS, MC, V.*

Resort

★★ **KALALOCH LODGE.** *157151
Hwy 101 (98331).* 360/962-2271; fax
306/962-3391. www.visitkalaloch.com.
*10 rms in lodge, 10 motel rms, 2
story, 44 cabins, 38 kits. No A/C. No
rm phones. June-mid-Oct: lodge rms:
S, D $89-$140; each addl $12; cabins
$150-$173; suites $140-$250; under 5
free; lower rates rest of yr. Crib free.
Pet accepted. Dining rm (public by
res) 5-9 pm. Coffee shop 7 am-9 pm.
Box lunches. Ck-out 11 am, ck-in 4
pm. Grocery. Gift shop. Fish/hunt
guides. Some refrigerators, fireplaces.
Some balconies. Cr cds: A, MC, V.*

B&B/Small Inn

★ **MANITOU LODGE BED &
BREAKFAST.** *813 Kilmer Rd (98331).
360/374-6295; fax 360/374-7495.
www.manitoulodge.com. 7 rms, 2 story.
No A/C. No rm phones. May-Oct: S,
D $100-$135; each addl $15; lower
rates rest of yr. Pet accepted, some
restrictions; $10/day. Complimentary
full bkfst; afternoon refreshments.
Ck-out 11 am, ck-in 4-8 pm. Exercise
equipt. Picnic tables. Amidst 10 acres
of rainforest. Cr cds: A, D, MC, V.*

Goldendale

Settled 1863 **Pop** 3,319 **Elev** 1,633 ft
Area code 509 **Zip** 98620
Information Greater Goldendale Area
Chamber of Commerce, Box 524;
509/773-3400

Agriculture, aluminum smelting, and
an assortment of small industries
comprise the major business of Goldendale, named for John J. Golden, a
pioneer settler.

What to See and Do

Brooks Memorial State Park. More
than 700 acres. Fishing; hiking, picnicking, camping (hookups). Standard fees. 12 mi N on US 97. Phone
509/773-4611.

Goldendale Observatory. Nation's
largest amateur-built Cassegrain telescope for public use; tours, demonstrations, displays, audiovisual
programs. (Apr-Sept, Wed-Sun; rest of
yr, schedule varies) 1602 Observatory
Dr. Phone 509/773-3141. **FREE**

Klickitat County Historical Museum.
Furniture and exhibits from early
days of Klickitat County, in 20-rm
restored mansion. Gift shop. (Apr-
Oct, daily; rest of yr, by appt) 127 W
Broadway. Phone 509/773-4303. ¢¢

Maryhill Museum of Art. Constructed
by Samuel Hill. Permanent exhibits
incl Rodin sculpture, European and
American paintings, Russian icons,
chess collection, French fashion
mannequins, Native American baskets and artifacts. (Mid-Mar-mid-Nov,
daily) 11 mi S on US 97, then 2 mi
W on WA 14; 35 Maryhill Museum
Dr. Phone 509/773-3733. ¢¢

Mount Adams Recreation Area.
Lakes, streams, forests; excellent fishing, bird hunting. Northwest of
town.

Special Event

Klickitat County Fair and Rodeo.
Fourth wkend Aug. Phone 509/773-
3900.

Motels/Motor Lodges

★ ★ **FARVUE MOTEL.** 808 E Simcoe
Dr (98620). 509/773-5881; toll-free
800/358-5881. 48 rms, 2 story. S, D
$49-$121; each addl $8. Crib free.
TV; cable. Heated pool. Restaurant 6
am-11 pm. Bar from 5 pm. Ck-out 11
am. Business servs avail. Free airport
transportation. Health club privileges. Refrigerators. View of Mt
Adams and Mt Hood. Cr cds: A, C,
D, DS, MC, V.
🄳 ⛵ 🏊 🔥

★ **PONDEROSA MOTEL.** 775 E
Broadway St (98620). 509/773-5842;
fax 509/773-4049. 28 rms, 2 story, 4
kits. S $38; D $45-$49; each addl $6;
kit. units $5 addl. Pet accepted. TV;
cable. Ck-out 11 am. Business servs
avail. Many refrigerators. Cr cds: A,
D, DS, MC, V.
🎣 🐾 📏 🏊 🔥

Hoquiam

(D-2) See also Aberdeen, Ocean Shores,
Westport

Settled 1859 **Pop** 8,972 **Elev** 10 ft
Area code 360 **Zip** 98550
Information Grays Harbor Chamber
of Commerce, 506 Duffy St,
Aberdeen 98520; 360/532-1924 or
800/321-1924
Web www.graysharbor.org

Twin city to Aberdeen, Hoquiam is
the senior community of the two
and the pioneer town of the Grays
Harbor region. A deepwater port 12
miles from the Pacific, it docks cargo
and fishing vessels, manufactures
wood products and machine tools,
and cans the harvest of the sea.

What to See and Do

Hoquiam's "Castle". A 20-rm mansion built in 1897 by lumber tycoon
Robert Lytle; antique furnishings;
oak-columned entry hall; authentic
Victorian atmosphere. (Summer,
Wed-Sat) 515 Chenault Ave. Phone
360/533-2005. ¢¢

Polson Park and Museum. (1924)
Restored 26-rm mansion; antiques;
rose garden. (June-Aug, Wed-Sun;
rest of yr, wkends) 1611 Riverside
Ave. Phone 360/533-5862.

B&B/Small Inn

★★ **LYTLE HOUSE BED & BREAKFAST.** *509 Chenault Ave (98550). 360/533-2320; fax 360/533-4025; toll-free 800/677-2320. www.lytlehouse. com.* 8 rms, 2 share bath, 2 with shower only, 3 story. No A/C. Mid-May-Oct: S $65-$100; D $85-$145; each addl $15; lower rates rest of yr. Crib free. TV; cable, VCR avail. Complimentary full bkfst; afternoon refreshments. Restaurant nearby. Ck-out 11 am, ck-in 4-8 pm. Luggage handling. Business servs avail. Built in 1897; antiques. Cr cds: A, MC, V.

☒ ☒

Issaquah

See also Bellevue, North Bend, Seattle

Pop 7,786 **Elev** 100 ft **Area code** 425 **Zip** 98027
Information Chamber of Commerce, 155 NW Gilman Blvd; 425/392-7024
Web www.issaquahchamber.com

Historic buildings and homes of Issaquah have been renovated and moved to a seven-acre farm site, called Gilman Village, where they now serve as specialty shops.

What to See and Do

Boehm's Chocolate Factory. The home of Boehm's Candies was built here in 1956 by Julius Boehm. The candy-making process and the Edelweiss Chalet, filled with artifacts, paintings, and statues, can be toured. The Luis Trenker Kirch'l, a replica of a 12th-century Swiss chapel, was also built by Boehm. Tours by appt (July-Aug). 255 NE Gilman Blvd. Phone 425/392-6652. **FREE**

Lake Sammamish State Park. Approx 430 acres. Swimming, fishing, boating (launch); hiking, picnicking. Standard fees. 2 mi W off I-90. Phone 425/455-7010.

Special Event

Salmon Days Festival. Welcomes return of Northwest salmon to original home. Phone 425/392-0661. First full wkend Oct.

Motel/Motor Lodge

★★ **HOLIDAY INN SEATTLE, ISSAQUAH.** *1801 12th Ave NW (98027). 425/392-6421; fax 425/391-4650; res 800/465-4329. www.holiday-inn.com.* 100 rms, 2 story. S, D $120-$135; each addl $7; under 17 free. Crib free. TV; cable (premium). Heated pool; wading pool, poolside serv. Complimentary coffee in rms. Restaurant 6 am-2 pm, 5-10 pm. Bar. Ck-out noon. Coin lndry. Meeting rms. Business servs avail. Cr cds: A, D, DS, JCB, MC, V.

☒ ☒ ☒

Kelso

(E-2) See also Longview

Founded 1847 **Pop** 11,820 **Elev** 40 ft
Information Chamber of Commerce, 105 Minor Rd; 360/577-8058

Kelso straddles the Cowlitz River and is an artery for the lumber industry. The river also yields a variety of fish from giant salmon to tiny smelt.

What to See and Do

Cowlitz County Historical Museum. Exhibits depict history of the area. (Tues-Sun; closed hols) 405 Allen St. Phone 360/577-3119. **Donation**

Seaquest State Park. Approx 300 acres. Hiking, picnicking, camping (hookups). Nearby is Silver Lake with fishing (about 10,000 fish are caught here every summer). Standard fees. 10 mi N on I-5 exit 49, then 5 mi E on WA 504. Phone 360/274-8633.

Volcano Information Center. Pictorial and scientific exhibits on the eruption of Mt St. Helens; 3-D narrated topographical display of the devastation. Also visitor information on surrounding area. (Daily) 105 Minor Rd, off I-5 exit 39. Phone 360/577-8058. **FREE**

Motels/Motor Lodges

★ **COMFORT INN.** *440 Three Rivers Dr (98626). 360/425-4600; fax 360/423-0762; res 800/228-5150.*

www.comfortinn.com. 57 rms, 2 story.
S $60-$85; D $65-$99; each addl $5;
under 18 free. Crib free. TV; cable
(premium). Indoor pool; whirlpool.
Complimentary continental bkfst.
Restaurant nearby. Ck-out noon.
Business servs avail. In-rm modem
link. Valet serv. Cr cds: A, D, DS, JCB,
MC, V.

⊡ ⌷ ⌷ ⌷

★ **MT ST. HELENS MOTEL.** *1340
Mount St. Helens Way, Castle Rock
(98611). 360/274-7721; fax 360/274-
7725. www.mtsthelensmotel.com.* 32
rms, 2 story. S $48-$55; D $63-$72;
each addl $5; under 6 free. Crib free.
Pet accepted; $6. TV; cable. Compli-
mentary continental bkfst. Restaurant adj 6 am-11 pm. Ck-out noon.
Coin lndry. Meeting rms. Some
refrigerators. Cr cds: A, C, D, DS,
MC, V.

⊡ ⌷ ⌷ ⌷ ⌷ SC

★★ **RED LION HOTEL.** *510 Kelso
Dr (98626). 360/636-4400, fax
360/425-3296; res 800/733-5466.
www.redlion.com.* 162 rms, 2 story. S,
D $61-$99; each addl $10; suites
$175; under 18 free; wkend rates.
Crib free. Pet accepted. TV; cable
(premium). Heated pool; wading
pool, whirlpool, poolside serv. Complimentary coffee in rms. Restaurant
6 am-10 pm, Fri, Sat to 11 pm. Bar
11-1:30 am; entertainment Sat. Ck-
out noon. Meeting rms. Business
servs avail. Exercise equipt. Cr cds: A,
C, D, DS, MC, V.

⊡ ⌷ ⌷ ⌷ ⌷ ⌷ SC

Kennewick

(E-6) *See also Pasco, Richland*

Founded 1892 **Pop** 42,155 **Elev** 380 ft
Area code 509
Information Chamber of Commerce,
3180 W. Clearwater Ave, Suite F,
99336; 509/736-0510

Huge hydroelectric dams harnessing
the lower stem of the Columbia
River have brought economic vitality
to the "Tri-Cities" of Kennewick,
Pasco, and Richland. On the south
bank of Lake Wallula and near the
confluence of the Columbia, Snake,
and Yakima rivers, Kennewick has
chemical and agricultural processing
plants. Irrigation of the 20,500-acre
Kennewick Highland project has
converted sagebrush into thousands
of farms, producing three cuttings of
alfalfa annually, corn, and beans.
Appropriately enough, this city with
the Native American name "winter
paradise" enjoys a brief winter and is
the center of the state's grape industry.

What to See and Do

Columbia Park. Approx 300 acres.
Waterskiing, fishing, boating
(ramps); 18-hole golf, driving range
(fee), tennis, picnicking, camping
(hookups; fee). Park open all yr
(daily). 2½ mi W on US 12 on Lake
Wallula, formed by McNary Dam.
Phone 509/585-4529. **FREE**

Two Rivers Park. Picnicking; boating
(ramp), swimming, fishing. Park
open all yr (Daily). 5 mi E, off Finley
Rd. Phone 509/783-3118. **FREE**

Motels/Motor Lodges

★ **KENNEWICK TRAVELODGE
INN & SUITES.** *321 N Johnson St
(99336). 509/735-6385; fax 509/736-
6631; res 888/515-6375. www.
travelodge.com.* 49 rms, 3 story. No
elvtr. May-Sept: S $47-$69; D $52-
$76; each addl $5; under 14 free;
lower rates rest of yr. Crib free. Pet
accepted, some restrictions; $5. TV;
cable (premium). Complimentary
continental bkfst. Complimentary
coffee in rms. Restaurant opp 8 am-
10 pm. Ck-out 11 am. Business servs
avail. In-rm modem link. Coin lndry.
Pool. Refrigerators, microwaves. Cr
cds: A, DS, MC, V.

⊡ ⌷ ⌷ ⌷ ⌷

★ **NENDELS INN.** *2811 W 2nd Ave
(99336). 509/735-9511; fax 509/735-
1944; toll-free 800/547-0106.* 104
rms, 3 story, 3 kits. S $45; D $50-
$53; each addl $5; kit. units $50;
under 12 free; higher rates boat race
wkends. Pet accepted; $5. TV; cable.
Heated pool. Complimentary continental bkfst. Restaurant nearby. Ck-
out 11 am. Business servs avail.

Some refrigerators. Cr cds: A, C, D, DS, ER, MC, V.

⬛ 🐾 🏊 🖥 🎩 SC

★★ **SILVER CLOUD INN - KEN-NEWICK.** *7901 W Quinault Ave (99336). 509/735-6100; fax 509/735-3084; res 800/205-6938. www.scinns. com.* 125 rms, 4 story, 30 suites. S $68-$89; D $78-$109; each addl $10; suites $70-$125; under 18 free; golf packages; higher rates boat races. Crib free. TV; cable (premium). 2 pools, 1 indoor; whirlpool. Complimentary continental bkfst. Complimentary coffee in rms. Restaurant open 24 hrs. Ck-out noon. Guest lndry. Meeting rms. Business servs avail. Exercise equipt. Refrigerators; some microwaves. Cr cds: A, C, D, DS, ER, MC, V.

⬛ 🏊 ⊀ 🖥 🎩 SC

★ **TAPADERA INN.** *300-A N Ely St (99336). 509/783-6191; fax 509/735-3854; res 800/722-8277.* 61 rms, 2 story. S, D $38-$70; each addl $7; under 13 free; higher rates hydro races. Crib free. Pet accepted; $5. TV; cable (premium). Heated pool. Complimentary coffee in lobby. Restaurant adj 6 am-11 pm. Ck-out noon. Coin lndry. Some refrigerators, microwaves. Cr cds: A, DS, MC, V.

⬛ 🐾 🏊 🖥 🎩

★★ **WESTCOAST TRI CITIES.** *1101 N Columbia Center Blvd (99336). 509/783-0611; fax 509/735-3087; toll-free 800/325-4000. www.westcoast hotels.com.* 162 rms, 2 story. S $77; D $87; each addl $5; suites $90-$280; studio rms $75-$85; golf plans. Crib $5. Pet accepted. TV; cable (premium). Pool; whirlpool. Coffee in rms. Restaurant 6:30 am-9 pm. Bar 11-2 am; entertainment Fri, Sat. Ck-out noon. Meeting rms. Business servs avail. In-rm modem link. Sundries. Gift shop. Airport, RR station, bus depot transportation. Health club privileges. Private patios, balconies. Cr cds: A, D, DS, MC, V.

⬛ 🐾 ⚓ ⊀ 🖥 🎩

La Conner

See also Anacortes, Mount Vernon

Pop 656 **Area code** 360 **Zip** 98257

Information Chamber of Commerce, PO Box 1610; 360/466-4778 or 888/642-9284

Web www.laconnerchamber.com

A picturesque town along the Swinomish Channel, La Conner is a popular destination for weekend travelers. Many of the town's homes and businesses are housed in the clapboarded structures built by its founders around the turn of the century. Numerous boutiques, galleries, and antique shops, some containing the works of local artists and craftspeople, line its streets.

What to See and Do

Museum of Northwest Art. Exhibits artist of the "Northwest School." (Tues-Sun; closed Jan 1, Thanksgiving, Dec 25) 121 S 1st St. Phone 360/466-4446. ¢¢

Skagit County Historical Museum. Exhibits depicting history of Skagit County. (Tues-Sun afternoons; closed Jan 1, Thanksgiving, Dec 25) 501 Fourth St. Phone 360/466-3365. ¢

B&Bs/Small Inns

★★ **THE HERON.** *117 Maple Ave (98257). 360/466-4626; fax 360/466-3254; toll-free 877/883-8899. www. theheron.com.* 12 rms, 3 story, 3 suites. No A/C. S, D $90- $100; suites $125-$150. TV. Complimentary full bkfst. Restaurant nearby. Ck-out 11 am, ck-in 3 pm. Whirlpool. Country-style inn. Game rm. Stone fireplace in parlor. Totally nonsmoking. Cr cds: A, MC, V.

⬛ ⚓ 🦮 🖥 🎩 SC

★★★ **KATYS INN.** *503 S 3rd (98257). 360/466-3366.* 5 rms, 2 story, 2 share bath. No A/C. No rm phones. S, D $72-$120; each addl $20. TV, VCR (movies) in one rm. Complimentary full bkfst; evening refreshments. Restaurant nearby. Ck-out 11 am, ck-in 4-6 pm. Luggage handling. Whirlpool. Many balconies. Picnic tables. Built in 1876; Victorian style. Cr cds: DS, MC, V.

🖥 🎩

★★★ **LACONNER COUNTRY INN.** *107 S Second St (98257). 360/466-3101; toll-free 888/466-4113. www.laconnerlodging.com.* 28 rms, 2 story. No A/C. S, D $102-

Lopez Island, Puget Sound

$112; each addl $20; under 13 free.
Crib free. TV; cable (premium).
Complimentary continental bkfst.
Dining rm 11.30 am-9 pm. Restaurant nearby. Ck-out 11 am, ck-in 3
pm. Meeting rms. Cedar lodge
building; many antiques, large fireplace in common area. Cr cds: A, D,
DS, MC, V.

Leavenworth

(C 5) *See also Cashmere, Wenatchee*

Founded 1892. **Pop** 1,692. **Elev** 1,165
ft **Area code** 509 **Zip** 98826
Information Chamber of Commerce,
PO Box 327; 509/548-5807
Web www.leavenworth.org

Surrounded by the Cascade Mountains, Leavenworth has an Old World
charm enhanced by authentic Bavarian architecture. Less than three
hours from Seattle, the village is a
favorite stop for people who enjoy
river rafting, hiking, bicycling, fishing, golf, or skiing. Two Ranger District offices of the Wenatchee
National Forest (see WENATCHEE)
are located here.

What to See and Do

Icicle Junction. Family fun park offers
18-hole Bavarian-theme miniature
golf, excursion train, bumper boats,
interactive arcade.
Party facilities. Fee
for each activity.
(Daily) Jct US 2 and
Icicle Rd. Phone
509/548-2400.

**National Fish
Hatchery.** Raises
chinook salmon
and steelhead.
Educational
exhibits. Fishing,
boat ramp; hiking,
interpretive trails,
picnicking, x-
country skiing.
(Daily; closed Dec
25) 3½ mi S on
Icicle Creek Rd.
Phone 509/548-
7641.

Nutcracker Museum. Displays more
than 5,000 nutcrackers. (May-Oct,
daily; rest of yr, wkends, also by
appt) 735 Front St. Phone 509/548-
4708. ¢¢

Stevens Pass Ski Area. Quad, four
triple, six double chairlifts; patrol,
school, rentals; restaurant, cafeteria,
bar; nursery. (Late Nov-mid-Apr,
daily) 36 mi NW on US 2. Phone
206/973-2441. ¢¢¢¢

Special Events

Bavarian Ice Fest. Snowshoe races,
dogsled rides. Fireworks. Mid-Jan.
Phone 509/548-5807.

Bavarian Maifest. Bandstand music,
grand march, Maypole dance, art,
chuck wagon breakfast. Early May.
Phone 509/548-5807.

Chamber Music Festival. Icicle Creek
Music Center. Professional chamber
music festival featuring classical, jazz,
bluegrass. Kayak and raft races.
Tours, booths, & more. Phone
509/548-6800. May.

Autumn Leaf Festival. Late Sept and
Early Oct. Phone 509/548-6348.

Christmas Lighting. Sleigh rides, sledding. Early and mid-Dec. Phone
509/548-5807.

Motels/Motor Lodges

★ ★ **BEST WESTERN ICICLE INN.**
*505 US 2 (98826). 509/548-7000; fax
509/548-7050; toll-free 800/558-2438.
www.icicleinn.com. 93 rms, 3 story. S,*

D $99-$109; each addl $10; suites $199; under 18 free. Crib free. TV; cable, VCR avail. Pool; whirlpool. Complimentary bkfst buffet. Coffee in rms. Restaurant 4:30-9:30 pm. Ck-out 11 am. Meeting rms. Business servs avail. In-rm modem link. Exercise equipt. Some refrigerators, microwaves. Game rm. Balconies. Bavarian-style architecture. Cr cds: A, C, D, DS, ER, JCB, MC, V.

🅳 🕭 🏋 ≈ 🕇 🔧 🔥

★★ **DER RITTERHOFF MOTOR INN.** *190 US 2 (98826). 509/548-5845; fax 509/548-4098; toll-free 800/255-5845. www.derritterhof.com.* 51 rms, 2 story, 6 kits. S $74; D $85; each addl $8; kit. units $85-$132; under 5 free. Crib free. Pet accepted. TV; cable. Heated pool; whirlpools. Restaurant opp 6 am-11 pm. Ck-out 11 am. Business servs avail. Putting green. X-country ski 1 mi. Lawn games. Private patios, balconies. Picnic table, grill. Cr cds: A, MC, V.

🅳 🔧 🏊 🕇 ≈ 🔧 🔥

★★ **ENZIAN MOTOR INN.** *590 US 2 (98826). 509/548-5269; fax 509/548-9319; toll-free 800/223-8511. www.enzianinn.com.* 104 rms, 2-4 story. S $90-$110; D $95-$115; each addl $10; suites $130-$205; under 6 free. Crib free. Pet accepted; $10. TV; cable. 2 pools, 1 indoor; whirlpools. Complimentary full bkfst. Restaurant nearby. Ck-out 11 am. Meeting rms. Putting green. Exercise equipt. Some balconies. Bavarian decor. Cr cds: A, C, D, DS, ER, MC, V.

🅳 🔧 🏊 🔧 🔥 🕇

★ **RODEWAY INN.** *185 US 2 (98826). 509/548-7992; fax 509/548-2193; res 800/693-1225. www. leavenworthwa.com.* 78 rms, 2 story, 4 suites. S, D $74-$134; suites $134-$174; hols 2-day min; higher rates special events; lower rates rest of yr. Crib free. Pet accepted; $10. TV; cable (premium). Complimentary continental bkfst. Complimentary coffee in rms. Restaurant adj 6 am-10 pm. Ck-out 11 am. Business servs avail. Refrigerators, microwaves. Some fireplaces. In-rm modem link. Downhill/x-country ski 1 mi. Indoor pool; whirlpool. Cr cds: A, D, DS, MC, V.

🅳 🔧 🏊 ≈ 🔧 🔥

★★ **SLEEPING LADY CONFERENCE RETREAT.** *7375 Icicle Rd (98826). 509/548-6344; fax 509/548-6312; res 800/574-2123. www.sleeping lady.com.* 46 rms, 2 story. Mar-mid-Nov: S $95-$202; D $284-$366; suites $366-$530; under 5 free; ski plans; higher rates Christmas season; lower rates rest of yr. Complimentary full bkfst. Complimentary coffee in rms. Bar 5:30-11 pm. Ck-out 11 am. Meeting rms. Business servs avail. In-rm modem link. Downhill ski 5 mi; x-country on site. Lawn games. Game rm. Sauna. Massage. Heated pool. Playground. Totally nonsmoking. Cr cds: A, DS, MC, V.

🅳 🕭 🏋 🏊 ≈ 🕇 🔧 🔥

B&Bs/Small Inns

★★ **ALL SEASONS RIVER INN.** *8751 Icicle Rd (98826). 509/548-1425; res 800/254-0555. www.allseasons riverinn.com.* 5 rms, 1 with shower only, 2 story, 3 suites. No rm phones. Oct-mid-Feb: S, D $115-$135; each addl $20; suites $145-$175; package plans; wkends, hols, Dec (2-day min); lower rates rest of yr. Adults only. TV in common rm; cable, VCR avail (movies). Complimentary full bkfst. Ck-out 11 am, ck-in 3 pm. X-country ski ½ mi. Game rm. Many in-rm whirlpools, fireplaces. Many balconies. Picnic tables. On river. Antiques. Totally nonsmoking. Cr cds: DS, MC, V.

🕭 🏊 🕇 🔧 🔧 🔥

★ **HAUS ROHRBACH PENSION.** *12882 Ranger Rd (98826). 509/548-7024; fax 509/548-5038; toll-free 800/548-4477. www.hausrohrbach. com.* 10 units, 2 share bath, 1-3 story, 5 suites. No elvtr. No rm phones. S, D $85-$110; each addl $20; suites $140-$175; wkly rates. Crib free. Heated pool; whirlpool. Complimentary full bkfst. Restaurant nearby. Ck-out 11 am, ck-in 2 pm. Free bus depot transportation. X-country ski 1 mi. Lawn games. Balconies. Picnic tables. Austrian chalet-style inn. At base of mountain. Totally nonsmoking. Cr cds: A, DS, MC, V.

🅳 🕭 🏋 🏊 ≈ 🔧 🔥

★★★ **MOUNTAIN HOME LODGE.** *8201 Mountain Home Rd (98826). 509/548-7077; fax 509/548-5008; res 800/414-2378. www.mthome.com.* 12

rms, 9 with shower only, 4 story. No rm phones. Mid-Nov-Mar: S $92-$242; D $260-$310; lower rates rest of yr. Adults only. TV in common rm; VCR avail (movies). Complimentary full bkfst. Restaurant from 6:30 pm. Rm serv 24 hrs. Ck-out noon, ck-in 3 pm. Business servs avail. Luggage handling. Gift shop. Lighted tennis. X-country ski on site. Pool; whirlpool. Game rm. Lawn games. Some fireplaces. Totally nonsmoking. Cr cds: DS, MC, V.

★★★ **RUN OF THE RIVER BED & BREAKFAST.** *9308 F. Leavenworth Rd (98826). 509/548-7171; toll-free 800/288-6491. www.runoftheriver.com.* 6 air-cooled rms. No rm phones. S, D $205-$245. Adults only. TV; cable. Complimentary full bkfst. Ck-out 11 am, ck-in 3 pm. Business servs avail. Gift shop. X country ski 2 mi. Mtn bicycles, snowshoes. Whirlpool. Refrigerators. Balconies. Picnic tables. Hand-hewn log furnishings and construction. Decks with views of forest and mountains; on bank of Icicle River. Totally nonsmoking. Cr cds: DS, MC, V.

Restaurant

★★ **LORRAINE'S EDEL HAUS.** *320 Ninth St (98826). 509/548-4412.* Hrs: 5-9 pm. Res accepted. Continental menu. Wine, beer. A la carte entrees: dinner $11.95-$23.95. Child's menu. Specialties: king salmon, filet mignon, puttanesca. Parking. Outdoor dining. Cottage-style atmosphere. Totally nonsmoking. Cr cds: DS, MC, V.

[D]

Long Beach (E-I)

Pop 1,236 **Elev** 10 ft **Area code** 360
Zip 98631
Information Peninsula Visitors Bureau, PO Box 562; 360/642-2400 or 800/451-2542
Web www.funbeach.com

This seashore resort is on one of the longest hard sand beaches in the world, stretching 28 miles along a narrow peninsula, just north of where the Columbia River empties into the Pacific Ocean.

What to See and Do

Oysterville. Community founded in 1854; original settlers were lured by oysters found on tidal flats of Willapa Bay. Many original homes remain, as well as church and schoolhouse. 15 mi N via Sandridge Rd. Phone 360/642-2400.

Seascape scenic drive. 14 mi N from Seaview on WA 103, through Long Beach to Ocean Park.

State historic parks.

Fort Canby. (1864) More than 1,880 acres overlooking mouth of Columbia River. Strategic base from pioneer days through WWII. The Lewis and Clark Interpretive Center, built near an artillery bunker on a hillside, has exhibits depicting the historic expedition and the contributions made by Native American tribes; also multimedia presentations (Daily). Fishing; hiking, picnicking, camping (hookups). Standard fees. (Daily) 2 mi S on WA 100, in Ilwaco. Phone 360/642-3078.

Fort Columbia. More than 580 acres. Site of former coastal artillery corps post with Endicott period fortifications that protected mouth of Columbia River. Interpretive center in former barracks (Apr-Sept, daily) Also here is Columbia House, a former commander's residence. Hiking, picnicking. Grounds (daily). 11 mi SE on US 101. Phone 360/777-8755.

Motels/Motor Lodges

★★ **THE BREAKERS MOTEL & CONDO.** *26th and Hwy 103 (98631). 360/642-4414; fax 360/642-8772; toll-free 800/219-9833. www.breakers longbeach.com.* 124 rms, 3 story, 53 kits. No A/C. June-Labor Day: S, D $70-$99; suites $130-$225; kit. units $91; lower rates rest of yr. Crib free. Pet accepted; $10. TV; cable, VCR avail. Heated pool; whirlpool. Restaurant nearby. Ck-out 11 am. Meeting rm. Business servs avail. Some refrigerators. Private patios, balconies. Public golf adj. Cr cds: A, D, DS, MC, V.

★ **CHAUTAUQUA LODGE.** *304 14th St NW (98631). 360/642-4401; fax 360/642-2340; toll-free 800/869-8401. www.chautauqualodge.com.* 180 units, 3 story, 60 kits. No A/C. June-Sept: S, D $89-$99; each addl $5; suites $129-$159; kit. units $99-$109; lower rates rest of yr. Crib $2. Pet accepted, some restrictions; $8. TV, cable. Indoor pool; whirlpool, sauna. Complimentary coffee in rms. Restaurant adj 8 am-10 pm; winter from 11 am. Bar 4 pm-1 am. Ck-out 11 am. Coin lndry. Meeting rms. Business servs avail. Sundries. Rec rm. Refrigerators. Private patios, balconies. On beach. Cr cds: A, D, DS, MC, V.

★ **EDGEWATER INN.** *409 10th St (98631). 360/642-2311; fax 360/642-8018; toll-free 800/561-2456.* 84 rms, 3 story. Mid-May-Sept: S, D $79-$110; lower rates rest of yr. Crib $3. Pet accepted, some restrictions; $8. TV; cable (premium). Coffee in rms. Restaurant 11:30 am-10 pm; Sat, Sun from 8 am. Bar. Ck-out 11 am. Some refrigerators, microwaves. Ocean view. Cr cds: A, D, DS, MC, V.

★ **OUR PLACE AT THE BEACH.** *1309 South Blvd (98631). 360/642-3793; fax 360/642-3896; toll-free 800/538-5107.* 25 rms, 1-2 story, 4 kits. May-Oct: S, D $49-$59; each addl $5; kit. units $64-$89; some lower rates rest of yr. Crib $1. Pet accepted; $5. TV, cable (premium). Coffee in rms. Restaurant nearby. Ck-out 11 am. Meeting rms. Business servs avail. Exercise equipt; sauna, whirlpool. Refrigerators, microwaves. Picnic tables. Pathway to beach. Cr cds: A, C, D, DS, MC, V.

★★ **SHAMAN MOTEL.** *115 3rd St SW (98631). 360/642-3714; toll-free 800/753-3750. www.shamanmotel. com.* 42 rms, 2 story, 20 kits. No A/C. July-Aug: S, D $74-$94; kit. units $79-$99; lower rates rest of yr. Crib free. Pet accepted, some restrictions; $5. TV; cable, VCR avail (movies). Heated pool. Restaurant adj 7 am-11 pm. Ck-out 11 am. Business servs

avail. Some refrigerators, fireplaces (log supplied). Cr cds: A, C, D, DS, JCB, MC, V.

★ **SUPER 8.** *500 Ocean Beach Blvd (98631). 360/642-8988; fax 360/642-8986; res 888/478-3297. www.super8. com.* 50 rms, 3 story. No A/C. May-Sept: S $54-$89; D $59-$96; suites $84-$124; each addl $5; under 13 free; lower rates rest of yr. Crib free. TV; VCR (movies $2.50). Complimentary continental bkfst. Restaurant adj 7 am-10 pm. Ck-out noon. Coin lndry. Meeting rms. Business servs avail. Sundries. Cr cds: A, C, D, DS, JCB, MC, V.

B&Bs/Small Inns

★★★ **BOREAS BED & BREAKFAST.** *607 N Ocean Beach Blvd (98631). 360/642-8069; res 888/642-8069. www.boreasinn.com.* 5 rms, 2 story. No A/C. No rm phones. S, D $130-$140; each addl $15; wkends (2-day min), hols (3-day min). Complimentary full bkfst. Restaurant nearby. Ck-out 11 am, ck-in 4 pm. Luggage handling. 1920s beachhouse with antiques; library. Totally nonsmoking. Cr cds: A, D, DS, MC, V.

★★★ **THE INN AT ILWACO.** *120 Williams Ave NE, Ilwaco (98642). 360/642-8686; fax 360/642-8642; res 888/244-2523. www.longbeachlodging. com.* 9 rms, 2 story, 3 suites. No A/C. No rm phones. Apr-Nov: S, D $99; each addl $15; suites $149-$189; lower rates rest of yr. Complimentary full bkfst; afternoon refreshments. Restaurant nearby. Ck-out 11 am, ck-in 3 pm. Business servs avail. Free airport transportation. Health club privileges. Located in renovated church building. Totally nonsmoking. Cr cds: MC, V.

★★ **SCANDINAVIAN GARDENS INN BED & BREAKFAST.** *1610 California Ave SW (98631). 360/642-8877; fax 360/642-8764; toll-free 800/988-9277. www.longbeachwa.com.* 5 rms, 1 with shower only, 2 story, 1 suite. No A/C. No rm phones. S $115; D $135; each addl $15; suite $155. Children over 2 yrs only. Complimentary full bkfst. Complimentary coffee in library. Restaurant nearby. Ck-out 11 am, ck-in 3-6 pm. Business servs avail. Free airport transportation. Whirlpool. Sauna. Game rm. Some refrigerators. Each rm decorated to theme of different Scandinavian country. Totally nonsmoking. Cr cds: DS, MC, V.

Restaurants

★★ **SANCTUARY.** *794 US 101, Chinook (98631).* 360/777-8380. Hrs: 5-9 pm. Closed Mon, Tues. Res recommended. Serv bar. Dinner $10.50-$17.95. Child's meals. Specializes in fresh local seafood, pasta, lamb, beef, chicken. Outdoor dining. High ceiling, stained glass, soft lighting. Former church, built 1906. Cr cds: A, DS, MC, V.

★★ **SHOALWATER.** *4503 Pacific Hwy, Seaview (98644).* 360/642-4142. www.shoalwater.com. Specializes in oysters, salmon, regional meats. Own breads. Hrs: 11:30 am-3 pm, 5:30-9 pm; Closed Dec 25. Res accepted. No A/C. Bar opens 11:30 am. Lunch $4.25-$13.50, dinner $13.50-$24. Child's meals. Outdoor dining. Cr cds: A, D, DS, MC, V.

Longview

(E-2) *See also Chehalis, Kelso*

Settled 1923 **Pop** 31,499 **Elev** 21 ft
Area code 360 **Zip** 98632
Information Longview Area Chamber of Commerce, 1563 Olympia Way; 360/423-8400

Longview is the home of one of the largest forest products mills in the world. Factories produce pulp, fine and kraft papers, paper boxes, plywood, glassine, pig aluminum, concrete paint, caustic soda, and chlorine. The first planned city in the West, Longview is a deepwater port fed by six railroad systems and several highways. Fishing for steel-head, smelt, and salmon is excellent. Longview is situated between Seattle, Washington and Portland, Oregon.

What to See and Do

Lake Sacajawea Park. A 120-acre park with 60-acre lake; picnic areas, playgrounds; gardens, jogging, bike and fitness trail. Fishing, wildlife refuge. (Daily) Between Kessler and Nichols blvds, US 30 and WA 432.

Monticello Convention Site. Here residents of Washington met to petition the federal government to separate Washington Territory from Oregon. Olympia Way and Maple St.

Mount St. Helens Visitor Center. (See MOUNT ST. HELENS NATIONAL VOLCANIC MONUMENT) 10 mi N on I-5 to Castle Rock, then 5 mi E on WA 504.

Special Events

Cowlitz County Fair. Cowlitz County Expo Center. Exhibits, entertainment, carnival, pro rodeo. Last wk July. Phone 360/577-3121.

Rain Fest. Cowlitz County Expo Center. Wine tasting, exhibit booths, music. Early Oct. Phone 360/577-3121.

Marysville

(B-3) *See also Everett*

Settled 1872 **Pop** 10,328
Area code 360
Information The Greater Marysville Tulalip Chamber of Commerce, 4411 76th St NE, 98270; 360/659-7700

Natural surroundings, including lakes, rivers, and wooded countryside, make Marysville a popular spot for outdoor recreation.

What to See and Do

Tulalip Reservation. Within the community are St. Anne's Church (1904) with old mission bell, the Native American Shaker Church, and tribal community center. 6 mi NW via WA 506. Phone 360/651-4000.

Wenberg State Park. A 46-acre park. Swimming, fishing, boating (launch); picnicking, concession (summer), camping (some hookups). Standard fees. N via I-5 exit 206, 2 mi W to Lakewood Rd, then 3 mi N to E Lake Goodwin Rd, then S. Phone 360/652-7417.

Special Events

Strawberry Festival. Parade, art show, races. Phone 360/659-7664. Third wk June.

Home-Grown Festival. 3rd and State Sts. Open-air market, arts and crafts booths, street fair. Early Aug. Phone 360/659-4997.

Merrysville for the Holidays. Water-tower lighting, lighted holiday parade. Phone 360/651-5085. Early Dec.

Motel/Motor Lodge

★ **VILLAGE MOTOR INN.** *235 Beach Ave (98270). 360/659-0005; fax 360/658-0866; toll-free 877/659-0005.* 45 rms, 3 story, 6 suites. S $50-$57; D $55-$62; each addl $5; suites $75-$130; under 12 free; monthly rates. Pet accepted, some restrictions. TV; cable (premium). Complimentary continental bkfst. Complimentary coffee in rms. Restaurant adj. Ck-out 11 am. Meeting rms. Business servs avail. In-rm modem link. Valet serv. Refrigerators, microwaves avail. Cr cds: A, C, D, DS, MC, V.
🄳 🍴 🛄 🖼 🐾

Restaurant

★ **VILLAGE.** *220 Ash Ave (98270). 360/659-2305.* Hrs: 5 am-10 pm; Fri, Sat to midnight. Closed Dec 25. Bar. Bkfst $3.25-$7.50, lunch $4-$7, dinner $5-$12.95. Child's meals. Specializes in steak, seafood. Own pies. Cr cds: A, DS, MC, V.
🄳 SC

Moclips

Founded 1902 **Pop** 700 **Elev** 10 ft
Area code 360 **Zip** 98562
Information Washington Coast Chamber, 2602 WA 109, Ocean City

98569; 360/289-4552 or 800/286-4552
Web www.washingtoncoastchamber.org

Motels/Motor Lodges

★ **HI-TIDE CONDOMINIUM RESORT.** *4890 Railroad Ave (98162). 360/296-4142; fax 360/276-0156; toll-free 800/662-5477.* 25 kit. suites, 2 story. No A/C. Mid-June-mid-Oct: kit. suites $110-$175; each addl $10; under 11 free; wkly rates; lower rates rest of yr. Crib free. Pet accepted; $12/day. TV; cable, VCR avail. Restaurant nearby. Ck-out 11 am. Business servs avail. Lawn games. Fireplaces. Private patios, balconies. Cr cds: A, DS, MC, V.
🄳 🍴 🛄 🖼 🐾 SC

★★ **OCEAN CREST RESORT.** *4651 WA 109 (98562). 360/276-4465; fax 360/276-4149; toll-free 800/684-8439. www.oceancrestresort.com.* 45 rms, 1-3 story, 19 kits. (no oven in 5). No A/C. June-mid-Sept: S, D $55-$150; each addl $5.50-$11; kit. units $92-$130; lower rates rest of yr. Crib avail. Pet accepted. TV; cable, VCR avail (movies $2.50). Indoor pool; whirlpool. Restaurant 8 am-9 pm. Bar. Ck-out 11 am. Coin lndry. Business servs avail. Sundries. Exercise equipt; sauna. Fireplaces. Some balconies. On cliff overlooking ocean. Cr cds: A, DS, MC, V.
🍴 🏊 🎿 🖼 🐾

⛽

Moses Lake

(D-6) *See also Ephrata*

Settled 1910 **Pop** 11,235 **Elev** 1,060 ft
Area code 509 **Zip** 98837
Information Chamber of Commerce, 324 S Pioneer Way; 509/765-7888
Web www.moses-lake.com

Because of the water impounded by Grand Coulee Dam, the recreational and agricultural resources of this area have blossomed. Swimming, fishing, and hunting abound within a 25-mile radius. The city is also an important shipping and processing point for agricultural products.

What to See and Do

Moses Lake Museum and Art Center. Native American artifacts; regional artwork; local history. (Tues-Sat afternoons; closed hols) 3rd and Beach Sts. Phone 509/766-9395. **FREE**

Moses Lake Recreation Area. South and west of city. Phone 509/766-9240. **FREE** Incl

Cascade Park. Swimming, boating (launch), fishing, waterskiing; camping (fee). Park (Mid-Apr-mid-Oct, daily). Valley Rd and Cascade Valley. Phone 509/766-9240.

Moses Lake. 18 mi long. NW off I-90, WA 17. Phone 509/766-9240.

Moses Lake State Park. A 78-acre park with swimming, fishing, boating (launch); picnicking. (Daily) 2 mi W on I-90. Phone 509/766-9240.

Potholes Reservoir. Formed by O'Sullivan Dam (10 mi S). Swimming, boating, waterskiing, fishing. 14 mi SW off WA 17, I-90 on WA 170.

Potholes State Park. Approx 2,500 acres. Water sports, fishing, boat launch; hiking, picnicking, camping (hookups). Standard fees. 14 mi SW on WA 17 to WA 170.

Special Events

Spring Festival. Memorial Day wkend. Phone 509/765-8248.

Grant County Fair. Fairgrounds Rodeo. Five days mid-Aug. Phone 509/765-3581.

Motels/Motor Lodges

★ **BEST VALUE EL RANCHO MOTEL.** *1214 S Pioneer Way (98837).* 509/765-9173; fax 509/765-1137; toll-free 888/315-BEST. www.bestvalueinn.com. 20 rms, some with shower only, 9 kits. S, D $45-$65; each addl $5; kit. units $4 addl; higher rates: Spring Festival, concerts at Gorge. Crib $3.50. Pet accepted, some restrictions. TV; cable (premium), VCR avail (movies). Heated pool. Coffee in rms. Restaurant nearby. Ck-

out 11 am. Refrigerators. Cr cds: A, D, DS, MC, V.

★★ **BEST WESTERN HALLMARK INN AND CONFERENCE CENTER.** *3000 Marina Dr (98837).* 509/765-9211; fax 509/766-0493; res 888/488-4449. www.hallmarkinns.com. 161 rms, 2-3 story. S $69-$90; D $79-$109; each addl $5; suites $115-$140; under 13 free. Crib free. Pet accepted, some restrictions. TV; cable (premium), VCR avail. Pool; wading pool, whirlpool. Coffee in rms. Restaurant 7 am-10 pm. Bar 11:30-1:30 am; entertainment Mon-Sat. Ck-out noon. Coin lndry. Meeting rms. Business servs avail. Valet serv. Free airport transportation. Kayak, bicycle rentals. Tennis. Exercise equipt; sauna. Refrigerators; microwaves avail. Many private patios, balconies. On lake; dock. Cr cds: A, C, D, DS, ER, JCB, MC, V.

★ **INTERSTATE INN.** *2801 W Broadway (98837).* 509/765-1777; fax 509/766-9452. 30 rms, 2 story. S $39; D $49-$54; each addl $6; family, wkly rates. Crib $3.50. Pet accepted. TV; cable (premium), VCR avail. Indoor pool; whirlpool, sauna. Restaurant adj open 24 hrs. Ck-out 11 am. Business servs avail. Some refrigerators. Cr cds: A, D, DS, MC, V.

★ **MOSES LAKE MOTEL 6.** *2822 Wapato Dr (98837).* 509/766-0250; fax 509/766-7762; res 800/466-8356. www.motel6.com. 111 rms, showers only, 2 story. June-Sept: S $34-$45; D $36-$51; each addl $3; under 18 free; lower rates rest of yr. Crib free. Pet accepted. Pool. TV; cable (premium). Restaurant opp open 24 hrs. Ck-out noon. Cr cds: A, D, DS, MC, V.

★★ **SHILO INN.** *1819 E Kittleson (98837).* 509/765-9317; fax 509/765-5058; res 800/222-2244. www.shiloinn.com. 100 rms, 2 story. 6 kits. Late May-mid-Sept: S, D $66-$113; each addl $6; under 12 free; wkly rates; lower rates rest of yr. Crib free. Pet accepted; $7. TV; cable (premium). Indoor pool; whirlpool. Coffee in rms. Restaurant open 24 hrs. Serv bar (beer) 11-2 am. Ck-out noon. Coin lndry. Meeting rms. Business servs avail. Valet serv. Sundries. Gift shop. Free airport, bus depot transportation. Exercise equipt; sauna. Bathrm phones, refrigerators, microwaves, wet bars. Cr cds: A, D, DS, MC, V.

D 🐾 🛏 🔥 🚶

Mount Rainier National Park

See also Packwood

Majestic Mount Rainier, towering 14,411 feet above sea level and 8,000 feet above the Cascade Range of western Washington, is one of America's outstanding tourist attractions. More than two million people visit this 378-square-mile park each year to picnic, hike, camp, climb mountains, or simply admire the spectacular scenery along the many miles of roadways.

The park's various "life zones," which change at different elevations, support a wide array of plant and animal life. Douglas fir, red cedar, and western hemlock, some rising 200 feet into the air, thrive in the old-growth forests. In the summer, the subalpine meadows come alive with brilliant, multicolored wildflowers. These areas are home to more than 130 species of birds and 50 species of mammals. Mountain goats, chipmunks, and marmots are favorites among visitors, but deer, elk, bears, mountain lions, and other animals can also be seen here.

Mount Rainier is the largest volcano in the Cascade Range, which extends from Mount Garibaldi in southwestern British Columbia to Lassen Peak in northern California. The eruption of Mount St. Helens in 1980 gives a clue to the violent history of these volcanoes. Eruptions occurred at Mount Rainier as recently as the mid-1800s. Even today, steam emissions often form caves in the summit ice cap and usually melt the snow along the rims of the twin craters.

A young volcano by geologic standards, Mount Rainier was once a fairly symmetrical mountain rising about 16,000 feet above sea level.

But glaciers and further volcanic activity shaped the mountain into an irregular mass of rock. The sculpting action of the ice gave each face of the mountain its own distinctive profile. The glaciation continues today, as Mount Rainier supports the largest glacier system in the contiguous United States, with 35 square miles of ice and 26 named glaciers.

Much of the park's beauty can be attributed to the glaciers, which at one time extended far beyond the park boundaries. The moving masses of ice carved deep valleys separated by high, sharp ridges or broad plateaus. From certain vantages, the valleys accentuate the mountain's height. The glaciers are the source of the many streams in the park, as well as several rivers in the Pacific Northwest. The meltwaters also nourish the various plants and animals throughout the region.

Winters at Mount Rainier are legendary. Moist air masses moving eastward across the Pacific Ocean are intercepted by the mountain. As a result, some areas on the mountain commonly receive 50 or more feet of snow each winter. Paradise, at 5,400 feet in elevation, made history in 1971-1972, when it received 93 feet of snow, the heaviest snowfall ever recorded in this country; the three-story Paradise Inn is often buried up to its roof by snow. Because the mountain's summit is usually above the storm clouds, the snowfall there is not as great.

The park's transformation from winter wonderland to summer playground is almost magical. Beginning in June or July, the weather becomes warm and clear, although the mountain is occasionally shrouded in clouds. The snow at the lower elevations then disappears; meltwaters fill stream valleys and cascade over cliffs; wildflowers blanket the meadows, and visitors descend on the park for its many recreational activities.

There are several entrances to the park. The roads from the Nisqually entrance to Paradise and from the southeast boundary to Ohanapecosh are usually open year-round but may be closed temporarily during the winter. Following the first heavy snow, around November 1, all other roads are closed until May or June.

Mount Rainier

The entrance fee is $10 per vehicle. For further information contact Mount Rainier National Park, Tahoma Woods, Star Rte, Ashford 98304; phone 360/569-2211.

What to See and Do

Camping. Major campgrounds are located at Cougar Rock, Ohanapecosh, and White River, and have fireplaces, tables, water and sanitary facilities. Smaller campgrounds are at Sunshine Point and Ipsut Creek. No hookups; dump stations at Cougar Rock and Ohanapecosh only. All areas closed during winter exc Sunshine Point. Phone 800/365-2267. ¢¢¢¢

Carbon River. Located on the Pacific side of Mt Rainier, the Carbon River area receives the most rainfall and contains the most luxurious forests. In fact, much of the woodland here is considered temperate rainforest. The main road into Carbon River and the northwestern corner of the park leads from Carbonado into Ipsut Creek, a seasonal ranger station and campground.

Fishing. No license required. Fishing season is open in lakes and ponds late Apr-Oct, in rivers and streams late May-Nov. Heavy snowfall restricts access to all water Nov-May. Most lakes are usually not ice-free until early July; ice-fishing not permitted. Specific regulations and details on special closure areas are available at ranger stations.

Hiking. More than 250 mi of trails wind throughout the park, offering unspoiled views of Mt Rainier, glaciers, meadows, lakes, waterfalls, and deep valleys; many trails converge at Paradise and Sunrise; trails vary in degree of difficulty. The **Wonderland Trail**, a 93-mi trail that circles the mountain, is linked with several other trails in the park. A *Pictorial Map* (1986) of the park's topography and *50 Hikes in Mount Rainier National Park*, an illustrated book with maps and hiking details, are available for purchase. Hiking information centers (summer, daily) are located at Longmire and White River. Permit is required yr-round for overnight backpacking; available at ranger stations and visitor centers (fee).

Interpretive programs and walks. Programs, incl nature walks and eve slide shows, are offered at several locations. Schedules are posted in visitor centers and at other locations. (Late June-Labor Day)

Longmire. Longmire is often the first stop for visitors in this area of the park. Visitor center; lodging; cafe, limited groceries. Facilities usually open yr-round. Near the Nisqually entrance, in southwestern corner of park.

Mountain climbing. The park has many opportunities for climbers; one of the most popular climbs is the two-day trek to the summit of Mt Rainier. The guide service at Paradise conducts various programs for new and experienced climbers. Climbs should be attempted only by persons who are in good physical condition and have the proper equipment; deep crevasses and unstable ridges of lava are dangerous. All climbers must register with a park ranger (fee). Phone 360/569-2227.

Ohanapecosh. A preserve of rushing waters and dense old-growth forest. Some of the largest trees in the park—many over 1,000 yrs old—are here. The Grove of the Patriarchs, a cluster of massive conifers on an island in the Ohanapecosh River, is reached by bridge along a popular trail that starts near the Steven's Canyon Entrance Station. At the Ohanapecosh Visitor Center, exhibits tell the story of the lowland forest ecosystem, where Douglas fir, western hemlock, and red cedar trees reign supreme. In southeastern corner of park. Phone 360/569-2211.

Paradise. This is the most visited area of the park, featuring subalpine meadows covered with wildflowers, and hiking trails that provide views of Nisqually, Paradise, and Stevens glaciers. Visitor center with slide programs and films (May-mid-Oct, daily; rest of yr, wkends only); lodging (see MOTELS); cafe (summer, daily); snack bar (summer, daily; winter, wkends and hols only). The nearby Narada Falls drop 168 ft to Paradise River Canyon; viewpoints along stairway. Accessible from Nisqually entrance at southwestern corner of park, and from Stevens Canyon entrance at southeastern corner of park (summer only). Phone 360/569-2211.

Skiing.

    Crystal Mountain Resort. Three triple, two quad, three double chairlifts; patrol, school, rentals; restaurants, bars; day-care center, accommodations. Longest run 2½ mi; vertical drop 3,102 ft. (Nov-Apr, daily) Midweek, half-day, and twilight rates. Also summer season (late June-Labor Day): swimming, fishing; hiking, mountain biking, tennis, volleyball; chairlift rides to summit (fee); poolside cafe; accommodations. E via WA 410, then 6 mi E at 33914 Crystal Mtn Blvd, on northeastern boundary of Mt Rainier National Park, in Mt Baker-Snoqualmie National Forest. Phone 360/663-2265.

    Paradise area. X-country skiing is popular here; equipt rentals and lessons avail at Longmire. For further information contact park headquarters. Phone 360/569-2211.

    White Pass Village. Quad, triple, two double chairlifts, Pomalift, rope tow; patrol, school, rentals; accommodations, restaurant, bar, daycare, general store, service station. Longest run 2½ mi; vertical drop 1,500 ft. (Mid-Nov-mid-Apr, daily) X-country trails. On US 12, 12 mi E of Stevens Canyon (SE) entrance to the park. Phone 509/672-3100. ¢¢¢¢

Sunrise. On northeast side of mountain; accessible only July-mid-Sept. This is the highest point reached by paved road within Washington (6,400 ft). The drive to Sunrise is worth the time; the crowds are smaller, and this area offers spectacular views of the mountain and Emmons Glacier, the largest in the US outside Alaska. Visitor center, snack bar, picnic area.

✪ **Visitor centers.** Located at Longmire; at Paradise; at Sunrise (summer only); and at Ohanapecosh (summer only), near the Stevens Canyon entrance, in southeastern corner of park. All offer exhibits and publications.

Motels/Motor Lodges

★★ **THE NISQUALLY LODGE.** *31609 WA 706, Ashford (98304). 360/569-8804; fax 360/569-2435; res 888/674-3554. www.escapetothe mountains.com.* 24 rms, 2 story. May-Sept: S, D $69-$79; each addl $10; lower rates rest of yr. Crib $5. TV; cable, VCR avail. Playground. Complimentary continental bkfst. Restau-

rant adj 7 am-9 pm. Ck-out 11 am.
Whirlpool. Picnic tables. Totally non-
smoking. Cr cds: A, DS, MC, V.
[D] [≋]

★★ **PARADISE INN.** *PO Box 108,
Ashford (98304). 360/569-2275; fax
360/569-2770. www.guestservices.com/
rainier.* 117 rms, 95 baths, 2-4 story.
No A/C. No elvtr. No rm phones.
Late-May-early Oct: S, D $115-$146;
each addl $10; suites $161. Closed
rest of yr. Crib $10. Restaurant 7-9
am, noon-2 pm, 5:30-8:30 pm. Bar
noon-11 pm. Ck-out 11 am. Business servs avail. Bellhops. Sundries.
Gift shop. Naturalist programs
nightly. Shake-shingle mountain
lodge built with on-site timber in
1916. Totally nonsmoking. Cr cds:
A, D, DS, MC, V
[D] [⚓] [⚞] [≋] [🖐]

B&B/Small Inn

★★ **ALEXANDERS COUNTRY
INN.** *37515 WA 706E, Ashford
(98304). 360/569-2300; toll-free
800/654-7615. www.alexanders
countryinn.com.* 12 rms, 7 with
shower only, 3 story, 2 guest houses.
No A/C. No rm phones. May-Oct: S,
D $89-$110; each addl $15; guest
house $219; lower rates rest of yr.
Crib free. Complimentary full bkfst;
eve refreshments. Restaurant (see
also ALEXANDER'S COUNTRY INN).
Ck-out 11 am, ck-in 3 pm. Built in
1912. Totally nonsmoking. Cr cds:
MC, V.
[⚓] [≋] [🖐]

Restaurant

★★ **ALEXANDER'S COUNTRY
INN.** *37515 SR 706E, Ashford (98304).
360/569-2300. www.alexanders
countryinn.com.* Hrs: 7:30 am-9 pm.
Closed wkdays mid-Oct-mid-Apr. Res
accepted. Northwest regional menu.
Bkfst $5.50-$8.50; lunch $5.95-$9.95,
dinner $7.95-$18.95. Child's meals.
Specializes in seafood, steak, pie.
Country decor. Cr cds: MC, V.
[D]

Mount St. Helens National Volcanic Monument

*(From I-5 exit 68: 48 mi E on US 12 to
Randle, then S on Forest Service Rd 25;
from I-5 exit 21: approx 35 mi NE on
WA 503, Forest Service Rds 90, 25)*

In 1978, two geologists who had
been studying Mount St. Helens
warned that this youngest volcano in
the Cascade Range could erupt again
by the end of the century. On March
27, 1980, the volcano did just that,
ending 123 years of inactivity. Less
than two months later, on May 18, a
massive eruption transformed this
beautiful snowcapped mountain and
the surrounding forest into an eerie,
desolate landscape with few signs of
life.

The eruption sent a lateral blast of
hot ash and gases out across the land
at speeds up to 670 miles per hour,
flattening 150 square miles of forest
north of the volcano. An ash plume
rising 13 miles into the atmosphere
was spread eastward by the wind,
coating many cities in Washington,
Idaho, and Montana with a fine grit.
Rivers were choked with logs and
mud, huge logging trucks were top-
pled like small toys, and the mountain, having lost 1,300 feet of its
summit, was left with a gaping crater
2,000 feet deep, ½ mile wide, and a
mile long.

Among the 57 people missing or
killed by the eruption was 83-year-
old Harry Truman, who for many
years owned a lodge on Spirit Lake,
just north of the mountain. Truman
refused to heed evacuation warnings,
believing his "beloved mountain"
would not harm him; he and his
lodge are now beneath hundreds of
feet of mud and water.

The Monument, established in
1982, covers 110,000 acres within
the Gifford Pinchot National Forest
and provides a rare, natural laboratory in which scientists and visitors

can view the effects of a volcanic eruption. Despite the destruction, the return of vegetation and wildlife to the blast zone has been relatively rapid. Within just weeks of the eruption, small plants and insects had begun to make their way through the ash. Today, herds of elk and other animals, as well as fir trees and wildflowers, have taken a strong foothold here.

Forest Service Road 25, which runs north-south near the eastern boundary, provides access to views of the volcano. The roads are usually closed from approximately November-May because of snow; some roads are narrow and winding.

Visitors are advised to phone ahead for current road conditions. Although volcanic activity at Mount St. Helens has decreased greatly in the last few years, some roads into the Monument could be closed if weather conditions dictate.

For further information, including a map with the locations of various facilities and attractions, contact the Monument Headquarters, 42218 NE Yale Bridge Rd, Amboy 98601; phone 360/247-3900.

What to See and Do

Ape Cave. At 12,810 ft in length, cave is said to be one of the longest intact lava tubes in continental US. Downslope portion of cave, extending approx 4,000 ft, is the most easily traveled. Upslope portion, extending nearly 7,000 ft, is recommended only for visitors carrying the proper equipment. All visitors are advised to carry three sources of light and wear sturdy shoes or boots and warm clothing; cave is a constant 42°F. An information station is also here; lantern rentals avail seasonally. On Forest Service Rd 8303, in southern part of monument. Phone 360/247-3900.

Camping. There are no campgrounds within the Monument, but many public and private campgrounds are located nearby. Primitive camping is usually allowed throughout the Gifford Pinchot National Forest (see VANCOUVER).

Coldwater Ridge Visitor Center. Major interpretive center at 3,100 ft offers views directly into mouth of crater. Lodgelike building overlooks Coldwater Lake created by eruption landslide. Films and viewing area; displays focus on rebirth of nature. Bookstore, cafeteria, interpretive hikes. (Daily) 45 mi E of Castle Rock. Phone 360/274-2131.

Hiking. An extensive system of trails offers hikers impressive views of the volcano and surrounding devastated areas. Trails vary in degree of difficulty. Some trails are accessible to wheelchairs. Temperatures can be very warm along the trails due to a lack of shade; hikers are advised to carry water.

Interpretive walks and programs. Presented at several locations. Details are available at the information stations, Monument headquarters, or visitor centers.

Johnson Ridge Obervatory. At 4,200 ft. State-of-the-art interpretive displays focus on sequence of geological events that drastically altered the landscape and opened up a new era in the science of monitoring an active volcano and forecasting eruptions. Wide-screen theater presentation, interpretive exhibits, staffed

Mount St. Helens

information desk, bookstore. Views of the lava dome, crater, pumice plain, and landslide deposit. Visitors can take ½-mi walk on Eruption Trail. Interpretive talks and hikes in summer. (Daily) 52 mi E of Castle Rock. Phone 360/274-2131. ¢¢

⭐ **Mount St. Helens Visitor Center.** (Center cannot be reached directly from the northeast side Monument.) The center houses exhibits incl a walk-through model of the volcano, displays on the history of the mountain and the 1980 eruption, and volcano monitoring equipment. A 10-min slide program and a 22-min movie are shown several times daily, and special programs are held throughout the yr. Also here are volcano viewpoints and a nature trail along Silver Lake. (Daily; closed hols) Outside the Monument, off I-5 exit 49, 5 mi east of Castle Rock on WA 504. Contact 3029 Spirit Lake Hwy, Castle Rock 98611. Phone 360/274-2100. ¢¢

Summit climb. Climbers are allowed to hike to the summit; free climbing permits are issued on a limited basis. Climb should be attempted only by persons in good physical condition. For climbing information contact the headquarters. Phone 360/247-3961.

Visitor information stations. Located at Pine Creek, on Forest Service Rd 90 near the southeast side of the Monument; at Woods Creek, at the jct of Forest Service roads 25 and 76 near the northeast side of the Monument; and at Ape Cave. (Summer, daily; may remain open until Labor Day)

Volcano viewpoints. There are several viewpoints throughout the eastern side of the Monument, particularly along Forest Service Rd 99; this road leads to Windy Ridge, with a spectacular view of the volcano and Spirit Lake. Lahar Viewpoint, on Forest Service Rd 83, provides an excellent view of mud flow activity on the south side of the mountain. Off Forest Service Rd 99.

Mount Vernon

(B-3) See also Anacortes, La Conner, Sedro Woolley

Settled 1870 **Pop** 17,647 **Elev** 31 ft
Area code 360 **Zip** 98273
Information Chamber of Commerce, 117 N 1st St, #4, PO Box 1007; 360/428-8547
Web www.mvcofc.org

Developed by farmers and loggers, Mount Vernon is a major commercial center. Centrally located between Puget Sound and the North Cascades, the Skagit Delta's deep alluvial soil grows 125 varieties of produce including flowers and bulbs, fruit, and vegetables. Spring brings fields of daffodils, tulips, and irises to the country; a map of the fields is available at the Chamber of Commerce. The city is named for George Washington's plantation.

What to See and Do

Bay View State Park. Approx 25 acres. Sand beach (no swimming), picnicking, camping (hookups). Standard fees. Interpretive center nearby. 7 mi W via WA 20, then right on Bay View-Edison Rd. Phone 360/757-0227.

Hillcrest Park. Approx 30 acres with playgrounds, tennis and basketball courts, hiking trails, covered and open picnic facilities, barbecue pits. 13th St and Blackburn Rd, ½ mi E of I-5 to Cedardale Rd, ½ mi N to Blackburn Rd, then E ¼ mi. Phone 360/336-6213. **FREE**

Little Mountain. Observation area atop 934-ft mountain, providing view of Skagit Valley, Olympic Mtns, Mt Rainier, and San Juan Islands; surrounded by 480-acre forested park. Hiking, picnicking. (Daily) SE of city on Blackburn Rd W. Phone 360/336-6213.

Special Events

Tulip Festival. Festival planned around tulip fields as they bloom.

Tulip field tours, arts and crafts, exhibits. Apr. Phone 360/428-5959.

Skagit County Fair. Second wk Aug. Phone 360/336-9453.

Awesome Autumn Festival. Six wks of events incl a four-acre corn maze, arts and crafts fair, pumpkin festival. Sept-Oct. Phone 360/428-8547.

Motels/Motor Lodges

★★ **BEST WESTERN COLLEGE WAY INN.** *300 W College Way (98273). 360/424-4287; fax 360/424-6036; res 800/780-7234. www.best western.com.* 66 rms, 56 A/C, 2 story, 10 kits. Mid-June-Sept: S $69; D $79; each addl $5; kit. units $10 addl; under 12 free; lower rates rest of yr. Crib free. Pet accepted; $10. TV; cable (premium). Heated pool; whirlpool. Complimentary continental bkfst. Coffee in rms. Restaurant adj 7 am-11 pm. Ck-out noon. Meeting rm. Business servs avail. In-rm modem link. Health club privileges. Some refrigerators; microwaves avail. Private patios, balconies. Cr cds: A, C, D, DS, MC, V.
[D] [symbols] [SC]

★★ **BEST WESTERN COTTON TREE INN.** *2300 Market St (98273). 360/428-5678; fax 360/428-1844; res 800/780-7234. www.bestwestern.com.* 120 rms, 3 story. S $79-$89; D $89-$99; each addl $5; under 17 free; wkly rates, golf plan. Crib free. Pet accepted; $10. TV; cable (premium). Pool. Complimentary continental bkfst. Complimentary coffee in rms. Restaurant opp 4 am-9 pm. Bar noon-2 am. Ck-out noon. Coin lndry. Meeting rms. Business servs avail. In-rm modem link. Sundries. Valet serv. Health club privileges. Some refrigerators; microwaves avail. Cr cds: A, C, D, DS, MC, V.
[D] [symbols]

B&Bs/Small Inns

★★ **RAINBOW INN.** *12757 Chilberg Rd (98257). 360/466-4578; fax 360/466-3844; res 888/266-8879. www.rainbowinnbandb.com.* 8 rms, 3 share bath, 3 story. No rm phones. S $80-$100; D $105-$115; each addl $20. Complimentary full bkfst. Ck-out 11 am, ck-in 3-6 pm. Bus depot, RR station transportation. Whirlpool. Lawn games. Balconies. Picnic tables. Farmhouse (1907); view of moun-

tains. Totally nonsmoking. Cr cds: DS, MC, V.
[symbols] [SC]

★★ **THE WHITE SWAN GUEST HOUSE.** *15872 Moore Rd (98273). 360/445-6805. www.thewhiteswan. com.* 3 rms in house, 2 baths, 1 kit. cottage. No A/C. No rm phones. S $65-$70; D $75-$85; cottage (2-4 persons) $125-$165. Complimentary continental bkfst. Ck-out 11 am, ck-in 3 pm. Queen Anne-style farmhouse (ca 1890). Wood stove in parlor, wicker chairs on porch; sun deck on cottage. Totally nonsmoking. Cr cds: MC, V.
[symbols]

Neah Bay

(B-1) *See also Port Angeles*

Settled 1791 **Pop** 916 **Elev** 0 ft
Area code 360 **Zip** 98357
Web www.olympicpeninsula.com/in dex.htm

What to See and Do

Makah Cultural and Research Center. Exhibits on Makah and Northwest Coast Native Americans; 500-yr-old artifacts uncovered at the Ozette archaeological site, a Makah village dating back 2,000 yrs. Craft shop; dioramas; canoes; complete longhouse. (Memorial Day-mid-Sept, daily; rest of yr, Wed-Sun; closed Jan 1, Thanksgiving, Dec 25) WA 112, 1 mi E. Phone 360/645-2711. ¢¢

Newport

(B-8) *See also Spokane; also see Priest Lake Area, ID*

Settled 1890 **Pop** 1,691
Area code 509 **Zip** 99156
Information Chamber of Commerce, 325 W 4th St; 509/447-5812

A shopping, distribution, and lumbering center, Newport was born in Idaho. For a while there was a Newport on both sides of the state line, but the US Post Office interceded on behalf of the Washington community, which was the county seat of Pend Oreille County. Newport is known as "the city of flags"; flags from around the world are displayed on the main streets. A Ranger District office of the Colville National Forest (see COLVILLE) is located here.

What to See and Do

Historical Society Museum. In old railroad depot; houses historical artifacts of Pend Oreille County; two reconstructed log cabins. (Mid-May-Sept, daily) Washington and 4th Sts, in Centennial Plaza. Phone 509/447-5388. **Donation** Also here is

Big Wheel. Giant Corliss steam engine that for yrs powered the town's foremost sawmill. Flag display. A visitor information center is located here. Centennial Plaza. Phone 509/447-5812.

North Bend

(C-4) *See also Seattle*

Founded 1889 **Pop** 2,578 **Elev** 442 ft
Area code 425 **Zip** 98045
Information The Upper Snoqualmie Valley Chamber of Commerce, PO Box 357, 98045; 425/888-4440
Web cl.north-bend.wa.us

A gateway to Mount Baker-Snoqualmie National Forest—Snoqualmie section (see SEATTLE)—and a popular winter sports area, North Bend also serves as a shipping town for a logging, farming, and dairy region. A Ranger District office of the Mount Baker-Snoqualmie National Forest (see BELLINGHAM) is located here.

What to See and Do

Skiing.

    Alpental. Three double chairlifts, quad, three rope tows, platter pull; patrol, school, rentals; cafeteria, bar. Longest run 1½ mi; vertical drop 2,200 ft. (Hrs, fees same as for Summit West) Shuttle bus to Summit West, Summit East, and Summit Central (Fri nights, wkends,

and hols); tickets interchangeable. 17 mi SE on I-90, then 1 mi N on Alpental Rd. Phone 425/434-7669. ¢¢¢¢

    Summit Central. Two triple, six double chairlifts, five rope tows; patrol, school, rentals; x-country center; cafeteria, bar; day care center. Vertical drop 1,020 ft. (Mid-Nov-Apr, daily) Shuttle bus to Summit West, Summit East, and Alpental (Fri nights, wkends, and hols); tickets interchangeable. 18 mi SE on I-90 at Snoqualmie Pass. Phone 425/434-7669. ¢¢¢¢

    Summit East. Two double chairlifts; patrol, school, rentals; cafeteria, bar. Vertical drop 1,055 ft. Shuttle bus to Summit Central, Summit West, and Alpental. (Late Dec-mid-Mar; Fri, Sat and Sun) Tickets interchangeable. 19 mi SE on I-90, at Snoqualmie Pass. Phone 425/434-7669. ¢¢¢¢

    Summit West. Six double, two triple, quad chairlifts; two rope tows; 15 slopes and trails. Patrol, school, rentals; bar, restaurant, cafeteria; day care center. Vertical drop 900 ft. (Mid-Nov-Apr, daily) Intermediate chairs; half-day and eve rates. 17 mi SE on I-90. Phone 425/434-7669. ¢¢¢¢

Snoqualmie Falls. Perpetual snow in the Cascade Mtns feeds the 268-ft falls. Power plant; park area; trail to bottom of falls. Salish Lodge (see RESORT) overlooks falls. 4 mi NW via WA 202.

Snoqualmie Valley Historical Museum. Displays, rm settings of early pioneer life from 1890s; photos, Native American artifacts; logging exhibits; farm shed; reference material. Slide shows; changing exhibits. (Apr-mid-Dec, Thurs-Sun; tours by appt) 320 S North Bend Blvd. Phone 425/888-3200. **Donation**

Resort

★★★ **SALISH LODGE AND SPA.** *6501 Railroad Ave, Snoqualmie (98065). 425/888-2556; fax 425/888-2533; toll-free 800/826-6124. www.salishlodge.com.* 91 units, 4 story. S, D $229-$409; each addl $25; suites $500-$575; higher rates Fri, Sat and hols June-Sept. Crib free. TV; cable (premium), VCR. Complimentary

coffee in rms. Restaurant (see also
SALISH LODGE AND SPA DINING
ROOM). Rm serv. Bar 11-2 am. Ck-
out noon. Meeting rms. Business
servs avail. Concierge. Gift shop.
Golf privileges. Downhill/x-country
ski 20 mi. Exercise equipt; saunas.
Spa. Refrigerators, whirlpools, minibars, bathrm phones, fireplaces. Private patios, balconies. Library. Cr
cds: A, D, DS, JCB, MC, V.

Restaurant

★★★ **SALISH LODGE AND SPA
DINING ROOM.** *6501 Railroad Ave,
Snoqualmie (98065). 425/888-2556.
www.salishlodge.com.* Hrs: 7 am-10
pm. Res accepted. Bar 11-2 am;
entertainment Fri, Sat. Wine cellar.
Bkfst $12.95-$29.50, lunch $10.95-
$15.95, dinner $22-$42. Sun brunch
$12.95-$29.50. Child's meals. Specializes in multicourse country bkfst,
Northwest game, seafood. Valet parking. Overlooks Snoqualmie Falls. Cr
cds: A, D, DS, JCB, MC, V.

Oak Harbor

(B-3) *See also Anacortes, Coupeville,
Everett, Port Townsend*

Settled 1849 **Pop** 17,176 **Elev** 115 ft
Area code 360 **Zip** 98277
Information Chamber of Commerce
Visitor Information Center, 5506
Hwy 20, PO Box 883; 360/675-3535
Web www.whidbey.net/islandco

This trading center on Whidbey
Island was first settled by sea captains and adventurers and then in
the 1890s by immigrants from the
Netherlands who developed the rich
countryside. The town's name was
inspired by the oak trees that cloaked
the area when the first settlers
arrived and which have been preserved. Side roads lead to secluded
beaches and some excellent boating
and fishing with marinas nearby.

What to See and Do

Holland Gardens. Gardens of flowers
and shrubs surround blue and white
windmill; Dutch provincial flags,
tulips, and daffodils decorate gardens
during Holland Happening (see SPE-
CIAL EVENTS). (Daily) SE 6th Ave W
and Ireland St. **FREE**

Oak Harbor Beach Park. Authentic
Dutch windmill; picnicking, barbecue pit; 1,800-ft sand beach, lagoon
swimming, bathhouse, wading pools;
tennis, baseball diamonds, playground; illuminated trails. Camping
(hookups, dump station; fee). (Daily)
Phone 360/679-5551. **FREE**

Whidbey Island Naval Air Station.
Only active naval air station in the
Northwest. Guided group tours (min
ten persons); res required several
months in advance. Approx 5 mi N
on WA 20. Phone 360/257-2286.
FREE

Special Events

Holland Happening. Tulip show, arts
and crafts, Dutch buffet, carnival,
culture foodfest, square dance exhibition, parade. Late Apr. Phone
360/675-3755.

Whidbey Island Jazz Festival. Mid-
Aug. Phone 888/747-7777.

Motels/Motor Lodges

★★★ **AULD HOLLAND INN.**
*33575 WA 20 (98277). 360/675-2288;
fax 360/675-2817; toll-free 800/228-
0148. www.auldhollandinn.com.* 34
rms, 6 kits. May-Sept: S, D $59-$69;
each addl $5; suites $115-$149; kit.
units $5 addl; lower rates rest of yr.
Crib $5. TV; cable, VCR avail
(movies). Heated pool; whirlpool.
Playground. Complimentary continental bkfst. Restaurant 5-9 pm. Bar
from 4 pm. Ck-out 11 am. Coin
lndry. Business servs avail. Valet serv.
Tennis. Exercise equipt. Lawn games.
Refrigerators, microwaves; some fireplaces. Also 24 mobile homes. Cr
cds: A, C, D, DS, MC, V.

★★ **BEST WESTERN HARBOR
PLAZA.** *33175 WA 20 (98277).
360/679-4567; fax 360/675-2543; res
800/780-7234. www.bestwestern.com.*
80 rms, 3 story. July-Sept: S, D $79-
$129; each addl $10; under 17 free;
lower rates rest of yr. Crib free. Pet

accepted, some restrictions. TV; cable (premium). Heated pool; whirlpool. Complimentary continental bkfst. Coffee in rms. Restaurant adj 6 am-11 pm. Bar. Ck-out noon. Meeting rms. Business servs avail. In-rm modem link. Valet serv. Exercise equipt. Refrigerators, microwaves. Balconies. Cr cds: A, C, D, DS, MC, V.

[icons]

★★ **COACHMAN INN.** *32959 WA 20 (98277). 360/675-0727; fax 360/675-1419; toll-free 800/635-0043. www.thecoachmaninn.com.* 102 rms, 2-3 story, 47 kits. S $60; D $70; each addl (after 4th person) $5; suites $125-$175; kit. units $80-$95; under 12 free. Crib $5. TV, VCR avail. Heated pool; whirlpool. Playground. Complimentary continental bkfst. Complimentary coffee in rms. Restaurant opp open 24 hrs. Ck-out noon. Coin lndry. Business servs avail. Exercise equipt. Refrigerators; microwaves avail. Picnic table, grill. Cr cds: A, DS, MC, V.

[icons]

Ocean Shores

(D-1) *See also Aberdeen, Hoquiam, West-port*

Pop 2,301 **Elev** 21 ft **Area code** 360 **Zip** 98569

Information Chamber of Commerce, Box 382; 360/289-2451 or 800/762-3224

Web www.oceanshores.org

This 6,000-acre area at the southern end of the Olympic Peninsula is a seaside resort community with 6 miles of ocean beaches, 23 miles of lakes and canals, and 12 miles of bay front. Clamming, crabbing, and trout and bass fishing are popular.

What to See and Do

Pacific Paradise Family Fun Center. 36-hole miniature golf (fee); entertainment center; Paradise Lake (fee). 767 Minard Ave. Phone 360/289-9537.

Motels/Motor Lodges

★★ **CANTERBURY INN.** *643 Ocean Shores Blvd (98569). 360/289-3317; fax 360/289-3420; toll-free 800/562-6678. www.canterburyinn.com.* 44 kit. units, 3 story. No A/C. Apr-Sept: S, D $96-$114; each addl $10; suites $130-$200; under 14 free; lower rates rest of yr. Crib free. TV; cable. Indoor pool; whirlpool. Restaurant adj 4-9 pm. Ck-out noon. Meeting rm. Business servs avail. In-rm modem link. Sundries. Some fireplaces. Some patios, balconies. Totally nonsmoking. Cr cds: A, D, DS, MC, V.

[icons]

★★ **THE GREY GULL RESORT.** *647 Ocean Shores Blvd NW (98569). 360/289-3381; fax 360/289-3673; toll-free 800/562-9712. www.thegreygull.com.* 36 kit. apts, 3 story. No A/C. Apr-Sept, hols and wkends in winter: kit. apts $105-$120; each addl $5; suites $130-$345; under 16 free; some lower rates rest of yr. Crib free. Pet accepted, some restrictions. TV; cable. Heated pool; whirlpool, sauna. Complimentary coffee. Restaurant nearby. Ck-out noon, ck-in 4 pm. Coin lndry. Business servs avail. Refrigerators, fireplaces. Lanais, balconies. Cr cds: A, DS, MC, V.

[icons]

★★ **SHILO INN SUITES OCEAN SHORES BEACHFRONT RESORT.** *707 Ocean Shores Blvd NW (98569). 360/289-4600; fax 360/289-0355; res 800/222-2244. www.shiloinn.com.* 113 rms, 4 story. S, D $139-$229; each addl $15; under 12 free. Crib free. TV; cable (premium), VCR (movies). Indoor pool; whirlpool. Coffee in rms. Restaurant 7 am-9 pm. Bar to midnight. Ck-out noon. Meeting rms. Business servs avail. Sundries. Coin lndry. Exercise equipt; sauna. Refrigerators, microwaves, wet bars. Cr cds: A, C, D, DS, JCB, MC, V.

[icons]

Olympia

(D-2) *See also Centralia, Tacoma*

Founded 1850 **Pop** 33,840 **Elev** 100 ft
Area code 360
Information Olympia/Thurston
County Chamber of Commerce, 521
Legion Way SE, PO Box 1427, 98507-
1427; 360/357-3362
Web www.olympiachamber.com

As though inspired by the natural
beauties that surround it—Mount
Rainier and the Olympic Mountains
on the skyline and Puget Sound at its
doorstep—Washington's capital city
is a carefully groomed, parklike community. Although concentrating on
the business of government,
Olympia also serves tourists and the
needs of nearby military installa-
tions. It is a deep-sea port and a
manufacturer of wood products, plas-
tics, and mobile homes. The tiny village of Smithfield was chosen in
1851 as the site for a customhouse.
The US Collector of Customs prevailed on the citizens to rename the
community for the Olympic Mountains. Shortly afterwards, agitation to
separate the land north of the
Columbia from Oregon began. In
1853 the new territory was proclaimed, with Olympia as territorial
capital. The first legislature convened
here in 1854, despite Native American unrest that forced construction
of a stockade ringing the town. (The
15-foot wall was later dismantled
and used to plank the capital's
streets.) The Olympia metropolitan
area also includes the communities
of Lacey and Tumwater, the oldest
settlement in the state (1845) north
of the Columbia River. The city
today has a compact 20-square-block
business section and a variety of
stores, which attract shoppers from a
wide area.

What to See and Do

⭐ **Capitol Group.** On Capitol Way
between 11th and 14th Aves. Phone
360/586-8687. In 35-acre park overlooking Capitol Lake and Budd Inlet
of Puget Sound are

Capitol grounds. Grounds lined
with Japanese cherry trees attract
hundreds of visitors in the spring;
plantings are changed seasonally.
Also here is a replica of Tivoli Gardens Fountain in Copenhagen,
Denmark; sunken gardens, state
conservatory (Memorial Day-Labor
Day, daily); WWI and Vietnam
memorials. Grounds (daily).

Legislative Building. A 287-ft dome
with 47-ft lantern; Neoclassical
architecture; lavishly detailed interior. Closed, will reopen in Nov
2004. Phone 360/586-8687.

Library Building. Houses rare
books; murals, mosaics. (Mon-Fri;
closed hols)

Temple of Justice. Houses State
Supreme Court. (Mon-Fri; closed
hols)

Capitol Lake. Formed by dam at
point where fresh water of Deschutes
River empties into salt water of Budd
Inlet. From top of dam thousands of
salmon may be seen making their
way upstream during spawning season starting in mid-Aug. Boating,
bicycle and running trails, playground, picnic tables. (Daily) Phone
360/586-8687. **FREE**

Millersylvania State Park. More than
800 acres along Deep Lake. Swimming, fishing, boating; hiking, picnicking, camping (hookups).
Standard fees. 10 mi S off I-5. Phone
360/753-1519.

Mima Mounds Natural Area. Mounds
eight to ten feet high and 20 to 30
feet in diameter spread across miles
of meadows west of Olympia. Once
thought to be ancient burial chambers, they are now believed to be the
result of Ice Age freeze-thaw patterns.
Trails wind through 500-acre site.
Information kiosk, picnic area. Contact Washington Department of Natural Resources. I-5 S to exit 95
toward Littlerock (Hwy 121), then
128th Ave SW 1 mi to t-jct with
Waddell Creek Rd. Turn N 1 mi to
preserve. Phone 360/748-2383. **FREE**

Olympic National Forest. More than
632,000 acres. Picturesque streams
and rivers, winding ridges, rugged
peaks, deep canyons, tree-covered
slopes; rain forest, world's largest
stand of Douglas fir, public-owned
oyster beds; populous herd of Roosevelt elk. Swimming, fishing; hiking,
hunting, picnicking, camping (May-

Sept). NW of city, reached via US 101, exit 104. 1835 Black Lake Blvd SW, 98502-5623. Phone 360/956-2400.

Oyster beds. Big Skookum, Little Skookum, Mud, Oyster bays. Beds of rare Olympia oyster found only in South Puget Sound.

Percival Landing Park. Pleasant ½-mi walk along marina filled with pleasure crafts and seals. Observation tower; at south end is statue of The Kiss. Also Heritage Fountain, popular with children on summer days. On waterfront between Thurston St and 4th Ave. **FREE**

Priest Point Park. Playgrounds, hiking trails, picnic facilities in heavily wooded area with view of Olympic Mtns. (Daily) E Bay Dr, overlooks Budd Inlet. **FREE**

State Capital Museum. A 1920 Spanish-style stucco mansion houses art gallery; Native American art and culture exhibits; pioneer exhibits. (Tues-Sun, closed hols) 211 W 21st Ave. Phone 360/753-2580. ¢¢

State Capitol Campus. On Capitol Way between 11th and 14th aves. Phone 360/586-8687.

Tumwater Falls Park. Gentle walk (one mi) follows spectacular falls of the Deschutes River. Landscaped grounds, picnicking, playground. Good view of fall salmon run on man-made fish ladder. (Daily) South of city off I-5, 15 acres. Phone 360/943-2550. Adj is

> **Tumwater Valley Athletic Club.** 18-hole golf course. (All yr) Phone 360/943-9500.

Wolf Haven America. Wolf sanctuary on 75 acres; also home to 40 wolves no longer able to live in the wild. Interpretive center, tours, and ecology center. (May-Sept, daily; rest of yr, Wed-Sun; closed Jan and Feb) 3111 Offut Lake Rd. Phone 360/264-4695. ¢¢¢

Yahiro Gardens. Cooperative project between Olympia and sister city, Yashiro, Japan. Incl pagoda, bamboo grove, pond, and waterfall. (Daily, daylight hrs) At Plum St and Union Ave. **FREE**

Special Events

Olympia Farmers Market. 700 Capitol Way N. Incl fresh produce, baked goods, food booths, seafood, crafts. First wkend in Apr through Dec; wkends only in Apr, Nov, and Dec. Phone 360/352-9096.

Capital City Marathon and Relay. 8-km run, children's run, 5-10-km walk, wheelchair division. Wkend before Memorial Day wkend. Phone 360/786-1786.

Super Saturday. Evergreen State College. Arts, crafts, food fair. Early June. Phone 360/867-6000.

Lakefair. Capitol Lake. Parade, carnival midway, boating and swimming competition, naval vessel tours, flower shows. Mid July. Phone 360/943-7344.

Thurston County Fair. Fairgrounds in Lacey. Late July-early Aug. Phone 360/786-5453.

Motels/Motor Lodges

★★ **BEST WESTERN TUMWATER INN.** *5188 Capitol Blvd, Tumwater (98501). 360/956-1235; res 800/780-7234. www.bestwestern.com.* 89 rms, 2 story. June-Sept: S $68-$79; D $$81-$99; each addl $2; under 12 free; lower rates rest of yr. Crib $5. Pet accepted, some restrictions; $5. TV; cable. Complimentary continental bkfst. Restaurant opp open 24 hrs. Ck-out 11 am. Guest lndry. Meeting rms. Business servs avail. In-rm modem link. Exercise equipt; sauna. Refrigerators. Cr cds: A, C, D, DS, MC, V.

🄳 🛬 🁙 🖾 🔥 SC

★ **RAMADA INN GOVERNOR HOUSE.** *621 S Capitol Way (98501). 360/352-7700; fax 360/943-9349; toll-free 888/298-2054. www.ramada.com.* 123 rms, 8 story. S $130-$150; D $140-$160; each addl $10; suites $125-$190; kit. units $79-$89; under 18 free; higher rates Lakefair. Crib free. TV; cable. Heated pool; whirlpool. Restaurant 6:30 am-9 pm. Bar 11:30-midnight. Ck-out noon. Coin lndry. Meeting rms. Business servs avail. In-rm modem link. Exercise equipt; sauna. Refrigerators. Balconies. Cr cds: A, C, D, DS, ER, JCB, MC, V.

🄳 🛥 🁙 🖾 🔥 SC

Hall of Mosses in Hoh Rain Forest, Olympic National Park

★★ **WESTCOAST OLYMPIA HOTEL.** *2300 Evergreen Park Dr (98502). 360/943-4000; fax 360/357-6604. www.westcoasthotels.com.* 190 rms, 3 story. S $105; D $115; each addl $10; suites $150-$200; under 18 free; some wkend rates. Crib free. Pet accepted. TV; Cable (premium). Heated pool; whirlpool. Complimentary coffee in rms. Restaurant 6 am-11 pm; Sun 7 am-2 pm. Bar 11:30-1 am. Ck-out noon. Coin lndry. Meeting rms. In-rm modem link. Valet serv. Exercise equipt. Lawn games. Wet bar in some suites. Some private patios, balconies. Cr cds: A, DS, MC, V.

Restaurant

★★ **BUDD BAY CAFE.** *525 N Columbia St (98501). 360/357-6963. www.olywa.net/bbaycafe.* Hrs: 11 am-9 pm; Sun brunch 9:30 am-1 pm. Closed Dec 25. Res accepted. Bar to 2 am. Lunch $4.25-$12.95, dinner $5.95-$24.95. Sun brunch $18.95. Child's meals. Specializes in fresh seafood, pasta, prime rib. Outdoor dining. View of Budd Inlet and marina. Cr cds: A, DS, MC, V.

Olympic National Park

See also Forks, Port Angeles, Sequim

(119 mi NW of Olympia on US 101)

In these 1,442 square miles of rugged wilderness are such contrasts as the wettest climate in the contiguous United States (averaging 140-167 inches of precipitation a year) and one of the driest; seascapes and snow-cloaked peaks; glaciers and rain forests; elk and seals. With Olympic National Forest, State Sustained Yield Forest No. 1, much private land, and several American Indian reservations, the national park occupies the Olympic Peninsula, due west of Seattle and Puget Sound.

The Spanish explorer Juan Perez was the first European explorer who spotted the Olympic Mountains in 1774. However, the first major western land exploration did not take place until more than a century later. Since then, generations of adventurous tourists have rediscovered Mount Olympus, the highest peak (7,965 feet), several other 7,000-foot peaks, and hundreds of ridges and crests between 5,000 and 6,000 feet high. The architects of these ruggedly contoured mountains are glaciers, which have etched these heights for thousands of years. About 60 glaciers are still actively eroding these mountains—the largest three are on Mount Olympus.

From approximately November through March, the west side of the park is soaked with rain and mist, while the northeast side is the driest area on the West Coast except southern California. The yearly deluge creates a rain forest in the western valleys of the park. Here Sitka spruce, western hemlock, Douglas fir, and western red cedar grow to heights of 250 feet with eight-foot diameters. Mosses carpet the forest floor and climb tree trunks. Club moss drips from the branches.

Some 50 species of mammals inhabit this wilderness, including several thousand elk, Olympic marmot, black-tailed deer, and black bear. On the park's 60-mile strip of Pacific coastline wilderness, deer, bear, raccoon, and skunk can be seen; seals sun on the offshore rocks or plow through the water beyond the breakers. Mountain and lowland lakes sparkle everywhere. Lake Crescent is among the largest. Some roads are closed in winter.

What to See and Do

Camping. Limited to 14 days. Small camp trailers accommodated at most campgrounds. Campfire programs at some areas (July-Labor Day).

Fishing. Streams and lakes have game fish incl salmon, rainbow, Dolly Varden, eastern brook trout, steelhead, and cutthroat. No license required in the park; permit or punch card is necessary for steelhead and salmon. Contact Park Headquarters for restrictions. Phone 360/565-3130.

Hiking. Over 600 mi of trails. Obtain maps and trail guides in the park. Guided walks conducted July and Aug.

Mountain climbing. Something for everyone, from the novice to the experienced climber. Climbing parties must register at a ranger station.

Rain forests. Along Hoh, Queets, and Quinault river roads. Hall of Mosses

and Spruce Nature Trails and trail to Mt Olympus start at end of Hoh River Rd.

★ **Visitor Center.** Has information, natural history exhibits, displays of American Indian culture, orientation slideshow. (Daily) 3002 Mt Angeles Rd. From here, one can enter the park on Heart O' the Hills Pkwy to Hurricane Ridge (access maybe Nov-Apr). 3002 Mt Angeles Rd. Per vehicle ¢¢¢ Per person ¢¢ Here is

> **Skiing. Hurricane Ridge Winter Use Area.** Pomalift, intermediate, and beginner's runs; school, rentals; snack bar. (Late Dec-late Mar, Sat and Sun) Also snowshoeing and x-country ski trails.

Omak

(B-6) *See also Winthrop*

Settled 1900 **Pop** 4,117 **Elev** 837 ft
Area code 509 **Zip** 98841
Information Tourist Information Center, 401 Omak Ave; 509/826-4218 or 800/225-6625

This lumber town is the largest in the north central part of Washington and is also known for its production of apples and its many orchards. The name of the town and nearby lake and mountain is derived from a Native American word meaning "good medicine." Omak is the "baby's breath capital of the world," a flower much used commercially by florists.

What to See and Do

Conconully State Park. Approx 80 acres along Conconully Reservoir; swimming, fishing, boating; picnicking, snowmobiling, camping. Standard fees. (Daily) 5 mi N on US 97, then 10 mi NW on Conconully Hwy (unnumbered road). Phone 509/826-7408.

Okanogan National Forest. Nearly 1.75 million acres. In the northern part of the forest is 530,031-acre Pasayten Wilderness. In the southwestern part of the forest is 95,976-

acre Lake Chelan-Sawtooth Wilderness. Hunting and fishing are plentiful; picnicking and camping at 41 sites, most of which have trailer spaces; eight boating sites. Thirty-eight mi west of town at Methow Valley Airport, between Winthrop and Twisp, is the North Cascades Smokejumper Base; visitors welcome. One-mi paved wheelchair trail to Rainy Lake at Rainy Pass. Northeast and northwest of town, reached via US 97, WA 20. Contact Supervisor, 1240 S Second Ave, Okanogan 98840. Phone 509/826-3275.

Special Event

Stampede and Suicide Race. Rodeo events; horses and riders race down a cliff and across the Okanogan River. Western art show. Native American dance contests. Encampment with more than 100 teepees. Phone 509/826-1002. Second wknd Aug.

Motels/Motor Lodges

★ **CEDARS INN.** *1 Apple Way, Okanogan (98840). 509/422-6431; fax 509/422-4214. www.cedarsinn.com.* 78 rms, 3 story, 6 kits. No elvtr. S $56-$62; D, kit. units $62-$69; each addl $5; under 12 free; higher rates Stampede. Crib free. Pet accepted; $5. TV; cable, VCR avail (movies $1.50). Pool. Restaurant 6:30 am-10 pm. Bar 11 am-11:30 pm. Ck-out noon. Coin lndry. Meeting rms. Business servs avail. Cr cds: A, DS, MC, V.

[🅓] [🔌] [📶] [🐾] [SC]

★ **MOTEL NICHOLAS.** *527 E Grape Ave (98841). 509/826-4611; res 800/404-4611.* 21 rms. S $34-$36; D $42-$46; each addl $4; higher rates Stampede wk. Pet accepted; $3. TV; cable (premium). Complimentary coffee in rms. Restaurant nearby. Ck-out 11 am. Refrigerators, microwaves. City park opp. Cr cds: A, C, D, DS, MC, V.

[🔌] [📶] [🐾]

Orcas Island

(see San Juan Islands)

Othello

(D-6) *See also Moses Lake*

Pop 4,638 **Area code** 509 **Zip** 99344
Information Chamber of Commerce, 33 E Larch; 509/488-2683 or 800/684-2556
Web www.televar.com/chambers/othello

Another beneficiary of the Grand Coulee project, Othello had a population of only 526 in 1950. The Potholes Canal runs by the town, linking the Potholes Reservoir and the smaller Scooteney Reservoir.

Special Events

Sandhill Crane Festival. Wildlife Refuge. View migrating birds. Guided tours, wildlife workshops. Late Mar-early Apr. Phone 509/488-2668.

Adams County Fair. Carnival, entertainment, tractor pull, exhibits. Mid-Sept. Phone 509/488-2871.

Motels/Motor Lodges

★★ **BEST WESTERN LINCOLN INN.** *1020 E Cedar (99344). 509/488-5671; fax 509/488-5084; res 800/780-7231. www.bestwestern.com.* 50 rms, 2 story. S, D $61-$71; each addl $5; kit units $79-$99; higher rates hunting season, concerts at Gorge. Pet accepted; $10. TV; cable (premium), VCR. Pool. Complimentary continental bkfst. Coffee in rms. Restaurant opp 7 am-10 pm. Ck-out 11 am. Coin lndry. Business servs avail. Exercise equipt; sauna. Some refrigerators, microwaves. Cr cds: A, C, D, DS, MC, V.

[🔌] [📶] [📶] [🐾] [🏋]

★ **CABANA MOTEL.** *665 E Windsor St (99344). 509/488-2605; fax 509/488-0885; toll-free 800/442-4581.* 55 rms, 3 kit. units. S $40-$50; D $50-$60; each addl $5; kit. units $45-$70. Crib free. TV; cable (premium). Heated pool; whirlpool. Restaurant nearby. Ck-out 11 am. Some refrigerators, microwaves. Cr cds: A, DS, MC, V.

[📶] [📶] [🐾]

Packwood (E-4)

Pop 950 **Elev** 1,051 ft **Area code** 360
Zip 98361

Named for William Packwood, a colorful explorer who helped open this region, the town is a provisioning point for modern-day explorers of Mount Rainier National Park (see) and Snoqualmie and Gifford Pinchot national forests. A Ranger District office of the Gifford Pinchot National Forest (see VANCOUVER) is located here. The area abounds in edible wild berries and mushrooms; no permit is needed for picking. Winter and spring are popular with gamewatchers; elk, deer, bear, and goats can be spotted in the local cemetery as well as in the nearby parks.

What to See and Do

Goat Rocks Wilderness. 105,600 acres of alpine beauty with elevations from 3,000-8,200 ft. Jagged pinnacles rising above snowfields, cascading streams, mountain meadows with wildflowers; this is the home of the pika and mountain goat. East and south of town, in Gifford Pinchot National Forest.

Motels/Motor Lodges

★★ **COWLITZ RIVER LODGE.**
13069 US 12 (98361). 360/494-4444; fax 360/494-2075; res 888/881-0379. www.escapetothemountains.com. 32 rms, 2 story. June-Sept: S $46-$57; D $54-$67; each addl $5; under 6 free; lower rates rest of yr. Crib free. TV; cable. Complimentary continental bkfst. Restaurant opp 5 am-10 pm. Ck-out 11 am. Downhill ski 19 mi. Whirlpool. Cr cds: A, D, MC, V.

⬛ 🐾 ♨ 🏊 ⛱ 🔥

★ **CREST TRAIL LODGE.** *12729 US 12 (98361). 360/494-4944; fax 360/494-6629; res 800/477-5339. www.mountsthelens.com.* 27 rms, 2 story. July-Aug: S $48-$58; D $56-$66; each addl $5; under 7 free; ski plans; lower rates rest of yr. Crib $5. TV; cable, VCR avail (movies). Complimentary continental bkfst. Ck-out 11 am. Business servs avail. Valet serv. Sundries. Airport transportation. Downhill ski 19 mi; x-country ski 1 mi. Some refrigerators; microwaves avail. Picnic tables, grills. Cr cds: A, DS, MC, V.

⬛ 🐾 ♨ 🏊 ⛱ 🔥 **SC**

Pasco

(E-6) *See also Kennewick, Richland*

Founded 1880 **Pop** 20,337 **Elev** 381 ft
Area code 509 **Zip** 99301

Information Greater Pasco Area Chamber of Commerce, 1600 N 20th, Suite A, PO Box 550; 509/547-9755

Web www.pascochamber.org

One of the "tri-cities" (see KENNEWICK and RICHLAND), Pasco has been nurtured by transportation throughout its history. Still a rail, air, highway, and waterway crossroads, Pasco is enjoying increased farm and industrial commerce thanks to the Columbia Basin project.

What to See and Do

Kahlotus. Town redone in Old West atmosphere. Many of the businesses and buildings are museums in themselves. Near Palouse Falls (see DAYTON) and Lower Monumental Dam. 42 mi NE via US 395 and WA 260.

McNary Lock and Dam. Single-lift navigation lock. Dam is 7,365 ft long, 92 ft high, and is the easternmost of four multipurpose dams on the lower Columbia River between Portland, OR and Pasco. The Columbia River forms Lake Wallula here. The 61-mi long lake reaches beyond the Tri-Cities up to Ice Harbor Dam on Snake River. Developed parks with boating, marinas, waterskiing, swimming, fishing; picnicking and camping nearby. (Daily) 3 mi S of WA 14 in Umatilla, OR. For information contact Park Ranger, PO Box 1441, Umatilla, OR 97882. Phone 541/922-4388.

Preston Premium Wines. Self-guided tour of tasting rm, oak aging casks, storage tanks, and bottling line; park with picnic and play area, amphitheater, gazebo, pond. (Daily; closed hols) 5 mi N via US 395, watch for road sign. Phone 509/545-1990. **FREE**

Sacajawea State Park. Site where Lewis and Clark camped in 1805. Approx 280 acres. Swimming, fishing, boating (launch, dock); picnicking. (Daily) 2 mi SE off US 12. Phone 509/545-2361.

Special Events

Jazz Unlimited. Columbia Basin Community College. Phone 509/547-0511. Usually second and third wkend Apr.

Tri-Cities Water Follies. Events scheduled throughout month of July leading to hydroplane races on Columbia River on last wkend of month. Phone 509/547-5531 or 509/547-5563. July.

Fiery Food Festival. Phone 509/545-0738. Wkend after Labor Day.

Motel/Motor Lodge

★ **VINEYARD INN.** *1800 W Lewis St (99301). 509/547-0791; fax 509/547-8632; toll-free 800/824-5457.* 165 rms, 2 story, 44 kits. S $40.50-$48; D $50-$60; each addl $5; kit. units, studio rms $50-$60; under 12 free; higher rates hydro races. Crib $6. Pet accepted; $5/day. TV; cable (premium), VCR avail. Indoor pool; whirlpool. Complimentary continental bkfst. Ck-out 11 am. Coin lndry. Business servs avail. Airport, RR station, bus depot transportation. Cr cds: A, C, D, DS, MC, V.

Hotel

★★ **WESTCOAST HOTEL.** *2525 N 20th Ave (99301). 509/547-0701; fax 509/547-4278; res 800/325-4000. www.doubletreehotels.com.* 279 rms, 2-3 story. S, D $99-$125; each addl $10; suites $145-$200; under 18 free; some wkend rates. Crib free. Pet accepted. TV; cable. Heated pool; whirlpool, poolside serv. Coffee in rms. Restaurants. Bar 11-2 am; entertainment. Ck-out noon. Convention facilities. Business center. In-rm modem link. Bellhops. Valet serv. Sundries. Free airport, RR station, bus depot transportation. Exercise equipt.

Refrigerator, wet bar in some suites. Private patios, balconies. Cr cds: A, C, D, DS, MC, V.

Port Angeles

(B-2) *See also Neah Bay, Sequim*

Pop 17,710 **Elev** 32 ft **Area code** 360
Zip 98362
Information Chamber of Commerce, 121 E Railroad; 360/452-2363

Sitting atop the Olympic Peninsula, Port Angeles has the Olympic Mountains at its back and Juan de Fuca Strait at its shoreline; just 17 miles across the Strait is Victoria, British Columbia (see). Ediz Hook, a sandspit, protects the harbor and helps make it the first American port of entry for ships coming to Puget Sound from all parts of the Pacific; there is a US Coast Guard Air Rescue Station here. A Spanish captain who entered the harbor in 1791 named the village he found here Port of Our Lady of the Angels, a name that has survived in abbreviated form. The fishing fleet, pulp, paper and lumber mills, and tourism are its economic mainstays today.

Port Angeles is the headquarters for Olympic National Park (see). It is an excellent starting point for expeditions to explore the many faces of the peninsula.

What to See and Do

Ferry service to Victoria, BC Canada. (see) A 90-min trip; departs from Coho ferry terminal to Victoria's Inner Harbour. (Daily; summer, four trips; spring and fall, two trips; rest of yr, one trip) Contact Black Ball Transport Inc, 10777 Main St, Suite 106, Bellevue 98004. Phone 206/622-2222. ¢¢¢¢

Olympic National Park. (see) Headquarters, 600 Park Ave.

Olympic Raft and Guide Service. River rafting in Olympic National Park. Phone 360/452-1443.

Olympic Tours. Unique, interpretive sightseeing tours into Olympic

National Park (eight hrs). Res required. For schedule and fees contact PO Box 2201. Phone 360/457-3545.

Special Event

Clallam County Fair. Mid-Aug. Phone 360/417-2551.

Motels/Motor Lodges

★ **PORT ANGELES INN.** *111 E 2nd St (98362). 360/452-9285; fax 360/452-7935; toll-free 800/421-0706. www.portangelesinn.com.* 23 rms, 3 story. No A/C. June-Sept: S, D $79-$120; each addl $12; lower rates rest of yr. TV; cable (premium). Complimentary coffee in rms. Restaurant nearby. Ck-out 11 am. Business servs avail. Some balconies. Cr cds: A, C, D, DS, MC, V.
🛏 📶 🔥

★★ **RED LION HOTEL-PORT ANGELES.** *221 N Lincoln (98362). 360/452-9215; fax 360/452-4734; res 800/733-5466. www.redlion.com.* 186 rms, 2 story. No A/C. May-Sept: S $100-$140; D $115-$155; suites $150-$175; each addl $10; under 18 free; some lower rates rest of yr. Crib free. Pet accepted. TV; cable. Heated pool; whirlpool. Complimentary coffee in rms. Restaurant 5:30 am mid night. Ck-out noon. Sundries. Health club privileges. Private balconies. Overlooks harbor. Cr cds: A, DS, MC, V.
🅳 🐾 🛏 📶 🕴

★★ **UPTOWN INN.** *101 E 2nd St (98362). 360/457-9434; fax 360/457-5915; toll-free 800/858-3812. www.uptowninn.com.* 35 rms, 1-3 story, 4 kits. No A/C. June-Oct: S, D $89-$130; each addl $5; kit. units $125; under 12 free; wkly, monthly rates; lower rates rest of yr. Crib free. Pet accepted, some restrictions. TV; cable (premium). Complimentary continental bkfst. Complimentary coffee in rms. Restaurant nearby. Ck-out 11 am. Refrigerators, microwaves. Scenic view. Cr cds: A, DS, MC, V.
🐾 📶 🔥

Resort

★ **SOL DUC HOT SPRINGS.** *Sol Duc Rd and US 101 (98362). 360/327-*

3583; fax 360/327-3593. www.north olympic.com/solduc. 32 cottages (1-bedrm), 6 kits. No A/C. Mid-Mar-late Sept and Apr, Oct wkends: S, D $110; each addl $12.50; kit. cabins $100; under 4 free. Closed rest of yr. Crib $20. Pool; wading pool, mineral pools. Dining rm 7:30-10:30 am, 5-9 pm. Ck-out 11 am, ck-in 4 pm. Grocery. Gift shop. Massage. Picnic tables. Originally conceived as a European-style health spa (ca 1912). Mineral pools range in temperature from 98°-106°. Cr cds: A, DS, MC, V.
🅳 🏊 🛏 📶 🔥

B&Bs/Small Inns

★★★ **DOMAINE MADELEINE.** *146 Wildflower Ln (98362). 360/457-4174; fax 360/457-3037; toll-free 888/811-8376. www.domainemadeleine.com.* 5 rms, 1 with shower only, 2 story. Mid-Apr-mid-Oct: S $165-$175; D $175-$185; each addl $25; wkly rates; 2-day min wkends; lower rates rest of yr. Children over 12 yrs only. TV; cable (premium), VCR (movies). Complimentary full bkfst; afternoon refreshments. Ck-out 11 am, ck-in 4-6 pm. Luggage handling. Business servs avail. In-rm modem link. Airport, ferry transportation. Lawn games. Massage. Many in-rm whirlpools. Some refrigerators, microwaves. Picnic tables. Totally nonsmoking. Cr cds: A, DS, MC, V.
📶 🔥

★★ **FIVE SEASUNS BED & BREAKFAST.** *1006 S Lincoln St (98362). 360/452-8248; toll-free 800/708-0777. www.seasuns.com.* 4 rms, 2 share bath, 2 story. No A/C. No rm phones. Mid-May-mid-Oct: S $80-$85; D $135-$145; each addl $15; ski plans; lower rates rest of yr. Children over 12 yrs only. TV in common rm; cable, VCR avail (movies). Complimentary full bkfst; afternoon refreshments. Complimentary coffee in rms. Restaurant nearby. Ck-out 11 am, ck-in 4-6 pm. Luggage handling. Free airport transportation. Lawn games. Some balconies. Picnic tables, grills. Restored Dutch Colonial inn built in 1920s; pond, waterfall. Totally nonsmoking. Cr cds: A, DS, MC, V.
✈ 📶 🔥

★★ **MAPLE ROSE INN.** *112 Reservoir Rd (98363). 360/457-ROSE; fax 707/215-7585; res 800/570-2007. www.northolympic.com/maplerose.* 5 rms, 4 story, 3 suites. No A/C. No elvtr. May-Sept: S, D $79-$89; each addl $15; suites $127-$147; wkends, hols (2-day min); lower rates rest of yr. Pet accepted; $15. TV; cable (premium), VCR (movies). Complimentary full bkfst. Complimentary coffee in rms. Restaurant nearby. Ck-out 11 am, ck-in 3-6 pm. Business servs avail. In-rm modem link. Luggage handling. Free airport transportation. Exercise equipt. Massage. Whirlpool. Some in-rm whirlpools, refrigerators, microwaves. Some balconies. Picnic tables, grills. Contemporary country inn. Cr cds: A, DS, MC, V.
🔄 🕇 ➔ 🐾 SC

★★★ **TUDOR INN BED & BREAK-FAST.** *1108 S Oak St (98362). 360/452-3138. www.tudorinn.com.* 5 rms, 2 story. No A/C. No rm phones. Mid-May-mid-Oct: S $75-$85; D $125-$135; lower rates rest of yr. Children over 12 yrs only. TV in sitting rm; VCR avail (free movies). Complimentary full bkfst; afternoon refreshments. Ck-out 11 am, ck-in 4-7 pm. Downhill/x-country ski 16 mi. View of Olympic Mnts. Antiques, grand piano. English gardens. Totally nonsmoking. Cr cds: A, DS, MC, V.
🏊 ✈ ➔ 🔥

Restaurants

★★ **BELLA ITALIA.** *117-B E 1st St (98362). 360/457-5442. www.northolympic.com/bella.* Hrs: 11 am-11 pm; winter hrs may vary. Closed Thanksgiving, Dec 25. Res accepted. Italian menu. Bar. A la carte entrees: lunch $5-$10, dinner $6-$18. Child's meals. Specializes in crab cakes, fresh seafood, organic produce. Own pastries. Two dining rms divided by espresso and wine bar; windows overlook courtyard. Totally nonsmoking. Cr cds: A, D, DS, MC, V.
D

★★ **BUSHWHACKER.** *1527 E 1st St (98362). 360/457-4113.* Hrs: 5-10 pm; Fri, Sat to 11 pm; Sun 4:30-9 pm. Closed Thanksgiving, Dec 24, 25. Northwest menu. Bar 4:30 pm-1 am; Sat, Sun fron 5 pm. Dinner $6.95-

$19.95. Child's meals. Specializes in prime rib, salmon, halibut. Salad bar. Parking. Northwest decor. Cr cds: A, DS, MC, V.
D

★★★ **C'EST SI BON.** *23 Cedar Park Dr (98362). 360/452-8888.* Hrs: 5-11 pm. Closed Mon. Res accepted. Bar. Wine list. A la carte entrees: dinner $23-$25. Child's meals. Parking. Outdoor dining on terrace with gazebo and rose garden. Romantic atmosphere. Cr cds: A, DS, MC, V.
D

★ **LANDINGS.** *115 E Railroad Ave US 101 (98362). 360/457-6768.* Hrs: 7 am-9 pm; 6 am-10 pm in summer. Closed Jan 1, Dec 25. No A/C. Bar. Bkfst $3-$8, lunch, dinner $3-$12. Specializes in seafood, hamburgers. Parking. Outdoor dining. Cr cds: A, D, DS, MC, V.
D

★★★ **TOGA'S INTERNATIONAL CUISINE.** *122 W Lauridsen Blvd (98362). 360/452-1952.* Hrs: 5-10 pm. Closed Mon; hols; also Sept. Res required. No A/C. Continental menu. Dinner $16.95-$24.95. Child's menu. Specializes in beef fillets, prawns, lamb chops. Own baking. Outdoor dining. Intimate dining in private residence; windows offer mountain view. Totally nonsmoking. Cr cds: A, DS, MC, V.
D

Port Gamble

See also Port Ludlow, Seattle

Captain William Talbot, a native of Maine, discovered the vast Puget Sound timberlands and located what has become the oldest continuously operating sawmill in North America here. Spars for the ships of the world were a specialty. The community, built by the company and still owned by it, gradually developed a distinctive appearance because of its unusual (to this part of the country) New England architectural style.

The company, realizing an opportunity to preserve a bit of the past, has rebuilt and restored more than 30 homes, commercial buildings, and St. Paul's Episcopal Church. Replicas of gas lamps and underground wiring have replaced street lighting. The entire town has been declared a historic district.

What to See and Do

Hood Canal Nursery. Self-guided tour covers storage and maintenance building, soil mixing, pump house, and chemical storage, water reservoir, greenhouses with a capacity of 3½ million seedlings. (Mon-Fri) Western edge of town. Phone 360/297-7555. **FREE**

Kitsap Memorial State Park. Over 50 acres. Saltwater swimming, scuba diving, fishing, boating (mooring); hiking, picnicking, shelters, camping (dump station). Standard fees. 4 mi S on WA 3. Phone 360/779-3205.

Of Sea and Shore Museum. One of the largest shell collections in the country. Gift, book shop. (Daily; closed Jan 1, Thanksgiving, Dec 25) General Store Building, 3 Rainier Ave. Phone 360/297-2426. **FREE**

Port Gamble Historic Museum. Exhibits trace the history of the area and the timber company. Displays arranged in order of time: replica of old saw filing rm; San Francisco office, captain's cabin from ship; individual rms from hotels and houses; Forest of the Future exhibit. (May-Oct, daily) Downhill side of the General Store. Phone 360/297-8074. ¢¢

Port Ludlow

See also Port Gamble, Sequim

Settled 1878 **Pop** 500 **Elev** 0-30 ft
Area code 360 **Zip** 98365
Information Port Ludlow Olympic Peninsula Gateway Visitor Center, 93 Beaver Valley Rd, PO Box 65478; 360/437-0120
Web www.portludlowchamber.org

Resort

★★ **PORT LUDLOW RESORT & CONFERENCE CENTER.** *200*

Olympic Pl (98365). 360/437-2222; fax 360/437-2482; toll-free 800/732-1239. www.portludlowresort.com. 190 multiunits, 1-2 story, 44 kits. No A/C. May-Oct: S, D $85-$120; suites $140-$445; each addl $15; under 12 free; golf plan; lower rates rest of yr. TV; cable, VCR avail (movies $5.95). Heated pool; whirlpool, lifeguard. Playground. Supervised child's activities (June-Sept); ages 4-12. Dining rm 7 am-10 pm. Box lunches, picnics. Bar 11-2 am; entertainment Tues-Sat (wkends winter). Ck-out noon, ck-in 4 pm. Grocery. Coin lndry. Convention facilities. Business center. Gift shop. Free airport transportation. Tennis. 27-hole golf, greens fee $55, driving range, putting green. Marina; boats, motors, sailboats. Bicycles. Lawn games. Exercise equipt; sauna. Picnic tables. Cr cds: A, MC, V.

⬛⬛⬛⬛⬛⬛⬛⬛

B&B/Small Inn

★★★ **HERON BEACH INN.** *1 Heron Rd (98365). 360/437-0411; fax 360/437-0310. www.heronbeachinn. com.* 37 rms, 3 story, 3 suites. No A/C. June-Oct: S, D $155-$215; each addl $35; suites $300-$450; under 18 free; golf plan; hol rates; summer wkends (2-day min); lower rates rest of yr. Crib avail. Pet accepted, some restrictions; $50 deposit. TV; VCR (free movies). Complimentary continental bkfst. Complimentary coffee in rms. Restaurant (see also HERON BEACH INN DINING ROOM). Ck-out 11 am, ck-in after 3 pm. Luggage handling. Meeting rms. Business servs avail. In-rm modem link. 27-hole golf privileges; greens fee $50-$55, putting green, driving range. Lawn games. Refrigerators. Balconies. Built in 1994 to resemble estate in Maine. Views of Olympic and Cascade Mtns. On shore, beach. Totally nonsmoking. Cr cds: A, D, DS, MC, V.

⬛⬛⬛⬛⬛⬛⬛

Restaurant

★★★ **HERON BEACH INN DINING ROOM.** *1 Heron Rd (98365). 360/437-0411. www.heronbeachinn. com.* Hrs: 5:30-9:30 pm. Closed Mon-Tues (winter). Res accepted. Northwestern menu. Bar. Wine cellar. Dinner $12-$24. Child's meals. Specializes in fresh game and seafood. Own herbs. Views of bay, marina, and Olympic Mtns. Totally nonsmoking. Cr cds: A, D, DS, MC, V.

D

Port Townsend

(B-3) *See also Coupeville, Everett, Oak Harbor*

Settled 1851 **Pop** 7,001 **Elev** 100 ft
Area code 360 **Zip** 98368
Information Tourist Information Center, 2437 E Sims Way; 360/385-2722
Web www.ptchamber.org

Located on the Quimper Peninsula, at the northeast corner of the Olympic Peninsula, this was once a busy port city served by sailing vessels and sternwheelers. Captain George Vancouver came ashore in 1792 and named this spot Port Townshend, after an English nobleman. Port Townsend is a papermill town with boat building and farming.

What to See and Do

Rothschild House. (1868) Furnished in original style; flower and herb gardens. (May-Sept, daily; rest of yr, Sat, Sun, and hols only) Franklin and Taylor Sts. Phone 360/379-8076. ¢

State parks.

Fort Flagler. More than 780 acres. Saltwater swimming, scuba diving, fishing, boating (launch, mooring); hiking, picnicking, camping (res required Memorial Day-Labor Day). Nature study; forested areas, some military areas. Standard fees. 20 mi SE on Marrowstone Island. Phone 360/385-3701.

Fort Worden. Approx 430 acres. Home of Centrum Foundation, with poetry and visual arts symposiums; fiction writer's workshop; fiddletune, jazz, and folk dance festivals. 200 Battery Way, 1 mi N. Phone 360/344-4400. **FREE**

Old Fort Townsend (Historical). Approx 380 acres. Posted site of

fort established in 1856, abandoned in 1895. Swimming, scuba diving, bank fishing; hiking, picnicking, camping. (Mid-Apr-mid-Sept) Standard fees. 3 mi S on WA 20. Phone 360/385-4730.

Special Events

Jefferson County Fair. Agricultural and 4-H displays, livestock shows. Wkend mid-Aug. Phone 360/385-1013.

Wooden Boat Festival. Displays, classes, and lectures. First wkend after Labor Day. Phone 360/385-3628.

House Tours. Third wkend Sept. Phone 360/385-2722.

Motel/Motor Lodge

★★ **INN AT PORT HADLOCK.** *310 Alcohol Loop Rd, Port Hadlock (98339). 360/385-7030; fax 360/385-6955; toll-free 800/785-7030. www.innatport hadlock.com.* 28 rms, 3 story. Mid-May-mid-Oct: S, D $62-$200; each addl $10; suites $62-$250; under 14 free; wkly, monthly rates; lower rates rest of yr. Crib free. Pet accepted; $10. TV; cable (premium), VCR (movies $6). Restaurant. Bar. Ck-out 11 am. Meeting rms. Picnic tables. Former alcohol plant built 1910. Marina. Cr cds: A, DS, MC, V.

D

Hotel

★★ **PALACE.** *1004 Water St (98368). 360/385-0773; toll-free 800/962-0741. www.olympus.net/palace.* 15 rms, 2 story. No A/C. No rm phones. May-mid-Sept: S, D $69-$139; each addl $10; suites $109-$129; under 13 free; lower rates rest of yr. Crib free. Pet accepted. TV; cable. Complimentary continental bkfst. Restaurant 6:30 am-10 pm. Ck-out noon. Meeting rms. Coin lndry. Some refrigerators. Cr cds: A, DS, MC, V.

B&Bs/Small Inns

★★★ **ANN STARRETT MANSION VICTORIAN BED & BREAKFAST.** *744 Clay St (98368). 360/385-3205; fax 360/385-2976; toll-free 800/321-0644. www.starrettmansion.com.* 11 rms, 4 story. No A/C. Apr-Oct: S, D

$138-$185; each addl $25; suites $155-$225; kit. unit $185; lower rates rest of yr. TV in some rms; cable, VCR avail. Complimentary full bkfst. Restaurants nearby. Ck-out 11 am, ck-in 3-6 pm. Business servs avail. Antiques. Winding staircase; frescoed ceilings. View of Puget Sound, Mt Rainier, Cascades, and Olympics. Totally nonsmoking. Cr cds: A, DS, MC, V.

★★★ **CHANTICLEER INN.** *1208 Franklin St (98368). 360/385-6239; fax 360/385-3377; toll-free 800/858-9421. www.northolympic.com/chanticleer/.* 5 rms, 3 with shower only, 2 story. S $90-$140; D $95-$145; each addl $10. Children over 12 yrs only. Complimentary full bkfst; afternoon refreshments. Restaurant nearby. Ck-out 10:30 am, ck-in 3-6 pm. Luggage handling. Victorian house built in 1876; antiques. Totally nonsmoking. Cr cds: A, DS, MC, V.

★★ **THE ENGLISH INN.** *718 F St (98368). 360/385-5302; toll-free 800/254-5302. www.english-inn.com.* 5 rms, 1 with shower only, 2 story. No A/C. S $75-$85; D $95-$105; each addl $15. Children over 14 yrs only. TV in sitting rm; cable, VCR avail (free movies). Whirlpool. Complimentary full bkfst; afternoon refreshments. Ck-out 11 am, ck-in 3-6 pm. Free bus depot transportation. Built 1885; antiques. Rms named for British poets. Some rms with mountain view. Totally nonsmoking. Cr cds: MC, V.

★★★ **FW HASTINGS HOUSE OLD CONSULATE.** *313 Walker St (98368). 360/385-6753; fax 360/385-2097; toll-free 800/300-6753. www.oldconsulateinn.com.* 8 rms, 5 with shower only, 3 story, 3 suites. No rm phones. June-Sept: S, D $96-$140; each addl $45; suites $140-$195; wkends (2-day min); lower rates rest of yr. Children over 12 yrs only. TVs; cable, VCR avail. Whirlpool. Complimentary full bkfst; afternoon refreshments. Ck-out 11 am, ck-in 3-6 pm. Luggage handling. Business servs avail. Free airport transportation. Queen Anne Victorian house built in

1889; many antiques. Totally nonsmoking. Cr cds: MC, V.

★★★ **HOLLY HILL HOUSE B&B.** *611 Polk St (98368). 360/385-5619; toll-free 800/435-1454. www.hollyhillhouse.com.* 5 rms, 2 story, 1 suite. No A/C. No rm phones. S $78-$95; D $110; each addl $20; suite $145-$165. Children over 12 yrs only. Complimentary full bkfst; afternoon refreshments. Ck-out 10:30 am, ck-in 3-6 pm. Built 1872; antiques, stippled woodwork. Rare upside-down Camperdown elm on grounds. Totally nonsmoking. Cr cds: MC, V.

★★★ **JAMES HOUSE.** *1238 Washington St (98368). 360/385-1238; fax 360/379-5551; toll-free 800/385-1238. www.jameshouse.com.* 12 rms, 4 story. No A/C. May-Oct: S $90-$100; D $110-$135; suites $125-$165. Complimentary full bkfst; afternoon refreshments. Restaurant nearby. Ck-out 11 am, ck-in 3 pm. Fireplaces. Some balconies. Restored Victorian guest house (1889); period furniture. Parlors, library. Most rms with view of mountains, bay. Totally nonsmoking. Cr cds: A, DS, MC, V.

★★ **MANRESA CASTLE.** *7th and Sheridan (98368). 360/385-5750; fax 360/385-5883; toll-free 800/732-1281. www.manresacastle.com.* 40 rms, 3 story. No A/C. May-mid Oct: S $60-$70; D $70-$80; each addl $10; lower rates rest of yr. TV; cable (premium). Complimentary continental bkfst. Restaurant (see also MANRESA CASTLE). Bar 4-11 pm. Ck-out 11 am. Business servs avail. Castle built 1892; period furniture. View of bay from many rms. Cr cds: DS, MC, V.

★★★ **RAVENSCROFT.** *533 Quincy St (98368). 360/385-2784; fax 360/385-6724; toll-free 800/782-2691. www.ravenscroftinn.com.* 8 rms, 3 with shower only, 3 story, 2 suites. No A/C. Mid-May-mid-Oct: S, D $80-$190; suites $165-$175; 2-day min hols, special events; lower rates rest of yr. Children over 12 yrs only. TV in library; cable, VCR avail (free movies). Complimentary full bkfst; afternoon refreshments. Restaurants nearby. Ck-out 11 am, ck-in 3-6 pm. Business servs avail. Free airport transportation. Luggage handling. Croquet. Colonial decor; many antiques. Totally nonsmoking. Cr cds: A, DS, MC, V.

★★ **THE SWAN HOTEL.** *222 Monroe St (98368). 360/385-6122. www. theswanhotel.com.* 9 rms, 3 story, 5 kit. suites, 4 kit. cottages. May-Sept: kit. suites $105-$400; kit. cottages $85-$105; under 12 free; wkly rates; higher rates special events; lower rates rest of yr. Crib free. Pet accepted, some restrictions; $15 and daily fees. TV; cable, VCR avail (movies). Complimentary coffee in rms. Restaurant nearby. Ck-out 11 am, ck-in 3 pm. Meeting rms. Business servs avail. In-rm modem link. Refrigerators; microwaves avail. Some balconies. Cr cds: A, DS, MC, V.

All Suite

★★ **BISHOP VICTORIAN GUEST SUITES.** *714 Washington St (98368). 360/385-6122; res 800/824-4738. www.bishopvictorian.com.* 14 kit. suites, 7 with shower only, 3 story. No A/C. No elvtr. May-Sept: kit. suites $119; under 12 free; wkly rates; hols (2-day min); higher rates special events; lower rates rest of yr. Crib free. Pet accepted, some restrictions; $15. TV; cable, VCR avail (movies). Complimentary continental bkfst. Restaurant nearby. Ck-out 11 am, ck-in 3 pm. Business servs avail. In-rm modem link. Luggage handling. Health club privileges. Refrigerators, microwaves; many fireplaces. Built in 1890 as an office/warehouse; converted to English inn. Totally nonsmoking. Cr cds: A, DS, MC, V.

Restaurants

★★ **KHU LARB THAI.** *225 Adams St (98368). 360/385-5023.* Hrs: 11 am-9 pm; Fri, Sat to 10 pm. Res accepted. Thai menu. A la carte entrees: lunch, dinner $7.50-$12.95. Attractive decor using Thai objets d'art. Cr cds: MC, V.

★★★ **LONNY'S.** *2330 Washington St (98368). 360/385-0700. www. lonnys.com.* Hrs: from 5 pm. Closed Tues; hols. Res accepted. Contemporary Italian, American menu. Bar. Wine cellar. Dinner $10.95-$18.95. Child's menu. Specializes in fresh seafood, local produce. Own baking, pasta. Elegant dining in rustic Italian atmosphere. Totally nonsmoking. Cr cds: A, DS, MC, V.

★★★ **MANRESA CASTLE.** *7th and Sheridan Sts (98368). 360/385-5750. www.manresacastle.com.* Hrs: 6-9 pm; Sun brunch 9 am-1 pm; winter Wed-Sat from 5 pm. Closed Jan 1, Dec 25. Res accepted. No A/C. Bar from 4 pm. Dinner $9-$22. Sun brunch $3.25-$8.50. Child's menu. Specialties: curry chicken, fresh Northwest salmon. Own desserts. In 1892 castle; antique oak furnishings, ornate fireplace. Totally nonsmoking. Cr cds: DS, MC, V.

★★ **ORIGINAL OYSTER HOUSE.** *280417 US 101 (98368). 360/385-1785.* Hrs: 4-9 pm; Sun brunch from noon. Res accepted. Bar. Early-bird dinner $9.95 Mon-Fri 4-6 pm, dinner $10.95-$21. Child's menu. Specializes in Northwest cuisine. Parking. Outdoor dining. Overlooking Discovery Bay, beach. Cr cds: A, D, DS, MC, V.

★ **SILVERWATER CAFE.** *237 Taylor St (98368). 360/385-6448. www. silverwatercafe.com.* Hrs: 11:30 am-3 pm, 5-10 pm; Sun from 5 pm. Closed Thanksgiving, Dec 25. Northwestern menu. Bar. Wine, beer. Lunch $4.50-$7.50, dinner $7.50-$15. Child's menu. Specializes in fresh local seafood, vegetarian dishes. Own desserts. Totally nonsmoking. Cr cds: MC, V.

Pullman

(D-8) *See also Clarkston*

Settled 1881 **Pop** 23,478 **Elev** 2,351 ft **Area code** 509 **Zip** 99163

Information Chamber of Commerce, 415 N Grand Ave; 509/334-3565 or 800/365-6948

Web pullman-wa.com

A university town and an agricultural storage and shipping center in the fertile Palouse Hills, this community is named for George M. Pullman, the inventor-tycoon who gave his name to the railroad sleeping car.

What to See and Do

Parks. Kamiak Butte County Park. 10 mi N on WA 27. Timbered area with rocky butte rising 3,641 ft high, trails leading to summit. Approx 300 acres. Picnicking, hiking, interpretive programs (summer). Camping (Apr-Oct; fee). Park (all yr). **Wawawai County Park.** 17 mi SW. Boating, fishing; picnicking, hiking. Earth-sheltered home (afternoon tours, call for dates). Camping (Apr-Oct; fee). Park (all yr). 10 mi N on WA 27. Phone 509/397-6238. **FREE**

Washington State University. (1890) 17,000 students. East of town center. Guided tours at Admission Office, Lighty Building, Rm 370 (afternoon, daily). Phone 509/335-8633. On campus are

  Museum of Art. Exhibitions, lectures, films. (Sept-July, daily, hrs vary) Fine Arts Center. Phone 509/335-1910. **FREE**

  Pullman Summer Palace Theater. Daggy Hall. (Late June-early Aug) Phone 509/335-7236.

Special Event

National Lentil Festival. Food booths, arts and crafts, musical entertainment, parade. Late Aug. Phone 509/334-3565.

Motels/Motor Lodges

★ **AMERICAN TRAVEL INN.** *515 S Grand Ave (99163).* 509/334-3500; fax 509/334-0549. *www.palouse.net/ allamerican.* 35 rms, 2 story. Mid-May-Sept: S, D $45-$70; each addl $5; suites $59-$78; under 12 free; higher rates: graduation, football wkends, Mother's and Father's Day wkends. TV; cable. Pool. Restaurant adj 6 am-3 pm. Ck-out 11 am. Business servs avail. Cr cds: A, D, DS, MC, V.

D ⇌ ⋈ 🐾

★ **QUALITY INN.** *SE 1400 Bishop Blvd (99163).* 509/332-0500; fax 509/334-4271; res 800/228-5151. *www.qualityinn.com.* 66 rms, 2 story, 15 suites. S $59-$99; D $69-$99; each addl $7.50; suites $83-$138; under 18 free; higher rates college wkends. Crib free. Pet accepted. TV; cable (premium), VCR avail. Heated pool; whirlpool, sauna. Restaurant adj 11-2 am. Ck-out noon. Meeting rms. Business servs avail. In-rm modem link. Sundries. Airport transportation. Health club privileges. Coin lndry. Refrigerator in suites. Cr cds: A, D, DS, MC, V.

D 🐾 ⇌ ✈ ⋈ 🐾 SC

Puyallup

See also Enumclaw, Tacoma

Founded 1877 **Pop** 23,875 **Elev** 40 ft **Area code** 253
Information Chamber of Eastern Pierce County, 417 F. Pioneer, PO Box 1298, 98371; 253/845-6755
Web www.puyallupchamber.com

Puyallup freezes the farm produce from the fertile soil and mild climate of the valley between Mount Rainier and Tacoma. A $2 million bulb industry (iris, daffodils, tulips) was born in 1923 when it was discovered the valley was ideal for growing. Ezra Meeker crossed the plains by covered wagon and named this city Puyallup (meaning "generous people") after a tribe that lived in the valley; Puyallups still live in the area.

What to See and Do

Ezra Meeker Mansion. (1890) The 17-rm Victorian house of Ezra Meeker, pioneer, farmer, first town mayor, author, and preserver of the Oregon Trail. Six fireplaces, period furnishings, stained-glass windows, and hand-carved woodwork. (Mar-mid-Dec, Wed-Sun; closed Easter, Thanksgiving) 312 Spring St. Phone 253/848-1770. ¢

Pioneer Park. Life-size statue of Ezra Meeker. Playground; wading pool (summer). S Meridian St and Elm Pl. Phone 253/841-5457. **FREE**

Special Events

Ezra Meeker Community Festival.
Fine arts show, arts and crafts, entertainment; ice cream social at Meeker Mansion. Late June. Phone 253/848-1770.

Pierce County Fair. 6 mi S in Graham. Early Aug. Phone 253/847-4754.

Sumner Summer Festival. Early Aug. Phone 253/845-3182.

Western Washington Fair. Pacific Northwest's largest fair; incl three statewide youth fairs, livestock shows, agricultural and commercial exhibits, free entertainment, midway, rodeo, top-name grandstand acts. Seventeen days Sept. Phone 253/841-5045.

Quinault

Pop 350 **Elev** 221 ft **Area code** 360 **Zip** 98575

Information Grays Harbor Chamber of Commerce, 506 Duffy St, Aberdeen 98520; 360/532-1924 or 800/321-1924

Web www.graysharbor.org

Quinault, on the shore of Lake Quinault, is the south entrance to Olympic National Park (see). In the heart of Olympic National Forest, it is the gateway to any of three valleys, the Hoh, Queets, and Quinault, which make up the rain forest, a lush green ecological phenomenon. It also provides an entrance to the Enchanted Valley area of the park. The Quinault Reservation is two miles west.

A Ranger District office of the Olympic National Forest (see OLYMPIA) is located here.

Motel/Motor Lodge

★ ★ **LAKE QUINAULT LODGE.** *345 South Shore Rd (98525). 360/288-2900; toll-free 800/562-6672. www. visitlakequinault.com.* 92 rms, 1-3 story. No A/C. No rm phones. June-Sept: S, D $105-$180; each addl $10; under 5 free; lower rates rest of yr. Indoor pool; sauna. Restaurant 7 am-9:30 pm. Bar noon-11:30 pm. Ck-out 11 am. Meeting rms. Business servs avail. Gift shop. Boat rental. Lawn games. Game rm. Some fireplaces.

Some balconies. On lake, beach. Cr cds: A, DS, MC, V.

Quincy

(D-5) *See also Ellensburg, Ephrata, Wenatchee*

Settled 1892 **Pop** 3,738 **Elev** 1,301 ft **Area code** 509 **Zip** 98848

Information Quincy Valley Chamber of Commerce, 119 F St SE, PO Box 668; 509/787-2140

Web www.quincyvalley.org

Although there are only about eight inches of rain a year in this area, irrigation has turned the surrounding countryside green. Quincy processes and markets farm produce; more than 80 crops are grown in the area. Deposits of diatomaceous earth (soft chalky material used for fertilizers, mineral aids, and filters) are mined in the area and refined in Quincy. Fishing and game-bird hunting are good in the surrounding area.

What to See and Do

Crescent Bar Park. On Wanapum Reservoir in the Columbia River. Swimming, bathhouse, beaches, waterskiing, boating, fishing, marina; playground, picnicking, camping (Apr-Oct; hookups; fee), restaurants, putting green, shops, pro shop, grocery, nine-hole golf (fee), four tennis courts (fee). Park (all yr). 8 mi W off WA 28.

Special Event

Farmer Consumer Awareness Day. Quincy High School, 16 Sixth Ave SE. Free tours to dairies, processing plants, packing houses, farms, harvesting operations. Exhibits, food booths, arts and crafts, petting zoo, antique autos, farm equipment, games, parade, 2K and 5K run, entertainment. Second Sat Sept. Phone 509/787-3501.

Motel/Motor Lodge

★ **TRADITIONAL INNS.** *500 F St SW (98848). 509/787-3525; fax 509/787-3528. www.traditionalinns. com.* 24 rms, 2 story. S $54-$60; D $62-$68; under 13 free; wkly rates. Crib free. Pet accepted; $5. TV; cable. Complimentary coffee in lobby. Ck-out 11 am. Coin lndry. Refrigerators, microwaves. Cr cds: A, C, D, DS, MC, V.

Richland

(E-6) *See also Kennewick, Pasco*

Pop 32,315 **Elev** 360 ft **Area code** 509 **Zip** 99352

Information Chamber of Commerce, 710A George Washington Way, PO Box 637; 509/946-1651

Web www.richlandchamberof comm.com

Although one of the "tri-cities" (see KENNEWICK and PASCO), Richland has an entirely different personality, due to the 560-square-mile Hanford Works of the Department of Energy (DOE)—formerly the US Atomic Energy Commission. In 1943, Richland was a village of 250, dedicated to fruit cultivation. A year later Hanford was established by the government as one of four main development points for the atomic bomb—the others, Oak Ridge, Tennessee; Los Alamos, New Mexico; and the Argonne Laboratory, near Chicago. Hanford no longer is involved in the production of plutonium, and the more than 16,000 employees are now dedicated to environmental cleanup and safe disposal of nuclear and hazardous wastes. Important companies in Richland include Siemens's Nuclear Fuels Inc, Battelle Northwest, Boeing Computer Services, Washington Public Power Supply Service (WPPSS), Kaiser Engineers, and Fluor Daniel Hanford.

Once largely desert area, Richland today is surrounded by vineyards and orchards, thanks to irrigation from Grand Coulee Dam and the Yakima River Irrigation Projects. The city is at the hub of an area of spectacular scenery and outdoor activities within a short drive in any direction.

What to See and Do

CRESHT Museum. Displays, models, computer exhibits relating to US energy, science, and environmental topics. (Mon-Sat, Sun afternoon; closed hols) 95 Lee Blvd. Phone 509/943-9000. ¢¢

Special Events

Cool Desert Nights Car Show. June. Phone 509/697-5898.

NASCAR Auto Racing. June-Sept.

Columbia Cup. Hydroplane races. July. Phone 509/547-2203.

Benton-Franklin Fair and Rodeo. Franklin County Fairgrounds. Fair, parade, carnival. Aug. Phone 509/586-9211.

Motels/Motor Lodges

★ **BALI HAI MOTEL.** *1201 George Washington Way (99352). 509/943-3101; fax 509/943-6363.* 44 rms, 2 story. S $41-$50; D $46; each addl $5; studio rms $37-$45; under 12 free; higher rates hydroplane races. Crib free. Pet accepted; $5. TV; cable (premium). Pool; whirlpool. Complimentary coffee in rms. Restaurant adj 7 am-11 pm. Ck-out noon. Coin lndry. Business servs avail. Refrigerators, microwaves. Cr cds: A, C, D, DS, ER, MC, V.

★★ **BEST WESTERN TOWER INN & CONFERENCE CENTER.** *1515 George Washington (99352). 509/946-4121; fax 509/946-2222; res 800/780-7234. www.bestwestern.com.* 195 rms, 6 story. S $59-$89; D $79-$99, each addl $10; suites $99-$129; under 17 free. Crib free. Pet accepted. TV; cable (premium). Heated pool; wading pool, whirlpool, poolside serv. Complimentary full bkfst. Coffee in rms. Restaurant 6 am-2 pm, 5-9 pm. Bar; entertainment Thurs-Sat. Ck-out noon. Coin lndry. Meeting rms. Business servs avail. Bellhops. Valet serv.

Free airport, RR station, bus depot transportation. Saunas. Lawn games. Some refrigerators. Balconies. Cr cds: A, C, D, DS, ER, JCB, MC, V.

★ **DAYS INN.** 615 Jadwin Ave (99352). 509/943-4611; fax 509/946-2271; res 800/329-7466. www.daysinn.com. 98 rms, 2 story, 16 kits. S $58-$69; D $62-$79; each addl $5; kit. units $50-$53; under 12 free; higher rates summer boat race wkends. Crib free. Pet accepted; $5. TV; cable (premium). Heated pool. Complimentary continental bkfst. Restaurant nearby. Ck-out noon. Business servs avail. Refrigerators. Cr cds: A, D, DS, MC, V.

★★ **RED LION HOTEL.** 802 George Washington Way (99352). 509/946-7611; fax 509/943-8564; res 800/222-8733. www.redlion.com. 149 rms, 2 story. S, D $59-$88; each addl $10; under 18 free. Crib $5. Pet accepted. TV; cable. Heated pool; poolside serv. Coffee in rms. Restaurant 6 am-2 pm, 5-10 pm. Bar. Ck-out noon. Meeting rms. Bellhops. Valet serv. Sundries. Free airport, RR station, bus depot transportation. Boat dock. Private patios, balconies. Most rms with private lanais. Cr cds: A, C, D, DS, ER, JCB, MC, V.

★★ **SHILO INN.** 50 Comstock St (99352). 509/946-4661; fax 509/943-6741; res 800/222-2244. www.shiloinn.com. 150 rms, 2 story, 13 kits. Mid-May-mid-Sept: S, D $50-$199; each addl $10; under 13 free; higher rates hydroplane races; lower rates rest of yr. Crib free. Pet accepted; $7/day. TV; cable (premium). Heated pool; wading pool, whirlpool. Complimentary bkfst buffet. Coffee in rms. Restaurant 6 am-10 pm. Bar. Ck-out noon. Coin lndry. Meeting rms. Business servs avail. In-rm modem link. Valet serv. Airport, RR station, bus depot transportation. Exercise equipt. Refrigerators, microwaves; some wetbars. On 12 acres. Cr cds: A, D, DS, JCB, MC, V.

Restaurant

★ **R.F. MCDOUGALL'S.** 1705 Columbia Park Tr (99352). 509/735-6418.

Hrs: 11 am-11 pm. Closed Thanksgiving, Dec 25. Bar to 1 am. Lunch, dinner $3.50-$9.50. Specializes in hamburgers, pasta. Outdoor dining. Antique advertising signs in Western-style restaurant. Cr cds: A, MC, V.

Ritzville

(D-7) See also Moses Lake

Settled 1878 **Pop** 1,725 **Elev** 1,815 ft
Area code 509 **Zip** 99169
Information Chamber of Commerce, 201 W Railroad, PO Box 122; 509/659-1936

Special Events

Ritzville Blues Festival. Second Sat July. Phone 509/659-1936.

Wheat Land Communities Fair. Parade, rodeo. Labor Day wkend. Phone 509/659-0141.

Motel/Motor Lodge

★★ **LAQUINTA.** 1513 S Smittys Blvd (99169). 509/659-1007; fax 509/659-1025; res 800/531-5900. www.laquinta.com. 54 rms, 2 story. May-mid-Nov: S, D $59-$89; each addl $10; suites $99-$159; under 18 free; lower rates rest of yr. Crib free. Pet accepted. TV; cable (premium), VCR avail. Heated pool; whirlpool. Complimentary continental bkfst. Restaurant adj 5:30 am-11 pm. Ck-out 11 am. Coin lndry. Meeting rms. Business servs avail. Gift shop. Refrigerators avail. Cr cds: A, D, DS, ER, JCB, MC, V.

Restaurant

★★ **CIRCLE T INN.** 214 W Main St (99169). 509/659-0922. Hrs: 7 am-10 pm. Closed hols. Bar to 2 am. Bkfst $3.75-$6.50, lunch, dinner $4-$15.95. Specializes in homemade foods. Own desserts. Cr cds: MC, V.

San Juan Islands

See also Anacortes; also see Victoria, BC, Canada

Humpback whales frolic in the San Juan Islands area

These 172 islands nestled between the northwest corner of Washington and Vancouver Island, British Columbia, Canada, comprise a beautiful and historic area. Secluded coves, giant trees, fresh-water lakes, fishing camps, modest motels, numerous bed-and-breakfasts, and plush resorts characterize the four major islands. Over 500 miles of paved or gravel roads swing through virgin woodlands and along lovely shorelines. The islands are accessible by ferry from Anacortes (see).

San Juan Island gave birth in 1845 to the expansionist slogan "fifty-four forty or fight" and was the setting for the "pig war" of 1859, in which a British pig uprooted an American potato patch. The subsequent hostilities between the Islands' 7 British and 14 American inhabitants reached such proportions that eventually Kaiser Wilhelm I of Germany was called in to act as arbiter and settle the boundaries. During the 13 years of controversy, the pig was the only casualty. This island was the last place the British flag flew within the territorial United States. Friday Harbor, most westerly stop in the United States on San Juan Islands ferry tour, is county seat of San Juan.

What to See and Do

⭐ **San Juan Island.** Friday Harbor on eastern shore serves as base for salmon fleet; major commercial center of islands. Fishing lakes; camping facilities, golf, International Seaplane Base, and two airstrips are here. Also on San Juan is

San Juan Island National Historical Park. Commemorates settlement of boundary issue between the US and Great Britain. British Camp, 10 mi northwest of Friday Harbor on Garrison Bay, has restored blockhouse, commissary, hospital, formal garden, and barracks built during the British occupation. American Camp, 6 mi SE of Friday Harbor, has remains of redoubt, the American defensive earthwork; laundresses' and officers' quarters. Picnicking; information specialist at both camps (June-Sept, daily; rest of yr, Thurs-Sun). Office and information center in Friday Harbor, 1st and Spring sts (June-Aug, daily; May and Sept, Mon-Fri; closed rest of yr; closed hols) For further information contact Superintendent, Box 429, Friday Harbor 98250. Phone 360/378-2240.

The Whale Museum. Art and science exhibits document the lives of whales and porpoises in this area. (Daily; closed major hols) 62 1st St N in Friday Harbor. Phone 360/378-4710. ¢¢

Special Event

San Juan Jazz Festival. Friday Harbor and Roche Harbor. Phone 360/378-5240. Last wkend July.

Resorts

⭐⭐ **ROCHE HARBOR SEASIDE VILLAGE.** *248 Reuben Memorial Dr, Roche Harbor (98250). 360/378-2155; fax 360/378-6809; toll-free 800/451-8910. www.rocheharbor.com.* 20 hotel rms, 4 with bath, 3 story, 9 kit. cottages (2-bedrm), 25 condos (1-3-bedrm). No A/C. No elvtr. May-Oct:

S, D $79-$135; cottages $130-$195; condos $175-$265; under 6 free; lower rates rest of yr. Crib $7. TV in condo. Pool. Restaurant opp 5-10 pm. Bar 11-1 am; entertainment (June-Aug). Ck-out 11 am, ck-in 3 pm. Business servs avail. Grocery. Coin lndry. Meeting rms. Business center. Gift shop. Tennis. Swimming beach; boats. Hiking. Microwaves avail. Some balconies. Picnic area; grills. On harbor. Totally nonsmoking. Cr cds: A, MC, V.

★★★ **ROSARIO.** *1400 Rosario Rd, East Sound (98245). 360/376-2222; fax 360/376-3680; toll-free 800/562-8820. www.rosarioresort.com.* 86 rms, 33 suites, 2 with kit., 1-2 story. No A/C. June-mid-Oct: S, D $180-$200; each addl $20; suites $200-$400; kit. units $140-$280; under 12 free; lower rates rest of yr. Crib $5. TV. 3 pools, 1 indoor; whirlpool, poolside serv. Restaurant (by res) 7 am-2 pm, 6-10 pm. Box lunches, snacks. Bar 11-1 am. Ck-out 11 am, ck-in 4 pm. Grocery. Coin lndry. Meeting rms. Airport transportation. Tennis. Golf privileges. Boating (marina). Lawn games. Music rm; piano, organ concerts. Entertainment. Exercise rm; sauna. Some wet bars, fireplaces. Private patios, balconies. On 30-acre estate. Totally nonsmoking. Cr cds: A, D, DS, MC, V.

B&Bs/Small Inns

★★ **ARGYLE HOUSE BED & BREAKFAST.** *685 Argyle Ave, Friday Harbor (98250). 360/378-4084; res 800/624-3459. www.argylehouse.net.* 4 rms, shower only, 2 story, 1 guest house. No A/C. No rm phones. Mid-May-Sept: S $95-$125; D $95-$135; honeymoon cottage $135; wkly rates; lower rates rest of yr. Children over 10 yrs only. TV in common rm; cable, VCR avail (movies). Complimentary full bkfst; afternoon refreshments. Restaurant nearby. Ck-out 11 am, ck-in 3 pm. Luggage handling. Free airport transportation. Whirlpool. Lawn games. Picnic tables, grills. Built in 1910; country setting, gardens. Totally nonsmoking. Cr cds: MC, V.

★★★ **1891 FRIDAY'S HISTORICAL INN.** *35 First St, San Juan Island (98250). 360/378-5848; fax 360/378-2881; toll-free 800/352-2632. www.friday-harbor.com.* 15 rms, 4 share bath, 3 story. No A/C. No rm phones. June-Oct: S, D $90-$225; each addl $20; lower rates rest of yr. TV in some rms; cable (premium). Complimentary continental bkfst; afternoon refreshments. Restaurant nearby. Ck-out 11 am, ck-in 2 pm. Refrigerators; microwaves avail. Balconies. Built 1891. Antiques. Totally nonsmoking. Cr cds: MC, V.

★★ **HARRISON HOUSE SUITES.** *235 C St, Friday Harbor (98250). 360/378-3587; fax 360/378-2270; res 800/407-7933. www.san-juan-lodging.com.* 5 suites. No A/C. May-Sept: S, D $125-$300; under 2 free; wknds (2-day min); lower rates rest of yr. Crib free. TV; cable (premium), VCR (movies). Complimentary continental bkfst. Complimentary coffee in rms. Restaurant nearby. Rm serv 24 hrs. Ck-out 3 pm, ck-in 11 am. Business servs avail. In-rm modem link. Luggage handling. Free guest lndry. Free airport transportation. Massage. Heated pool; whirlpool. Refrigerators, microwaves; many in-rm whirlpools and private outdoor jacuzzis; some fireplaces. Many balconies. Built in 1904; eclectic furnishings. Totally nonsmoking. Cr cds: A, DS, MC, V.

★★★ **HILLSIDE HOUSE BED & BREAKFAST.** *365 Carter Ave, Friday Harbor (98250). 360/378-4730; fax 360/378-4715; toll-free 800/232-4730. www.hillsidehouse.com.* 7 rms, 2 with shower only, 3 story. No A/C. Some rm phones. May-Sept: S, D $100-$225; each addl $25; lower rates rest of yr. Complimentary full bkfst. Restaurant nearby. Ck-out 11 am, ck-in 3 pm. Business servs avail. Luggage handling. Near ocean. Gardens with fountains. Cr cds: A, DS, MC, V.

★★★ **INN AT SWIFTS BAY.** *856 Port Stanley Rd, Lopez Island (98261). 360/468-3636; fax 360/468-3637; toll-free 800/903-9536. www.swiftsbay.com.* 5 air-cooled rms, 2 story. No rm phones. S, D $95-$185. No children under 16. TV in den; VCR. Complimentary full bkfst; afternoon refreshments. Ck-out 11 am, ck-in 3-7 pm. Exercise equipt; sauna. Whirlpool. Refrigerators, fireplaces. Tudor-style inn in cedar grove; quiet atmosphere. Totally nonsmoking. Cr cds: MC, V.

★★ **ORCAS HOTEL.** *PO Box 155, Orcas (98280). 360/376-4300; toll-free 888/672-2792. www.orcashotel.com.* 12 air-cooled rms, 7 with bath, 3 story. No rm phones. May-Oct: S, D $79-$198; each addl $15; lower rates rest of yr. Complimentary continental bkfst. Restaurant 8-11:30 am, 5-8:30 pm. Bar 11 am-10 pm. Ck-out 11 am, ck-in 1:30 pm. Business servs avail. Balconies. Victorian hotel built in 1904. View of island's ferry landing. Totally nonsmoking. Cr cds: A, MC, V.

★★ **PANACEA BED AND BREAKFAST.** *595 Park St, Friday Harbor (98250). 360/378-3757; fax 360/378-8543; res 800/639-2762. www.panaceainn.com.* 4 rms, 2 with shower only. No A/C. No rm phones. May-Oct: S, D $135-$165; lower rates rest of yr. Children over 17 yrs only. TV; cable. Complimentary full bkfst. Ck-out 10 am, ck-in 2 pm. Some in-rm whirlpools. Picnic tables, grills. Craftsman-style home built in 1907. Totally nonsmoking. Cr cds: MC, V.

★★ **SAN JUAN INN.** *50 Spring St W, Friday Harbor (98250). 360/378-2070; fax 360/378-2027; toll-free 800/742-8210. www.sanjuaninn.com.* 9 rms, 2 story. No A/C. Mid-May-mid-Oct: S, $65-$75; D $70-$105; suites $180-$205; wkly rates off season; lower rates rest of yr. Children over 7 yrs only. Complimentary continental bkfst. Ck-out 11 am, ck-in 2 pm. Restored inn; built 1873. Totally nonsmoking. Cr cds: A, DS, MC, V.

★★ **TUCKER HOUSE BED & BREAKFAST.** *260 B St, Friday Harbor (98250). 360/378-2783; fax 360/378-8775; res 800/965-0123. www.tuckerhouse.com.* 6 rms, 3 share bath, 2 story, 2 kit. units. No A/C. No rm phones. May-mid-Oct: S, D $135-$225; each addl $20; wkly rates; lower rates rest of yr. Crib free. Pet

accepted, some restrictions; $15. TV; cable, VCR avail (movies). Complimentary full bkfst. Complimentary coffee in rms. Ck-out 11 am, ck-in 3 pm. Picnic tables. Victorian home built in 1898. Totally nonsmoking. Cr cds: MC, V.

★★★ **TURTLEBACK FARM INN.** *1981 Crow Valley Rd, East Sound (98245). 360/376-4914; fax 360/376-5329. www.turtlebackinn.com.* 11 air-cooled rms, 2 story. Rm phones avail. S, D $90-$225; each addl $25. Complimentary full bkfst; afternoon refreshments. Ck-out 11 am. Some refrigerators, fireplaces. Overlooks eighty acres of farmland. Totally nonsmoking. Cr cds: DS, MC, V.

★★★ **WINDSONG BED & BREAKFAST.** *213 Deer Harbor Rd, Orcas (98280). 360/376-5257; fax 360/376-4453. www.windsonginn.com.* 4 air-cooled rms, 3 with shower only. No rm phones. May-Oct: S $100-$125; D $110-$135; each addl $25; wkends, hols (2-day min); lower rates rest of yr. Children over 14 yrs only. TV in common rm; cable (premium), VCR avail (movies). Complimentary full bkfst. Complimentary coffee in rms. Ck-out 11 am, ck-in 2-5 pm. Luggage handling. Airport transportation. Whirlpool. Many fireplaces. Picnic tables, grills. Built in 1917 as a grammar school; first inn on Orcas Island. Totally nonsmoking. Cr cds: MC, V.

Cottage Colony

★★★ **LOPEZ FARM COTTAGES.** *555 Fisherman Bay Rd, Lopez Island (98261). 360/468-3555; fax 360/468-3966. www.lopezfarmcottages.com.* 4 kit. units, shower only. May-Oct: S, D $125; each addl $25; lower rates rest of yr. Complimentary continental bkfst. Ck-out 11 am, ck-in 3-7 pm. Grocery, coin lndry, package store 1½ mi. Free airport transportation. Hiking. Spa. Whirlpool. Refrigerators, microwaves, wet bars, fireplaces. On historic family farm. Totally nonsmoking. Cr cds: MC, V.

Restaurants

★ ★ ★ **CHRISTINA'S.** *310 Main, East Sound (98245). 360/376-4904. www.christinas.net.* Hrs: 5:30-10 pm. Closed Dec 25; also 1st 3 wks in Nov and Jan. Res accepted. Bar from 4 pm. Wine list. A la carte entrees: dinner $14.50-$26.50. Child's meals. Specializes in fresh Northwest seafood. Street parking. Outdoor dining. Extensive woodwork in several dining areas; large deck overlooks water. Cr cds: A, D, DS, MC, V.

★ ★ **DOWNRIGGERS.** *10 Front St (98250). 360/378-2700.* Hrs: 11 am-10 pm. Res accepted. Bar. Lunch $4.95-$12.95, dinner $8.95-$25.95. Specializes in fresh local seafood, steak, pasta. Outdoor dining. Several dining levels with views of harbor. Totally nonsmoking. Cr cds: A, MC, V.
[D]

Seattle (C-3)

Founded 1852 **Pop** 516,259 **Elev** 125 ft **Area code** 206

Information Seattle-King County Convention & Visitors Bureau, 520 Pike St, Suite 1300, 98101; 206/461-5840

Web www.seeseattle.org

Suburbs Bellevue, Bremerton, Everett, Issaquah, Marysville, Port Gamble, Tacoma. (See individual alphabetical listings.)

Seattle has prospered from the products of its surrounding forests, farms, and waterways, serving as provisioner to Alaska and the Orient. Since the 1950s it has acquired a new dimension from the manufacture of jet airplanes, missiles, and space vehicles—which, along with tourism, comprise the city's most important industries.

The Space Needle, which dominated Seattle's boldly futuristic 1962 World's Fair, still stands, symbolic of the city's forward-looking character. The site of the fair is now the Seattle Center. Many features of the fair have been made permanent.

Seattle is on Elliott Bay, nestled between Puget Sound, an inland-probing arm of the Pacific Ocean, and Lake Washington, a 24-mile stretch of fresh water. The city sprawls across hills and ridges, some of them 500 feet high, but all are dwarfed by the Olympic Mountains to the west and the Cascades to the east. Elliott Bay, Seattle's natural harbor, welcomes about 2,000 commercial deep-sea cargo vessels a year. From Seattle's piers, ships wind their way 125 nautical miles through Puget Sound and the Strait of Juan de Fuca, two-thirds of them Orient-bound, the others destined for European, Alaskan, and Eastern ports.

On the same latitude as Newfoundland, Seattle is warmed by the Japan Current, shielded by the Olympics from excessive winter rains, and protected by the Cascades from midcontinent winter blasts. Only twice has the temperature been recorded at 100°F; there isn't a zero on record.

Five families pioneered here and named the town for a friendly Native American chief. The great harbor, and the timber surrounding it, made an inviting combination; shortly thereafter a sawmill and a salmon-canning plant were in operation.

Seattle's famous Public Market Center

Soon wagon trains were rolling to Seattle through Snoqualmie Pass, a tempting 3,022 feet, lower than any other in the Northwest.

Isolated at the fringe of the continent by the vast expanse of America, Seattle enjoyed great expectations but few women, an obvious threat to the growth and serenity of the community. Asa Mercer, a civic leader and first president of the Territorial University, went East and persuaded 11 proper young women from New England to sail with him around the Horn to Seattle to take husbands among the pioneers. This venture in long distance matchmaking proved so successful that Mercer returned East and recruited 100 Civil War widows. Today many of Seattle's families proudly trace their lineage to these women.

When a ship arrived from Alaska with a "ton of gold" in 1897, the great Klondike Gold Rush was on, converting Seattle into a boomtown—the beginning of the trail to fortune. Since then Seattle has been the natural gateway to Alaska because of the protected Inside Passage; the commercial interests of the two remain tightly knit. Another major event for Seattle was the opening of the Panama Canal in 1914, a tremendous stimulant for the city's commerce.

Additional Visitor Information

For additional accommodations, see SEATTLE-TACOMA INTERNATIONAL AIRPORT AREA, which follows SEATTLE.

Transportation

Airport. Seattle-Tacoma International Airport. Information: 206/433-5312. Lost and Found: 206/433-5312.

Car Rental Agencies. See IMPOR TANT TOLL-FREE NUMBERS.

Public Transportation. Metro Transit System, phone 206/553-3000.

Rail Passenger Service. Amtrak 800/872-7245.

What to See and Do

Alki Beach. Site where Seattle's first settlers built cabins; monument; scenic views; lighthouse at Alki Point

(adj); boat ramp on Harbor Ave SW; concessions. Alki Ave SW and 59th Ave SW, Southwest Side. **FREE**

⭐ **Boeing Field—King County International Airport.** Observation Park has viewing, picnicking facilities. Southeast Side. Phone 206/296-7380. Also here is

> **Museum of Flight.** Exhibits on aviation pioneers, industry. Spectacular Great Gallery focuses on modern flight, incl Space Age; more than 40 aircraft on display, incl A-12 Blackbird. Adj is Red Barn (1909), original Boeing Aircraft Manufacturing Building, featuring exhibits emphasizing aviation from its beginnings through the 1930s. (Daily; closed Thanksgiving, Dec 25) Phone 206/764-5720.

Carkeek Park. Approx 190 acres on Puget Sound. Beach, picnic area; model airplane meadow, hiking trail (one mi). (Daily) NW 110th St, Northwest Side. **FREE**

Charles and Emma Frye Art Museum. Collection of American and European paintings from late 19th century; art competitions; traveling and changing exhibits. (Tues-Sun; closed Thanksgiving, Dec 25) 704 Terry Ave, at Cherry St, Downtown. Phone 206/622-9250. **FREE**

Discovery Park. More than 500 acres of urban wilderness on the Magnolia bluff. Former US Army post. Nature trails, meadows, forests, cliffs, and beaches (no swimming). Picnicking, playground, tennis. Visitor center (daily; closed hols). Indian Cultural Center (Mon-Fri). Park (daily). Guided nature walks (Sat). 3801 W Government Way, Northwest Side. Phone 206/386-4236. **FREE**

Evergreen Floating Bridge. Almost 1½ mi long; connects downtown Seattle with Bellevue (see). On WA 520, near Montlake Pl, Southeast Side.

Ferry trips and cruises.

> **Argosy Harbor Cruise.** One-hr narrated harbor tour. (Daily) From Pier 55, foot of Seneca St. Phone 206/623-1445.

> **Ferry trips.** Access to Olympic Peninsula, a number of interesting ferry trips. Seattle Ferry Terminal, Colman Dock, foot of Madison St.

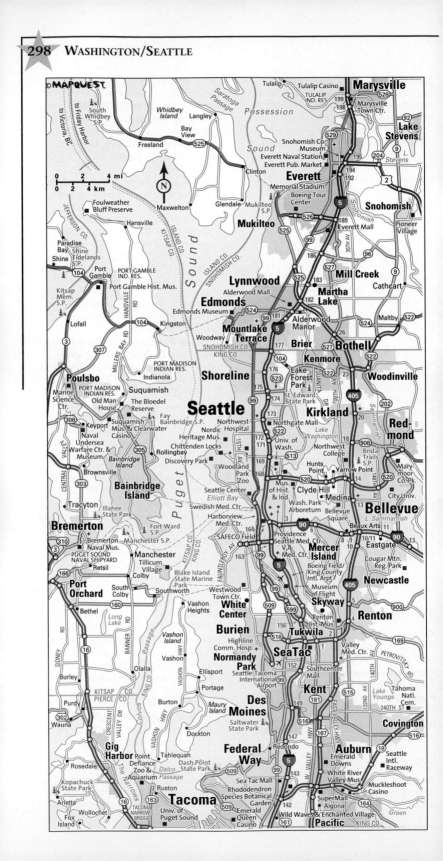

Contact Washington State Ferries, Colman Dock, 98104. Phone 206/464-6400. ¢¢¢¢

Gallant Lady Cruises. Six-day inclusive summer cruises to San Juan Islands; also extended cruises along British Columbia. Depart from Lake Union. For prices, schedule, contact PO Box 1250, Vashon 98070. Phone 206/463-2073.

Tillicum Village. Narrated harbor cruise; baked-salmon dinner; stage show. (May-mid-Oct, daily; rest of yr, Sat; hrs vary) Res advised. Blake Island State Park. Excursion from Pier 55/56, foot of Seneca St. Phone 206/443-1244. ¢¢¢¢¢

Freeway Park. Five-acre park features dramatic water displays. Free concerts (summer, Mon). (Daily) 6th and Seneca, Downtown.

Gas Works Park. Views of downtown and Lake Union in 20-acre park. Towers of an old gas plant and imaginative reuse of industrial machinery. More than 26,000 boats/yr pass here to the ship canal. Your shadow marks the time on 28-ft sundial at top of Kite Hill. Kite-flying mound, picnic shelter, play barn, promenade. (Daily) 2101 N Northlake Way at Meridian N, Northwest Side. Phone 206/684-4075. **FREE**

Golden Gardens. Saltwater swimming beach (no lifeguards; water temperature 54°F in summer); boat ramp (adj to Shilshole Bay Marina); picnic areas with views of Sound, mountains; volleyball courts. Teen activity center. (Daily) 8499 Seaview Ave NW, Northwest Side. Phone 206/684-4075. **FREE**

Green Lake Park. Two swimming beaches (Mid-June-early Sept, daily), indoor pool (Mon-Sat; fee), wading pool (May-Sept, daily), fishing pier, boat rentals; tennis, three-mi pedestrian and bicycle path around lake, picnic and playfield areas, playground, pitch 'n' putt golf, concessions. Aurora Ave (WA 99), between N 65th and 72nd Sts, Northwest Side. Phone 206/684-4075. **FREE**

International District. Asian community with shops, restaurants, and the Nippon Kan Theatre, a national historic site at Kobe Park, where a giant lantern overlooks the terraced community gardens. Southeast of Downtown, 4th Ave to I-5 and Yesler to S Dearborn Sts, Downtown.

Klondike Gold Rush National Historical Park-Seattle Unit. Visitor center in historic Pioneer Square District. Details gold rush stampede of 1897-1898; displays, photomurals, artifacts, slide and film programs; gold-panning demonstrations. (Daily; closed Jan 1, Thanksgiving, Dec 25) 117 S Main St, Southwest Side. Phone 206/553-7220.

Lake Union. Boatyards, seaplane moorages, houseboat colonies on lake. Seen from George Washington Memorial Bridge, Northwest Side.

Lake Washington Canal. Chittenden Locks raise and lower boats to link salt and fresh water anchorages. More than 400,000 passengers and six million tons of freight pass through annually. Commodore Park and a salmon ladder with viewing windows are on the S side. Can be seen from Seaview Ave NW or NW 54th St, Northwest Side.

Lake Washington Floating Bridge. Can be seen from Lake Washington Blvd and Lakeside Ave. Connects downtown Seattle with Mercer Island via I-90.

Lincoln Park. Trails, picnic areas, tennis; beach, bathhouse, saltwater pool (Mid-June-early Sept, daily; fee), wading pool (June-Sept, daily); fitness trail. (Daily) 8011 Fauntleroy Ave SW, Southwest Side. **FREE**

Mount Baker-Snoqualmie National Forest. Snoqualmie Section. Incl several ski areas (see MOUNT RAINIER NATIONAL PARK and NORTH BEND); eight wilderness areas; picnic and campsites, fishing, hunting. More than one million acres. East and south of city, reached via I-90. Contact Outdoor Recreation Information Center, 915 2nd Ave, Suite 442, 98174. Phone 425/775-9702.

Museum of History and Industry. History of Seattle and Pacific Northwest; exhibits change frequently. (Daily; closed Jan 1, Thanksgiving, Dec 25) 2700 24th Ave E, on N side of WA 520, just S of Husky Stadium, Southeast Side. Phone 206/324-1125. ¢¢¢

Myrtle Edwards/Elliott Bay. One mi of shoreline; paved bike trail; views of Puget Sound, the Olympic Peninsula, and oceangoing vessels; Seamen's Memorial and a granite and concrete sculpture. North of Pier 70, Northwest Side.

Nordic Heritage Museum. Center for Scandinavian community in Pacific Northwest. Represents all five Scandinavian countries. Historical exhibits; art gallery; performing arts. (Tues-Sat, also Sun afternoon) 3014 NW 67th St, Northwest Side. Phone 206/789-5707. ¢¢

⭐ **Pike Place Market.** Oldest continuously operating farmers market in the country. Buy anything from artichokes to antiques. More than 225 permanent shops, restaurants; handcrafts. (Daily; closed hols) First Ave and Pike St, in nine-acre historical district, Downtown. Phone 206/682-7453. **FREE**

Pioneer Square. Restored buildings of early Seattle now house galleries, shops, and restaurants. Bounded by 1st Ave, James St, and Yesler Way, Downtown.

Professional sports.

  Seattle Mariners (MLB). Safeco Field, 1250 1st Ave S. Phone 206/346-4000.

  Seattle Seahawks (NFL). Washington State Football/Soccer Stadium. Phone 425/827-9777.

  Seattle SuperSonics (NBA). Key Arena, First Ave N between Thomas and Republican. Phone 206/283-DUNK.

Schmitz Park. Section of forest as it was when first settlers arrived. Admiral Way SW and SW Stevens St, E of Alki Ave, Southwest Side. **FREE**

The Seattle Aquarium. Features 400,000-gallon underwater viewing dome; re-created Puget Sound habitats with tide that ebbs and flows; tropical Pacific exhibit; marine mammal exhibits of seals and sea otters. (Daily) Pier 59, Waterfront Park, Downtown. Phone 206/386-4300. ¢¢¢

Seattle Art Museum. Collection of Asian art and Chinese jades; modern art; ethnic art, including the Katherine White Collection of African art; changing exhibits. (Tues-Sun; closed Jan 1, Thanksgiving, Dec 25). 100 University St, Downtown. Phone 206/654-3255. ¢¢¢

Seattle Asian Art Museum. This branch of the Seattle Art Museum features collection of Asian art incl

Japanese, Chinese, and Korean collections. Japanese collection is one of top five in US. (Tues-Sun; closed Jan 1, Thanksgiving, Dec 25) 1400 E Prospect St, Volunteer Park. Phone 206/654-3206. ¢¢

⭐ **Seattle Center.** Site of 1962 World's Fair. 305 Harrison St, Downtown. Phone 206/684-7200. Its 74 acres incl

  Center House. Three floors of specialty shops, restaurants, conference facilities, administrative offices. (Daily) Phone 206/684-7200.

  Fun Forest Amusement Park. Rides (fees), games in parklike setting. (June-Labor Day, daily; Mar-June and early Sept-Nov, Fri-Sun) Phone 206/728-1585. **FREE**

  International Fountain. Music and light show. (Daily)

  Monorail. Provides a scenic 90-second ride between Center House and Westlake Center, Downtown. Legacy of 1962 World's Fair, the Swedish-built train makes frequent runs throughout the day. (Daily, closed Jan 1, Thanksgiving, Dec 25) ¢¢

  Pacific Science Center. More than 200 hands-on exhibits plus IMAX Theater, live science demonstrations, planetarium shows, laser light shows, and special events. Science playground. (Daily; closed Thanksgiving, Dec 25) 200 2nd Ave N. Phone 206/443-2001. ¢¢¢¢

  Seattle Center Opera House, Playhouse, Arena, Key Arena. The Opera House is home of the Seattle Opera Association, Pacific Northwest Ballet, and Seattle Symphony. Bagley Wright Theatre is home of Seattle Repertory Theatre. Phone 206/443-2222.

  Space Needle. A 605-ft tower. At 520-ft level, visitors can take in spectacular view from observation deck. Shops, lounge, and displays on observation deck; glass elevators. Two revolving restaurants at 500 ft; no elevator charge when dining. (Daily) Phone 800/937-9582. ¢¢¢¢

Seattle University. (1891) 4,800 students. Landscaped urban campus with more than 1,000 varieties of exotic flowers, trees and shrubs; water fountain sculpture by George

Tsutakawa. Tours of campus. 900 Broadway. Phone 206/296-6000.

Seward Park. Swimming beach (Mid-June-early Sept, daily), bathhouse; picnic and play areas, tennis; amphitheater; Japanese lantern and *torii* (Japanese arch); fish hatchery. (Daily) Occupies peninsula off Lake Washington Blvd S and S Orcas St, Southeast Side. **FREE**

Shilshole Bay Marina. Moorage for 1,500 boats, fuel, repairs, launching ramp, marine supplies; restaurants. 7001 Seaview Ave NW, Northwest Side. Phone 206/728-3385.

Sightseeing tours.

 Gray Line bus tours. 4500 W Marginal Way SW, 98106. Phone 206/624-5077.

 Underground Tour. Informative, humorous lecture and guided walking tour of five-blk area where street level was raised 8-35 ft after the Seattle fire of 1889, leaving many storefronts and some interiors intact underground; 90-min tour goes both above and below ground. (Daily; closed hols; advanced res recommended) 610 1st Ave. Phone 206/682-4646. ¢¢¢

Smith Cove. Navy ships at anchor; Seattle Annex, Naval Supply Center along north side of W Garfield St. Can be seen from Elliott Ave and W Garfield St, Northwest Side.

University of Washington. (1861) 34,400 students. Visitor Information Center, 4014 University Way NE. A 694-acre campus with 128 major buildings, stadium. Special exhibits in Henry Art Gallery (daily exc Mon; closed hols; fee). Thomas Burke Memorial-Washington State Museum (Tues-Sun; closed hols; free); Henry Suzzallo Library. Meany Hall for the Performing Arts, three theaters; health sciences research center and teaching hospital; Waterfront Activities Center; Washington Park Arboretum. Parking fee. Main entrance, 17th Ave NE and NE 45th St, Northeast Side. Phone 206/543-9198.

Volunteer Park. Tennis, play area, wading pool (June-Sept, daily), picnic area; conservatory (daily), formal gardens; observation deck in water tower (520 ft) with view of mountains, city, Puget Sound (Daily). 1247 15th Ave E, Northeast Side. **FREE**

Warren G. Magnuson Park. Approx 200 acres; one-mi shoreline. Swimming beach (Mid-July-early Sept, daily); picnicking, playfield, small boat launch ramp, concessions. Fee for some activities. (Daily) NE 65th and Sand Point Way NE, Northeast Side.

Washington Park Arboretum. Arboretum Dr E winds over 200 acres containing more than 5,000 species of trees and shrubs from all parts of world. Rhododendrons, cherries, azaleas (Apr-June). Arboretum open daily all yr. Tours (Jan-Nov, Sun). On both sides of Lake Washington Blvd, between E Madison and Montlake, Southeast Side. Phone 206/543-8800. **FREE** Within is

 Japanese Garden. Ornamental plants, glassy pools, 12-tier pagoda, and teahouse. Tea ceremony. 1502 Lake Washington Blvd E. Phone 206/684-4725. ¢

⭐ **Waterfront Drive.** Or take higher level Alaskan Way Viaduct along a parallel route to view harbor, sound, mountains. A trolley runs the length of the waterfront and continues into Pioneer Square and the International District. Follow Alaskan Way along Elliott Bay to see ships of many nations docked at piers.

Wing Luke Museum. Commemorates Asian and Pacific Asian culture and history in the Pacific Northwest. Notable exhibits focus on the culture clash between Chinese and white settlers in the 1880s and Japanese internment during WWII. (Tues-Sun) 407 7th Ave S. Phone 206/623-5124. ¢¢

Woodland Park Zoological Gardens. Displays more than 1,000 specimens, many in natural habitats, incl nocturnal house, African savanna, and Asian primates exhibits. Children's zoo. (Daily) Phinney Ave N between N 50th and N 59th Sts, on WA 99, I-5 N 50th St exit, southwest of Green Lake, Northwest Side. Phone 206/684-4800. ¢¢¢

Special Events

A Contemporary Theater (ACT). One of the major resident theaters in the country, ACT is a professional (Equity) theater. Tues-Sun. "A Christmas Carol," in Dec. 700 Union St.

May-Nov. Phone 206/878-3285 or 206/292-7676.

Pacific Northwest Arts Fair. 4 mi E in Bellevue. Art exhibits, handicrafts. Late July. Phone 206/363-2048.

Seafair. Citywide marine festival. Regattas, speedboat races, shows at Aqua Theater, parades, sports events, exhibits. Late July-early Aug. Phone 206/728-0123.

Motels/Motor Lodges

★★ **BEST WESTERN EXECUTIVE INN.** *200 Taylor Ave N (98109). 206/448-9444; fax 206/441-7929; toll-free 800/351-9444. www.bwexec-inn. com.* 123 rms, 5 story. July-Sept: S $119-$142; D $134-$157; each addl $15; under 18 free; lower rates rest of yr. Crib free. TV; cable. Complimentary coffee in rms. Restaurant 6:30 am-10 pm; wkends from 7 am. Bar 11-midnight. Ck-out noon. Meeting rms. Business servs avail. Valet serv. Sundries. Exercise equipt. Whirlpool. Some refrigerators. Cr cds: A, C, D, DS, JCB, MC, V.

D ⬛ ⬛

★ **BEST WESTERN LOYAL INN.** *2301 Eighth Ave (98121). 206/682-0200; fax 206/467-8984; res 800/937-8376. www.bestwestern.com.* 91 rms, 4 story. July-Sept: S $98; D $139; each addl $6; suites $185; under 12 free; lower rates rest of yr. Crib $3. TV; cable. Complimentary continental bkfst. Ck-out noon. Coin lndry. Business servs avail. Sauna. Whirlpool. Some refrigerators, wet bars; microwaves avail. Cr cds: A, D, DS, MC, V.

D ⬛

★★ **BEST WESTERN PIONEER SQUARE HOTEL.** *77 Yesler Way (98104). 206/340-1234; fax 206/467-0707; toll-free 800/800-5514. www. pioneersquare.com.* 75 rms, 4 story. S $119-$189; D $139-$209; each addl $20; under 12 free. Crib free. TV; cable, VCR avail. Complimentary continental bkfst. Ck-out 11 am. Meeting rms. Business servs avail. Bellhops. Valet serv. Health club privileges. In restored building (1914). Cr cds: A, C, D, DS, ER, JCB, MC, V.

D ⬛ ⬛ ⬛ SC

★ **HAMPTON INN & SUITES SEATTLE.** *700 Fifth Ave N (98109). 206/282-7700; fax 206/282-0899; res 800/426-7866. www.hamptoninn-*

suites.com. 198 rms, 6 story, 74 suites. June-Sept: S $139; D $149; each addl $10; suites $159; under 18 free; lower rates rest of yr. Crib avail. Parking garage. TV; cable, VCR avail. Complimentary continental bkfst, coffee in rms, newspaper, toll-free calls. Restaurant nearby. Ck-out noon, ck-in 3 pm. Meeting rm. Business center. Dry cleaning, coin lndry. Exercise rm. Cr cds: A, C, D, DS, ER, JCB, MC, V.

D ⬛ ⬛ SC ⬛

★ **LA QUINTA INN.** *2224 8th Ave (98121). 206/624-6820; fax 206/467-6926; toll-free 800/437-4867. www. laquinta.com.* 72 rms, 7 story. May-Aug: S, D $139-$169; each addl $10; suites $145-$185; under 18 free. Crib free. Pet accepted; $50. TV; cable. Complimentary bkfst. Coffee in rms. Ck-out 1 pm. Meeting rms. Business servs avail. Sundries. Exercise equipt; sauna. Whirlpool. Refrigerators; microwaves. Many balconies. Cr cds: A, C, D, DS, JCB, MC, V.

D ⬛ ⬛ ⬛ ⬛ SC

★★ **LA QUINTA INN.** *2824 S 188th St (98188). 206/241-5211; fax 206/246-5596. www.laquinta.com.* 143 rms, 6 story. Late May-Sept: S $89; D $99-$109; each addl $6; lower rates rest of yr; under 18 free. Crib free. Pet accepted, some restrictions. TV; cable (premium). Pool; whirlpool. Complimentary continental bkfst. Ck-out noon. Coin lndry. Meeting rm. Business servs avail. Sundries. Free airport transportation. Exercise equipt. Cr cds: A, D, DS, MC, V.

⬛ ⬛ ⬛ ⬛ ⬛

★ **SIXTH AVENUE INN.** *2000 6th Ave (98121). 206/441-8300; fax 206/441-9903; res 888/627-8290. www.sixthavenueinn.com.* 167 rms, 5 story, no ground floor rms. Mid-May-mid-Oct: S $99-$169; D $111-$181; each addl $12; suites $150; under 17 free. Crib free. TV; cable (premium). Restaurant 6:30 am-10 pm. Rm serv 7 am-9 pm. Bar 11 am-midnight. Ck-out noon. Meeting rms. Business servs avail. In-rm modem link. Valet serv. Sundries. Cr cds: A, C, D, JCB, MC, V.

⬛ ⬛ SC

★ **TRAVELERS INN.** *4710 Lake Washington Blvd, Renton (98056). 425/228-2858; fax 425/228-3055; toll-*

UNDER AND ABOVE GROUND IN DOWNTOWN SEATTLE

Begin in Seattle's Pioneer Square district, the city's original downtown, which was built in the 1890s (after a disastrous fire) as money from the Yukon Gold Rush started pouring in. The architecture is amazingly harmonious (one architect was responsible for nearly 60 major buildings in a ten-block radius) and graciously restored. The area also features the Underground tour (see SIGHTSEEING TOURS) and many galleries, cafes, and antique shops. A collection of totem poles can be found in tree-lined Occidental Park and in Pioneer Square itself.

Continue across Alaskan Way (or take Waterfront Trolley, a vintage street car that runs from Pioneer Square to the waterfront to Pike Place Market) to the waterfront. Walk along the harbor, watching ferries dart to and fro, or take a boat tour (see FERRY TRIPS AND CRUISES). Stop at the Seattle Aquarium, located in Waterfront Park at Pier 59, then stop for clam chowder at Ivar's, located at Pier 54.

Continue north, recrossing Alaskan Way, and climb to Pike Place Market, eight stories above the harbor on a bluff. There are two ways to do this: there's an elevator hidden at the base of the market, or you can take the Harbor Stairs, a new cascade of steps flanked by shops and gardens. The Pike Place Market is Seattle's most interesting destination, an old-fashioned public market (built around 1910) in a warrenlike building with three floors of food, baked goods, ethnic shops, fresh fish, and crafts. You could spend hours here. Also in the Market are some of Seattle's best-loved restaurants; many of them have great views over the harbor to the islands and Olympic Mountains to the west. Just down the street is the new Seattle Art Museum, with its excellent collection of Northwest Native Art.

---

free 888/596-4777. www.travelers innrenton.com. 117 rms, 2-3 story. No elvtr. S $54; D $58; each addl $4; suites $63.99-$79.99; under 18 free. Crib free. TV; cable (premium). Heated pool. Complimentary continental bkfst. Restaurant adj open 24 hrs. Bar 11-2 am. Ck-out 11 am. Coin lndry. Business servs avail. Cr cds: A, D, DS, MC, V.
🅳 ⬧ 🏊 🛏 🏃 🔄 ⬧

★ **UNIVERSITY INN.** 4140 Roosevelt Way NE (98105). 206/632-5055; fax 206/547-4937; toll-free 800/733-3855. www.universityinnseattle.com. 102 rms, 4 story. June-Sept: S $102-$117; D $112-$127; suites $129-$139; each addl $10; under 18 free. Pet accepted; fee. Crib free. TV; cable (premium). Heated pool. Complimentary continental bkfst. Restaurant (see also PORTAGE BAY CAFE). Ck-out noon. Coin lndry. Meeting rms. Business servs avail. Valet serv. Exercise equipt. Cr cds: A, D, DS, MC, V.
🅳 ⬧ 🏊 🏃 🔄

Hotels

★★★ **ALEXIS.** 1007 First Ave (98104). 206/624-4844; fax 206/621-9009; toll-free 800/426-7033. www. alexishotel.com. 109 rms, 6 story. S, D $295-$335; suites $525-$825; under 12 free; some wkend rates. Crib free. Pet accepted. Covered valet parking $23/day. TV; cable (premium), VCR avail. Restaurant 6:30 am-3 pm (see also PAINTED TABLE). Rm serv 24 hrs. Bar 11 am-midnight. Ck-out noon. Meeting rms. Business servs avail. In-rm modem link. Concierge. Shopping arcade. Steam rm. Massage. Refrigerators; some bathrm phones; microwaves avail. Wet bar, minibar, beverages, whirlpool in suites. Eight wood-burning fireplaces. Some balconies. Cr cds: A, C, D, DS, JCB, MC, V.
🅳 ⬧ ⬧ 🔄 ⬧

★★★ **BEST WESTERN UNIVERSITY TOWER HOTEL.** 4507 Brooklyn Ave NE (98105). 206/634-2000; fax 206/547-6029; toll-free 800/899-0251. www.universitytowerhotel.com. 155 rms, 16 story. June-Sept: S $109-$129; D $129-$149; each addl $10; under 14 free; lower rates rest of yr.

Crib free. TV; cable. Restaurant. Bar. Ck-out noon. Meeting rms. Business servs avail. View of mountains, lakes, city. 2 blks from University of WA campus. Cr cds: A, D, DS, MC, V.

D ⊠ 🐾 SC

★ **CAMLIN HOTEL.** *1619 9th Ave and Pine St (98101).* *206/682-0100; fax 206/682-7415; res 800/325-4000. www.camlinhotel.com.* 132 rms, 36 A/C, 4-10 story. S, D $83-$114; each addl $10; suites $175; under 18 free. Crib free. TV; cable. Pool. Restaurant 7-10:30 am, 11:30 am-2 pm, 5-10 pm; Sat, Sun 7:30-11:30 am, 5-10 pm. Bar 11:30 am-midnight; Sat, Sun 5 pm-midnight; entertainment Tues-Sat. Ck-out noon. Business servs avail. Some balconies. Motor entrance on 8th Ave. Cr cds: A, D, DS, JCB, MC, V.

D ⊷ ⊠ 🐾

★★ **CROWNE PLAZA.** *1113 Sixth Ave (98101).* *206/464-1980; fax 206/340-1617; toll-free 800/521-2762. www.crowneplaza.com.* 415 rms, 34 story. June-Oct: S, D $240; each addl $20; suites $260-$525; under 18 free; wkend rates; lower rates rest of yr. Crib free. Covered valet parking $22. TV; cable (premium), VCR avail. Coffee in rms. Restaurant 6 am-10 pm. Bar 11-2 am. Ck-out noon. Meeting rms. Business servs avail. Concierge. Exercise equipt. Refrigerators avail. Luxury level. Cr cds: A, D, DS, JCB, MC, V.

D 🏃 ⊠ 🐾

★★★ **THE EDGEWATER.** *2411 Alaskan Way; Pier 67 (98121).* *206/728-7000; fax 206/441-4119; toll-free 800/624-0670. www.edgewater hotel.com.* 236 rms, 4 story. S, D $219-$329; each addl $15; suites $750-$1,500; under 18 free. Crib free. Valet parking (fee). TV; cable (premium). Coffee in rms. Restaurant 6:30 am-11 pm. Bar 11-1:30 am; entertainment Tues-Sat. Ck-out noon. Meeting rms. Business center. Bellhops. Valet serv. Gift shop. Exercise equipt. Guest bicycles. Minibars. Some balconies. Built entirely over water; adj to ferry terminal. Cr cds: A, C, D, DS, ER, MC, V.

D 🏃 ⊠ 🐾 SC 🏃

★★★ **ELLIOTT GRAND HYATT SEATTLE.** *721 Pine St (98101).* *206/262-0700; fax 206/774-6120; res*

800/233-1234. www.hyatt.com. 425 rms, 30 story. S, D $330-$395; each addl $20; under 17 free. Crib avail. TV; cable (premium), VCR avail. Complimentary coffee, newspaper in rms. Restaurant 6 am-10 pm. Ck-out noon. Meeting rms. Business center. Gift shop. Exercise rm. Some refrigerators, minibars. Cr cds: A, C, D, DS, JCB, MC, V.

D 🏃 🐾 🐾 🏃

★★ **EXECUTIVE PACIFIC PLAZA HOTEL.** *400 Spring St (98104).* *206/623-3900; toll-free 800/426-1165. www.pacificplazahotel.com.* 155 rms, 8 story. S, D $89-$114; under 18 free; wkend rates. Crib free. Garage parking $14 in/out. TV; cable. Complimentary continental bkfst. Ck-out 11 am. Business servs avail. Cr cds: A, D, DS, JCB, MC, V.

⊠ 🐾

★★★★ **FOUR SEASONS HOTEL SEATTLE.** *411 University St (98101).* *206/621-1700; fax 206/682-9633; toll-free 800/223-8772. www.fourseasons. com.* Listed on the National Registry of Historic Places, this property was built in 1924 as the Olympic Hotel and has been meticulously restored to original Italian-Renaissance splendor. The 240-room, 210-suite destination has three restaurants, including the stunning Georgian dining room, Shucker's Oyster Bar and The Garden, and its own retail annex with 14 boutiques. 450 rms, 13 story. S $225-$255; D $265-$295; each addl $30; suites $330-$1,250; under 18 free; wkend rates. Crib free. Valet parking $26. TV; cable (premium), VCR avail (movies). Indoor pool; whirlpool, poolside serv. Restaurant (see also THE GEORGIAN). Rm serv 24 hrs. Bar 11-1 am. Ck-out 1 pm. Convention facilities. Business center. In-rm modem link. Concierge. Shopping arcade. Barber, beauty shop. Airport transportation. Exercise equipt; sauna. Health club privileges. Massage. Bathrm phones, minibars; some refrigerators. Cr cds: A, D, DS, ER, JCB, MC, V.

⊷ 🏃 ⊠ 🐾 🏃

★★★ **HILTON SEATTLE.** *1301 6th Ave (98101).* *206/624-0500; fax 206/682-9029; toll-free 800/774-1500. www.hilton.com.* 237 rms, 28 story. S $165-$210; D $185-$230; each addl $20; suites $310-$475; under 18 free;

some wkend rates. Crib free. Garage $19. TV; cable (premium). Complimentary coffee in rms. Restaurants 6 am-10 pm. Rm serv 24 hrs. Ck-out 1 pm. Meeting rms. Business servs avail. Concierge. Gift shop. Exercise equipt. Refrigerators, minibars. View of Puget Sound. Cr cds: A, C, D, DS, ER, JCB, MC, V.

D 木 ≥ 🔥

★★★ **HOTEL MONACO.** *1101 4th Ave (98101). 206/621-1770; fax 206/621-7779; toll-free 800/945-2240. www.monaco-seattle.com.* 189 rms, 11 story, 45 suites. May-Sept: S $310; D $325; suites $255-$900; under 18 free; lower rates rest of yr. Crib free. Pet accepted. Valet parking $24. TV; cable (premium), VCR. Complimentary coffee in rms. Restaurant (See SAZERAC). Rm serv 24 hrs. Bar 11:30 am-midnight. Ck-out noon. Meeting rms. Business center. Valet serv. Concierge. Gift shop. Exercise equipt. Health club privileges. Bathrm phones, refrigerators, minibars; some in-rm whirlpools. Cr cds: A, C, D, DS, ER, MC, V.

D ➜ 木 ≥ 🔥 🏃

★★★ **HOTEL VINTAGE PARK.** *1100 Fifth Ave (98101). 306/624 8000; fax 206/623-0568 www.vintage park.com.* 126 rms, 11 story. S $185-$205; D $200-$220; suites $215-$375; under 18 free; wkend rates; package plans. Crib free. Pet accepted. Valet parking $24. TV; cable, VCR avail. Complimentary coffee in lobby. Restaurant (see also TULIO). Rm serv 24 hrs. Ck-out noon. Business servs avail. Concierge. Exercise equipt delivered to rms. Health club privileges. Bathrm phones, minibars. Wine tasting (Northwest wines) in lobby nightly. Cr cds: A, D, DS, JCB, MC, V.

D ➜ 木 ≥ 🔥

★★★ **INN AT THE MARKET.** *86 Pine St (98101). 206/443-3600; fax 206/448-0631; toll-free 800/446-4484. www.innatthemarket.com.* 65 rms, 4-8 story, 10 suites. May-Oct: S, D $160-$170; each addl $15; suites $250-$350; under 16 free; lower rates rest of yr. Crib free. Parking $17; valet. TV; cable (premium), VCR avail. Complimentary coffee in rms. Ck-out noon. Meeting rm. Business servs avail. Shopping

arcade. Beauty shop. Health club privileges. Bathrm phones, refrigerators; microwaves in suites. Cr cds: A, C, D, DS, ER, MC, V.

D ≥ 🔥

★★ **INN AT VIRGINIA MASON.** *1006 Spring St (98104). 206/583-6453; fax 206/223-7545; toll-free 800/283-6453.* 79 rms, 9 story. No A/C. S, D $115-$135; suites $165-$245. TV; cable (premium). Ck-out noon. Business servs avail. English country-style apartment house (1928); Queen Anne-style furnishings. Totally nonsmoking. Cr cds: A, D, DS, JCB, MC, V.

D ≥ 🔥

★★★ **MAYFLOWER PARK HOTEL.** *405 Olive Way (98101). 206/623-8700; fax 206/382-6997; toll-free 800/426 5100. www.mayflowerpark com.* 171 rms, 12 story. S, D $115-$220; each addl $15; suites $175-$350; mini-suites $175-$245; under 18 free. Crib free. Covered valet parking $21. TV; cable (premium). Restaurant 6:30 am-10 pm. Rm serv 24 hrs. Bar 11:30-2 am. Ck-out noon. Meeting rms. Business servs avail. Exercise rm. Health club privileges. Cr cds: A, C, D, DS, JCB, MC, V.

D 木 ≥ 🔥 SC

★★ **THE PARAMOUNT.** *734 Pine St (98101). 206/292-9500; fax 206/292-8610. www.westcoasthotels.com/ paramount.* 146 rms, 11 story. May-Oct: S $230, each addl $20; suites $425; under 18 free. Crib free. Valet parking $18; garage parking. TV; cable (premium). Complimentary coffee in rms. Restaurant 7-1 am. Bar. Ck-out noon. Meeting rms. Business servs avail. In-rm modem link. Exercise equipt. Refrigerators; some in-rm whirlpools; fireplace in suites. Cr cds: A, C, D, DS, MC, V.

D 木 ≥ 🔥

★★★ **RENAISSANCE MADISON HOTEL.** *515 Madison St (98104). 206/583-0300; fax 206/624-8125; res 800/468-3571. www.renaissancehotels. com.* 553 rms, 28 story. S, D $139-$179; suites $199-$800; wkend rates. Crib free. Covered parking $18. TV; cable, VCR avail. Indoor pool; whirlpool. Restaurant 6:30 am-10 pm; Fri, Sat to 11 pm (see also PREGO). Rm serv 24 hrs. Bars 11-2 am. Ck-out noon. Convention facilities. Business center. Concierge. Barber, beauty shop. Gift shop. Exercise equipt. Health club privileges. Free local transportation. Minibars. Luxury level. Cr cds: A, C, D, DS, ER, JCB, MC, V.

⬛ 🏊 🏋 ⛵ 🔥 SC 🏃

★★★ **SHERATON SEATTLE HOTEL & TOWERS.** *1400 Sixth Ave (98101).* 206/621-9000; fax 206/621-8441; toll-free 800/625-5144. *www.sheraton.com.* 840 units, 35 story. S $169-$209, D $189-$229; suites $275-$600; under 17 free; wkend rates. Crib free. Valet parking $22. TV; cable (premium), VCR avail. Indoor pool; whirlpool. Complimentary coffee in rms. Restaurant 6 am-10 pm. Rm serv 24 hrs. Bar. entertainment. Ck-out noon. Convention facilities. Business center. Concierge. Barber. Exercise rm; sauna. Minibars; some bathrm phones. Rms with original Northwest art. Luxury level. Cr cds: A, C, D, DS, ER, JCB, MC, V.

⬛ 🏊 🏋 ⛵ 🏃

★★ **SILVER CLOUD INN UNIVERSITY VILLAGE.** *5036 25th Ave NE (98105).* 206/526-5200; fax 206/522-1450; res 800/551-7207. *www.silvercloud.com.* 180 rms, 4 story. July-Oct: S, D $125-$135; each addl $10; suites $117-$145; under 12 free; lower rates rest of yr. Crib free. TV; cable (premium). Indoor pool; whirlpool. Complimentary continental bkfst. Restaurant nearby. Ck-out noon. Meeting rms. Business center. Guest lndry avail. Exercise equipt. Refrigerators, microwaves avail. Cr cds: A, C, D, DS, JCB, MC, V.

⬛ 🏊 🏋 ⛵ SC 🏃

★★★ **SORRENTO.** *900 Madison St (98104).* 206/622-6400; fax 206/343-6155; toll-free 800/426-1265. *www.hotelsorrento.com.* 34 rms, 7 story, 42 suites. S $215; D $240; each addl $25; under 16 free. Crib free. Pet accepted. Covered parking; valet $24. TV; VCR avail. Stereo and CD Players. Restaurant (see also HUNT CLUB). Bar 11:30-2 am. Thurs/Fri/Sat night complimentary Jazz in Fireside Room. Ck-out noon, ck-in 4 pm. Meeting rms. Business servs avail. Concierge. Airport transportation avail. Complimentary Towncar transfers throughout Downtown area.

Exercise rm. Massage. Refrigerators; bathrm phones in suites; microwaves avail. Turndown service nightly. Cr cds: A, D, DS, ER, JCB, MC, V.

⬛ 🏋 ⛵

★★ **SUMMERFIELD SUITES BY WYNDHAM.** *1011 Pike St (98101).* 206/682-8282; fax 206/682-5315; res 800/996-3426. *www.wyndham.com.* 193 units, 9 story. Studios $125-$190; S, D $119-$199; under 18 free. Crib $10. Valet parking $18. TV; cable (premium), VCR avail. Heated pool; whirlpool. Complimentary continental bkfst. Complimentary coffee in rms. Ck-out noon. Coin lndry. Meeting rms. Business servs avail. Gift shop. Exercise equipt. Refrigerators, microwaves. Cr cds: A, C, D, DS, JCB, MC, V.

⬛ 🏊 🏋 ⛵ 🔥

★★ **WARWICK HOTEL.** *4th and Lenora st (98121).* 206/443-4300; fax 206/441-9488; toll-free 800/426-9280. *www.warwickhotels.com.* 229 units, 19 story. May-Oct: S, D $240; each addl $10; suites $275-$385; under 18 free; lower rates rest of yr. Crib free. Covered valet parking $18. TV; cable, VCR avail. Indoor pool; whirlpool. Restaurant 6:30 am-2 pm, 5-10 pm. Rm serv 24 hrs. Bar 11-2 am. Ck-out noon. Meeting rms. Business servs avail. Exercise equipt; sauna. Bathrm phones. Fireplace in lobby. Cr cds: A, C, D, DS, ER, JCB, MC, V.

⬛ 🏊 🏋 ⛵ 🔥 SC

★★ **THE WESTIN SEATTLE.** *1900 Fifth Ave (98101).* 206/728-1000; fax 206/728-2259; res 888/625-5144. *www.westin.com.* 891 rms, 40-47 story. S $149-$250; D $164-$275; each addl $25; suites $295-$1,200; under 18 free; wkend rates. Crib free. Garage $21. TV; cable; VCR avail. Heated pool; whirlpool. Restaurants (see also ROY'S). Rm serv 24 hrs. Bar; entertainment. Ck-out noon. Convention facilities. Business center. Concierge. Gift shop. Exercise rm. Refrigerators, minibars. Sun deck. Tower rms with panoramic view. Cr cds: A, C, D, DS, ER, JCB, MC, V.

⬛ 🍴 🍸 ⛵ 🏊 🏋 ⛵ 🔥 🏃

★★★ **W SEATTLE.** *1112 4th Ave (98101).* 206/264-6000; fax 206/264-6100. *www.whotels.com.* Since this hotel is designed for style-conscious, tech-savvy business travelers, rooms offer CD players, high-speed Internet access, and cordless phones at a well-equipped work station. Dream up desires to test the "whatever you want, whenever you want it" service motto. The lobby, adjacent bar, and dining room are new contenders in the 'now' scene of Seattle. 426 rms, 26 story, 9 suites. May-Oct: S $395; D $415; each addl $20; under 17 free; lower rates rest of yr. Crib avail. Pet accepted. Valet parking avail. TV; cable (premium), VCR avail, CD avail. Complimentary coffee in rms, newspaper, toll-free calls. Restaurant. 24-hr rm serv. Bar 11 am-midnight; Fri, Sat to 2 am. Ck-out noon, ck-in 3 pm. Meeting rms. Business center. Bellhops. Concierge. Dry cleaning. Exercise rm. Cr cds: A, C, D, DS, ER, JCB, MC, V.

B&Bs/Small Inns

★★ **CHAMBERED NAUTILUS BED & BREAKFAST.** *5005 22nd Ave NE (98105). 206/522-2536; fax 206/528-0898; toll-free 800/545-8459. www.chamberednautilus.com.* 6 rms, 3 story. No A/C. Rm phones avail. S $79-$110; D $84-$115; each addl $15. Complimentary full bkfst; afternoon refreshments. Restaurant nearby. Ck-out 11 am, ck-in 4-6 pm. Business servs avail. Street parking. Sundeck. Georgian Colonial house (1915); library/sitting rm with fireplace. Cr cds: A, MC, V.

★★ **CHELSEA STATION BED & BREAKFAST.** *4915 Linden Ave N (98103). 206/547-6077; fax 206/632-5107; toll-free 800/400-6077.* 8 rms, 2 story, 6 suites. No A/C. June-Sept: S $84-$109; D $95; each addl $10; suites $119; lower rates rest of yr. Children over 12 yrs only. Complimentary full bkfst; afternoon refreshments. Restaurants nearby. Ck-out 11 am, ck-in 3 pm. Business servs avail. In-rm modem link. Street parking. Microwaves avail. Colonial-style brick house (1929); antiques. Near Woodland Park Zoo. Totally non-smoking. Cr cds: A, C, D, DS, ER, JCB, MC.

★★ **GASLIGHT INN.** *1727 15th Ave (98122). 206/325-3654; fax 206/328-4803. www.gaslight-inn.com.* 16 rms, 4 with shower only, 3 share bath, 3 story, 7 suites. No A/C. Some rm phones. S $98; D $108; suites $128-$148; some wkly rates. TV; cable. Heated pool; poolside serv. Complimentary continental bkfst; afternoon refreshments. Restaurant nearby. Ck-out 11 am, ck-in 3-6 pm. Business servs avail. In-rm modem link. Luggage handling. Refrigerators. Picnic tables. Two buildings; one built 1906. Antiques. Cr cds: A, MC, V.

★★ **HILL HOUSE BED & BREAKFAST.** *1113 E John St (98102). 206/720-7161; fax 206/323-0772; res 800/720-7161. www.seattlebnb.com.* 5 rms, 2 share bath, 2 suites. No A/C. Some rm phones. Mid-May-mid-Nov: S $75-$95; D $100-$120; suites $115; wkly rates; wkends, hols (2-4 day min); lower rates rest of yr. Children over 12 yrs only. TV in suites; cable (premium). Complimentary full bkfst. Restaurant nearby. Ck-out 11 am, ck-in (by appt). In-rm modem link. Restored 1903 Victorian inn. Cr cds: A, D, DS, MC, V.

★★ **INN AT HARBOR STEPS.** *1221 1st Ave (98101). 206/748-0973; fax 206/748-0533; res 888/728-8910. www.foursisters.com.* 25 rms, 2 story. S, D $160-$220; each addl $20; hol rates. Crib free. TV; cable, VCR avail. Complimentary full bkfst; afternoon refreshments. Complimentary coffee in rms. Restaurant. Ck-out noon, ck-in 3 pm. Business servs avail. Luggage handling. Indoor pool; whirlpool. In-rm whirlpools, refrigerators, fireplaces. Balconies. Ocean and garden views. Cr cds: A, C, D, ER, JCB, MC, V.

★ **PRINCE OF WALES BED & BREAKFAST.** *133 13th Ave E (98102). 206/325-9692; fax 206/322-6402; toll-free 800/327-9692. www.uspan.com/sbba.* 4 rms, 2 with shower only, 3 story. Apr-Oct: S, D $99-$125; lower rates rest of yr. Children over 3 yrs only. Complimentary full bkfst; afternoon refreshments. Restaurant nearby. Ck-out 11 am, ck-in 4-6 pm. Business servs avail. Microwaves avail. Built in 1903; furnished with antiques. Totally nonsmoking. Cr cds: DS, MC, V.

★★★ **SALIBURY HOUSE BED & BREAKFAST.** *750 16th Ave E (98112). 206/328-8682; fax 206/720-1019. www.salisburyhouse.com.* 4 rms, 3 with shower only, 2 story. No A/C. No rm phones. May-Oct: S $75-$115; D $85-$125; each addl $15; lower rates rest of yr. Children over 12 yrs only. Complimentary full bkfst. Restaurants nearby. Ck-out 11 am, ck-in 4-6 pm. Business servs avail. In-rm modem link. Built 1904; wraparound porch. Many antiques. Totally nonsmoking. Cr cds: A, MC, V.

Seattle skyline

Restaurants

★★★ **AL BOCCALINO.** *1 Yesler Way (98104). 206/622-7688. www.alboccalino.com.* Hrs: 11:30 am-2 pm, 5-10 pm; Mon from 5 pm; Fri to 10:30 pm; Sat 5-10:30 pm; Sun 5-9:30 pm. Closed hols. Res accepted. No A/C. Italian menu. Lunch $8-$12.50, dinner $12-$21. Specializes in fresh seafood, rissotto, veal chop. Bistro atmosphere. Cr cds: A, D, MC, V.

★★★ **ANDALUCA.** *407 Olive Way (98101). 206/382-6999. www.andaluca.com.* Hrs: 6:30 am-2:30 pm, 5-10 pm; Fri, Sat to 11 pm; Sun 7 am-noon. Res accepted. Bar 11:30 am-closing. Bkfst $5-$11, lunch

$7.50-$15, dinner $15-$30. Specializes in Northwestern cuisine with Mediterranean influence. Cr cds: A, D, DS, MC, V.

★★★ **ASSAGGIO RISTORANTE.** *2010 Fourth Ave (98121). 206/441-1399.* Hrs: 11:30 am-2:30 pm, 5-10:30 pm; Fri to 11 pm; Sat 5-11 pm. Closed Sun; hols. Res accepted. Italian menu. Serv bar. Lunch $8.95-$14.95, dinner $9.95-$20.95. Specializes in seafood, risotto. Outdoor dining. Italian decor. Totally nonsmoking. Cr cds: A, D, DS, MC, V.

★ **ATLAS FOODS.** *2820 NE University Village (98105). 206/522-6025. www.chowfoods.com.* Specializes in pastries, desserts. Hrs: 9 am-10 pm. Res accepted. Wine list. Lunch $4.25-$9.75; dinner $5.50-$15.25. Child's menu. Entertainment. Cr cds: MC, V.

★★ **BANDOLEONE.** *2241 Eastlake Ave E (98102). 206/329-7559. www.bandoleone.net.* Hrs: 5-11 pm; Fri, Sat 11:30 pm; Sat, Sun brunch 9 am-2:30 pm. Closed Thanksgiving, Dec 24, 25. Res accepted. Latin American menu. Bar to 2 am. Dinner $8.50-$15.95. Sat, Sun brunch $4.50-$6.95. Child's meals. Specialties: ancho chile-marinated chicken, Jamaican jerk rack of lamb, pistachio-crusted Chilean sea bass. Own pastries. Latino music Sun. Validated parking. Outdoor dining. Casual, eclectic decor with original artwork. Cr cds: A, DS, MC, V.

★★★★ **BRASA.** *2107 3rd Ave (98121). 206/728-4220. www.brasa.com.* Rich fabrics, terrazzo walkways, and iron create the ambiance for a Mediterranean-inspired meal at this hip restaurant. The daily-changing menu offers rustic, earthy flavors from the wood-fired oven such as roast suckling pig and braised lamb with Moroccan chutney. Wildly cre-

ative desserts complete the evening. Specializes in roast suckling pig, squid ink risotto. Hrs: 5-10:30 pm; Fri, Sat to midnight. Closed hols. Res accepted. Wine, beer. Dinner $16-$29. Entertainment. Cr cds: A, C, D, MC, V.
D

★★ **BROOKLYN SEAFOOD, STEAK & OYSTER HOUSE.** *1212 Second Ave (98101). 206/224-7000.* Hrs: 11 am-10 pm; Sat 4:30-10:30 pm; Sun to 10 pm. Closed Dec 25. Res accepted. Bar. A la carte entrees: lunch $7-$14, dinner $12-$33. Child's meals. Specializes in seafood, steak. Oyster bar. Valet parking (dinner). Patio/courtyard dining. In 1890s building; artwork. Cr cds: A, D, DS, MC, V.
D

★ **BUCA DI BEPPO.** *701 N 9th Ave (98109). 206/244-2288. www. bucadibeppo.com.* Hrs: 5-10 pm; Fri to 11 pm; Sat, Sun from 4 pm. Closed Thanksgiving, Dec 24, 25. Res accepted Sun-Thurs. Italian menu. Bar. A la carte entrees: dinner $7.95-$19.95. Specialties: chicken cacciatore, tiramisu. Outdoor dining. Eclectic decor; mural on dome ceiling; some seating in kitchen. Totally nonsmoking. Cr cds: A, D, DS, MC, V.
D

★ **BURRITO LOCO.** *9211 Holman Rd NW (98117). 206/783-0719.* Hrs: 11 am-10 pm. Closed hols. Mexican menu. Wine, beer. Lunch $3.25-$4.75, dinner $7.50-$8.95. Child's meals. Specialties: chile relleno, chicken en mole, tacos de carnitas. Outdoor dining. Colorful Mexican decor. Totally nonsmoking. Cr cds: A, DS, MC, V.
D

★★ **CAFE CAMPAGNE.** *1600 Post Alley (98101). 206/728-2233.* Hrs: 8 am-10 pm; Fri, Sat to 11 pm; Sun brunch 8 am-3 pm. Closed hols. Res accepted. French menu. Bar. Bkfst $6.95-$12.95, lunch $5.95-$17, dinner $8.95-$17. Sun brunch $6.95-$17. Specialties: traditional cassoulet, house-made sausages. French bistro decor. Cr cds: A, D, MC, V.
D

★★ **CAFE FLORA.** *2901 E Madison (98112). 206/325-9100. www.cafeflora. com.* Hrs: 11:30 am-2:30 pm, 5:30-10 pm; Sat from 5 pm; Sun 5-9 pm; Sat, Sun brunch 9 am-2 pm. Closed Mon; hols. Vegetarian menu. Wine, beer. Lunch $6.95-$9.95, dinner $9.95-$14.95. Sat, Sun brunch $5.95-$9.95. Child's meals. Specialties: Oaxca tacos, portabello Wellington, wheat-berry burgers. Two large rms, one with stone fountain, decorated with original works of art. Totally nonsmoking. Cr cds: MC, V.
D

★★★ **CAFE LAGO.** *2305 24th Ave E (98112). 206/329-8005.* Hrs: 5-9:30 pm; Fri, Sat to 10 pm. Closed major hols; also 4th wk in Aug. Res accepted. Italian menu. Wine. A la carte entrees: dinner $10-$21. Specializes in pasta, wood-fired pizza, grilled fish. Trattoria atmosphere. Totally nonsmoking. Cr cds: A, DS, MC, V.
D

★★ **CAMPAGNE.** *86 Pine St (98101). 206/728-2800.* French cuisine menu. Specializing in regional French dishes. Specialties: rack of lamb, daily fish entrees. Dinner. Hrs: 5:30-10 pm. Closed Jan 1, Thanksgiving, Dec 25. Res accepted. Bar to 2 am. A la carte entrees: dinner $26-$35. Outdoor dining. Cr cds: A, D, MC, V.
D

★★★ **CANLIS.** *2576 Aurora Ave N (98109). 206/283-3313. www.canlis. com.* Hrs: 5:30-10:30 pm. Closed Sun; hols. Res accepted. Extensive wine list. Dinner $20-$34. Specializes in seafood, steak. Own sauces. Piano bar from 7 pm. Valet parking. Fireplace. Open-hearth grill. Panoramic view of Lake Union, Cascade Mtns. Formal dining. Family-owned. Jacket. Cr cds: A, D, DS, MC, V.
D

★★ **CARMELITA.** *7314 Greenwood Ave N (98103). 206/706-7703. www. carmelita.net.* Hrs: 5-10 pm; Fri, Sat to 10:45 pm; Sat, Sun brunch 9 am-1:30 pm. Closed Mon; Jan 1, Dec 24, 25. No A/C. Vegetarian menu. Bar. Dinner $8.50-$13.95. Sat, Sun brunch $8.95. Child's meals. Specializes in vegetarian and vegan fare with

Mediterranean influences. Own baking, pasta. Outdoor dining. Eclectic furnishings decorate this large dining area with high ceilings. Totally nonsmoking. Cr cds: MC, V.
[D]

★★★ **CASCADIA.** *2328 1st Ave (98121). 206/448-8884. www.cascadia restaurant.com.* Specializes in wild salmon, mint cured rack of lamb, sweet corn and squash ravioli. Hrs: 5-10 pm; Fri, Sat to 10:30 pm. Closed Sun; hols. Res accepted. Wine, beer. Dinner $20-$30. Child's menu. Entertainment: pianist Wed-Sat. Cr cds: A, D, DS, MC, V.
[D]

★★★ **CHEZ SHEA.** *94 Pike St (98101). 206/467-9990. www. chezshea.com.* Hrs: 4:30 pm-midnight. Closed Mon; most major hols. Res accepted. Contemporary American menu. Bar. A la carte entrees: dinner $6-$12. Complete meals: 4-course dinner $39. Child's meals. Specializes in seafood. Contemporary decor. Totally nonsmoking. Cr cds: A, MC, V.

★★ **CHINOOK'S.** *1900 W Nickerson (98119). 206/283-4665. www. anthonys.com.* Hrs: 11 am-10 pm; Fri to 11 pm; Sat 7:30 am-11 pm; Sun 7:30 am-10 pm. Closed Thanksgiving, Dec 25. Bar to midnight. Complete meals: bkfst $4.95-$9.95. Lunch $14.95, dinner $25.95. Child's meals. Specializes in Northwest seafood, salmon, halibut. Parking. Outdoor dining. On Fisherman's Wharf. Nautical decor. Cr cds: A, MC, V.
[D]

★★ **CHUTNEY'S.** *519 1st Ave N (98109). 206/284-6799.* Hrs: 11:30 am-2:30 pm, 5-10 pm; Fri, Sat to 10:30 pm; Sun from 5 pm. Res accepted. Indian menu. Bar. Lunch, dinner $8.95-$16.95. Specialties: tandoori items, tikka masala, curried mussels. Own baking. Indian prints and carved deities decorate walls. Totally nonsmoking. Cr cds: A, D, DS, MC, V.
[D]

★ **CUCINA! CUCINA!.** *901 Fairview Ave N (98109). 206/447-2782. www. cucinacucina.com.* Hrs: 11:30-2 am. Closed Thanksgiving, Dec 25. Res accepted (lunch). Italian menu. Bar. A la carte entrees: lunch $4.95-

$10.95, dinner $4.95-$14.95. Child's meals. Specializes in pizza, pasta, salads. Valet parking. Outdoor dining. Bicycles hang from ceiling in lounge. Cr cds: A, D, DS, MC, V.
[D]

★★★ **DAHLIA LOUNGE.** *2001 Fourth Ave (98121). 206/682-4142. www.tomdouglas.com.* Hrs: 11:30 am-2:30 pm, 5:30-10 pm; Fri to 11 pm; Sat 5:30-11 pm; Sun 5-9 pm. Closed hols. Res accepted. Lunch $6.50-$12, dinner $9.95-$22. Child's meals. Specializes in crab cakes, salmon, duck. Eclectic decor. Cr cds: A, DS, MC, V.
[D]

★ **DOONG KONG LAU.** *9710 Aurora Ave N (98103). 206/526-8828.* Hrs: 11 am-10 pm. Res accepted. Chinese menu. Lunch $3.95-$5.95, dinner $5.95-$10.95. Specializes in northern Hakka cuisine. Parking. Chinese prints, fish tanks. Cr cds: A, D, DS, MC, V.
[⌐]

★★ **DRAGON FISH ASIAN CAFE.** *722 Pine St (98101). 206/467-7777. www.dragonfishcafe.com.* Specializes in chicken lettuce cup, five-spice salmon. Hrs: 7-2 am. Closed Thanksgiving, Dec 25. Res accepted. Wine, beer. A la carte entrees: Bkfst $7-$9; Lunch $6.95-$11.95; dinner $8.95-$16.90. Cr cds: A, C, D, DS, JCB, MC, V.
[D] [⌐]

★★ **DULCES LATIN BISTRO.** *1430 34th Ave (98122). 206/322-5453. www.dulceslatinbistro.com.* Hrs: 5-10 pm; Sun to 9 pm. Closed Mon; hols. Res accepted. Continental menu. Bar. Dinner $14.25-$18.50. Complete meal: dinner $25. Specialties: chiles rellenos, roasted red pepper ravioli, paella Valenciana. Own pasta, pastries. Classical guitarist Wed, Thurs, Sun. Bistro decor with deep gold and bronze accents; completely separate cigar rm. Cr cds: A, DS, MC, V.
[D] [⌐]

★★★ **EARTH AND OCEAN.** *1112 Fourth Ave (98101). 206/264-6060. www.whotels.com.* Hrs: 6:30 am-10:30 pm; Sat, Sun from 7:30 pm. Res accepted. Wine, beer. Bkfst $6-$12; lunch $7-$30; dinner $18-$27.

Child's menu. Entertainment. Cr cds: A, C, D, DS, JCB, MC, V.

D

★★★ **EL GAUCHO.** 2505 1st Ave (98121). 206/728-1337. Hrs: 5 pm-1 am; Sun to 11 pm. Closed hols. Res accepted. Continental menu. Bar to 2 am. Wine cellar. A la carte entrees: dinner $13-$30. Specialties: flaming shish kabob, chateaubriand, Angus steak. Own pastries. Pianist. Valet parking. Former union hall for merchant seamen; formal, elegant dining. Cr cds: A, MC, V.

D

★★ **ELLIOTT'S OYSTER HOUSE.** 1201 Alaskan Way (98101). 206/623-4340. www.elliottsoysterhouse.com. Hrs: 11 am-11 pm; Fri, Sat to midnight; winter hrs: 11 am-10 pm; Fri, Sat to 11 pm. Res accepted. Bar. Lunch $5.95-$15.95, dinner $10.95-$29.95. Child's meals. Specializes in Pacific salmon, fresh Dungeness crab, fresh oysters. Outdoor dining. View of bay. Cr cds: A, D, DS, MC, V.

D SC

★★★ **ETTA'S SEAFOOD.** 2020 Western Ave (98121). 206/443-6000. www.tomdouglas.com. Hrs: 11:30 am-10 pm; Fri to 11 pm; Sat 9 am-11 pm; Sun 9 am-10 pm. Closed hols. Res accepted. Bar to 1 am. Lunch $5-$28, dinner $8-$30. Child's meals. Specializes in Northwestern seafood. Two dining rms. Totally nonsmoking. Cr cds: A, D, DS, JCB, MC, V.

D

★★★ **FLYING FISH.** 2234 1st Ave (98121). 206/728-8595. www.flyingfish seattle.com. Hrs: 5 pm-1 am. Closed hols. Res accepted. Bar to 2 am. Dinner $12-$17. Specialties: Thai crab cakes, whole fried snapper in lemon grass marinade. Outdoor dining. Eclectic decor. Totally nonsmoking. Cr cds: A, D, MC, V.

D

★ **FOUR SEAS.** 714 S King St (98104). 206/682-4900. www.fourseas. com. Hrs: 10 am-midnight; Fri, Sat to 2 am. Res accepted. Cantonese, Mandarin menu. Bar. Lunch $5.75-$8.35, dinner $5.25-$15.95. Specialties: Hong Kong-style dim sum, garlic spareribs, moo goo gai pan. Parking.

Hand-carved Asian screens. Cr cds: A, D, DS, MC, V.

D ⬛

★★ **F.X. MCRORY'S STEAK, CHOP & OYSTER HOUSE.** 419 Occidental Ave S (98104). 206/623-4800. www. mickmchughs.com. Hrs: 11:30 am-2 pm, 5-10 pm; Sat noon-11 pm; Sun from 3 pm. Closed hols. Res accepted. Bar. Lunch $8-$15, dinner $13-$40. Child's meals. Specializes in steak, oysters, prime rib. Oyster bar. Outdoor dining. 1920s atmosphere. Cr cds: A, D, DS, MC, V.

D ⬛

★★★ **GENEVA.** 1106 Eighth Ave (98101). 206/624-2222. www.geneva restaurant.com. Hrs: 5-10 pm. Closed Sun, Mon; hols. Res accepted. Continental menu. Serv bar. Wine list. A la carte entrees: dinner $19-$28. Specializes in rack of lamb, crab cakes, calf's liver. Outdoor dining. Intimate dining in European atmosphere. Totally nonsmoking. Cr cds: A, MC, V.

★★★★ **THE GEORGIAN.** 411 University St (98101). 206/621-7889. www.fourseasons.com. Located in the Four Seasons Hotel Seattle, this Italian Renaissance-style dining room has romantic appeal with its exquisite chandeliers, vaulted ceilings, and lovely piano music. Showy, intricately prepared cuisine highlights the Pacific Northwest's seasonal ingredients and is complemented by an extensive, over-the-top wine list and attentive service. Come for breakfast (served until 1 pm on Sundays), lunch, or dinner. Own baking. Menu changes seasonally. Hrs: 6:30 am-2:30 pm, 5:30-10 pm; Fri to 10:30 pm; Sat 7 am-2:30 pm, 5:30-10:30 pm. Res accepted. Bar. Wine cellar. Valet parking. Cr cds: A, D, DS, ER, JCB, MC, V.

D ⬛

★ **HIRAM'S AT THE LOCKS.** 5300 34th St NW (98107). 206/781-2024. www.hiramsatthelocks.com. Specializes in steak, seafood. Hrs: 4-10 pm; Sat, Sun 11 am-10 pm. Closed Thanksgiving, Dec 25. Res accepted. Wine, beer. Lunch $7.95-$14.95; dinner $16.95-$48.95. Entertainment. Cr cds: A, D, DS, JCB, MC, V.

D SC

★★★ **HUNT CLUB.** *900 Madison St (98104). 206/343-6156. www.hotel sorrento.com.* Hrs: 7 am-2:30 pm, 5:30-10 pm. Res accepted. Bar from 11:30 am. A la carte entrees: bkfst $6-$10, lunch $9-$18, dinner $18-$30. Free valet parking. Cr cds: A, DS, MC, V.
D

★★ **IL BISTRO.** *93A Pike St (98101). 206/682-3049. www.savvydiner.com.* Hrs: 5:30-10 pm; Fri, Sat to 11 pm. Closed hols. Res accepted. Italian menu. Bar to 2 am. A la carte entrees: dinner $13.95-$36.95. Specializes in fresh seafood, pasta, rack of lamb. Valet parking Thurs-Sat. Outdoor dining. Original art. Cr cds: A, MC, V.
D

★★★ **IL TERRAZZO CARMINE.** *411 1st Ave S (98104). 206/467-7797.* Hrs: 11:30 am-2:30 pm, 5:30-10 pm; Fri, Sat to 11 pm. Closed Sun; hols. Res accepted. Italian menu. Bar. Lunch $10-$16, dinner $9.50-$28. Specialties: osso buco, venison ravioli. Outdoor dining. Elegant decor. Totally nonsmoking. Cr cds: A, D, DS, MC, V.
D

★ **IVAR'S ACRES OF CLAMS.** *Pier 54 (98104). 206/624-6852. www.ivars. net.* Hrs: 11 am-10 pm; Fri, Sat to 11 pm. Closed Thanksgiving, Dec 25. Res accepted. Bar. Lunch $6.95-$13.95, dinner $10.95-$19.95. Child's meals. Specializes in Northwestern king salmon, oven-roasted seafood brochettes, Dungeness crab-topped prawns. On pier with windows overlooking waterfront; collection of old photos of the area. Cr cds: A, MC, V.
D ⊟

★★ **IVAR'S INDIAN SALMON HOUSE.** *401 NE Northlake Way (98105). 206/632-0767.* Hrs: 11:30 am-2:30 pm, 4:30-10 pm; Fri to 11 pm; Sat noon-3:30 pm, 4-11 pm; Sun 3:30-10 pm; Sun brunch 10 am-2 pm. Closed Thanksgiving, Dec 25. Res accepted. Bar. Lunch $7-$15, dinner $13-$25. Sun brunch $14.95. Child's meals. Specializes in smoked salmon. Parking. Outdoor dining. Indian long house decor. View of lake. Family-owned. Cr cds: A, MC, V.
D

★ **JITTERBUG.** *2114 N 45th St (98103). 206/547-6313.* Hrs: 8 am-10 pm; Fri, Sat to 11 pm; June-Aug to 11 pm. Closed hols. Bar. Bkfst $2-$8.25, lunch $4-$8.25, dinner $8.25-$15.75. Child's meals. Specialties: Italian farmhouse egg rumble, charmoula chicken sandwich, transcontinental tango. Own pasta, pastries. Lively atmosphere; counter service. Cr cds: MC, V.
D

★★★ **KASPAR'S.** *19 W Harrison St (98119). 206/298-0123. www.uspan. com.* Hrs: 5-10 pm; Fri, Sat to 11 pm. Closed Sun, Mon; Jan 1, July 4. Res accepted. Bar. A la carte entrees: dinner $13-$25. Child's meals. Specializes in Northwestern cuisine, vegetarian dishes, smoked salmon. Own ice cream and sorbets. Valet parking. 2 levels. Totally nonsmoking. Cr cds: MC, V.
D

★★★ **LAMPREIA RESTAURANT.** *2400 First Ave (98121). 206/443-3301.* Italian, Mediterranean menu. Specializes in seasonal dishes using local fare. Own pasta. Menu changes weekly. Hrs: 5-11 pm. Closed Sun, Mon; Thanksgiving, Dec 25. Res accepted. Bar. World-class wine cellar. A la carte entrees: dinner $19-$35. Tasting seafood menu $58-$90. Modern, classical decor and elegant atmosphere. Totally nonsmoking. Cr cds: A, MC, V.
D

★★★ **LE GOURMAND.** *425 NW Market St (98107). 206/784-3463.* Hrs: 5:30-11 pm. Closed Sun-Tues; Easter, Thanksgiving, Dec 24, 25. Res accepted. French, American menu. Wine, beer. Complete meals: dinner $28-$48. Specialties: poached salmon with gooseberry and dill sauce, roast duckling with black currant sauce. Original artwork. Totally nonsmoking. Cr cds: A, MC, V.

★★ **MADISON PARK CAFE.** *1807 42nd Ave E (98112). 206/324-2626. www.madisonparkcafe.citysearch.com.* Hrs: 5-9 pm; Fri, Sat to 10 pm; Sat, Sun 8 am-2 pm. Closed Mon; hols. Res accepted. No A/C. Continental menu. Wine, beer. Bkfst $2.50-$8.95, dinner $12.95-$16.95. Child's meals. Specializes in fresh seasonal pastas and seafoods, homemade

Experience Music Project

$5.50-$17, dinner $8.25-$24. French family supper Mon-Fri: $13.25-$30. Sun brunch $2.50-$15. Specializes in French-style Northwest seafood. French marketplace decor; antiques. View of bay, mountains. Cr cds: A, D, DS, MC, V.
D

★★ **MCCORMICK & SCHMICK'S.** *1103 1st Ave (98101). 206/623-5500. www. mccormickandschmicks.com.* Hrs: 11:30 am-11 pm; Sat 4:30-11 pm; Sun 5-10 pm; summer hrs vary. Closed Thanksgiving, Dec 25. Res accepted. Bar to 12:30 am; Fri, Sat to 1:30 am; Sun to 11:30 pm. Lunch $4.95-$12.75, dinner $9.95-$20. Specializes in fresh seafood. Beamed ceilings, Irish bar. Original art. Cr cds: A, DS, MC, V
D

★★★ **MCCORMICK'S FISH HOUSE.** *722 4th Ave (98104). 206/682-3900.* Hrs: 11:30 am-11 pm; Fri to midnight; Sat 4:30 pm-midnight; Sun from 4:30 pm. Closed Memorial Day, Thanksgiving, Dec 25. Res accepted. Bar. Lunch $6.95-$15, dinner $6.95-$22. Specializes in fresh seafood. Oyster bar. Outdoor dining. Vintage 1920s and 30s atmosphere; tin ceilings. Cr cds: A, D, DS, MC, V.
D

★★ **METROPOLITAN GRILL.** *820 Second Ave (98104). 206/624-3287.* Hrs: 11 am-3:30 pm, 5-11 pm; Sat from 4:30 pm; Sun 4:30-10 pm. Closed Thanksgiving. Res accepted. Bar. Wine list. Lunch $6.95-$15.95, dinner $10.95-$27.95. Child's meals. Specialties: 28-day aged prime steak, Northwest seafood dishes. Cr cds: A, D, DS, MC, V.
D

bkfst pastries. Own pasta, pastries. Outdoor dining. French bistro atmosphere in converted house; brick courtyard. Totally nonsmoking. Cr cds: A, MC, V.

★ **MALAY SATAY HUT.** *212 12th Ave S (98144). 206/324-4091 www. sidewalk.com.* Specializes in Indian bread, satay, curry meats. Hrs: 11 am-11 pm. Res required. Wine, beer. Lunch $5.25-$16.95; dinner $7-$25. Cr cds: MC, V.
D

★★ **MARCO'S.** *2510 First Ave (98121). 206/441-7801.* Hrs: 11:30 am-2 pm, 5:30-11 pm; Fri, Sat to midnight; Sun from 5:30 pm. Closed hols. Res accepted. Continental menu. Bar. Lunch $6.95-$10.95, dinner $10.95-$19.95. Child's meals. Specializes in jerk chicken, fried sage leaves. Outdoor dining. Eclectic decor. Cr cds: A, MC, V.
D

★★ **MAXIMILIEN-IN-THE-MARKET.** *81A Pike Pl (98101). 206/682-7270. www.maximilien restaurant.com.* Hrs: 7:30 am-10 pm; Sun brunch 9:30 am-4 pm. Closed Jan 1, Thanksgiving, Dec 25. Res accepted. French menu. Bar. Lunch

★★★ **NIKKO RESTAURANT.** *1900 5th Ave (98101). 206/322-4641. www. nikkorestaurant.com.* Specializes in sushi, sukiyaki, shabu shabu. Hrs: 11:15 am-2 pm, 5:30-10 pm. Closed Sun; hols. Res accepted. Wine, beer. Lunch $6.75-$19; dinner $16.95-$50. Entertainment. Cr cds: A, D, JCB, MC, V.

★★★ **NISHINO.** *3130 E Madison (98112). 206/322-5800.* Hrs: 5:30-10:30 pm; Sun to 9:30 pm. Closed some major hols. Res accepted. Japanese menu. Serv bar. Dinner $4-$16. Complete meal: dinner $45-$60. Specializes in omakase, sushi. Outdoor dining. Rooftop dining. Totally nonsmoking. Cr cds: A, MC, V.
D

★★★ **THE PAINTED TABLE.** *1007 First Ave (98104). 206/624-3646. www.alexishotel.com.* Hrs: 7-10 am, 11:30 am-2 pm, 5-10 pm; Sat, Sun 8 am-noon, 5:30-10 pm. Res required (dinner). Bar. Wine list. Specializes in Northwest cuisine. Valet parking. Totally nonsmoking. Cr cds: A, D, DS, JCB, MC, V.

★★★ **PALACE KITCHEN.** *2030 5th Ave (98121). 206/448-2001. www.tomdouglas.com.* Hrs: 11:30 am-2:30 pm, 5 pm-1 am. Closed hols. Res accepted. Bar. Wine list. Lunch $9-$14, dinner $18-$24. Child's meals. Specializes in applewood-grilled rotisserie dishes. Own baking, pasta. Central kitchen and bar dominate dining rm. Cr cds: A, D, DS, MC, V.
D

★★ **PALISADE.** *2601 W Marina Pl (98199). 206/285-1000. www.plaisadeseattle.com.* Specializes in cedar-plank roasted salmon, Dungeness crab, stuffed wood-oven roasted halibut. Hrs: 11:30 am-9:30 pm; Sat noon-10 pm; Sun 10 am-9 pm. Res accepted. Wine list. Lunch $7.99-$17.99; dinner $20-$55. Brunch $17-$22. Child's menu. Entertainment. Fish pond runs through part of restaruant. Cr cds: A, D, MC, V.
D �’

★★★ **PALOMINO.** *1420 Fifth Ave (98101). 206/623-1300. www.palomino.com.* Hrs: 11:15 am-10:30 pm; Tues, Thurs to 11:30 pm; Fri to 12:30 am; Sat 11-12:30 am; Sun 4-10 pm. Closed hols. Res accepted. Mediterranean menu. Lunch $6.95-$15.95, dinner $7.95-$19.95. Specializes in grilled salmon, spit-roasted chicken, wood oven-roasted prawns. Parking. Original art, exotic African wood. Overlooking atrium. Cr cds: A, D, DS, MC, V.
D

★★ **PARAGON.** *2125 Queen Anne Ave N (98109). 206/283-4548.* Hrs: 5-11 pm. Closed Dec 25. Res accepted. Contemporary American menu. Bar 4 pm-2 am. Dinner $10.95-$21. Specializes in risotto, seafood. Bistro decor. Entertainment. Totally nonsmoking. Cr cds: A, D, MC, V.
D

★★ **PIATTI.** *2800 NE University Village (94941). 206/524-9088. www.piatti.com.* Hrs: 11:30 am-10 pm; Fri, Sat to 11 pm. Closed Dec 25. Res accepted. Italian menu. Bar. Lunch, dinner $6.95-$19.95. Child's meals. Specializes in regional Italian cuisine. Outdoor dining. Casual decor. Totally nonsmoking. Cr cds: A, D, MC, V.
D

★★ **PINK DOOR.** *1919 Post Alley (98101). 206/443-3241.* Hrs: 11:30 am-2:30 pm, 5:30-10 pm. Closed Mon; hols. Res accepted. No A/C. Italian menu. Bar to 11:30 pm; Fri, Sat to 1 am. Lunch $10-$14, dinner $12-$18. Child's meals. Specializes in rustic Italian dishes. Own baking, pasta. Entertainment. Outdoor dining. Eclectic decor with cherubs, mirrors and a swing; patio offers water view. Totally nonsmoking. Cr cds: A, MC, V.

★★★ **PLACE PIGALLE.** *81 Pike St (98101). 206/624-1756.* Hrs: 11:30 am-3 pm, 5:30-10 pm; Fri to 11 pm; Sat 11:30 am-3:30 pm, 6-10:30 pm. Closed Sun; hols. Res accepted. Northwest regional menu. Bar. Lunch $9-$18, dinner $15-$25. Specialties: rabbit reminiscence, seafood in tamarind broth, duck bijoux. Overlooks Elliott Bay. Casual decor. Cr cds: A, D, MC, V.

★★ **PONTI SEAFOOD GRILL.** *3014 3rd Ave N (98109). 206/284-3000. www.pontiseafoodgrill.com.* Hrs: 11:30 am-2:30 pm, 5-10 pm; Fri, Sat to 11 pm; Sun from 10 am; early-bird dinner 5-6 pm. Closed Jan 1, July 4, Dec 25. Res accepted. Eclectic menu. A la carte entrees: lunch $14.95, dinner $15.95-$25.95. Child's meals. Specializes in Pacific rim seafood. Valet parking. Patio dining. Formal dining in attractive surroundings. View of Lake Washington Canal. Cr cds: A, D, MC, V.
D

★ **PORTAGE BAY CAFE.** *4130 Roosevelt Way NE (98105).* *206/547-8230.* Hrs: 7:30 am-4 pm; Sat, Sun from 8 am. Closed Jan 1, Dec 25. Res accepted. Child's meals. Specialties: cafe linguine, blackened salmon. Outdoor dining. Bright, contemporary decor with floor-to-ceiling windows. Totally nonsmoking. Cr cds: A, MC, V.
D

★★ **PREGO.** *515 Madison St (98104).* *206/583-0300.* Hrs: 5-10 pm. Closed Sun, Mon; Dec 25. Res accepted. Italian menu. Bar. Lunch $7-$28, dinner $11-$25. Specializes in seafood, pasta. Original Matisse art. Views of skyline, Puget Sound. Cr cds: A, D, DS, MC, V.
D

★★ **QUEEN CITY GRILL.** *2201 1st Ave (98121).* *206/443-0975.* *www. queencitygrill.com.* Hrs: 11:30 am-11 pm; Fri to midnight; Sat 4:30 pm-midnight; Sun 4:30-11 pm. Closed Jan 1, Easter, Thanksgiving, Dec 24-25. Res accepted. Bar. Wine cellar. A la carte entrees: lunch, dinner $15-$25. Child's meals. Specialties: pan-seared Chilean sea bass with chili-lime butter, grilled ahi tuna, aged Colorado Angus steak. Own pasta, desserts. Exposed brick walls, original artwork, and mahogany woodwork accent this dining rm. Cr cds: A, D, DS, MC, V.
D ⬧

★★★ **RAY'S BOATHOUSE.** *6049 Seaview Ave NW (98107).* *206/789-3770.* *www.rays.com.* Hrs: 11:30 am-2 pm, 5-10 pm. Closed Jan 1, Dec 25. Res accepted. Bar to midnight. Wine cellar. Lunch $5.95-$9.95, dinner $10.95-$25. Child's meals. Specializes in Northwest seafood. Valet parking. Outdoor dining. View of Olympic Mts. Cr cds: A, D, DS, MC, V.
D

★★★★ **ROVER'S.** *2808 E Madison St (98112).* *206/325-7442.* *www.rovers-seattle.com.* Recognized as one of the Pacific Northwest's best chefs, owner Thierry Rautureau serves regionally inspired, contemporary cuisine with French accents at this relaxed, homey restaurant. The wine list's 300 selections constantly change, as do the seasonal offerings presented in both regular and vegetarian five-course and eight-course degustation menus. The country house setting is awash in yellow, an appropriate color given the staff's sunny disposition and their friendly service. Specializes in seafood, Northwest game, vegetarian dishes. Hrs: 5:30-11 pm. Closed Sun, Mon; hols. Res required. Extensive wine list. Complete meals: dinner $59.50, $69.50, $97.50. Entertainment. Cr cds: A, D, MC, V.
D

★★ **ROY'S.** *1900 5th Ave (98101).* *206/256-7697.* *www.roysrestaurant. com.* Hrs: 6-10:30 am, 11:30 am-2 pm, 5-9:30 pm. Res accepted. Continental menu. Bar from 5 pm. Wine cellar. Complete meal: bkfst $8.75-$15.75. Bkfst $3.75-$9.75, lunch $4.25-$14, dinner $14.95-$23.95. Child's meals. Specializes in fresh seafood with Pacific Rim influence. Own desserts. Multileveled, semicircular dining rm. Totally nonsmoking. Cr cds: A, D, DS, MC, V.
D

★★ **RUTH'S CHRIS STEAK HOUSE.** *800 5th Ave (98104).* *206/624-8524.* *www.ruthschris steakhouse.com.* Hrs: 5-10 pm. Closed hols. Res accepted. Bar. A la carte entrees: dinner $16-$29.95. Specializes in steak, seafood. Valet parking. Cr cds: A, D, DS, MC, V.
D

★★★ **SAZERAC.** *1101 4th Ave (98101).* *206/624-7755.* *www.monaco seattle.com.* Hrs: 7am-10 pm; Fri to 11:00 pm; Sat 9am-2:30 pm, 5-11 pm; Sun 9 am-2:30 pm, 5-9 pm. Res accepted. Bar. Wine list. Bkfst $5.95-$14, lunch $8.95-$17, dinner $14.95-$25. Child's meals. Specialty: honey-glazed cedar plank salmon on collard greens. Own baking, pasta. Valet parking. Totally nonsmoking. Cr cds: A, D, DS, MC, V.

★★ **SERAFINA.** *2043 Eastlake Ave E (98102).* *206/323-0807.* *www.serafinas eattle.com.* Hrs: 11:30 am-2 pm, 5:30-10 pm; Fri to 11 pm; Sat 5:30-11 pm; Sun 5:30-10 pm. Closed hols. Res accepted. Italian menu. Bar. A la carte entrees: lunch $2.95-$8.95, dinner $7.95-$17.95. Specializes in rustic Italian dishes. Entertainment. Outdoor dining in European courtyard. Murals. Cr cds: MC, V.

D

★★ **SHIRO'S.** *2401 2nd Ave (98121).* *206/443-9844.* Hrs: 11:30 am-1:45 pm, 5:30-10 pm; Sat from 5:30 pm. Closed Sun; hols. Res accepted. Japanese menu. Wine, beer. Lunch $6.95-$14.50, dinner $16-$19.50. Specializes in sushi, full Japanese dinners. Casual decor with large windows, sushi bar. Totally nonsmoking. Cr cds: A, MC, V.

D

★★ **SPACE NEEDLE.** *219 4th Ave N (98109).* *206/905-2100.* *www.space needle.com.* Hrs: 8 am-11 pm; Sun brunch to 3 pm. Res accepted. Bar 11 am-midnight. Bkfst $9.95-$14.95, lunch $14.95-$19.95, dinner $20.95-$31.95. Sun brunch $17.95-$21.95. Child's meals. Specializes in regional dishes. Valet parking. Revolving dining rm. Family-owned. Totally nonsmoking. Cr cds: A, D, DS, MC, V.

D

★★ **STELLA'S TRATTORIA.** *4500 9th Ave NE (98105).* *206/633-1100.* Open 24 hrs. Sun brunch 4 am-3 pm. Closed Thanksgiving, Dec 25. Italian, Amer menu. Bkfst $2.95-$6, lunch $6-$8.50, dinner $7-$13. Sun brunch $2.95-$8. Child's meals. Outdoor dining. Lively atmosphere. Totally nonsmoking. Cr cds: A, DS, MC, V.

D SC

★★★ **SZMANIA'S MAGNOLIA.** *3321 W McGraw (98199).* *206/284-7305.* *www.szmanias.com.* Hrs: 5-9:30 pm; Fri, Sat to 10 pm; Sun 4:30-9 pm. Closed Mon; hols. Res accepted. Continental menu. Bar. Wine list. Dinner $9-$20. Child's meals. Specializes in German dishes, seasonal Pacific Northwest regional dishes. Parking. Fireplace; open kitchen. Totally nonsmoking. Cr cds: A, D, MC, V.

D

★ **TRATTORIA MITCHELLI.** *84 Yesler Way (98104).* *206/623-3883.* Hrs: 7-4 am; Mon to 11 pm; Sat from 8 am; Sun 8 am-11 pm. Closed Dec 25. Res accepted Sun-Thurs. Italian menu. Bar 11-2 am. Bkfst $2.75-$8.75, lunch $4.95-$9.95, dinner $6.75-$14.50. Complete meals: lunch (Mon-Fri) $4.95. Child's meals. Spe-

cializes in pizza, pasta, chicken. Outdoor dining. Antique furnishings. Cr cds: A, DS, MC, V.

D ⬓

★★★ **TULIO RISTORANTE.** *1100 5th Ave (98101).* *206/624-5500.* *www.vintagepark.com.* Hrs: 7-10 am, 11:30 am-2:30 pm, 5-10 pm; Sat 8 am-noon, 5-11 pm; Sun to 10 pm. Closed hols. Res accepted. Italian menu. Bar. Wine cellar. A la carte entrees: bkfst $5-$12, lunch $9-$16, dinner $9-$27. Child's meals. Valet parking. Outdoor dining. Open view of wood-burning pizza oven. Cr cds: A, D, DS, MC, V.

★★★ **UNION BAY CAFE.** *3515 NE 45th St (98105).* *206/527-8364.* Hrs: 5-10 pm; Sun 4:30-9 pm. Closed Mon; hols. Res accepted. Wine list. A la carte entrees: dinner $14-$24. Specializes in fresh seafood, organic produce, free-range chicken. Own pastries. Outdoor dining. Intimate dining in two dining rms with original artwork, wine and flower displays. Totally nonsmoking. Cr cds: A, D, DS, MC, V.

D

★★★ **UNION SQUARE GRILL.** *621 Union St (98101).* *206/224-4321.* Hrs: 11 am-3 pm, 5-10 pm; Fri, Sat to midnight. Closed hols. Res accepted. Bar. Wine list. Lunch $6.95-$15.95, dinner $15.95-$29.95. Specializes in steaks, chops, Northwestern seafood. Valet parking. Several dining areas; mahogany furnishings, dividers. Cr cds: A, D, DS, MC, V.

D

★★★ **WILD GINGER.** *1401 Third Ave (98101).* *206/623-4450.* Hrs: 11:30 am-3 pm, 5-11 pm; Fri 5 pm-midnight; Sat to midnight; Sun 4:30-11 pm. Closed Thanksgiving, Dec 25. Res accepted. Southeast Asian, Chinese menu. Bar. Lunch $6.95-$12.95, dinner $9.95-$19.95. Specializes in fresh seafood, curry. Satay bar. Near Pike Place Market. Cr cds: A, D, DS, MC, V.

D ⬓

Seattle-Tacoma International Airport Area (C-3)

(See also Seattle, Tacoma)

Services and Information

Information. 206/433-5312.

Lost and Found. 206/433-5312.

Airlines. Aeroflot, Air Canada, Alaska Airlines, America West, American, Asiana, British Airways, Canadian Airlines International, China Eastern, Continental, Delta, Eva Airways, Frontier Airlines, Hawaiian Airlines, Martinair Holland, Northwest, Reno Air, SAS, Southwest, Swissair, TWA, United, USAir, Western Pacific Airlines.

Motels/Motor Lodges

★ **BEST WESTERN AIRPORT EXE-CUTEL.** *20717 International Blvd, Seattle (98198). 206/878-3300; fax 206/824-9000; res 800/780-7234. www.bestwestern.com.* 138 rms, 3 story. June-Sept: S $69-$99; D $79-$119; each addl $6; suites $213-$325; under 18 free; lower rates rest of yr. Crib free. TV; cable (premium). Indoor pool; whirlpool. Complimentary continental bkfst. Complimentary coffee in rms. Restaurant 6-11 am, 5-10 pm. Bar 5-10 pm. Ck-out noon. Meeting rms. Business servs avail. In-rm modem link. Bellhops. Free airport transportation. Exercise equipt; sauna. Cr cds: A, D, DS, ER, JCB, MC, V.

★★ **BEST WESTERN EXECUTIVE INN.** *31611 20th Ave S, Federal Way (98003). 253/941-6000; fax 253/941-9500; toll-free 800/648-3311. www.bestwestern.com.* 112 rms, 3 story. Mid-June-mid-Sept: S, D $99-$129; each addl $10; under 12 free; lower rates rest of yr. Crib free. Pet accepted; $25. TV; cable (premium). Heated pool; whirlpool. Restaurant. Bar. Ck-out noon. Meeting rms. Business center. In-rm modem link. Bellhops. Valet serv. Free airport transportation. Health club privi-leges. Cr cds: A, C, D, DS, ER, JCB, MC, V.

★ **CLARION HOTEL SEA-TAC.** *3000 S 176th St, Seattle (98188). 206/242-0200; fax 206/242-1998; toll-free 800/252-7466. www.clarionhotel.com.* 211 rms, 3 story. June-Oct: S $60-$89; D $70-$99; each addl $10; under 18 free. Crib free. TV; cable (premium), VCR avail. Complimentary coffee in rms. Restaurant 6 am-2 pm, 5-10 pm. Rm serv. Bar from 4 pm. Ck-out noon. Meeting rms. Business center. In-rm modem link. Coin lndry. Free airport transportation. Exercise equipt. Indoor pool; whirlpool. Some refrigerators, microwaves. Cr cds: A, D, DS, JCB, MC, V.

★ **COMFORT INN & SUITES SEA-TAC-SEATTLE.** *19333 International Blvd, Sea Tac (98188). 206/878-1100; fax 206/878-8678. www.comfortinnseatac.com.* 119 rms, 4 story. S, D $59-$150; each addl $10; suites $79-$150; under 18 free. Crib free. TV; cable (premium). Complimentary continental bkfst. Restaurant adj open 24 hrs. Ck-out noon. Meeting rms. In rm modem link. Bellhops. Sundries. Free covered parking. Free airport transportation. Exercise equipt. Whirlpool. Refrigerator in suites. Cr cds: A, C, D, DS, ER, JCB, MC, V.

★★ **DOUBLETREE HOTEL.** *18740 International Blvd, Seattle (98188). 206/246-8600; fax 206/431-8687; toll-free 800/222-8733. www.doubletreehotels.com.* 850 rms, 14 story. S, D $69-$189; suites $139-$779; under 18 free; wkend rates; lower rates rest of yr. Crib free. TV; cable. Heated pool; poolside serv. Coffee in rms. Restaurant. Rm serv 6 am-midnight. Bars 11:30-2 am; entertainment. Ck-out noon. Convention facilities. Business center. In-rm modem link. Bellhops. Concierge. Sundries. Gift shop. Barber, beauty shop. Free airport transportation. Exercise equipt. Private patios, balconies. Cr cds: A, C, D, DS, JCB, MC, V.

★★ **HOLIDAY INN SEATAC AIRPORT.** *17338 International Blvd, Seat-*

tle (98188). 206/248-1000; fax 206/242-7089. www.holiday-inn.com. 260 rms, 12 story. S $109-$139; D $119-$169; suites $200-$250; each addl $10; family, wkend rates. Crib free. TV; cable (premium). Indoor pool; whirlpool. Restaurant 6 am-1:30 pm, 5-10 pm. Bar 11 am-11 pm. Ck-out noon. Coin lndry. Meeting rms. Business servs avail. In-rm modem link. Bellhops. Sundries. Gift shop. Free airport transportation. Exercise equipt. Microwaves avail. Revolving rooftop dining rm. Cr cds: A, C, D, DS, JCB, MC, V.

★★★ RED LION HOTEL SEATTLE AIRPORT. 205 Strander Blvd, Seattle (98188). 206/246-8220; fax 206/575-4749; res 800/733-5466. www.redlion. com. 198 rms, 2 story. S, D $75-$135; each addl $10; suites $105-$175; under 18 free; wkend, seasonal rates. Crib free. TV; cable (premium). Heated pool; poolside serv. Restaurant 6 am-11 pm. Rm serv 6-11 pm. Bar 2-11 pm. Ck-out noon. Meeting rms. Business servs avail. Bellhops. Valet serv. Microwaves avail. Some private patios. Cr cds: A, DS, MC, V.

★ RED ROOF INN. 16838 International Blvd, Seattle (98188). 206/248-0901; fax 206/242-3170; res 800/843-7663. www.redroof.com. 152 rms, 3 story. June-Sept: S, D $70-$87; each addl $5; suites $80; under 18 free; lower rates rest of yr. Crib free. Pet accepted. TV; cable (premium). Ck-out noon. Business servs avail. In-rm modem link. Sundries. Free airport transportation. Coin lndry. Exercise equipt. Balconies. Cr cds: A, D, DS, ER, JCB, MC, V.

★ TRAVELODGE. 2900 S 192nd St, Seattle (98188). 206/241-9292; fax 206/242-0681; toll-free 800/393-1856. www.travelodge.com. 106 rms, 3 story. May-Aug: S, D $39-$60; each addl $5; under 18 free; lower rates rest of yr. Crib free. TV; cable (premium). Complimentary coffee in rms. Restaurant adj open 24 hrs. Ck-out noon. Coin lndry. Business servs avail. In-rm modem link. Free airport transportation. Sauna. Cr cds: A, C, D, DS, ER, MC, V.

★★ WESTCOAST-SEA-TAC HOTEL. 18220 International Blvd, Seattle (98188). 206/246-5535; fax 206/246-9733; toll-free 800/426-0670. www.westcoasthotels.com. 146 rms, 5 story. S $95-$105; D $105-$109; each addl $10; under 18 free; some wkend rates. Crib free. TV; cable (premium). Pet accepted. Heated pool; whirlpool, poolside serv. Restaurant 6 am-10 pm. Bar 11:30-2 am. Ck-out noon. Meeting rms. Business servs avail. Bellhops. Valet serv. Free valet parking. Free airport transportation. Exercise rm; sauna. Cr cds: A, D, DS, MC, V.

Hotels

★★★ HILTON. 17620 Pacific Hwy S, Seattle (98188). 206/244-4800; fax 206/248-4499; res 800/445-8667. www.seattleairport.hilton.com. 396 rms, 6 suites, 4 story. S, D $79-$224; suites $159-$929; under 18 free; wkend rates. Crib $10. Pet accepted; $50. Self parking $14. TV; cable (premium), VCR avail. Internet. Heated pool; whirlpool, poolside serv. Complimentary coffee in rms. Restaurant 6 am-11 pm. Bar 11 am-midnight. Ck-out noon. Meeting rms. Business center 24 hrs. In-rm modem link. Gift shop. Concierge. Bellhops. Valet serv. Sundries. Free airport transportation. Exercise equipt. Minibars. Some private patios. Garden setting. Cr cds: A, C, D, DS, ER, JCB, MC, V.

★★★ MARRIOTT AIRPORT SEA-TAC. 3201 S 176th St, Seattle (98188). 206/241-2000; fax 206/248-0789; toll-free 800/228-9290. www.marriott.com. 459 rms. 5 suites, S, D $89-$169; suites $220; under 18 free; wkend rates. Overnight parking $12. Crib free. Pet accepted. TV; cable (premium). Heated indoor pool; whirlpool, poolside serv. Restaurant 6 am-10 pm. Bar 11-1 am. Coffee in rms. Ck-out 1 pm. Convention facilities. Business center. In-rm modem link. Bellhops. Valet serv. Gift shop. Free airport transportation. Exercise equipt; sauna. Massage. Game rm. Luxury level. Cr cds: A, C, D, DS, ER, JCB, MC, V.

★★ **RADISSON HOTEL.** *17001 Pacific Hwy S, Seattle (98188). 206/244-6000; fax 206/246-6835; res 800/333-3333. www.radisson.com/ seattlewa.* 308 rms, 3 story. June-Sept: S, D $99-$139; suite $179-$299; each addl $10; under 18 free; wkend rates. Crib free. TV; cable (premium). Heated pool; poolside serv. Coffee in rms. Restaurant 6 am-11 pm. Bar 4 pm-1 am. Ck-out noon. Convention facilities. Business servs avail. Valet serv. In-rm modem link. Bellhops. Sundries. Gift shop. Free airport transportation. Exercise equipt; sauna. Some balconies. Cr cds: A, C, D, DS, JCB, MC, V.

[D] [≈] [⚒] [SC] [≈] [⊼]

★ **WYNDHAM SEATTLE-TACOMA AIRPORT.** *18118 Pacific Hwy S, Seattle (98188). 206/244-6666; fax 206/244-6679, res 800/996-3426. www.wyndham.com.* 204 rms, 7 story. S, D $79-$180; each addl $20. Crib avail. Indoor pool. TV; cable (premium). VCR avail. Complimentary coffee, newspaper in rms. Restaurant 6 am-10 pm. Ck-out noon. Meeting rms. Business center. Gift shop. Exercise rm. Some refrigerators, minibars. Cr cds: A, C, D, DS, MC, V.

[D] [≈] [⊼] [≈] [⚒] [⊼]

All Suite

★★ **DOUBLETREE GUEST SUITES.** *16500 Southcenter Pkwy, Seattle (98188). 206/575-8220; fax 206/575-4743; toll-free 800/222-8733. www.doubletree.com.* 221 suites, 8 story. Mid-July-mid-Sept: S, D $99-$229; each addl $15; under 18 free; wkend, seasonal rates. Crib free. TV; cable (premium). Heated indoor pool; outdoor pool privileges in summer; whirlpool. Coffee in rms. Restaurant 6 am-10 pm; wkends 7 am-10 pm. Bar 2-11 pm. Ck-out noon. Meeting rms. Business servs avail. Coin lndry. Valet serv. Sundries. Free airport transportation. Exercise equipt; sauna. Racquetball. Refrigerators, wet bars. Microwaves avail. Atrium lobby. Cr cds: A, D, JCB, MC, V.

[D] [≈] [≈] [⚒] [⊼]

Restaurant

★★ **SEAPORTS.** *18740 Pacific Hwy S, Seattle (98188). 206/246-8600.* Hrs: 11:30 am-10 pm; Sun 9 am-2 pm (brunch). Closed Dec 25. Res accepted. Continental menu. Bar to 2 am. Lunch $11.95-$17.95, dinner $17.95-$39.95. Sun brunch $17.95. Child's meals. Specialties: tableside Caesar salad, tableside steak Diane. Valet parking. Elegant, multilevel dining areas offer views of mountains or airport. Family-owned. Cr cds: A, C, D, DS, ER, JCB, MC, V.

[D]

Sedro Woolley

(A-3) *See also Anacortes, Bellingham, Mount Vernon*

Founded 1889 **Pop** 6,031 **Elev** 509 ft
Area code 360 **Zip** 98284
Information Chamber of Commerce, 714-B Metcalf St; 360/855-1841 or 888/225-8365
Web www.sedro-woolley.com

A thick growth of cedar once cloaked the Skagit River Valley, but it has been replaced with fertile farms, for which Sedro Woolley is the commercial center. Lumbering is still one of the main industries. The town represents the merger of the town of Sedro (Spanish for "cedar") and its onetime rival, Woolley, named for its founder.

A Ranger District station of the Mount Baker-Snoqualmie National Forest (see BELLINGHAM, SEATTLE) is located here.

What to See and Do

Lake Whatcom Railway. A seven-mi, round-trip steam train ride in antique Northern Pacific passenger cars through countryside. (July-Aug, Sat and Tues; Dec, Sat only; rest of yr, charter trips) 11 mi N on WA 9, in Wickersham. Phone 360/595-2218. ¢¢¢

North Cascades National Park. Authorized in 1968, this 504,781-

acre area has beautiful alpine scenery, deep glaciated canyons, more than 300 active glaciers, and hundreds of jagged peaks and mountain lakes. It is adj to the 576,865-acre Glacier Peak Wilderness dominated by 10,541-ft-high Glacier Peak and to Ross Lake and Lake Chelan National Recreation Areas. Camping along WA 20 in Ross Lake area (June-Sept, fee); fishing; climbing, hiking, backpacking (by permit). 50 mi E on WA 20 (portions of this road are closed in winter). Contact 2105 Hwy 20. Phone 360/856-5700.

Seattle City Light Skagit Hydroelectric Project. 4½-hr tours incl 560-ft ride up mountain on incline lift, 4½-mi boat ride to Ross Dam and Powerhouse (tour) and return by boat to Diablo; family-style dinner. (Late June-Labor Day, Mon, Thurs-Sun) Res and advance payment required. Single 90-min tour also avail. (July-Labor Day, Thurs-Mon) 62 mi E of I-5/Mt Vernon on WA 20 (North Cascades Hwy) in Diablo, in Ross Lake National Recreation Area. Contact Skagit Tours, Seattle City Light, 1015 3rd Ave, Seattle 98104. Phone 206/684-3030. ¢¢¢¢ Self-guided mini-tours at Ross Lake National Recreation Area incl

    Gorge Powerhouse/Ladder Creek Falls and Rock Gardens. Begins at Gorge Powerhouse, Newhalem; self-guided tour of powerhouse, walk through Gorge Rock Gardens to Ladder Creek Falls. Gardens lighted at night. (Late June-Labor Day, daily) **FREE**

    Newhalem Visitor Information Center. Information on Skagit Project and National Park/Recreation Area. (Mid-June-Labor day, daily) **FREE**

    Trail of the Cedars. (45 min) Informative nature walk on south bank of Skagit River. Begins at end of Main St, Newhalem. **FREE**

Swimming, hiking, camping, boating, fishing, windsurfing. Also fishing in Skagit River. Clear Lake. 3 mi S on WA 9. RV sites in town.

Special Events

Woodfest. Woodcarvers displaying their craft. Second wkend May. Phone 360/855-1841.

Loggerodeo. Logging contests, rodeos, parades. One wk late June-early July. Phone 360/855-1129.

Santa's City of Lights. Parade, tree lighting. First wkend Dec. Phone 360/855-1841.

Sequim

(B-2) *See also Neah Bay, Port Angeles, Port Townsend*

Pop 3,616 **Elev** 183 ft **Area code** 360 **Zip** 98382
Information Sequim-Dungeness Valley Chamber of Commerce, 1192 E Washington St, PO Box 907; 360/683-6197 or 800/737-8462
Web www.cityofsequim.com

Sequim (pronounced SKWIM) is a Native American name meaning "quiet water."

What to See and Do

Dungeness Recreation Area. Approx 200 acres. Camping (Feb-Oct; fee). Access to Dungeness National Wildlife Refuge. (Daily) Clallam County Park, 6 mi NW. Phone 360/683-5847.

Olympic Game Farm. Wild animals; guided walking tour (summer; drive-through rest of yr). Endangered species breeding program. (Daily) 6 mi NW. Phone 360/683-4295.

Sequim Bay State Park. Along Sequim Bay. Swimming, scuba diving, fishing, clamming, boating (dock); hiking, tennis, ballpark, picnicking, camping (hookups). Standard fees. 4 mi SE on US 101. Phone 360/683-4235.

Special Event

Irrigation Festival. Oldest community festival in the state; celebrates the bringing of water to the Sequim Prairie. Picnics, parades, flower shows, contests. First full wk May. Phone 360/683-6197.

Motels/Motor Lodges

★ **ECONO LODGE.** *801 E Washington St (98382). 360/683-7113; res*

800/446-6900. www.econolodge.com.
43 rms, 2 story. May-Sept: S $55-$79;
D $65-$89; each addl $6; under 18
free; lower rates rest of yr. Crib free.
Pet accepted. TV; cable, VCR avail
(movies). Complimentary continental bkfst. Restaurant opp 6:30 am-10
pm. Ck-out 11 am. Guest lndry. Business servs avail. Lawn games. Refrigerators, microwaves. Cr cds: A, C, D,
DS, MC, V.

★★ **SEQUIM BAY LODGE.** 268522
US 101 (59730). 360/683-0691; fax
360/683-3748; toll-free 800/622-0691.
54 rms, 1 with shower only, 36 with
A/C, 3 story, 14 suites. No elvtr. May-
Sept: S $79-$100; D $89-$113; each
addl $8; suites $99-$139; under 12
free; lower rates rest of yr. Crib free.
Pet accepted. TV; cable. Heated pool.
Complimentary continental bkfst.
Complimentary coffee in rms.
Restaurant adj 4-9 pm. Ck-out 11
am. Meeting rms. Business servs
avail. 9-hole putting course. Lawn
games. Refrigerator in suites. Balconies. Picnic tables. Cr cds: A, C, D,
DS, MC, V.

B&Bs/Small Inns

★★ **DIAMOND POINT INN.** 241
Sunshine Dr, Gardiner (98382).
360/797-7720; fax 360/797-7723; res
888/797-0393. 6 rms, 2 share bath, 2
story. No A/C. No rm phones. Apr-
Sept: S, D $75-$125; each addl $20;
lower rates Oct-Nov, Feb-Mar. Closed
rest of yr. Children over 5 yrs only.
Complimentary full bkfst. Ck-out 11
am, ck-in 3 pm. Business servs avail.
Luggage handling. Whirlpool. Lawn
games. Some refrigerators. Picnic
tables, grills. Surrounded by 10 acres
of evergreens. Totally nonsmoking.
Cr cds: MC, V.

★★★ **GREYWOLF INN.** 395 Keeler
Rd (98382). 360/683-5889; fax
360/683-1487; toll-free 800/914-9653.
www.greywolfinn.com. 5 rms, 2 story.
No A/C. 1 rm phone. June-Oct: S
$65-$130; D $85-$100; each addl
$20; lower rates rest of yr. Children
over 12 yrs only. TV; VCR avail (free
movies). Complimentary full bkfst;

afternoon refreshments. Ck-out
11:30 am, ck-in 4 pm. Business servs
avail. Bus depot transportation. Gift
shop. Exercise equipt. Whirlpool. Picnic tables, grills. Theme oriented rms
with many antiques. Totally nonsmoking. Cr cds: A, DS, MC, V.

★★ **GROVELAND COTTAGE BED
& BREAKFAST.** 4861 Sequim Dungeness Way (98382). 360/683-3565; fax
360/683-5181; res 800/879-8859.
www.northolympic.com/groveland. 4
rms, 2 story. No A/C. June-Oct: S
$70-$100; D $80-$110; each addl
$15; wkly rates; lower rates rest of yr.
Children over 12 yrs only. TV; cable,
VCR (free movies). Complimentary
full bkfst. Complimentary coffee in
rms. Restaurant nearby. Ck-out noon,
ck-in 3 pm. Meeting rm. Business
servs avail. Picnic tables. Former merchant's residence (1886); many
antiques, Oriental rugs. Library/sit-
ting rm. Totally nonsmoking. Cr cds:
A, DS, MC, V.

Restaurants

★★ **DUNGENESS INN.** 1965 Wood-
cock (98382). 360/683-3331. www.
dungenessgcc.com. Hrs: Mon-Wed 7
am-4 pm; Thurs-Fri 7 am-8 pm; Sat
to 4 pm, Sun to 2 pm. Closed Dec
25. Res accepted. Bar. Bkfst $2.75-
$9.95, lunch $3.75-$8.95, dinner
$6.95-$18.95, Sun brunch $11.95.
Child's meals. Specializes in seafood,
steak. Two-level dining with windows offering panoramic view of golf
course. Totally nonsmoking. Cr cds:
DS, MC, V.

★ **MOON PALACE.** 323 E Washington (98382). 360/683-6898. Hrs:
11:30 am-8:30 pm; Fri to 9 pm; Sat 3-
9 pm; Sun noon-8 pm. Closed Mon;
hols. Res accepted. Chinese menu.
Bar from 2 pm. Lunch $4.75-$5.95,
dinner $5.95-$11. Sun lunch buffet
$5.95. Specializes in Cantonese,
mandarin dishes. Parking. Asian
decor. Cr cds: A, DS, MC, V.

★★ **PARADISE.** 703 N Sequim Ave
(98382). 360/683-1977. Hrs: 11 am-9
pm. Closed Mon; July 4, Thanksgiving, Dec 25. Res accepted. Bar. Lunch

$4.75, dinner $13.95-$18.95. Specializes in steak, seafood, pasta. Parking. Many plants. Etched-glass booth dividers. Cr cds: A, DS, MC, V.

D

Snohomish

(B-3) *See also Everett, Marysville*

Settled 1853 **Pop** 6,499 **Elev** 64 ft
Area code 360 **Zip** 98290
Information Chamber of Commerce, 127 Ave A, Waltz Building, PO Box 135, 98291; 360/568-2526
Web ci.snohomish.wa.us

Snohomish is sustained by dairy farms, tourism, and retail trade. The Boeing plant that manufactures 747s and 767s (see EVERETT) is nearby. Snohomish claims to be the antique capital of the Pacific Northwest, boasting 450 dealers and many specialty shops.

What to See and Do

Blackman Museum. Restored 1878 Victorian house; vintage furnishings. (June-Sept, daily; Mar-May and Oct-Dec, Wed-Sun afternoons; closed rest of yr) 118 Ave B. Phone 360/568-5235. ¢ Nearby is

Old Snohomish Village. Six authentic pioneer buildings moved here incl general store (ca 1910) and weaver's shop, which displays antique looms. (June-Sept, daily; rest of yr, by appt) 2nd and Pine sts. Phone 360/568-5235. ¢

Star Center Antique Mall. More than 165 antique shops housed in a former armory. Restaurant, children's play area. (Daily) 829 2nd St. Phone 360/568-2131.

Stevens Pass Ski Area. Road goes past Eagle Falls. (See LEAVENWORTH) 53 mi E on US 2.

Walking tour of historical houses. Contact Chamber of Commerce, 116 Ave B, Waltz Building, for brochure. Phone 360/568-2526. **FREE**

Soap Lake

(C-6) *See also Coulee Dam, Ephrata*

Pop 1,149 **Elev** 1,075 ft
Area code 509 **Zip** 98851
Information Soap Lake Chamber of Commerce, PO Box 433; 509/246-1821
Web www.soaplakecoc.org

The minerals and salts in Soap Lake (Native American name *Smokiam*, or "healing waters") give the community status as a health resort. They also whip into a soaplike foam that lines the shoreline on windy days. This is the south entrance to the Grand Coulee, the 50-mile channel of the prehistoric Columbia River.

Motel/Motor Lodge

★★ **NOTARAS LODGE.** *13 Canna St (98851). 509/246-0462; fax 509/246-1054. www.notaraslodge.com.* 12 rms, 3 kit. units, 2 story. May-Sept: S $58; D $65; each addl $7; suites $91-$125; under 6 free; lower rates rest of yr. Pet accepted; $40 refundable and $10/day. TV; cable. Restaurant 11 am-10 pm. Ck-out 11 am. Refrigerators, microwaves; some in-rm whirlpools. Balconies. Picnic tables. Cr cds: DS, MC, V.

D ⌐ ⋈ ⚶

Restaurant

★★ **DON'S.** *14 Canna St (98851). 509/246-1217.* Hrs: 11 am-10 pm; Fri to 11 pm; Sat 4-11 pm; Sun from 4 pm. Closed Dec 25. Bar. Lunch $4-$10.95, dinner $5.95-$18.95. Specializes in steak, seafood, Greek dishes. Own baking. Collection of Louie Leininger photos. Cr cds: MC, V.

D ⌐

Spokane

(C-8) *See also Cheney*

Settled 1871 **Pop** 177,196 **Elev** 1,898 ft **Area code** 509

Information Spokane Area Visitor Information Center, 801 W Riverside, #301, 99201; 509/624-1341

Web www.visitspokane.com

Spokane (Spo-KAN) is the booming center of the vast, rich "Inland Northwest," an area including eastern Washington, northern Idaho, northeastern Oregon, western Montana, and southern British Columbia. A large rail center, the Spokane area also produces wheat, apples, hops, silver, gold, zinc, and lead. Spokane boasts more than 6,500 commercial and industrial firms. Thanks to the surrounding mountain ranges, Spokane enjoys what it likes to term New Mexico's climate in the winter and Maine's in the summer. The city itself is in a saucerlike setting amid pine-green hills with the Spokane River running through its 52 square miles.

Long a favorite Native American hunting and fishing ground, Spokane began as a sawmill, powered by Spokane Falls. This village, the name meaning "children of the sun," was the only point in a 400-mile-long north-south range of mountains where railroads could cross the Rockies and reach the Columbia Basin. Railroading sparked the city's early growth. The Coeur d'Alene gold fields in Idaho helped finance Spokane's continuing development and helped it to survive an 1889 fire that nearly leveled the city. Farming, lumbering, mining, and railroading aided Spokane's growth during the first decade of the century.

In 1974, the Havermale and Cannon islands in the Spokane River were the site of EXPO 74. The area has since been developed as Riverfront Park.

What to See and Do

Auto tour.

Cathedral of St. John the Evangelist. (Episcopal) Magnificent sandstone Gothic structure; stained-glass windows by Boston's Connick Studios; wood and stone carvings. Tours (Mon, Tues, Thurs, Sat-Sun; Sun after services). Recitals on 49-bell carillon (Thurs, Sun); also recitals on Aeolian-Skinner organ (schedule varies). 127 E 12th Ave. Phone 509/838-4277.

Cheney Cowles Museum. Houses collections of regional history and Native American culture. Fine Arts Gallery has changing art exhibits. Adj is **Campbell House** (1898), a restored mansion of Spokane's "age of elegance." 2316 W 1st Ave. Phone 509/456-3931. ¢¢

Children's Museum. Children are permitted to touch, encouraged to make noise and create. Weather exhibit; hydroelectric power station; music, art; regional and cultural history. (Tues-Sat) 110 N Post. Phone 509/624-5437. ¢¢

Cliff Park. Built around old volcanic island; Review Rock, half acre at base, offers highest point in city for viewing. (Daily) 13th Ave and Grove St. **FREE**

Comstock Park. Picnicking, tennis courts. Pool (Mid-June-Aug, daily; fee). Park (Daily). 29th Ave and Howard St. **FREE**

Flour Mill. (1890) When it was built it was the most modern mill west of the Mississippi River. Today it is the home of boutiques, designer shops, galleries, restaurants. Overlooks Spokane River. (Daily) W 621 Mallon, adj to Riverfront Park north entrance. **FREE**

⭐ **Loop drive.** A 33-mi city drive to major points of interest; route, marked with "city drive" signs, begins at Sprague Ave and Stevens St. Among points incl are

Manito Park. Duncan Formal Gardens (May-Sept, daily); conservatory (Daily; closed Jan 1, Dec 25). Davenport Memorial Fountain with changing formations in ten-min cycle (May-Sept, daily); Japanese, lilac, and rose gardens (Apr-Oct, daily). Duck pond; picnicking. Grand Blvd at 18th Ave. Phone 509/625-6622. **FREE**

Riverfront Park. A 100-acre recreational park features outdoor amphitheater, IMAX theater, opera house, game rm. Spokane River runs through park; suspension bridges over Spokane River; foot bridges; skyride over falls. Miniature golf; roller coaster, carousel. Children's petting zoo. Ponds; ice rink. Restaurant, vending carts, picnicking. Some fees. Spokane Falls Blvd from Division St to Post St. Phone 509/625-6600. **FREE**

Spokane Falls. Viewed from Bridge Ave at Monroe St or foot of Lincoln St. Spokane River roars over rocks in series of cascades; illuminated at night. Adj is

Finch Arboretum. Approx 70 acres; incl Corey Glen Rhododendron Gardens, creek, 2,000 specimen plantings of ornamental trees and shrubs. (Daily) 3404 W Woodland Blvd, off Sunset Blvd. Phone 509/624-4832. **FREE**

Gonzaga University. (1887) 4,700 students. Rodin sculptures on display. In center of campus is Bing Crosby's gift to his *alma mater,* Crosby Student Center; Academy Award Oscar, gold records, certificates, trophies on display in Crosbyana Room (daily). Tours of campus (incl Crosby Center and St. Aloyisius Church; by appt). Boone Ave and Addison St. Phone 509/328-4220.

Mount Spokane State Park. More than 13,000 acres; incl Mt Spokane (5,881 ft), with excellent view from summit, and Mt Kit Carson (5,306 ft). Hiking and bridle trails, downhill skiing, x-country skiing, snowmobiling (special parking permit required), picnicking, camping. Standard fees. 25 mi NE on WA 206. Phone 509/456-4169.

Riverside State Park. Approx 7,300 acres along Spokane River. Fishing, boating (launch); hiking, equestrian area, snowmobiling, picnicking, camping. Also 600-acre off-road vehicle area; outdoor stoves; interpretive center. Standard fees. 6 mi NW via Downriver Dr. Phone 509/456-3964.

Skiing. Mount Spokane. Five double chairlifts; patrol, school, rentals; cafeteria, bar; lodge, daycare. Longest run 1½ mi; vertical drop 2,000 ft. (Dec-mid-Apr, Wed-Sun) 30 mi NE on WA 206, in Mt Spokane State Park. Phone 509/238-2220.

Wyvern Cellars. Tour and tasting of Gold Medal wines. Picnicking. (Daily; closed Jan 1, Dec 25) 7217 W Westbow. Phone 509/455-7835. **FREE**

Special Events

Ag Expo. Convention Center. Agricultural fair. Mid-Jan. Phone 509/459-4108.

Horse racing. Playfair Race Course. N Altamont and E Main Sts. Wed, Fri-Sun, hols. Phone 509/534-0505. July-mid-Nov.

Spokane Interstate Fair. Interstate Fairgrounds. Broadway and Havana sts. Phone 509/477-1766. Nine days mid-Sept.

Spokane Civic Theatre. 1020 N Howard. Live productions. Phone 509/325-1413. Thurs-Sun, Oct-mid-June.

Motels/Motor Lodges

★ **BUDGET INN.** *110 E 4th Ave (99202). 509/838-6101; fax 509/624-0733; res 800/325-4000. www.west coasthotels.com.* 153 rms, 6 story. S, D $39.99-$53.99; each addl $10; suites $69; under 18 free. Crib free. Pet accepted. TV; cable. Heated pool. Bar. Ck-out noon. Coin lndry. Meeting rms. Business servs avail. Free airport, RR station, bus depot transportation. Cr cds: A, D, DS, MC, V.
🄳 🔁 ⤫ 🛫 🖼 🔥

★ **COMFORT INN VALLEY.** *905 N Sullivan Rd, Veradale (99037). 509/924-3838; fax 509/921-6976; res 800/228-5150. www.choice international.com.* 76 rms, 2 story, 13 suites. May-Sept: S $59-$69; D $64-$74; each addl $5; suites $75-$109; under 18 free; lower rates rest of yr. Crib free. Pet accepted, some restrictions; $15/day. TV; cable. Pool; whirlpool. Complimentary continental bkfst. Restaurant nearby. Ck-out 11 am. Coin lndry. Meeting rms. Business servs avail. Refrigerator in suites. Cr cds: A, C, D, DS, MC, V.
🄳 🔁 🖼 🖼

★★ **COURTYARD BY MARRIOTT.** *N 401 Riverpoint Blvd (99202). 509/456-7600; fax 509/456-0969; res 800/321-2211. www.courtyard.com.* 149 rms, 3 story. S, D $99; suites $129; under 18 free; wkly rates. Crib free. TV. Indoor pool; whirlpool.

Complimentary coffee in rms. Restaurant 6:30-10 am. Bar 5-10 pm. Ck-out noon. Coin lndry. Meeting rms. Business servs avail. Valet serv. Exercise equipt. Refrigerator in suites. Balconies. Cr cds: A, D, DS, MC, V.

★ **DAYS INN AIRPORT.** *4212 W Sunset Blvd (99224). 509/747-2021; fax 509/747-5950; res 800/329-7466.* 132 rms, 2 story. S, D $65; each addl $5; under 18 free. Crib free. Pet accepted, some restrictions; $10. TV. Ck-out noon. Meeting rms. Business servs avail. In-rm modem link. Coin lndry. Complimentary continental bkfst. Free airport, RR station, bus depot transportation. Heated pool. Picnic tables, grills. Cr cds: A, C, D, DS, MC, V.

★★ **DOUBLETREE HOTEL.** *1100 N Sullivan Rd (99037). 509/924-9000; fax 509/922-4965; res 800/222-8733. www.doubletreevalley.com.* 236 rms, 2-3 story. S $79-99; D $89-$109; each addl $10; under 18 free. Crib $10. Pet accepted, some restrictions. Heated pool; whirlpool, poolside serv. Coffee in rms. Restaurant 6 am-11 pm. Bar 2 pm-midnight; entertainment Fri-Sat. Ck-out noon. Meeting rms. Business servs avail. Bellhops. Sundries. Barber, beauty shop. Free airport trans-

portation. Exercise equipt. Some bathrm phones, refrigerators. Private patios, balconies. Cr cds: A, C, D, DS, JCB, MC, V.

★ **MOTEL 6.** *1919 N Hutchinson Rd (99212). 509/926-5399; fax 509/928-5974; res 800/466-8356. www.motel6. com.* 92 rms, 2 story. June-Sept: S $45-$95; D $55-$95; each addl $6; under 18 free; lower rates rest of yr. Crib free. TV; cable (premium). Complimentary coffee in lobby. Ck-out noon. Meeting rm. Business servs avail. Microwaves avail. Cr cds: A, D, DS, MC, V.

★ **QUALITY INN VALLEY SUITES.** *8923 E Mission Ave (99212). 509/928-5218; res 800/228-5151. www.spokane qualityinn.com.* 127 rms, 3-4 story, 52 suites. June-Oct: S, D $87; suites $119-$300; under 18 free; golf, package plans; lower rates rest of yr. Crib $5. TV; cable (premium), VCR avail (movies). Indoor pool; whirlpool. Complimentary full bkfst. Coffee in rms. Ck-out 11 am. Coin lndry. Meeting rms. Business center. Gift shop. Exercise equipt; sauna. Refrigerators, microwaves. Balconies. Picnic tables. Cr cds: A, D, DS, JCB, MC, V.

Spokane Falls

★ **RAMADA INN AIRPORT.** *Spokane International Airport (99219). 509/838-5211; fax 509/838-1074; res 800/272-6232. www.ramada.com.* 168 rms, 2 story. S $69-$88; D $79-$95; each addl $8; suites $185-$225; kit units $175; studio rms $85; under 18 free. Crib free. Pet accepted. TV; cable. 2 pools, 1 indoor; whirlpool. Coffee in rms. Restaurant 6 am-11 pm. Bar; entertainment Thurs-Sat. Ck-out noon. Business servs avail. Bellhops. Valet serv. Sundries. Free airport transportation. Exercise equipt. Cr cds: A, C, D, DS, ER, MC, V.

🔊 🐾 🏊 🎿 🏃 ⛷ 🔥 SC

★ **SHANGRI-LA.** *2922 W Government Way (99224). 509/747-2066; fax 509/456-8696; toll-free 800/234-4941.* 20 (1-3 rm) units, 2 story, 8 kits. S $42-$45; D $47-$50; each addl $5; kit units $50-$75. Crib free. Pet accepted. TV; cable, VCR avail. Heated pool. Playground. Complementary continental bkfst. Coffee in rms. Restaurant nearby. Ck-out 11 am. Business servs avail. Free airport transportation. Health club privileges. Some refrigerators. Picnic tables. Cr cds: A, C, D, DS, MC, V.

🐾 🛎 🎿 🏊 ⛷ 🔥

★★ **SHILO INN HOTEL.** *923 E 3rd Ave (99202). 509/535-9000; fax 509/535-5740; res 800/222-2244. www.shiloinn.com.* 105 rms, 5 story. S, D $55-$119; each addl $8; under 12 free. Crib free. Pet accepted; $10/day. TV; cable (premium). Indoor pool. Complimentary full bkfst. Coffee in rms. Restaurant 6:30 am-10 pm. Bar 11:30 am-11 pm. Ck-out noon. Meeting rms. Business servs avail. In-rm modem link. Free airport transportation. Exercise equipt; sauna. Guest lndry. Refrigerators. Cr cds: A, C, D, DS, JCB, MC, V.

D 🐾 🏊 🏃 ⛷ 🔥

★ **SUPER 8 MOTEL.** *N 2020 Argonne Rd (99212). 509/928-4888; fax 509/928-4888; res 800/800-8000. www.super8.com.* 181 rms, 3 story. May-Sept: S $50-$55; D $55-$65; each addl $5; under 13 free; lower rates rest of yr. Crib free. Pet accepted, $25 refundable deposit. TV; cable (premium). Complimentary continental bkfst. Restaurant adj open 24 hrs. Ck-out 11 am. Meeting rms. Business servs avail. Coin lndry.

Microwaves avail. Cr cds: A, C, D, DS, MC, V.

🐾 ⛷ 🔥

★ **TRADE WINDS NORTH MOTEL.** *3033 N Division St (99207). 509/326-5500; fax 509/328-1357; res 800/621-8593.* 63 rms, 3 story. No elvtrs. May-Sept: S, D $64-$74; each addl $4; under 18 free; lower rates rest of yr. Crib $3. Pet accepted, some restrictions. TV; cable (premium). Indoor pool. Complimentary continental bkfst. Ck-out noon. Business servs avail. Balconies. Cr cds: A, C, D, DS, MC, V.

🐾 🏊 ⛷ 🔥 SC

★ **TRAVELODGE.** *33 W Spokane Falls Blvd (99201). 509/623-9727; fax 509/623-9737; res 888/824-0292. www.spokanetravelodge.com.* 80 rms, 4 story. May-Sept: S $60-$70; D $65-$85; each addl $10; suites $129.95-$179.95; under 18 free; lower rates rest of yr. Crib free. Pet accepted, some restrictions; $10/day. Free garage parking. TV; cable (premim). Complimentary continental bkfst. Complimentary coffee in rms. Restaurant nearby. Ck-out 11 am. Meeting rm. Business servs avail. Coin lndry. Exercise equipt. Some refrigerators, microwaves. Some balconies. Cr cds: A, C, D, DS, JCB, MC, V.

D 🐾 🏃 ✈ ⛷ 🔥 SC

★★ **WESTCOAST RIVER INN.** *N 700 Division St (99202). 509/326-5577; fax 509/326-1120. www.westcoasthotels.com.* 245 rms, 2 story. S, D $63-$130; each addl $10; suites $190-$240; under 17 free. Crib free. Pet accepted, some restrictions. TV; cable. 2 heated pools; wading pool, whirlpool, poolside serv. Coffee in rms. Restaurant 6 am-10 pm. Bar 11-2 am; entertainment Fri, Sat. Ck-out noon. Meeting rms. Business servs avail. Sundries. Airport, RR station, bus depot transportation. Tennis. Refrigerators avail. On river. Cr cds: A, C, D, DS, MC, V.

D 🐾 🎿 🏊 ⛷ 🔥

Hotels

THE DAVENPORT HOTEL. *(Too new to be rated) 10 S Post St (99201). 509/455-8888; fax 509/624-4455; toll-free 800/899-1482. www.thedavenporthotel.com.* 284 rms, 14 story, 24 suites.

S, D $145-$160; suites from $180.
Self, valet parking avail. Pet accepted.
TV; cable (premium). Indoor lap pool;
whirlpool. Restaurant. Rm serv 24 hrs.
Bar. Ck-out noon. Meeting rms. 24-hr
business center. In-rm modem link.
Concierge. Gift shop. Barber, beauty
shop. Valet serv. Exercise rm; sauna.
Spa. Credit crds: A, D, DS, JCB, MC, V

★★ **DOUBLETREE HOTEL
SPOKANE CITY CENTER.** *322 N
Spokane Falls Ct (99201). 509/455-
9600; fax 509/455-6285; res 800/222-
8733. www.doubletreehotels.com.* 375
rms, 15 story. S, D $109-$169; suites
$199-$500; under 18 free; some
wkend rates; higher rates for special
events; lower rates rest of yr. Crib
free. Valet parking. TV; cable (premium). Pool. Restaurant 6:30 am-10
pm. Entertainment. Ck-out noon.
Convention facilities. Concierge. Free
airport, RR station, bus depot transportation. Exercise equipt. Wet bar in
some suites. On river in park. Cr cds:
A, DS, MC, V.

★ **WESTCOAST RIDPATH HOTEL.**
*515 W Sprague Ave (99201). 509/838-
2711; fax 509/747-6970; res 800/325-
4000. www.westcoasthotels.com.* 350
rms, 3-12 story. S, D $69-$99; each
addl $10; suites $115-$180; under 18
free; wkend rates. Crib free. Pet
accepted. TV; cable, VCR avail. Heated
pool; poolside serv. Restaurant. Bar 11-2 am; entertainment
Mon-Sat. Ck-out noon. Meeting rms.
Business servs avail. In-rm modem
link. Drugstore. Barber. Garage parking. Free airport, RR station, bus
depot transportation. Exercise rm.
Some bathrm phones. Private patios,
balconies, sun deck. Cr cds: A, D, DS,
MC, V.

B&Bs/Small Inns

★★★ **ANGELICA'S BED & BREAK-
FAST.** *1321 W 9th Ave (99204).
509/624-5598; res 800/987-0053.
www.angelicasbb.com.* 4 rms, 3 story.
No elvtr. No rm phones. D $100-
$125. Children over 12 yrs only. TV;
cable (premium), VCR avail (movies).
Complimentary full bkfst. Ck-out 11
am, ck-in 4-7 pm. Business servs

avail. In-rm modem link. Lawn
games. Microwaves avail. Built in
1907. Totally nonsmoking. Cr cds: A,
MC, V.

★★★ **FOTHERINGHAM HOUSE.**
*2128 W 2nd Ave (99204). 509/838-
1891; fax 509/838-1807. www.
fotheringham.net.* 4 air-cooled rms, 1
with shower only, 3 share baths. No
A/C. No rm phones. S, D $105. Chil-
dren over 12 yrs only. Complimentary full bkfst. Restaurant adj 11:30
am-9 pm. Ck-out 11 am, ck-in 2-4
pm. Queen Anne-style house built
1891 for mayor of Spokane. Many
antiques. Totally nonsmoking. Cr
cds: A, DS, MC, V.

★★★ **MARIANNA STOLTZ
HOUSE BED & BREAKFAST.** *427 E
Indiana Ave (99207). 509/483-4316;
fax 509/483-6773; res 800/978-6587.
www.mariannastoltzhouse.com.* 4 rms,
2 with shower only, 2 share bath, 2
story. No rm phones. S $79; D $89;
each addl $10; under 12 free; some
wkends (2-day min). Children over 4
yrs only. TV; cable, VCR avail. Complimentary full bkfst. Ck-out 11 am,
ck-in 3 pm. Free airport transportation. Health club privileges. Built in
1908; antiques. Totally nonsmoking.
Cr cds: A, DS, MC, V.

Restaurants

★ **CHAPTER XI.** *105 E Mission Ave
(99202). 509/326-0466.* Hrs: 11:30
am-10 pm; Fri to 11 pm; Sat 4-11
pm; Sun 4-10 pm. Closed Thanksgiving, Dec 25. Bar. Lunch $6-$10, dinner $6-$25. Specializes in prime rib,
stuffed shrimp, mud pie. Salad bar.
Cr cds: A, C, DS, MC, V.

★★ **CLINKERDAGGER.** *621 W Mallon (99201). 509/328-5965.* Hrs: 11:15
am-2:30 pm, 5-9 pm; Fri, Sat 5-10
pm; Sun 4-9 pm. Closed July 4, Dec
25. Res accepted. Bar to midnight. A
la carte entrees: lunch $5.95-$12.95,
dinner $12.95-$22. Child's meals.
Specializes in prime rib, fish. Parking.
Outdoor dining. Converted flour
mill; shops inside. Overlooks

Spokane Falls. Cr cds: A, C, D, DS, ER, MC, V.

★ **OLD SPAGHETTI FACTORY.** *152 S Monroe St (99204). 509/624-8916. www.osf.com.* Hrs: 4:30-9:30 pm; Fri, Sat to 10:30 pm; Sun 4-9 pm. Closed Thanksgiving, Dec 24, 25. Italian menu. Bar. Complete meal: dinner $5-$9. Specializes in fettucine, tortellini, spaghetti dishes. Converted warehouse. Cr cds: A, D, DS, MC, V.

★ ★ ★ **PATSY CLARK'S.** *2208 W 2nd Ave (99204). 509/838-8300. www.nwadv.com/patsy-clarks.* Hrs: 11:30 am-1:45 pm, 5-8 pm; Fri to 9 pm; Sat 5-9 pm; Sun 5-8 pm; Sun brunch 10 am-1:30 pm. Res accepted. International menu. Bar. A la carte entrees: lunch $10-$16, dinner $24-$36. Sun brunch $25. Specializes in seafood, steak, wild game. Menu changes seasonally. Own baking. Pianist. Valet parking. Mansion designed and built in 1898 by Kirkland K. Cutter for prominent mining tycoon, Patrick "Patsy" Clark. Furnished with antiques, handmade furniture, Tiffany stained glass. Cr cds: A, MC, V.

Sunnyside

(E-5) *See also Richland, Toppenish*

Founded 1893 **Pop** 11,238 **Elev** 743 ft **Area code** 509 **Zip** 98944

Information Chamber of Commerce, 520 S 7th St, PO Box 329; 509/837-5939 or 800/457-8089

Web www.sunnysidechamber.com

This is the home of one of the first irrigation projects of more than 100,000 acres in the state. Its selection as a site for a large settlement of the Christian Cooperative movement brought growth and prosperity to this community. Irrigation continues to bring rich crops to the fields that circle the city.

The town is aptly named. Sunnyside averages over 300 days of sunshine every year with mild winters and dry summers.

What to See and Do

Darigold Dairy Fair. Tours of cheese-making plant. (Daily; closed hols) 400 Alexander Rd. Phone 509/837-4321. **FREE**

Tucker Cellars Winery. Wine tasting. (Daily) Yakima Valley Hwy and Ray Rd. Phone 509/837-8701.

Washington Hills Cellar. Wine tasting. (Daily) 111 E Lincoln.

Tacoma (C-3)

Settled 1868 **Pop** 176,664 **Elev** 250 ft **Area code** 253

Information Tacoma-Pierce County Visitor & Convention Bureau, 1119 Pacific Ave, 5th floor, PO Box 1754, 98402; 253/627-2836 or 800/272-2662

Web www.traveltacoma.com

In its gemlike setting on Puget Sound, midway between Seattle and Olympia, Tacoma maintains its wood and paper products and its shipping traditions. Its harbor is a port of call for merchant vessels plying the oceans of the world. Backed by timber, shipping facilities, and low-cost water and power, more than 500 industries produce lumber, plywood, paper, millwork, furniture, foodstuffs, beverages, chemicals, and clothing. Major railroad and ship-building yards are also located here. Health care is a major employer, and high-tech industry continues to grow rapidly. The nearest metropolitan center to Mount Rainier National Park (see), Tacoma is a base for trips to Olympic National Park (see) and Puget Sound. Mild weather keeps parks and gardens green throughout the year.

In 1833 the Hudson's Bay Company built its second post (Fort Nisqually) on the North Pacific Coast in the forest, 18 miles south of the present site of Tacoma. In 1841 Charles Wilkes, commander of a US expedition, began a survey of Puget Sound from this point and named the bay around which Tacoma is built Commencement Bay. When the rails of the Northern Pacific reached tidewater here late in 1873, they sparked the industrial growth of the city.

What to See and Do

Emerald Downs. Thoroughbred horse racing. (Late June-early Nov, Wed-Sun) 15 mi NE on I-5 to Auburn. Phone 253/288-7700. ¢¢

Enchanted Village. Family entertainment park with rides for all ages; wax museum, antique toy and doll museum. Live entertainment. Concessions. (Mid-May-Labor Day, daily; early Apr-mid-May and Sept after Labor Day, wkends) 36201 Enchanted Pkwy S in Federal Way. Phone 253/661-8000. ¢¢¢¢ Also here is

> **Wild Waves Water Park.** A 24,000-sq-foot wave pool with body and mat surfing in ocean-size waves; raging river ride; adult activity pool; four giant water slides with flashing lights and music, two speed slides; spas; children's pool. Game rm; raft rentals. (Memorial Day wkend-Labor Day wkend, daily) Admission incl entry to Enchanted Village. Phone 253/661-8000. ¢¢¢¢

Ferry. Point Defiance to Vashon Island. Contact Washington State Ferries, Seattle Ferry Terminal, Colman Dock, Seattle 98104. Phone 206/464-6400. ¢¢

Fort Lewis. Army center of the Northwest, home of I Corps, the Seventh Infantry Division, and associated support units. Approx 86,000 acres with military buildings and living quarters. Museum with exhibits on Northwest military history (Wed-Sun). 11 mi SW on I-5. Phone 253/967-7206.

McChord AFB. The 62nd Airlift Wing and 446th Aircraft Wing (Reserves) are based here. Tours (Tues and Thurs; res required one month in advance). Museum (Tues-Sun, afternoons). 8 mi SW on I-5. Phone 253/982-2485.

Mount Rainier National Park. (see) Nisqually entrance, approx 56 mi SE on WA 7.

Narrows Bridge. Fifth-longest span for a suspension bridge in US (2,800 ft). Total length: 5,450 ft between anchorages. Successor to "Galloping Gertie," which collapsed in 1940, four months and seven days after it had officially opened. W on Olympic Blvd; WA 16.

Northwest Trek. One-hr naturalist-guided and narrated tram tour takes visitors on 5½-mi ride through 600-acre wilderness and wildlife preserve, where native Northwest animals may be seen roaming free in their natural habitat; self-guided nature walks through wetlands and forest animal exhibits; nature trails incl barrier-free trail; children's discovery center. Theater with 14-min film on history of facility. (Mar-Oct, daily; rest of yr, Fri-Sun and selected hols) 32 mi SE via I-5, WA 512, 161. Phone 360/832-6117. ¢¢

Pacific Lutheran University. (1890) 3,500 students. Swimming pool. Nine-hole golf course open to public; 11 mi SW on I-5. Off I-5, exit 127. Phone 253/535-7430. On campus are

> **Robert Mortvedt Library.** African tribal art. (Mon-Sat) Phone 253/535-7500. **FREE**

> **University Gallery.** Changing art exhibits (Mon-Fri). Rune stones sculpture on campus mall. Ingram Hall. Phone 253/535-7573.

Pioneer Farm. Replica of an 1887 homestead with animals; log cabin, barn, trading post, and other outbuildings; furnished with turn-of-the-century antiques. "Hands on" program; guided tours. (Mid-June-Labor Day, daily; Mar-mid-June and after Labor Day-Thanksgiving, Sat and Sun only) 35 mi SE via WA 7, in the Ohop Valley. Phone 360/832-6300.

★ **Point Defiance Park.** Approx 700 acres of dense forest, clay cliffs, driftwood-covered gravel beaches, and formal gardens. On bold promontory, nearly surrounded by water. Boating, fishing, swimming; hiking, picnicking. Park (daily). 6 mi N, entrance at N 54th and Pearl sts. **FREE** In the park are

> **Boathouse Marina.** Bait and tackle shop. Boat and motor rentals. Moorage. Restaurant. Gift shop. (Daily; closed Thanksgiving, Dec 25) Phone 253/591-5325.

> **Camp Six Logging Exhibit (Western Forest Industries Museum).** Reconstructed steam logging camp

POINT DEFIANCE PARK

One of Tacoma's preeminent attractions, this 700-acre park, flanked by the waters of Puget Sound, contains a wealth of gardens, the city zoo and aquarium, and a number of recreational and historic sites. The park includes 14 miles of hiking trails, which wind through groves of old-growth forests and lead to sheltered beaches. The main paved road through the park is called Five Mile Drive; on Saturday this scenic road remains closed to motor vehicles until 1 pm, though it's open to cyclists, joggers, and inline skaters.

Enter the park at Pearl Street and follow signs to the parking area at the Vashon Island Ferry. From here, watch as the ferries cross to and from Vashon Island, an agricultural island in the misty distance. Walk past the tennis courts, and follow the path to the garden area.

Formal gardens are abundant at Point Defiance Park and are maintained cooperatively by members of local garden clubs, with help from Tacoma's Metropolitan Park District. Park gardens include the Japanese Garden, with a Torii Gate and Shinto Shrine received as a gift from Kitakyushu, Tacoma's sister city in Japan. Also found here are iris gardens, dahlia test gardens, herb gardens, and a rhododendron garden that is a blaze of color in May. Just past the zoo entrance on Five Mile Drive is the civic Rose Garden, established in 1895, with more than an acre of bushes, many of heirloom varieties. The Northwest Native Garden, located near the Pearl Street entrance, presents a collection of indigenous plants ranging from trees to grasses.

Just past the main garden area is the Point Defiance Zoo and Aquarium. Often considered one of the best in the United States, the Point Defiance Zoo is unusual in that it focuses primarily on species from the Pacific Rim, including polar bears, musk ox, and Arctic fox. Peer at coastline mammals through the underwater windows at Rocky Shores. No less than 30 huge sharks swim among tropical fish and eels in the lagoon at Discovery Reef Aquarium. Elephants and apes and other zoo favorites are housed in the Southeast Asia complex.

set amid virgin timber. Dolbeer Donkey steam engine (one of two in existence), 110-ft spar pole, restored water wagon, bunkhouses. (Jan-Oct, Wed-Sun) Logging train ride (Apr-Sept, Sat, Sun, and hols). A 90-ton shay steam locomotive operates in summer (wkends and hols). Santa train (three wkends Dec). Phone 253/752-0047. ¢

Five-Mile Drive. Around Point Defiance Park. Contains old growth forest with some 200-ft-high Douglas firs, variety of other evergreens, deciduous trees, shrubs. Scenic views of Puget Sound, Olympic and Cascade mountains, Narrows Bridge. Drive closed to motor vehicles Sat mornings for cycling and walking.

Fort Nisqually. (1833) Restored fur-trading outpost of Hudson's Bay Company reflects period of English control when fur pelts were used as currency. Purchased by US in 1869, moved to this site in 1937. Two remaining buildings of original outpost are the Factor's House (1853) and the Granary (1843), oldest existing building in state; eight other buildings reconstructed according to original specifications using handmade hardware, lumber. Living history presentations. Fee for some special events. (Memorial Day-Labor Day, daily; rest of yr, Wed-Sun) Phone 253/591-5339. ¢

Gardens. Formal gardens in park incl an AARS rose garden, Japanese Garden, Northwest Native garden, Pacific Northwest dahlia trial garden, rhododendron garden, and seasonal annual displays. **FREE**

Never Never Land. Sculptured storybook characters in ten-acre forest setting. Each wkend storybook characters visit and special events take place. (May-Aug, daily; Apr and Sept, wkends only) Phone 253/591-5845. ¢¢

From the zoo, follow trails north into the wild heart of the park. Point Defiance has been a public park for almost 125 years, and vast sections of it preserve old-growth forest and virgin meadowlands. Heading north, stop at Owens Beach to explore the shoreline—or take in the sun along the sandy strand. Farther west, past a viewpoint onto Vashon Island, is Mountaineer Tree, a massive fir tree nearly 450 years old. The western edge of the park is at Gig Harbor Viewpoint, which overlooks the Tacoma Narrows, a constricted, surging strait between Point Defiance and the Kitsap Peninsula.

Round the cap and walk south along the western flank of the park. From here, watch for vistas onto the Tacoma Narrows Bridge. At a mile in length, it is the fifth longest span in North America. The present bridge replaced the infamous "Galloping Gertie" bridge that collapsed at this site during a wind storm in 1940.

At the southwest corner of the park are a number of attractions. If you have kids in tow, they may enjoy Never Never Land, a ten-acre, storyland theme park in an outdoor forest setting. Wooded paths lead to oversized sculpted figures of nursery rhyme characters. On summer weekends, kids can meet real costumed characters.

Adjacent is Fort Nisqually Historic Site. In 1833, the Hudson's Bay Company trading post at Fort Nisqually was established 17 miles south of Tacoma near DuPont. This restoration of the original fort includes the factor's house, granary, trade store, blacksmith shop, laborer's quarters, and stockade, all furnished to reflect life on the frontier in the 1850s. Docents in period clothing demonstrate blacksmithing, spinning, beadwork, and black powder.

Walk back toward the main park entrance, stopping by Camp 6 Logging Museum, an open-air logging museum and reconstruction of a pioneer logging camp. On spring and summer weekends, hitch a ride on a logging train with a steam locomotive.

Back at the ferry terminal, refresh yourself with a stop at the Boathouse Grill, located above the marina with views over Vashon Island and the Olympic mountain peaks.

Point Defiance Zoo & Aquarium. Zoo has polar bear complex, musk ox habitat, tundra waterfowl, elephants, beluga whales, walrus, seals, and otters; World of Adaptions, Southeast Asia Complex, and "The Farm." Aquarium and 38 perimeter displays with hundreds of Pacific Northwest marine specimens. Reef Aquarium features sharks and other South Pacific sea life. (Daily; closed Thanksgiving, Dec 25) 5400 N Pearl St. Phone 253/591-5337.

St. Peter's Church. (1873) Episcopal. Oldest church in city; the organ came around Cape Horn in 1874; half-ton bell, also shipped around the Horn, is mounted on tower beside church. (Sun; also by appt) 2910 Starr St, at N 29th St. Phone 253/272-4406.

Tacoma Art Museum. Permanent collection; changing exhibits; children's gallery with hands-on art activities. (Tues-Sun; closed Jan 1, Dec 25) 12th St and Pacific Ave. Phone 253/272-4258. ¢¢

Tacoma Nature Center. Approx 50 acres of marshland, forest, thickets, and ponds providing a wildlife haven in heart of urbanized Tacoma. Nature trails, observation shelters; natural science library. Interpretive center; lectures and workshops. Park (daily). 1919 S Tyler St. Phone 253/591-6439. **FREE**

Totem Pole. One of the tallest in US, carved from 105-ft cedar tree by Alaskan Native Americans; located in Firemen's Park with view of Commencement Bay and the Port of Tacoma. 9th and A Sts.

University of Puget Sound. (1888) 2,800 students. 37 Tudor Gothic buildings on 72-acre campus. Many free cultural events, art gallery, theater, recital hall. University is older than state. 1500 N Warner St. Phone 253/879-3100. Also here is

James R. Slater Museum of Natural History. Thompson Hall. Displays research specimens, particularly of Pacific Northwest flora and fauna; more than 11,000 birds, 4,600 egg sets; reptiles, amphibians, mammals, and pressed plants. (Mon-Fri by appt; closed hols) **FREE**

Washington State History Museum. Exhibits incl collections of pioneer, Native American, and Alaskan artifacts and detail the history of the state and its people. Interactive, introductory, and changing exhibits. Indoor and outdoor theaters. Museum cafe and shop. (Memorial Day-Labor Day, daily; rest of yr, Tues-Sun; closed hols) 1911 Pacific Ave. Phone 888/238-4373. ¢¢ Adj is

Union Station. Built in 1911 by Northern Pacific Railroad, the station, with its 98-ft-high dome, has been restored. Now home to the federal courthouse. The rotunda houses the largest single exhibit of sculptured glass by Tacoma native Dale Chihuly. (Mon-Fri; closed hols) Phone 253/396-1768. **FREE**

Wright Park. More than 800 trees of 100 varieties in one of finest arboretums in Pacific Northwest. W. W. Seymour Botanical Conservatory, located in park at S 4th and Gsts, contains tropical plants, seasonal displays, and a botanical gift shop. 6th Ave and I St. Phone 253/591-5330. **FREE**

Special Events

Daffodil Festival. In Tacoma and Puyallup Valley. Flower show, coronation, four-city floral parade of floats, marine regatta, bowling tournament. Phone 253/627-6176. Two wks Apr.

Taste of Tacoma. Point Defiance Park. Entertainment, arts and crafts. Phone 206/232-2982. Early July.

Tacoma Little Theater. 210 N I St. Five shows, incl comedies, dramas, and musicals. Phone 253/272-2281. Sept-June.

Tacoma Symphony Orchestra. 727 Commerce St. For details phone 253/272-7264. Late Sept-early Apr.

Motels/Motor Lodges

★ **BEST INN & SUITES.** *3100 Pacific Hwy E, Fife (98424). 253/922-9520; fax 253/922-2002; toll-free 877/982-3781. www.bestinnhotel.com.* 115 rms, 2 story. S $40-$58; D $48-$65; each addl $7.70; suites $56.99-$64.99; under 17 free. Crib free. Pet accepted. TV; cable (premium). Heated pool. Complimentary coffee in lobby. Restaurant opp 6 am-10 pm. Ck-out 11 am. Guest lndry. Business servs avail. In-rm modem link. Health club privileges. Refrigerator in suites. Cr cds: A, DS, MC, V.
[icons]

★★ **BEST WESTERN TACOMA INN.** *8726 S Hosmer St (98444). 253/535-2880; fax 253/537-8379; res 800/780-7234. www.bwtacomainn. com.* 149 rms, 2 story, 8 kits. S, D $69-$79; each addl $6; kit. units $78-$84; under 12 free. Crib free. Pet accepted, some restrictions; $20. TV; cable (premium). Heated pool; poolside serv. Playground. Complimentary coffee in rms. Restaurant 6:30 am-10:30 pm. Bar 11-2 am; entertainment. Ck-out noon. Coin lndry. Meeting rms. Business servs avail. In-rm modem link. Valet serv. Putting green. Exercise equipt. Some refrigerators; microwaves avail. Private patios, balconies. Cr cds: A, C, D, DS, ER, JCB, MC, V.
[icons]

★ **DAYS INN.** *6802 Tacoma Mall Blvd (98409). 253/475-5900; fax 253/475-3540; toll-free 800/329-7466. www.daysinn.com.* 123 rms, 2 story. S, D $70-$89; each addl $10; suites $165; under 12 free. Crib free. Pet accepted. TV; cable (premium). Heated pool. Complimentary coffee in lobby. Restaurant 6:30 am-10 pm; Sat from 8 am; Sun 8 am-9 pm. Ck-out 11 am, ck-in 3 pm. Meeting rms. Business center. In-rm modem link. Valet serv. Health club privileges. Refrigerator; microwaves avail. Cr cds: A, C, D, DS, ER, JCB, MC, V.
[icons]

★★ **LA QUINTA INN.** *1425 E 27th St (98421). 253/383-0146; fax 253/627-3280; res 800/531-5900. www.laquinta.com.* 157 rms, 7 story. S $74-$110; D $82-$118; each addl $5; under 18 free. Crib free. Pet accepted. TV; cable (premium). Heated pool;

whirlpool. Complimentary continental bkfst. Restaurant 6:30 am-2 pm; 5-10 pm. Bar. Ck-out noon. Coin lndry. Meeting rms. Business center. In-rm modem link. Valet serv. Sundries. Exercise equipt. Microwaves avail. View of both Mt Rainier and Commencement Bay. Cr cds: A, C, D, DS, MC, V.

🅳 🐾 ⚓ 🏋 🎿 🔥 SC 🚶

★★ **ROYAL COACHMAN INN, INC.** *5805 Pacific Hwy E (98424). 253/922-2500; fax 253/922-6443; toll-free 800/422-3051. www.royalcoachman inn.com.* 94 rms, 2 story. S, D $65-$71; each addl $7; suites $140; kit. units $95-$130; under 12 free. Crib free. Pet accepted; $25 refundable. TV; cable (premium), VCR avail. Coffee in rms. Ck-out noon. Coin lndry. Meeting rms. Business servs avail. Some refrigerators, microwaves, in-rm whirlpools. Cr cds: A, C, D, DS, ER, JCB, MC, V.

🅳 🐾 ⚓ 🔥

★★ **SHILO INN.** *7414 S Hosmer (98408). 253/475-4020; fax 253/475-1236; res 800/222-2244. www. shiloinns.com.* 132 rms, 4 story, 11 kits. S, D $69-$125; each addl $10; under 12 free. Crib avail. Pet accepted; $10. TV; cable (premium), VCR (movies $3). Indoor pool; whirlpool. Complimentary continental bkfst. Restaurant opp 6 am-11 pm. Ck-out noon. Coin lndry. Meeting rms. In-rm modem link. Valet serv. Exercise equipt; sauna, steam rm. Bathrm phones, refrigerators, microwaves. Cr cds: A, DS, MC, V.

🐾 ⚓ 🏋 🎿 🔥

Hotel

★★★ **SHERATON.** *1320 Broadway Plaza (98402). 253/572-3200; fax 253/591-4105; toll-free 800/845-9466. www.sheratontacoma.com.* 319 rms, 26 story. S $140-$155; D $150-$165; each addl $10; suites $265-$450; under 12 free. wknd rates. Crib free. Pet accepted. TV; cable (premium), VCR avail. Pool privileges; whirlpool. Complimentary coffee in rms. Restaurant 6 am-11 pm (see also ALTEZZO). Bar to 2 am; entertainment Wed-Sat. Ck-out noon. Convention facilities. Business center. In-rm modem link. Concierge. Shop-

ping arcade. Barber, beauty shop. Sauna. Health club privileges. Minibars; some bathrm phones, refrigerators. Dramatic 4-level skylit winter garden lobby. Luxury level. Cr cds: A, C, D, DS, ER, JCB, MC, V.

🅳 🐾 🏋 🎿 🔥 🚶 ⚓

B&Bs/Small Inns

★★★ **CHINABERRY HILL.** *302 Tacoma Ave N (98403). 253/272-1282; fax 253/272-1335. www.chinaberry hill.com.* 5 rms, 3 story, 1 guest house. No A/C. No rm phones. S $100; D $110; each addl $25; guest house $200; wkly rates. Children over 12 yrs only (any age allowed in guest house). TV in some rms; cable (premium), VCR avail (movies). Complimentary full bkfst; afternoon refreshments. Restaurant nearby. Ck-out 11 am, ck-in 4-6 pm. Business servs avail. In rm modem link. Luggage handling. Health club privileges. Whirlpool. Refrigerators; many in-rm whirlpools. Victorian inn built in 1889; antiques. Totally nonsmoking. Cr cds: A, MC, V.

🎿 🔥

★★★ **COMMENCEMENT BAY BED & BREAKFAST.** *3312 N Union Ave (98407). 253/752-8175; fax 253/759-4025; toll-free 800/406-4088. www. great-views.com.* 3 rms, 4 story. Apr-Oct: S, D $100-$110; lower rates rest of yr. Children over 12 yrs only. TV; cable (premium), VCR (free movies). Complimentary full bkfst. Restaurant nearby. Ck-out 11 am, ck-in 4-6 pm. Luggage handling. Business servs avail. Exercise equipt. Massage. Whirlpool. Mountain bikes. Game rm. Microwaves avail. Colonial house built in 1937. Cr cds: A, DS, MC, V.

⚡ 🏋 🎿 🔥 SC 🚶

★ **KEENAN HOUSE BED AND BREAKFAST.** *2610 N Warner St (98407). 253/752-0702; fax 253/756-0822.* 3 rms, 2 with bath, 2 story. No A/C. No rm phones. S $65-$70; D $70-$75; wkly rates. Crib free. TV in sitting rm. Complimentary full bkfst. Restaurant nearby. Ck-out 11 am, ck-in 2 pm. Street parking. Picnic tables. One Victorian house (ca 1890);

antiques. Totally nonsmoking. Cr
cds: MC, V.

★★★ **VILLA BED & BREAKFAST.**
*705 N 5th St (98403). 253/572-1157;
fax 253/572-1805; toll-free 888/572-
1157. www.villabb.com.* 4 rms, 1 with
shower only, 2 story. No A/C. Guest
phone avail. S, D $90-$145; each
addl $15; wkly rates. Children over
12 yrs only. TV; cable (premium).
Complimentary full bkfst. Ck-out
noon, ck-in 3-9 pm. Business servs
avail. In-rm modem link. Italianate
villa built 1925; landscaped grounds;
antiques. Totally nonsmoking. Cr
cds: Λ, MC, V.

Restaurants

★★★ **ALTEZZO RISTORANTE.**
*1320 Broadway Plaza (98402).
253/591-4155.* Hrs: 5:30-10 pm; Fri,
Sat to 11 pm. Res accepted. Italian
menu. Bar. Wine list. À la carte
entrees: dinner $9.95-$21.50. Own
baking. Valet parking. Penthouse
dining; view of bay and mountains.
Cr cds: A, D, DS, MC, V.
D

★★★ **CLIFF HOUSE.** *6300 Marine
View Dr (98422). 253/927-0400.
www.cliffhouserestaurant.com.* Hrs:
11:30-1 am. Closed Dec 25. Res
accepted. Bar. Lunch $6.95-$14, dinner $12.95-$25.95. Specializes in
European, Northwestern cuisine.
Tableside cooking. Built on cliff; view
of Commencement Bay and Mt
Rainier. Cr cds: A, D, DS, MC, V.

★★ **COPPERFIELD'S.** *8726 S Hosmer St (98444). 253/531-1500. www.
bwtacomainn.com.* Hrs: 6:30 am-10:30
pm; Sun brunch 9 am-2 pm. Res
accepted. Bar. Bkfst $2.50-$13.95,
lunch $4.25-$7.25, dinner $6.50-
$14.95. Sun brunch $13.95. Specializes in salmon, prime rib, pasta.
Parking. Gardenlike setting; wicker
furniture. Cr cds: A, DS, MC, V.
D

★★ **HARBOR LIGHTS.** *2761 Ruston
Way (98402). 253/752-8600.* Hrs: 11
am-11 pm; Fri to 2 am; Sat noon-2
am; Sun 2-9 pm. Closed most major
hols. Res accepted. Bar. Lunch $5-
$9.50, dinner $9.50-$32. Child's
meals. Specializes in steak, seafood,

veal. Parking. Outdoor dining.
Marine view. Family-owned. Cr cds:
A, DS, MC, V.
D

★★ **JOHNNY'S DOCK.** *1900 E D St
(98421). 253/627-3186. www.johnnys
dock.com.* Hrs: 10 am-9 pm; Fri, Sat
to 10 pm. Res accepted. Bar. Bkfst
$5.50-$7.95, lunch $5.95-$12.95,
dinner $10.95-$24.95. Child's meals.
Specializes in steak, seafood. Parking. Outdoor dining. Waterfront
view; moorage. Family-owned.
Totally nonsmoking. Cr cds: A, D,
DS, MC, V.
D

★★★ **LOBSTER SHOP SOUTH.**
*4015 Ruston Way (98402). 253/927-
1513. www.lobstershop.com.* Hrs: 4:30-
9 pm; Fri, Sat to 10:30 pm; Sun to 9
pm; early-bird dinner Sun-Fri 4:30-
5:30 pm; Sun brunch 9:30 am-1:30
pm, dinner 3:30-9 pm. Closed Dec
25. Res accepted. Bar. Wine list. A la
carte entrees: dinner $9.95-$25.95.
Sun brunch $15.95. Child's meals.
Specializes in steak, seafood, Aus-
tralian lobster. Own pastries. Parking.
Outdoor dining. Cr cds: A, D, DS,
MC, V.
D

Toppenish

(E-5) *See also Sunnyside, Yakima*

Pop 7,419 **Elev** 755 ft **Area code** 509
Zip 98948

Information Chamber of Commerce,
PO Box 28; 509/865-3262 or
800/569-3982

Web www.toppenish.org

Toppenish is a Native American word
meaning "people from the foot of
the hills." The Yakama Indian
Agency is here, and the nearby million-acre Yakama Reservation is an
important tourist attraction. The cultural differences offer good opportunities for sightseeing and dining. The
Toppenish area produces hops, fruits,
vegetables, and dairy products. Average rainfall is only about eight
inches a year, but irrigation makes
the countryside bloom.

What to See and Do

Fort Simcoe Historical State Park.
200 acres. Restoration of fort established 1856 to protect treaty lands from land-hungry settlers and to guard military roads. Five original buildings restored; interpretive center with army and Native American relics. Picnicking, hiking. Park (Apr-Sept, daily; rest of yr, wkends and hols). 28 mi W on WA 220, Fort Rd. Phone 509/874-2372.

Historical Murals. Painted on downtown buildings. For map or guided tour contact Mural Society, 5A Toppenish Ave. Phone 509/865-6516.

Yakama Nation Cultural Center.
Located on ancestral grounds of the Yakamas. Incl museum depicting history of the Yakama Nation, library, theater, and restaurant. (Daily; closed Dec 25) S on US 97, Phone 509/865-2800. ¢¢

Special Events

Native American Celebrations. Most at Yakama Reservation in White Swan, 23 mi W on WA 220. For details and locations phone 509/865-2800. **Yakama Nation Treaty Day, Powwow Rodeo.** (Phone 509/865-2800) Early June at fairgrounds. **Bull-O-Rama.** Early July.

Silver Spur PRCA Rodeo. Early July. Phone 509/248-7160.

Old-Fashioned Melodrama. Yakama Nation Cultural Center Theatre. Boo and hiss at the villain, cheer the hero. Late July-early Aug. Phone 509/865-5719.

Western Art Show. Downtown. Three-day art show, cowboy poetry. Late Aug. Phone 800/569-3982.

Union

See also Bremerton

Settled 1858 **Pop** 600 **Elev** 10 ft
Area code 360 **Zip** 98592

This resort town at the curve of the Hood Canal almost became the saltwater terminus of the Union Pacific Railroad, but the failure of a British bank was a blow to Union's commercial future. There are public beaches,

a marina, free launching sites, and a golf course in town.

What to See and Do

Lake Cushman State Park. Approx 600 acres. Swimming, fishing, boating (launch, fee); hiking trails, picnicking, camping (Apr-Nov; hookups). Standard fees. 5 mi SW via WA 106, 5 mi N via US 101 to Hoodsport, then 7 mi NW via Lake Cushman Rd. Phone 360/877-5491.

Tollie Shay Engine and Caboose #7. Refurbished three-cylinder locomotive and Simpson logging caboose with coal-burning stove and unique side-door design. Caboose used by Shelton-Mason County Chamber of Commerce as office and tourist information center. (Daily; closed hols) 5 mi W on WA 106, 10 mi S on US 101 in Shelton. Phone 360/426-2021. **FREE**

Twanoh State Park. 182 acres along Hood Canal. Swimming, scuba diving, boating (launch, dock), fishing, clamming; hiking, picnicking, camping (hookups). Standard fees. 12 mi E on WA 106, off US 101. Phone 360/275-2222.

Vancouver

(F-3) Also see Portland, OR

Founded 1824 **Pop** 46,380 **Elev** 89 ft
Area code 360
Information Greater Vancouver Chamber of Commerce, 1101 Broadway, Suite 120, 98660; 360/694-2588
Web www.vancouverusa.com

Vancouver treasures a national historic site, Fort Vancouver, now completely encircled by the city. The fort served as a commercial bastion for the Hudson's Bay Company, whose vast enterprises stretched far to the north and across the sea to Hawaii, bringing furs from Utah and California and dominating coastal trade well up the shoreline to Alaska. Around the stockaded fort, the company's cultivated fields and pastures extended for miles; drying sheds, mills, forges, and shops made it a pioneer metropolis. This community was a major stake in Britain's claim for all the territory north of the Columbia River, but by the treaty of 1846, Fort Vancouver became American. Settlers began to take over the Hudson's Bay Company lands, and an Army post was established here in 1849, continuing to the present day. In 1860, all of Fort Vancouver was turned over to the US Army.

The city is on the Columbia River, just north of Portland, Oregon. Vancouver has a diversified industrial climate, which includes electronics, paper products, fruit packing, malt production, and the manufacture of textiles, furniture, and machinery. The Port of Vancouver, one of the largest on the West Coast, is a deepwater seaport handling a wide range of commodities.

What to See and Do

Clark County Historical Museum. Exhibits incl 1890s store, doctor's office, printing press, doll collection, dioramas of area history, Native American artifacts; railroad exhibit; genealogical and historical research libraries. (Tues-Sat; closed hols) 1511 Main St. Phone 360/695-4681. **FREE**

☒ Fort Vancouver National Historic Site. Over 150 acres. After extensive research and excavation, the fort has been partially reconstructed by the National Park Service. Now at the fort site: Chief Factor's house, kitchen, wash house, stockade wall, gates, the bastion, bake house, blacksmith shop, and trade shop-dispensary. Visitor center has museum exhibiting artifacts, information desk, video presentations. Tours, interpretive talks, and living history programs are offered. (Daily; closed hols) 1501 E Evergreen Blvd. Phone 360/696-7655.

Gifford Pinchot National Forest. Forest's 1,379,000 acres incl 12,326-ft Mt Adams; 8,400-ft Mt St. Helens (see MOUNT ST. HELENS NATIONAL VOLCANIC MONUMENT); and 180,600 acres distributed among seven wilderness areas. Picnicking, hiking, swimming, fishing, boating; camping, hunting. Some fees. NE of city, reached via WA 14, 25, 503. Contact Public Affairs Assistant, PO Box 8944, 98668. Phone 360/750-5001.

Officers' Row. Self-guided walking tour of 21 turn-of-the-century houses; two open to public.

Pearson Air Museum. At M. J. Murdock Aviation Center, one of the oldest operating airfields in the nation. Vintage aircraft and flying memorabilia. (Tues-Sun; closed hols) 1115 E Fifth St. Phone 360/694-7026. ¢

Motels/Motor Lodges

★ **BEST INN AND SUITES.** *7001 NE Hwy 99 (98665). 360/696-0516; fax 360/693-8343; res 888/696-0516. www.bestinn.com.* 72 kit. suites, 2 story. S $54-$64; D $59-$71; each addl $5; under 18 free. Crib free. Pet accepted, some restrictions; $10. TV; cable (premium). Heated pool; whirlpool. Complimentary continental bkfst. Restaurant nearby. Ck-out noon. Coin lndry. Business servs avail. Health club privileges. Some balconies. Cr cds: A, D, DS, MC, V.
D 🐾 🕑 🖎 🖎 SC 🖎

★ **COMFORT INN.** *13207 NE 20th (98686). 360/574-6000; fax 360/573-3746; res 800/228-5150. www.comfortinn.com.* 58 rms, 2 story. S $62-$72; D $79-$89; each addl $5; suites $119; under 18 free. Crib $3. TV; cable (premium). Indoor pool; whirlpool. Complimentary continental bkfst. Restaurant opp 6:30 am-9 pm. Ck-out 11 am. Coin lndry. Meeting rms. Business servs avail. In-rm modem link. Exercise equipt. Refrigerators. Cr cds: A, C, D, DS, JCB, MC, V.
🖎 🕇 🖎 🖎

★★ **COMFORT SUITES.** *4714 NE 94th Ave (98662). 360/253-3100; fax 360/253-7998; res 800/517-4000. www.comfortsuites.com.* 68 suites, 2 story. S $76-$86; D $81-$91; each addl $5; under 18 free. Crib free. TV; cable (premium). Indoor pool; whirlpool. Complimentary continental bkfst. Complimentary coffee in rms. Restaurant nearby. Ck-out noon. Meeting rms. Business servs avail. Valet serv Mon-Fri. Airport transportation. Exercise equipt. Health club privileges. Refrigerators, microwaves; some in-rm whirlpools. Cr cds: A, C, D, DS, JCB, MC, V.
D 🕑 🖎 🕇 🖎 🖎

★ **DAYS INN.** *221 NE Chkalov Dr (98684).* 360/256-7044; fax 360/256-1231; toll-free 800/426-5110. www.daysinn.com. 117 rms, 2 story. S $49; D $54; each addl $5; suites $79-$95; under 18 free. Crib free. Pet accepted; $10. TV; cable (premium). Indoor pool; whirlpool. Complimentary continental bkfst. Complimentary coffee in rms. Restaurant 6 am-10 pm. Ck-out noon. Meeting rms. Business servs avail.Valet serv. Free airport transportation. Cr cds: A, DS, MC, V.
🔁 🏊 🔌 🔥 🐾

★ **FERRYMAN'S INN.** *7901 NE 6th Ave (98665).* 360/574-2151; fax 360/574-9644. 134 rms, 2 story, 9 kit. S $54-$65; D $63-$78; each addl $5; suites $65-$90.50; kit. units $65-$70; under 12 free. Crib $5. Pet accepted; $3. TV; cable (premium). Heated pool. Restaurant adj open 24 hrs. Ck-out noon. Meeting rms. Business servs avail. Cr cds: A, C, D, DS, JCB, MC, V.
D 🔁 🏊 🔌 🔥

★★ **HOLIDAY INN EXPRESS.** *9107 NE Vancouver Mall Dr (98662).* 360/253-5000; fax 360/253-3137; toll-free 800/465-4329. www.holiday-inn.com. 56 rms, 2 story. S $65-$75; D $70-$80; each addl $5; under 18 free; special events (2-3 day min). Crib avail. TV; cable (premium). Complimentary continental bkfst. Ck-out noon. Sundries. Indoor pool; whirlpool. Health club privileges. Cr cds: A, C, D, DS, ER, JCB, MC, V.
D 🏊 🔌 🔥 SC

★★ **RED LION HOTEL.** *100 Columbia St (98660).* 360/694-8341; fax 360/694-2023; toll-free 800/222-8733. www.redlion.com. 160 rms, 2-3 story. S $79-$89; D $89-$99; suites $185-$339; under 18 free; wkend rates. Crib free. Pet accepted; $20. TV; cable. Heated pool. Coffee in rms. Restaurant 6 am-10 pm. Bar 11-2 am; entertainment Tues-Sun. Ck-out noon. Meeting rms. Business servs avail. In-rm modem link. Bellhops. Valet serv. Free airport transportation. Health club privileges. Some private patios, balconies. Overlooks river. Cr cds: A, C, D, DS, ER, JCB, MC, V.
D 🔁 🏊 ✈ 🔌 🔥

★★ **SHILO INN.** *13206 NE Hwy 99 (98686);* res 800/222-2244. 360/573-0511; fax 360/573-0396. www.shiloinns.com. 66 rms, 2 story, 6 kits. S, D $49.95-$109.95; each addl $10; kit. units $69-$99; under 13 free. Crib free. Pet accepted; $10. TV; cable (premium). Indoor pool; whirlpool. Complimentary continental bkfst. Restaurant adj 11:30 am-10:30 pm. Bar. Ck-out noon. Coin lndry. Meeting rms. Business servs avail. Sauna, steam rm. Health club privileges. Refrigerators. Cr cds: A, D, DS, JCB, MC, V.
D 🔁 🏊 🔌 🔥 🐾

Resort

★★★ **THE HEATHMAN LODGE.** *7801 NE Greenwood Dr (98662).* 360/254-3100; fax 360/254-6100; res 888/475-3100. www.heathmanlodge.com. 143 rms, 4 story, 22 suites. S, D $119; suites $159-$550; family rates. Crib free. TV; cable (premium), VCR avail. Complimentary coffee in rms. Restaurant 7 am-10 pm. Bar to 11 pm; pianist wkends. Ck-out noon. Meeting rms. Business center. In-rm modem link. Concierge. Gift shop. Lndry servs. Exercise equipt; sauna. Indoor pool; whirlpool. Bathrm phones, refrigerators, microwaves; some in-rm whirlpools, fireplaces in suites. Many balconies. Cr cds: A, C, D, DS, JCB, MC, V.
D 🏊 ✈ 🔌 🔥 🐾 ✦

Walla Walla

(E-7) *See also Dayton (Columbia County)*

Founded 1859 **Pop** 26,478 **Elev** 949 ft
Area code 509 **Zip** 99362

Information Chamber of Commerce, 29 E Sumach, PO Box 644; 509/525-0850 or 877/998-4748

Web www.wwchamber.com

Walla Walla Valley was first the site of a Native American trail and then an avenue for exploration and settlement of the West. Lewis and Clark passed through the area in 1805. Fur traders followed and Fort Walla

Walla was established in 1818 as a trading post at the point where the Walla Walla and Columbia rivers meet. One of the key figures in the area's history was Dr. Marcus Whitman, a medical missionary, who in 1836 founded the first settler's home in the Northwest—a mission seven miles west of present-day Walla Walla. The Whitmans were killed by Native Americans in 1847. No successful settlement was made until after the Indian Wars of 1855-1858.

In 1859 the city became the seat of Walla Walla County, which then included half of present-day Washington, all of Idaho, and ¼ of Montana. It also had the first railroad in the Northwest, first bank in the state, first meat market and packing plant, and first institution of higher learning.

Walla Walla means "many waters," but local enthusiasts will tell you this is "the city they liked so much they named it twice." Agriculture is the major industry, with wheat the most important crop and green peas the second. Industries concentrate chiefly on food processing. The Walla Walla onion is known nationwide for its sweetness; a festival is held each July to honor the important crop. A Ranger District office of the Umatilla National Forest (see CLARKSTON, also see PENDLETON, OR) is located here.

What to See and Do

Fort Walla Walla Park. Camping (dump station; fee). (Apr-Sept, daily; limited facilities rest of yr) Dalles Military Rd. 1 mi W of WA 125, W edge of town. Phone 509/527-3770. Also in park is Audubon Society Nature Walk, outdoor amphitheater, andflfl

Fort Walla Walla Museum Complex. Fourteen original and replica buildings from mid-1800s. Schoolhouse, homestead cabin, railroad depot, blockhouse, doctor's office, blacksmith shop; largest horse-era agricultural museum in the West. Tours (Apr-Oct, by appt). Complex (Apr-Oct, Tues-Sun). Phone 509/525-7703.

Pioneer Park. A 58-acre park with horticultural displays, exotic game bird display, playground, tennis courts, picnicking. Division and Alder sts. Phone 509/527-4527. **FREE**

Whitman Mission National Historic Site. The memorial shaft, erected in 1897, overlooks the site of the mission established by Dr. Marcus and Narcissa Whitman in 1836. A self-guided trail with audio stations leads to mission grounds, Old Oregon Trail, memorial shaft, and grave. Visitor center, museum; cultural demonstrations (summer, wkends). (Daily; closed some hols) 7 mi W on US 12, then ¾ mi S. Phone 509/522-6360.

Motels/Motor Lodges

★ **HOWARD JOHNSON EXPRESS INN.** *325 E Main (99362). 509/529-4360; fax 509/529-7463; res 800/446-4656. www.hojo.com.* 85 rms, 2 story. S, D $78-$128; under 18 free. Crib free. Pet accepted. TV; cable (premium). Pool; whirlpool. Complimentary continental bkfst. Coffee in rms. Ck-out noon. Free lndry facilities. Meeting rms. Business servs avail. In-rm modem link. Exercise equipt; sauna. Some refrigerators. Some private patios, balconies. Cr cds: A, D, DS, MC, V.

★ **TRAVELODGE.** *421 E Main St (99362). 509/529-4940; fax 509/529-4943; res 800/578-7878. www.travelodge.com.* 39 rms, 2 story. S $47; D $53-$58; each addl $5; under 17 free. Crib free. TV; cable (premium). Pool; whirlpool. Coffee in rms. Restaurant nearby. Ck-out noon. Business servs avail. Refrigerators. Cr cds: A, C, D, DS, ER, MC, V.

B&B/Small Inn

★★ **GREEN GABLES INN.** *922 Bonsella St (99362). 509/525-5501; res 888/525-5501. www.greengablesinn. com.* 5 rms, 1 guest house. No rm phones. S, D $105-$135; guest house $135; each addl $35; higher rates special events. Children over 12 yrs only. Crib free. TV; cable, VCR avail. Complimentary full bkfst. Ck-out 11 am, ck-in 3 pm. In-rm modem link. Lawn games. Refrigerators. Some balconies. Picnic tables. Built in 1909; period antiques. Cr cds: A, DS, MC, V.

Restaurant

★ **RED APPLE.** *57 E Main St (99362). 509/525-5113.* Open 24 hrs. Bar. Bkfst $1.95-$6.95, lunch $3.50-$6.95, dinner $5.95-$12.95. Specializes in steak, seafood. Salad bar. Entertainment Fri-Sun. Parking.

Wenatchee

(C-5) See also Cashmere, Leavenworth

Founded 1888 **Pop** 21,756 **Elev** 727 ft
Area code 509

Information Wenatchee Chamber of Commerce, 300 S Columbia, PO Box 850, 98807; 509/662-2116 or 800/572-7753

Web www.wenatchee.org

The apple blossoms in the spring and the sturdy red of the grown fruit in the fall are the symbols of this community. Nestled among the towering mountains are fertile, irrigated valleys where residents care for the orchards. Cherries, pears, peaches, and apricots are also grown here. With the establishment in 1952 of a huge aluminum smelter and casting plant, Wenatchee no longer has an economy based only on agriculture. The headquarters of the Wenatchee National Forest is located here.

What to See and Do

North Central Washington Museum. Cultural Center; restored, operational 1919 Wurlitzer pipe organ; Great Northern Railway model; fine art gallery; apple industry exhibit; first trans-Pacific flight (Japan to Wenatchee) exhibit; archaeological and Native American exhibits. (Feb-Dec, daily; rest of yr, Mon-Fri; closed hols) 127 S Mission St. Phone 509/664-3340. ¢¢

Rocky Reach Dam. Visitors Center with underwater fish viewing gallery; theater. Powerhouse has Gallery of the Columbia and Gallery of Electricity; changing art exhibits. Landscaped grounds; picnic and play areas. (Daily; closed Dec 25; also Jan-mid-Feb) On Columbia River. 7 mi N on US 97A. Phone 509/663-7522. **FREE**

Skiing. Mission Ridge Ski Area. Four double chairlifts, two rope tows; patrol, school, rentals; snowmaking; cafeteria; child care. Vertical drop 2,200 ft. (Dec-mid-Apr) Half-day rates. Limited x-country trails. 7500 Mission Ridge Rd. Phone 509/663-6543. ¢¢¢¢

Squilchuck State Park. This 287-acre park offers day use and group camping. (Mar-Nov) Standard fees. 9 mi SW on Squilchuck Rd. Phone 509/664-6373.

Wenatchee National Forest. Approx two million forested, mountainous acres lying west of Columbia River. Trail system leads to jagged peaks, mountain meadows, sparkling lakes. Fishing; hunting, picnicking, winter sports (also see LEAVENWORTH), many developed campsites (some fees). Forest map avail (fee). North, south, and west of town. Contact Supervisor, 215 Melody Ln, 98801-5933. Phone 509/662-4335.

Special Event

Washington State Apple Blossom Festival. Parades, carnival, arts and crafts, musical productions; "Ridge to River Relay." Phone 509/662-3616. Last wkend Apr-first wkend May.

Motels/Motor Lodges

★★ **HOLIDAY LODGE.** *610 N Wenatchee (98801). 509/663-8167; toll-free 800/722-0852.* 59 rms, 2 story. S $40-$60; D $42-$60; each addl $5; under 12 free; higher rates: Apple Blossom season, some hols. Crib $5. Pet accepted, some restrictions. TV; cable (premium), VCR avail. Heated pool; whirlpool. Complimentary continental bkfst. Restaurant nearby. Ck-out noon. Coin lndry. Business servs avail. Exercise equipt; sauna. Some refrigerators, microwaves. Cr cds: A, C, D, DS, MC, V.

★★ **MICKEY O'REILLEY'S INN AT THE RIVER.** *580 Valley Mall Pkwy, East Wenatchee (98802). 509/884-1474; fax 509/884-9179; toll-free*

800/922-3199. www.mickeyoreillys.
com. 55 rms, 2 story. S, D $57-$82;
each addl $5; under 12 free. Crib
free. TV; cable. Heated pool; whirlpool. Complimentary continental
bkfst. Restaurant 11 am-10 pm. Bar
11-2 am. Ck-out 11 am. Business
servs avail. Some refrigerators, microwaves. Some balconies. View of
mountains. Cr cds: A, DS, MC, V.

★ **ORCHARD INN.** 1401 N Miller St
(98801). 509/662-3443; fax 509/665-
0715; res 800/368-4571. 103 rms, 3
story. May-Aug: S $50-$55; D $55-
$65; each addl $5; suites $70-$75;
under 13 free; package plans; higher
rates special events; lower rates rest
of yr. Crib free. Pet accepted; some
restrictions. TV; cable (premium).
Complimentary coffee in lobby.
Restaurant opp open 24 hrs. Ck-out
11 am. Meeting rms. Business servs
avail. Sundries. Downhill ski 12 mi;
x-country ski 10 mi. Pool; whirlpool.
Some refrigerators, microwaves. Picnic tables. Cr cds: A, DS, MC, V.

★★ **RED LION HOTEL
WENATCHEE.** 1225 N Wenatchee
Ave (98801). 509/663-0711; fax
509/662-8175; res 800/222-8733.
www.redlion.com. 149 rms, 3 story. S
$79-$84; D $89-$99; each addl $10;
under 18 free; wkend rates. Crib free.
Pet accepted. TV; cable. Heated pool;
whirlpool, poolside serv. Coffee in
rms. Restaurant 6 am-10 pm. Bar
noon-2 am; entertainment Mon-Sat.
Ck-out noon. Meeting rms. Business
servs avail. In-rm modem link. Sundries. Free airport, bus depot transportation. Exercise equipt. Balconies.
Cr cds: A, C, D, DS, ER, JCB, MC, V.

★ **TRAVELODGE.** 1004 N Wenatchee
Ave (98801). 509/662-8165; res
888/515-6375. www.travelodge.com. 49
rms, 2 story. May-Oct: S $59; D $79;
under 18 free; package plans; higher
rates special events; lower rates rest
of yr. Crib free. TV; cable, VCR avail
(movies). Complimentary continental bkfst. Complimentary coffee in
rms. Restaurant adj open 24 hrs. Ck-
out 11 am. Business servs avail. Sundries. Coin lndry. Downhill ski 12
mi. Pool; whirlpool. Some refrigera-

tors, microwaves. Cr cds: A, C, D, DS,
ER, JCB, MC, V.

Hotel

★★ **WESTCOAST WENATCHEE
CENTER.** 201 N Wenatchee Ave
(98801). 509/662-1234; fax 509/662-
0782; res 800/426-0670. www.
westcoasthotels.com. 147 rms, 9 story.
S $87-$99; D $95-$104; each addl
$10; suites $135-$200; under 18 free;
ski rates; higher rates Apple Blossom
Festival. Crib free. Pet accepted; $50
deposit. TV. Indoor/outdoor pool;
whirlpool, poolside serv. Coffee in
rms. Restaurant 6:30 am-9 pm. Bar
11-2 am; entertainment Wed-Sat. Ck-
out noon. Guest lndry. Meeting rms.
Business servs avail. Free airport, RR
station, bus depot transportation.
Downhill ski 12 mi. Exercise equipt.
Some refrigerators. Cr cds: A, D, DS,
MC, V.

Westport

(D-1) See also Aberdeen, Hoquiam,
Ocean Shores

Settled 1858 **Pop** 1,892 **Elev** 12 ft
Area code 360 **Zip** 98595

Information Westport-Grayland
Chamber of Commerce, 2985 S Mon-
tesano St, PO Box 306, 98595-0306;
360/268-9422 or 800/345-6223

Near the tip of a sandy strip of land
separating Grays Harbor from the
Pacific, Westport is home to probably
the largest sports fishing fleet in the
Northwest. Pleasure and charter
boats take novice and experienced
anglers alike across Grays Harbor Bay
into the Pacific for salmon fishing in
the summer and deep-sea fishing
nearly all year. In the winter, commercial fleets set their pots for crab
and have their catch processed at
one of Westport's large canneries.
Whale-watching excursions operate
from March to May.

What to See and Do

Grays Harbor Lighthouse. (1900) Tallest lighthouse on West Coast (107 ft). Ocean Ave.

Maritime Museum. Shipwreck and Coast Guard memorabilia; also on grounds are Coast Guard vessel *U/B 41332* and Whale Display House. (June-Sept, Wed-Sun afternoons, also hols) 2201 Westhaven Dr. Phone 360/268-0078. **Donation**

Twin Harbors State Park. More than 150 acres. Surf fishing, clamming, whale-watching; hiking, picnicking, camping (hookups; res advised Memorial Day-Labor Day). Ocean swimming permitted, but hazardous. Standard fees. 3 mi S on WA 105. Phone 360/268-9717.

Westport Aquarium. Large tank aquariums, performing seals. (Feb-Oct, daily; Nov, wkends; closed hols) 321 Harbor St. Phone 360/268-0471. ¢¢

Winthrop

(B-5) *See also Omak*

Pop 302 **Elev** 1,760 ft **Area code** 509 **Zip** 98862

Information Chamber of Commerce, Information Office, 202 Hwy 20, PO Box 39; 509/996-2125 or 888/463-8469

Web www.winthropwashington.com

Redesigning the entire town on an Old West theme has transformed it into the "Old Western town of Winthrop," complete with annual events in the same vein.

Fifty-five miles west on the North Cascades Highway (WA 20) is North Cascades National Park (see SEDRO WOOLLEY). A Ranger District office of the Okanogan National Forest (see OMAK) is located here.

What to See and Do

Shafer Museum. Log house built by town founder, Guy Waring (1897). Incl early farming and mining implements. (Memorial Day-Sept, daily) Castle Ave. Phone 509/996-2712. **FREE**

Motel/Motor Lodge

★ **THE WINTHROP INN.** *960 Hwy 20 (98862). 509/996-2217; fax 509/996-3923; res 800/444-1972. www.winthropinn.com.* 30 rms, 2 story. May-Oct: S $50-$75; D $55-$75; each addl $5; under 12 free; higher rates hols; lower rates rest of yr. Crib free. Pet accepted, some restrictions; $7. TV. Pool; whirlpool. Complimentary coffee in lobby. Restaurant nearby. Ck-out 11 am. Business servs avail. In-rm modem link. Downhill ski 15 mi; x-country ski on site. Picnic tables. Refrigerators, microwaves. Private patios, balconies. Cr cds: A, DS, MC, V.

⬛⬛⬛⬛⬛

Resort

★★★ **SUN MOUNTAIN LODGE.** *Patterson Lake Rd (98862). 509/996-2211; fax 509/996-3133; toll-free 800/572-0493. www.sunmountain lodge.com.* 102 rms, 2-3 story, 13 kit. cottages. Mid-June-mid-Oct: S, D $175-$230; each addl $20; suites $290-$610; kit. cottages $155-$205; under 13 free; higher rates: wkends (2-night min) and hols (3-night min); lower rates rest of yr. Crib free. 2 pools; whirlpool, poolside serv. Playground. Supervised children activities (July-Labor Day); ages 5-10. Complimentary coffee in rms. Restaurant (see also THE DINING ROOM). Rm serv 7 am-10 pm. Bar. Ck-out noon, ck-in 4:00 pm. Meeting rms. Business servs avail. Concierge. Gift shop. Tennis. X-country ski on site. Exercise equipt. Spa. Rec rm. Lawn games. Stables. Hiking, bicycle trails. Refrigerators in rms. Balconies. Picnic tables. Cr cds: A, D, MC, V.

⬛⬛⬛⬛⬛⬛⬛⬛⬛⬛

Restaurant

★★★ **THE DINING ROOM.** *Patterson Lake Rd (98862). 509/996-2211. www.sunmountainlodge.com.* Hrs: 7:30 am-8:30 pm; Fri, Sat to 9 pm. Res accepted. Wine list. Bar from 2 pm. Bkfst $4, lunch $6.50-$12, dinner $15-$32. Child's meals. Specialties:

wild mushroom strudel, tenderloin mignon. Cr cds: A, D, MC, V.

Yakima

(D-5) *See also Ellensburg, Toppenish*

Settled 1861 **Pop** 54,827 **Elev** 1,068 ft
Area code 509
Information Yakima Valley Visitors & Convention Bureau, 10 N 9th St, 98901; 509/248-2021
Web www.yakima.org

Yakima (YAK-e-ma) County ranks first in the United States in production of apples, hops, sweet cherries, and winter pears. Irrigation was started as early as 1875, when early settlers dug crude canals. Orchards and farms replaced sagebrush and desert. The city takes its name from the Yakama Nation, whose reservation lies to the south. There are about 300 days of sunshine annually, with an average yearly rainfall of eight inches.

What to See and Do

Ahtanum Mission. Founded in 1852, destroyed in Yakama Native American Wars, rebuilt in 1867; site of oldest irrigated apple orchards in valley (1872). 9 mi SW on unnumbered roads.

Historic North Front Street. Called "birthplace of Yakima" this two-block section of downtown has restaurants and shopping.

Painted Rocks. Historic Yakima Nation pictographs. 7 mi NW on US 12.

Skiing. White Pass Village. 55 mi NW on US 12, in Mt Baker-Snoqualmie National Forest. (See MOUNT RAINIER NATIONAL PARK)

Yakima Interurban Trolley Lines. Trolley cars make trips around city and surrounding countryside. Boarding at car barns at 3rd Ave and W Pine St. (May-mid-Oct wkends; also evening rides July, Aug) 307 W Pine St. Phone 509/575-1700. ¢¢

Yakima Sportsman State Park. Approx 250 acres. Picnicking, camping (hookups). Standard fees. 3 mi E on WA 24, Keyes Rd. Phone 509/575-2774.

Yakima Valley Museum. Exhibits relating to history of Yakima valley; Yakima Nation; fruit industry. Collection of horse-drawn vehicles. (Tues-Sun; closed hols) 2105 Tieton Dr, in Franklin Park. Phone 509/248-0747. ¢¢

Special Events

Chocolate Fantasy. Chocolate manufacturers from across the nation showcase candy, cookies, and pies; sampling, "chocolate bingo." Mid-Mar. Phone 509/575-6062.

Spring Barrel Tasting. Area wineries participate. Last wkend Apr. Phone 800/258-7270.

Central Washington State Fair and Rodeo. Fairgrounds. Phone 509/248-7160. Late Sept-early Oct.

Yakima Meadows Racetrack. Fairgrounds. Thoroughbred racing. Pari-mutuel wagering. For schedule phone 509/248-7160.

Fruit orchards of Yakima

Motels/Motor Lodges

★★ **DOUBLETREE HOTEL YAKIMA.** *1507 N First St (98901). 509/248-7850; fax 509/575-1694; res 800/222-8733. www.doubletreehotels.com.* 208 rms, 2 story. S, D $69-$94; each addl $10; suites $135-$300; under 18 free. Crib free. Pet accepted. TV; cable. 2 heated pools; whirlpool, poolside serv. Coffee in rms. Restaurant 6 am-11 pm. Bar; entertainment Thurs-Sat. Ck-out noon. Meeting rms. Business servs avail. Bellhops. Valet serv. Sundries. Exercise equipt. Some bathrm phones, refrigerators. Private patios, balconies. Cr cds: A, D, DS, MC, V.

D ◆ ≈ 大 ✕ ⬚ 🐾 SC

★★ **OXFORD INN.** *1603 E Yakima Ave (98901). 509/457-4444; fax 509/453-7593. www.oxfordsuites.com.* 96 rms, 4 story, 6 kits. S $59; D $65-$71; each addl $8; under 12 free; kit. units $69-$75. Crib free. TV; cable, VCR avail. Heated pool; whirlpool. Complementary continental bkfst. Bar 11-2 am. Ck-out noon. Coin lndry. Meeting rms. In-rm modem link. Sundries. Many refrigerators. Private patios, balconies. View of river. Cr cds: A, C, D, DS, ER, MC, V.

D ≈ ⬚ 🐾 SC

★ **QUALITY INN OF YAKIMA.** *12 E Valley Mall Blvd (98903). 509/248-6924; fax 509/575-8470; res 800/228-5151. www.qualityinn.com.* 86 rms, 2 story. S $59-$64; D $69-$74; each addl $10; under 18 free. Pet accepted; $10. TV; cable. Heated pool. Complimentary continental bkfst. Restaurant adj open 24 hrs. Ck-out 11 am. Business servs avail. Some refrigerators. Sun deck. Cr cds: A, D, DS, MC, V.

D ◆ ≈ ⬚ 🐾

★★ **WESTCOAST YAKIMA CENTER HOTEL.** *607 E Yakima Ave (98901). 509/248-5900; fax 509/575-8975; res 800/325-4000. www. westcoasthotels.com.* 153 rms, 2 story. June-Oct: S $92-$97; D $102-$107; suites $150-$200; each addl $10; under 12 free; lower rates rest of yr. Crib free. Pet accepted; $10. TV; cable (premium). 2 pools; poolside serv. Coffee in rms. Restaurant 6:30 am-10 pm. Bar 11-2 am; entertainment. Ck-out noon. Meeting rms. Business center. In-rm modem link. Valet serv. Sundries. Airport, bus depot transportation. Health club privileges. Some refrigerators. Private patios, balconies. Cr cds: A, D, DS, MC, V.

D ◆ ≈ ⬚ 大

★★ **WESTCOAST YAKIMA GATEWAY HOTEL.** *9 N 9th St (98901). 509/452-6511; fax 509/457-4931; res 800/325-4000. www.westcoasthotels. com.* 171 rms, 2-3 story, 8 kits. S $65-$75; D $75-$85; each addl $10; suites $120-$200; under 13 free. Crib free. Pet accepted. TV; cable (premium), VCR avail. Heated pool; poolside serv. Coffee in rms. Restaurant 6:30 am-9 pm. Bar. Ck-out noon. Coin lndry. Meeting rms. Business servs avail. In-rm modem link. Free airport transportation. Some refrigerators. Some private patios, balconies. Cr cds: A, D, DS, MC, V.

D ◆ ≈ ⬚ 🐾

Restaurant

★★ **DELI DE PASTA.** *7 N Front St (98901). 509/453-0571.* Hrs: 11:30 am-8:30 pm; Fri, Sat to 9:30 pm. Closed hols. Res accepted. Italian menu. Wine, beer. Lunch $5.95-$12.95, dinner $10.95-$21.95. Specializes in seafood, steak, gourmet pasta dishes. Outdoor dining. Small, intimate dining area. Totally nonsmoking. Cr cds: A, MC, V.

D

WYOMING

From the high western plateaus of the Great Plains, the state of Wyoming stretches across the Continental Divide and into the Rocky Mountains. This is a land of scenic beauty and geographic diversity; mountain ranges, grasslands, and desert can all be found within Wyoming's borders.

The first Europeans to explore this region were French; brothers Louis and Francés François Verendrye trapped here in 1743. The first American to enter what is now Yellowstone National Park was John Colter, a member of the Lewis and Clark expedition, who was here during the winter of 1807-1808. The 1820s saw a number of trappers and fur traders become established in the area. The territory became the site of important stops along the pioneer trails to the West Coast in the 1840s-1860s.

The pioneer trails across Wyoming allowed pioneers to cross the rugged spine of the Rocky Mountains on an easy grade, following grass and water over the Continental Divide. Of the approximately 350,000 individuals who made their way along the various westward trails, some 21,000 died en route, claimed by disease, accidents, and mountain snow. After 1847 thousands of Mormons came along the Mormon Trail to join Brigham Young's settlement at Salt Lake. The situation improved dramatically for those bound for the West when the Union Pacific Railroad pushed across Wyoming during 1867-1869. The "iron horse" made the journey considerably safer and easier, not to mention faster. Permanent settlement of the West then began in earnest.

The hard existence wrought from a sometimes inhospitable land bred a tough, practical people who recognized merit when they saw it. While still a territory, Wyoming in 1869 became the first area in the United States to grant women the right to vote. Subsequently, Wyomingites were the first in the nation to appoint a woman justice of the peace, the first to select women jurors, and the first to elect a woman, Nellie Tayloe Ross in 1924, governor. This reputation has earned Wyoming the nickname "the equality state."

The civic-mindedness of its

Population: 453,588
Area: 96,988 square miles
Elevation: 3,100-13,804 feet
Peak: Gannett Peak (between Fremont and Sublette Counties)
Entered Union: July 10, 1890 (44th state)
Capital: Cheyenne
Motto: Equal Rights
Nickname: Equality State, Cowboy State
Flower: Indian Paintbrush
Bird: Meadowlark
Tree: Cottonwood
Fair: August 9-16, 2003, in Douglas
Time Zone: Mountain
Website: www.state.wy.us

Old Faithful Geyser

citizens spread beyond the political arena with equal vigor. Wyoming introduced the nation's first county library system and instituted a public education system that today ranks among the finest in the United States.

Cattle and sheep outnumber people by more than five to one in Wyoming, which is the least populated state in the country. It is, therefore, easy to see how the cowboy has become such a prominent symbol here. The "bucking horse" insignia has appeared on Wyoming license plates since 1936. It also appears in various versions on road signs, storefronts, and newspapers.

Mineral extraction is the principal industry in Wyoming, which has the largest coal resources in the country. Tourism and recreation ranks second, with approximately four million visitors per year entering the state. Generally, they come to visit the numerous national parks, forests, and monuments. But Wyoming offers a wide range of attractions, from abundant camping to rustic guest ranching, all set among some of the finest natural beauty to be found in the nation.

The country's first national park (Yellowstone), first national monument (Devils Tower), and first national forest (Shoshone) are all located in Wyoming.

When to Go/Climate

Wyoming's climate is relatively cool and dry, though spring can be wet in the lower elevations and winter actually can be dangerous. Blizzards are frequent and have been known to arise from November through June. Temperatures can vary greatly on any given day in both spring and fall.

AVERAGE HIGH/LOW TEMPERATURES (°F)

CHEYENNE

Jan 38/15	May 65/39	Sept 71/44
Feb 41/18	June 74/48	Oct 60/34
Mar 45/22	July 82/55	Nov 47/24
Apr 55/30	Aug 80/53	Dec 39/17

LANDER

Jan 31/8	May 66/40	Sept 72/44
Feb 37/14	June 77/49	Oct 60/34
Mar 46/22	July 86/56	Nov 43/20
Apr 56/31	Aug 84/54	Dec 32/9

Parks and Recreation Finder

Directions to and information about the parks and recreation areas below are given under their respective town/city sections. Please refer to those sections for details.

NATIONAL PARK AND RECREATION AREAS

Key to abbreviations. I.H.S. = International Historic Site; I.P.M. = International Peace Memorial; N.B. = National Battlefield; N.B.P. = National Battlefield Park; N.B.C. = National Battlefield and Cemetery; N.C.A. = National Conservation Area; N.E.M. = National Expansion Memorial; N.F. = National Forest; N.G. = National Grassland; N.H.P. = National Historical Park; N.H.C. = National Heritage Corridor; N.H.S. = National Historic Site; N.L. = National Lakeshore; N.M. = National Monument; N.M.P. = National Military Park; N.Mem. = National Memorial; N.P. = National Park; N.Pres. = National Preserve; N.R.A. = National Recreational Area; N.R.R. = National Recreational River; N.Riv. = National River; N.S. = National Seashore; N.S.R. = National Scenic Riverway; N.S.T. = National Scenic Trail; N.Sc. = National Scientific Reserve; N.V.M. = National Volcanic Monument.

CALENDAR HIGHLIGHTS

JUNE

Plains Indian PowWow (Cody). People from tribes throughout the western plains states and Canada gather to compete. Dancing and singing; ceremonial and traditional tribal dress.

JULY

Legend of Rawhide (Lusk). Live show performed since 1946. Concert, dances, trade show, golf tournament, gun show, parade, pancake breakfast.

1838 Mountain Man Rendezvous (Riverton). Council fire, primitive shoots, hawk and knife throw, games, food. Camping available. Phone 307/856-7306.

Central Wyoming Fair and Rodeo (Casper). Fairgrounds. Phone 307/235-5775.

Red Desert Round-Up (Rock Springs). One of the largest rodeos in the Rocky Mountains region.

Cheyenne Frontier Days (Cheyenne). Frontier Park arena. One of the country's most famous rodeos; originated in 1897. Parades, carnivals; USAF *Thunderbirds* flying team; pancake breakfast; entertainment, square dancing nightly.

AUGUST

Gift of the Waters Pageant (Thermopolis). Hot Springs State Park. Commemorates the deeding of the world's largest mineral hot springs from the Shoshone and Arapahoe to the people of Wyoming in 1896. Pageant features Native American dances, parade, buffalo barbecue.

SEPTEMBER

Jackson Hole Fall Arts Festival (Jackson). Three-week celebration of the arts featuring special exhibits in more than 30 galleries, demonstrations, special activities. Also dance, theater, mountain film festival, Native American arts, and culinary arts. Phone 307/733-3316.

Place Name	Listed Under
Bighorn Canyon N.R.A.	LOVELL
Bighorn N.F.	SHERIDAN
Bridger-Teton N.F.	JACKSON, PINEDALE
Devils Tower N.M.	same
Flaming Gorge N.R.A.	GREEN RIVER
Fort Laramie N.H.S.	same
Fossil Butte N.M.	KEMMERER
Grand Teton N.P.	same
Medicine Bow N.F.	LARAMIE
Shoshone N.F.	CODY
Thunder Basin N.G.	DOUGLAS
Yellowstone N.P.	same

STATE PARK AND RECREATION AREAS

Key to abbreviations. I.P. = Interstate Park; S.A.P. = State Archaeological Park; S.B. = State Beach; S.C.A. = State Conservation Area; S.C.P. = State Conservation Park; S.Cp. = State Campground; S.F. = State Forest; S.G. = State Garden; S.H.A. = State Historic Area; S.H.P. = State Historic Park; S.H.S. = State Historic Site; S.M.P. = State Marine Park; S.N.A. = State Natural Area; S.P. = State Park; S.P.C. = State Public Campground; S.R. = State Reserve; S.R.A. = State Recreation

Area; S.Res. = State Reservoir; S.Res.P. = State Resort Park; S.R.P. = State Rustic Park.

Place Name	Listed Under
Boysen S.P.	THERMOPOLIS
Buffalo Bill S.P.	CODY
Curt Gowdy S.P.	CHEYENNE
Edness K Wilkins S.P.	CASPER
Glendo S.P.	WHEATLAND
Guernsey S.P.	same
Hot Springs S.P.	THERMOPOLIS
Keyhole S.P.	GILLETTE
Seminoe S.P.	RAWLINS
Sinks Canyon S.P.	LANDER

Water-related activities, hiking, various other sports, picnicking, and visitor centers, as well as camping, are available in many of these areas. State parks are open all year, but some facilities may be closed November-March. Entrance fee per vehicle $5 nonresident, $2 resident; nonresident annual entrance pass $40, overnight camping $12. Entrance fee for state historical sites, $2. Camping is limited to 14 days per site unless otherwise posted (no reservations); $9/vehicle/ night. Pets under control. Further information may be obtained from Wyoming State Parks and Historic Sites,122 W 25th, Herschler Building 1-E, Cheyenne 82002; phone 307/777-6323.

SKI AREAS

Place Name	Listed Under
Hogadon Ski Area	CASPER
Jackson Hole Ski Resort	JACKSON
Sleeping Giant Ski Area	CODY
Snow King Ski Resort	JACKSON
Snowy Range Ski Area	LARAMIE

FISHING AND HUNTING

For anglers there are 16,000 miles of fishing streams, 270,000 acres of fishing lakes, and 90 fish varieties, among which are 22 game fish. Throughout Wyoming pronghorn antelope, moose, elk, black bear, whitetail and mule deer, and bighorn sheep roam the mountain ranges and meadows, which are open to hunters.

Nonresident hunting and fishing license for one elk and one season of fishing: $410. Nonresident deer permit: $220; bighorn sheep permit (one male): $1,510; moose permit (one bull): $1,010; bird license: $50; turkey: $50; small game (cottontail) license: $50; (one-day, $15); nonresident fishing license: annual $65 (one-day, $10). Most hunting licenses must be applied for well in advance of the hunting season and are issued via computer drawing. January 31 is the deadline for elk applications, February 28 for bighorn sheep and moose, March 15 for deer and antelope. Persons missing date may apply for any leftover licenses. All license holders except for those purchasing a one-day or five-day fishing license must purchase a conservation stamp for $10 before hunting or fishing; one-time fee/person/year.

Visitors may take a self-guided tour of the visitor center in the headquarters office building, 5400 Bishop Blvd, Cheyenne.

Further information can be obtained from the State of Wyoming Game and Fish Department, 5400 Bishop Blvd, Cheyenne 82006; phone 307/777-4600.

Driving Information

Safety belts are mandatory for all persons in front seat of vehicle. Children under three years or under 40 pounds in weight must be in an approved safety seat. For further information phone 307/772-0824.

INTERSTATE HIGHWAY SYSTEM

The following alphabetical listing of Wyoming towns in *Mobil Travel Guide* shows that these cities are within ten miles of the indicated Interstate highways. A highway map, however, should be checked for the nearest exit.

Highway Number	Cities/Towns within ten miles
Interstate 25	Buffalo, Casper, Cheyenne, Douglas, Sheridan, Wheatland.
Interstate 80	Cheyenne, Evanston, Green River, Laramie, Rawlins, Rock Springs.
Interstate 90	Buffalo, Gillette, Sheridan.

Additional Visitor Information

Detailed visitor information is distributed by Wyoming Business Council Tourism Division, I-25 at College Dr, Cheyenne 82002; 307/777-7777 or 800/225-5996. There are several welcome centers in Wyoming; visitors will find the information provided at these stops most helpful in planning their stay in the state. Their locations are as follows: in the northern central part of Wyoming, N on I-90 in Sheridan; at the lower eastern corner, on I-25, S of I-80 in Cheyenne; on the western side, near Grand Teton National Park, on US 89 in Jackson; and in central Wyoming in Casper on Center St, S of I-25 (Mon-Fri); I-80 E at exit 6 in Evanston; I-80, 10 mi E of Laramie (late May-mid-October); on I-90 in Sundance (late May-mid-October).

DRIVING THE OLD OREGON TRAIL

Between 1843 and 1860, an estimated 53,000 pioneers trekked across the North American continent on the Oregon Trail. This resolute group journeyed up the North Platte River and across Wyoming's Great Divide Basin before crossing the Continental Divide at South Pass, from whence they followed the Snake and Columbia rivers to Oregon. Modern highways parallel the Oregon Trail much of the distance across the state, and many of the same landmarks greet today's travelers.

Begin the tour on Highway 26 near Torrington. Fort Laramie was constructed at the confluence of the North Platte and Laramie rivers, first as a fur trading post, then as a military fort to protect the influx of white settlers from the local Native Americans. Today, the many buildings of the original fort complex have been reconstructed by the national park service and serve as a fascinating reminder of frontier life. Thirteen buildings stand around a central parade ground, many filled with period artifacts. The Fort Laramie Museum and Visitor Center houses artifacts, uniforms, and weapons from the fort's heyday.

Just west of Fort Laramie on Highway 26 is Guernsey, where the Register Cliff State Historic Site preserves a sandstone bluff on which migrating pioneers left initials, dates, and other messages carved in stone. The pioneer graveyard near the site is testimony to the incredible hardships of this epic trek. Continue west on I-25 through Douglas, with a town center dominated by a statue of a jackalope, and then on to Glenrock.

Casper, Wyoming's largest city, didn't exist during Oregon Trail days, but the ford on the North Platte River made this a hub for the many trails that brought pioneers to the West. The Oregon, Mormon, Pony Express, California, and Pioneer trails all converged here. Fort Casper was established in 1855 by the army to protect migrating settlers from hostile Indians and over the years served as a military fort, Pony Express station, trading post, and stage stop. The fort was reconstructed during the 1930s by the Civilian Conservation Corps (CCC) according to the original floor plans. Today, the fort buildings serve as museums of the frontier West, complete with living history activities that demonstrate daily life in the 19th century. Also near Casper, the National Historic Trails Interpretive Center, a BLM facility that commemorates the pioneer trails that intersect at Casper.

From Casper, follow Highway 220 west. Independence Rock was named by pioneer William Sublette, who spent July 4, 1830, camped here. Independence Rock became a landmark for Oregon Trail pioneers, who knew that if they reached Independence Rock by July 4, they would get across the mountains to Oregon before snowfall. The pioneers also chiseled names and dates into the rock—among the names carved here are Jesuit missionary Father DeSmet and Mormon leader Brigham Young.

A few miles west of Independence Rock is another landmark of the Oregon Trail. Here the Sweetwater River carves a narrow chasm through a high rock outcrop. Called Devil's Gate, the cleft is nearly 400 feet high, but only 30 feet across at its base. Only the most foolhardy pioneers attempted to brave the raging river as it passed through Devil's Gate.

At Muddy Gap, follow Highway 287 west across a desolate desert basin. Roadside markers tell the harrowing story of Oregon Trail pioneers as they passed through this high-elevation wasteland. Follow Highway 28 south as it climbs steadily toward South Pass. Unlike many Rocky Mountain passes, South Pass is not a high mountain divide. Rather, it's a high desert plateau covered by sagebrush and short prairie grasses—ideal for Oregon Trail pioneers and their wagon trains.

As the road climbs up to the pass, it passes two historic gold rush ghost towns from the 1870s. Atlantic City, a near-ghost town, still boasts the Mercantile, a steakhouse and saloon that's been serving the locals for over a century. South Pass City preserves 39 acres of abandoned buildings from the days when gold rush fever brought thousands of residents to this lofty corner of Wyoming. **(APPROX 340 MI)**

THE BIG HORN MOUNTAIN SCENIC LOOP

This loop tour departs from Cody, a Wild West town if there ever was one, and travels east across the arid plains to the Big Horn Mountains. This fault-block range rises up precipitously to tower 13,000 feet above the neighboring rangeland. The route passes geological curiosities and sacred Native American sites before dropping back down to traverse the dramatic Big Horn Canyon on its way back to Cody.

Cody is named for Buffalo Bill Cody, the showman famous for his traveling Wild West Show. The town was established in 1895, and though he didn't help found it, Cody was brought in shortly thereafter to promote the town. As befits a showman's adoptive home, the town of Cody became a Wild West tourist destination overnight.

Be sure to visit the complex of downtown museums and galleries that comprise the Buffalo Bill Historical Center, particularly the Whitney Gallery of Western Art, which contains one of the world's foremost collections of 19th-century Western art. As you leave Cody's too-perfect Wild West town center, consider a detour to Old Trail Town, west of town off Highway 20. This open-air museum preserves a collection of 26 historic frontier structures in their authentic state. Included are the actual cabins lived in by the likes of Butch Cassidy, plus the saloons, schoolhouses, and ranch houses that represented everyday life for frontier pioneers.

Travel east of Cody on Highway 14, leaving behind the Yellowstone foothills to cross the increasingly barren ranchland of the Big Horn Basin. The gray, sparsely vegetated buttes and badlands that increasingly dominate the landscape are remnants of volcanic ash deposits from Yellowstone's ancient volcanoes. Dunes of ash built up here over millions of years; these are now mined for bentonite, a source material of cement.

Two things characterize this arid prairie: oil, made evident by the rise and fall of rigs scattered to the horizon, and dinosaurs. To get an idea of the plant and reptile Eden that once existed here, stop in Greybull (pronounced "Grable") to visit the Greybull Museum. For a small regional museum, this institution houses an impressive number of significant fossils, including a five-foot-diameter ammonite and the remnants of a cycad tree forest from 120 million years ago.

Eight miles east of Greybull, on the Red Gulch/Alkali National Back Country Byway, is another important paleontological destination. The Red Gulch Dinosaur Tracksite preserves hundreds of dinosaur tracks left in oozy ocean shoreline mud about 167 million years ago. These tracks were only discovered in 1997 and are, worldwide, some of the only known tracks from the Middle Jurassic Era.

East of the town of Shell, Highway 14 begins to climb up through a wonderland of red hoodoos—the result of iron-rich ash deposits—to the near-vertical face of the Big Horn Mountains. This unusual mountain range was formed by uplifts along vertical fault lines: One side of the fault line has been pushed up over two miles into the sky, whereas the other dropped into the Big Horn Basin. The road climbs steeply up the red cliffs, eventually passing through dense forests and—even in

midsummer—snowfields. Stop at the Shell Falls Viewpoint to gawk at Shell Creek as it tumbles into an extremely narrow canyon cut through limestone and granite.

The top of the Big Horns is a series of rolling mountain peaks flanked by vast alpine meadows, which in summer is spangled with wildflowers and tiny ponds of snowmelt. Watch for beaver dams in the coursing streambeds. Moose and elk are frequently seen in these high-country marshes.

At Burgess Junction, turn west onto Highway 14A. The road begins to drop back down the western face of the Big Horn range. Midway down the mountainside is a side road leading to the Medicine Wheel National Historic Landmark, a fascinating ritual site built by ancient Paleo-Indians. Perhaps dating back 10,000 years, this large ring of rocks with 28 radiating spokes aligned around a central hub is thought to be a Native American Stonehenge. Scientists believe the Medicine Wheel was used to make astronomical calculations and predictions. The Medicine Wheel is a one-mile hike from the parking area.

Continue the descent of the Big Horns, again reaching arid basin land. The road traverses the now-dammed Big Horn River in its awe-inspiring canyon. Turn north on Highway 37 to catch glimpses of the canyon—over 1,000 feet deep in places—threaded by the blue waters of the lake. To the north rise the Pryor Mountains, home to one of the West's last free-ranging herds of wild horses.

From Big Horn Canyon, return east along Highway 14A through Lovell and Powell to Cody. **(APPROX 200 MI)**

Afton

(D-1) *See also Alpine*

Pop 1,394 **Elev** 6,239 ft
Area code 307 **Zip** 83110
Information Chamber of Commerce,
PO Box 1097; 307/883-2759 or
800/426-8833
Web www.starvalleychamber.com

An arch across Main Street composed
of 3,000 elk horns marks the
entrance to the town of Afton. For
anglers and big-game hunters there
are outfitters and experienced guides
here who rarely send their clients
home empty-handed. Afton is
located in Star Valley, which is noted
for its dairy industry. A Ranger District office of the Bridger-Teton
National Forest (see JACKSON) is
located here.

What to See and Do

Bridger-Teton National Forest. (see
JACKSON).
Fishing. Excellent brown trout and
cutthroat trout fishing year-round on
Salt River (within 2½ mi).
Intermittent spring. Spring flows out
of mountain for about 18 min, then
stops completely for the same period.
The theory behind this phenomenon
is that a natural siphon exists from
an underground lake. Canyon suit-
able for hiking or horseback riding.
Horses, guides avail. 7 mi E up Swift
Creek Canyon.
Outfitting and Big Game Hunting.
Inquire at the Chamber of Com-
merce.

Motels/Motor Lodges

★★ **HI-COUNTRY INN.** *689 S
Washington (83110). 307/885-3856;
fax 307/885-9318; toll-free 866/299-
1727.* 30 rms. No A/C. S $45-$50; D
$50-$55; each addl $5. Crib free. Pet
accepted, some restrictions. TV;
cable. Heated pool; whirlpool. Complimentary coffee in lobby. Restaurant adj 6 am-10 pm. Ck-out 11 am.
X-country ski 12 mi. Cr cds: A, C, D,
DS, MC, V.

★ **MOUNTAIN INN MOTEL.** *83542
US Hwy 89 (83110). 307/886-3156;*
fax 307/885-3156; toll-free 800/682-
5356. 20 rms. No A/C. Mid-May-mid-
Oct: S, D $55-$80; each addl $5;
lower rates rest of yr. Crib $5. Pet
accepted, some restrictions; $5/day.
TV; cable (premium). Heated pool;
whirlpool. Sauna. Restaurant nearby.
Ck-out 11 am. Cr cds: A, C, D, DS,
MC, V.

Alpine

(D-1) *See also Afton, Jackson*

Pop 200 **Elev** 5,600 ft **Area code** 307
Zip 83128

The Palisades Reservoir, just south of
town, offers fishing, boating, and
tent and trailer camping.

Motels/Motor Lodges

★★ **BEST WESTERN FLYING SAD-
DLE LODGE.** *118878 Jct Hwy 89 &
26 (83128). 307/654-7561; fax
307/654-7563; toll-free 800/780-7234.
www.bestwestern.com.* 20 rms, 6 cottages. June-Oct: S, D $60-$150; each
addl $5. Closed rest of yr. Crib free.
TV; cable (premium), VCR avail (free
movies). Heated pool; whirlpools.
Restaurant 7-11 am, 5-10 pm. Serv
bar. Ck-out 11 am. Business servs
avail. Sundries. Tennis. Some in-rm
whirlpools, refrigerators. Western
decor. On Snake River. Cr cds: A, C,
D, DS, MC, V.

★ **ROYAL RESORT.** *Jct US 26 and 89
(83128). 307/654-7545; fax 307/654-
7546; toll-free 800/343-6755. www.
royal-resort.com.* 45 rms, 3 story. S, D
$39-$85; each addl $7; under 12 free.
Crib $10. Pet accepted. TV; cable
(premium); VCR avail (movies). Playground. Ck-out 11 am. Meeting rm.
Gift shop. X-country ski on site.
Whirlpool. Some refrigerators, minibars. Some balconies. Cr cds: A, D,
DS, MC, V.

Buffalo

(B-5) *See also Sheridan*

Founded 1884 **Pop** 3,302 **Elev** 4,640 ft **Area code** 307 **Zip** 82834
Information Chamber of Commerce, 55 N Main; 307/684-5544 or 800/227-5122
Web www.buffalowyo.com

Buffalo began as a trading center at the edge of Fort McKinney, one of the last of the old military posts. In 1892, trouble erupted here between big cattlemen and small ranchers with their allies, the nesters, in the Johnson County Cattle War. Several people were killed before Federal troops ended the conflict.

Located at the foot of the Big Horn Mountains, Buffalo attracts many tourists, hunters, and anglers; the economy is dependent on tourism, as well as lumber, minerals, and cattle. A Ranger District office of the Bighorn National Forest (see SHERIDAN) is located in Buffalo.

What to See and Do

Fort Phil Kearny Site. Cavalry post was the scene of a clash between Sioux, Arapahoe, Cheyenne, and US soldiers; site of Fetterman and Wagon Box battles; visitor center. (Mid-May-Sept, daily) 13 mi N on US 87. Phone 307/684-7629. ¢

Johnson County-Jim Gatchell Memorial Museum. Collection of Native American artifacts, local and regional history, pioneer equipment; natural history display. (April 15-Dec 23, hrs vary) 100 Fort St, adj to courthouse. Phone 307/684-9331. ¢¢

Special Event

Johnson County Fair and Rodeo. Features working cowhands; parade. Rodeo held last 3 days of fair. Phone 307/684-7357. 2nd wk Aug.

Motels/Motor Lodges

★ **CANYON MOTEL.** *997 Fort St (82834).* 307/684-2957; toll-free 800/231-0742. 18 rms, 3 kits. S $42, D $50; each addl $3; kit. units $50-$55. Crib free. Pet accepted. TV; cable. Complimentary coffee in rms. Restaurant nearby. Ck-out 11 am. Airport transportation. Picnic tables. Cr cds: A, DS, MC, V.
🐾 ⛷ 🐾 SC

★ **COMFORT INN.** *65 US 16 E (82834).* 307/684-9564; toll-free 800/228-5150. www.comfortinn.com. 41 rms, 2 story. Late June-mid-Aug: S, D $79.95-$94.95; each addl $5; under 18 free; lower rates rest of yr. Crib $5. Pet accepted, some restrictions. TV; cable (premium). Complimentary continental bkfst. Restaurant nearby. Ck-out 11 am. Whirlpool. Cr cds: A, C, D, DS, JCB, MC, V.
🐾 ⛷ 🐾

★★ **THE RANCH AT UCROSS.** *2673 US Hwy 14 E, Clearmont (82835).* 307/737-2281; fax 307/737-2211; toll-free 800/447-0194. www.blairhotels.com. 31 rms, 2 story. S, D $159; each addl $20; under 18 free. Pet accepted. Heated pool. Complimentary full bkfst. Restaurant 6:30-9 am, 11:30 am-1 pm, 7-9 pm. Bar 5-9 pm. Ck-out 1 pm. Meeting rm. Business servs avail. Bellhops. Sundries. Gift shop. Tennis. On creek. Cr cds: MC, V.
🐾 🐾 🐾 🐾 🐾 ⛷ 🐾

★ **WYOMING MOTEL.** *610 E Hart St (82834).* 307/684-5505; toll-free 800/666-5505. www.buffalowyoming.com/wyomotel/. 27 rms, 5 kit. June-Oct: S $24-$67; D $35-$88; each addl $8; kit. unit $60-$145; lower rates rest of yr. Pet accepted. TV; cable (premium). Heated pool; whirlpool. Restaurant adj 6 am-10:30 pm. Ck-out 11 am. Picnic tables. Cr cds: A, C, D, DS, MC, V.
🐾 ⛷ 🐾 🐾

Guest Ranch

★★★ **PARADISE.** *283 Hunter Creek Rd (82834).* 307/684-7876; fax 307/684-7380. www.paradiseranch.com. 18 kit. cabins. AP, July-Aug: S $1,650/wk; D $2,800/wk; each addl $1,400/wk; ages 6-12, $1,550/wk; under 6, $850/wk; lower rates June-Sept. Closed rest of yr. Crib free. Heated pool; whirlpool. Playground.

Free supervised child's activities. Complimentary coffee in cabins. Dining rm, sittings 7:30-8:30 am, 12:30 pm, 7 pm. Lunch rides. Cookouts. Bar 5-10 pm. Ck-out 10 am, ck-in 3 pm. Lndry facilities in most cabins. Package store 16 mi. Meeting rms. Free airport transportation. Lawn games. Entertainment. Fishing guides. Fireplaces. Private patios. Picnic tables.

D 🗢 🏕 🌊 🎿 🔥

Restaurant

★ **COLONEL BOZEMAN'S.** *675 E Hart St (82834). 307/684-5555.* Hrs: 11 am-10 pm. Closed Dec 25. Lunch $5.99-$10.99, dinner $9.99-$18.99. Child's meals. Specializes in pasta, steaks, Mexican dishes. Cr cds: A, D, MC, V.

D 🍴

Casper

(D-5) See also Douglas

Founded 1888 **Pop** 46,742 **Elev** 5,140 ft **Area code** 307

Information Chamber of Commerce Visitor Center, 500 N Center St, PO Box 399, 82602; 307/234-5311 or 800/852-1889

Web www.casperwyoming.org

Before oil was discovered, Casper was a railroad terminus in the cattle-rich Wyoming hinterlands, where Native Americans and emigrants on the Oregon Trail had passed before. Casper was known as an oil town after the first strike in 1890 in the Salt Creek Field, site of the Teapot Dome naval oil reserve that caused a top-level government scandal in the 1920s. World War I brought a real boom and exciting prosperity. A half-million dollars in oil stocks was traded in hotel lobbies every day; land prices skyrocketed and rents inflated while oil flowed through some of the world's biggest refineries. The crash of 1929 ended the speculation, but oil continued to flow through feeder lines to Casper. Oil continues to contribute to the area's economy; also important are tourism, agriculture, light manufacturing, coal, bentonite, and uranium mining.

What to See and Do

Casper Mountain and Beartrap Meadow Parks. Nordic ski trails (fee). Snowmobile trails (registration required), mountain bike trails. Picnicking, camping (fee), shelters (res required). (Daily) 10 mi S. Phone 307/235-9311. Located on the mountain is

Lee McCune Braille Trail. Flora, fauna, and geology are the focus of this trail (⅓ mi) geared for both the sighted and the visually impaired. The self-guided loop trail has signs in both Braille and English at 36 interpretive stations. Safety ropes are provided for guidance. **FREE**

Casper Planetarium. Three one-hr shows every eve. (Early June-early Sept and Thanksgiving-Dec 24, daily) 904 N Poplar St. Phone 307/577-0310. ¢¢

Devil's Gate. Pioneer landmark noted by emigrants moving W on the Oregon and Mormon Trails. Church of Jesus Christ of Latter-Day Saints interpretive center tells of the 1856 Martin's Cove disaster, in which as many as 145 people died when confronted by an early, severe winter. Hiking. (Daily; closed Dec 25) 63 mi S on WY 220. Phone 307/328-2953. **FREE**

Edness K. Wilkins State Park. Approx 300 acres on the Oregon Trail, bordered by the historic Platte River. Day-use park. Swimming pond, fishing; hiking paths, picnicking. 4 mi E via I-25, Hat Six exit on US 87. Phone 307/577-5150. ¢¢

🔲 **Fort Caspar Museum and Historic Site.** On grounds of restored fort; exhibits of Platte Bridge Station/Fort Caspar, Oregon Trail, pony express, Mormon Trail, military artifacts, city of Casper, central Wyoming. (Mid-May-mid-Sept, daily; rest of yr, Mon-Fri, Sun) Fort buildings closed in winter. 4001 Fort Caspar Rd. Phone 307/235-8462.

Hogadon Ski Area. Two double chairlifts, Pomalift; patrol, school, rentals; snowmaking; cafeteria. Longest run ¾ mi; vertical drop 600 ft. (Late

Nov-mid-Apr, Wed-Sun, hols; closed Dec 25) 11 mi S via WY 251 at 1800 E K St. Phone 307/235-8499. ¢¢¢¢

Independence Rock. "Register of the Desert," 193 ft high. Inscribed with more than 50,000 pioneer names, some dating back more than 100 yrs. Many names are obscured by lichen or worn away. 45 mi SW on WY 220. Phone 800/645-6233.

Nicolaysen Art Museum & Discovery Center. Changing and permanent exhibits. (Tues-Sun; closed hols) 400 E Collins Dr. Phone 307/235-5247. **FREE**

Special Event

Central Wyoming Fair and Rodeo. Fairgrounds, W of city. Phone 307/235-5775. Mid-July.

Motels/Motor Lodges

★ **COMFORT INN.** *480 Lathrop Rd, Evansville (82636).* 307/235-3038; res 800-228-5150. www.comfortinn.com. 56 rms, 2 story. June-Sept: S, D $70-$95; each addl $5; suites $85-$95; under 18 free; lower rates rest of yr. Crib free. Pet accepted, some restrictions. TV; cable (premium). Complimentary continental bkfst, newspaper. Coffee in rms. Restaurant nearby. Ck-out 11 am. Business servs avail. In-rm modem link. Heated indoor pool; whirlpool. Refrigerator, microwave in suites. Cr cds: A, D, DS, MC, V.
🅳 ⌨ 🛏 ▧ 🐾 **SC**

★★ **HAMPTON INN.** *400 West F St (82601).* 307/235-6668; fax 307/235-2027; toll-free 800/426-7866. www.hamptoninn.com. 122 rms, 2 story. S $65-$69; D $75-$79; under 18 free. Crib free. TV; cable (premium). Heated pool; sauna. Complimentary continental bkfst. Coffee in rms. Ck-out 11 am. Business servs avail. Valet serv. Free airport transportation. Downhill ski 7 mi. Cr cds: A, D, DS, MC, V.
🅳 ▨ 🛏 ✈ ▧ 🐾 **SC**

★★ **HOLIDAY INN.** *300 West F St (82601).* 307/235-2531; fax 307/473-3100; toll-free 877/576-8636. www.holiday-inn.com. 200 rms, 12 suites, 2 story. S, D $94-$99; each addl $10; suites $150-$175; under 18 free. Crib free. Pet accepted, some restrictions. TV; cable (premium). Indoor pool;

whirlpool. Restaurant 6 am-2 pm, 5-10 pm. Rm serv. Bar. Ck-out noon. Coin lndry. Meeting rms. Business servs avail. Sundries. Free airport, bus depot transportation. Downhill/x-country ski 7 mi. Exercise equipt; sauna. On river. Cr cds: A, C, D, DS, ER, JCB, MC, V.
🅳 ⌨ 🛏 🏋 ✈ ▧ 🐾 🔥

Hotel

★★ **RADISSON HOTEL CASPER.** *800 N Poplar St (82601).* 307/266-6000; fax 307/473-1010. www.radisson.com. 229 rms, 6 story. S, D $84; suites $90-$175; under 18 free. Crib free. Pet accepted. TV; cable (premium). Indoor pool; whirlpool. Coffee in rms. Restaurant 6 am-10 pm. Bar 11-1:30 am. Ck-out noon. Meeting rms. Business servs avail. Sundries. Beauty shop. Gift shop. Free airport transportation. Downhill/x-country ski 7 mi. Some in-rm whirlpools. Cr cds: A, C, D, DS, JCB, MC, V.
🅳 ⌨ 🏋 ✈ ▧ 🐾 🔥

B&B/Small Inn

★★ **HOTEL HIGGINS.** *416 W Birch St, Glenrock (82637).* 307/436-9212; fax 307/436-9213; toll-free 800/458-0144. www.hotelhiggins.com. 6 rms, 2 story, 2 suites. S, D $56-$80; each addl $7-$15; suites $80. Crib avail. Street parking. TV; cable. Complimentary continental bkfst. Restaurant. Bar. Baggage handling. Ck-out 11 am, ck-in 3 pm. Cr cds: A, DS, MC, V.
🅳 ▧ 🔥

Restaurants

★★★ **PAISLEY SHAWL.** *416 W Birch St, Glenrock (82637).* 307/436-9212. www.hotelhiggins.com. Hrs: 11:30 am-1:30 pm, 6-9:30 pm. Closed hols. Res accepted. Continental menu. Bar. A la carte entrees: lunch $5-$9, dinner $12-$28. Complete meals: dinner $28. Specialties: steak, pork tenderloin. Own baking. Outdoor dining. In 1916 building; turn-of-the-century decor. Cr cds: A, D, DS, MC, V.
🅳 🍴

★★ **SILVER FOX.** *3422 S Energy Ln (82604).* 307/235-3000. Hrs: 5-9:30

pm; Fri, Sat to 10 pm. Closed Sun; Dec 25. Res accepted. Continental menu. Bar. Dinner $8.95-$35.95. Child's meals. Specializes in veal, fettucine, prime rib. Picture windows with mountain view. Cr cds: A, D, DS, MC, V.

D ⊒

Cheyenne

(F-7) *See also Laramie*

Founded 1867 **Pop** 50,008 **Elev** 6,098 ft **Area code** 307 **Zip** 82001

Information Cheyenne Convention & Visitors Bureau, 309 W Lincolnway; 307/778-3133 or 800/426-5009

Web www.cheyenne.org

Cheyenne was named for an Algonquian tribe that roamed this area. When the Union Pacific Railroad reached what is now the capital and largest city of Wyoming on November 13, 1867, there was already a town. Between July of that year and the day the tracks were actually laid, 4,000 people had set up living quarters and land values soared. Professional gunmen, soldiers, promoters, trainmen, gamblers, and confidence men enjoying quick money and cheap liquor gave the town the reputation of being "hell on wheels." Two railways and three transcontinental highways made it a wholesale and commodity jobbing point, the retail and banking center of a vast region. Cheyenne is the seat of state and county government. Agriculture, light manufacturing, retail trade, and tourism support the economy of the area.

What to See and Do

Cheyenne Botanic Gardens. Wildflower, rose gardens, lily pond, community garden. (Mon-Fri; wkends, hols, afternoons) 710 S Lions Park Dr. Phone 307/637-6458. **Donation**

Cheyenne Frontier Days Old West Museum. Incl collections of clothing, weapons, carriages, Western art. Gift shop. (Daily; closed hols) (See SPECIAL EVENTS) 4610 N Carey Ave. Phone 307/778-7290. ¢¢

⭐ **Cheyenne Street Railway Trolley.** Two-hr historic tour of major attractions. (Mid-May-mid Sept, daily) 309 W Lincolnway, Convention & Visitors Bureau. Phone 307/778-3133. ¢¢¢

Curt Gowdy State Park. The foothills of a mountain range separating Cheyenne and Laramie create the park formation. Two reservoirs provide trout fishing (no swimming); boating (ramps). Hiking. Picnicking. Camping (standard fees). 26 mi W on Happy Jack Rd (WY 210). Phone 307/632-7946. ¢¢

Historic Governors' Mansion. (1904) Residence of Wyoming's governors from 1905-1976; first governors' mansion in the nation to be occupied by a woman, Nellie Tayloe Ross (1925-1927). (Tues-Sat; closed hols) 300 E 21st St. Phone 307/777-7878. **FREE**

Holliday Park. One of world's largest steam locomotives, 4000-type U.P.R.R., on grounds. Tennis. Picnicking, lighted horseshoe pit. Morrie Ave and 19th St. Phone 307/637-6423. **FREE**

State Capitol. (1887) Beaux-arts building with murals in Senate and House chambers by Allen T. True. Ceiling of each chamber is of stained glass. Guided tours (Mon-Fri; closed hols). Head of Capitol Ave. Phone 307/777-7220. **FREE**

Warren AFB. Museum traces history of base from 1867-pre-

Plains Indian Dancer, Frontier Days

sent (Mon-Fri; also by appt). (See SPECIAL EVENTS) W on Randall Ave. Phone 307/773-2980. **FREE**

Special Events

Old fashioned Melodrama. Atlas Theater. Phone 307/638-6543. July-mid-Aug.

Cheyenne Frontier Days. Frontier Park Arena, N on Carey Ave. One of country's most famous rodeos; originated in 1897. Parades, carnivals; USAF *Thunderbirds* flying team; pancake breakfast; entertainment, square dancing nightly. Phone 800/227-6336. Last full wk July.

Laramie County Fair. Frontier Park. Incl livestock and farm exhibits. Phone 307/633-4534. Early Aug.

Motels/Motor Lodges

★★ **BEST WESTERN HITCHING POST INN RESORT & CONFERENCE CENTER.** *1700 W Lincolnway (82001).* 307/638-3301; toll-free 800/221-0125. www.hitchingpostinn. com. 166 rms, 1-2 story. June-Labor Day: S $79-$99; D $89-$109; each

addl $6; suites $85-$160; under 12 free; lower rates rest of yr. Crib free. Pet accepted. TV; cable (premium). 2 pools, 1 indoor; whirlpool. Playground. Restaurants 5:30 am-11 pm. Bar noon-2 am; entertainment. Ck-out noon. Coin lndry. Meeting rms. Business center. Bellhops. Gift shop. Free airport, RR station, bus depot transportation. Exercise rm; sauna, steam rm. Game rm. Bathrm phones, refrigerators. Private patios, balconies. Cr cds: A, C, D, DS, MC, V.

★ **CHEYENNE SUPER 8.** *1900 W Lincolnway (82001).* 307/635-8741; res 800/800-8000. www.super8.com. 61 rms, 3 story. No elvtr. May-Sept: S $47.88; D $52.98-$55.98; each addl $6; under 18 free; lower rates rest of yr. Crib free. Pet accepted, some restrictions. TV; cable (premium). Restaurant adj open 24 hrs. Ck-out 11 am. Cr cds: A, C, D, DS, ER, JCB, MC, V.

★ **COMFORT INN.** *2245 Etchepare Dr (82007).* 307/638-7202; fax

A GOOD 'OL FRONTIER TOWN

Cheyenne grew up with the arrival of the railroad in 1867—going from a population of zero to three thousand in five months. By 1880, 10,000 people made their home here. This rapid growth produced an unusual unity of architectural design. Cheyenne has one of the best-preserved frontier town centers in Wyoming.

Begin a walking tour at the Wyoming Transportation Museum, 15th Street and Capitol Avenue. Formerly the depot for the Union Pacific Railway, this massive structure of stone and brick surmounted by a bell tower, was built in 1886. The building now serves as a railway museum.

Walk north to 16th Street, the city's main street during the frontier era. Many of the handsome redbrick storefronts from the 1880s are still in use. Stop by the Old Town Square, a pedestrian-friendly, two-block area with boutique shopping and reenactments of Old West activities, including a nightly "shoot-out" with gunslingers in period garb. The Cheyenne Visitors and Convention Bureau is adjacent to the square at 309 West 16th Street.

At the corner of 16th Street and Central Avenue is the Historic Plains Hotel (1600 Central Avenue). Built in 1910, this grand old hotel has a wonderfully atmospheric lobby and one of the oldest restaurants and bars in the state. The Plains is a favorite watering hole for Wyoming's political movers and shakers.

Walk up Capitol Avenue, past opulent, late-Victorian state office buildings and storefronts, with the state capitol building looming in the distance. Turn on 17th Street, and walk east to Lexies Cafe (216 East 17th), a Cheyenne dining institution. This period restaurant is located in the city's oldest structure, the luxurious 1880s home of Erasmus Nagle. In summer there's al fresco dining against the backdrop of the town's historic district.

Continue north along House Street, past more historic homes, to the Historic Governor's Mansion (200 East 21st Street). Built in 1904, this beautifully preserved sandstone structure was the home of Wyoming's governors until 1977. Today, free tours of the building focus on period furnishings and artifacts.

Head west on 23rd Avenue. The Wyoming State Museum (2301 Central Avenue), is the state's foremost history museum, telling Wyoming's story from the era of the dinosaurs through to the present, with especially good exhibits on the state's Native American and early settlement history. The museum also houses the state's art collection, rich in late 19th-century Western art.

Continue one block west to Capitol Avenue and turn north. The Wyoming Arts Council Gallery (2320 Capitol Avenue) is housed in an 1880s carriage house and is dedicated to mounting the works of contemporary Wyoming artists.

The Wyoming State Capitol Building, at 24th and Capitol Avenue, with its gleaming 24-karat gold leaf dome and feints toward French Renaissance architectural style, has dominated Cheyenne's skyline since 1888. The interior is equally grandiose, with marble floors, mahogany woodwork, and banks of stained glass. Free tours lead through the legislative chambers, or visitors can explore the building's art, historical displays, and huge stuffed buffalo (the state's symbol) on their own.

From there, continue south along Capitol Avenue, turning west at 18th Street. The Nelson Museum of the West (1714 Carey Avenue), offers 11,000 square feet of exhibits focusing on Native America and the Old West. One block farther south, at Carey and 16th, is Cheyenne's farmers market, where local growers sell produce on Saturday mornings.

307/635-8560; toll-free 800/228-5150. www.comfortinn.com. 77 rms, 2 story. June-Aug: S, D $79.99; under 18 free. Crib free. Pet accepted. TV; cable (premium). Heated pool. Complimentary continental bkfst. Restaurant opp open 24 hrs. Ck-out noon. Coin lndry. Meeting rm. Business servs avail. Cr cds: A, C, D, DS, MC, V.

D ⊘ ⊠ ⊠ ⊠ SC

★ **DAYS INN.** 2360 W Lincolnway (82001). 307/778-8877; fax 307/778-8697; res 800/325-2525. www.daysinn.com. 72 rms, 2 story. May-Sept: S, D $60-$75; each addl $5; suites $75-$80; lower rates rest of yr. Crib free. Pet accepted, some restrictions. TV; cable (premium). Complimentary continental bkfst. Restaurant adj open 24 hrs. Ck-out noon. Meeting rm. Business servs avail. Whirlpool. Exercise equipt, sauna. Cr cds: A, C, DS, MC, V.

D ⊘ ⊠ SC ⊼

★★ **FAIRFIELD INN.** 1415 Stillwater Ave (82001). 307/637-4070; res 800/228-2800. www.fairfieldinn.com. 62 rms, 3 story, 8 suites. May-Sept: S $63; D $74.95; each addl $6; suites $74.95-$89.95; under 18 free; higher rates Cheyenne Frontier Days; lower rates rest of yr. Crib free. TV; cable (premium). Indoor pool; whirlpool. Complimentary continental bkfst. Restaurant nearby. Ck-out noon. Meeting rms. Business servs avail. Refrigerator in some suites. Cr cds: A, D, DS, MC, V.

D ⊠ ⊠ ⊠

★★ **LA QUINTA INN.** 2410 W Lincolnway (82009). 307/632-7117; fax 307/638-7807; toll-free 800/531-5900. www.laquinta.com. 105 rms, 3 story. June-Aug: S $72.99; D $78.99; each addl $5; under 18 free; lower rates rest of yr. Crib free. Pet accepted. TV; cable (premium). Pool. Complimentary continental bkfst. Coffee in rms. Ck-out noon. Sundries. Cr cds: A, C, D, DS, MC, V.

D ⊘ ⊠ ⊠ ⊠ SC

★★★ **LITTLE AMERICA HOTEL.** 2800 W Lincolnway (82009). 307/775-8400; fax 307/775-8425; toll-free 800/235-6396. www.littleamerica.com/cheyenne. 188 rms, 2 story. S $91; D $99; each addl $10; suites $109;

under 12 free. Crib free. TV; cable (premium). Pool. Restaurants; entertainment Thurs-Sat. Ck-out noon. Coin lndry. Meeting rms. Business center. Bellhops. Shopping arcade. Free airport, RR station, bus depot transportation. 9-hole golf, putting green. Exercise equipt. Many bathrm phones, refrigerators. Private patios, balconies. Cr cds: A, C, D, DS, MC, V.

D ⊠ ⊠ ⊼ ⊠ ⊠ SC ⊼

B&B/Small Inn

★★★ **A DRUMMOND'S RANCH BED & BREAKFAST.** 399 Happy Jack Rd (82007). 307/634-6042. www.adrummond.com. 4 rms, 2 share bath, 2 story. No A/C. Mid-May-mid-Sept: S, D $150-$160; each addl $20; under 8 free, wkly rates, MAP avail, lower rates rest of yr. Crib free. TV in sitting rm, VCR avail (free movies). Playground. Complimentary full bkfst. Ck-out 11 am, ck-in 4 pm. Business servs avail. X-country ski 8 mi. Whirlpool. Bicycle rentals. Llama treks. Totally nonsmoking. Cr cds: MC, V.

⊠ ⊠ ⊠ ⊠ ⊠

Restaurant

★ **POOR RICHARD'S.** 2233 E Lincolnway (82001). 307/635-5114. Hrs: 11 am-2:30 pm, 5-10 pm; Fri, Sat to 11 pm; Sat brunch 11 am-2:30 pm; Sun 5-10 pm. Closed Dec 25, Thanksgiving. Bar to 11 pm. Lunch $4.95-$7.95, dinner $8-$29.50. Sat brunch $4.75-$7.25. Child's meals. Specializes in steak, fresh seafood. Salad bar. Patio dining. Cr cds: A, D, DS, MC, V.

D

Cody (B-3)

Founded 1896 **Pop** 7,897 **Elev** 5,002 ft **Area code** 307 **Zip** 82414

Information Cody Country Chamber of Commerce, 836 Sheridan Ave; 307/587-2777

Web www.codychamber.org

Buffalo Bill Cody founded this town, gave it his name, and devoted time and money to its development. He built a hotel and named it after his daughter Irma, arranged for a railroad spur from Montana and, with the help of his friend Theodore Roosevelt, had what was then the world's tallest dam constructed just west of town.

Cody is located 52 miles east of Yellowstone National Park (see); everyone entering Yellowstone from the east must pass through here, making tourism an important industry. A Ranger District office of the Shoshone National Forest is located here.

Buffalo Bill Historical Center, Cody

What to See and Do

⭐ **Buffalo Bill Historical Center.** Five-museum complex; gift shops. (Apr-Oct, daily; Nov-Mar, Tues-Sun) (See SPECIAL EVENTS) 720 Sheridan Ave. Phone 307/587-4771. ¢¢¢¢¢ Admission incl

Buffalo Bill Museum. Personal and historical memorabilia of the great showman and scout incl guns, saddles, clothing, trophies, gifts, and posters. Phone 307/857-4771.

Cody Firearms Museum. More than 5,000 projectile arms on display. Comprehensive collection begun in 1860 by Oliver Winchester. Phone 307/587-4771.

Plains Indian Museum. Extensive displays of memorabilia and artifacts representing the people of the Plains tribes and their artistic expressions; clothing, weapons, tools, and ceremonial items. Phone 307/587-4771.

Whitney Gallery of Western Art. Paintings, sculpture; major collection and comprehensive display of western art by artists from the early 1800s through today. Phone 307/857-4771.

Buffalo Bill State Park. Wildlife is abundant in this area. Fishing; boating (ramps, docks). Picnicking. Primitive camping. 13 mi W on US 14, 16, 20, on Buffalo Bill Reservoir. Phone 307/587-9227. ¢¢¢ Camping ¢¢; Along the adj reservoir is

Buffalo Bill Dam and Visitor Center. (1910) A 350-ft dam, originally called the Shoshone Dam. The name was changed in 1946 to honor Buffalo Bill, who helped raise money for its construction. The Visitor Center has a natural history museum, dam overlook, gift shop. (May-Sept, daily) East end of reservoir. Phone 307/527-6076. **FREE**

Shoshone National Forest. This 2,466,586-acre area is one of the largest in the national forest system. Incl magnificent approach route (Buffalo Bill Cody's Scenic Byway) to the east gate of Yellowstone National Park (see) along north fork of the Shoshone River. The Fitzpatrick, Popo Agie, North Absaroka, Washakie, and a portion of the Absaroka-Beartooth wilderness areas all lie within its boundaries. Incl outstanding lakes, streams, big-game herds, mountains, and some of the largest glaciers in the continental US. Fishing; hunting. Camping. Stan-

dard fees. 808 Meadow Lane Ave.
Phone 307/527-6241.

Shoshone river trips.

River Runners. Whitewater trips;
90-min-half-day trips. (June-Labor
Day, daily) 1491 Sheridan Ave.
Phone 307/527-7238. ¢¢¢¢

Wyoming River Trips. Ninety-min-
half-day trips. (Mid-May-late Sept,
daily) 1701 Sheridan Ave, located
at Holiday Inn Complex. Phone
307/587-6661. ¢¢¢¢

Skiing. Sleeping Giant Ski Area.
Chairlift, T-bar; patrol, school,
rentals; snack bar. Longest run ¾ mi;
vertical drop 600 ft. (Dec-mid-Apr,
Fri-Sun, hols; closed Dec 25) X-coun-
try trails, snowmobiling. 46 mi W on
US 14, 16, 20 at 349 Yellowstone
Hwy. Phone 307/587-4044. ¢¢¢¢

**Trail Town & the Museum of the Old
West.** Twenty-four reconstructed
buildings dating from 1879-1899 and
cemetery on site of Old Cody City
along the original wagon trails.
Buildings incl cabin used as rendezvous for Butch Cassidy and the
Sundance Kid and cabin of Crow
scout Curley, the only one of General Custer's troops that escaped
from the Battle of Little Bighorn.
Cemetery incl remains of Jeremiah
"Liver-eating" Johnson. (Mid-May-
mid-Sept, daily) 2 mi W on Yellowstone Hwy. Phone 307/587-5302. ¢¢

**Wyoming Vietnam Veteran's Memor-
ial.** Black granite memorial lists
names of state residents who died or
are missing in action in Vietnam. Off
US 16/20 W of the airport. Phone
307/587-2297.

Yellowstone National Park. (see) 52
mi W on US 14, 16, 20.

Special Events

Cowboy Songs and Range Ballads.
Buffalo Bill Historical Center. Early
Apr. Phone 307/578-4028.

Cody Nite Rodeo. Stampede Park.
Phone 307/587-2777. Nightly, June-
last Sat in Aug.

Plains Indian PowWow. People from
tribes throughout the western plains
states and Canada gather to compete. Dancing and singing; ceremonial and traditional tribal dress.
Phone 307/587-4034. Late June.

Cody Stampede. Rodeo; parade.
Phone 307/587-2777. Early July.

Frontier Festival. Buffalo Bill Historical Center. Demonstrations of pioneer skills, cooking crafts; musical
entertainment. Mid-July. Phone
307/587-4771.

Yellowstone Jazz Festival. Elks Club
lawn. Phone 307/754-6307. Mid-July.

Buffalo Bill Festival. City Park. Old
West celebration; chili cook-off, kid-
die festival. Phone 307/587-9227.
Mid-Aug.

Motels/Motor Lodges

★ **ABSAROKA MOUNTAIN
LODGE.** *1231 E Yellowstone Hwy,
Wapiti (82414). 307/587-3963,
absarokamtlodge.com.* 16 cabins. No
A/C. AP, June-Aug: S, D $76-$135;
lower rates May and Sept. Closed
rest of yr. Crib $6. Playground. Din-
ing rm 7:30-9:30 am, 6-8:30 pm. Bar
6-10:30 pm. Ck-out 11 am, ck-in 2
pm. Lawn games. Refrigerators avail.
Picnic tables. Log cabins; western
decor. Totally nonsmoking. Cr cds:
DS, MC, V.

★ **BILL CODY RANCH.** *2604-MG
Yellowstone Hwy (82414). 307/587-
6271; fax 307/587-6272; toll-free
800/615-2934. www.billcodyranch.com.*
14 cabins. No A/C. May-Sept: S, D
$115; each addl $10; wkly rates,
package plans; lower rates May-mid-
June, late Aug-Sept. Closed rest of yr.
Dining rm 7:30-9 am, 6-8 pm. Bar 6-
10 pm. Entertainment Mon. Ck-out
10 am. River rafting. Chuck wagon
cookout. Private porches. Cr cds: DS,
MC, V.

★ **COMFORT INN BUFFALO BILL
VILLAGE.** *1601 Sheridan Ave (82414).
307/587-5556; fax 307/527-7757; toll-
free 800/527-5544. www.blairhotels.
com.* 75 rms, 2 story. June-mid-Sept:
S, D $59-$149; each addl $6; under
19 free; lower rates rest of yr. Crib
free. TV; cable. Pool. Complimentary
continental bkfst. Restaurant adj 6
am-10 pm. Ck-out noon. Business
servs avail. Free airport transportation. Cr cds: A, C, D, DS, JCB, MC, V.

★ **DAYS INN.** *524 Yellowstone Ave (82414). 307/527-6604; fax 307/527-7341; res 800/325-2525. www.daysinn. com.* 52 rms, 2 story. Mid-May-Oct: S $115; D $125-$135; suites $150; each addl $10; under 12 free; lower rates rest of yr. Crib free. TV; cable (premium). Indoor pool; whirlpool. Complimentary continental bkfst. Restaurant nearby. Ck-out 11 am. Coin lndry. Cr cds: A, D, DS, MC, V.

[icons]

★★ **ELEPHANT HEAD LODGE.** *1170 Yellowstone Hwy, Wapiti (82450). 307/587-3980; fax 307/527-7922. www.elephantheadlodge.com.* 12 cabins. No A/C. Mid-May-mid-Oct: S, D $90-$130; AP avail. Closed rest of yr. Pet accepted. Playground. Dining rm 7:30-9:30 am, 11:30 am-1:30 pm, 6:30-8:30 pm. Bar 5:30-10 pm. Ck-out. Hiking, nature trails. Picnic tables, grills. On river in Shoshone National Forest. Trail rides avail. Totally non-smoking. Cr cds: A, DS, MC, V.

[icons]

★★ **HOLIDAY INN.** *1701 Sheridan Ave (82414). 307/587-3654; fax 307/527-7757; toll-free 800/527-5544. www.holidayinn.com.* 83 rms, 2 story. Mid-June-Aug: S, D $59-$149; under 19 free; lower rates rest of yr. Crib free. TV; cable. Pool. Restaurant 6 am-10 pm. Bar 4-11 pm. Ck-out noon. Meeting rms. Business servs avail. In-rm modem link. Valet serv. Sundries. Exercise equipt. Free airport transportation. Bathrm phones. Cr cds: A, C, D, DS, JCB, MC, V.

[icons]

★ **KELLY INN.** *2513 Greybull Hwy (82414). 307/527-5505; fax 307/527-5001. www.kellyinns.com.* 50 rms, 2 story. June-mid-Sept: S $75; D $92; each addl $5; lower rates rest of yr. Crib free. Pet accepted. TV; cable. Complimentary continental bkfst. Restaurant nearby. Ck-out 11 am. Coin lndry. Business servs avail. Free airport transportation. Whirlpool, sauna. Cr cds: A, D, DS, MC, V.

[icons]

★ **SHOSHONE LODGE RESORT & GUEST RANCH.** *349 Yellowstone Hwy (82414). 307/587-4044; fax 307/587-2681. shoshonelodge.com.* 16 cabins, 3 kits. (no equipt). No A/C. No rm phones. May-Oct: S, D $100-$135; each addl $10; kit. units $20 addl. Closed rest of yr. Crib $2. Dining rm 7-9 am, noon-1:30 pm, 6-8 pm. Ck-out 10 am. Coin lndry. Sundries. Lawn games. Downhill/x-country ski opp. Cookouts. Fireplace in lodge. Most cabins have porches. Cr cds: A, D, DS, MC, V.

[icons]

★ **VALLEY GOFF CREEK.** *995 Yellowstone Hwy (82414). 307/587-3753.* 17 cabins. No A/C. Mid-May-mid-Oct: S $75; D $95; each addl $5; duplex cabins $150-$200; lower rates rest of yr. Crib $5. Pet accepted. TV in main lodge. Dining rm 7-9:30 am, 5-8 pm. Bar noon-11 pm. Ck-out 11 am. Sundries. White water rafting. Lawn games. Private patios. Picnic tables. Trail rides. Cr cds: A, MC, V.

[icons]

Guest Ranches

★ **BLACKWATER CREEK RANCH.** *1516 N Fork Hwy (82414). 307/587-5201; toll-free 888/243-1607. www. blackwatercreekranch.com.* 15 cabins. No A/C. AP: S $1,150/wk; D $2,300/wk; under 10, $1,050/wk. Pool. Dining rm 7:30-8:30 am, 12:30-1:30 pm, 6:30-7:30 pm; closed mid-Sept-June. Cookouts. Bar. Ck-out 9:30 am, ck-in after 2 pm. Free airport transportation. Whitewater rafting. Horseback riding. Guided trips to Cody and Yellowstone. Hiking. Rodeos. Rec rm. Whirlpool. Lawn games. Square dancing. Picnic tables. On Shoshone River and Blackwater Creek. Cr cds: MC, V.

[icons]

★★★ **DOUBLE DIAMOND X RANCH.** *3453 Southfork Rd (82414). 307/527-6276; fax 307/587-2708; toll-free 800/833-7262. www.ddxranch. com.* 12 units, 5 cabins, 7 rms in lodge. AP, Mid-June-mid-Sept, wkly: S, D $1,500-$1,700; children 6-14 $880-$1,275; under 6, $700; lower rates May-mid-June, mid-Sept-Oct. Closed rest of yr. Indoor pool; whirlpool. Supervised children's activities (June-Sept). Cookouts. Ck-out 11 am. Guest lndry. Meeting rms. Gift shop. Hiking. Entertainment nightly in summer. Square dancing. Fishing/hunting trips. Fly fishing instruction. On south fork of Shoshone River. Cr cds: MC, V.

[icons]

★★ RIMROCK DUDE RANCH.

2728 Northfork Hwy (82414).
307/587-3970; fax 307/527-5014; toll-free 800/208-7468. www.rimrockranch.com. 9 cabins, 1-2 bedrms. No A/C.
June-Aug, wkly: S $1,500; D $1,350, children $975. Closed rest of yr. Crib free. Pool. Dining rm. Cookouts.
Free airport transportation. Pack trips. Guided trip to Yellowstone Park. Float trip on Shoshone River.
Clean and store. Rec rm. Refrigerators; some fireplaces, porches. Cr cds: MC, V.

★★ SEVEN D RANCH. *774 Sunlight Rd (82414). 307/587-3997; fax 307/587-9885. www.7dranch.com.* 11 cabins (1-4-bedrm). No A/C. No rm phones. AP, June-Aug, wkly: D $1,510/person; each addl $1,200/person; under 12, $1,125/person; lower rates Sept. Closed rest of yr. Supervised children's activities (June-Aug). Dining rm in lodge. Box lunches, cookouts. Ck-out 9:30 am, ck-in 3 pm. Guest lndry. Airport transportation. Horse corrals. Pack trips. Hiking. Trap shooting. Square dancing. Lawn games. Rec rm. Fishing/hunting guides. On creek in Shoshone National Forest.

★★ UXU RANCH. *1710 Yellowstone Hwy, Wapiti (82450). 307/587-2143; fax 307/587-7390; toll-free 800/373-9027. www.uxuranch.com.* 11 cabins. No A/C. No rm phones. AP: wkly: S $1,475; D $2,375; each addl $1,275; ages 3-5 $525; under 3 free. Closed Oct-May. Playground. Supervised children's activities. Restaurant 8-9 am, 12:30-1:30 pm, 7:30-8:30 pm. Bar noon-11 pm; entertainment. Ck-out 11 am. Gift shop. Rec rm. Lawn games. Rustic former logging camp in forest setting. Cr cds: MC, V.

Restaurants

★★★ FRANCA'S ITALIAN DINING. *1421 Rumsey Ave (82414). 307/587-5354.* Hrs: 6-10 pm. Closed Mon, Tues; mid-Jan-mid-May. Res accepted. Italian menu. Wine list. Dinner $14.50-$29. Specializes in homemade ravioli, focaccine bread, fresh seafood. Menu changes nightly.

Own desserts. Elegant decor. Totally nonsmoking.
🅳

★★ MAXWELL'S. *937 E Sheridan St (82414). 307/527-7749.* Hrs: 11 am-9 pm. Closed Sun; hols. Res accepted. Italian, American menu. Serv bar. Lunch $5.50-$7, dinner $10-$20. Child's meals. Specializes in pasta, steaks, chicken. Outdoor dining. Cr cds: A, D, MC, V.
🅳

★★ STEFAN'S. *1367 Sheridan Ave (82414). 307/587-8511.* Hrs: 7 am-10 pm; Fri, Sat to 11 pm; Sun 7 am-2 pm, 4-10 pm. Closed Jan 1, Thanksgiving, Dec 25. Res accepted. Wine, beer. Bkfst $3.95-$10.95, lunch $2.95-$7.95, dinner $6.50-$22.50. Child's meals. Specialties: stuffed filet mignon, homemade ravioli, fresh seafood pasta. Street parking. Garden decor; potted plants. Totally nonsmoking. Cr cds: A, DS, MC, V.
🅳

Devils Tower National Monument

The nation's first national monument, Devils Tower was set aside for the American people by President Theodore Roosevelt in 1906. Located on 1,347 acres approximately five miles west of the Black Hills National Forest, this gigantic landmark rises from the prairie like a giant tree stump. Sixty million years ago volcanic activity pushed molten rock toward the earth's surface. As it cooled Devils Tower was formed. Towering 1,267 feet above the prairie floor and Ponderosa pine forest, the flat-topped formation appears to change hue with the hour of the day and glows during sunsets and in moonlight.

The visitor center at the base of the tower offers information about the area, a museum, and a bookstore (April-October, daily). A self-guided trail winds around the tower for nature and scenery lovers. There are

Devils Tower

picnicking and camping facilities with tables, fireplaces, water, and restrooms (April-October). Contact Superintendent, PO Box 10, Devils Tower 82714; phone 307/467-5283. ¢¢-¢¢¢

Douglas

(D-6) See also Casper

Founded 1886 **Pop** 5,076 **Elev** 4,842 ft **Area code** 307 **Zip** 82633
Information Douglas Area Chamber of Commerce, 121 Brownfield Rd; 307/358-2950
Web www.jackalope.org

Cattlemen were attracted here by plentiful water and good grass. Homesteaders gradually took over, and agriculture became dominant. The town was named for Stephen Douglas, Lincoln's celebrated debating opponent. A Ranger District office for the Medicine Bow National

Forest (see LARAMIE) is located in Douglas.

What to See and Do

Fort Fetterman State Museum. Located on a plateau above the valleys of LaPrele Creek and the North Platte River. Museum in restored officers' quarters; additional exhibits in ordinance warehouse. Picnic area. (Memorial Day-Labor Day, daily) 10 mi NW on WY 93 at Fort Fetterman State Historic Site. Phone 307/358-2864.

Medicine Bow National Forest. S of town on WY 91 or WY 94 (see LARAMIE).

Thunder Basin National Grassland. Approx 572,000 acres; accessible grasslands, sagebrush, and some ponderosa pine areas. Bozeman and Texas trails cross parts of the grasslands. Large herds of antelope, mule deer; sage grouse. Hunting. N on WY 59. Phone 307/358-4690.

Wyoming Pioneer Memorial Museum. Large collection of pioneer and Native American artifacts; guns; antiques. (June-Sept, Mon-Sat; rest of yr, Mon-Fri; closed winter hols) State Fairgrounds, W end of Center St. Phone 307/358-9288. **FREE**

Special Events

High Plains Old Time Country Music Show & Contest. Douglas High School Auditorium. 307/358-2950. Late Apr.

Jackalope Days. Carnival, entertainment, exhibitors. Usually 3rd wkend June. Phone 307/358-2950.

Wyoming State Fair and Rodeo. Incl rodeo events, horse shows, exhibits. Phone 307/358-2398. Aug 20-27.

Motel/Motor Lodge

★ ★ **BEST WESTERN DOUGLAS INN.** *1450 Riverbend Dr (82633). 307/358-9790; fax 307/358-6251; res 800/344-2113. www.bwdouglas.com.* 116 rms, 2 story. S, D $69-$150; each addl $10; suites $150; under 18 free.

Crib avail. Pet accepted, some restrictions. TV; cable; VCR, DVD avail; $25. Heated indoor pool; whirlpool; poolside serv. Complimentary continental bkfst. Coffee in rms. Restaurant 6 am-2 pm, 5-10 pm. Bar. Ck-out 11 am. Coin lndry. Valet serv. Meeting rms. Business servs avail. In-rm modem link. Exercise equipt, sauna. Airport transportation. Hiking trail. Picnic facilities. Cr cds: A, C, D, DS, MC, V.

D ☜ ⬤ ⬛ ⅄ ⬛ ⬛ SC

Dubois

(C-2) *See also Grand Teton National Park*

Founded 1886 **Pop** 895 **Elev** 6,940 ft
Area code 307 **Zip** 82513
Information Chamber of Commerce, 616 W Ramshorn St, PO Box 632; 307/455-2556
Web www.duboiswyoming.org

On the Wind River, 56 miles from Grand Teton National Park (see), Dubois is surrounded on three sides by the Shoshone National Forest. The Wind River Reservation (Shoshone and Arapahoe) is a few miles east of town. Dubois, in ranching and dude ranching country, is a good vacation headquarters. There are plentiful rockhounding resources, and a large herd of Bighorn sheep roam within five miles of town. A Ranger District office of the Shoshone National Forest (see CODY) is located here.

What to See and Do

Big-game hunting. For elk, deer, moose, bear, and mountain sheep.

Fishing. For six varieties of trout in nearby streams. 907 Ramshorn, off US 26, 287. Phone 307/455-3429. ¢

National Bighorn Sheep Interpretive Center. Major exhibit, "Sheep Mtn," features full-size bighorns and the plants and animals that live around them. Other exhibits promote education, research, and conservation of the sheep and their habitats. (Memo-

rial Day-Labor Day, daily; winter hrs vary) 907 Ramshorn, off US 26, 287. Phone 307/455-3429. ¢

Wind River Historical Center. Exhibits and displays depicting natural and social history of the Wind River Valley; incl Native American, wildlife and archaeological displays; also Scandinavian tie-hack industries. (Mid-May-mid-Sept, daily; rest of yr, by appt) W on US 26, 287 at 909 W Ramshorn. Phone 307/455-2284. **Donation**

Motel/Motor Lodge

★ **SUPER 8.** *1414 Warm Springs Dr (82513). 307/455-3694; fax 307/455-3640; res 800/800-8000. www.super8. com.* 34 rms, 2 story. July-Aug: S $45.88; D $48.88-$60.88; suite $85; each addl $5; under 12 free; lower rates rest of yr. Crib free. Pet accepted. TV; cable (premium). Whirlpool. Complimentary coffee. Ck-out 11 am. Cr cds: A, C, D, DS, MC, V.

D ☜ ⬛ ⬛

Guest Ranches

★ **ABSAROKA RANCH.** *US 26/287 (82513). 307/455-2275. www. dteworld.com/absaroka.* 4 cabins. AP (1-wk min), mid-June-mid-Sept: $1,150/person; family rates; lower rates early June-mid-June. Closed rest of yr. 10 percent serv charge. Crib free. Supervised children's activities. Dining rm. Cookouts. Box lunches. Ck-out 11 am, ck-in 2 pm. Horse stables. Guided hiking. Sauna. Lawn games. Game rm. On creek. Totally nonsmoking. Cr cds: A, DS, MC, V.

⬤ ⅄ ⬛ ⬛

★★★ **BROOKS LAKE LODGE.** *458 Brooks Lake Rd (82513). 307/455-2121. www.brookslake.com.* 6 rms in main bldg, 6 cabins (1- and 2-bedrm). Late June-late Sept, 3-day min: S, D $250-$450; each addl $195; family rates; wkly rates; lower rates late Sept, Jan-Mar. Closed rest of yr. Crib free. Whirlpool. Complimentary coffee in cabins; full bkfst, lunch, dinner. Restaurant 7:30-9 am, 1 pm sitting, 7:30 pm sitting. Box lunches. Picnics, cookouts. Bar 6-10 pm; entertainment. Ck-out 11 am, ck-in 3 pm. Guest lndry. Gift shop.

Meeting rms. Business servs avail. Boats. X-country ski on site. Horse stables. Snowmobiles, tobogganing, tubing. Hiking. Lawn games. Some refrigerators, minibars. Picnic tables. Cr cds: A, MC, V.

★★ **LAZY L & B RANCH.** *1072 E Fork Rd (82513). 307/455-2839; fax 307/455-2634; toll-free 800/453-9488. www.ranchweb.com/lazyl&b.* 12 cabins. AP (1-wk min), Memorial Day-Sept: S $970-$1,050 person; under 13 yrs $1,050. Closed rest of yr. Pet accepted. Heated pool. Supervised children's activities (May-Aug). Dining rm. Cookouts. Ck-out Sat 10 am, ck-in Sun 1 pm. Coin lndry. Gift shop. Airport transportation. River swimming. Hiking. Hayrides. Children's petting farm. Lawn games. Rec rm. 1,800 acres on mountain range bordering Shoshone National Forest. Totally nonsmoking.

Evanston

(F-1) *See also Green River, Kemmerer*

Settled 1869 **Pop** 10,903 **Elev** 6,748 ft
Area code 307 **Zip** 82930
Information Chamber of Commerce, 36 10th St, PO Box 365, 82931-0365; 307/783-0370 or 800/328-9708
Web www.etownchamber.com

Coal from the mines at Almy, six miles north of Evanston, supplied trains of the Union Pacific Railroad, which operated a roundhouse and machine shop in Evanston beginning in 1871. By 1872, the mines employed 600 men.

While cattle and sheep ranching remain important industries, the discovery of gas and oil has triggered a new "frontier" era for the town. Evanston is also a trading center and tourist stopping point.

What to See and Do

Fort Bridger State Museum. Museum in barracks of partially restored fort named for Jim Bridger, scout and explorer. Pioneer history and craft demonstrations during summer; restored original buildings. (May-

Sept, daily; rest of yr, wkends; closed mid-Dec-Feb) Picnicking. (See SPECIAL EVENTS) 30 mi E on I-80, at Fort Bridger State Historic Site. Phone 307/782-3842. ¢

Special Events

Horse Racing. Wyoming Downs. 12 mi N on WY 89. Thoroughbred and quarter horse racing. Parimutuel wagering. Wkends and hols. Phone 307/789-0511. Memorial Day-Labor Day.

Chili Cook-off. Uinta County fairgrounds. Phone 800/328-9708. Usually third Sat June.

Uinta County Fair. Fairgrounds, US 30 E. 4-H, FFA exhibits; carnival, food. Phone 307/783-0313. First full wk Aug.

Cowboy Days. PRCA rodeo with carnival, entertainment, parade, exhibits, booths, cookouts. Labor Day wkend. Phone 800/328-9708.

Mountain Man Rendezvous. Fort Bridger State Museum (see). Black powder gun shoot, Native American dancing, exhibits, food. Labor Day wkend. Phone 307/789-3613.

Motels/Motor Lodges

★★ **BEST WESTERN DUNMAR INN.** *1601 Harrison Dr (82930). 307/789-3770; fax 307/789-3758; toll-free 800/654-6509. www.bestwestern.com.* 165 rms. May-Sept: S $79; D $85-$99; each addl $6; under 18 free; lower rates rest of yr. Crib $6. TV; cable. Heated pool. Restaurant 5:30 am-10 pm. Bar 11-2 am. Ck-out noon. Meeting rms. Gift shop. Exercise equipt. Bathrm phones; some refrigerators, wet bars. Cr cds: A, C, DS, JCB, MC, V.

★ **PRAIRIE INN MOTEL.** *264 Bear River Dr (82920). 307/789-2920.* 31 rms, 1 story. S $40-$50; D $50-$70; each addl $6. Crib avail; TV; cable (premium). Pet accepted, some restrictions, fee. Complimentary continental bkfst, toll-free calls. Restaurant nearby. Ck-out 11 am, ck-in 1 pm. Golf, 9 holes. Tennis. Cr cds: A, C, D, DS, MC, V.

Fort Laramie National Historic Site

See also Torrington

Fort Laramie played an important role in much of the history of the Old West. It was one of the principal fur-trading forts in the Rocky Mountain region from 1834-1849 and one of the the most important army posts on the Northern plains from 1849-1890. The first stockade built here, owned at one time by Jim Bridger and his fur-trapping partners, was Fort William, located on the strategic route to the mountains later to become the Oregon, California and Mormon trails. In 1041, the decaying Fort William was replaced with an adobe-walled structure called Fort John on the Laramie River.

Gillette

(B-6) *See also Buffalo, Devils Tower National Monument*

Pop 17,635 **Elev** 4,608 ft
Area code 307
Information Convention & Visitors Bureau, 1810 S Douglas Hwy #A, 82718; 307/686-0040 or 800/544-6136
Web www.visitgillette.net

What to See and Do

Keyhole State Park. Within sight of Devils Tower (see). Surrounding mountains form the western boundary of the Black Hills. Antelope, deer, and wild turkeys are common to this area. Reservoir is excellent for water sports. Swimming, fishing, boating (ramps, marina); picnicking, lodging, camping, tent and trailer sites (standard fees). 45 mi E via I-90, then 6 mi N on Pine Ridge Rd. Phone 307/756-3596. ¢¢

Tours. Coal Mines. Res recommended. (Memorial Day-Labor Day,

daily) 1810 S Douglas Hwy. Phone 307/686-0040. **FREE**

Motels/Motor Lodges

★★ **BEST WESTERN TOWER WEST LODGE.** *109 N US 14 & 16 (82716). 307/686-2210; fax 307/682-5105; res 800/528-1234. www. bestwestern.com.* 190 rms, 2 story. S $65; D $80; each addl $5; suites $125-$150; under 12 free. Crib free. Pet accepted, some restrictions. TV; cable. Indoor pool; whirlpool. Complimentary coffee in rms. Restaurant 6 am-10 pm. Rm serv to 9 pm. Bar; entertainment. Ck-out noon. Coin lndry. Meeting rm. Business servs avail. Bellhops. Valet serv. Free airport transportation. Exercise equipt; sauna. Game rm. Refrigerators avail. Cr cds: A, C, D, DS, MC, V.

★★ **CLARION INN.** *2009 S Douglas Hwy (82718). 307/686-3000; fax 307/686-4018; toll-free 800/686-3368. www.clarioninn.com.* 159 rms, 13 suites, 3 story. July-mid-Sept: S, D $90; suites $120-$150; under 18 free; lower rates rest of yr. Crib free. Pet accepted. TV; cable (premium). Indoor pool; whirlpool. Coffee in rms. Restaurant 6 am-2 pm; 5-10 pm. Bar 1 pm-2 am; entertainment Wed-Sat. Ck-out 11 am. Coin lndry. Meeting rms. Business center. Valet serv. Gift shop. Free airport transportation. Exercise equipt; sauna. Game rm. Rec room. Cr cds: A, C, D, DS, MC, V.

Restaurant

★ **HONG KONG.** *1612 W 2nd St (82716). 307/682-5829.* Hrs: 11 am-9:30 pm. Closed Dec 25. Res accepted. Chinese menu. Serv bar. Lunch $5-$5.750, dinner $5-$22.50. Specializes in Hunan beef, lemon chicken. Cr cds: A, D, DS, MC, V.

Grand Teton National Park

See also Dubois, Jackson, Yellowstone National Park

These rugged, block-faulted mountains began to rise about nine million years ago, making them some of the youngest on the continent. Geologic and glacial forces combined to buckle and sculpt the landscape into a dramatic setting of canyons, cirques, and craggy peaks that cast their reflections across numerous clear alpine lakes. The Snake River winds gracefully through Jackson Hole ("hole" being the old fur trapper's term for a high-altitude valley surrounded by mountains).

John Colter passed through the area during 1807-08. French-Canadian trappers in the region thought the peaks resembled breasts and applied the French word *teton* to them.

Entering from the north, from Yellowstone National Park (see), US 89/191/287 skirts the eastern shore of Jackson Lake to Colter Bay, continuing to Jackson Lake Junction, where it turns eastward to the entrance at Moran Junction (at US 26). The Teton Park Road begins at Jackson Lake Junction and borders the mountains to Jenny Lake, then continues to park headquarters at Moose. US 89/191/26 parallels Teton Park Road on the east side of the Snake River to the south entrance from Moran Junction. All highways have a continuous view of the Teton Range, which runs from north to south. US 26/89/191 is open year-round from Jackson to Flagg Ranch, two miles south of Yellowstone

National Park's South Gate, as is US 26/287 to Dubois. Secondary roads and Teton Park Road are open May-October.

The park is open year-round (limited in winter), with food and lodging available in the park from mid-May through September and in Jackson (see). There are three visitor centers with interpretive displays: Moose Visitor Center (daily; closed Dec 25); Colter Bay Visitor Center & Indian Arts Museum (mid-May-late September, daily); and Jenny Lake Visitor Center (June-Labor Day). Ranger-led hikes are available (mid-June-mid-September, daily; inquire for schedule), and self-guided trails are marked. A 24-hour recorded message gives information on weather; phone 307/739-3611.

The park can be explored by various means. There is hiking on more than 200 miles of trails. Corrals at Jackson Lake Lodge and Colter Bay have strings of horses accustomed to rocky trails; pack trips can be arranged. Boaters and anglers can enjoy placid lakes or wild streams; the Colter Bay, Signal Mountain,

The awe-inspiring mountains of Grand Teton N.P.

and Leek's marinas have ramps, guides, facilities, and rentals. Climbers can tackle summits via routes of varying difficulty; the more ambitious may take advantage of Exum School of Mountaineering and Jackson Hole Mountain Guides classes that range from a beginner's course to an attempt at conquering the 13,770-foot Grand Teton, considered a major North American climbing peak.

Horses, boats, and other equipment can be rented. Bus tours, an airport, auto rentals, general stores, and guide services are available. Five National Park Service campgrounds are maintained: Colter Bay, Signal Mountain, Jenny Lake, Lizard Creek, and Gros Ventre (fee). Slide-Illustrated talks on the park and its features are held each night (mid-June-Labor Day) at the amphitheaters at Colter Bay, Signal Mountain, and Gros Ventre.

Many river and lake trips are offered. Five-, ten-, and twenty-mile trips on rubber rafts float the Snake River. Visitors can choose an adventure to suit their individual tastes (see JACKSON). A self-guided trail tells the story of Menor's Ferry (1894) and the Maude Noble Cabin. Jenny Lake has boat trips and boat rentals. Jackson Lake cruises are available, some reaching island hideaways for breakfast cookouts. Boat rentals also are available at Jackson Lake. The Grand Teton Lodge Company offers a full-day, guided combination bus and boat trip covering major points of interest in the park (June-mid-September); phone 307/543-2811.

A tram with a vertical lift of 4,600 feet operates at Teton Village, rising from the valley floor to the top of Rendezvous Peak, just outside the park's southern boundary (see JACKSON).

The Chapel of the Transfiguration, located in Moose, is a log chapel with a large picture window over the altar framing the mountains. (Daily; services held late May-September)

The park is home to abundant wildlife, including pronghorn antelope, bighorn sheep, mule deer, elk, moose, grizzly and black bear, coyote, beavers, marmots, bald eagles, and trumpeter swans. Never approach or feed any wild animal. Do not pick wildflowers.

A park boat permit is required. A Wyoming fishing license is required for any fishing and may be obtained at several locations in the park. Camping permits are required for backcountry camping.

Grand Teton and Yellowstone national parks admission is $20/car. Contact Superintendent, PO Drawer 170, Moose 83012; phone 307/739-3399 or 307/739-3600 (recording).

CCInc Auto Tape Tours. This 90-minute cassette offers a mile-by-mile self-guided tour of the park. Written by informed guides, it provides information on history, points of interest, and flora and fauna of the park. Tapes may be purchased directly from CCInc, PO Box 227, 2 Elbrook Dr, Allendale, NJ 07401; phone 201/236-1666 or from the Grand Teton Lodge Company, phone 307/543-2811. ¢¢¢¢

Motels/Motor Lodges

★ **COLTER BAY VILLAGE & CABINS.** *Grand Teton National Park, Moran (83013). 307/543-3100; fax 307/543-3143; toll-free 800/628-9988. www.gtlc.com.* 166 cabins, 146 with shower only, 9 share bath. No A/C. No rm phones. S, D $35-$125; each addl $8.50; under 12 free. Closed Oct-mid-May. Crib free. Restaurant 6:30 am-10 pm. Ck-out 11 am, ck-in 4 pm. Coin lndry. Gift shop. Grocery store. Airport transportation. Boat rentals, river and lake cruises. On Jackson Lake; marina. Cr cds: A, C, D, DS, MC, V.

🄳 ⬤ ⚒ ⊠ 🦶

★★ **COWBOY VILLAGE RESORT.** *US 26/287, Moran (83013). 307/543-2847; fax 307/543-2391; toll-free 800/962-4988. www.cowboyvillage. com.* 89 units, 3 story, 54 kit. cabins. No A/C. No elvtr. Mid-Nov-mid-Apr: S $241/person; D $211/person; suites $233/person; cabins $239/person; under 13, $40; lower rates June-mid-Oct. Closed rest of yr. TV; cable (premium). Dining rm 7 am-9:30 pm. Rm serv. Bar noon-midnight. Ck-out 11 am. Coin lndry. Sundries. Gift shop. Free airport transportation in winter. X-country ski on site. Snowmobiling. Whirlpools. Rec rm. Cabins have private porches, picnic tables, grills. Cr cds: A, DS, MC, V.

⬛ 🔥 ➤ ➤ ➤ 🔥

★★ DORNAN'S SPUR RANCH CABINS. *10 Moose Jct, Moose (83012). 307/733-2415; fax 307/733-3544. www.dornans.com.* 12 kit. cabins. No A/C. June-Oct: 1-bdrm $130-$160 (up to 4); 2-bdrm $190 (up to 6); lower rates rest of yr. Restaurant adj 7 am-9 pm. Ck-out 11 am. Totally nonsmoking. Cr cds: A, DS, MC, V.

⬛ 🔥 ➤ ➤ 🔥

★★★ GRAND TETON NATIONAL PARK/JACKSON LAKE. *N Jackson Lake Lodge; N US 89, Moran (83013). 307/543-3100; fax 307/543-3143. www.gtlc.com.* 385 rms, 3 story. Mid-May-mid-Oct: S, D $154-$225; each addl $8.50; suites $350-$565; under 12 free. Closed rest of yr. Crib free. Heated pool; lifeguard. Dining rms 6 am-10:30 pm. Box lunches. Bar 11-1 am; entertainment Mon-Sat. Ck-out 11 am. Convention facilities. Business servs avail. Airport transportation. Bellhops. Concierge. Shopping arcade. Nightly programs July-Aug. Eve cookout rides. Float trips. Fly fishing, instruction. Many private patios, balconies. Grand lobby has 2 fireplaces, 60-ft picture window. View of Mt Moran, Grand Tetons. Cr cds: A, C, D, DS, MC, V.

🔥 ➤ ➤ ➤ 🔥

★★ HATCHET RESORT. *Hwy 287, Moran (83013). 307/543-2413; fax 307/543-2034. www.hatchetresort.com.* 22 cabins. No A/C. Memorial Day-Labor Day: S, D $80; each addl $5. Closed rest of yr. Pet accepted; $20. Restaurant 6:30 am-9:30 pm. Ck-out 10 am. Gift shop. Sundries. Picnic tables. Totally nonsmoking. Cr cds: A, DS, MC, V.

➤ 🔥 ➤ 🔥

★★ SIGNAL MOUNTAIN LODGE. *Inner Park Rd, Moran (83013). 307/543-2831; fax 307/543-2569; toll-free 800/672-6012. www.signalmtn lodge.com.* 79 cabins, 1-2 story, 30 kits. No A/C. Mid-May-mid-Oct: S, D $92-$215; kit. units $172. Closed rest of yr. Pet accepted, some restrictions. Crib free. Restaurant 7 am-10 pm in season. Bar noon-midnight. Ck-out 11 am. Meeting rms. Gift shop. Gro-

cery store. Some refrigerators, fireplaces. Private patios, balconies. Marina; boat rentals; guided fishing trips. Scenic float trips on Snake River. On lake; campground adj. Cr cds: A, DS, MC, V.

➤ 🔥 ➤ 🔥

Guest Ranches

★★★ GROS VENTRE RIVER RANCH. *18 Gros Ventre Rd, Moose (83011). 307/733-4138; fax 307/733-4272. www.grosventreriverranch.com.* 8 cabins, 4 kits. No A/C. No rm phones. AP, mid-June-Aug, wkly: S $1,190-$1,600; D $2,380-$3,200; each addl $1,000; lower rates rest of yr. Closed Nov, Apr. Crib free. TV in rec rm; VCR. Playground. Dining rm in lodge. Box lunches, cookouts. Ck-out 10 am, ck-in 3 pm. Meeting rms. Free airport transportation. Swimming in pond. Canoes. Hiking. Mountain bikes. Lawn games. Rec rm. Some fireplaces. On 160 acres.

🔥 🔥 🔥

★★★ JENNY LAKE LODGE. *Grand Teton National Park, Moran (83013). 307/733-4647. www.gtlc.com.* 37 cabins. No A/C. No rm phones. MAP, June-early Oct: S, D $619. Closed rest of yr. Crib free. Restaurant (see also JENNY LAKE LODGE DINING ROOM). Serv bar. Ck-out 11 am, ck-in 4 pm. Bellhops. Gift shop. Airport transportation. Bicycles; trail rides. Golf, tennis, and swimming privileges nearby. Some refrigerators. Wood stove in suites, lounge. Private patios. Totally nonsmoking. Cr cds: A, D, MC, V.

⬛ 🔥 ➤ 🔥 ➤ ➤ 🔥

★★★★ LOST CREEK RANCH. *#1 Old Ranch Rd, Moose (83012). 307/733-3435; fax 307/733-1954. www.lostcreek.com.* Complimentary transfers from Jackson Hole Airport to this lodge and spa located between Grand Teton National Park and Bridger Teton Forest. Rates for the 10 cabins and 20 rooms, available May through October, include meals. Consider visiting in the fall when the leaves are breathtaking and nearby fly-fishing is at its peak. 10 cabins, 7 with kit. No A/C. AP, June-mid-Oct, wkly rates: 1-4 persons $4,670-$10,450; each addl $860; under 6 free. Closed rest of yr. Crib free. Heated pool; whirlpool. Super-

vised children's activities (June-Aug). Coffee in cabins. Dining rm sittings: bkfst 7:30-8:30 am, lunch 12:30 pm, dinner 7 pm (children's dinner at 6 pm if desired). Ck-out 10 am, ck-in 3 pm. Free lndry serv. Meeting rms. Business servs avail. Airport transportation. Tennis. Hayrides. Exercise rm; sauna, steam rm. Spa. Massage. Lawn games. Entertainment. Game rm. Scenic float trips. Riding instruction avail. Refrigerators, fireplaces. Private porches. Picnic tables. Totally nonsmoking. Cr cds: A, MC, V.

★★★ **MOOSE HEAD RANCH.** *Hwy 89, Moose (83012). 307/733-3141; fax 307/739-9097.* 14 cabins, 1-2 bedrm. No A/C. No rm phones. AP (incl riding), mid-June-Aug (5-day min): S $400; D $500; under 6, $150; 2-bedrm house (up to 6 people) $1,350-$1,850. Closed rest of yr. Crib free. Complimentary coffee in cabins. Dining rm 8-9 am, 12:30-1:30 pm, 7-8 pm. Cookouts. Meeting rm. Free airport transportation. Horseback riding instruction, trips; hiking trails. Fly fishing, instruction. Rec rm. Lawn games. Refrigerators. Some fireplaces in cabins. Private porches. Library. On 120 acres; series of manmade trout ponds.

Cottage Colony

★★ **FLAGG RANCH RESORT.** *Hwy 89, Moran (83013). 307/543-2861; fax 307/543-2356; res 800/443-2311. www.flaggranch.com.* 92 cabins. No A/C. Late June-Aug: S, D $139-$145; each addl $10; under 18 free; lower rates rest of yr. Crib free. Pet accepted; $5. Complimentary coffee in rms. Restaurant 7 am-10 pm. Bar 3-11 pm. Ck-out 11 am, ck-in 4 pm. Meeting rms. Business servs avail. Bellhops. Concierge. Gift shop. Grocery store. Cr cds: A, DS, MC, V.

Restaurant

★★★ **JENNY LAKE LODGE DINING ROOM.** *Inner Loop Rd, Moose (83012). 307/733-4647. www.gtlc. com.* Hrs: 6:30-9 am, noon-1:30 pm, 6-8:45 pm. Closed Oct-May. Res required. No A/C. Serv bar. Wine list. Complete meals: bkfst $13.50, lunch $7-$9, dinner $42.50. Buffet: dinner (Sun) $42.50. Child's meals. Specialties: range-fed buffalo, fresh Pacific salmon, Rocky Mtn trout. Classical musicians. Dining in restored cabin. Totally nonsmoking. Cr cds: A, MC, V.

Unrated Dining Spot

MOOSE CHUCK WAGON. *10 Moose Jct, Moose (83012). 307/733-2415. www.dornans.com.* Hrs: 7-11 am, noon-3 pm, 5-8 pm. No A/C. Closed Sept-May. A la carte entrees: bkfst $4.25-$6.25, lunch $3.35-$6.75. Buffet: dinner $12. Specializes in beef and barbecue cooked over wood fires. Outdoor dining; inside giant teepees when raining. View of Tetons, Snake River. Family-owned. Cr cds: A, D, MC, V.

Green River

(F-2) See also Evanston, Kemmerer, Rock Springs

Settled 1862 **Pop** 12,711 **Elev** 6,109 ft
Area code 307 **Zip** 82935
Information Chamber of Commerce, 541 E Flaming Gorge Way, Suite E; 307/875-5711
Web www.grchamber.com

Green River, seat of Sweetwater County, is known as the trona (sodium sesquicarbonate) capital of the world. As early as 1852, Jim Bridger guided Captain Howard Stansbury on a Native American trail through the area. By 1862, a settlement here consisted mainly of the overland stage station, located on the east bank of the Green River. In 1868, Major John Wesley Powell started from here on his expedition of the Green and Colorado rivers. This point of departure is now known as Expedition Island. The Green River, one of Wyoming's largest, is the northern gateway to the Flaming Gorge National Recreation Area.

What to See and Do

Flaming Gorge National Recreation Area. This area, administered by the US Forest Service, surrounds Flaming Gorge Reservoir in Wyoming (see ROCK SPRINGS) and Utah. Firehole campground and Upper Marsh Creek boat ramp are on the east shore of the reservoir; two other sites (Buckboard Crossing and Squaw Hollow) are on the west shore. Lucerne, Buckboard Crossing, Firehole, and Antelope Flats have camping and boat-launching ramps. Upper Marsh Creek and Squaw Hollow are boat ramp sites only. (Check road conditions locally before traveling during winter or wet periods.) There is usually ice fishing Jan-Mar. The Flaming Gorge Dam, administered by the US Bureau of Reclamation, the headquarters, three visitor centers, and several other recreation sites are located along the south half of the loop in Utah. Campground fees; res required for group sites. S on WY 530 or US 191. For information contact District Ranger, Box 279, Manila, UT 84046. Phone 435/784-3445.

Sweetwater County Historical Museum. Historical exhibits on southwestern Wyoming; Native American, Chinese, and pioneer artifacts; photographic collection. (July-Aug, Mon-Sat; rest of yr, Mon-Fri; closed hols) Courthouse, 3 E Flaming Gorge Way. Phone 307/872-6435. **FREE**

Motel/Motor Lodge

★★★ **LITTLE AMERICA HOTEL.** I-80 exit 68, Little America (82929). 307/875-2400; fax 307/872-2666; toll-free 800/634-2401. www.littleamerica. com. 140 rms, 18 with shower only, 2 story. May-Sept: S $63; D $69; each addl $6; suites $85; under 12 free; lower rates rest of yr. Crib free. TV; cable (premium). Heated pool. Playground. Restaurant open 24 hrs. Bar 2:30 pm-1 am. Ck-out noon. Meeting rms. Business center. Sundries. Shopping arcade. Coin lndry. Exercise equipt. Some refrigerators. Some balconies. Cr cds: A, C, D, DS, MC, V.
⊠ 🏃 ⊠ 🐾 SC 🏃

Greybull

(B-4) *See also Lovell*

Pop 1,789 **Elev** 3,788 ft
Area code 307 **Zip** 82426
Information Chamber of Commerce, 521 Greybull Ave; 307/765-2100
Web www.greybull.com

Just north of town are the rich geological sites Sheep Mountain and Devil's Kitchen. Sheep Mountain looks like a natural fortress surrounded by flatland when seen from the Big Horn Mountains. A Ranger District office of the Bighorn National Forest (see SHERIDAN) is located here.

What to See and Do

Greybull Museum. History and fossil displays; Native American artifacts. (June-Labor Day, Mon-Sat; Apr-May and Sept-Oct, Mon-Fri afternoons; rest of yr, Mon, Wed, and Fri afternoons; closed Jan 1, Thanksgiving, Dec 25) 325 Greybull Ave, PO Box 348, 82426. Phone 307/765-2444. **FREE**

Special Event

Days of '49 Celebration. Parades, rodeo, running races, demolition derby. Concert, dances. Second wkend June. Phone 307/765-9619.

Jackson

(C-1) *See also Alpine, Grand Teton National Park, Pinedale*

Pop 4,472 **Elev** 6,234 ft
Area code 307 **Zip** 83001
Information Jackson Hole Area Chamber of Commerce, 990 W Broadway, PO Box 550; 307/733-3316
Web jacksonholechamber.com

Jackson, uninhibitedly western, is the key town for the mountain-rimmed, 600-square-mile valley of Jackson Hole, which is surrounded by mountain scenery, dude ranches, national parks, big game, and other vacation attractions. Jackson Hole is one of the most famous ski resort areas in the country, known for its spectacular views and its abundant ski slopes. It has three Alpine ski areas, five Nordic ski areas, and miles of groomed snowmobile trails. Annual snowfall usually exceeds 38 feet, and winter temperatures average around 21°F. The Jackson Hole area, which includes Grand Teton National Park, the town of Jackson, and much of the Bridger-Teton National Forest, has all the facilities and luxuries necessary to accommodate both the winter and summer visitor. Jackson Hole offers winter sports, boating, chuck wagon dinner shows, live theater productions, symphony concerts, art galleries, rodeos, horseback riding, mountain climbing, fishing, and several white-water and scenic float trips. Two Ranger District offices of the Bridger-Teton National Forest are located in Jackson.

What to See and Do

Bridger-Teton National Forest. With more than 3.3 million acres, the forest literally surrounds the town of Jackson. Bridger-Teton was the site of one of the largest earth slides in US history, the Gros Ventre Slide (1925), which dammed the Gros Ventre River (to a height of 225 ft and a width of nearly ½ mi), forming Slide Lake, which is approx three mi long. There are scenic drives along the Hoback River Canyon, the Snake River Canyon, and in Star Valley. Unspoiled backcountry incl parts of Gros Ventre, Teton, and Wind River ranges along the Continental Divide and the Wyoming Range. Teton Wilderness (557,311 acres) and Gros Wilderness (247,000 acres) are accessible on foot or horseback. Swimming, fishing, rafting; hiking, mountain biking, winter sports areas, camping (fee). Also in the forest is Bridger Wilderness (see PINEDALE). Fishing, boating; big-game hunting. For further information contact Forest Supervisor, 340 N Cache, PO Box 1888. Phone 307/739-5500.

Gray Line bus tours. For information on tours in Jackson, Grand Teton, and Yellowstone national parks contact PO Box 411. Phone 307/733-4325.

Jackson Hole Historical Society & Museum. Fur trade exhibit. Research library. (Daily) 105 Mercill Ave. Phone 307/733-9605. **FREE**

Jackson Hole Museum. Regional museum of early West, local history and archeology. (Late May-Sept, daily) 105 N Glenwood. Phone 307/733-9605. ¢¢

National Elk Refuge. This 25,000-acre refuge is the winter home of thousands of elk and many waterfowl. Visitor center with slide show, exhibits, and horse-drawn sleigh rides (mid-Dec-Mar, daily). 2 mi N of town. Phone 307/733-9212.

National Wildlife Art Museum. Art museum with large collection of North American wildlife paintings and sculpture; traveling exhibits, special programs. Overlooks National Elk Refuge. (Daily) Rungus Rd, N of town. Phone 307/733-5771. ¢¢¢

River excursions.

Barker-Ewing Float Trips. Ten-mi scenic trips on the Snake River, within Grand Teton National Park. Res necessary. Phone 307/733-1800. ¢¢¢¢

Lewis and Clark Expeditions. Scenic 3½- and 6-hr whitewater float trips through Grand Canyon of Snake River. (June-mid-Sept, daily) 335 N Cache. Phone 307/733-4022. ¢¢¢¢

Mad River Boat Trips, Inc. Three-hr whitewater Snake River Canyon trips (daily). Also combination scenic/whitewater trips, lunch/dinner trips. Res suggested. Phone 307/733-6203. ¢¢¢¢

Solitude Float Trips. Five- and ten-mi scenic trips within Gand Teton National Park. Res suggested. Phone 307/733-2871.

Triangle X Float Trips. Trips incl ten-mi floats; sunrise and eve wildlife floats; also cookout supper floats. Most trips originate at Triangle X Ranch. (May-Oct) On the Snake River in Grand Teton National Park. Phone 307/733-5500. ¢¢¢¢

Skiing.

Aerial Tramway. Makes 2½-mi ride to top of Rendezvous Mtn for spectacular views. Free guided nature hike. (Late May-early Oct) Phone 307/733-2291. ¢¢¢

Jackson Hole Mountain Resort.
2½-mi aerial tramway, six quad, or double chairlifts, two surface tows; patrol, school, rentals; bar, restaurants, cafeterias; daycare; lodging. Longest run 4½ mi; vertical drop 4,139 ft. (Dec-mid-Apr, daily) X-country trails. Also summer swimming, tennis, horseback riding, hiking. 12 mi NW at 3395 McCollister Dr, in Teton Village. Phone 307/733-2292. ¢¢¢¢¢

Snow King Ski Resort. Triple, two double chairlifts, surface tow; school, rental/repair shop; snack bar, resort facilities. Longest run nearly one mi; vertical drop 1,571 ft. (Nov-Mar, daily) Six blks south of Town Square. ¢¢¢¢¢

Teton Mountain Bike Tours. Guided mountain bike tours for all ability levels. Mountain bike, helmet, transportation, and local guides. Day, multiday, and customized group tours avail. Phone 800/733-0788.

Teton Wagon Train & Horse Adventure. Four-day guided covered wagon trip between Yellowstone and Grand Teton national parks (see). Activities incl hiking, horseback riding, swimming, and canoeing. Meals, tents, and sleeping bags incl. (Mid-June-late Aug) Phone 307/734-6101. ¢¢¢¢¢ Also avail is

Covered Wagon Cookout & Wild West Show. Ride covered wagons to outdoor dining area; eating area covered in case of rain. Western entertainment. Departs from Bar-T-Five Corral (late May-mid-Sept, Mon-Sat). Phone 307/733-5386.

Wagons West. Covered wagon treks through the foothills of the Tetons. Gentle riding horses, chuck-wagon meals, campfire entertainment. Special guided horseback treks and hiking trips into surrounding mountains. Two-, four-, and six-day furnished trips. (June-Labor Day, Mon-Sat) Res necessary. Depart from motels in Jackson. Phone 307/886-9693. ¢¢¢¢¢

Special Events

The Shootout. Town Square. Real-life Western melodrama. Mon-Sat eves, Memorial Day wkend-Labor Day. Phone 307/733-3316.

Jackson Hole Rodeo. Snow King Ave. Phone 307/733-2805. Sat, Memorial Day-Aug 31.

Grand Teton Music Festival. 12 mi NW in Teton Village. Symphony and chamber music concerts. Virtuoso orchestra of top professional musicians from around the world. Many different programs of chamber music and orchestral concerts. Phone 307/733-3050 or 307/733-1128 (box office). Early July-late Aug.

Jackson Hole Fall Arts Festival. Three-wk celebration of the arts featuring special exhibits in more than 30 galleries, demonstrations, special activities. Also dance, theater, mountain film festival, Native American arts, and culinary arts. Phone 307/733-3316. Mid-Sept-early Oct.

Motels/Motor Lodges

★★★ **ALPENHOF LODGE.** *3255 W Village Dr, Teton Village (83025). 307/733-3242; fax 307/739-1516; toll-free 800/732-3244. www.alpenhoflodge. com.* 43 rms, 4 story. No A/C. Mid-June-Aug: S, D $125-$185; each addl $15; suites $235-$388; higher rates winter season. Closed mid-Oct-Nov and Apr-mid-May. Crib $10. TV; cable (premium). Heated pool; whirlpool. Rm serv 7:30 am-10 pm. Bar. Ck-out 11 am, ck-in 3 pm. Coin lndry. Bellhops. Downhill/x-country ski in and out lodge. Sauna. Massage. Some private balconies. Sun deck. Fireplace in lounge. Cr cds: A, C, D, DS, MC, V.

⬛⬛⬛⬛⬛⬛

★ **ANTLER INN.** *43 W Pearl St (83001). 307/733-2535; fax 307/733-4158. townsquareinns.com.* 110 rms, 1-2 story, 2 suites. June-mid-Sept: S $76-$98; D $80-$102; each addl $5; suites $120; family rm (up to 6 persons) $122; lower rates rest of yr. Crib free. Pet accepted, some restrictions. TV; cable (premium). Restaurant opp 7 am-10 pm. Ck-out 11 am. Coin lndry. Meeting rm. Business servs avail. In-rm modem link. Downhill/x-country ski 12 mi. Exercise equipt; sauna. Whirlpool. Some fireplaces, in-rm whirlpools. Many refrigerators; microwaves avail. Cr cds: A, C, D, DS, MC, V.

⬛⬛⬛⬛⬛⬛⬛

★★ **BEST WESTERN INN.** *3345 W McCollister Dr, Jackson Hole (83025). 307/739-2311; toll-free 800/842-7666. www.bestwestern.com.* 83 rms, 4 story. Late June-Labor Day, late Dec-Feb: S $189; D $179-$249; under 12 free; lower rates rest of yr. Crib free. TV; cable. Restaurant 7:30-10 am, 5-10 pm. Bar 11 am-midnight. Ck-out 11 am. Meeting rms. Business servs avail. In-rm modem link. Sundries. Coin lndry. Outdoor pool; whirlpool, poolside serv. Downhill/ x-country ski 12 mi. Game rm. Some fireplaces, microwaves. Cr cds: A, C, D, DS, MC, V.

★★ **BEST WESTERN INN.** *80 Scott Ln (83002). 307/739-9703; fax 307/739-9168; toll-free 800/458-3866. www.bestwestern.com.* 154 rms, 3 story. Mid-June-mid-Sept: S, D $199; each addl $10; under 12 free; ski plan; lower rates rest of yr. Crib free. TV; cable, VCR (movies). Indoor/outdoor pool; whirlpools. Complimentary full bkfst. Complimentary coffee in rms. Restaurant nearby. Ck-out 11 am. Coin lndry. Meeting rms. Business servs avail. In-rm modem link. Bellhops. Gift shop. Valet serv. Downhill/x-country ski 12 mi. Sauna. Health club privileges. Refrigerators, microwaves, minibars. Cr cds: A, C, D, DS, MC, V.

★★ **BUCKRAIL LODGE.** *110 E Karns Ave (83001). 307/733-2079; fax 307/734-1663. www.buckraillodge.com.* 12 rms. No A/C. No rm phones. Mid-June-mid-Sept: S, D $75-$110; each addl $5; lower rates May-mid-June and mid-Sept-mid-Oct. Closed rest of yr. Crib $5. TV; cable (premium). Restaurant nearby. Ck-out 11 am. Whirlpool. Picnic table, grill. Downhill/x-country ski 10 mi. Totally nonsmoking. Cr cds: A, DS, MC, V.

★ **DAYS INN.** *350 S US 89 (83001). 307/733-0033; fax 307/730-0044; res 800/325-2525. www.daysinn.com.* 90 rms, 3 story. June-Labor Day: S, D $149-$209; each addl $10; suites $169-$209; under 12 free; lower rates rest of yr. Crib free. TV; cable (premium). Complimentary continental bkfst. Coffee in rms. Restaurant adj. Ck-out 11 am. Sauna. Whirlpool. Some in-rm whirlpools, refrigerators, fireplaces; microwaves avail. Cr cds: A, D, DS, MC, V.

★ **FLAT CREEK.** *1935 N US 89 (83002). 307/733-5276; toll-free 800/438-9338. www.flatcreekmotel. com.* 73 rms, 2 story, 12 kit. units. July-Aug: S $52-$95; D $59-$113; kit. units $125; lower rates rest of yr. Crib $5. Pet accepted. TV; cable. Complimentary continental bkfst. Ck-out 11 am. Coin lndry. Sauna. Whirlpool. Refrigerators, microwaves. Cr cds: A, C, D, DS, MC, V.

An elk snacks on lush Wyoming greenery

★ **4 WINDS.** *150 N Millward St (83001). 307/733-2474; fax 307/734-2796; toll-free 800/228-6461. www. jacksonholefourwinds.com.* 21 rms, 1-2 story. June-Labor Day: S, D $85-$105; each addl $5; lower rates mid-late May-mid-June, after Labor Day-mid-Oct. Closed rest of yr. TV; cable (premium). Complimentary coffee in lobby. Restaurant adj 7 am-10 pm. Ck-out 11 am. Picnic tables, grill. City park, playground adj. Cr cds: A, DS, MC, V.

★ **HITCHING POST LODGE.** *460 E Broadway (83001). 307/733-2606; fax 307/733-8221.* 33 rms in cabins, 16 kit. units. No A/C. Mid-June-mid-

Sept: S $78 D $88-$92; kit. units $149-$179; each addl $5; lower rates rest of yr. Crib free. TV; cable (premium). Pool. Complimentary continental bkfst. Restaurant nearby. Ck-out 11 am. Coin lndry. Whirlpool. Refrigerators, microwaves. Picnic tables. Cr cds: DS, MC, V.

★ **QUALITY 49'ER INN & SUITES.**
330 W Pearl St (83001). 307/733-7550; fax 307/733-2002; toll-free 800/451-2980. townsquareinns.com. 148 rms, 1-2 story. June-Sept: S $70-$115; D $74-$119; each addl $4; suites $130-$230; lower rates rest of yr. Crib free. Pet accepted, some restrictions. TV; cable (premium). Complimentary continental bkfst. Restaurant nearby. Ck-out 11 am. Meeting rm. In-rm modem link. Downhill/x-country ski 12 mi. Exercise equipt. Health club privileges. Whirlpool. Some in-rm whirlpools, refrigerators, microwaves, fireplaces. Cr cds: A, C, D, DS, ER, JCB, MC, V.

★★ **RED LION WYOMING INN.**
930 W Broadway (83002). 307/734-0035; fax 307/734-0037; toll-free 800/844-0035. www.wyoming-inn.com. 73 rms, 3 story, 4 kit. units. July-Aug: S, D $179-$249; each addl $10; kit. units $209; under 13 free; lower rates rest of yr. Pet accepted. TV; cable. Complimentary continental bkfst. Coffee in rms. Restaurant nearby. Ck-out 11 am. Free guest lndry. Meeting rm. Business servs avail. Free airport transportation. Some refrigerators, fireplaces, whirlpools. Totally non-smoking. Cr cds: A, DS, MC, V.

★★★ **RUSTY PARROT LODGE.**
175 N Jackson St (83001). 307/733-2000; fax 307/733-5566; res 800/458-2004. www.rustyparrot.com. 30 rms, 3 story, 1 suite. Dec-Mar, June-Sept: S, D $280-$329; each addl $30; suites $500; children $30; under 12 free; lower rates rest of yr. Crib avail, fee. Parking lot. TV; cable (premium). Complimentary full bkfst, newspaper, toll-free calls. Restaurant nearby. Ck-out 11 am, ck-in 4 pm. Bellhops. Concierge. Dry cleaning. Gift shop. Exercise privileges, whirlpool. Golf. Tennis. Downhill skiing. Bike rentals. Hiking trails. Cr cds: A, C, D, DS, MC, V.

★★★ **SNOW KING RESORT.** *400 E Snow King Ave (83001). 307/733-5200; fax 307/733-4086; toll-free 800/522-5464. www.snowking.com.* 204 rms, 15 suites, 7 story. Late May-late Sept: S, D $115-$205; each addl $10; suites $220-$380; under 14 free; ski plan; lower rates rest of yr. Crib free. Pet accepted, some restrictions. TV; cable. Heated pool; whirlpools, poolside serv. Restaurants 6:30 am-10 pm. Bar noon-2 am. Ck-out noon. Coin lndry. Meeting rms. Business servs avail. Bellhops. Valet serv. Concierge. Sundries. Gift shop. Barber, beauty shop. Free airport transportation. Alpine slide. Exercise equipt; sauna. Massage. Downhill ski adj; x-country ski 5 mi. Game rm. Located at foot of Snow King Mtn. Cr cds: A, C, D, DS, MC, V.

★★★ **SPRING CREEK RANCH.**
1800 Spirit Dance Rd (83001). 307/733-8833; toll-free 800/443-6139. www.springcreekresort.com. 117 rms, some kits. S, D $250; each addl $15; studio rms $275; condo units $450-$1,000; under 12 free; package plans. TV; cable (premium), VCR avail (movies). Heated pool; whirlpool. Complimentary coffee in rms. Restaurant 7:30 am-10 pm. Rm serv 7:30-10 am, noon-2 pm, 6-10 pm. Bar. Ck-out 11 am. Meeting rms. Business servs avail. Bellhops. Valet serv. Concierge. Sundries. Gift shop. Airport transportation. Tennis. Downhill ski 12 mi; x-country ski. Lawn games. Refrigerators, fireplaces; microwaves avail. Private decks, balconies with view of Tetons. Picnic tables. Cr cds: A, DS, MC, V.

★★ **TRAPPER INN.** *235 N Cache Dr (83001). 307/733-2648; fax 307/739-9351; toll-free 800/341-8000. www.trapperinn.com.* 54 rms, 2 story. June-mid-Sept: S, D $58-$134; each addl $7; under 12 free; higher rates special events; lower rates rest of yr. Crib free. TV; cable (premium). Complimentary coffee in rms. Restaurant nearby. Ck-out 11 am. Coin lndry. Meeting rm. Whirlpools. Refrigerators; many microwaves. Cr cds: A, C, D, JCB, MC, V.

★★★ **THE WORT HOTEL.** *50 N Glenwood St, Jackson Hole (83001).*

307/733-2190; fax 307/733-2067; toll-free 800/322-2727. www.worthotel.com. 60 units, 2 story. Mid-June-mid-Sept: S, D $140-$220; each addl $15; suites $240-$440; under 12 free; lower rates rest of yr. TV; cable (premium). Restaurant 7 am-10 pm. Bar 11-2 am. Ck-out 11 am. Meeting rms. Business servs avail. Bellhops. Valet serv. Downhill/x-country ski 15 mi. Exercise equipt. Whirlpools. Renovated 1940s hotel. Old West decor. Cr cds: A, D, DS, MC, V.

🄳 ⬧ ⬧ 🛪 ⬧ ⬧ 🆂🄲

Resorts

★★ **JACKSON HOLE RESORT.** 3535 N Wilson Rd, Wilson (83014). 307/733-3990; fax 307/733-5551. www.jhrl.com. 117 condo units. No A/C. June-Sept: 1-bedrm $140-$160; 2-bedrm $150-$170; 3-bedrm $150-$300; 4-bedrm $200-$380; house $255-$910; min stay required; higher rates Dec 25; lower rates rest of yr. Crib $10. TV; cable. Heated pool; whirlpool. Dining rm 6-10 pm. Bar 4 pm-2 am. Ck-out 11 am. Guest lndry. Meeting rms. Beauty shop. Downhill/x-country ski 4 mi. Exercise rm; sauna, steam rm. Massage. Refrigerators, microwaves, fireplaces. Private patios, balconies. Cr cds: A, DS, MC, V.

🄳 ⬧ ⬧ ⬧ ⬧ ⬧ ⬧ 🛪

★★★ **TETON PINES.** 3450 N Clubhouse Dr (83002). 307/733-1005, fax 307/733-2860; toll-free 800/238-2223. www.tetonpines.com. 16 suites. Mid-June-Sept: S, D $180-$495; 2-bedrm $895; golf plan; lower rates rest of yr. Crib free. TV; cable, VCR avail. Pool; whirlpool. Complimentary continental bkfst. Coffee in rms. Restaurant (see also TETON PINES). Ck-out 11 am, ck-in 4 pm. Grocery ½ mi. Coin lndry 7 mi. Package store ½ mi. Meeting rms. Business servs avail. Bellhops. Free airport transportation. Tennis, pro. 18-hole golf, greens fee $50-$150, pro, putting green, driving range. Downhill ski 5 mi; x-country ski on site, rentals. Health club privileges. Refrigerators, wet bars, microwaves; some fireplaces. Cr cds: A, D, V.

🄳 ⬧ ⬧ 🛪 ⬧ ⬧ ⬧ 🛪 ⬧ ⬧

B&Bs/Small Inns

★★ **DAVY JACKSON.** 85 Perry Ave (83001). 307/739-2294; fax 307/733-9704; toll-free 800/584-0532. www.davyjackson.com. 12 rms, 3 story. June-Sept: S, D $199-$239; each addl $15; under 12 free; lower rates rest of yr. Crib free. TV; cable. Complimentary full bkfst; afternoon refreshments. Restaurant nearby. Ck-out noon, ck-in 3 pm. Whirlpool. Some in-rm whirlpools, fireplaces. Victorian decor; many antiques. Cr cds: A, DS, MC, V.

🄳 ⬧ ⬧ ⬧ ⬧ 🆂🄲

★★★ **THE HUFF HOUSE INN BED & BREAKFAST.** 240 E Deloney (83001). 307/733-4164; fax 307/739-9091. www.jacksonwyomingbnb.com. 7 rms, 2 with shower only, some A/C, 2 story. Feb-Mar, June-Sept: S, D $109-$215 (2-day min); each addl $20; lower rates rest of yr. TV; cable, VCR avail (movies). Complimentary full bkfst. Restaurant nearby. Ck-out 11 am, ck-in 3 pm. Luggage handling. Downhill/x-country ski 1 mi. Game rm. Some in-rm whirlpools. Victorian house built in 1917. Totally nonsmoking. Cr cds: DS, MC, V.

⬧ ⬧ ⬧ ⬧ ⬧

★★★ **THE WILDFLOWER INN.** 3725 N Teton Village Rd (83001). 307/733-4710; fax 307/739-0914. www.jacksonholewildflower.com. 5 rms, 1 suite, 2 story. A/C. S, D $200-$320; suite $320; each addl $50; under 12 free. TV; cable (premium). Complimentary full bkfst. Restaurant nearby. Ck-out 11 am, ck-in 3-5 pm. Concierge serv. Downhill ski 4 mi. Whirlpool. Log house on 3 acres; pond; mountain views. Totally nonsmoking. Cr cds: MC, V.

⬧ ⬧ ⬧

Restaurants

★★★ **THE ALPENHOF DINING ROOM.** 3255 W Village Dr, Teton Village (83025). 307/733-3242. www.alpenhoflodge.com. Own baking. Hrs: 7:30-10:30 am, 6-9:30 pm. Closed early Apr-mid-May and mid-Oct-early Dec. Res accepted. Bar. Wine list. Bkfst $3-$7.95, dinner $16-$30;

Dinner for 2: $55-$61. Child's menu. Parking. Cr cds: A, D, DS, MC, V.

★★ **ANTHONY'S.** *62 S Glenwood (83001). 307/733-3717.* Hrs: 5:30-9:30 pm. Closed Thanksgiving, Dec 25. Italian menu. Bar. Dinner $10-$18. Specializes in lemon chicken, Cajun fettuccine, homemade bread. Art Deco Italian decor. Totally non-smoking. Cr cds: A, D, MC, V.

D

★★★ **BLUE LION.** *160 N Millward St (83001). 307/733-3912. www. bluelionrestaurant.com.* Hrs: 5:30-10 pm. Res accepted. Continental menu. Bar. Dinner $15-$25. Specializes in fresh seafood, lamb, fresh elk. Own baking. Outdoor dining; bi-level deck. In renovated old house. Herb garden. Cr cds: A, DS, MC, V.

★★★ **CADILLAC GRILLE.** *55 N Cache (83001). 307/733-3279.* Hrs: 11:30 am-2:30 pm, 5:30-9:30 pm. Res accepted. Bar. A la carte entrees: lunch $4.95-$10.95. Dinner $14-$28. Child's meals. Specializes in wild game, steak, fresh seafood, wood-oven pizza. Own baking. Contemporary art decor. Cr cds: A, MC, V.

D

★★ **CALICO.** *2650 Teton Village Rd (83025). 307/733-2460. www.calico restaurant.com.* Hrs: 5-10 pm. Bar to midnight. Dinner $9.75-$18.95. Child's menu. Specializes in pasta, pizza, seafood. Old West decor. Cr cds: A, MC, V.

D

★ **JEDEDIAH'S.** *135 E Broadway (83001). 307/733-5671.* Hrs: 7 am-2 pm; also 5:30-9 pm; winter hrs vary. Closed Thanksgiving, Dec 25. Res accepted. Bkfst $2.95-$8.95, lunch $4.50-$8.50, dinner $8-$17. Child's menu. Specialties: sourdough pancakes, buffalo burgers, sourdough carrot cake. Rustic decor in old house (1910); Western antiques. Cr cds: A, D, MC, V.

D SC

★★ **MILLION DOLLAR COWBOY STEAK HOUSE.** *25 N Cache St (83001). 307/733-4790.* Hrs: 5:30-10 pm, Fri, Sat to 11 pm; Closed Thanksgiving, Dec 25; Apr-early May, Nov. Bar. Dinner $18-$30. Specializes in steak, fresh seafood, wild game.

Knotty pine furnishings, Western decor. Cr cds: A, DS, MC, V.

D

★★ **OFF BROADWAY.** *30 S King St (83001). 307/733-9777.* Hrs: 5:30-10 pm. Closed Dec 25. Res accepted. Serv bar. Dinner $11.95-$22.95. Child's meals. Specializes in fresh seafood, pasta, elk medallions, Thai dishes. Outdoor dining. Totally non-smoking. Cr cds: A, MC, V.

SC

★★★ **RANGE.** *225 N Cacat St (83001). 307/733-5481.* Hrs: 5:30-10 pm. Res accepted. Bar. Dinner $16-$31. Child's meals. Specialties: medallions of elk, breast of turkey, Sonoma free-range cornish game hen. Metropolitan high plains decor. Cr cds: A, MC, V.

D

★★★ **SNAKE RIVER GRILL.** *84 E Broadway (83001). 307/733-0557. www.snakerivergrill.com.* Hrs: 5:30-10:30 pm. Closed Dec 25; Apr-mid-May, Nov-early Dec. Res accepted. Wine list. Dinner $17.95-$34.95. Child's menu. Specialties: fresh ahi tuna, roast elk loin. Upscale Western ranch decor and atmosphere; stone fireplace. Cr cds: A, DS, MC, V.

D

★★★ **STRUTTING GROUSE.** *Jackson Hole Golf and Tennis Club (83001). 307/733-7788. www.gtlc.com.* Hrs: 11:30 am-9:30 pm. Closed Oct-mid-May. Res accepted. Bar. A la carte entrees: lunch $5-$8.50, dinner $15.95-$22.95. Specializes in fresh salmon, bison medallions, venison sausage. Parking. Outdoor dining (lunch). Western decor; gardens. View of golf course, mountains. Cr cds: A, DS, MC, V.

D

★★ **SWEETWATER.** *King and Pearl Sts (83001).* Hrs: 11:30 am-3 pm, 5:30-10 pm. Closed Thanksgiving, Dec 25. Res accepted. Greek, Amer menu. Bar. Lunch $7.25-$8.50, dinner $14.95-$19.95. Child's meals. Specializes in lamb, seafood, Greek phyllo pies. Outdoor dining. Western decor. In log house built by pioneers. Totally nonsmoking. Cr cds: A, D, MC, V.

D

★★★ **TETON PINES.** *3450 N Clubhouse Dr (83001).* 307/733-1005. *www.tetonpines.com.* Hrs: 11:30 am-2:30 pm, 6-9 pm. Closed Sun. Res accepted. Bar. Lunch $4.75-$11.75, dinner $16-$29. 15 percent serv charge. Specializes in wild game, fresh seafood, steak. Parking. Outdoor dining. View of Tetons. Paintings of local scenes displayed. Cr cds: A, MC, V.

D

★★ **VISTA GRANDE.** *2550 Teton Village Rd (83001).* 307/733-6964. Hrs: 5:30-10 pm. Closed part of Nov. Mexican menu. Bar. Dinner $7.50-$14.95. Child's meals. Parking. Mexican decor. Outdoor dining. View of mountains. Totally nonsmoking. Cr cds: A, MC, V.

D

Unrated Dining Spots

BAR J. *4200 Bar J Chuckwagon Rd (83014).* 307/733-3370. *www.barj chuckwagon.com.* Sittings: 7:30 pm (dinner), 8:30 pm (show). Closed Oct-May. Res accepted. Complete meals: dinner $16-$24; children 4-8 yrs, $6. Specializes in barbecue-chuck wagon dinner with beef, chicken, steak. Western stage show. On working cattle ranch. Cr cds: DS, MC, V.

D

THE BUNNERY. *130 N Cache St (83001).* 307/733-5474. Hrs: 7 am-9 pm. Closed Thanksgiving, Dec 25. Wine, beer. Bkfst $5-$8, lunch $5-$8, dinner $6.95-$9.95. Child's menu. Specializes in whole grain waffles, broiled sandwiches. Own baking. Cr cds: MC, V.

D SC

Kemmerer

(E-1) *See also Evanston, Green River*

Pop 3,020 **Elev** 6,959 ft
Area code 307 **Zip** 83101
Information Chamber of Commerce, 800 Pine Ave; 307/877-9761
Web www.kemmerer.org

A Ranger District office of the Bridger-Teton National Forest (see JACKSON) is located here.

What to See and Do

Fossil Butte National Monument. On 8,198 acres is one of the most extensive concentrations of fossilized aquatic vertebrates, plants, and insects (some 50 million yrs old) in the US. (Daily) 11 mi W on US 30 N. Phone 307/877-4455.

Lander

(D-3) *See also Riverton*

Settled 1875 **Pop** 7,023 **Elev** 5,360 ft
Area code 307 **Zip** 82520
Information Chamber of Commerce, 160 N 1st St; 307/332-3892 or 800/433-0662
Web www.landerchamber.org

Lander was once called the place where the rails end and the trails begin. Wind River Range, surrounding the town, offers hunting and fishing, mountain climbing, and rock hunting. The annual One-Shot Antelope Hunt opens the antelope season and draws celebrities and sports enthusiasts from all over the country. Sacajawea Cemetery (burial place of Lewis and Clark's Shoshone guide) is located in Fort Washakie, 15 mi NW on US 287. A Ranger District office of the Shoshone National Forest (see CODY) is located in Lander.

What to See and Do

Fremont County Pioneer Museum. Seven exhibit rms and outdoor exhibit area document the pioneer, ranching, Native American, and business history of the area. (Mon-Fri, also Sat afternoons) 1445 W Main St. Phone 307/332-4137.

Sinks Canyon State Park. In a spectacular canyon, amid unspoiled Rocky Mtn beauty, lies the middle fork of the Popo Agie River, which disappears into a cavern and rises again several hundred yards below in a crystal-clear, trout-filled spring pool. Abundant wildlife in certain seasons. Visitor center; observation points. Fishing (exc in the Rise of the Sinks). Hiking, nature trails. Groomed x-country ski and snowmobile trails nearby. Limited tent and trailer sites (standard fees); other sites nearby. 7 mi SW on WY 131. Phone 307/332-6333.

South Pass City. An example of a once-flourishing gold mining town. During the gold rush of 1868-1872, 1,200 people lived here. Women were first given equal suffrage by a territorial act introduced from South Pass City and passed in Cheyenne on December 10, 1869. The town is currently being restored and has more than 20 historic buildings on display (mid-May-Sept, daily). 33 mi S on WY 28, then 3 mi W. Phone 307/332-3684. ¢

Motels/Motor Lodges

★★ **BEST WESTERN INN AT LAN-DER.** *260 Grand View Dr (82520). 307/332-2847; fax 307/332-2760; toll-free 800/780-7234. www.bestwestern. com.* 100 rms, 2 story. May-Sept: S $70; D $85; each addl $5; under 12 free; lower rates rest of yr. Crib $5. TV; cable. Heated pool; whirlpool. Complimentary continental bkfst. Restaurant nearby. Ck-out 11 am. Meeting rms. Free airport transportation. Exercise equipt. Some refrigerators. Cr cds: A, D, DS, MC, V.

★★ **BUDGET HOST PRONG-HORN.** *150 E Main St (82520). 307/332-3940; fax 307/332-2651; toll-free 800/283-4678. www.budgethost.com.* 55 rms, 2 story. May-Sept: S $42-$54; D $58-$74; each addl $5; suites $65; under 12 free; lower rates rest of yr. Crib $5. Pet accepted, some restrictions. TV; cable (premium). Complimentary continental bkfst. Restaurant 6 am-10 pm. Rm serv. Ck-out 11 am. Coin lndry. Meeting rms. Exercise equipt. Whirlpool. Some refrigerators. On river. Cr cds: A, C, D, DS, MC, V.

Laramie

(F-6) *See also Cheyenne*

Founded 1868 **Pop** 26,687 **Elev** 7,165 ft **Area code** 307 **Zip** 82070

Information Albany County Tourism Board, 210 Custer; 307/745-4195 or 800/445-5303

Web www.laramie-tourism.org

Laramie had a rugged beginning as a lawless leftover of the westward-rushing Union Pacific. The early settlement was populated by hunters, saloonkeepers, and brawlers. When the tracks pushed on, Laramie stabilized somewhat, but for six months vigilantes were the only law enforcement available against desperate characters who operated from town. Reasonable folk finally prevailed; schools and businesses sprang up, and improved cattle breeds brought prosperity. A Ranger District office of the Medicine Bow National Forest is located here.

What to See and Do

Laramie Plains Museum. Victorian mansion (1892); each rm finished in a different wood; collections incl antique furniture, toys, china, ranching memorabilia, Western artifacts. Special seasonal displays. (Tues-Sat) 603 Ivinson Ave. Phone 307/742-4448. ¢¢

Lincoln Monument. World's largest bronze head (12½ ft high, 3½ tons), by Robert Russin of the University of Wyoming. 8 mi SE on I-80.

Medicine Bow National Forest. The more than one million acres incl the Snowy Range Scenic Byway; one 30-mi stretch on WY 130, west from Centennial, is particularly scenic with elevations as high as 10,800 ft at Snowy Range Pass. Winter sports areas, picnic grounds, camping (fee), commercial lodges. W on WY 130, SW on WY 230, E on I-80 or N via US 30, WY 34, I-25, local roads. For further information contact the Forest Supervisor, 2468 Jackson St. Phone 307/745-2300.

Skiing. Snowy Range Ski Area. Triple, three double chairlifts, T-bar; 25

EXPLORING LARAMIE

Laramie has an oddly bifurcated nature: born of the railroad boom that followed the nation's first transcontinental railway, the town preserves the rough-around-the-edges feel of an Old West frontier town. Since 1887, Laramie has also been the home of the University of Wyoming, for many years the state's only center of higher education, which gives the town a patina of sophistication lacking in other Wyoming towns of this size. Laramie's well-preserved Victorian architecture and a comparative wealth of art and museums make it an excellent town to explore on foot.

Start a walking tour of Laramie on the steps of the town's city hall (406 Ivinson Street). Just to the north is St. Matthews Cathedral (104 South 4th Street), an imposing Neo-Gothic Episcopal church with an attached English-style garden. The church was constructed with funds donated by Edward Ivinson, one of the town's original settlers, who made his fortune on real estate and banking. Two of the church's impressive stained-glass windows memorialize the lives of Mr. and Mrs. Ivinson.

The Ivinson's 1892 home is also among the town's landmarks. Now operated as the Laramie Plains Museum (603 Ivinson), this Queen Anne Victorian home was slated to be demolished (and the land used for a parking lot) before citizens raised money to turn it into a museum. The Ivinson mansion houses a valuable collection of household items from Laramie's pioneer days. Also on the spacious landscaped grounds are a carriage house and a one-room log schoolhouse.

Continue east on Ivinson Street to the campus of the University of Wyoming, beginning at 9th Street. This oasis of well-tended lawns and huge spruce trees contains a number of worthwhile museums and handsome university buildings, many constructed of the local yellow sandstone. At the corner of Ivinson and 10th Street is Old Main, the university's original structure from 1887. An imposing building fronted by columns and capped by a bell tower, Old Main is now office to the university president.

Head north on 10th Street past classroom buildings to university's Geology Museum, near 10th and Clark streets. The museum has a major collection of Wyoming rocks and minerals, as well as some impressive fossils. Highlights include a mounted Apatasaurus (Brontosaurus) skeleton (one of only five in the world) and "Big Al," the most complete Allosaurus fossil ever found. A life-sized, copper-clad statue of Tyrannosaurus rex marks the museum's entrance.

Walk a block east to Prexy's Pasture, the heart of the University of Wyoming campus. This large, grassy area was originally a pasture where the university's first president kept his personal herd of cattle. Today, it's the place to hang out in the sun, kick around a hacky sack, and toss Frisbees.

Continue southeast on the campus to the Anthropology Museum, near the corner of Ivinson and 14th streets. The museum has an excellent set of exhibits on the history and prehistory of Wyoming's Native Americans.

Walk north one block to University Street, where across a meadow of manicured lawn, the school's sororities and fraternities face each other. Head east, past the Fine Arts Center, then north to the Centennial Complex. This imposing structure, fashioned to resemble a six-story tipi, houses both the American Heritage Center, one of the finest museums in the state, and the University Art Museum. Unlike many large collections of art in the American West, this museum focuses on 20th-century and contemporary art.

runs; school, rentals, snowmaking; guided snowmobile tours; cafeteria, bar. Vertical drop 1,000 ft; longest run two mi. X-country trails nearby. (Mid-Nov-mid-Apr, daily) 32 mi W on WY 130 (Snowy Range Rd). ¢¢¢¢

University of Wyoming. (1886) 11,057 students. The state's only four-yr university. Its campus has the highest elevation of any in the US. The UW Visitor Information Center, 1408 Ivinson Ave, has displays, community and campus literature. Between 9th and 30th sts, 1 blk N of US 30 (Grand Ave). Phone 307/766-4075. On campus are

American Heritage Center & Art Museum. Nine galleries feature display of paintings, graphics, and sculpture from the 16th century to the present. Manuscripts, rare books, artifacts relating to Wyoming and the West. Research facilities. (Tues-Sun; closed hols) 2111 Willet Dr. Phone 307/766-6622.

Geological Museum. Houses rocks, minerals, vertebrate, invertebrate, mammal, and plant fossils, incl one of five brontosaurus skeletons in the world. (Mon-Fri) S. K. Knight Geology Building. Phone 307/766-4218. **FREE**

Wyoming Territorial Prison and Old West Park. Western heritage park with living history programs. Frontier town, Territorial Prison, US Marshals' Museum (fee), dinner theater (fee), playground, gift shop. (May-Sept, daily) 975 Snowy Range Rd, just off I-80. Phone 745/616-1580. ¢

Vedauwoo. Sightseeing, camping, and climbing amid rock formations on the Medicine Bow National Forest. (Daily) Fee for camping. 21 mi SE of Laramie. Phone 800/280-2267. **FREE**

Motels/Motor Lodges

★ **CAMELOT MOTEL.** *523 S Adams St (82070). 307/721-8860; toll-free 866/721-8395.* 33 rms, 2 story. S $45; D $55-$65; each addl $5. Crib $3. TV; cable. Restaurant opp open 24 hrs. Ck-out 11 am. Coin lndry. Cr cds: A, C, D, DS, MC, V.
D ⊠ 🐾 SC

★ **ECONO LODGE.** *1370 McCue St (82072). 307/745-8900; fax 307/745-5806; res 800/446-6900. www.econo*

lodge.com. 51 rms, 2 story. June-Aug: S, D $75-$95; each addl $10; suites $100; under 13 free; lower rates rest of yr. Crib free. TV; cable. Indoor pool. Complimentary continental bkfst. Restaurant nearby. Ck-out 11 am. Meeting rm. Cr cds: A, D, DS, MC, V.
D 👤 🏊 ⊠ ⊠ 🐾

★★ **HOLIDAY INN.** *2313 Soldier Springs Rd (82070). 307/742-6611; fax 307/745-8371; toll-free 800/465-4329. www.holiday-inn.com.* 100 rms, 2 story. Mid-May-mid-Sept: S $80; D $80-$120; each addl $8; under 18 free; lower rates rest of yr. Crib free. Pet accepted. TV; cable (premium). Indoor pool; whirlpool. Coffee in rms. Restaurant 6 am-10 pm. Bar. Ck-out noon. Coin lndry. Meeting rms. Gift shop. Free airport transportation. Cr cds: A, C, D, DS, MC, V.
D 🐾 ⊠ ⊠ 🐾 SC

★★ **HOWARD JOHNSON INN.** *1555 Snowy Range Rd (82070). 307/742-8371; fax 307/742-0884. www.hojo.com.* 112 rms, 2 story. Mid-May-mid-Sept: S, D $60-$120; each addl $6; under 12 free; higher rates special events; lower rates rest of yr. Crib $6. Pet accepted; $10. TV; cable. Heated indoor pool; whirlpool. Complimentary full bkfst. Restaurant 6 am-10 pm. Bar 8-2 am. Coffee in rms. Ck-out noon. Coin lndry. Meeting rms. In-rm modem link. Gift shop. Free airport, RR station, bus depot transportation. Cr cds: A, C, D, DS, MC, V.
D 🐾 ⊠ ⊠ 🐾

Lovell

(B-3) *See also Greybull*

Pop 2,131 **Elev** 3,837 ft
Area code 307 **Zip** 82431
Information Lovell Area Chamber of Commerce, 287 E Main, PO Box 295; 307/548-7552
Web www.lovellchamber.com

A Ranger District office of the Bighorn National Forest (see SHERIDAN) is located here.

What to See and Do

Bighorn Canyon National Recreation Area. The focus of the area is 71-mi-long Bighorn Lake, created by the Yellowtail Dam in Fort Smith, MT. Boats may travel through Bighorn Canyon, which cuts across the northern end of the Bighorn Mtns in north-central Wyoming and south-central Montana. The solar-powered Bighorn Canyon Visitor Center is in Lovell on US 14A (daily). The Fort Smith Visitor Contact Station is in Ft Smith, MT (daily). Both centers are closed Jan 1, Thanksgiving, Dec 25. Recreational and interpretive activities are avail at both ends of the area. Fishing, boating, picnicking, camping. South entrance 2 mi E on US 14A, then 8 mi N on WY 37. For further information contact Bighorn Canyon Visitor Center, Hwy 14A E. Phone 307/548-2251. Adj and accessible from town is

Pryor Mountain Wild Horse Range. This 32,000-acre refuge, established in 1968, provides a sanctuary for wild horses descended from Native American ponies and escaped farm and ranch horses. Administered jointly by the National Park Service and the Bureau of Land Management. Phone 406/896-5223.

Special Event

Mustang Days. Parade, rodeo, exhibits, entertainment, dancing, barbecue, seven-mi run. Late June. Phone 307/548-7552.

Motel/Motor Lodge

★ **SUPER 8 MOTEL.** 595 E Main (82431). 307/548-2725; toll-free 800/800-8000. www.super8.com. 34 rms, 2 story. S $44.88; D $57.88; each addl $3; lower rates rest of yr; under 12 free. Crib free. Pet accepted. TV; cable (premium). Restaurant adj 6 am-9:30 pm. Ck-out 11 am. Cr cds: A, C, D, DS, MC, V.
🄳 🐾 🔀 🔥 SC

Restaurant

★ **BIG HORN.** 605 E Main St (82431). 307/548-6811. Hrs: 6 am-10 pm. Closed Jan 1, Dec 25. Bar. Bkfst $2.75-$7.50, lunch $2.50-$5.75, dinner $5-$15. Child's menu. Specializes in seafood, steak. Salad bar. Cr cds: A, C, D, DS, MC, V.
🄳 SC 🔀

Lusk

(D-7) *See also Douglas*

Founded 1886 **Pop** 1,504 **Elev** 5,015 ft **Area code** 307 **Zip** 82225
Information Chamber of Commerce, PO Box 457; 307/334-2950 or 800/223-LUSK
Web www.luskwyoming.com

Raising livestock has always been important in Lusk; fine herds of Simmental, Angus, and sheep are the local pride. Hunting is excellent for deer and antelope.

What to See and Do

Stagecoach Museum. Relics of pioneer days, Native American artifacts; stagecoach. (Mon-Sat) 322 S Main. Phone 307/334-3444. ¢

Special Events

Legend of Rawhide. Live show performed since 1946. Concert, dances, trade show, golf tournament, gun show, parade, pancake bkfst. Second wkend July. Phone 307/334-2950.

Senior Pro Rodeo. Labor Day wkend. Phone 307/334-2950.

Motels/Motor Lodges

★ **BEST VALUE INN COVERED WAGON MOTEL.** 730 S Main St (82225). 307/334-2836; fax 307/334-2977. www.bestvalueinn.com. 51 rms. Mid-June-mid-Oct: S $66-$99; D $82-$115; each addl $5; suite $155; lower rates rest of yr. Crib $2. TV; cable. Indoor pool; whirlpool. Playground. Complimentary coffee in lobby. Restaurant nearby. Ck-out 11 am. Coin lndry. Meeting rm. Sauna. Cr cds: A, C, D, DS, MC, V.
🄳 🛏 🔀 🔥 SC

★★ **BEST WESTERN PIONEER.** 731 S Main (82225). 307/334-2640; fax 307/334-2660; toll-free 800/528-1234. www.bestwestern.com. 30 rms. S $63; D $71; each addl $4. Crib $4. TV; cable.

Pool. Complimentary coffee in lobby. Restaurant nearby. Ck-out 11 am. Cr cds: A, C, D, DS, MC, V.

Newcastle (C-7)

Founded 1889 **Pop** 3,003 **Elev** 4,317 ft **Area code** 307 **Zip** 82701

Information Newcastle Area Chamber of Commerce, 1323 Washington, PO Box 68; 307/746-2739 or 800/835-0157

Web www.newcastle.1wyo.net

Originally a coal mining town, Newcastle is now an oil field center with its own refinery. It is also a tourist center, with fishing, hunting, and recreational facilities nearby. A Ranger District office of the Black Hills National Forest is located here.

What to See and Do

Anna Miller Museum. Museum of Northeastern Wyoming, housed in stone cavalry barn. Log cabin from Jenney Stockade, oldest building in the Black Hills, and an early rural schoolhouse. More than 100 exhibits. (Mon-Fri, Sat by appt) Delaware and Washington Park. Phone 307/746-4188. **FREE**

Beaver Creek Loop Tour. Self-guided driving tour designed to provide the opportunity to explore a diverse and beautiful country. 45-mi tour covering 23 marked sites. Phone 307/746-2739. **FREE**

Pinedale

(D-2) *See also Jackson*

Settled 1878 **Pop** 1,181 **Elev** 7,175 ft **Area code** 307 **Zip** 82941

Information Chamber of Commerce, 32 E Pine, PO Box 176; 307/367-2242

Web www.pinedaleonline.com/chamber

Pinedale is a place where genuine cowboys can still be found, and cattle drives still occur. Mountains, conifer and aspen forests, and lakes and rivers combine to make this a beautiful vacation area. There are fossil beds in the area, and rockhounding is popular. Cattle and sheep are raised on nearby ranches. A Ranger District office of the Bridger-Teton National Forest (see JACKSON) is located in Pinedale.

What to See and Do

Bridger-Teton National Forest. Lies along the Wind River Range, east, north, and west of town. Fishing; hunting, hiking, camping (fee). In forest is

Bridger Wilderness. Approx 400,000 acres of mountainous terrain entered only by foot or horseback. Trout fishing in snow-fed streams and more than 1,300 mountain lakes; hunting for big game. Backpacking. Permits required for some activities. Pack trips arranged by area outfitters.

Hunting. In-season hunting for elk, moose, deer, bear, antelope, mountain bighorn sheep, birds, and small game in surrounding mountains and mesas.

Museum of the Mountain Man. Houses exhibits on fur trade, western exploration, early history. (May-Oct, daily) Henick St, exit 191, Fremont Lake Rd. Phone 307/367-4101. ¢¢

⭐ **Scenic Drives. Skyline.** Up into the mountains 14 mi the fauna changes from sagebrush to an alpine setting. Lakes, conifers, beautiful mountain scenery; wildlife often seen. **Green River Lakes.** N via WY 352 to the lakes with Square Top Mtn in the background; popular with photographers. Wooded campground, trails, backpacking.

Water sports. Fishing for grayling, rainbow, mackinaw, brown trout, golden, and other trout in most lakes and rivers; ice-fishing, mostly located north of town. Swimming, waterskiing, boating, sailing regattas, float trips on New Fork and Green rivers.

Winter recreation. X-country skiing, groomed snowmobile trails, ice-fishing, skating.

Special Event

Green River Rendezvous. Rodeo grounds, Sublette County. Noted historical pageant commemorating the meeting of fur trappers, mountain men, and Native Americans with the Trading Company's wagon trains at Fort Bonneville. Mid-July. Phone 307/367-2242.

Motel/Motor Lodge

★★ **BEST WESTERN INN.** *850 W Pine St (82941). 307/367-6869; fax 307/367-6897; res 800/528-1234. www.bestwestern.com.* 58 rms, 2 story. June-Labor Day: S, D $99; suites $125; under 12 free; lower rates rest of yr. Crib $5. Pet accepted. TV; cable. Indoor pool; whirlpool. Sauna. Complimentary continental bkfst. Restaurant nearby. Ck-out 11 am. Meeting rms. In-rm modem link. Exercise equipt. Some refrigerators. Cr cds: A, C, D, DS, MC, V.

Restaurant

★★ **MCGREGOR'S PUB.** *21 N Franklin St (82941). 307/367-4443.* Hrs: 11:30 am-2 pm, 5-10 pm; Sat, Sun from 5:30 pm. Closed hols. Res accepted. No A/C. Bar. Lunch $4.95-$7.99, dinner $12.95-$29.95. Child's menu. Specializes in prime rib, scallops, pasta. Own desserts, bread. Contemporary ranch decor. Cr cds: A, D, DS, MC, V.

Rawlins

(F-4) *See also Lander, Thermopolis*

Founded 1867 **Pop** 9,380 **Elev** 6,755 ft **Area code** 307 **Zip** 82301

Information Rawlins-Carbon County Chamber of Commerce, 519 W Cedar, PO Box 1331; 307/324-4111 or 800/228-3547

Web w3.trib.com/~rcccoc/

Rawlins, a division point of the Union Pacific Railroad, is located 20 miles east of the Continental Divide. In 1867, General John A. Rawlins, Chief of Staff of the US Army, wished for a drink of cool, clear water. Upon finding the spring near the base of the hills and tasting it, he said, "If

anything is ever named after me, I hope it will be a spring of water." The little oasis was named Rawlins Springs, as was the community that grew up beside it. The city name was later shortened to Rawlins.

What to See and Do

Carbon County Museum. Houses artifacts of mining and ranching ventures. (Schedule varies) 9th and Walnut sts. Phone 307/328-2740. **Donation**

Seminoe State Park. Seminoe Dam impounds a 27-mi-long reservoir surrounded by giant white sand dunes and sagebrush. Pronghorn antelope and sage grouse inhabit area. Swimming, fishing (trout, walleye), boating (ramps); hiking, picnicking, tent and trailer sites (standard fee). 6 mi E on I-80 to Sinclair, then 35 mi N on County Rd 351. Phone 307/320-3043.

Wyoming Frontier Prison. Located on 49 acres, construction was begun in 1888. The prison operated from 1901-1981. Tours (fee). (Memorial Day-Labor Day, daily; rest of yr, by appt) 5th and Walnut. Phone 307/324-4422. ¢

Special Event

Carbon County Fair and Rodeo. Fairgrounds, Rodeo Park off Spruce St. Incl parades, exhibits, livestock, contests, demolition derby, old-timer rodeo. Second full wk Aug. Phone 307/324-6866.

Motels/Motor Lodges

★ **DAYS INN.** *2222 E Cedar St (82301). 307/324-6615; toll-free 888/324-6615. www.daysinn.com.* 118 rms, 2 story. June-mid-Sept: S $65; D $79; each addl $5; under 18 free; lower rates rest of yr. Crib free. Pet accepted. TV; cable (premium). Pool. Complimentary continental bkfst. Coffee in rms. Restaurant 11 am-2 pm, 5-9 pm. Bar 5 pm-2 am. Ck-out noon. Coin lndry. Meeting rms. Business servs avail. Cr cds: A, C, D, DS, MC, V.

★ **SLEEP INN.** *1400 Higley Blvd (82301). 307/328-1732; fax 307/328-0412; res 800/753-3746. www.sleepinn.*

com. 81 rms, many with shower only, 2 story. June-Sept: S $53; D $58-$63; each addl $5; under 18 free; lower rates rest of yr. Crib free. TV; cable (premium), VCR avail (movies $3.50). Complimentary continental bkfst. Restaurant adj open 24 hrs. Ck-out 11 am. Meeting rms. Business servs avail. Sauna. Cr cds: A, DS, MC, V.

Riverton

(D-3) *See also Lander, Thermopolis*

Founded 1906 **Pop** 9,202 **Elev** 4,964 ft **Area code** 307 **Zip** 82501

Information Chamber of Commerce, 213 Main St; 307/856-4801 or 800/325-2732

Web www.rivertonchamber.org

Riverton is the largest city in Fremont County. Resources extracted from the region include natural gas, oil, iron ore, timber, and phosphate. Irrigation from the Wind River Range has placed 130,000 acres under cultivation, on which barley, alfalfa hay, beans, sunflowers, and grain are grown. The town is surrounded by the Wind River Reservation, where Arapaho and Shoshone live.

What to See and Do

Riverton Museum. Shoshone and Arapaho displays; mountain man display. General store, drugstore, post office, saloon, homesteader's cabin, church, bank, dentist's office, parlor, school, beauty shop. Clothing, quilts, cutters, buggies. 700 E Park St. Phone 307/856-2665. **FREE**

Special Events

Wild West Winter Carnival. Depot Building. Phone 307/856-4801. Early Feb.

State Championship Old-time Fiddle Contest. 21 mi NE via US 26, 789 in Shoshoni. Divisional competition. Late May. Phone 307/856-4801.

1838 Mountain Man Rendezvous. Council fire, primitive shoots, hawk and knife throw, games, food. Camp-

ing avail. Phone 307/856-7306. Early July. Phone 307/325-2732.

Fremont County Fair & Rodeo. First full wk Aug. Phone 800/325-2732.

Powwows. Shoshone and Arapaho tribal powwows are held throughout the summer. Phone 307/856-4801.

Motels/Motor Lodges

★★ **HOLIDAY INN.** *900 E Sunset Dr (82501).* 307/856-8100; fax 307/856-0266; toll-free 877/857-4834. *www. holiday-inn.com.* 121 rms, 2 story. S, D $79; each addl $6; under 19 free. Pet accepted. TV; cable. Indoor pool; poolside serv. Restaurant 6 am-10 pm. Bar 4 pm-2 am. Ck-out noon. Coin lndry. Meeting rms. Sundries. Beauty shop. Airport transportation. Bathrm phones. Cr cds: A, C, D, DS, JCB, MC, V.

★★ **SUNDOWNER STATION.** *1616 N Federal Blvd (82501).* 307/856-6503; toll-free 800/874-1116. 61 rms, 2 story. S $54; D $60; each addl $4; under 12 free. Crib free. Pet accepted. TV; cable. Sauna. Restaurant 5:30 am-10 pm. Bar 4-11 pm. Ck-out 11 am. Meeting rms. Sundries. Free airport transportation. Balconies. Cr cds: A, DS, MC, V.

Rock Springs

(F-3) *See also Green River*

Pop 19,050 **Elev** 6,271 ft **Area code** 307 **Zip** 82901

Information Rock Springs Chamber of Commerce, 1897 Dewar Dr, PO Box 398, 82902; 307/362-3771 or 800/46-DUNES

Web www.rockspringswyoming.net

Rock Springs traces its roots to a spring, which offered an ideal camping site along a Native American trail and, later, a welcome station on the Overland Stage route. Later still, Rock Springs became a supply station that provided millions of tons of coal to the Union Pacific Railroad. Noted for its multiethnic heritage, the town's first inhabitants were primarily Welsh and English immigrants brought in by the railroad and coal companies. West of town are large deposits of trona (sodium sesquicarbonate), used in the manufacture of glass, phosphates, silicates, soaps, and baking soda.

What to See and Do

Flaming Gorge Reservoir. This man-made lake, fed by the Green River, is 90 mi long with approx 375 mi of shoreline, which ranges from low flats to cliffs more than 1,500 ft high. Surrounded by a national recreation area (see GREEN RIVER), the reservoir offers excellent fishing. SW via I-80.

Special Events

Desert Balloon Rally. Early July. Phone 307/362-3771.

Red Desert Round-Up. One of the largest rodeos in the Rocky Mtns region. Late July. Phone 307/352-6789.

Sweetwater County fair. Late July-early Aug. Phone 307/362-3771.

Motels/Motor Lodges

★ **COMFORT INN.** *1670 Sunset Dr (82901).* 307/382-9490; *fax 307/382-7333; res 800/228-5150. www. comfortinn.com.* 103 rms. Mid-May-mid-Sept: S $68; D $74; each addl $6; lower rates rest of yr. Crib $5. Pet accepted; $6. TV; cable (premium). Heated pool; whirlpool. Playground. Complimentary continental bkfst. Restaurant adj. Ck-out 11 am. Coin lndry. Business servs avail. Bathrm phones. Cr cds: A, D, DS, MC, V.

★★ **HOLIDAY INN.** *1675 Sunset Dr (82901).* 307/382-9200; *fax 307/362-1064; res 800/465-4329. www.holiday-inn.com.* 114 rms, 4 story. May-Sept: S, D $83; under 18 free; lower rates rest of yr. Crib free. Pet accepted. TV; cable (premium). Indoor pool; wading pool, whirlpool, poolside serv. Restaurant 6 am-2 pm, 5-10 pm. Bar 11-2 am, Sun noon-10 pm. Ck-out noon. Coin lndry. Meeting rms. Business servs avail. Bellhops. Airport transportation. Balconies. Cr cds: A, D, DS, JCB, MC, V.

★ **RAMADA LIMITED.** *2717 Dewar Dr (82901).* 307/362-1770; *fax 307/362-2830; res 888/298-2054. www.ramada.com.* 130 rms, 2 story. May-early Sept: S, D $65-$90; each addl $6; suites $85; under 18 free; higher rates special events; lower rates rest of yr. Crib avail. Pet accepted. TV; cable (premium). Complimentary continental bkfst. Complimentary coffee in rms. Restaurant adj open 24 hrs. Ck-out noon. Meeting rms. Business servs avail. Bellhops. Heated pool. Cr cds: A, DS, MC, V.

Restaurant

★ **LOG INN.** *#12 Purple Sage Rd (82901).* 307/362-7166. Hrs: 5:30-10 pm; Closed hols. Res accepted. Bar. Dinner $11.50-$25. Specializes in deep-fried lobster, barbecued ribs, blackened prime rib steaks. Log building; rustic decor. Cr cds: A, D, DS, MC, V.

Sheridan

(B-4) *See also Buffalo*

Founded 1882 **Pop** 13,900 **Elev** 3,745 ft **Area code** 307 **Zip** 82801

Information Convention and Visitors Bureau, PO Box 707; 307/672-2485 or 800/453-3650

Web www.sheridanwyoming.com

Sheridan, named for General Philip Sheridan, was not settled until the Cheyenne, Sioux, and Crow were subdued after a series of wars in the region. While the land, rich with grass, was ideal for grazing livestock, ranchers only moved in their herds after the tribes were driven onto reservations. For years the town had a reputation for trouble because of rustling and boundary disputes. Nevertheless, the first dude ranch in history was established near Sheridan in 1904.

Today, the town is a tourist center with dude ranches, hotels and motels, and sporting facilities. The nearby Big Horn Range, once a favored hunting ground of Native Americans, is rich in big game and fishing. A Ranger District office of the Bighorn National Forest is located in Sheridan.

What to See and Do

❌ **Bighorn National Forest.** The Big Horn Mtns rise abruptly from the arid basins below to elevations of more than 13,000 ft. Fallen City, a jumble of huge rock blocks, is viewed from US 14, as are Sibley Lake and Shell Canyon and Falls. From Burgess Junction, US 14A passes by Medicine Mtn, site of the "medicine wheel," an ancient circular structure. US 16 features Meadowlark Lake and panoramic views of Tensleep Canyon and the 189,000-acre Cloud Peak Wilderness. Forest has resorts, campgrounds (fee); backpacking and horseback trails; skiing at Antelope Butte Ski Area (60 mi W on US 14) and High Park Ski Area (40 mi E of Worland). Fishing; hunting, x-country skiing, snowmobiling. More than 1,100,000 acres west and south of town, traversed by three scenic byways; US 14 (Bighorn Scenic Byway), US 14A (Medicine Wheel Passage), and US 16 (Cloud Peak Skyway). Contact the Forest Supervisor, 2013 Eastside 2nd St. Phone 307/674-2600.

Bradford Brinton Memorial. Historic ranch house built in 1892; purchased in 1923 by Bradford Brinton and enlarged to its present 20 rms. Contains collections and furnishings that make this a memorial to the art and history of the West. More than 600 oils, watercolors, and sketches by American artists incl Russell and Remington. Also bronzes, prints and rare books, ranch equipment, saddles, and Native American artifacts. (Mid-May-Labor Day, daily; also early Dec-Dec 24) 7 mi S on US 87, then 5 mi SW on WY 335. Phone 307/672-3173. ¢

King's Saddlery Museum. Collection of saddles; also Western memorabilia, Native American artifacts, old photographs, carriages. (Mon-Sat; closed hols) 184 N Main St, behind store. Phone 307/672-2702. **FREE**

Main Street Historic District. Take a walking tour of Sheridan, which boasts the largest collection of original late-1800s and early-1900s buildings in the state. Phone 307/672-8881. **FREE**

Trail End Historic Center. Home of John B. Kendrick, Governor of Wyoming (1915-1917), later US Senator (1917-1933). Historical and family memorabilia. Mansion of Flemish-Revival architecture; beautifully carved and burnished woodwork is outstanding. Botanical specimens on landscaped grounds. (Apr-Dec 14, daily; closed Veterans' Day, Thanksgiving) 400 Clarendon Ave adj to Kendrick Park. Phone 307/674-4589. ¢

Special Events

Sheridan-Wyo PRCA Rodeo. Carnival and parade. Mid-July. Phone 307/672-9084.

Sheridan County Rodeo. Phone 303/672-2079. Second wkend Aug. Phone 307/672-2079.

Motels/Motor Lodges

★★ **BEST WESTERN SHERIDAN CENTER.** *612 N Main St (82801). 307/674-7421; fax 307/672-3018; toll-free 800/780-7234. www.bestwestern. com.* 138 rms, 2 story. June-Aug: S $69.95; D $79.95; each addl $6; under 12 free; lower rates rest of yr. Crib free. TV; cable. 2 pools, 1 indoor; whirlpool. Complimentary coffee in rms. Restaurant 6:30 am-9:30 pm. Bar noon-midnight. Ck-out 11 am. Meeting rms. Valet serv. Sundries. Free airport, bus depot transportation. Game rm. Some balconies. Cr cds: A, C, D, DS, MC, V.
🏊 ⛷ 🐾 **SC**

★ **DAYS INN.** *1104 Brundage Ln (82801). 307/672-2888; toll-free 800/325-2525. www.daysinn.com.* 46 rms, 2 story. June-Aug: S, D $88-$110; each addl $5; suites $100-$150; under 12 free; lower rates rest of yr. Crib free. TV; cable (premium). Indoor pool; whirlpool. Sauna. Complimentary continental bkfst. Restaurant nearby. Ck-out 11 am. Coin lndry. Meeting rms. Near airport. Cr cds: A, D, DS, MC, V.

[D] [symbols]

★★ **HOLIDAY INN.** *1809 Sugarland Dr (82801). 307/672-8931; fax 307/672-6388; toll-free 877/672-4011. www.holiday-inn.com.* 212 rms, 5 story. S, D $72-$99; suites $135-$200. Crib free. Pet accepted. TV; cable. Indoor pool; whirlpool, poolside serv. Coffee in rms. Restaurant 6 am-10 pm. Bar 4 pm-1:45 am. Ck-out noon. Coin lndry. Meeting rms. Business servs avail. Bellhops. Sundries. Gift shop. Beauty shop. Airport, bus depot transportation. Exercise equipt; sauna. Game rm. Putting green. Basketball. Some refrigerators. Picnic area. Cr cds: A, DS, MC, V.

[D] [symbols] [SC]

B&B/Small Inn

★★★ **SPAHN'S BIG HORN MOUNTAIN BED & BREAKFAST.** *70 Upper Hideaway Ln (82833). 307/674-8150. www.bighorn-wyoming.com.* 3 lodge rms, 2 cabins. No A/C. Mid-June-mid-Aug: S $90-$135; D $85-$140; each addl $25, lower rates rest of yr. Complimentary full bkfst. Ck-out 11 am, ck-in 4-8 pm. Balconies. Antiques. Wildlife trips. Totally nonsmoking. Cr cds: A, MC, V

[symbols]

Teton Village (C-1)

(see Jackson)

Thermopolis

(C-3) *See also Riverton*

Founded 1897 **Pop** 3,247 **Elev** 4,326 ft **Area code** 307 **Zip** 82443

Information Chamber of Commerce, 119 S 6th St, PO Box 768; 307/864-3192 or 800/786-6772

Web www.thermopolis.com

The world's largest mineral hot spring is at Thermopolis, which lies in a beautiful section of Big Horn Basin where canyons, tunnels, and buttes abound. The town is surrounded by rich irrigated farm and grazing land.

What to See and Do

Boysen State Park. Surrounded by the Wind River Reservation. Boysen Reservoir is 18 mi long and 3 mi wide. Beach on eastern shore, water-skiing, fishing for trout and walleye (all yr), boating (ramp, marina); picnicking, restaurant, lodging, tent and trailer sites (standard fees). 20 mi S on US 20. Phone 307/876-2772.

Hot Springs County Museum and Cultural Center. Home of "Hole-in-the-Wall" bar. Displays of arrowheads, minerals, gems; petroleum industry; country schoolhouse; agricultural building; railroad caboose; also period inns and costumes. (Memorial Day-Labor Day, daily; rest of yr, Mon-Sat; closed Jan 1, Thanksgiving, Dec 25) 7th and Broadway. Phone 307/864-5183. ¢¢

Hot Springs State Park. Beautiful terraces and mineral cones. Big Horn Spring, a hot mineral spring, pours out millions of gallons every 24 hrs at 135°F. The warm waters pour into the Big Horn River. Mineral swimming pools, indoor and outdoor, public bathhouse (massage avail). Terrace walks. Picnicking, playgrounds. Campgrounds nearby. A state buffalo herd is also quartered here. Across the Big Horn River, 1 mi N on US 20. Phone 307/864-2176.

Wind River Canyon. Formations visible in canyon walls range from early to recent geologic ages. Whitewater rafting (fee). S on US 20.

Wyoming Dinosaur Center. Exhibits mounted dinosaurs and dioramas, fossils, guided tours of excavation sites. (Daily) Carter Ranch Rd. Phone 307/864-2997. ¢¢

Special Events

Gift of the Waters Pageant. Hot Springs State Park. Commemorates the deeding of the world's largest mineral hot springs from the Shoshone and Arapahoe to the people of Wyoming in 1896. Pageant features Native American dances, parade, buffalo barbecue. First wkend Aug. Phone 800/786-6772.

Currier & Ives Winter Festival. Downtown. Town is decorated in 19th-century holiday style. Christmas choir, sleigh rides. Beard contest; cookie contest. Nov-Dec. Phone 800/786-6772.

Motels/Motor Lodges

★★ **COMFORT INN.** *100 N Rd 11, Worland (82401). 307/347-9898; fax 307/347-6734; res 800/228-5150. www.comfortinn.com.* 50 rms, 2 story. Mid-June-mid-Aug: S $56-$80; D $64-$100; each addl $10; suites $130-$160; under 18 free; family rates; lower rates rest of yr. Crib avail. Pet accepted, some restrictions; $10. TV; cable (premium), VCR avail (movies). Complimentary continental bkfst. Restaurant nearby. Ck-out 11 am. Meeting rms. Business servs avail. Coin lndry. Airport transportation. Exercise equipt; sauna. Health club privileges. Indoor pool; whirlpool. Some in-rm whirlpools. Cr cds: A, C, D, DS, ER, JCB, MC, V.

⬛ 🔧 🐾 ⛓ ⌷ 🏋 ⬜ 🔥

★ **SUPER 8.** *Ln 5 Hwy 20 S (82443). 307/864-5515; fax 307/864-5447; res 800/800-8000. www.super8.com.* 52 rms, 2 story. June-Sept: S $76.88; D $80.88; each addl $5; suite $150; under 10 free; lower rates rest of yr. Crib $5. TV; cable (premium). Indoor pool; whirlpool. Complimentary coffee in lobby. Restaurant nearby. Ck-out 11 am. Meeting rms. Coin lndry. Cr cds: A, C, D, DS, MC, V.

⬛ 🔧 🐾 ⌷ ⬜ 🔥

Torrington (E-7)

Pop 5,651 **Elev** 4,098 ft
Area code 307 **Zip** 82240
Information Goshen County Chamber of Commerce, 350 W 21st Ave; 307/532-3879 or 800/577-3555
Web www.go-goshen.com

The town was a way station for the Oregon Trail, the Texas Trail, the Mormon Trail, and the pony express. It is now a livestock marketing center.

What to See and Do

Fort Laramie National Historic Site. (see) 20 mi NW on US 26, then W on WY 160; 3 mi SW of town of Fort Laramie.

Homesteader's Museum. Historical items from the area's homesteading, ranching and settlement period (1830-1940). Ranch collection, furnished homestead shack; artifacts, photographs, archaeological materials. Changing exhibits. (Summer, daily; winter, Mon-Fri; closed hols). 495 Main St. Phone 307/532-5612. **Donation**

Western History Center. Exhibits on prehistory, archeology, paleontology. Tours to dig sites (fee). (Tues-Sun, also by appt) 5 mi W of Hwy 26. Phone 307/837-3052. **Donation**

Special Events

Goshen County Fair & Rodeo. Mid-Aug. Phone 307/532-2525.

Septemberfest. Early Sept. Phone 307/532-3879.

Motel/Motor Lodge

★ **SUPER 8.** *1548 Main St (82240). 307/532-7118; toll-free 800/800-8000. www.super8.com.* 56 rms, 3 story. No elvtr. June-Sept: S $50; D $65; each addl $5; lower rates rest of yr. Crib $5. TV; cable. Indoor pool; whirlpool. Complimentary coffee in lobby. Restaurant opp 5:30 am-10 pm. Ck-out 11 am. Meeting rm. Cr cds: A, D, DS, MC, V.

⬛ ⌷ ⬜ 🔥

Wheatland

(E-6) *See also Cheyenne, Torrington*

Pop 3,271 **Elev** 4,748 ft
Area code 307 **Zip** 82201
Information Platte County Chamber of Commerce, 65 16th St, PO Box 427; 307/322-2322
Web www.plattechamber.com

The southern edge of Medicine Bow National Forest (see LARAMIE) is 20 miles west.

What to See and Do

Glendo State Park. Rising out of Glendo Resevoir's east side at Sandy Beach are a series of sand dunes, some reaching from the Great Divide Basin to the sand hills in Nebraska. Chips, scrapers, and arrowheads dating back 8,000 yrs are sometimes found. Abundant wildlife. Near historic crossings. Swimming, waterskiing, fishing, boating (marina, ramp, rentals); hunting, picnicking, restaurant, grocery, lodging, tent and trailer sites (standard fees). N on I-25. Phone 307/735-4433.

Guernsey State Park. On the shores of Guernsey Reservoir; high bluffs surround the park with Laramie Peak on the west. Surrounding area is rich in historical interest incl the Oregon Trail. Museum (mid-May-Labor Day, daily; free) has exhibits on early settlers, the Oregon Trail, geology. Park offers swimming, waterskiing; camping (standard fees). Some facilities may be closed Nov-Apr. 12 mi N on I-25, then 12 mi E on US 26, then N on WY 317. Phone 307/836-2334. ¢¢

Special Events

Chugwater Chili Cookoff. Diamond Guest Ranch. Music, dancing, food. Family activities. Phone 307/422-3564. Second Sat June. Phone 800/972-4454.

Guernsey Old Timer's & Street Dance. Parade, barbecue. Early July. Phone 307/322-2322.

Summer Fun Fest & Antique Tractor Pull. Second Sat July. Phone 307/322-2322.

Platte County Fair and Rodeo. Incl parade, livestock sale, barbecue, pig wrestling. Early Aug. Phone 307/322-9504.

Motel/Motor Lodge

★★ **BEST WESTERN TORCHLITE INN.** *1809 N 16th St (82201). 307/322-4070; fax 307/322-4072; res 800/528-1234. www.bestwestern.com.* 50 rms, 2 story. S, D $40-$75; each addl $5. Crib $8. Pet accepted; $5. TV; cable (premium). Restaurant opp. Heated pool. Coffee in rms. Ck-out 11 am. Business servs avail. In-rm modem link. Airport transportation.

Health club privileges. Refrigerators. Cr cds: A, D, DS, MC, V.

Yellowstone National Park

See also Cody

In 1872, the US Congress set aside more than 3,000 square miles of wilderness in the Wyoming Territory, establishing the world's first national park. More than a century later, Yellowstone boasts a marvelous list of sights, attractions, and facilities: A large freshwater lake, the highest in the nation (7,733 feet); a waterfall almost twice as high as Niagara; a dramatic, 1,200-foot-deep river canyon; and the world's most famous geyser—Old Faithful.

Most of the park has been left in its natural state, preserving the area's beauty and delicate ecological balance. The widespread fires at Yellowstone in 1988 were the greatest ecological event in the more than 100-year history of the park. Although large areas of forest land were affected, park facilities and attractions remained generally undamaged. Yellowstone is one of the world's most successful wildlife sanctuaries. Within its boundaries live a variety of species, including grizzly and black bears, elk, deer, pronghorn, and bison. Although it is not unusual to encounter animals along park roads, they are more commonly seen along backcountry trails and in more remote areas. Never approach, feed, or otherwise disturb any wild animal. Visitors should stay in their cars with the windows up if approached by wildlife. Animals may look friendly but are unpredictable.

The Grand Loop Road, a main accessway within the park, winds approximately 140 miles past many major points of interest. Five miles south of the North Entrance is Mammoth Hot Springs, the park headquarters and museum (year-round). The visitor center provides a general overview of the history of the park. High terraces with water spilling from natural springs are nearby. Naturalist-guided walks are conducted on boardwalks over the terraces (summer).

The Norris Geyser Basin is 21 miles directly south of Mammoth Hot Springs. The hottest thermal basin in the world provides a multitude of displays; springs, geysers, mud pots, and steam vents hiss, bubble, and erupt in a showcase of thermal forces at work. The visitor center has self-explanatory exhibits and dioramas (June-Labor Day, daily). A self-guided trail (2½ miles) offers views of the Porcelain and Back basins from boardwalks (mid-June-Labor Day). The Museum of the National Park Ranger is also nearby.

At Madison, 14 miles southwest of Norris, the West Entrance Road (US 20/91 outside the park) joins the Grand Loop Road. Heading south of Madison, it is a 16-mile trip to Old Faithful. Along the route are four thermal spring areas; numerous geysers, mud pots, and pools provide an appropriate prologue to the spectacle ahead. Old Faithful has not missed a performance in the more than 100 years since eruptions were first recorded. Eruptions occur on the average of every 75 minutes, although intervals have varied from 30 to 120 minutes. A nearby visitor center provides information, exhibits, and a film and slide program (May-October, mid-December-mid-March, daily).

From Old Faithful it is 17 miles east to West Thumb. Yellowstone Lake, the highest natural freshwater lake in the United States, is here. Early explorers thought that the shape of the lake resembled a hand-with the westernmost bay forming its thumb. A variety of rare species of waterfowl make their home along its 110 miles of shoreline. The 22-mile road from the South Entrance on the John D. Rockefeller, Jr., Memorial Parkway (US 29/287 outside the park) meets the Grand Loop Road here.

Northeast of West Thumb, about 19 miles up the western shore of Yellowstone Lake, the road leads to Lake Village and then to Fishing Bridge. Although fishing is not permitted at Fishing Bridge (extending one mile downstream, to the north and one-quarter mile upstream, to the south of Fishing Bridge), the numerous lakes and rivers in the park make Yellowstone an angler's paradise. At Fishing Bridge the road splits—27 miles east is the East Entrance from US 14/16/20, 16 miles north is Canyon Village. Canyon Village is near Upper Falls (109-ft drop) and the spectacular Lower Falls (308-ft drop). The colorful and awesome Grand Canyon of the Yellowstone River can be viewed from several points; there are self-guided trails along the rim and naturalist-led walks (summer). Groomed cross-country ski trails are open in winter. Museum (mid-May-late September, daily).

Morning Glory Pool, Yellowstone National Park

Sixteen miles north of Canyon Village is Tower. Just south of Tower Junction is the 132-foot Tower Fall, which can best be observed from a platform at the end of the path leading from the parking lot. The Northeast Entrance on US 212 is 29 miles east of Tower; Mammoth Hot Springs is 18 miles west.

The rest of the park is wilderness, with more than 1,100 miles of marked foot trails. Some areas may be closed for resource management purposes; inquire at one of the visitor centers in the area before hiking in backcountry. Guided tours of the wilderness can be made on horseback, horse rentals are available at Mammoth Hot Springs, Roosevelt, and Canyon Village.

Do not pick wildflowers or collect any natural objects. Read all regulations established by the National Park Service and comply with them—they are for the protection of all visitors as well as for the protection of park resources.

Recreational vehicle campsites are available by reservation at Fishing Bridge RV Park (contact TW Recreational Services, Inc, at 307/344-7901 for general information or 307/344-7311 for reservations). During July and August, demand often exceeds supply and many sites are occupied by mid-morning. Overnight vehicle camping or stopping outside designated campgrounds is not permitted. Reservations for Bridge Bay, Canyon, Madison, Grant Village, as well as Fishing Bridge RV Park. There are seven additional National Park Service campgrounds at Yellowstone; these are operated on a first-come, first-served basis, so it is advisable to arrive early to secure the site of your choice. Campfires are prohibited except in designated areas or by special permit obtained at ranger stations. Backcountry camping is available by permit only, no more than 48 hours in advance, in person, at ranger stations. Backcountry sites can be reserved for a $15 fee.

Fishing in Yellowstone National Park requires a permit. Anglers 16 years and older require a $10/ten-day or $20/season permit. Rowboats, powerboats, and tackle may be rented at Bridge Bay Marina. Permits are also required for all vessels (seven-day permit: motorized, $10; nonmotorized, $5) and must be obtained in person at any of the following locations: South Entrance, Bridge Bay Marina, Mammoth Visitor Center, Grant Village Visitor Center, Lake Ranger Station, and Lewis Lake Campground. Information centers near Yellowstone Lake are located at Fishing Bridge and Grant Village (both Memorial Day-Labor Day, daily).

At several locations there are visitor centers, general stores for provisions, photo shops, service stations, tent and trailer sites, hotels, and lodges. There are bus tours through the park from mid-June to Labor Day (contact Xanterra Parks and Resorts at 307/344-7311). Cars can be rented in some of the gateway communities.

CCInc Auto Tape Tours, two 90-minute cassettes, offer a mile-by-mile self-guided tour of the park. Written in cooperation with the National Park Service, it provides information on geology, history, points of interest, and flora and fauna. Tapes may be obtained at gift shops throughout the park. Tapes also may be purchased directly from CCInc, PO Box 227, 2 Elbrook Dr, Allendale, NJ 07401; phone 201/236-1666. ¢¢¢

TourGuide Self-Guided Car Audio Tours. Produced in cooperation with the National Park Service, this system uses the random-access capability of CD technology to instantly select narration on topics like wildlife, ecology, safety, history, and folklore. Visitors rent a self-contained player (about the size of a paperback book) that plugs into a car's cigarette lighter and broadcasts an FM signal to its radio. A screen on the unit displays menus of chapters and topics, which may be played in any order for an individualized, narrated auto tour (total running time approximately five hours). Players may be rented by contacting Xanterra Parks and Resorts at 301/344-7311. For further information contact TIS, Inc, 1018 Burlington Ave, Suite 101, Missoula, MT 59801; phone 406/549-3800 or 800/247-1213. Per day ¢¢¢¢

The official park season is May 1-October 31. However, US 212 from

Red Lodge, Montana to Cooke City, Montana (outside the Northeast Entrance) is not open to automobiles until about May 30 and closes about October 1. In winter, roads from Gardiner to Mammoth Hot Springs and to Cooke City, Montana are kept open, but the road from Red Lodge is closed; travelers must return to Gardiner to leave the park. The west, east, and south entrances are closed to automobiles from November 1 to about May 1, but are open to over-snow vehicles from mid-December-mid-March. Dates are subject to change. For current road conditions and other information, phone park headquarters at 307/344-7381. Entrance permit, $20/vehicle/visit, good for seven days to Yellowstone and Grand Teton.

Note: Weather conditions or conservation measures may dictate the closing of certain roads and recreational facilities. In winter, inquire before attempting to enter the park.

Motels/Motor Lodges

★ **CANYON LODGE CABINS.** *PO Box 165 (82190). 307/344-7311; fax 307/344-7456. www.travelyellowstone. com.* 300 rms in 6 bldgs, 2 story. No A/C. Late May-Sept: S, D $85-$105; each addl $10; under 12 free. Closed rest of yr. Restaurant 6:30 am-10 pm. Bar 5 pm-midnight. Ck-out 11 am. Coin lndry. Meeting rms. Gift shop. On lake. Cr cds: A, D, MC, V.
[D] [≈] [🔥]

★★ **CASCADE LODGE AT CANYON VILLAGE.** *Yellowstone National Park (82190). 307/344-7311; fax 307/344-7456. www.ynp-lodges.com.* 35 rms, 3 story. No A/C. No elvtr. No rm phones. Early June-mid-Sept: S, D $130; each addl $10; under 11 free. Crib avail. Restaurant nearby. Ck-out 11 am. Sundries. Gift shop. Coin lndry. Cr cds: A, D, DS, JCB, MC, V.
[D] [≈] [🔥]

Hotels

★★★ **LAKE YELLOWSTONE HOTEL.** *Yellowstone National Park (82190). 307/344-7311; fax 307/344-7456. www.travelyellowstone.com.* 194 rms. No A/C. Late May-late Sept: S, D $100-$170; each addl $10; suite $390; under 12 free. Closed rest of yr. Crib free. Restaurant (see also LAKE YELLOWSTONE DINING ROOM). No rm serv. Bar 11:30 am-midnight. Ck-out 11 am. Overlooks Yellowstone Lake. Cr cds: A, D, MC, V.
[≈] [🔥]

★ **MAMMOTH HOT SPRINGS HOTEL AND CABINS.** *PO Box 165 (82190). 307/344-7311; fax 307/344-7456. www.travelyellowstone.com.* 97 rms, 69 baths, 4 story, 126 cabins, 75 baths. No A/C. Late May-mid-Sept: S, D $45-$115; each addl $10; suites $255; cabins $120; under 12 free; lower rates rest of yr. Closed Oct-Nov and Mar-Apr. Crib free. Restaurant opp 7 am-10 pm. No rm serv. Bar 11:30 am-midnight. Ck-out 11 am. Meeting rm. Gift shop. X-country ski on site. Cr cds: A, DS, MC, V.
[≈] [🔥]

★★ **OLD FAITHFUL INN.** *PO Box 165 (82190). 307/344-7311; fax 307/344-7456. www.travelyellowstone. com.* 325 rms, 246 baths, 1-4 story. No A/C. Many rm phones. Early May-mid-Oct: S, D $55-$150; each addl $9; suites $330; under 12 free. Closed rest of yr. Crib free. Restaurant 6:30-10 am, 11:30 am-2:30 pm, 5-9:45 pm. No rm serv. Bar 11:30 am-midnight. Ck-out 11 am. Some refrigerators. Some rms have view of Old Faithful. Historic log structure (1904). Cr cds: A, D, MC, V.
[≈] [🔥]

Restaurant

★★ **LAKE YELLOWSTONE DINING ROOM.** *Yellowstone National Park (82190). 307/344-7311. www. ynp-lodges.com.* Hrs: 6:30-10:30 am, 11:30 am-2:30 pm, 5-10 pm. Closed Oct-May. Res accepted. Bar 11:30 am-11:30 pm. Bkfst $2.75-$5.95, lunch $3.75-$8.95, dinner $10.95-$18.95. Buffet: bkfst $6.75. Child's meals. Specializes in sauteed salmon, seared sea scallops, roasted tenderloin. String quartet or pianist. Overlooks lake. Totally nonsmoking. Cr cds: A, D, DS, MC, V.
[D]

CANADA

Just north of the United States, with which it shares the world's longest undefended border, lies Canada, the world's largest country in terms of land area. Extending from the North Pole to the northern border of the United States and including all the islands from Greenland to Alaska, Canada's area encompasses nearly four million square miles (10.4 million square kilometers). The northern reaches of the country consist mainly of the Yukon and Northwest territories, which make up the vast, sparsely populated Canadian frontier.

Population: 31,006,347
Area: 6,181,778 square miles (9,970,610 square kilometers)
Peak: Mount Logan, Yukon Territory, 19,850 feet (6,050 meters)
Capital: Ottawa
Speed Limit: 50 or 60 MPH (80 or 100 KPH), unless otherwise indicated

Jacques Cartier erected a cross at Gaspé in 1534 and declared the establishment of New France. Samuel de Champlain founded Port Royal in Nova Scotia in 1604. Until 1759 Canada was under French rule. In that year, British General Wolfe defeated French General Montcalm at Québec and British possession followed. In 1867 the British North America Act established the Confederation of Canada, with four provinces: New Brunswick, Nova Scotia, Ontario, and Québec. The other provinces joined later. Canada was proclaimed a self-governing Dominion within the British Empire in 1931. The passage in 1981 of the Constitution Act severed Canada's final legislative link with Great Britain, which had until that time reserved the right to amend the Canadian Constitution.

Today, Canada is a sovereign nation—neither a colony nor a possession of Great Britain. Since Canada is a member of the Commonwealth of Nations, Queen Elizabeth II, through her representative, the Governor-General, is the nominal head of state. However, the Queen's functions are mostly ceremonial with no political power or authority. Instead, the nation's chief executive is the prime minister; the legislative branch consists of the Senate and the House of Commons.

Vermillion Lake, Banff National Park

Visitor Information

Currency. The American dollar is accepted throughout Canada, but it is advisable to exchange your money into Canadian currency upon arrival. Banks and currency exchange firms typically give the best rate of exchange, but hotels and stores will also convert it for you with purchases. The Canadian monetary system is based on dollars and cents, and rates in *Mobil Travel Guide* are given in Canadian currency. Generally, the credit cards you use at home are also honored in Canada.

Goods and Services Tax (GST). Most goods and services in Canada are subject to a 7 percent tax. Visitors to Canada may claim a rebate of the GST paid on *short-term accommodations* (hotel, motel, or similar lodging) and on *most consumer goods* purchased to take home. Rebates may be claimed for cash at participating Canadian Duty Free shops or by mail. For further information and a brochure detailing rebate procedures and restrictions contact Visitors' Rebate Program, Revenue Canada, Summerside Tax Center, Summerside, PE C1N 6C6; phone 902/432-5608 or 800/66-VISIT (in Canada).

Driving in Canada. Your American driver's license is valid in Canada; no special permit is required. In Canada the liter is the unit of measure for gasoline. One US gallon equals 3.78 liters. Traffic signs are clearly understood and in many cities are bilingual. All road speed limits and mileage signs have been posted in kilometers. A flashing green traffic light gives vehicles turning left the right-of-way, like a green left-turn arrow. The use of safety belts is generally mandatory in all provinces; consult the various provincial tourism bureaus for specific information.

Holidays. Canada observes the following holidays, and these are indicated in text: New Year's Day, Good Friday, Easter Monday, Victoria Day (usually third Monday May), Canada Day (July 1), Labour Day, Thanksgiving (second Monday October), Remembrance Day (November 11), Christmas, and Boxing Day (December 26). See individual provinces for information on provincial holidays.

Liquor. The sale of liquor, wine, beer, and cider varies from province to province. Restaurants must be licensed to serve liquor, and in some cases liquor may not be sold unless it accompanies a meal. Generally there are no package sales on holidays. Minimum legal drinking age also varies by province. **Note:** It is illegal to take children into bars or cocktail lounges.

Daylight Saving Time. Canada observes Daylight Saving Time beginning the first Sunday in April through the last Sunday in October, except for most of the province of Saskatchewan, where Standard Time is observed year-round.

Tourist information is available from individual provincial and territorial tourism offices (see Border Crossing Regulations in MAKING THE MOST OF YOUR TRIP).

PROVINCE OF ALBERTA

With a history of ancient indigenous civilizations, missionary settlements, fur trading, "gold fever," and frontier development, Alberta thrives today as a vital industrial, agricultural, and recreational center. It possesses the widest variety of geographical features of any province in Canada, including a giant plateau "badlands" rich in dinosaur fossils, rolling prairie, and vast parkland. All along its western border are the magnificent Canadian Rockies.

Pop 2,513,100 **Land area** 246,423 square miles (661,185 square kilometers)
Capital Edmonton
Web www.discoveralberta.com

Information Travel Alberta, Box 2500, Edmonton T5J 2Z4; 780/427-4321 or 800/661-8888

Easily accessible from Montana, you can enter Alberta from Waterton Lakes National Park and drive north to Calgary, where you'll intersect with the Trans-Canada Highway and enjoy a variety of attractions. The view of the Rockies from the Calgary Tower and the excitement of the Calgary Stampede are not to be missed.

From Calgary drive northwest to Banff, Lake Louise, and Jasper National Park for some of the finest mountain scenery, outdoor activities, resorts, and restaurants on the continent.

Heading due north from Calgary visit Red Deer, a town famous for agriculture, oil, and its beautiful parkland setting. Farther north is the provincial capital, Edmonton. A confident, multicultural city, it is noted for its oil, its "gold rush" past, and its parks, cultural activities, magnificent sports facilities, and rodeos. Northwest of Edmonton, Alberta provides paved access to "Mile 0" of the Alaska Highway at Dawson Creek, British Columbia. There is also paved access to the Northwest Territories—Canada's "frontier" land.

Drive southeast from Calgary and enter an entirely different scene: cowboy and Indian territory. Fort Macleod brings you back to the early pioneer days. Lethbridge is famous for its replica of the most notorious 19th-century whiskey fort—Fort Whoop-Up—and the Nikka Yuko Japanese Gardens. Farther east visit Medicine Hat, known for its parks, pottery, and rodeos. Alberta is truly a vacation destination for all seasons and tastes.

Alberta observes Mountain Standard Time and Daylight Saving Time in summer. Hunting is not permitted in national or provincial parks and a separate fishing license is required. For information on hunting and fishing in other areas of the province contact the Fish and Wildlife Division, Department of Forestry, Lands, and Wildlife, 9920 108th St, Edmonton T5K 2C9.

In addition to national holidays, Alberta observes Heritage Day (first Monday August) and Family Day (third Monday February).

Safety belts are mandatory for all persons anywhere in vehicle. Children under six years or under 40 pounds in weight must be in an approved child safety seat. For further information phone 780/427-8901.

THE ICEFIELD PARKWAY

One of the most famous mountain highways in the world, the Icefield Parkway travels between Lake Louise and Jasper, along the crown of the Canadian Rockies. The scenery is absolutely dramatic: soaring peaks still under the bite of glaciers; turquoise green lakes surrounded by deep forests; roaring waterfalls; and, at the very crest of the drive, the Columbia Icefield, the largest nonpolar icecap in the world. Besides the scenery, there are activities and opportunities for recreation. A number of lakeside lodges offer canoe rentals, short horseback trail rides, whitewater rafting trips, and trips onto the Columbia Snowfield in specially designed snowcoaches. Wildlife is also abundant: mountain goats, mountain sheep, elk, moose, and bears are frequently sighted. **(APPROX 142 MI; 229 KM.)**

CANADIAN ROCKIES SCENERY

Much of this route is along expressways, so this is hardly a back road. Yet, on the edge of the Canadian prairies, the journey from Calgary up the Bow River valley and into the vastness of the Canadian Rockies is one of dramatically fast and beautiful geological transitions. From Calgary, Highway 1 heads west, passing long-established ranches. Consider a stop at the Western Heritage Center at the historic Cochrane Ranch. The Rockies rise up fully grown from the prairies. One minute you're in ranch country, the next you're inside a narrow mountain valley surrounded by 10,000-foot-high peaks. At Canmore, Highway 1 enters Banff National Park, Canada's oldest national park. The town of Banff is a wonderfully scenic mountain town that's also one of the most cosmopolitan small communities in North America (Banff is apparently the single-most popular destination in Canada for foreign visitors). The setting is totally unlikely (how did they fit a town in between all these incredible mountain peaks?), and the amenities are superb. You'll find first-class hotels and dining, as well as the hiking, climbing, fishing, and rafting that you expect in the Rockies. Lake Louise and its smaller cousin, Morraine Lake, are both incredibly beautiful spots: eerily green lakes nestled in a glacial basin directly below the peaks of the Continental Divide. Again, the facilities are great. The Chateau Lake Louise, sitting at the lake's edge, is one of the most famous hotels in Canada. **(APPROX 112 MI; 180 KM.)**

Banff

(F-3) *See also Calgary, Lake Louise*

Pop 6,800 **Elev** 4,538 ft (1,383 m)
Area code 403
Information Banff-Lake Louise Tourism Bureau, PO Box 1298, T1L 1B3; 403/762-8421
Web www.banfflakelouise.com

Banff came to be because of the popularity of the hot springs in the area. The Banff Hot Springs Reservation was created in 1885 and by 1887 had become Rocky Mountains Park. Today we know this vast recreation area as Banff National Park, offering the visitor activity all year, plus the beauty of the Rocky Mountains.

Banff comes alive each summer with its music and drama festival at Banff Centre. In winter the Rockies provide some of the best skiing on the North American continent, including helicopter, downhill, and cross-country. The town of Banff itself has exciting nightlife, sleigh rides, Western barbecues, and indoor recreational activities. The area offers sightseeing gondola rides, boat and raft tours, concerts, art galleries, museums, hot springs, ice field tours, hiking, and trail rides.

What to See and Do

Cave and Basin Centennial Centre. The birthplace of Canada's national park system and a national historic site. Hot springs, cave, exhibits, trails, theater (Daily; closed Jan 1, Dec 25). W on Cave Ave. Phone 403/762-1557. ¢¢

Natural History Museum. More than 60 displays, slide and film shows depicting the national parks; prehistoric life, precious stones, trees and flowers, origins of the earth, and formations of mountains and caves. (Daily; closed Dec 25) 112 Banff Ave, upstairs at Clock Tower Mall. Phone 403/762-4652. **FREE**

Sightseeing tours.

  CCInc Auto Tape Tours. This 90-min cassette offers a mi-by-mi self-guided tour. Written by informed guides, it provides information on history, glaciers, points of interest, and flora and fauna of the area. Tapes are avail at The Thunderbird on Banff Ave, opp the park Information Center. Rental incl player and tape: Banff tour or combination Banff/Jasper. Tapes also may be purchased directly from CCInc, PO Box 227, 2 Elbrook Dr, Allendale, NJ 07401. Phone 201/236-1666. ¢¢¢

Rocky Mountain Raft Tours. One-hr round-trip excursions (four trips daily); also three-hr round-trips (two trips daily). Trip durations approx; incl transportation time to departure site. (June-mid-Sept) For schedule and fees contact Rocky Mtn Raft Tours, PO Box 1771, T0L 0C0. Phone 403/762-3632.

Special Event

Banff Festival of the Arts St Julien Rd. Mainstage productions and workshops in opera, ballet, music theater, drama, concerts, poetry reading, visual arts. Some events free. For information contact The Banff Centre Box Office, PO Box 1020, T0L 0C0. June-Aug. Phone 800/413-8368.

Motels/Motor Lodges

★ **AKAI MOTEL.** *1717 Mountain Ave, Canmore (T1W 2W1). 403/678-4664; fax 403/678-4775; toll free 877/900-2524.* 41 kit. units. July-Aug: S $75; D $80-$85; each addl $5; under 12 free; family rates; package plans; lower rates rest of yr. Crib free. Pet accepted, some restrictions. TV; cable. Complimentary coffee in lobby. Restaurant nearby. Ck-out 11 am. Bellhops. Downhill ski 15 mi; x-country ski 3 mi. Picnic tables. Cr cds: A, D, ER, MC, V.

D 🔄 🖇 🈁 🐾

★★ **BANFF PARK LODGE.** *222 Lynx St (T1L 1K5). 403/762-4433; fax 403/762-3553; toll-free 800/661-9266. www.banffparklodge.com.* 211 rms, 3 story. June-Sept: S, D $261-$322; each addl $15; suites $382; under 16 free; lower rates rest of yr; ski plans. TV; cable (premium). Heated pool; whirlpool, steam rms. Restaurant 7 am-midnight. Bar; entertainment Mon-Sat. Coffee, tea in rms. Ck-out 11 am. Business servs avail. In-rm modem link. Meeting rms. Bellhops. Shopping arcade. Barber, beauty shop. Concierge. Valet serv. Heated underground parking. Downhill/x-country ski 2 mi. Some refrigerators, whirlpools, fireplaces. Private patios, balconies. Cr cds: A, D, ER, JCB, MC, V.

⊡ ⬤ ⬤ ⬤ ⬤ ⬤ ⬤ ⬤ SC

★★ **BANFF VOYAGER INN.** 555 Banff Ave (T0L 0C0). 403/762-3301; fax 403/762-4131; toll-free 800/879-1991. www.banffvoyagerinn.com. 88 rms, 2 story. No A/C. June-Sept: S, D $115-$164; each addl $15; under 17 free; ski plans; lower rates rest of yr. Crib free. TV; cable (premium). Heated pool; whirlpool, sauna. Restaurant 7-11 am, 5:30-9:30 pm. Bar 11-2 am. Ck-out 11 am. Meeting rms. Business servs avail. Downhill/country ski 2 mi. Balconies. Cr cds: A, MC, V.

⬤ ⬤ ⬤ ⬤ ⬤

★★ **BEST WESTERN GREEN GABLES INN.** 1602 2nd Ave, Canmore (T1W 1M8). 403/678-5488; fax 403/678-2670; toll-free 800/661-2133. www.bestwestern.com. 61 rms, 4 story, 10 kit. units. June-mid-Sept: S, D $159-$179; each addl $10; kit. units $149; under 17 free; ski plans; lower rates rest of yr. Crib free. TV; cable (premium). Complimentary coffee in rms. Restaurant 7 am-2 pm, 5-10 pm (see also CHEZ FRANCOIS). Bar 5-10 pm. Whirlpool; steam rm. Ck-out 11 am. Meeting rms. Business servs avail. Valet serv. In-rm modem link. Downhill ski 15 mi; x-country ski 2 mi. Exercise equipt. Some whirlpools, fireplaces. Refrigerators. Balconies. Cr cds: A, C, D, DS, ER, MC, V.

⊡ ⬤ ⬤ ⬤ ⬤ ⬤ ⬤ ⬤ SC

★★ **BEST WESTERN SIDING 29 LODGE.** 453 Marten St (T0L 0C0). 403/762-5575; fax 403/762-8866; res 800/528-1234. www.bestwesternbanff.com. 57 rms, 3 story, 10 suites. No A/C. July-Aug: S, D $183-$203; suites $219-$304; lower rates rest of yr. Crib free. Pet accepted. TV; cable. Indoor pool; whirlpool. Complimentary continental bkfst. Restaurant opp 7-11 am, 5-11 pm. Ck-out 11 am. Business servs avail. Downhill ski 5 mi; x-country ski 2 mi. Some refrigerators. Heated underground parking. Some balconies, whirlpools. Cr cds: A, C, D, DS, ER, JCB, MC, V.

⊡ ⬤ ⬤ ⬤ ⬤ ⬤ SC

★★ **BREWSTER'S MOUNTAIN LODGE.** 208 Caribou St (T0L 0W0). 403/762-2900; fax 403/762-2970; toll-free 888/762-2900. www.brewster adventures.com. 73 rms, 2 story, 19 suites. Mid-June-mid-Oct: S, D $189-$229; each addl $15; suites $275-$350; under 18 free; family rates; package plans; lower rates rest of yr. Crib avail. TV; cable (premium). Restaurant nearby. Ck-out 11 am. Meeting rms. Business servs avail. In-rm modem link. Bellhops. Sundries. Shopping arcade. Heated underground parking. Downhill/x-country ski 5 mi. Sauna. In-rm whirlpool, refrigerator in suites. Some balconies. Cr cds: A, MC, V.

⊡ ⬤ ⬤ ⬤ SC

★★★ **BUFFALO MOUNTAIN LODGE.** 700 Tunnel Mountain Rd (T0L 0C0). 403/609-6150; fax 403/609-6158; toll-free 800/661-1367. www.crmr.com. 108 rms, 20 kit. units. No A/C. Early June-late Sept: S, D $222; kit. units $235-$255; each addl $25; under 12 free; ski plan. Crib free. TV; cable, VCR avail. Complimentary coffee, tea in rms. Restaurant 7 am-10 pm. Bar 11 am-11 pm. Ck-out 11 am. Meeting rms. Business servs avail. Bellhops. Downhill/x-country ski 3 mi. Steam rm. Whirlpool. Some refrigerators, microwaves, fireplaces. Balconies. Cr cds: A, D, ER, MC, V.

⬤ ⬤ ⬤ ⬤

★★ **CASTLE MOUNTAIN CHALETS.** Jct Hwy 1-A, 93 S (T0L 0C0). 403/522-2783; fax 403/762-8629. www.castlemountain.com. 21 kit. cottages, 12 suites. No A/C. June-Sept S, D $249-$329; each addl $10; under 17 free; lower rates rest of yr; package plans. Crib $5. Pet accepted; $20. TV; cable, VCRs. Restaurant nearby. Ck-out 10:30 am. Coin lndry. Gift shop. Grocery store. Downhill ski 20 mi; x-country ski on site. Exercise equipt. Some in-rm whirlpools, fireplaces, microwaves. Grills. Library. Cr cds: A, MC, V.

⊡ ⬤ ⬤ ⬤ ⬤ ⬤

★ **CHARLTON'S CEDAR COURT.** 513 Banff Ave (T1L 1B4). 403/762-4485; fax 403/762-4415; toll-free 800/661-1225. www.charltonresorts.com. 63 rms, 3 story, 16 kits. June-Sept: S, D $189-$219; each addl $25;

kit. units $150; under 16 free; lower rates rest of yr; package plans. Crib free. TV; cable. Heated indoor pool; whirlpool, steam rm. Complimentary coffee, tea in rms. Restaurant nearby 6:30-10:30 am, 5:30-9:30 pm. Bar. Ck-out 11 am. Meeting rms. Business servs avail. Free covered parking. Downhill ski 2 mi; x-country ski 1 mi. Fireplaces. Cr cds: A, D, ER, JCB, MC, V.

★ ★ **DYNASTY INN.** *501 Banff Ave (T0L 0C0). 403/762-8844; fax 403/762-4418; toll-free 800/667-1464. www.dynastyinn.com.* 99 rms, 3 story. Mid-June late Sept: S, D $155-$205; each addl $15; under 12 free; family suites; ski plan; lower rates rest of yr. Crib free. Garage parking. TV; cable. Restaurant 7-10 am. Ck-out 11 am. Business servs avail. Bellhops. Downhill/x-country ski 3 mi. Sauna, steam rm. Some whirlpools, fireplaces. Many balconies. Cr cds: MC, V.

★ **HIDDEN RIDGE RESORT.** *901 Coyote Dr (T0L 0C0). 403/762-3544; fax 403/760-8287; toll-free 800/661-1372. www.bestofbanff.com.* 83 kit. units, 1-2 story. No A/C. June-Sept: S, D $199-$228; each addl $15; under 16 free; package plans; higher rates Dec 25, lower rates rest of yr. Crib free. TV; cable. Complimentary coffee in rms. Restaurant nearby. Ck-out 11 am. Business servs avail. Whirlpool. Downhill/x-country ski 5 mi. Free shuttle. Fireplaces. Balconies. Picnic tables. Grills. Cr cds: A, D, DS, ER, JCB, MC, V.

★ ★ **HIGH COUNTRY INN.** *419 Banff Ave (T1L 1A7). 403/762-2236; fax 403/762-5084; toll-free 800/293-5142. www.banffhighcountryinn.com.* 70 rms, 3 story. June-Sept: S, D $79-$150; suites $220; each addl $10; under 12 free; lower rates rest of yr. Crib $5. TV; cable. Heated indoor pool; whirlpools. Sauna. Restaurant 7:30-10:30 am; 5:30-10:30 pm (see also TICINO). Coffee in rms. Ck-out 11 am. Meeting rms. Business servs avail. Free garage parking. Downhill/x-country ski 2 mi. Refrigerators.

Some microwaves, fireplaces. Many balconies. Cr cds: A, MC, V.

★ ★ **INNS OF BANFF.** *600 Banff Ave (T0L 0C0). 403/762-4581; fax 403/762-2434; toll-free 800/661-1272. www.innsofbanff.com.* 180 rms, 4 story. June-Sept: S, D $220-$245; each addl $20; under 16 free; ski plans; lower rates rest of yr. Crib free. TV; cable. Sauna. Indoor pool; whirlpool. Restaurant 7 am-2 pm, 6-10 pm. Bar 5-10 pm. Ck-out 11 am. Meeting rms. Business servs avail. Massage. Beauty shop. Underground parking. Bellhops. Gift shop. Downhill/x-country ski 2 mi. Refrigerators. Balconies. Scenic mountain location. Cr cds: A, D, ER, JCB, MC, V.

★ ★ **IRWIN'S MOUNTAIN INN.** *429 Banff Ave (T0L 0C0). 403/762-4566; fax 403/762-8220; toll-free 800/661-1721. www.irwinsmountaininn.com.* 65 rms, 3 story. No A/C. June-Sept: S, D $144-$174; each addl $10; suites $174; under 16 free; lower rates rest of yr. Crib free. TV; cable (premium). Whirlpool. Complimentary coffee in rms. Restaurant 7-11 am, 5-11 pm. Ck-out 11 am. Meeting rms. Business servs avail. Gift shop. Valet serv. Coin lndry. Downhill ski 5 mi; x-country ski 1 mi. Exercise equipt; sauna, steam rm. Massage. Refrigerators, microwaves avail. Some whirlpools. Game rm. Local and ski transportation. Underground parking. Cr cds: A, MC, V.

★ ★ **NORQUAY'S TIMBERLINE INN.** *1 Norquay Rd (T0L 0C0). 403/762-2281; fax 403/762-8331; res 877/762-2281. www.banfftimberline. com.* 52 rms, 2 story. No A/C. June-early Oct: S, D $76-$86; each addl $15; suites $102-$112; kit. chalet $285; under 16 free; MAP avail; lower rates rest of yr; 2-day min. (late Dec-early Jan). Pet accepted; $15/day. TV; cable. Dining rm 7 am-10 pm. Ck-out 11 am. Meeting rms. Business servs avail. Valet serv. Downhill/x-country ski ½ mi. Outdoor whirlpool. Some refrigerators, fireplaces. Balconies. Cr cds: A, MC, V.

Banff Avenue

★★★ **QUALITY RESORT - CHATEAU CANMORE.** *1720 Bow Valley Trl, Canmore (T1W 2X3). 403/678-6699; fax 403/678-6954; res 800/261-8551. www.chateaucanmore. com.* 120 suites, 3 story. July-Oct: S, D $175; kit. units $195; package plans; under 18 free; lower rates rest of yr. Crib free. TV, cable; VCR (movies). Indoor pool; whirlpool. Sauna. Playground. Supervised children's activities (July-Aug); ages 7-15. Complimentary coffee in rms. Restaurant 6 am-11 pm. Bar to 1 am. Ck-out 11 am. Meeting rms. Business servs avail. Exercise rm. Valet serv. Lighted tennis. Spa. Massage. Downhill ski 18 mi; x-country ski 1 mi. Bicycles rental. Refrigerators, microwaves. Some balconies, fireplaces. Cr cds: A, DS, ER, JCB, MC, V.

★ **RED CARPET INN.** *Banff Ave (T0L 0C0). 403/762-4184; fax 403/762-4894; toll-free 800/563-4609. www. motels.ab.ca/m/redcrpet.html.* 52 rms, 3 story. June-Sept: S $110-$125; D $140-$160; lower rates rest of yr. Crib avail. Pet accepted. TV; VCR avail. Restaurant adj 7 am-11 pm. Coffee in rms. Business servs avail. Free garage parking. 2 whirlpools (winter only). Balconies. Cr cds: A, MC, V.

★ **RUNDLE MOUNTAIN LODGE.** *1723 Bow Valley Tr, Canmore (T1W 1L7). 403/678-5322; fax 403/678-5813; toll-free 800/661-1610. www. rundlemountain.com.* 61 rms, 2 story, 14 suites, 18 kit. units. No A/C. Mid-June-early-Sept: S, D $125-$160; condo $250; each addl $10; under 18 free; suites $275-$295; kit. units $143; family, wkly rates; ski plans; lower rates rest of yr. Crib free. TV; cable. Heated indoor pool; outdoor whirlpool. Playground. Complimentary coffee in rms. Restaurant 7 am-10 pm. Ck-out 11 am. Coin lndry. Meeting rms. Refrigerators. Some whirlpools, fireplaces. Picnic tables. Cr cds: A, D, ER, MC, V.

★★ **RUNDLESTONE LODGE.** *537 Banff Ave (T1L 1A6). 403/762-2201; fax 403/762-4501; toll-free 800/661-8630. www.rundlestone.com.* 95 rms, 3 story, 20 suites. June-Sept: S, D $155-$195; each addl $10; suites $175-$310; under 5 free; lower rates rest of yr. TV; cable. Ck-out 11 am. Restaurant 7-11 am, 5:30-11 pm. Coffee in rms. Coin lndry. Valet serv. Meeting rms. Business servs avail. Bellhops. Exercise equipt. Whirlpool. Balconies. Garage parking. Cr cds: A, C, D, DS, ER, MC, V.

★ ★ **TUNNEL MOUNTAIN RESORT.** *Tunnel Mtn Rd and Tunnel Mtn Dr (T0L 0C0). 403/762-4515; fax 403/762-5183; toll-free 800/661-1859. www.tunnelmountain.com.* 24 kit. condo units, 2 story, 50 kit. chalets. No A/C. June-Sept: S, D $208-$279; each addl $15; under 14 free; lower rates rest of yr. Crib free. TV; cable (premium), VCR avail. Sauna. Indoor pool; whirlpools. Steam rm. Complimentary coffee in rms. Restaurant nearby. Ck-out 11 am. Meeting rm. Business servs avail. Exercise equipt. Some fireplaces, whirlpools. Downhill ski 5 mi; x-country ski 1 mi. Picnic tables, grills. Balconies. Cr cds: A, DS, MC, V.

Hotels

★ ★ **BANFF CARIBOU LODGE.** *521 Banff Ave (T0L 0C0). 403/762-5887; fax 403/760-8287; toll-free 800/563-8764. www.banffcaribouproperties.com.* 200 rms, 4 story. June-Oct: S, D $100-$195; each addl $15; suites $275-$335; under 16 free; hol rates; ski plans; lower rates rest of yr. Crib avail. TV; cable (premium). Playground. Coffee in rms. Restaurant 6:30 am-11 pm. Bar. Ck-out 11 am. Gift shop. Meeting rm. Business servs avail. Downhill ski 2 mi; x-country ski 1 mi. Exercise equipt; sauna. 3 whirlpools; steam rm. Massage. Some balconies. Free garage parking. Cr cds: A, D, DS, ER, JCB, MC, V.

★ ★ **BANFF INTERNATIONAL HOTEL.** *333 Banff Ave (T0L 0C0). 403/762-5666; fax 403/760-3281; toll-free 800/665-5666. www.banffinternational.com.* 165 rms, 3 story. No A/C. June-Sept: S, D $220-$270; each addl $20; under 16 free; lower rates rest of yr. TV; cable; VCR (movies). Restaurant 7-10:30 am. No rm serv. Bar. Coffee, tea in rms. Business servs avail. Gift shop. Free covered parking. Concierge. Valet serv. Downhill/x-country ski 1 mi. Whirl-

pool. Sauna. Steam rm. Cr cds: A, JCB, MC, V.

★ ★ **BANFF PTARMIGAN INN.** *337 Banff Ave (T0L 0C0). 403/762-2207; fax 403/760-8287; toll-free 800/661-8310. www.banffcaribouproperties.com.* 134 rms, 3 story. No A/C. June-Sept: S, D $100-$195; each addl $15; suites $275; under 16 free; ski plans; lower rates rest of yr. Free garage parking. TV; cable. Restaurant 7 am-11 pm. Bar 11:30 am-midnight. Ck-out 11 am. Meeting rms. Business servs avail. Exercise rm. Gift shop. Downhill/x-country ski 2 mi. Sauna. Whirlpools. Spa. Balconies. Cr cds: A, D, JCB, MC, V.

★ ★ **MOUNT ROYAL.** *138 Banff Ave (T1L 1A7). 403/762-3331; fax 403/762-8938; toll-free 800/267-3035. www.mountroyalhotel.com.* 136 rms, 3-4 story. June-early Oct: S, D $270-$295; each addl $15; suites $285-$475; under 16 free; ski plans; lower rates rest of yr. Crib free. Pet accepted, some restrictions. TV; cable. Restaurant 7 am-10 pm. Bar 11:30-1 am. Ck-out 11 am. Coffee in rms. Meeting rms. Coin lndry. Shopping arcade. Beauty shop. Airport transportation. Downhill/x-country ski 5 mi. Exercise equipt; sauna. Health club privileges. Some refrigerators, wet bars, whirlpools, fireplaces, DVDs, stereo systems. Cr cds: A, D, JCB, MC, V.

★ ★ **RADISSON HOTEL AND CONFERENCE CENTER.** *511 Bow Valley Tr, Canmore (T1W 1N7). 403/678-3625; fax 403/678-3765; res 800/333-3333. www.radisson.com.* 224 rms, 3 story. Late June-early Sept: S, D $159-$179; each addl $10; suites $219; under 16 free; lower rates rest of yr. Crib free. Pet accepted. TV; cable. Playground. Indoor pool; whirlpool, steam rm. Restaurant 6:30 am-2 pm. Rm serv 6:30 am-10 pm. Bar to midnight. Ck-out 11 am. Coffee, tea in rms. Coin lndry. Valet serv. Meeting rms. Business servs avail. Exercise equipt. Gift shop. Downhill ski 14 mi, x-country ski 2 mi. Some whirlpools, fireplaces. Balconies. Cr cds: A, D, DS, ER, JCB, MC, V.

Resorts

★★ **BANFF ROCKY MOUNTAIN RESORT.** *1029 Banff Ave (T1L 1A2). 403/762-5531; fax 403/762-5166; toll-free 800/661-9563. www.rocky mountainresort.com.* 171 units, 2 story. Mid-June-mid-Sept: S, D $213-$315; condos $220-$290; each addl $15; under 18 free; higher rates Christmas hol; lower rates rest of yr; package plans. Crib free. Pet accepted. TV, cable. Indoor pool; whirlpool. Playground. Supervised children's activities. Restaurant 7-11 am, 6-9:30 pm. Rm serv 3-10 pm. Bar 11-1 am. Ck-out 11 am. Meeting rms. Business servs avail. Coin lndry. Valet serv. Tennis. Squash. Down-hill/x-country ski 2 mi. Exercise rm; sauna. Massage. Refrigerators, fire-places. Some whirlpools, kitch-enettes. Balconies. Picnic tables, grill. Cr cds: A, D, DS, ER, JCB, MC, V.

★★ **DOUGLAS FIR RESORT.** *Tunnel Mtn Rd (T1L 1B2). 403/762-5591; fax 403/762-8774; toll-free 800/661-9267. www.douglasfir.com.* 133 units, 3 story, 9 chalets. No A/C. S, D $115-$228; each addl $15; suites, chalets $155-$408; under 15 free. TV; cable. Indoor pool; whirlpools, waterslides. Ck-out 11 am. Coin lndry. Grocery store. Business servs avail. Under-ground parking. Tennis. Downhill ski 5 mi; x-country ski adj. Exercise equipt; saunas, steam rm. Refrigera-tors, microwaves, fireplaces. Game rms. Private patios, balconies. Picnic tables, grills. Gazebo. Cr cds: A, D, ER, MC, V.

★★★ **THE FAIRMONT BANFF SPRINGS.** *405 Spray Ave (T1L 1J4). 403/762-2211; fax 403/762-4447; toll-free 800/866-5577. www.fairmont.com.* 770 rms, 9 story. No A/C. June-Aug: S, D $325-$390; each addl $21; suites $540-$975; under 18 free; lower rates rest of yr; package plans. Crib free. Pet accepted; $25. Garage $20/day, valet $20. TV; cable. 2 pools, 1 indoor; 2 whirlpools. Restaurant (see also BANFF SPRINGS). Bar 3:30 pm-1 am. Coffee, tea in rms. Ck-out noon. Convention facilities. Business cen-

ter. Concierge. Shopping arcade. Bar-ber, beauty shop. Valet serv. Tennis, pro. 27-hole golf, greens fee $75-$150, pro, putting green, driving range. Downhill ski 2 mi. Exercise rm; sauna. Spa. Massage. Bowling. Horseback riding. Rec rm. Minibars. Picnic tables. Cr cds: A, C, D, DS, ER, JCB, MC, V.

★★★ **RIMROCK RESORT.** *301 Mountain Ave (T1L 1J2). 403/762-3356; fax 403/762-4132; toll-free 800/661-1587. www.rimrockresort.com.* 346 rms, 9 story, 21 suites. May-Oct: S, D $280-$385; each addl $20; suites $450-$690; under 18 free; package plans; lower rates rest of yr. Crib free. Garage parking $6; valet $10; free self parking. TV; cable. Indoor pool; whirlpool, poolside serv. Restaurant (see also THE PRIMROSE). Rm serv 24 hrs. Bar. Coffee in rms. Ck-out noon. Convention facilities. Business servs avail. Valet serv. Concierge. Shopping arcade. Downhill ski 3 mi; x-country ski on site. Exercise rm; sauna. Squash. Massage. Health club privileges. Minibars. Balconies Cr cds: A, D, DS, ER, JCB, MC, V.

B&Bs/Small Inns

★★ **BANFF AVE INN.** *433 Banff Ave (T0L 0C0). 403/762-4499; fax 403/760-3166; toll-free 888/762-4499. www.banffaveinn.com.* 14 rms, 3 story. No elvtr. Mid-June-Sept: S, D $159-$219; each addl $10; under 12 free; ski plans; lower rates rest of yr. TV; cable. Complimentary coffee in lobby. Restaurant 7-10:30 am, 5:30-10:30 pm. Ck-out 11 am, ck-in 4 pm. Luggage handling. Downhill/x-coun-try ski 10 mi. Many in-rm whirlpools, fireplaces. Many bal-conies. Contemporary decor. Totally nonsmoking. Cr cds: A, MC, V.

★★ **THE LADY MACDONALD COUNTRY INN.** *1201 Bow Valley Tr, Canmore (T1W 1P5). 403/678-3665; fax 403/678-9714; toll-free 800/567-3919. www.ladymacdonald.com.* 12 rms, 2 story. No A/C. June-Sept and Dec hols: D $155-$225; each addl $10; under 12 free; lower rates rest of yr. TV; cable (premium). Complimen-tary full bkfst. Restaurant adj open 24 hrs. Ck-out 11 am. Luggage handling. Spa adj. Downhill ski 10 mi; x-country ski 2 blks. Many fireplaces. Some whirlpools. Victorian-style architecture; Shaker pine furniture. Cr cds: A, MC, V.

Cottage Colony

★ **KANANASKIS GUEST RANCH.** *Hwy 1X, Seebe (TOL 1X0). 403/673-3737; fax 403/673-2100; res 800/691-5085. www.brewsteradventures.com.* 33 cabins (1-2-bcdrm). No A/C. May-mid-Oct: D $89-$104; each addl $29-$49; golf packages; under 12 free. Closed rest of yr. Crib free. TV lounge. Dining rm 7:30-10:30 am, 6-8:30 pm. MAP. Box lunches. Barbecues. Bar 4 pm-1 am. Ck-out 11 am, ck-in 4 pm. Grocery nearby. Meeting rms. Business servs avail. Gift shop, Golf. Hiking. Trail rides. Whitewater rafting. Lawn games. Whirlpool. Picnic tables. On Bow River. Cr cds: A, MC, V.

Restaurants

★★ **BALKAN.** *120 Banff Ave (TOL 0C0). 403/762-3454.* Hrs: 11 am-11 pm. Closed Dec 25. Res accepted. Greek, American menu. Lunch $6.95-$12, dinner $10.99-$23. Child's meals. Own desserts. Greek wall hangings, statues. Cr cds: A, C, D, DS, ER, MC, V.

★★★ **BANFF SPRINGS.** *405 Spray Ave (TOL 0C0). 403/762-2211.* Res accepted. No A/C. Bar noon-midnight. Child's meals. Own baking. Entertainment. Valet parking. Alberta Dining Room: 7-10 am, 6-9 pm; Sun brunch 11 am-2 pm. Continental menu. Complete meals: bkfst $16. Dinner $22-$45. Sun brunch $23.95. Rob Roy: 6-10 pm. A la carte entrees: dinner $22-$45. Specializes in steak, flambeed desserts. Waldhaus: noon-10 pm. German menu. Lunch $7-$15, dinner $16-$27. Specializes in fondues, schnitzel. Historical castle, built 1888. View of mountains. Cr cds: A, D, DS, MC, V.

★★ **THE BISTRO.** *229 Wolf St (TOL 0C0). 403/762-8900. www.info-pages.*

com/bistro. Hrs: noon-11 pm. Res accepted. Continental menu. Lunch $6.75-$17, dinner $14-$20. Child's meals. Specializes in seafood, steak, European style cuisine. Parking. Modern decor. Cr cds: C.

★★ **BUFFALO MOUNTAIN LODGE DINING ROOM.** *Tunnel Mtn Rd (TOL 0C0). 403/760-4485. www.crmr. com.* Specializes in medallion of ranch elk with nectarine relish, port wine sauce, Yukon potato hash, medallions of wild caribou. Hrs: 6:30 am-10 pm. Res required. Wine list. Lunch $6-$19; dinner $21-$33. Child's menu. Entertainment. Cozy, lodge style dining with exposed beams and fieldstone fireplace. Cr cds: A, D, ER, MC, V.

★ **CABOOSE STEAK AND LOBSTER.** *Lynx and Elk Sts (TOL 0C0). 403/762-3622.* Hrs: 5-10 pm. Closed Dec 25. Res accepted. Bar 9 pm-2 am. A la carte entrees: dinner $15-$30. Specializes in prime rib, steak, seafood. Salad bar. Parking. Antiques and memorabilia from the railroad era. Porter's cart used as salad bar. Cr cds: D, ER, MC, V.

★★ **CHEZ FRANCOIS.** *1604 2nd Ave, Canmore (T1W 1M8). 403/678-6111.* Hrs: 6:30 am-2 pm, 5-11 pm; Sun brunch 11 am-3 pm. Res accepted. French menu. Bar. Bkfst $3.95-$8.50, lunch $5.50-$12.95, dinner $13.95-$22.95. Sun brunch $6.50-$12.95. Child's meals. Specialties: braised duck, poached fresh salmon, rack of lamb. Parking. Outdoor dining. Cr cds: A, D, DS, MC, V.

★★ **GIORGIO'S TRATTORIA.** *219 Banff Ave (TOL 0C0). 403/762-5114.* Hrs: 5-10 pm. Northern Italian menu. Bar. A la carte entrees: dinner $12.50-$26.25. Specializes in veal, pasta, lamb. Cr cds: MC, V.

★★★ **LE BEAUJOLAIS.** *212 Buffalo St (TOL 0C0). 403/762-2712. www. info-pages.com/bistro.* Hrs: 6-11 pm. Res accepted. Air-cooled. French menu. Wine cellar. A la carte entrees: dinner $26-$33. Complete meals:

dinner $43-$50. Child's meals. Specializes in rack of lamb, Alberta beef. Own baking. Scenic view of mountains. Cr cds: MC, V.

★★ **PEPPERMILL.** *726 9th St, Canmore (T1W 2V1). 403/678-2292.* Hrs: 5-10 pm. Closed Tues; Dec 25; also Nov. Res accepted. Swiss menu. Complete meal: dinner $12-$24. Child's meals. Specializes in pepper steak, seafood. Swiss atmosphere. Casual decor. Cr cds: A, MC, V.

[D] [⊸]

★★★ **THE PRIMROSE.** *Mountain Ave (T0L 0C0). 403/762-3356.* Hrs: 6:30 am-2 pm, 6-10 pm. Res accepted. Continental menu. Bar. Wine list. Bkfst $7.75-$14.75, lunch $8-$23.75, dinner $15.50-$25. Buffet: bkfst $13. Child's meals. Specializes in pasta, veal, seafood. Valet parking. Large windows provide beautiful view. Cr cds: A, C, D, DS, ER, MC, V.

[D] [⊸]

★★ **SINCLAIR'S.** *637 8th St, Canmore (T1W 2B1). 403/678-5370.* Hrs: 11 am-10 pm. Res accepted. No A/C. Continental menu. Liquor, wine, beer. Lunch $8-$12, dinner $10-$20. Child's meals. Specialties: fresh glazed salmon, char-broiled lamb chops, seared halibut steak. Street parking. Outdoor dining. View of mountains; original artwork. Fireplace. Cr cds: A, D, DS, ER, MC, V.

[D]

★★★ **TICINO.** *415 Banff Ave (T0L 0C0). 403/762-3848. www.ticino restaurant.com.* Hrs: 7:30 am-10:30 pm. Res accepted. Swiss, Italian menu. Wine list. A la carte entrees: dinner $12-$26. Child's meals. Specializes in veal dishes, beef and cheese fondue, pasta. European atmosphere. Family-owned. Cr cds: A, C, D, DS, ER, MC, V.

[D] [SC] [⊸]

Unrated Dining Spot

CLASSICO. *Rimrock Resort Hotel, Mountain Ave (T0L 0C0). 403/762-1840. www.rimrockresort.com.* Hrs: 6-10 pm; closed Mon. Bar. Limited bar menu available after 11 pm. Continental menu. Prix fixe: $75; tasting menu $95. Valet parking. Wine list. Mountain views. Private room avail. Cr cds: A, D, JCB, MC, V.

[D] [⊸]

Calgary

(F-4) *See also Banff*

Founded 1875 **Pop** 720,000
Elev 3,439 ft (1,049 m)
Area code 403
Information Convention and Visitors Bureau, 237 8th Ave SE, Rm 200, T2G 0K8; 403/263-8510 or 800/661-1678
Web www.visitor.calgary.ab.ca

Calgary, called "the gateway to the Canadian Rockies," was founded in 1875 by the North West Mounted Police at the confluence of the Bow and Elbow rivers. Surrounding the city are fertile farmlands and, to the west, the rolling foothills of the Rockies. It is partially due to this lush land that ranching and grain farming have played such a large part in the development of the city. In fact Calgary is a principal centre for Canada's agri-businesses.

Calgary is also the major oil center in Canada. Since 1914 the petroleum industry has centered its activities here. Today more than 85 percent of Canada's oil and gas producers are headquartered in Calgary. As a result, Calgary has experienced a phenomenal growth rate. But the city has retained some of its earlier "small town" atmosphere, and Calgarians are still noted for their warmth and hospitality.

Site of the 1988 Olympic Winter Games, Calgary offers a broad array of pursuits for outdoors enthusiasts, ranging from its numerous golf courses to hiking and whitewater rafting in its foothills and alpine environs. Cultural activities abound as well and Calgary also provides its share of nightlife.

What to See and Do

Calaway Park. Amusement park with 25 rides, attractions, entertainment, games, shops, concessions. (July-Aug, daily; late May-June and Sept-Oct, wkends) 6 mi (10 km) W via Hwy 1, Springbank exit. Phone 403/240-3822. ¢¢¢¢

Calgary Science Centre. Discovery Dome, astronomy displays, exhibitions, observatory, and self-guided tours; science and technology demonstrations. Souvenir shop, snack bar. Admission varies with program. (Tues-Sun; Jul & Aug, daily; closed Dec 25) 7th Ave and 11th St SW. Phone 403/268-8300. ¢¢¢

⭐ **Calgary Tower.** A 626-ft (191-m) tower with a spectacular view of Calgary and the Rocky Mtns; revolving restaurant (see PANORAMA), observation terrace, lounge, souvenir shop. (Daily) 101 9th Ave SW. Phone 403/266-7171. ¢¢¢

The Calgary Zoo, Botanical Garden and Prehistoric Park. One of Canada's largest zoos, with more than 900 animals; botanical garden; Canadian Wilds (25 acres) features Canadian ecosystems populated by their native species. Prehistoric Park. (Daily) St. George's Island, 1300 Zoo Rd NE. Phone 403/232-9300 or 403/232-9372. ¢¢¢¢

Canada Olympic Park. Premiere site of XV Olympic Winter Games. Olympic Hall of Fame and Museum. Winter sports facilities incl double, two triple chairlifts, T-bar, ski school, rentals; snowmaking. Snowboarding. Winter facilities (Nov-Apr, daily). Tours, special events (all yr). Trans-Canada Hwy and Bowfort Rd NW. Phone 403/247-5452. ¢¢¢¢

Devonian Gardens. Approx 2½ acres (1¼ hectares) of indoor vegetation in the heart of the city; waterfalls, fountains, ponds with rainbow trout, goldfish, and koi; seating for concerts; art displays; playground; reflecting pool. Below the gardens are stores and restaurants. (Daily) 7th Ave between 2nd and 3rd sts SW. Phone 403/268-2300. **FREE**

Eau Claire Market and Prince's Island Park. Market is a two-story warehouse, containing boutique shops, fish, meat, vegetable, and fruit stands, restaurants and bars, and four-screen cinema. Also incl IMAX Theatre (phone 403/974-4629). Prince's Island Park is located on an island in the Bow River, lined with cottonwood trees and inhabited by Canada geese. Near 2nd Ave SW and 3rd St SW. Phone 403/264-6450.

Energeum. Public visitor center that involves guests in the story of Alberta's energy resources. Hands-on exhibits cover geology, exploration, conservation, and more; 1958 limited-edition Buick; theater with films, demonstrations, special events. (June-Aug, Sun-Fri; rest of yr, Mon-Fri) 640 5th Ave SW. Phone 403/297-4293. **FREE**

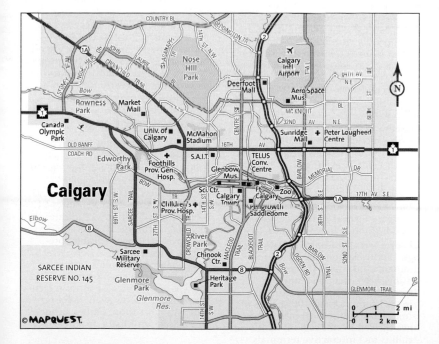

© MAPQUEST

EPCOR Centre for Performing Arts. Four theaters noted for their excellent acoustics house the Calgary Philharmonic, Theatre Calgary, and other performing arts. Guided tours avail. 205-8 Ave SE. Phone 403/294-7455. **FREE**

Fort Calgary Historic Park. (1875) Riverside park of 40 acres (16 hectares), site of original North West Mounted Police (NWMP) fort, at confluence of Bow and Elbow rivers. Abandoned in 1914, the site of the fort is now being rebuilt. Interpretive center focuses on NWMP, Calgary history. Exhibit hall, audiovisual presentation, Discovery Room. Excellent views of rivers and St. George's Island. Adj is **Deane House** (1906), restored and open to public as restaurant; guided tours (by appt; phone 403/269-7747). (Daily) 750 9th Ave SE. Phone 403/290-1875. ¢¢¢

Glenbow Museum. Museum, art gallery, library, and archives. Regional, national, and international fine arts; displays of native cultures of North America and the development of the West; mineralogy, warriors, African and personal adornment. (Daily; closed hols) 130 9th Ave SE. ¢¢¢

Heritage Park Historical Village. Recreates life in western Canada before 1914. More than 150 exhibits; steam train, paddlewheeler, horse-drawn wagon and electric streetcars, wagon rides, antique midway. (Mid-May-early Sept, daily; mid-Sept-early Oct, wkends and hols) 1900 Heritage Dr SW. Phone 403/268-8500 or 403/259-1900. ¢¢¢

Museum of the Regiments. One of North America's largest military museums, honors four Calgary Regiments. Films. Traveling art exhibits. (Thurs-Tues) 4520 Crowchild Tr SW. Phone 403/974-2850. ¢¢

Professional sports team.

   Calgary Flames (NHL). Pengrowth Saddledome. Phone 403/777-4630.

🔲 **Royal Tyrrell Museum of Paleontology.** World's largest display of dinosaurs in state-of-the-art museum setting. More than 35 complete dinosaur skeletons; "Paleoconservatory" with more than 100 species of tropical and subtropical plants that once thrived in this region; hands-on exhibits incl interactive terminals and games throughout. Souvenir shop, cafeteria. Inquire locally about summer bus service from Calgary. (Late May-Labour Day, daily; rest of yr, Tues-Sun; also Mon hols; closed Dec 25) 80 mi (128 km) NE via Hwy 9 in Drumheller. Phone 403/823-7707. ¢¢¢

Spruce Meadows. One of North America's finest equestrian facilities. Devoted to hosting the best show jumping tournaments on the continent, training young riders and young horses, and breeding a super sport horse by crossing the North American Thoroughbred with the German Hanoverian. (Daily; closed Jan 1, Dec 25) (See SPECIAL EVENTS) Fee during tournaments. 3 mi (5 km) SW via Hwy 22X. Phone 403/974-4200. ¢¢

Special Events

Calgary Winter Festival. Music, entertainment, sports competitions, children's activities, carnival, dance. Eleven days mid-Feb. Phone 403/543-5480.

Spruce Meadows. Only internationally sanctioned outdoor horse jumping show held in North America; offers the world's richest show jumping purse. June-Sept. Phone 403/974-4200.

Calgary Stampede. Stampede Park. "The World's Greatest Outdoor Show." Parade, rodeo, chuck wagon races, stage shows, exhibition, square dances, marching bands, vaudeville shows. Ten days early July. Phone 403/261-0101 or 661/126-0800.

Motels/Motor Lodges

★★ **BEST WESTERN HOSPITALITY INN.** *135 Southland Dr SE (T2J 5X5). 403/278-5050; toll-free 800/780-7234. www.bestwestern.com/ca/ hospitalityinn.* 260 rms, 8 story. S, D $149-$164; each addl $5; suites $139-$299; under 17 free; wkend rates Oct-May. Crib free. Pet accepted, some restrictions. TV; cable (premium). Heated indoor pool; whirlpool, waterslide. Coffee in rms. Restaurant 6:30 am-11 pm. Bar 11-2 am. Ck-out noon. Convention facilities. Business servs avail. Valet serv. Bellhops. Gift shop. Barber, beauty shop. Some minibars. Some private patios, balconies. Cr cds: A, C, D, DS, ER, MC, V.

[icons]

★★ **BEST WESTERN PORT O' CALL HOTEL.** *1935 McKnight Blvd NE (T2E 6V4). 403/291-4600; fax 403/250-6827; toll-free 800/661-1161. www.portocallinn.com.* 201 rms, 7 story. S, D $139; suites $220; each addl $5; wkend rates Oct-Apr; under 17 free. TV; cable. Indoor pool; whirlpool. Coffee, tea in rms. Restaurant 6:30 am-10 pm; Sat 7 am-10 pm; Sun, hols 7 am-2 pm. Sun brunch 10 am-2 pm. Rm serv 6:30 am-midnight; Sun, hols 7 am-10 pm. Bar 11-1 am. Ck-out noon. Meeting rms. Business servs avail. Gift shop. Barber, beauty shop. Free heated garage parking. Free airport transportation. Exercise equipt; steam rm. Some minibars, fireplaces, whirlpools. Balconies. Luxury level Cr cds: A, C, D, DS, ER, JCB, MC, V.

[icons]

★★ **BLACKFOOT INN.** *5940 Blackfoot Tr SE (T2H 2B5). 403/252-2253; fax 403/252-3574; toll-free 800/661-1151. www.blackfootinn.com.* 200 rms, 7 story. S, D $127-$160; each addl $10; suite $179; under 16 free; monthly rates. Crib free. Pet accepted. TV; cable, VCR (movies). Heated pool; whirlpool, poolside serv. Coffee in rms. Restaurant 6 am-midnight. Bar 11-1:30 am; entertainment Mon-Fri. Ck-out noon. Meeting rms. Business center. Bellhops. Sundries. Gift shop. Exercise equipt; sauna. Minibars. Cr cds: A, D, ER, MC, V.

[icons]

★ **COMFORT INN & SUITE MOTEL VILLAGE.** *2369 Banff Tr NW (T2M 4L2). 403/289-2581; fax 403/284-3897; res 800/228-5150. www.comfortinn.com.* 70 rms, 2 story. Apr-Sept: S, D $99-$149; each addl $10; under 16 free; wkend rates; lower rates rest of yr. Crib $5. TV; cable. Sauna. Heated indoor pool; whirlpool, waterslide. Complimentary continental bkfst. Coffee in rms. Restaurant adj 24 hrs. Ck-out 11 am. Business servs avail. Exercise equipt. Refrigerators, microwaves in suites. Some balconies. Cr cds: A, D, DS, MC, V.

[icons]

★ **DAYS INN - CALGARY WEST.** *1818 16th Ave NW (Trans-Can Hwy 1) (T2M 0L8). 403/289-1961; fax 403/289-3901; toll-free 800/661-9564. www.daysinn.com.* 130 rms, 4 story. Mid-June-Sept: S, D $65-$130; suites $130-$170; each addl $10; under 16 free; higher rates special events; lower rates rest of yr. Crib free. Pet accepted. TV; cable (premium), VCR avail. Heated pool; poolside serv. Coffee in rms. Restaurant 6:30 am-11:30 pm; pianist in dining rm Thurs-Sun. Bar 11-1:30 am. Ck-out 11 am. Meeting rms. Business servs avail. Bellhops. Gift shop. Airport transportation. Balconies. Cr cds: A, C, D, DS, ER, JCB, MC, V.

[icons]

★★ **GLENMORE INN & CONVENTION CENTER.** *2720 Glenmore Tr SE (T2I 2E6). 403/279-8811; fax 403/236-8035; toll-free 800/661-3163. www.glenmoreinn.com.* 169 rms, 2 story. June-Aug: S, D $104-$119; each addl $10; suite $189; under 18 free; lower rates rest of yr. Crib free. TV; cable (premium), VCR avail. Whirlpool. Coffee in rms. Restaurant 6:30 am-11 pm. Bar 11-1 am. Ck-out noon. Convention facilities. Business servs avail. Gift shop. Valet serv. Exercise equipt; sauna. Some whirlpools, wet bars. Cr cds: A, DS, MC, V.

[icons]

★★ **HAMPTON INN & SUITES - CALGARY AIRPORT.** *2420 37th Ave NE (T2E 8S6). 403/250-4667; fax 403/250-5788; res 800/426-7866. www.hamptoninn-suites.com.* 72 rms, 4 story, 32 kit. units. S $109-$114; D $114-$119; suites $134-$139; kit. units $134-$159; under 18 free; wkend rates; higher rates special events. Crib free. TV; cable (premium), VCR avail. Complimentary continental bkfst. Complimentary coffee in rms. Restaurant nearby. Ck-out 11 am. Meeting rms. Business servs avail. In-rm modem link. Bellhops. Valet serv. Sundries. Coin lndry. Free airport, RR station transportation. Exercise equipt. Massage. Indoor pool. Some refrigerators, microwaves. Cr cds: A, C, D, DS, ER, JCB, MC, V.

[icons]

★★ **HOLIDAY INN AIRPORT.** *1250 McKinnon Dr NE (T2E 7T7). 403/230-1999; fax 403/277-2623; toll-free 877/519-7113. www.holiday-inn.com/calgary-apt.* 170 rms, 5 story. S, D $149-$159; each addl $10; under 18 free. Pet accepted. TV; cable. Indoor pool. Coffee, tea in rms. Restaurant 6:30 am-10 pm. Bar 11-1 am. Ck-out noon. Meeting rms. Business center. In-rm modem link. Gift shop. Free airport transportation. Coin lndry. Valet serv. Exercise equipt; sauna. Cr cds: A, C, D, DS, JCB, MC, V.

[icons]

★★ **HOLIDAY INN EXPRESS.** *2227 Banff Tr NW (T2M 4L2). 403/289-6600; fax 403/289-6767; res 800/465-4329. www.holiday-inn.com.* 62 rms, 3 story. S, D $89-$115; each addl $10; suites $100-$175; under 18 free. Crib free. Pet accepted, some restrictions. TV; cable. Whirlpool. Complimentary coffee, tea maker in rms. Complimentary continental bkfst. Restaurant adj. Ck-out noon. Meeting rms. Business servs avail. Coin lndry. In-rm modem link. Sauna. Cr cds: A, D, DS, ER, JCB, MC, V.

[icons]

★★ **HOLIDAY INN - MACLEOD TRAIL SOUTH.** *4206 Macleod Trl S (T2G 2R7). 403/287-2700; fax 403/243-4721; toll-free 800/661-1889. www.calgaryholidayinn.com.* 150 rms, 4 story. May-Sept: S, D $114-$131; each addl $5; under 18 free; wknd, wkly rates; lower rates rest of yr. Crib free. Pet accepted, some restrictions; $20. TV; cable (premium). Heated indoor pool; whirlpool. Coffee, tea in rms. Restaurant 7 am-10 pm. Bar 11 am-midnight. Ck-out noon. In-rm modem link. Coin lndry. Meeting rms. Business servs avail. Exercise equipt. Health club privileges. Bellhops. Valet serv. Cr cds: A, C, D, DS, JCB, MC, V.

[icons]

★ **QUALITY HOTEL & CONFERENCE CENTRE.** *3828 Macleod Tr (T2G 2R2). 403/243-5531; fax 403/243-6962; toll-free 800/361-3422. www.qualityinn.com.* 134 rms, 3 story. S, D $10-$149; suites $119-$129; each addl $10; under 18 free. Crib free. Pet accepted; $10. TV; cable (premium). Heated indoor pool; whirlpool. Coffee in rms. Restaurants

7 am-10 pm. Bar 11-2 am; closed Sun. Ck-out noon. Coin lndry. Meeting rms. Business servs avail. Exercise equipt. Bellhops in summer. Valet serv Mon-Fri. Gift shop. Some refrigerators, microwaves. Luxury level. Cr cds: A, C, D, DS, ER, JCB, MC, V.

[icons]

★ **QUALITY INN MOTEL VILLAGE.** *2359 Banff Tr NW (1A) (T2M 4L2). 403/289-1973; fax 403/282-1241; toll-free 800/661-4667. www.qualityinnmotelvillage.com.* 105 rms, 2 story. July-Sept: S, D $99-$129; suites $139-$209; under 18 free; higher rates: Calgary Stampede, 1st 2 wks July; lower rates rest of yr. Free garage parking. Crib free. Pet accepted. TV; cable (premium); VCR (movies). Indoor pool; whirlpool, waterslide. Complimentary continental bkfst. Coffee in rms. Restaurant 7 am-2 pm, 5-10 pm. Bar 10-2 am. Ck-out 11 am. Meeting rms. Business servs avail. Exercise equipt; sauna, steam rm. Balconies. Refrigerators, microwaves. Casino. Cr cds: A, D, DS, ER, MC, V.

[icons]

★ **TRAVELODGE CALGARY SOUTH.** *7012 Macleod Tr S (T2H 0L3). 403/253-1111; fax 403/253-2879; res 800/578-7878. www.travelodge.com.* 62 rms, 2 story. June-Oct: S, D $82-$95; each addl $8; under 18 free; lower rates rest of yr. Crib free. TV; cable (premium); VCR avail (movies). Pool. Complimentary coffee in rms. Restaurant nearby. Business servs avail. Ck-out noon. Refrigerators. Microwaves avail; $3/day. Cr cds: A, D, DS, JCB, MC, V.

[icons]

Hotels

★★ **CARRIAGE HOUSE INN.** *9030 Macleod Tr S (T2H 0M4). 403/253-1101; fax 403/259-2414; toll-free 800/661-9566. www.carriagehouse.net.* 157 rms, 10 story. S, D $105-$135; each addl $10; suites $205-$245; under 18 free. Crib free. Pet accepted, some restrictions; $5. TV; cable (premium). Heated pool; whirlpool, poolside serv. Coffee in rms. Restaurant 7 am-11 pm. Bar 11-2 am. Ck-out noon. Meeting rms. Business servs avail. In-rm modem link. Gift shop. Sauna. Health club privileges.

Calgary skyline

Valet serv. Minibars. Some whirlpools. Bakery. Cr cds: A, D, DS, ER, JCB, MC, V.

★ **THE COAST PLAZA HOTEL & CONFERENCE CENTRE.** *1316 33rd St NE (T2A 6B6). 103/248-8888; fax 403/248-0749; toll-free 800/661-1464. www.calgaryplaza.com.* 248 rms, 7 and 12 story. S, D $132-$175; each addl $15; suites $293; under 18 free. Crib free. Pet accepted; $20. TV; cable, VCR avail. Heated indoor pool; whirlpool. Complimentary coffee, tea in rms. Restaurant 6:30 am-2 pm, 5-10 pm. Rm serv 24 hrs. Bar 11:30-2 am. Ck-out noon. Convention facilities. Business servs avail. Concierge. Bellhops. Valet serv. Gift shop. Free airport transportation. Exercise equipt; sauna. Refrigerators, microwaves avail. Luxury level. Cr cds: A, D, DS, ER, MC, V.

★★ **DELTA BOW VALLEY.** *209 4th Ave SE (T2G 0C6). 403/266-1980; fax 403/205-5460; toll-free 800/268-1133. www.deltabowvalley.com.* 398 rms, 25 story. S, D $209-$224; each addl $15; suites $249-$265; under 18 free; wkend, family rates. Pet accepted. Garage $6, valet $8. TV; cable (pre-

mium). Indoor pool; whirlpool, poolside serv. Supervised children's activities (wkends), ages 3-16. Coffee in rms. Restaurant 5:30 am-10 pm. Rm serv 24 hrs. Bar 11:30-1 am; pianist Mon-Fri. Ck-out 11 am. Convention facilities. Business servs avail. Gift shop. Concierge. Exercise equipt; sauna. Many minibars. Sundeck. Canadian artwork on display. Overlooks river. Cr cds: A, C, D, DS, ER, JCB, MC, V.

★★ **DELTA CALGARY AIRPORT.** *2001 Airport Rd NE (T2E 6Z8). 403/291-2600; fax 403/250-8722; toll-free 800/268-1133. www.deltahotels. com.* 296 rms, 8 story. S, D $169-$189; each addl $20; suites $269-$370; under 18 free. Pet accepted, some restrictions. Indoor pool; whirlpool. Coffee, tea in rms. Restaurant (see also ATRIUM STEAKHOUSE). Rm serv 24 hrs. Bar 11-1 am; Sun 11 am-midnight. Ck-out noon. Convention facilities. Business center. Concierge. Bellhops. Gift shop. Exercise equipt; sauna. Minibars; some whirlpools. Atrium. Cr cds: A, C, D, DS, ER, JCB, MC, V.

★★★ DELTA LODGE AT KANANASKIS. *209 4th Ave SE, Kananaskis (T0L 2H0). 403/591-7711; fax 403/591-7770; toll-free 888/244-8666. www.deltahotels.com.* 321 air-cooled rms, 3 story. S, D $299; each addl $20; suites $340-$550; under 18 free; ski plans. Crib free. Pet accepted; $100/stay. Covered parking $8; valet parking $12. TV; cable. Indoor pool; indoor/outdoor whirlpool. Restaurant. Bar; entertainment. Ck-out noon. Convention facilities. Business center. Concierge. Bellhops. Shopping arcade. Barber, beauty shop. Tennis. 36-hole golf course; greens fee, pro, putting green, driving range. Downhill ski 1 mi; x-country ski on site. Exercise equipt; sauna, steam rm. Game rm. Rec rm. Minibars; some bathrm phones, whirlpools, fireplaces, minibars. Private patios, balconies. Cr cds: A, D, DS, ER, JCB, MC, V.

★★★ THE FAIRMONT PALLISER. *133 9th Ave SW (T2P 2M3). 403/262-1234; fax 403/260-1260; res 800/441-1414. www.fairmont.com.* 405 rms, 12 story. S, D $240-$300; each addl $25; suites $400-$900; under 18 free. Crib free. Pet accepted; $25. TV; cable (premium), VCR avail. Indoor pool; whirlpool. Coffee, tea in rms. Restaurant (see also RIMROCK). Rm serv 24 hrs. Bar 11-2 am. Ck-out noon. Convention facilities. Business center. In-rm modem link. Self parking $18. Valet parking $20. Concierge. bellhops. Gift shop. Barber, beauty shop. Valet serv. Airport transportation. Exercise rm; steam rm. Spa. Massage. Minibars; refrigerators, microwaves avail. Luxury level. Cr cds: A, C, D, DS, ER, JCB, MC, V.

★ HAWTHORN HOTEL & SUITES. *618 5th Ave SW (T2P 0M7). 403/263-0520; fax 403/298-4888; toll-free 800/661-1592. www.hawthorncalgary.com.* 301 air-cooled kit. suites, 28 story. S, D $145-$210; each addl $15; under 18 free. TV; cable. Pool. Complimentary bkfst buffet. Coffee in rms. Restaurant 7 am-11 pm. Bar from noon. Ck-out noon. Coin lndry. Valet serv. Meeting rms. Airport transportation. Business servs avail. Gift shop. Exercise equipt; sauna, steam rm. Refrigerators. Cr cds: A, C, D, DS, MC, V.

★★★ HYATT REGENCY CALGARY. *700 Centre St (T2G 5P6). 403/717-1234; fax 403/537-4444. www.hyatt.com.* 355 rms, 21 story. S, D $89-$224; each addl $20; under 17 free. Crib avail. TV; cable (premium), VCR avail. Self parking $14, valet parking $18. Indoor pool; whirlpool. Complimentary coffee, tea, newspaper in rms. Restaurant 6:30 am-2 pm, 5-10 pm. Rm serv 24 hrs. Bar 11 am-midnight; Fri, Sat 11-1 am. Ck-out noon. Meeting rms. Business center. In-rm modem link. Gift shop. Exercise rm; steam rm. Some refrigerators, minibars. Sundeck. Cr cds: A, C, D, DS, MC, V.

★★ INTERNATIONAL HOTEL OF CALGARY. *220 4th Ave SW (T2P 0H5). 403/265-9600; fax 403/265-6949; toll-free 800/637-7200. www.intlhotel.com.* 247 suites, 35 story. S, D $149-$252; under 16 free; wkend rates. Crib free. Garage $7. TV; cable (premium), VCR avail. Indoor pool; whirlpool. Coffee in rms. Restaurant 6:30 am-11 pm. Bar 11-1 am. Ck-out 1 pm. Meeting rms. Business servs avail. Valet serv. Concierge. Gift shop. Barber. Exercise equipt; sauna. Massage. Some refrigerators, minibars. Balconies. Cr cds: A, C, D, ER, MC, V.

★★★ JOHN PALLISER MANOR. *Hwy 40 and Trans-Can Hwy 1 (T0L 2B0). 403/591-7711; fax 403/591-7770.* 68 air-cooled rms, 3 story. S, D $295; each addl $20; suites $340-$550; under 18 free; ski plans. Crib free. Garage $4. TV; cable. Indoor/outdoor pool; whirlpool. Restaurant 6:30 am-9:30 pm. Bar. Ck-out noon. Meeting rms. Concierge. Tennis. 36-hole golf; greens fee, pro, putting green, driving range. Downhill ski 1 mi; x-country ski on site. Exercise equipt; sauna. Bathrm phones, minibars. Private patios, balconies. Cr cds: A, D, DS, ER, JCB, MC, V.

★★ KANANASKIS MOUNTAIN LODGE. *Kananaskis Village, Kananaskis Village (T0L 2H0).*

403/591-7500; fax 403/591-7633; res 888/591-7501. www.kananaskis mountainlodge.com. 94 rms, 3 story. S, D $170-$270; each addl $20; suites $230-$270; under 18 free; ski, golf plans. Crib free. Pet accepted; $25. TV; cable (premium). Indoor pool; whirlpool, steam rm. Restaurant 7 am-10 pm. Bar. Ck-out 11 am. Meeting rms. Business servs avail. Gift shop. Free covered parking. Tennis. 36-hole golf; greens fee, putting green, driving range. Spa. Massage. Downhill ski 4 mi. Private patios, balconies. Refrigerators; some fireplaces. Cr cds: A, D, DS, ER, MC, V.

★★★ MARRIOTT HOTEL CAL-GARY. 110 9th Ave SE (T2G 0N6) 403/266-7331; fax 403/262-1961; toll-free 800/896-6878. www.marriott.com/marriott/yycdt. 384 rms, 23 story. S, D $157-$188; each addl $20; suites $245-$399; under 18 free; family, wkend rates; higher rates special events. Crib free. Pet accepted. Garage $11-$17/day. TV; cable (premium). Heated indoor pool; whirlpool, poolside serv. Coffee in rms. Restaurant 6:30 am-2 pm, 5-10 pm; Sat, Sun 7 am-10 pm. Rm serv 6:30 am-midnight. Bar 11 am-midnight. Ck-out noon. Convention facilities. Gift shop. Business center. Concierge. Exercise equipt; sauna. Luxury level. Cr cds: A, D, DS, JCB, MC, V.

★★ RADISSON HOTEL CALGARY AIRPORT. 2120 16th Ave NE (T2E 1L4). 403/291-4666; fax 403/291-6498; res 800/333-3333. www.radisson.com. 185 rms, 10 story. S, D $99-$159; each addl $10; suites $279; under 12 free. Crib free. Pet accepted. TV; cable (premium). Indoor pool; whirlpool. Coffee in rms. Restaurant 6:30 am-11:30 pm; Sat, Sun 7 am-11 pm; Sun brunch 10 am-2 pm. Bar 11-2 am; entertainment. Ck-out 11 am. Meeting rms. Business center. Gift shop. Free airport transportation. Exercise equipt. Some refrigerators. Balconies. Cr cds: A, D, DS, ER, JCB, MC, V.

★★★ SHERATON CAVALIER. 2620 32nd Ave NE (T1Y 6B8). 403/291-0107; fax 403/291-2834; toll-free 800/325-3535. www.sheraton-calgary.com. 306 rms, 8 story. S, D $179-$229; each addl $10; suites $219-$350; under 18 free. Crib free. TV; cable (premium). Indoor pool; wading pool, whirlpools, poolside serv. Coffee in rms. Restaurant 5:30 am-10:30 pm; Sun 5-9 pm. Rm serv 24 hrs. Bar 11-12:30 am. Ck-out noon. Convention facilities. Business center. Gift shop. Concierge. Bellhops. Free airport transportation. Game rm. Exercise equipt; sauna. Refrigerators, microwaves, minibars. Some whirlpools. Luxury level. Cr cds: A, C, D, ER, MC, V.

★★★ WESTIN CALGARY. 320 4th Ave SW (T2P 2S6). 403/266-1611; fax 403/233-7471; toll-free 800/937-8461. www.westin.com. 525 rms, 17 and 19 story. S, D $255-$349; each addl $20; suites $285-$700; under 18 free; wkend rates. Crib free. Pet accepted, some restrictions. TV; cable (premium), VCR avail. Indoor pool; whirlpool, poolside serv. Coffee in rms. Restaurants. Rm serv 24 hrs. Bar 11:30-1 am. Ck-out 1 pm. Convention facilities. Business servs avail. In-rm modem link. Valet serv. Concierge. Shopping arcade. Indoor valet parking. Exercise equipt; sauna. Minibars. Cr cds: A, C, D, DS, ER, JCB, MC, V.

Guest Ranch

★★ RAFTER SIX RANCH RESORT. Hwy 1 and S Ranch Rd, Seebe (T0L 1X0). 403/673-3622; fax 403/673-3961; res 888/267-2624. www.raftersix.com. 18 rms in 3-story lodge, 8 cabins, 4 chalets. No A/C. AP: S, D $415-$740; 2-day min. TV in sitting rm. Heated pool; whirlpool. Playground. Dining rm 7:30 am-9 pm. Bar 4 pm-midnight. Ck-out noon. Coin lndry. Meeting rms. Business servs avail. Gift shop. Hiking. Hayrides. Entertainment. Horseback riding, chuck wagon bkfst, barbecues. Wilderness camping facilities. Lawn games. Some fireplaces. Balconies. Rustic; authentic Western Canadian ranch decor, furnishings; original Indian design door murals. Cr cds: A, MC, V.

Restaurants

★★ **ATRIUM STEAKHOUSE.** *2001 Airport Rd NE (T2E 6Z8). 403/291-2600.* Hrs: 5-10 pm; Terrace from 5 pm. Sun brunch (Atrium) 11 am-2 pm. Res accepted. Bar 11-1 am. Atrium: Continental menu. Dinner $18-$26. Sun brunch $18.95. Specializes in Alberta beef, fresh salmon, linguini Calabrese. Parking. Bright atmosphere; fresh flowers. Totally nonsmoking. Cr cds: A, D, ER, MC, V.
[D] [SC]

★★★ **THE BELVEDERE.** *107 8th Ave SW (T2P 1B4). 403/265-9595.* Specializes in Arctic char with citrus honey and sake, sesame spinach and sticky coconut rice. Hrs: 11:30 am-midnight; Sat 5 pm-midnight. Closed Sun. Res accepted. Wine list. Lunch $14-$18; dinner $22-$36. View of the Calgary tower. Cr cds: A, D, ER, MC, V.
[D]

★ **CAESAR'S STEAK HOUSE.** *512 4th Ave SW (T2P 0J6). 403/264-1222.* Hrs: 11 am-midnight; Sat from 4:30 pm. Closed Sun; hols. Res accepted. Continental menu. Bar. Wine list. Lunch $8-$18, dinner $18-$35. Specializes in steak, seafood, ribs. Valet parking. Greco-Roman motif; marble pillars, statues. Cr cds: A, D, MC, V.
[D] [⊒]

★★ **HY'S CALGARY STEAK HOUSE.** *316 4th Ave SW (T2P 0H8). 403/263-2222.* Hrs: 11:30 am-2:30 pm, 5-11 pm; Sun 5-10 pm. Closed hols. Res accepted. Continental menu. Bar to 11:30 pm. Lunch $9.50-$17.95, dinner $17.95-$29.50. Specializes in steak. Parking. Rustic decor; antiques. Family-owned. Cr cds: A, D, MC, V.
[D] [⊒]

★★ **INN ON LAKE BONAVISTA.** *747 Lake Bonavista Dr SE (T2J 0N2). 403/271-6711.* Hrs: 11:30 am-2 pm, 5-11 pm; Sun 5-9 pm; Sun brunch 10:30 am-2 pm. Res accepted. French, continental menu. Bar. Wine list. A la carte entrees: lunch $7.50-$14.50, dinner $17-$32. Sun brunch $18.95. Child's meals. Specializes in Alberta beef, fresh seafood. Entertain-ment Tues-Sat. Outdoor dining. On lake. Cr cds: A, C, D, DS, ER, MC, V.
[D] [SC] [⊒]

★★ **THE KEG STEAKHOUSE AND BAR.** *7104 MacLeod Trl S (T2H 0L3). 403/253-2534. www.kegsteakhouse. com.* Hrs: 11:30 am-2:30 pm, 4-10:30 pm; Fri, Sat to 11 pm; Sun to 9:30 pm. Closed Dec 25. Res accepted Sun-Thurs. Bar. Lunch $6.99-$13.99, dinner $12.99-$26.99. Child's meals. Specializes in prime rib, steak. Patio dining. 4-tier dining area; 2 fireplaces. Cr cds: A, C, D, DS, ER, MC, V.
[D] [⊒]

★★★ **MAMMA'S.** *320 16th Ave NW (T2M 0H6). 403/276-9744.* Hrs: 11:30 am-2 pm, 5-11 pm. Closed Sun. Res required. Italian menu. Wine cellar. Lunch $7.95-$14.95, dinner $9.95-$24.95. Specializes in pasta, veal, game birds. Own baking. Parking. Formal dining rm with chandeliers. Italian paintings. Cr cds: A, C, D, DS, ER, MC, V.
[D] [⊒]

★ **MESCALERO.** *1315 1st St SW (T2R 0V5). 403/266-3339.* Hrs: 11:30 am-midnight; Sun brunch 11 am-3 pm. Closed Dec 25. Res accepted. Mexican, Southwestern menu. Bar. A la carte entrees: lunch $5-$13, dinner $5-$26. Sun brunch $8-$12. Specializes in Tex-Mex, wild game, fresh seafood. Parking. Outdoor dining. Rustic decor; imported Southwestern furnishings. Cr cds: A, D, ER, MC, V.
[D] [⊒]

★★★ **PANORAMA.** *101 9th Ave SW (T2P 1J9). 403/266-7171. www.calgary tower.com.* Hrs: 8 am-3 pm, 5-10 pm. Res accepted. Continental menu. Bar 11:30 am-midnight. Complete meals: bkfst $11, lunch $10-$15, dinner $17-$26. Child's meals. Specializes in prime rib, tenderloin steak, fresh seafood. Revolving restaurant atop Calgary Tower; panoramic view of city, mountains (fee). Cr cds: A, D, MC, V.
[D] [⊒]

★★ **QUINCY'S ON SEVENTH.** *609 7th Ave SW (T2P 0Y9). 403/264-1000. www.quincysonseventh.com.* Hrs: 11 am-11 pm; Sat, Sun from 5 pm. Closed hols. Res accepted. Bar. A la carte entrees: lunch $12.95-$18, dinner $19-$35. Child's meals. Specializes in steak, prime rib. Antique furnishings. Cr cds: A, C, D, DS, ER, MC, V.

★ **REGENCY PALACE.** *328 Centre St SE (T2G 2B8). 403/777-2288.* Hrs: 10 am-11 pm. Res accepted. Chinese menu. Bar. Lunch $4.95-$14.95, dinner $7.95-$15.95. Specializes in duck, chicken, seafood. Salad bar. Outdoor dining. Asian decor. Cr cds: A, C, D, DS, ER, MC, V.

★ ★ ★ **THE RIMROCK ROOM.** *133 9th Ave SW (T2P 2M3). 403/262-1234. www.cphotels.ca.* Hrs: 6:30 am-10 pm; Sun brunch 10:30 am-2:30 pm. Res accepted. Continental menu. Bar 11:30-1:30 am. Bkfst $8-$12, lunch $12-$19, dinner $24-$30. Sun brunch $22.95. Child's meals. Specializes in Alberta beef, Alberta lamb, wild game. Valet parking. Formal atmosphere. Cr cds: A, C, D, DS, ER, MC, V.

★ ★ **RIVER CAFE.** *Prince's Island Park (T2G 0K7). 403/261-7670.* Hrs: 11 am-11 pm; Sat, Sun from 10 am. Sat, Sun brunch 10 am-3 pm. Closed Dec 25; also Jan. Res accepted. Bar. Lunch $8-$20, dinner $17-$35. Sat, Sun brunch $5-$15. Specialties: cedar-planked Arctic char, Alberta caribou, seafood pasta. Outdoor dining. Canadian Northwoods decor. Totally nonsmoking. Cr cds: A, D, MC, V.

★ ★ ★ **SEASONS.** *1029 Banff Ave, Kananaskis Village (T0L 0C0). 403/762-5531. www.rockymountain resort.com.* Specializes in marinated lamb kabobs, salmon florentine. Hrs: 7 am-10 pm. Res accepted. Wine, beer. Dinner $18-$22. Child's menu. Entertainment. View of the Rocky Mts. Cr cds: A, D, DS, ER, JCB, MC, V.

★ **SILVER DRAGON.** *106 3rd Ave SE (T2G 0B6). 403/264-5326.* Hrs: 10:30-1 am; Fri, Sat to 2 am; Sun 9:30 am-10 pm. Res accepted; required Sat, Sun. Chinese menu. Wine. Lunch $6-$15, dinner $10-$30. Specializes in Cantonese, Peking-style cuisine.

Oriental decor. Family-owned. Cr cds: A, D, MC, V.

★ ★ **SMUGGLER'S INN.** *6920 MacLeod Trl (T2H 0L3). 403/253-5355. www.smugglers-inn.com.* Hrs: 11:30 am-midnight; Fri, Sat to 1 am; Sun 4:30-11 pm; Sun brunch 10 am-2 pm. Closed Jan 1, Dec 25. Res accepted. Continental menu. Bar to 2 am. Complete meals: lunch $6-$10. Dinner $7-$25. Specializes in Alberta beef, seafood, prime rib. Salad bar. Entertainment. Parking. Patio dining. Rustic atmosphere; antique furnishings. Family-owned. Cr cds: A, D, DS, MC, V.

★ ★ **TEATRO.** *200 8th Ave SE (T2G 0K7). 403/290-1012. www.teatro-rest. com.* Hrs: 11:30 am-11 pm, Sat 5 pm-midnight; Sun 5-10 pm. Closed Jan 1, Dec 24, 25. Res accepted. Italian menu. Bar. A la carte entrees: lunch $10-$16, dinner $18-$30. Specialties: lobster and scallop lasagna, rack of lamb, Italian market cuisine. Parking. Outdoor dining. In old Dominion Bank bldg (1911). Cr cds: A, C, D, DS, ER, MC, V.

Unrated Dining Spot

CONSERVATORY. *209 4th Ave SE (T2G 0C6). 403/266-1980.* Amer cuisine. Hrs: 5:30-10 pm. Dinner: $11.50-$22.95. Child's meals. Valet parking. Cr cds: A, D, MC, V.

Edmonton <small>(D-5)</small>

Settled 1795 **Pop** 854,200 **Elev** 2,192 ft (671 m) **Area code** 780

Information Edmonton Tourism, 9797 Jasper Ave NW, T5J 1N9; 780/426-4715 or 800/463-4667

Web www.tourism.ede.org

As capital of a province whose economic mainstays are petroleum and agriculture, Edmonton has all the brash confidence of its position as a major supplier of one of the world's most sought-after resources, yet traces of the practical reticence nurtured by its past still linger.

The first Fort Edmonton, established in 1795, was named for Edmonton, England, now a suburb of London. The fort was relocated several times before its fifth site location near the present Alberta Legislature Building. With the close of the fur trade era, a settlement grew up around the fort and became the nucleus of the city. The sixth fort, a reconstruction from the fur-trading days, is now a major attraction in the city's river valley.

In the 1890s Edmonton became a major supply depot for the gold rush to the Yukon, since it was on the All-Canadian Route to the Klondike. Thousands of men stopped for days, weeks, or months before making the final 1,500-mile (2,400-kilometer) trip to Yukon gold. Many decided to stay in the town, turning a quiet village into a prosperous city. Each July the city returns to the colorful era of the gold rush for ten days of fun and frolic called Edmonton's Klondike Days (see SPECIAL EVENTS).

Edmonton prides itself in having more park area per capita than any other city in Canada. The park area winds along the banks of the North Saskatchewan River, Edmonton's most prominent physical characteristic. Capital City Recreation Park encompasses 3,000 acres (1,214 hectares) with 18 miles (29 kilometers) of biking and hiking trails along the river valley.

What to See and Do

Alberta Legislature Building. Tours of historic structure. Interpretive Centre incl displays of Alberta's history and legislature. Cafeteria. (Daily; closed hols) 108 St and 97 Ave. Phone 780/427-7362. **FREE**

Citadel Theatre. Five-theater complex located in downtown Edmonton is one of Canada's finest centers for the performing arts. Glass-enclosed atrium area; waterfall, plants. Three theater series (Sept-May). 9828 101 A Ave.

Commonwealth Stadium. Built for the XI Commonwealth Games; seating capacity is 61,356. Home of the Canadian Football League Edmonton Eskimos. The Stadium Recreation Centre houses gym, weights, and racquetball and squash courts. 11000 Stadium Rd. Phone 780/944-7400. ¢¢

Devonian Botanic Garden. Approx 200 acres (80 hectares) incl alpine and herb gardens, peony collection, and native plants; outstanding five-acre Japanese garden; nature trails; aspen and jackpine forests; lilac garden; butterfly pavilion; orchid greenhouse. Concession. (May-Sept, daily) 6 mi W via Yellowhead Hwy 16, then 9 mi S on Hwy 60. Phone 780/987-3054. ¢¢¢

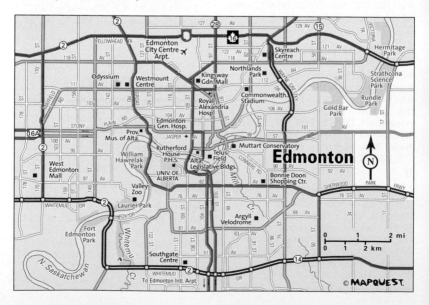

© MAPQUEST

Edmonton Queen Riverboat. Riverboat runs along the North Saskatchewan River, which travels through many local parks. Packages incl brunch (Sun), dinner, or cruise only. 9734 98th Ave. Phone 780/424-2628. ¢¢¢¢

Elk Island National Park of Canada. Forests, meadowlands, quiet lakes, and beaver ponds form an island in an area developed by man. A 75-sq-mi sanctuary for many species; moose, elk, deer, trumpeter swans, beaver, and coyote; large herd of plains bison and a small herd of rare wood bison; more than 200 species of birds. Camping (summer), hiking, golfing, x-country skiing. Visitor center and Interpretive Theatre (summer, wkends). Park (all yr). 28 mi (45 km) E on Yellowhead Hwy 16. ¢¢

Fort Edmonton Park. Canada's largest historical park is a re-creation of four sites of historic Edmonton incl Fort Edmonton, the Hudson's Bay Company Trading Post that gave the city its name, 1885 Street, 1905 Street, and 1920 Street. Demonstrations of artifacts and skills of earlier times by costumed interpreters. Steam train and streetcar rides. (Victoria Day-Labour Day, daily; rest of yr, days vary) Whitemud and Fox Drs. Phone 780/496-8787. ¢¢¢ Adj is

John Janzen Nature Centre. Natural history events and programs; hands-on exhibits; active beehive, gopher colony, and nature trails; nature shop. (Daily; closed Dec 25) Phone 780/496-2939. ¢

Kinsmen Sports Centre. Built for the XI Commonwealth Games. Swimming, diving; weight training, all types of racquet sports. Children under eight must be accompanied by an adult. 9100 Walterdale Hill. Phone 780/496-7300. ¢¢

Muttart Conservatory. Glass pyramids house controlled growing environments: tropical, arid, and temperate. A fourth pyramid is a floral showcase, which is changed every few wks. (Daily) 98 Ave and 96A St. Phone 780/496-8755. ¢¢

★ **Odyssium.** Multipurpose facility incl 275-seat IMAX theatre; largest dome theatre, the Margaret Zeidler Star Theatre; six exhibit galleries dealing with latest discoveries in science, astronomy, and space exploration; artifacts (moon rock, telescopes). Challenger Learning Centre lets visitors cooperate in teams to complete a space flight simulation. Book, gift store. (Daily; closed Dec 25) Varied fees for general admission and IMAX films. 11211 142 St, in Coronation Park. Phone 780/451-3344.

Parks. Capital City Recreation Park, winding through the city's river valley, is one of Canada's most extensive park systems. Bicycle, walking, and x-country ski trails link the major parks, where barbecue, picnic facilities, public restrms, and food concessions may be found. Contact River Valley Parks, Phone 780/496-7275.

Professional sports team.

Edmonton Oilers (NHL). Skyreach Centre, 11230 110 St. Phone 403/414-4000.

Provincial Museum of Alberta. Contains excellent displays reflecting the many aspects of Alberta's heritage. Exhibits on natural and human history, incl aboriginal peoples, wildlife, geology, live insects, dinosaurs, and Ice Age mammals. (Daily; closed Dec 24-25) 12845 102 Ave. Phone 780/453-9100. ¢¢

★ **Reynolds-Alberta Museum.** Interprets the mechanization of ground and air transportation, agriculture, and selected industries in Alberta from the turn of the 20th century. More than 100 major artifacts in museum building, hangar, and on 156-acre grounds. Displays incl vintage steam-powered farm equipment, automobiles, and aircraft; multimedia orientation show (17 min). (Daily; closed Jan 1, Dec 24-25) Approx 40 mi (64 km) S via Hwy 2A in Wetaskiwin. Phone 780/361-1351. ¢¢¢ Also here is

Canada's Aviation Hall of Fame. More than 100 aviators have been inducted into the hall of fame; many artifacts. Vintage planes, free-standing exhibits; videos, large aviation library. Phone 403/361-1351.

University of Alberta. 30,000 students. One of Canada's largest major research universities; 18 faculties and many research institutes. Tours (by appt). 114 St and 89 Ave. Phone 780/492-2325. On campus is

Rutherford House. (1911) Jacobean Revival home was residence of Alberta's first premier. Restored and refurnished to reflect lifestyle of post-Edwardian era. Costumed interpreters reenact life in 1915 with activities such as baking on wood stove, historical dramas, craft demonstrations, and musical performances. (Daily; closed Jan 1, Dec 25) Phone 780/427-3995. ¢¢

Valley Zoo. Features a wide variety of birds and mammals, fish, and reptiles. Train, merry-go-round, pony and camel rides; gift shop. (Daily) 134 St and Buena Vista Rd. Phone 780/496-8787. ¢¢

✪ West Edmonton Mall. Mi-long (1.6-km) shopping and entertainment complex with more than 800 stores and services; 110 eating establishments, 26 movie theaters, aquarium, dolphin shows; 80-ft (24-m) replica of Spanish galleon, four submarines, water park with wave pool and water slides, bungee-jumping, ice-skating rink, casino, Galaxyland amusement park with 14-story looping rollercoaster, 18-hole miniature golf course, IMAX Theatre. (Daily) 8770 170 St. Phone 780/444-5200.

Special Events

Jazz City Festival. Jazz concerts, workshops, outdoor events. Late June-early July. Phone 780/432-7166.

Edmonton's Klondike Days. Entertainment, exhibits, midway, parade; events incl Sourdough Raft Race, Sunday promenade, band extravaganza, chuckwagon races. Mid-late July. Northlands Park, 116 Ave and 73 St. Phone 780/471-7210.

Heritage Festival. William Hawrelak Park. More than 40 ethnic groups show Alberta's multicultural heritage in pageantry of color and music. Early Aug. 10715 124 St. Phone 780/488-3378.

Folk Music Festival. Three days of music at Alberta's largest outdoor music festival. Mid-Aug. Phone 780/429-1899.

Fringe Theatre Event. Old Strathcona district. Dance, music, plays, mime, mask, street entertainers; more than 700 performances. Mid-late Aug. Phone 780/448-9000.

Canadian Finals Rodeo. Edmonton Coliseum. Professional indoor rodeo to decide national championships. Mid-Nov. Northlands Park, 116 Ave and 73 St. Phone 780/471-7210.

Motels/Motor Lodges

★★ BEST WESTERN CEDAR PARK INN. *5116 Calgary Tr N (T6H 2H4). 780/434-7411; fax 780/437-4836; res 800/780-7234. www.bestwestern.com.* 190 rms, 5 story. S, D $94-$109; each addl $7; suites $149-$160; under 18 free; family rates. Crib free. Pet accepted, some restrictions. TV; cable. Heated indoor pool. Coffee in rms. Restaurant 7 am-11 pm; also 24-hr snack shop. Bar 11:30-1 am. Ck-out noon. Meeting rms. Business servs avail. In-rm modem link. Coin lndry. Gift shop. Free airport transportation. Exercise equipt; sauna. Cr cds: A, C, D, DS, ER, MC, V.
D 🐾 ⌕ 🏋 ✈ ⊠ **SC**

★★ BEST WESTERN CITY CENTRE INN. *11310 109th St (T5G 2T7). 780/479-2042; fax 780/474-2204; toll-free 800/666-5026. www.bestwestern. com.* 109 rms, 2 story. S $69-$89; D $79-$99; suites $125; under 17 free; wknd rates. Crib free. TV; cable (premium), VCR avail (movies). Heated indoor pool; whirlpool, waterslide. Restaurant open 24 hrs. Bar. Coffee in rms. Coin lndry. Ck-out noon. Meeting rms. Business servs avail. Exercise equipt; sauna. Some balconies, whirlpools. Cr cds: A, C, D, DS, ER, MC, V.
D ⌕ ⊠ 🐾 **SC** 🏋

★ CHATEAU LOUIS HOTEL & CONFERENCE CENTRE. *11727 Kingsway (T5G 3A1). 780/452-7770; fax 780/454-3436; toll-free 800/661-9843. www.chateaulouis.com.* 145 rms, 3 story. S $79; D $89; each addl $10; suites $120-$279; wknd rates; under 12 free. Crib $3. Pet accepted, some restrictions. TV; cable. Complimentary coffee in rms. Restaurant 6 am-midnight; Sat from 7 am; Sun, hols from 8 am. Rm serv 24 hrs. Bars 11-2 am; entertainment. Ck-out noon. Meeting rms. Business servs avail. Valet serv. Some minibars, whirlpools. Cr cds: A, C, D, ER, MC, V.
D 🐾 ✈ ⊠ 🐾

★★ **DAYS INN NISKU INN AND CONFERENCE CENTER.** *1101 4th St (T5J 2T2). 780/955-7744; fax 780/955-7743; toll-free 800/661-6966. www.daysinnedmontonairport.com.* 156 rms, 2 story. S, D $98-$108; each addl $10; suites $119-$199; under 18 free; wkend rates. Crib free. Pet accepted, some restrictions. TV; cable. Indoor pool; whirlpool. Coffee, tea in rms. Restaurant 6 am-midnight. Bar 11:30-2 am. Ck-out noon. Meeting rms. In-rm modem link. Valet serv. Sundries. Gift shop. Barber, beauty shop. Exercise equipt. Free airport transportation. Courtyard atrium. Cr cds: A, D, ER, MC, V.

★★ **EXECUTIVE ROYAL INN WEST EDMONTON.** *10010 178th St (T5S 1T3). 780/484-6000; fax 780/489-2900; toll-free 800/661-4879. www.royalinn.com.* 238 rms, 4 story. S, D $90-$152; each addl $8. Crib free. TV; cable. Coffee, tea in rms. Restaurants 6:30 am-10 pm. Bar noon 1 am. Ck-out 11 am. Meeting rms. Business center. In-rm modem link. Bellhops. Valet serv. Sundries. Gift shop. Exercise equipt; steam rm, massage. 2 whirlpools. Refrigerators avail; some in-rm whirlpools. Cr cds: A, D, ER, MC, V.

★★ **HOLIDAY INN PALACE.** *4235 Calgary Tr N (T6J 5H2). 780/438-1222; fax 780/430-0906; toll free 800/565-1222. www.holiday-inn.com.* 136 rms, 5 story, 40 suites. S, D $180-$200; suite $200-$270. TV; cable. Pet accepted; $10. Restaurant. Bar. Ck-out 11 am. Meeting rms. Business servs avail. Valet serv. Gift shop. Beauty shop. Free airport transportation. Exercise equipt; sauna, steam rm. Coffee in rms. Some in-rm whirlpools; refrigerators avail. Balconies. Cr cds: A, C, D, DS, ER, JCB, MC, V.

★ **RAMADA INN.** *5359 Calgary Tr (T6H 4J9). 780/434-3431; fax 780/437-3714; res 800/661-9030. www.ramada.ca.* 122 rms, 7 story. S, D $79-$89; each addl $5; suites $79-$109; under 18 free. Crib free. TV; cable. Indoor pool; wading pool, whirlpool. Restaurant 6:30 am-9 pm. Rm serv. Bar to 2 am. Coffee in rms.

Complimentary bkfst. Ck-out 11 am. Meeting rms. Business servs avail. Valet serv. Coin lndry. Exercise equipt. Free airport transportation. Some balconies. Cr cds: A, C, D, DS, JCB, MC, V.

★★ **WEST HARVEST INN.** *17803 Stony Plain Rd (T5S 1B4). 780/484-8000; fax 780/486-6060; toll-free 800/661-6993.* 161 rms, 3 story. S $65-$75; D $75-$85; each addl $10; under 16 free. Crib free. TV; cable. Coffee in rms. Restaurant 7 am-10:30 pm. Ck-out 11 am. Meeting rms. Business servs avail. Barber, beauty shop. Some refrigerators, in-rm whirlpools. Cr cds: A, D, ER, MC, V.

Hotels

★★★ **COAST TERRACE INN.** *4440 Calgary Trl N (T6H 5C2). 780/437-6010; fax 780/431-5801; toll-free 888/837-7223. www.coastterraceinn.com.* 235 rms, 4 story. S, D $150; suites $185-$250; under 18 free; wkend rates; package plans. Pet accepted, some restrictions. TV; cable. Heated indoor pool; whirlpool. Coffee in rms. Restaurant 6:30 am-10 pm. Rm serv 24 hrs. Bar 11:30-1 am; entertainment. Ck-out noon. Meeting rms. Business servs avail. Bellhops. Gift shop. Valet serv. Underground parking. Exercise equipt; sauna, steam rm. Racquetball court. Minibars; some in-rm whirlpools. Balconies. Luxury level. Cr cds: A, D, ER, MC, V.

★★★ **CROWNE PLAZA CHATEAU LACOMBE.** *10111 Bellamy Hill (T5J 1N7). 780/428-6611; fax 780/425-6564; res 800/661-8801. www.chateaulacombe.com.* 307 rms, 24 story. S, D $160; each addl $15; suites $190-$350; under 18 free; wkend rates. Crib free. Pet accepted, some restrictions. TV; cable. Coffee in rms. Restaurant 6:30 am-9 pm; Fri, Sat to 11 pm (see also LA RONDE). Bar 11-1 am. Ck-out 1 pm. Meeting rms. Business servs avail. Valet serv. Gift shop. Garage parking; valet. Exercise equipt. Minibars. Some balconies.

Luxury level. Cr cds: A, C, D, DS, ER, JCB, MC, V.

D 🍴 🏋 🏊 🔥 SC

★★★ DELTA CENTRE SUITES.
10222 102nd St (T5J 4C5). 780/429-3900; fax 780/428-1566; toll-free 800/268-1133. www.deltahotels.com. 169 rms, 7 story, 126 suites. S, D $169; each addl $15; suites $220-$250; under 18 free; wkend rates. Crib free. Valet parking $12. TV; cable, VCR avail. Coffee in rms. Restaurant (see also COCOA'S). Bar 11 am-midnight, Sun to 11 pm. Ck-out noon. Free lndry facilities. Meeting rms. Business center. In-rm modem link. Concierge. Barber, beauty shop. Exercise equipt; steam rm. Miniature golf. Minibars; many refrigerators; microwaves avail. Cr cds: A, C, D, DS, ER, JCB, MC, V.

D 🍴 🏋 🏊 🔥 🏃

★★ DELTA EDMONTON SOUTH.
4404 Gateway Blvd (T6H 5C2). 780/434-6415; fax 780/426-0562; toll-free 800/268-1133. www.deltahotels. com. 237 rms, 11 story. S, D $159; each addl $10; suites $150-$325; under 18 free. Crib free. TV; cable. Heated indoor pool; whirlpool. Coffee, tea in rms. Restaurants 6 am-11 pm. Rm serv 24 hrs. Bar 11:30 am-midnight; Fri, Sat 11:30-2 am; entertainment. Ck-out noon. Meeting rms. Business center. In-rm modem link. Free indoor parking; valet. Gift shop. Exercise equipt; sauna. Many refrigerators. Cr cds: A, C, D, DS, ER, JCB, MC, V.

D 🚭 🏋 🏊 🔥 🏃

★★★ THE FAIRMONT HOTEL MACDONALD.
10065 100th St (T5J 0N6). 780/424-5181; fax 780/429-6481; toll-free 800/441-1414. www. fairmont.com. Originally built in 1915 during the era of grand hotels in Canada, the MacDonald has been fully restored to its original old-world elegance. High on the banks of the North Saskatchewan River and only minutes from the Shaw Convention Center and the city's main cultural attractions, this French chateau-style hotel has a first-class, fully equipped health club, squash courts, swimming pool and whirlpools, and a fully equipped 24-hour business centre. 198 rms, 8 story. S, D $129-$269; each addl $20; suites $359-$659; under 18 free; wkend rates. Crib free.

Pet accepted, some restrictions. Valet parking. TV; cable (premium). Indoor pool; wading pool, whirlpool, poolside serv. Restaurant (see HARVEST ROOM). Rm serv 24 hrs. Bar 11-1 am. Ck-out 1 pm. Meeting rms. Business center. In-rm modem link. Concierge. Gift shop. Exercise rm; sauna, steam rm. Massage. Sun deck. Game rm. Minibars. Cr cds: A, DS, MC, V.

D 🚭 🏊 🏋 🏃 🔥

★★ FANTASYLAND HOTEL.
17700 87th Ave (P5T 4V4). 780/444-3000; fax 780/444-3294; toll-free 800/737-3783. www.fantasylandhotel. com. 354 rms, 12 story. Mid-June-early Sept: S, D $165-$210; each addl $10; suites, theme rms $195-$225; under 18 free; lower rates rest of yr. Crib free. Some covered parking; valet $6.50. TV; cable. Restaurant 7 am-11 pm. Rm serv 24 hrs. Bar noon-1 am. Ck-out 11 am. Convention facilities. Business center. Concierge. Shopping arcade. Barber, beauty shop. Exercise equipt. Mall attractions incl indoor amusement park, water park, movie theaters. Cr cds: A, D, ER, JCB, MC, V.

D 🏋 🏊 🔥 🏃

★★ INN ON 7TH.
10001 107th St (T5J 1J1). 780/429-2861; toll-free 800/661-7327. www.innon7th.com. 172 rms, 14 story. S $85; D $95; suites $170; each addl $10; under 12 free. Crib free. Pet accepted; $10/day. TV; cable (premium). Coffee in rms. Restaurant 6:30 am-9 pm. Bar 11 am-9 pm. Ck-out 11 am. Meeting rms. Business servs avail. Exercise equipt. Cr cds: A, C, D, DS, ER, MC, V.

D 🚭 🏋 🏊 🔥

★★ MAYFIELD INN AND SUITES.
16615 Mayfield Rd (T5P 5K8). 780/484-0821; fax 780/486-1634; toll-free 800/661-9804. www.mayfieldinn edmonton.com. 327 rms, 10 story, 105 suites, 10 kits. S, D $109; each addl $10; suites $149-$299; kit. units $149; under 16 free; wkend rates. Crib free. Pet accepted. TV; cable (premium). Heated pool; whirlpool. Complimentary bkfst buffet. Coffee in rms. Restaurant 6:30 am-11 pm. Bar; entertainment. Ck-out 1 pm. Meeting rms. Business servs avail. In-rm modem link. Barber, beauty shop. Airport transportation. Exercise rm; sauna, steam rm. Racquetball courts.

Dinner theater. Cr cds: A, C, D, DS, ER, JCB, MC, V.

★★★ SHERATON GRANDE. *10235 101st St (T5J 3E9). 780/428-7111; fax 780/441-3098; toll-free 800/263-9030. www.sheratonedmonton.com.* 313 rms, 26 story. S, D $155; each addl $20; suites $209-$249. Crib free. Pet accepted. TV; cable (premium), VCR avail. Heated pool. Coffee in rms. Restaurant 6:30 am-11 pm. Rm serv 24 hrs. Bar 11:30-2 am; entertainment. Ck-out noon. Meeting rms. Business center. Concierge. Shopping arcade. Valet parking. X-country ski 2 mi. Minibars; some bathrm phones. Atrium lobby; garden lounge. Connected by walkway to Edmonton Centre. Cr cds: A, C, D, ER, MC, V.

★ TOWER ON THE PARK. *9715 110th St (T5K 2M1). 780/488-1626; fax 780/488-0659; toll-free 800/720-2179. toweronthepark.com.* 98 kit. suites, 14 story. 1-bedrm $100; 2-bedrm $110; wkly, monthly rates. Crib $5. Pet accepted. TV; cable. Complimentary continental bkfst. Coffee in rms. Ck-out noon. Meeting rms. Business servs avail. Covered parking. Lndry facilities. Balconies. Italian marble, mirrored lobby. Cr cds: A, D, ER, MC, V.

★★★ WESTIN EDMONTON. *10135 100th St (T5J 0N7). 780/426-3636; fax 780/428-1454; res 800/937-8461. www.westin.com.* 413 rms, 12-20 story. S, D $175-$255; each addl $20; suites $400-$800; under 12 free; wkend rates. Crib free. Valet parking $17, garage $13. TV; cable. Heated pool. Coffee in rms. Restaurant 6:30 am-11 pm. Rm serv 24 hrs. Bar 11-1 am. Ck-out 1 pm. Meeting rms. Business center. Exercise equipt; sauna. Massage. Refrigerators, minibars; some bathrm phones and TVs. Luxury level. Cr cds: A, C, D, DS, ER, JCB, MC, V.

Restaurants

★ CHIANTI CAFE. *10501 82nd Ave (T6E 2A3). 780/439-9829.* Hrs: 11 am-11 pm; Fri, Sat to midnight.

Closed Dec 25. Res accepted. Italian menu. Bar. Lunch, dinner $4.50-$15.95. Specializes in pasta, veal, chicken. Outdoor patio dining. Renovated historic post office building. Cr cds: A, D, DS, MC, V.

★★ COCOA'S. *10222 102nd St (T5J 4C5). 780/429-3900. www.deltahotels.com.* Hrs: 6:30 am-10 pm; Sat, Sun from 7 am; Sun brunch 10 am-2 pm. Res accepted. Continental menu. Bar 11-1 am. Bkfst $6.95-$12.95, lunch $7.25-$11.95, dinner $11.95-$24.95. Sun brunch $14.95. Child's meals. Specialties: grilled Alberta bison, rack of lamb, fresh maritime seafood chowder. Valet parking. Art Deco decor; atrium skylight. Cr cds: A, DS, ER, MC, V.

★ FIORE. *8715 109th St (T6G 2L5). 780/439-8466.* Hrs: 11 am-11 pm; Sat to midnight; Sun to 10 pm. Closed Dec 25. Res accepted. Italian menu. Bar. Lunch $5-$8.50; dinner $8-$15. Child's meals. Specializes in pasta, seafood. Outdoor dining. Casual decor. Cr cds: A, D, ER, MC, V.

★★★ HARVEST ROOM. *10065 100th St (T5J 0N6). 780/424-5181.* Hrs: 6:30 am-2 pm, 5:30-10 pm; Sat, Sun 7 am-11 pm; Sun brunch 10:30 am-1:30 pm. Res accepted. Canadian menu. Bar 11:30-1 am; Sun to midnight. Wine cellar. Bkfst $7.75-$11.95, lunch $9-$15. A la carte entrees: dinner $19-$28. Buffet: lunch $12. Sun brunch $24. Child's meals. Specialties: cream of wild mushroom and artichoke soup, lamb loin with rosemary, fresh British Columbia salmon on cedar plank. Valet parking. Terrace dining overlooking Saskatchewan River and city. Elegant dining in historic hotel. Cr cds: A, C, D, DS, ER, MC, V.

★★ HY'S STEAK LOFT. *10013 101A Ave (T5J 0C3). 780/424-4444. www.hyssteakhouse.com.* Hrs: 11:30 am-2 pm, 5-10 pm; Sat 5-11 pm; Sun 5-9 pm. Closed hols. Res accepted. Continental menu. Bar 11:30 am-midnight; Sat from 5 pm; Sun 5-10 pm. Wine cellar. A la carte entrees: lunch $10-$18, dinner $19-$35. Spe-

cializes in Alberta beef. Elegant dining. Cr cds: A, D, MC, V.
D [image]

★ **JAPANESE VILLAGE.** *10126 100th St (T5J 0N8). 780/422-6083. www. japanesevillage.bc.ca.* Hrs: 11:30 am-2 pm, 5-10:30 pm; Fri, Sat 5-11 pm; Sun 4:30-10 pm. Closed Victoria Day, Nov 11, Dec 24 and 25. Res accepted. Japanese menu. Serv bar. Lunch $7-$10, dinner $7-$17. Complete meals: dinner $18-$35. Child's meals. Specializes in sushi, tempura, Teppanyaki cooking. Cr cds: A, C, D, DS, ER, MC, V.
D [image]

★★ **LA BOHEME.** *6427 112th Ave (T5W 0N9). 780/474-5693. www. laboheme.ca.* Hrs: 11 am-11 pm; Sun to 9 pm. Closed Dec 25. Res required. French, Moroccan menu. Bar. A la carte entrees: lunch, dinner $15-$28. Complete meals: dinner $22-$32. Sun brunch $13.75. Specializes in seafood, lamb. Own pastries. Parking. Outdoor dining. Romantic European atmosphere. Guest rms avail. Cr cds: A, D, DS, MC, V.
D [image]

★★★ **L'ANJOU.** *10643 123rd St (T5N 1P3). 780/482-7178.* Hrs: 6-9 pm. Closed Sun-Tues; hols. Res required. French country menu. Bar. Complete meals: dinner $37-$45. Parking. Five-course meal only Fri, Sat. Specialties: stuffed chicken breast, roast duck breast, grilled halibut with mango salsa. French country decor. Cr cds: D, MC, V.
D

★★★ **LA RONDE.** *10111 Bellamy Hill (T5J 1N7). 780/428-6611.* Hrs: 5:30-10:30 pm; Sun brunch 10:30 am-2 pm. Res accepted. Bar. A la carte entrees: dinner $20-$35. Sun brunch $24. Child's meals. Specializes in Alberta beef, fresh fish. Parking. Revolving restaurant with panoramic view of city. Cr cds: A, D, DS, MC, V.
D SC [image]

★★ **LA SPIGA.** *10133 125th St (T5N 1S7). 780/482-3100.* Hrs: 11:30 am-2 pm, 5-11 pm; Sat 5 pm-midnight. Closed Sun; hols. Res accepted. Northern Italian menu. Serv bar. A la carte entrees: dinner $11.95-$22.95.

Specializes in rack of lamb, pasta. Own desserts. Parking. Outdoor dining. Mansion built 1915; beamed ceilings; fireplace. Cr cds: ER, MC, V.
D [image]

Unrated Dining Spot

CREPERIE. *10220 103rd St (T5J 0Y8). 780/420-6656. www.thecreperie.com.* Hrs: 11:30 am-11 pm; Fri to midnight; Sat noon-midnight; Sun 5-10 pm. Closed Dec 25. Res accepted; required Fri, Sat. French menu. Bar. A la carte entrees: lunch $6-$10, dinner $6-$14. Child's meals. Specializes in crepes, country French dishes. Menu changes twice wkly. Cr cds: A, MC, V.
[image]

Fort Macleod

(H-5) *See also Lethbridge*

Settled 1874 **Pop** 3,139 **Elev** 3,105 ft (1,046 m) **Area code** 403

Information Tourism Action Committee, PO Box 1959, T0L 0Z0; 403/553-2500 or 403/553-3204

Web www.town.fortmacleod.ab.ca

Fort Macleod was the first North West Mounted Police post in Alberta, named in honor of Colonel James F Macleod, who led the force on its march westward. The fort was successful in stamping out the illegal whiskey trade that had flourished previously in the area. Today the region has an abundance of mixed and grain farming.

What to See and Do

Fort Museum. Museum complex depicts history of North West Mounted Police, Plains tribes, and pioneer life in Fort Macleod, the first outpost in the Canadian west. A special feature is the Mounted Patrol Musical Ride (July-Sept, four times daily). (May-Oct, daily; rest of yr, Mon-Fri; closed hols) 25th St and 3rd Ave. Phone 403/553-4703. ¢¢

Head-Smashed-In Buffalo Jump Interpretive Centre. Buffalo jump site dating back approx 6,000 yrs. Interpretive tours, theater, cafeteria.

(Daily; closed Easter, Dec 25) 2 mi (3 km) N on Hwy 2, then 10 mi (16 km) W on Spring Point Rd (S-785) Phone 403/553-2731. ¢¢

Remington Carriage Museum. Displays one of the largest collections of horse-drawn vehicles in North America: over 200 carriages, wagons, and sleighs. Gallery has interactive displays, audiovisual productions, carriage factory. (Daily) 35 mi S on Hwy 2 at 623 Main St in Cardston. Phone 403/653-5139. ¢¢

Special Events

Powwow and Tipi Village. Celebration features open tipi village, traditional native dances, games, food. Third wkend July. At Head-Smashed-In Buffalo Jump. Phone 403/553-2731.

Santa Claus Parade and Festival. One of the oldest and largest Santa Claus parades west of Toronto. Last Sat in Nov. Phone 403/553-2500.

Motel/Motor Lodge

★ **SUNSET MOTEL.** Box 398, 104 Hwy 3W (TOL 0Z0). 403/553-4448; fax 403/553-2784; res 888/554-2784. 22 rms, 3 kits. June-Sept: S $54; D $60; each addl $5; kit. units $76-$90; lower rates rest of yr. Crib free. Pet accepted. TV; cable. Restaurant nearby. Ck-out 11 am. Refrigerators. Cr cds: A, D, DS, ER, MC, V.

Restaurant

★★★ **COBBLESTONE MANOR.** 173 7th Ave W, Cardston (TOK 0K0). 403/653-1519. Hrs: 4:30-10 pm. Closed early Jan-Mar; Sun Oct-Dec, Apr-mid-May. Res accepted. British, Amer menu. Complete meals: dinner $10.95-$19.95. Child's meals. Specializes in steaks, soups, home-style cooking. Own baking. Historic house (1889) built of rock with inlaid panels of fine wood from all over the world; antique furniture and woodwork. Cr cds: MC, V.

D

Jasper National Park

179 mi (287 km) N on Hwy 93.

Established in 1907 and located in the Canadian Rockies, Jasper is one of Canada's largest and most scenic national parks. In its more than 4,200 square miles (10,878 square kilometers) are waterfalls, lakes, canyons, glaciers, and wilderness areas filled with varied forms of wildlife, in the midst of which is the resort town of Jasper.

Jasper has year-round interpretive programs, trips, and campfire talks. There are also guided wilderness trips, a sky tram, skating, skiing, ice climbing, and rafting and cycling trips. The park, the Rockies, and the resort atmosphere of Jasper make this trip enjoyable any time of the year.

What to See and Do

Miette Hot Springs. Pool uses natural hot mineral springs. Lodge (phone 403/866-3750). (Mid-May early Sept) Contact Canadian Parks Service, PO Box 10, Jasper, T0E 1E0. 38 mi (61 km) E of Jasper via Hwy 16, Pocahontas jct. ¢¢

Sightseeing tours.

Boat cruise. Maligne Tours, Ltd. Narrated cruise (1½-hr) on Maligne Lake to world-famous Spirit Island. (June-Sept, daily) Fishing supplies and boat rentals. Whitewater raft trips. 30 mi (48 km) S of Jasper via Hwy 16, Maligne Rd exit. Phone 780/852-3370. ¢¢¢¢

Jasper Tramway. Two 30-passenger cars take 1¼ mi (2 km) trip up Whistlers Mtn. Vast area of alpine tundra at summit; hiking trails, picnicking; restaurant, gift shop. (Apr-mid-Oct, daily) 4 mi (6 km) S of Jasper, exit Jasper-Banff Hwy to Whistlers Mtn Rd. Phone 780/852-3093. ¢¢¢¢

Other tours. Various tours are offered by bus, raft, gondola, and "snocoach" to Lake Louise, Jasper, Calgary, Banff, and the Athabasca Glacier. For further information contact Brewster Transportation and Tours, PO Box 1140, Banff, T0L 0C0. Phone 780/762-6700.

Skiing. Marmot Basin. Quad, triple, three double chairlifts, two T-bars; patrol, school, rentals; repair shop; nursery, three cafeterias, bar. Vertical drop 3,000 ft (897 m). (Early Dec-late Apr) 13 mi (19 km) S of Jasper via Icefield Pkwy (93A). Phone 780/852-3816. ¢¢¢¢

Motels/Motor Lodges

★★ **ALPINE VILLAGE.** *Hwy 93A N; Box 610, Jasper (T0E 1E0). 780/852-3285. www.alpinevillagejasper.com.* 37 log cabins, 5 lodge suites, 29 kits. No A/C. S, D $80-$140; each addl $10; suites, kit. units $140-$200. Closed mid-Oct-Apr. TV; cable. Playground. Coffee in rms. Ck-out 11 am. Many fireplaces. Grills. Whirlpool. Cr cds: MC, V.
🄳 ⛄ 🐾

★ **AMETHYST LODGE.** *200 Connaught Dr (T0E 1E0). 780/852-3394; fax 780/852-5198. www.mtn-park-lodges.com.* 97 rms, 3 story. June-Sept: S, D $165-$220; each addl $10; under 15 free; lower rates rest of yr. Pet accepted, some restrictions. TV; cable (premium). Complimentary coffee in rms. Restaurant 6:30 am-10 pm. Bar 5 pm-midnight. Ck-out 11 am. Meeting rms. Business center. Free RR station, bus depot transportation. Downhill/x-country ski 15 mi. 2 whirlpools. Balconies. Cr cds: A, D, ER, JCB, MC, V.
🄳 🐾 📠 🌊 🐾 🏃

★★★ **CHARLTON'S CHATEAU JASPER.** *96 Geikie St (T0E 1E0). 780/852-5644; fax 780/852-4860; toll-free 800/661-9323. www.charlton resorts.com.* 119 rms, 3 story. Early June-late Sept: S, D $315; each addl $25; under 18 free; lower rates rest of yr. Crib free. TV; cable, VCR avail. Indoor pool; whirlpool. Complimentary coffee in rms. Restaurants 7 am-10 pm (see also LE BEAUVALLON). Bar 11 am-midnight; entertainment. Ck-out 11 am. Meeting rms. Business servs avail. Bellhops. Sundries. Free underground parking. Free RR station, bus depot transportation. Downhill/x-country ski 15 mi. Some whirlpools. Cr cds: A, C, D, DS, ER, JCB, MC, V.
🄳 🌊 🌊 🌊 🐾 SC

★★ **LOBSTICK LODGE.** *94 Geikie St, Jasper (T0E 1E0). 780/852-4431; fax 780/852-4142; toll-free 888/852-7737. www.mtn-park-lodges.com.* 139 rms, 3 story, 43 kits. No A/C. June-Sept: S, D $99-$202; each addl $10; suites, kit. units $190; under 15 free; MAP avail; ski plans; lower rates rest of yr. Crib free. Pet accepted, some restrictions. TV; cable (premium). Sauna, steam rm. Heated pool; whirlpools. Restaurant 6:30-11:30 am, 5-10 pm. Bar 5 pm-midnight. Ck-out 11 am. Coin lndry. Business servs avail. Downhill/x-country ski 15 mi. Cr cds: A, D, ER, JCB, MC, V.
🄳 🐾 📠 🌊 🐾 🌊 🐾

★★ **MARMOT LODGE.** *86 Connaught Dr (T0E 1E0). 780/852-4471; fax 403/852-3280; toll-free 888/852-7737. www.mtn-park-lodges.com.* 107 rms, 47 A/C, 2 story, 32 kits. June-Sept: S, D $162-$182; each addl $10; suites $178-$325; under 16 free; ski plan; lower rates rest of yr. Pet accepted, some restrictions. TV; cable. Heated pool; whirlpool. Sauna. Restaurant 6:30-11 am, 5-10 pm. Bar 5 pm-1 am. Ck-out 11 am. Coin lndry. Meeting rm. Business servs avail. Valet serv. RR station, bus depot transportation. Downhill/x-country ski 15 mi. Fireplace in some kit. units. Private patios, balconies. Grills. Ski waxing rm and lockers in winter. Cr cds: A, D, ER, JCB, MC, V.
🄳 🐾 🌊 🌊 🐾 🐾

★ **OVERLANDER MOUNTAIN LODGE.** *PO Box 6118, Hinton (T7V 1X5). 780/866-2330; fax 780/866-2332. www.overlander-mtn-lodge.com.* 40 rms, 12 with shower only, 2 story. No A/C. No rm phone. May-Oct: S, D $100-$150; each addl $20; lower rates rest of yr. Crib free. Complimentary coffee in rms. Restaurant 7:30-10:30 am, 5:30-9:30 pm. Ck-out 11 am. Meeting rms. Business servs avail. X-country ski 15 mi. Some refrigerators, fireplaces. Some balconies. Cr cds: A, DS, MC, V.
🌊 🐾

★★ **SAW RIDGE HOTEL & CONFERENCE CENTER.** *82 Connaught Dr, Jasper (T0E 1E0). 780/852-5111; fax 780/852-5942; toll-free 800/661-6427. www.sawridge.com/jasper.* 154 rms, 3 story. June-Sept: S, D $209; each addl $20; suites $240-$280; under 18 free; lower rates rest of yr;

MAP avail. Crib free. TV; cable (premium). Indoor pool; whirlpools. Restaurant 6:30 am-10:30 pm. Bar 4:30 pm-2 am. Ck-out 11 am. Meeting rms. Business servs avail. Valet serv. Free RR station, bus depot transportation. Sauna. Downhill/x-country ski 5 mi. Some refrigerators; whirlpool in suites. Balconies. Ski lockers. Cr cds: A, DS, MC, V.

Resort

★★★ **THE FAIRMONT JASPER PARK LODGE.** *Old Lodge Rd, Jasper (T0E 1E0). 780/852-3301; fax 780/852-5107.* 450 units, 6 cabins. No A/C. Late May-mid-Oct: S, D $299-$419; each addl $25; under 18 free; MAP avail; lower rates rest of yr. Crib free. Pet accepted. TV; cable. Heated pool; whirlpool. Supervised children's activities; ages 2 and up. Dining rm (see also EDITH CAVELL). Box lunches. Bar 11:30-1 am. Ck-out noon, ck-in 4 pm. Business servs avail. Shopping arcade. Airport, RR station, bus depot transportation. Tennis. 18-hole golf, greens fee $45-$75, putting green. Swimming. Rowboats, canoes. Whitewater rafting. Downhill ski 15 mi; x-country ski on site. Bicycles. Lawn games. Soc dir; entertainment, movies. Barber, beauty shop. Rec rm. Game rm. Exercise rm; sauna, steam rm. Massage. Fishing guides. Minibars; fireplaces. Many private patios, balconies. Cr cds: A, D, DS, ER, JCB, MC, V.

Restaurants

★★★ **EDITH CAVELL DINING ROOM.** *82 Connaught Dr, Jasper (T0E 1E0). 780/852-6073.* Hrs: 6-9 pm. Res accepted. French menu. Bar. Dinner $55-$65. Complete meals: dinner $59. Child's meals. Specialties: wild mushroom chowder, beef tenderloin. Entertainment. Jacket. Cr cds: A, D, MC, V.

★ **L & W.** *Patricia St (T0E 1E0). 780/852-4114.* Hrs: 11 am-midnight. Closed Nov. Greek, American menu. Bar. A la carte entrees: bkfst $5-

$8.25, lunch $5-$10.25, dinner $9-$16. Child's meals. Specializes in pasta, pizza, Alberta prime rib. Salad bar. Parking. Outdoor dining. Garden-like setting. Family-owned. Cr cds: MC, V.

★★★ **LE BEAUVALLON.** *96 Geikie St (T0E 1E0). 780/852-5644. www. charltonresorts.com.* Hrs: 7 am-1 pm, 5:30-9:30 pm; summer 6:30 am-2 pm, 5:30-10 pm; Sun brunch 10:30 am-1:30 pm. Res accepted. Continental menu. Bar. Bkfst $8-$14, lunch $9-$14, dinner $18-$38. Buffet: dinner (late May-Sept) $21. Sun brunch $15. Child's meals. Specializes in game, beef, seafood. Own baking. Harpist. Parking. Cr cds: A, DS, ER, MC, V.

★ **SOMETHING ELSE.** *621 Patricia (T0E 1E0). 780/852-3850.* Hrs: 11 am-11 pm. Greek, Italian, American menu. Serv bar. Lunch $6-$10, dinner $10-$20. Child's meals. Own pizza. Outdoor dining. Open kitchen. Cr cds: A, D, MC, V.

★ **TOKYO TOM'S PLACE.** *410 Connaught Dr (T0E 1E0). 780/852-3780.* Hrs: noon-10:30 pm; Oct-mid-May 5-10 pm. Closed Dec 25. Res accepted. Japanese menu. Bar. A la carte entrees: lunch, dinner $5.95-$20.95. Specializes in sushi, deep fried tempura, sukiyaki. Cr cds: A, D, MC, V.

★★ **TONQUIN PRIME RIB.** *100 Juniper (T0E 1E0). 780/852-4966.* Hrs: 7-10:30 am, 5-11 pm. Res accepted; required in season. Continental menu. Bar 4 pm-2 am. Buffet: bkfst $8.50-$9.50. A la carte entrees: dinner $14-$24.95. Child's meals. Specializes in prime rib, seafood. Parking. Outdoor dining. Views of mountains. Cr cds: A, D, DS, ER, MC, V.

Lake Louise

(F-3) *See also Banff*

Pop 1,600 **Elev** 5,018 ft (1,520 m)
Area code 403

Lake Louise

Information Banff-Lake Louise Tourism Bureau, PO Box 1298, T0L 0C0; 403/762-8421; or Parks Canada Lake Louise Info Centre; 403/522-3833

In the heart of the Canadian Rockies, Lake Louise is probably best known as one of the finest year-round resort towns in this area, along with Banff (see) and Jasper. The Rockies provide miles of summer hiking trails, natural beauty for the photographer, and excellent skiing for a great part of the year. Lake Louise also provides the resort atmosphere of nightlife and fun. During the summer, be sure to view the town from the gondola. The ride takes you to Mount Whitehorn where there is a lodge, and you can hike, picnic, explore, and relax. Other popular activities include canoeing, fishing, climbing, biking, riding, tennis, and sightseeing tours.

Motels/Motor Lodges

★ **DEER LODGE.** *109 Lake Louise Dr (T0L 1E0). 403/522-3991; fax 403/522-4222.* 73 rms, 3 story. Some rm phones. June-Sept: S, D $155-$220; each addl $25; under 12 free; lower rates rest of yr. Crib free. Dining rm 7-11 am, 6-10 pm. Bar 11 am-midnight. Ck-out 11 am. Business servs avail. Downhill ski 3 mi; x-country ski adj. Sauna. Outdoor whirlpool. Some balconies. Former trading camp (1921); rustic setting. Cr cds: A, D, ER, MC, V.

★ ★ **EMERALD LAKE LODGE.** *1 Emerald Lake Rd, Field (V0A 1G0). 250/343-6321; fax 250/343-6724; toll-free 800/663-6336.* 85 suites in 24 cabin-style bldgs, 2 story. No A/C. June-Sept: suites $275-$455; under 12 free; ski plans; lower rates rest of yr. Crib free. Restaurant 6-11 pm. Bar. Ck-out 11 am. Meeting rms. Business servs avail. X-country ski on site; rentals. Sauna. Whirlpool. Boat rentals. Ice rink (winter). Game rm. Fireplaces. Private balconies. Picnic tables. On Emerald Lake in Canadian Rockies; canoeing. Cr cds: A, D, ER, MC, V.

★ ★ **MOUNTAINEER LODGE.** *101 Village Rd (T0L 1E0). 403/522-3844; fax 403/522-3902. www.mountaineerlodge.com.* 78 rms in motel and lodge, 2 story. June-Sept: S $80-$160; D $85-$170; each addl $10; suites $180-$260; under 10 free; lower rates rest of year. Crib avail. TV; cable (premium). Complimentary coffee in rms. Restaurant nearby. Ck-out 11 am, ck-in 4 pm. Cr cds: A, MC, V.

Hotel

★★★ **POST HOTEL.** *200 Pipestone Rd (TOL 1E0). 403/522-3989; fax 403/522-3966; toll-free 800/661-1586. www.posthotel.com.* First known in 1942 as the Lake Louise Ski Lodge, this Alpine-style chalet enjoys a splendid Canadian Rockies location in Banff National Park, just five minutes from the lake and ski area. Luxurious rooms are outfitted with goose-down comforters, slate floors, wood-burning fireplaces, and Jacuzzi tubs. The nationally recognized continental dining room is housed in the hotel's original log building. 98 units, 3 story, 5 kit. units, 2 cottages. S, D $240-$341; suites $440-$520; kit. units $385-$462; cottages $310-$340; ski plans. Closed Nov. Crib free. TV; cable (premium), VCR avail. Sauna, steam rm. Indoor pool; whirlpool. Restaurant (see also POST HOTEL DINING ROOM). No rm serv. Bar noon-midnight; entertainment. Ck-out 11 am. Meeting rms. Business servs avail. Concierge. Bus depot transportation. Downhill/x-country ski 1 mi. Many in-rm whirlpools, fireplaces. Private patios, balconies. Picnic tables. On river. Cr cds: A, MC, V.

🄳 ⬛ ⬛ ⬛ ⬛ ⬛ ⬛ ⬛

Resorts

★★ **BAKER CREEK CHALETS.** *Hwy 1A, Bow Valley Pkwy (TOL 1E0). 403/522-3761; fax 403/522-2270. www.bakercreek.com.* 33 units, 11 with shower only, 27 with kits., 25 chalets (1- or 2-bdrm). S $85-$165; D $155-$240; chalets $115-$225; family rates; lower rates winter. Crib $15. Restaurant 8 am-11 pm. Box lunches. Bar. Ck-out 11 am, ck-in 3 pm. Gift shop. Grocery, coin lndry 7 mi. Downhill ski 7 mi; x-country ski on site. Hiking. Refrigerators. Balconies. Picnic tables. Near river. Cr cds: MC, V.

⬛ ⬛ ⬛ ⬛

★★★ **THE FAIRMONT CHATEAU LAKE LOUISE.** *111 Lake Louise Dr (TOL 1E0). 403/522-3511; fax 403/522-3834; toll-free 800/441-1414. www.fairmont.com.* 497 rms, 8 story. Mid-May-mid-Oct: S, D $244-$545; each addl $20; suites $703-$1,353; under 18 free; lower rates rest of yr.

Pet accepted; $20. Covered parking $6/day. TV; cable. Indoor pool; whirlpool. 6 dining rms (see also WALLISER STUBE and VICTORIA DINING ROOM). Bars noon-2 am; entertainment. Ck-out noon. Convention facilities. Business servs avail. Shopping arcade. Airport transportation. Downhill ski 5 mi; x-country ski on site. Exercise equipt; steam rm. Sleigh rides, ice-skating. Minibars. Some balconies. Resortlike hotel on Lake Louise, surrounded by rolling lawns and large flower gardens. Cr cds: A, D, DS, ER, JCB, MC, V.

🄳 ⬛ ⬛ ⬛ ⬛ ⬛ ⬛ ⬛ ⬛ ⬛

★ **PARADISE LODGE AND BUNGALOWS.** *105 Lake Louise Dr (TOL 1E0). 403/522-3595; fax 403/522-3987. www.paradiselodge.com.* 24 rms in lodge, 21 cabins (shower only). No rm phones. June-Sept: suites $200-$250; cabins $145-$165; kit. cabins $165-$175; lower rates May and Oct. Closed rest of yr. Crib free. TV; cable. Playground. Restaurant nearby. Ck-out 11 am, ck-in 4 pm. Business servs avail. Refrigerators. Balconies. Picnic tables. Cr cds: MC, V.

🄳 ⬛ ⬛ ⬛

Restaurants

★★★★ **POST HOTEL DINING ROOM.** *200 Pipestone Rd (TOL 1E0). 403/522-3989. www.posthotel.com.* Located five minutes from the lake and ski area, this continental dining room is housed in the hotel's original log building and boasts a beautiful, fieldstone fireplace. Creative, internationally influenced preparations of fish, Alberta beef, and rack of lamb, caribou, venison, and veal are served in the Alpine-chalet ambiance, complimented by more than 900 wine selections. Specializes in veal, caribou strip loin, rack of lamb. Hrs: 7 am-9 pm. Closed mid-Oct-early-Dec. Res accepted. Wine list. Lunch $9.50-$23.50; dinner $27.50-$37.50. Child's menu. Entertainment: pianist. Cr cds: A, MC, V.

🄳

★★★ **VICTORIA DINING ROOM.** *111 Lake Louise Dr (TOL 1E0). 403/522-3511.* Hrs: 7-9 am, 11 am-1:30 pm, 6-9 pm. Res accepted. No A/C. Continental menu. Wine list.

Bar from noon. Buffet: bkfst $16, lunch $21. Complete meals: dinner $28-$49. Child's meals. Specializes in prime rib, salmon, rack of lamb. Own baking. Entertainment. Valet parking. Totally nonsmoking. Cr cds: A, C, D, DS, ER, MC, V.

D SC

★★ **WALLISER STUBE.** *111 Lake Louise Dr (T0L 1E0). 403/522-3511.* Hrs: 6-11 pm. Res accepted. No A/C. Swiss Alpine menu. Bar. Complete meals: dinner $25-$50. Child's meals. Specialties: cheese and beef fondues, game. Swiss decor. Cr cds: A, D, DS, ER, MC, V.

D

Lethbridge

(H-5) *See also Fort Macleod*

Settled 1870 **Pop** 60,610 **Elev** 2,983 ft (909 m) **Area code** 403
Information Lethbridge Tourism Bureau, 2805 Scenic Dr, T1K 5B7; 800/661-1222
Web www.albertasouth.com

Lethbridge, in Chinook Country, sits amid ranchland and irrigated farms. The chinook, an Alberta winter phenomenon, is a warm wind that reportedly can raise temperatures as much as 40 degrees within ten minutes.

Originally known to the Blackfoot as *Sik-okotoks* or "place of black rocks," Lethbridge was named after William Lethbridge, first president of the North-West Coal & Navigation Company. Among the many beautiful parks and gardens are the Brewery Gardens at the western edge of town; Indian Battle Park, site of the last battle between Native American nations in North America (1870), today a semi-wilderness; and Henderson Lake Park.

In 1869 traders from the United States came north and built so-called "whiskey forts." One of the most notorious was Fort Whoop-Up near Lethbridge. The arrival of the North West Mounted Police in 1874 soon stamped out this illegal whiskey trade. The city has rebuilt this fort, and the flag that signaled the arrival of the latest load of whiskey is now the official flag of Lethbridge.

What to See and Do

Alberta Birds of Prey Centre. Living museum featuring hawks, owls, falcons, and other birds of prey from Alberta and around the world. Interpretive center has educational displays, wildlife art. Daily flying demonstrations; picnicking. (May-mid-Oct, daily, weather permitting) Approx 5 mi (8 km) E via Crowsnest Hwy (Hwy 3), on 16 Ave in Coaldale. ¢¢

Fort Whoop-Up. This is a replica of the original fort, a major whiskey trading post in southern Alberta in the 1870s. Interpretive gallery, theater; tours. (Mid-May-Sept, daily; rest of yr, Tues-Fri, Sun afternoons) In Indian Battle Park. Phone 403/329-0444. ¢¢

Nikka Yuko Japanese Garden. Built to commemorate Canada's Centennial in 1967, the authentic garden is a symbol of Japanese-Canadian friendship. Buildings and bridges were built in Japan and reassembled in Lethbridge. The garden is an art form of peace and tranquility. (Mid-May-late Sept, daily) Henderson Lake Park. Phone 403/328-3511. ¢¢

Sir Alexander Galt Museum. Displays relate to early development of area. Featured exhibits incl indigenous culture, pioneer life, civic history, coal mining, farming history, irrigation, ethnic displays. Video presentations. (Daily; closed hols) W end 5th Ave S. Phone 403/320-3898. **FREE**

Special Events

"Ag-Expo" Agricultural Exposition. Early Mar.

International Air Show. Aug. Phone 800/661-1222.

Whoop-Up Days. Fair, exhibitions, horse racing, rodeo, grandstand show. Early Aug.

Motel/Motor Lodge

★★ **BEST WESTERN HEIDELBERG INN.** *1303 Mayor Magrath Dr (T1K 2R1). 403/329-0555; fax 403/328-8846; toll-free 800/528-1234. www. bestwestern.com.* 66 rms, 9 story. S $87-$92; D $94-$97; each addl $5; under 18 free. Crib free. TV; cable, VCR avail. Coffee in rms. Restaurant 6 am-11 pm. Bar 4 pm-1:30 am. Ckout noon. Valet serv. Sundries. Exercise equipt; sauna. Cr cds: A, C, D, DS, ER, JCB, MC, V.

🅳 🧖 ✈ 🏊 🔥

Hotel

★★★ **LETHBRIDGE LODGE.** *320 Scenic Dr (T1J 4B4). 403/328-1123; fax 403/328-0002; toll-free 800/661-1232. www.lethbridgelodge.com.* 120 rms, 4 story, 28 suites. S $109-$129; D $119-$139; each addl $10; suites $119-$149; under 18 free. Crib free. Pet accepted, some restrictions, fee. TV; cable. Coffee in rms. Restaurant 6:30 am-11 pm. Bar. Ck-out noon. Cr cds: A, C, D, DS, ER, JCB, MC, V.

🅳 🍴 🏊 🔥 **SC**

Restaurants

★★★ **COCO PAZZO.** *1264 3rd Ave S (T1J 0J9). 403/329-8979.* Hrs: 11 am-11 pm; Fri, Sat to midnight; Sun 5-9 pm. Closed hols. Res accepted. Italian menu. Bar. Lunch $4.95-$7.95, dinner $7.25-$16.50. Child's meals. Specializes in wood-fired pizza, Alberta beef. Outdoor dining. Casual Italian café dining. Cr cds: A, MC, V.

🅳

★★ **NEW DYNASTY.** *103 7th St S (T1J 2G1). 403/328-1212.* Hrs: 11 am-midnight; Fri, Sat to 2 am; Sun to 9:30 pm. Closed Dec 25. Res accepted. Chinese menu. Bar. Lunch $5-$8, dinner $8-$12. Child's meals. Specialties: shredded ginger beef, moo shu pork, shrimp and scallops with bacon wrap. Modern Oriental decor. Cr cds: A, D, DS, ER, MC, V.

🅳

★★★ **SVEN ERICKSEN'S.** *1715 Mayor Magrath Dr (T1K 2R7). 403/328-7756.* Hrs: 11 am-midnight; Sun 10 am-9 pm; Sun brunch to 1:30 pm. Closed Dec 25, 26. Res accepted. Bar. Lunch $5-$8.50. Complete meals: dinner $10-$32. Sun brunch $6.95-$11.95. Child's meals. Specializes in prime rib, seafood, roast beef. Own baking. Entertainment Sat. Provincial decor; display of old photos, Lethbridge memorabilia; antique clock. Family-owned. Cr cds: A, ER, MC, V.

🅳 **SC**

Medicine Hat (G-7)

Settled 1883 **Pop** 42,929 **Elev** 2,365 ft (721 m) **Area code** 403

Information Medicine Hat & District Convention and Visitors Bureau, 8 Gehring Rd SE, PO Box 605, T1A 7G5; 403/527-6422 or 800/481-2822

Web www.albertasouth.com/town/medhat.html

The city of Medicine Hat is famous for its industries. Rich in clays and natural gas, the area was a natural site for brick, tile, and petrochemical plants. Its hot summer temperatures make it ideal for market gardens and greenhouses. There are many beautiful parks and excellent recreational facilities.

The name Medicine Hat is a translation of the Blackfoot name *Saamis* meaning "headdress of a medicine man." Supposedly a Cree medicine man lost his war bonnet in the river during a fight between the Cree and Blackfoot.

Natural gas was discovered here in 1883, and in 1909 the huge Bow Island gas field was founded. Because of these gas fields, the British poet Rudyard Kipling referred to the early settlement as "the town with all hell for a basement." Medicine Hat came into being with the arrival of the Canadian Pacific Railway.

What to See and Do

Cypress Hills Provincial Park. Oasis of mixed deciduous and coniferous forests in the middle of a predominantly grassland region. At a maximum elevation of 4,810 ft (1,466 m) above sea level, the hills are the highest point in Canada between the Rocky Mtns and Labrador. The area offers a swimming beach, boating, canoeing, fishing; camping (fee), golf course, hiking trails, and nature interpretive programs. E on Trans-Canada Hwy 1, then S on Hwy 41. For further information contact PO Box 12, Elkwater T0J 1C0. Phone 403/893-3777. **FREE** Fort Walsh National Historic Park is nearby.

⭐**Dinosaur Provincial Park.** A UNESCO World Heritage Site. Discoveries of extensive fossil concentrations in this area in the late 1800s led to the designation of this area as a provincial park. More than 300 complete skeletons have been recovered for display in museums worldwide. The 22,000-acre park consists mainly of badlands; large areas have restricted access and can be seen only on interpretive tours. Facilities incl canoeing, fishing; interpretive trails, dinosaur displays (at their actual site of discovery) along public loop drive. Picnicking. Camping (firewood and water provided). Guided tours and hikes, amphitheater events and talks (summer; fee; inquire in advance). A field station of the Royal Tyrell Museum of Paleontology in Drumheller is located here; also John Ware Cabin, with displays. Park (daily). Field station (Mid-May-mid-Oct, daily; rest of yr, Mon-Fri). Some fees. Approx 25 mi (40 km) W on Hwy 1, then N on Hwy 884, W on Hwy 544. Phone 403/378-4342.

Medicine Hat Museum and Art Gallery. Displays depict the history of the Canadian West, featuring pioneer items, local fossils, relics, and Native artifacts. The archives contain a large collection of photographs and manuscripts. (Daily; closed Jan 1, Good Friday, Dec 25) 1302 Bomford Crescent SW. Phone 403/527-6266 or 403/526-0486. **FREE**

Special Event

Exhibition and Stampede. Stampede Park. Cattle and horse shows, professional rodeo, midway rides. First wkend Aug. Phone 403/527-1234.

Motels/Motor Lodges

★ ★ **BEST WESTERN INN.** *722 Redcliff Dr (T1A 5A3).* 403/527-3700; fax 403/526-8689; toll-free 800/528-1234. www.bestwestern.com. 110 rms, 2 story, 24 suites, 11 kits. S $69; D $75-$79; suites $119; kit. units $73-$83. Crib $3. Pet accepted. TV; cable (premium). 2 indoor pools; whirlpools. Complimentary continental bkfst. Restaurant adj 6 am-10:30 pm. Bar. Ck-out 11 am. Coin lndry. Meeting rms. Business servs avail. Sundries. Exercise equipt; sauna. Game rm. Refrigerators, microwaves. Cr cds: A, C, D, DS, ER, MC, V.
⧉ 🐾 ⛱ 🐂 🛟 🔥 SC

★ ★ ★ **MEDICINE HAT LODGE.** *1051 Ross Glen Dr SE (T1B 3T8).*

403/529-2222; fax 403/529-1538; toll-free 800/661-8095. www.medhatlodge.com. 190 rms, 4 story. S $89-$109; D $99-$119; suites $125-$265; under 18 free. Crib free. Pet accepted. TV; cable, VCR avail. Indoor pool; wading pool, whirlpool. Coffee in rms. Restaurant 6:30 am-11 pm. Bar noon-1 am. Ck-out noon. Meeting rms. Business servs avail. In-rm modem link. Bellhops. Sundries. Gift shop. Barber, beauty shop. Exercise equipt; sauna. Game rm. Balconies. Cr cds: A, C, D, DS, ER, JCB, MC, V.
⧉ 🐾 ⛱ 🐂 🛟 🔥 SC

★ **SUPER 8.** *1280 Trans-Canada Way SE (T1B 1J5).* 403/528-8888; fax 403/526-4445; res 800/800-8000. www.super8.com. 70 rms, 3 story, 8 kit. units. Late June-early Sept: S $59.88; D $63.88-$68.88; each addl $4; suite $114.88; kit. units $78.88; under 12 free; wkly rates; higher rates Exhibition and Stampede; lower rates rest of yr. Crib free. Pet accepted. TV; cable. Indoor pool; whirlpool. Complimentary continental bkfst. Restaurant opp open 24 hrs. Ck-out 11 am. Business servs avail. Cr cds: A, D, DS, ER, JCB, MC, V.
⧉ 🐾 ⛱ 🛟 🔥

★ **TRAVELODGE.** *1100 Redcliff Dr SW (T1A 5E5).* 403/527-2275; fax 403/526-7842; toll-free 800/442-8729. www.travelodge.com. 129 rms, 2 story. S $79; D $71-89. Crib free. TV; cable (premium). Heated pool; wading pool, whirlpool. Coffee in rms. Restaurant 6 am-11 pm; Sun 7 am-9 pm. Bar 11-2 am. Ck-out noon. Meeting rms. Business servs avail. Valet serv. Exercise equipt; sauna. Some refrigerators. Cr cds: A, D, DS, ER, MC, V.
⧉ ⛱ 🐂 🛟 🔥 SC 🐂

Red Deer (E-5)

Settled 1885 **Pop** 58,252 **Elev** 2,816 ft (860 m) **Area code** 403

Information Visitor & Convention Bureau, Greater Red Deer Visitor Centre at Heritage Ranch, PO Box 5008, T4N 3T4; 403/346-0180 or 800/215-8946

Web www.tourismreddeer.net/guide

The city of Red Deer sits in the valley of the Red Deer River, which winds through the lush green parkland of central Alberta. Sylvan and Pine lakes are among the popular recreational lakes surrounding the city. Agriculture and the petroleum industry are the mainstays of the economy. To the west is the David Thompson Highway, leading through the foothills into Alberta's Canadian Rockies and Banff National Park (see BANFF).

In the early 1870s the Calgary-Edmonton Trail crossed the river at a point known as Red Deer Crossing. With the coming of the railway, traffic increased and a trading post and stopping place were established. When the Northwest Rebellion broke out in 1885, a small regiment was stationed at Fort Normandeau. A reconstruction of this fort stands near Red Deer.

The river was originally called *Waş-ka-soo See-pi*, the Cree word for elk, because of the abundance of these animals. Early Scottish fur traders thought the elk were related to the red deer of their native land, hence the present name for the river and city.

What to See and Do

Fort Normandeau. Rebuilt 1885 army fort and interpretive center with displays of cultural history. Slide program, living history interpreters. (May-Sept, daily) Picnic area, canoe launch. (See SPECIAL EVENTS) 2 mi (3 km) W off Hwy 2 on 32nd St. Phone 403/346-2010 or 403/347-7550. **Donation**

Red Deer and District Museum. Displays cover prehistory and early settlement of Red Deer; changing exhibits. Also here are Heritage Square and Red Deer and District Archives. (Daily; extended hrs July early Sept; closed Jan 1, Dec 25) 4525 47 A Ave, adj to Recreation Centre. Phone 403/309-8405. **Donation**

Skiing. Canyon Ski Area. Triple, double chairlifts, two T-bars, handle tow; nordic jump; patrol, school, rentals; snowmaking; day lodge; bar, cafeteria. Longest run ½ mi (1 km); vertical drop 500 ft (164 m). (Nov-Mar, daily) X-country skiing. 6 mi (10 km) E on Ross St. Phone 403/346-5580. ¢¢¢¢

Waskasoo Park. Large River Valley park extending throughout city. Incl 47 mi (75 km) of bicycle and hiking trails, equestrian area, fishing, canoeing, water park, 18-hole golf. Picnicking (shelters). Campground (fee). Natural and cultural history interpretive centers; other attractions located within park. Fee for activities. (Daily) Phone 403/342-8159. **FREE**

Special Events

Fort Normandeau Days. Fort Normandeau. Native American ceremonies and dances, parade, children's activities. Late May. Phone 403/346-2010.

Highland Games. Westerner Park. Last Sat June.

Westerner Days. Fair and exhibition, midway, livestock shows, chuckwagon races. Mid-July.

Motels/Motor Lodges

★★ **HOLIDAY INN EXPRESS.** *2803 50th Ave (T4R 1H1). 403/343-2112; fax 403/340-8540; toll-free 800/223-1993. www.hiexpress.com/reddeer-exab.* 92 rms, 2 story. S, D $94-$104; each addl $6; suites $140; under 18 free. Crib free. TV; cable (premium). Pool; whirlpool. Coffee in rms. Ck-out 11 am. Business servs avail. In-rm modem link. Downhill ski 10 mi; x-country ski 3 mi. Exercise equipt; sauna. Some refrigerators. Picnic tables. Courtyard. Cr cds: A, D, DS, ER, JCB, MC, V.

⬛ 🏊 🛏 🍴 🎿 ⛷ SC

★ **NORTH HILL INN.** *7150 50th Ave (T4N 6A5). 403/343-8800; fax 403/342-2334; toll-free 800/662-7152. www.northhillinnreddeer.com.* 117 rms, 3 story. S $72; D $75-$85; under 18 free; wkend rates. Crib free. Pet accepted, some restrictions. TV; cable (premium). Heated pool; whirlpool. Coffee in rms. Restaurant 6 am-10 pm. Bar. Ck-out 11 am. Meeting rms. Business center. Exercise equipt; sauna. Downhill ski 10 mi; x-country ski 3 mi. Cr cds: A, D, ER, MC, V.

⬛ 🍽 🎿 🛏 🍴 ⛷ 🏊 🚶

★ **TRAVELODGE.** *2807 50th Ave (T4R 1H6). 403/346-2011; fax 403/346-1075; toll-free 888/383-2344. www.travelodge.com.* 136 rms, 3 story, 10 kits. S $69; D $75; suites $120. Crib avail. Pet accepted, some restrictions. TV; cable. Indoor pool; whirlpool. Restaurant 6:30 am-1 pm, 5-10 pm. Ck-out 11 am. Business servs avail. In-rm modem link. Coin lndry. Downhill ski 10 mi; x-country ski 3 mi. Cr cds: A, D, DS, ER, MC, V.

D 🐾 🖼 🚫 🔥 🎿

Hotels

★★ **BLACK KNIGHT INN.** *2929 50th Ave (T4R 1H1). 403/343-6666; fax 780/340-8970; toll-free 800/661-8793. www.blackknightinn.com.* 98 rms, 8 story. S, D $88; each addl $10; suites $105-$175; under 18 free. Crib free. TV; cable (premium). Heated pool; whirlpool. Coffee in rms. Restaurant 6:30 am-10 pm. Bar 11-1 am. Ck-out noon. Meeting rms. Business servs avail. Gift shop. Downhill ski 10 mi; x-country ski 3 mi. Whirlpool in some suites. Cr cds: A, D, ER, MC, V.

D 🎿 🎿 🖼 🚫 🖐

★★ **CAPRI HOTEL - CONVENTION & TRADE CENTRE.** *3310 Gaetz Ave (T4N 3X9). 403/346-2091; fax 403/346-4790; toll-free 800/662-7197. www.capricentre.com.* 155 rms, 9 story, 16 kits. S, D $110; each addl $15; kit. units $150-$350; under 18 free. TV; cable. Heated pool; whirlpool. Coffee in rms. Restaurant 6 am-midnight. Bar 11-2 am. Ck-out noon. Meeting rms. Shopping arcade. Barber, beauty shop. Downhill ski 10 mi; x-country ski 3 mi. Exercise equipt; sauna, steam rm. Some refrigerators. Some balconies. Cr cds: A, C, D, DS, ER, MC, V.

D 🏋 🎿 🖼 🏊 🧍 🖐 🔥

★★ **HOLIDAY INN RED DEER.** *6500 67th St (T3P 1A2). 403/342-6567; fax 403/343-3600; res 800/661-4961. www.holiday-inn.com.* 97 rms, 4 story. S, D $89; suites $99-$179; under 18 free. Crib free. Pet accepted. TV; cable (premium). Complimentary coffee in rms. Restaurant 6 am-10 pm; Bar 10-2 am. Ck-out 11 am. Business center. Barber, beauty shop. Downhill ski 10 mi; x-country ski 2 mi. Exercise equipt; sauna. Massage. Whirlpool. Cr cds: A, DS, MC, V.

D 🐾 🎿 🧍 🚫 🖐 SC 🧍

Restaurant

★ **HOULIHAN'S.** *6791 Gaetz Ave #11 (T4N 4C9). 403/342-0330.* Hrs: 11 am-10 pm; Wed-Thurs to 10:30 pm; Fri to 11 pm; Sat 4:30-11 pm. Closed Sun; hols. Res accepted Mon-Thurs. Bar. Lunch $5-$9, dinner $12-$40. Child's meals. Specializes in prime rib, beef Wellington, seafood. Various dining levels with fountain in center. Cr cds: A, D, DS, ER, MC, V.

D 🔄

Waterton Lakes National Park

30 mi SW on Hwy 3, then on Hwy 6

Waterton Lakes National Park was established in 1895, taking its name from the lakes in the main valley which were named for the 19th-century English naturalist Squire Charles Waterton. In 1932 it was linked with Glacier National Park in Montana (see); the whole area is now known as Waterton-Glacier International Peace Park. This park contains 203 square miles (526 square kilometers) on the eastern slope of the Rocky Mountains, just north of the US-Canadian border.

Travelers from the United States can reach the park via the Chief Mountain Highway along the east edge of Glacier National Park (Mid-May-mid-September). The trails are well-maintained and afford an introduction to much of the scenery that is inaccessible by car. Whether by foot, car, or boat, exploring the park and its many wonders will make the trip most worthwhile.

The Red Rock Parkway goes from the town of Waterton Park to Red Rock Canyon after branching off Alberta Highway 5. A buffalo paddock is located on Highway 6, just inside the northeastern park boundary. Also from the town of Waterton Park, you can drive to Cameron Lake via the Akamina Parkway. Separate fees are charged at most parks.

Prince of Wales Hotel, Waterton Lakes National Park

Motels/Motor Lodges

★★ ASPEN VILLAGE INN. *111 Windflower Ave, Waterton Lakes National Park (T0K 2M0). 403/859-2255; fax 403/859-2033. www.aspenvillageinn.com.* 37 rms, 1-2 story, 2 suites, 12 kit. units. No A/C. No elvtr. Mid-May-Oct: S, D $122-$193; each addl $10; suites $159-$215; kit. units $126-$174; under 16 free; lower rates Easter-mid-June and Oct-Thanksgiving. Closed rest of yr. Crib $10. TV. Playground. Complimentary coffee in rms. Restaurant adj 7:30 am-10 pm. Ck-out 11 am. Gift shop. Sundries. Whirlpool. Grills. Cr cds: A, D, DS, ER, MC, V.

★★ CRANDALL MOUNTAIN LODGE. *102 Mtn View Rd Box 114, Waterton Lakes National Park (T0K 2M0). 403/859-2288. www.crandell mountainlodge.com.* 17 rms, 2 story, 8 kit. units. No A/C. No rm phones. June-Sept: S, D $129-$199; each addl $10; kit. units $128-$188; hols (2-day min); lower rates rest of yr. Crib $7. TV. Playground. Coffee in rms. Restaurant opp 7:30 am-10 pm. Ck-out 10 am. Some fireplaces. Cr cds: DS, MC, V.

★★★ KILMOREY. *Box 100, 117 Evergreen Ave, Waterton Lakes National Park (T0K 2M0). 403/859-2334; fax 403/859-2342; toll-free 888/859-8669. www.watertonpark.com.* 23 rms, 3 story, 3 suites. No A/C. No elvtr. No rm phones. S, D $86-$133; each addl $10; suites $117-$171; under 16 free. TV in lobby. Dining rm 7:30 am-10 pm. Ck-out 11 am, ck-in 3 pm. Country-style inn built in 1923. On Emerald Bay in Waterton Park. Cr cds: A, D, DS, ER, MC, V.

Hotel

★ PRINCE OF WALES. *117 Evergreen Ave, Waterton Lakes National Park (T0K 2M0). 403/859-2231; fax 403/859-2630.* 87 rms, 7 story. No A/C. S $169-$221; D $175-$227; each addl $15; under 12 free. Closed late Sept-mid May. Crib free. Dining rm 6:30-9:30 am, 11:30 am-2 pm, 5-9 pm. Tearoom 2-5 pm. Bar 11:30 am-midnight. Ck-out 11 am. Bellhops. Gift shop. Large, gabled inn (built 1927) overlooking lake and mountains. Cr cds: A, MC, V.

PROVINCE OF BRITISH COLUMBIA

This huge territory, with its mixture of climate, geography, products, and people, began its modern history in 1843 while under British control. In 1871 British Columbia joined the Confederation and its steady progression can be traced through fur trading and gold rushes to urban development. Bordered on the south by Washington and on the north by the Yukon, the province has a wide range of weather conditions, from the balmy warm breezes in Victoria to cold arctic winds in the far north. Thus many recreational possibilities, including skiing, sailing, swimming, spelunking, and river rafting, can be enjoyed.

Vacation choices range from shopping for indigenous art, to gold panning, to flying over the magnificent wilderness of the Queen Charlotte Islands. No trip to British Columbia would be complete without a visit to Vancouver and Victoria. International in character, Vancouver boasts all the attractions of a modern city while preserving its vital past. Museums, galleries, parks, gardens, and fine dining blend well with beaches and marinas in this lovely peninsular city.

Victoria, the capital, is located on Vancouver Island and is noted for its many gardens and parks. Victoria offers sights that include the Parliament buildings, the Royal British Columbia Museum with its Natural History Gallery, and reconstructed areas that reflect the past.

Rogers Pass

Pop 3,100,000 (est) **Land area** 344,817 square miles (893,073 square kilometers) **Capital** Victoria **Web** www.travel.bc.ca

Information Tourism British Columbia, Parliament Buildings, Victoria V8W 1X4; 250/387-1642 or 800/435-5622

Most of British Columbia is on Pacific Standard Time and observes Pacific Daylight Saving Time in summer. Tourists should note that there is strong anti-litter legislation in British Columbia which applies to boaters and hikers, as well as drivers and pedestrians.

In addition to national holidays, British Columbia observes British Columbia Day (first Monday August).

Safety belts are mandatory for all persons anywhere in vehicle. Children under 40 pounds in weight must be in an approved passenger restraint anywhere in vehicle: 20-39 pounds may use an approved safety seat facing forward if in parents' or guardians' vehicle, or a regulation safety belt if in someone else's vehicle; under 20 pounds must be in an approved safety seat facing rear.

DISCOVERING VANCOUVER'S WESTERN COAST

Only one paved road reaches the open ocean on Vancouver's western coast, which is an area of primordial beauty, tempestuous climate, abundant wildlife, and vast wilderness beaches. From Parksville on the island's east coast, Highway 4 passes a number of popular destinations, including a butterfly zoo and roaring Englishman Falls, before cresting Vancouver Island's central mountain range. Provincial parks protect Cathedral Grove, an old-growth forest preserve with millennium-old cedars and firs. Highway 4 reaches Port Alberni, where travelers can opt to take a day-long mail-boat trip out to far-flung communities scattered along Alberni Inlet. Highway 4 continues to Ucluelet, a fishing village and popular departure point for whale-watching trips onto the Pacific and sea-kayak trips to the Broken Group Islands (part of Pacific Rim National Park). The road to Tofino passes long beaches and rugged island-flecked shorelines, most of which are preserved in Pacific Rim National Park. Tofino, at the end of the road, occupies a narrow peninsula between rocky, forested islands in churning seas. Once a backwoods village, Tofino is now one of the top resort destinations in British Columbia, with native art galleries and world-class hotels and restaurants. From Tofino, boat or float plane trips lead out to even more remote destinations, including shoreline hot springs on a remote island. (**APPROX 107 MI; 173 KM.**)

ADVENTURES IN THE CANADIAN ROCKIES

This route parallels the western slopes of the Canadian Rockies along the Columbia River. Stirring mountain scenery mixes with great outdoor recreation, especially if you're a golfer. Highway 95 follows what's called the Rocky Mountain Trench, a broad U-shaped valley carved between the jagged peaks of the Rockies and the somewhat lower, but equally spectacular, peaks of the Selkirk, Columbia, and Purcell ranges. Besides miles and miles of mountain vistas, other highlights include Fairmont and Radium Hot Springs; a good railway museum at Cranbrook; Fort Steele, a reconstructed frontier town from the 1880s with summer interpretive programs and classic melodramas in the opera house; and the Columbia Wetlands, a 100-mile-long wildlife refuge that preserves the habitat of moose, coyote, mink, beaver, and hundreds of varieties of migrating birds. At Golden, travelers can enjoy a whitewater rafting trip in the Kicking Horse River, one of Canada's most thrilling rivers for rafters. (**APPROX 154 MI; 248 KM.**)

Kamloops (E-6)

Pop 64,048 **Elev** 1,181 ft (360 m)
Area code 250
Information Chamber of Commerce and Visitor Information Centre, 1290 W Trans-Canada Hwy, V2C 6R3; 250/374-3377 or 800/662-1994
Web www.city.kamloops.bc.ca

Kamloops is located at the junction of the North and South Thompson rivers and is a trade center for a farming, mining, ranching, lumbering, and fruit-growing region. Kamloops trout are world famous; there are some 200 lakes within 60 miles (96 kilometers) of the city.

What to See and Do

Kamloops Museum and Archives. Natural history; Shuswap culture; fur trade; Gold Rush eras. (Tues-Sat; summer hrs vary) 207 Seymour St. Phone 250/828-3576. **Donation**

Kamloops Wildlife Park. More than 300 animals, both native and international. Nature trail. Miniature railroad (seasonal, fee). Park (daily). 11 mi (18 km) E, at 9077 E Dallas Dr. For further information contact PO Box 698, V2C 5L7. Phone 250/573-3242. ¢¢¢

Secwepemc Native Heritage Park. Located on the Kamloops Reserve, park interprets culture and heritage of the Secwepemc people. Incl archaeological site, full-scale winter village model, indoor museum exhibits, native arts and crafts. Tours avail. (Summer, daily; rest of yr, Mon-Fri) N across Yellowhead Bridge, then 1st right. Phone 250/828-9801. ¢¢¢

Special Event

International Air Show. Concession, beer garden. Mid-July. Fulton Field. Phone 250/554-0700.

Motels/Motor Lodges

★★★ **THE COAST CANADIAN INN.** *339 St. Paul St (V2E 1J7). 250/372-5201; fax 250/372-9363.* 94 rms, 5 story. May-Sept: S $120; D $130; each addl $10; under 18 free; ski plans; lower rates rest of yr. Crib free. Pet accepted. TV; cable (premium), VCR avail (movies). Pool. Restaurant 6:30 am-10 pm. Rm serv 24 hrs. Bar 1 pm-1 am; entertainment Mon-Sat. Ck-out noon. Meeting rms. Business center. In-rm modem link. Bellhops. Exercise equipt. Health club privileges. Mini-bars. Cr cds: A, D, DS, JCB, MC, V.
🄳 🌊 ☎ 🏋 ➤ 🛇 SC 🏋

★ **DAYS INN.** *1285 W Trans Canada Hwy (V2E 2J7). 250/374-5911; fax 250/374-6922; toll-free 800/561-5002. www.daysinn.com.* 60 rms. June-Sept: S $99; D $109; each addl $10; suites $125-$250; kits. $150-$250; under 12 free; lower rates rest of yr. Crib free. Pet accepted, some restrictions. TV; cable (premium), VCR avail. Heated pool; whirlpool. Restaurant 7 am-9 pm. Ck-out noon. Meeting rms. Business servs avail. Refrigerators. Cr cds: A, D, ER, JCB, MC, V.
🄳 🌊 ☎ 🏋 ➤ 🛇 🏋

★★ **EXECUTIVE INN - KAMLOOPS.** *540 Victoria St (V2C 2B2). 250/372-2281; fax 250/372-1125; toll-free 800/663-2837. www.kamloops.com/executiveinn.* 151 rms, 5 story. May-Sept: S $105-$139; D $115-$149; each addl $10; suites $150-$250; under 14 free; lower rates rest of yr. Crib $10. TV; cable (premium). Coffee in rms. Restaurant 6 am-10 pm. Bar noon-1 am Mon-Sat. Ck-out noon. Meeting rms. Business servs avail. Health club privileges. Casino. Cr cds: A, D, DS, ER, JCB, MC, V.
🄳 ☎ 🏋 🏊 ➤ 🏋

★★ **HOSPITALITY INN.** *500 W Columbia St (V2C 1K6). 250/374-4164; fax 250/374-6971; toll-free 800/663-5733.* 77 rms, 2 story, 15 kits. June-Sept: S $92.50; D $96.50; each addl $6; kit. units $6 addl; under 12 free; lower rates rest of yr. Crib $6. TV; cable (premium). Sauna. Pool; whirlpool. Restaurant 7 am-10 pm. Ck-out 11 am. Meeting rms. Business servs avail. Refrigerators. Private patios. Cr cds: A, D, DS, ER, JCB, MC, V.
☎ 🏋 ➤ 🏋

★ **HOWARD JOHNSON PANORAMA INN.** *610 W Columbia St (V2C 1L1). 250/374-1515; fax 250/374-4116; toll-free 800/663-3813. www.hojo.com.* 94 rms, 2-3 story, 11 suites, 40 kits. May-Sept: S $79-$85; D $85-$89; each addl $8; suites $95-

$125; kits. $8 addl; under 12 free; lower rates rest of yr. Crib free. TV; cable. Sauna. Heated pool; whirlpool. Coffee in rms. Restaurant 8 am-10 pm. Ck-out noon. Business servs avail. In-rm modem link. Private balconies. View of city. Cr cds: A, D, DS, ER, MC, V.

D ⌇ ⌁ ⛧ SC

★ **KAMLOOPS CITY CENTER TRAVELODGE.** *430 Columbia St (V2C 2T5). 250/372-8202; fax 250/372-1459; toll-free 800/578-7878. www.travelodge.com.* 68 rms, 2 story. May-Oct: S, D $84-$94; each addl $5; under 13 free; lower rates rest of yr. Crib free, TV; cable, VCR avail. Sauna. Heated pool; whirlpool. Restaurant 7 am-9 pm. Ck-out 11 am. Meeting rm. Business servs avail. Health club privileges. Cr cds: A, C, D, ER, MC, V.

D ⌇ ⌁ ⛧ SC

★ **RAMADA INN- KAMLOOPS.** *555 W Columbia St (V2C 1K7). 250/374-0358; fax 250/374-0691; toll-free 800/663-2832. www.ramada.com.* 90 rms, 3 story, 12 kits. May-Sept: S $109; D $119; each addl $10; suites $100-$175; kit. units $10 addl; under 18 free; lower rates rest of yr. Crib free. TV; cable (premium), VCR avail. Sauna. Pool; whirlpool. Restaurant 7 am-10 pm. Bar; entertainment. Ck-out 11 am. Meeting rms. Business servs avail. Valet serv. Health club privileges. Refrigerators. Cr cds: A, D, DS, ER, JCB, MC, V.

D ⌁ ⛧ ⌇ ⛧

★ ★ **SAGE BRUSH MOTEL.** *660 W Columbia St (V2C 1L1). 250/372-3151; fax 250/372-2983; toll-free 888/218-6116.* 60 rms, 2 story, 30 kits. May-mid-Sept: S $50-$55; D $55-$65; each addl $5; kit. units $5 addl; higher rates hols; lower rates rest of yr. TV; cable (premium). Sauna. Heated pool; whirlpool. Restaurant 7 am-11 pm. Ck-out 11 am. Business servs avail. Refrigerators. Cr cds: A, MC, V.

⌇ ⌁ ⛧ SC

★ ★ **STAY 'N SAVE.** *1325 Columbia St W (V2C 6P4). 250/374-8877; fax 250/372-0507.* 83 rms, 3 story, 25 kit. units. S, D $109-$119; each addl $10; suites $120; kit. units $99-$130; under 16 free; ski plans. Crib free.

Pet accepted. TV; cable. Heated pool; whirlpool. Complimentary coffee in lobby. Ck-out 11 am. Coin lndry. Meeting rms. Business servs avail. In-rm modem link. Valet serv. X-country ski 15 mi. Exercise equipt; sauna. Picnic tables. Cr cds: A, D, MC, V.

D ⌁ ⌇ ⛧ ⌇ ⌇ ⌇ ⌇ ⌇

Kelowna

(E-6) *See also Penticton*

Pop 78,000 **Elev** 1,129 ft (344 m)
Area code 250
Information Visitors and Convention Bureau, 544 Harvey Ave, V1Y 6C9; 250/861-1515 or 800/663-4345
Web www.kelownachamber.org.

Kelowna is located on the shores of Okanagan Lake between Penticton (see) and Vernon, 80 miles (128 kilometers) north of the US border. The name Kelowna is a corruption of an indigenous word for grizzly bear. The history of Europeans in the area dates back to the fur brigades in the 19th century. Father Pandosy established a mission here in 1858. The apple trees that were planted by him were the beginning of one of the largest fruit-growing districts in Canada.

The Civic Centre complex, located in downtown Kelowna, includes government buildings, community theater, a curling rink, regional library, and centennial museum. The city also has 31 parks, seven on the lakeshore. Among the facilities in these parks are soccer fields, lawn bowling greens, and tennis courts.

Kelowna is a playground at almost any time of year. Water sports, golf, cricket, curling, baseball, and skiing are only a few of the sports played in the area. The winter highlight is the annual Snowfest.

Special Events

Snowfest. "Smockey" game, Light Up Parade, polar bear dip, snowshoe relay, belly flop contest. Late Jan.
Okanagan Wine Festival. Races, ethnic events, baking contest, dance,

wine tasting (also see PENTICTON). May and Oct. Phone 250/861-6654.

Black Mountain Rodeo Golf Tournament. Mid-May. Phone 250/763-7888.

Kelowna Regatta. Mid-July.

Motels/Motor Lodges

★★ **ACCENT INNS.** *1140 Harvey Ave (V1Y 6E7). 250/862-8888; fax 250/862-8884; toll-free 800/663-0298.* 101 rms, 3 story, 12 suites, 26 kits. Mid-May-Sept: S $79-$119; D $89-$129; each addl $10; suites $120; kit. units $109; under 16 free; lower rates rest of yr. Crib free. Pet accepted. TV; cable. Heated pool; whirlpool. Restaurant adj 7 am-10 pm. Ck-out 11 am. Coin lndry. Meeting rms. Business servs avail. Exercise equipt; sauna. Cr cds: A, D, ER, MC, V.

[D] [symbols] SC

★★ **BEST WESTERN INN.** *2402 Hwy 97N (V1X 4J1). 250/860-1212; fax 250/860-0675; toll-free 888/860-1212. www.bestwestern.com/ca/innkelowna.* 147 rms, 2 story, 30 suites. May-Sept: S, D $139-$239; each addl $10; under 18 free; ski; lower rates rest of yr. Crib free. TV; cable (premium). Heated pool; whirlpools. Complimentary coffee in rms. Restaurant 7 am-10 pm. Bar. Ck-out 11 am. Business servs avail. Tennis. Refrigerators. Private patios, balconies. Cr cds: A, D, DS, MC, V.

[D] [symbols] SC

★★ **BEST WESTERN VERNON LODGE.** *3914 32nd St, Vernon (V1T 5P1). 250/545-3385; fax 250/545-7156; res 800/663-4422. www.rpbhotels.com/vernon/verindex.html.* 131 rms, 3 story. S $79-$99; D $89-$109; each addl $10; suites $109-$160; under 13 free. Crib avail. TV; cable (premium). Heated pool; whirlpool. Restaurant 6:30 am-5 pm; dining rm 5-10 pm. Bar. Ck-out noon. Meeting rms. Business servs avail. Valet serv. Sundries. Downhill/x-country ski 14 mi. Balconies. Cr cds: A, C, D, DS, ER, JCB, MC, V.

[D] [symbols] SC

★★ **HOLIDAY INN EXPRESS.** *2429 Hwy 97 N (V1X 4J2). 250/763-0500; fax 250/763-7555; toll-free 800/465-0200. www.hiexpress.com/kelownabc.* 120 rms, 4 story. May-Oct: S, D $99-$139; each addl $10; suites $229;

under 19 free; golf plans; lower rates rest of yr. Crib free. TV; cable (premium). Indoor pool; whirlpool. Complimentary continental bkfst. Coffee in rms. Restaurant 6 am-8:30 pm. Ck-out noon. Meeting rm. Business center. In-rm modem link. Bellhops. Valet serv. Exercise equipt. Some in-rm whirlpools. Cr cds: A, C, D, DS, ER, JCB, MC, V.

[D] [symbols] SC

★★★ **RAMADA LODGE.** *2170 Harvey Ave (V1Y 6G8). 250/860-9711; fax 250/860-3173; toll-free 800/665-2518. rpbhotels.com.* 135 rms, 3 story, 39 suites. Mid-May-mid-Sept: S, D $99-$119; each addl $10; suites $110-$199; under 19 free; ski, golf plans; lower rates rest of yr. Crib free. Pet accepted. TV; cable (premium). Indoor pool; whirlpool. Complimentary coffee in rms. Restaurant open 24 hrs. Bar 11-1 am. Ck-out noon. Meeting rms. Business servs avail. Valet serv. Sundries. Some covered parking. Exercise equipt. 18-hole golf 4 mi. Some in-rm whirlpools. Cr cds: A, C, D, DS, ER, JCB, MC, V.

[D] [symbols] SC

★ **SANDMAN HOTEL.** *2130 Harvey Ave (V1Y 6J8). 250/860-6409; fax 250/860-7377; toll-free 888/526-1988. www.sandman.ca.* 120 rms, 3 story. S $77-$87; D $85-$89; each addl $5; kit. units $10 addl; under 12 free. Crib free. Pet accepted, some restrictions. TV; cable. Sauna. Pool; whirlpool. Restaurant open 24 hrs. Bar 11-1 am. Ck-out noon. Meeting rms. Business servs avail. Sundries. Refrigerators. Balconies. Cr cds: A, C, D, DS, ER, JCB, MC, V.

[symbols] SC

★★ **VILLAGE GREEN HOTEL & CASINO.** *4801 27th St, Vernon (V1T 4Z1). 250/542-3321; fax 250/549-4252; toll-free 800/663-4433. www.villagegreen.bc.ca.* 138 rms, 2-6 story. S $75-$89; D $83-$99; each addl $10; suites $120-$210; under 13 free. Crib free. TV; cable (premium). Sauna. 2 heated pools; whirlpool, poolside serv. Restaurant 6 am-10 pm. Bar noon-1 am; entertainment. Ck-out noon. Meeting rms. Business servs avail. Bellhops. Valet serv. Sundries. Downhill/x-country ski 12 mi. Refrigerators. Private patios, balconies. Cr cds: A, C, D, DS, ER, JCB, MC, V.

 (icons)

Hotel

★★★ **COAST CAPRI HOTEL.** *1171 Harvey Ave (Hwy 97) (V1Y 6E8). 250/860-6060; fax 250/762-3430; toll-free 800/663-1144. www.coasthotels. com.* 185 rms, 4-7 story. May-Sept: S $125-$135; D $135-$145; each addl $10; suites $205; under 18 free; ski, golf plans; lower rates rest of yr. Crib free. Pet accepted. TV; cable, VCR avail. Heated pool; whirlpool, poolside serv. Coffee in rms. Restaurant 6:30 am-10 pm. Rm serv 24 hrs. Bar. Ck-out noon. Meeting rms. Business center. In-rm modem link. Drugstore. Barber, beauty shop. Health club privileges. Balconies. Cr cds: A, C, D, ER, MC, V.

(icons)

Nanaimo

(F-4) *See also Vancouver, Victoria*

Founded 1874 **Pop** 47,069 **Elev** 100 ft (30 m)
Information Tourism Nanaimo, Beban House, 2290 Bowen Rd, V9T 3K7; 250/756-0106 or 800/663-7337
Web www.tourismnanaimo.com

Nanaimo is located on Vancouver Island off the west coast of British Columbia, a main entry port for ferries from Vancouver and Horseshoe Bay. Because of its location it serves as a fine starting point to other attractions on the island as well as being a vacation highlight in itself. The name comes from the indigenous term "Sne-ny-mos" that referred to the gathering of the tribes. In 1849 coal was discovered and was mined here for 100 years.

What to See and Do

Bastion. Built in 1853 as a Hudson's Bay Company fort. Now a museum; cannon firing ceremony (summer months at noon). Restored to original appearance. (July-Aug) Front and Bastion sts. Along harbor basin below is

Queen Elizabeth Promenade. Named to commemorate the vessel and landing of the first miner-colonists in the area (1854); boardwalk offers pleasant view of waterfront and tidal lagoon.

Bowen Park. Swimming pool (fee); tennis courts, fitness circuit, game fields, picnic shelters, recreation complex, lawn bowling; totem poles, rose garden, rhododendron grove, petting farm, duck ponds, fish ladder. 500 Bowen Rd. Phone 250/755-5200. ¢¢

Cyber City. Adventure park with laser tag, go-carts, paintball, miniature golf, virtual reality arcade, spaceball. Restaurant. (Daily) 1815 Bowen Rd. Phone 250/755-1828. **FREE**

Ferry trips. BC Ferries. Service between Nanaimo and Horseshoe Bay, north of Vancouver (1½ hrs); or Duke Point and Tsawassen, south of Vancouver, near US border (two hrs). For current schedule and fare information contact BC Ferry Corporation, 1112 Fort St, Victoria, V8V 4V2; phone 250/669-1211 (Vancouver) or 250/386-3431 (Victoria).

Nanaimo Art Gallery and Exhibition Centre. Gallery with changing exhibits of art, science, and history. (Mon-Sat; closed hols) On Malaspina College campus Phone 250/755-8790. **Donation**

Totem pole

Nanaimo District Museum. Walk-in replica of coal mine; turn-of-the-century shops, restored miner's cottage; dioramas; Chinatown display; changing exhibits. Tours avail. (May-Aug, daily; rest of yr, Tues-Sat; closed hols) 100 Cameron St. Phone 250/753-1821. ¢

Newcastle Island Provincial Marine Park. Boat docking (fee); camping (fee), hiking and bicycle trails, picnicking; pavilion with historical displays, concession (May-Sept). Dance and barbecue events in summer. No land vehicle access. Access by foot/passenger ferry from Maffeo Sutton Park (May-mid-Oct; fee); private boat rest of yr. Phone 250/754-7893. **FREE**

Petroglyph Park. Established to preserve the many ancient indigenous rock carvings. 2 mi (3 km) S on Trans-Canada Hwy 1. Phone 250/391-2300.

Special Events

Polar Bear Swim. Prizes for all participants; free ice cream, bananas, and suntan lotion. Jan 1. Phone 250/756-5200.

Nanaimo Marine Festival. Bathtub race (third or fourth Sun July) across the Straits of Georgia to Vancouver; many other events. Begins one wk prior to race day. Phone 250/753-7223.

Vancouver Island Exhibition. Beban Park. Early or mid-Aug. Phone 250/758-3247.

Motels/Motor Lodges

★ **DAYS INN HARBOURVIEW.** *809 Island Hwy S (V9R 5K1).* 250/754-8171; *fax 250/754-8557; res 800/325-2525. www.daysinn.com.* 79 rms, 2 story, 16 kits. June-Sept: S $95; D $115; each addl $10; suites $145; kit. units $85-$115; under 12 free; lower rates rest of yr. Crib free. Pet accepted; $7/day. TV; cable (premium), VCR avail. Indoor pool; whirlpool. Restaurant 7 am-9:30 pm. Ck-out 11 am. Coin lndry. Meeting rms. Business servs avail. Sundries. Some refrigerators. Overlooking Nanaimo's inner harbour. Cr cds: A, D, DS, ER, JCB, MC, V.
🄳 ⬚ 🐾 ⛱ ⬚ 🖐

★ **HOWARD JOHNSON HARBOUR SIDE HOTEL.** *1Terminal Ave (V9R 5R4).* 250/753-2241; *fax 250/753-6522; toll-free 800/663-7322. www. hojo.com.* 101 rms, 3 story. S, D $80-$110; each addl $10; suites $150; under 18 free; wkend rates. Crib free. TV; cable, VCR avail. Heated pool. Restaurant 6:30 am-9 pm. Bar 11:30-1:30 am. Ck-out noon. Meeting rms. Business servs avail. Valet serv. Sundries. Health club privileges. Cr cds: A, C, D, DS, ER, MC, V.
🐾 ⬚ ⬚ 🖐 **SC**

Hotel

★★ **COAST BASTION INN.** *11 Bastion St (V9R 2Z9).* 250/753-6601; *fax 250/753-4155. www.coasthotels.com.* 179 rms, 14 story. Mid-May-mid-Sept: S $140-$165, D $150-$175; each addl $10; suites $198-$208; under 18 free; package plans; lower rates rest of yr. Crib free. Pet accepted. TV; cable (premium). Restaurant 6:30 am-9 pm. Bar 11:30-1 am. Ck-out 11 am. Meeting rms. Business servs avail. Barber, beauty shop. Exercise equipt; sauna. Whirlpool. Many minibars. Balconies. Ocean 1 blk; swimming. Cr cds: A, D, DS, ER, JCB, MC, V.
🄳 🐾 🐾 ⛱ 🏃 ⬚ 🖐

Resorts

★★★ **FAIRWINDS SCHOONER COVE RESORT & MARINA.** *3521 Dolphin Dr, Nanoose Bay (V9P 9J7).* 250/468-7691; *fax 250/468-5744; toll-free 800/663-7060. www.fairwinds. bc.ca.* 31 units. May-Oct: S, D $154; each addl $10; under 12 free; lower rates rest of yr. TV; cable, VCR avail (movies). Pool; whirlpool. Dining rm 7 am-9 pm. Box lunches. Ck-out noon. Grocery. Coin lndry. Meeting rms. Business servs avail. Tennis. 18-hole golf privileges opp, greens fee $60, pro, driving range. Boats (rentals). 405-slip marina. Balconies. Picnic tables. Extensive landscaping; outstanding views. Cr cds: A, D, DS, ER, MC, V.
🄳 🐾 🏃 🐾 ⬚ ⬚ 🖐 **SC**

★★★ **KINGFISHER OCEANSIDE RESORT AND SPA.** *4330 S Island Hwy, Courtenay (V9N 8R9).* 250/338-1323; *fax 250/338-0058; toll-free 800/663-7929. www.kingfisher*

resortspa.com. 27 rms, 2 story, 36 suites. S, D $100-$150. Crib avail. Pet accepted, fee. Parking garage. Pool, whirlpool. TV; cable (premium), VCR avail, CD avail. Complimentary coffee in rms, newspaper, toll-free calls. Restaurant 7 am-10 pm. Bar. Ck-out 11 am, ck-in 3 pm. Meeting rms. Business center. Concierge. Dry cleaning, coin lndry. Gift shop. Exercise equipt, sauna, steam rm. Golf, 18 holes. Tennis. Downhill skiing. Beach access. Hiking trail. Picnic facilities. Cr cds: A, D, DS, MC, V.

Cottage Colony

★★ **YELLOW POINT LODGE**. *3700 Yellow Point Rd, Ladysmith (V9G 1E8). 250/245-7422; fax 250/245-7411. www.yellowpointlodge.com*. 9 rms in main bldg, 4 story, 44 cottages, 19 with bath. No A/C. No elvtr. No rm phones. AP, May-Sept: S, D $115-$190; each addl $64; suites $177; higher rates Christmas hols; lower rates rest of yr. Children over 14 yrs only. Saltwater pool; whirlpool. Complimentary continental bkfst. Dining rm, 3 sittings: 8:30-9:30 am, 12:30 pm, 6:30 pm. Serv bar 11 am-11 pm. Ck-out noon, ck-in 3 pm. Coin lndry 8 mi. Meeting rms. Grocery 5 mi. Package store. Airport, RR station, bus depot transportation. Tennis. Sauna. Beach; ocean swimming. Kayaks. Bicycles. Lawn games. Rec rm. Some refrigerators. Balconies. Picnic tables. Surrounded by 180 acres of preserved private forest; on Straits of Georgia. Cr cds: A, MC, V.

Restaurants

★★★ **KINGFISHER RESTAURANT**. *4330 S Island Hwy, Courtenay (Z9N 8H9). 250/334-9600. www.kingfisher-resort-.com*. Specializes in salmon, oysters, halibut. Hrs: 7:30 am-9 pm. Res accepted. Wine, beer. Lunch $5.95-$9.95; dinner $11.95-$21.95. Child's menu. Entertainment. Cr cds: A, D, DS, ER, JCB, MC, V.

[D] [SC]

★★ **THE MAHLE HOUSE RESTAURANT**. *2104 Hemer Rd (V9X 1L8). 250/722-3621. www.island.net/~mahle/*. Menu changes wkly. Hrs: 5-9 pm.

Closed Mon, Tues. Res accepted. Wine, beer. Dinner $13.95-$26.95. Entertainment. Own vegetables. Old Victorian house. Cr cds: A, MC, V.

[D]

★★ **OLD HOUSE RESTAURANT**. *1760 Riverside Ln, Courtenay (V9N 8C7). 250/338-5406*. Specializes in steak, Paradise Meadows chicken breast, prime rib. Hrs: 11:30 am-9 pm; Fri, Sat to 9:30 pm. Closed Dec 25, Labor Day. Res accepted. Lunch $7.95-$11.95; dinner $10.95-$22.95. Child's menu. Entertainment. On the Courtney River, beautiful grounds. Cr cds: A, D, ER, MC, V.

★ **THE RESTAURANT AT TIGH-NA-MARA RESORT**. *1095 E Island Hwy, Parksville (V9P 2E5). 250/248-2333. www.tigh-na-mara.com*. Specializes in rack of lamb, salmon. Hrs: 7:30 am-9:30 pm; Sun from 10 am. Res accepted. Wine list. Lunch $8.95-$12.95; dinner $15.95-$26.95. Brunch $9.95-$17.95. Child's menu. Rustic atmosphere. Cr cds: A, D, ER, MC, V.

[D]

Penticton

(F-6) *See also Kelowna*

Pop 23,181 **Elev** 1,150 ft (351 m)
Area code 250
Information Visitor InfoCentre, 888 Westminster Ave W, V2A 8R2; 250/492-4103 or 800/663-5052
Web www.penticton.org

Penticton is situated between the beautiful Okanagan and Skaha lakes on an alluvial plain. Beyond the lakes are fertile orchard lands and rolling hills. Penticton is famous for its peaches and other fruits. Because of its prime location, Penticton is sometimes called the land of peaches and beaches. Grape-growing and wine-making have become very important in the Okanagan Valley, producing some very fine wines.

What to See and Do

Agriculture Canada Research Station. Beautiful display of ornamental gardens; canyon view; picnicking. Guided tours (daily). 6 mi (10 km) N on Hwy 97. Phone 250/494-7711. **Donation ¢**

Dominion Radio Astrophysical Observatory. Guided tours (July-Aug, Sun). Visitor Centre (daily). 9 mi (15 km) SW via Hwy 97, 5½ mi (9 km) S on White Lake Rd. Phone 250/493-2277. **FREE**

Penticton Museum. Collection of Salish artifacts; taxidermy, ghost town, and pioneer exhibits. Changing exhibits. At 1099 Lakeshore Dr W are two historic 1914 steamships: SS *Sicamous*, a 200-ft sternwheeler, and SS *Naramata*, a 90-ft steam tug (donation). (Mon-Sat; closed hols) 785 Main St. Phone 250/490-2451. **FREE**

Wonderful Water World. Waterpark has waterslides, miniature golf, slot car racing on 110-ft track. Concessions, picnic area. Campground on site. (Late May-Labour Day, daily) 225 Yorkton Ave. Phone 250/493-8121. **¢¢¢¢**

Special Events

Midwinter Breakout. Festival for the entire family. Second and third wk Feb. Phone 250/493-4055.

Okanagan Wine Festival. Wine tasting, grape stomping, seminars, and dinners (also see KELOWNA). Late Apr-early May; late Sept-mid-Oct. Phone 250/861-6654.

British Columbia Square Dance Jamboree. Street dancing; dancing under the stars on perhaps North America's largest outdoor board floor. Early Aug. In King's Park. Phone 250/493-4055.

Peach Festival. Parade, entertainment, family events. Mid-Aug. Phone 250/493-7384.

Ironman Canada Championship Triathlon. Qualifier for Hawaiian Ironman. Late Aug.

Motels/Motor Lodges

★★ **BEL-AIR MOTEL.** *2670 Skaha Lake Rd (V2A 6G1). 250/492-6111; fax 250/492-8035; toll-free 800/766-5770. www.belairmotel.bc.ca.* 42 rms, 2 story, 16 kits. Mid-June-mid-Sept: S $69-$79; D $69-$89; each addl $5;

kit. units $84-$98; lower rates rest of yr. Pet accepted. TV; cable (premium). Sauna. Heated pool; whirlpool. Restaurant nearby. Ck-out 11 am. Coin lndry. Picnic tables, grills. Cr cds: A, MC, V.
🐾 🏊 ✈ 🎿 🔥

★★ **BEST WESTERN INN AT PENTICTON.** *3180 Skaha Lake Rd, Penticton (V2A 6G4). 250/493-0311; fax 250/493-5556; res 800/668-6746. www.bestwestern.com.* 67 rms, 2 story, 24 kits. Mid-June-mid-Sept: S $109-$189; D $119-$189; each addl $10; kit. units $139-$189; suites $189-$275; under 18 free; lower rates rest of yr. Crib $10. TV; cable (premium). 2 pools, 1 indoor; whirlpool. Playground. Restaurant 7 am-9 pm. Ck-out 11 am. Coin lndry. Business servs avail. In-rm modem link. Valet serv. Refrigerators. Picnic tables. Cr cds: A, D, DS, ER, JCB, MC, V.
🐾 🏊 ✈ 🎿 🔥

★ **RAMADA COURTYARD INN.** *1050 Eckhardt Ave W (V2A 2C3). 250/492-8926; fax 250/492-2778; toll-free 800/665-4966. www.ramada.com.* 50 rms. Mid-May-mid-Sept: S, D $95; each addl $10; under 12 free; lower rates rest of yr. Pet accepted, some restrictions. TV; cable (premium). Heated pool. Restaurant nearby. Bar. Ck-out 11 am. Coin lndry. Meeting rms. Business servs avail. Valet serv. Lawn games. Some refrigerators, fireplaces. Private patios. Picnic tables, grill. Cr cds: A, D, DS, ER, MC, V.
🐾 🏊 🎿 🔥

★★ **SANDMAN HOTEL.** *939 Burnaby Ave W (V2A 1G7). 250/493-7151; fax 250/493-3767; toll-free 888/648-1118. www.sandman.ca.* 141 rms, 3 story. Mid-May-Sept: S $71; D $81; each addl $5; under 16 free; lower rates rest of yr. Crib free. TV; cable (premium). Indoor pool; whirlpool. Restaurant open 24 hrs. Bar noon-1 am. Ck-out noon. Meeting rms. Business servs avail. Valet serv. Sundries. Cr cds: A, C, D, DS, ER, JCB, MC, V.
🧖 🏊 🎿 🐾 SC

★★ **SPANISH VILLA.** *890 Lakeshore Dr W (V2A 1C1). 250/492-2922; toll-free 800/552-9199.* 60 rms, 1-2 story, 45 kits. Mid-June-Sept: S $58-$108; D $68-$118; each addl $20; suites, kit. units $80-$150; under 12 free; lower rates rest of yr. Crib $5. TV; cable.

Indoor pool. Playground. Ck-out 11 am. Coin lndry. Meeting rms. Business servs avail. In-rm modem link. Free airport transportation. Refrigerators. Private patios. Opp beach. Cr cds: A, C, D, DS, ER, JCB, MC, V.

D ⊷ ⊠ ⚲ **SC**

★ **TRAVELODGE.** *950 Westminster Ave (B2A 1L2). 250/492-0225; fax 250/493-8340; toll-free 800/578-7878. www.travelodge.com.* 34 rms, 3 story. Mid-May-mid-Sept: S, D $85-$105; each addl $8; kit. units $8 addl; under 17 free; lower rates rest of yr. TV; cable (premium). Sauna. 2 pools, heated; whirlpool. Restaurant 7 am-1:30 pm. Ck-out noon. Meeting rms. Refrigerators. Private patios, balconies. Picnic tables. Cr cds: A, C, D, ER, MC, V.

D ⚷ ⛄ ⊷ ✕ ⊠ ⚲

Hotel

★ ★ ★ **PENTICTON LAKESIDE RESORT AND CONFERENCE CEN- TER.** *21 Lakeshore Dr W (V2A 7M5). 250/493-8221; fax 250/493-0607; toll-free 800/663-9400. www.rpbhotels.com.* 204 rms, 6 story. July-Aug: S, D $175-$195; each addl $15; under 16 free; golf plans; lower rates rest of yr. Crib free. Pet accepted, some restrictions. TV; cable (premium). Indoor pool; whirlpool. Supervised children's activities (late May-Labor Day); ages 3-14. Restaurant 7 am-11 pm. Bar noon-2 am; seasonal entertainment. Meeting rms. Business servs avail. In rm modem link. Gift shop. Beauty shop. Golf privileges. Downhill/x-country ski 20 mi. Exercise rm; sauna. Balconies. On Okanagan Lake; swimming, boat rides. Cr cds: A, C, D, DS, ER, MC, V.

D ⚷ ⚷ ⛄ ⛷ ⊷ ⋀ ⊠ ⚲

Revelstoke (E-7)

Pop 5,544 **Elev** 1,499 ft (457 m)
Area code 250

Information Chamber of Commerce, 204 Campbell Ave, PO Box 490, V0E 2S0, phone 250/837-5345 or 800/487-1493; or visit the Travel Information Centre, Trans-Canada Hwy 1 and BC 23 N, 250/837-3522

Web www.revelstokecc.bc.ca

Located in the towering Monashee and Selkirk ranges of the Columbia Mountains between the scenic Rogers and Eagle passes, Revelstoke is the gateway to Mount Revelstoke National Park, with Glacier National Park just to the east. Visitors may enjoy many activities all year. Especially popular is the skiing; with an annual average of 40 feet (13 meters) of snow, Revelstoke offers multiple opportunities for downhill, cross-country, cat helicopter, ski touring adventures, and snowmobiling. Tennis, fishing, hiking, golfcaving, mountaineering, and swimming are also available throughout this exciting alpine city.

What to See and Do

Beardale Castle Miniatureland. Indoor attraction constructed in a European-style village setting. Hand-crafted authentic miniature exhibits incl prairie town, Swiss mountain village, and medieval German village, each with a model railway running through it. Also animated toyland exhibits. (May-Sept, daily) 26 mi (42 km) W via Trans-Canada Hwy 1 at Craigellachie. Phone 250/836-2268. ¢¢

Provincial Building and Court House. (1912) Provincial building contains the original oak staircase connecting the three floors and basement; courtrm same as when built; marble walls in foyer; pillars; lighted dome. Tour (Mon-Fri, by appt; closed hols). 1123 W 2nd St. Phone 250/837-7636. **FREE**

Three Valley Gap. Historic ghost town (guided tours; fee); lake. Lodging, restaurant. Cowboy show (Mon; fee). (Mid-Apr-mid-Oct, daily) 12 mi (19 km) W on Trans Canada Hwy 1. Phone 250/837-2109. ¢¢¢

Special Events

Revelstoke Sno Fest. Outhouse races, parade, casino, dances, entertainment, x-country skiing, downhill races, sno pitch, ice sculpture, snow golf tournaments. Jan. Phone 250/837-9351.

Revelstoke Mountain Arts Festival. Theatre, music, children's events. Third wkend Sept. Phone 250/837-5345.

Motels/Motor Lodges

★★ **BEST WESTERN WAYSIDE INN.** *1901 La Forme Blvd (V0E 2S0). 250/837-6161; fax 250/837-5460; toll-free 800/663-5307. www.bestwestern. com.* 88 rms, 2 story, 25 kits. S $89-$129; D $99-$139; each addl $6-$8; suites $190; under 12 free. Crib free. TV; cable (premium). Saunas. Indoor pool; whirlpool. Coffee in rms. Restaurant 6:30 am-9 pm. Bar. Ck-out noon. Meeting rms. Business servs avail. Downhill/x-country ski 5 mi. Some refrigerators. Cr cds: A, C, D, DS, ER, JCB, MC, V.

⬛ 🏊 🛒 🎿 🔥

★ **CANYON MOTOR INN.** *1911 Fraser Dr (V0E 2S0). 250/837-5221; fax 250/837-3160; toll-free 877/837-5221.* 40 rms, 1-2 story, 12 kits. May-Oct: S $44-$76; D $50-$100; each addl $7; kit. units $7 addl; lower rates rest of yr. Crib free. Pet accepted. TV; cable. Restaurant 6 am-9 pm. Ck-out 11 am. Coin lndry. Meeting rms. Sundries. Downhill/x-country ski 5 mi. Sauna. Whirlpool. Refrigerators. Private patios, balconies. Picnic tables. Cr cds: A, C, D, DS, ER, JCB, MC, V.

⬛ 🐾 🛎 🛒 🍳 ✈ 🎿 🔥

★ **SANDMAN INN.** *1891 Fraser Dr (V0E 2S0). 250/837-5271; fax 250/837-2032; toll-free 800/726-3626.* 83 rms, 2 story, 10 kits. S $94; D $94-$104; each addl $5; kit. units $10 addl; under 18 free. Crib free. TV; cable (premium). Sauna. Heated pool; whirlpool. Restaurant open 24 hrs. Bar 4 pm-1 am. Ck-out 11 am. Meeting rms. Business servs avail. Valet serv. Downhill/x-country ski 5 mi. Refrigerators. Balconies. Cr cds: A, C, D, DS, ER, JCB, MC, V.

🏊 🛒 🎿 🔥 **SC**

★★★ **THREE VALLEY LAKE CHATEAU.** *Trans-Canada Hwy #1 (V0E 2S0). 250/837-2109; fax 250/837-5220; toll-free 888/667-2109. www.3valley.com.* 200 rms, 2-6 story. No A/C. Mid-Apr-mid-Oct: S $85-$105; D $95-$120; each addl $4; suites $120-$230; family rates. Closed rest of yr. Crib free. TV. Heated pool; whirlpool. Restaurants 7 am-9 pm. Ck-out 11 am. Meeting rms. Sundries. Rec rm. Private patios, balconies. On lake. Cr cds: A, D, ER, MC, V.

⬛ 🛒 🎿 🔥

Restaurant

★ **FRONTIER.** *1 mi W on Trans-Can Hwy 1 and Hwy 23N (V0E 2S0). 250/837-5119.* Hrs: 5 am-10 pm. Continental, Canadian menu. Serv bar. Bkfst $1.75-$9.95, lunch $2.75-$9.95, dinner $4.25-$16.95. Child's meals. Specializes in steak, chicken. Salad bar (dinner). Rustic; view of mountains. Cr cds: D, DS, MC, V.

⬛

Vancouver

(F-4) *See also Nanaimo, Victoria*

Settled 1886 **Pop** 456,000 **Elev** 38 ft (12 m) **Area code** 604

Information Tourism Vancouver Info-Centre, 200 Burrard St, V6C 3L6; 604/683-2000

Web www.tourismvancouver.com

Surrounded by the blue waters of the Strait of Georgia and backed by the mile-high peaks of the Coast Range, Vancouver enjoys a natural setting surpassed by few other cities on this continent. The waters that wash the city's shores protect it from heat and cold, making it a pleasant place to visit all year.

Captain George Vancouver, searching these waters for the Northwest Passage, sailed into Burrard Inlet and landed here in 1792. Fur traders, gold prospectors, and other settlers soon followed. In 1886 Vancouver was incorporated as a city, only to be destroyed by fire several months later. The city was rebuilt by the end of that same year. In the next four years rail transportation from the east, along with the traffic of sailing vessels of the Canadian Pacific fleet, assured the future of its growth. Today Vancouver is one of Canada's largest cities—a major seaport, cultural center, tourist spot, and gateway to Asia.

Vancouver's population is primarily English, but its large number of ethnic groups—including Germans, French, Scandinavians, Dutch, Chinese, and Japanese—give the city an international flavor. Tourism, logging, mineral extraction equipment, marine supplies, chemical and petroleum products, and machine tools are among the city's major industries.

Vancouver is on the Canadian mainland, not on Vancouver Island as some people think. The downtown area, which includes many of the points of interest which follow, is a "peninsula on a peninsula:" it juts out from the rest of Vancouver into Burrard Inlet, making it an especially attractive spot with beaches and marinas within easy walking distance of the city's busy heart. To the north across Burrard Inlet is North Vancouver; to the south is the mouth of the Fraser River and the island municipality of Richmond; to the east is Burnaby, and beyond that, the Canadian mainland.

For Border Crossing Regulations see MAKING THE MOST OF YOUR TRIP.

Additional Visitor Information

There are many more interesting things to see and do in Vancouver and the suburbs of Burnaby and New Westminster to the east, Richmond to the south, North Vancouver, and West Vancouver. The Tourism Vancouver InfoCentre has pamphlets, maps, ferry schedules, and additional information at Plaza Level, Waterfront Centre, 200 Burrard St, V6C 3L6; phone 604/683-2000.

Vancouver Public Library

What to See and Do

Burnaby Village Museum. Living museum of the period before 1925, with costumed attendants; more than 30 full-scale buildings with displays and demonstrations. (Daily; closed Jan 5-May 4) 6501 Deer Lake Ave in Burnaby, 9 mi (15 km) E. ¢¢¢

Capilano Suspension Bridge and Park. Park flanks one mi (1.6 km) of the canyon through which the Capilano River flows. A 450-ft (137-m) gently swaying footbridge spans the canyon at a height of 230 ft (70 m). Park contains gardens, walking trail, trout ponds, living forest exhibit, totem poles, and large Trading Post. Guided tours; native wood carver on site; Story Centre; restaurants. (Daily; closed Dec 25) N on Capilano Rd in N Vancouver. Phone 604/985-7474. ¢¢¢¢

Chinatown. This downtown area is the nucleus of the third-largest Chinese community in North America (only San Francisco's and New York's are larger). At the heart lies the Chinese Market where 100-yr-old duck eggs may be purchased; herbalists promise cures with roots and powdered bones. The Dr. Sun Yat-Sen Classical Chinese Garden provides a beautiful centerpiece. Chinese shops display a variety of items ranging from cricket cages to cloisonné vases. Offices of three Chinese newspapers, and one of the world's narrowest buildings, are located within the community's borders. Resplendent Asian atmosphere offers fine examples of Chinese architecture, restaurants, and nightclubs. East Pender St between Gore and Carrall sts.

Dr. Sun-Yet-sen Classical Garden. Unique to the Western hemisphere, garden was originally built in China ca AD 1492; transplanted to Vancouver for Expo '86. (Daily) 578 Carrall St. Phone 604/689-7133. ¢¢¢

Exhibition Park. Approx 165 acres (70 hectares). Concert, convention, entertainment facilities.

Thoroughbred racing (late spring-early fall) and Playland Amusement Park (Apr-June, wkends; July-Oct, daily; also eves). Hastings St between Renfrew and Cassiar sts. Phone 604/253-2311.

Fort Langley National Historic Site. Restoration of Hudson's Bay Company post built in 1840 on the Fraser River; reconstructed palisade, bastion, and four buildings plus one original building. Demonstrations of fur trade activities and period crafts of 1858. (Mar-Oct, daily; Nov-Feb, hrs vary; closed Jan 1, Dec 25, 26) 35 mi (48 km) E off Trans-Canada Hwy 1 or BC 7. ¢¢

Gallery at Ceperley House. Monthly exhibitions of local, national, and international artists. Collection of contemporary Canadian works on paper. Housed in Ceperley Mansion, overlooking Deer Lake and the surrounding gardens. (Tues-Sun) 6344 Deer Lake Ave in Burnaby. Phone 604/291-9441. **Donation**

★ **Gastown.** The original heart of Vancouver, named for "Gassy Jack" Deighton, who opened a saloon here in 1867. Restored late 19th- and early 20th-century buildings now house antique shops, boutiques, art galleries, coffeehouses, restaurants, and nightclubs. Historic landmarks, cobblestone streets, and unique steam clock. Area bounded by Alexander, Columbia, Water, and Cordova Sts. Adj is

Harbour Centre-The Lookout. Glass elevators to 360° viewing deck 553 ft (167 m) above street level; multimedia presentation, historical displays, tour guides. (Daily; closed Dec 25) 555 W Hastings St. Phone 604/689-0421. Deck ¢¢¢

Gordon Southam Observatory. (Fri-Sat eves and hols, weather permitting) Phone 604/738-7827. **FREE**

Granville Island. Originally dredged for industrial purposes in 1913 from the False Creek Tidal Flats, now restored to retain flavor of boom-

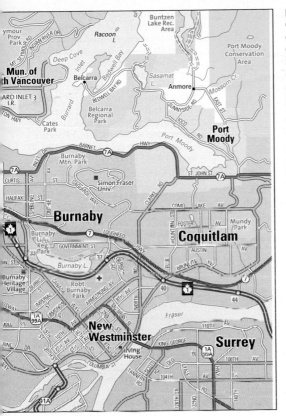

Maritime Museum. Changing maritime exhibits highlighting exploration, marine industries, model ships, and a harbor. Restored Arctic schooner *St. Roch*, first ship to navigate the Northwest Passage both ways; open to the public. (May-Sept daily; rest of yr, Tues-Sun; closed Dec 25) Foot of Cypress St. ¢¢

Old Hastings Mill. (ca 1865) One of few buildings remaining after fire of 1886; now houses indigenous artifacts, memorabilia of Vancouver's first settlers. (June-mid-Sept, daily; rest of yr, Sat and Sun afternoons) 1575 Alma Rd. Phone 604/734-1212. **FREE**

Pacific Space Centre. Visitors experience a journey through the night sky, backward or forward in time, or a search for other worlds. Shows are dramatic, informative, easy to understand. Shows (summer, daily; rest of yr, Tues-Sun). 1100 Chestnut St. Phone 604/738-4431. ¢¢¢

Professional sports.

Vancouver Canucks (NHL). General Motors Place, 800 Griffiths Way. Phone 604/899-GOAL.

Queen Elizabeth Park. Observation point affords view of city, harbor, and mountains; Bloedel Conservatory has more than 100 free-flying birds; tropical, desert, and seasonal displays. (Daily; closed Dec 25) Off Cambie St and W 33rd Ave ¢¢

***Samson V* Maritime Museum.** Last steam-powered paddlewheeler to operate on the Fraser River now functions as a floating museum. Displays focus on the various paddlewheelers and paddlewheeler captains that have worked the river, and on river-related activities. (Daily; May 1-June 30, Sat-Sun, hols;) Moored on the Fraser River at the Westminster Quay Market in New Westminster,

town industry. Public Market area houses many specialty shops. Electronic irrigation has helped Norway and red maples, which are cultivated here to adapt to the saline soil. Parks, supervised playground, craft studios, an art college, tennis, theaters. Harbor tours. (Daily) 37-acre (15-hectare) area in heart of city, beneath south end of Granville Bridge. Phone 604/666-5784.

Industrial tours. The Tourism Vancouver Travel InfoCentre has information on avail tours.

Irving House Historic Centre. (1864) Fourteen rms of period furniture 1864-90. Adj is **New Westminster Museum**, on back of property, which has displays on local history, household goods, May Day memorabilia. (May-mid-Sept, Tues-Sun; rest of yr, Sat and Sun; closed Jan 1, Dec 25, 26) 302 Royal Ave, in New Westminster, 12 mi (19 km) S via Hwy 1A. Phone 604/527-4640. **Donation**

12 mi (19 km) S via Hwy 1A. Phone 604/522-6891.

Sightseeing trips.

British Columbia Ferry Corp. Trips to Nanaimo (two hrs) or to Swartz Bay near Victoria (1½ hrs); both destinations are on Vancouver Island. Terminals at Horseshoe Bay, north of Vancouver via Trans-Canada Hwy 1 and Tsawwassen near US border, south of Vancouver via Hwy 99, 17. For current schedule and fare information contact BC Ferry Corporation, 1112 Fort St, Victoria V8V 4V2. ¢¢¢¢

Gray Line sightseeing tours. Contact 255 E 1st Ave, V5T 1A7. Phone 604/879-3363.

Grouse Mountain tramway. Phone 604/984-0661.

Harbour Cruises Ltd. Boat/train excursion (6½ hrs); also sunset dinner cruises; harbor tours, private charters. (May-Sept) Departures from northern foot of Denman St.

SeaBus Harbour Ride. Makes 15-min crossing on twin-hulled catamaran vessels every 15 min (30 min eves and Sun). Part of regional public transit system. Operates between Waterfront Station and Lonsdale Quay, across Burrard Inlet. Phone 604/953-3333. ¢¢

Simon Fraser University. (1965) 20,000 students. Located on Burnaby Mtn; architecturally outstanding buildings. Original campus was completed in only 18 months. Hrly guided tours (July-Aug, daily; free) 10 mi (16 km) E off BC 7A (Hastings St) in Burnaby. Phone 604/291-3111.

Ski areas.

Cypress Mountain Ski Area. Four double chairlifts, two quad; patrol, school, rentals; cafeteria. X-country trails; hiking trails. Snowshoe/winter hiking trail. Vertical drop 1,750 ft. (Dec-mid-Apr, daily) Provincial park offers spectacular views of Vancouver and the surrounding area and an accessible old-growth forest; scenic lookouts; picnic areas; hiking, self-guided interpretive trails. Park (all yr, daily). 7½ mi (12 km) NW via BC 99, in Cypress Provincial Park. Phone 604/926-5612. Ski area ¢¢¢¢

Grouse Mountain. All-yr recreational facility. Aerial tramway, high-speed quad, four double chairlifts, two T-bars, three rope tows; 13 runs; patrol, school, rentals; lounge, restaurants. (Dec-mid-Apr, daily) Night skiing. Skyride (all yr; fee). Playground, hiking trails. "Our Spirit Soars" multimedia presentation; logging shows; helicopter tours, chairlift rides, horse-drawn wagon rides. 8 mi (13 km) N at 6400 Nancy Greene Way (top of Capilano Rd) in North Vancouver. Phone 604/980-9311. ¢¢¢¢

Seymour Ski Country. Three double chairlifts, rope tow; night skiing; patrol, school, rentals; cafeteria. (Mid-Nov-Apr, daily) X-country and snowshoe trails (Dec-Mar, daily). Chairlift also operates July-Aug (Daily). Mt Seymour Provincial Park is a large semi-wilderness with scenic roadside viewpoints overlooking Vancouver; picnic areas; hiking, self-guided interpretive trails. Park (all yr, daily). 9 mi (15 km) NE off Mt Seymour Pkwy, in Mt Seymour Provincial Park. Phone 604/736-4431. ¢¢¢¢

Stanley Park. Approx 1,000 acres (405 hectares) of beautifully landscaped gardens, lakes, totem poles, trails; swimming pool and sand beaches; golf, tennis. Children's farmyard (fee), miniature train (daily; fee). Horse-drawn tours avail from AAA Horse and Carriage Ltd (May-mid-Oct; phone 604/681-5115). Northwest of downtown. Phone 604/257-8400.

Vancouver Aquarium. One of the largest in North America; more than 8,000 marine and freshwater animals from around the world in five major viewing areas; killer whales, Beluga whales; Amazon Rain Forest gallery; North Pacific and Tropical galleries. (Daily) Phone 604/268-9900. ¢¢¢

University of British Columbia. (1915) 34,869 students. The 990-acre (401-hectare) campus features museums, galleries (some fees), many spectacular gardens; almost 400 buildings complement the natural grandeur of the area. Free guided campus tours (May-Aug). Beautifully situated on scenic Point Grey. 8 mi

(13 km) SW via Burrard St, 4th Ave. Phone 604/822-2211. Inclflfl

Frederic Wood Theatre. Summer stock and winter main stage productions. Phone 604/822-2678.

Museum of Anthropology. World-renowned collection of artifacts from many cultures, with emphasis on art of first peoples of the Northwest Coast. **Great Hall** displays 30-ft totem poles and huge feast dishes; **Masterpiece Gallery** contains intricate works in gold, silver, wood, and stone; unique European ceramics collection; outdoor exhibit area has replicas of traditional Haida buildings. "Visible storage" concept allows 90 percent of the museum's collection to be viewed at all times. Changing exhibits; public programs. Guided tours (free exc if by appt). (July-Aug, daily; rest of yr, Tues-Sun; closed Dec 25, 26) Free admission Tues. 6393 NW Marine Dr. ¢¢

UBC Botanical Garden. Seven separate areas incl Asian, Physick, B.C. Native, Alpine, and Food gardens. (Daily; closed Jan 1, Dec 25) 6804 SW Marine Dr. Phone 604/822-9666. **Nitobe Garden**, authentic Japanese tea garden located behind Asian Centre (mid-Mar-early Oct, daily; rest of yr, Mon-Fri). Phone 604/822-6038. 6804 SW Marine Dr. ¢¢

Vancouver Art Gallery. Changing exhibits of contemporary and historical art, featuring masterworks of Emily Carr. Guided tours (by appt). Fine arts library. Restaurant, gift shop. (June-Sept, daily; rest of yr, Wed-Mon; closed Jan 1, Dec 25) 750 Hornby St. ¢¢

Vancouver Museum. One of Canada's largest civic museums. Decorative arts, Vancouver history, Northwest Coast indigenous culture, and touring exhibits. (Daily; closed Dec 25) 1100 Chestnut St, 1½ mi (2½ km) SW via Burrard, Cypress sts. Phone 604/736-4431. ¢¢

VanDusen Botanical Garden. Approx 55 acres (22 hectares) of flowers and exotic plants. Seasonal displays, mountain views, restaurant. (Daily; closed Dec 25) 5251 Oak St. Phone 604/878-9274. ¢¢

Whale watching tours. Whale-watching boats line both the Wharf St waterfront and Inner Harbour. Half-day tours display marine life, incl orcas, sea lions, seals, and porpoises. Victoria Marine Adventures (phone 250/995-2211) and Prince of Whales (phone 250/383-4884) are two of the finer tour companies.

Special Events

Christmas events. Christmas Carol Ship and lighted ship parade; New Year's Day Polar Bear swim.

Hyack Festival. 12 mi (19 km) S via Hwy 1A in New Westminster. Commemorates birthday of Queen Victoria, held yearly since 1871; 21-gun salute; band concerts, parade, carnival, sports events. Phone 604/522-6894. Ten days mid-May.

International Bathtub Race. Thirty-four-mi (55-km) race from Nanaimo to Vancouver. Phone 800/663-7337. Third or fourth Sun July.

Symphony of Fire. English Bay Beach. Intl fireworks comeptition accompanied with music. July. Phone 604/683-2000.

Pacific National Exhibition Annual Fair. Exhibition Park. Second-largest fair in Canada. Hundreds of free exhibits, major theme event, concerts, thrill shows, world championship timber show; petting zoo, thoroughbred horse racing, commercial exhibits, roller coaster, agricultural shows, horse shows, livestock competitions, horticultural exhibits. Phone 604/253-2311. Usually mid-Aug-early Sept.

Queen Elizabeth Theatre and Playhouse and Orpheum Theatre. A symphony orchestra, opera company, and many theater groups present productions around town, especially at the Queen Elizabeth Theatre and Playhouse and Orpheum Theatre. Consult local paper for details. Phone 604/683-2000.

Motels/Motor Lodges

★★ **ACCENT INNS.** *10551 St Edward Dr, Richmond (V6X 3L8). 604/273-3311; fax 604/273-9522; toll-free 800/663-0298. www.accentinns. com.* 206 rms, 3 story. Mid-May-Sept: S $89-$124; D $99-$134; each addl $10; suites $120-$130; kits. $10 addl; under 16 free; lower rates rest of yr.

Crib free. Pet accepted. TV; cable, VCR avail (movies free). Complimentary coffee in rms. Restaurant 6:30 am-11 pm. Ck-out 11 am. Coin lndry. Meeting rms. Business servs avail. Valet serv. Free airport transportation. Exercise equipt. Whirlpool. Cr cds: A, D, ER, JCB, MC, V.

[D] [icons] [SC]

★★ **BEST WESTERN ABERCORN INN.** *9260 Bridgeport Rd, Richmond (V6X 1S1). 604/270-7576; fax 604/270-0001; toll-free 800/663-0085. www.abercorn-inn.com.* 98 rms, 3 story. June-Sept: S $99-$129; D $109-$139; each addl $15; under 17 free; higher rates special events; lower rates rest of yr. Crib free. TV; cable. Complimentary coffee in rms. Restaurant 6:30 am-10 pm. Bar 11-1 am. Ck-out noon. Meeting rms. Business servs avail. In-rm modem link. Concierge. Free airport transportation. Health club privileges. Minibars. Cr cds: A, D, DS, ER, JCB, MC, V.

[D] [icons] [SC]

★★ **BEST WESTERN CHATEAU GRANVILLE.** *1100 Granville St (V6Z 2B6). 604/669-7070; fax 604/669-4928; toll-free 800/663-0575. www.bestwestern.com.* 148 rms, 15 story, 90 suites. May-Oct: S, D $133-$180; each addl $20; under 16 free; wkend rates; lower rates rest of yr. Crib free. Covered parking $7. TV; cable (premium). Restaurant 7 am-10 pm. Bar noon-1 am. Ck-out 11 am. Meeting rms. Business servs avail. Refrigerators. Private patios, balconies. Cr cds: A, C, D, DS, ER, JCB, MC, V.

[D] [icons]

★★ **BEST WESTERN EXHIBITION PARK.** *3475 E Hastings St (V5K 2A5). 604/294-4751; fax 604/294-1269; toll-free 877/296-4751. www.bestwestern.com.* 58 rms, 3 story, 22 suites. June-Sept: S, D $99-$185; each addl $10; suites $180-$220; under 12 free; higher rates some special events; lower rates rest of yr. TV, VCR avail (movies). Complimentary continental bkfst. Complimentary coffee. Restaurant adj 6:30 am-11 pm. Ck-out noon. Business servs avail. In-rm modem link. Coin lndry. Sundries. Free parking. Sauna. Whirlpool. Refrigerators. Cr cds: A, C, D, DS, ER, MC, V.

[D] [icons] [SC]

★★ **BEST WESTERN KINGS INN.** *5411 Kingsway, Burnaby (V5H 2G1). 604/438-1383; fax 604/438-2954; toll-free 800/211-1122. www.bestwestern.com.* 137 rms, 2 story. May-Sept: S, D $129; each addl $10; suites, kit. units $130-$135; under 12 free; lower rates rest of yr. Crib free. TV; cable. Pool.

DISCOVERING DOWNTOWN VANCOUVER

Vancouver is one of the most cosmopolitan cities in the world, and part of its considerable charm is the wonderful mix of people from all around the globe. Downtown Vancouver remains very dynamic, and a wander through the people-thronged streets is a great way to catch the energy of this city. Start at the Vancouver Art Gallery, which is the old City Hall. Walk up Robson Street, the city's primary boutique street, lined with all sorts of tiny shops, cafes, galleries, and food markets: this is a very busy place, and you'll hear dozens of languages in the bustle of the crowds. Grab a table at a coffee shop, and watch the world—literally—go by. Continue to Denman Street, and turn south (left). Denman is another busy commercial street, but less international. Here you'll find remnants of aging hippie Vancouver—bookstores, veggie restaurants, and little corner markets—rubbing shoulders with upscale twenty-something cocktail bars and tattoo parlors for middle-class teenagers. Denman terminates at English Beach, where you can relax on the sand and enjoy the views of Vancouver's West Side across English Bay. Follow the seawall west (right) and, after a couple of blocks, enter Stanley Park, Vancouver's fantastic 1,000-acre park filled with old-growth forests, winding paths, and a number of tourist destinations. Of these, Vancouver Aquarium, reached by a forest path from the southern part of the park, is a must-see. One of the best in North America, it features performing orcas and porpoises, as well as ecosystem tanks from waters around the world. Nearby is Vancouver's small zoo, mostly of interest to children; stop and watch the sea otters play.

Complimentary coffee in rms. Restaurant 7 am-9 pm. Bar 11 am-midnight. Ck-out noon. Coin lndry. Meeting rms. Business servs avail. Sundries. Health club privileges. Game rm. Cr cds: A, C, D, DS, ER, JCB, MC, V.

⬛ 🏊 📶 🔥

★★ **BEST WESTERN SANDS.** *1755 Davie St (Z6G 1W5). 604/682-1831; fax 604/682-3546; toll-free 800/663-9400. rpbhotels.com.* 121 rms, 5 story. May-Oct: S, D $149-$239; each addl $15; suites $219-$305; under 12 free; lower rates rest of yr. Crib free. TV; cable. Restaurant 7-11 am. Rm serv 8 am-9 pm. Bars noon-2 am. Ck-out noon. Meeting rms. Business servs avail. In-rm modem link. Bellhops. Valet serv. Exercise equipt; sauna. Balconies. Cr cds: A, C, D, DS, ER, MC, V.

⬛ 🏋 ✈ 📶 🔥 SC

★★ **BILTMORE HOTEL.** *395 Kingsway (V5T 3J7). 604/872-5252, fax 604/874-3003; toll-free 800/663-5713.* 100 rms, 7 story. Apr-Oct: S, D $79-$110; each addl $8; under 12 free; lower rates rest of yr. Crib free. TV; cable. Pool. Coffee in rms. Restaurant 6:30 am-8 pm; Sat from 7 am; Sun 8 am-2 pm. Bar noon-2 am. Ck-out 11 am. Meeting rms. Business servs avail. Cr cds: A, D, ER, MC, V.

⬛ 🏊 📶 🔥

★★ **DELTA TOWN AND COUNTRY.** *6005 Hwy 17, Delta (V4K 5B8). 604/946-4404; fax 604/946-5916; toll-free 888/777-1266. www.deltainn.com.* 48 rms, 2 story. May-late Oct: S, D $99; each addl $15; suites $160; under 16 free; lower rates rest of yr. Crib free. TV. Pool. Complimentary coffee in rms. Restaurant 6 am-10 pm. Ck-out 11 am. Meeting rms. Business servs avail. In-rm modem link. Gift shop. Lighted tennis. Lawn games. Exercise equipt. Cr cds: A, D, ER, MC, V.

🛏 🏋 🎿 🏊 🏋 📶 🔥 SC

★★ **EXECUTIVE AIRPORT PLAZA HOTEL.** *7311 Westminster Hwy, Richmond (V6X 1A3). 604/278-5555; fax 604/278-0255; toll-free 800/663-2878. executiveinnhotels.com.* 153 units, 3 story, 30 kit. units. May-Sept: S $99-$129; D $99-$149; each addl $10; suites $139-$209; under 13 free; lower rates rest of yr. Crib free. TV; cable (premium), VCR avail. Indoor pool. Coffee in rms. Restaurant 5:30 am-10 pm. Bar 5 pm-midnight. Ck-out noon. Meeting rms. Business center. In-rm modem link. Bellhops. Gift shop. Free airport transportation. Health club privileges. Many refrigerators; some in-rm whirlpools. Cr cds: A, D, ER, MC, V.

⬛ 🏊 ✈ 📶 🔥 SC 🏃

★★ **HAMPTON INN.** *8811 Bridgeport Rd, Richmond (V6X 1R9). 604/232-5505; fax 604/232-5508. www.hamptoninn-vancover.com.* 111 rms, 5 story. May-Sept: S, D $120-$140; each addl $10; suites $270; under 17 free; lower rates rest of yr. Crib avail. Parking lot. TV; cable (premium), VCR avail. Complimentary continental bkfst, coffee in rms, newspaper, toll-free calls. Restaurant nearby. Ck-out noon, ck-in 3 pm. Meeting rm. Business center. Bellhops. Dry cleaning. Free airport transportation. Exercise equipt. Golf. Hiking trail. Video games. Cr cds: A, C, D, DS, ER, MC, V.

⬛ 🛎 🏌 🏋 ✈ 🏊 🔥 🏃

★ **HOWARD JOHNSON EXPRESS INN & SUITES.** *13245 King George Hwy, Surrey (V3T 2T3). 604/588-0181; fax 604/588-0180; res 877/588-0181. www.hojo.com.* 54 rms, 2 story. May-Sept: S $60-$70; D $65-$75; each addl $6; suites $95; under 18 free; lower rates rest of yr. Crib avail. TV; cable (premium). Complimentary coffee in rms. Ck-out 11 am. Coin lndry. Cr cds: A, C, D, DS, ER, MC, V.

⬛ 📶 🔥

★ **QUALITY HOTEL - DOWNTOWN.** *1335 Howe St (V6Z 1R7). 604/682-0229; fax 604/662-7566; toll-free 800/663-8474. www.qualityhotel vancouver.com.* 157 rms, 7 story, 25 suites. May-Sept: S $79-$139; D $89-$139; each addl $20; suites $199-$229; under 18 free; lower rates rest of yr. Crib free. Pet accepted. Garage $6. TV; cable. Pool. Coffee in rms. Restaurant 7 am-10 pm. Bar 11:30-1 am. Ck-out 11 am. Meeting rms. Business servs avail. Bellhops. Valet serv. Some refrigerators. Cr cds: A, C, D, DS, ER, JCB, MC, V.

⬛ 🐾 🏊 📶 🔥 SC

Hotels

★★ **BLUE HORIZON.** *1225 Robson St (V6E 1C3). 604/688-1411; fax 604/688-4461; toll-free 800/663-1333. www.bluehorizonhotel.com.* 214 rms, 31 story. May-Oct: S $99-$199, D $109-$199; each addl $15; suites $175-$300; under 17 free; lower rates rest of yr. Crib free. Covered parking $9. TV; cable (premium). Indoor pool; whirlpool. Coffee in rms. Restaurant 6:30 am-10 pm. No rm serv. Bar noon-2 am. Ck-out 11 am. Meeting rms. Business servs avail. In-rm modem link. Exercise equipt; sauna. Refrigerators, minibars. Balconies. Cr cds: A, D, ER, MC, V.
[D] [≈] [↑] [≡] [♨]

★★★ **COAST PLAZA SUITE HOTEL.** *1763 Comox St (V6G 1P6). 604/688-7711; fax 604/688-5934; toll-free 800/663-1144. www.coasthotels. com.* 269 rms, 35 story, 190 kits. Some A/C. May-Oct: S $245-$315; D $285-$355; each addl $20; suites $295-$425; under 18 free; package plans. Crib free. TV; cable (premium), VCR avail. Indoor pool. Restaurants 6:30 am-10 pm. Rm serv 24 hrs. Bar 11:30-2 am. Ck-out noon. Coin lndry. Meeting rms. Business servs avail. In-rm modem link. Concierge. Shopping arcade. Valet parking. Free downtown transportation. Exercise rm; sauna. Refrigerators, minibars. Balconies. Luxury level. Cr cds: A, D, DS, ER, JCB, MC, V.
[D] [≈] [↑] [≡] [♨] [SC]

★★ **CROWNE PLAZA HOTEL GEORGIA VANCOUVER.** *801 W Georgia St (V6C 1P7). 604/682-5566; fax 604/642-5579; toll-free 800/663-1111. www.hotelgeorgia.bc.ca.* 313 rms, 12 story. May-Oct: S, D $229-$329; each addl $20; suites $400; under 16 free; lower rates rest of yr. Crib free. Garage $12. TV; cable (premium). Coffee in rms. Restaurant 6:30 am-10 pm. Bars 11:30-1:30 am; entertainment. Ck-out noon. Meeting rms. Business center. Shopping mall adj. Exercise equipt. Health club privileges. Cr cds: A, D, DS, ER, JCB, MC, V.
[D] [↑] [≡] [♨] [⚡]

★★ **DELTA VANCOUVER AIRPORT HOTEL AND MARINA.** *3500 Cessna Dr, Richmond (V7B 1C7). 604/278-* 1241; fax 604/276-1975; toll-free 800/268-1133. www.deltahotels.com. 415 rms, 11 story. May-Sept: S, D $300; each addl $20; suites $395-$495; under 18 free; lower rates rest of yr. Crib free. TV; cable, VCR avail. Heated pool; poolside serv in season. Restaurant 6 am-10:30 pm. Bars 11-1 am. Ck-out 1 pm. Business center. In-rm modem link. Concierge. Gift shop. Airport transportation. Exercise equipt. Health club privileges. On Fraser River; marina. Cr cds: A, D, DS, ER, JCB, MC, V.
[D] [≈] [↑] [✈] [≡] [♨] [SC] [⚡]

★★ **EMPIRE LANDMARK HOTEL & CONFERENCE CENTRE.** *1400 Robson St (V6G 1B9). 604/687-0511; fax 604/687-2801; toll-free 800/830-6144. www.asiastandard.com.* 358 rms, 42 story. May-Oct: S $100-$180; D $120-$200; each addl $20; suites $350-$450; under 18 free. Crib free. TV; cable (premium). Restaurant (see also CLOUD 9). Rm serv 6 am-11 pm. Bar. Ck-out noon. Meeting rms. Business center. In-rm modem link. Exercise equipt; sauna. Whirlpool. Some refrigerators. Balconies. Beach 4 blks. Cr cds: A, D, DS, ER, JCB, MC, V.
[D] [↑] [≡] [♨] [⚡]

★★★ **ENGLISH BAY INN.** *1968 Comox St (V6G 1R4). 604/683-8002. www.englishbayinn.com.* 7 rms. S,D $117-$220. Complimentary full bkfst Cr cds: A, D, DS, ER, JCB, MC, V.
[≡] [♨]

★★ **EXECUTIVE INN HOTEL AND CONFERENCE CENTER.** *4201 Lougheed Hwy, Burnaby (V5C 3Y6). 604/298-2010; fax 604/298-1123; toll-free 800/590-3932. www.executiveinn hotels.com.* 125 suites, 4 story. May-Sept: S, D $115-$160; each addl $10; under 12 free; wknd rates; lower rates rest of yr. Crib free. TV; cable (premium), VCR avail. Pool; whirlpool. Complimentary coffee in rms. Restaurant 6:30 am-10 pm. Bar 11 am-11 pm. Ck-out noon. Meeting rms. Business center. In-rm modem link. Health club privileges. Exercise equipt. Refrigerators. Balconies. Cr cds: A, D, MC, V.
[D] [≈] [↑] [≡] [♨] [⚡]

★★★ THE FAIRMONT HOTEL VANCOUVER. *900 W Georgia St (V6C 2W6). 604/684-3131; fax 604/662-1929; toll-free 800/441-1414. www.fairmont.com.* 550 rms, 14 story. Late Apr-early Oct: S $180-$340; D $205-$365; each addl $25; suites $305-$1,830; family, wkend rates; lower rates rest of yr. Pet accepted. TV; cable (premium), VCR avail. Indoor pool; wading pool, whirlpool. Restaurant 6 am-10 pm. Rm serv 24 hrs. Bars 11-1 am; entertainment. Ck-out noon. Meeting rms. Business center. In-rm modem link. Concierge. Shopping arcade. Beauty salon. Exercise rm; sauna. Refrigerator in suites. Luxury level. Cr cds: A, D, DS, ER, JCB, MC, V.

★★★ THE FAIRMONT VANCOUVER AIRPORT. *3111 Grant McConachie Way (V7B 1X9). 604/207-5200; fax 604/248-3219; toll-free 800/676-8922. www.fairmont.com.* Not the stereotypical airport hotel, this elegant property has 392 technology-friendly and very comfortable guest rooms for busy international travelers. Rooms include complimentary high-speed Internet access and portable phones. Floor-to-ceiling soundproof windows offer great views of the mountains and Georgia Straits. This elegant full-service hotel offers a fully-equipped exercise room, spa, dining room and lounge, and full concierge service. 392 rms, 14 story, 2 suites. May-Oct: S, D $189-$299; each addl $20; suites $600, under 17 free; lower rates rest of yr. Crib avail. Pet accepted, fee. Valet parking avail. Indoor pool, whirlpool. TV; cable (premium), VCR avail, CD avail. Complimentary coffee in rms, newspaper. Restaurant 6:30 am-11 pm. Rm serv 24 hrs. Bar. Ck-out noon, ck-in 3 pm. Conference center, meeting rms. Business center. Bellhops. Concierge. Dry cleaning. Gift shop. Salon/barber. Exercise rm, sauna. Bike rentals. Video games. Cr cds: A, D, DS, ER, JCB, MC, V.

★★★ THE FAIRMONT WATERFRONT. *900 Canada Pl Way (V6C 3L5). 604/691-1991; fax 604/691-1838; toll-free 800/527-4727. www.fairmont.com.* 489 rms, 25 story. S, D $225-$375; each addl $20; under 17 free. Crib avail. Heated pool. TV; cable (premium), VCR avail. Complimentary coffee, newspaper in rms. Restaurant 6 am-10 pm. Ck-out noon. Meeting rms. Business center. Gift shop. Exercise rm. Some refrigerators, minibars. Cr cds: A, C, D, DS, MC, V.

★★★★ FOUR SEASONS HOTEL VANCOUVER. *791 W Georgia St (V6C 2T4). 604/689-9333; fax 604/689-3466; toll-free 800/819-5053. www.fourseasons.com.* Located amidst the fine shops of the Pacific Centre, within walking distance of the convention centre, theatres, and other sports and entertainment facilities, this elegant hotel is noted for impeccable service and a renewed commitment to guest satisfaction. Relax with nightly entertainment in the Garden Terrace, lounge at the pool, or dine in the nationally recognized Chartwell. The 21,333 square feet of meeting space and complimentary downtown transportation are great amenities for business guests. 385 rms, 28 story. May-Oct: S, D $315-$465; each addl $30; suites $450-$2,500; under 18 free; wkend rates; lower rates rest of yr. Crib free. Pet accepted. Garage $21/day. TV; cable (premium), VCR (movies). Heated pool; whirlpool. Restaurant 6:30 am-11 pm (see also CHARTWELL). Rm serv 24 hrs. Bar 11:30-1 am. Ck-out noon. Meeting rms. Business center. In-rm modem link. Concierge. Shopping arcade. Tennis privileges. Downhill ski 10 mi. Exercise rm; sauna. Shuffleboard. Minibars. Cr cds: A, C, D, DS, ER, JCB, MC, V.

★★ GEORGIAN COURT HOTEL. *773 Beatty St (V6B 2M4). 604/682-5555; fax 604/682-8830; toll-free 800/663-1155. www.georgiancourt.com.* 180 rms, 12 story. May-Oct: S $115-$190; D $135-$210; each addl $20; suites $210-$450; under 18 free; lower rates rest of yr. Crib free. Pet accepted, some restrictions. Parking $8. TV; cable (premium). Coffee in rms. Restaurant (see also WILLIAM

TELL). Bar. Ck-out 1 pm. Meeting rms. Business servs avail. In-rm modem link. Concierge. Gift shop. Exercise equipt; sauna. Whirlpool. Bathrm phones, minibars. Italian marble in bathrms. Cr cds: A, D, ER, JCB, MC, V.

Gassy Jack Statue, Gastown

★★★ **HILTON VANCOUVER AIR-PORT.** *5911 Minoru Blvd (V6X 4C7). 604/273-6336; toll-free 800/445-8667.* 237 rms, 10 story. S, D $175-$275; each addl $20; under 17 free. Crib avail. Heated pool. TV; cable (premium). Complimentary coffee, newspaper in rms. Restaurant 6 am-10 pm. Ck-out noon. Meeting rms. Business center. Gift shop. Exercise rm. Cr cds: A, C, D, DS, MC, V.

★★★ **HILTON VANCOUVER METROTOWN.** *6083 McKay Ave (V5H 2W7). 604/438-1200; toll-free 800/445-8667. www.hilton.com.* 750 rms, 32 story. S, D $195-$325; under 17 free. Crib avail. TV; cable (premium). Indoor pool; whirlpool. Restaurant 6:30 am-10 pm. Bar to midnight. Ck-out noon, ck-in 4 pm. Meeting rms. Business center. In-rm modem link. Concierge. Exercise equipt. Minibars; many refrigerators in suites. Cr cds: A, C, D, DS, MC, V.

★★ **HOLIDAY INN.** *711 W Broadway (V5Z 3Y2). 604/879-0511; fax 604/872-7520; toll-free 800/465-4329. holidayinnvancouver.com.* 196 rms, 16 story. May-Oct: S $169-$189; D $179-$209; each addl $20; suites $275-$325; under 18 free; wkend rates; lower rates rest of yr. Crib free. Pet accepted, some restrictions. TV; cable. Indoor pool. Coffee in rms. Restaurant 7 am-10 pm. Bar 11-1 am. Ck-out noon. Meeting rms. Business servs avail. In-rm modem link. Gift shop. Exercise rm; sauna. Refrigerator in suites. Balconies. Cr cds: A, D, DS, ER, JCB, MC, V.

★★ **HOLIDAY INN HOTEL & SUITES DOWNTOWN.** *1110 Howe S (V6Z 1R2). 604/684-2151; fax 604/684-4736; res 800/465-4329. www.atlific.com.* 245 rms, 7 story. May-Oct: S, D $189; each addl $10; suites $199-$299; under 18 free; lower rates rest of yr. Crib free. Valet parking $8.95. TV; cable (premium). Indoor pool. Complimentary coffee. Restaurant 6:30 am-10 pm. Rm serv 24 hrs. Bars 11-2 am. Ck-out noon. Meeting rms. Business center. Concierge. Gift shop. Game rm. Exercise equipt; sauna. Health club privileges. Some refrigerators. Balconies. Cr cds: A, C, D, DS, ER, JCB, MC, V.

★★ **HOLIDAY INN VANCOUVER AIRPORT.** *10720 Cambie Rd, Richmond (V6X 1K8). 604/821-1818; fax 604/821-1819; toll-free 888/831-3388. www.hi-airport.bc.ca.* 162 rms, 6 story, 1 suite. May-Sept: S, D $139; each addl $10; suite $279; under 18 free; lower rates rest of yr. Crib avail. Parking garage. TV; cable (DSS), VCR avail, CD avail. Complimentary coffee in rms, toll-free calls. Restaurant 6:30 am-midnight. Bar. Ck-out noon. Meeting rms. Business center. Bell-hops. Concierge. Dry cleaning. Free airport transportation. Exercise equipt, whirlpool. Golf. Supervised children's activities. Video games. Cr cds: A, D, DS, ER, JCB, MC, V.

[icons]

★★★ **HYATT REGENCY VANCOU-VER.** *655 Burrard St (V6C 2R7). 604/683-1234; fax 604/689-3707. www.vancouver.hyatt.com.* 645 rms, 34 story. Apr-Oct: S, D $139-$269; each addl $35; suites $795-$1,295; under 18 free; wkend rates; lower rates rest of yr. Crib free. Garage parking $18.50. TV; cable, VCR. Heated pool. Restaurant 6:30 am-10 pm. Bars 11-1 am. Ck-out noon. Convention facilities. Business center. In-rm modem link. Concierge. Shopping arcade. Exercise equipt; sauna. Health club privileges. Some bathrm phones. Some balconies. Luxury level. Cr cds: A, C, D, DS, ER, JCB, MC, V.

[icons]

★★★ **MARRIOTT VANCOUVER AIRPORT.** *7571 Westminster Hwy (V6X 1A3). 604/276-2112; 800/228-9290. www.marriott.com.* 237 rms, 18 story. S, D $159-$189; each addl $20; under 17 free. Crib avail. Pool. TV; cable (premium). Complimentary coffee, newspaper in rms. Restaurant 6 am-10 pm. Ck-out noon. Meeting rms. Business center. Exercise rm. Cr cds: A, C, D, DS, MC, V.

[icons]

★★★★ **THE METROPOLITAN HOTEL.** *645 Howe St (V6C 2Y9). 604/687-1122; fax 604/602-7846; toll-free 800/667-2300. www.metropolitan. com.* Located in the heart of Vancouver's financial, shopping, and entertainment district, this property surrounds guests with classic Asian art collectibles, as the hotel was constructed according to the art of Feng Shui. The golden Chinese Temple Carving located in the lobby is a specially commissioned gilt Chinese temple screen placed there by the Feng Shui Master to bring prosperity to the hotel. 197 units, 18 story. May-Oct: S $235-$280; D $265-$310; each addl $20; suites $509-$2,000; under 18 free; wkend rates. Crib free. Pet accepted. Covered parking $16. TV; cable (premium), VCR avail. Indoor pool; whirlpool, poolside serv. Complimentary coffee, tea in rms. Restaurant 6:30 am-11 pm. Rm serv 24 hrs. Bar 11:30-1 am. Ck-out 1 pm. Convention facilities. Business center. In-rm modem link. Concierge. Exercise rm; sauna, steam rm. Bathrm phones, refrigerators. Private patios, balconies. Library. Artwork, antiques; elaborate floral arrangements. Elegant Asian touches. Cr cds: A, D, ER, JCB, MC, V.

[icons]

★★ **PACIFIC PALISADES.** *1277 Robson St (V6E 1C4). 604/688-0461; fax 604/688-4374; toll-free 800/663-1815. www.pacificpalisadeshotel.com.* 233 suites, 20-23 story. May-Oct: S, D $225-$390; each addl $30; suites $250-$800; under 16 free; lower rates rest of yr. Crib free. Parking $22. TV; cable, VCR avail. Indoor pool; whirlpool. Restaurant 7 am-10 pm. Rm serv 24 hrs. Bar 11:30-1 am; entertainment Thurs-Sat. Ck-out noon. Meeting rms. Business center. In-rm modem link. Concierge. Garage parking. Exercise rm; sauna. Some balconies. Cr cds: A, D, DS, JCB, MC, V.

[icons]

★★★ **THE PAN PACIFIC VANCOUVER.** *300-999 Canada Pl (V6C 3B5). 604/662-8111; fax 604/685-8690; toll-free 800/937-1515. www. panpacific.com.* This downtown waterfront property shares a complex with the World Trade Centre and Convention Centre. All 504 rooms and suites have a clean, Asian-influenced design and large windows with harbour, mountain, or city views. All rooms are equipped with a computer and high-speed Internet access. The soaring atrium lobby contains the lounge, the all-day restaurant and, on the second level, the award-winning Five Sails dining room. Stunning architecture and elegant Asian-influenced interiors make this a popular meeting spot for both locals and visitors alike. 506 rms, 23 story. Mid-Apr-late Oct: S, D, studios $385-$515; each addl $30; suites $525-$2,000; under 18 free; wkend rates; lower rates rest of yr. Crib free. Pet accepted. Garage $20; valet. TV; cable, VCR avail. Heated pool; whirlpool. Restaurant 6:30 am-11 pm (see also FIVE SAILS). Rm serv 24 hrs. Bar 11:30-1 am. Ck-out 1 pm. Convention facilities. Business center. In-rm modem link. Concierge. Shopping arcade. Barber, beauty shop. Exercise rm; sauna, steam rm. Massage. Bathrm phones, refrigerators; some in-rm steam baths. Cr cds: A, D, ER, JCB, MC, V.

D ◐ ▱ 🕇 ◲ ▥ 🕇

★★ **RADISSON HOTEL BURNABY.** *4331 Dominion St, Burnaby (V5G 1C7). 604/430-2828; fax 604/430-9230; toll-free 800/667-6116. www. radisson.com.* 275 rms, 21 story. S $131; D $141; each addl $10; suites $175-$1,000; under 18 free. Crib free. TV; cable. 2 pools, 1 indoor; poolside serv. Restaurant 6:30 am-10 pm. Bar 11-1 am. Ck-out noon. Meeting rms. Business center. In-rm modem link. Gift shop. Barber. Free covered parking. Exercise equipt. Refrigerators. Balconies. Cr cds: A, C, D, ER, MC, V.

D ▱ 🕇 ▥ ▥ SC 🕇

★★★ **RADISSON PRESIDENT HOTEL AND SUITES.** *8181 Cambie Rd, Richmond (V6X 3X9). 604/276-8181; fax 604/279-8381; toll-free 800/333-3333. www.radisson.com.* 184 rms, 11 story. S, D $205; each addl $15; suites $165-$370; under 18 free. Crib free. TV; cable (premium), VCR avail. Indoor pool. Complimentary coffee in rms. Restaurant 6:30 am-2 pm, 5-10 pm. Rm serv 24 hrs. Bar to midnight. Ck-out 1 pm. Meeting rms. Business servs avail. In-rm modem link. Barber, beauty shop. Free airport transportation. Exercise equipt. Refrigerators. Cr cds: A, D, DS, JCB, MC, V.

D ▱ ✈ ▥ ▥ 🕇

★★★ **RENAISSANCE VANCOUVER HOTEL HARBOURSIDE.** *1133 W Hastings (V6E 3T3). 604/689-9211; fax 604/689-4358. www.renaissance vancouver.com.* This hotel is located on the waterfront overlooking Vancouver Harbor, Burrard Inlet, and the North Shore Mountains and is easy walking distance to the Robson Street and the Pacific Center shopping area. 489 rms, 19 story. May-Oct: S, D $160-$215; each addl $25; suites $260-$320; under 18 free; lower rates rest of yr. Crib free. Pet accepted. Covered parking $15. TV; cable (premium). Indoor pool. Restaurant 6:30 am-11 pm. 2 bars; entertainment Mon-Sat. Ck-out

noon. Convention facilities. Business servs avail. In-rm modem link. Exercise equipt; sauna. Minibars; refrigerators. Balconies. Cr cds: A, C, D, DS, ER, JCB, MC, V.

D ◐ ✦ ⬚ ▱ 🕇 ▥ ▥

★★★ **SHERATON GUILFORD HOTEL.** *15269 104th Ave (V3R 1N5). 604/582-9288. www.sheratonguilford. com.* 278 rms, 18 story. S, D $125-$275; each addl $20; under 17 free. Crib avail. TV; cable (premium), VCR avail. Complimentary coffee, newspaper in rms. Restaurant 6 am-10 pm. Ck-out noon. Meeting rms. Business center. Gift shop. Exercise rm. Some refrigerators. Cr cds: A, C, D, MC, V.

🕇 🕇 ▥

★★★ **SHERATON SUITES LE SOLEIL.** *567 Hornby St (V6C 2E8). 604/632-3000; fax 604/632-3001; toll-free 877/632-3030. www.lesoleilhotel. com.* In the heart of the city's financial and business districts sits this charming 122-suite boutique hotel. The stunning lobby boasts 30-foot gilded ceilings, crystal chandeliers, and a Louis XVI-style collection of imported Italian furniture. Complimentary bottled water and fruit upon arrival are welcome surprises, and the property's restaurant, a cool hot spot, offers an eclectic Asian-Mediterranean cuisine. 122 suites. Mid-Oct-Apr: S $165; suites $600. May-mid-Oct: S $200; suites $1,000. Cribs. TV. Restaurant. Rm serv 24 hrs. Valet. Concierge. Business center. Cr cds: A, D, ER, MC, V.

D ▥ ▥ 🕇

★★★ **SHERATON VANCOUVER WALL CENTRE.** *1088 Burrard St (V6Z 2R9). 604/331-1000; toll-free 800/325-3535. www.sheraton.com.* 736 rms, 25 story. S, D $275-$475; each addl $20; under 17 free. Crib avail. Indoor pool. TV; cable (premium), VCR avail. Complimentary coffee, newspaper in rms. Restaurant 6 am-10 pm. Ck-out noon. Meeting rms. Business center. Gift shop. Exercise rm. Spa. Some refrigerators, minibars. Cr cds: A, C, D, DS, MC, V.

▱ 🕇 🕇 ▥

★★★★ **THE SUTTON PLACE HOTEL.** *845 Burrard St (V6Z 2K6).*

604/682-5511; fax 604/682-5513; toll-free 800/961-7555. www.suttonplace. com. Antiques and beautiful floral displays welcome guests in the elegant lobby of this downtown Vancouver hotel. This European-style hotel is located near businesses, arts, and shopping. It offers 397 guest rooms and suites, a fitness center with indoor pool and tennis facilities, beaches, and winter skiing. 397 rms, 21 story, 47 suites. Mid-Apr-Oct: S $195-$395; D $215-$415; each addl $20; suites $445-$1,500; under 18 free; lower rates rest of yr. Crib free. Garage, valet parking $15. TV; cable (premium), VCR avail (movies). Indoor pool; whirlpool, poolside serv. Restaurant 6:30 am-11 pm. Rm serv 24 hrs. Bar 11:30-1:30 am; entertainment. Ck-out noon. Convention facilities. Business center. In-rm modem link. Concierge. Gift shop. Exercise rm; sauna, steam rm. Massage. Bathrm phones, refrigerators. Sun deck. Cr cds: A, C, D, DS, ER, JCB, MC, V.

⬛ 🛗 〰 🎿 ⛷ 🏋 〰 🖐 🏃

★★★ **WEDGEWOOD.** 845 Hornby St (V6Z 1V1). 604/689-7777; fax 604/608-5348; toll-free 800/663-0666. www.wedgewoodhotel.com. 89 rms, 14 story. May-Nov: S $179-$200; D $199-$220; each addl $20; suites $400-$520; under 14 free; wkend rates; package plans; lower rates rest of yr. Crib free. Garage $15. TV; cable (premium), VCR avail. Complimentary coffee in rms. Restaurant (see also BACCHUS). Rm serv 24 hrs. Bar noon-2 am; entertainment. Ck-out 1 pm. Meeting rms. Business center. Exercise equipt; sauna. Refrigerators. Private patios, balconies. Old World charm. Cr cds: A, C, D, DS, ER, JCB, MC, V.

⬛ 🛗 〰 🏋 〰 🖐 🏃

★★★ **THE WESTIN GRAND VANCOUVER.** 433 Robson St (V6B 6L9). 604/602-1999; toll-free 888/625-5144. www.westingrandvancouver.com. This property resides in the entertainment district within walking distance of Yaletown's clubs and restaurants and Robson Street shopping. Rooms are decorated in black and beige tones with a contemporary style, and Grandview Floors (30 and 31) have wonderful city views. All of the rooms are suites, with a small live/work area, a kitchenette with microwave oven, two televisions (one with Internet access), and a bathroom that has a separate bathtub and shower. 31 story, 207 suites. June-Oct: suites $329; each addl $25; under 18 free; lower rates rest of yr. Crib avail, CD avail. Complimentary coffee in rms, newspaper. Restaurant 6:30 am-10 pm. Rm serv 24 hrs. Bar. Ck-out noon, ck-in 3 pm. Meeting rms. Business center. Bellhops. Concierge. Dry cleaning. Gift shop. Exercise equipt, sauna, steam rm. Golf. Downhill skiing. Beach access. Bike rentals. Supervised children's activities. Hiking trail. Picnic facilities. Video games. Cr cds: A, D, ER, MC, V.

⬛ 🛗 〰 🎿 ⛷ 🏋 〰 🖐 🏃

Resort

★★ **DELTA PACIFIC RESORT AND CONFERENCE CENTER.** 10251 St. Edwards Dr, Richmond (V6X 2M9). 604/278-9611; fax 604/276-1121; toll-free 800/268-1133. www.deltapacific. bc.ca. 438 rms, 2, 15 and 21 story. Apr-Oct: S, D $200-$300; each addl $15; suites $299-$1,000; under 18 free; lower rates rest of yr. Crib free. Pet accepted. TV; cable. 3 pools, 1 indoor; whirlpool, poolside serv. Playground. Supervised children's activities; ages 5-12. Complimentary coffee in rms. Restaurants 6:30 am-11 pm. Rm serv 24 hrs. Bar 11-1 am. Ck-out noon. Convention facilities. Business center. In-rm modem link. Gift shop. Beauty shop. Golf privileges. Lighted and indoor tennis. Exercise rm; sauna. Massage. Squash courts. Private patios, balconies. Cr cds: A, C, D, ER, JCB, MC, V.

⬛ 🍴 🛗 〰 🏋 〰 🖐 🏃

B&Bs/Small Inns

★★ **BEAUTIFUL BED AND BREAKFAST.** 428 W 40th Ave (V5Y 2R4). 604/327-1102; fax 604/327-2299. www.beautifulbandb.bc.ca. 5 rms, 3 share bath, 2 story. No A/C. No rm phones. Apr-Oct: S $76-$85; D $95-$210; each addl $15-$25; lower rates rest of yr. Children over

14 yrs only. TV; cable. Complimentary full bkfst. Restaurant nearby. Ck-out 11 am, ck-in 5-6 pm. Business servs avail. Downhill/x-country ski 10 mi. Balconies. Colonial-style house with sculpture gardens. Totally nonsmoking.

★★★ **RIVER RUN COTTAGES.** *4551 River Rd W, Ladner (V4K 1R9). 604/946-7778; fax 604/940-1970. www.riverruncottages.com.* 4 cottages, 1 story. June-Sept: S, D $130-$210; each addl $20; under 5 free; lower rates rest of yr. Pet accepted. Complimentary full bkfst. Restaurants nearby. Ck-out noon, ck-in 4 pm. Luggage handling. Business servs avail. Bicycles, kayaks avail. On river. Totally nonsmoking. Cr cds: MC, V.

★★ **WEST END GUEST HOUSE.** *1362 Haro St (V6E 1G2). 604/681-2889; fax 604/688-8812; toll-free 888/546-3327. westendguesthouse.com.* 8 air-cooled rms, 3 story. S $70-$105; D $135-$225. Children over 12 yrs only. TV; cable. Complimentary full bkfst; afternoon refreshments. Restaurant nearby. Ck-out 11 am, ck-in 3 pm. Business servs avail. Former residence (1906) of one of first photographers in Vancouver. Period furnishings. Totally nonsmoking. Cr cds: A, DS, MC, V.

All Suite

★★★ **DELTA VANCOUVER SUITES.** *550 W Hastings St (V6B 1L6). 604/689-8188; fax 604/605-8881. www.deltahotels.com.* 225 rms, 22 story. S, D $175-$325; each addl $20; under 17 free. Crib avail. Indoor pool. TV; cable (premium), VCR avail. Complimentary coffee, newspaper in rms. Restaurant 6 am-10 pm. Ck-out noon. Meeting rms. Business center. Gift shop. Exercise rm. Some refrigerators, minibars. Cr cds: A, C, D, DS, MC, V.

Restaurants

★★ **A KETTLE OF FISH.** *900 Pacific (V6X 2E3). 604/682-6853. www.andersonsrestaurants.com.* Hrs: 11:30 am-2 pm, 5:30-9:30 pm; Fri, Sat 5:30-10 pm. Closed Jan 1, Dec 24 eve, 25, 26. Res accepted. Serv bar. Complete meals: lunch $6.95-$12.95, dinner $14.95-$32. Specializes in fresh seafood. English country garden atmosphere. Cr cds: A, D, MC, V.
D

★★ **ALLEGRO CAFI.** *888 Nelson St (V6J 2H1). 604/683-8485.* Specializes in rack of lamb, chicken, seafood. Hrs: 11:30 am-10 pm; Sat, Sun 5-9 pm. Closed hols. Res accepted. Wine list. Lunch $8-$10; dinner $14-$19. Entertaiment. Cr cds: A, D, ER, MC, V.
D

★★ **AQUA RIVA.** *30-200 Gramble St (V6C 1S4). 604/683-5599. www.aquariva.com.* Specializes in wood-grilled Pacific salmon, wood-roasted rack of lamb, coriander crusted rack of prawns. Hrs: 11:30 am-10 pm; Fri, Sat to 10:30 pm; Sun 11 am-10 pm. Closed hols. Res accepted. Wine list. Lunch $10.95-$14.95; dinner $17.50-$28.95. Brunch $9.95-$13.95. Mountain view. Cr cds: A, D, ER, MC, V.
D

★★ **ARIA.** *433 Robson St (V6B 6L9). 604/647-2521. www.westingrandvancouver.com.* Menu changes seasonally. Hrs: 6:30 am-11 pm; Thurs, Fri to midnight; Sat 7 am-midnight; Sun 7 am-11 pm. Res accepted. Wine, beer. Lunch $5-$18; dinner $18-$27. Brunch $5-$18. Child's menu. Entertainment. Cr cds: A, D, DS, ER, JCB, MC, V.
D

★★★ **BACCHUS.** *845 Hornby St (V6Z 1V1). 604/689-7777. www.travel.bc.ca/w/wedgewood.* Hrs: 6:30 am-11 pm. Res accepted. Northern Italian menu. Bar from 11 am. Wine list. Bkfst $6.95-$12.25, lunch $12-$17, dinner $14-$30. Sun brunch $5-$14. Specializes in lamb, seafood. Pianist exc Sun. Valet parking. European decor; many antiques and original artwork. Jacket (dinner). Cr cds: A, D, DS, ER, MC, V.
D

★★★★ **BISHOP'S.** *2183 W 4th Ave (V6K 1N7). 604/738-2025. www.bishopsonline.com.* With chef Dennis Green in the kitchen and founder John Bishop as the ever-genial host, this contemporary American restaurant is still highly regarded after sixteen years in business. Noted for fresh, simple preparations, dishes highlighting local ingredients are artfully presented, not overly contrived, and combine well with the predominantly West Coast wine list. The space is a stylish showroom for Bishop's Canadian art collection. Seafood menu. Specializes in contemporary Pacific Northwest cuisine. Hrs: 5:30-11 pm; Sun to 10 pm. Closed Dec 24-26. Res accepted. Wine list. Dinner $8-$34. Cr cds: A, D, ER, MC, V.

D

★★ **CAFE DE PARIS.** *761 Dennan St (V6G 2L6). 604/687-1418.* Specializes in bouillabaisse, cassoulet, rabbit Hrs: 11:30 am-2 pm, 5:30-10 pm; Sun 5-9 pm. Closed Dec 25. Res accepted. Wine, beer. Lunch $10.50-$17.95; dinner $24-$34. Brunch $9.95-$17.95. Cr cds: A, MC, V.

D

★★ **CAFFE DE MEDICI.** *1025 Robson St (V6E 1A9). 604/669-9322. www.medici.cc.* Specializes in scallops wrapped with prawn, crusted rack of lamb. Hrs: 11:30 am-10:30 pm; Sat noon-11 pm; Sun 5-11 pm. Closed Dec 25. Res accepted. Wine list. Lunch $14.95-$18.95; dinner $25.95-$32.95. Entertainment. Covered patio terrace. Cr cds: A, D, DS, ER, JCB, MC, V.

D

★★ **CANNERY.** *2205 Commissioner St (V5L 1A4). 604/254-9606. www. canneryseafood.com.* Hrs: 11:30 am-2:30 pm, 5:30-10 pm; Sat 5:30-10:30 pm; Sun 5:30-10 pm. Closed Dec 24-26. Res accepted. Bar. Wine list. A la carte entrees: lunch $8.95-$15.95, dinner $17.95-$31.95. Child's meals. Specializes in fresh seafood, mesquite-grilled dishes. Parking. Nautical motif; view of harbor.

Totally nonsmoking. Cr cds: A, D, ER, MC, V.

★ **CAPILANO HEIGHTS.** *5020 Capilano Rd (V7R 4K7). 604/987-9511.* Hrs: noon-10 pm; Sat from 4:30 pm; Sun 4:30-9 pm. Closed Dec 25, 26. Res accepted. Chinese menu. Bar. A la carte entrees: lunch $7-$17, dinner $10-$20. Specialties: prawns and broccoli with black bean sauce, Peking duck (24-hr notice). Parking. Cr cds: A, MC, V.

D

★★ **CHARTHOUSE.** *3866 Bayview, Richmond (V7E 4R7). 604/271-7000. www.charthouse.ca.* Hrs: 11:30 am-10 pm. Closed Dec 25. Res accepted. Lunch $5.95-$10.95, dinner $10.95-$21.95. Child's meals. Specializes in seafood, beef. Outdoor dining. Casual decor. Cr cds: MC, V.

D

Pacific Rim National Park, Vancouver Island

★★★ **CHARTWELL.** *791 W Georgia St (V6C 2T4). 604/844-6715. www. fourseasons.com.* Seasonal menu. Specializes in Salt Spring Island lamb. Own baking. Hrs: 6:30 am-2:30 pm, 5:30-10 pm; Fri, Sat 6:30-11:30 am, 5:30-11pm; Sun 6:30 am-10 pm. Res accepted. Bar. Wine cellar. A la carte entrees: bkfst $9-$19, lunch $17-$23, dinner $18-$39. Parking. Cr cds: D, DS, ER, MC, V.

D

★★ **CHEZ MICHEL.** *1373 Marine Dr (V7T 1B6). 604/926-4913.* Hrs: 11:30 am-2 pm, 5:30-10:30 pm. Closed Sun; major hols. Res required.

French menu. Wine, beer. Lunch $9.95-$11.95, dinner $12.95-$21.95. Specialties: prawns Nicoise, rack of lamb au jus, bouillabaisse. Parking. French art on display. View of English Bay and Burrard Inlet. Cr cds: A, D, MC, V.

★★★ **CINCIN ITALIAN WOOD GRILL.** *1154 Robson St (V6E 1V5). 604/688-7338. www.cincin.net.* Hrs: 11:30 am-midnight; Sat, Sun 5 pm-midnight. Res accepted. Wine list. Lunch $12.50-$16.50; dinner $14-$37. Entertainment. Cr cds: A, D, ER, MC, V.

★ **CLOUD 9.** *1400 Robson St (V6G 1B9). 604/687-0511. www.empire landmark.com.* Hrs: 6:30 am-10 pm; Sun from 7 am; Sun brunch 11 am-2 pm. Res accepted. Continental menu. Bar. Bkfst $7.50-$15. A la carte entrees: lunch $8-$15, dinner $17-$40. Sun brunch $14-$25. Child's meals. Specializes in fresh seafood, baked salmon. Parking. Revolving dining rm on 42nd floor of hotel. Cr cds: A, C, D, ER, MC, V.
Ⓓ

★★★ **C RESTAURANT.** *1600 Howe St (V6O 2L9). 604/681-1164. www. crestaurant.com.* Specializes in smoked octopus, bacon-wrapped scallops. Hrs: 11:30 am-11 pm; Sat 5:30-11 pm. Res accepted. Wine list. Lunch $12-$30; dinner $21-$39. Brunch $12-$30. Entertainment. Cr cds: A, D, ER, MC, V.
Ⓓ

★★ **DELILAH'S.** *1789 Comox St (V6G 1P5). 604/687-3424.* Hrs: 5:30 pm-1 am. Closed Dec 24-26. Continental menu. Bar. Wine list. Complete meals: dinner 2-course $18.50, 5-course $29. Specializes in rack of lamb, grilled salmon. Eclectic decor with Art Nouveau touches. Ceilings painted in oils by local artist. Cr cds: A, D, ER, MC, V.
Ⓓ

★★★ **DIVA AT THE MET.** *645 Howe St (V6C 2Y9). 604/602-7788. www. divamet.com.* Pacific Northwestern seafood menu. Specialties: Alaskan black cod, grilled Atlantic lobster tail with octopus bacon, paillard of veal with wild mushrooms, Stilton cheesecake. Hrs: 6:30-11 am, 11:30 am-2:30 pm, 6-10 pm; Thurs-Sat to 11 pm. Sun brunch 11 am-2:30 pm. Res recommended. Bar; lounge. Extensive wine list. Cr cds: A, D, DS, MC, V.
Ⓓ

★★ **DUNDARAVE PIER.** *150 25th St (V7B 4H8). 604/922-1414. www.beach housewestvan.com.* Hrs: 11:30 am-11 pm; Sat, Sun from 10:30 am; summer hrs vary; Sun brunch 10:30 am-5 pm. Res accepted. Bar. A la carte entrees: lunch $8.95-$13.95, dinner $9.95-$21. Sun brunch $17-$29. Child's meals. Specializes in rack of lamb, pasta, fresh seafood. Valet parking. Heated outdoor patio. View of ocean and Vancouver Bay. Cr cds: A, MC, V.
Ⓓ

★★ **FISH AND COMPANY.** *655 Burrard St (V6C 2R7). 604/639-4770. www.hyatt.com.* Specializes in kettle of "stoertebecker," traditional Northern German fish soup, Pacific Rim plate, lamb, salmon, halibut. Hrs: 6:30-10 pm. Res accepted. Wine list. Dinner $10.50-$23. Child's menu. Entertainment. Overlooking downtown Vancouver. Cr cds: A, D, ER, JCB, MC, V.
Ⓓ

★★ **FISH HOUSE IN STANLEY PARK.** *8901 Stanley Park Dr (V6G 3E2). 604/681-7275. www.fishhouse stanleypark.com.* Specializes in Northwest seafood bowl, grilled tuna steak Diane. Hrs: 11:30 am-10 pm; Sun 11 am-10 pm. Res accepted. Wine list. Lunch $10.95-$21.95; dinner $16.95-$59.95. Brunch $9.95-$21.95. Child's menu. Entertainment. Cr cds: A, D, ER, JCB, MC, V.
Ⓓ

★★★ **FIVE SAILS.** *300-999 Canada Pl (V6C 3B5). 604/662-8111. www. panpac.com.* Pacific Rim cuisine. Own baking. Hrs: 6-11 pm. Res accepted. Bar. Wine list. A la carte entrees: dinner $38-$45. Valet parking. Cr cds: A, D, MC, V.
Ⓓ

★★ **FLEURI.** *845 Burrard St (V6Z 2K6). 604/642-2900.* Continental menu. Specialties: seared Dungeness crab cake, oolong tea-steamed sea bass, broiled Alberta beef tenderloin, rack of lamb, chocoholic buffet. Hotel parking. Hrs: 6 am-11 pm. High tea 2:30-5 pm Mon-Sat. Sun

brunch 11 am-2 pm. A la carte entrees: $15.50-$39. Brunch $27.95. Bar 11:30-1 am; Sun 4:30 pm-midnight. Extensive wine list. Classic Europeon decor. Cr cds: A, ER, MC, V.
D

★★★ **GLOBE @ YVR.** *Vancouver International Airport (V7B 1X9). 604/248-3281. www.fairmont.com.* Specializes in seared halibut, Asian vegetables, roasted duck confit. Hrs: 6-11 pm. Res accepted. Wine, beer. Lunch $9-$15.50; dinner $20-$29. Child's menu. Entertainment: pianist. Overlooks North Shore Mts, watch planes take off and land, panoramic view. Cr cds: A, C, D, ER, JCB, MC, V.
D **SC**

★★★ **GOTHAM STEAKHOUSE AND COCKTAIL BAR.** *615 Seymour St (V6B 3K3). 604/605-8282. www. gothamsteakhouse.com.* Specializes in filet mignon, porterhouse. Hrs: 11:30 am-3 pm, 5-10 pm. Closed Dec. 25. Res accepted. Wine, beer. Lunch $13.95-$18.95; dinner $24.95-$49.95. Entertainment. Cr cds: A, D, ER, MC, V.
D

★ **GRANVILLE SUSHI.** *2526 Granville St (V6H 3G8). 604/738-0388.* Specializes in teriyaki, sushi, sashimi. Hrs: 11:30 am-2:30 pm, 5-10 pm; Fri, Sat 5-11 pm; Sun 11 am-2:30 pm, 5-10 pm. Res accepted. Wine, beer. Lunch $5.25-$12.50; dinner $6.25-$20. Entertainment. Cr cds: V.
D

★ **HART HOUSE ON DEER LAKE.** *6664 Deer Lake Ave, Burnaby (V5E 4H3). 604/298-4278. www.harthouse restaurant.com.* Specializes in beef, fish. Hrs: 11:30 am-2 pm, 5:30-10 pm. Closed Mon. Res accepted. Wine, beer. Lunch $12-$16; dinner $16-$28. Entertainment. Overlooking lake. Cr cds: A, D, MC, V.
D

★ **HY'S ENCORE.** *637 Hornby St (V6C 2G3). 604/683-7671. www. hyssteakhouse.com.* Hrs: 11:30 am-10:30 pm; Sat, Sun from 5:30 pm. Bar. A la carte entrees: lunch $10-$22. Complete meals: dinner $26-

$40. Specializes in steak. Baronial decor. Cr cds: A, D, MC, V.
D

★★★ **IL GIARDINO DI UMBERTO RISTORANTE.** *1382 Hornby St (V6Z 1W5). 604/669-2422. www.umberto. com.* Specializes in rack of lamb, osso buco, filet of veal. Hrs: noon-11 pm; Sat from 5:30 pm. Closed Sun; hols. Res accepted. Wine list. A la carte entrees: lunch $9-$15, dinner $14-$30. Entertainment. Valet parking. In converted Victorian house (1896). Italian, Tuscan decor. Cr cds: A, C, D, DS, ER, JCB, MC, V.
D

★★ **IMPERIAL CHINESE SEAFOOD RESTAURANT.** *355 Burrard St (V6C 2G8). 604/688-8191. www.imperialrest.com.* Hrs: 11 am-11 pm; Sat, Sun from 10:30 am. Res accepted. Wine list. Lunch $3.30-$40; dinner $12.50-$52. Entertainment. Cr cds: D, ER, MC, V.
D

★★★★ **LA BELLE AUBERGE.** *4856 48th Ave, Ladner (V4K 1V2). 604/946-7717. www.labelleauberge.com.* Since 1980, the acclaimed Chef Bruno Marti's restaurant has combined the old (circa 1900s farmhouse with Victorian decor) with the new (his marvelous contemporary interpretations of classic French cuisine). Menu changes seasonally. Hrs: 6 pm-midnight. Closed Mon. Res accepted. Wine, beer. Dinner $26-$33. Entertainment. Cr cds: A, C, D, ER, MC, V.

★★★ **LA TERRAZZA.** *1088 Cambie St (V6B 6J5). 604/899-4449. www. laterrazza.ca.* Contemporary menu. Specialties: rack of lamb, salmon. Hrs: 5-11 pm; Fri, Sat to midnight. Closed hols. Res accepted. Wine list. Dinner $16-$29. Totally nonsmoking. Setting is an impressive rm with burnt sienna walls and murals, massive windows, and vaulted ceilings. Cr cds: A, D, ER, MC, V.
D

★★★ **LE CROCODILE.** *909 Burrard St (V7Z 2N2). 604/669-4298.* Hrs: 11:30 am-2 pm, 5:30-10 pm; Sat from 5:30 pm. Closed Sun; hols. Res accepted. French, Continental menu. Serv bar. Wine list. A la carte entrees: lunch $9.50-$16.95, dinner $22-$34.

Specializes in veal, salmon. Own baking. Own ice cream. Valet parking. Outdoor dining. Modern French decor; antiques. Cr cds: A, D, MC, V.
D

★★★★ **LUMIERE.** *2551 W Broadway (V6K 2E9). 604/739-8185.* Easily one of the most sophisticated dining experiences in Vancouver, this comfortable restaurant affords a terrific contemporary French meal. Chef/owner Robert Feenie has studied with the best chefs, and his cooking shows it. The freshest seasonal produce is perfectly prepared. The service is professional and very warm, making this a delightful dining experience. Specializes in vegetarian and seafood tasting menu. Hrs: 5:30-10:30 pm. Closed Mon; hols. Res accepted. Dinner $80-$120. Cr cds: A, D, ER, MC, V.
D

★★ **MONK MCQUEENS.** *601 Stamps Landing (D5Z 3Z1). 604/877-1351. www.monkmcqueens.com.* Specializes in smoked Alaskan black cod, ahi tuna steak. Hrs: 5:30-10 pm. Res accepted. Wine list. Dinner $19-$40. Child's menu. Entertainment: Thurs-Sat jazz, blues. Cr cds: A, MC, V.

★★ **MONTRI 'S THAI.** *3629 W Broadway (3V6 R2B). 604/738-9888.* Hrs: 5-11 pm. Res accepted. Wine, beer. Dinner $9.95-$14.95. Cr cds: MC, V.
D

★★ **PAPI'S RISTORANTE ITALIANO.** *12251 Number 1 Rd, Richmond (V7E 1T6). 604/275-8355.* Hrs: 11 am-2 pm, 5-9 pm; Fri, Sat 5-10 pm. Res accepted. Wine, beer. Lunch $8-$14; dinner $14-$27. Cr cds: A, D, MC, V.
D

★★★ **PICCOLO MONDO.** *850 Thurlow St (V6E 1W2). 604/688-1633. www.piccolomondoristorante.com.* Hrs: noon-2 pm, 6-10 pm; Sat from 6 pm. Closed Sun. Res accepted. Italian menu. Bar. Lunch $12-$18, dinner $15-$33. Specialties: tortellini della Nonna, osso buco, bollito misto. Extensive wine selection. Cr cds: A, D, MC, V.

★★ **PINK PEARL.** *1132 E Hastings St (V6A 1S2). 604/253-4316. www.pink*

pearl.com. Hrs: 9 am-9 pm; Fri, Sat to 11 pm. Res accepted. Chinese menu. Bar 11 am-midnight. A la carte entrees: bkfst, lunch $6-$14, dinner $14-$28. Specialties: Peking duck, spiced crab. Parking. Very large dining area. Cr cds: A, D, MC, V.
D

★★★ **PRESIDENT CHINESE SEAFOOD RESTAURANT.** *8181 Cambie Rd, Richmond (V6X 3X9). 604/279-1997.* Specializes in Peking duck, crispy fried pigeon. Hrs: 8:30 am-3 pm, 5-10 pm. Res accepted. Wine, beer. Dinner $12-$50. Cr cds: A, D, MC.
D

★★★ **PROVENCE.** *4473 W 10th Ave (V6R 2H2). 604/222-1980. www. provencevancouver.com.* Specializes in bouillabaisse, tiger prawns. Hrs: 11:30 am-10 pm; Fri to 11 pm; Sat 10 am-11 pm ; Sun 10 am-10 pm. Res accepted. Wine list. Lunch $8.75-$15.95; dinner $13.50-$25. Brunch $7.50-$14.95. Cr cds: A, D, ER, MC, V.
D

★★★ **QUATTRO ON FOURTH.** *2611 W 4th (V6K 1P8). 604/734-4444. www.quattro-ristorante.com.* Specializes in antipasta platters, pasta combination platter. Hrs: 5-11 pm. Closed Dec 24-27. Res accepted. Wine list. Dinner $15.95-$32.95. Entertainment. Cr cds: A, D, MC, V.
D

★ **RAINCITY GRILL.** *1193 Denman St (V6G 2N1). 604/685-7337. www. raincitygrill.com.* Specializes in grilled Caesar salad, albacore tuna sashimi. Hrs: 5-10 pm; Sat, Sun 10:30 am-2:30 pm, 5-10 pm. Closed Dec 24, 25. Res accepted. Wine list. Lunch $11-$16; dinner $18-$30. Brunch $10-$18. Cr cds: A, D, ER, MC, V.

★★ **SEASON'S RESTAURANT.** *33rd and Cambie (V6G 3E7). 604/874-8008. www.seasonsinthepark.com.* Specialties: Pacific Northwest salmon, lemon pie. Hrs: 11:30 am-10 pm. Closed Dec 25. Res accepted. Wine list. Lunch $9-$25; dinner $12-$26. Brunch $9-$22. Child's menu. Cr cds: A, MC, V.
D

Black bear

★★ **SHANGHAI CHINESE BISTRO.**
1124 Alberni St (V6E 1A5). 604/683-8322. Specializes in general Tao chicken, Mongolian beef. Hrs: 11:30 am-11 pm; Fri, Sat to midnight. Closed Dec 25. Res accepted. Wine, beer. Lunch, dinner $11-$17. Handmade noodle show. Cr cds: A, D, JCB, MC, V.
D

★★ **SHIJO JAPANESE RESTAURANT.** *1926 W 4th Ave, Suite 202 (V6J 1M5). 604/732-4676.* Specializes in sushi. Hrs: noon-2 pm, 5:30-10 pm; Sat, Sun 5:30-10 pm. Res accepted. Wine list. Lunch $8.50, dinner $25. Cr cds: A, D, JCB, MC, V.
D

★★★ **STAR ANISE.** *1485 W 12th Ave (V6H 1M6). 604/737-1485.* Hrs: 11:30 am-2:30 pm, 5:30-11 pm; summer hrs vary. Closed Dec 24-26. Res accepted. Northwestern menu. Bar. Wine cellar. Lunch $12-$14, dinner $18-$30. Specializes in local seafood, game. Own desserts. Parking. Elegant dining. Art by local artists. Cr cds: A, D, MC, V.
D

★★★ **SUN SUI WAH SEAFOOD RESTAURANT.** *3888 Main St (V5V 3N9). 604/872-8822. www.sunsuiwah. com.* Specializes in squab, seafood. Hrs: 10:30 am-10:30 pm; Fri, Sat from 10 am. Res accepted. Wine,

beer. Lunch $2.75-$15; dinner $20-$30. Cr cds: A, ER, MC, V.
D

★★ **TAMA SUSHI.** *1595 W Broadway, Suite 200 (V6J 1W6). 604/738-0119.* Specializes in spicy tuna sashimi, lobster sashimi, tama chili prones. Hrs: 11:30 am-2 pm, 5-10:15 pm; Fri, Sat to 10:45 pm. Res accepted. Wine list. Lunch $2.10-$19.25; dinner $2.10-$25.50. Tatami rum (Japanese-style rms). Cr cds: A, D, MC, V.
D

★★ **TEAHOUSE.** *7501 Stanley Park Dr (V6G 3E7). 604/669-3281. www. vancouverdine.com.* Hrs: 11:30 am-2:30 pm, 5:30-10 pm; Sun from 10:30 am. Closed Dec 25. Res accepted. Continental, West coast menu. Wine cellar. A la carte entrees: lunch $11.75-$17.95, dinner $21-$29. Sat, Sun brunch $11-$15. Specializes in seafood, poultry. Own baking. Outdoor dining. Glass conservatory; view of harbor. Cr cds: A, MC, V.
D

★★★ **TOJO'S.** *777 W Broadway #202 (V5Z 4J7). 604/872-8050. www. tojos.com.* Hrs: 5-10:30 pm. Closed Sun. Res accepted. Japanese menu. Bar. Dinner $15-$28. Complete meals: dinner $45-$100. Specializes in traditional Japanese dishes. Sushi bar. Parking. Patio dining with view of Japanese garden. Tatami rms avail. Cr cds: A, DS, MC, V.

★★ **TOP OF VANCOUVER.** *555 W Hastings (V6B 4N4). 604/669-2220.* Hrs: 11:30 am-2:30 pm, 5-10 pm; summer to 11 pm; Sun brunch to 3 pm. Res accepted. Bar. A la carte entrees: lunch $14-$56, dinner $21-$56. Sun brunch $34.95. Child's meals. Specializes in local seafood, pasta. Revolving restaurant 550 ft above street level. Cr cds: A, D, DS, MC, V.
D

★★★ **UMBERTO'S.** *1380 Hornby St (V6Z 1W5). 604/687-6316. www. umberto.com.* Hrs: noon-11 pm, Sat from 6 pm. Closed Mon; Jan 1, Dec 25. Res accepted. Northern Italian menu. No A/C. Serv bar. Wine list. A la carte entrees: dinner $14-$30. Specialties: rack of lamb, osso buco, filet of veal. Valet parking. Outdoor dining. In converted Victorian house (1896); Italian, Tuscan decor. Cr cds: A, D, MC, V.

★★★ **VILLA DEL LUPO.** *869 Hamilton St (V6B 2R7). 604/688-7436. www.villadellupo.com.* Specializes in lamb osso buco. Hrs: 5:30-10:30 pm. Res accepted. Extensive wine list. Dinner $18.95-$29.95. Entertainment. Cr cds: A, D, ER, MC, V.

★★★ **WILLIAM TELL.** *765 Beatty St (V6B 2M4). 604/688-3504. www. williamtell.bc.ca.* Hrs: 6:30 am-9:30 pm; Sun 6:30 am-noon, 5:30-8 pm. Res accepted. Swiss, Continental menu. Bar. Bkfst $6.50-$9.50, lunch $6-$13.25, dinner $18.75-$28. Specializes in veal, fresh seafood. Own baking, ice cream. Valet parking. European decor. Cr cds: A, D, DS, MC, V.
D

★★★ **ZINFANDELLS.** *1355 Hornby St (V6Z 1W7). 604/681-4444.* Hrs: 5-10 pm. Wine, beer. Dinner $17-$25. Cr cds: A, MC, V.
D ⊐

Unrated Dining Spots

GREENS AND GOURMET. *2681 W Broadway (V6K 2G2). 604/737-7373.* Hrs: 9 am-10 pm. Closed Dec 25. International health food menu. Juice bar. Wine, beer. Bkfst, lunch $4.95-$7.95, dinner $4.95-$10.95. Specialties: Greek moussaka, spinach pie, vegetarian dishes. Salad bar. Parking. California-style dining. Totally nonsmoking. Cr cds: MC, V.
D SC

TAPASTREE. *1829 Robson St (V6G 1E4). 604/606-4680. www.tapastree. net.* Specializes in beef, fish. Hrs: 11:30 am-2 pm, 5:30-10 pm. Closed Mon. Res accepted. Wine, beer. Lunch $12-$16; dinner $16-$28. Overlooking lake. Cr cds: A, D, ER, MC, V.
D

TRUE CONFECTIONS. *866 Denman St (V6G 2L8). 604/682-1292. www.true confections.ca.* Hrs: 1 pm-midnight; Fri, Sat to 1:30 am. Dessert menu. Wine, beer. A la carte entrees: lunch, dinner $3.50-$10. Specialties: devil's food cake with marshmallow icing,

white chocolate raspberry cheesecake. 13-ft refrigerated display case filled daily with fresh cakes, pies and other desserts. Outdoor dining (May-Oct). Totally nonsmoking. Cr cds: A, DS, MC, V.

Vancouver Island

(F-4) See also Nanaimo, Vancouver, Victoria

Southwest of mainland and accessible by ferry, aircraft, and jet catamaran.

The largest of the Canadian Pacific Coast Islands, Vancouver Island stretches almost 300 miles (480 kilometers) along the shores of western British Columbia. It is easily accessible by ferry from the city of Vancouver on the mainland as well as from other parts of British Columbia and the state of Washington. With most of its population located in the larger cities on the eastern coast, much of the island remains a wilderness and is very popular with outdoor enthusiasts.

The Vancouver Island Mountain Range cuts down the middle of the island, providing spectacular snow-capped scenery, fjords, and rocky coastal cliffs. Several provincial parks are dedicated to the preservation of wildlife: Columbia black-tailed deer and eagles are common to the southern tip; Roosevelt elk, black bears, and cougars inhabit the northern forests; and whales, sea lions, and seals are found along the shores. The surrounding ocean, as well as the inland lakes and rivers, offers anglers some of the world's best salmon and trout. Among the variety of activities to enjoy are sailing, canoeing, boating, scuba diving, camping, climbing, and caving.

The southern portion of the island contains more than half the island's total population and includes Victoria (see), British Columbia's capital city. Here, countryside resembles rural Britain with its rolling farmland, rows of hedges, and colorful flower gardens. Spain claimed the Sooke Inlet in the 18th century, giving the familiar Spanish names to much of the area. Later, British farmers arrived as well as thousands of prospectors looking for gold. A spectacular and demanding coastal trail—the West Coast Trail, which runs from Port Renfrew to Bamfield—and countless paths through Pacific rain forests traverse East Sooke Park on the southwest coast. On the southeast coast, Malahat Drive on the Island Highway provides a dramatic panorama of the Gulf Islands and the Saanich Peninsula. Inland is the Cowichan Valley, with many lakes and rivers teeming with fish. Whippletree Junction in Duncan is a reminder of the role played by Asian settlers in the island's mining and railway construction history. Just outside of Duncan are the British Columbia Forest Museum and Demonstration Forest and the Native Heritage Centre.

Island-hopping is pleasant in the Gulf Islands, located in the sheltered waters of the Strait of Georgia. These beautiful, isolated islands have become home to many artists. Salt Spring, the largest island, has a traditional market on Saturday in the town of Ganges where handmade crafts are featured.

Nanaimo (see) is the dominant town in the central region, an area known for excellent sandy beaches and beautiful parks. The spectacular waterfalls found on Englishman River and the natural caves in Horne Lake Provincial Park on the Qualicum River are worth a special trip. MacMillan Provincial Park contains the famous Cathedral Grove and features Douglas fir trees 800 years old with circumferences of 30 feet (9 meters). In the center of the island is the Alberni Valley, named for the Spanish sea captain who landed at the port in 1791 searching for gold and native treasures along the coast. Located in the valley are several parks with excellent swimming and fishing, the tallest falls found in North America—Della Falls—and a bird sanctuary and fish hatchery. From Port Alberni the mountain highway winds its way to the peaceful fishing village of Tofino, the northern boundary of the Long Beach section of the Pacific Rim National Park. The park encompasses 80 miles (129 kilometers) of rugged

shoreline: Long Beach, only seven miles (11 kilometers) is the best-known and most easily accessible; south of Long Beach lies the Broken Island Group of Barkley Sound, 98 islands clustered in a huge bay surrounded by the Mackenzie Mountains; and south of Barkley Sound is the famous West Coast Lifesaving Trail of 45 miles (77 kilometers), originally a route to civilization for shipwrecked sailors, now a test of strength and endurance for experienced hikers. The Pacific Rim is especially popular among amateur naturalists who enjoy watching the whales and other sea life.

Settlements along the northern coast are primarily lumber towns or small villages. Cumberland, which once had the largest Chinese population in Canada, began as a coal mining town. A popular area among sports enthusiasts is Forbidden Plateau and Mount Washington, excellent for skiing and hiking. The Campbell River is where the famous Tyee and Coho salmon are found in abundance. The Quinsam River fish hatchery keeps the area well-stocked. Inland from Campbell River is the largest untouched wilderness area on the island—Strathcona Provincial Park. In the center of the park is the Golden Hinde, the island's highest peak (more than 7,000 feet/2,200 meters). Much of the rugged, mountainous wilderness is a wildlife sanctuary, but it also accommodates campers, hikers, climbers, and canoe and kayak enthusiasts. Nootka Sound, on the west coast, discovered by Captain Cook, remains pristine, with few towns and no roads along the coast. On the east coast, a major highway runs north of Kelsey Bay. Although this section of the north island is more heavily populated, it is still able to preserve its wilderness character. Visiting the tiny villages in this section is like stepping back in time to the days of the first settlers. Cape Scott, at the northernmost tip of the island, can be reached by a hiking trail that winds through Cape Scott Provincial Park, a stormy coastal wilderness with magnificent forests and various wildlife.

Adding to the beauty of Vancouver Island is its moderate climate, especially in the south where the land is protected from the open sea by mainland British Columbia on the southeast and Washington state on the southwest. On the west coast, however, winter storms can be bitter, and there is much rainfall throughout the year. All in all, Vancouver Island is an exciting place to visit, with its fascinating terrain, sparkling waters, abundant wildlife, and delightful people.

Victoria

(F-4) See also Nanaimo, Vancouver

Founded 1843 **Pop** 64,379 **Elev** 211 ft (64 m) **Area code** 250
Information Tourism Victoria, 812 Wharf St, V8W 1T3; 250/953-2033 or 800/663-3883
Web www.tourismvictoria.com

Bordered by Juan de Fuca Strait on one side and majestic mountains on the other, Victoria is situated on the southeast tip of Vancouver Island. Established in 1843 as a trading post of the Hudson's Bay Company, the city was later called Fort Victoria. In the late 1850s Victoria became the provisioning and outfitting base for miners on their way to British Columbia's goldfields. In 1866 Vancouver Island was administratively linked with the mainland; Victoria became the provincial capital in 1871.

A major port with two harbors—the outer for ocean shipping and cruising, and the inner for coastal shipping, pleasure boats, ferries to the US mainland, amphibian aircraft, and fishing—Victoria has a distinctly English flavor with many Tudor-style buildings and a relaxed way of life. It is a center of Pacific Northwest indigenous culture.

Victoria is a city of parks and gardens; even the five-globed Victorian lampposts are decorated with baskets of flowers in summer. One may take a horse-drawn carriage or double-decker bus tours through many historic and scenic landmarks; inquire locally for details. In winter, temperatures rarely go below 40°F (4°C). Victoria's climate is Canada's most moderate, making it a delightful place to visit any time of year.

What to See and Do

Art Gallery of Greater Victoria. Said to be the finest collection of Japanese art in Canada. Major holdings of Asian ceramics and paintings. Canadian and European art, with focus on prints and drawings. Decorative arts. Lectures, films, concerts. Only Shinto shrine outside of Japan is located here. Japanese garden, bonsai. Gift shop. (Daily; closed hols) 1040 Moss St. Phone 250/384-4101. ¢¢

BC Forest Museum. Logging museum; old logging machines and tools, hands-on exhibits, logging camp, 1½-mi (2.4 km) steam railway ride, sawmill, films, nature walk, picnic park, snack bar, gift shop. (May-Sept, daily) 40 mi (64 km) N on Hwy 1, near Duncan. Phone 250/715-1113.

Beacon Hill Park. Approx 180 acres (75 hectares) with lakes, wildfowl sanctuary, children's petting farm, walks and floral gardens, cricket pitch; world's second-tallest totem pole; beautiful view of the sea. For a list of additional recreational areas contact Tourism Victoria. From Douglas St to Cook St, between Superior St and waterfront. Phone 250/361-0370. **FREE**

Butchart Gardens. Approx 50 acres (20 hectares). The "Sunken Garden" was created in the early 1900s by the Butcharts on the site of their depleted limestone quarry with topsoil brought in by horse-drawn cart. Already a tourist attraction by the 1920s, the gardens now incl the Rose, Japanese, and Italian gardens; also Star Pond, Concert Lawn, Fireworks Basin, Ross Fountain, and Show Greenhouse. Subtly illuminated at night (mid-June-mid-Sept). Fireworks (July-Aug, Sat eves). Restaurants; seed and gift store. 13 mi (21 km) N on Benvenuto Ave, near Brentwood Bay. Phone 250/652-4422. ¢¢¢¢

Carr House. (1863) Italianate birthplace of famous Canadian painter/author Emily Carr. Ground floor restored to period. (Mid-May-Oct, daily; rest of yr, by appt) 207 Government St. Phone 250/383-5843. ¢¢

Centennial Square. Incl fountain plaza; Elizabethan knot garden of herbs and flowers. Occasional noontime concerts. Douglas and Pandora sts.

Craigdarroch Castle. (1890) Historic house museum with beautifully crafted wood, stained glass; furnished with period furniture and artifacts. (Daily; closed Jan 1, Dec 25, 26) 1050 Joan Crescent. Phone 250/592-5323. ¢¢

Craigflower Farmhouse & Schoolhouse Historic Site. Farmhouse built in 1856 in simple Georgian style. 1854 schoolhouse is oldest in western Canada. Some original furnishings. (May-Oct) Craigflower Rd at Admirals Rd, 4 mi (6 km) NW. Phone 250/383-4627. ¢¢

Dominion Astrophysical Observatory. Public viewing through 72-in (183-cm) telescope; display galleries (Mon-Fri). Tours (Apr-Oct, Sat eves). 10 mi (16 km) NW at 5071 W Saanich Rd. **FREE**

Empress Hotel. Historically famous building constructed by Canadian Pacific Railroad in 1908 and restored in 1989. Victorian in tradition, incl afternoon tea and crumpets served in the lobby. 721 Government St. Also here are

Crystal Garden. Glass building formerly housed the largest saltwater pool in the British Empire. Tropical gardens, waterfall, fountain, aviary, monkeys, free-flying butterflies, exotic fish pool; restaurant, shops. (Daily) 713 Douglas St, behind Empress Hotel. Phone 250/953-8816. ¢¢¢

Miniature World. More than 80 miniature, 3-D scenes of fact, fiction, and history. Two large doll houses; very large rail diorama; villages; world's smallest operational sawmill. (Daily; closed Dec 25) 649 Humboldt St, at Empress Hotel. Phone 250/385-9731. ¢¢

Ferry trips. Black Ball Transport, Inc: between Victoria, BC, and Port Angeles, WA (see), car ferry, phone 250/386-2202; **Washington State Ferries:** between Sidney, BC, and Anacortes, WA, phone 250/381-1551; **British Columbia Ferry Corp:** between Victoria and British Columbia mainland or smaller island destinations, car ferry, phone 250/386-3431 or 604/669-1211 (Vancouver).

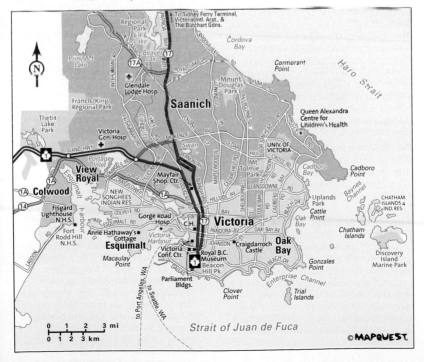

Fort Rodd Hill and Fisgard Lighthouse National Historic Site. A coastal artillery fort from 1895-1956; casemated barracks, gun and searchlight positions, loopholed walls. Grounds (daily; closed Dec 25). Historic lighthouse (1860) adj. For further information contact the Superintendent, 603 Fort Rodd Hill Rd, V9C 2W8. 8 mi (13 km) W, then ½ mi (1 km) S of BC 1A. Phone 250/478-5849. ¢¢

Hatley Castle. (Royal Roads University, 1908) Once the private estate of James Dunsmuir, former Lieutenant Governor of British Columbia. Buildings are noted for their beauty, as are the grounds, with their Japanese, Italian, and rose gardens. Grounds (daily). 6 mi (10 km) W via Trans-Canada Hwy 1 and 1A, Colwood exit, on Hwy 14 (Sooke Rd) in Colwood. Phone 250/391-2511. ¢¢

Helmcken House. (1852) Second-oldest house in British Columbia; most furnishings are original. Extensive 19th-century medical collection. (May-Oct, daily; rest of yr, by appt) 10 Elliot Sq. Phone 250/361-0021. ¢¢

Maritime Museum. Located in Old Provincial Courthouse. Depicts rich maritime heritage of the Pacific Northwest from early explorers through age of sail and steam; Canadian naval wartime history; large collection of models of ships used throughout the history of British Columbia. The *Tilikum,* a converted dugout that sailed from Victoria to England during the years 1901-1904, is here. Captain James Cook display. (Daily; closed Jan 1, Dec 25) 28 Bastion Sq. Phone 250/385-4222. ¢¢

Pacific Undersea Gardens. Underwater windows for viewing of more than 5,000 marine specimens; scuba diver shows. (Daily; closed Dec 25) 490 Belleville St. Phone 250/382-5717. ¢¢¢

Parliament Buildings. Built in 1893-1897 mostly of native materials, beautifully illuminated at night; houses British Columbia's Legislative Assembly. Guided tours (mid-June-Labour Day, daily; rest of yr, Mon-Fri; closed hols exc summer). Foreign language tours. Advance notice suggested for group tours. 501 Belleville St, at Inner Harbour Phone 250/387-3046. **FREE**

Point Ellice House Museum. (1861) Original Victorian setting, furnishings. Afternoon tea served in restored garden. (May-mid Sept; daily) Pleasant St, off Bay St. Phone 250/380-6506. ¢¢

Royal British Columbia Museum. Exhibits incl natural and human history, indigenous history, and art; recreation of a turn-of-the-century town. Natural history gallery, "Living Land-Living Sea" depicts natural history of British Columbia from Ice Age-present. (Daily; closed Dec 25, Jan 1) 675 Belleville St. Phone 250/356-7226. Nearby are

  Carillon. Bells made in Holland; presented to the province by citizens of Dutch descent. Concerts; inquire locally for private tour.

  Thunderbird Park. Collection of authentic totem poles and indigenous carvings, representing the work of the main Pacific Coastal tribes. Indigenous carvers may be seen at work in the Carving Shed (May-Sept).

Royal London Wax Museum. More than 250 figures in theatrical settings. (Daily; closed Dec 25) 470 Belleville St, downtown on Inner Harbour Phone 250/388-4461. ¢¢¢

Sightseeing tours.

  Capital City Tally-Ho and Sightseeing Company. English horse-drawn carriage sightseeing tours: of city highlights, departing from Inner Harbour beside Parliament Buildings; or past Victorian homes and through 200-acre (81-hectare) Beacon Hill Park and its extensive flower gardens (departs from Menzies and Belleville Sts). Fully narrated. (Apr-Sept, daily) 8615 Ebor Ter. Phone 250/383-5067.

  Gray Line bus tours. Several bus tours of Victoria and vicinity are offered (all yr). Contact 700 Douglas St, V8W 2B3. Phone 250/388-5248. ¢¢¢¢

  Scenic Drives. North. Malahat Dr (Trans-Canada Hwy 1), a continuation of Victoria's Douglas St, through Goldstream Park over Malahat Dr to Mill Bay, Cowichan Bay, Duncan, and the BC Forest Museum. **North.** On the continuation of Victoria's Blanshard St (Hwys 17 and 17A) through rural communities, pastoral valleys known as the Saanich Peninsula where on 50 acres (20 hectares) of manicured lawns, ponds, fountains, and formal gardens bloom the world-famous Butchart Gardens. **North.** Around the seashore along Dallas Rd through beautiful, traditionally English residential areas to Beach Dr, Oak Bay, and beyond to Cordova Bay. **West.** Leave the city behind on Trans-Canada Hwy 1 to Hwy 14, which winds through rural communities to the village of Sooke, where the population is still engaged in fishing, clamming, and logging. Unspoiled beaches, hiking trails, rocky seashores are accessible from this West Coast road. Continuation on Hwy 14 will lead to Jordan River and to Port Renfrew, with its beautiful Botanical Beach.

Motels/Motor Lodges

★ **ACCENT INN.** *3233 Maple St (V8X 4Y9). 250/475-7500; fax 250/475-7599. www.accentinns.com.* 117 rms, 3 story. July-Aug: S $84-$129; D $94-$134; each addl $10; suites $120-$130; under 16 free; golf plans; lower rates rest of yr. Crib free. Pet accepted, some restrictions. TV; cable. Complimentary coffee in rms. Restaurant 6:30 am-10 pm. Ck-out 11 am. Coin lndry. Meeting rms Business servs avail. In-rm modem link. Health club privileges. Cr cds: A, D, ER, MC, V.

🄳 🔌 💫 🔥 SC

★★ **BEST WESTERN CARLTON PLAZA.** *642 Johnson St (V8W 1M6). 250/388-5513; fax 250/388-5343; toll-free 800/663-7241. www.bestwestern carlton.com.* 103 rms, 6 story, 47 kit. suites. May-mid-Oct: S, D $159-$209; each addl $20; kit. suites $179-$209; under 18 free; wkly rates; lower rates rest of yr. Crib free. Garage parking; valet $9. TV; cable (premium). Complimentary coffee in rms. Restaurant 7 am-3 pm. Ck-out 11 am. Coin lndry. In-rm modem link. Shopping arcade. Barber, beauty shop. Health club privileges. Cr cds: A, DS, MC, V.

🄳 💫

★★ **BEST WESTERN INNER HARBOR.** *412 Quebec St (V8V 1W5). 250/384-5122; fax 250/384-5113; res 800/528-5122. www.bestwestern.com.* 74 rms, 7 story. Mid-May-mid-Oct: S $94-$140; D $110-$160; each addl $20; suites $190-$355; under 12 free; lower rates rest of yr. Crib free. TV; cable, VCR avail. Heated pool; whirlpool. Complimentary continental bkfst. Restaurant nearby. Ck-out 11 am. Coin lndry. Sauna. Refrigerators, microwaves. Cr cds: A, D, DS, MC, V.

🄳 🔌 🔥 💫 💫 💫

★ **DAYS INN ON THE HARBOUR.** *427 Belleville St (V8V 1X3). 250/386-3451; fax 250/386-6999; toll-free 800/665-3024. www.daysinnvictoria. com.* 71 rms, 4 story, 18 kit. units. No A/C. July-Sept: S, D $173-$213; kit. units $213-$250; under 12 free; family, wkly rates; lower rates rest of yr. Crib $10. TV; cable, VCR avail (movies). Complimentary coffee in rms. Restaurant 7 am-10 pm. Bar noon to 1.30 am. Ck-out noon. Business servs avail. Valet serv. Heated pool; whirlpool. Refrigerator, microwave in kit. units. Cr cds: A, D, DS, ER, JCB, MC, V.

💫 💫 💫 SC

★★ **EMBASSY INN.** *520 Menzies St (V8V 2H4). 250/382-8161; fax 250/382-4224; toll-free 800/268-8161.* 103 rms, 3-4 story, 70 A/C, 45 kits. July-Sept: S, D $139-$170; each addl $20; suites $169-$195; kit. units $10 addl; under 16 free; lower rates rest of yr. Crib free. TV; cable (premium). Heated pool. Complimentary coffee in rms. Restaurant 7 am-9:30 pm. Bar from 11 am. Ck-out 11 am. Coin lndry. Business center. In-rm modem link. Valet serv. Sundries. Free parking. Microwaves avail. Cr cds: A, D, ER, MC, V.

🄳 🔌 💫 ✈ 💫 💫 SC 🏃

★★ **HOLIDAY INN.** *3020 Blanshard St (V5V 4E4). 250/382-4400; fax 250/382-4053; toll-free 800/465-4329. www.holiday-inn.com.* 122 rms, 3 story. June-Sept: S, D $79-$159; each addl $20; suites $180-$200; under 18 free; lower rates rest of yr. Crib free. TV; cable (premium). Complimentary coffee in rms. Restaurant 6:30 am-10 pm. Bar 11-1 am. Ck-out noon. Coin lndry. Meeting rms. Business servs avail. In-rm modem link. Valet serv. Sundries. Gift shop. Barber, beauty shop. Exercise equipt; sauna. Whirlpool. Refrigerator, microwave, wet bar in suites. Balconies. Cr cds: A, D, DS, ER, JCB, MC, V.

★★ **HOTEL GRAND PACIFIC.** *463 Belleville St (V8V 1X3). 250/386-2421; fax 250/383-7603. www.hotel grandpacific.com.* 308 rms, 10 story. June-Sept: S, D $145-$165; kit. units $160-$180; under 18 free; golf plans; lower rates rest of yr. Crib free. Pet accepted, some restrictions. TV; cable, VCR avail. Complimentary coffee in rms. Restaurant 6:30 am-10 pm. Bar 11-1 am. Ck-out 11 am. Meeting rms. Business servs avail. In-rm modem link. Bellhops. Valet serv. Sundries. Free garage parking. Exercise equipt; sauna. Massage. Indoor pool; wading pool, whirlpool. Opp ocean. Cr cds: A, D, DS, ER, JCB, MC, V.

★ **PAUL'S MOTOR INN.** *1900 Douglas St (V8T 4K8). 250/382-9231; fax 250/384-1435; toll-free 866/333-7285. www.paulsmotorinn.com.* 78 rms, 2 story. No A/C. May-Sept: S, D $74-$119; each addl $10; under 12 free; lower rates rest of yr. Crib free. TV; cable. Restaurant open 24 hrs. Ck-out noon. Meeting rms. Business servs avail. Cr cds: A, ER, MC, V.

★ **RAMADA HUNTINGDON MANOR.** *330 Quebec St (V8V 1W3). 250/381-3456; fax 250/382-7666; toll-free 800/663-7557. www.bctravel.com/ huntingdon.* 116 rms, 40 A/C, 3 story, 58 kits. Mid-June-mid-Sept: S, D $179-$239; each addl $15; suites $199-$239; kit. units $10 addl; under 18 free; wkly rates; lower rates rest of yr. Crib free. TV; cable. Coffee in rms. Restaurant 7 am-10 pm. Bar 3-10 pm. Ck-out 11 am. Coin lndry. Meeting rms. Business servs avail. Sauna. Massage. Whirlpool. Refrigerators, microwaves. Some private patios, balconies. Opp harbor. Cr cds: A, DS, MC, V.

★★ **ROYAL SCOT INN.** *425 Quebec St (V8V 1W7). 250/388-5463; fax 250/388-5452.* 150 kit. suites, 4 story. No A/C. Mid-May-Sept: S, D $130-$305; each addl $15; under 16 free; wkly, monthly rates; lower rates rest of yr. TV; cable, VCR avail (movies $2.50). Indoor pool; whirlpool. Complimentary coffee in rms. Restaurant 7 am-9 pm. Ck-out 11 am. Coin lndry. Meeting rms. Business servs avail. Bellhops. Valet serv. Gift shop. Free covered parking. Exercise equipt; sauna. Rec rm. Some bathrm phones; microwaves. Balconies. Cr cds: A, MC, V.

Hotels

★★★ **THE BEDFORD REGENCY.** *1140 Government St (V8W 1Y2). 250/384-6835; fax 250/386-8930; toll-free 800/665-6500. www.victoriabc.*

Strait of Juan De Fuca, Victoria, British Columbia

com/accom/bedford.html. 40 rms, 12 with shower only, 6 story. No A/C. May-early Oct: S, D $165-$215; each addl $20; under 16 free; lower rates rest of yr. Crib $15. TV; cable (premium). Continental bkfst. Restaurant 7-11 am. No rm serv. Bar 11:30 am-midnight. Ck-out 11 am. Meeting rms. Business servs avail. Some in-rm whirlpools, fireplaces. Cr cds: A, D, ER, MC, V.

★★ CHATEAU VICTORIA. 740 Burdett Ave (V8W 1B2). 250/382-4221; fax 250/380-1950; toll-free 800/663-5891. www.chateauvictoria.com. 60 rms, 118 suites, some A/C, 19 story, 49 kits. May-mid-Oct: S $117; D $147; each addl $15; suites $210-$260; under 18 free; package plans; lower rates rest of yr. Crib free. TV; cable (premium); VCR avail (movies). Indoor pool, whirlpool. Complimentary coffee in rms. Restaurants 6:30 am-10 pm. Bar 11:30 am-midnight. Ck-out 11 am. Meeting rms. Business servs avail. In-rm modem link. Free parking. Exercise equipt. Microwaves avail. Cr cds: A, C, D, DS, ER, JCB, MC, V.

★★★ COAST HARBOURSIDE HOTEL & MARINA. 146 Kingston St (V9B 5X3). 250/360-1211; fax 250/360-1418. 132 rms, 10 story. May-Oct: S $275; D $305; each addl $20; suites $270-$600; under 18 free; lower rates rest of yr. Crib free. Pet accepted. TV; cable, VCR avail. 2 pools, 1 indoor; whirlpool. Complimentary coffee in rms. Restaurant (see also BLUE CRAB BAR AND GRILL). Rm serv 24 hrs. Bar. Ck-out noon. Meeting rms. Business servs avail. In-rm modem link. Concierge. Sundries. Valet serv. Exercise equipt; sauna. Refrigerators; microwaves avail. Balconies. Cr cds: A, D, DS, ER, JCB, MC, V.

★★★ DELTA VICTORIA OCEAN POINTE RESORT AND SPA. 45 Songhees Rd (V9A 6T3). 250/360-2999; fax 250/360-1041; toll-free 800/667-4677. wwwdeltahotels.com. 250 rms, 8 story, 7 suites. Mid-May-mid-Oct: S, D $200; each addl $15; suites $395-$650; kits. avail; under 18 free; wkly, wkend, hol rates; lower

rates rest of yr. Crib free. Pet accepted. TV; cable, VCR avail. Indoor pool; whirlpool, poolside serv. Restaurants 7:30 am-10 pm (see also THE VICTORIAN). Rm serv 24 hrs. Bar 11-1 am. Ck-out noon. Meeting rms. Business center. In-rm modem link. Concierge. Gift shop. Beauty shop. Lighted tennis. Exercise rm; sauna. Spa. Minibars; microwaves avail. Balconies. On harbor. Cr cds: A, D, DS, ER, JCB, MC, V.

★★ EXECUTIVE HOUSE. 777 Douglas St (V8W 2B5). 250/388-5111; fax 250/385-1323; toll-free 800/663-7001. executivehouse.com. 179 rms, 17 story, 100 kits. No A/C. May-mid-Oct: S, D $99-$195; each addl $15; kit. units $15 addl; suites $195-$595; under 18 free; lower rates rest of yr. Pet accepted, $15/day. Garage $2. TV; cable. Complimentary coffee. Restaurant 7 am-10 pm. Bars 11-1 am; entertainment. Ck-out noon. Meeting rm. Business servs avail. Exercise equipt; sauna, steam rm. Massage. Whirlpool. Many refrigerators; some bathrm phones. Private patios, balconies. Cr cds: A, DS, MC, V.

★★★ THE FAIRMONT EMPRESS. 721 Government St (V8W 1W5). 250/384-8111, fax 250/381-1331; toll-free 800/441-1414. vvv.com/empress/. 480 rms, 7 story. No A/C. Mid-May-Sept: S, D $279-$329; each addl $25; suites $405-$1,700; under 18 free; lower rates rest of yr. Crib free. Garage $14.50. TV; cable (premium), VCR avail. Indoor pool; whirlpool, wading pool. Restaurants 7 am-10 pm. Bar 11:30-1 am; entertainment Mon-Sat. Ck-out 11 am. Convention facilities. Business servs avail. In-rm modem link. Shopping arcade. Exercise equipt; sauna. Minibars; some refrigerators. Opened in 1908. Cr cds: A, C, D, DS, ER, JCB, MC, V.

★★ HARBOUR TOWERS. 345 Quebec St (V8V 1W4). 250/385-2405; fax 250/360-2313; toll-free 800/663-5896. www.harbourtowers.com. 184 rms, 12 story, 49 kits. No A/C. June-mid-Oct: S, D $179-$600; each addl $15; suites $309-$500; under 16 free; lower rates rest of yr. Crib free. Garage parking $2/day. TV; cable (premium). Indoor pool; whirlpool. Complimentary coffee in rms. Restaurant 6:30 am-10 pm. Rm serv 24 hrs. Bar 11-1 am; Sat noon-2 am. Ck-out 11 am. Meeting rms. Business center. In-rm modem link. Gift shop. Airport transportation. Exercise equipt; sauna. Refrigerators, minibars, microwaves. Balconies. Luxury level. Cr cds: A, D, JCB, MC, V.

D 🛏 🦮 🛏 🔥 🎿

★★ **LAUREL POINT INN.** *680 Montreal St (V8V 1Z8). 250/386-8721; fax 250/386-9547; toll-free 800/663-7667. www.laurelpoint.com.* 200 rms, 3 story. No A/C. June-Sept, mid-Dec-early Jan: S, D $279-$329; each addl $25; suites $244-$399; lower rates rest of yr. Crib free. TV; cable, VCR avail. Restaurant 7-10:30 am, 2:30-9 pm. Bar from 11:30 am. Ck-out noon. Meeting rms. Business servs avail. In-rm modem link. Tennis, golf adj. Some refrigerators, bathrm phones. Some balconies. Tudor-style hotel (1927); some four poster beds, many antiques. On beach. Cr cds: A, D, DS, ER, JCB, MC, V.

D 🛏 🦮 🔥

★★★ **THE MAGNOLIA HOTEL & SUITES.** *623 Courtney St (V8W 1B8). 250/381-0999; toll-free 877/624-6654. www.magnoliahotel.com.* 64 rms, 7 story. May-Sept: S, D $285; each addl $20; under 12 free; lower rates rest of yr. Crib avail. Valet parking avail. TV; cable (premium), VCR avail. Complimentary continental bkfst, coffee in rms, newspaper. Restaurant 11:30 am-10 pm. Bar. Ck-out noon, ck-in 3 pm. Meeting rms. Business servs avail. Bellhops. Dry cleaning. Some refrigerators, minibars. Cr cds: A, D, DS, JCB, MC, V.

D 🛏 🦮

★★★ **OAK BAY BEACH AND MARINE RESORT.** *1175 Beach Dr (V8S 2N2). 250/598-4556; toll-free 800/668-7758. www.oakbaybeachhotel.com.* 50 rms, 3 story. No A/C. June-Sept, mid-Dec-early Jan: S, D $198-$225; each addl $25; suites $260-$475; lower rates rest of yr. Crib free. TV; cable, VCR avail. Restaurant 7 am-9 pm. Bar from 11:30 am. Ck-out noon. Meeting rms. Business servs avail. In-rm modem link. Tennis, golf adj. Some refrigerators, bathrm phones. Some balconies. Tudor-style hotel (1927); some four

poster beds, many antiques. On beach. Cr cds: A, D, ER, JCB, MC, V.

🛏 🦮 🛏 🎿 🔥

★★ **QUEEN VICTORIA INN.** *655 Douglas St (V8V 2P9). 250/386-1312; fax 250/381-4312; toll-free 800/663-7007. www.queenvictoriainn.com.* 146 rms, 7 story, 20 suites, 84 kit. units. No A/C. June-Sept: S, D $85-$165 each addl $25; suites $190-$215; kit. units $10 addl; under 15 free; lower rates rest of yr. Crib free. Garage parking $3/day. TV; cable (premium). Indoor pool. Restaurant 6:30 am-9 pm. Ck-out noon. Business servs avail. Some bathrm phones. Balconies. Cr cds: A, C, D, DS, ER, JCB, MC, V.

D 🛏 🔥

★★★ **SWANS SUITE HOTEL.** *506 Pandora Ave (V8W 1N2). 250/361-3310; fax 250/361-3491; toll-free 800/668-7926. www.swanshotel.com.* 29 rms, 4 story. No A/C. July-Sept: S, D $165-$175; each addl $20; under 12 free; lower rates rest of yr. Crib $15. Garage $8. TV; cable, VCR avail (movies $3.50). Complimentary coffee in rms. Restaurant 7-1 am. Bar 11:30-2:30 am; entertainment Sun-Thurs. Ck-out noon. Coin lndry. Meeting rms. Business servs avail. Refrigerators, microwaves. Some balconies. Brewery, beer and wine shop on premises. Cr cds: A, D, DS, MC, V.

D 🛏 🔥

★★★ **VICTORIA REGENT.** *1234 Wharf St (V8W 3H9). 250/386-2211; fax 250/386-2622; toll-free 800/663-7472. www.victoriaregent.com.* 45 rms, 8 story, 30 suites. July-Sept: S, D $249-$369; each addl $20; suites $219-$695; under 16 free; wkly rates in winter; golf, package plans. TV; cable (premium), VCR avail. Complimentary continental bkfst. Restaurant 7 am-11 pm. Ck-out noon. Meeting rms. Business servs avail. In-rm modem link. Free covered parking. Health club privileges. Refrigerators, microwaves; some fireplaces, in-rm whirlpools. Balconies. Marina. View of Inner Harbour and city. Cr cds: A, D, DS, ER, JCB, MC, V.

D 🛏 🔥

Resorts

★★★★ **THE AERIE RESORT.** *600 Ebedora Ln, Malahat (V0R 2L0). 250/743-7115; fax 250/743-4766; res 800/518-1933. www.aerie.bc.ca.* This Mediterranean-style resort and spa is 30 minutes from Victoria in the mountains of Southern Vancouver Island. The ten-acre, parklike property of manicured grounds and breathtaking views is home to clusters of white buildings nestled along the green mountainside holding 29 rooms and suites. After a nature-filled day, relax in the Wellness and Beauty Centre or dine on Northwest-influenced French cuisine. 10 rms, 3 story, 13 suites. May-Sept: S, D $285; suites $495; lower rates rest of yr. Parking lot. Indoor pool; whirlpool. TV; cable (premium). Complimentary full bkfst, coffee in rms, newspaper. Restaurant (see also THE AERIE DINING ROOM). Bar. Meeting rms. Business servs avail. Bellhops Concierge. Dry cleaning. Gift shop. Sauna. Golf. Tennis. Hiking trail. Picnic facilities. Cr cds: A, D, ER, MC, V.
🐾 🛠 🏋 🎣 ⛱ 🖥 🐕

B&Bs/Small Inns

★★★ **ABIGAIL'S HOTEL.** *906 McClure St (V8V 3E7). 250/388-5363; fax 250/388-7787; toll-free 800/561-6565. www.abigailshotel.com.* 22 rms, 4 story. No A/C. No elvtr. S $119-$219; D $159-$349 each addl $30. Complimentary full bkfst; afternoon refreshments. Restaurant nearby. Ck-out 11 am, ck-in 3 9 pm. Business servs avail. In-rm modem link. Gift shop. Some refrigerators, fireplaces. Renovated Tudor-style building (1930). Antiques. Flower garden. Totally nonsmoking. Cr cds: A, MC, V.
🐾 🖥 🐕

★★ **ANDERSEN HOUSE.** *301 Kingston St (V8V 1V5). 250/388-4565; fax 250/388-4563. www.islandnet. com/~andersen/.* 5 rms, 3 with shower only, 3 story, 2 suites, 1 kit. unit. No A/C. Mid-May-mid-Oct: S $145-$185; D $155-$195; each addl $35; suites $165-$205; lower rates rest of yr. Children over 12 yrs only. TV in some rms; cable. Complimentary full bkfst. Complimentary coffee in rms.

Restaurant nearby. Ck-out 11 am, ck-in 1 pm. Luggage handling. Street parking. Some refrigerators. Some balconies. Picnic tables. Built in 1891; eclectic mix of antiques and modern art. A 1927 motor yacht is avail as guest rm. Totally nonsmoking. Cr cds: MC, V.
🖥 🐕

★★★ **BEACONSFIELD INN.** *998 Humboldt St (V8V 2Z8). 250/384-4044; fax 250/384-4052. www. beaconsfieldinn.com.* 9 rms, 4 story. No A/C. No elvtr. Rm phones avail. Mid-June-Sept: S, D $219-$359; each addl $65. Complimentary full bkfst; afternoon refreshments. Restaurant nearby. Ck-out 11 am, ck-in 3 pm. Business servs avail. Restored Edwardian mansion (1905); period antique furnishings, stained glass, mahogany floors. Library. Totally nonsmoking. Cr cds: MC, V.
🅳 🐾 🛠 🖥 🐕

★★★★ **HASTINGS HOUSE.** *160 Upper Ganges Rd, Salt Spring (V8K 2S2). 250/537-2362; toll-free 800/661-9255. www.hastingshouse.com.* Nestled on Salt Spring Island, one of British Columbia's beautiful Gulf Islands, this retreat is both tranquil and romantic. Five different buildings, including a barn with hayloft suite, make up the accommodations, and all are decorated in warm, country-house style. Dining is found in the main house, where guests can enjoy breakfast, afternoon refreshments, and formal dinner. The dining room provides seasonal French cuisine featuring fresh local ingredients and herbs and vegetables from the gardens. Salt Spring Island lamb is a special feature of the house and should not be missed. 17 rms. Mar-Apr, Mid-Oct-Dec 20 $360-$410; May-mid-June, Dec 21-29 $350-$450; mid-June-mid-Oct $400-$500; ages 16 and over only. Restaurant. Ck-out 11 am, ck-in 1:30 pm. Golf. Tennis. Hiking. Biking. Fishing. Cr cds: A, MC, V.
🅳 🐾 🛠 🏋 🎣 ✕ 🖥 🐕

★★★ **HATERLEIGH HERITAGE INN.** *243 Kingston St (V8V 1V5). 250/384-9995; fax 250/384-1935. www.haterleigh.com.* 6 rms, 2 story. No rm phones. June-mid-Oct: S, D $150-$195; lower rates rest of yr.

Complimentary full bkfst; afternoon refreshments. Restaurant nearby. Ck-out 11 am, ck-in 4 pm. Luggage handling. Built in 1901; antiques. Health club privileges. Many in-rm whirlpools. Totally nonsmoking. Cr cds: MC, V.

★★ **HOLLAND HOUSE.** *595 Michigan St (V8V 1S7). 250/384-6644; fax 250/384-6117; toll-free 800/335-3466. www.hollandhouse.victoria.bc.ca.* 14 rms, 3 story. No A/C. May-Oct: S $75-$100; D $145-$250; each addl $25; lower rates rest of yr. Children over 10 yrs only. TV; cable. Complimentary full bkfst. Ck-out 11 am, ck-in 2 pm. Business servs avail. Some fireplaces. Balconies. Many antique furnishings; 4-poster beds. Totally nonsmoking. Cr cds: A, MC, V.

★★★ **OLDE ENGLAND INN.** *429 Lampson St (V9A 5Y9). 250/388-4353; fax 250/382-8311. www.oldeengland inn.com.* 53 rms, 3 story, 6 kits. No A/C. No elvtr. Apr-Oct: S, D $129-$349; each addl $15; lower rates rest of yr. Crib $10. TV; cable. Restaurant 8 am-10 pm. Ck-out 11 am. Business servs avail. Luggage handling. Microwaves avail. Tudor-style mansion (1909); many antiques, incl canopied beds used by European monarchs. Replica of Shakespeare's 16th-century birthplace on grounds. Cr cds: A, MC, V.

★★★ **PRIOR HOUSE B&B INN.** *620 St. Charles (V8S 3N7). 250/592-8847; fax 250/592-8223; toll-free 877/924-3300. www.priorhouse.com.* 6 air-cooled rms, 3 story. Some rm phones. June-Oct: S, D $210-$295; each addl $35; 2-day min wkends, Aug; lower rates rest of yr. Complimentary full bkfst; afternoon refreshments. Restaurant nearby. Ck-out 11 am, ck-in 4 pm. Business servs avail. Lawn games. Fireplaces; microwave avail. Balconies. Edwardian mansion (1912) built by King's representative. Crystal chandeliers, oak woodwork. Totally nonsmoking. Cr cds: MC, V.

★★★ **SOOKE HARBOUR HOUSE.** *1528 Whiffen Split Rd, Sooke (V0S 1N0). 250/642-3421; fax 250/642-6988; res 800/889-9688. www.sooke harbourhouse.com.* 28 rms, 4 story. No A/C. Apr-Oct: S $290-$555; each addl $35; under 12 free; lower rates rest of yr. Closed 3 wks Jan. Crib free. Pet accepted; $20. TV avail; cable (premium), VCR avail (movies). Restaurant (see also SOOKE HARBOUR HOUSE). Ck-out noon, ck-in 3 pm. Luggage handling. Business servs avail. Massage. Refrigerators; balconies. On ocean. Totally nonsmoking. Cr cds: A, D, MC, V.

★★★★ **THE WICKANINNISH INN.** *Osprey Ln at Chesterman Beach, Tofino (V0R 2Z0). 250/725-3100; fax 250/725-3110; res 800/333-4604. www.wickinn.com.* Along the rocky, wooded coastline of Vancouver Island's west shore sits this weathered cedar inn marking the gateway to Pacific Rim National Park. All 46 guest rooms have fireplaces, private balconies, and floor-to-ceiling windows with panoramic coast and ocean views. Visit Ancient Cedars Spa or have a private treatment on the sea-washed rocks. Take morning constitutionals, hike the trails in the temperate rain forest, or enjoy sunset walks on Chesterman Beach. End the day with a dinner at the resort's Pointe Restaurant, perched high above the crashing waves of the Pacific Ocean. 46 rms, 3 story, S, D $220-$360; each addl $20; under 12 free. Crib free, rollaway beds $20. TV; cable (premium), VCR avail. Coffee in rms. Restaurant 8-11 am, 11:30 am-2 pm, 5-9 pm. Lounge 2-9 pm. Ck-out noon, ck-in 3 pm. Meeting rm. In-rm modem link. Golf nearby. Hiking trails, beach. Spa, steam rm. Mini-bars. Fireplaces in all rms. Balconies. Wooden building with natural surroundings. Environmentally sensitive. Cr cds: A, C, D, ER, JCB, MC, V.

Restaurants

★★★★ **THE AERIE DINING ROOM.** *600 Ebedora Ln, Malahat (V0R 2L0). 250/743-7115. www.aerie. bc.ca.* Located in the Mediterranean-inspired resort and spa of the same name, this renowned dining room has absolutely stunning views of the fjordlike Sound and the waters of the Georgia Strait. Chef Christophe

Letard presents Northwest-inspired French cuisine in each of the three menus offered each day: five-course prix fixe, a market tasting menu, plus a full a la carte option. Specializes in fresh seafood, lamb, game. Hrs: 6 pm-midnight. Res accepted. Bar. Dinner a la carte entrees: $30-$40. Complete meals: $95. Parking. Cr cds: A, D, MC, V.
D

★★★ **ANTOINE'S.** *2 Centennial Sq (V8W 1P7).* 250/384-7055. Hrs: 11:30 am-2 pm, 5:30-10 pm. Closed Jan 1. Res required. Continental menu. Bar. Wine list. A la carte entrees: lunch $12-$19, dinner $22-$30. Complete meals: dinner $22-$45. Specializes in local seafood. Parking. Overlooks large fountain in Centennial Sq. Cr cds: A, MC, V.

★★ **BLUE CRAB BAR AND GRILL.** *146 Kingston (V8V 1V4).* 250/480-1999. Hrs: 6:30 am-11 pm; Sun brunch 11 am-2:30 pm; early-bird dinner 5-6:30 pm. Res accepted. Seafood menu. Bar 11-1 am. Bkfst $5-$9.25, lunch $8.50-$14.25, dinner $20-$30. Sun brunch $10. Child's meals. Specializes in fresh local seafood. Contemporary decor; view of harbor and skyline. Totally non-smoking. Cr cds: A, D, DS, MC, V.
D

★★ **CAFE BRIO.** *944 Fort St (V8V 3K2).* 250/383-0009. www.cafe-brio. com. Specializes in confit of duck. Hrs: 11:45 am-10 pm; Sat-Mon 5:30-10 pm. Closed Dec 25; 1st wk in Jan. Res accepted. Wine list. Lunch $6-$12; dinner $13-$28. Child's menu. Entertainment. Italian Tuscan patio. Cr cds: A, MC, V.
D

★★ **CAMILLE'S.** *45 Bastion Sq (V8W 1J1).* 250/381-3433. www.camilles restaurant.com. Hrs: 5:30-10 pm. Closed Jan 1, Dec 24, 25. Res accepted. Bar. Dinner $17-$23. Specializes in seafood. Entertainment. Romantic atmosphere. Cr cds: A, MC, V.

★★★ **DEEP COVE CHALET.** *11190 Chalet Rd (V8L 4R4).* 250/656-3541. www.deepcovechalet.com. Hrs: noon-2:30 pm, 5:30-10 pm. Closed Mon. Res accepted. French menu. Bar. Wine cellar. Lunch $15-$35, dinner

$20.50-$70. Complete meals: lunch $15-$22, dinner $20-$40. Many daily specials. Pianist Fri, Sat. Parking. Outdoor dining. View of Deep Cove Bay. Built in 1914; originally tea-house for a railroad station. Cr cds: A, MC, V.
D

★★★ **EMPRESS ROOM.** *721 Government St (V8W 1W5).* 250/384-8111. www.fairmont.com. Specializes in roasted rack of lamb, fresh seasonal fish. Hrs: 5:30-9 pm. Closed Mon, Tues in Nov & Feb. Res accepted. Wine list. Dinner $22-$56. Entertainment: harpist. Cr cds: A, D, DS, MC, V.
D

★★ **GATSBY MANSION.** *309 Belleville St (V8V 1X2).* 250/388-9191. www.bctravel.com/huntingdon/gatsby.ht ml. Hrs: 7 am-10 pm. Res accepted. Continental menu. Serv bar. Bkfst, lunch $4.95-$8.95, dinner $14.95-$23.95. Specializes in seafood, steak, poultry. Parking. Outdoor dining. Restored 3-story mansion (1897); antiques; garden. Cr cds: A, D, DS, MC, V.

★★★ **HERALD STREET CAFFE.** *546 Herald St (V8W 1S6).* 250/381-1441. Hrs: 11:30 am-3 pm, 5:30-10:30 pm; Mon, Tues from 5:30 pm; Fri, Sat to midnight; Sun brunch 11 am-3 pm. Res accepted. Eclectic menu. Bar. Lunch $8-$15, dinner $11.95-$32.95. Sun brunch $8.50-$10.95. Specializes in seafood. Eclectic decor. Cr cds: A, D, DS, ER, MC, V.
D

★★ **HUGO'S GRILL.** *619 Courtney St (V8W 1B8).* 250/920-4844. www. hugoslounge.com. Closed Dec 25. Res accepted. Wine, beer. Lunch $5.95-$12.95; dinner $9.95-$30.95. Entertainment. Cr cds: A, JCB, MC, V.
D

★★ **IL TERRAZZO.** *555 Johnson St (V8W 1M2).* 250/361-0028. www. ilterrazzo.com. Hrs: 11:30 am-3:30 pm, 5-11 pm; Fri, Sat to midnight; Sun 5-10 pm. Closed Jan 1, Dec 25. Res accepted. No A/C. Italian menu. Bar. A la carte entrees: lunch $7.95-$11.95, dinner $13.95-$21.95. Child's meals. Specializes in wood oven-baked meats and game, North-

ern Italian dishes. Own baking, pasta. Outdoor dining. Two-level dining area features fireplaces, wood-fired pizza oven. Cr cds: MC, V.
D

★ **INDIA TANDOORI HUT.** *1548 Fort St (V8S 5J2).* 250/370-1880. Hrs: 11 am-2 pm, 5-9:30 pm; Sat brunch to 2 pm. Closed Dec 25. Res accepted. No A/C. East Indian menu. Bar. A la carte entrees: lunch $5-$18, dinner $11-$19. Sat brunch $7.99. Specialties: tandoori chicken, lamb curry, chicken marsala. Own baking. Outdoor dining. Colorful Indian decor. Cr cds: MC, V.
D SC

★★ **J & J WONTON NOODLE HOUSE.** *1012 Fort St (V8V 3K4).* 250/383-0680. Hrs: 11 am-2:30 pm, 4:30-8:30 pm. Closed Sun, Mon; hols. Chinese menu. Bar. Lunch $3.95-$11, dinner $5.95-$16.95. Child's meals. Specialties: spicy beef or chicken noodle soup, sizzling hot pan prawns, spicy tofu hot pot. Own baking, noodles. Casual Chinese decor. Totally nonsmoking. Cr cds: MC, V.
D

★★ **JAPANESE VILLAGE STEAK AND SEAFOOD HOUSE.** *734 Broughton St (V8W 1E1).* 250/382-5165. *www.japanesevillage.bc.ca.* Hrs: 11:30 am-2 pm, 5-10:30 pm; Sat 5-11:30 pm; Sun 5-10 pm. Closed hols. Res accepted. Japanese menu. Serv bar. Complete meals: lunch $6.50-$11.50, dinner $16.50-$34.50. Child's meals. Specialties: teppan-style steak, salmon, lobster. Entertainment Sun eves. Tableside cooking, sushi bar. Japanese decor. Cr cds: A, C, D, DS, ER, MC, V.
D

★★ **THE MARINA.** *1327 Beach Dr (V8S 2N4).* 250/598-8555. *www. marinarestaurnt.com.* Hrs: 11:30 am-10 pm; Fri, Sat to 11 pm; Sun from 10 am; Sun brunch to 2:30 pm. Closed Dec 25. Res accepted. Continental menu. Bar. Wine list. Lunch $7.25-$15.95, dinner $9.95-$29.95. Sun brunch $26.95. Child's meals. Specialties: roasted oysters, seafood hot pot. Own baking. Outdoor dining. Two-level dining area with large

windows overlooking marina. Cr cds: A, D, DS, MC, V.
D

★★★★ **RESTAURANT MATISSE.** *512 Yates St (V8W 1K8).* 250/480-0883. *www.restaurantmatisse.com.* Original artwork covers the exposed red-brick walls, and the scent of fresh flowers fills the air at this downtown, very traditional French restaurant steps from the Inner Harbour. The atmosphere is further enhanced by nostalgic French Chanteuse. Chef Ludovic Renaud offers specialties from his native France on the a la carte and prix fixe menus. The host/co-owner matches each course with wines from the wine menu if desired. Classic French menu. Specializes in lobster bisque, creme brulee, bouillabaisse. Hrs: 11:30 am-midnight; Sat, Sun 5 pm-midnight. Res accepted. Extensive wine list. Dinner $18.75-$27.95. Child's menu. Entertainment. Cr cds: A, MC, V.
D SC

★★★ **SOOKE HARBOUR HOUSE.** *1528 Whiffen Spit Rd, Sooke Harbour (V0S 1N0).* 250/642-3421. *www.sooke harbourhouse.com.* Continental menu. Specializes in fresh seafood. Hrs: 5:30-9:30 pm. Res accepted. Bar. A la carte entrees Apr-Oct: dinner $20-$30, $100/couple; winter 4-course $55. Cr cds: D, DS, MC, V.
D

★★ **SPINNAKER'S BREW PUB.** *308 Catherine St (V9A 3S8).* 250/386-2739. *www.spinnakers.com.* Hrs: 7 am-11 pm. Res accepted. No A/C. Bar from 10 am. Bkfst $1.99-$8.95, lunch $4.50-$11.95, dinner $4.50-$14.95. Child's meals. Specializes in pasta, pot pies, fish and chips. Own baking, pasta. Jazz, blues Fri, Sat. Outdoor dining. Views of harbor and city skyline; brewing vats can be seen from bar. Cr cds: A, D, MC, V.
D

★★★ **THE VICTORIAN.** *45 Songhees Rd (V9A 6T3).* 250/360-5800. *www. oprhotel.com.* Hrs: 6-10:30 pm. Closed Sun; also 1st 3 wks Jan. Res accepted. Bar 11-1 am. A la carte entrees: dinner $21-$27. Complete meals: dinner $39-$49. Child's meals. Specializes in fresh seafood, rack of lamb. Valet parking. View of Inner and Outer

Harbour. Totally nonsmoking. Cr cds: A, D, MC, V.

D

★ **WHITE HEATHER TEA ROOM.** *1885 Oak Bay Ave (V8R 1C6). 250/595-8020.* Specializes in grilled focaccia sandwiches, homemade soups, tarts, crepes, high tea. Hrs: 9:30 am-5 pm; Sun 10 am-5 pm. Closed Mon. Res accepted. Wine, beer. Lunch $6.95-$8.95. Entertainment. Cr cds: MC, V.

D

Whistler

(F-4) *See also Vancouver*

Pop 4,500 **Elev** 2,200 ft
Area code 604
Information Whistler Resort Association, 4010 Whistler Way, V0N 1B4; 604/932-3928 or 800/944-7853; or the Activity & Information Centre; 604/932-2394
Web www.whistler-resort.com

The winning combination of Blackcomb and Whistler mountains makes this an internationally famous ski area. It is also a popular summer vacation area. Five lakes dot the valley in Whistler, offering ample opportunity to fish, swim, boardsail, canoe, kayak, sail, or waterski; all of the lakes are accessible by the Valley Trail network that winds its way through Whistler.

The alpine slopes for a time give way to extensive hiking and mountain biking trails, but even in summer there is skiing to be found; Whistler is where enthusiasts will find the only lift-serviced, summertime public glacier skiing in North America.

What to See and Do

Ski areas.

Blackcomb. Six high-speed quad chairlifts (one covered), three triple chairlifts, three handletows, two T-bars, platter lift, magic carpet lift. More than 100 runs; longest run seven mi, vertical drop 5,280 ft. Glacier skiing (Mid-June-Aug, weather permitting). High-speed gondola. Phone 604/687-1032.

Whistler. Six high-speed quad, double, two triple chairlifts, two handletows, two T-bars, platter pull. More than 100 runs; longest run seven mi, vertical drop 5,020 ft. Two high-speed gondolas. Phone 604/687-1032.

Motels/Motor Lodges

★★ **BEST WESTERN LISTEL WHISTLER HOTEL.** *4121 Village Green (V0N 1B4). 604/932-1133; fax 604/932-8383; toll-free 800/663-5472. www.listelhotel.com.* 98 rms, 3 story. Mid-Dec-mid-Apr: S, D $99-$299; each addl $40; suites $495; family rates; ski, golf plans; higher rates New Year's hols; lower rates rest of yr. Crib free. Parking $8; valet. TV; cable. Sauna. Heated pool; whirlpool. Restaurant 7-10 am, 6-10 pm. Bar 6 pm-midnight. Ck-out 10 am. Coin lndry. Meeting rms. Business servs avail. Bellhops. Sundries. Gift shop. Downhill/x-country ski adj. Refrigerators; bathrm phone in suites. Cr cds: A, D, DS, ER, JCB, MC, V.

D ♣ ✈ ☉ ⚗ ≈ ✕ ▨ 🔥

★★ **CRYSTAL LODGE.** *4154 Village Green (V0N 1B0). 604/932-2221; fax 604/932-2635; toll-free 800/667-3363. www.crystal-lodge.com.* 137 rms, 2-3 story, 40 kit. suites. Late Jan-Apr: S, D $115-$220; each addl $25; kit. suites $250-$270; suites from $450; ski, golf plans; higher rates Christmas hols; lower rates rest of yr. Crib free. Garage parking $7. TV; cable, VCR avail. Heated pool; whirlpools, steam rm, poolside serv. Restaurant 7 am-10 pm. Bar noon-1 am; entertainment. Ck-out 10 am. Coin lndry. Meeting rms. Business servs avail. Bellhops. Valet serv. Concierge. Shopping arcade. Airport, RR station transportation. Downhill/x-country ski adj. Cr cds: A, DS, ER, JCB, MC, V.

D ☉ ⚗ ≈ ▨ 🔥

Hotel

★★★ **PAN PACIFIC LODGE.** *4320 Sundial Crescent (V0N 1S4). 604/905-2999; toll-free 888/905-9995. www. panpac.com.* 8 story, 121 suites. Dec-

Out for a stroll

Mar; suites $309; lower rates rest of yr. Crib avail. TV; cable (premium), VCR avail. Complimentary coffee in rms, newspaper. Restaurant 7 am-2 pm. Bar. Ck-out 11 am, ck-in 3 pm. Meeting rm. Business center. Bellhops. Concierge. Dry cleaning, coin lndry. Gift shop. Exercise equipt. Golf. Tennis, 8 courts. Downhill skiing. Bike rentals. Supervised children's activities. Video games. Cr cds: A, C, D, DS, ER, JCB, MC, V.

Resorts

★★ DELTA WHISTLER RESORT.
4050 Whistler Way (V0N 1B4). 604/932-1982; fax 604/932-7332; toll-free 800/515-4050. www.delta-whistler. com. 292 rms, 8 story, 99 kit. units. Early Dec-mid-Apr: S, D $289-$409; each addl $30; suites $470-$595; kit. units $390; family rates; ski, golf plans; higher rates Christmas hols; lower rates rest of yr. Crib free. Pet accepted. Garage parking $12. TV; cable (premium). Pool; whirlpool, poolside serv. Complimentary coffee. Restaurant 6 am-10 pm. Bar 11-1 am. Ck-out 11 am. Coin lndry. Convention facilities. Business servs avail. Concierge. Shopping arcade. Indoor tennis, pro. Downhill/x-country ski adj. Exercise equipt; steam rm. Minibars; some bathrm phones. Cr cds: A, D, ER, JCB, MC, V.

★★★ THE FAIRMONT CHATEAU WHISTLER. *4599 Chateau Blvd (V0N 1B4). 604/938-8000; fax 604/938-2055; toll-free 800/606-8244. www. chateauwhistlerresort.com.* 342 rms, 10-12 story. Mid-Dec-mid-May: S, D $350-$375; each addl $30; suites $475-$1,100; under 17 free; ski, golf plans; higher rates Christmas hols; lower rates rest of yr. Crib free. Pet accepted; $10. Valet parking $15. TV; cable. Indoor/outdoor pool; whirlpool, poolside serv. Supervised children's activities (June-Sept). Restaurants 7 am-11 pm. Rm serv 24 hrs. Bar 11 am-midnight; entertainment. Ck-out 11 am. Meeting rms. Concierge. Shopping arcade. Tennis, pro. 18-hole golf, greens fee $109 (incl cart), pro, putting green. Downhill/x-country ski adj. Exercise equipt; sauna. Refrigerators avail. Minibars; some bathrm phones. Cr cds: A, D, DS, JCB, MC, V.

★★★ SUMMIT LODGE. *4359 Main St (V0N 1B4). 604/932-2778; toll-free 888/913-8811. www.summitlodge.com.* 81 rms, 4 story. Dec-Mar, July-Sept: S, D $425; each addl $20; under 18 free; lower rates rest of yr. Crib avail. Pet accepted, fee. Parking garage. Pool; whirlpool. TV; cable (premium), VCR avail. Complimentary continental bkfst, coffee in rms, newspaper. Restaurant 7 am-11 pm. Ck-out 11 am, ck-in 4 pm. Meeting rms. Business center. Bellhops. Concierge. Dry cleaning, coin lndry. Free airport transportation. Sauna. Downhill skiing. Exercise rm. Some refrigerators, minibars. Cr cds: A, D, DS, ER, MC, V.

★★★ THE WESTIN RESORT AND SPA. *4090 Whistler Way (V0N 1B4). 604/905-5000; toll-free 888/634-5577. www.westinwhistler.net.* This resort and spa is nestled at the foot of the famed Whistler Mountain. This all-suite hotel has fully equipped kitchenettes, extra large bathrooms with soaker tubs, a full range of in-room amenities, business-friendly work stations, and the usual electronics, including video checkout. Aubergine Grill with summer terrace, the FireRock Lounge, 24-hour room service, and a state-of-the-art spa add to the enjoyment of this luxurious property. Combining business with pleasure? The Westin offers full conference facilities with on-site business services. 419 suites,

11 story. Dec-Apr, July-Sept: S, D $250-$300; each addl $30; suites $2,500; under 18 free; lower rates rest of yr. Crib avail. Valet parking avail. Indoor/outdoor pools, lap pool, whirlpool. TV; cable (premium). Complimentary coffee in rms, newspaper. Restaurant. Rm serv 24 hrs. Bar. Ck-out noon, ck-in 4 pm. Meeting rms. Business servs avail. Bellhops. Concierge. Dry cleaning, coin lndry. Gift shop. Salon/barber. Exercise rm, sauna, steam rm. Golf, 18 holes. Tennis, 4 courts. Downhill skiing. Supervised children's activities. Hiking trail. Video games. Cr cds: A, DS, MC, V.

Restaurants

★ ★ ★ **BEAR FOOT BISTRO.** *4121 Village Green (V0N IB4). 604/932-3433. www.bearfootbistro.com.* Only a hard day of skiing can justify this four-hour, decadent feast for the senses. Chef Brock Windsor directs ten chefs in handcrafting each of eight courses from a huge range of rare, high-quality ingredients including caribou and pheasant. Add to this one of the most beautiful locations in North America and the result is a truly standout dining experience. Hrs: 5:30-11 pm. Res accepted. Wine list. Dinner $16-$50. Child's menu. Entertainment: jazz Mon-Sat. Cr cds: A, C, D, DS, ER, JCB, MC, V.

★ ★ ★ **LA RUA.** *4557 Blackcomb Way (V0N 1B0). 604/932-5011. www.laruarestaurante.com.* Hrs: 5:30-11 pm. Res required. Continental menu. Bar. Wine cellar. Dinner $13.95-$29.95. Specializes in Northwestern cuisine, seafood. Parking. Outdoor dining. Formal dining in Mediterranean-style decor; many antiques. Jacket. Totally nonsmoking. Cr cds: A, DS, MC, V.

★ ★ **RIMROCK CAFE.** *2117 Whistler Rd (V0N 1B0). 604/932-5565. www.rimrockwhistler.com.* Hrs: 6-10 pm. Res accepted. No A/C. Bar. Dinner $16-$25. Specializes in fresh Northwest seafood, oysters. Parking. Outdoor dining. Works of local artists. Built

on and around a very large rock. Cr cds: A, D, ER, MC, V.

★ ★ ★ **RISTORANTE ARAXI.** *4222 Village Sq (V0N 1B4). 604/932-4540. www.araxi.com.* Hrs: 10:30 am-3 pm, 5:30-10:30 pm. Res accepted. Italian menu. Bar. 11-12:30 am. Wine list. A la carte entrees: lunch $8-$14.95, dinner $10.50-$29.95. Specializes in fresh seafood, live lobster, local game. Own baking. Outdoor dining. Mediterranean decor. Cr cds: A, D, MC, V.

★ **SUSHI VILLAGE.** *4272 Mountain Sq (V0N 1B4). 604/932-3330.* Hrs: noon-2:30 pm, 5-10 pm; summer hrs vary. Japanese menu. Bar. Complete meals: lunch $7.95-$13.25, dinner $7.95-$31.25. Specialties: sushi, chicken teriyaki, Sushi bar. Tatami rms or traditional dining facilities. Cr cds: A, D, MC, V.

★ ★ **TRATTORIA DI UMBERTO.** *4417 Sundial Pl (V0N 1B0). 604/932-5858. www.umberto.com.* Hrs: noon-2:30 pm, 5:30-10 pm. Res accepted. Italian menu. Bar. Lunch $5-$15, dinner $5-$26. Child's meals. Specialties: rack of lamb, prawns sauteed in tomato and garlic sauce, Tuscan cuisine. Outdoor dining. Large tile mosaic imported from the Vatican. Cr cds: A, D, ER, MC, V.

★ ★ ★ **VAL D'ISERE.** *4314 Main St, #8 (V0N 1B0). 604/932-4666. www.valdisere-restaurant.com.* Hrs: 5:30-10:30 pm. Closed mid-Oct-mid-Nov. Res accepted. No A/C. French country menu. Wine list. Dinner $14.50-$22.50. Specialties: venison, Alsace-style onion pie. Overlooks large courtyard. Cr cds: A, D, ER, MC, V.

★ ★ ★ **WILDFLOWER RESTAURANT.** *4599 Chateau Blvd (V0N 1B4). 604/938-2033. www.chateauwhistler.ca.* Specializes in seafood. Hrs: 7 am-10 pm. Res accepted. Wine list. Lunch $13-$18; dinner $18-$42. Brunch $38. Child's menu. Entertainment. Cr cds: A, D, DS, ER, JCB, MC, V.

PROVINCE OF MANITOBA

Manitoba is the most eastern of Canada's three prairie provinces. The capital city, Winnipeg, houses more than half of the province's population. Much of the remainder of the province is unspoiled recreational area. Entry into Manitoba can be made from Ontario on the east, Saskatchewan on the west, or from Minnesota and North Dakota on the south.

Many summer festivals are held that reflect the varied ethnic settlements in the province. Most representative of all ethnic backgrounds is Folklorama, a festival of the nations, which takes place in Winnipeg in August.

Pop 1,026,241 **Land area** 211,470 square miles (547,705 square kilometers) **Capital** Winnipeg **Web** www.travelmanitoba. com

Information Travel Manitoba, Department RK9, 155 Carlton St, 7th Floor, Winnipeg R3C 3H8; 204/945-3777 or 800/665-0040, extension RK9

Manitoba is also known for its 12 provincial parks and numerous recreation and heritage parks. Riding Mountain National Park is located near Dauphin. Fishing is good from May to September and water-related activities can be enjoyed in the many resorts and beaches on Lake Winnipeg, Lake Manitoba, and lakes in the provincial parks.

Outstanding attractions in Winnipeg include the zoo in Assiniboine Park, the Forks National Historic Site, the Manitoba Museum of Man and Nature, and the Winnipeg Art Gallery. The internationally acclaimed Royal Winnipeg Ballet,

"Wheat City," Brandon

the Winnipeg Symphony Orchestra, the Manitoba Opera, and the Manitoba Theatre Centre have made Winnipeg a mecca for all who enjoy fine music and theater.

Manitoba observes Central Standard Time and Daylight Saving Time in summer.

In addition to national holidays, Manitoba observes Civic Holiday (first Monday August).

Seat belts are mandatory for all persons anywhere in vehicle. Children under five years or 50 pounds in weight must be in an approved safety seat anywhere in vehicle. For further information phone 204/945-4603.

EXPLORING CENTRAL CANADA

The LaVerendrye Trail follows the path of the LaVerendrye brothers, French explorers who traveled across central Canada and the United States in the 1700s on foot and canoe. The route begins along the east side of Lake Winnipeg, a portion of lake shore with an abundance of beaches. Grand Beach Provincial Park provides miles of sandy relaxation and swimming along the lake; the natural dunes tower nearly 30 feet. The route continues past more beach resorts and parks to the mouth of the Winnipeg River, part of the river "highway" system used by the early French voyageurs. Turn to follow the river toward St. Georges, a French-speaking community along the river with a rebuilt fur-trading fort. At Seven Sisters Falls, turn and enter Whiteshell Provincial Park, which preserves thick spruce forests, rock-lined lakes, waterfalls, and the wildlife of the Great North Woods. In spring and summer, Alfred Hole Goose Sanctuary, near Rennie, is filled with young geese. Along park hiking trails, you may notice native petroforms, rock formations in the shape of snakes or turtles, constructed as sacred sites by early Native Americans. In the eastern portion of Whiteshell Park are more lakes, including Falcon Lake, with a number of excellent resorts and public beaches, and West Hawk Lake, which was formed by the impact of a meteorite. With a depth of 380 feet, the lake is popular with scuba divers. (**APPROX 103 MI; 167 KM.**)

WATER ACTIVITIES NEAR WINNIPEG

This route leaves Winnipeg to travel north along the western shores of Lake Winnipeg, the continent's seventh-largest lake. The southern part of the lake is flanked by hardwood forests and lined with beautiful white sand beaches. In the summer, provincial parks are popular with sunbathers, swimmers, and picnickers. Gimli, a small farming and fishing village, was settled almost exclusively by Icelandic settlers in the late 19th century; for many years it was capital of a semiautonomous region known as the Republic of New Iceland. The historic town still celebrates its Icelandic heritage in a series of summer festivals. An hour farther north is Hecla Island, also part of New Iceland, now preserved as Hecla/Grindstone Provincial Park. The island—which once was a fishing community—is linked to the mainland by a bridge and has a number of hiking trails through wildlife habitats. Nearby resorts rent canoes, cross-country skis, and other recreational gear. Island beaches are also popular for sunbathers and swimmers. (**APPROX 73 MI; 117 KM.**)

Brandon (G-2)

Pop 42,000 **Elev** 1,342 ft (409 m)
Area code 204
Information Brandon Chamber of Commerce, 1043 Rossler Ave, R7A 0L5; 204/728-3287 or 888/799-1111
Web www.brandon.com/chamber

Brandon has been named the "Wheat City" in honour of its rich agricultural heritage and reputation as a prosperous farming community. It is also the setting for the province's largest agricultural fairs.

What to See and Do

Commonwealth Air Training Plan Museum. Display of WWII aircraft, vehicles; photos, uniforms, flags, and other mementos of Air Force training conducted in Canada (1940-45) under the British Commonwealth Air Training Plan. (Daily) McGill Field, Hangar #1. Phone 204/727-2444. ¢¢

Special Events

Royal Manitoba Winter Fair. Keystone Centre. Manitoba's largest winter fair. Equestrian events, heavy horses, entertainment. Late Mar. Phone 204/726-3500.

Manitoba Summer Fair. Keystone Centre. Competition, children's entertainment, midway, dancing. June. Phone 204/726-3500.

Manitoba Fall Fair. Keystone Centre. Manitoba's largest livestock show and sale; tractor pull, rodeo. Nov. Phone 204/726-3500.

Motels/Motor Lodges

★★ **COLONIAL INN.** *1944 Queens Ave (R7B 0T1). 204/728-8532; fax 204/727-5969; toll-free 800/665-6373. colonialinn.mb.ca.* 86 rms, 2 story. S $54.95; D $65.95. Crib free. TV; cable, VCR avail (movies). Indoor pool; wading pool, whirlpool. Coffee in rms. Restaurant 6 am-9 pm; Sun 7 am-8 pm. Ck-out noon. Business servs avail. In-rm modem link. Valet serv. Cr cds: A, D, ER, MC, V.
[D] [symbols]

★ **COMFORT INN.** *925 Middleton Ave (R7C 1A8). 204/727-6232; fax 204/727-2246. www.choicehotels.ca.* 81

rms, 2 story. Apr-Oct: S $79-$85; D $89-$95; each addl $4; under 18 free; wkend rates; lower rates rest of yr. Crib free. Pet accepted. TV; cable. Complimentary coffee in lobby. Complimentary newspaper. Restaurant nearby. Ck-out 11 am. Business servs avail. In-rm modem link. Sundries. Valet serv. Cr cds: A, C, D, DS, ER, JCB, MC, V.
[D] [symbols] [SC]

★ **REDWOOD MOTOR INN.** *345 18th St N (R7A 6Z2). 204/728-2200; fax 204/725-4758; toll-free 877/728-2200.* 61 rms. S $56.95; D $66.95. Crib free. TV; cable, VCR avail (movies). Indoor pool; whirlpool. Complimentary continental bkfst. Restaurant nearby. Ck-out noon. Business servs avail. In-rm modem link. Sundries. Cr cds: A, C, D, ER, MC, V.
[D] [symbols]

★★ **THE ROYAL OAK INN & SUITES.** *3130 Victoria Ave (R7B 0N2). 204/728-5775; fax 204/726-2709; toll-free 800/852-2709. www.royaloakinn. com.* 96 rms, 60 suites, 2 story. S $89.99; D, suites $109.99-$114.99; package plans. Pet accepted. TV; cable, VCR avail (movies). Indoor pool; wading pool, whirlpool, poolside serv. Restaurant 7 am-10 pm; Sun 8 am-10 pm. Bar 11-2 am. Ck-out noon. Coin lndry. Meeting rms. Business servs avail. Valet serv. Sundries. RR station, bus depot transportation. Exercise equipt. Cr cds: A, D, ER, MC, V.
[D] [symbols]

★★★ **VICTORIA INN.** *3550 Victoria Ave (R7B 2R4). 204/725-1532; fax 204/727-8282. www.victoriainn.ca.* 131 rms, 10 suites, 2 story. S, D $89.99; suites $99.99; studio rms $75-$125; under 18 free; package plans. Crib free. Pet accepted. TV; cable. Indoor pool; whirlpool, poolside serv. Restaurant 7 am-10 pm; Sun 8 am-9 pm. Bar 11:30-2 am. Ck-out noon. Valet serv. Meeting rms. Business servs avail. In-rm modem link. Sundries. Exercise equipt; sauna. Poolside balconies. Cr cds: A, D, ER, MC, V.
[D] [symbols] [SC]

B&B/Small Inn

★ **THE CASTLE.** *149 2nd Ave SW, Minnedosa (R0J 1E0). 204/867-2830. www.minnedosa.com/castleb&b.* 4 rms, 1 shared bath, 3 story. S $47-$65; D $63-$99; each addl $5; suites $99. Complimentary full bkfst. Restaurants nearby. Ck-out noon, ck-in 2 pm. Downhill ski 5 mi; x-country 2 mi. Built in 1901; antiques, art collection. Totally nonsmoking. Cr cds: A, MC, V.

Restaurant

★★★ **KOKONAS.** *1011 Rosser Ave (R7A 1A0). 204/727-4395. www. kokonas.com.* Hrs: 4:30-11 pm; Sat from 11:30 am; Sun 5-9 pm. Res accepted. Continental menu. Bar to 1 am. Lunch $5.25-$10.95, dinner $8.95-$29.95. Lunch buffet $8.95. Specializes in steak, seafood. Nightly prime rib buffet. Salad bar. Own pastries. Cr cds: A, D, DS, MC, V.

Turtle Mountain Provincial Park

See also Brandon

(Adjacent to International Peace Garden on US-Canada border)

Turtle Mountain is one of Manitoba's smaller provincial parks, with 47,000 acres (19,020 hectares) of forested hills, ponds, and lakes. Its lakes provide a good environment for western painted turtle, beaver, muskrat, and mink. Arbor and Eagle islands have stands of elm, oak, and ash that have not been touched by fire, thereby remaining excellent examples of mature deciduous forests. Swimming, hiking trails, interpretive programs, fishing, and boating are available, as well as snowmobile and cross-country skiing trails and a winter day-use area at Lake Adam. Camping (primitive and improved) at Lake Adam, Lake William, and Lake Max

campgrounds (hookups, dump stations).

Not far from the park is the town of Boissevain, where the annual Canadian Turtle Derby is held in mid-July. A large statue of Tommy Turtle welcomes the visitor at the south end of town. For further information phone 204/534-7204.

Winnipeg (G-4)

Pop 650,000 **Elev** 915 ft (279 m)
Area code 204
Information Tourism Winnipeg, 279 Portage Rd, R3B 2B4; 204/943-1970 or 800/665-0204
Web www.tourism.winnipeg.mb.ca

Winnipeg, the provincial capital, is situated in the heart of the continent and combines the sophistication and friendliness of east and west. The city offers much for any visitor, including relaxing cruises on the Assiniboine and Red rivers, Rainbow Stage summer theater in Kildonan Park, the Manitoba Theatre Centre, the Winnipeg Symphony, the Manitoba Opera, and the renowned Royal Winnipeg Ballet. Sports fans will enjoy the Blue Bombers in football and the Manitoba Moose hockey team. Shopping, nightlife, gourmet restaurants—Winnipeg has it all.

What to See and Do

Assiniboine Park. A 376-acre (152-hectare) park features colorful English and formal gardens; the Leo Mol Sculpture Garden; conservatory with floral displays; duck pond; playgrounds; picnic sites; cricket and field hockey area; refreshment pavilion; miniature train; bicycle paths; fitness trail. **Assiniboine Park Zoo** has collection of rare and endangered species, tropical mammals, birds, and reptiles; children's discovery area featuring variety of young animals (daily). Park (daily). 2355 Corydon Ave. Phone 204/986-3989. **FREE**

Birds Hill Provincial Park. A 8,275-acre (3,350-hectare) park situated on a glacial formation called an *eskar*. Large population of whitetail deer;

Winnipeg

© MAPQUEST

many orchid species. Interpretive, hiking, bridle, and bicycle trails; rollerblading path; snowshoe, snowmobile, and x-country skiing trails (winter). Interpretive programs. Swimming; camping and picnicking at 81½-acre (33-hectare) lake (seasonal). Riding stables (phone 204/222-1137). (Daily) 8 mi N on Hwy 59. Phone 204/222-9151. Per vehicle (May-Sept) ¢¢

✪ **Centennial Centre.** Complex incl concert hall, planetarium, Museum of Man and Nature, Manitoba Theatre Centre Building. 555 Main St. Here are

> **Manitoba Museum of Man and Nature.** Eight galleries interpret Manitoba's human and natural history: Orientation; Earth History (geological background); Grasslands (prairie); Arctic-Subarctic; Boreal Forest; *Nonsuch* (full-size replica of a 17th-century ship); and Urban. (Victoria Day-Labour Day, daily; rest of yr, Tues-Sun) 190 Rupert Ave. ¢¢¢ Also here is

> **Planetarium.** Circular, multipurpose audiovisual theater. Wide

variety of shows; subjects incl cosmic catastrophes and the edge of the universe. In the **Science Gallery**, visitors can learn about science through hands-on exhibits (separate admission fee). (Same days as museum) ¢¢

"Dalnavert". Restored Victorian residence (1895) of Sir Hugh John Macdonald, premier of Manitoba, depicting lifestyle and furnishings of the period. Gift shop. Guided tours (Mar-Dec, Tues-Thurs, Sat and Sun; rest of yr, Sat and Sun only) 61 Carlton St. Phone 204/943-2835. ¢¢

The Forks National Historic Site. Situated on 10 acres at the confluence of the Red and Assiniboine rivers. Riverside promenade; walkways throughout. Historical exhibits, playground; evening performances. Special events. (May-Sept) Grounds (all yr). Adj area open in winter for skating, cross-country skiing. Pioneer Blvd, opp Water and Pioneer Aves at Provencher Bridge. Phone 204/983-2007 or 204/983-5988. **FREE**

Legislative Building. Example of neoclassical architecture. Grounds contain statues of Queen Victoria, Lord Selkirk, George Cartier. Tours (June-Aug, Mon-Fri; Sept-June, by appt) Broadway and Osborne. Phone 204/945-5813. **FREE**

Lower Fort Garry National Historic Site of Canada. Hudson's Bay Co fur trade post restored to the 1850s. Original buildings; blacksmith shop, farmhouse, Ross cottage, furloft, Governor's house, sales shop; indigenous encampment. Visitor center with exhibits and artifacts of the fur trade society; costumed tour guides. Restaurant, gift shop. (Mid-May-Labour Day, daily) 20 mi (32 km) N on Hwy 9. Phone 204/785-6050. ¢¢

Oak Hammock Marsh Wildlife Management Area. More than 8,000 acres (3,238 hectares) of marshland and grassland wildlife habitat. Attracts up to 300,000 ducks and geese during spring (Apr-mid-May) and fall migration (Sept-Oct). Nature trails; picnic sites, marsh boardwalk, viewing mounds, drinking water. Conservation center with displays, interpretive programs (daily; fee). 14 mi (23 km) N via Hwy 7 or 8, then 5 mi (8 km) to Hwy 67. Phone 204/467-3300. **FREE**

Ross House. (1854) Oldest bldg in the original city of Winnipeg; first post office in western Canada. Displays and period-furnished rms depict daily life in the Red River Settlement. (June-Aug, Wed-Sun) 140 Meade St N, between Euclid and Sutherland Aves. Phone 204/947-0559. **FREE**

Royal Canadian Mint. (1976) One of the world's most modern mints; striking glass tower, landscaped interior courtyard. Tour allows viewing of coining process; coin museum. (Early May-late Aug, Mon-Fri; closed hols) 520 Lagimodière Blvd. Phone 204/257-3359. ¢

St.-Boniface Museum. (1846) Housed in oldest structure in the city, dating to the days of the Red River Colony; largest oak log construction in North America. 494 ave Taché. Phone 204/237-4500.

Seven Oaks House Museum. Oldest habitable house in Manitoba (1851). Log construction, original furnishings, housewares. Adjoining bldgs incl general store, post office. (Mid-June-Sept, daily; mid-May-mid-June,

Sat and Sun) Rupertsland Ave, in West Kildonan area. Phone 204/339-7429 or 204/986-3031. ¢

Sightseeing tours.

Paddlewheel/River Rouge boat and bus tours. Floating restaurant, moonlight dance, and sightseeing cruises (May-Sept); also guided tours on double-decker buses. Bus/cruise combinations avail. Contact PO Box 3930, Postal Station B, R2W 5H9. Phone 204/942-4500. ¢¢¢¢

Winnipeg Art Gallery. Canada's first civic gallery (1912). Eight galleries present changing exhibitions of contemporary, historical, and decorative art, plus North America's largest collection of Inuit art. (Summer, daily; rest of yr, Tues-Sun; closed hols) Programming incl tours, lectures, films, concerts. Restaurant. 300 Memorial Blvd. Phone 204/786-6641. ¢¢

Special Events

Festival du Voyageur. In St.-Boniface, Winnipeg's "French Quarter." Winter festival celebrating the French-Canadian voyageur and the fur trade era. Phone 204/237-7692. Ten days mid-Feb.

Red River Exhibition. Large event encompassing grandstand shows, band competitions, displays, agricultural exhibits, parade, entertainment, midway, petting zoo, shows, food. Late June-early July. Phone 204/888-6990.

Winnipeg Folk Festival. Birds Hill Provincial Park, 8 mi N on Hwy 59. More than 100 regional, national, and international artists perform; nine stages; children's village; evening concerts. Juried crafts exhibit and sale; international food village. Early July. Phone 204/231-0096.

Folklorama. Multicultural festival featuring up to 40 pavilions. Singing, dancing, food, cultural displays. Aug. Pavilions throughout city.

Winnipeg Symphony Orchestra. Centennial Concert Hall. Classical, pops, and children's concerts. Phone 204/949-3999. Sept-May.

Canada's Royal Winnipeg Ballet. Centennial Concert Hall. Performs mix of classical and contemporary ballets. Phone 204/956-2792. Oct-May.

Manitoba Opera Association. Portage Place. Nov-May. Phone 204/942-7479.

Motels/Motor Lodges

★★ **BEST WESTERN VICTORIA INN.** *1808 Wellington Ave, Winnipeg (R3H 0G3). 204/786-4801; fax 204/786-1329; toll-free 800/928-4067. www.bestwestern.com.* 288 rms, 5 story. S $79; D $84; suites $175; under 16 free. Crib free. Pet accepted. TV; cable. 1 indoor; whirlpool, poolside serv. Restaurant 7 am-11 pm. Bar 11:30-1 am. Ck-out noon. Meeting rms. Business servs avail. In-rm modem link. Bellhops. Gift shop. Free airport transportation. Some refrigerators. Cr cds: A, DS, MC, V.

(icons)

★ **COMFORT INN.** *1770 Sargent Ave, Winnipeg (R3H 0C8). 204/783-5627; fax 204/783-5661; toll-free 800/228-5150. www.hotelchoice.com.* 81 rms, 2 story. Mid-June-mid-Sept: S, D $85-$95; each addl $10; under 18 free; wkend rates; lower rates rest of yr. Crib free. Pet accepted. TV; cable. Complimentary coffee in lobby. Continental bkfst avail. Restaurant nearby. Ck-out 11 am. Business servs

avail. In-rm modem link. Valet serv. Cr cds: A, C, D, DS, MC, V.

(icons)

★★ **COUNTRY INN AND SUITES.** *730 King Edward St, Winnipeg (R3H 1B4). 204/783-6900; fax 204/775-7197. www.countryinns.com.* 77 units, 3 story, 36 suites. S $65-$95; D $75-$105; each addl $10; under 18 free; wkend rates. Crib free. Pet accepted, some restrictions. TV; cable (premium), VCR (free movies). Complimentary coffee in rms. Complimentary continental bkfst. Restaurant adj 7 am-11 pm. Ck-out noon. Coin lndry. Business servs avail. Sundries. Valet serv. Refrigerators. Cr cds: A, C, D, DS, MC, V.

(icons)

★★ **HOLIDAY INN.** *1330 Pembina Hwy, Winnipeg (R3T 2B4). 204/452-4747; fax 204/284-2751; toll-free 800/423-1337. www.hi-winnipeg.mb.ca.* 170 rms, 11 story. S $159; D $179; each addl $10; suites $250; under 19 free; wkend rates. Crib free. Pet accepted. TV; cable, VCR avail. Indoor pool; wading pool, whirlpool, poolside serv. Coffee in rms. Restaurant 6:30 am-11 pm; wkend hrs vary. Bar from 11:30 am. Ck-out noon. Coin lndry. Meeting rms. Business servs avail. In-rm

Legislative Building, Winnipeg

modem link. Bellhops. Valet serv. Sundries. Free airport transportation. Exercise equipt. Cr cds: A, C, D, DS, ER, JCB, MC, V.

[icons]

★ **HOWARD JOHNSON HOTEL.** *1740 Ellice Ave, Winnipeg (R2K 0R2). 204/775-7131; fax 204/788-4685; toll-free 800/665-8813. hojo.com.* 155 rms, 5 story. S, D $54-$72; each addl $10; under 16 free; package plans. Crib $10. TV; cable. Sauna. Indoor pool; whirlpool, poolside serv. Restaurant 7 am-9 pm. Bar 11-2 am; entertainment. Ck-out noon. Coin lndry. Meeting rms. Business servs avail. Bellhops. Gift shop. Free airport transportation. Cr cds: A, D, MC.

[icons]

Hotels

★★ **CHARTER HOUSE.** *330 York Ave, Winnipeg (R3C 0N9). 204/942-0101; fax 204/956-0665; toll-free 800/782-0175.* 90 rms, 5 story. S, D $65-$125; under 18 free; wkly, wkend rates. Crib $10. Pet accepted. TV; cable, VCR avail (movies). Restaurant 7 am-11 pm. Bar 11-2 am. Ck-out 11 am. Meeting rms. Business servs avail. In-rm modem link. Balconies. Cr cds: A, C, D, DS, MC, V.

[icons]

★★ **DELTA WINNIPEG.** *350 St Mary Ave, Winnipeg (R3C 3J2). 204/942-0551; fax 204/943-8702. www.deltahotels.com.* 392 rms, 18 story. S $155; D $165; each addl $15; suites $195-$485; under 18 free. Crib avail. TV; cable (premium). 2 pools, 1 indoor; whirlpool; wading pool. Complimentary coffee in rms. Restaurants 6:30-1 am. 24-hr rm serv. Ck-out noon. Coin lndry. Meeting rms. Business servs. In-rm modem link. Airport transportation. Exercise rm; sauna. Refrigerators. Balconies. Luxury level. Cr cds: A, D, DS, ER, MC, V.

[icons]

★★★ **THE FAIRMONT WINNIPEG.** *2 Lombard Pl (R3B 0Y3). 204/957-1300. www.fairmont.com.* 340 rms, 20 story. S, D $175-$275; each addl $20; under 17 free. Crib avail. TV; cable (premium), VCR avail. Complimentary coffee, newspaper in rms.

Restaurant 6 am-10 pm. Ck-out noon. Meeting rms. Business center. Gift shop. Exercise rm. Some refrigerators, minibars. Cr cds: A, C, D, DS, MC, V.

[icons]

★★ **HOLIDAY INN AIRPORT WEST.** *2520 Portage Ave, Winnipeg (R3J 3T6). 204/885-4478; fax 204/831-5734; toll-free 800/465-4329. www.holiday-inn.com/winnipeg-arpt.* 226 rms, 15 story, 8 kits. S $139; D $149; each addl $10; suites $145-$186; under 19 free; wkend rates. Crib free. TV; cable. Indoor pool; wading pool, whirlpool, poolside serv, lifeguard. Supervised children's activities, ages 3-11. Coffee in rms. Restaurant 6:30 am-11 pm. Bar 11:30-2 am; entertainment. Ck-out 1 pm. Coin lndry. Meeting rms. Business center. In-rm modem link. Free airport transportation. Game rm. Exercise equipt; sauna. Some minibars; refrigerators. Some balconies. Cr cds: A, D, DS, ER, JCB, MC, V.

[icons]

★★ **RADISSON DOWNTOWN.** *288 Portage Ave, Winnipeg (R3C 0B8). 204/956-0410; fax 204/947-1129; toll-free 800/333-3333. www.radisson.com.* 272 rms, 29 story. S, D $129-$199; each addl $15; suites $229; under 18 free; wkend rates. Crib free. Pet accepted. Garage parking $9.63. TV; cable (premium), VCR avail (movies). Indoor pool; poolside serv. Coffee in rms. Restaurant 6:30 am-10 pm; Sat, Sun from 7 am. Rm serv 24 hrs. Bars 11:30-1 am. Ck-out 1 pm. Meeting rms. Business center. In-rm modem link. Concierge. Gift shop. Exercise equipt; sauna. Minibars. Cr cds: A, D, DS, ER, JCB, MC, V.

[icons]

★★ **RADISSON SUITE HOTEL WINNIPEG AIRPORT.** *1800 Wellington Ave, Winnipeg (R3H 1B2). 204/783-1700; fax 204/786-6588; toll-free 800/333-3333. www.radisson.com/ winnipegca_airport.* 149 suites, 6 story. S $139; D $189; each addl $15; under 17 free; wkend and hol rates. Crib free. TV; cable. 2 pools, 1 indoor; whirlpool, poolside serv. Complimentary continental bkfst. Complimentary coffee in rms. Restaurant 7 am-10 pm. Rm serv 24 hrs. Bar 11:30

am-midnight. Ck-out noon. Meeting rms. Business servs avail. Gift shop. Free airport transportation. Exercise equipt; sauna. Refrigerators, wet bars. Cr cds: A, D, DS, ER, MC, V.

D ⟆ 🏋 ⟆ 🐾 SC

★★★ **SHERATON WINNIPEG HOTEL.** *161 Donald St, Winnipeg (R3C 1M3). 204/942-5300; fax 204/943-7975; toll-free 800/463-6400. www.sheraton.com.* 271 rms, 21 story. S $130-$145; D $140-$155; under 18 free; wkend rates. Crib free. Pet accepted. Underground parking, valet $9/day. TV; cable (premium). Indoor pool; whirlpool. Coffee in rms. Restaurant 6:30 am-11 pm. Rm serv 24 hrs. Bar 11-1 am. Ck-out noon. Convention facilities. Business servs avail. In-rm modem link. Concierge. Gift shop. Sauna. Health club privileges. Many refrigerators. Many balconies. Cr cds: A, D, MC, V.

D 🐾 ⟆ ⟆ 🐾

Restaurants

★★ **AMICI.** *326 Broadway, Winnipeg (R3C 0S5). 204/943-4997. www. amiciwpg.com.* Hrs: 11:30 am-2 pm, 5-10 pm; Sat from 5 pm. Closed Sun; hols. Res accepted. Italian menu. Bar to 11 pm. Lunch $9.50-$18.50, dinner $15-$38. Child's meals. Specializes in veal, wild boar, rack of lamb. Contemporary decor. Cr cds: A, D, MC, V.

D

★★ **HY'S STEAK LOFT.** *216 Kennedy, Winnipeg (R3C 1T1). 204/942-1000. www.hyssteakhouse. com.* Hrs: 5-11 pm; Fri, Sat to midnight; Sun to 9 pm. Closed hols. Res accepted. Bar 4 pm-midnight; Sat from 5 pm. Wine list. Dinner $21.95-$45. Specializes in steak, seafood. Bi-level dining; Old English decor. Cr cds: A, D, ER, MC, V.

⊒

★★ **ICHIBAN JAPANESE STEAK-HOUSE AND SUSHI BAR.** *189 Carlton St, Winnipeg (R3C 3H7). 204/925-7400.* Hrs: 4:30-10 pm. Fri, Sat to 10:30 pm. Closed hols. Res accepted. Japanese menu. Bar 4:30-10 pm, Fri, Sat to 10:30. Dinner $17.95-$35. Specialties: Imperial dinner, Empress dinner, sushi. Teppanyaki

cooking. Japanese garden atmosphere. Cr cds: A, D, MC, V.

D SC ⊒

ATTRACTION LIST

Attraction names are listed in alphabetical order followed by a symbol identifying their classification and then city. The symbols for classification are: [S] for Special Events and [W] for What to See and Do.

Aberdeen Museum of History [W] Aberdeen, WA

A.C. Gilbert's Discovery Village [W] Salem, OR

A Contemporary Theater (ACT) [S] Seattle, WA

Adam East Museum [W] Moses Lake, WA

Adams County Fair [S] Othello, WA

Aerial Fire Depot [W] Missoula, MT

Aerial Tramway [W] Jackson, WY

Ag Expo [S] Spokane, WA

"Ag-Expo" Agricultural Exposition [S] Lethbridge, AB

Agriculture Canada Research Station [W] Penticton, BC

Agriculture-Farm Show [S] Kalispell, MT

Ahtanum Mission [W] Yakima, WA

Alberta Birds of Prey Centre [W] Lethbridge, AB

Alberta Legislature Building [W] Edmonton, AB

Albertson College of Idaho [W] Caldwell, ID

Alder House II [W] Lincoln City, OR

Alexander Blockhouse [W] Coupeville, WA

Alki Beach [W] Seattle, WA

Alpental [W] North Bend, WA

Alta Lake [W] Chelan, WA

Amazing May [S] Grants Pass, OR

American Advertising Museum [W] Portland, OR

American Falls Dam [W] American Falls, ID

American Heritage Center & Art Museum [W] Laramie, WY

American Musical Jubilee [S] Ontario, OR

Anaconda's Old Works [W] Anaconda, MT

Anna Miller Museum [W] Newcastle, WY

Annual Moon Tree Country Run [S] Cave Junction, OR

Anthony Lakes Ski Area [W] Baker City, OR

Ape Cave [W] Mount St. Helens National Volcanic Monument, WA

Appaloosa Museum and Heritage Center [W] Moscow, ID

Apple Blossom Festival [S] Chelan, WA

Apple Days [S] Cashmere, WA

Archie Bray Foundation, The [W] Helena, MT

Argosy Harbor Cruise [W] Seattle, WA

Armed Forces Day Parade [S] Bremerton, WA

Armitage County Park [W] Eugene, OR

Arroyo Park [W] Bellingham, WA

Art Gallery of Greater Victoria [W] Victoria, BC

Art Museum of Missoula [W] Missoula, MT

Art on the Green [S] Coeur d'Alene, ID

Arts Chateau [W] Butte, MT

Arts in the Park [S] Shoshone, ID

Asotin County Fair [S] Clarkston, WA

Asotin County Museum [W] Clarkston, WA

Assiniboine Park [W] Winnipeg, MB

Astoria Column [W] Astoria, OR

Astoria Regatta [S] Astoria, OR

Astoria-Warrenton Crab and Seafood Festival [S] Astoria, OR

Auto racing [S] Everett, WA

Auto tour [W] Spokane, WA

Auto tour [W] Wallace, ID

Auto tours [W] Lewiston, ID

Autumn Leaf Festival [S] Leavenworth, WA

Avalanche Creek [W] Glacier National Park, MT

Avery Park [W] Corvallis, OR

Awesome Autumn Festival [S] Mount Vernon, WA

Azalea Festival [S] Brookings, OR

Azalea Park [W] Brookings, OR

Bach Festival [S] Eugene, OR

Balanced Rock [W] Buhl, ID

Bald Eagle Conference [S] Klamath Falls, OR

Ballon Roundup [S] Miles City, MT

Bandon Museum [W] Bandon, OR

Banff Festival of the Arts [S] Banff, AB

Bannack Days [S] Dillon, MT

Bannack State Park [W] Dillon, MT

Bannock County Fair and Rodeo [S] Pocatello, ID

Bannock County Historical Museum [W] Pocatello, ID

Barbershop Ballad Contest [S] Forest Grove, OR

Barbershop Concert and Salmon Barbecue [S] Anacortes, WA

Barker-Ewing Float Trips [W] Jackson, WY

Basque Museum and Cultural Center [W] Boise, ID

Bastion [W] Nanaimo, BC

Battle Rock Wayside [W] Port Orford, OR

Bavarian Ice Fest [S] Leavenworth, WA

Bavarian Maifest [S] Leavenworth, WA

Bay Area Fun Festival [S] Coos Bay, OR

Bay View State Park [W] Mount Vernon, WA

BC Forest Museum [W] Victoria, BC

Beacon Hill Park [W] Victoria, BC

Beardale Castle Miniatureland [W] Revelstoke, BC

Bear Lake [W] Montpelier, ID

Bear Lake County Fair and Rodeo [S] Montpelier, ID

Bear Lake State Park [W] Montpelier, ID

Bear's Paw Battleground [W] Chinook, MT

Beartooth Highway (National Forest Scenic Byway) [W] Red Lodge, MT

Beaver Creek Loop Tour [W] Newcastle, WY

Beaver Creek Park [W] Havre, MT

Beaver Dick [W] Rexburg, ID

Beaverhead County Fair & Jaycee Rodeo [S] Dillon, MT

Beaverhead County Museum [W] Dillon, MT

Beaverhead National Forest [W] Dillon, MT

Beekman House [W] Jacksonville, OR

Belfair [W] Bremerton, WA

Bellevue Art Museum [W] Bellevue, WA

Bellevue Botanical Garden [W] Bellevue, WA

Belly River Country [W] Glacier National Park, MT

Benewah, Round, and Chatcolet lakes [W] St. Marie's, ID

Benson State Recreation Area [W] Portland, OR

Benton County Fair and Rodeo [S] Corvallis, OR

Benton County Historical Museum [W] Corvallis, OR

Benton-Franklin Fair and Rodeo [S] Richland, WA

Berkeley Pit [W] Butte, MT

Beverly Beach [W] Newport, OR

Big Arm Unit [W] Polson, MT

Bigfork Art and Cultural Center [W] Bigfork, MT

Bigfork Summer Playhouse [S] Bigfork, MT

Big-game hunting [W] Dubois, WY

Big Hole Basin [W] Anaconda, MT

Big Hole National Battlefield [W] Anaconda, MT

Big Hole National Battlefield [W] Hamilton, MT

Bighorn Canyon National Recreation Area [W] Hardin, MT

Bighorn Canyon National Recreation Area [W] Lovell, WY

Bighorn National Forest [W] Sheridan, WY

Big Mountain Ski and Summer Resort [W] Whitefish, MT

Big Sky Resort [W] Big Sky (Gallatin County), MT

Big Sky Water Slide [W] Columbia Falls, MT

Big Spring Creek [W] Lewistown, MT

Big Springs [W] Ashton, ID

Big Wheel [W] Newport, WA

Bingham County Historical Museum [W] Blackfoot, ID

Birch Bay State Park [W] Blaine, WA

Birds Hill Provincial Park [W] Winnipeg, MB

Bitterroot National Forest [W] Hamilton, MT

Blackberry Arts Festival [S] Coos Bay, OR

Blackberry Festival [S] Bremerton, WA

Blackcomb [W] Whistler, BC

Blackfoot Pride Days [S] Blackfoot, ID

Blackman Museum [W] Snohomish, WA

Black Mountain Rodeo Golf Tournament [S] Kelowna, BC

Blaine County Fair [S] Chinook, MT

Blaine County Museum [W] Chinook, MT

Blake Island [W] Bremerton, WA

Bloedel Donovan Park [W] Bellingham, WA

Bloomington Lake [W] Montpelier, ID

Blossom Festival [S] Hood River, OR

Blue River Dam and Lake [W] McKenzie Bridge, OR

Boat cruise. Maligne Tours, Ltd [W] Jasper National Park, AB

Boathouse Marina [W] Tacoma, WA

Boating [W] Burley, ID

Boatnik Festival [S] Grants Pass, OR

Boat tours [W] Everett, WA

Boat trips [W] Gold Beach, OR

Boehm's Chocolate Factory [W] Issaquah, WA

Boeing Everett Facility [W] Everett, WA

Boeing Field—King County International Airport [W] Seattle, WA

Bogachiel State Park [W] Forks, WA

Bogus Basin Ski Resort [W] Boise, ID

Bohemia Mining Days Celebration [S] Cottage Grove, OR

Boise Art Museum [W] Boise, ID

Boise Basin Museum [W] Idaho City, ID

Boise National Forest [W] Boise, ID

Boise National Forest [W] Idaho City, ID

Boise River Festival [S] Boise, ID

Boise Tour Train [W] Boise, ID

Bonner County Historical Society Museum [W] Sandpoint, ID

Bonneville Lock & Dam [W] Hood River, OR

Bonneville Museum [W] Idaho Falls, ID

Boot Hill [W] Idaho City, ID

Boot Hill [W] Virginia City, MT

Boothill Cemetery [W] Billings, MT

Border Days [S] Grangeville, ID

Borst Blockhouse [W] Centralia, WA

Boulevard Park [W] Bellingham, WA

Bowdoin National Wildlife Refuge [W] Malta, MT

Bowen Park [W] Nanaimo, BC

Boysen State Park [W] Thermopolis, WY

Bradford Brinton Memorial [W] Sheridan, WY

Bremerton Naval Museum [W] Bremerton, WA

Bridger Bowl Ski Area [W] Bozeman, MT

Bridger Raptor Festival [S] Bozeman, MT

Bridger-Teton National Forest [W] Afton, WY

Bridger-Teton National Forest [W] Jackson, WY

Bridger-Teton National Forest [W] Pinedale, WY

Bridger Wilderness [W] Pinedale, WY

British Columbia Ferry Corp [W] Vancouver, BC

British Columbia Square Dance Jamboree [S] Penticton, BC

Britt Musical Festivals [S] Jacksonville, OR

Brooks Memorial State Park [W] Goldendale, WA

Brownlee Dam [W] Weiser, ID

Brundage Mountain Ski Area [W] McCall, ID

Bruneau Canyon [W] Mountain Home, ID

Bucking Horse Sale [S] Miles City, MT

Buffalo Bill Dam and Visitor Center [W] Cody, WY

Buffalo Bill Festival [S] Cody, WY

Buffalo Bill Historical Center [W] Cody, WY

Buffalo Bill Museum [W] Cody, WY

Buffalo Bill State Park [W] Cody, WY

Buffalo Bus Lines [W] West Yellowstone, MT

Bullards Beach State Park [W] Bandon, OR

Burnaby Village Museum [W] Vancouver, BC

Bush Barn Art Center [W] Salem, OR

Bush House [W] Salem, OR

Butchart Gardens [W] Victoria, BC

Butte Creek Mill [W] Medford, OR

Butte Vigilante Rodeo [S] Butte, MT

Buzzard Day [S] Glendive, MT

Calaway Park [W] Calgary, AB

Caldwell Exchange Youth Rodeo [S] Caldwell, ID

Calgary Flames (NHL) [W] Calgary, AB

Calgary Science Centre [W] Calgary, AB

Calgary Stampede [S] Calgary, AB

Calgary Tower [W] Calgary, AB

Calgary Winter Festival [S] Calgary, AB

Calgary Zoo, Botanical Garden and Prehistoric Park, The [W] Calgary, AB

Callahan Ridge Winery [W] Roseburg, OR

Camping [W] Mount Rainier National Park, WA

Camping [W] Mount St. Helens National Volcanic Monument, WA

Camping [W] Olympic National Park, WA

Camping. Libby Ranger District; [W] Libby, MT

Camp Putt Adventure Golf Park [W] Eugene, OR

Camp Six Logging Exhibit (Western Forest Industries Museum) [W] Tacoma, WA

Canada Olympic Park [W] Calgary, AB

Canada's Aviation Hall of Fame [W] Edmonton, AB

Canada's Royal Winnipeg Ballet [S] Winnipeg, MB

Canadian Finals Rodeo [S] Edmonton, AB

C&M Stables [W] Florence, OR

Canyon County Fair [S] Caldwell, ID

Canyon County Historical Society Museum [W] Nampa, ID

Canyon Ferry State Park [W] Helena, MT

Cape Arago [W] Coos Bay, OR

Cape Blanco State Park [W] Port Orford, OR

Cape Lookout State Park [W] Tillamook, OR

Cape Perpetua Campground [W] Yachats, OR

Cape Perpetua Visitor Center [W] Yachats, OR

Cape Sebastian State Park [W] Gold Beach, OR

Capes Scenic Loop Drive to Cape Meares and Oceanside [W] Tillamook, OR

Capilano Suspension Bridge and Park [W] Vancouver, BC

Capital City Marathon and Relay [S] Olympia, WA

Capital City Tally-Ho and Sightseeing Company [W] Victoria, BC

Capitol grounds [W] Olympia, WA

Capitol Group [W] Olympia, WA

Capitol Lake [W] Olympia, WA

Capitol Mall [W] Salem, OR

Carbon County Fair and Rodeo [S] Rawlins, WY

Carbon County Museum [W] Rawlins, WY

Carbon River [W] Mount Rainier National Park, WA

Caribou National Forest [W] Montpelier, ID

Caribou National Forest [W] Pocatello, ID

Carillon [W] Victoria, BC

Carkeek Park [W] Seattle, WA

Carl G. Washburne Memorial [W] Florence, OR

Carmen-Smith Hydroelectric Development [W] McKenzie Bridge, OR

Carr House [W] Victoria, BC

Cascade Dam Reservoir [W] McCall, ID

Cascade Park [W] Moses Lake, WA

Casper Mountain and Beartrap Meadow Parks [W] Casper, WY

Casper Planetarium [W] Casper, WY

Cassia County Fair and Rodeo [S] Burley, ID

Cassia County Historical Museum [W] Burley, ID

Castle Museum [W] Lewiston, ID

Cathedral of St. Helena [W] Helena, MT

Cathedral of St. John the Evangelist [W] Spokane, WA

Catherine Creek State Park [W] La Grande, OR

Cave and Basin Centennial Centre [W] Banff, AB

CCInc Auto Tape Tours [W] Banff, AB

Celilo Park [W] The Dalles, OR

Centennial Centre [W] Winnipeg, MB

Centennial Square [W] Victoria, BC

Center House [W] Seattle, WA

Central Montana Horse Show, Fair, Rodeo [S] Lewistown, MT

Central Washington State Fair and Rodeo [S] Yakima, WA

Central Washington University [W] Ellensburg, WA

Central Wyoming Fair and Rodeo [S] Casper, WY

Challis National Forest [W] Challis, ID

Chamber Music Festival [S] Leavenworth, WA

Chamber Music Northwest [S] Portland, OR

Champoeg State Historic Area [W] Newberg, OR

Chariot Races [S] Jerome, ID

Charles and Emma Frye Art Museum [W] Seattle, WA

Charles M. Russell National Wildlife Refuge [W] Lewistown, MT

Charleston Marina Complex [W] Coos Bay, OR

Charlie Russell Chew-Choo [S] Lewistown, MT

Chateau Lorane Winery [W] Cottage Grove, OR

Chateau Ste. Michelle [W] Bellevue, WA

Chelan County Fair [S] Cashmere, WA

Chelan County Historical Museum [W] Cashmere, WA

Cheney Cowles Museum [W] Spokane, WA

Cheney Historical Museum [W] Cheney, WA

Cheyenne Botanic Gardens [W] Cheyenne, WY

Cheyenne Frontier Days Old West Museum [W] Cheyenne, WY

Cheyenne Frontier Days [S] Cheyenne, WY

Cheyenne Street Railway Trolley [W] Cheyenne, WY

Chief Black Otter Trail [W] Billings, MT

Chief Joseph Days [S] Joseph, OR

Chief Victor Days [S] Hamilton, MT

Children's Museum [W] Portland, OR

Children's Museum [W] Spokane, WA

Chili Cook-off [S] Evanston, WY

Chinatown [W] Vancouver, BC

Chocolate Fantasy [S] Yakima, WA

Chouteau County Fair [S] Fort Benton, MT

Christmas Dickens Festival [S] Kellogg, ID

Christmas events [S] Vancouver, BC

Christmas Lighting [S] Leavenworth, WA

Chuckanut Drive [W] Bellingham, WA

Chugwater Chili Cookoff [S] Wheatland, WY

Citadel Theatre [W] Edmonton, AB

City of Rocks National Reserve [W] Burley, ID

City recreation areas [W] Bellingham, WA

Civic Field Athletic Complex [W] Bellingham, WA

Clallam County Fair [S] Port Angeles, WA

Clark County Historical Museum [W] Vancouver, WA

Clarno Unit [W] John Day, OR

Classic melodramas [S] Virginia City, MT

Classic Wooden Boat Show and Crab Feed [S] Depoe Bay, OR

Clearwater National Forest [W] Lewiston, ID

Cliff Park [W] Spokane, WA

Cline Falls [W] Redmond, OR

Clymer Museum of Art [W] Ellensburg, WA

C.M. Russell Museum Complex and Original Log Cabin Studio [W] Great Falls, MT

Cody Firearms Museum [W] Cody, WY

Cody Nite Rodeo [S] Cody, WY

Cody Stampede [S] Cody, WY

Coeur d'Alene Greyhound Park [W] Coeur d'Alene, ID

Coldwater Creek on the Cedar Street Bridge [W] Sandpoint, ID

Coldwater Ridge Visitor Center [W] Mount St. Helens National Volcanic Monument, WA

Collage of Culture [S] Madras, OR

Collier Memorial State Park and Logging Museum [W] Klamath Falls, OR

Colorama Festival & PWRA Rodeo [S] Coulee Dam, WA

Columbia County Fair [S] Dayton (Columbia County), WA

Columbia Crest Winery [W] Umatilla, OR

Columbia Cup [S] Richland, WA

Columbia Gorge [W] Hood River, OR

Columbia Gorge Discovery Center [W] The Dalles, OR

Columbia Park [W] Kennewick, WA

Columbia River Maritime Museum [W] Astoria, OR

Colville National Forest [W] Colville, WA

Colville PRCA Rodeo [S] Colville, WA

Colville Tribal Museum [W] Coulee Dam, WA

Commonwealth Air Training Plan Museum [W] Brandon, MB

Commonwealth Stadium [W] Edmonton, AB

Community Theater [W] McMinnville, OR

Comstock Park [W] Spokane, WA

Conconully State Park [W] Omak, WA

Concours d'Elegance [S] Forest Grove, OR

Conrad Mansion [W] Kalispell, MT

Cool Desert Nights Car Show [S] Richland, WA

Cooley's Gardens [W] Silverton, OR

Coos County Historical Society Museum [W] North Bend, OR

Copper King Mansion [W] Butte, MT

Copper Village Museum and Arts Center [W] Anaconda, MT

Cornwall Park [W] Bellingham, WA

Cottage Grove Lake [W] Cottage Grove, OR

Cottage Grove Museum [W] Cottage Grove, OR

Cougar Dam and Lake [W] McKenzie Bridge, OR

Council Crest Park [W] Portland, OR

Country Museum/Restored Train Station [W] Silverton, OR

Cove Palisades State Park, The [W] Madras, OR

Covered Bridges [W] Cottage Grove, OR

Covered Wagon Cookout & Wild West Show [W] Jackson, WY

Cowboy Days [S] Evanston, WY

Cowboy Poet Festival [S] St. Anthony, ID

Cowboy Songs and Range Ballads [S] Cody, WY

Cowlitz County Fair [S] Longview, WA

Cowlitz County Historical Museum [W] Kelso, WA

Craigdarroch Castle [W] Victoria, BC

Craigflower Farmhouse & Schoolhouse Historic Site [W] Victoria, BC

Cranberry Festival [S] Bandon, OR

Crater Rock Museum [W] Medford, OR

Crescent Bar Park [W] Quincy, WA

CRESHT Museum [W] Richland, WA

Cross Channel Swim [S] Hood River, OR

Crow Fair [S] Hardin, MT

Crown Point [W] Portland, OR

Crystal Garden [W] Victoria, BC

Crystal Mountain Resort [W] Mount Rainier National Park, WA

Crystal Springs Rhododendron Garden [W] Portland, OR

Currier & Ives Winter Festival [S] Thermopolis, WY

Curry County Fair [S] Gold Beach, OR

Curry County Historical Museum [W] Gold Beach, OR

Curt Gowdy State Park [W] Cheyenne, WY

Custer County Art Center [W] Miles City, MT

Custer National Forest [W] Hardin, MT

Cut Bank [W] Glacier National Park, MT

CWU Library [W] Ellensburg, WA

Cyber City [W] Nanaimo, BC

Cypress Hills Provincial Park [W] Medicine Hat, AB

Cypress Mountain Ski Area [W] Vancouver, BC

Dabney [W] Portland, OR

Daffodil Festival [S] Tacoma, WA

Dalles Dam and Reservoir, The [W] The Dalles, OR

"Dalnavert" [W] Winnipeg, MB

Daly Mansion [W] Hamilton, MT

Darigold Dairy Fair [W] Sunnyside, WA

Darlingtonia [W] Florence, OR

Da Vinci Days [S] Corvallis, OR

Dawson County Fair and Rodeo [S] Glendive, MT

Days of '49 Celebration [S] Greybull, WY

Dayton Depot Festival [S] Dayton (Columbia County), WA

Deadman's Basin Fishing Access Site [W] Harlowton, MT

Dean Creek Elk Viewing Area [W] Reedsport, OR

Deception Pass State Park [W] Anacortes, WA

Deer Flat National Wildlife Refuge [W] Nampa, ID

Deerlodge National Forest [W] Butte, MT

Deerlodge National Forest [W] Deer Lodge, MT

Deming Logging Show [S] Bellingham, WA

Depoe Bay Park [W] Depoe Bay, OR

Depot Center [W] Livingston, MT

Deschutes County Fair and Rodeo [S] Redmond, OR

Desert Balloon Rally [S] Rock Springs, WY

Devil's Elbow [W] Florence, OR

Devil's Gate [W] Casper, WY

Devil's Lake State Park [W] Lincoln City, OR

Devil's Punch Bowl [W] Newport, OR

Devonian Botanic Garden [W] Edmonton, AB

Devonian Gardens [W] Calgary, AB

Dinosaur Provincial Park [W] Medicine Hat, AB

Discovery Basin [W] Anaconda, MT

Discovery Center of Idaho [W] Boise, ID

Discovery Park [W] Seattle, WA

Dominion Astrophysical Observatory [W] Victoria, BC

Dominion Radio Astrophysical Observatory [W] Penticton, BC

Dorena Lake [W] Cottage Grove, OR

Douglas County Fair [S] Roseburg, OR

Douglas County Museum of History and Natural History [W] Roseburg, OR

Drag Races [S] Lewistown, MT

Drews Reservoir [W] Lakeview, OR

Driving Tour In Deschutes National Forest [W] Bend, OR

Dr. Sun-Yet-sen Classical Garden [W] Vancouver, BC

Dumas Brothel Museum [W] Butte, MT

Dungeness Recreation Area [W] Sequim, WA

Eagle Island State Park [W] Boise, ID

Eagle Watch [S] Helena, MT

Eastern Idaho State Fair [S] Blackfoot, ID

Eastern Montana Fair [S] Miles City, MT

Eastern Oregon Museum [W] Baker City, OR

Eastern Oregon University [W] La Grande, OR

Eastern Washington University [W] Cheney, WA

East Linn Museum [W] Sweet Home, OR

Eau Claire Market and Prince's Island Park [W] Calgary, AB

Ecola State Park [W] Cannon Beach, OR

Edmonton Oilers (NHL) [W] Edmonton, AB

Edmonton Queen Riverboat [W] Edmonton, AB

Edmonton's Klondike Days [S] Edmonton, AB

Edness K. Wilkins State Park [W] Casper, WY

1838 Mountain Man Rendezvous [S] Riverton, WY

Elk Island National Park of Canada [W] Edmonton, AB

Elmore County Historical Foundation Museum [W] Mountain Home, ID

Elmo Unit [W] Polson, MT

Emerald Downs [W] Tacoma, WA

Emigrant Gulch [W] Livingston, MT

Emigrant Springs State Park [W] Pendleton, OR

Empress Hotel [W] Victoria, BC

Enchanted Forest [W] Salem, OR

Enchanted Village [W] Tacoma, WA

End of the Oregon Trail Interpretive Center [W] Oregon City, OR

Energeum [W] Calgary, AB

EPCOR Centre for Performing Arts [W] Calgary, AB

Evergreen Floating Bridge [W] Seattle, WA

Exhibition and Stampede [S] Medicine Hat, AB

Exhibition Park [W] Vancouver, BC

Experimental Breeder Reactor Number 1 (EBR-1) [W] Arco, ID

Ezra Meeker Community Festival [S] Puyallup, WA

Ezra Meeker Mansion [W] Puyallup, WA

Face Rock State Park [W] Bandon, OR

Fairhaven District [W] Bellingham, WA

Fairhaven Park [W] Bellingham, WA

Fall Creek Dam and Lake [W] Eugene, OR

Fall Festival [S] Corvallis, OR

Farewell Bend [W] Ontario, OR

Farmer Consumer Awareness Day [S] Quincy, WA

Farmers Market [S] Buhl, ID

Farragut State Park [W] Coeur d'Alene, ID

Favell Museum of Western Art and Native American Artifacts [W] Klamath Falls, OR

Federation Forest State Park [W] Enumclaw, WA

Ferndale [W] Bellingham, WA

Ferry [W] Tacoma, WA

Ferry service to Victoria, BC Canada [W] Port Angeles, WA

Ferry trips [W] Seattle, WA

Ferry trips [W] Victoria, BC

Ferry trips and cruises [W] Seattle, WA

Ferry trips. BC Ferries [W] Nanaimo, BC

Festival du Voyageur [S] Winnipeg, MB

Festival of Free-Flight [S] Lakeview, OR

Festival of Nations [S] Red Lodge, MT

Festival of Quilts [S] Gold Beach, OR

Fiddlers' Hall of Fame [W] Weiser, ID

Fields Spring State Park [W] Clarkston, WA

Fiery Food Festival [S] Pasco, WA

Finch Arboretum [W] Spokane, WA

Finley Point Unit [W] Polson, MT

Firemen's Lake [W] Redmond, OR

Fishing [W] Afton, WY

Fishing [W] Dubois, WY

Fishing [W] Glendive, MT

Fishing [W] Mount Rainier National Park, WA

Fishing [W] Olympic National Park, WA

Fishing [W] Port Orford, OR

Fishing [W] Twin Falls, ID

Fishing and hunting [W] Ontario, OR

Fishing, camping. Martinsdale, Harris and North Fork lakes [W] Harlowton, MT

Fishing, swimming, boating, camping [W] Mountain Home, ID

Five-Mile Drive [W] Tacoma, WA

Flaming Geyser State Park [W] Enumclaw, WA

Flaming Gorge National Recreation Area [W] Green River, WY

Flaming Gorge Reservoir [W] Rock Springs, WY

Flathead Lake [W] Kalispell, MT

Flathead Lake Biological Station, The University of Montana [W] Bigfork, MT

Flathead Lake Cruise [W] Polson, MT

Flathead Lake State Park [W] Bigfork, MT

Flathead Lake State Park [W] Polson, MT

Flathead Music Festival [S] Kalispell, MT

Flathead National Forest [W] Kalispell, MT

Flattop Mountain [W] Glacier National Park, MT

Flavel House [W] Astoria, OR

Fleet of Flowers Ceremony [S] Depoe Bay, OR

Flerchinger Vineyards [W] Hood River, OR

Flinn's Heritage Tours [W] Albany, OR

Flour Mill [W] Spokane, WA

Fogarty Creek State Park [W] Depoe Bay, OR

Folklorama [S] Winnipeg, MB

Folk Music Festival [S] Edmonton, AB

Forest Park [W] Portland, OR

Forks National Historic Site, The [W] Winnipeg, MB

Fort Assinniboine [W] Havre, MT

Fort Bridger State Museum [W] Evanston, WY

Fort Calgary Historic Park [W] Calgary, AB

Fort Canby [W] Long Beach, WA

Fort Casey State Park [W] Coupeville, WA

Fort Caspar Museum and Historic Site [W] Casper, WY

Fort Clatsop National Memorial [W] Astoria, OR

Fort Columbia [W] Long Beach, WA

Fort Dalles Museum [W] The Dalles, OR

Fort Dalles Rodeo [S] The Dalles, OR

Fort Edmonton Park [W] Edmonton, AB

Fort Fetterman State Museum [W] Douglas, WY

Fort Flagler [W] Port Townsend, WA

Fort Henry Trading Post Site [W] St. Anthony, ID

Fort Langley National Historic Site [W] Vancouver, BC

Fort Laramie National Historic Site [W] Torrington, WY

Fort Lewis [W] Tacoma, WA

Fort Maginnis [W] Lewistown, MT

Fort Museum [W] Fort Macleod, AB

Fort Nisqually [W] Tacoma, WA

Fort Normandeau [W] Red Deer, AB

Fort Normandeau Days [S] Red Deer, AB

Fort Owen State Park [W] Hamilton, MT

Fort Peck Dam and Lake [W] Glasgow, MT

Fort Peck Summer Theater [S] Glasgow, MT

Fort Phil Kearny Site [W] Buffalo, WY

Fort Rodd Hill and Fisgard Lighthouse National Historic Site [W] Victoria, BC

Fort Sherman Museum [W] Coeur d'Alene, ID

Fort Simcoe Historical State Park [W] Toppenish, WA

Fort Spokane [W] Coulee Dam, WA

Fort Stevens State Park [W] Astoria, OR

Fort Union Trading Post National Historic Site [W] Sidney, MT

Fort Vancouver National Historic Site [W] Vancouver, WA

Fort Walla Walla Museum Complex [W] Walla Walla, WA

Fort Walla Walla Park [W] Walla Walla, WA

Fort Whoop-Up [W] Lethbridge, AB

Fort Worden [W] Port Townsend, WA

Fossil Butte National Monument [W] Kemmerer, WY

Foster Lake [W] Sweet Home, OR

Founders' Day [S] Cashmere, WA

Founders Day Corn Roast [S] Forest Grove, OR

Frederic Wood Theatre [W] Vancouver, BC

Freeway Park [W] Seattle, WA

Fremont County Fair [S] St. Anthony, ID

Fremont County Fair & Rodeo [S] Riverton, WY

Fremont County Pioneer Museum [W] Lander, WY

Fremont County Pioneer Days [S] St. Anthony, ID

Fremont National Forest [W] Lakeview, OR

Fringe Theatre Event [S] Edmonton, AB

Frontier Festival [S] Cody, WY

Frontier Gateway Museum [W] Glendive, MT

Frontier Montana [W] Deer Lodge, MT

Frontier Town [W] Helena, MT

Fun Forest Amusement Park [W] Seattle, WA

Gallant Lady Cruises [W] Seattle, WA

Gallatin County Fair [S] Bozeman, MT

Gallatin National Forest [W] Bozeman, MT

Gallery at Ceperley House [W] Vancouver, BC

Gallery I [W] Ellensburg, WA

Gallery of Art [W] Cheney, WA

Gardens [W] Tacoma, WA

Gardiner Summer Series Rodeo [S] Gardiner, MT

Gastown [W] Vancouver, BC

Gas Works Park [W] Seattle, WA

Gates of the Mountains [W] Helena, MT

Geological Museum [W] Laramie, WY

George Fox University [W] Newberg, OR

Georgetown Lake [W] Anaconda, MT

Geyser and Hot Springs [W] Lakeview, OR

Geyser Park [W] Billings, MT

Ghost towns and Sapphire mines [W] Anaconda, MT

Giant Springs State Park and State Trout Hatchery [W] Great Falls, MT

Gifford Pinchot National Forest [W] Vancouver, WA

Gift of the Waters Pageant [S] Thermopolis, WY

Gilbert's Brewery [W] Virginia City, MT

Ginkgo/Wanapum State Park [W] Ellensburg, WA

Glacier Jazz Stampede [S] Kalispell, MT

Glacier Maze [W] Columbia Falls, MT

Glacier National Park [W] Kalispell, MT

Glacier National Park [W] Whitefish, MT

Glacier Raft Co [W] Glacier National Park, MT

Glenbow Museum [W] Calgary, AB

Glendo State Park [W] Wheatland, WY

Goat Rocks Wilderness [W] Packwood, WA

Gold Collection [W] Helena, MT

Goldendale Observatory [W] Goldendale, WA

Golden Gardens [W] Seattle, WA

Gold Hill [W] Idaho City, ID

Gonzaga University [W] Spokane, WA

Good Nations Powwow [S] Hamilton, MT

Gordon Southam Observatory [W] Vancouver, BC

Gorge Powerhouse/Ladder Creek Falls and Rock Gardens [W] Sedro Woolley, WA

Goshen County Fair & Rodeo [S] Torrington, WY

Governor's Cup Marathon [S] Helena, MT

Grand Canyon in miniature [W] Challis, ID

Grand Coulee Dam [W] Coulee Dam, WA

Grand Targhee Ski and Summer Resort [W] Driggs, ID

Grand Teton Music Festival [S] Jackson, WY

Granite Park [W] Glacier National Park, MT

Grant County Fair [S] Moses Lake, WA

Grant County Fair and Rodeo [S] John Day, OR

Grant County Historical Museum [W] John Day, OR

Grant County Pioneer Village and Museum [W] Ephrata, WA

Grant-Kohrs Ranch National Historic Site [W] Deer Lodge, MT

Grants Pass Museum of Art [W] Grants Pass, OR

Granville Island [W] Vancouver, BC

Grasshopper Glacier [W] Cooke City, MT

Gray Line bus tours [W] Jackson, WY

Gray Line bus tours [W] Portland, OR

Gray Line bus tours [W] Seattle, WA

Gray Line bus tours [W] Victoria, BC

Gray Line bus tours [W] West Yellowstone, MT

Gray Line sightseeing tours [W] Vancouver, BC

Grays Harbor Historical Seaport [W] Aberdeen, WA

Grays Harbor Lighthouse [W] Westport, WA

Great Columbia Crossing Bridge Run [S] Astoria, OR

Greatest of the Grape [S] Roseburg, OR

Great Northern Fair [S] Havre, MT

Great Northern Whitewater [W] Glacier National Park, MT

Great Salmon BalloonFest, The [S] Salmon, ID

Green Lake Park [W] Seattle, WA

Green River Gorge Conservation Area [W] Enumclaw, WA

Green River Rendezvous [S] Pinedale, WY

Greybull Museum [W] Greybull, WY

Greyhound Racing [S] Portland, OR

Grizzly Wolf & Discovery Center [W] West Yellowstone, MT

Grotto—The National Sanctuary of Our Sorrowful Mother [W] Portland, OR

Grouse Mountain [W] Vancouver, BC

Grouse Mountain tramway [W] Vancouver, BC

Guernsey Old Timer's & Street Dance [S] Wheatland, WY

Guernsey State Park [W] Wheatland, WY

Guy W. Talbot [W] Portland, OR

Harbour Centre-The Lookout [W] Vancouver, BC

Harbour Cruises Ltd [W] Vancouver, BC

Harlowtown Rodeo [S] Harlowton, MT

Harney County Fair, Rodeo and Race Meet [S] Burns, OR

Harney County Historical Museum [W] Burns, OR

Harriman State Park [W] Ashton, ID

Harris Beach [W] Brookings, OR

Hatfield Marine Science Center of Oregon State University [W] Newport, OR

Hatley Castle [W] Victoria, BC

Hat Rock State Park [W] Umatilla, OR

Havre Beneath the Streets [W] Havre, MT

Havre Festival Days [S] Havre, MT

Hawaiian Luau [S] Forest Grove, OR

Headquarters Visitor Information Center [W] Sun Valley Area, ID

Head-Smashed-In Buffalo Jump Interpretive Centre [W] Fort Macleod, AB

H. Earl Clack Memorial Museum [W] Havre, MT

Heceta Head Lighthouse [W] Florence, OR

Heise Hot Springs [W] Idaho Falls, ID

Helena National Forest [W] Helena, MT

Hell Creek State Park [W] Glasgow, MT

Hellgate Jetboat Excursions [W] Grants Pass, OR

Hell's Canyon Adventures [W] Weiser, ID

Hell's Canyon Dam [W] Weiser, ID

Hell's Canyon Excursions [W] Lewiston, ID

Hell's Canyon National Recreation Area [W] Grangeville, ID

Hells Canyon National Recreation Area [W] Joseph, OR

Hell's Canyon National Recreation Area [W] Weiser, ID

Hell's Gate State Park [W] Lewiston, ID

Helmcken House [W] Victoria, BC

Hendricks Park Rhododendron Garden [W] Eugene, OR

Henry Estate Winery [W] Roseburg, OR

Henry's Lake State Park [W] Ashton, ID

Heritage Days [S] Columbia Falls, MT

Heritage Days [S] Grants Pass, OR

Heritage Festival [S] Edmonton, AB

Heritage Museum [W] Libby, MT

Heritage Park Historical Village [W] Calgary, AB

Herrett Center [W] Twin Falls, ID

Heyburn State Park [W] St. Marie's, ID

High Desert Museum, The [W] Bend, OR

Highland Games [S] Red Deer, AB

Highland Games Festival [S] Glasgow, MT

High Plains Old Time Country Music Show & Contest [S] Douglas, WY

High School Rodeo [S] Salmon, ID

Hiking [W] Mount Rainier National Park, WA

Hiking [W] Mount St. Helens National Volcanic Monument, WA

Hiking [W] Olympic National Park, WA

Hilgard Junction State Recreation Area [W] La Grande, OR

Hillcrest Park [W] Mount Vernon, WA

Hillcrest Vineyard [W] Roseburg, OR

Historical Murals [W] Toppenish, WA

Historical Museum at Fort Missoula [W] Missoula, MT

Historical points of 19th-century gold mining. Maiden [W] Lewistown, MT

Historical Society Museum [W] Newport, WA

Historic Claquato Church [W] Chehalis, WA

Historic Deepwood Estate [W] Salem, OR

Historic Governors' Mansion [W] Cheyenne, WY

Historic Hughes House [W] Port Orford, OR

Historic Interior Homes Tours [S] Albany, OR

Historic North Front Street [W] Yakima, WA

Hockaday Center for the Arts [W] Kalispell, MT

Hogadon Ski Area [W] Casper, WY

Holiday Parade of Christmas Ships [S] Portland, OR

Holland Gardens [W] Oak Harbor, WA

Holland Happening [S] Oak Harbor, WA

Holliday Park [W] Cheyenne, WY

Holmes Family Home [W] Oregon City, OR

Holter Museum of Art [W] Helena, MT

Home-Grown Festival [S] Marysville, WA

Homesteader's Museum [W] Torrington, WY

Honeywood Winery [W] Salem, OR

Hood Canal Nursery [W] Port Gamble, WA

Hood River County Fair [S] Hood River, OR

Hood River County Museum [W] Hood River, OR

Hood River Valley Harvest Fest [S] Hood River, OR

Hood River Valley Sternwheeler Days [S] Hood River, OR

Hood River Vineyards [W] Hood River, OR

Hoover-Minthorn House Museum [W] Newberg, OR

Hoquiam's "Castle" [W] Hoquiam, WA

Horse Racing [S] Evanston, WY

Horse racing [S] Jerome, ID

Horse racing [S] Portland, OR

Horse racing [S] Spokane, WA

Hot Springs County Museum and Cultural Center [W] Thermopolis, WY

Hot Springs State Park [W] Thermopolis, WY

House Tours [S] Port Townsend, WA

Howell Territorial Park and The Bybee House [W] Portland, OR

Hoyt Arboretum [W] Portland, OR

Hughes River Expeditions [W] Weiser, ID

Hult Center [W] Eugene, OR

Humbug Mountain State Park [W] Port Orford, OR

Hungry Horse Dam and Power Plant [W] Columbia Falls, MT

Hunting [W] Pinedale, WY

Hunt moss agates [W] Glendive, MT

Hyack Festival [S] Vancouver, BC

Ice Harbor Lock and Dam [W] Pasco, WA

Icicle Junction [W] Leavenworth, WA

Idaho Black History Museum [W] Boise, ID

Idaho Botanical Gardens [W] Boise, ID

Idaho Centennial Carousel [W] Rexburg, ID

Idaho Falls [W] Idaho Falls, ID

Idaho International Folk Dance Festival [S] Rexburg, ID

Idaho Museum of Natural History [W] Pocatello, ID

Idaho Panhandle National Forests—Coeur d'Alene [W] Coeur d'Alene, ID

Idaho Panhandle National Forests—Kaniksu [W] Priest Lake Area, ID

Idaho Panhandle National Forests—St. Joe [W] St. Marie's, ID

Idaho Powerboat Regatta [S] Burley, ID

Idaho Repertory Theater [S] Moscow, ID

Idaho Shakespeare Festival [S] Boise, ID

Idaho State Historical Museum [W] Boise, ID

Idaho State University [W] Pocatello, ID

Illahee [W] Bremerton, WA

Independence Rock [W] Casper, WY

Indian Springs [W] American Falls, ID

Industrial tour. Rainier Brewing Company [W] Seattle, WA

Industrial tours [W] Vancouver, BC

Interagency Aerial Fire Control Center [W] West Yellowstone, MT

Intermittent spring [W] Afton, WY

International Air Show [S] Kamloops, BC

International Air Show [S] Lethbridge, AB

International Bathtub Race [S] Vancouver, BC

International District [W] Seattle, WA

International Fountain [W] Seattle, WA

International Peace Arch [W] Blaine, WA

International Wildlife Film Festival [S] Missoula, MT

Interpretive programs and walks [W] Mount Rainier National Park, WA

Interpretive walks and programs [W] Mount St. Helens National Volcanic Monument, WA

Irish Days [S] Lakeview, OR

Ironman Canada Championship Triathlon [S] Penticton, BC

Irrigation Festival [S] Sequim, WA

Irving House Historic Centre [W] Vancouver, BC

Jackalope Days [S] Douglas, WY

Jackson County Fair [S] Medford, OR

Jackson F. Kimball State Park [W] Klamath Falls, OR

Jackson Hole Fall Arts Festival [S] Jackson, WY

Jackson Hole Historical Society & Museum [W] Jackson, WY

Jackson Hole Mountain Resort [W] Jackson, WY

Jackson Hole Museum [W] Jackson, WY

Jackson Hole Rodeo [S] Jackson, WY

Jacksonville Museum [W] Jacksonville, OR

James R. Slater Museum of Natural History [W] Tacoma, WA

Japanese Garden [W] Portland, OR

Japanese Garden [W] Seattle, WA

Jasper Tramway [W] Jasper National Park, AB

Jazz City Festival [S] Edmonton, AB

Jazz Unlimited [S] Pasco, WA

Jedediah Smith Mountain Man Rendezvous [S] Grants Pass, OR

Jefferson County Fair [S] Port Townsend, WA

Jefferson County Museum [W] Madras, OR

Jefferson State Stampede [S] Klamath Falls, OR

Jerome County Fair & Rodeo [S] Jerome, ID

Jerome County Historical Museum [W] Jerome, ID

Jerry's Rogue River Jet Boat Trips [W] Gold Beach, OR

Jessie M. Honeyman Memorial [W] Florence, OR

John Day Fossil Beds National Monument [W] John Day, OR

John Day Locks and Dam [W] Biggs, OR

John Inskeep Environmental Learning Center [W] Oregon City, OR

John Janzen Nature Centre [W] Edmonton, AB

John Scharff Migratory Bird Festival [S] Burns, OR

Johnson County Fair and Rodeo [S] Buffalo, WY

Johnson County-Jim Gatchell Memorial Museum [W] Buffalo, WY

Johnson Ridge Obervatory [W] Mount St. Helens National Volcanic Monument, WA

Josephine County Air Fair [S] Grants Pass, OR

Josephine County Fair [S] Grants Pass, OR

Joseph P. Stewart State Park [W] Medford, OR

Julia Davis Park [W] Boise, ID

Junior Rodeo [S] Lakeview, OR

Kahlotus [W] Pasco, WA

Kamloops Museum and Archives [W] Kamloops, BC

Kamloops Wildlife Park [W] Kamloops, BC

Kam Wah Chung and Co Museum [W] John Day, OR

Keller Heritage Center [W] Colville, WA

Kelowna Regatta [S] Kelowna, BC

Kendall Skyline Drive [W] Dayton (Columbia County), WA

Kerbyville Museum [W] Cave Junction, OR

Keyhole State Park [W] Gillette, WY

King County Fair [S] Enumclaw, WA

Kingdome, The [W] Seattle, WA

King's Saddlery Museum [W] Sheridan, WY

Kinsmen Sports Centre [W] Edmonton, AB

Kitsap County Fair and Stampede [S] Bremerton, WA

Kitsap County Historical Society Museum [W] Bremerton, WA

Kitsap Memorial State Park [W] Port Gamble, WA

Kittitas County Fair & Rodeo [S] Ellensburg, WA

Klamath County Baldwin Hotel Museum [W] Klamath Falls, OR

Klamath County Fair [S] Klamath Falls, OR

Klamath County Museum [W] Klamath Falls, OR

Klamath Memorial Powow and Rodeo [S] Klamath Falls, OR

Klickitat County Fair and Rodeo [S] Goldendale, WA

Klickitat County Historical Museum [W] Goldendale, WA

Klondike Gold Rush National Historical Park-Seattle Unit [W] Seattle, WA

Knight Library [W] Eugene, OR

Kootenai National Forest [W] Libby, MT

Kootenai National Wildlife Refuge [W] Bonners Ferry, ID

Kootenai River Days [S] Bonners Ferry, ID

Lake Chelan [W] Chelan, WA

Lake Chelan [W] Chelan, WA

Lake Chelan Rodeo [S] Chelan, WA

Lake Coeur d'Alene [W] Coeur d'Alene, ID

Lake Coeur d'Alene Cruises, Inc [W] Coeur d'Alene, ID

Lake County Fair and Roundup [S] Lakeview, OR

Lake cruises [W] Chelan, WA

Lake Cushman State Park [W] Union, WA

Lakefair [S] Olympia, WA

Lake Gillette Recreation Area [W] Colville, WA

Lake Lowell [W] Nampa, ID

Lake McDonald [W] Glacier National Park, MT

Lake Owyhee [W] Ontario, OR

Lake Padden Park [W] Bellingham, WA

Lake Pend Oreille [W] Sandpoint, ID

Lake Roosevelt National Recreation Area [W] Coulee Dam, WA

Lake Sacajawea Park [W] Longview, WA

Lake Sammamish State Park [W] Issaquah, WA

Lake Sylvia State Park [W] Aberdeen, WA

Lake Umatilla [W] Biggs, OR

Lake Union [W] Seattle, WA
Lakeview Park [W] Nampa, ID
Lake Washington Canal [W] Seattle, WA
Lake Washington Floating Bridge [W] Seattle, WA
Lake Whatcom Railway [W] Sedro Woolley, WA
Lane County Fair [S] Eugene, OR
Lane County Historical Museum [W] Eugene, OR
LaPine [W] Bend, OR
Laramie County Fair [S] Cheyenne, WY
Laramie Plains Museum [W] Laramie, WY
Larrabee State Park [W] Bellingham, WA
Laser Light Festival [S] Coulee Dam, WA
Last Chance Stampede and Fair [S] Helena, MT
Last Chance Tour Train [W] Helena, MT
Latah County Fair [S] Moscow, ID
Latah County Historical Society [W] Moscow, ID
Lava Butte and Lava River Cave [W] Bend, OR
Lava Hot Springs [W] Lava Hot Springs, ID
Lavas, The [W] Idaho Falls, ID
Lawrence Park [W] Kalispell, MT
Lee McCune Braille Trail [W] Casper, WY
Legend of Rawhide [S] Lusk, WY
Legislative Building [W] Olympia, WA
Legislative Building [W] Winnipeg, MB
Lemhi County Fair & Rodeo [S] Salmon, ID
Lewis and Clark [W] Portland, OR
Lewis and Clark Caverns State Park [W] Three Forks, MT
Lewis and Clark College [W] Portland, OR
Lewis and Clark Expeditions [W] Jackson, WY
Lewis and Clark National Forest [W] Great Falls, MT
Lewis and Clark National Historical Trail Interpretive Center [W] Great Falls, MT
Lewis and Clark Trail State Park [W] Dayton (Columbia County), WA

Lewis County Historical Museum [W] Chehalis, WA
Lewiston Round-Up [S] Lewiston, ID
Libby Dam [W] Libby, MT
Liberty Orchards Company, Inc [W] Cashmere, WA
Library Building [W] Olympia, WA
Lincoln County Fair [S] Shoshone, ID
Lincoln County Historical Society Museums. Log Cabin Museum [W] Newport, OR
Lincoln Monument [W] Laramie, WY
Lincoln Park [W] Seattle, WA
Linfield College [W] McMinnville, OR
Lionel Hampton/Chevron Jazz Festival [S] Moscow, ID
Lithia Park [W] Ashland, OR
Little Bighorn Days [S] Hardin, MT
Little Mountain [W] Mount Vernon, WA
Loeb [W] Brookings, OR
Logger Days [S] Libby, MT
Loggerodeo [S] Sedro Woolley, WA
Lolo National Forest [W] Missoula, MT
Longest Dam Run [S] Glasgow, MT
Longmire [W] Mount Rainier National Park, WA
Lookout Pass Ski Area [W] Wallace, ID
Lookout Point and Dexter Dams and Lakes [W] Eugene, OR
Loop drive [W] Spokane, WA
Lost Creek State Park [W] Anaconda, MT
Lost Lake [W] Hood River, OR
Lower Fort Garry National Historic Site of Canada [W] Winnipeg, MB
Lower Mesa Falls [W] Ashton, ID
Loyalty Days and Sea Fair Festival [S] Newport, OR
Lucky Peak State Park [W] Boise, ID
Lummi Stommish [S] Bellingham, WA
Luna House Museum [W] Lewiston, ID
Lynden Pioneer Museum [W] Bellingham, WA
Madison Buffalo Jump State Monument [W] Three Forks, MT

Madison River Canyon Earthquake Area [W] West Yellowstone, MT

Mad River Boat Trips, Inc [W] Jackson, WY

Mail Boat Whitewater Trips [W] Gold Beach, OR

Main Street Historic District [W] Sheridan, WY

Makah Cultural and Research Center [W] Neah Bay, WA

Makoshika [W] Glendive, MT

Malad Gorge State Park [W] Jerome, ID

Malheur County Fair [S] Ontario, OR

Malheur National Forest [W] John Day, OR

Malheur National Wildlife Refuge [W] Burns, OR

Malmstrom AFB [W] Great Falls, MT

Manitoba Fall Fair [S] Brandon, MB

Manitoba Museum of Man and Nature [W] Winnipeg, MB

Manitoba Opera Association [S] Winnipeg, MB

Manitoba Summer Fair [S] Brandon, MB

Manito Park [W] Spokane, WA

Manty Shaw Fiddlers' Jamboree [S] Shoshone, ID

Many Glacier Area [W] Glacier National Park, MT

Marine Discovery Tours [W] Newport, OR

Maritime Heritage Center [W] Bellingham, WA

Maritime Museum [W] Vancouver, BC

Maritime Museum [W] Victoria, BC

Maritime Museum [W] Westport, WA

Marshall Mountain Ski Area [W] Missoula, MT

Maryhill Museum of Art [W] Goldendale, WA

Mary L. Gooding Memorial Park [W] Shoshone, ID

Marysville Ghost Town [W] Helena, MT

Massacre Rocks Rendezvous [S] American Falls, ID

Massacre Rocks State Park [W] American Falls, ID

Maverick Mountain Ski Area [W] Dillon, MT

Mayer State Park [W] The Dalles, OR

McCall Folk Music Festival [S] McCall, ID

McChord AFB [W] Tacoma, WA

McIntosh Apple Days [S] Hamilton, MT

McLoughlin House National Historic Site [W] Oregon City, OR

McNary Lock and Dam [W] Pasco, WA

McNary Lock and Dam [W] Umatilla, OR

Medicine Bow National Forest [W] Douglas, WY

Medicine Bow National Forest [W] Laramie, WY

Medicine Hat Museum and Art Gallery [W] Medicine Hat, AB

Merrysville for the Holidays [S] Marysville, WA

Middle Fork of the Salmon Wild and Scenic River [W] Challis, ID

Midwinter Breakout [S] Penticton, BC

Miette Hot Springs [W] Jasper National Park, AB

Migratory Bird Refuge [W] Klamath Falls, OR

Millersylvania State Park [W] Olympia, WA

Milo McIver State Park [W] Oregon City, OR

Mima Mounds Natural Area [W] Olympia, WA

Mineral collecting [W] Newport, OR

Mineral collecting [W] Prineville, OR

Mineral Museum [W] Butte, MT

Miner's Jubilee [S] Baker City, OR

Miniature World [W] Victoria, BC

Minnetonka Cave [W] Montpelier, ID

Mission Mill Museum [W] Salem, OR

Missoula Carousel [W] Missoula, MT

Missoula Public Library [W] Missoula, MT

Missouri Headwaters State Park [W] Three Forks, MT

MonDak Heritage Center [W] Sidney, MT

Monorail [W] Seattle, WA

Montana Cowboy Poetry Gathering [S] Lewistown, MT
Montana Fair [S] Billings, MT
Montana Governor's Cup Walleye Tournament [S] Glasgow, MT
Montana Historical Society Museum [W] Helena, MT
Montana Pro Rodeo Circuit Finals [S] Great Falls, MT
Montana Raft Company & Glacier Wilderness Guides [W] Glacier National Park, MT
Montana Snowbowl [W] Missoula, MT
Montana State University [W] Bozeman, MT
Montana Tech of the University of Montana [W] Butte, MT
Montana Territorial Prison [W] Deer Lodge, MT
Montana Traditional Dixieland Jazz Festival [S] Helena, MT
Montana Winter Fair [S] Bozeman, MT
Monticello Convention Site [W] Longview, WA
Moses Lake [W] Moses Lake, WA
Moses Lake Recreation Area [W] Moses Lake, WA
Moses Lake State Park [W] Moses Lake, WA
Moss Mansion [W] Billings, MT
Mount Adams Recreation Area [W] Goldendale, WA
Mountain climbing [W] Mount Rainier National Park, WA
Mountain climbing [W] Olympic National Park, WA
Mountaineers' Forest Theater [S] Bremerton, WA
Mountain Man Rendezvous [S] Evanston, WY
Mount Bachelor Ski Area [W] Bend, OR
Mount Baker-Snoqualmie National Forest [W] Bellingham, WA
Mount Baker-Snoqualmie National Forest [W] Seattle, WA
Mount Hood-Columbia Gorge Loop Scenic Drive [W] Portland, OR
Mount Hood Jazz Festival [S] Portland, OR
Mount Hood National Forest [W] Hood River, OR
Mount Hood National Forest [W] The Dalles, OR

Mount Hood Scenic Railroad [W] Hood River, OR
M-K Nature Center [W] Boise, ID
Mount Rainier National Park [W] Tacoma, WA
Mount Spokane State Park [W] Spokane, WA
Mount St. Helens Visitor Center [W] Longview, WA
Mount St. Helens Visitor Center [W] Mount St. Helens National Volcanic Monument, WA
Mount Tabor Park [W] Portland, OR
Moyie Falls [W] Bonners Ferry, ID
Mud Mountain Dam [W] Enumclaw, WA
Mukilteo [W] Everett, WA
Multnomah County Fair [S] Portland, OR
Multnomah Falls [W] Portland, OR
Museum of Anthropology [W] Cheney, WA
Museum of Anthropology [W] Vancouver, BC
Museum of Art [W] Eugene, OR
Museum of Art [W] Pullman, WA
Museum of Flight [W] Seattle, WA
Museum of History and Industry [W] Seattle, WA
Museum of Montana Wildlife and Hall of Bronze [W] Browning, MT
Museum of North Idaho [W] Coeur d'Alene, ID
Museum of Northwest Art [W] La Conner, WA
Museum of the Mountain Man [W] Pinedale, WY
Museum of the Northern Great Plains [W] Fort Benton, MT
Museum of the Plains Indian [W] Browning, MT
Museum of the Regiments [W] Calgary, AB
Museum of the Rockies [W] Bozeman, MT
Museum of the Upper Missouri River [W] Fort Benton, MT
Music and Art Festival [S] Chehalis, WA
Music Festival [S] Red Lodge, MT
Mustang Days [S] Lovell, WY
Muttart Conservatory [W] Edmonton, AB

Myrtle Edwards/Elliott Bay [W] Seattle, WA

Nanaimo Art Gallery and Exhibition Centre [W] Nanaimo, BC

Nanaimo District Museum [W] Nanaimo, BC

Nanaimo Marine Festival [S] Nanaimo, BC

Narrows Bridge [W] Tacoma, WA

NASCAR Auto Racing [S] Richland, WA

National Bighorn Sheep Interpretive Center [W] Dubois, WY

National Bison Range [W] Polson, MT

National Elk Refuge [W] Jackson, WY

National Fish Hatchery [W] Ennis, MT

National Fish Hatchery [W] Leavenworth, WA

National Historic Oregon Trail Interpretive Center [W] Baker City, OR

National Lentil Festival [S] Pullman, WA

National Oldtime Fiddlers' Contest [S] Weiser, ID

National Western Art Show and Auction [S] Ellensburg, WA

National Wildlife Art Museum [W] Jackson, WY

Native American Celebrations [S] Toppenish, WA

Natural History Museum [W] Banff, AB

Neptune State Park [W] Yachats, OR

Nevada City [W] Virginia City, MT

Nevada City Depot [W] Virginia City, MT

Never Never Land [W] Tacoma, WA

Newberry National Volcanic Monument [W] Bend, OR

Newcastle Island Provincial Marine Park [W] Nanaimo, BC

Newell House Museum [W] Newberg, OR

Newhalem Visitor Information Center [W] Sedro Woolley, WA

Nez Perce County Fair [S] Lewiston, ID

Nez Perce National Forest [W] Grangeville, ID

Nez Perce National Historical Park [W] Lewiston, ID

Nicolaysen Art Museum & Discovery Center [W] Casper, WY

Night Rodeo [S] Caldwell, ID

Nikka Yuko Japanese Garden [W] Lethbridge, AB

Ninepipe and Pablo National Wildlife Refuges [W] Polson, MT

Nordicfest [S] Libby, MT

Nordic Heritage Museum [W] Seattle, WA

North American Native American Days Powwow [S] Browning, MT

North Cascades National Park [W] Bellingham, WA

North Cascades National Park [W] Sedro Woolley, WA

North Central Washington Museum [W] Wenatchee, WA

Northeast Montana Fair and Rodeo [S] Glasgow, MT

Northeast Washington Fair [S] Colville, WA

Northern Idaho Fair [S] Coeur d'Alene, ID

Northern International Livestock Exposition [S] Billings, MT

Northern Pacific Depot Railroad Museum [W] Wallace, ID

Northwest Cherry Festival [S] The Dalles, OR

Northwest Montana Fair and Rodeo [S] Kalispell, MT

Northwest Trek [W] Tacoma, WA

NRA/MRA Rodeo [S] Big Timber, MT

Nutcracker Museum [W] Leavenworth, WA

Oak Hammock Marsh Wildlife Management Area [W] Winnipeg, MB

Oak Harbor Beach Park [W] Oak Harbor, WA

Oaks Amusement Park [W] Portland, OR

Oasis Bordello Museum [W] Wallace, ID

Oasis Park [W] Ephrata, WA

Obon Festival [S] Ontario, OR

Ochoco Lake Campground [W] Prineville, OR

Ochoco National Forest [W] Prineville, OR

Odyssium [W] Edmonton, AB

Officers' Row [W] Vancouver, WA

Official Rogue River Mail Boat Hydro-Jet Trips [W] Gold Beach, OR

Of Sea and Shore Museum [W] Port Gamble, WA

Ohanapecosh [W] Mount Rainier National Park, WA

Okanagan Wine Festival [S] Kelowna, BC

Okanagan Wine Festival [S] Penticton, BC

Okanogan National Forest [W] Omak, WA

Oktubberfest [S] Grangeville, ID

Old Aurora Colony Museum, The [W] Oregon City, OR

Old fashioned Melodrama [S] Cheyenne, WY

Old Fashioned Melodrama [S] Toppenish, WA

Old Fort Hall Replica [W] Pocatello, ID

Old Fort Townsend (Historical) [W] Port Townsend, WA

Old Hastings Mill [W] Vancouver, BC

Old Idaho Penitentiary [W] Boise, ID

Old Mission State Park [W] Kellogg, ID

Old No. 1 [W] Butte, MT

Old Snohomish Village [W] Snohomish, WA

Olmstead Place State Park-Heritage Site [W] Ellensburg, WA

Olympia Farmers Market [S] Olympia, WA

Olympic Game Farm [W] Sequim, WA

Olympic National Forest [W] Olympia, WA

Olympic National Park [W] Forks, WA

Olympic National Park [W] Port Angeles, WA

Olympic National Park [W] Port Angeles, WA

Olympic Raft and Guide Service [W] Port Angeles, WA

Olympic Van Tours, Inc [W] Port Angeles, WA

Ona Beach [W] Newport, OR

Ontario [W] Ontario, OR

Oregon Cabaret Theatre [S] Ashland, OR

Oregon Caves National Monument [W] Cave Junction, OR

Oregon Caves National Monument [W] Grants Pass, OR

Oregon Coast Aquarium [W] Newport, OR

Oregon Coast Music Festival [S] Coos Bay, OR

Oregon Connection/House of Myrtlewood, The [W] Coos Bay, OR

Oregon Dunes National Recreation Area [W] North Bend, OR

Oregon Dunes National Recreation Area [W] Reedsport, OR

Oregon Folklife Festival [S] Corvallis, OR

Oregon History Center [W] Portland, OR

Oregon Jamboree, The [S] Sweet Home, OR

Oregon Museum of Science and Industry [W] Portland, OR

Oregon Shakespeare Festival [S] Ashland, OR

Oregon State Fair [S] Salem, OR

Oregon State University [W] Corvallis, OR

Oregon Trail Living History Park [W] The Dalles, OR

Oregon Trail Regional Museum [W] Baker City, OR

Oregon Trail Rendezvous Pageant [S] Montpelier, ID

Oregon Vortex Location of the House of Mystery, The [W] Jacksonville, OR

Oregon Zoo [W] Portland, OR

Original Governor's Mansion [W] Helena, MT

Oswald West State Park [W] Cannon Beach, OR

Other tours [W] Jasper National Park, AB

Our Lady of the Rockies [W] Butte, MT

Outfitting and Big Game Hunting [W] Afton, WY

Owen Municipal Rose Garden [W] Eugene, OR

Owyhee Canyon [W] Ontario, OR

Oxbow Dam [W] Weiser, ID

Oyster beds [W] Olympia, WA

Oysterville [W] Long Beach, WA

Pacific Lutheran University [W] Tacoma, WA

Pacific National Exhibition Annual Fair [S] Vancouver, BC

Pacific Northwest Arts Fair [S] Seattle, WA

Pacific Northwest Sled Dog Championship Races [S] Priest Lake Area, ID

Pacific NW Scottish Highland Games [S] Enumclaw, WA

Pacific Paradise Family Fun Center [W] Ocean Shores, WA

Pacific Science Center [W] Seattle, WA

Pacific Space Centre [W] Vancouver, BC

Pacific Undersea Gardens [W] Victoria, BC

Pacific University [W] Forest Grove, OR

Pack trips into Idaho primitive areas [W] McCall, ID

Paddlewheel/River Rouge boat and bus tours [W] Winnipeg, MB

Painted Hills Unit [W] John Day, OR

Painted Rocks [W] Yakima, WA

Painted Rocks State Park [W] Hamilton, MT

Paisley [W] Lakeview, OR

Palouse River Canyon [W] Dayton (Columbia County), WA

Panorama Point [W] Hood River, OR

Paradise [W] Mount Rainier National Park, WA

Paradise area [W] Mount Rainier National Park, WA

Pari-mutuel Horse Racing [S] Grants Pass, OR

Paris Gibson Square Museum of Art [W] Great Falls, MT

Park County Museum [W] Livingston, MT

Parks [W] Edmonton, AB

Parks [W] Rexburg, ID

Parks. Airport [W] Blackfoot, ID

Parks. Kamiak Butte County Park [W] Pullman, WA

Parliament Buildings [W] Victoria, BC

Paul Bunyan Days [S] St. Marie's, ID

Paxson Paintings [W] Missoula, MT

Payette National Forest [W] McCall, ID

Peace Arch Celebration [S] Blaine, WA

Peach Festival [S] Penticton, BC

Pear Blossom Festival [S] Medford, OR

Pearson Air Museum [W] Vancouver, WA

Pebble Creek Ski Area [W] Pocatello, ID

Pendleton Round-up [S] Pendleton, OR

Pendleton Woolen Mills [W] Pendleton, OR

Peninsula Park and Community Center [W] Portland, OR

Penticton Museum [W] Penticton, BC

Percival Landing Park [W] Olympia, WA

Perrine Memorial Bridge [W] Twin Falls, ID

Peter Paddlefish Day [S] Sidney, MT

Petersen Rock Gardens [W] Redmond, OR

Peter Skene Ogden Wayside [W] Redmond, OR

Peter Yegen, Jr.—Yellowstone County Museum [W] Billings, MT

Petroglyph Park [W] Nanaimo, BC

Petroglyphs [W] Clarkston, WA

Phillips County Museum [W] Malta, MT

Pickles & Ice Cream Festival Street Fair [S] Enumclaw, WA

Pictograph Cave State Park [W] Billings, MT

Pierce County Fair [S] Puyallup, WA

Pike Place Market [W] Seattle, WA

Pilot Butte [W] Bend, OR

Pine Mount Observatory [W] Bend, OR

Pioneer Cabin [W] Helena, MT

Pioneer Farm [W] Tacoma, WA

Pioneer Mother's Memorial Log Cabin [W] Newberg, OR

Pioneer Park [W] Puyallup, WA

Pioneer Park [W] Walla Walla, WA

Pioneer Square [W] Seattle, WA

Pittock Mansion [W] Portland, OR

Plains Indian Museum [W] Cody, WY

Plains Indian PowWow [S] Cody, WY

Planetarium [W] Winnipeg, MB

Platte County Fair and Rodeo [S] Wheatland, WY

Playmill Theater [S] West Yellowstone, MT

Point Defiance Park [W] Tacoma, WA

Point Defiance Zoo & Aquarium [W] Tacoma, WA

Point Ellice House Museum [W] Victoria, BC

Polar Bear Swim [S] Nanaimo, BC

Police Historical Museum [W] Portland, OR

Polson-Flathead Historical Museum [W] Polson, MT

Polson Park and Museum [W] Hoquiam, WA

Pomerelle Ski Area [W] Burley, ID

Ponderosa State Park [W] McCall, ID

Port Gamble Historic Museum [W] Port Gamble, WA

Portland Art Museum [W] Portland, OR

Portland Center Stage [S] Portland, OR

Portland Fire (WNBA) [W] Portland, OR

Portland Marathon [S] Portland, OR

Portland Rose Festival [S] Portland, OR

Portland Saturday Market [W] Portland, OR

Portland Scottish Highland Games [S] Portland, OR

Portland State University [W] Portland, OR

Portland Trailblazers (NBA) [W] Portland, OR

Potholes Reservoir [W] Moses Lake, WA

Potholes State Park [W] Moses Lake, WA

Powell County Museum [W] Deer Lodge, MT

Powell County Territorial Days [S] Deer Lodge, MT

Powwow and Tipi Village [S] Fort Macleod, AB

Powwows [S] Riverton, WY

Prehistoric Gardens [W] Gold Beach, OR

Preston Estate Vineyards [W] Pasco, WA

Priest Lake [W] Priest Lake Area, ID

Priest Lake State Park [W] Priest Lake Area, ID

Priest Point Park [W] Olympia, WA

Priest River [W] Priest Lake Area, ID

Professional sports [W] Portland, OR

Professional sports [W] Seattle, WA

Professional sports [W] Vancouver, BC

Professional sports team [W] Calgary, AB

Professional sports team [W] Edmonton, AB

Provincial Building and Court House [W] Revelstoke, BC

Provincial Museum of Alberta [W] Edmonton, AB

Pryor Mountain Wild Horse Range [W] Lovell, WY

Pullman Summer Palace Theater [W] Pullman, WA

Quarter Horse Show [S] Kalispell, MT

Queen Elizabeth Park [W] Vancouver, BC

Queen Elizabeth Promenade [W] Nanaimo, BC

Queen Elizabeth Theatre and Playhouse and Orpheum Theatre [S] Vancouver, BC

"Race to the Sky" Dog Sled Races [S] Helena, MT

Rafting. Yellowstone Raft Company [W] Gardiner, MT

Rainbow Falls State Park [W] Chehalis, WA

Rain Fest [S] Longview, WA

Rain forests [W] Olympic National Park, WA

Range Rider of the Yellowstone [W] Billings, MT

Range Riders Museum and Pioneer Memorial Hall [W] Miles City, MT

Ravalli County Fair [S] Hamilton, MT

Real Oregon Gift, The [W] North Bend, OR

Recreation areas [W] Everett, WA

Red Deer and District Museum [W] Red Deer, AB

Red Desert Round-Up [S] Rock Springs, WY

Red Eagle Lake [W] Glacier National Park, MT

Redfish Lake Visitor Center [W] Stanley, ID

Red Lodge Mountain Ski Area [W] Red Lodge, MT

Red River Exhibition [S] Winnipeg, MB

Reeder's Alley [W] Helena, MT

Remington Carriage Museum [W] Fort Macleod, AB

Rendezvous [S] Colville, WA

Rendezvous in the Park [S] Moscow, ID

Restored buildings [W] Virginia City, MT

Revelstoke Mountain Arts Festival [S] Revelstoke, BC

Revelstoke Sno Fest [S] Revelstoke, BC

Reynolds-Alberta Museum [W] Edmonton, AB

Rhododendron Festival [S] Florence, OR

Richland County Fair and Rodeo [S] Sidney, MT

Ripley's—Believe It or Not [W] Newport, OR

Ritzville Blues Festival [S] Ritzville, WA

River excursions [W] Jackson, WY

River Expeditions [W] Stanley, ID

Riverfront Park [W] Spokane, WA

Riverfront Park [W] The Dalles, OR

River Rafting [W] Glacier National Park, MT

River rafting, backpack, fishing, and pack trips [W] Salmon, ID

River Rafting. Flathead Raft Company [W] Polson, MT

River rafting. Salmon River Outfitters [W] McCall, ID

River Runners [W] Cody, WY

Riverside State Park [W] Spokane, WA

Riverton Museum [W] Riverton, WY

River trips. Yellowstone Raft Company [W] Big Sky (Gallatin County), MT

Robbers' Roost [W] Virginia City, MT

Robert Mortvedt Library [W] Tacoma, WA

Rockhounding. Richardson's Recreational Ranch [W] Madras, OR

Rocky Boy Powwow [S] Havre, MT

Rocky Mountain College [W] Billings, MT

Rocky Mountain Raft Tours [W] Banff, AB

Rocky Mountain Research Station Fire Sciences Laboratory [W] Missoula, MT

Rocky Mountain River Tours [W] Pocatello, ID

Rocky Reach Dam [W] Wenatchee, WA

Rodeo Days [S] Cheney, WA

Rodeo Days [S] Livingston, MT

Rogue River National Forest [W] Medford, OR

Rogue River Raft Trips [W] Grants Pass, OR

Rooster Rock [W] Portland, OR

Rosalie Whyel Museum of Doll Art [W] Bellevue, WA

Roseburg Graffiti Week [S] Roseburg, OR

Ross House [W] Winnipeg, MB

Ross Park [W] Pocatello, ID

Rothschild House [W] Port Townsend, WA

Round Lake State Park [W] Sandpoint, ID

Royal British Columbia Museum [W] Victoria, BC

Royal Canadian Mint [W] Winnipeg, MB

Royal London Wax Museum [W] Victoria, BC

Royal Manitoba Winter Fair [S] Brandon, MB

Royal Tyrrell Museum of Paleontology [W] Calgary, AB

Ruins of Old Fort Benton [W] Fort Benton, MT

Rutherford House [W] Edmonton, AB

Sacajawea State Park [W] Pasco, WA

Saddle Mt State Park [W] Seaside, OR

Sage and Sun Festival [S] Ephrata, WA

Sagebrush Days [S] Buhl, ID

Sage Riders Rodeo [S] Umatilla, OR

St. Anthony Sand Dunes [W] St. Anthony, ID

St.-Boniface Museum [W] Winnipeg, MB

Ste. Chapelle Winery and Vineyards [W] Caldwell, ID

St. Francis Xavier Church [W] Missoula, MT

St. Joe Baldy Mountain [W] St. Marie's, ID

St. Joe River [W] Coeur d'Alene, ID

St. Joe River [W] St. Marie's, ID

St Mary Lake [W] Glacier National Park, MT

St. Mary's Mission [W] Hamilton, MT

St. Michael's Episcopal Cathedral [W] Boise, ID

St. Patrick's Irish Festival [S] Portland, OR

St. Paul's Episcopal Church [W] Virginia City, MT

St. Paul's Mission [W] Colville, WA

St. Peter's Church [W] Tacoma, WA

Salem Art Fair and Festival [S] Salem, OR

Salmon Bake [S] Depoe Bay, OR

Salmon Days Festival [S] Issaquah, WA

Salmon Harbor [W] Reedsport, OR

Salmon National Forest [W] Salmon, ID

Salmon River [W] Stanley, ID

Salmon River Days [S] Salmon, ID

Salty Sea Days [S] Everett, WA

Samson V Maritime Museum [W] Vancouver, BC

Samuel Benn Park [W] Aberdeen, WA

Samuel H. Boardman [W] Brookings, OR

Sandcastle Contest [S] Cannon Beach, OR

Sand Dunes Frontier [W] Florence, OR

Sandhill Crane Festival [S] Othello, WA

Sandpoint Public Beach [W] Sandpoint, ID

San Juan Island [W] San Juan Islands, WA

San Juan Island National Historical Park [W] San Juan Islands, WA

San Juan Islands Trip [W] Anacortes, WA

San Juan Jazz Festival [S] San Juan Islands, WA

Santa Claus Parade and Festival [S] Fort Macleod, AB

Santa's City of Lights [S] Sedro Woolley, WA

Sarah Spurgeon Art Gallery [W] Ellensburg, WA

Sawtooth Mountain Mamas Arts and Crafts Fair [S] Stanley, ID

Sawtooth National Forest [W] Bellevue, ID

Sawtooth National Forest [W] Burley, ID

Sawtooth National Recreation Area [W] Stanley, ID

Sawtooth National Recreation Area [W] Sun Valley Area, ID

Sawtooth Quilt Festival [S] Stanley, ID

Sawtooth Twin Falls Ranger District [W] Twin Falls, ID

Sawtooth Valley and Stanley Basin [W] Stanley, ID

Sawtooth Wilderness [W] Stanley, ID

Scandinavian Midsummer Festival [S] Astoria, OR

Scenic Beach [W] Bremerton, WA

Scenic drives [W] Coeur d'Alene, ID

Scenic Drives. North [W] Victoria, BC

Scenic Drives. Skyline [W] Pinedale, WY

Schaefer County Park [W] Centralia, WA

Schafer State Park [W] Aberdeen, WA

Schminck Memorial Museum [W] Lakeview, OR

Schmitz Park [W] Seattle, WA

Scoggin Valley Park and Hagg Lake [W] Forest Grove, OR

SeaBus Harbour Ride [W] Vancouver, BC

Seafair [S] Seattle, WA

Seafood and Wine Festival [S] Newport, OR

Sea Lion Caves [W] Florence, OR

Seaquest State Park [W] Kelso, WA

Seascape scenic drive [W] Long Beach, WA

Seaside Aquarium [W] Seaside, OR

Seattle Aquarium, The [W] Seattle, WA

Seattle Art Museum [W] Seattle, WA

Seattle Asian Art Museum [W] Seattle, WA

Seattle Asian Art Museum [W] Seattle, WA

Seattle Center [W] Seattle, WA

Seattle Center Opera House, Playhouse, Arena, Key Arena [W] Seattle, WA

Seattle City Light Skagit Hydroelectric Project [W] Sedro Woolley, WA

Seattle Mariners (MLB) [W] Seattle, WA

Seattle Seahawks (NFL) [W] Seattle, WA

Seattle SuperSonics (NBA) [W] Seattle, WA

Seattle University [W] Seattle, WA

Secwepemc Native Heritage Park [W] Kamloops, BC

Sehome Hill Arboretum [W] Bellingham, WA

Semiahmoo Park [W] Blaine, WA

Seminoe State Park [W] Rawlins, WY

Senior Pro Rodeo [S] Lusk, WY

Septemberfest [S] Torrington, WY

Sequim Bay State Park [W] Sequim, WA

Seven Oaks House Museum [W] Winnipeg, MB

Seward Park [W] Seattle, WA

Seymour Ski Country [W] Vancouver, BC

Shafer Museum [W] Winthrop, WA

Sheep Rock Unit [W] John Day, OR

Sheridan County Rodeo [S] Sheridan, WY

Sheridan-Wyo PRCA Rodeo [S] Sheridan, WY

Shilshole Bay Marina [W] Seattle, WA

Shipwreck Day [S] Anacortes, WA

The Shootout [S] Jackson, WY

Shore Acres [W] Coos Bay, OR

Shoshone-Bannock Indian Festival [S] Blackfoot, ID

Shoshone-Bannock Indian Festival [S] Pocatello, ID

Shoshone Falls [W] Twin Falls, ID

Shoshone Falls Park [W] Twin Falls, ID

Shoshone Indian Ice Caves [W] Shoshone, ID

Shoshone National Forest [W] Cody, WY

Shoshone river trips [W] Cody, WY

Showdown Ski Area [W] White Sulphur Springs, MT

Sierra Silver Mine Tour [W] Wallace, ID

Sightseeing tours [W] Banff, AB

Sightseeing tours [W] Jasper National Park, AB

Sightseeing tours [W] Seattle, WA

Sightseeing tours [W] Victoria, BC

Sightseeing tours [W] West Yellowstone, MT

Sightseeing tours [W] Winnipeg, MB

Sightseeing trips [W] Vancouver, BC

Silver Falls State Park [W] Silverton, OR

Silver Mountain Ski Area [W] Kellogg, ID

Silver Spur PRCA Rodeo [S] Toppenish, WA

Silverwood Theme Park [W] Coeur d'Alene, ID

Simon Fraser University [W] Vancouver, BC

Sinks Canyon State Park [W] Lander, WY

Sir Alexander Galt Museum [W] Lethbridge, AB

Siskiyou National Forest [W] Grants Pass, OR

Siuslaw National Forest [W] Corvallis, OR

Siuslaw Pioneer Museum [W] Florence, OR

"62" Day Celebration [S] John Day, OR

Skagit County Fair [S] Mount Vernon, WA

Skagit County Historical Museum [W] La Conner, WA

Skagit Valley Tulip Festival [S] Anacortes, WA

Ski areas [W] Missoula, MT

Ski areas [W] Vancouver, BC

Ski areas [W] Whistler, BC

Ski Bluewood [W] Dayton (Columbia County), WA

Skiing [W] Jackson, WY

Skiing [W] Mount Rainier National Park, WA

Skiing [W] North Bend, WA

Skiing. Canyon Ski Area [W] Red Deer, AB

Skiing. Hurricane Ridge Winter Use Area [W] Olympic National Park, WA

Skiing. Lost Trail Powder Mountain [W] Hamilton, MT

Skiing. Marmot Basin [W] Jasper National Park, AB

Skiing. Mission Ridge Ski Area [W] Wenatchee, WA

Skiing. Mount Ashland Ski Area [W] Ashland, OR

Skiing. Mount Baker Ski Area [W] Bellingham, WA

Skiing. Mount Spokane [W] Spokane, WA

Skiing. Schweitzer Mountain Resort [W] Sandpoint, ID

Skiing. Spout Springs. Ski Bluewood [W] Pendleton, OR

Skiing. White Pass Village [W] Yakima, WA

Skiing. Willamette Pass Ski Area [W] Eugene, OR

Ski to Sea Festival [S] Bellingham, WA

Sleeping Giant Ski Area [W] Cody, WY

smART Festival [S] St. Marie's, ID

Smith Cove [W] Seattle, WA

Smith Rock [W] Redmond, OR

Smokejumper Center [W] Missoula, MT

Snake River Heritage Center [W] Weiser, ID

Snake River Stampede [S] Nampa, ID

Snoqualmie Falls [W] North Bend, WA

Snoqualmie Valley Historical Museum [W] North Bend, WA

Snowfest [S] Kelowna, BC

Snowhaven [W] Grangeville, ID

Snow King Ski Resort [W] Jackson, WY

Snowy Range Ski Area [W] Laramie, WY

Soldier Mountain Ski Area [W] Mountain Home, ID

Solitude Float Trips [W] Jackson, WY

Sorosis Park [W] The Dalles, OR

South Bannock County Historical Center [W] Lava Hot Springs, ID

South Beach [W] Newport, OR

Southern Oregon History Center [W] Medford, OR

South Hills Ridgeline Trail [W] Eugene, OR

South Pass City [W] Lander, WY

South Slough National Estuarine Research Reserve [W] Coos Bay, OR

Southwest Washington Fair [S] Centralia, WA

Space Needle [W] Seattle, WA

Spencer Butte Park [W] Eugene, OR

Sperry and Grinnell Glaciers [W] Glacier National Park, MT

Spokane Civic Theatre [S] Spokane, WA

Spokane Falls [W] Spokane, WA

Spokane Interstate Fair [S] Spokane, WA

Spring Barrel Tasting [S] Yakima, WA

Spring Craft Fair [S] Roseburg, OR

Spring Festival [S] Moses Lake, WA

Spring Festival [S] Priest Lake Area, ID

Spring Flower, Art, & Clam Chowder Festival [S] Gold Beach, OR

Spruce Meadows [W] Calgary, AB

Spruce Meadows [S] Calgary, AB

Squilchuck State Park [W] Wenatchee, WA

Stagecoach Museum [W] Lusk, WY

Stampede and Suicide Race [S] Omak, WA

Stanley Park [W] Vancouver, BC

Star Center Antique Mall [W] Snohomish, WA

State Capital Museum [W] Olympia, WA

State Capitol [W] Boise, ID

State Capitol [W] Cheyenne, WY

State Capitol [W] Helena, MT

State Capitol [W] Salem, OR

State Capitol Campus [W] Olympia, WA

State Championship Old-time Fiddle Contest [S] Riverton, WY

State Fair [S] Great Falls, MT

State historic parks [W] Long Beach, WA

State parks [W] Bremerton, WA

State parks [W] Brookings, OR

State parks [W] Chelan, WA

State parks [W] Coos Bay, OR

State parks [W] Florence, OR

State parks [W] Newport, OR

State parks [W] Ontario, OR

State parks [W] Port Townsend, WA

State parks [W] Portland, OR

State parks [W] Redmond, OR

State parks and recreation areas [W] Bend, OR

Steamboat Rock State Park [W] Coulee Dam, WA

Steens Mountain Rim Run [S] Burns, OR

Sternwheeler Columbia Gorge [W] Portland, OR

Stevens Crawford Heritage House [W] Oregon City, OR

Stevens Pass Ski Area [W] Leavenworth, WA

Stevens Pass Ski Area [W] Snohomish, WA

Stock Car Racing [S] Hermiston, OR

Strawberry Festival [S] Marysville, WA

Succor Creek Canyon [W] Caldwell, ID

Summer [W] Sun Valley Area, ID

Summer Band Concert Series [S] Pocatello, ID

Summer Celebration [S] Fort Benton, MT

Summerfest [S] St. Anthony, ID

Summer Fun Fest & Antique Tractor Pull [S] Wheatland, WY

Summit Central [W] North Bend, WA

Summit climb [W] Mount St. Helens National Volcanic Monument, WA

Summit East [W] North Bend, WA

Summit West [W] North Bend, WA

Sumner Summer Festival [S] Puyallup, WA

Sumpter Valley Railroad [W] Baker City, OR

Sunflower Days [S] Clarkston, WA

Sunrise [W] Mount Rainier National Park, WA

Sunrise Festival of the Arts [S] Sidney, MT

Sunset Bay [W] Coos Bay, OR

Sunshine Mine Disaster Memorial [W] Kellogg, ID

Sun Valley Resort. Year-round activities [W] Sun Valley Area, ID

Super Saturday [S] Olympia, WA

Swan Lake [W] Bigfork, MT

Sweet Home Rodeo, The [S] Sweet Home, OR

Sweet Pea Festival [S] Bozeman, MT

Sweetwater County fair [S] Rock Springs, WY

Sweetwater County Historical Museum [W] Green River, WY

Swimming, hiking, camping, boating, fishing, windsurfing [W] Sedro Woolley, WA

Symphony of Fire [S] Vancouver, BC

Table Rock [W] Boise, ID

Tacoma Art Museum [W] Tacoma, WA

Tacoma Little Theater [S] Tacoma, WA

Tacoma Nature Center [W] Tacoma, WA

Tacoma Symphony Orchestra [S] Tacoma, WA

Targhee National Forest [W] Ashton, ID

Taste of Chelan Street Fair [S] Chelan, WA

Taste of Tacoma [S] Tacoma, WA

Tautphaus Park [W] Idaho Falls, ID

Temple of Justice [W] Olympia, WA

Teton Flood Museum [W] Rexburg, ID

Teton Mountain Bike Tours [W] Jackson, WY

Teton Wagon Train & Horse Adventure [W] Jackson, WY

Theatre West [W] Lincoln City, OR

Thompson-Hickman Memorial Museum [W] Virginia City, MT

Thoroughbred racing [S] Boise, ID

Three Island Crossing State Park [W] Mountain Home, ID

Three Valley Gap [W] Revelstoke, BC

Threshing Bee and Antique Equipment Show [S] Ellensburg, WA

Thunder Basin National Grassland [W] Douglas, WY

Thunderbird Park [W] Victoria, BC

Thundering Seas [W] Depoe Bay, OR

Thurston County Fair [S] Olympia, WA

Tillamook County Fair [S] Tillamook, OR

Tillamook County Pioneer Museum [W] Tillamook, OR

Tillamook Dairy Parade and Rodeo [S] Tillamook, OR

Tillicum Beach Campground [W] Yachats, OR

Tillicum Village [W] Seattle, WA

Tollie Shay Engine and Caboose #7 [W] Union, WA

Top of the World Bar [S] Red Lodge, MT

Totem Pole [W] Everett, WA

Totem Pole [W] Tacoma, WA

Tours. Coal Mines [W] Gillette, WY

Tou Velle State Park [W] Medford, OR

Towe Ford Museum [W] Deer Lodge, MT

Trail End Historic Center [W] Sheridan, WY

Trail of the Cedars [W] Sedro Woolley, WA

Trail Town & the Museum of the Old West [W] Cody, WY

Trenner Memorial Park [W] American Falls, ID

Triangle X Float Trips [W] Jackson, WY

Tri-Cities Water Follies [S] Pasco, WA

Tri-County Fair [S] Deer Lodge, MT

Trips into Hell's Canyon [W] Weiser, ID

Tucker Cellars Winery [W] Sunnyside, WA

Tulalip Reservation [W] Marysville, WA

Tulip Festival [S] Mount Vernon, WA

Tumalo [W] Bend, OR

Tumalo Falls [W] Bend, OR

Tumwater Falls Park [W] Olympia, WA

Tumwater Valley Athletic Club [W] Olympia, WA

Turkey Rama [S] McMinnville, OR

Turnbull National Wildlife Refuge [W] Cheney, WA

Turner Mountain Ski Area [W] Libby, MT

Turns of the Brick [W] La Grande, OR

Twanoh State Park [W] Union, WA

Twenty-Five Mile Creek [W] Chelan, WA

Twin Bridges [W] Rexburg, ID

Twin Falls [W] Twin Falls, ID

Twin Falls County Fair and Magic Valley Stampede [S] Buhl, ID

Twin Falls County Fair and Magic Valley Stampede [S] Twin Falls, ID

Twin Falls Park [W] Twin Falls, ID

Twin Harbors State Park [W] Westport, WA

Two Medicine Valley [W] Glacier National Park, MT

Two Rivers Park [W] Kennewick, WA

Tyee Wine Cellars [W] Corvallis, OR

UBC Botanical Garden [W] Vancouver, BC

Uinta County Fair [S] Evanston, WY

Ukiah-Dale Forest State Park [W] Pendleton, OR

Umatilla Indian Reservation [W] Pendleton, OR

Umatilla Marina Park [W] Umatilla, OR

Umatilla National Forest [W] Clarkston, WA

Umatilla National Forest [W] Pendleton, OR

Umpqua Discovery Center [W] Reedsport, OR

Umpqua Lighthouse State Park [W] Reedsport, OR

Umpqua National Forest [W] Roseburg, OR

Umpqua Valley Roundup [S] Roseburg, OR

Underground Tour [W] Seattle, WA

Undersea Gardens [W] Newport, OR

Union County Fair [S] La Grande, OR

Union Station [W] Tacoma, WA

Unity Lake State Park [W] Baker City, OR

University Gallery [W] Tacoma, WA

University of Alberta [W] Edmonton, AB

University of British Columbia [W] Vancouver, BC

University of Great Falls [W] Great Falls, MT

University of Idaho [W] Moscow, ID

University of Montana [W] Missoula, MT

University of Oregon [W] Eugene, OR

University of Puget Sound [W] Tacoma, WA

University of Washington [W] Seattle, WA

University of Wyoming [W] Laramie, WY

Upper Mesa Falls [W] Ashton, ID

USS Turner Joy [W] Bremerton, WA

Valley Art Center [W] Clarkston, WA

Valley Bronze of Oregon [W] Joseph, OR

Valley County Pioneer Museum [W] Glasgow, MT

Valley of the Rogue State Park [W] Grants Pass, OR

Valley Zoo [W] Edmonton, AB

Vancouver Aquarium [W] Vancouver, BC

Vancouver Art Gallery [W] Vancouver, BC

Vancouver Canucks (NHL) [W] Vancouver, BC

Vancouver Grizzlies (NBA) [W] Vancouver, BC

Vancouver Island Exhibition [S] Nanaimo, BC

Vancouver Museum [W] Vancouver, BC

VanDusen Botanical Garden [W] Vancouver, BC

Vedauwoo [W] Laramie, WY

Veteran's Day Parade [S] Albany, OR

Vintage Celebration [S] Newberg, OR

Virginia City-Madison County Historical Museum [W] Virginia City, MT

Visitor Center [W] Anaconda, MT

Visitor Center [W] Missoula, MT

Visitor Center [W] Newberg, OR

Visitor Center [W] Olympic National Park, WA

Visitor centers [W] Mount Rainier National Park, WA

Visitor information stations [W] Mount St. Helens National Volcanic Monument, WA

Volcano Information Center [W] Kelso, WA

Volcano viewpoints [W] Mount St. Helens National Volcanic Monument, WA

Volunteer Park [W] Seattle, WA

Wadopana Powwow [S] Wolf Point, MT

Wagon Days [S] Sun Valley Area, ID

Wagons West [W] Jackson, WY

Wahkpa Chu'gn [W] Havre, MT

Walking tour of historical houses [W] Snohomish, WA

Wallace District Mining Museum [W] Wallace, ID

Wallowa Lake State Park [W] Joseph, OR

Wallowa Lake Tramway [W] Joseph, OR

Wallowa-Whitman National Forest [W] Baker City, OR

Wanapum Dam Heritage Center [W] Ellensburg, WA

War Bonnet Roundup [S] Idaho Falls, ID

Warhawk Air Museum [W] Caldwell, ID

Warren AFB [W] Cheyenne, WY

Warren G. Magnuson Park [W] Seattle, WA

Wasco County Historical Museum [W] The Dalles, OR

Washington Hills Cellar [W] Sunnyside, WA

Washington Park [W] Anacortes, WA

Washington Park [W] Portland, OR

Washington Park Arboretum [W] Seattle, WA

Washington State Apple Blossom Festival [S] Wenatchee, WA

Washington State History Museum [W] Tacoma, WA

Washington State University [W] Pullman, WA

Waskasoo Park [W] Red Deer, AB

Waterfront Drive [W] Seattle, WA

Waterfront Festival [S] Anacortes, WA

Water sports [W] Pinedale, WY

Water Tower in Johns Landing [W] Portland, OR

Wax Works [W] Newport, OR

Wayfarers Unit [W] Bigfork, MT

Wayne Estes Memorial Tournament [S] Anaconda, MT

Wenatchee National Forest [W] Wenatchee, WA

Wenberg State Park [W] Marysville, WA

West Coast Game Park [W] Bandon, OR

West Edmonton Mall [W] Edmonton, AB

Western Art Show [S] Toppenish, WA

Western Days [S] Twin Falls, ID

Westerner Days [S] Red Deer, AB

Western Heritage Center [W] Billings, MT

Western History Center [W] Torrington, WY

Western Idaho Fair [S] Boise, ID

Western Montana Fair & Rodeo [S] Missoula, MT

Western Montana Quarter Horse Show [S] Missoula, MT
Western Rendezvous of Art [S] Helena, MT
Western Washington Fair [S] Puyallup, WA
Western Washington University [W] Bellingham, WA
Westport Aquarium [W] Westport, WA
West Salem Waterfront Parade [S] Salem, OR
Westward Ho! Sternwheeler [W] Florence, OR
Whale Museum, The [W] San Juan Islands, WA
Whale of an Art and Wine Festival [S] Gold Beach, OR
Whale watching tours [W] Vancouver, BC
Whatcom Falls Park [W] Bellingham, WA
Whatcom Museum of History and Art [W] Bellingham, WA
Wheat Land Communities Fair [S] Ritzville, WA
Whidbey Island Jazz Festival [S] Oak Harbor, WA
Whidbey Island Naval Air Station [W] Oak Harbor, WA
Whistler [W] Whistler, BC
White Bird Hill [W] Grangeville, ID
Whitefish Lake [W] Whitefish, MT
Whitefish State Park [W] Whitefish, MT
White Pass Village [W] Mount Rainier National Park, WA
Whitewater rafting [W] Eugene, OR
Whitewater Rafting. Sun Country Tours [W] Bend, OR
Whitman Mission National Historic Site [W] Walla Walla, WA
Whitney Gallery of Western Art [W] Cody, WY
Whoop-Up Days [S] Lethbridge, AB
Wild Blackberry Festival [S] Cave Junction, OR
Wild Horse Stampede [S] Wolf Point, MT
Wildlife Safari [W] Roseburg, OR
Wildlife Safari Wildlights [S] Roseburg, OR
Wild River Adventures [W] Glacier National Park, MT

Wild Waves Water Park [W] Tacoma, WA
Wild West Day [S] Bigfork, MT
Wild West Winter Carnival [S] Riverton, WY
Willamette Falls Locks [W] Oregon City, OR
Willamette National Forest [W] Eugene, OR
Willamette Science and Technology Center [W] Eugene, OR
Willamette Stone [W] Portland, OR
Willamette University [W] Salem, OR
William M. Tugman State Park [W] Reedsport, OR
Wind River Canyon [W] Thermopolis, WY
Wind River Historical Center [W] Dubois, WY
Wine & Food Classic [S] McMinnville, OR
Wine & Food Festival [S] Bandon, OR
Winema National Forest [W] Klamath Falls, OR
Wineries [W] Roseburg, OR
Winery tours [W] Hood River, OR
Wing Luke Museum [W] Seattle, WA
Winnipeg Art Gallery [W] Winnipeg, MB
Winnipeg Folk Festival [S] Winnipeg, MB
Winnipeg Symphony Orchestra [S] Winnipeg, MB
Winter [W] Sun Valley Area, ID
Winter Carnival [S] McCall, ID
Winter Carnival [S] Red Lodge, MT
Winter Carnival [S] Sandpoint, ID
Winter Carnival [S] Whitefish, MT
Winter recreation [W] Pinedale, WY
Wolf Haven America [W] Olympia, WA
Wonderful Water World [W] Penticton, BC
Wooden Boat Festival [S] Port Townsend, WA
Woodfest [S] Sedro Woolley, WA
Woodland Park [W] Kalispell, MT
Woodland Park Zoological Gardens [W] Seattle, WA
World Center for Birds of Prey [W] Boise, ID
World Forestry Center [W] Portland, OR

World Museum of Mining and 1899 Mining Camp [W] Butte, MT

World Snowmobile Expo [S] West Yellowstone, MT

Wright Park [W] Tacoma, WA

Wyoming Dinosaur Center [W] Thermopolis, WY

Wyoming Frontier Prison [W] Rawlins, WY

Wyoming Pioneer Memorial Museum [W] Douglas, WY

Wyoming River Trips [W] Cody, WY

Wyoming State Fair and Rodeo [S] Douglas, WY

Wyoming Territorial Prison and Old West Park [W] Laramie, WY

Wyoming Vietnam Veteran's Memorial [W] Cody, WY

Wyvern Cellars [W] Spokane, WA

Xanterra Parks & Resorts [W] West Yellowstone, MT

Yachats State Recreation Area [W] Yachats, OR

Yahiro Gardens [W] Olympia, WA

Yakama Nation Cultural Center [W] Toppenish, WA

Yakima Interurban Trolley Lines [W] Yakima, WA

Yakima Meadows Racetrack [S] Yakima, WA

Yakima Sportsman State Park [W] Yakima, WA

Yakima Valley Museum [W] Yakima, WA

Yamhill County Fair & Rodeo [S] McMinnville, OR

Yaquina Bay [W] Newport, OR

Yaquina Head [W] Newport, OR

Yellow Bay Unit [W] Bigfork, MT

Yellowstone Art Museum [W] Billings, MT

Yellowstone Bear World [W] Rexburg, ID

Yellowstone IMAX Theatre [W] West Yellowstone, MT

Yellowstone Jazz Festival [S] Cody, WY

Yellowstone National Park [W] Cody, WY

Yellowstone Rendezvous Marathon Ski Race [S] West Yellowstone, MT

Yesterday's Playthings [W] Deer Lodge, MT

Youth Horse Show [S] Kalispell, MT

Zoo Boise [W] Boise, ID

ZooMontana [W] Billings, MT

LODGING LIST

Establishment names are listed in alphabetical order followed by a symbol identifying their classification and then city and state. The symbols for classification are: [AS] for All Suites, [BB] for B&Bs/Small Inns, [CAS] for Casinos, [CC] for Cottage Colonies, [CON] for Villas/Condos, [CONF] for Conference Centers, [EX] for Extended Stays, [HOT] for Hotels, [MOT] for Motels/Motor Lodges, [RAN] for Guest Ranches, and [RST] for Resorts

ABERDEEN MANSION BED AND BREAKFAST [BB] *Aberdeen, WA*

ABIGAIL'S HOTEL [BB] *Victoria, BC*

ABSAROKA LODGE [MOT] *Gardiner, MT*

ABSAROKA MOUNTAIN LODGE [MOT] *Cody, WY*

ABSAROKA RANCH [RAN] *Dubois, WY*

ACCENT INN [MOT] *Victoria, BC*

ACCENT INNS [MOT] *Kelowna, BC*

ACCENT INNS [MOT] *Vancouver, BC*

A CREEKSIDE INN THE MARQUEE HOUSE [BB] *Salem, OR*

ADOBE RESORT MOTEL [MOT] *Yachats, OR*

A DRUMMOND'S RANCH BED & BREAKFAST [BB] *Cheyenne, WY*

AERIE RESORT, THE [RST] *Victoria, BC*

AIRPORT INN [MOT] *Sun Valley Area, ID*

AKAI MOTEL [MOT] *Banff, AB*

ALDERWOOD INN HOTEL [MOT] *Portland, OR*

ALEXANDERS COUNTRY INN [BB] *Mount Rainier National Park, WA*

ALEXIS [HOT] *Seattle, WA*

ALL SEASONS RIVER INN [BB] *Leavenworth, WA*

ALPENHOF LODGE [MOT] *Jackson, WY*

ALPINE VILLAGE [MOT] *Jasper National Park, AB*

AMERICAN INN [MOT] *Hardin, MT*

AMERICAN TRAVEL INN [MOT] *Pullman, WA*

AMERITEL INN [MOT] *Idaho Falls, ID*

AMERITEL INN [MOT] *Pocatello, ID*

AMERITEL INN-TWIN FALLS [MOT] *Twin Falls, ID*

AMETHYST LODGE [MOT] *Jasper National Park, AB*

ANACORTES INN [MOT] *Anacortes, WA*

ANCHOR BAY INN [MOT] *Reedsport, OR*

ANDERSEN HOUSE [BB] *Victoria, BC*

ANGELICA'S BED & BREAKFAST [BB] *Spokane, WA*

ANGEL POINT GUEST SUITES [BB] *Kalispell, MT*

ANN STARRETT MANSION VICTORIAN BED & BREAKFAST [BB] *Port Townsend, WA*

ANTLER INN [MOT] *Jackson, WY*

APPLETON INN BED & BREAKFAST [BB] *Helena, MT*

ARGYLE HOUSE BED & BREAKFAST [BB] *San Juan Islands, WA*

ASPEN VILLAGE INN [MOT] *Waterton Lakes National Park, AB*

ASTORIA DUNES MOTEL [MOT] *Astoria, OR*

AULD HOLLAND INN [MOT] *Oak Harbor, WA*

AVERILL'S FLATHEAD LAKE LODGE [RAN] *Bigfork, MT*

BAD ROCK COUNTRY BED & BREAKFAST [BB] *Columbia Falls, MT*

BAKER CREEK CHALETS [RST] *Lake Louise, AB*

BALI HAI MOTEL [MOT] *Richland, WA*

BANFF AVE INN [BB] *Banff, AB*

BANFF CARIBOU LODGE [HOT] *Banff, AB*

BANFF INTERNATIONAL HOTEL [HOT] *Banff, AB*

BANFF PARK LODGE [MOT] *Banff, AB*

BANFF PTARMIGAN INN [HOT] *Banff, AB*

BANFF ROCKY MOUNTAIN RESORT [RST] *Banff, AB*

BANFF VOYAGER INN [MOT] *Banff, AB*

BARRISTER BED & BREAKFAST [BB] *Helena, MT*

BAY BRIDGE MOTEL [MOT] *North Bend, OR*

BAYSHORE MOTOR INN [MOT] *Astoria, OR*

BEACONSFIELD INN [BB] *Victoria, BC*

BEAR PAW COURT [MOT] *Chinook, MT*

BEAUTIFUL BED AND BREAKFAST [BB] *Vancouver, BC*

BEDFORD REGENCY, THE [HOT] *Victoria, BC*

BEL-AIR MOTEL [MOT] *Penticton, BC*

BELLEVUE CLUB HOTEL [HOT] *Bellevue, WA*

BENSON HOTEL [HOT] *Portland, OR*

BEST INN [MOT] *Missoula, MT*

BEST INN AND CONFERENCE CENTER [MOT] *Missoula, MT*

BEST INN & SUITES [MOT] *Coeur d'Alene, ID*

BEST INN AND SUITES [MOT] *Eugene, OR*

BEST INN & SUITES [MOT] *Medford, OR*

BEST INN & SUITES [MOT] *Roseburg, OR*

BEST INN & SUITES [MOT] *Tacoma, WA*

BEST INN AND SUITES [MOT] *Vancouver, WA*

BEST INN & SUITES CASCADE PARK [MOT] *Vancouver, WA*

BEST REST INN [MOT] *Boise, ID*

BEST VALUE EL RANCHO MOTEL [MOT] *Moses Lake, WA*

BEST VALUE INN COVERED WAGON MOTEL [MOT] *Lusk, WY*

BEST WESTERN [MOT] *Ontario, OR*

BEST WESTERN [MOT] *Reedsport, OR*

BEST WESTERN ABERCORN INN [MOT] *Vancouver, BC*

BEST WESTERN AIRPORT EXECUTEL [MOT] *Seattle-Tacoma Intl Airport Area, WA*

BEST WESTERN AIRPORT MOTOR INN [MOT] *Boise, ID*

BEST WESTERN BARD'S INN [MOT] *Ashland, OR*

BEST WESTERN BELLEVUE INN [MOT] *Bellevue, WA*

BEST WESTERN BILLINGS [MOT] *Billings, MT*

BEST WESTERN BREMERTON INN [MOT] *Bremerton, WA*

BEST WESTERN BUCK'S T-4 LODGE [MOT] *Big Sky (Gallatin County), MT*

BEST WESTERN BURLEY INN & CONVENTION CENTER [MOT] *Burley, ID*

BEST WESTERN BY MAMMOTH HOT SPRINGS [MOT] *Gardiner, MT*

BEST WESTERN CANYON SPRINGS PARK HOTEL [MOT] *Twin Falls, ID*

BEST WESTERN CARLTON PLAZA [MOT] *Victoria, BC*

BEST WESTERN CASCADIA INN [MOT] *Everett, WA*

BEST WESTERN CEDAR PARK INN [MOT] *Edmonton, AB*

BEST WESTERN CHATEAU GRANVILLE [MOT] *Vancouver, BC*

BEST WESTERN CITY CENTRE INN [MOT] *Edmonton, AB*

BEST WESTERN CLOVER CREEK INN [MOT] *Montpelier, ID*

BEST WESTERN COLLEGE WAY INN [MOT] *Mount Vernon, WA*

BEST WESTERN COTTON TREE INN [MOT] *Idaho Falls, ID*

BEST WESTERN COTTON TREE INN [MOT] *Mount Vernon, WA*

BEST WESTERN COTTON TREE INN [MOT] *Pocatello, ID*

BEST WESTERN COTTON TREE INN [MOT] *Rexburg, ID*

BEST WESTERN DOUGLAS INN [MOT] *Douglas, WY*

BEST WESTERN DOUGLAS INN [MOT] *Roseburg, OR*

BEST WESTERN DUNMAR INN [MOT] *Evanston, WY*

BEST WESTERN ENTRADA LODGE [MOT] *Bend, OR*

BEST WESTERN EXECUTIVE INN [MOT] *Seattle, WA*

BEST WESTERN EXECUTIVE INN [MOT] *Seattle-Tacoma Intl Airport Area, WA*

BEST WESTERN EXHIBITION PARK [MOT] *Vancouver, BC*

BEST WESTERN FLYING SADDLE LODGE [MOT] *Alpine, WY*

BEST WESTERN FOOTHILLS MOTOR INN [MOT] *Mountain Home, ID*

BEST WESTERN GARDEN VILLA MOTEL [MOT] *Roseburg, OR*

BEST WESTERN GRAND MANOR INN [MOT] *Corvallis, OR*

BEST WESTERN GRAND MANOR [MOT] *Eugene, OR*

BEST WESTERN GRANT CREEK INN [MOT] *Missoula, MT*

BEST WESTERN GRANTREE INN [MOT] *Bozeman, MT*

BEST WESTERN GRANTS PASS INN [MOT] *Grants Pass, OR*

BEST WESTERN GREEN GABLES INN [MOT] *Banff, AB*

BEST WESTERN HALLMARK INN AND CONFERENCE CENTER [MOT] *Moses Lake, WA*

BEST WESTERN HAMILTON INN [MOT] *Hamilton, MT*

BEST WESTERN HARBOR PLAZA [MOT] *Oak Harbor, WA*

BEST WESTERN HEIDELBERG INN [MOT] *Lethbridge, AB*

BEST WESTERN HERITAGE INN [MOT] *Great Falls, MT*

BEST WESTERN HITCHING POST INN RESORT & CONFERENCE CENTER [MOT] *Cheyenne, WY*

BEST WESTERN HOLIDAY MOTEL [MOT] *Coos Bay, OR*

BEST WESTERN HOOD RIVER INN [MOT] *Hood River, OR*

BEST WESTERN HORIZON INN [MOT] *Medford, OR*

BEST WESTERN HOSPITALITY INN [MOT] *Calgary, AB*

BEST WESTERN HOTEL [MOT] *Helena, MT*

BEST WESTERN ICICLE INN [MOT] *Leavenworth, WA*

BEST WESTERN INN [MOT] *Bellingham, WA*

BEST WESTERN INN [MOT] *Jackson, WY*

BEST WESTERN INN [MOT] *Jackson, WY*

BEST WESTERN INN [MOT] *Kelowna, BC*

BEST WESTERN INN [MOT] *Lakeview, OR*

BEST WESTERN INN [MOT] *Medicine Hat, AB*

BEST WESTERN INN [MOT] *Pinedale, WY*

BEST WESTERN INN AT LANDER [MOT] *Lander, WY*

BEST WESTERN INN AT PENTICTON [MOT] *Penticton, BC*

BEST WESTERN INN AT THE MEADOWS [MOT] *Portland, OR*

BEST WESTERN INN AT THE ROGUE [MOT] *Grants Pass, OR*

BEST WESTERN INNER HARBOR [MOT] *Victoria, BC*

BEST WESTERN KENTWOOD LODGE [MOT] *Sun Valley Area, ID*

BEST WESTERN KINGS INN [MOT] *Vancouver, BC*

BEST WESTERN KLAMATH INN [MOT] *Klamath Falls, OR*

BEST WESTERN KWATAQNUK RESORT [RST] *Polson, MT*

BEST WESTERN LAKEWAY INN [MOT] *Bellingham, WA*

BEST WESTERN LINCOLN INN [MOT] *Othello, WA*

BEST WESTERN LINCOLN SANDS [MOT] *Lincoln City, OR*

BEST WESTERN LISTEL WHISTLER HOTEL [MOT] *Whistler, BC*

BEST WESTERN LOYAL INN [MOT] *Seattle, WA*

BEST WESTERN LUPINE INN [MOT] *Red Lodge, MT*

BEST WESTERN MCCALL [MOT] *McCall, ID*

BEST WESTERN NEW KINGS INN [MOT] *Salem, OR*

BEST WESTERN NEW OREGON MOTEL [MOT] *Eugene, OR*

BEST WESTERN OCEAN VIEW RESORT [MOT] *Seaside, OR*

BEST WESTERN OLYMPIC INN [MOT] *Klamath Falls, OR*

BEST WESTERN OUTLAW HOTEL [MOT] *Kalispell, MT*

BEST WESTERN PARADISE INN [MOT] *Dillon, MT*

BEST WESTERN PARK CENTER [MOT] *Enumclaw, WA*

BEST WESTERN PIER POINT INN [MOT] *Florence, OR*

BEST WESTERN PIONEER [MOT] *Lusk, WY*

BEST WESTERN PIONEER SQUARE HOTEL [MOT] *Seattle, WA*

BEST WESTERN PONDEROSA INN [MOT] *Billings, MT*

BEST WESTERN PONY SOLDIER INN [MOT] *Albany, OR*

BEST WESTERN PONY SOLDIER INN [MOT] *Medford, OR*

BEST WESTERN PONY SOLDIER INN AIRPORT [MOT] *Portland, OR*

BEST WESTERN PORT O' CALL HOTEL [MOT] *Calgary, AB*

BEST WESTERN RAMA INN [MOT] *Redmond, OR*

BEST WESTERN RIVERTREE INN [MOT] *Clarkston, WA*

BEST WESTERN ROCKY MOUNTAIN LODGE [MOT] *Whitefish, MT*

BEST WESTERN SAFARI INN [MOT] *Boise, ID*

BEST WESTERN SALBASGEON INN AND SUITES [MOT] *Reedsport, OR*

BEST WESTERN SANDS [MOT] *Vancouver, BC*

BEST WESTERN SAWTOOTH INN [MOT] *Jerome, ID*

BEST WESTERN SHERIDAN CENTER [MOT] *Sheridan, WY*

BEST WESTERN SIDING 29 LODGE [MOT] *Banff, AB*

BEST WESTERN SUNRIDGE INN [MOT] *Baker City, OR*

BEST WESTERN TACOMA INN [MOT] *Tacoma, WA*

BEST WESTERN TETON WEST [MOT] *Driggs, ID*

BEST WESTERN TORCHLITE INN [MOT] *Wheatland, WY*

BEST WESTERN TOWER INN & CONFERENCE CENTER [MOT] *Richland, WA*

BEST WESTERN TOWER WEST LODGE [MOT] *Gillette, WY*

BEST WESTERN TUMWATER INN [MOT] *Olympia, WA*

BEST WESTERN TYROLEAN LODGE [MOT] *Sun Valley Area, ID*

BEST WESTERN UMATILLA HOUSE [MOT] *The Dalles, OR*

BEST WESTERN UNIVERSITY INN [MOT] *Moscow, ID*

BEST WESTERN UNIVERSITY TOWER HOTEL [HOT] *Seattle, WA*

BEST WESTERN VERNON LODGE [MOT] *Kelowna, BC*

BEST WESTERN VICTORIA INN [MOT] *Winnipeg, MB*

BEST WESTERN VILLAGE GREEN [MOT] *Cottage Grove, OR*

BEST WESTERN VISTA INN [MOT] *Boise, ID*

BEST WESTERN WALLACE INN [MOT] *Wallace, ID*

BEST WESTERN WAR BONNET INN [MOT] *Miles City, MT*

BEST WESTERN WAYSIDE INN [MOT] *Revelstoke, BC*

BEST WESTERN WINDSOR INN [MOT] *Ashland, OR*

BEST WESTERN YELLOWSTONE INN & CONFERENCE CENTER [MOT] *Livingston, MT*

BIG SKY RESORT [RST] *Big Sky (Gallatin County), MT*

BILL CODY RANCH [MOT] *Cody, WY*

BILLINGS INN, THE [MOT] *Billings, MT*

BILTMORE HOTEL [MOT] *Vancouver, BC*

BISHOP VICTORIAN GUEST SUITES [AS] *Port Townsend, WA*

BLACK BUTTE RANCH [RST] *Bend, OR*

BLACKFOOT INN [MOT] *Calgary, AB*

BLACK KNIGHT INN [HOT] *Red Deer, AB*

BLACKWATER CREEK RANCH [RAN] *Cody, WY*

BLUE HORIZON [HOT] *Vancouver, BC*

BOISE CENTER GUEST LODGE [MOT] *Boise, ID*

BOREAS BED & BREAKFAST [BB] *Long Beach, WA*

BOZEMAN'S WESTERN HERITAGE INN [MOT] *Bozeman, MT*

BREAKERS MOTEL & CONDO, THE [MOT] *Long Beach, WA*
BREWSTER'S MOUNTAIN LODGE [MOT] *Banff, AB*
BROOKS LAKE LODGE [RAN] *Dubois, WY*
BUCKRAIL LODGE [MOT] *Jackson, WY*
BUDGET HOST PRONGHORN [MOT] *Lander, WY*
BUDGET INN [MOT] *Great Falls, MT*
BUDGET INN [MOT] *Spokane, WA*
BUFFALO BILL VILLAGE (CABINS) [MOT] *Cody, WY*
BUFFALO MOUNTAIN LODGE [MOT] *Banff, AB*
CABANA MOTEL [MOT] *Othello, WA*
CAMELOT MOTEL [MOT] *Laramie, WY*
CAMLIN HOTEL [HOT] *Seattle, WA*
CAMPBELL - A CITY INN, THE [BB] *Eugene, OR*
CAMPBELL'S RESORT CONFERENCE CENTER [MOT] *Chelan, WA*
CAMPUS INN [MOT] *Eugene, OR*
CANTERBURY INN [MOT] *Ocean Shores, WA*
CANYON LODGE CABINS [MOT] *Yellowstone National Park, WY*
CANYON MOTEL [MOT] *Buffalo, WY*
CANYON MOTOR INN [MOT] *Revelstoke, BC*
CAPRI HOTEL - CONVENTION & TRADE CENTRE [HOT] *Red Deer, AB*
CAPTAIN WHIDBEY INN [BB] *Coupeville, WA*
CARRIAGE HOUSE INN [HOT] *Calgary, AB*
CARVEL RESORT MOTEL [MOT] *Chelan, WA*
CASCADE LODGE AT CANYON VILLAGE [MOT] *Yellowstone National Park, WY*
CASTLE, THE [BB] *Brandon, MB*
CASTLE MOUNTAIN CHALETS [MOT] *Banff, AB*
CEDAR LODGE MOTOR INN [MOT] *Medford, OR*
CEDARS INN [MOT] *Omak, WA*
CEDARWOOD INN [MOT] *Ashland, OR*

CENTENNIAL INN, THE [BB] *Dillon, MT*
CHAMBERED NAUTILUS BED & BREAKFAST [BB] *Seattle, WA*
CHANDLERS BED BREAD TRAIL INN [BB] *Joseph, OR*
CHANNEL HOUSE [BB] *Depoe Bay, OR*
CHANNEL HOUSE BED & BREAKFAST [BB] *Anacortes, WA*
CHANTICLEER INN [BB] *Ashland, OR*
CHANTICLEER INN [BB] *Port Townsend, WA*
CHARLTON'S CEDAR COURT [MOT] *Banff, AB*
CHARLTON'S CHATEAU JASPER [MOT] *Jasper National Park, AB*
CHARTER HOUSE [HOT] *Winnipeg, MB*
CHATEAU LOUIS HOTEL & CONFERENCE CENTRE [MOT] *Edmonton, AB*
CHATEAU VICTORIA [HOT] *Victoria, BC*
CHAUTAUQUA LODGE [MOT] *Long Beach, WA*
CHELSEA STATION BED & BREAKFAST [BB] *Seattle, WA*
CHESTNUT TREE INN [MOT] *Portland, OR*
CHEYENNE SUPER 8 [MOT] *Cheyenne, WY*
CHICO HOT SPRINGS RESORT [MOT] *Livingston, MT*
CHINABERRY HILL [BB] *Tacoma, WA*
CIMARRON MOTOR INN [MOT] *Klamath Falls, OR*
CLARION HOTEL SEA-TAC [MOT] *Seattle-Tacoma Intl Airport Area, WA*
CLARION INN [MOT] *Gillette, WY*
C'MON INN [MOT] *Billings, MT*
COACHMAN INN [MOT] *Oak Harbor, WA*
COAST BASTION INN [HOT] *Nanaimo, BC*
COAST CANADIAN INN, THE [MOT] *Kamloops, BC*
COAST CAPRI HOTEL [HOT] *Kelowna, BC*
COAST HARBOURSIDE HOTEL & MARINA [HOT] *Victoria, BC*

COAST PLAZA HOTEL & CONFERENCE CENTRE, THE [HOT] *Calgary, AB*
COAST PLAZA SUITE HOTEL [HOT] *Vancouver, BC*
COAST TERRACE INN [HOT] *Edmonton, AB*
COEUR D'ALENE - A RESORT ON THE LAKE, THE [RST] *Coeur d'Alene, ID*
COEUR D'ALENE INN & CONFERENCE CENTER [MOT] *Coeur d'Alene, ID*
COHO INN [MOT] *Lincoln City, OR*
COLONIAL INN [MOT] *Brandon, MB*
COLTER BAY VILLAGE & CABINS [CC] *Grand Teton National Park, WY*
COLUMBIA GORGE HOTEL [HOT] *Hood River, OR*
COLUMBIA RIVER INN [BB] *Astoria, OR*
COLUMBIA RIVER INN [MOT] *Coulee Dam, WA*
COMFORT INN [MOT] *Big Sky (Gallatin County), MT*
COMFORT INN [MOT] *Billings, MT*
COMFORT INN [MOT] *Boise, ID*
COMFORT INN [MOT] *Bozeman, MT*
COMFORT INN [MOT] *Brandon, MB*
COMFORT INN [MOT] *Buffalo, WY*
COMFORT INN [MOT] *Casper, WY*
COMFORT INN [MOT] *Cheyenne, WY*
COMFORT INN [MOT] *Gardiner, MT*
COMFORT INN [MOT] *Grants Pass, OR*
COMFORT INN [MOT] *Great Falls, MT*
COMFORT INN [MOT] *Helena, MT*
COMFORT INN [MOT] *Idaho Falls, ID*
COMFORT INN [MOT] *Kelso, WA*
COMFORT INN [MOT] *Livingston, MT*
COMFORT INN [MOT] *Miles City, MT*
COMFORT INN [MOT] *Pocatello, ID*
COMFORT INN [MOT] *Red Lodge, MT*
COMFORT INN [MOT] *Rexburg, ID*
COMFORT INN [MOT] *Rock Springs, WY*

COMFORT INN [MOT] *The Dalles, OR*
COMFORT INN [MOT] *Thermopolis, WY*
COMFORT INN [MOT] *Vancouver, WA*
COMFORT INN [MOT] *West Yellowstone, MT*
COMFORT INN [MOT] *Winnipeg, MB*
COMFORT INN & SUITE MOTEL VILLAGE [MOT] *Calgary, AB*
COMFORT INN & SUITES SEA-TAC-SEATTLE [MOT] *Seattle-Tacoma Intl Airport Area, WA*
COMFORT INN BUFFALO BILL VILLAGE [MOT] *Cody, WY*
COMFORT INN OF BUTTE [MOT] *Butte, MT*
COMFORT INN OF DILLON [MOT] *Dillon, MT*
COMFORT INN OF HAMILTON [MOT] *Hamilton, MT*
COMFORT INN TWIN FALLS [MOT] *Twin Falls, ID*
COMFORT INN VALLEY [MOT] *Spokane, WA*
COMFORT SUITES [MOT] *Vancouver, WA*
COMMENCEMENT BAY BED & BREAKFAST [BB] *Tacoma, WA*
CONNIE'S HAWTHORN INN [MOT] *Sandpoint, ID*
COTTONWOOD INN [MOT] *Glasgow, MT*
COULEE HOUSE MOTEL [MOT] *Coulee Dam, WA*
COUNTRY INN AND SUITES [MOT] *Winnipeg, MB*
COUNTRY WILLOWS BED & BREAKFAST INN [BB] *Ashland, OR*
COURTYARD BY MARRIOTT [MOT] *Beaverton, OR*
COURTYARD BY MARRIOTT [MOT] *Portland, OR*
COURTYARD BY MARRIOTT [MOT] *Spokane, WA*
COWBOY VILLAGE RESORT [MOT] *Grand Teton National Park, WY*
COWLITZ RIVER LODGE [MOT] *Packwood, WA*
COYOTE ROADHOUSE INN [BB] *Bigfork, MT*
COZY COVE BEACH FRONT RESORT [MOT] *Lincoln City, OR*

CRANDALL MOUNTAIN LODGE [MOT] *Waterton Lakes National Park, AB*

CRATER LAKE LODGE [MOT] *Crater Lake National Park, OR*

CREST MOTEL [MOT] *Astoria, OR*

CREST TRAIL LODGE [MOT] *Packwood, WA*

CROWNE PLAZA [HOT] *Portland, OR*

CROWNE PLAZA [HOT] *Seattle, WA*

CROWNE PLAZA CHATEAU LACOMBE [HOT] *Edmonton, AB*

CROWNE PLAZA HOTEL GEORGIA VANCOUVER [HOT] *Vancouver, BC*

CRYSTAL LODGE [MOT] *Whistler, BC*

CUSTER HOUSE BED & BREAKFAST [BB] *Seaside, OR*

DAVY JACKSON [BB] *Jackson, WY*

DAYS INN [MOT] *Bellingham, WA*

DAYS INN [MOT] *Billings, MT*

DAYS INN [MOT] *Bozeman, MT*

DAYS INN [MOT] *Butte, MT*

DAYS INN [MOT] *Cheyenne, WY*

DAYS INN [MOT] *Cody, WY*

DAYS INN [MOT] *Coeur d'Alene, ID*

DAYS INN [MOT] *Glendive, MT*

DAYS INN [MOT] *Jackson, WY*

DAYS INN [MOT] *Jerome, ID*

DAYS INN [MOT] *Kalispell, MT*

DAYS INN [MOT] *Kamloops, BC*

DAYS INN [MOT] *Portland, OR*

DAYS INN [MOT] *Portland, OR*

DAYS INN [MOT] *Rawlins, WY*

DAYS INN [MOT] *Richland, WA*

DAYS INN [MOT] *Sheridan, WY*

DAYS INN [MOT] *Tacoma, WA*

DAYS INN [MOT] *West Yellowstone, MT*

DAYS INN AIRPORT [MOT] *Spokane, WA*

DAYS INN - CALGARY WEST [MOT] *Calgary, AB*

DAYS INN HARBOURVIEW [MOT] *Nanaimo, BC*

DAYS INN NISKU INN AND CONFERENCE CENTER [MOT] *Edmonton, AB*

DAYS INN OF GREAT FALLS [MOT] *Great Falls, MT*

DAYS INN ON THE HARBOUR [MOT] *Victoria, BC*

DAYS INN PONDEROSA [MOT] *Burns, OR*

DAYS INN PORTLAND SOUTH [MOT] *Portland, OR*

DEER CROSSING BED & BREAKFAST [BB] *Hamilton, MT*

DEER LODGE [MOT] *Lake Louise, AB*

DELTA BOW VALLEY [HOT] *Calgary, AB*

DELTA CALGARY AIRPORT [HOT] *Calgary, AB*

DELTA CENTRE SUITES [HOT] *Edmonton, AB*

DELTA EDMONTON SOUTH [HOT] *Edmonton, AB*

DELTA LODGE AT KANANASKIS [HOT] *Calgary, AB*

DELTA PACIFIC RESORT AND CONFERENCE CENTER [RST] *Vancouver, BC*

DELTA TOWN AND COUNTRY [MOT] *Vancouver, BC*

DELTA VANCOUVER AIRPORT HOTEL AND MARINA [HOT] *Vancouver, BC*

DELTA VANCOUVER SUITES [AS] *Vancouver, BC*

DELTA WHISTLER RESORT [RST] *Whistler, BC*

DELTA WINNIPEG [HOT] *Winnipeg, MB*

DER RITTERHOFF MOTOR INN [MOT] *Leavenworth, WA*

DESERT INN [MOT] *Nampa, ID*

DIAMOND POINT INN [BB] *Sequim, WA*

DOCK OF THE BAY MOTEL [MOT] *Lincoln City, OR*

DOMAINE MADELEINE [BB] *Port Angeles, WA*

DORNAN'S SPUR RANCH CABINS [MOT] *Grand Teton National Park, WY*

DOUBLE DIAMOND X RANCH [RAN] *Cody, WY*

DOUBLETREE [HOT] *Boise, ID*

DOUBLETREE CLUB HOTEL - BOISE [HOT] *Boise, ID*

DOUBLETREE GUEST SUITES [AS] *Seattle-Tacoma Intl Airport Area, WA*

DOUBLETREE HOTEL [HOT] *Bellevue, WA*

DOUBLETREE HOTEL [MOT] *Seattle-Tacoma Intl Airport Area, WA*

DOUBLETREE HOTEL [MOT]
Spokane, WA
DOUBLETREE HOTEL COLUMBIA
RIVER [HOT] *Portland, OR*
DOUBLETREE HOTEL JANTZEN
BEACH [HOT] *Portland, OR*
DOUBLETREE HOTEL
MISSOULA/EDGEWATER
[HOT] *Missoula, MT*
DOUBLETREE HOTEL RIVERSIDE
[HOT] *Boise, ID*
DOUBLETREE HOTEL SPOKANE
CITY CENTER [HOT]
Spokane, WA
DOUBLETREE HOTEL YAKIMA
[MOT] *Yakima, WA*
DOUBLETREE PORTLAND -
LLOYD CENTER [HOT]
Portland, OR
DOUGLAS FIR RESORT [RST] *Banff,
AB*
DREAMERS LODGE MOTEL [MOT]
John Day, OR
D SANDS MOTEL [MOT] *Lincoln
City, OR*
DYNASTY INN [MOT] *Banff, AB*
EAGLE CREST RESORT [RST]
Redmond, OR
EBB TIDE MOTEL [MOT] *Seaside,
OR*
ECONO LODGE [MOT] *Boise, ID*
ECONO LODGE [MOT] *Laramie,
WY*
ECONO LODGE [MOT] *Pendleton,
OR*
ECONO LODGE [MOT] *Sequim, WA*
ECONOMY INN [MOT] *Hermiston,
OR*
ECONOMY INN [MOT] *Pendleton,
OR*
EDGEWATER, THE [HOT] *Seattle,
WA*
EDGEWATER INN [MOT] *Long
Beach, WA*
EDGEWATER RESORT [MOT]
Sandpoint, ID
1891 FRIDAY'S HISTORICAL INN
[BB] *San Juan Islands, WA*
ELDORADO INN [MOT] *Baker City,
OR*
ELEPHANT HEAD LODGE [MOT]
Cody, WY
ELKHORN RESORT [RST] *Sun Valley
Area, ID*
ELKINS ON PRIEST LAKE [RST]
Priest Lake Area, ID
ELLENSBURG INN [MOT]
Ellensburg, WA

ELLIOTT GRANT HYATT SEATTLE
[HOT] *Seattle, WA*
EL WESTERN RESORT [MOT] *Ennis,
MT*
EMBARCADERO RESORT HOTEL
[MOT] *Newport, OR*
EMBASSY INN [MOT] *Victoria, BC*
EMBASSY SUITES DOWNTOWN
[AS] *Portland, OR*
EMERALD LAKE LODGE [MOT]
Lake Louise, AB
EMILY A. BED & BREAKFAST, THE
[BB] *Missoula, MT*
EMPIRE LANDMARK HOTEL &
CONFERENCE CENTRE
[HOT] *Vancouver, BC*
ENGLISH BAY INN [HOT]
Vancouver, BC
ENGLISH INN, THE [BB] *Port
Townsend, WA*
ENZIAN MOTOR INN [MOT]
Leavenworth, WA
EXECUTIVE AIRPORT PLAZA
HOTEL [MOT] *Vancouver, BC*
EXECUTIVE HOUSE [HOT]
Victoria, BC
EXECUTIVE INN HOTEL AND
CONFERENCE CENTER
[HOT] *Vancouver, BC*
EXECUTIVE INN - KAMLOOPS
[MOT] *Kamloops, BC*
EXECUTIVE PACIFIC PLAZA
HOTEL [HOT] *Seattle, WA*
EXECUTIVE ROYAL INN WEST
EDMONTON [MOT]
Edmonton, AB
FAIRFIELD INN [MOT] *Billings, MT*
FAIRFIELD INN [MOT] *Bozeman,
MT*
FAIRFIELD INN [MOT] *Cheyenne,
WY*
FAIRFIELD INN [MOT] *Great Falls,
MT*
FAIRFIELD INN [MOT] *Helena, MT*
FAIRFIELD INN [MOT] *Portland,
OR*
FAIRFIELD INN [MOT] *West
Yellowstone, MT*
FAIRFIELD INN & SUITES [MOT]
Beaverton, OR
FAIRMONT BANFF SPRINGS, THE
[RST] *Banff, AB*
FAIRMONT CHATEAU LAKE
LOUISE, THE [RST] *Lake
Louise, AB*
FAIRMONT CHATEAU WHISTLER,
THE [RST] *Whistler, BC*

FAIRMONT EMPRESS, THE [HOT]
Victoria, BC
FAIRMONT HOTEL MACDONALD,
THE [HOT] Edmonton, AB
FAIRMONT HOTEL VANCOUVER,
THE [HOT] Vancouver, BC
FAIRMONT HOT SPRINGS RESORT
[RST] Anaconda, MT
FAIRMONT JASPER PARK LODGE,
THE [RST] Jasper National
Park, AB
FAIRMONT PALLISER, THE [HOT]
Calgary, AB
FAIRMONT VANCOUVER
AIRPORT, THE [HOT]
Vancouver, BC
FAIRMONT WATERFRONT, THE
[HOT] Vancouver, BC
FAIRMONT WINNIPEG, THE
[HOT] Winnipeg, MB
FAIRWINDS SCHOONER COVE
RESORT & MARINA [RST]
Nanaimo, BC
FAN MOUNTAIN INN [MOT] Ennis,
MT
FANTASYLAND HOTEL [HOT]
Edmonton, AB
FARVUE MOTEL [MOT] Goldendale,
WA
FERRYMAN'S INN [MOT]
Vancouver, WA
5TH AVENUE SUITES HOTEL
[HOT] Portland, OR
FIRESIDE MOTEL [MOT] Yachats,
OR
FIVE SEASUNS BED & BREAKFAST
[BB] Port Angeles, WA
FLAGG RANCH RESORT [CC]
Grand Teton National Park,
WY
FLAGSHIP INN [MOT] Bremerton,
WA
FLAMINGO MOTEL [MOT] Coeur
d'Alene, ID
FLAT CREEK [MOT] Jackson, WY
FLERY MANOR [BB] Grants Pass,
OR
FLYING ARROW RESORT [MOT]
Joseph, OR
FLYING M RANCH [RAN]
McMinnville, OR
FOREST GROVE INN [MOT] Forest
Grove, OR
FORKS MOTEL [MOT] Forks, WA
FORT THREE FORKS [MOT] Three
Forks, MT

FOTHERINGHAM HOUSE [BB]
Spokane, WA
FOUR POINTS BY SHERATON
PORTLAND DOWNTOWN
[MOT] Portland, OR
FOUR SEASONS HOTEL SEATTLE
[HOT] Seattle, WA
FOUR SEASONS HOTEL
VANCOUVER [HOT]
Vancouver, BC
4 WINDS [MOT] Jackson, WY
FOX HOLLOW BED & BREAKFAST
[BB] Bozeman, MT
FRANKLIN STREET STATION BED
& BREAKFAST INN [BB]
Astoria, OR
FW HASTINGS HOUSE OLD
CONSULATE [BB] Port
Townsend, WA
GALLATIN GATEWAY [BB]
Bozeman, MT
GASLIGHT INN [BB] Seattle, WA
GEARHART BY THE SEA RESORT
[MOT] Seaside, OR
GEORGIAN COURT HOTEL [HOT]
Vancouver, BC
GILBERT INN BED & BREAKFAST
[BB] Seaside, OR
GLENMORE INN & CONVENTION
CENTER [MOT] Calgary, AB
GOLDSMITH'S BED & BREAKFAST
INN [BB] Missoula, MT
GOOD MEDICINE LODGE [BB]
Whitefish, MT
GOVERNOR HOTEL [HOT]
Portland, OR
GRAND TARGHEE [RST] Driggs, ID
GRAND TETON NATIONAL
PARK/JACKSON LAKE [MOT]
Grand Teton National Park,
WY
GRANDVIEW LODGE AND
RESORT [RST] Priest Lake
Area, ID
GRAY WOLF INN & SUITES [MOT]
West Yellowstone, MT
GREEN GABLES INN [BB] Walla
Walla, WA
GREENWOOD INN [MOT]
Beaverton, OR
GREY GULL RESORT, THE [MOT]
Ocean Shores, WA
GREY WHALE INN [BB] Cannon
Beach, OR
GREYWOLF INN [BB] Sequim, WA

GROS VENTRE RIVER RANCH [RAN] *Grand Teton National Park, WY*

GROUSE MOUNTAIN LODGE [RST] *Whitefish, MT*

GROVELAND COTTAGE BED & BREAKFAST [BB] *Sequim, WA*

GUEST HOUSE BED & BREAKFAST COTTAGES [BB] *Coupeville, WA*

HALLMARK RESORT [MOT] *Cannon Beach, OR*

HAMPTON INN [MOT] *Bellingham, WA*

HAMPTON INN [MOT] *Bend, OR*

HAMPTON INN [MOT] *Bozeman, MT*

HAMPTON INN [MOT] *Casper, WY*

HAMPTON INN [MOT] *Idaho Falls, ID*

HAMPTON INN [MOT] *Kalispell, MT*

HAMPTON INN [MOT] *Missoula, MT*

HAMPTON INN [MOT] *Portland, OR*

HAMPTON INN [MOT] *Vancouver, BC*

HAMPTON INN & SUITES - CALGARY AIRPORT [MOT] *Calgary, AB*

HAMPTON INN & SUITES SEATTLE [MOT] *Seattle, WA*

HARBOR VIEW MOTEL [MOT] *Bandon, OR*

HARBOUR INN [MOT] *Coupeville, WA*

HARBOUR TOWERS [HOT] *Victoria, BC*

HARRISON HOUSE BED & BREAKFAST [BB] *Corvallis, OR*

HARRISON HOUSE SUITES [BB] *San Juan Islands, WA*

HASTINGS HOUSE [BB] *Victoria, BC*

HATCHET RESORT [MOT] *Grand Teton National Park, WY*

HATERLEIGH HERITAGE INN [BB] *Victoria, BC*

HAUS ROHRBACH PENSION [BB] *Leavenworth, WA*

HAWTHORN HOTEL & SUITES [HOT] *Calgary, AB*

HAWTHORN INN & SUITES [MOT] *Portland, OR*

HAWTHORN INN AND SUITES [MOT] *Walla Walla, WA*

HEARTHSTONE INN [MOT] *Cannon Beach, OR*

HEATHMAN HOTEL, THE [HOT] *Portland, OR*

HEATHMAN LODGE, THE [RST] *Vancouver, WA*

HERON, THE [BB] *La Conner, WA*

HERON BEACH INN [BB] *Port Ludlow, WA*

HERON HAUS [BB] *Portland, OR*

HI-COUNTRY INN [MOT] *Afton, WY*

HIDDEN RIDGE RESORT [MOT] *Banff, AB*

HIGH COUNTRY INN [MOT] *Banff, AB*

HIGH COUNTRY MOTEL [MOT] *Cooke City, MT*

HILANDER MOTEL & STEAK HOUSE [MOT] *Mountain Home, ID*

HILLCREST MOTEL [MOT] *Moscow, ID*

HILL HOUSE BED & BREAKFAST [BB] *Seattle, WA*

HILLSIDE HOUSE BED & BREAKFAST [BB] *San Juan Islands, WA*

HILLS RESORT [RST] *Priest Lake Area, ID*

HILLTOP INN [MOT] *Billings, MT*

HILTON [HOT] *Eugene, OR*

HILTON [HOT] *Seattle-Tacoma Intl Airport Area, WA*

HILTON HOTEL BELLEVUE [HOT] *Bellevue, WA*

HILTON PORTLAND [HOT] *Portland, OR*

HILTON SEATTLE [HOT] *Seattle, WA*

HILTON VANCOUVER AIRPORT [HOT] *Vancouver, BC*

HILTON VANCOUVER METROTOWN [HOT] *Vancouver, BC*

HITCHING POST LODGE [MOT] *Jackson, WY*

HI-TIDE CONDOMINIUM RESORT [MOT] *Moclips, WA*

HI-TIDE MOTEL [MOT] *Seaside, OR*

HOLIDAY INN [MOT] *Boise, ID*

HOLIDAY INN [MOT] *Bozeman, MT*

HOLIDAY INN [MOT] *Casper, WY*

HOLIDAY INN [HOT] *Great Falls, MT*

HOLIDAY INN [MOT] *Laramie, WY*

HOLIDAY INN [MOT] *Ontario, OR*

HOLIDAY INN [MOT] *Pocatello, ID*

HOLIDAY INN [MOT] *Riverton, WY*

HOLIDAY INN [MOT] *Rock Springs, WY*
HOLIDAY INN [HOT] *Vancouver, BC*
HOLIDAY INN [MOT] *Victoria, BC*
HOLIDAY INN [MOT] *Winnipeg, MB*
HOLIDAY INN AIRPORT [MOT] *Calgary, AB*
HOLIDAY INN AIRPORT WEST [HOT] *Winnipeg, MB*
HOLIDAY INN EXPRESS [MOT] *Bozeman, MT*
HOLIDAY INN EXPRESS [MOT] *Calgary, AB*
HOLIDAY INN EXPRESS [MOT] *Eugene, OR*
HOLIDAY INN EXPRESS [MOT] *Florence, OR*
HOLIDAY INN EXPRESS [MOT] *Helena, MT*
HOLIDAY INN EXPRESS [MOT] *Kelowna, BC*
HOLIDAY INN EXPRESS [MOT] *Klamath Falls, OR*
HOLIDAY INN EXPRESS [MOT] *Miles City, MT*
HOLIDAY INN EXPRESS [MOT] *Missoula, MT*
HOLIDAY INN EXPRESS [MOT] *Red Deer, AB*
HOLIDAY INN EXPRESS [MOT] *Vancouver, WA*
HOLIDAY INN EXPRESS GRANTS PASS [MOT] *Grants Pass, OR*
HOLIDAY INN EXPRESS-PARKSIDE [MOT] *Butte, MT*
HOLIDAY INN GRAND MONTANA [HOT] *Billings, MT*
HOLIDAY INN HOTEL & SUITES DOWNTOWN [HOT] *Vancouver, BC*
HOLIDAY INN - MACLEOD TRAIL SOUTH [MOT] *Calgary, AB*
HOLIDAY INN OF SHERIDAN [MOT] *Sheridan, WY*
HOLIDAY INN PALACE [MOT] *Edmonton, AB*
HOLIDAY INN PARKSIDE [MOT] *Missoula, MT*
HOLIDAY INN RED DEER [HOT] *Red Deer, AB*
HOLIDAY INN SEATAC AIRPORT [MOT] *Seattle-Tacoma Intl Airport Area, WA*
HOLIDAY INN SEATTLE, ISSAQUAH [MOT] *Issaquah, WA*
HOLIDAY INN SUNSPREE RESORT [MOT] *West Yellowstone, MT*
HOLIDAY INN VANCOUVER AIRPORT [HOT] *Vancouver, BC*
HOLIDAY LODGE [MOT] *Wenatchee, WA*
HOLIDAY MOTOR INN [MOT] *Ontario, OR*
HOLLAND HOUSE [BB] *Victoria, BC*
HOLLY HILL HOUSE B&B [BB] *Port Townsend, WA*
HOOSIER'S MOTEL & BAR [MOT] *Cooke City, MT*
HOSPITALITY INN [MOT] *Kamloops, BC*
HOSPITALITY INN [MOT] *Seattle, WA*
HOTEL GRAND PACIFIC [MOT] *Victoria, BC*
HOTEL HIGGINS [BB] *Casper, WY*
HOTEL MCCALL [BB] *McCall, ID*
HOTEL MONACO [HOT] *Seattle, WA*
HOTEL VINTAGE PARK [HOT] *Seattle, WA*
HOWARD JOHNSON [MOT] *Lewiston, ID*
HOWARD JOHNSON EXPRESS INN [MOT] *Billings, MT*
HOWARD JOHNSON EXPRESS INN [MOT] *Coeur d'Alene, ID*
HOWARD JOHNSON EXPRESS INN & SUITES [MOT] *Vancouver, BC*
HOWARD JOHNSON EXPRESS INN [MOT] *Walla Walla, WA*
HOWARD JOHNSON HARBOUR SIDE HOTEL [MOT] *Nanaimo, BC*
HOWARD JOHNSON HOTEL [MOT] *Winnipeg, MB*
HOWARD JOHNSON INN [MOT] *La Grande, OR*
HOWARD JOHNSON INN [MOT] *Laramie, WY*
HOWARD JOHNSON PANORAMA INN [MOT] *Kamloops, BC*
HOWARD JOHNSON PLAZA HOTEL [MOT] *Everett, WA*
HUFF HOUSE INN BED & BREAKFAST, THE [BB] *Jackson, WY*
HYATT REGENCY BELLEVUE [HOT] *Bellevue, WA*
HYATT REGENCY CALGARY [HOT] *Calgary, AB*

HYATT REGENCY VANCOUVER [HOT] *Vancouver, BC*

IDAHO COUNTRY INN [BB] *Sun Valley Area, ID*

IDAHO HERITAGE INN [BB] *Boise, ID*

IDAHO ROCKY MOUNTAIN RANCH [RAN] *Stanley, ID*

IMPERIAL HOTEL [MOT] *Portland, OR*

INDIAN LODGE MOTEL [MOT] *Joseph, OR*

INN AMERICA [MOT] *Boise, ID*

INN AMERICA [MOT] *Nampa, ID*

INN AMERICA - A BUDGET MOTEL [MOT] *Lewiston, ID*

INN AT CENTRALIA [MOT] *Centralia, WA*

INN AT HARBOR STEPS [BB] *Seattle, WA*

INN AT ILWACO, THE [BB] *Long Beach, WA*

INN AT LANGLEY [BB] *Coupeville, WA*

INN AT NESIKA BEACH [BB] *Gold Beach, OR*

INN AT OTTER CREST [MOT] *Depoe Bay, OR*

INN AT PORT HADLOCK [MOT] *Port Townsend, WA*

INN AT SPANISH HEAD [MOT] *Lincoln City, OR*

INN AT SWIFTS BAY [BB] *San Juan Islands, WA*

INN AT THE DALLES [MOT] *The Dalles, OR*

INN AT THE MARKET [HOT] *Seattle, WA*

INN AT VIGINIA MASON [HOT] *Seattle, WA*

INN OF THE SEVENTH MOUNTAIN, THE [RST] *Bend, OR*

INN OF THE WHITE SALMON [BB] *Hood River, OR*

INN ON 7TH [HOT] *Edmonton, AB*

INNS OF BANFF [MOT] *Banff, AB*

INTERMOUNTAIN LODGE [MOT] *Driggs, ID*

INTERNATIONAL HOTEL OF CALGARY [HOT] *Calgary, AB*

INTERSTATE INN [MOT] *Moses Lake, WA*

IRWIN'S MOUNTAIN INN [MOT] *Banff, AB*

IVY CHAPEL INN BED & BREAKFAST [BB] *Ephrata, WA*

IZAAK WALTON INN [BB] *West Glacier Area, MT*

JACKSON HOLE RESORT [RST] *Jackson, WY*

JACKSONVILLE INN [BB] *Jacksonville, OR*

JACOBSON'S COTTAGES [MOT] *East Glacier Area, MT*

JAMES HOUSE [BB] *Port Townsend, WA*

JENNY LAKE LODGE [RAN] *Grand Teton National Park, WY*

JOHN DAY SUNSET INN [MOT] *John Day, OR*

JOHN PALLISER MANOR [HOT] *Calgary, AB*

JORGENSON'S INN AND SUITES [MOT] *Helena, MT*

KAH-NEE-TA LODGE [RST] *Madras, OR*

KALALOCH LODGE [RST] *Forks, WA*

KALISPELL GRAND HOTEL [HOT] *Kalispell, MT*

KAMLOOPS CITY CENTER TRAVELODGE [MOT] *Kamloops, BC*

KANANASKIS GUEST RANCH [CC] *Banff, AB*

KANANASKIS MOUNTAIN LODGE [HOT] *Calgary, AB*

KANDAHAR LODGE [MOT] *Whitefish, MT*

KATYS INN [BB] *La Conner, WA*

KEENAN HOUSE BED AND BREAKFAST [BB] *Tacoma, WA*

KELLY INN [MOT] *Cody, WY*

KELLY INN [MOT] *West Yellowstone, MT*

KENNEWICK TRAVELODGE INN & SUITES [MOT] *Kennewick, WA*

KILMOREY [MOT] *Waterton Lakes National Park, AB*

KINGFISHER OCEANSIDE RESORT AND SPA [RST] *Nanaimo, BC*

KNIGHTS INN [MOT] *Ashland, OR*

KNIGHTS INN [MOT] *Medford, OR*

KNOB HILL INN [HOT] *Sun Valley Area, ID*

KOOTENAI VALLEY MOTEL [MOT] *Bonners Ferry, ID*

LACONNER COUNTRY INN [BB] *La Conner, WA*

LADY MACDONALD COUNTRY INN, THE [BB] *Banff, AB*

LAKE MCDONALD LODGE [HOT] *West Glacier Area, MT*

LAKE QUINAULT LODGE [MOT] *Quinault, WA*

LAKESIDE INN [MOT] *Sandpoint, ID*

LAKEVIEW LODGE [MOT] *Lakeview, OR*

LAKE YELLOWSTONE HOTEL [HOT] *Yellowstone National Park, WY*

LAQUINTA [MOT] *Ritzville, WA*

LA QUINTA INN [MOT] *Caldwell, ID*

LA QUINTA INN [MOT] *Cheyenne, WY*

LA QUINTA INN [MOT] *Seattle, WA*

LA QUINTA INN [MOT] *Tacoma, WA*

LA QUINTA INN AND SUITES ALBANY [MOT] *Albany, OR*

LAUREL POINT INN [HOT] *Victoria, BC*

LAZY L & B RANCH [RAN] *Dubois, WY*

LETHBRIDGE LODGE [HOT] *Lethbridge, AB*

LITTLE AMERICA HOTEL [MOT] *Cheyenne, WY*

LITTLE AMERICA HOTEL [MOT] *Green River, WY*

LITTLE CREEK COVE [MOT] *Newport, OR*

LIVINGSTON SUPER 8 [MOT] *Livingston, MT*

LOBSTICK LODGE [MOT] *Jasper National Park, AB*

LONE MOUNTAIN [RAN] *Big Sky (Gallatin County), MT*

LOPEZ FARM COTTAGES [CC] *San Juan Islands, WA*

LOST CREEK RANCH [RAN] *Grand Teton National Park, WY*

LOVE'S RIVERVIEW LODGE [MOT] *Hood River, OR*

LYTLE HOUSE BED & BREAKFAST [BB] *Hoquiam, WA*

MAGNOLIA HOTEL & SUITES, THE [HOT] *Victoria, BC*

MALLORY HOTEL [HOT] *Portland, OR*

MALTANA [MOT] *Malta, MT*

MAMMOTH HOT SPRINGS HOTEL AND CABINS [HOT] *Yellowstone National Park, WY*

MANITOU LODGE BED & BREAKFAST [BB] *Forks, WA*

MANRESA CASTLE [BB] *Port Townsend, WA*

MAPLE ROSE INN [BB] *Port Angeles, WA*

MARCLAIR INN [MOT] *Tillamook, OR*

MARIANNA STOLTZ HOUSE BED & BREAKFAST [BB] *Spokane, WA*

MARINA CAY RESORT & CONFERENCE CENTER [RST] *Bigfork, MT*

MARINA VILLAGE INN [HOT] *Everett, WA*

MARK IV MOTOR INN [MOT] *Moscow, ID*

MARK SPENCER HOTEL PORTLAND [HOT] *Portland, OR*

MARMOT LODGE [MOT] *Jasper National Park, AB*

MARRIOTT AIRPORT SEA-TAC [HOT] *Seattle-Tacoma Intl Airport Area, WA*

MARRIOTT DOWNTOWN PORTLAND [HOT] *Portland, OR*

MARRIOTT HOTEL CALGARY [HOT] *Calgary, AB*

MARRIOTT PORTLAND CITY CENTER [HOT] *Portland, OR*

MARRIOTT VANCOUVER AIRPORT [HOT] *Vancouver, BC*

MAYFIELD INN AND SUITES [HOT] *Edmonton, AB*

MAYFLOWER PARK HOTEL [HOT] *Seattle, WA*

MCCALL HOUSE BED & BREAKFAST [BB] *Ashland, OR*

MCMENAMINS EDGEFIELD [BB] *Portland, OR*

MEADOW LAKE [RST] *Columbia Falls, MT*

MEDICINE HAT LODGE [MOT] *Medicine Hat, AB*

METROPOLITAN HOTEL, THE [HOT] *Vancouver, BC*

MICKEY O'REILLEY'S INN AT THE RIVER [MOT] *Wenatchee, WA*

MIDWAY INN [MOT] *Bremerton, WA*

MONEY SAVER MOTEL [MOT] *Florence, OR*

MOOSE HEAD RANCH [RAN] *Grand Teton National Park, WY*

MORRISON'S ROGUE RIVER LODGE [MOT] *Grants Pass, OR*

MOSES LAKE MOTEL 6 [MOT]
Moses Lake, WA
MOTEL 6 [MOT] Bend, OR
MOTEL 6 [MOT] Bozeman, MT
MOTEL 6 [MOT] Coeur d'Alene, ID
MOTEL 6 [MOT] Ontario, OR
MOTEL 6 [MOT] Spokane, WA
MOTEL 6 GARDINER [MOT]
Gardiner, MT
MOTEL DEL ROGUE [MOT] Grants
Pass, OR
MOTEL NICHOLAS [MOT] Omak,
WA
MOTEL ORLEANS [MOT] Corvallis,
OR
MOUNTAINEER LODGE [MOT]
Lake Louise, AB
MOUNTAIN HOME LODGE [BB]
Leavenworth, WA
MOUNTAIN INN MOTEL [MOT]
Afton, WY
MOUNTAIN PINE [MOT] East
Glacier Area, MT
MOUNTAIN SKY GUEST RANCH
[RAN] Livingston, MT
MOUNTAIN VILLAGE LODGE
[MOT] Stanley, ID
MOUNT ASHLAND INN [BB]
Ashland, OR
MOUNT BACHELOR VILLAGE
RESORT [MOT] Bend, OR
MOUNT ROYAL [HOT] Banff, AB
MOUNT ST. HELENS MOTEL
[MOT] Kelso, WA
MY PARENTS ESTATE BED &
BREAKFAST [BB] Colville, WA
NENDELS INN [MOT] Kennewick,
WA
NENDELS INN [MOT] Yakima, WA
NINE QUARTER CIRCLE RANCH
INC. [RAN] Big Sky (Gallatin
County), MT
NISQUALLY LODGE, THE [MOT]
Mount Rainier National Park,
WA
NORDIC MOTEL [MOT] Lincoln
City, OR
NORQUAY'S TIMBERLINE INN
[MOT] Banff, AB
NORTHGATE INN [MOT] Challis,
ID
NORTH HILL INN [MOT] Red Deer,
AB
NOTARAS LODGE [MOT] Soap
Lake, WA
OAK BAY BEACH AND MARINE
RESORT [HOT] Victoria, BC

OAK HILL BED & BREAKFAST [BB]
Ashland, OR
OCEAN CREST RESORT [MOT]
Moclips, WA
OCEAN POINTE RESORT AND SPA
[RST] Victoria, BC
O'DUACHAIN COUNTRY INN [BB]
Bigfork, MT
OLDE ENGLAND INN [BB] Victoria,
BC
OLD FAITHFUL INN [HOT]
Yellowstone National Park, WY
OLYMPIC INN [MOT] Aberdeen,
WA
ORANGE STREET BUDGE MOTOR
INN MISSOULA [MOT]
Missoula, MT
ORCAS HOTEL [BB] San Juan
Islands, WA
ORCHARD INN [MOT] Wenatchee,
WA
OREGON CAVES LODGE [MOT]
Cave Junction, OR
OUR PLACE AT THE BEACH [MOT]
Long Beach, WA
OVERLANDER MOUNTAIN
LODGE [MOT] Jasper
National Park, AB
OWYHEE PLAZA HOTEL [MOT]
Boise, ID
OXFORD INN [MOT] Yakima, WA
PACIFIC 9 MOTOR INN [MOT]
Eugene, OR
PACIFIC INN MOTEL [MOT] Forks,
WA
PACIFIC PALISADES [HOT]
Vancouver, BC
PALACE [HOT] Port Townsend, WA
PANACEA BED AND BREAKFAST
[BB] San Juan Islands, WA
PAN PACIFIC LODGE [HOT]
Whistler, BC
PAN PACIFIC VANCOUVER, THE
[HOT] Vancouver, BC
PARADISE [RAN] Buffalo, WY
PARADISE INN [MOT] Livingston,
MT
PARADISE INN [MOT] Mount
Rainier National Park, WA
PARADISE LODGE AND
BUNGALOWS [RST] Lake
Louise, AB
PARAMOUNT, THE [HOT] Seattle,
WA
PAUL'S MOTOR INN [MOT]
Victoria, BC
PEDIGRIFT HOUSE B&B [BB]
Ashland, OR

PELICAN SHORES INN [MOT]
    Lincoln City, OR
PENTICTON LAKESIDE RESORT
    AND CONFERENCE CENTER
    [HOT] Penticton, BC
PEPPERTREE INN [MOT] Beaverton,
    OR
PHOENIX INN [MOT] Eugene, OR
PHOENIX INN [MOT] Portland, OR
PHOENIX INN [MOT] Portland, OR
PHOENIX INN [MOT] Salem, OR
PHOENIX INN TIGARD [MOT]
    Beaverton, OR
PINE LODGE [MOT] Whitefish, MT
PINE MEADOW INN [BB] Grants
    Pass, OR
PLAZA SUITE HOTEL [HOT] Boise,
    ID
POCATELLO SUPER 8 [MOT]
    Pocatello, ID
POLLARD HOTEL [HOT] Red Lodge,
    MT
PONDEROSA MOTEL [MOT]
    Goldendale, WA
PORT ANGELES INN [MOT] Port
    Angeles, WA
PORTLAND'S WHITE HOUSE BED
    AND BREAKFAST [BB]
    Portland, OR
PORT LUDLOW RESORT &
    CONFERENCE CENTER [RST]
    Port Ludlow, WA
POST HOTEL [HOT] Lake Louise, AB
PRAIRIE INN MOTEL [MOT]
    Evanston, WY
PRINCE OF WALES [HOT] Waterton
    Lakes National Park, AB
PRINCE OF WALES BED &
    BREAKFAST [BB] Seattle, WA
PRIOR HOUSE B&B INN [BB]
    Victoria, BC
QUALITY 49'ER INN & SUITES
    [MOT] Jackson, WY
QUALITY HOTEL & CONFERENCE
    CENTRE [MOT] Calgary, AB
QUALITY HOTEL - DOWNTOWN
    [MOT] Vancouver, BC
QUALITY INN [MOT] Baker City,
    OR
QUALITY INN [MOT] Bellingham,
    WA
QUALITY INN [MOT] Billings, MT
QUALITY INN [MOT] Clarkston,
    WA
QUALITY INN [MOT] Lincoln City,
    OR
QUALITY INN [MOT] Pullman, WA

QUALITY INN [MOT] The Dalles,
    OR
QUALITY INN AIRPORT SUITES
    [MOT] Boise, ID
QUALITY INN & SUITES [MOT]
    Klamath Falls, OR
QUALITY INN MOTEL VILLAGE
    [MOT] Calgary, AB
QUALITY INN OF YAKIMA [MOT]
    Yakima, WA
QUALITY INN VALLEY SUITES
    [MOT] Spokane, WA
QUALITY RESORT - CHATEAU
    CANMORE [MOT] Banff, AB
QUEEN VICTORIA INN [HOT]
    Victoria, BC
RADISSON DOWNTOWN [HOT]
    Winnipeg, MB
RADISSON HOTEL [HOT] Portland,
    OR
RADISSON HOTEL [HOT] Seattle-
    Tacoma Intl Airport Area, WA
RADISSON HOTEL AND
    CONFERENCE CENTER
    [HOT] Banff, AB
RADISSON HOTEL BURNABY
    [HOT] Vancouver, BC
RADISSON HOTEL CALGARY
    AIRPORT [HOT] Calgary, AB
RADISSON HOTEL CASPER [HOT]
    Casper, WY
RADISSON NORTHERN HOTEL
    [HOT] Billings, MT
RADISSON PRESIDENT HOTEL
    AND SUITES [HOT]
    Vancouver, BC
RADISSON SUITE HOTEL
    WINNIPEG AIRPORT [HOT]
    Winnipeg, MB
RAFTER SIX RANCH RESORT
    [RAN] Calgary, AB
RAINBOW INN [BB] Mount Vernon,
    WA
RAINBOW RANCH [MOT] Big Sky
    (Gallatin County), MT
RAINBOW VALLEY LODGE [MOT]
    Ennis, MT
RAMADA COURTYARD INN [MOT]
    Penticton, BC
RAMADA HUNTINGDON MANOR
    [MOT] Victoria, BC
RAMADA INN [MOT] Beaverton, OR
RAMADA INN [MOT] Bellingham,
    WA
RAMADA INN [MOT] Bozeman, MT
RAMADA INN [MOT] Butte, MT

RAMADA INN [MOT] *Edmonton, AB*

RAMADA INN [MOT] *Portland, OR*

RAMADA INN [MOT] *Wenatchee, WA*

RAMADA INN AIRPORT [MOT] *Spokane, WA*

RAMADA INN AT ROSE QUARTER [MOT] *Portland, OR*

RAMADA INN GOVERNOR HOUSE [MOT] *Olympia, WA*

RAMADA INN- KAMLOOPS [MOT] *Kamloops, BC*

RAMADA LIMITED [MOT] *Billings, MT*

RAMADA LIMITED [MOT] *Rock Springs, WY*

RAMADA LODGE [MOT] *Kelowna, BC*

RANCH AT UCROSS, THE [MOT] *Buffalo, WY*

RAVENSCROFT [BB] *Port Townsend, WA*

RED CARPET INN [MOT] *Banff, AB*

RED LION HOTEL [MOT] *Coos Bay, OR*

RED LION HOTEL [MOT] *Kelso, WA*

RED LION HOTEL [MOT] *Lewiston, ID*

RED LION HOTEL [MOT] *Pendleton, OR*

RED LION HOTEL [MOT] *Richland, WA*

RED LION HOTEL [MOT] *Vancouver, WA*

RED LION HOTEL EUGENE [MOT] *Eugene, OR*

RED LION HOTEL MEDFORD [MOT] *Medford, OR*

RED LION HOTEL-PORT ANGELES [MOT] *Port Angeles, WA*

RED LION HOTEL SALEM [MOT] *Salem, OR*

RED LION HOTEL SEATTLE AIRPORT [MOT] *Seattle-Tacoma Intl Airport Area, WA*

RED LION HOTEL WENATCHEE [MOT] *Wenatchee, WA*

RED LION INN [MOT] *Aberdeen, WA*

RED LION INN [MOT] *Astoria, OR*

RED LION INN [MOT] *Missoula, MT*

RED LION INN [MOT] *Yakima, WA*

RED LION INN NORTH [MOT] *Bend, OR*

RED LION WYOMING INN [MOT] *Jackson, WY*

REDMOND INN [MOT] *Redmond, OR*

RED ROOF INN [MOT] *Seattle-Tacoma Intl Airport Area, WA*

REDWOOD MOTEL [MOT] *Grants Pass, OR*

REDWOOD MOTOR INN [MOT] *Brandon, MB*

RENAISSANCE MADISON HOTEL [HOT] *Seattle, WA*

RENAISSANCE VANCOUVER HOTEL HARBOURSIDE [HOT] *Vancouver, BC*

RESIDENCE INN BY MARRIOTT [EX] *Bellevue, WA*

RESIDENCE INN BY MARRIOTT [EX] *Boise, ID*

RESIDENCE INN BY MARRIOTT [EX] *Portland, OR*

RESIDENCE INN BY MARRIOTT [EX] *Portland, OR*

RESORT AT GLACIER, THE [MOT] *East Glacier Area, MT*

RESORT SEMIAHMOO [RST] *Blaine, WA*

RESTON HOTEL [MOT] *Medford, OR*

RIMROCK DUDE RANCH [RAN] *Cody, WY*

RIMROCK RESORT [RST] *Banff, AB*

RIVERBEND INN [MOT] *Coeur d'Alene, ID*

RIVER HOUSE MOTEL [MOT] *Florence, OR*

RIVERHOUSE RESORT, THE [MOT] *Bend, OR*

RIVER PLACE HOTEL [HOT] *Portland, OR*

RIVER ROCK LODGE [MOT] *Big Sky (Gallatin County), MT*

RIVER RUN COTTAGES [BB] *Vancouver, BC*

RIVERSHORE HOTEL [MOT] *Oregon City, OR*

RIVERSIDE INN [MOT] *Grants Pass, OR*

RIVER STREET INN, THE [BB] *Sun Valley Area, ID*

RIVERVIEW INN [MOT] *Lewiston, ID*

RIVIERA [MOT] *Biggs, OR*

ROCHE HARBOR SEASIDE VILLAGE [RST] *San Juan Islands, WA*

ROCK CREEK RESORT [RST] *Red Lodge, MT*

ROCK SPRINGS GUEST RANCH [RAN] *Bend, OR*
RODEWAY INN [MOT] *Ashland, OR*
RODEWAY INN [MOT] *Boise, ID*
RODEWAY INN [MOT] *Leavenworth, WA*
ROGUE REGENCY INN [MOT] *Medford, OR*
ROGUE VALLEY MOTEL [MOT] *Grants Pass, OR*
ROMEO INN BED & BREAKFAST [BB] *Ashland, OR*
ROOSEVELT, THE [BB] *Coeur d'Alene, ID*
ROSARIO [RST] *San Juan Islands, WA*
ROSE BRIAR HOTEL [BB] *Astoria, OR*
ROYAL 7 [MOT] *Bozeman, MT*
ROYAL COACHMAN INN, INC. [MOT] *Tacoma, WA*
ROYAL MOTOR INN [MOT] *La Grande, OR*
ROYAL OAK INN & SUITES, THE [MOT] *Brandon, MB*
ROYAL RESORT [MOT] *Alpine, WY*
ROYAL SCOT INN [MOT] *Victoria, BC*
ROYAL VIEW MOTOR HOTEL [MOT] *Grants Pass, OR*
RUNDLE MOUNTAIN LODGE [MOT] *Banff, AB*
RUNDLESTONE LODGE [MOT] *Banff, AB*
RUN OF THE RIVER BED & BREAKFAST [BB] *Leavenworth, WA*
RUSTY PARROT LODGE [MOT] *Jackson, WY*
SACAJAWEA SELECT INN [MOT] *Lewiston, ID*
SAFARI MOTOR INN, INC [MOT] *McMinnville, OR*
SAGE BRUSH MOTEL [MOT] *Kamloops, BC*
SALIBURY HOUSE BED & BREAKFAST [BB] *Seattle, WA*
SALISH LODGE AND SPA [RST] *North Bend, WA*
SANDERS - HELENA'S BED & BREAKFAST, THE [BB] *Helena, MT*
SANDLAKE COUNTRY INN [BB] *Tillamook, OR*
SANDMAN HOTEL [MOT] *Kelowna, BC*

SANDMAN HOTEL [MOT] *Penticton, BC*
SANDMAN INN [MOT] *Revelstoke, BC*
SANDPOINT QUALITY INN [MOT] *Sandpoint, ID*
SAN JUAN [BB] *San Juan Islands, WA*
SAW RIDGE HOTEL & CONFERENCE CENTER [MOT] *Jasper National Park, AB*
SCANDINAVIAN GARDENS INN BED & BREAKFAST [BB] *Long Beach, WA*
SCHOONERS COVE OCEAN FRONT MOTEL [MOT] *Cannon Beach, OR*
SEA QUEST BED & BREAKFAST [BB] *Yachats, OR*
SEQUIM BAY LODGE [MOT] *Sequim, WA*
SEVEN D RANCH [RAN] *Cody, WY*
SHAMAN MOTEL [MOT] *Long Beach, WA*
SHAMROCK LODGETTES [MOT] *Yachats, OR*
SHANGRI-LA [MOT] *Spokane, WA*
SHANICO INN [MOT] *Corvallis, OR*
SHARLYN MOTEL [MOT] *Ephrata, WA*
SHERATON [HOT] *Billings, MT*
SHERATON [HOT] *Tacoma, WA*
SHERATON CAVALIER [HOT] *Calgary, AB*
SHERATON GRANDE [HOT] *Edmonton, AB*
SHERATON GUILFORD HOTEL [HOT] *Vancouver, BC*
SHERATON PORTLAND AIRPORT HOTEL [HOT] *Portland, OR*
SHERATON SEATTLE HOTEL & TOWERS [HOT] *Seattle, WA*
SHERATON SUITES LE SOLEIL [HOT] *Vancouver, BC*
SHERATON VANCOUVER WALL CENTRE [HOT] *Vancouver, BC*
SHERATON WINNIPEG HOTEL [HOT] *Winnipeg, MB*
SHILO INN [MOT] *Bend, OR*
SHILO INN [MOT] *Coeur d'Alene, ID*
SHILO INN [MOT] *Eugene, OR*
SHILO INN [MOT] *Grants Pass, OR*
SHILO INN [MOT] *Helena, MT*
SHILO INN [MOT] *Idaho Falls, ID*
SHILO INN [MOT] *Moses Lake, WA*

SHILO INN [MOT] *Nampa, ID*
SHILO INN [MOT] *Newberg, OR*
SHILO INN [MOT] *Newport, OR*
SHILO INN [MOT] *Portland, OR*
SHILO INN [MOT] *Portland, OR*
SHILO INN [MOT] *Richland, WA*
SHILO INN [MOT] *Salem, OR*
SHILO INN [MOT] *Seaside, OR*
SHILO INN [MOT] *Tacoma, WA*
SHILO INN [MOT] *Tillamook, OR*
SHILO INN [MOT] *Twin Falls, ID*
SHILO INN [MOT] *Vancouver, WA*
SHILO INN AIRPORT [MOT] *Boise, ID*
SHILO INN HOTEL [MOT] *Spokane, WA*
SHILO INN OCEANFRONT RESORT [MOT] *Lincoln City, OR*
SHILO INN PORTLAND AIRPORT [MOT] *Portland, OR*
SHILO INN RIVERSIDE [MOT] *Boise, ID*
SHILO INN SEASIDE EAST [MOT] *Seaside, OR*
SHILO INN SUITES [MOT] *Astoria, OR*
SHILO INN SUITES [MOT] *Nampa, ID*
SHILO INN SUITES HOTEL [MOT] *Klamath Falls, OR*
SHILO INN SUITES OCEAN SHORES BEACHFRONT RESORT [MOT] *Ocean Shores, WA*
SHIP HARBOR INN [MOT] *Anacortes, WA*
SHORE CLIFF INN [MOT] *Gold Beach, OR*
SHOSHONE LODGE RESORT & CUEST RANCH [MOT] *Cody, WY*
SHUMWAY MANSION [BB] *Bellevue, WA*
SIGNAL MOUNTAIN LODGE [MOT] *Grand Teton National Park, WY*
SILVER CLOUD INN [MOT] *Bellevue, WA*
SILVER CLOUD INN-BELLEVUE [HOT] *Bellevue, WA*
SILVER CLOUD INN - KENNEWICK [MOT] *Kennewick, WA*
SILVER CLOUD INN PORTLAND [HOT] *Portland, OR*
SILVER CLOUD INN UNIVERSITY VILLAGE [HOT] *Seattle, WA*
SILVER FOREST [BB] *Bozeman, MT*

SILVERHORN MOTOR INN & RESTAURANT [MOT] *Kellogg, ID*
SILVER SPUR MOTEL [MOT] *Burns, OR*
SIXTH AVENUE INN [MOT] *Seattle, WA*
SKAMANIA LODGE [RST] *Hood River, OR*
SLEEPING LADY CONFERENCE RETREAT [MOT] *Leavenworth, WA*
SLEEP INN [MOT] *Billings, MT*
SLEEP INN [MOT] *Boise, ID*
SLEEP INN [MOT] *Missoula, MT*
SLEEP INN [MOT] *Mountain Home, ID*
SLEEP INN [MOT] *Rawlins, WY*
SLEEPY HOLLOW MOTEL [MOT] *McKenzie Bridge, OR*
SNOW KING RESORT [MOT] *Jackson, WY*
SOL DUC HOT SPRINGS [RST] *Port Angeles, WA*
SONNY'S MOTEL [MOT] *Madras, OR*
SOOKE HARBOUR HOUSE [BB] *Victoria, BC*
SORRENTO [HOT] *Seattle, WA*
SPAHN'S BIG HORN MOUNTAIN BED & BREAKFAST [BB] *Sheridan, WY*
SPANISH VILLA [MOT] *Penticton, BC*
SPRINDRIFT MOTOR INN [MOT] *Brookings, OR*
SPRING CREEK RANCH [MOT] *Jackson, WY*
STAGECOACH INN [MOT] *West Yellowstone, MT*
STAGECOACH INN MOTEL [MOT] *Salmon, ID*
STAGE LODGE [BB] *Jacksonville, OR*
STANG MANOR BED & BREAKFAST [BB] *La Grande, OR*
STARDUST MOTEL [MOT] *Wallace, ID*
STATEHOUSE INN [HOT] *Boise, ID*
STAY 'N SAVE [MOT] *Kamloops, BC*
STEIGER HAUS BED & BREAKFAST [BB] *McMinnville, OR*
STRATFORD INN [MOT] *Ashland, OR*
SUMMERFIELD SUITES BY WYNDHAM [HOT] *Seattle, WA*
SUMMIT LODGE [RST] *Whistler, BC*

SUNDOWNER MOTEL [MOT]
Caldwell, ID
SUNDOWNER STATION [MOT]
Riverton, WY
SUN MOUNTAIN LODGE [RST]
Winthrop, WA
SUNRIVER RESORT [RST] Bend, OR
SUNSET MOTEL [MOT] Bonners
Ferry, ID
SUNSET MOTEL [MOT] Fort
Macleod, AB
SUNSET OCEANFRONT
ACCOMMODAT [MOT]
Bandon, OR
SUN VALLEY RESORT [RST] Sun
Valley Area, ID
SUPER 8 [MOT] Boise, ID
SUPER 8 [MOT] Dubois, WY
SUPER 8 [MOT] Klamath Falls, OR
SUPER 8 [MOT] Long Beach, WA
SUPER 8 [MOT] Medicine Hat, AB
SUPER 8 [MOT] Missoula, MT
SUPER 8 [MOT] Missoula, MT
SUPER 8 [MOT] Montpelier, ID
SUPER 8 [MOT] Moscow, ID
SUPER 8 [MOT] Ontario, OR
SUPER 8 [MOT] Red Lodge, MT
SUPER 8 [MOT] Rexburg, ID
SUPER 8 [MOT] Thermopolis, WY
SUPER 8 [MOT] Torrington, WY
SUPER 8 LIONSHEAD RESORT
[MOT] West Yellowstone, MT
SUPER 8 MOTEL [MOT] Baker City,
OR
SUPER 8 MOTEL [MOT] Big Timber,
MT
SUPER 8 MOTEL [MOT] Billings,
MT
SUPER 8 MOTEL [MOT] Butte, MT
SUPER 8 MOTEL [MOT] Coeur
d'Alene, ID
SUPER 8 MOTEL [MOT] Deer Lodge,
MT
SUPER 8 MOTEL [MOT] Dillon, MT
SUPER 8 MOTEL [MOT] Hardin, MT
SUPER 8 MOTEL [MOT] Helena, MT
SUPER 8 MOTEL [MOT] Kellogg, ID
SUPER 8 MOTEL [MOT] Lewiston,
ID
SUPER 8 MOTEL [MOT] Lewistown,
MT
SUPER 8 MOTEL [MOT] Lovell, WY
SUPER 8 MOTEL [MOT] Sandpoint,
ID
SUPER 8 MOTEL [MOT] Spokane,
WA

SUPER 8 MOTEL [MOT] Whitefish,
MT
SUPER 8 TETON WEST [MOT]
Driggs, ID
SUPER 8 WILSONVILLE [MOT]
Portland, OR
SURFRIDER RESORT [MOT] Depoe
Bay, OR
SURFSAND RESORT HOTEL [MOT]
Cannon Beach, OR
SURFSIDE MOTEL [MOT]
Rockaway, OR
SUTTON PLACE HOTEL, THE
[HOT] Vancouver, BC
SWAN HOTEL, THE [BB] Port
Townsend, WA
SWANS SUITE HOTEL [HOT]
Victoria, BC
SWAN VALLEY SUPER 8 MOTEL
[MOT] Bigfork, MT
SWEET BRIER INN, THE [MOT]
Portland, OR
SWIFTCURRENT MOTOR INN
[MOT] East Glacier Area, MT
TAMARACK LODGE [MOT] Sun
Valley Area, ID
TAPADERA BUDGET INN [MOT]
Walla Walla, WA
TAPADERA INN [MOT] Kennewick,
WA
TAPADERA MOTEL [MOT]
Pendleton, OR
TETON MOUNTAIN VIEW LODGE
[MOT] Driggs, ID
TETON PINES [RST] Jackson, WY
TETON RIDGE RANCH [RAN]
Driggs, ID
WOODS HOUSE BED &
BREAKFAST, THE [BB]
Ashland, OR
THREE VALLEY LAKE CHATEAU
LTD. [MOT] Revelstoke, BC
TIKI LODGE [MOT] Salem, OR
TIMBERS MOTEL [MOT] Bigfork,
MT
TLC INN [MOT] Bozeman, MT
TOLOVANA INN [MOT] Cannon
Beach, OR
TOUVELLE HOUSE BED &
BREAKFAST [BB] Jacksonville,
OR
TOWER ON THE PARK [HOT]
Edmonton, AB
TOWN & COUNTRY MOTEL
[MOT] Bonners Ferry, ID
TOWNHOUSE INN [MOT] Havre,
MT

TOWN HOUSE INN OF GREAT FALLS [MOT] *Great Falls, MT*

TRADE WINDS NORTH MOTEL [MOT] *Spokane, WA*

TRADITIONAL INNS [MOT] *Quincy, WA*

TRAPPER INN [MOT] *Jackson, WY*

TRAVELERS INN [MOT] *Bellingham, WA*

TRAVELERS INN [MOT] *Seattle, WA*

TRAVELODGE [MOT] *Eugene, OR*

TRAVELODGE [MOT] *Hillsboro, OR*

TRAVELODGE [MOT] *Medicine Hat, AB*

TRAVELODGE [MOT] *Missoula, MT*

TRAVELODGE [MOT] *Penticton, BC*

TRAVELODGE [MOT] *Portland, OR*

TRAVELODGE [MOT] *Red Deer, AB*

TRAVELODGE [MOT] *Roseburg, OR*

TRAVELODGE [MOT] *Seattle-Tacoma Intl Airport Area, WA*

TRAVELODGE [MOT] *Spokane, WA*

TRAVELODGE [MOT] *Walla Walla, WA*

TRAVELODGE [MOT] *Wenatchee, WA*

TRAVELODGE CALGARY SOUTH [MOT] *Calgary, AB*

TRAVELODGE NEW REDMOND HOTEL [MOT] *Redmond, OR*

TRAVELODGE SUITES [MOT] *Forest Grove, OR*

TRIPLE CREEK RANCH [RAN] *Hamilton, MT*

TUCKER HOUSE BED & BREAKFAST [BB] *San Juan Islands, WA*

TUDOR INN BED & BREAKFAST [BB] *Port Angeles, WA*

TUNNEL MOUNTAIN RESORT [MOT] *Banff, AB*

TURTLEBACK FARM INN [BB] *San Juan Islands, WA*

TU TU' TUN LODGE [MOT] *Gold Beach, OR*

UNIVERSITY INN [MOT] *Boise, ID*

UNIVERSITY INN [MOT] *Seattle, WA*

UPTOWN INN [MOT] *Port Angeles, WA*

UXU RANCH [MOT] *Cody, WY*

VAGABOND LODGE HOOD RIVER [MOT] *Hood River, OR*

VALLEY GOFF CREEK [MOT] *Cody, WY*

VALLEY RIVER INN [MOT] *Eugene, OR*

VAL-U INN [MOT] *Missoula, MT*

VAL-U INN MOTEL [MOT] *Bellingham, WA*

VICTORIA INN [MOT] *Brandon, MB*

VICTORIA REGENT [HOT] *Victoria, BC*

VILLA BED & BREAKFAST [BB] *Tacoma, WA*

VILLAGE GREEN HOTEL & CASINO [MOT] *Kelowna, BC*

VILLAGE INN [MOT] *Challis, ID*

VILLAGE INN [HOT] *East Glacier Area, MT*

VILLAGE INN MOTEL [MOT] *Cashmere, WA*

VILLAGE MOTOR INN [MOT] *Marysville, WA*

VILLAGE SQUIRE MOTEL [MOT] *Redmond, OR*

VINEYARD INN [MOT] *Pasco, WA*

VINTAGE PLAZA [HOT] *Portland, OR*

VOSS INN [BB] *Bozeman, MT*

WALLOWA LAKE LODGE [MOT] *Joseph, OR*

WARWICK HOTEL [HOT] *Seattle, WA*

WATERFRONT CENTRE [HOT] *Vancouver, BC*

WEASKU INN [BB] *Grants Pass, OR*

WEDGE MOUNTAIN INN [MOT] *Cashmere, WA*

WEDGEWOOD [HOT] *Vancouver, BC*

WELCOME MOTOR INN [MOT] *Everett, WA*

WESTCOAST BELLEVUE HOTEL [MOT] *Bellevue, WA*

WESTCOAST HOTEL [HOT] *Pasco, WA*

WESTCOAST KALISPELL CENTER [MOT] *Kalispell, MT*

WESTCOAST OLYMPIA HOTEL [MOT] *Olympia, WA*

WEST COAST PARKCENTER SUITES [MOT] *Boise, ID*

WESTCOAST POCATELLO HOTEL [MOT] *Pocatello, ID*

WESTCOAST RIDPATH HOTEL [HOT] *Spokane, WA*

WESTCOAST RIVER INN [MOT] *Spokane, WA*

WESTCOAST-SEA-TAC HOTEL [MOT] *Seattle-Tacoma Intl Airport Area, WA*

WESTCOAST SILVERDALE HOTEL [MOT] *Bremerton, WA*

WESTCOAST TEMPLIN'S RESORT [MOT] *Coeur d'Alene, ID*

WESTCOAST TRI CITIES [MOT]
Kennewick, WA
WESTCOAST WENATCHEE
CENTER [HOT] Wenatchee,
WA
WESTCOAST YAKIMA CENTER
HOTEL [MOT] Yakima, WA
WESTCOAST YAKIMA GATEWAY
HOTEL [MOT] Yakima, WA
WEST END GUEST HOUSE [BB]
Vancouver, BC
WEST HARVEST INN [MOT]
Edmonton, AB
WESTIN CALGARY [HOT] Calgary,
AB
WESTIN EDMONTON [HOT]
Edmonton, AB
WESTIN GRAND VANCOUVER,
THE [HOT] Vancouver, BC
WESTIN PORTLAND, THE [HOT]
Portland, OR
WESTIN RESORT AND SPA, THE
[RST] Whistler, BC
WESTIN SALISHAN LODGE [RST]
Lincoln City, OR
WESTIN SEATTLE, THE [HOT]
Seattle, WA
WHALER MOTEL [MOT] Newport,
OR
WHITE SWAN GUEST HOUSE, THE
[BB] Mount Vernon, WA
WICKANINNISH INN, THE [BB]
Victoria, BC
WILDFLOWER INN, THE [BB]
Jackson, WY
WILLOWS LODGE [RST] Issaquah,
WA

WILLOW SPRINGS MOTEL [MOT]
Cheney, WA
WINCHESTER INN &
RESTAURANT, THE [BB]
Ashland, OR
WINDMILL INN [MOT] Medford,
OR
WINDMILL INN & SUITES [MOT]
Ashland, OR
WINDMILL INN OF ROSEBURG
[MOT] Roseburg, OR
WINDSONG BED & BREAKFAST
[BB] San Juan Islands, WA
WINTHROP INN, THE [MOT]
Winthrop, WA
WOODMARK HOTEL ON LAKE
WASHINGTON [HOT]
Bellevue, WA
WOODSMAN MOTEL AND CAFE
[MOT] McCall, ID
WORT HOTEL, THE [MOT] Jackson,
WY
W SEATTLE [HOT] Seattle, WA
WYNDHAM SEATTLE-TACOMA
AIRPORT [HOT] Seattle-
Tacoma Intl Airport Area, WA
WYOMING MOTEL [MOT] Buffalo,
WY
YELLOW POINT LODGE [CC]
Nanaimo, BC
YELLOWSTONE SUPER 8 [MOT]
Gardiner, MT
YELLOWSTONE VILLAGE INN
[MOT] Gardiner, MT
YE OLDE COLONIAL MOTOR INN
[MOT] Ontario, OR

RESTAURANT LIST

Establishment names are listed in alphabetical order followed by a symbol identifying their classification and then city and state. The symbols for classification are: [RES] for Restaurants and [URD] for Unrated Dining Spots.

AERIE DINING ROOM, THE [RES]
    Victoria, BC
A KETTLE OF FISH [RES]
    Vancouver, BC
AL-AMIR LEBANESE RESTAURANT
    [RES] Portland, OR
AL BOCCALINO [RES] Seattle, WA
ALESSANDRO'S [RES] Portland, OR
ALESSANDRO'S [RES] Salem, OR
ALEXANDER'S COUNTRY INN
    [RES] Mount Rainier
    National Park, WA
ALEXIS [RES] Portland, OR
ALLEGRO CAFI [RES] Vancouver,
    BC
ALPENHOF DINING ROOM, THE
    [RES] Jackson, WY
ALTEZZO RISTORANTE [RES]
    Tacoma, WA
AMBROSIA [RES] Eugene, OR
AMICI [RES] Winnipeg, MB
ANDALUCA [RES] Seattle, WA
ANTHONY'S [RES] Jackson, WY
ANTOINE'S [RES] Victoria, BC
AQUA RIVA [RES] Vancouver, BC
ARIA [RES] Vancouver, BC
ASHLAND BAKERY & CAFE [RES]
    Ashland, OR
ASSAGGIO RISTORANTE [RES]
    Seattle, WA
ATLAS FOODS [RES] Seattle, WA
ATRIUM STEAKHOUSE [RES]
    Calgary, AB
ATWATER'S [RES] Portland, OR
BACCHUS [RES] Vancouver, BC
BALKAN [RES] Banff, AB
BANDOLEONE [RES] Seattle, WA
BANDON BOATWORKS [RES]
    Bandon, OR
BANFF SPRINGS [RES] Banff, AB
BANGKOK CUISINE [RES]
    Sandpoint, ID
BARCLAY II [RES] Anaconda, MT
BAR J [URD] Jackson, WY
BAY HOUSE [RES] Lincoln City,
    OR
BEAR FOOT BISTRO [RES]
    Whistler, BC

BELVEDERE, THE [RES] Calgary,
    AB
BEVERLY'S [RES] Coeur d'Alene,
    ID
BIGFORK INN [RES] Bigfork, MT
BIG HORN [RES] Lovell, WY
BILLY'S RESTAURANT [RES]
    Aberdeen, WA
BISHOP'S [RES] Vancouver, BC
BISTRO, THE [RES] Banff, AB
BLACK RABBIT [RES] Portland, OR
BLUE CRAB BAR AND GRILL [RES]
    Victoria, BC
BLUE LION [RES] Jackson, WY
BOAT SHED [RES] Bremerton, WA
BOODLES [RES] Bozeman, MT
BRASA [RES] Seattle, WA
BREWHOUSE TAP ROOM & GRILL
    [RES] Portland, OR
BRIDGES RESTAURANT [RES]
    Aberdeen, WA
BROOKLYN SEAFOOD, STEAK &
    OYSTER HOUSE [RES]
    Seattle, WA
BUCA DI BEPPO [RES] Seattle, WA
BUDD BAY CAFE [RES] Olympia,
    WA
BUFFALO MOUNTAIN LODGE
    DINING ROOM [RES] Banff,
    AB
BUGATTI'S [RES] Portland, OR
BUNNERY, THE [URD] Jackson,
    WY
BURRITO LOCO [RES] Seattle, WA
BUSH GARDEN [RES] Portland, OR
BUSHWHACKER [RES] Port
    Angeles, WA
CABOOSE STEAK AND LOBSTER
    [RES] Banff, AB
CADILLAC GRILLE [RES] Jackson,
    WY
CAESAR'S STEAK HOUSE [RES]
    Calgary, AB
CAFE AZUL [RES] Portland, OR
CAFE BRIO [RES] Victoria, BC

BELLA ITALIA [RES] Port Angeles,
    WA

CAFE CAMPAGNE [RES] Seattle, WA
CAFE DE PARIS [RES] Vancouver, BC
CAFE DES AMIS [RES] Portland, OR
CAFE EDELWEISS [RES] Big Sky (Gallatin County), MT
CAFE FLORA [RES] Seattle, WA
CAFE JUANITA [RES] Bellevue, WA
CAFE LAGO [RES] Seattle, WA
CAFE LANGLEY [RES] Coupeville, WA
CAFE NAVARRO [RES] Eugene, OR
CAFFE DE MEDICI [RES] Vancouver, BC
CALICO [RES] Jackson, WY
CAMILLE'S [RES] Victoria, BC
CAMP 18 [RES] Seaside, OR
CAMPAGNE [RES] Seattle, WA
CANLIS [RES] Seattle, WA
CANNERY [RES] Vancouver, BC
CAPILANO HEIGHTS [RES] Vancouver, BC
CAPRIAL'S BISTRO [RES] Portland, OR
CARMELITA [RES] Seattle, WA
CASA DE BLANCA [RES] Ellensburg, WA
CASCADIA [RES] Seattle, WA
C'EST SI BON [RES] Port Angeles, WA
CHANDLER'S RESTAURANT [RES] Sun Valley Area, ID
CHANTERELLE [RES] Eugene, OR
CHAPTER XI [RES] Spokane, WA
CHART HOUSE [RES] Portland, OR
CHARTHOUSE [RES] Vancouver, BC
CHARTWELL [RES] Vancouver, BC
CHATEAULIN [RES] Ashland, OR
CHATHAMS LIVINGSTON BAR AND GRILL [RES] Livingston, MT
CHEZ FRANCOIS [RES] Banff, AB
CHEZ JEANNETTE [RES] Lincoln City, OR
CHEZ MICHEL [RES] Vancouver, BC
CHEZ SHEA [RES] Seattle, WA
CHIANTI CAFE [RES] Edmonton, AB
CHINOOK'S [RES] Seattle, WA
CHRISTINA'S [RES] San Juan Islands, WA
CHUCKANUT MANOR [RES] Bellingham, WA

CHUTNEY'S [RES] Seattle, WA
CIMMIYOTTI'S [RES] Pendleton, OR
CINCIN ITALIAN WOOD GRILL [RES] Vancouver, BC
CIRCLE T INN [RES] Ritzville, WA
CLASSICO [URD] Banff, AB
CLAWSON WINDWARD INN [RES] Florence, OR
CLIFF HOUSE [RES] Tacoma, WA
CLINKERDAGGER [RES] Spokane, WA
CLOUD 9 [RES] Vancouver, BC
COBBLESTONE MANOR [RES] Fort Macleod, AB
COCOA'S [RES] Edmonton, AB
COCO PAZZO [RES] Lethbridge, AB
COLONEL BOZEMAN'S [RES] Buffalo, WY
COLUMBIA RIVER COURT DINING ROOM [RES] Hood River, OR
CONSERVATORY [URD] Calgary, AB
CONSERVATORY RESTAURANT, THE [RES] Nanaimo, BC
COPPERFIELD'S [RES] Tacoma, WA
COTTAGE [RES] Cottage Grove, OR
COUSIN'S [RES] The Dalles, OR
COUVRON [RES] Portland, OR
COYOTE RIVERHOUSE [RES] Bigfork, MT
CREPERIE [URD] Edmonton, AB
C RESTAURANT [RES] Vancouver, BC
CUCINA! CUCINA! [RES] Seattle, WA
DAHLIA LOUNGE [RES] Seattle, WA
DAN & LOUIS OYSTER BAR [RES] Portland, OR
DEEP COVE CHALET [RES] Victoria, BC
DELI DE PASTA [RES] Yakima, WA
DELILAH'S [RES] Vancouver, BC
DEPOT [RES] Missoula, MT
DINING ROOM, THE [RES] Winthrop, WA
DINING ROOM AT SALISHAN, THE [RES] Lincoln City, OR
DIVA AT THE MET [RES] Vancouver, BC
DON'S [RES] Soap Lake, WA
DOOGER'S [RES] Cannon Beach, OR

DOOGER'S SEAFOOD & GRILL [RES] Seaside, OR

DOONG KONG LAU [RES] Seattle, WA

DORY COVE [RES] Lincoln City, OR

DOWNRIGGERS [RES] San Juan Islands, WA

DRAGON FISH ASIAN CAFE [RES] Seattle, WA

DULCES LATIN BISTRO [RES] Seattle, WA

DUNDARAVE PIER [RES] Vancouver, BC

DUNGENESS INN [RES] Sequim, WA

EARTH AND OCEAN [RES] Seattle, WA

EDDIE'S SUPPER CLUB [RES] Great Falls, MT

EDITH CAVELL DINING ROOM [RES] Jasper National Park, AB

EL GAUCHO [RES] Seattle, WA

ELLIOTT'S OYSTER HOUSE [RES] Seattle, WA

EMPRESS ROOM [RES] Victoria, BC

ERNESTO'S ITALIAN RESTAURANT [RES] Bend, OR

ESPARZA'S TEX MEX CAFE [RES] Portland, OR

ESPLANADE AT RIVERPLACE [RES] Portland, OR

ETTA'S SEAFOOD [RES] Seattle, WA

EVERGREEN BISTRO [RES] Ketchum, ID

EXCELSIOR INN [RES] Eugene, OR

FENDERS [RES] Whitefish, MT

FERNANDO'S HIDEAWAY [RES] Portland, OR

FIORE [RES] Edmonton, AB

FIORELLA'S [RES] Klamath Falls, OR

FIRST AVENUE WEST [RES] Kalispell, MT

FIRST PLACE [RES] Big Sky (Gallatin County), MT

FISH AND COMPANY [RES] Vancouver, BC

FISH HOUSE IN STANLEY PARK [RES] Vancouver, BC

FIVE SAILS [RES] Vancouver, BC

FLEURI [RES] Vancouver, BC

FLOATING RESTAURANT [RES] Sandpoint, ID

FLYING FISH [RES] Seattle, WA

FOUR SEAS [RES] Seattle, WA

FRANCA'S ITALIAN DINING [RES] Cody, WY

FRONTIER [RES] Revelstoke, BC

FRONTIER PIES RESTAURANT [RES] Rexburg, ID

F.X. MCRORY'S STEAK, CHOP & OYSTER HOUSE [RES] Seattle, WA

GABLES [RES] Corvallis, OR

GALLATIN GATEWAY INN [RES] Bozeman, MT

GATSBY MANSION [RES] Victoria, BC

GENEVA [RES] Seattle, WA

GENOA [RES] Portland, OR

GEORGE HENRY'S [RES] Billings, MT

GEORGIAN, THE [RES] Seattle, WA

GIORGIO'S TRATTORIA [RES] Banff, AB

GLACIER VILLAGE [RES] East Glacier Area, MT

GLOBE @ YVR [RES] Vancouver, BC

GOTHAM STEAKHOUSE AND COCKTAIL BAR [RES] Vancouver, BC

GOVINDA'S VEGETARIAN BUFFET [URD] Eugene, OR

GRAND, THE [RES] Big Timber, MT

GRANVILLE SUSHI [RES] Vancouver, BC

GREAT WALL [RES] Billings, MT

GREENLEE'S [RES] Red Lodge, MT

GREENS AND GOURMET [URD] Vancouver, BC

GRETCHEN'S [RES] Sun Valley Area, ID

HARBOR LIGHTS [RES] Tacoma, WA

HART HOUSE ON DEER LAKE [RES] Vancouver, BC

HARVEST ROOM [RES] Edmonton, AB

HEATHMAN [RES] Portland, OR

HERALD STREET CAFFE [RES] Victoria, BC

HERBFARM, THE [RES] Issaquah, WA

HERON BEACH INN DINING ROOM [RES] Port Ludlow, WA

HIGGINS [RES] Portland, OR

HILLTOP HOUSE [RES] North Bend, OR

HIRAM'S AT THE LOCKS [RES]
    Seattle, WA
HONG KONG [RES] Gillette, WY
HOULIHAN'S [RES] Red Deer, AB
HUBER'S CAFE [RES] Portland, OR
HUGO'S GRILL [RES] Victoria, BC
HUNT CLUB [RES] Seattle, WA
HYDRA [RES] Sandpoint, ID
HY'S CALGARY STEAK HOUSE
    [RES] Calgary, AB
HY'S ENCORE [RES] Vancouver,
    BC
HY'S STEAK LOFT [RES]
    Edmonton, AB
HY'S STEAK LOFT [RES] Winnipeg,
    MB
ICHIBAN JAPANESE STEAKHOUSE
    AND SUSHI BAR [RES]
    Winnipeg, MB
IL BISTRO [RES] Seattle, WA
IL FORNAIO [RES] Portland, OR
IL GIARDINO DI UMBERTO
    RISTORANTE [RES]
    Vancouver, BC
IL TERRAZZO [RES] Victoria, BC
IL TERRAZZO CARMINE [RES]
    Seattle, WA
IMPERIAL CHINESE SEAFOOD
    RESTAURANT [RES]
    Vancouver, BC
INDIA TANDOORI HUT [RES]
    Victoria, BC
INN ON LAKE BONAVISTA [RES]
    Calgary, AB
IRON HORSE [RES] Coeur d'Alene,
    ID
IVANO'S RISTORANTE [RES]
    Sandpoint, ID
IVAR'S ACRES OF CLAMS [RES]
    Seattle, WA
IVAR'S INDIAN SALMON HOUSE
    [RES] Seattle, WA
IVY HOUSE [URD] Portland, OR
JACKSONVILLE INN [RES]
    Jacksonville, OR
JADE GARDEN [RES] Helena, MT
JAKERS [RES] Idaho Falls, ID
JAKER'S [RES] Twin Falls, ID
JAKER'S STEAK, RIBS & FISH
    HOUSE [RES] Great Falls, MT
JAKE'S FAMOUS CRAWFISH [RES]
    Portland, OR
JAKE'S GRILL [RES] Portland, OR
JALAPENO'S [RES] Sandpoint, ID
J & J WONTON NOODLE HOUSE
    [RES] Victoria, BC

JAPANESE VILLAGE [RES]
    Edmonton, AB
JAPANESE VILLAGE STEAK AND
    SEAFOOD HOUSE [RES]
    Victoria, BC
JEDEDIAH'S [RES] Jackson, WY
JENNY LAKE LODGE DINING
    ROOM [RES] Grand Teton
    National Park, WY
JIMMY D'S CAFE [RES] Coeur
    d'Alene, ID
JITTERBUG [RES] Seattle, WA
JOHN BOZEMAN'S BISTRO [RES]
    Bozeman, MT
JOHNNY'S DOCK [RES] Tacoma,
    WA
JULIANO'S [RES] Billings, MT
KASPAR'S [RES] Seattle, WA
KEG STEAKHOUSE AND BAR, THE
    [RES] Calgary, AB
KHU LARB THAI [RES] Port
    Townsend, WA
KINGFISHER RESTAURANT [RES]
    Nanaimo, BC
KOKONAS [RES] Brandon, MB
KWAN ORIGINAL CUISINE [RES]
    Salem, OR
LA BELLE AUBERGE [RES]
    Vancouver, BC
LA BOHEME [RES] Edmonton, AB
LAKE YELLOWSTONE DINING
    ROOM [RES] Yellowstone
    National Park, WY
LAMPREIA RESTAURANT [RES]
    Seattle, WA
LANDINGS [RES] Port Angeles, WA
L & W [RES] Jasper National Park,
    AB
L'ANJOU [RES] Edmonton, AB
LA RONDE [RES] Edmonton, AB
LA RUA [RES] Whistler, BC
LA SPIGA [RES] Edmonton, AB
LA TERRAZZA [RES] Vancouver,
    BC
L'AUBERGE [RES] Portland, OR
LEAF & BEAN COFFEE HOUSE
    [URD] Bozeman, MT
LE BEAUJOLAIS [RES] Banff, AB
LE BEAUVALLON [RES] Jasper
    National Park, AB
LE CROCODILE [RES] Vancouver,
    BC
LE GOURMAND [RES] Seattle, WA
LE GREC [RES] Vancouver, BC
LOBSTER SHOP SOUTH [RES]
    Tacoma, WA

LOG CABIN CAFE [RES] Cooke City, MT

LOG CABIN INN [RES] McKenzie Bridge, OR

LOG INN [RES] Rock Springs, WY

LONDON GRILL [RES] Portland, OR

LONE MOUNTAIN RANCH DINING ROOM [RES] Big Sky (Gallatin County), MT

LONNY'S [RES] Port Townsend, WA

LORD BENNETT'S [RES] Bandon, OR

LORRAINE'S EDEL HAUS [RES] Leavenworth, WA

LUMIERE [RES] Vancouver, BC

LYDIA'S [RES] Butte, MT

MACARONI'S [RES] Ashland, OR

MACKENZIE RIVER PIZZA [URD] Bozeman, MT

MADISON PARK CAFE [RES] Seattle, WA

MAHLE HOUSE RESTAURANT, THE [RES] Nanaimo, BC

MALAY SATAY HUT [RES] Seattle, WA

MAMMA'S [RES] Calgary, AB

MANDARIN COVE [RES] Portland, OR

MANRESA CASTLE [RES] Port Townsend, WA

MARCO'S [RES] Seattle, WA

MARINA [RES] Bellingham, WA

MARINA, THE [RES] Victoria, BC

MARY MC CRANK'S DINNER HOUSE [RES] Chehalis, WA

MATTHEW'S TASTE OF ITALY [RES] Billings, MT

MAXIMILIEN-IN-THE-MARKET [RES] Seattle, WA

MAXWELL'S [RES] Cody, WY

MAZZI'S ITALIAN-SICILIAN FOOD [RES] Portland, OR

MCCORMICK & SCHMICK'S [RES] Seattle, WA

MCCORMICK'S FISH HOUSE [RES] Seattle, WA

MCCULLY HOUSE [RES] Jacksonville, OR

MCGREGOR'S PUB [RES] Pinedale, WY

MEADOWS [RES] Bend, OR

MESCALERO [RES] Calgary, AB

METROPOLITAN GRILL [RES] Seattle, WA

MICHAEL'S LANDING [RES] Corvallis, OR

MILFORD'S FISH HOUSE [RES] Boise, ID

MILLION DOLLAR COWBOY STEAK HOUSE [RES] Jackson, WY

MILL STEAKS & SPIRITS [RES] McCall, ID

MON DESIR DINING INN [RES] Medford, OR

MONK MCQUEENS [RES] Vancouver, BC

MONTRI 'S THAI [RES] Vancouver, BC

MOON PALACE [RES] Sequim, WA

MOOSE CHUCK WAGON [URD] Grand Teton National Park, WY

MORTONS OF CHICAGO [RES] Portland, OR

MRS. BEASLEY'S [RES] Redmond, OR

MURATA [RES] Portland, OR

NEW DYNASTY [RES] Lethbridge, AB

NICHOLS STEAK HOUSE [RES] Ontario, OR

NIKKO RESTAURANT [RES] Seattle, WA

NISHINO [RES] Seattle, WA

NORTH BANK [RES] Eugene, OR

NOR'WESTER SEAFOOD [RES] Gold Beach, OR

OFF BROADWAY [RES] Jackson, WY

OLD HOTEL, THE [RES] Dillon, MT

OLD HOUSE RESTAURANT [RES] Nanaimo, BC

OLD PINEY DELL [RES] Red Lodge, MT

OLD SPAGHETTI FACTORY [RES] Portland, OR

OLD SPAGHETTI FACTORY [RES] Spokane, WA

ONATI-THE BASQUE RESTAURANT [RES] Boise, ID

ON BROADWAY [RES] Helena, MT

OREGON ELECTRIC STATION [RES] Eugene, OR

ORIGINAL OYSTER HOUSE [RES] Port Townsend, WA

ORIGINAL PANCAKE HOUSE [URD] Portland, OR

ORITALIA [RES] Portland, OR

PAINTED TABLE, THE [RES] Seattle, WA

PAISLEY SHAWL [RES] Casper, WY

PALACE KITCHEN [RES] Seattle, WA

PALEY'S PLACE [RES] Portland, OR

PALISADE [RES] Seattle, WA

PALOMINO [RES] Seattle, WA

PANHANDLE RESTAURANT [RES] Bonners Ferry, ID

PANORAMA [RES] Calgary, AB

PAPA HAYDN [URD] Portland, OR

PAPI'S RISTORANTE ITALIANO [RES] Vancouver, BC

PARADISE [RES] Sequim, WA

PARAGON [RES] Seattle, WA

PATSY CLARK'S [RES] Spokane, WA

PAVILION TRATTORIA [RES] Beaverton, OR

PAZZO RISTORANTE [RES] Portland, OR

PEPPERMILL [RES] Banff, AB

PERRY'S ON FREMONT [URD] Portland, OR

PIATTI [RES] Seattle, WA

PICCOLO MONDO [RES] Vancouver, BC

PIER 11 FEED STORE [RES] Astoria, OR

PINE ROOM CAFE [RES] Burns, OR

PINE TAVERN [RES] Bend, OR

PINK DOOR [RES] Seattle, WA

PINK PEARL [RES] Vancouver, BC

PLACE PIGALLE [RES] Seattle, WA

PLAINFIELD'S MAYUR [RES] Portland, OR

POINTE, THE [RES] Vancouver, BC

POLARIS [RES] Bellevue, WA

PONTI SEAFOOD GRILL [RES] Seattle, WA

POOR RICHARD'S [RES] Cheyenne, WY

POOR RICHARDS [RES] Portland, OR

PORTAGE BAY CAFE [RES] Seattle, WA

PORTLAND STEAK & CHOPHOUSE [RES] Portland, OR

PORTSIDE [RES] Coos Bay, OR

POST HOTEL DINING ROOM [RES] Lake Louise, AB

PREGO [RES] Seattle, WA

PRESIDENT CHINESE SEAFOOD RESTAURANT [RES] Vancouver, BC

PRIMROSE, THE [RES] Banff, AB

PROVENCE [RES] Vancouver, BC

QUATTRO ON FOURTH [RES] Vancouver, BC

QUEEN CITY GRILL [RES] Seattle, WA

QUINCY'S ON SEVENTH [RES] Calgary, AB

RAINCITY GRILL [RES] Vancouver, BC

RANGE [RES] Jackson, WY

RAY'S BOATHOUSE [RES] Seattle, WA

RED APPLE [RES] Walla Walla, WA

RED STAR TAVERN & ROAST HOUSE [RES] Portland, OR

REGENCY PALACE [RES] Calgary, AB

RESTAURANT AT TIGH-NA-MARA RESORT, THE [RES] Nanaimo, BC

RESTAURANT MATISSE [RES] Victoria, BC

REX [RES] Billings, MT

R.F. MCDOUGALL'S [RES] Richland, WA

RHEINLANDER [RES] Portland, OR

RICK'S CAFE AMERICAN AT THE FLICKS [RES] Boise, ID

RIMROCK CAFE [RES] Whistler, BC

RIMROCK ROOM, THE [RES] Calgary, AB

RINGSIDE [RES] Portland, OR

RINGSIDE EAST [RES] Portland, OR

RISTORANTE ARAXI [RES] Whistler, BC

RIVER CAFE [RES] Calgary, AB

ROOSTER'S LANDING [RES] Clarkston, WA

ROSZAK'S FISH HOUSE [RES] Bend, OR

ROVER'S [RES] Seattle, WA

ROY'S [RES] Seattle, WA

RUTH'S CHRIS STEAK HOUSE [RES] Seattle, WA

SALISH LODGE AND SPA DINING ROOM [RES] North Bend, WA

SALMON RIVER COFFEE SHOP [RES] Salmon, ID

SALTY'S ON THE COLUMBIA [RES] Portland, OR

SAM'S SUPPER CLUB [RES] Glasgow, MT

SANCTUARY [RES] Long Beach, WA

SAUCEBOX [RES] Portland, OR

SAYLER'S OLD COUNTRY KITCHEN [RES] Beaverton, OR
SAYLER'S OLD COUNTRY KITCHEN [RES] Portland, OR
SAZERAC [RES] Seattle, WA
SEAPORTS [RES] Seattle-Tacoma Intl Airport Area, WA
SEASONS [RES] Calgary, AB
SEASON'S RESTAURANT [RES] Vancouver, BC
SERAFINA [RES] Seattle, WA
SHANGHAI CHINESE BISTRO [RES] Vancouver, BC
SHANGHAI TO TOKYO RESTAURANT & BAR [RES] Beaverton, OR
SHIJO JAPANESE RESTAURANT [RES] Vancouver, BC
SHIP INN [RES] Astoria, OR
SHIRO'S [RES] Seattle, WA
SHOALWATER [RES] Long Beach, WA
SHOWTHYME [RES] Bigfork, MT
SILVER DRAGON [RES] Calgary, AB
SILVER FOX [RES] Casper, WY
SILVERWATER CAFE [RES] Port Townsend, WA
SINCLAIR'S [RES] Banff, AB
SMUGGLER'S INN [RES] Calgary, AB
SNAKE RIVER GRILL [RES] Jackson, WY
SNOW GOOSE GRILLE [RES] East Glacier Area, MT
SOMETHING ELSE [RES] Jasper National Park, AB
SOOKE HARBOUR HOUSE [RES] Victoria, BC
SPACE NEEDLE [RES] Seattle, WA
SPAGHETTINI'S [RES] Butte, MT
SPANISH PEAKS BREWERY [RES] Bozeman, MT
SPAZZO MEDITERRANEAN GRILL [RES] Bellevue, WA
SPINNAKER'S BREW PUB [RES] Victoria, BC
STAR ANISE [RES] Vancouver, BC
STEFAN'S [RES] Cody, WY
STELLA'S TRATTORIA [RES] Seattle, WA
STONEHOUSE [RES] Helena, MT
STRUTTING GROUSE [RES] Jackson, WY
SUN SUI WAH SEAFOOD RESTAURANT [RES] Vancouver, BC

SUSHI VILLAGE [RES] Whistler, BC
SVEN ERICKSEN'S [RES] Lethbridge, AB
SWAGAT INDIAN CUISINE [RES] Portland, OR
SWEETWATER [RES] Jackson, WY
SWEETWATERS [RES] Eugene, OR
SYLVIA'S [RES] Portland, OR
SZMANIA'S MAGNOLIA [RES] Seattle, WA
TAMA SUSHI [RES] Vancouver, BC
TAPASTREE [URD] Vancouver, BC
TEAHOUSE [RES] Vancouver, BC
TEATRO [RES] Calgary, AB
TETON PINES [RES] Jackson, WY
THIRD FLOOR FISH CAFE [RES] Bellevue, WA
THREE BEAR [RES] West Yellowstone, MT
TICINO [RES] Banff, AB
TOGA'S INTERNATIONAL CUISINE [RES] Port Angeles, WA
TOJO'S [RES] Vancouver, BC
TOKYO TOM'S PLACE [RES] Jasper National Park, AB
TONQUIN PRIME RIB [RES] Jasper National Park, AB
TONY'S [RES] Bend, OR
TOP OF VANCOUVER [RES] Vancouver, BC
TRATTORIA DI UMBERTO [RES] Whistler, BC
TRATTORIA MITCHELLI [RES] Seattle, WA
TRUE CONFECTIONS [URD] Vancouver, BC
TULIO RISTORANTE [RES] Seattle, WA
TYPHOON! [RES] Portland, OR
UMBERTO'S [RES] Vancouver, BC
UNION BAY CAFE [RES] Seattle, WA
UNION SQUARE GRILL [RES] Seattle, WA
UPTOWN CAFE [RES] Butte, MT
VAL D'ISERE [RES] Whistler, BC
VICTORIA DINING ROOM [RES] Lake Louise, AB
VICTORIAN, THE [RES] Victoria, BC
VILLA DEL LUPO [RES] Vancouver, BC
VILLAGE [RES] Marysville, WA
VISTA GRANDE [RES] Jackson, WY
WALKER'S GRILL [RES] Billings, MT

WALLISER STUBE [RES] Lake Louise, AB
WARM SPRINGS RANCH RESTAURANT [RES] Sun Valley Area, ID
WESLEY STREET [RES] Nanaimo, BC
WESTSIDE BAKERY & CAFE [URD] Bend, OR
WHALE'S TALE [RES] Newport, OR
WHEELHOUSE [RES] Bandon, OR
WHITE HEATHER TEA ROOM [RES] Victoria, BC
WHOLE FAMDAMILY [RES] Lewistown, MT
WIDMER GASTHAUS [RES] Portland, OR
WILDFLOWER RESTAURANT [RES] Whistler, BC
WILD GINGER [RES] Seattle, WA
WILDWOOD [RES] Portland, OR

WILLIAM TELL [RES] Vancouver, BC
WINCHESTER COUNTRY INN [RES] Ashland, OR
WINDBAG SALOON [RES] Helena, MT
WINTERBORNE [RES] Portland, OR
YACHT CLUB BROILER [RES] Bremerton, WA
YANKEE POT ROAST [RES] Grants Pass, OR
YELLOWSTONE MINE [RES] Gardiner, MT
ZENON CAFE [RES] Eugene, OR
ZIMORINO RED PIES OVER MONTANA [RES] Missoula, MT
ZINFANDELLS [RES] Vancouver, BC

CITY INDEX

Notes

Notes

Notes

Mobil Travel Guides

Please check the guides you would like to order:

☐ 0-7627-2619-9
California
$18.95

☐ 0-7627-2618-0
Florida
$18.95

☐ 0-7627-2612-1
Great Lakes
Illinois, Indiana, Michigan,
Ohio, Wisconsin
$18.95

☐ 0-7627-2610-5
Great Plains
Iowa, Kansas, Minnesota,
Missouri, Nebraska, North
Dakota, Oklahoma, South
Dakota
$18.95

☐ 0-7627-2613-X
Mid-Atlantic
Delaware, Maryland,
Pennsylvania, Virginia,
Washington D.C., West
Virginia
$18.95

☐ 0-7627-2614-8
**New England and Eastern
Canada**
Connecticut, Maine, Massachu-
setts, New Hampshire, Rhode
Island, Vermont, Canada
$18.95

☐ 0-7627-2616-4
New York/New Jersey
$18.95

☐ 0-7627-2611-3
Northwest
Idaho, Montana, Oregon, Wash-
ington, Wyoming, Canada
$18.95

☐ 0-7627-2615-6
Southeast
Alabama, Arkansas, Georgia, Ken-
tucky, Louisiana, Mississippi,
North Carolina, South Carolina,
Tennessee
$18.95

☐ 0-7627-2617-2
Southwest
Arizona, Colorado, Nevada, New
Mexico, Texas, Utah
$18.95

Please ship the books above to:

Name: _____

Address: _____

City:_____ State _____ Zip _____

Total Cost of Book(s)	$_____	☐ Please charge my credit card.
Shipping & Handling	$_____	☐ Discover ☐ Visa
(Please add $3.00 for first book $1.50 for each additional book)		☐ MasterCard ☐ American Express
Add 8.75% sales tax	$_____	Card #_____
Total Amount	$_____	Expiration _____
☐ My Check is enclosed.		Signature _____

Please mail this form to: **Mobil Travel Guides
1460 Renaissance Drive Suite 401
Park Ridge, IL 60068**

Mobil
Travel Guide®

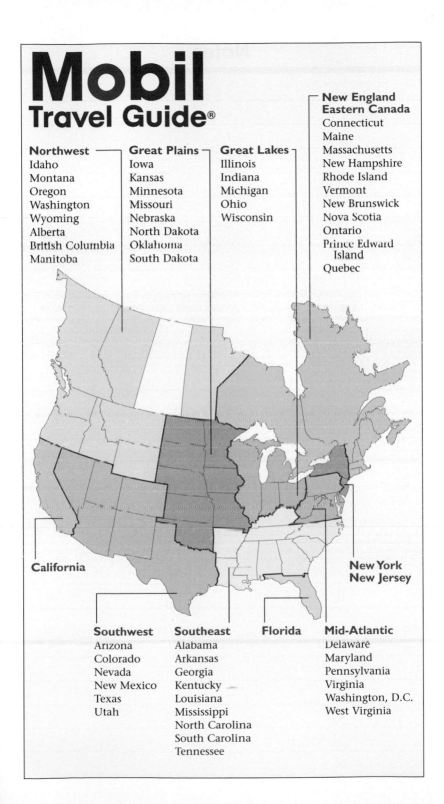

New England
Eastern Canada
Connecticut
Maine
Massachusetts
New Hampshire
Rhode Island
Vermont
New Brunswick
Nova Scotia
Ontario
Prince Edward
  Island
Quebec

Northwest
Idaho
Montana
Oregon
Washington
Wyoming
Alberta
British Columbia
Manitoba

Great Plains
Iowa
Kansas
Minnesota
Missouri
Nebraska
North Dakota
Oklahoma
South Dakota

Great Lakes
Illinois
Indiana
Michigan
Ohio
Wisconsin

California

New York
New Jersey

Southwest
Arizona
Colorado
Nevada
New Mexico
Texas
Utah

Southeast
Alabama
Arkansas
Georgia
Kentucky
Louisiana
Mississippi
North Carolina
South Carolina
Tennessee

Florida

Mid-Atlantic
Delaware
Maryland
Pennsylvania
Virginia
Washington, D.C.
West Virginia

Notes

Add your opinion!

Help make the Guides even more useful. Tell us about your experiences with the hotels and restaurants listed in the Guides (or ones that should be added).

Find us on the Internet at **www.mobiltravelguide.com/feedback**

Or copy the form below and mail to Mobil Travel Guides, 1460 Renaissance Drive, Suite 401, Park Ridge, IL 60068. All information will be kept confidential.

Your name _____   Were children with you on trip? ☐ Yes ☐ No

Street _____   Number of people in your party _____

City/State/Zip _____   Your occupation _____

Establishment name_____   ☐ Hotel ☐ Resort ☐ Restaurant
☐ Motel ☐ Inn ☐ Other

Street_____ City_____ State _____

Do you agree with our description? ☐ Yes ☐ No   If not, give reason_____

Please give us your opinion of the following: 2003 Guide rating _____ ★

Decor	Cleanliness	Service	Food	Check your suggested rating
☐ Excellent	☐ Spotless	☐ Excellent	☐ Excellent	☐ ★
☐ Good	☐ Clean	☐ Good	☐ Good	☐ ★★
☐ Fair	☐ Unclean	☐ Fair	☐ Fair	☐ ★★★
☐ Poor	☐ Dirty	☐ Poor	☐ Poor	☐ ★★★★
				☐ ★★★★★

Date of visit _____   First visit? ☐ Yes ☐ No   ☐ ✔ unusually good value

Comments _____

Establishment name_____   ☐ Hotel ☐ Resort ☐ Restaurant
☐ Motel ☐ Inn ☐ Other

Street_____ City_____ State _____

Do you agree with our description? ☐ Yes ☐ No   If not, give reason_____

Please give us your opinion of the following: 2003 Guide rating _____ ★

Decor	Cleanliness	Service	Food	Check your suggested rating
☐ Excellent	☐ Spotless	☐ Excellent	☐ Excellent	☐ ★
☐ Good	☐ Clean	☐ Good	☐ Good	☐ ★★
☐ Fair	☐ Unclean	☐ Fair	☐ Fair	☐ ★★★
☐ Poor	☐ Dirty	☐ Poor	☐ Poor	☐ ★★★★
				☐ ★★★★★

Date of visit _____   First visit? ☐ Yes ☐ No   ☐ ✔ unusually good value

Comments _____

Notes